African Development
Indicators
2000

The World
Washington,

Cover design by Patrick Fagan/Patricia Hord Graphik Design

This volume was prepared by the Operational Quality and Knowledge Services of the Africa Regional Office at the World Bank.

ISSN 1020-2927
ISBN 0-8213-4386-6

Contents

Prices

Commodity Trade

Table des matières

15. Indicateurs du bien-être des ménages: revue de pays choisis   379

Graphiques

Acknowledgments

This volume was produced by the Operational Quality and Knowledge Services of the Africa Region, in collaboration with the Development Data Group of the Development Economics Vice Presidency.

The volume was prepared by a team led by Vildan Verbeek-Demiraydin and comprising Ronnie Hammad, and Joan Pandit. Maria Cristina Germany provided valuable guidance. Tariqul Khan updated and managed the systems programs. The chapters on national accounts, balance of payments, trade, and government finance draw heavily on the work of World Bank country desks. The chapters on power, communication and transportation, labor force and social indicators tap the World Bank's World Development Indicators database. The chapter on environment was prepared with data from the World Resources Institute. The chapter on privatization of public enterprises was provided by Oliver C. Campbell-White. The chapter on household welfare indicators was provided by the Institutional and Social Policy Group of the Africa Region, with the financial support of the Norwegian and Belgian Trust Funds. Nicki Marrian provided assistance in editing and production of the volume. Gaudencio Dizon desktopped the text.

In addition, many World Bank staff provided information on their countries or related to their economic or sectoral specialties. Other staff aided and advised on the design and content of this volume.

Preface

African Development Indicators 2000 continues the data publication series started by the World Bank in 1989 with *African Economic and Financial Data* (published jointly with the United Nations Development Programme), followed by *African Development Indicators 1992, 1994–95, 1996, 1997,* and *1998/99.* These data volumes are intended to provide Africans and those interested in Africa with a consistent and convenient set of data to monitor development programs and aid flows in the region. Each successive volume provides access to more focused information and represents an improvement in the quality and availability of the data.

The data in this volume derive from a variety of sources. In most cases, the original source is national statistical services in Africa. In addition, many international agencies collect or compile data on Africa and organize national data in a standardized framework. This volume draws heavily from such sources. The data have been supplemented by World Bank staff estimates to help address problems of missing or inconsistent data from standard sources. Some of the estimation methods used here differ from methods used in other sources. Throughout the volume, in introductions to chapters or in technical notes, such differences in methodologies are discussed.

In the tradition of the first six volumes, this data collection is intended to serve as a prime source of information on Africa. Its wide dissemination to African and non-African analysts and policymakers will contribute to a better understanding of Africa and to development on that continent.

John Roome
Director, Operational Quality
and Knowledge Services
Africa Region

Acronyms and Abbreviations

ADB	African Development Bank	CPI	Consumer price index
ADI	*African Development Indicators*	DAC	Development Assistance Committee of the OECD
AEFD	*African Economic and Financial Data* (UNDP/World Bank 1989)	DDG	Development Data Group, World Bank
AFESD	Arab Fund for Economic and Social Development	DRS	Debtor Reporting System (World Bank)
BADEA	Arab Bank for Economic Development in Africa	ECA	Economic Commission for Africa
		FAO	UN Food and Agriculture Organization
BIS	Bank for International Settlements	f.o.b.	Free on board
CDIAC	Carbon Dioxide Information Analysis Center	GDI	Gross domestic investment
		GDP	Gross domestic product
CFA	Communauté Financière Africaine (franc zone)	GDS	Gross domestic savings
		GFS	*Government Finance Statistics* (IMF)
CIDA	Canadian International Development Agency	GNFS	Goods and nonfactor services
		GNP	Gross national product
c.i.f.	Cost, insurance, freight	GNS	Gross national savings
CITES	Convention on International Trade in Endangered Species of Wild Flora and Fauna	IBRD	International Bank for Reconstruction and Development
		ICP	International Comparison Project
CMEA	Council for Mutual Economic Assistance	IDA	International Development Association
		IEA	International Energy Agency
COMTRADE	Commodity Trade database (United Nations)	IFAD	International Fund for Agricultural Development

IFS	*International Financial Statistics* (IMF)	SNA	System of national accounts
ILO	International Labour Organization	UNCTAD	United Nations Conference on Trade and Development
IMF	International Monetary Fund		
ISIC	UN International Standard Industrial Classification	UNDP	United Nations Development Programme
ITU	International Telecommunications Union	UNECE	United Nations Economic Commission for Europe
IUCN	International Union for Conservation of Nature and Natural Resources	UNEP	United Nations Environment Programme
LIBOR	London interbank offered rate		
LIMIC	Low-income and middle-income countries	UNESCO	United Nations Education, Scientific, and Cultural Organization
MBO	Management employee buyout	UNFPA	
METMIN	Metals and minerals database (World Bank)		
ODA	Official development assistance	UNHCR	United Nations High Commissioner for Refugees
OECD	Organization for Economic Cooperation and Development	UNICEF	United Nations Children's Fund
OPEC	Organization of Petroleum Exporting Countries	UNIDO	United Nations Industrial Development Organization
ORT	Oral rehydration therapy	UNSO	United Nations Statistical Office
PE	Public enterprise	UNSTAT	United Nations Statistical Department
SAF	Structural adjustment facility	UNTA	United Nations Technical Assistance
SDA	Social dimensions of adjustment	WFP	World Food Programme
SDR	Special drawing right	WHO	World Health Organization
SIMA	Statistical Information Management and Analysis Database (World Bank)	WRI	World Resources Institute
SITC	UN Standard International Trade Classification	ZIMCO	Zambia Industrial and Mining Corporation

Introduction

The task of monitoring Africa's development progress and aid flows requires basic empirical data that can be readily used by analysts. This publication—which is the sixth in a series that began with the *African Economic and Financial Data (AEFD)* and was followed by *African Development Indicators (ADI) 1992, 1994–95, 1996, 1997,* and *1998/99*—is meant to provide a starting point to fulfill that task.

This volume has been able to extend the work of the previous volumes in this series. In particular:

- Most macroeconomic data (in particular, national accounts, balance of payments, government finance statistics, and trade) reflect data maintained by World Bank country desks, often referred to as operational data. These data are often more up to date and offer better country coverage than the data stored in the Bank's central files, SIMA, which were used in publications before 1998. SIMA is a large database that contains some, but not all, data produced by Bank staff—operational and other—and some, but not all, data produced by UN agencies.
- The chapter on household welfare indicators has been improved, with new countries added.

- The coverage of many of the data series has been improved, reflecting improvements in the underlying data series, as well as estimates made by Bank staff.
- New purchasing power parity (PPP) indicators have been added.

However, substantial data gaps remain, notably in areas such as public enterprises, gender, and labor. Strengthening the statistical capacity in African countries is an ongoing process, and greater efforts and institutional support will be required if substantial improvements are to be made.

This volume presents the available relevant data for 1970–98, grouped into 15 chapters: background data; national accounts; prices and exchange rates; money and banking; external sector; external debt and related flows; government finance; agriculture; power, communications, and transportation; public enterprises; labor force and employment; aid flows; social indicators; environmental indicators; and household welfare indicators. Chapter 14 (environmental indicators) was once again taken from the World Resources Institute's *World Resources 1998–99.* Chapter 15 (household welfare indicators) is presented on a country basis.

1

Each chapter begins with a brief introduction on the nature of the data, followed by a set of charts, statistical tables, and technical notes. These define the indicators and identify specific sources.

A companion CD-rom (expected to be available by the end of 1999 through the World Bank) will provide year-by-year time series of most chapters back to 1970. These series will provide analysts with data needed to help place the most recent years in an historical context.

The data in this volume incorporate numerous revisions to those published previously in the series. There are several reasons for this.

- Many of the data that were based on estimates in the earlier volumes have been replaced with updated actual data or improved estimates. In most cases, these reflect revisions made by the original reporting authorities or sources, but it also includes corrections of errors in previous volumes.

- Data series expressed in constant U.S. dollars and exchange rates use a base year of 1995; previous *ADI*s were based on 1987 exchange rates and prices; and *AEFD* used 1980 exchange rate and prices.

- Some series expressed in constant prices have been revised as a result of updated or revised deflators.

- As in the 1998/99 volume, macroeconomic data reflect country desk information. The difference is most noticeable in the chapter on government finance, as figures reflect consolidated government data instead of only central government data.

Considerable effort has been made to standardize and to harmonize related data sets drawn from diverse sources. Because statistical methods, coverage, practices, and definitions differ widely among sources, full comparability cannot be assured, and the indicators must be interpreted with care. In addition, the statistical systems in many developing economies are still weak, and this affects the availability and reliability of the data they report. Moreover, intercountry and intertemporal comparisons always involve complex technical problems, which have no full and unequivocal solution.

The data are drawn from sources thought to be the most authoritative, but many data sources are subject to considerable margins of error. To provide reasonably timely data required for meaningful monitoring, the World Bank, the International Monetary Fund (IMF), and other agencies sometimes make estimates on the basis of available secondary information to fill critical gaps in national reporting, especially for the most recent years, when data cannot be readily produced by national statistical sources. Nonetheless, data gaps exist for many indicators, and some countries are covered only sporadically.

Readers are urged to take these limitations into account in using the data and interpreting the indicators, particularly when making comparisons across economies. Weaknesses in the data point to the need for strengthened statistical systems throughout the region.

As a visual aid to data interpretation and cross-country comparisons, figures for selected indicators are included. As with time series, the figures should also be interpreted with caution, in particular in cross-country analysis, because countries with missing data are excluded from the charts.

As in the three previous publications, this volume contains a special chapter on household welfare indicators. The data in this chapter all come directly from national household surveys. A number of improvements have been made to the layout of the country tables, including the complete standardization of the table formats and the inclusion of selective welfare indicators. In the tables, all indicators are presented by urban and rural expenditure quintiles, which makes it possible to make comparisons within a country between poor and non-poor household groups.

Throughout this volume (except when otherwise stated), the symbol ".." indicates that data are not available or not applicable. A zero (0) indicates either zero value or an insignificant value, that is, less than one-half of the smallest unit shown. The symbol "MR" indicates "most recent year available."

In chapter 13, columns headed by a period (for example, 1992–95) show data for the latest available year in the period.

To facilitate cross-country comparisons, values of many national series have been converted from the national currencies to U.S. dollars, using the *World Bank Atlas* methodology.

Indicators in this volume generally follow standard definitions as far as possible and cover years through 1998, depending on the chapter. Data for 1998 are preliminary and therefore may not be internally consistent within and across accounts, and may not be available for all countries. Because data are continually updated, the statistics here may be different from those in other publications.

Shares and ratios are always calculated using current price series; when gross domestic product (GDP) is used as the denominator for these calculations, it is always expressed at market prices (except in Figure 2-3).

In all but the last chapter, the data are arranged by indicator to facilitate cross-country comparisons. For country-specific work, data can be arranged to show all indicators together for each country.

In this volume, the statistical tables are usually arranged as time series, by country and by country groups. The largest country group is All Africa, consisting of two subgroups: North Africa and Sub-Saharan Africa (including South Africa). In turn, the Sub-Saharan Africa group is shown excluding South Africa and Nigeria. These two subgroups correspond to the Sub-Saharan Africa and Sub-Saharan Africa excluding Nigeria groups shown in the *AEFD* and *ADI 1992*, where South Africa was listed separately.

Annual data shown for country groups are totals, averages, or medians for the countries included in the group, as indicated on the table. These group aggregates can be either simple (arithmetic)—where missing data are not imputed—or gap-filled—where weights are used to adjust group totals for missing countries. In the latter case, when values are missing for a country or a year, estimates are made to maintain the same country composition of the groups through time. However, the implicit estimated values for the countries with missing data are not shown separately in the tables. These gap-fill estimates are made, and the aggregate statistics shown, only if the countries for which data are available for a given year account for at least two-thirds of the full group, as defined by benchmarks in 1995. This procedure is standard for many World Bank statistical publications.

Most group averages are weighted according to the relative importance of the countries in the group total for that indicator, based on simple addition across countries when the indicator is expressed in reasonably comparable units. Group averages for analytical ratios (for example, imports to GDP) can be either weighted or simple (arithmetic). Usually they are calculated from the group totals for both the numerator and the denominator, which is analytically equivalent to calculating weighted averages, where the weight for each country is its share in the group total for the denominator. Sometimes, however, when it is appropriate to treat the experiences of different countries equally in determining a representative value for the group, these group averages are arithmetic, that is, each country is assigned equal weight.

Period averages—shown for 1975–84, 1985–89, and 1990 to most recent year—are calculated from time series (levels, ratios, growth rates, or medians) for both countries and country groups. They are either simple averages or average annual percentage growth rates. These growth rates always use the least-squares method and are usually computed from real-term series. In this publication, the least-squares growth rates are computed using the level for the year before the first year shown in the label. The least-squares growth rate, r, is estimated by fitting a least-squares linear regression trend line to the logarithmic annual values of the variable in the relevant period. More specifically, the regression equation takes the form: $\log X_t = a + bt + e_t$, where this is equivalent to the logarithmic transformation of the compound growth rate equation, $X_t = X_o (1 + r)^t$. In these equations X is the variable, t is time, and $a = \log X_o$ and $b = \log (1 + r)$ are the parameters to be estimated; e is the error term. If b^* is the least-squares estimate of b, then the annual average growth rate, r, is obtained as [anti log ($b*$)] − 1 and multiplied by 100 to express it in percentage terms. The least-squares growth rate dampens the influence of exceptional values, particularly at the end points. Least-square growth rates are calculated only if more than two-thirds of consecutive data—carrying the same sign—are present in the time series.

Throughout this volume, data for Ethiopia include Eritrea up to 1992, except when otherwise indicated. Zaire's name has been changed to Democratic Republic of the Congo.

1

Selected Background Data

The first two tables of the volume provide selected indicators, including a series on population, as background to the data in the rest of the volume. Table 1-1 provides a comparative view, across indicators, of some of the more important indicators for all countries in the most recent year for which relatively complete information is available.

1-1. Basic indicators

	Population mid-1998 (millions)	Land area (thousands of square km.)	GNP per capita		Life expectancy at birth (years)	School enrollment				Total net ODA per capita
			Atlas dollars	Av. annual percentage growth		Primary		Secondary		
			1998	1988-98	1997	1980	1995-96	1980	1995-96	1997
SUB-SAHARAN AFRICA	628.3	23628	513	-0.6	51	78	..	15	..	23
excluding South Africa	587.0	22407	316	-0.2	50	77	..	15	..	24
excl. S.Africa & Nigeria	465.7	21497	320	-0.5	49	68	63	14	17	30
Angola	12.0	1247	340	-8.5	46	..	..	21	..	37
Benin	6.0	111	380	0.9	53	67	78	16	17	39
Botswana	1.6	567	3600	3.4	47	91	108	19	65	81
Burkina Faso	10.7	274	240	0.8	44	18	40	3	..	35
Burundi	6.6	26	140	-3.7	42	26	51	3	..	19
Cameroon	14.3	465	610	-4.4	57	98	..	18	..	36
Cape Verde	0.4	4	1060	1.1	68	114	..	8	..	273
Central African Republic	3.5	623	300	-1.5	45	71	..	14	..	27
Chad	7.4	1259	230	1.5	49	..	58	..	10	31
Comoros	0.5	2	370	-2.5	60	86	75	22	21	54
Congo, Democratic Rep. of	48.2	2267	110	-9.3	51	92	..	24	..	4
Congo, Republic of	2.8	342	690	-2.2	48	141	114	74	53	99
Côte d'Ivoire	14.5	318	700	-0.2	47	75	71	19	24	31
Djibouti	0.7	23	..	..	50	37	39	12	14	136
Equatorial Guinea	0.4	28	1060	9.8	50	135	..	..	..	58
Eritrea	3.9	101	200	2.2	51	..	53	..	20	33
Ethiopia	61.3	1000	100	0.7	43	37	38	9	12	11
Gabon	1.2	258	4170	0.5	52	..	..	..	..	35
Gambia, The	1.2	10	340	-0.9	53	53	77	11	25	35
Ghana	18.5	228	390	1.5	60	79	..	41	..	28
Guinea	7.1	246	540	2.4	46	36	48	17	12	55
Guinea-Bissau	1.2	28	160	0.2	44	68	..	6	..	110
Kenya	29.3	569	350	-0.3	52	115	85	20	24	16
Lesotho	2.1	30	570	1.3	56	104	108	18	31	46
Liberia	3.0	96	..	..	47	48	..	22	..	33
Madagascar	14.6	582	260	-1.2	57	130	92	..	16	59
Malawi	10.5	94	200	0.8	43	60	89	5	17	34
Mali	10.6	1220	250	0.5	50	26	45	8	10	44
Mauritania	2.5	1025	410	0.8	53	37	79	11	16	102
Mauritius	1.2	2	3700	4.1	71	93	107	50	65	36
Mozambique	16.9	784	210	2.7	45	..	60	5	7	58
Namibia	1.7	823	1940	1.5	56	..	131	..	61	102
Niger	10.1	1267	190	-2.0	47	25	29	5	7	35
Nigeria	121.3	911	300	1.3	54	109	..	18	..	2
Rwanda	8.1	25	230	-4.6	40	63	..	3	..	75
São Tomé and Principe	0.1	1	270	-1.6	64	..	..	..	..	242
Senegal	9.0	193	530	-0.1	52	46	68	11	16	49
Seychelles	0.1	0	6450	3.1	71	..	..	..	..	194
Sierra Leone	4.9	72	140	-5.7	37	52	..	14	..	27
Somalia	9.1	627	..	..	47	22	..	9	..	12
South Africa	41.3	1221	2880	-0.5	65	90	131	..	94	12
Sudan	28.3	2376	290	2.3	55	50	51	16	21	7
Swaziland	1.0	17	1400	1.4	60	103	118	38	54	30
Tanzania	32.1	884	210	1.2	48	93	66	3	5	31
Togo	4.5	54	330	-1.5	49	118	120	33	27	29
Uganda	20.9	200	310	3.7	42	50	74	5	12	41
Zambia	9.7	743	330	-0.9	43	90	89	16	..	65
Zimbabwe	11.7	387	610	-0.2	55	85	119	8	49	29
NORTH AFRICA	133.9	5738	1536	0.9	68	84	100	41	64	22
Algeria	30.0	2382	1570	-1.6	70	95	108	33	63	8
Egypt, Arab Republic	61.4	995	1250	2.5	66	73	101	51	75	32
Libya	5.3	1760	..	..	70	125	..	76	..	2
Morocco	27.8	446	..	0.7	67	83	86	26	39	17
Tunisia	9.4	155	2150	2.4	70	102	117	27	65	21
ALL AFRICA	762.2	29367	688	-0.2	54	79	78	20	..	23

Note: 1998 data are preliminary (see page 3).

1-2. Population

| | Millions of people | | | | | | | | | | | Average annual percentage growth | | |
	1980	1989	1990	1991	1992	1993	1994	1995	1996	1997	1998	75-84	85-89	90-MR
SUB-SAHARAN AFRICA	380.74	493.71	508.34	523.16	538.22	550.12	563.83	579.18	595.40	612.30	628.29	3.0	2.9	2.7
excluding South Africa	353.16	459.22	473.14	487.23	501.53	512.65	525.54	540.06	555.48	571.70	586.97	3.0	2.9	2.7
excl. S.Africa & Nigeria	282.01	365.71	376.93	388.24	399.64	407.75	417.53	428.78	440.92	453.80	465.72	3.0	2.9	2.6
Angola	7.02	8.94	9.23	9.59	9.94	10.29	10.63	10.97	11.32	11.66	12.00	2.7	2.8	3.3
Benin	3.46	4.59	4.74	4.88	5.03	5.18	5.33	5.48	5.63	5.80	5.97	2.9	3.2	2.9
Botswana	0.91	1.24	1.28	1.31	1.35	1.39	1.43	1.46	1.50	1.53	1.56	3.6	3.5	2.6
Burkina Faso	6.96	8.67	8.88	9.09	9.31	9.53	9.76	9.99	10.23	10.47	10.73	2.4	2.4	2.4
Burundi	4.13	5.31	5.46	5.60	5.75	5.89	6.02	6.16	6.29	6.43	6.58	2.5	2.9	2.4
Cameroon	8.66	11.16	11.47	11.80	12.13	12.47	12.82	13.18	13.55	13.94	14.33	2.8	2.9	2.8
Cape Verde	0.29	0.33	0.34	0.35	0.35	0.36	0.37	0.38	0.39	0.40	0.41	1.0	1.9	2.3
Central African Republic	2.31	2.87	2.94	3.01	3.08	3.15	3.22	3.29	3.35	3.42	3.48	2.4	2.4	2.2
Chad	4.48	5.62	5.75	5.89	6.06	6.25	6.46	6.71	6.94	7.15	7.35	2.4	2.4	3.1
Comoros	0.34	0.42	0.43	0.44	0.46	0.47	0.48	0.49	0.50	0.52	0.53	..	2.6	2.6
Congo, Democratic Rep. of	27.01	36.16	37.36	38.60	39.87	41.16	42.49	43.85	45.25	46.71	48.22	3.1	3.4	3.2
Congo, Republic of	1.67	2.16	2.22	2.28	2.35	2.42	2.49	2.56	2.63	2.71	2.78	2.9	2.9	2.9
Côte d'Ivoire	8.19	11.28	11.64	12.00	12.37	12.75	13.13	13.53	13.89	14.21	14.49	3.9	3.4	2.9
Djibouti	0.28	0.49	0.52	0.53	0.55	0.57	0.58	0.60	0.62	0.64	0.65	6.7	6.1	3.1
Equatorial Guinea	0.22	0.35	0.35	0.36	0.37	0.38	0.39	0.40	0.41	0.42	0.43	2.4	3.4	2.5
Eritrea	2.38	3.05	3.14	3.22	3.31	3.39	3.48	3.57	3.67	3.77	3.88	2.6	3.0	2.7
Ethiopia	37.72	49.34	51.18	52.95	54.79	53.30	54.89	56.53	58.23	59.75	61.27	2.8	3.2	2.2
Gabon	0.69	0.93	0.96	0.99	1.02	1.05	1.07	1.10	1.13	1.15	1.18	3.2	3.4	2.6
Gambia, The	0.64	0.88	0.92	0.96	1.00	1.04	1.08	1.11	1.15	1.18	1.22	3.1	4.1	3.6
Ghana	10.74	14.43	14.87	15.31	15.76	16.20	16.64	17.08	17.52	17.98	18.46	2.3	3.5	2.8
Guinea	4.46	5.59	5.76	5.93	6.09	6.26	6.43	6.59	6.76	6.92	7.08	1.7	2.8	2.7
Guinea-Bissau	0.80	0.96	0.97	0.99	1.01	1.03	1.06	1.09	1.11	1.14	1.16	3.7	2.3	2.2
Kenya	16.63	22.79	23.55	24.30	25.05	25.78	26.51	27.22	27.92	28.61	29.29	3.8	3.5	2.8
Lesotho	1.35	1.68	1.72	1.76	1.80	1.84	1.89	1.93	1.97	2.01	2.06	2.5	2.5	2.3
Liberia	1.88	2.39	2.44	2.48	2.54	2.60	2.66	2.73	2.81	2.89	2.97	3.2	2.3	2.5
Madagascar	8.87	11.31	11.63	11.89	12.20	12.55	12.92	13.30	13.72	14.15	14.59	2.6	2.8	2.9
Malawi	6.18	8.22	8.51	8.74	8.99	9.24	9.49	9.76	10.02	10.28	10.53	3.2	3.4	2.8
Mali	6.59	8.22	8.46	8.70	8.95	9.20	9.45	9.71	9.99	10.29	10.60	2.2	2.7	2.8
Mauritania	1.55	1.97	2.03	2.08	2.14	2.20	2.27	2.33	2.39	2.46	2.53	2.5	2.8	2.8
Mauritius	0.97	1.05	1.06	1.07	1.08	1.10	1.11	1.12	1.13	1.15	1.16	1.4	0.8	1.2
Mozambique	12.10	14.04	14.15	14.42	14.69	15.01	15.42	15.82	16.23	16.63	16.95	2.7	1.0	2.2
Namibia	1.03	1.31	1.35	1.39	1.42	1.46	1.50	1.54	1.58	1.62	1.66	2.7	2.8	2.7
Niger	5.59	7.49	7.73	7.99	8.26	8.55	8.84	9.15	9.47	9.80	10.14	3.3	3.2	3.4
Nigeria	71.15	93.50	96.20	98.98	101.88	104.89	108.01	111.27	114.57	117.90	121.26	3.1	3.0	2.9
Rwanda	5.16	6.79	6.95	7.15	7.35	7.54	6.23	6.40	6.73	7.90	8.11	3.3	3.0	1.0
São Tomé and Principe	0.09	0.11	0.12	0.12	0.12	0.13	0.13	0.13	0.14	0.14	0.14	1.5	2.8	2.7
Senegal	5.54	7.13	7.33	7.51	7.70	7.90	8.11	8.33	8.56	8.79	9.03	2.9	2.8	2.7
Seychelles	0.06	0.07	0.07	0.07	0.07	0.07	0.07	0.08	0.08	0.08	0.08	1.4	0.7	1.5
Sierra Leone	3.24	3.91	4.00	4.09	4.19	4.29	4.40	4.51	4.63	4.75	4.85	2.0	2.2	2.5
Somalia	5.85	7.28	7.77	8.15	8.38	8.47	8.41	8.20	8.48	8.77	9.08	5.5	2.3	1.8
South Africa	27.58	34.49	35.20	35.93	36.69	37.47	38.28	39.12	39.91	40.60	41.32	2.3	2.5	2.1
Sudan	18.68	23.56	24.06	24.57	25.08	25.59	26.10	26.62	27.16	27.74	28.35	3.1	2.4	2.1
Swaziland	0.57	0.75	0.77	0.79	0.82	0.85	0.87	0.90	0.93	0.96	0.99	3.2	3.2	3.2
Tanzania	18.58	24.69	25.47	26.28	27.10	27.94	28.79	29.65	30.49	31.32	32.13	3.2	3.2	3.0
Togo	2.62	3.41	3.51	3.64	3.75	3.87	3.99	4.11	4.23	4.34	4.46	2.8	3.0	3.1
Uganda	12.81	15.77	16.33	16.89	17.46	18.03	18.60	19.17	19.74	20.32	20.90	2.4	2.6	3.2
Zambia	5.74	7.55	7.78	8.02	8.26	8.50	8.74	8.98	9.21	9.44	9.67	3.4	3.0	2.8
Zimbabwe	7.01	9.47	9.75	10.02	10.28	10.53	10.78	11.01	11.24	11.47	11.69	3.1	3.3	2.4
NORTH AFRICA	88.35	111.46	114.07	116.64	119.19	121.68	124.12	126.53	128.96	131.39	133.88	2.7	2.5	2.0
Algeria	18.67	24.39	25.01	25.63	26.25	26.85	27.45	28.06	28.68	29.32	29.98	3.1	2.8	2.3
Egypt, Arab Republic	40.88	51.26	52.44	53.62	54.78	55.93	57.06	58.18	59.27	60.35	61.40	2.5	2.5	2.0
Libya	3.04	4.30	4.42	4.53	4.64	4.75	4.86	4.97	5.08	5.20	5.33	4.5	3.4	2.4
Morocco	19.38	23.56	24.04	24.52	25.00	25.47	25.93	26.39	26.85	27.31	27.81	2.3	2.2	1.8
Tunisia	6.38	7.96	8.16	8.34	8.51	8.67	8.81	8.94	9.08	9.22	9.36	2.6	2.5	1.8
ALL AFRICA	469.09	605.17	622.40	639.80	657.41	671.79	687.95	705.71	724.35	743.69	762.17	2.9	2.8	2.5

Note: 1998 data are preliminary (see page 3).

8

Figure 1-1. Development diamonds for all African countries, 1997 (or most recent available year)

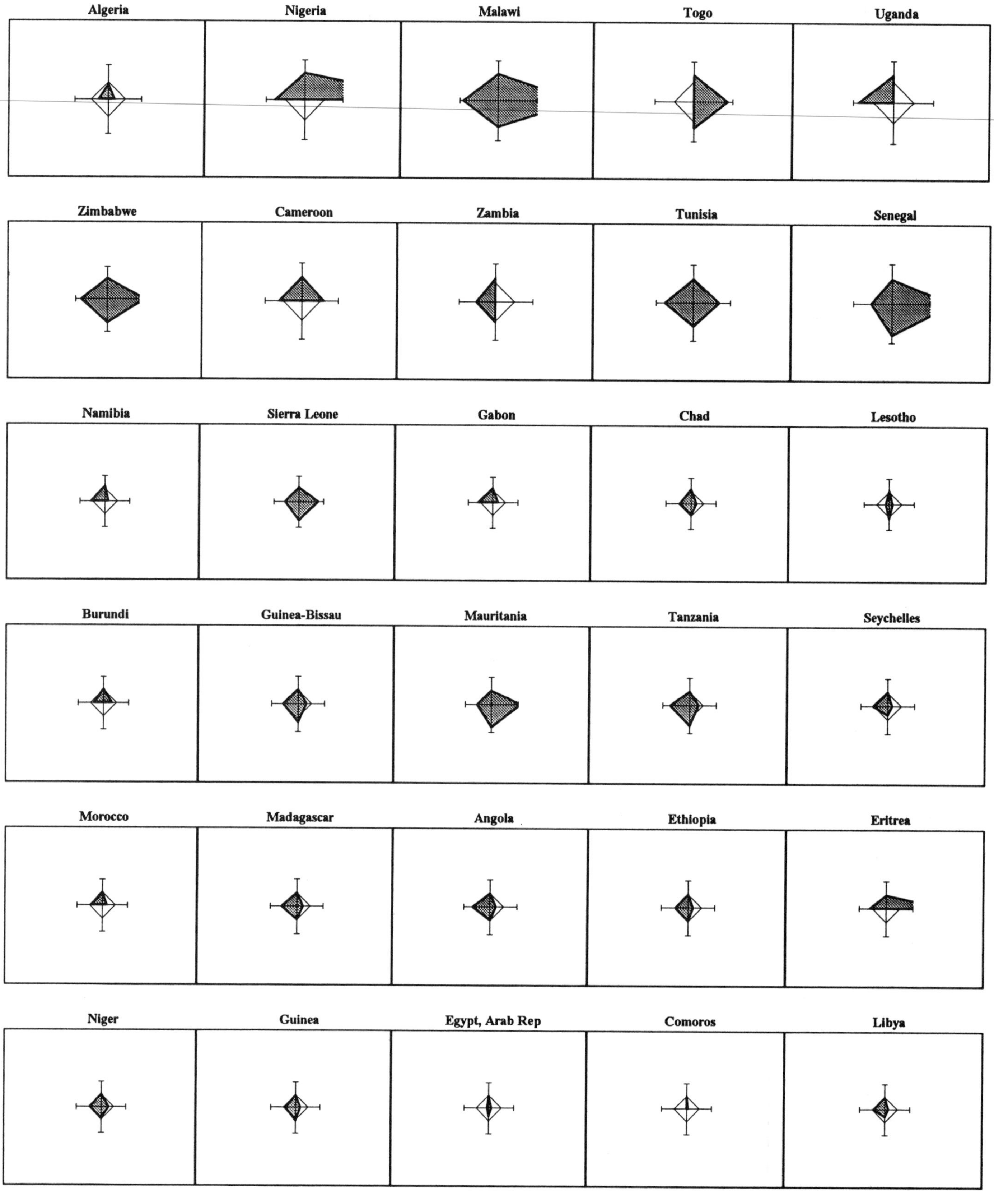

Algeria Nigeria Malawi Togo Uganda

Zimbabwe Cameroon Zambia Tunisia Senegal

Namibia Sierra Leone Gabon Chad Lesotho

Burundi Guinea-Bissau Mauritania Tanzania Seychelles

Morocco Madagascar Angola Ethiopia Eritrea

Niger Guinea Egypt, Arab Rep Comoros Libya

(Graph to be continued on the following page.)

Figure 1-1. (continued)

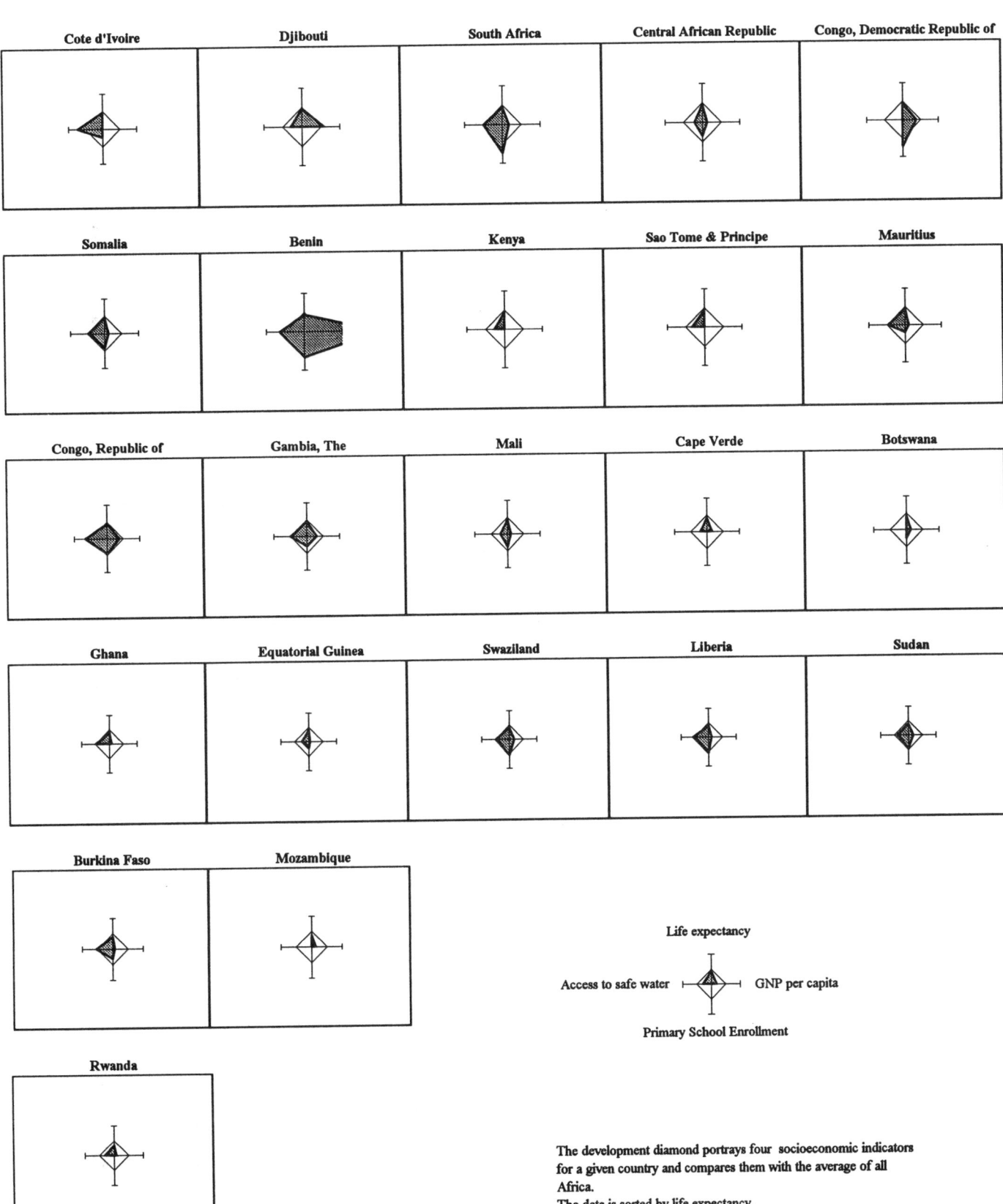

The development diamond portrays four socioeconomic indicators for a given country and compares them with the average of all Africa.
The data is sorted by life expectancy.

Figure 1-2.   Selected basic indicators, 1998*

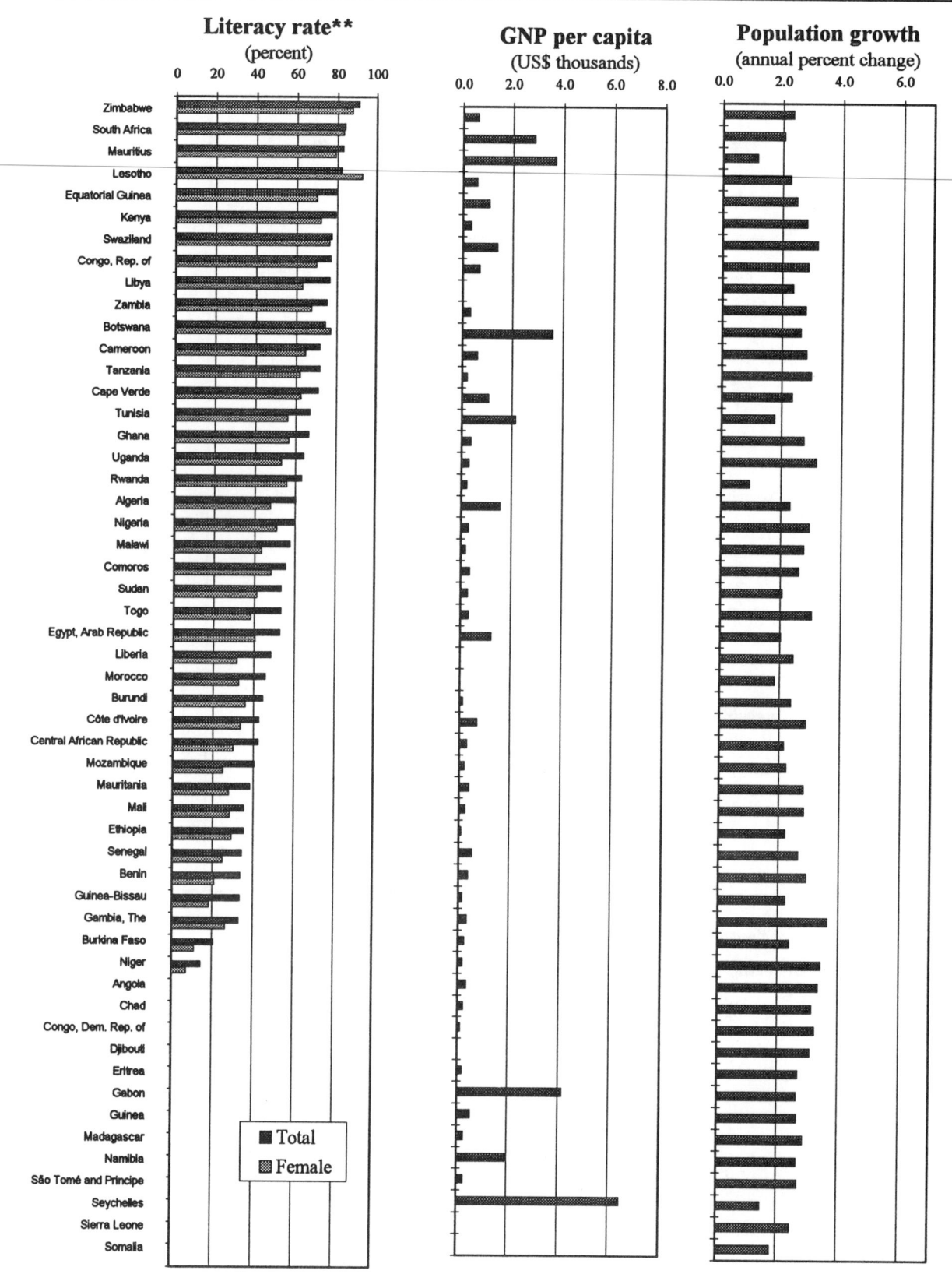

* Or most recent year available.
** Sorted by total literacy rate.

Technical Notes

Tables

Table 1-1. Basic indicators. The data for this table are from the World Bank's Economic and Social Database (BESD), except for official development assistance (ODA), which are from the OECD, Geographical Distribution of Financial Flows to Developing Countries database (see technical notes to Chapter 12). Regional aggregates for GNP per capita, life expectancy, and education are weighted by population.

Population estimates for mid-1998 are World Bank estimates. These are usually projections from the most recent population censuses or surveys (mostly from 1980–98). Refugees not permanently settled in the country of asylum are generally considered to be part of the population of their country of origin (see technical notes to Tables 13-1, 13-4, and 13-5).

Land area refers to the land surface area of a country, excluding inland waters.

GNP per capita figures in U.S. dollars are calculated according to the *World Bank Atlas* method described below. GNP measures the total domestic and foreign value added claimed by residents. It comprises GDP (defined in the note for Table 2-5) plus net factor income from abroad, which is the income residents receive from abroad for factor services (labor and capital) less similar payments made to nonresidents who contributed to the domestic economy. The data are from the Food and Agriculture Organization (FAO).

The *World Bank Atlas* method uses a three-year average of conversion factors to convert GNP data, expressed in different national currencies, to a common denomination, conventionally U.S. dollars. The *Atlas* conversion factor for any year is the average of the official exchange rate (Table 3-4) or alternative conversion factor (Table 3-6) for that year and for the two preceding years, after adjusting them for differences in relative inflation between that country and the United States. This three-year average smoothes fluctuations in prices and exchange rates for each country. The resulting GNP in U.S. dollars is divided by the midyear population for the latest of the three years to derive GNP per capita.

The following formulas describe the procedures for computing the conversion factor for year t:

$$e_{t-2,t}^* = \frac{1}{3}\left[e_{t-2}\left(\frac{P_t}{P_{t-2}}\bigg/\frac{P_t^\$}{P_{t-2}^\$}\right) + e_{t-1}\left(\frac{P_t}{P_{t-1}}\bigg/\frac{P_t^\$}{P_{t-1}^\$}\right) + e_t\right]$$

and for calculating per capita GNP in U.S. dollars for year t:

$$Y_t^\$ = (Y_t/N_t) + e_{t-2,t}^*$$

where Y_t = current GNP (local currency) for year t, P_t = GNP deflator for year t, e = average annual exchange rate or alternative conversion factor (local currency to the US dollar) for year t, N_t = midyear population for year t, and $P_t^\$$ = US GNP deflator for year t.

Growth rates of GNP per capita for this table are shown in real terms. They have been calculated by the least-squares method using constant GNP per capita series in 1995 prices in national currency (World Bank, BESD). See also technical notes for Table 2-19.

Life expectancy at birth indicates the number of years a newborn infant would live if prevailing patterns of mortality at the time of its birth were to remain the same throughout its life. Figures are World

Bank estimates based on data from the UN Population Division, the UN Statistical Office, and national statistical offices.

Primary school enrollment is the ratio of children of all ages enrolled in primary school to the population of children of primary school age. While many countries consider the primary school age to be 6 to 11 years, others use different age groups. These different country practices are also reflected in the ratios. Gross enrollment may be reported in excess of 100 percent if some pupils are younger or older than the country's standard range of primary school age. In practice, enrollment does not necessarily equal attendance, nor does it remain constant throughout the year. Data are from the United Nations Education, Scientific, and Cultural Organization (UNESCO).

Secondary school enrollment is the ratio of children of all ages enrolled in secondary schools to the population of children of secondary school age. The definition of secondary school age differs among countries. It is most commonly considered to be 12 to 17 years. Data are from UNESCO.

Total net ODA per capita consists of net disbursements of loans and grants from all official sources on concessional financial terms, divided by the midyear population for the corresponding year (see the technical notes to Chapter 12).

Table 1-2. Population. Average annual percentage growth shown in this table was calculated using the least-squares method.

Statistical background for the population estimates is available in the UN Population and Vital Statistics Report and the World Bank's *World Population Projections* (World Bank 1994–95) (see also the technical notes to Chapter 13).

Figures

The following indicators have been used to derive the figures in this chapter.

Figure 1-1. Life expectancy (Table 1-1); access to safe water (Table 13-10); GNP per capita (Table 2-19); primary school enrollment (Table 1-1).

Figure 1-2. Literacy rate (Table 13-13); GNP per capita (Table 2-19); population growth (Table 1-2).

Methodology used for regional aggregations and period averages in chapter 1

Table	Aggregations[a] (1)	(2)	(3)	(4)	(6)	Period averages[b] (2)	(3)
Table 1-1							
Column 1	x						
Column 2	x						
Column 3				x			
Column 4				x			x
Column 5					x		
Column 6					x		
Column 7					x		
Column 8					x		
Column 9					x		
Column 10		x					
Table 1-2	x					x	

Note: Regional aggregations are shown in the rows for Sub-Saharan Africa, North Africa, and All Africa. Period averages are shown in column 4 for Table 1-1 and in the last three columns for Table 1-2. This table shows only the methodologies used in this chapter.

a. Regional aggregations: (1) simple total; (2) simple total of the first indicator divided by the simple total of the second indicator (same country coverage); (3) simple total of the gap-filled indicator; (4) simple total of the gap-filled main indicator divided by the simple total of the gap-filled secondary indicator; (5) simple total of the first gap-filled main indicator less the simple total of the second gap-filled main indicator, all divided by the simple total of the secondary indicator; (6) weighted total (by population); (7) median; (8) no aggregation; (9) simple arithmetic mean.

b. Period averages: (1) arithmetic mean (using the same series as shown in the table, i.e., ratio if the rest of the table is shown as ratio, level if the rest of the table is shown as level, growth rate if the rest of the table is shown as growth rate); (2) least-squares growth rate (using main indicator); (3) least-squares growth rate (using main indicator in constant terms, with the rest of the table in current terms).

2

National Accounts

National accounts data provide the broadest picture of a nation's economic performance. National accounts provide information on the structure of production in the form of gross domestic product (GDP) and its components by industrial origin, GDP and its components by expenditure, and information on a nation's economic relations with the outside world. These are the key statistics for assessing a nation's economic condition at a given point in time or the trends in a nation's economic performance over time. Moreover, national accounts data provide a quantitative basis for forecasting and policymaking and as such are used widely both by analysts and policymakers.

GDP and its components by industrial origin are compiled following the widely used System of National Accounts (SNA). The SNA methodology accounts for virtually all activities pertinent to the production of goods and the provision of services in an economy by residents and nonresidents, regardless of the allocation to domestic and foreign claims. GDP does not account for the depreciation of fixed capital.

There are three methods of compiling GDP figures: income, expenditure, and production methods. Because of technical and resource constraints, the income method is not used in most developing countries. In this volume, GDP and its components by industrial origin are compiled using the production method. The three components of GDP by industrial origin are value added in agriculture, value added in industry, and value added in services. (See the technical notes at the end of this chapter.) The national accounts are constructed in national currencies and in current prices. Figures reported in this chapter are, however, in U.S. dollars, usually converted from national currency series at the official exchange rate. If the official exchange rate is significantly different from the prevailing market rate or shows extreme volatility, the local currency is converted into U.S. dollars by using an alternative conversion factor. The conversion factors used for this purpose are presented in Table 3-6. Reporting currencies in a common denominator facilitates cross-country comparisons and aggregations in country groups.

In addition, estimates of GDP and its components by industrial origin are converted into constant prices. Reporting figures in constant prices is essential for monitoring real changes in the structure of production and for analyzing relations among prices, production, employment, and so forth.

Constant price series in U.S. dollars use a 1995 base

year and are converted from national currency series using 1995 exchange rates. To establish a common base year for all countries, national accounts in national currencies at constant prices based on years other than 1995 have been partially rebased to 1995 by rescaling constant price series of components of GDP.

Using a single base year raises problems when there are profound structural changes or significant changes in relative prices. For example, values expressed in constant U.S. dollars necessarily reflect the exchange rates prevailing during the base year. Where subsequent exchange rate changes have been substantial, as they have for many African countries since 1980, comparisons among countries and aggregate trends will be affected. For this reason alone, the data should be used with considerable caution.

Monitoring resource allocations across sectors in any given point in time requires the use of current prices. Accordingly, in addition to GDP in constant prices, GDP in current prices is provided. Following GDP in current prices are components of GDP by expenditure. Data on consumption, investment, and savings are constructed using the SNA's convention. Conceptually, all income is either consumed or saved, and as such the sum of total consumption and gross domestic saving equals GDP.

When viewed from a production point of view, by definition savings equals investment. Investment measures additions to fixed assets of an economy, whether it represents additions to the stock of capital or merely replenishes depreciated capital stock, plus net changes in the level of inventories. It is financed either through domestic savings or by drawing on the savings of foreigners. Data on gross domestic investment and gross domestic savings thus shed light not only on the nature of the domestic inter-temporal resource allocation but also on the size of the resource gap. Gross national savings, however, indicates the amount of savings generated by the residents of a nation.

Although this volume includes a chapter on international trade, the fact that balance of payments is an integral part of the national accounts warrants the inclusion of the resource balance and its components in this chapter. Moreover, a closer examination of the fifth edition of the IMF's *Balance of Payments Manual* (1993) reflects differences in concepts, definitions, and classifications from the UN's SNA guidelines. For instance, in the SNA, factor services rendered by residents of another country are excluded from goods and services, but this practice is not universally followed. The tables on resource balance, and on values of exports (f.o.b.) and imports (c.i.f.) of goods and nonfactor services in current U.S. dollars provide a comprehensive and systematic framework for macroeconomic analysis in general. Those interested in a more specialized and rigorous study of international trade transactions should use the data provided in Chapter 5.

The rate of growth of real domestic product is an important indicator of economic progress and as such is widely monitored. Because these growth rates are calculated from national series, they are suitable for both cross-country comparisons and trend analysis for individual countries. Aggregate values and trends, however, reflect the choice of the base year, as explained above.

Gross national income per capita, which is GDP per capita adjusted for changes in international terms of trade and which include net factor income from abroad, and total consumption per capita are also widely monitored indicators of economic progress. When expressed in current U.S. dollars to facilitate comparison and aggregation, however, the values for these indicators necessarily reflect exchange rate fluctuations as well as underlying economic and demographic changes. These indicators may be used with caution for cross-country comparison during any single year. They require special attention when used for trend analysis.

Data for Chapter 2 are from the World Bank's country desks. Estimates are based on data obtained from national sources, usually collected by World Bank staff who review the quality of national accounts data and, in some instances, help adjust national series.

2-1. Gross domestic product, real

	Millions of U.S. dollars, constant 1995 prices											Average annual percentage growth		
	1980	1989	1990	1991	1992	1993	1994	1995	1996	1997	1998	75-84	85-89	90-MR
SUB-SAHARAN AFRICA	251,635	295,722	298,506	300,046	296,119	298,469	305,288	317,661	332,734	344,022	350,718	2.2	2.3	2.0
excluding South Africa	124,070	150,304	153,590	156,656	155,815	156,425	158,629	166,454	175,263	182,630	188,486	1.9	3.3	2.5
excl. S. Africa & Nigeria	100,786	127,363	128,728	130,592	128,971	128,981	131,164	138,315	145,919	152,232	157,550	2.5	3.0	2.4
Angola	..	6,172	6,155	6,196	5,878	4,481	4,544	5,059	5,644	6,075	5,844	..	4.7	-0.9
Benin	1,253	1,581	1,632	1,709	1,778	1,840	1,921	2,009	2,121	2,242	2,343	3.8	1.5	4.5
Botswana	1,542	3,771	4,043	4,346	4,476	4,565	4,729	4,969	5,314	5,686	6,027	11.5	10.6	4.9
Burkina Faso	1,444	2,033	2,002	2,201	2,256	2,238	2,265	2,355	2,496	2,614	2,776	3.6	4.4	3.4
Burundi	720	1,076	1,114	1,169	1,177	1,110	1,076	1,000	914	918	959	3.8	5.1	-2.5
Cameroon	6,319	9,335	8,765	8,431	8,170	7,908	7,711	7,965	8,364	8,790	9,233	8.5	-0.1	-0.1
Cape Verde	..	351	354	359	371	386	401	420	438	451	469	..	5.1	3.5
Central African Republic	964	1,092	1,069	1,063	994	998	1,047	1,122	1,076	1,132	1,185	0.4	0.7	1.0
Chad	787	1,168	1,073	1,278	1,404	1,294	1,426	1,441	1,494	1,555	1,681	-1.9	4.9	4.2
Comoros	167	212	223	211	229	236	223	215	214	214	216	..	1.3	-0.2
Congo, Democratic Rep. of	8,458	9,883	9,234	8,457	7,569	6,549	6,294	6,338	6,281	5,923	6,101	-0.3	1.7	-5.6
Congo, Republic of	1,294	2,052	2,070	2,120	2,175	2,153	2,035	2,116	2,250	2,207	2,295	9.2	-1.0	1.0
Côte d'Ivoire	8,566	9,299	9,198	9,201	9,179	9,163	9,343	9,992	10,681	11,317	11,957	2.2	2.0	2.9
Djibouti	..	..	..	550	548	527	511	491	466	468	471	..	..	-2.7
Equatorial Guinea	..	114	117	116	128	137	144	164	212	373	..	..	1.4	13.0
Eritrea	..	..	..	..	521	508	558	574	612	661	681	..	..	5.2
Ethiopia	..	5,012	5,134	4,893	4,636	5,256	5,446	5,779	6,410	6,787	6,716	..	2.9	4.1
Gabon	3,566	4,054	4,264	4,525	4,378	4,482	4,636	4,959	5,147	5,358	5,465	-0.2	-1.4	3.3
Gambia, The	241	332	344	355	367	378	379	382	390	410	429	4.3	3.3	2.5
Ghana	4,233	5,070	5,238	5,515	5,729	6,014	6,211	6,461	6,758	7,042	7,362	-1.1	5.2	4.2
Guinea	..	2,801	2,908	2,986	3,113	3,249	3,517	3,672	3,840	4,023	4,207	..	4.0	4.8
Guinea-Bissau	134	205	217	228	231	236	243	254	266	281	202	2.1	3.1	1.7
Kenya	5,612	8,024	8,360	8,481	8,413	8,443	8,665	9,047	9,422	9,619	9,791	4.7	5.9	2.2
Lesotho	419	613	638	642	665	691	781	852	960	1,037	1,000	4.5	7.8	6.7
Liberia	..	..	..	..	..	..	..	..	..	..	..	..	..	..
Madagascar	3,048	3,115	3,212	3,009	3,045	3,109	3,108	3,160	3,228	3,343	3,473	-0.2	2.3	1.0
Malawi	1,035	1,218	1,287	1,400	1,297	1,423	1,277	1,465	1,621	1,703	1,755	3.2	1.9	3.9
Mali	1,987	2,148	2,108	2,142	2,321	2,271	2,319	2,468	2,559	2,729	2,827	2.3	0.8	3.3
Mauritania	865	904	888	911	926	977	1,022	1,068	1,118	1,169	1,210	1.6	0.1	3.7
Mauritius	1,738	2,910	3,119	3,251	3,453	3,641	3,789	3,967	4,183	4,393	4,628	3.6	7.7	5.2
Mozambique	2,006	2,016	2,036	2,136	1,963	2,134	2,294	2,392	2,562	2,852	3,194	..	6.0	5.0
Namibia	2,456	2,663	2,630	2,903	3,085	3,024	3,227	3,336	3,434	3,494	3,546	..	2.3	3.5
Niger	1,833	1,837	1,813	1,859	1,738	1,762	1,833	1,881	1,946	2,010	2,179	2.0	4.2	1.7
Nigeria	22,357	22,980	24,864	26,046	26,806	27,396	27,423	28,109	29,318	30,373	30,920	-0.7	5.0	3.0
Rwanda	1,655	2,073	2,024	1,973	2,089	1,919	969	1,326	1,486	1,648	1,813	6.8	3.5	-3.6
São Tomé and Principe	..	43	42	43	43	44	45	45	46	47	48	..	3.5	1.3
Senegal	3,084	4,031	4,188	4,171	4,263	4,169	4,289	4,493	4,744	4,989	5,272	2.1	3.5	2.7
Seychelles	314	404	441	453	485	515	511	508	532	555	568	3.6	5.2	3.5
Sierra Leone	1,035	1,100	1,118	1,028	929	930	962	866	909	726	731	2.0	0.8	-4.4
Somalia	..	..	..	..	..	..	..	..	..	..	..	..	..	..
South Africa	127,413	145,228	144,766	143,292	140,230	141,959	146,550	151,117	157,391	161,331	162,212	2.4	1.4	1.5
Sudan	4,271	4,784	4,763	5,049	5,298	5,525	5,748	7,194	7,482	7,983	8,383	2.6	0.9	7.3
Swaziland	591	1,022	1,113	1,141	1,155	1,193	1,234	1,267	1,317	1,366	1,393	3.3	9.9	3.2
Tanzania	..	4,234	4,464	4,664	4,249	4,768	4,834	4,958	5,160	5,367	5,552	..	..	2.9
Togo	1,186	1,320	1,317	1,308	1,256	1,050	1,226	1,309	1,437	1,499	1,484	2.1	3.4	1.7
Uganda	..	3,853	4,102	4,330	4,478	4,851	5,161	5,756	6,278	6,576	6,944	..	3.4	7.1
Zambia	3,160	3,521	3,505	3,503	3,442	3,677	3,550	3,470	3,695	3,822	3,746	0.2	2.3	0.9
Zimbabwe	4,490	6,458	6,909	7,291	6,632	6,721	7,180	7,134	7,654	7,901	8,028	3.0	4.2	2.1
NORTH AFRICA	106,005	151,470	156,519	159,729	162,848	163,594	169,919	172,459	183,626	188,475	197,493	6.2	3.0	2.8
Algeria	31,582	41,504	40,964	40,473	41,120	40,216	39,746	41,256	42,824	43,381	45,536	5.5	0.8	0.9
Egypt, Arab Republic	29,370	47,321	50,019	50,558	52,800	54,321	56,466	59,100	62,061	65,469	68,743	8.3	4.1	4.1
Libya	..	..	..	..	..	..	..	..	..	..	..	..	..	..
Morocco	21,590	30,315	31,492	33,680	32,323	31,996	35,310	32,986	36,986	36,232	37,681	4.7	4.8	2.2
Tunisia	10,475	13,772	14,867	15,448	16,653	17,018	17,579	17,987	19,259	20,302	21,337	5.3	2.4	4.6
ALL AFRICA	360,137	448,895	456,478	461,060	459,848	462,992	475,961	491,234	517,302	533,574	548,909	3.3	2.5	2.3

Note: 1998 data are preliminary (see page 3).

2-2. Value added in agriculture

	Millions of U.S. dollars, constant 1995 prices											Average annual percentage growth		
	1980	1989	1990	1991	1992	1993	1994	1995	1996	1997	1998	75-84	85-89	90-MR
SUB-SAHARAN AFRICA	41,033	49,845	50,181	51,483	48,761	51,177	51,804	52,781	56,775	58,471	59,630	0.7	4.3	2.1
excluding South Africa	35,292	42,428	43,350	44,333	43,722	44,795	44,871	47,391	49,970	51,484	52,754	0.7	3.7	2.5
excl. S. Africa & Nigeria	..	35,200	35,780	36,474	35,642	36,624	36,463	38,711	40,960	42,070	43,219	..	3.0	2.3
Angola	..	732	730	721	524	279	307	388	447	490	505	..	0.5	-5.5
Benin	361	532	534	581	601	617	673	684	732	774	826	3.0	4.6	5.1
Botswana	161	199	206	210	212	209	203	198	198	207	220	-3.8	13.2	0.2
Burkina Faso	458	636	594	717	725	735	733	754	810	800	844	1.0	4.6	3.3
Burundi	358	468	494	505	520	499	448	421	427	429	450	2.0	4.1	-1.8
Cameroon	2,131	2,729	2,701	2,593	2,749	2,782	2,868	3,119	3,350	3,603	3,847	4.5	0.6	4.2
Cape Verde	..	59	54	39	38	37	30	31	31	33	35	..	..	-5.9
Central African Republic	408	455	454	465	470	482	487	516	538	573	597	0.6	1.1	3.1
Chad	319	398	336	451	520	406	515	505	519	558	583	-1.0	5.1	4.9
Comoros	58	82	86	86	86	88	84	83	83	83	84	..	3.7	-0.2
Congo, Democratic Rep. of	2,332	2,922	2,998	3,082	3,178	3,238	3,211	3,584	3,659	3,623	3,688	1.7	2.5	2.8
Congo, Republic of	159	220	224	205	219	200	207	221	232	234	242	3.4	4.8	1.1
Côte d'Ivoire	2,365	2,434	2,550	2,587	2,627	2,629	2,639	2,880	2,930	3,059	2,993	2.7	3.0	2.5
Djibouti	..	..	..	..	..	..	..	..	..	..	..	..	..	..
Equatorial Guinea	..	70	70	66	64	64	73	83	95	115	..	..	0.1	6.0
Eritrea	..	..	..	..	..	..	..	..	..	..	..	..	..	..
Ethiopia	..	..	..	..	..	..	..	..	..	..	..	..	..	..
Gabon	431	463	460	464	461	455	448	398	397	417	395	..	0.8	-2.0
Gambia, The	95	100	97	98	96	91	97	99	96	98	102	3.0	-2.4	0.2
Ghana	1,132	1,195	1,171	1,239	1,224	1,252	1,275	1,323	1,392	1,452	1,529	0.2	2.3	2.8
Guinea	..	600	621	643	667	700	736	761	795	836	878	..	4.1	4.3
Guinea-Bissau	59	101	104	109	110	117	123	132	141	151	125	-2.6	3.4	4.0
Kenya	1,660	2,297	2,377	2,360	2,281	2,207	2,275	2,384	2,490	2,520	2,560	4.1	4.4	1.1
Lesotho	95	116	108	74	69	88	101	81	125	126	132	-5.1	6.4	3.4
Liberia	..	..	..	..	..	..	..	..	..	..	..	..	..	..
Madagascar	729	882	900	905	920	950	946	963	987	1,006	1,005	0.2	2.8	1.5
Malawi	272	313	312	352	264	404	285	394	532	553	568	2.2	1.2	7.7
Mali	765	935	924	874	1,007	921	991	1,080	1,093	1,124	1,142	3.2	8.9	2.8
Mauritania	160	203	190	204	209	228	238	250	252	265	281	2.9	4.5	4.3
Mauritius	230	314	345	338	360	336	311	337	351	364	406	-2.5	1.3	1.6
Mozambique	..	789	798	766	626	760	710	833	923	994	1,064	..	7.3	3.7
Namibia	224	249	277	304	285	299	346	354	372	343	326	..	3.2	3.5
Niger	577	666	646	728	673	678	747	756	757	763	901	1.1	5.4	2.8
Nigeria	6,432	7,434	7,748	8,022	8,187	8,298	8,498	8,809	9,169	9,556	9,699	-3.0	6.4	2.9
Rwanda	749	803	782	828	871	740	437	484	543	585	638	5.6	1.1	-5.0
São Tomé and Principe	..	20	22	19	19	16	12	12	12	12	13	..	19.3	-7.0
Senegal	661	798	873	829	843	799	873	881	947	926	910	-1.2	4.5	1.5
Seychelles	28	23	27	26	22	20	22	21	21	22	22	-2.8	-2.5	-1.9
Sierra Leone	317	424	419	394	333	335	356	363	444	444	405	7.9	0.9	0.6
Somalia	..	..	..	..	..	..	..	..	..	..	..	..	..	..
South Africa	5,448	7,047	6,544	6,836	4,973	6,167	6,652	5,326	6,603	6,781	6,701	0.2	7.6	-0.1
Sudan	..	..	..	..	..	..	..	..	..	..	..	..	..	..
Swaziland	161	204	197	209	168	158	165	157	194	182	187	-1.4	2.5	-1.1
Tanzania	..	1,737	1,818	1,900	1,739	1,987	2,039	2,120	2,222	2,292	2,355	..	..	3.6
Togo	285	429	442	437	442	469	468	494	575	601	585	2.8	4.3	4.1
Uganda	..	2,065	2,173	2,235	2,213	2,419	2,462	2,607	2,718	2,748	2,800	..	2.7	3.6
Zambia	580	811	738	777	520	874	423	564	560	531	499	0.5	5.6	-5.2
Zimbabwe	685	875	981	991	761	968	1,039	960	1,162	1,141	1,177	-0.1	1.2	3.3
NORTH AFRICA	16,193	22,268	22,272	25,025	21,994	21,617	24,690	21,309	27,093	24,529	26,921	2.3	5.4	1.7
Algeria	2,584	3,803	3,450	3,982	4,066	3,887	3,456	3,974	4,821	4,165	4,483	3.6	7.2	2.2
Egypt, Arab Republic	6,302	8,040	8,263	8,465	8,631	8,846	9,185	9,451	9,742	10,076	10,252	2.8	2.7	2.8
Libya	..	..	..	..	..	..	..	..	..	..	..	..	..	..
Morocco	5,032	7,665	7,282	8,862	5,588	5,328	8,599	4,820	8,587	6,387	8,047	1.3	10.0	-0.4
Tunisia	1,504	1,700	2,215	2,524	2,661	2,527	2,275	2,049	2,654	2,733	2,856	1.2	-1.2	3.4
ALL AFRICA	57,136	72,297	72,629	76,817	70,947	72,910	76,775	74,151	84,179	83,122	86,791	1.2	4.7	2.0

Note: 1998 data are preliminary (see page 3).

2-3. Value added in industry

	Millions of U.S. dollars, constant 1995 prices											Average annual percentage growth		
	1980	1989	1990	1991	1992	1993	1994	1995	1996	1997	1998	75-84	85-89	90-MR
SUB-SAHARAN AFRICA	82,964	93,389	93,511	92,353	90,790	89,674	90,911	93,575	96,764	100,149	101,421	2.3	1.7	1.0
excluding South Africa	39,086	44,794	45,582	46,173	45,640	44,449	44,521	45,444	47,992	50,246	52,048	1.8	2.9	1.4
excl. S. Africa & Nigeria	24,480	33,493	33,517	32,992	32,397	31,283	31,751	32,520	34,504	36,365	38,234	..	3.3	1.2
Angola	..	3,282	3,257	3,323	3,284	2,729	3,049	3,339	3,741	4,043	4,251	..	8.1	2.8
Benin	134	219	237	248	269	272	285	293	306	320	322	5.4	-1.9	4.3
Botswana	760	2,006	2,070	2,171	2,151	2,139	2,179	2,266	2,419	2,540	2,690	15.9	8.3	2.9
Burkina Faso	415	559	548	550	577	566	579	581	600	663	735	1.6	4.8	2.6
Burundi	142	214	230	251	259	217	203	168	146	145	147	8.9	3.7	-6.3
Cameroon	1,478	2,976	2,773	2,590	2,321	2,221	1,901	1,855	1,939	2,088	2,248	18.2	0.7	-4.0
Cape Verde	..	74	78	84	89	71	77	81	83	88	91	..	..	1.5
Central African Republic	191	206	205	201	190	192	217	227	201	194	201	1.4	0.6	0.0
Chad	88	224	241	209	206	181	174	208	213	239	274	-2.0	2.5	1.1
Comoros	25	19	20	19	28	31	30	27	27	27	28	..	-9.0	4.6
Congo, Democratic Rep. of	2,768	3,128	2,536	2,032	1,424	1,218	1,192	1,069	1,069	1,022	..	-2.0	0.3	-13.3
Congo, Republic of	483	837	874	870	894	929	901	949	965	849	878	11.5	-0.3	0.5
Côte d'Ivoire	1,406	1,942	1,805	1,821	1,878	1,891	1,909	1,999	2,252	2,461	2,747	6.5	6.5	4.1
Djibouti	..	..	..	..	..	..	..	..	..	..	..	..	..	..
Equatorial Guinea	..	13	15	17	29	35	35	44	84	237	..	..	6.4	37.2
Eritrea	..	..	..	..	..	..	..	..	..	..	..	..	..	..
Ethiopia	..	..	..	..	..	..	..	..	..	..	..	..	..	..
Gabon	1,859	2,069	2,410	2,215	2,173	2,264	2,469	2,597	2,655	2,679	2,714	..	-1.7	2.9
Gambia, The	31	43	45	46	47	48	46	44	46	47	48	3.1	10.6	0.6
Ghana	596	620	663	687	730	769	796	829	868	923	947	-7.5	9.1	4.8
Guinea	..	1,154	1,187	1,200	1,207	1,246	1,286	1,169	1,271	1,327	1,388	..	3.3	1.6
Guinea-Bissau	18	23	26	26	26	28	28	29	30	30	16	3.2	-3.5	-0.7
Kenya	769	1,081	1,132	1,161	1,160	1,162	1,184	1,226	1,268	1,294	1,311	4.7	5.2	2.0
Lesotho	84	149	162	175	190	190	236	279	312	315	276	13.4	14.1	9.2
Liberia	..	..	..	..	..	..	..	..	..	..	..	..	..	..
Madagascar	455	395	393	391	387	400	396	402	410	427	446	-2.9	2.8	1.2
Malawi	181	224	245	254	260	241	247	255	264	267	281	2.7	3.7	1.7
Mali	199	278	297	335	352	365	369	398	432	526	565	1.6	1.4	7.6
Mauritania	168	254	237	238	235	272	280	297	297	295	291	0.6	3.7	2.8
Mauritius	361	814	882	932	997	1,052	1,106	1,154	1,222	1,281	1,347	3.6	13.0	5.6
Mozambique	..	406	369	381	359	352	373	425	483	599	736	..	-4.5	6.6
Namibia	910	799	718	836	915	816	890	932	948	980	992	..	1.6	3.0
Niger	368	320	331	328	310	315	317	325	347	361	370	10.4	-4.1	1.4
Nigeria	13,605	11,492	12,217	13,265	13,309	13,210	12,845	13,009	13,591	14,005	14,005	0.0	2.1	1.7
Rwanda	363	438	448	346	395	347	173	288	334	389	427	7.4	0.3	-1.8
São Tomé and Principe	..	5	7	7	8	8	9	9	8	9	7	..	7.4	3.9
Senegal	551	823	870	859	902	880	876	961	1,031	1,099	1,196	3.7	4.9	3.8
Seychelles	49	65	72	85	81	91	94	115	126	153	156	2.0	3.4	10.3
Sierra Leone	245	249	320	238	243	238	241	193	235	134	156	-3.1	2.2	-6.5
Somalia	..	..	..	..	..	..	..	..	..	..	..	..	..	..
South Africa	43,795	48,462	47,833	46,144	45,128	45,170	46,307	48,026	48,714	49,873	49,431	2.6	0.7	0.6
Sudan	..	..	..	..	..	..	..	..	..	..	..	..	..	..
Swaziland	128	307	360	356	377	387	408	428	437	464	477	4.4	23.3	4.4
Tanzania	..	621	659	700	634	687	679	678	694	740	790	..	..	1.9
Togo	277	285	273	292	270	190	241	290	306	313	322	1.5	6.2	1.7
Uganda	..	412	437	472	512	555	627	754	879	979	1,092	..	6.4	12.1
Zambia	1,358	1,476	1,518	1,482	1,639	1,496	1,274	1,096	1,098	1,194	1,143	-1.0	2.6	-4.1
Zimbabwe	1,502	2,001	2,085	2,117	1,990	1,875	2,024	1,829	1,899	1,933	1,973	-1.0	5.4	-0.8
NORTH AFRICA	38,633	52,327	54,274	55,790	56,721	56,305	57,673	60,107	60,574	61,871	64,796	6.4	2.0	2.1
Algeria	12,858	16,105	16,063	16,332	16,333	15,590	15,273	15,688	14,464	13,683	14,469	5.3	-0.4	-1.7
Egypt, Arab Republic	9,157	14,267	15,038	15,835	16,073	16,431	17,327	18,195	19,089	19,967	20,909	11.0	4.2	4.2
Libya	..	..	..	..	..	..	..	..	..	..	..	..	..	..
Morocco	7,170	9,025	9,826	9,884	10,118	10,015	10,415	10,882	11,407	12,088	12,536	3.6	3.1	3.3
Tunisia	2,945	4,121	4,211	4,348	4,650	4,791	4,949	5,224	5,418	5,718	5,975	7.1	2.6	4.3
ALL AFRICA	122,620	146,384	148,275	148,421	147,606	146,046	148,596	153,624	157,427	162,191	166,203	3.5	1.8	1.3

Note: 1998 data are preliminary (see page 3).

2-4. Value added in services

	Millions of U.S. dollars, constant 1995 prices											Average annual percentage growth		
	1980	1989	1990	1991	1992	1993	1994	1995	1996	1997	1998	75-84	85-89	90-MR
SUB-SAHARAN AFRICA	109,172	138,644	140,531	141,879	142,273	142,361	146,173	152,470	159,490	164,420	168,139	3.1	2.5	2.2
excluding South Africa	46,907	60,155	61,610	62,869	63,413	62,879	64,381	67,003	70,343	73,191	75,593	2.8	3.2	2.5
excl. S. Africa & Nigeria	43,551	55,984	56,700	57,859	58,000	57,113	58,607	61,111	64,195	66,843	68,886	2.9	2.8	2.3
Angola	..	1,984	1,992	1,984	1,942	1,426	1,200	1,332	1,459	1,549	1,170	..	2.3	-5.5
Benin	783	833	867	881	907	953	958	1,033	1,080	1,148	1,192	3.8	0.4	4.1
Botswana	618	1,557	1,761	1,959	2,111	2,215	2,346	2,504	2,698	2,941	3,120	10.8	13.8	7.6
Burkina Faso	493	769	795	834	863	846	859	876	934	1,008	1,053	8.9	4.0	3.2
Burundi	166	272	303	310	315	308	298	285	252	253	258	6.2	4.1	-1.9
Cameroon	2,621	3,492	3,194	3,143	3,036	2,872	2,915	2,991	3,093	3,147	3,212	6.7	-0.9	-0.6
Cape Verde	..	215	218	231	239	279	294	308	324	329	343	..	..	6.0
Central African Republic	335	389	360	337	280	269	289	320	276	296	315	0.3	1.0	-2.3
Chad	391	748	731	752	777	693	714	696	716	743	770	-0.5	6.8	-0.1
Comoros	85	111	117	105	115	117	109	104	103	103	104	..	2.0	-1.2
Congo, Democratic Rep. of	3,690	4,195	3,957	3,512	3,031	2,131	1,926	1,685	1,551	1,274	..	-0.5	2.1	-14.6
Congo, Republic of	644	988	968	1,042	1,059	1,026	926	945	1,051	1,115	1,166	9.3	-2.7	1.3
Côte d'Ivoire	4,859	4,989	4,876	4,815	4,675	4,640	4,807	5,113	5,531	5,836	6,314	1.0	-0.2	2.7
Djibouti	..	..	..	..	..	..	..	..	..	..	..	..	..	..
Equatorial Guinea	..	23	24	26	30	32	32	34	38	51	..	..	6.5	8.9
Eritrea	..	..	..	..	..	..	..	..	..	..	..	..	..	..
Ethiopia	..	..	..	..	..	..	..	..	..	..	..	..	..	..
Gabon	1,327	1,560	1,476	1,849	1,757	1,779	1,756	1,964	2,080	2,230	2,308	..	-1.7	4.5
Gambia, The	117	149	160	159	170	190	186	188	198	212	220	4.7	1.9	4.3
Ghana	1,936	2,962	3,214	3,385	3,678	3,953	4,133	4,309	4,480	4,632	4,842	0.1	7.8	5.5
Guinea	..	1,102	1,156	1,196	1,286	1,348	1,530	1,742	1,784	1,870	1,952	..	4.5	7.2
Guinea-Bissau	54	80	86	92	93	90	91	93	96	102	67	10.0	5.7	-0.1
Kenya	2,112	3,263	3,409	3,531	3,635	3,714	3,842	4,046	4,256	4,387	4,478	5.9	5.6	3.6
Lesotho	171	249	268	278	289	303	325	355	377	402	422	5.5	6.3	6.1
Liberia	..	..	..	..	..	..	..	..	..	..	..	..	..	..
Madagascar	1,605	1,540	1,602	1,489	1,506	1,539	1,547	1,571	1,604	1,678	1,763	0.1	1.8	1.2
Malawi	463	592	631	668	673	638	630	647	613	666	669	3.3	3.7	0.6
Mali	694	837	831	826	851	879	857	871	921	956	992	1.6	0.0	1.9
Mauritania	353	352	365	371	382	373	387	400	439	486	512	2.1	3.6	4.0
Mauritius	878	1,383	1,467	1,540	1,639	1,750	1,882	1,994	2,112	2,225	2,127	5.4	7.4	5.6
Mozambique	..	664	705	822	796	801	1,025	939	958	1,026	1,126	..	10.0	5.5
Namibia	1,060	1,300	1,319	1,418	1,500	1,508	1,564	1,609	1,691	1,733	1,791	..	0.7	3.7
Niger	889	851	837	803	754	769	769	800	842	886	908	-0.1	7.6	0.9
Nigeria	3,488	4,450	5,117	5,222	5,580	5,884	5,910	6,049	6,317	6,530	6,873	1.5	7.6	4.2
Rwanda	405	770	743	768	781	801	338	527	581	638	710	11.2	6.7	-3.1
São Tomé and Principe	..	22	18	20	20	22	24	25	26	26	28	..	-2.3	4.0
Senegal	1,858	2,405	2,442	2,479	2,517	2,488	2,535	2,651	2,768	2,968	3,175	3.1	2.8	2.8
Seychelles	241	318	343	344	382	403	395	372	384	380	390	-1.1	6.1	1.8
Sierra Leone	382	369	337	327	291	287	291	248	313	241	263	2.5	-3.3	-3.6
Somalia	..	..	..	..	..	..	..	..	..	..	..	..	..	..
South Africa	61,528	77,615	78,106	78,261	78,149	78,707	80,977	84,600	88,269	90,397	91,792	3.2	2.0	2.1
Sudan	..	..	..	..	..	..	..	..	..	..	..	..	..	..
Swaziland	187	319	340	357	370	390	396	409	412	425	453	5.7	4.3	3.5
Tanzania	..	1,587	1,640	1,699	1,567	1,772	1,763	1,790	1,847	1,909	1,954	..	..	2.3
Togo	635	611	608	583	547	389	519	524	554	585	576	2.0	1.5	-0.5
Uganda	..	1,191	1,268	1,367	1,467	1,571	1,693	1,917	2,082	2,200	2,345	..	3.2	8.2
Zambia	1,215	1,202	1,227	1,216	1,296	1,267	1,880	1,811	2,043	2,111	2,120	1.5	-0.1	8.1
Zimbabwe	2,088	2,817	3,032	3,185	3,200	3,220	3,324	3,518	3,687	3,809	3,792	5.4	3.7	3.3
NORTH AFRICA	41,889	65,206	67,620	69,331	72,332	73,292	75,642	78,109	82,961	88,133	92,582	7.6	3.5	3.8
Algeria	9,079	13,094	12,975	12,874	13,316	13,155	13,478	13,771	15,613	17,371	19,210	5.7	1.8	4.1
Egypt, Arab Republic	12,046	22,273	23,389	24,086	24,607	25,268	26,018	27,328	28,849	30,682	32,374	11.0	4.3	4.0
Libya	..	..	..	..	..	..	..	..	..	..	..	..	..	..
Morocco	9,925	14,388	15,053	15,857	16,777	16,754	17,075	17,285	17,768	18,086	17,831	6.7	4.0	2.4
Tunisia	6,006	7,928	8,402	8,516	9,287	9,659	10,344	10,714	11,159	11,827	12,486	5.7	3.2	5.2
ALL AFRICA	151,761	204,552	208,800	211,821	215,099	216,110	222,269	231,085	242,928	252,936	261,024	4.3	2.8	2.7

Note: 1998 data are preliminary (see page 3).

2-5. Gross domestic product, nominal

	Millions of U.S. dollars, current prices											Annual average		
	1980	*1989*	*1990*	*1991*	*1992*	*1993*	*1994*	*1995*	*1996*	*1997*	*1998*	*75-84*	*85-89*	*90-MR*
SUB-SAHARAN AFRICA	264,428	270,041	296,979	302,717	304,433	288,004	281,391	317,661	329,943	344,712	333,328	199,908	240,127	311,019
excluding South Africa	185,439	174,549	185,410	182,796	174,044	157,580	145,459	166,454	187,043	197,261	200,201	140,050	161,357	177,361
excl. S.Africa & Nigeria	114,501	150,793	156,979	155,540	141,238	136,300	121,786	138,315	151,638	157,243	158,662	94,732	137,602	146,411
Angola	..	9,298	10,268	12,197	5,780	5,286	4,060	5,059	7,618	7,482	6,648	..	7,572	7,155
Benin	1,405	1,502	1,845	1,878	1,624	2,106	1,497	2,009	2,208	2,141	2,306	1,035	1,413	1,957
Botswana	1,105	3,108	3,630	4,177	4,145	4,544	4,591	4,969	5,507	5,343	5,690	905	2,168	4,733
Burkina Faso	1,709	2,363	2,765	2,788	1,996	2,049	1,854	2,355	2,538	2,382	2,581	1,311	2,038	2,367
Burundi	920	1,114	1,132	1,167	1,086	975	923	1,000	900	957	949	778	1,136	1,010
Cameroon	6,741	11,140	11,152	12,434	11,396	11,891	7,854	7,965	9,109	9,115	8,736	5,630	10,942	9,961
Cape Verde	..	268	305	319	358	331	347	420	425	426	453	..	257	376
Central African Republic	797	1,269	1,488	1,404	1,434	1,299	853	1,122	1,070	1,004	1,057	619	1,150	1,192
Chad	1,033	1,342	1,609	1,774	1,781	1,384	1,179	1,441	1,637	1,603	1,740	921	1,167	1,572
Comoros	124	199	250	247	266	264	186	215	213	194	196	113	176	226
Congo, Democratic Rep. of	..	9,020	9,348	9,086	8,206	8,975	7,158	6,338	5,869	6,101	6,964	7,884	8,163	7,561
Congo, Republic of	1,706	2,390	2,799	2,725	2,933	1,919	1,769	2,116	2,526	2,304	1,961	1,452	2,182	2,339
Côte d'Ivoire	10,175	9,757	10,796	10,493	11,153	10,405	7,666	9,992	10,700	10,251	11,041	7,172	9,247	10,278
Djibouti	..	401	425	456	470	471	487	491	485	500	..	..	376	473
Equatorial Guinea	..	112	132	131	154	152	126	164	259	498	456	104	107	230
Eritrea	..	..	..	..	437	409	510	574	631	655	650	..	..	552
Ethiopia	..	7,988	6,842	5,321	5,568	6,249	4,894	5,779	6,010	6,381	6,544	5,603	7,356	5,954
Gabon	4,279	4,186	5,952	5,403	5,592	4,381	4,191	4,959	5,781	5,152	5,518	3,211	3,609	5,214
Gambia, The	241	284	317	317	347	366	363	382	392	407	424	181	236	368
Ghana	4,445	5,249	5,886	6,600	6,413	5,966	5,440	6,461	6,927	6,884	7,501	3,762	5,150	6,453
Guinea	..	2,432	2,818	3,015	3,285	3,279	3,435	3,672	3,959	3,918	3,615	..	2,230	3,444
Guinea-Bissau	111	213	244	257	226	237	236	254	271	269	206	131	165	244
Kenya	7,265	8,341	8,533	8,043	8,002	4,977	7,148	9,047	9,220	10,572	11,579	5,550	7,641	8,569
Lesotho	369	512	622	585	661	701	759	852	860	950	792	279	371	754
Liberia	1,117	1,202	..	..	..	..	..	..	..	..	..	987	1,143	..
Madagascar	4,042	2,498	3,081	2,677	3,001	3,371	2,977	3,160	3,995	3,546	3,749	3,057	2,724	3,284
Malawi	1,238	1,522	1,803	2,204	1,800	2,071	1,173	1,465	2,270	2,519	1,688	1,018	1,266	1,888
Mali	1,787	2,008	2,421	2,423	2,846	2,672	1,854	2,468	2,654	2,509	2,694	1,285	1,776	2,505
Mauritania	814	1,085	1,135	1,130	1,191	944	1,027	1,068	1,094	1,098	989	740	972	1,075
Mauritius	1,132	2,182	2,642	2,831	3,189	3,195	3,503	3,967	4,299	4,173	4,202	990	1,747	3,556
Mozambique	3,526	2,314	2,512	2,496	1,955	2,103	2,267	2,392	2,842	3,438	3,893	3,457	3,293	2,655
Namibia	2,262	2,253	2,444	2,578	2,931	2,730	3,075	3,336	3,189	3,280	3,108	2,002	1,900	2,963
Niger	2,509	2,180	2,481	2,327	2,345	1,606	1,564	1,881	1,990	1,854	2,048	1,725	2,008	2,011
Nigeria	64,202	23,844	28,472	27,313	32,710	21,353	23,663	28,109	35,299	39,856	41,353	42,093	23,750	30,903
Rwanda	1,163	2,410	2,584	1,912	2,038	1,971	750	1,326	1,392	1,863	2,082	1,091	2,123	1,769
São Tomé and Principe	43	46	50	57	46	48	50	45	45	44	41	32	50	47
Senegal	2,986	4,626	5,698	5,500	6,027	5,430	3,642	4,493	4,807	4,529	4,836	2,364	4,110	4,996
Seychelles	147	308	369	375	434	469	483	508	508	539	537	112	244	469
Sierra Leone	1,199	1,181	897	807	691	771	928	866	942	823	647	1,044	1,081	819
Somalia	604	1,092	917	..	..	..	..	..	..	..	..	677	989	917
South Africa	80,544	95,962	111,997	120,243	130,533	130,448	135,820	151,117	143,031	147,617	133,462	61,201	79,315	133,807
Sudan	7,617	15,779	13,167	11,410	6,402	7,895	8,169	7,194	7,208	10,069	10,366	7,964	15,971	9,098
Swaziland	582	725	860	881	970	988	1,062	1,267	1,228	1,313	1,210	435	563	1,087
Tanzania	..	4,774	4,220	4,750	4,903	4,550	4,213	4,958	5,838	7,065	7,917	..	4,432	5,379
Togo	1,136	1,353	1,628	1,602	1,693	1,234	983	1,309	1,473	1,501	1,510	813	1,161	1,437
Uganda	1,245	5,252	4,304	3,322	2,858	3,220	3,997	5,756	6,049	6,298	6,775	2,117	5,097	4,731
Zambia	3,884	3,995	3,288	3,377	3,183	3,274	3,347	3,470	3,286	3,932	3,352	3,159	2,781	3,390
Zimbabwe	6,679	8,286	8,784	8,642	6,752	6,564	6,891	7,134	8,545	8,388	5,908	5,993	6,939	7,512
NORTH AFRICA	124,880	145,342	163,135	141,521	153,847	157,751	159,506	172,459	193,707	199,580	211,010	97,282	144,086	172,502
Algeria	42,345	54,937	61,902	46,301	49,116	49,762	42,063	41,256	46,061	47,072	49,585	34,782	59,855	48,124
Egypt, Arab Republic	22,913	39,648	43,130	36,971	41,857	47,197	51,898	59,100	67,651	75,605	78,097	20,312	37,154	55,723
Libya	35,545	21,864	..	..	..	..	..	..	..	..	..	24,534	22,902	..
Morocco	18,821	22,847	25,825	27,836	28,451	26,801	30,351	32,986	36,673	33,514	..	13,468	18,731	30,305
Tunisia	8,742	10,102	12,291	13,075	15,575	14,663	15,650	17,987	19,589	18,937	22,041	6,901	9,465	16,645
ALL AFRICA	387,241	416,439	461,023	447,012	460,210	446,659	441,373	491,234	523,705	544,561	540,998	295,795	385,545	484,086

Note: 1998 data are preliminary (see page 3).

2-6. Total consumption

	Percentage of GDP											*Annual average*		
	1980	*1989*	*1990*	*1991*	*1992*	*1993*	*1994*	*1995*	*1996*	*1997*	*1998*	*75-84*	*85-89*	*90-MR*
SUB-SAHARAN AFRICA	71.5	80.6	82.1	81.8	87.0	85.5	83.5	83.8	82.3	83.6	85.2	76.1	79.8	83.9
excluding South Africa	73.4	82.6	82.6	81.3	89.8	88.3	84.6	86.5	82.8	84.3	87.4	76.9	81.4	85.3
excl. S. Africa & Nigeria	79.6	84.1	85.0	83.4	93.0	89.9	85.7	87.4	86.7	85.6	86.7	78.6	81.4	87.0
Angola	..	73.0	70.4	83.9	98.3	74.8	67.3	84.3	79.8	74.8	87.5	..	76.1	80.1
Benin	105.1	96.6	94.5	94.1	95.8	94.8	90.5	90.0	92.0	90.2	92.6	100.0	97.0	92.7
Botswana	65.6	56.8	62.9	62.3	64.8	63.9	61.1	59.4	56.6	62.6	64.9	69.8	50.8	62.1
Burkina Faso	105.8	92.9	92.3	93.9	93.0	95.0	95.7	94.7	91.2	89.5	87.6	101.7	97.6	92.6
Burundi	100.6	96.7	105.4	104.2	105.1	104.5	107.7	104.8	97.6	96.1	101.2	95.9	96.7	102.9
Cameroon	78.3	79.9	79.3	78.0	83.5	82.4	82.1	80.4	80.9	79.4	79.8	76.9	77.1	80.6
Cape Verde	..	90.1	87.2	101.9	102.3	104.0	106.4	114.5	107.0	104.6	105.1	..	92.4	103.7
Central African Republic	108.9	97.7	100.6	97.4	100.4	98.2	94.0	100.1	99.3	96.4	95.6	101.6	99.2	98.0
Chad	108.7	112.1	103.1	107.7	108.3	108.8	105.6	102.7	103.2	103.4	100.6	107.2	113.5	104.8
Comoros	110.1	107.0	103.2	97.9	101.6	97.1	105.9	106.9	106.1	102.6	105.0	106.5	102.5	102.9
Congo, Democratic Rep. of	89.9	85.0	90.7	98.2	93.9	96.0	89.4	85.9	86.6	91.0	..	89.5	86.7	91.5
Congo, Republic of	64.3	72.2	76.2	81.4	75.6	76.4	73.4	71.6	65.7	64.8	73.5	73.9	76.8	73.2
Côte d'Ivoire	79.6	88.1	88.7	89.6	89.3	90.6	77.6	81.1	78.9	77.0	75.8	75.7	81.6	83.2
Djibouti	..	..	..	110.2	118.6	111.0	111.3	108.7	107.7	106.2	..	..	..	110.5
Equatorial Guinea	..	..	120.1	107.2	97.8	101.0	81.2	77.6	75.4	66.8	80.0	92.4		89.7
Eritrea	..	..	..	..	131.3	124.6	135.4	131.5	131.0	117.4	129.0	..	..	128.6
Ethiopia	..	92.1	92.8	97.3	97.0	94.4	94.6	92.0	95.3	91.4	93.7	93.6	92.8	94.3
Gabon	39.4	69.1	63.1	59.5	65.3	63.3	54.7	55.8	53.2	51.7	56.8	41.9	67.7	58.2
Gambia, The	94.2	89.9	89.3	89.4	90.7	96.0	97.7	99.1	97.9	95.2	93.7	95.7	92.4	94.3
Ghana	95.1	94.4	94.5	92.7	98.7	93.4	87.4	88.3	88.1	90.2	86.8	93.7	94.5	91.1
Guinea	..	81.5	82.3	82.0	88.8	88.9	87.7	82.9	85.0	80.7	80.7	..	83.6	84.3
Guinea-Bissau	100.9	98.3	97.2	96.8	96.8	93.0	96.1	101.2	98.2	97.2	108.9	103.0	100.1	98.4
Kenya	86.6	86.8	85.5	9.0	86.8	76.8	80.4	88.4	87.5	91.9	93.3	83.0	83.4	77.7
Lesotho	159.3	146.5	130.5	149.4	145.5	133.2	114.6	116.9	101.8	109.8	142.7	173.6	167.1	127.1
Liberia	72.7		..	..	..	..	..	..	..	..	..	76.7	83.6	..
Madagascar	101.4	90.2	93.7	99.3	96.6	97.5	96.6	96.4	93.7	96.3	94.7	98.0	94.2	96.1
Malawi	89.2	95.3	90.3	85.8	99.3	100.9	91.7	91.9	99.2	97.9	99.3	84.4	90.0	95.2
Mali	98.9	94.3	93.6	93.6	95.6	93.6	92.9	92.2	92.6	89.7	89.9	99.8	99.9	92.6
Mauritania	103.1	89.4	95.6	90.3	94.0	93.9	89.3	94.4	92.5	91.6	92.0	104.9	90.8	92.6
Mauritius	89.5	76.2	76.4	75.1	73.9	75.5	76.6	76.8	76.1	75.9	75.8	81.5	74.5	75.8
Mozambique	110.6	115.6	112.3	111.2	117.2	122.4	113.9	101.9	101.6	98.4	98.3	110.4	110.2	108.6
Namibia	63.2	86.5	82.4	90.8	87.9	90.4	83.1	87.2	86.5	85.8	81.2	90.7	88.5	86.1
Niger	85.4	93.0	98.8	95.5	95.7	96.7	100.0	99.6	96.9	96.8	96.7	91.6	92.1	97.4
Nigeria	68.6	74.7	70.6	70.7	76.5	79.8	79.4	81.8	66.5	78.1	88.2	78.5	82.3	76.8
Rwanda	95.8	97.7	93.8	96.7	98.8	100.1	154.5	111.6	109.8	107.7	107.3	93.2	94.7	108.9
São Tomé and Principe	114.9	139.0	..	127.3	128.3	128.8	114.0	120.1	119.7	116.0	90.9	109.0	121.3	118.1
Senegal	105.0	93.6	91.1	94.1	92.6	94.5	90.4	88.7	88.1	86.7	84.9	98.9	96.2	90.1
Seychelles	72.9	70.2	79.7	81.3	82.4	81.6	77.9	76.5	60.4	77.7	88.0	75.7	69.9	78.4
Sierra Leone	..	93.7	83.9	82.7	83.1	86.6	88.9	101.8	105.5	..	101.3	98.9	96.1	91.7
Somalia	112.9	106.9	112.5	..	..	..	..	..	..	..	..	111.4	94.4	112.5
South Africa	68.6	78.5	82.4	83.1	83.9	82.4	82.1	80.9	82.1	83.2	83.1	75.6	78.0	82.6
Sudan	97.9		..	..	..	..	..	..	..	..	100.0	94.2	92.1	100.0
Swaziland	93.5	88.1	79.6	81.8	81.4	73.7	74.0	71.0	81.2	80.5	80.8	84.0	82.3	78.2
Tanzania	..	102.7	100.8	97.8	98.5	102.4	101.0	98.0	96.4	94.6	94.0	..	99.7	98.2
Togo	76.8	92.7	85.3	91.0	93.4	100.1	93.3	88.1	91.6	91.6	92.5	78.6	92.4	91.9
Uganda	100.4	99.0	99.4	99.3	99.6	98.9	95.7	92.9	95.2	92.1	94.3	95.9	97.0	96.4
Zambia	80.7	96.2	83.4	91.6	100.0	91.0	90.7	91.9	91.3	90.7	94.7	81.1	85.1	91.7
Zimbabwe	86.2	83.3	82.6	84.2	89.0	79.0	77.7	77.6	73.9	80.0	80.2	84.8	81.0	80.5
NORTH AFRICA	59.6	77.1	78.1	76.3	77.3	79.9	81.9	81.9	80.7	79.3	81.1	64.6	75.4	79.6
Algeria	56.9	70.7	72.5	63.3	67.6	72.2	73.0	71.5	67.4	65.5	66.6	61.1	69.2	68.9
Egypt, Arab Republic	84.8	82.7	83.9	86.8	84.6	86.8	88.6	87.6	89.2	87.0	89.9	84.6	84.3	87.2
Libya	43.1	..	..	..	..	..	..	..	..	..	..	53.5	..	..
Morocco	86.3	81.7	80.8	82.8	83.2	83.0	84.7	85.8	83.9	83.2	81.6	87.1	81.8	83.2
Tunisia	76.0	79.4	80.0	79.0	77.7	78.3	78.5	79.3	76.5	75.8	76.3	75.8	78.4	77.9
ALL AFRICA	68.2	79.4	80.7	80.0	83.9	83.6	82.9	83.1	81.8	82.1	83.8	72.9	77.8	82.4

Note: 1998 data are preliminary (see page 3). Since 1994, Nigeria's ratios are distorted because the official exchange rate used by the Government for oil exports and oil value added is significantly over-valued.

2-7. General government consumption

	Percentage of GDP											Annual average		
	1980	1989	1990	1991	1992	1993	1994	1995	1996	1997	1998	75-84	85-89	90-MR
SUB-SAHARAN AFRICA	13.9	16.0	17.3	18.1	19.0	18.4	17.6	16.5	16.5	16.5	16.0	14.7	15.9	17.3
excluding South Africa	13.9	14.3	15.9	17.0	18.0	16.9	15.1	14.7	14.1	13.8	13.2	14.3	14.6	15.4
excl. S. Africa & Nigeria	15.4	15.0	16.1	17.9	17.9	16.8	15.3	15.5	15.5	15.2	13.8	14.8	15.0	16.0
Angola	..	28.4	34.5	45.2	41.9	41.5	40.1	50.4	50.0	51.6	39.1	..	31.5	43.8
Benin	8.6	11.1	11.0	10.8	10.7	10.3	10.1	11.2	10.7	10.4	9.7	9.9	14.1	10.6
Botswana	19.6	21.2	23.8	24.7	26.4	28.5	28.2	28.1	27.4	23.2	24.9	20.5	22.3	26.1
Burkina Faso	10.4	14.0	14.9	14.6	15.8	15.2	17.4	15.9	15.1	14.6	14.7	12.8	14.2	15.4
Burundi	9.2	10.2	10.8	10.8	10.0	12.8	12.7	13.4	13.6	14.5	11.1	10.3	9.7	12.2
Cameroon	9.7	10.8	12.8	13.3	12.8	12.8	10.0	8.6	8.4	8.2	9.2	9.7	10.8	10.7
Cape Verde	..	16.0	17.5	17.9	28.9	31.0	37.9	31.7	29.5	20.1	19.1	..	16.0	26.0
Central African Republic	15.1	15.4	14.9	16.3	16.9	15.0	17.5	15.2	9.6	10.9	11.7	15.0	15.9	14.2
Chad	..	16.1	10.9	9.4	9.7	10.6	10.9	9.0	9.0	7.2	6.8	12.0	14.7	9.3
Comoros	30.9	27.6	16.5	17.5	15.8	15.1	16.7	17.2	15.2	14.0	11.6	29.7	27.4	15.5
Congo, Democratic Rep. of	..	10.1	11.5	13.3	21.7	15.4	4.4	4.9	5.7	8.5	..	6.6	9.7	10.7
Congo, Republic of	17.6	19.5	13.8	21.0	21.1	21.2	16.2	13.0	10.6	19.2	14.3	17.3	20.5	16.7
Côte d'Ivoire	16.9	18.3	16.8	16.4	17.4	16.4	13.0	11.9	12.1	11.6	10.8	16.5	16.2	14.1
Djibouti	..	..	..	32.0	44.2	44.1	40.1	38.3	33.5	27.9	..	..	..	37.2
Equatorial Guinea	..	27.5	39.7	34.2	29.4	39.3	15.3	16.4	19.8	11.0	20.9	28.3	27.4	25.1
Eritrea	..	..	..	..	32.9	36.6	43.2	46.7	45.0	32.6	48.0	..	..	40.7
Ethiopia	..	18.7	18.5	15.5	10.1	10.6	12.5	11.8	11.7	11.4	14.3	15.3	16.0	12.9
Gabon	13.2	14.2	13.4	14.3	15.5	15.3	12.0	14.1	13.0	14.0	14.9	14.5	20.9	14.0
Gambia, The	31.2	11.1	10.7	10.8	11.4	11.9	12.2	11.5	12.9	11.3	9.9	36.6	12.0	11.4
Ghana	11.2	9.8	9.3	9.5	12.1	14.4	13.7	12.1	12.0	12.4	10.3	9.9	10.1	11.8
Guinea	..	11.7	11.9	9.7	11.4	11.1	7.5	7.3	7.1	6.9	6.9	..	11.4	8.9
Guinea-Bissau	27.7	11.2	10.3	10.6	9.0	7.1	7.1	6.4	6.6	7.0	9.3	23.6	12.5	8.2
Kenya	19.8	17.9	18.7	17.0	16.1	16.7	15.2	14.8	16.1	16.2	16.1	18.4	18.1	16.3
Lesotho	25.8	16.6	14.6	20.3	20.9	20.0	20.1	20.8	16.6	27.8	21.7	21.5	22.1	20.3
Liberia	16.3	..	..	..	..	..	..	..	..	..	..	15.8	19.0	
Madagascar	12.1	8.8	8.0	8.7	8.3	7.9	6.9	6.7	6.1	7.6	6.1	11.1	8.9	7.4
Malawi	19.3	17.1	15.7	12.0	14.1	13.0	31.8	18.2	13.3	12.7	14.3	16.4	18.0	16.1
Mali	11.5	10.4	9.4	10.7	11.4	11.5	11.1	13.7	13.3	14.4	12.8	11.0	11.8	12.0
Mauritania	39.9	20.1	22.4	32.0	16.3	16.3	15.1	14.5	14.2	13.7	13.8	39.8	21.7	17.6
Mauritius	14.1	12.3	11.8	11.7	11.5	12.1	12.5	12.1	12.2	11.9	8.9	13.5	11.7	11.6
Mozambique	12.2	11.3	11.6	10.6	12.6	11.7	12.9	7.8	7.2	7.4	9.3	14.2	11.3	10.1
Namibia	16.7	27.2	29.4	32.4	34.3	33.7	30.3	31.1	31.3	31.3	25.5	24.7	28.8	31.0
Niger	10.4	15.7	15.0	15.5	17.5	15.8	16.0	14.0	11.3	13.7	12.7	11.5	12.9	14.6
Nigeria	12.1	10.4	15.1	12.2	18.4	17.5	14.3	11.1	8.0	8.5	10.7	14.4	12.5	12.9
Rwanda	12.5	12.7	10.1	12.1	12.9	11.6	8.3	11.0	12.1	10.7	11.0	14.7	12.6	11.1
São Tomé and Principe	23.6	45.5	34.6	58.1	31.3	31.1	33.4	43.1	43.4	45.1	39.8	20.6	44.2	40.0
Senegal	20.3	15.6	14.7	13.5	15.4	14.7	13.2	12.1	10.8	10.3	9.9	17.2	15.6	12.7
Seychelles	28.7	32.9	27.7	28.2	30.4	29.8	29.6	29.3	29.1	27.9	26.7	28.5	34.5	28.7
Sierra Leone	20.9	9.3	9.9	9.4	10.3	11.2	11.1	14.0	11.0	9.7	8.4	12.3	9.0	10.5
Somalia	15.6	..	..	..	..	..	..	..	..	..	..	19.8	..	
South Africa	14.3	19.2	19.7	19.8	20.2	20.1	20.0	18.3	19.4	19.8	20.2	15.7	18.8	19.7
Sudan	16.0	..	..	..	..	..	..	..	..	..	0.0	12.1	13.0	0.0
Swaziland	19.1	15.6	18.5	19.6	17.7	24.2	23.2	20.7	22.6	27.1	20.0	20.6	18.4	21.5
Tanzania	..	16.3	17.0	18.4	19.3	19.5	18.1	16.1	13.2	10.0	8.8	..	15.7	15.6
Togo	22.4	13.8	14.2	14.2	12.4	16.1	13.2	12.1	11.7	10.2	11.3	20.0	15.2	12.8
Uganda	..	7.0	7.5	8.8	9.7	9.8	10.3	9.8	10.3	10.4	9.6	10.8	9.3	9.6
Zambia	25.5	13.7	19.0	31.8	15.0	18.4	14.0	14.0	12.5	11.3	10.8	25.7	19.9	16.3
Zimbabwe	18.5	18.7	19.4	16.1	24.2	14.9	16.7	18.0	17.1	17.1	16.9	16.9	22.1	17.8
NORTH AFRICA	12.0	15.4	14.6	14.1	14.8	14.9	14.4	14.3	13.4	13.4	..	13.8	16.3	14.2
Algeria	13.8	16.9	16.2	15.0	17.2	17.4	16.8	15.7	14.1	14.4	11.0	13.8	17.5	15.3
Egypt, Arab Republic	15.7	12.6	11.3	11.2	10.4	10.2	10.3	10.7	10.4	10.2	10.3	19.5	14.9	10.5
Libya	21.8	..	..	..	..	..	..	..	..	..	..	27.8	..	
Morocco	18.3	15.7	15.5	15.2	16.4	18.1	17.1	17.4	16.7	17.9	..	18.9	15.6	16.8
Tunisia	14.5	17.3	16.4	16.6	16.0	16.3	16.5	16.9	15.6	15.6	15.0	15.7	17.1	16.1
ALL AFRICA	13.1	15.8	16.4	16.8	17.6	17.2	16.5	15.8	15.4	15.4	14.7	14.3	16.0	16.2

Note: 1998 data are preliminary (see page 3). Since 1994, Nigeria's ratios are distorted because the official exchange rate used by the Government for oil exports and oil value added is significantly over-valued.

2-8. Gross domestic investment

	Percentage of GDP											Annual average		
	1980	1989	1990	1991	1992	1993	1994	1995	1996	1997	1998	75-84	85-89	90-MR
SUB-SAHARAN AFRICA	20.2	15.8	14.2	17.0	14.7	16.2	17.5	18.5	17.7	17.4	17.8	20.0	15.1	16.8
excluding South Africa	19.1	15.6	15.8	20.6	17.0	18.1	19.4	18.8	18.7	18.8	19.5	19.6	15.3	18.5
excl. S. Africa & Nigeria	18.1	15.3	16.0	20.1	15.7	17.3	19.3	19.3	20.2	19.6	19.3	18.0	15.4	18.5
Angola	..	12.2	11.7	12.9	3.6	26.4	23.2	25.0	22.7	23.8	24.5	..	14.8	19.3
Benin	15.2	11.8	14.2	14.5	13.8	15.4	15.8	19.6	17.1	18.5	16.2	17.7	12.6	16.1
Botswana	36.8	31.0	31.7	30.4	28.6	26.6	26.9	26.9	25.8	26.7	25.3	32.9	25.0	27.7
Burkina Faso	17.0	21.6	20.6	20.6	21.1	19.8	17.4	20.6	26.5	27.0	28.6	20.2	21.7	22.5
Burundi	13.9	16.5	14.5	14.4	15.0	15.7	10.6	9.6	12.1	8.1	7.8	14.3	15.9	12.0
Cameroon	21.0	17.1	17.8	16.7	14.3	16.5	15.3	14.5	15.4	16.2	18.4	25.1	22.6	16.1
Cape Verde	..	43.6	43.1	29.0	37.8	35.5	41.5	34.8	33.5	30.3	32.6	..	39.5	35.4
Central African Republic	7.0	11.5	12.3	12.4	12.2	10.2	11.7	7.2	4.4	9.0	13.5	10.5	12.5	10.3
Chad	3.3	6.8	13.6	5.5	6.2	8.2	13.1	13.1	13.8	14.7	12.6	3.2	6.6	11.2
Comoros	33.2	17.4	19.7	20.3	22.2	20.6	21.0	19.9	18.9	21.3	19.8	33.4	24.2	20.4
Congo, Democratic Rep. of	10.0	14.3	9.0	5.6	6.9	1.8	7.9	9.4	7.1	7.1	8.1	12.7	13.7	7.0
Congo, Republic of	35.8	14.1	15.9	20.5	21.6	29.5	54.5	36.6	60.5	26.0	35.1	36.2	22.4	33.3
Côte d'Ivoire	26.5	8.9	6.7	7.4	6.9	8.3	12.5	13.5	13.4	16.0	18.2	23.6	11.8	11.4
Djibouti	..	..	..	14.4	19.1	17.3	11.7	8.6	9.2	9.5	..	..	..	12.8
Equatorial Guinea	..	..	17.4	50.7	24.2	22.0	67.8	71.4	107.4	61.3	84.6	13.9	..	56.3
Eritrea	..	..	..	..	5.4	15.1	17.8	19.2	29.3	40.9	40.9	..	..	24.1
Ethiopia	..	13.5	11.8	9.9	9.2	14.2	15.2	16.4	19.1	19.1	18.2	13.7	14.7	14.8
Gabon	27.5	26.3	21.7	26.5	22.4	22.4	21.9	22.7	22.8	26.3	32.3	42.9	35.7	24.3
Gambia, The	26.7	20.4	22.3	21.9	22.2	21.0	18.1	20.2	21.6	17.6	19.8	19.7	17.1	20.5
Ghana	5.6	13.2	14.4	15.9	12.8	22.2	24.0	20.0	21.5	24.1	22.9	6.9	10.8	19.8
Guinea	..	17.2	17.5	18.1	17.4	17.8	19.5	20.6	19.6	21.6	22.2	..	16.1	19.4
Guinea-Bissau	28.2	39.0	29.9	31.0	48.4	30.9	21.8	22.3	23.0	21.7	11.3	23.8	35.6	26.7
Kenya	24.5	20.6	19.7	92.3	13.7	17.7	16.4	17.5	16.8	15.4	14.4	21.1	20.3	24.9
Lesotho	42.5	60.6	70.7	80.2	78.3	75.0	80.3	83.2	89.2	85.5	48.6	35.1	49.9	76.8
Liberia	27.3	..	..	..	..	..	..	..	..	..	..	23.8	9.2	..
Madagascar	15.0	13.4	17.0	8.2	11.3	11.4	10.9	10.9	11.6	11.9	13.3	10.2	10.9	11.8
Malawi	24.7	21.2	19.7	20.2	19.9	15.2	29.3	16.6	12.4	12.3	13.7	25.3	17.3	17.7
Mali	15.5	21.7	23.0	22.8	21.9	21.8	25.9	22.8	22.9	20.6	20.9	14.8	20.1	22.5
Mauritania	22.9	16.8	17.9	17.9	20.5	22.0	14.5	16.0	19.2	17.5	21.0	23.3	23.6	18.5
Mauritius	20.7	31.1	30.9	28.7	29.3	30.7	32.3	25.7	25.1	27.6	26.1	25.3	26.6	28.5
Mozambique	5.9	14.8	15.6	16.0	15.6	12.7	19.8	22.8	19.1	19.1	20.4	5.8	10.3	17.9
Namibia	29.3	16.3	27.4	18.1	21.2	16.1	23.1	20.7	22.5	19.8	19.0	22.0	13.1	20.9
Niger	28.1	13.7	8.1	9.2	5.4	5.7	10.4	7.5	9.6	10.8	10.4	18.2	13.7	8.6
Nigeria	21.3	17.7	14.7	23.4	21.8	23.3	19.6	16.1	12.8	15.3	20.0	22.3	15.1	18.6
Rwanda	16.1	13.4	14.7	14.0	13.9	15.2	4.3	8.6	10.3	10.0	9.9	14.8	15.4	11.2
São Tomé and Principe	34.2	28.4	..	31.4	38.7	38.1	45.1	59.3	50.2	49.7	51.6	33.4	25.1	45.5
Senegal	11.7	11.9	13.8	12.9	14.8	14.1	16.2	16.9	17.4	18.7	19.7	13.1	11.8	16.1
Seychelles	38.3	27.1	24.6	22.3	21.2	28.7	26.2	30.3	50.9	36.0	22.5	33.5	23.6	29.2
Sierra Leone	..	9.8	9.4	10.5	8.2	7.7	7.9	5.6	9.3	..	8.1	3.2	6.5	8.4
Somalia	42.4	30.3	15.5	..	..	..	..	..	..	..	..	27.1	28.5	15.5
South Africa	23.4	16.5	11.8	11.9	12.0	14.0	15.6	18.2	16.5	15.7	15.6	21.3	14.9	14.6
Sudan	14.7	..	..	..	..	..	..	..	..	..	0.0	16.0	13.0	0.0
Swaziland	30.3	23.2	19.6	20.6	26.1	26.6	32.1	34.1	30.1	33.9	12.3	31.6	21.6	26.2
Tanzania	..	17.4	22.6	26.2	26.8	26.1	24.9	21.9	18.0	16.3	16.0	..	20.1	22.1
Togo	28.4	16.5	26.6	17.1	15.8	7.6	10.4	16.1	16.4	14.9	14.2	29.8	17.1	15.5
Uganda	6.2	11.1	12.7	15.2	15.9	15.2	14.6	16.2	16.2	16.0	15.1	7.2	9.8	15.2
Zambia	23.3	10.8	17.3	11.0	11.9	15.0	13.5	13.9	14.9	14.5	14.3	22.3	14.7	14.1
Zimbabwe	16.9	15.0	17.4	19.1	20.2	22.8	24.2	25.1	25.9	26.2	21.2	16.7	16.9	22.4
NORTH AFRICA	28.2	28.5	28.2	25.7	24.8	23.5	23.0	23.1	20.9	21.4	22.7	31.1	28.2	23.7
Algeria	39.1	29.0	29.3	31.0	30.0	29.2	31.7	32.2	26.2	25.7	27.0	41.5	30.6	29.1
Egypt, Arab Republic	27.5	31.8	28.8	21.2	18.2	16.2	16.6	17.5	16.6	17.7	19.5	29.9	28.6	19.1
Libya	22.1	..	..	..	..	..	..	..	..	..	..	26.3	..	..
Morocco	24.2	23.7	25.2	22.7	23.2	22.5	21.3	20.7	19.8	20.6	21.7	26.5	23.1	22.0
Tunisia	29.4	23.9	27.1	26.0	29.2	29.2	24.5	24.8	25.2	26.6	25.5	31.2	25.0	26.5
ALL AFRICA	22.3	20.0	18.8	19.5	17.9	18.6	19.4	20.0	18.8	18.8	19.6	23.2	19.7	19.0

Note: 1998 data are preliminary (see page 3). Since 1994, Nigeria's ratios are distorted because the official exchange rate used by the Government for oil exports and oil value added is significantly overvalued.

2-9. Gross public investment

	\multicolumn{11}{c}{*Percentage of GDP*}		\multicolumn{3}{c}{*Annual average*}	
	1980	*1989*	*1990*	*1991*	*1992*	*1993*	*1994*	*1995*	*1996*	*1997*	*1998*	*75-84*	*85-89*	*90-MR*
SUB-SAHARAN AFRICA	..	6.8	6.5	8.4	6.6	5.5	5.5	5.4	5.4	5.6	5.8	7.9	7.0	6.1
excluding South Africa	..	..	6.0	10.2	7.7	6.6	7.0	6.6	6.4	6.6	6.1	..	..	7.0
excl. S. Africa & Nigeria	..	5.8	5.9	10.0	6.2	5.8	6.6	6.4	6.2	6.0	6.1	..	6.3	6.6
Angola	..	..	..	..	..	..	..	..	..	..	..	..	..	..
Benin	..	8.0	7.4	7.4	6.6	7.1	9.3	10.4	7.5	7.5	5.4	..	9.1	7.6
Botswana	12.5	..	..	..	..	..	..	..	..	13.9	13.7	12.1	..	13.8
Burkina Faso	..	5.4	4.4	6.3	10.1	8.9	8.0	10.4	12.2	14.1	13.8	..	7.6	9.8
Burundi	12.8	14.7	12.5	12.0	11.7	12.4	9.0	8.3	10.4	5.0	5.0	14.1	13.6	9.6
Cameroon	4.4	6.1	5.5	4.0	2.7	1.8	1.3	1.2	0.5	1.0	2.0	4.7	9.0	2.2
Cape Verde	..	15.0	12.1	17.9	28.9	31.0	37.9	31.7	29.5	27.7	24.8	..	18.9	26.8
Central African Republic	3.7	6.0	4.7	7.2	7.5	6.2	10.3	10.3	2.4	5.2	9.5	4.7	6.3	7.0
Chad	..	6.5	13.3	5.2	5.9	7.6	9.0	9.1	8.9	8.8	6.4	2.8	6.3	8.2
Comoros	23.2	8.0	5.2	4.6	10.9	7.2	10.4	6.9	6.2	6.3	6.1	23.3	14.2	7.1
Congo, Democratic Rep. of	5.1	5.4	4.0	2.6	2.8	0.9	0.6	4.4	2.5	2.5	2.8	3.9	4.9	2.6
Congo, Republic of	..	2.7	5.6	4.7	4.7	7.1	12.8	9.3	18.3	8.3	9.7	..	11.1	9.0
Côte d'Ivoire	11.4	4.4	3.6	3.4	3.8	3.7	4.1	4.2	4.3	4.8	5.1	10.5	4.4	4.1
Djibouti	..	..	..	9.2	9.3	8.2	5.6	3.7	4.0	4.3	..	..	..	6.3
Equatorial Guinea	..	..	10.5	13.4	10.1	8.9	4.1	1.9	1.2	4.4	7.5	..	..	6.9
Eritrea	..	..	..	..	3.6	14.1	10.5	11.1	15.4	18.9	16.9	..	..	12.9
Ethiopia	..	8.1	5.7	4.3	3.2	5.0	7.1	7.5	7.5	8.3	7.6	..	6.9	6.2
Gabon	5.3	4.2	3.9	5.2	5.3	5.1	5.6	5.1	5.9	7.2	10.9	15.8	5.9	6.0
Gambia, The	..	6.4	7.4	7.7	7.8	7.5	7.0	10.0	12.9	8.4	5.9	13.8	7.6	8.3
Ghana	..	7.8	7.5	8.3	10.3	11.1	13.3	14.0	13.3	12.4	11.3	2.5	7.0	11.3
Guinea	..	8.3	9.2	7.0	6.7	6.2	5.5	5.9	5.0	6.1	5.8	..	7.4	6.4
Guinea-Bissau	..	30.3	21.5	23.2	28.4	24.6	20.4	15.2	14.8	17.8	6.2	..	29.6	19.1
Kenya	10.1	7.8	9.4	82.6	7.1	8.0	8.5	7.4	6.4	6.4	5.5	8.8	7.6	15.7
Lesotho	..	..	43.3	52.0	51.8	46.9	54.2	..	..	15.6	14.1	20.0	..	39.7
Liberia	..	..	..	..	..	..	..	..	..	..	..	..	..	..
Madagascar	..	9.7	7.9	5.9	7.6	7.8	6.2	6.0	6.7	6.3	7.2	6.4	7.0	6.8
Malawi	17.5	7.6	8.0	8.3	10.2	8.4	15.3	9.2	6.6	7.1	11.0	13.6	8.2	9.4
Mali	..	9.8	10.5	12.1	9.5	9.3	13.0	9.4	9.0	8.1	9.2	..	10.2	10.0
Mauritania	..	5.1	5.6	3.8	3.4	4.3	4.3	3.8	4.1	3.8	4.3	..	6.7	4.2
Mauritius	8.4	7.1	11.4	8.2	9.6	7.9	9.1	8.0	9.3	7.2	3.2	7.9	7.9	8.2
Mozambique	7.6	12.4	12.0	11.4	12.8	12.3	14.0	12.0	10.5	10.7	9.3	10.4	8.6	11.7
Namibia	15.1	5.7	7.8	7.3	9.7	8.1	8.3	7.6	8.0	7.8	7.3	13.2	7.3	8.0
Niger	20.4	9.6	7.4	3.7	3.9	4.2	6.6	5.4	4.6	5.8	5.5	13.8	8.5	5.2
Nigeria	..	..	..	11.4	13.4	10.7	8.9	7.0	6.7	8.6	6.0	..	..	9.1
Rwanda	12.2	5.4	5.9	7.0	7.4	7.6	2.7	7.9	9.2	8.2	6.5	13.7	10.2	6.9
São Tomé and Principe	..	26.4	..	24.4	24.9	20.4	26.9	41.1	32.0	32.5	33.2	..	21.6	29.4
Senegal	5.5	4.2	4.1	4.6	5.2	4.2	5.0	5.2	5.2	5.6	5.8	4.1	4.0	5.0
Seychelles	..	..	8.2	12.9	9.4	11.2	7.5	6.8	10.2	10.0	0.0	16.3	7.6	8.5
Sierra Leone	..	3.1	3.5	4.4	4.7	5.3	4.4	2.6	3.3	..	3.8	3.2	3.0	4.0
Somalia	..	..	..	..	..	..	..	..	..	..	..	..	..	..
South Africa	13.0	7.7	7.0	6.1	5.2	4.4	4.1	4.3	4.4	4.5	5.4	13.0	8.1	5.1
Sudan	6.9	..	..	..	..	..	..	..	..	..	..	5.6	3.0	..
Swaziland	11.8	6.7	7.2	12.1	12.2	10.3	9.3	6.3	5.6	4.9	5.5	13.1	8.8	8.1
Tanzania	..	3.5	3.1	1.7	2.7	4.2	3.7	3.2	3.6	2.6	3.7	..	6.0	3.2
Togo	20.2	7.4	7.3	4.5	3.5	2.3	2.3	3.5	2.8	2.0	4.0	12.2	10.2	3.6
Uganda	..	5.4	6.2	7.4	7.4	6.7	5.4	5.4	6.4	5.9	5.5	..	4.4	6.3
Zambia	..	..	6.2	7.8	6.7	4.5	7.0	7.0	5.9	5.2	7.7	..	..	6.4
Zimbabwe	1.8	2.9	3.4	3.5	3.8	3.6	3.1	2.9	2.7	3.0	1.8	2.9	3.3	3.1
NORTH AFRICA	..	9.9	8.9	7.5	8.0	8.7	7.6	7.2	6.8	6.9	..	..	11.2	7.7
Algeria	..	10.2	8.2	6.1	6.8	8.7	7.9	7.4	6.9	7.4	7.1	..	11.2	7.4
Egypt, Arab Republic	..	10.5	10.2	9.2	8.5	7.1	6.1	5.6	5.5	5.6	6.3	..	12.6	7.1
Libya	19.4	..	..	..	..	..	..	..	..	..	..	21.1	..	..
Morocco	..	..	7.3	6.2	7.1	7.9	6.7	7.0	6.5	6.1	..	..	..	6.8
Tunisia	15.0	10.0	11.0	10.2	12.0	15.3	13.7	12.3	11.8	12.4	..	17.2	11.4	12.3
ALL AFRICA	..	8.0	7.5	8.1	7.0	6.6	6.3	6.0	5.9	6.1	6.3	..	8.5	6.6

Note: 1998 data are preliminary (see page 3). Since 1994, Nigeria's ratios are distorted because the official exchange rate used by the Government for oil exports and oil value added is significantly over-valued.

2-10. Gross private investment

					Percentage of GDP							Annual average		
	1980	1989	1990	1991	1992	1993	1994	1995	1996	1997	1998	75-84	85-89	90-MR
SUB-SAHARAN AFRICA	8.6	9.6	9.7	10.5	9.6	10.7	11.4	11.4	11.3	11.6	12.0	9.9	9.3	10.9
excluding South Africa	..	8.0	8.1	10.2	9.0	11.0	11.8	11.2	10.8	11.5	12.7	7.8	8.1	10.7
excl. S. Africa & Nigeria	..	8.0	9.0	9.9	9.1	10.8	12.0	11.7	12.1	12.8	12.3	..	8.5	11.1
Angola	..	1.8	1.6	10.6	0.0	19.8	28.4	14.1	4.7	21.0	23.0	..	9.3	13.7
Benin	..	4.5	6.0	6.1	6.7	7.9	6.2	6.9	9.1	11.0	10.7	..	4.5	7.8
Botswana	19.1	..	..	..	..	..	..	..	..	11.2	9.9	14.1	..	10.6
Burkina Faso	..	15.4	15.3	14.2	13.2	10.7	14.1	13.0	13.6	13.8	14.9	..	13.0	13.6
Burundi	1.1	1.9	2.7	2.9	2.8	2.9	1.6	1.4	1.8	2.2	2.1	1.5	2.7	2.3
Cameroon	15.6	12.0	11.9	12.7	11.6	14.7	14.0	13.3	14.9	15.2	16.4	24.2	12.1	13.8
Cape Verde	..	28.6	31.0	11.1	8.9	4.5	3.6	3.1	4.0	2.6	7.8	..	20.6	8.5
Central African Republic	3.2	4.3	6.7	4.7	4.4	3.3	1.4	-3.1	2.0	3.8	4.0	4.1	5.3	3.0
Chad	..	0.3	0.3	0.3	0.4	0.6	4.1	3.9	4.9	5.9	6.1	0.1	0.3	3.0
Comoros	5.3	6.4	6.7	14.3	9.2	9.8	9.5	11.5	12.5	13.6	13.8	5.4	5.7	11.2
Congo, Democratic Rep. of	3.7	7.9	8.9	3.5	4.3	1.4	7.0	5.3	4.6	..	..	5.8	8.3	5.0
Congo, Republic of	..	11.8	11.6	15.0	15.9	21.8	40.1	25.0	41.0	16.5	24.1	..	11.4	23.4
Côte d'Ivoire	13.0	5.9	4.9	5.1	4.7	4.1	7.0	8.7	9.6	11.2	13.1	12.3	7.1	7.6
Djibouti	..	..	..	5.1	9.7	9.1	6.2	4.9	5.3	5.2	..	..	..	6.5
Equatorial Guinea	..	..	..	..	..	13.1	63.7	69.5	106.1	57.0	77.1	..	..	64.4
Eritrea	..	..	..	..	1.8	1.0	7.3	8.2	13.9	22.0	24.0	..	..	11.2
Ethiopia	..	5.4	6.2	5.6	6.0	9.2	8.0	9.0	11.6	10.8	10.6	..	8.9	8.6
Gabon	21.4	21.8	17.6	20.9	16.7	17.8	15.4	16.6	16.9	19.1	21.4	24.0	29.8	18.0
Gambia, The	..	14.0	14.9	14.2	14.4	13.5	11.1	10.2	8.6	9.2	13.9	7.4	9.5	12.2
Ghana	..	5.4	6.9	7.5	2.4	12.7	9.3	7.1	7.3	10.8	10.9	4.4	3.7	8.3
Guinea	..	8.9	8.3	10.0	9.8	10.6	11.1	13.1	13.0	13.2	13.4	..	8.7	11.4
Guinea-Bissau	..	8.7	8.4	7.8	20.0	6.3	1.4	7.1	8.3	7.0	5.2	..	10.0	7.9
Kenya	8.2	7.5	6.8	7.7	6.2	8.9	7.5	9.7	9.9	8.1	8.0	8.1	7.8	8.1
Lesotho	..	..	28.0	28.6	26.9	28.1	26.0	..	..	69.9	34.5	7.1	..	34.6
Liberia	..	..	..	..	..	..	..	..	..	..	..	..	..	..
Madagascar	..	3.7	6.9	4.6	3.7	3.7	4.7	4.9	5.0	5.6	6.1	2.2	3.9	5.0
Malawi	4.7	9.0	8.6	8.7	6.9	4.6	11.7	4.9	3.2	2.7	-0.3	7.0	6.0	5.7
Mali	..	11.9	12.4	10.7	12.4	12.5	13.0	13.4	13.9	12.5	11.7	..	9.9	12.5
Mauritania	..	11.8	12.4	14.1	17.1	17.7	10.2	12.2	15.1	13.7	16.7	..	16.9	14.3
Mauritius	14.9	19.0	19.2	20.4	18.3	20.6	21.7	16.3	16.8	20.0	22.1	15.3	15.0	19.5
Mozambique	-1.7	2.4	3.6	4.7	2.8	0.4	5.8	10.8	8.6	8.3	11.1	-4.5	1.7	6.2
Namibia	10.9	10.4	12.6	8.2	10.5	13.4	12.7	14.0	15.5	12.9	12.0	7.9	7.1	12.4
Niger	5.1	3.9	4.0	4.1	1.9	1.9	2.3	1.8	4.7	4.8	4.7	3.6	2.4	3.4
Nigeria	..	8.3	3.8	12.0	8.3	12.5	10.7	9.1	6.1	6.7	14.0	5.2	6.1	9.2
Rwanda	..	8.0	8.7	7.0	6.5	7.6	..	0.7	1.1	1.8	3.4	..	7.8	4.6
São Tomé and Principe	..	2.0	..	7.0	13.8	17.7	18.2	18.2	18.2	17.2	18.4	..	2.0	16.1
Senegal	7.7	9.0	8.8	9.3	9.2	9.7	11.1	11.7	12.2	13.1	13.8	8.3	8.4	11.0
Seychelles	..	..	14.8	8.4	11.5	15.6	17.9	23.6	40.6	25.8	14.3	5.4	14.9	19.2
Sierra Leone	..	6.7	5.9	6.1	3.6	2.4	3.5	3.0	6.0	..	4.3	..	5.7	4.3
Somalia	..	..	..	..	..	..	..	..	..	..	..	..	..	..
South Africa	12.9	12.5	12.2	11.0	10.4	10.3	11.0	11.6	11.8	11.9	11.1	13.9	11.8	11.3
Sudan	3.8	..	..	..	..	..	..	..	..	..	..	8.0	8.3	..
Swaziland	13.3	15.4	11.7	7.5	13.0	15.5	21.9	27.0	23.6	28.2	6.2	17.2	11.5	17.2
Tanzania	..	13.5	19.2	24.2	23.9	21.6	20.9	18.5	14.3	13.5	12.1	..	15.9	18.7
Togo	8.0	10.4	18.0	13.5	12.6	8.7	5.0	10.1	12.2	11.4	9.7	8.0	7.6	11.3
Uganda	..	5.7	6.5	7.8	8.5	8.5	9.2	10.0	10.5	10.3	9.7	..	5.4	9.0
Zambia	..	1.5	7.2	3.5	3.8	7.0	6.3	6.6	8.6	7.9	5.6	9.0	4.1	6.3
Zimbabwe	12.3	11.1	14.8	17.1	18.6	19.9	18.7	22.9	19.5	23.4	19.1	13.3	11.7	19.4
NORTH AFRICA	..	17.1	16.8	16.0	15.3	14.0	14.7	14.9	13.8	14.6	..	12.9	15.6	15.0
Algeria	22.8	15.8	17.6	19.0	19.4	18.4	21.0	22.1	20.4	19.6	19.9	25.3	16.8	19.7
Egypt, Arab Republic	..	20.1	16.7	13.1	10.5	9.2	10.5	10.9	10.5	12.1	13.1	7.1	13.3	11.8
Libya	1.8	..	..	..	..	..	..	..	..	..	..	3.6	..	..
Morocco	..	..	16.7	16.0	15.3	14.9	14.0	14.5	13.0	14.6	..	..	..	14.9
Tunisia	13.3	12.5	13.4	13.9	15.2	12.8	13.3	11.9	11.4	12.1	..	13.2	12.2	13.0
ALL AFRICA	..	12.1	12.1	12.2	11.4	11.8	12.6	12.6	12.2	12.6	13.1	11.4	11.5	12.3

Note: 1998 data are preliminary (see page 3). Since 1994, Nigeria's ratios are distorted because the official exchange rate used by the Government for oil exports and oil value added is significantly over-valued.

2-11. Gross domestic savings

	Percentage of GDP											Annual average		
	1980	1989	1990	1991	1992	1993	1994	1995	1996	1997	1998	75-84	85-89	90-MR
SUB-SAHARAN AFRICA	28.5	19.4	17.9	18.2	13.0	14.5	16.5	16.2	17.7	16.4	14.8	23.9	20.2	16.1
excluding South Africa	26.6	17.4	17.4	18.7	10.2	11.7	15.4	13.5	17.2	15.7	12.6	23.1	18.6	14.7
excl. S. Africa & Nigeria	20.4	15.9	15.0	16.6	7.0	10.1	14.3	12.6	13.3	14.4	13.3	21.4	18.6	13.0
Angola	..	27.0	29.6	16.1	1.7	25.2	32.7	15.7	20.2	25.2	12.5	..	23.9	19.9
Benin	-5.1	3.4	5.5	5.9	4.2	5.2	9.5	10.0	8.0	9.8	7.4	0.0	3.0	7.3
Botswana	34.4	43.2	37.1	37.7	35.2	36.1	38.9	40.6	43.4	37.4	35.1	30.2	49.2	37.9
Burkina Faso	-5.8	7.1	7.7	6.1	7.0	5.0	4.3	5.3	8.8	10.5	12.4	-1.7	2.4	7.4
Burundi	-0.6	3.3	-5.4	-4.2	-5.1	-4.5	-7.7	-4.8	2.4	3.9	-1.2	4.1	3.3	-2.9
Cameroon	21.7	20.1	20.7	22.0	16.5	17.6	17.9	19.6	19.1	20.6	20.2	23.1	22.9	19.4
Cape Verde	..	9.9	12.8	-1.9	-2.3	-4.0	-6.4	-14.5	-7.0	-4.6	-5.1	..	7.6	-3.7
Central African Republic	-8.9	2.3	-0.6	2.6	-0.4	1.8	6.0	-0.1	0.7	3.6	4.4	-1.6	0.8	2.0
Chad	-8.7	-12.1	-3.1	-7.7	-8.3	-8.8	-5.6	-2.7	-3.2	-3.4	-0.6	-7.2	-13.5	-4.8
Comoros	-10.1	-7.0	-3.2	2.1	-1.6	2.9	-5.9	-6.9	-6.1	-2.6	-5.0	-6.5	-2.5	-2.9
Congo, Democratic Rep. of	10.1	15.0	9.3	1.8	6.1	4.0	10.6	14.1	13.4	9.0	..	10.5	13.3	8.5
Congo, Republic of	35.7	27.8	23.8	18.6	24.4	23.6	26.6	28.4	34.3	35.2	26.5	26.1	23.2	26.8
Côte d'Ivoire	20.4	11.9	11.3	10.4	10.7	9.4	22.4	18.9	21.2	23.0	24.2	24.3	18.4	16.8
Djibouti	..	..	..	-10.2	-18.6	-11.0	-11.3	-8.7	-7.7	-6.2	..	..	..	-10.5
Equatorial Guinea	..	..	-20.1	-7.2	2.2	-1.0	18.8	22.4	24.6	33.2	20.0	7.6	..	10.3
Eritrea	..	..	..	..	-31.3	-24.6	-35.4	-31.5	-31.0	-17.4	-29.0	..	..	-28.6
Ethiopia	..	7.9	7.2	2.7	3.0	5.6	5.4	8.0	4.7	8.6	6.3	6.4	7.2	5.7
Gabon	60.6	30.9	36.9	40.5	34.7	36.7	45.3	44.2	46.8	48.3	43.2	58.1	32.3	41.8
Gambia, The	5.8	10.1	10.7	10.6	9.3	4.0	2.3	0.9	2.1	4.8	6.3	4.3	7.6	5.7
Ghana	4.9	5.6	5.5	7.3	1.3	6.6	12.6	11.7	11.9	9.8	13.2	6.3	5.5	8.9
Guinea	..	18.5	17.7	18.0	11.2	11.1	12.3	17.1	15.0	19.3	19.3	..	16.4	15.7
Guinea-Bissau	-0.9	1.7	2.8	3.2	3.2	7.0	3.9	-1.2	1.8	2.8	-8.9	-3.0	-0.1	1.6
Kenya	13.4	13.2	14.5	91.0	13.2	23.2	19.6	11.6	12.5	8.1	6.7	17.0	16.6	22.3
Lesotho	-59.3	-46.5	-30.5	-49.4	-45.5	-33.2	-14.6	-16.9	-1.8	-9.8	-42.7	-73.6	-67.1	-27.1
Liberia	27.3	..	..	..	..	..	..	..	..	..	..	23.3	16.4	..
Madagascar	-1.4	9.8	6.3	0.7	3.4	2.5	3.4	3.6	6.3	3.7	5.3	2.0	5.8	3.9
Malawi	10.8	4.7	9.7	14.2	0.7	-0.9	8.3	8.1	0.8	2.1	0.7	15.6	10.0	4.8
Mali	1.1	5.7	6.4	6.4	4.4	6.4	7.1	7.8	7.4	10.3	10.1	0.2	0.1	7.4
Mauritania	-3.1	10.6	4.4	9.7	6.0	6.1	10.7	5.6	7.5	8.4	8.0	-4.9	9.2	7.4
Mauritius	10.5	23.8	23.6	24.9	26.1	24.5	23.4	23.2	23.9	24.1	24.2	18.5	25.5	24.2
Mozambique	-10.6	-15.6	-12.3	-11.2	-17.2	-22.4	-13.9	-1.9	-1.6	1.6	1.7	-10.4	-10.2	-8.6
Namibia	36.8	13.5	17.6	9.2	12.1	9.6	16.9	12.8	13.5	14.2	18.8	9.3	11.5	13.9
Niger	14.6	7.0	1.2	4.5	4.3	3.3	0.0	0.4	3.1	3.2	3.3	8.4	7.9	2.6
Nigeria	31.4	25.3	29.4	29.3	23.5	20.2	20.6	18.2	33.5	21.9	11.8	21.5	17.7	23.2
Rwanda	4.2	2.3	6.2	3.3	1.2	-0.1	-54.5	-11.6	-9.8	-7.7	-7.3	6.8	5.3	-8.9
São Tomé and Principe	-14.9	-39.0	..	-27.3	-28.3	-28.8	-14.0	-20.1	-19.7	-16.0	9.1	-9.0	-21.3	-18.1
Senegal	-5.0	6.4	8.9	5.9	7.4	5.5	9.6	11.3	11.9	13.3	15.1	1.1	3.8	9.9
Seychelles	27.1	29.8	20.3	18.7	17.6	18.4	22.1	23.5	39.6	22.3	12.0	24.3	30.1	21.6
Sierra Leone	..	6.3	16.1	17.3	16.9	13.4	11.1	-1.8	-5.5	..	-1.3	1.1	3.9	8.3
Somalia	-12.9	-6.9	-12.5	..	..	..	..	..	..	..	..	-11.4	5.6	-12.5
South Africa	31.4	21.5	17.6	16.9	16.1	17.6	17.9	19.1	17.9	16.8	16.9	24.4	22.0	17.4
Sudan	2.1	..	..	..	..	..	..	..	..	..	0.0	5.8	7.9	0.0
Swaziland	6.5	11.9	20.4	18.2	18.6	26.3	26.0	29.0	18.8	19.5	19.2	16.0	17.7	21.8
Tanzania	..	-2.7	-0.8	2.2	1.5	-2.4	-1.0	2.0	3.6	5.4	6.0	..	0.3	1.8
Togo	23.2	7.3	14.7	9.0	6.6	-0.1	6.7	11.9	8.4	8.4	7.5	21.4	7.6	8.1
Uganda	-0.4	1.0	0.6	0.7	0.4	1.1	4.3	7.1	4.8	7.9	5.7	4.1	3.0	3.6
Zambia	19.3	3.8	16.6	8.4	0.0	9.0	9.3	8.1	8.7	9.3	5.3	18.9	14.9	8.3
Zimbabwe	13.8	16.7	17.4	15.8	11.0	21.0	22.3	22.4	26.1	20.0	19.8	15.2	19.0	19.5
NORTH AFRICA	40.4	22.9	21.9	23.7	22.7	20.1	18.1	18.1	19.3	20.7	18.9	35.4	24.6	20.4
Algeria	43.1	29.3	27.5	36.7	32.4	27.8	27.0	28.5	32.6	34.5	33.4	38.9	30.8	31.1
Egypt, Arab Republic	15.2	17.3	16.1	13.2	15.4	13.2	11.4	12.4	10.8	13.0	10.1	15.4	15.7	12.8
Libya	56.9	..	..	..	..	..	..	..	..	..	..	46.5	..	..
Morocco	13.7	18.3	19.2	17.2	16.8	17.0	15.3	14.2	16.1	16.8	18.4	12.9	18.2	16.8
Tunisia	24.0	20.6	20.0	21.0	22.3	21.7	21.5	20.7	23.5	24.2	23.7	24.2	21.6	22.1
ALL AFRICA	31.8	20.6	19.3	20.0	16.1	16.4	17.1	16.9	18.2	17.9	16.2	27.1	22.2	17.6

Note: 1998 data are preliminary (see page 3). Since 1994, Nigeria's ratios are distorted because the official exchange rate used by the Government for oil exports and oil value added is significantly over-valued.

2-12. Gross national savings

	Percentage of GDP											Annual average		
	1980	1989	1990	1991	1992	1993	1994	1995	1996	1997	1998	75-84	85-89	90-MR
SUB-SAHARAN AFRICA	24.1	15.7	13.7	14.6	9.9	11.4	13.6	13.2	14.6	13.7	12.1	20.5	17.0	13.0
excluding South Africa	22.1	13.5	13.0	14.7	6.7	8.1	11.8	9.8	13.8	13.0	9.9	20.1	15.4	11.2
excl. S. Africa & Nigeria	16.4	12.7	11.6	13.4	4.3	7.0	11.6	9.2	10.0	11.4	10.7	18.0	15.9	9.9
Angola	..	10.7	9.0	-2.8	-35.8	-10.4	-13.4	-35.8	-23.0	-16.6	-33.4	..	13.6	-18.0
Benin	2.3	10.0	12.0	11.7	9.2	10.8	13.1	13.0	11.8	13.0	10.2	4.9	7.3	11.7
Botswana	36.3	42.3	37.7	43.9	40.7	45.0	35.5	39.3	44.4	38.4	35.3	34.0	44.4	40.0
Burkina Faso	0.1	12.5	16.9	13.9	14.9	13.9	15.6	14.9	16.6	17.4	18.1	1.5	10.2	15.8
Burundi	4.6	10.4	3.5	6.3	4.2	7.6	6.6	6.7	5.5	7.7	3.0	7.5	7.9	5.7
Cameroon	6.3	16.9	16.1	16.3	12.4	11.3	11.2	13.7	13.0	14.9	15.9	13.4	20.5	13.9
Cape Verde	..	37.2	41.5	27.4	34.3	27.3	28.0	20.3	25.6	27.4	25.9	..	29.0	28.6
Central African Republic	-8.5	-1.7	-4.2	-0.7	0.1	1.8	6.1	0.0	-1.5	1.7	3.9	-3.8	-1.9	0.8
Chad	-8.6	-6.9	2.2	-2.6	-2.8	-7.7	0.4	0.0	-0.9	-2.9	0.2	-7.2	-6.4	-1.6
Comoros	0.9	19.6	14.9	19.4	14.9	24.2	9.3	8.8	9.6	9.1	6.7	13.0	22.2	13.0
Congo, Democratic Rep. of	..	..	..	-6.5	5.0	-4.2	-1.2	1.1	0.6	-3.5	..	..	..	-1.2
Congo, Republic of	..	10.2	6.6	1.9	10.9	9.4	16.6	9.7	8.7	13.1	10.9	38.0	14.0	9.7
Côte d'Ivoire	..	..	..	..	..	..	..	..	..	..	..	..	..	..
Djibouti	..	..	..	-4.9	-16.1	-3.4	-5.6	-1.5	-0.5	-0.5	..	..	..	-4.6
Equatorial Guinea	..	..	-22.0	-13.6	-3.4	-3.5	10.8	15.7	12.7	31.4	9.6	..	..	4.2
Eritrea	..	..	..	..	27.6	43.3	57.8	29.9	32.5	65.0	25.6	..	..	40.2
Ethiopia	..	9.8	9.0	4.4	5.9	9.7	9.9	14.9	11.4	12.0	10.3	7.9	9.5	9.7
Gabon	..	22.3	24.2	28.2	18.4	21.4	29.9	25.9	28.3	31.0	28.7	..	21.8	26.2
Gambia, The	5.1	9.0	5.3	9.3	11.4	6.3	4.8	3.9	4.9	7.0	9.1	4.0	9.0	6.9
Ghana	4.5	7.2	7.0	8.8	3.6	9.1	17.6	15.8	15.8	15.1	18.2	5.9	5.8	12.3
Guinea	..	8.3	8.2	10.7	4.9	5.8	7.9	11.5	11.0	15.1	15.0	..	7.2	10.0
Guinea-Bissau	..	7.7	15.3	6.8	10.6	9.8	9.4	4.7	6.6	12.3	-3.4	..	13.3	8.0
Kenya	10.7	10.0	11.2	87.1	9.2	17.8	16.2	12.1	14.4	10.4	9.3	13.9	13.7	20.9
Lesotho	-193.3	-8.7	12.0	10.2	16.5	21.1	55.4	59.8	72.9	47.9	14.5	-226.2	12.5	34.5
Liberia	..	..	..	..	..	..	..	..	..	..	..	..	..	..
Madagascar	-3.1	10.4	9.2	0.1	3.9	3.6	1.5	1.2	5.4	6.2	6.1	1.1	5.6	4.1
Malawi	..	..	..	..	..	..	..	..	2.7	2.2	-6.0	..	..	-0.4
Mali	1.9	12.8	15.1	16.6	14.3	14.9	18.1	13.6	12.9	13.3	13.1	1.0	7.5	14.7
Mauritania	3.7	28.4	6.1	10.1	14.1	12.5	12.4	7.8	17.5	18.6	18.6	3.4	21.0	13.1
Mauritius	8.4	26.8	26.1	28.2	29.3	27.7	25.6	25.5	25.7	26.2	24.8	17.4	26.7	26.6
Mozambique	..	..	..	..	..	..	..	..	..	..	..	..	..	..
Namibia	..	18.9	29.1	23.5	24.2	20.7	26.2	25.3	25.6	25.6	29.4	15.6	15.9	25.5
Niger	17.1	8.3	-2.1	1.9	2.8	3.5	-4.5	-3.6	0.3	0.8	-2.7	11.7	11.0	-0.4
Nigeria	..	16.9	19.4	20.5	16.7	11.2	11.6	11.1	27.8	17.3	6.0	20.6	17.0	15.7
Rwanda	13.3	2.7	11.3	12.3	6.2	4.3	-2.8	7.5	5.6	2.4	•1.1	15.5	8.8	5.3
São Tomé and Principe	-7.5	-30.7	..	-21.9	-29.6	-32.1	-12.2	-20.8	-25.1	-3.7	21.5	-4.2	-16.9	-15.5
Senegal	-7.4	2.3	6.0	2.9	5.8	2.3	9.3	10.3	10.4	11.7	14.0	-3.2	-0.6	8.1
Seychelles	23.5	27.9	21.7	20.2	19.5	19.6	21.8	21.6	40.1	23.3	10.7	19.6	27.4	22.1
Sierra Leone	..	2.8	6.9	12.6	9.5	7.7	1.4	-5.2	-2.3	..	3.6	0.2	1.1	4.3
Somalia	..	..	..	..	..	..	..	..	..	..	..	..	..	..
South Africa	27.3	18.0	13.7	13.8	13.5	15.1	15.6	16.8	15.2	14.1	..	20.2	18.1	14.6
Sudan	3.9										-6.2	7.9	10.7	-6.2
Swaziland	20.9	19.9	39.1	38.4	41.3	47.0	39.2	46.3	39.1	41.1	40.7	27.7	31.5	41.4
Tanzania	..	4.5	6.5	7.3	8.0	5.4	6.8	-0.6	1.5	3.7	..	..	9.9	4.8
Togo	27.2	9.5	18.2	12.2	8.8	0.8	3.9	11.3	8.8	9.1	8.3	24.8	9.4	9.0
Uganda	..	1.9	0.6	1.4	2.1	3.6	10.3	11.9	11.0	12.7	13.2	5.9	3.8	7.4
Zambia	..	..	..	..	..	..	..	..	..	..	..	..	..	..
Zimbabwe	..	..	..	..	..	..	..	..	..	..	..	..	..	..
NORTH AFRICA	36.6	17.6	20.8	16.9	18.1	16.0	14.6	15.0	16.8	18.8	17.4	31.4	19.9	17.2
Algeria	40.8	29.6	26.6	34.6	31.0	26.6	26.3	25.9	29.4	32.0	31.6	37.4	30.6	29.3
Egypt, Arab Republic	..	22.2	30.9	14.7	26.2	21.4	17.2	18.8	16.3	19.7	16.8	..	21.8	20.2
Libya	..	..	..	..	..	..	..	..	..	..	..	..	..	..
Morocco	16.9	20.2	24.4	21.3	..	..	..	..	..	..	..	16.5	21.6	22.8
Tunisia	25.1	20.8	21.7	21.5	21.3	20.0	20.2	20.0	22.4	23.6	23.1	24.7	21.5	21.5
ALL AFRICA	28.4	17.7	17.4	17.2	14.1	14.4	15.0	14.8	16.1	16.3	14.9	23.8	19.5	15.6

Note: 1998 data are preliminary (see page 3). Since 1994, Nigeria's ratios are distorted because the official exchange rate used by the Government for oil exports and oil value added is significantly over-valued.

2-13. Resource balance

	Percentage of GDP											*Annual average*		
	1980	1989	1990	1991	1992	1993	1994	1995	1996	1997	1998	75-84	85-89	90-MR
SUB-SAHARAN AFRICA	2.9	0.4	2.0	0.3	-1.0	-1.5	-1.1	-1.8	0.5	-1.0	-3.4	-1.7	0.6	-0.8
excluding South Africa	0.6	-2.2	-0.4	-2.9	-5.0	-5.9	-4.3	-4.2	-0.2	-2.7	-6.7	-3.7	-2.6	-3.6
excl. S. Africa & Nigeria	-6.1	-3.7	-3.1	-4.5	-6.5	-6.3	-5.3	-5.5	-5.1	-5.1	-6.1	-5.1	-3.6	-5.3
Angola	..	14.7	17.9	3.2	-1.9	-1.3	9.5	-9.3	-2.5	1.4	-12.0	..	9.1	0.6
Benin	-20.3	-8.4	-8.7	-8.6	-9.5	-10.1	-6.2	-9.6	-9.1	-8.7	-8.8	-17.8	-9.5	-8.8
Botswana	-2.4	12.2	5.3	7.3	6.6	9.5	12.0	13.7	17.6	10.6	9.8	-2.8	24.2	10.3
Burkina Faso	-22.9	-14.5	-12.9	-14.5	-14.1	-14.8	-13.1	-15.3	-17.7	-16.5	-16.2	-21.8	-19.3	-15.0
Burundi	-14.5	-13.2	-19.9	-18.6	-20.0	-20.2	-18.2	-14.4	-9.6	-4.2	-9.0	-10.2	-12.6	-14.9
Cameroon	0.8	3.0	2.9	5.4	2.2	1.1	2.6	5.1	3.7	4.4	1.8	-2.0	0.3	3.2
Cape Verde	..	-33.8	-30.3	-30.9	-40.1	-39.5	-47.9	-49.3	-40.5	-34.9	-37.8	..	-31.9	-39.0
Central African Republic	-15.9	-9.2	-12.9	-9.8	-12.6	-8.3	-5.7	-7.3	-3.7	-5.4	-9.1	-12.0	-11.7	-8.3
Chad	-11.9	-18.8	-16.7	-13.2	-14.5	-16.9	-18.8	-15.8	-17.0	-18.2	-13.2	-10.3	-20.1	-16.0
Comoros	-43.2	-24.4	-22.9	-18.2	-23.8	-17.7	-26.9	-26.8	-24.9	-23.8	-24.8	-39.8	-26.7	-23.3
Congo, Democratic Rep. of	0.1	0.7	0.3	-3.7	-0.8	2.2	2.7	4.8	6.3	1.9	..	-2.2	-0.4	1.7
Congo, Republic of	-0.1	13.7	7.9	-1.9	2.8	-5.9	-27.9	-8.2	-26.1	9.2	-8.7	-10.2	0.8	-6.5
Côte d'Ivoire	-6.2	3.0	4.6	3.0	3.8	1.1	9.8	5.4	7.7	7.0	6.0	0.7	6.6	5.4
Djibouti	..	..	..	-24.6	-37.6	-28.2	-23.0	-17.2	-16.9	-15.7	..	..	..	-23.3
Equatorial Guinea	..	-32.2	-37.4	-57.9	-22.0	-23.0	-48.9	-49.0	-82.8	-28.2	..	-6.3	-28.6	-43.7
Eritrea	..	..	..	..	-36.6	-39.7	-53.1	-50.8	-60.3	-58.3	-69.9	..	..	-52.7
Ethiopia	..	-5.6	-4.6	-7.2	-6.2	-8.6	-9.8	-8.5	-14.4	-10.5	-11.9	-7.4	-7.5	-9.1
Gabon	33.1	4.6	15.2	14.0	12.3	14.2	23.4	21.5	24.0	21.9	10.9	15.2	-3.4	17.5
Gambia, The	-20.9	-10.2	-11.7	-11.3	-12.9	-17.0	-15.9	-19.2	-19.5	-12.8	-13.5	-15.4	-9.5	-14.9
Ghana	-0.7	-7.6	-9.0	-8.6	-11.5	-15.6	-11.3	-8.3	-9.6	-14.3	-9.7	-0.6	-5.3	-10.9
Guinea	..	1.3	0.2	-0.1	-6.2	-6.7	-7.2	-3.5	-4.6	-2.3	-2.9	..	0.2	-3.7
Guinea-Bissau	-29.1	-37.3	-27.1	-27.8	-45.2	-23.8	-17.9	-23.5	-21.3	-18.8	-20.2	-27.2	-35.6	-25.1
Kenya	-11.1	-7.4	-5.2	-1.3	-0.5	5.5	3.1	-5.9	-4.3	-7.4	-7.7	-4.1	-3.7	-2.6
Lesotho	-101.8	-107.1	-101.2	-129.6	-123.8	-108.2	-94.9	-100.1	-91.0	-95.3	-91.2	-108.6	-117.0	-103.9
Liberia	0.0	..	..	..	..	..	..	..	..	..	..	-0.5	7.2	..
Madagascar	-16.4	-3.6	-10.7	-7.5	-7.9	-8.9	-7.5	-7.3	-5.3	-8.2	-8.0	-8.2	-5.1	-7.9
Malawi	-14.0	-16.4	-10.1	-6.0	-19.2	-16.1	-21.0	-8.5	-11.5	-10.2	-13.0	-9.7	-7.2	-12.9
Mali	-14.4	-16.1	-16.6	-16.4	-17.4	-15.4	-18.9	-15.1	-15.5	-10.3	-10.8	-14.6	-20.0	-15.1
Mauritania	-26.0	-6.3	-13.6	-8.2	-14.5	-15.9	-3.8	-10.4	-11.7	-9.2	-13.0	-28.2	-14.4	-11.1
Mauritius	-10.3	-7.3	-7.2	-3.8	-3.3	-6.2	-8.9	-2.5	-1.3	-3.5	-2.0	-6.8	-1.1	-4.3
Mozambique	-16.5	-30.4	-27.9	-27.3	-32.8	-35.1	-33.7	-24.7	-20.6	-17.4	-18.8	-16.2	-20.5	-26.5
Namibia	7.5	-2.9	-9.8	-8.9	-9.0	-6.5	-6.2	-7.9	-9.0	-5.5	-0.2	-12.7	-1.6	-7.0
Niger	-13.5	-6.7	-6.9	-4.7	-1.1	-2.4	-10.3	-7.1	-6.5	-7.6	-7.1	-9.8	-5.8	-6.0
Nigeria	10.2	7.5	14.6	5.9	1.7	-3.1	1.0	2.1	20.7	6.5	-8.2	-0.8	2.6	4.6
Rwanda	-11.9	-11.1	-8.5	-10.7	-12.7	-15.3	-58.8	-20.2	-20.1	-17.7	-17.2	-8.0	-10.1	-20.1
São Tomé and Principe	-49.1	-67.4	-66.7	-58.6	-67.0	-66.9	-59.1	-79.5	-69.9	-65.6	-42.5	-42.4	-46.4	-64.0
Senegal	-16.7	-5.4	-4.9	-6.9	-7.4	-8.6	-6.7	-5.6	-5.5	-5.4	-4.6	-12.0	-8.0	-6.2
Seychelles	-11.2	2.6	-4.3	-3.6	-3.6	-10.3	-4.0	-6.8	-11.3	-13.7	-10.5	-9.2	6.5	-7.6
Sierra Leone	-10.0	-3.5	6.7	6.7	8.7	5.7	3.2	-7.4	-14.8	-3.0	-9.5	-8.0	-2.6	-0.4
Somalia	-55.3	-37.2	-28.0	..	..	..	..	..	..	..	..	-38.5	-22.9	-28.0
South Africa	8.0	5.0	5.8	5.0	4.0	3.7	2.3	0.9	1.4	1.1	1.2	3.0	7.1	2.8
Sudan	-12.6	..	..	..	..	..	..	..	..	..	0.0	-10.2	-5.1	0.0
Swaziland	-23.8	-11.3	0.8	-2.4	-7.5	-0.3	-6.1	-5.2	-11.3	-14.5	6.9	-15.6	-3.9	-4.4
Tanzania	..	-20.1	-23.4	-24.0	-25.3	-28.5	-25.9	-19.8	-14.4	-10.9	-9.9	..	-19.9	-20.2
Togo	-5.3	-9.2	-11.9	-8.1	-9.2	-7.7	-3.7	-4.2	-8.0	-6.5	-6.7	-8.4	-9.6	-7.3
Uganda	-6.6	-10.1	-12.1	-14.5	-15.5	-14.1	-10.4	-9.0	-11.5	-8.1	-9.4	-3.1	-6.8	-11.6
Zambia	-4.0	-7.0	-0.7	-2.6	-11.9	-6.0	-4.2	-5.8	-6.2	-5.2	-9.0	-3.4	0.3	-5.7
Zimbabwe	-3.2	1.6	0.1	-3.3	-9.3	-1.7	-1.9	-2.7	0.2	-6.2	-1.4	-1.5	2.1	-2.9
NORTH AFRICA	8.2	-1.1	-1.1	4.0	3.7	2.2	0.5	0.9	4.0	5.0	..	0.8	-0.6	2.4
Algeria	4.0	0.3	-1.8	5.6	2.3	-1.4	-4.7	-3.7	6.4	8.8	6.4	-2.7	0.2	2.0
Egypt, Arab Republic	-12.4	-14.5	-12.7	-8.0	-2.8	-3.0	-5.2	-5.1	-5.8	-4.7	-9.3	-14.5	-12.9	-6.3
Libya	34.8	..	..	..	..	..	..	..	..	..	..	20.1	..	..
Morocco	-10.5	-5.4	-5.9	-5.6	-6.4	-5.5	-6.0	-6.5	-3.7	-3.8	-3.2	-13.6	-5.0	-5.2
Tunisia	-5.4	-3.3	-7.0	-5.0	-6.9	-7.5	-3.0	-4.1	-1.7	-2.5	-1.8	-7.0	-3.4	-4.4
ALL AFRICA	4.0	-0.3	0.6	0.9	0.0	-0.8	-1.0	-1.3	1.3	0.6	-2.2	-1.4	-0.1	-0.2

Note: 1998 data are preliminary (see page 3). Since 1994, Nigeria's ratios are distorted because the official exchange rate used by the Government for oil exports and oil value added is significantly over-valued.

2-14. Exports of goods and nonfactor services, nominal

	Millions of U.S. dollars, current prices											Annual average		
	1980	1989	1990	1991	1992	1993	1994	1995	1996	1997	1998	75-84	85-89	90-MR
SUB-SAHARAN AFRICA	80,966	67,416	78,713	74,620	78,642	72,217	77,778	91,394	101,909	102,675	90,632	51,325	58,573	85,398
excluding South Africa	52,971	42,288	51,495	47,694	50,889	44,212	47,712	56,744	66,736	66,239	56,226	33,826	36,140	54,216
excl. S.Africa & Nigeria	31,664	34,602	39,155	37,604	37,056	34,194	37,908	44,366	49,754	49,984	46,860	24,251	30,693	41,876
Angola	..	3,144	3,980	3,697	3,975	2,849	3,465	3,493	5,043	5,147	3,795	..	2,615	3,938
Benin	323	302	402	459	388	478	411	544	559	532	537	244	395	479
Botswana	550	1,849	2,012	2,228	1,997	2,132	2,214	2,470	2,980	2,501	2,560	453	1,407	2,344
Burkina Faso	173	244	352	337	202	237	244	306	276	267	356	126	214	286
Burundi	81	109	89	116	95	88	95	129	50	96	57	86	125	91
Cameroon	1,898	2,334	2,251	2,487	2,341	2,032	1,734	2,055	2,204	2,443	2,343	1,615	2,226	2,210
Cape Verde	..	47	56	47	49	48	61	83	101	132	137	..	44	79
Central African Republic	201	214	220	176	165	182	205	229	185	196	168	145	194	192
Chad	175	198	234	224	209	195	190	309	262	271	375	143	173	252
Comoros	11	30	36	49	48	53	38	46	42	30	32	15	29	42
Congo, Democratic Rep. of	..	2,299	2,758	1,852	1,369	1,017	1,620	1,805	1,650	1,463	..	2,051	2,105	1,692
Congo, Republic of	1,024	1,160	1,502	1,228	1,257	849	1,115	1,252	1,726	1,774	1,236	782	996	1,327
Côte d'Ivoire	3,561	3,126	3,421	3,149	3,559	2,991	3,291	4,109	5,014	4,777	4,752	2,701	3,301	3,896
Djibouti	..	..	..	249	201	233	215	200	200	207	..	..	..	215
Equatorial Guinea	..	41	42	42	58	58	70	91	201	489	..	34	39	131
Eritrea	..	..	..	..	88	139	144	171	200	201	129	..	..	153
Ethiopia	..	734	535	304	251	521	489	786	785	1,011	1,034	560	640	635
Gabon	2,770	1,917	2,740	2,554	2,577	2,136	2,585	2,916	3,474	3,295	2,823	1,877	1,603	2,789
Gambia, The	103	156	190	202	219	213	182	172	183	184	216	77	117	196
Ghana	376	879	993	1,120	1,105	1,068	1,225	1,583	1,727	1,655	2,004	336	850	1,387
Guinea	..	756	870	694	637	640	598	757	715	773	813	..	660	722
Guinea-Bissau	14	19	24	26	11	21	39	30	28	56	31	12	16	30
Kenya	2,030	1,923	2,234	2,200	2,154	2,326	2,644	2,967	3,020	2,977	2,851	1,533	1,782	2,597
Lesotho	74	84	87	89	133	157	167	183	219	309	265	44	59	179
Liberia	614	..	..	..	..	..	..	..	..	..	..	508	466	..
Madagascar	539	461	512	480	496	516	656	762	819	773	796	415	406	646
Malawi	307	299	447	513	418	334	350	424	515	613	549	258	293	463
Mali	263	334	415	442	439	423	405	520	524	640	636	175	290	494
Mauritania	261	489	465	498	448	413	431	525	516	435	407	255	455	460
Mauritius	579	1,401	1,724	1,780	1,912	1,899	2,018	2,370	2,749	2,586	2,586	471	1,092	2,180
Mozambique	383	190	205	279	271	278	317	363	428	438	456	275	155	337
Namibia	1,712	1,269	1,232	1,371	1,514	1,522	1,612	1,722	1,709	1,726	1,961	1,210	1,078	1,596
Niger	617	362	372	327	393	251	258	323	337	300	333	397	385	322
Nigeria	18,859	7,795	12,366	10,165	13,816	10,062	9,881	12,449	16,995	16,286	9,712	8,898	5,563	12,415
Rwanda	168	148	145	140	113	102	48	67	83	144	109	144	179	106
São Tomé and Principe	20	11	8	11	10	10	12	9	11	12	14	13	11	11
Senegal	803	1,234	1,450	1,358	1,403	1,203	1,272	1,543	1,587	1,488	1,559	775	1,035	1,429
Seychelles	100	201	230	219	243	257	250	271	317	365	366	77	157	280
Sierra Leone	213	142	215	213	215	192	270	164	163	116	142	154	124	188
Somalia	200	84	90	..	..	..	..	..	..	..	..	142	64	90
South Africa	28,267	25,173	27,327	26,997	27,844	28,034	30,099	34,703	35,306	36,549	34,384	17,752	22,450	31,249
Sudan	806	..	..	..	..	..	..	..	..	..	0	782	871	0
Swaziland	404	712	660	709	761	838	837	1,052	999	1,075	1,228	290	444	906
Tanzania	..	506	509	536	563	707	821	1,120	1,271	1,245	1,248	..	456	891
Togo	580	537	545	536	456	301	300	453	483	521	509	401	498	456
Uganda	242	418	312	248	250	227	349	679	724	826	697	258	483	479
Zambia	1,608	1,071	1,180	1,169	1,149	1,046	1,175	1,306	1,109	1,248	984	1,138	946	1,152
Zimbabwe	1,561	1,934	2,009	2,064	1,838	2,016	2,384	2,721	3,116	3,192	2,379	1,211	1,631	2,413
NORTH AFRICA	47,067	37,147	48,161	48,637	51,423	50,525	49,761	57,280	62,010	64,888	..	31,402	33,024	54,086
Algeria	14,541	10,224	14,425	13,346	12,195	10,880	9,966	11,325	14,077	14,681	14,580	10,568	9,996	12,831
Egypt, Arab Republic	6,992	7,094	8,647	10,284	12,150	13,071	11,904	13,506	13,650	15,251	13,011	5,294	6,161	12,386
Libya	23,523	..	..	..	..	..	..	..	..	..	..	13,757	..	..
Morocco	3,273	5,409	6,849	6,716	7,161	7,123	7,555	9,090	9,503	9,342	..	2,584	4,527	7,917
Tunisia	3,518	4,480	5,353	5,278	6,158	5,931	7,021	8,031	8,188	8,251	9,167	2,441	3,504	7,042
ALL AFRICA	123,466	103,551	124,786	120,716	127,357	119,623	125,070	146,000	161,291	164,455	148,823	79,966	90,560	137,569

Note: 1998 data are preliminary (see page 3)

2-15. Imports of goods and nonfactor services, nominal

	Millions of U.S. dollars, current prices											Annual average		
	1980	1989	1990	1991	1992	1993	1994	1995	1996	1997	1998	75-84	85-89	90-MR
SUB-SAHARAN AFRICA	73,271	66,251	72,814	73,764	81,817	76,579	80,751	96,964	100,159	106,289	102,047	54,389	57,327	87,910
excluding South Africa	51,855	46,055	52,190	53,022	59,561	53,575	53,939	63,738	67,024	71,623	69,593	38,967	40,452	60,474
excl. S.Africa & Nigeria	38,606	40,218	44,099	44,563	46,245	42,847	44,335	51,909	57,489	57,963	56,510	29,265	35,703	49,551
Angola	..	1,773	2,140	3,303	4,088	2,915	3,079	3,964	5,235	5,042	4,590	..	1,900	3,818
Benin	608	428	563	621	543	692	505	736	761	719	740	433	531	653
Botswana	576	1,469	1,818	1,924	1,723	1,700	1,665	1,791	2,010	1,932	2,005	459	900	1,841
Burkina Faso	564	587	709	743	483	540	488	666	725	660	775	413	596	643
Burundi	214	256	314	333	312	285	264	273	137	136	142	175	267	244
Cameroon	1,847	2,002	1,931	1,820	2,087	1,904	1,532	1,646	1,867	2,041	2,185	1,696	2,209	1,890
Cape Verde	..	137	148	146	192	179	227	290	273	280	308	..	126	227
Central African Republic	327	330	411	314	346	290	253	311	225	250	264	220	327	296
Chad	298	450	503	458	467	429	411	537	540	562	603	240	404	501
Comoros	64	78	93	94	111	99	88	103	95	76	81	60	75	94
Congo, Democratic Rep. of	..	2,241	2,730	2,192	1,438	818	1,424	1,504	1,281	1,350	..	2,059	2,140	1,592
Congo, Republic of	1,026	832	1,282	1,280	1,176	962	1,609	1,425	2,387	1,561	1,407	872	963	1,454
Côte d'Ivoire	4,190	2,835	2,927	2,832	3,136	2,874	2,538	3,570	4,188	4,055	4,087	2,714	2,742	3,356
Djibouti	..	..	..	361	378	366	327	284	282	285	..	..	..	326
Equatorial Guinea	..	77	92	118	92	93	132	171	416	629	..	49	72	218
Eritrea	..	..	..	..	248	301	415	463	580	583	583	..	..	453
Ethiopia	..	1,183	851	686	595	1,059	969	1,276	1,652	1,682	1,810	973	1,191	1,175
Gabon	1,354	1,725	1,837	1,798	1,890	1,513	1,603	1,847	2,089	2,165	2,220	1,338	1,717	1,885
Gambia, The	153	185	227	237	263	275	239	246	260	236	273	108	140	251
Ghana	407	1,278	1,522	1,685	1,845	2,000	1,842	2,121	2,393	2,640	2,732	360	1,124	2,086
Guinea	..	724	864	697	841	860	844	887	896	861	919	..	658	852
Guinea-Bissau	46	98	90	97	113	77	81	89	86	107	72	48	75	90
Kenya	2,837	2,540	2,679	2,302	2,193	2,051	2,420	3,503	3,417	3,756	3,742	1,791	2,087	2,896
Lesotho	450	632	717	847	951	915	888	1,036	1,002	1,215	988	353	487	951
Liberia	614	..	..	..	..	..	..	..	..	..	..	514	387	..
Madagascar	1,202	550	842	681	733	817	878	994	1,031	1,064	1,094	691	542	904
Malawi	480	549	629	646	764	667	597	549	777	870	769	352	392	696
Mali	520	657	816	838	935	834	754	892	934	899	928	364	635	870
Mauritania	473	557	619	591	620	563	470	636	643	536	536	463	591	579
Mauritius	695	1,561	1,915	1,887	2,017	2,098	2,330	2,469	2,803	2,732	2,668	541	1,122	2,324
Mozambique	965	894	906	959	913	1,017	1,080	955	1,014	1,038	1,186	836	711	1,008
Namibia	1,542	1,334	1,472	1,600	1,778	1,700	1,802	1,984	1,995	1,908	1,966	1,452	1,127	1,801
Niger	957	508	545	436	418	291	420	457	466	441	479	569	495	439
Nigeria	12,324	5,998	8,203	8,559	13,248	10,719	9,646	11,858	9,688	13,677	13,115	8,996	4,898	10,968
Rwanda	307	417	364	345	372	404	488	334	363	474	467	237	397	401
São Tomé and Principe	41	42	42	44	41	42	41	46	42	41	31	27	33	41
Senegal	1,301	1,486	1,728	1,740	1,851	1,668	1,515	1,796	1,851	1,730	1,780	1,070	1,340	1,740
Seychelles	117	193	246	233	259	306	270	306	375	438	422	89	141	317
Sierra Leone	334	183	155	158	155	148	240	228	302	140	203	238	153	192
Somalia	534	490	346	..	..	..	..	..	..	..	..	400	296	346
South Africa	21,838	20,380	20,886	21,014	22,585	23,240	26,973	33,386	33,340	34,900	32,733	15,866	17,053	27,673
Sudan	1,763	..	..	..	..	..	..	..	..	..	0	1,606	1,697	0
Swaziland	543	794	653	730	834	840	901	1,117	1,138	1,265	1,145	371	458	958
Tanzania	..	1,465	1,498	1,676	1,805	2,003	1,912	2,103	2,113	2,012	2,034	..	1,327	1,906
Togo	640	661	738	665	612	396	337	508	601	619	610	471	609	565
Uganda	324	950	834	729	694	682	763	1,199	1,417	1,335	1,335	364	873	999
Zambia	1,764	1,351	1,203	1,258	1,527	1,244	1,317	1,506	1,311	1,454	1,286	1,249	941	1,345
Zimbabwe	1,771	1,800	2,002	2,348	2,463	2,130	2,516	2,912	3,100	3,709	2,463	1,342	1,481	2,627
NORTH AFRICA	36,840	38,702	49,890	43,041	45,777	46,988	48,954	55,715	54,232	54,911	59,542	29,995	33,838	51,006
Algeria	12,847	10,038	15,529	10,738	11,048	11,557	11,940	12,855	11,144	10,534	11,426	10,816	9,883	11,863
Egypt, Arab Republic	9,822	12,827	14,109	13,234	13,325	14,488	14,604	16,544	17,562	18,820	20,301	8,159	10,934	15,888
Libya	11,167	..	..	..	..	..	..	..	..	..	..	8,634	..	..
Morocco	5,247	6,641	8,384	8,271	8,986	8,590	9,377	11,243	10,862	10,622	..	4,372	5,378	9,542
Tunisia	3,986	4,815	6,220	5,926	7,237	7,033	7,492	8,766	8,525	8,719	9,557	2,950	3,813	7,719
ALL AFRICA	108,012	104,856	122,150	116,678	127,573	123,287	129,447	152,562	154,480	161,460	160,476	83,199	91,019	138,679

Note: 1998 data are preliminary (see page 3).

2-16. Exports of goods and nonfactor services, real

| | Millions of U.S. dollars, constant 1995 prices | | | | | | | | | | | Average annual percentage growth | | |
	1980	1989	1990	1991	1992	1993	1994	1995	1996	1997	1998	75-84	85-89	90-MR
SUB-SAHARAN AFRICA	66,219	74,406	77,184	76,863	79,329	79,724	84,787	91,394	100,280	105,150	105,112	1.0	2.9	4.4
excluding South Africa	42,271	46,883	49,202	48,894	50,656	49,633	53,406	56,744	62,429	65,206	64,226	1.2	3.0	4.0
excl. S. Africa & Nigeria	28,265	38,194	39,732	38,973	40,407	39,785	42,850	44,366	48,590	51,214	51,446	2.7	3.1	3.6
Angola	..	2,282	2,614	2,052	4,425	2,643	3,878	3,493	3,736	4,081	3,745	..	1.9	6.4
Benin	730	529	484	602	726	733	579	544	638	652	646	4.0	-2.4	1.9
Botswana	..	2,255	2,249	2,328	2,171	2,142	2,285	2,470	2,876	3,019	3,170	..	10.7	4.1
Burkina Faso	335	271	375	387	333	398	287	306	311	355	393	4.7	-0.2	0.8
Burundi	54	90	95	115	136	114	96	129	65	132	121	4.7	0.2	1.1
Cameroon	1,456	2,976	2,684	2,574	2,710	2,263	2,014	2,055	2,176	2,426	2,540	14.0	-1.5	-2.3
Cape Verde	..	61	65	53	50	56	70	83	104	111	140	..	..	10.4
Central African Republic	144	126	124	123	108	126	239	229	211	293	295	-0.4	0.0	12.4
Chad	190	291	255	246	237	253	254	309	276	322	415	-0.3	5.2	3.8
Comoros	8	23	23	36	33	43	39	46	48	50	50	..	10.2	9.2
Congo, Democratic Rep. of	2,008	3,721	3,684	3,054	1,779	1,621	1,499	1,805	2,083	1,833	2,095	4.2	1.0	-7.0
Congo, Republic of	718	1,216	1,306	1,046	1,114	1,117	1,218	1,252	1,427	1,583	1,692	10.1	2.2	3.9
Côte d'Ivoire	3,073	3,720	4,116	3,796	3,787	3,386	4,093	4,109	5,031	5,262	5,175	8.5	0.7	4.0
Djibouti	..	..	..	..	..	..	..	..	..	..	..	..	..	..
Equatorial Guinea	..	27	23	25	30	41	89	91	184	573	..	..	-1.8	44.4
Eritrea	..	..	..	..	105	173	158	171	194	203	135	..	..	4.7
Ethiopia	..	829	812	619	329	605	708	786	824	1,244	1,127	..	1.6	6.2
Gabon	1,629	2,149	2,400	2,470	2,533	2,851	2,979	2,916	3,161	3,276	3,186	0.7	0.4	4.6
Gambia, The	113	186	207	214	218	213	185	172	179	183	193	7.3	-1.2	-1.4
Ghana	883	979	1,040	1,136	1,167	1,366	1,428	1,583	1,954	1,946	2,226	-9.4	11.3	9.8
Guinea	..	622	651	671	626	699	655	757	744	727	815	..	6.6	2.6
Guinea-Bissau	24	15	20	25	13	19	38	30	28	55	35	-1.8	5.8	12.1
Kenya	1,572	2,058	2,522	2,491	2,472	3,251	3,213	2,967	3,102	2,683	2,528	-0.2	5.6	2.4
Lesotho	122	164	141	153	146	171	179	183	239	285	330	6.3	17.3	9.0
Liberia	..	..	..	..	..	..	..	..	..	..	..	..	..	..
Madagascar	784	542	620	646	623	657	723	762	781	645	652	-4.1	0.3	2.2
Malawi	353	319	398	419	407	386	426	424	494	558	566	2.7	-1.7	5.3
Mali	242	347	368	415	443	457	489	520	535	769	779	8.9	2.7	9.0
Mauritania	366	500	445	452	371	323	456	525	522	433	471	5.8	-0.3	0.8
Mauritius	802	1,710	1,851	1,930	1,996	2,156	2,220	2,370	2,607	2,720	2,848	3.8	15.5	5.8
Mozambique	269	139	146	187	233	322	383	363	430	422	450	..	2.7	15.5
Namibia	1,389	1,322	1,079	1,530	1,619	1,771	1,612	1,722	1,838	1,885	1,922	..	1.7	5.1
Niger	380	313	316	303	288	276	303	323	329	326	355	-1.3	-1.3	1.4
Nigeria	12,962	8,797	9,571	10,005	10,337	9,940	10,656	12,449	13,913	14,082	12,910	-2.9	2.3	5.2
Rwanda	153	195	188	174	159	138	55	67	93	105	92	6.5	1.8	-10.0
São Tomé and Principe	..	8	6	7	8	8	10	9	12	17	19	..	10.1	11.9
Senegal	932	1,390	1,447	1,455	1,351	1,318	1,439	1,543	1,576	1,601	1,684	0.5	2.8	2.0
Seychelles	..	293	299	318	300	318	339	271	341	368	380	..	21.7	2.4
Sierra Leone	149	98	249	259	251	198	276	164	128	96	175	-17.2	13.4	-3.6
Somalia	..	..	..	..	..	..	..	..	..	..	..	..	..	..
South Africa	24,198	27,581	28,055	28,040	28,750	30,142	31,448	34,703	37,914	40,005	40,917	0.7	2.8	5.1
Sudan	..	..	..	..	..	..	..	..	..	..	..	..	..	..
Swaziland	468	1,017	1,010	1,018	972	997	1,023	1,052	1,104	1,140	1,175	2.6	20.3	1.7
Tanzania	..	527	574	572	549	763	913	1,120	1,279	1,122	979	..	..	10.6
Togo	603	543	500	504	434	323	357	453	466	501	500	4.6	4.2	-0.5
Uganda	..	366	385	363	420	401	528	679	863	1,118	952	..	1.2	14.3
Zambia	1,663	1,235	1,101	1,207	1,733	1,445	1,361	1,306	1,368	1,569	1,451	-2.9	-2.9	2.2
Zimbabwe	997	1,508	1,580	1,741	1,806	2,065	2,484	2,721	2,791	3,007	2,844	5.4	5.5	8.8
NORTH AFRICA	28,923	43,761	47,148	47,442	51,281	53,660	53,960	57,280	59,537	63,432	67,366	3.7	6.4	4.6
Algeria	7,239	10,560	10,919	10,821	11,243	11,029	10,654	11,325	12,130	13,195	14,052	1.9	3.0	2.7
Egypt, Arab Republic	6,537	9,782	10,481	10,830	12,228	13,113	12,477	13,506	13,718	14,051	15,179	5.5	7.1	4.6
Libya	..	..	..	..	..	..	..	..	..	..	..	..	..	..
Morocco	3,553	5,664	6,821	6,841	7,331	8,175	8,495	9,090	9,832	10,452	10,827	3.3	7.8	7.1
Tunisia	3,855	6,045	6,311	6,255	6,757	6,985	7,895	8,031	7,925	8,761	9,283	5.6	10.5	5.0
ALL AFRICA	95,348	116,536	122,307	122,196	127,992	130,348	136,111	146,000	157,517	165,979	169,132	1.7	3.9	4.5

Note: 1998 data are preliminary (see page 3).

2-17. Imports of goods and nonfactor services, real

	Millions of U.S. dollars, constant 1995 prices											Average annual percentage growth		
	1980	*1989*	*1990*	*1991*	*1992*	*1993*	*1994*	*1995*	*1996*	*1997*	*1998*	*75-84*	*85-89*	*90-MR*
SUB-SAHARAN AFRICA	95,976	79,344	78,881	80,534	83,662	84,197	88,033	96,964	105,114	111,576	112,952	1.5	-0.8	4.6
excluding South Africa	74,252	57,229	58,128	59,336	61,311	59,932	59,712	63,738	69,014	73,544	74,115	3.0	-2.0	3.0
excl. S. Africa & Nigeria	44,158	48,112	47,938	47,971	49,700	48,490	49,127	51,909	56,098	59,529	58,947	..	2.4	2.6
Angola	..	1,689	2,032	1,676	4,158	2,472	3,449	3,964	3,878	3,998	3,170	..	-2.2	9.4
Benin	1,119	464	678	720	814	819	539	736	767	795	850	2.8	-6.6	3.8
Botswana	..	2,126	2,245	2,075	1,912	1,741	1,729	1,791	1,954	2,131	2,269	..	14.0	-0.2
Burkina Faso	547	592	687	740	706	763	545	666	732	738	779	3.2	4.3	1.5
Burundi	193	218	250	262	254	257	274	273	131	169	224	8.4	-4.1	-3.4
Cameroon	1,284	1,832	2,016	2,085	1,681	1,694	1,745	1,646	1,863	2,226	2,410	10.5	-3.7	1.6
Cape Verde	..	175	172	164	199	209	262	290	281	276	304	..	..	7.8
Central African Republic	319	298	287	306	329	286	305	311	222	291	298	3.0	2.8	-1.0
Chad	380	675	638	593	584	559	469	537	563	640	689	-4.0	7.9	-0.3
Comoros	102	106	104	106	121	115	98	103	99	96	97	..	-3.2	-1.4
Congo, Democratic Rep. of	2,103	5,230	3,949	3,678	2,270	1,473	1,101	1,504	1,421	1,386	1,515	4.2	9.5	-13.9
Congo, Republic of	1,244	1,200	1,346	1,379	1,228	1,548	1,771	1,425	2,456	1,744	1,587	8.0	-11.9	4.8
Côte d'Ivoire	4,160	3,176	2,877	3,013	3,089	3,030	3,077	3,570	3,927	4,162	4,297	3.2	-0.1	4.4
Djibouti	..	..	..	..	..	..	..	..	..	..	..	..	..	..
Equatorial Guinea	..	70	54	68	52	60	165	171	427	783	..	..	12.6	36.9
Eritrea	..	..	..	..	277	338	449	463	607	642	669	..	..	16.3
Ethiopia	..	1,441	1,158	1,250	1,088	1,333	1,174	1,276	1,545	1,573	1,758	..	3.0	3.3
Gabon	2,091	2,283	2,175	2,133	2,157	2,253	1,896	1,847	2,281	2,624	2,426	4.0	-9.2	0.9
Gambia, The	337	224	251	264	274	273	242	246	256	236	247	5.3	0.1	-0.1
Ghana	1,946	1,509	1,588	1,747	1,863	2,177	2,180	2,121	2,395	2,747	2,976	-9.8	9.9	7.5
Guinea	..	820	900	904	881	931	860	887	870	897	921	..	4.9	0.5
Guinea-Bissau	99	123	104	117	130	98	96	89	84	104	74	0.1	-5.9	-4.3
Kenya	2,110	1,978	2,044	1,953	1,907	2,552	2,981	3,503	3,566	3,654	3,502	-3.9	9.4	9.0
Lesotho	770	1,034	974	1,080	1,059	1,000	954	1,036	1,090	1,220	1,239	7.2	4.2	1.9
Liberia	..	..	..	..	..	..	..	..	..	..	..	..	..	..
Madagascar	1,892	766	1,008	820	841	960	970	994	1,035	1,113	1,124	-3.2	-5.1	3.6
Malawi	698	627	646	643	739	682	618	549	788	882	863	-2.1	2.2	3.1
Mali	505	811	880	905	969	893	833	892	961	1,049	1,125	7.0	2.6	2.6
Mauritania	471	542	568	547	553	517	473	636	609	538	612	2.9	-3.4	1.0
Mauritius	952	1,999	2,225	2,190	2,253	2,417	2,548	2,469	2,681	2,876	2,970	-1.1	20.6	4.1
Mozambique	1,501	1,107	1,036	1,058	1,139	1,390	1,134	955	976	983	1,220	..	1.2	-0.4
Namibia	1,865	1,943	1,733	1,824	1,904	1,889	2,006	1,984	2,156	1,968	2,053	..	3.7	1.5
Niger	743	438	416	338	315	319	493	457	456	478	509	4.9	-3.1	3.3
Nigeria	27,928	9,229	10,254	11,378	11,631	11,458	10,640	11,858	12,947	14,036	15,125	5.8	-15.1	4.5
Rwanda	200	280	237	436	448	519	665	334	355	507	531	10.4	-0.1	5.9
São Tomé and Principe	..	50	48	50	45	47	43	46	41	43	36	..	5.3	-2.8
Senegal	1,603	1,936	1,996	1,891	1,969	1,880	1,711	1,796	1,872	1,928	2,083	2.3	1.3	0.0
Seychelles	..	197	228	222	249	325	279	306	388	448	469	..	14.2	10.1
Sierra Leone	284	123	214	191	161	173	246	228	237	118	250	-13.4	19.9	2.9
Somalia	..	..	..	..	..	..	..	..	..	..	..	..	..	..
South Africa	22,395	22,455	21,144	21,597	22,752	24,600	28,558	33,386	36,295	38,249	39,041	-1.4	2.8	8.2
Sudan	..	..	..	..	..	..	..	..	..	..	..	..	..	..
Swaziland	716	1,151	1,160	1,185	1,240	1,328	1,091	1,117	1,164	1,220	899	8.8	7.9	-1.5
Tanzania	..	1,718	1,771	1,817	1,605	2,024	2,088	2,103	2,079	1,711	1,454	..	..	-0.1
Togo	761	840	864	784	688	467	387	508	607	735	750	6.0	5.7	-2.7
Uganda	..	774	763	727	716	692	772	1,199	1,355	1,382	1,425	..	7.3	9.1
Zambia	2,484	1,583	1,472	1,455	1,939	1,466	1,413	1,506	1,452	1,731	1,588	-10.7	3.8	0.2
Zimbabwe	989	1,388	1,575	2,008	2,510	2,195	2,639	2,912	2,779	3,831	3,082	3.7	3.1	10.0
NORTH AFRICA	52,058	50,674	51,424	48,391	50,377	50,818	52,675	55,715	53,221	55,328	61,242	4.8	-5.0	1.9
Algeria	18,588	16,435	14,824	12,171	12,731	11,878	12,603	12,855	11,145	11,780	12,868	5.1	-10.1	-2.5
Egypt, Arab Republic	16,885	14,253	14,775	14,948	14,253	15,385	15,675	16,544	16,801	17,123	19,807	4.5	-5.9	3.1
Libya	..	..	..	..	..	..	..	..	..	..	..	..	..	..
Morocco	5,376	7,398	8,419	8,636	9,692	9,584	9,931	11,243	10,788	10,964	11,858	1.5	7.6	4.8
Tunisia	5,316	6,852	7,584	7,157	7,998	8,217	8,504	8,766	8,461	9,198	9,776	8.5	2.0	3.5
ALL AFRICA	147,545	129,621	129,848	128,701	133,801	134,767	140,478	152,562	158,650	167,310	174,310	2.7	-2.4	3.7

Note: 1998 data are preliminary (see page 3).

2-18. GDP growth

	Percent annual change											Average annual percentage growth		
	1980	*1989*	*1990*	*1991*	*1992*	*1993*	*1994*	*1995*	*1996*	*1997*	*1998*	*75-84*	*85-89*	*90-MR*
SUB-SAHARAN AFRICA	5.7	2.9	0.9	0.5	-1.3	0.8	2.3	4.1	4.7	3.4	1.9	2.2	2.3	2.0
excluding South Africa	1.4	3.4	2.2	2.0	-0.5	0.4	1.4	4.9	5.3	4.2	3.2	1.9	3.3	2.5
excl. S.Africa & Nigeria	0.6	2.7	1.1	1.4	-1.2	0.0	1.7	5.5	5.5	4.3	3.5	2.5	3.0	2.4
Angola	..	0.4	-0.3	0.7	-5.1	-23.8	1.4	11.3	11.6	7.6	-3.8	..	4.7	-0.9
Benin	6.8	-2.9	3.2	4.7	4.0	3.5	4.4	4.6	5.5	5.7	4.5	3.8	1.5	4.5
Botswana	11.7	9.1	7.2	7.5	3.0	2.0	3.6	5.1	6.9	7.0	6.0	11.5	10.6	4.9
Burkina Faso	0.8	0.9	-1.5	10.0	2.5	-0.8	1.2	4.0	6.0	4.7	6.2	3.6	4.4	3.4
Burundi	1.0	1.3	3.5	5.0	0.7	-5.7	-3.1	-7.0	-8.6	0.4	4.5	3.8	5.1	-2.5
Cameroon	-2.0	-1.8	-6.1	-3.8	-3.1	-3.2	-2.5	3.3	5.0	5.1	5.0	8.5	-0.1	-0.1
Cape Verde	..	5.7	0.7	1.4	3.3	4.2	3.8	4.7	4.3	3.0	4.0	..	5.1	3.5
Central African Republic	-4.5	2.0	-2.1	-0.6	-6.4	0.3	4.9	7.2	-4.1	5.2	4.7	0.4	0.7	1.0
Chad	-6.0	5.3	-8.1	19.1	9.9	-7.8	10.2	1.0	3.7	4.1	8.1	-1.9	4.9	4.2
Comoros	..	-3.2	5.1	-5.4	8.5	3.0	-5.3	-3.9	-0.4	0.0	1.0	..	1.3	-0.2
Congo, Democratic Rep. of	2.2	-1.3	-6.6	-8.4	-10.5	-13.5	-3.9	0.7	-0.9	-5.7	3.0	-0.3	1.7	-5.6
Congo, Republic of	17.6	2.6	0.9	2.4	2.6	-1.0	-5.5	4.0	6.3	-1.9	4.0	9.2	-1.0	1.0
Côte d'Ivoire	-11.0	2.9	-1.1	0.0	-0.2	-0.2	2.0	7.0	6.9	6.0	5.7	2.2	2.0	2.9
Djibouti	..	..	..	..	-0.3	-3.9	-2.9	-4.0	-5.1	0.5	0.7	..	..	-2.7
Equatorial Guinea	..	-1.2	3.3	-1.1	10.7	6.3	5.1	14.3	29.1	76.1	..	..	1.4	13.0
Eritrea	..	..	..	..	..	-2.5	9.8	2.9	6.7	7.9	3.0	..	..	5.2
Ethiopia	..	1.1	2.5	-4.7	-5.3	13.4	3.6	6.1	10.9	5.9	-1.0	..	2.9	4.1
Gabon	2.6	8.5	5.2	6.1	-3.3	2.4	3.4	7.0	3.8	4.1	2.0	-0.2	-1.4	3.3
Gambia, The	6.3	5.9	3.6	3.1	3.4	3.0	0.2	0.9	2.2	4.9	4.7	4.3	3.3	2.5
Ghana	0.5	5.1	3.3	5.3	3.9	5.0	3.3	4.0	4.6	4.2	4.6	-1.1	5.2	4.2
Guinea	..	2.7	3.8	2.7	4.3	4.3	8.3	4.4	4.6	4.7	4.6	..	4.0	4.8
Guinea-Bissau	-16.0	6.1	6.1	5.1	1.1	2.1	3.2	4.4	4.6	5.9	-28.1	2.1	3.1	1.7
Kenya	5.6	4.7	4.2	1.4	-0.8	0.4	2.6	4.4	4.1	2.1	1.8	4.7	5.9	2.2
Lesotho	-2.7	12.7	4.0	0.7	3.5	4.0	12.9	9.1	12.7	8.0	-3.6	4.5	7.8	6.7
Liberia	..	..	..	..	..	..	..	..	..	..	..	..	..	..
Madagascar	0.8	4.1	3.1	-6.3	1.2	2.1	0.0	1.7	2.1	3.6	3.9	-0.2	2.3	1.0
Malawi	0.4	1.3	5.7	8.7	-7.3	9.7	-10.2	14.7	10.7	5.1	3.1	3.2	1.9	3.9
Mali	-4.3	11.8	-1.9	1.6	8.3	-2.2	2.1	6.4	3.7	6.7	3.6	2.3	0.8	3.3
Mauritania	3.4	4.8	-1.8	2.6	1.7	5.5	4.6	4.5	4.7	4.5	3.5	1.6	0.1	3.7
Mauritius	-10.1	4.5	7.2	4.3	6.2	5.4	4.1	4.7	5.4	5.0	5.3	3.6	7.7	5.2
Mozambique	..	6.5	1.0	4.9	-8.1	8.7	7.5	4.3	7.1	11.3	12.0	..	6.0	5.0
Namibia	..	1.6	-1.2	10.4	6.3	-2.0	6.7	3.4	2.9	1.8	1.5	..	2.3	3.5
Niger	-2.2	0.9	-1.3	2.5	-6.5	1.4	4.0	2.6	3.4	3.3	8.4	2.0	4.2	1.7
Nigeria	4.2	7.2	8.2	4.8	2.9	2.2	0.1	2.5	4.3	3.6	1.8	-0.7	5.0	3.0
Rwanda	9.0	0.0	-2.4	-2.5	5.9	-8.1	-49.5	36.8	12.1	10.9	10.0	6.8	2.9	-3.6
São Tomé and Principe	..	3.1	-2.2	1.5	0.7	1.1	2.2	2.0	1.5	1.0	2.5	..	3.5	1.3
Senegal	-3.3	-1.4	3.9	-0.4	2.2	-2.2	2.9	4.7	5.6	5.2	5.7	2.1	3.5	2.7
Seychelles	-4.2	10.3	9.0	2.8	7.2	6.2	-0.8	-0.6	4.7	4.3	2.3	3.6	5.2	3.5
Sierra Leone	4.8	5.0	1.6	-8.0	-9.6	0.1	3.5	-10.0	5.0	-20.2	0.7	2.0	0.8	-4.4
Somalia	..	..	..	..	..	..	..	..	..	..	..	..	..	..
South Africa	9.2	2.4	-0.3	-1.0	-2.1	1.2	3.2	3.1	4.2	2.5	0.5	2.4	1.4	1.5
Sudan	1.5	2.8	-0.4	6.0	4.9	4.3	4.0	25.2	4.0	6.7	5.0	2.6	0.9	7.3
Swaziland	10.7	9.1	8.9	2.5	1.3	3.3	3.5	2.7	3.9	3.7	2.0	3.3	9.9	3.2
Tanzania	..	3.9	5.4	4.5	-8.9	12.2	1.4	2.6	4.1	4.0	3.4	..	..	2.9
Togo	14.6	4.1	-0.2	-0.7	-4.0	-16.4	16.8	6.8	9.7	4.3	-1.0	2.1	3.4	1.7
Uganda	..	6.4	6.5	5.6	3.4	8.3	6.4	11.5	9.1	4.7	5.6	..	3.4	7.1
Zambia	3.0	-1.0	-0.5	0.0	-1.7	6.8	-3.4	-2.3	6.5	3.4	-2.0	0.2	2.3	0.9
Zimbabwe	14.4	5.2	7.0	5.5	-9.0	1.3	6.8	-0.7	7.3	3.2	1.6	3.0	4.2	2.1
NORTH AFRICA	6.2	4.0	3.3	2.1	2.0	0.5	3.9	1.5	6.5	2.6	4.8	6.2	3.0	2.8
Algeria	0.9	4.9	-1.3	-1.2	1.6	-2.2	-1.2	3.8	3.8	1.3	5.0	5.5	0.8	0.9
Egypt, Arab Republic	10.0	5.0	5.7	1.1	4.4	2.9	3.9	4.7	5.0	5.5	5.0	8.3	4.1	4.1
Libya	..	..	..	..	..	..	..	..	..	..	..	..	..	..
Morocco	9.1	2.5	3.9	6.9	-4.0	-1.0	10.4	-6.6	12.1	-2.0	4.0	4.7	4.8	2.2
Tunisia	7.4	1.7	8.0	3.9	7.8	2.2	3.3	2.3	7.1	5.4	5.1	5.3	2.4	4.6
ALL AFRICA	5.8	3.2	1.7	1.0	-0.3	0.7	2.8	3.2	5.3	3.1	2.9	3.3	2.5	2.3

Note: 1998 data are preliminary (see page 3).

2-19. GNP per capita

	U.S. dollars, Atlas method											Annual average		
	1980	*1989*	*1990*	*1991*	*1992*	*1993*	*1994*	*1995*	*1996*	*1997*	*1998*	*75-84*	*85-89*	*90-MR*
SUB-SAHARAN AFRICA	624	566	552	552	551	533	514	522	531	539	513	524	511	534
excluding South Africa	481	396	380	369	349	319	289	289	299	315	316	404	372	325
excl. S.Africa & Nigeria	403	428	408	395	365	340	306	308	314	324	320	337	390	342
Angola	..	860	840	930	600	380	220	250	210	260	340	..	867	448
Benin	410	360	360	380	370	380	340	350	360	380	380	313	326	367
Botswana	1,210	2,330	2,780	3,090	3,330	3,350	3,230	3,510	3,610	3,660	3,600	1,026	1,652	3,351
Burkina Faso	260	290	290	320	290	240	210	220	240	250	240	198	242	256
Burundi	220	230	220	220	210	180	160	150	140	140	140	186	246	173
Cameroon	650	1,070	970	910	920	900	730	660	620	620	610	599	996	771
Cape Verde	..	880	880	900	1,000	990	990	1,030	1,070	1,090	1,060	..	880	1,001
Central African Republic	340	470	470	470	460	440	360	350	300	320	300	271	392	386
Chad	240	270	250	300	340	250	230	210	210	230	230	220	222	250
Comoros	370	520	540	530	620	610	490	440	410	400	370	348	420	490
Congo, Democratic Rep. of	620	230	220	210	200	190	160	150	130	110	110	451	238	164
Congo, Republic of	880	1,000	1,020	1,030	1,110	900	730	660	660	690	690	831	1,052	832
Côte d'Ivoire	1,140	850	800	780	800	760	680	670	680	710	700	856	798	731
Djibouti	..	..	..	..	..	..	..	..	..	..	..	..	..	..
Equatorial Guinea	..	340	350	340	400	420	370	390	470	1,050	1,060	..	340	539
Eritrea	..	..	..	..	..	..	180	180	200	230	200	..	..	198
Ethiopia	..	170	160	120	110	120	110	110	110	110	100	135	162	117
Gabon	4,750	4,550	4,750	5,100	5,050	4,480	4,060	3,860	4,010	4,160	4,170	4,301	3,980	4,404
Gambia, The	380	310	320	330	350	350	340	350	340	340	340	297	282	340
Ghana	430	400	390	410	430	410	380	370	380	400	390	356	404	396
Guinea	..	430	440	480	530	530	540	540	570	570	540	..	435	527
Guinea-Bissau	150	210	220	250	240	230	220	220	230	230	160	179	182	222
Kenya	450	400	370	340	330	250	240	260	320	340	350	340	366	311
Lesotho	440	530	560	540	600	610	640	670	710	680	570	394	436	620
Liberia	620		..	..	..	..	..	..	..	..	..	523	470	..
Madagascar	450	230	240	220	230	240	240	240	250	250	260	349	270	241
Malawi	190	170	190	230	220	250	170	180	190	220	200	162	164	206
Mali	270	280	270	270	320	300	260	250	240	260	250	201	226	269
Mauritania	540	570	540	530	540	490	470	450	460	440	410	472	508	481
Mauritius	1,240	2,230	2,430	2,610	2,960	3,080	3,180	3,420	3,710	3,800	3,700	1,071	1,646	3,210
Mozambique	..	170	170	170	140	140	140	140	160	180	210	240	246	161
Namibia	..	1,700	1,820	2,000	2,110	2,010	2,120	2,220	2,200	2,110	1,940	1,653	1,396	2,059
Niger	440	330	310	300	290	240	210	190	200	200	190	318	288	237
Nigeria	710	270	270	270	290	240	220	210	240	280	300	599	292	258
Rwanda	250	370	370	320	310	260	150	200	200	210	230	207	330	250
São Tomé and Principe	540	460	400	400	390	370	350	340	330	290	270	407	460	349
Senegal	530	690	720	710	780	710	590	550	530	540	530	436	558	629
Seychelles	2,110	4,510	5,070	5,240	5,930	6,330	6,440	6,460	6,750	6,910	6,450	1,646	3,344	6,176
Sierra Leone	380	300	260	210	160	160	170	170	200	160	140	318	296	181
Somalia	110	150	120	..	..	..	..	..	..	..	..	133	140	120
South Africa	2,540	2,850	2,890	3,050	3,320	3,460	3,610	3,740	3,760	3,690	2,880	2,133	2,376	3,426
Sudan	480	740	610	560	350	300	270	300	270	270	290	427	656	358
Swaziland	970	1,000	1,200	1,210	1,290	1,260	1,220	1,380	1,470	1,520	1,400	817	868	1,328
Tanzania	..	..	190	180	160	180	160	160	170	190	210	..	..	178
Togo	440	430	430	430	440	340	320	310	320	350	330	325	340	363
Uganda	..	430	340	260	200	190	190	250	290	320	310	125	324	261
Zambia	630	430	450	400	370	390	360	350	370	370	330	562	332	377
Zimbabwe	950	900	920	910	740	670	650	630	690	700	610	865	808	724
NORTH AFRICA	1,313	1,396	1,406	1,260	1,296	1,247	1,293	1,324	1,420	1,474	1,536	1,073	1,372	1,362
Algeria	2,080	2,590	2,400	2,050	1,980	1,790	1,660	1,580	1,530	1,500	1,570	1,771	2,670	1,784
Egypt, Arab Republic	520	780	850	690	760	770	860	980	1,080	1,200	1,250	483	762	938
Libya	10,460	5,670	..	..	..	..	..	..	..	..	..	7,927	6,034	..
Morocco	990	980	1,030	1,100	1,090	1,060	1,170	1,120	1,300	1,260	..	726	792	1,141
Tunisia	1,360	1,310	1,430	1,490	1,700	1,690	1,740	1,830	1,940	2,110	2,150	1,092	1,244	1,787
ALL AFRICA	749	720	709	684	688	665	656	667	690	704	688	623	673	683

Note: 1998 data are preliminary (see page 3).

National Accounts

2-20. Total consumption per capita

| | Current U.S. dollars | | | | | | | | | | | Annual average | | |
	1980	1989	1990	1991	1992	1993	1994	1995	1996	1997	1998	75-84	85-89	90-MR
SUB-SAHARAN AFRICA	497	441	480	473	492	447	417	460	456	471	452	400	410	461
excluding South Africa	386	314	324	305	312	271	234	267	279	291	298	307	303	287
excl. S.Africa & Nigeria	323	347	354	334	329	301	250	282	298	297	295	266	324	304
Angola	..	759	783	1,066	571	384	257	389	537	480	484	..	678	550
Benin	426	316	368	362	309	386	254	330	361	333	358	300	316	340
Botswana	800	1,429	1,791	1,978	1,985	2,090	1,968	2,023	2,082	2,182	2,366	670	928	2,052
Burkina Faso	260	253	287	288	199	204	182	223	226	203	211	193	239	225
Burundi	224	203	219	217	198	173	165	170	140	143	146	179	219	175
Cameroon	609	798	771	822	784	786	503	486	544	519	486	491	799	633
Cape Verde	..	723	778	937	1,033	949	994	1,261	1,165	1,111	1,155	..	720	1,042
Central African Republic	375	432	508	454	467	405	249	342	317	283	290	274	416	368
Chad	251	268	289	324	318	241	193	221	244	232	238	223	245	255
Comoros	406	505	597	545	594	548	410	466	448	383	388	343	450	487
Congo, Democratic Rep. of	..	212	227	231	193	209	151	124	112	119	..	231	209	171
Congo, Republic of	658	800	961	971	943	606	522	592	630	551	518	587	818	699
Côte d'Ivoire	989	762	823	784	805	740	453	599	607	555	577	671	715	660
Djibouti	..	..	..	943	1,015	924	930	888	844	835	..	..	..	911
Equatorial Guinea	..	..	451	388	408	406	263	319	477	792	846	446	..	483
Eritrea	..	..	..	..	173	150	198	211	225	204	216	..	..	197
Ethiopia	..	149	124	98	99	111	84	94	98	98	100	130	148	101
Gabon	2,438	3,110	3,915	3,249	3,584	2,655	2,141	2,519	2,735	2,312	2,654	1,944	2,794	2,863
Gambia, The	354	291	308	295	315	338	330	341	335	328	326	272	269	324
Ghana	393	343	374	399	402	344	286	334	348	345	353	326	360	354
Guinea	..	355	403	417	479	466	469	462	498	457	412	..	348	451
Guinea-Bissau	141	219	244	251	216	213	214	237	239	229	193	180	179	226
Kenya	378	318	310	30	277	148	217	294	289	340	369	280	299	253
Lesotho	436	446	471	496	533	506	462	517	445	518	548	358	378	500
Liberia	433		..	..	..	..	..	..	..	..	..	408	411	..
Madagascar	462	199	248	224	238	262	223	229	273	241	243	340	241	242
Malawi	179	176	191	216	199	226	113	138	225	240	159	140	148	190
Mali	268	230	268	261	304	272	182	235	246	219	229	196	225	246
Mauritania	541	492	536	490	522	402	405	433	423	409	360	502	470	442
Mauritius	1,049	1,585	1,909	1,993	2,181	2,198	2,412	2,716	2,887	2,760	2,748	847	1,254	2,423
Mozambique	322	190	199	192	156	172	167	154	178	203	226	300	259	183
Namibia	1,389	1,484	1,492	1,687	1,807	1,687	1,700	1,885	1,742	1,734	1,519	1,651	1,350	1,695
Niger	384	271	317	278	272	182	177	205	204	183	195	281	260	224
Nigeria	619	191	209	195	245	162	174	207	205	264	301	464	223	218
Rwanda	216	347	349	259	274	262	186	231	227	254	276	196	312	257
São Tomé and Principe	556	573	..	612	480	490	439	414	397	368	262	394	567	433
Senegal	566	607	708	689	725	649	406	478	495	447	455	428	579	561
Seychelles	1,667	3,121	4,196	4,308	4,986	5,267	5,086	5,163	4,006	5,392	6,014	1,427	2,480	4,935
Sierra Leone	..	283	188	163	137	156	188	195	214	..	135	398	278	172
Somalia	116	160	133	..	..	..	..	..	..	..	..	136	137	133
South Africa	2,004	2,184	2,622	2,782	2,986	2,867	2,914	3,125	2,941	3,025	2,686	1,655	1,873	2,883
Sudan	399	..	..	..	..	..	..	..	..	..	366	405	679	366
Swaziland	964	856	889	907	963	861	901	1,000	1,074	1,103	989	662	645	965
Tanzania	..	199	167	177	178	167	148	164	185	213	232	..	184	181
Togo	334	368	395	401	422	319	230	281	319	316	313	246	332	333
Uganda	98	330	262	195	163	177	206	279	292	286	306	153	333	241
Zambia	546	509	352	386	385	350	347	355	325	378	328	455	334	356
Zimbabwe	822	730	744	726	585	492	497	503	562	585	406	724	629	567
NORTH AFRICA	842	1,005	1,116	926	998	1,036	1,053	1,116	1,212	1,204	1,279	704	1,023	1,104
Algeria	1,291	1,592	1,795	1,144	1,265	1,337	1,118	1,052	1,083	1,051	1,102	1,115	1,792	1,216
Egypt, Arab Republic	476	640	690	599	647	732	806	890	1,018	1,090	1,143	417	641	846
Libya	5,040	..	..	..	..	..	..	..	..	..	..	4,325	..	..
Morocco	838	792	867	940	947	874	991	1,073	1,147	1,021	..	608	674	982
Tunisia	1,041	1,008	1,205	1,238	1,422	1,324	1,394	1,595	1,651	1,559	1,796	820	969	1,465
ALL AFRICA	563	546	598	559	587	556	532	579	591	601	595	459	524	578

Note: 1998 data are preliminary (see page 3).

Figure 2-1.   Gross domestic product, 1998*

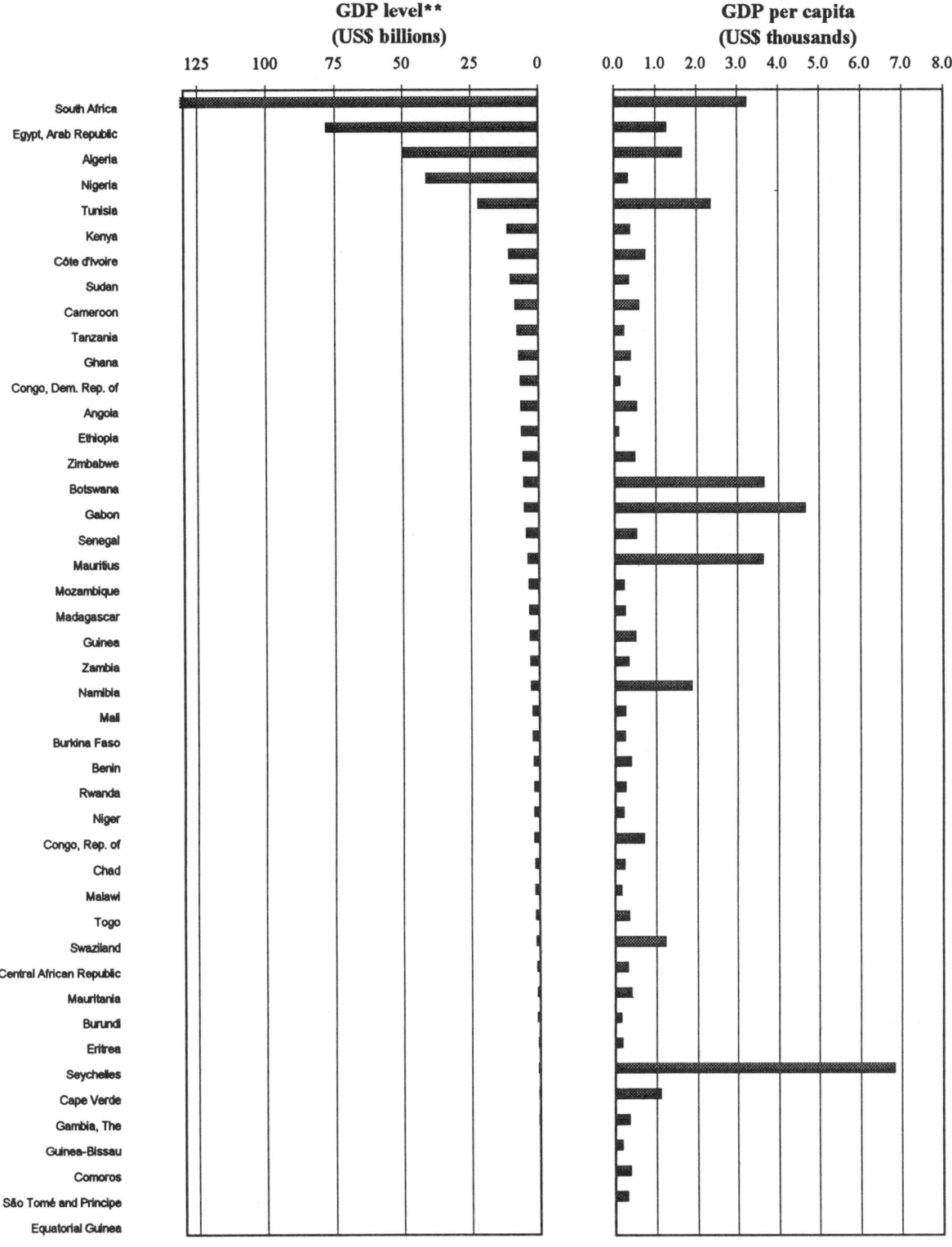

38

Figure 2-2. GDP and export growth rates, average 1992-98*

(average annual percent change)

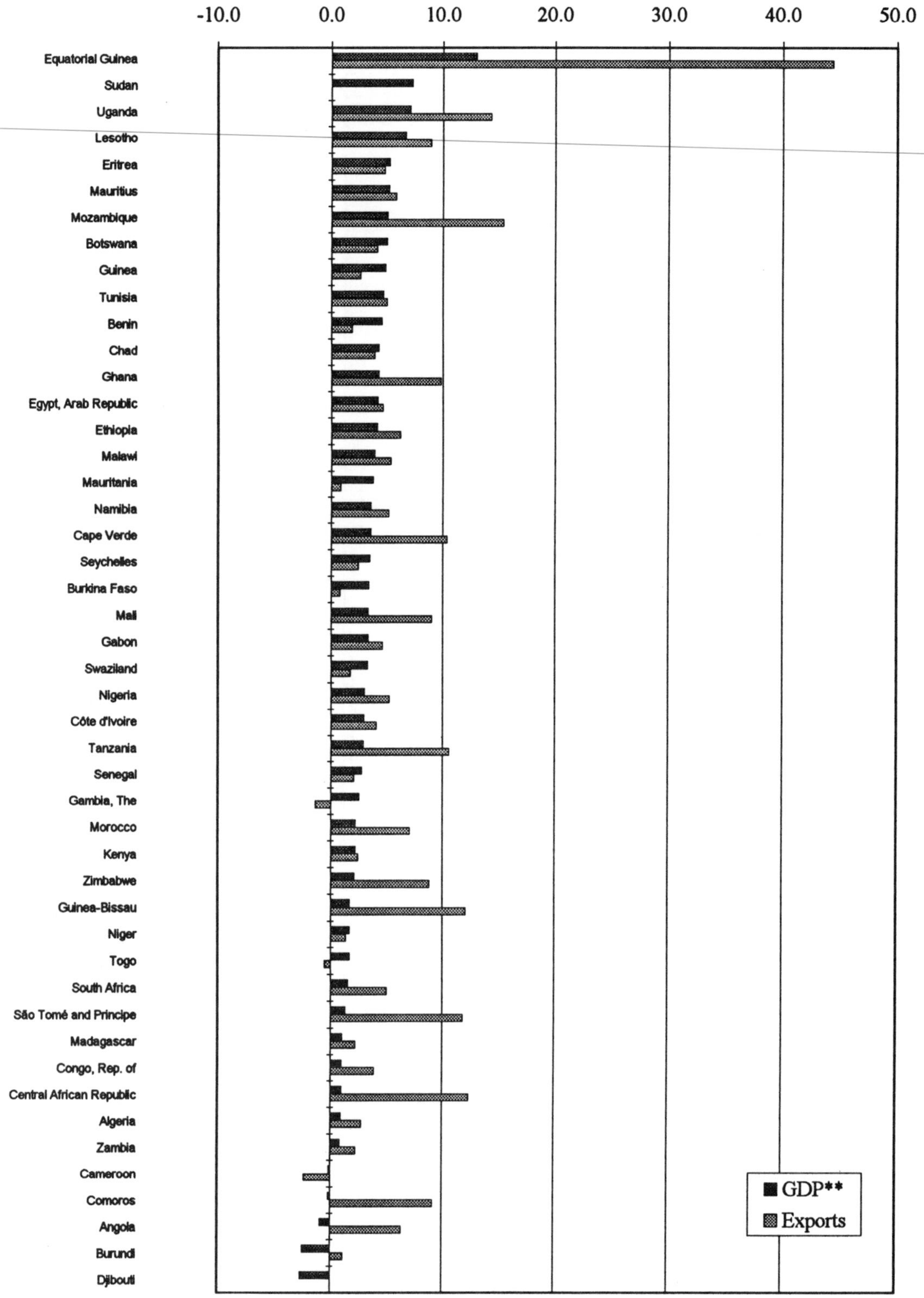

| | GDP** | Exports |

*Or most recent year available.

** Sorted by GDP.

Figure 2-3. Composition of GDP, 1998*

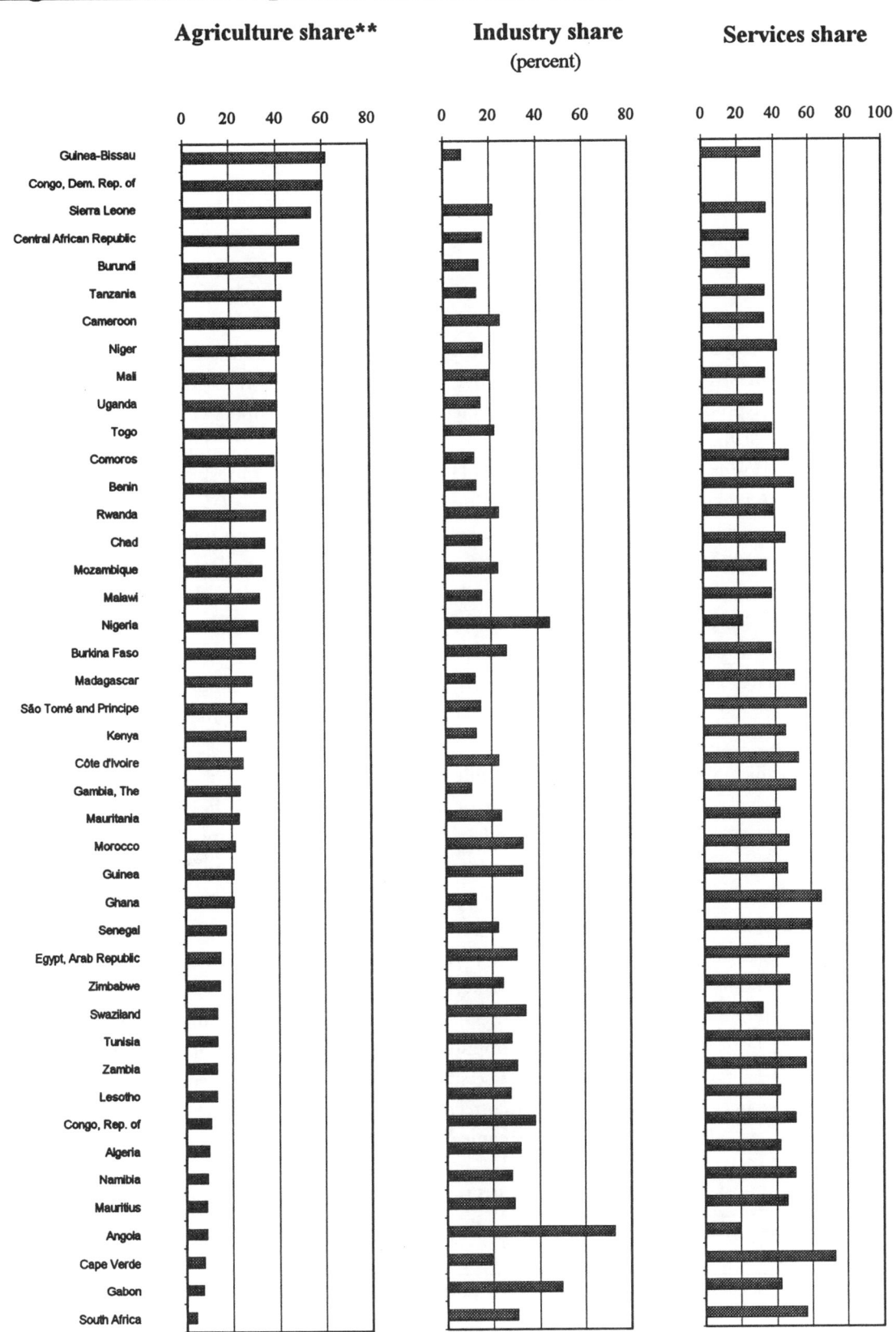

Agriculture share

Industry share
(percent)

Services share

* Or most recent year available ** Sorted by agriculture share.

Note: Nigeria's shares are distorted because of official exchange rate over-valuation affecting oil exports and oil value added.

Technical Notes

Tables

Table 2-1. Gross domestic product, real. Gross domestic product (GDP) measures the total output of goods and services for final use produced by residents and nonresidents, regardless of the allocation to domestic and foreign claims (World Bank country desks). It is calculated without making deductions for depreciation of "manmade" assets or depletion and degradation of natural resources. In this table, GDP figures are shown at market prices (also known as purchaser values) and have been converted to U.S. dollars using constant (1995) exchange rates. For a few countries where the official exchange rate does not reflect effectively the rate applied to actual foreign exchange transactions, an alternative currency conversion factor has been used (Table 3-6). The sum of the components of GDP by industrial origin (presented in this volume in the form of value added) will not normally equal total GDP for several reasons. First, components of GDP by expenditure are individually rescaled and summed to provide a partially rebased series for total GDP. Second, total GDP is shown at purchaser value, while value added components are conventionally reported at producer prices. As explained above, the former excludes net indirect taxes, while the latter includes indirect taxes. Third, certain items, such as imputed bank charges, are added in total GDP.

Table 2-2. Value added in agriculture. Value added in agriculture is shown at factor cost (World Bank country desks). It comprises the gross output of forestry, hunting, and fishing less the value of their intermediate inputs. However, for Botswana, Cameroon, Chad, Congo, Gabon, Guinea, Madagascar, Mali, Morocco, Niger, Rwanda, Senegal, Togo, Zaire, and Zambia it is shown at market prices, that is, including intermediate inputs.

Table 2-3. Value added in industry. Value added in industry is shown at factor cost (World Bank country desks). It comprises the gross output of mining, manufacturing, construction, electricity, water, and gas, less the value of their intermediate inputs. However, for Botswana, Cameroon, Chad, Congo, Gabon, Guinea, Madagascar, Mali, Morocco, Niger, Rwanda, Senegal, Togo, Zaire, and Zambia it is shown at market prices, that is, including intermediate inputs.

Table 2-4. Value added in services. Also shown at factor cost, this table consists of the gross output of all other branches of economic activity, including government, less the value of their intermediate inputs (World Bank country desks). However, for Botswana, Cameroon, Chad, Congo, Gabon, Guinea, Madagascar, Mali, Morocco, Niger, Rwanda, Senegal, Togo, Zaire, and Zambia it is shown at market prices, that is, including intermediate inputs. Other items, such as imputed bank service charges (which are difficult to assess in the same fashion for all countries) and any corrections for statistical discrepancies, are not included.

Table 2-5. Gross domestic product, nominal. This table, presented at market prices, is obtained by converting national currency GDP series in current prices (World Bank country desks) to U.S. dollars at official annual exchange rates (Table 3-4; see also the note for Table 2-1). GDP growth rates are presented in real terms.

Table 2-6. Total consumption. Total consumption is the sum of private consumption (World Bank country desks) and general government consumption (Table 2-7). Private consumption, not separately shown here, is the value of all goods and services purchased or received as income in kind by households and nonprofit institutions. It excludes purchases of dwellings, but includes imputed rent for owner-occupied dwellings. In practice, it includes any statistical discrepancy in the use of resources.

Table 2-7. General government consumption. This indicator includes all current expenditure for purchases of goods and services by all levels of government, including capital expenditure on national defense and security (World Bank country desks). Other capital expenditure by government is included in investment.

Tables 2-8, 2-9, and 2-10. Gross domestic, public, and private investment. Gross domestic investment (GDI) consists of gross domestic fixed capital formation plus net changes in the level of inventories (World Bank country desks). GDI comprises outlays by the public sector (Table 2-9) and the private sector (Table 2-10). Examples include improvements in land, dwellings, machinery, and other equipment. For some countries the sum of gross private investment and gross public investment does not add up to gross domestic investment due to statistical discrepancies.

Table 2-11. Gross domestic savings. Gross domestic savings (GDS) is calculated by deducting total consumption (Table 2-6) from gross domestic product in current prices (Table 2-5).

Table 2-12. Gross national savings. Gross national savings (GNS) is the sum of gross domestic savings (Table 2-11), net factor income from abroad (World Bank country desks) and net private transfers from abroad (Table 5-5). The estimate here also includes net public transfers from abroad (Table 5-6).

Table 2-13. Resource balance. The table indicates the difference between exports f.o.b. (Table 2-14) and imports c.i.f. (Table 2-15) of goods and nonfactor services (or the difference between GDS and GDI). The resource balance is shown as a share of GDP in U.S. dollars at current prices (Table 2-5).

Tables 2-14 and 2-15. Exports and imports of goods and nonfactor services, nominal. Data for exports and imports of goods and nonfactor services are from the World Bank country desks and refer to all goods and nonfactor services (GNFS) provided to, or by, the rest of the world, including merchandise, freight, insurance, travel, and other nonfactor services. The value of factor services, such as investment income, interest, and labor income, is not included. These series are generally estimated on the basis of foreign trade statistics from customs declarations. They are not fully comparable with the series from the balance of payments, which are based on changes in ownership between residents of a country and the rest of the world. Exports, as well as imports of GNFS, are shown in current U.S. dollars.

Tables 2-16 and 2-17. Exports and imports of goods and nonfactor services, real. These are defined as in Tables 2-14 and 2-15, but expressed in constant 1995 U.S. dollars.

Table 2-18. GDP growth. This table (World Bank country desks) provides average annual growth rates calculated from GDP at constant 1995 prices (Table 2-1).

Table 2-19. GNP per capita. Figures presented here (World Bank country desks) are calculated using the *World Bank Atlas* method, as described in the technical notes for Table 1-1; they are similar in concept to GNP per capita in current prices, except that the use of three-year averages of exchange rates smoothes out sharp fluctuations from year to year.

Table 2-20. Total consumption per capita. This table is obtained by dividing total consumption at current U.S. dollars (Table 2-6) by the corresponding midyear population (Table 1-2).

Figures

The following indicators have been used to derive the figures in this chapter.

Figure 2-1. Gross domestic product (Table 2-5); GDP per capita (Tables 1-2 and 2-5).

Figure 2-2. GDP growth (Table 2-1); export growth (Table 2-16).

Figure 2-3. Value added in agriculture (Table 2-2); value added in industry (Table 2-3); value added in services (Table 2-4); gross domestic product (Table 2-1).

Methodology used for regional aggregations and period averages in chapter 2

Table	Aggregations[a] (3)	(4)	(5)	Period averages[b] (1)	(2)
2-1	x				x
2-2	x				x
2-3	x				x
2-4	x				x
2-5	x			x	
2-6		x		x	
2-7		x		x	
2-8		x		x	
2-9		x		x	
2-10		x		x	
2-11		x		x	
2-12		x		x	
2-13			x	x	
2-14	x			x	
2-15	x			x	
2-16	x				x
2-17	x				x
2-18	x				x
2-19		x		x	
2-20		x		x	

Note: Regional aggregations are shown in the rows for Sub-Saharan Africa, North Africa, and All Africa. Period averages are shown in the last three columns. This table shows only the methodologies used in this chapter.

    a. Regional aggregations: (1) simple total; (2) simple total of the first indicator divided by the simple total of the second indicator (same country coverage); (3) simple total of the gap-filled indicator; (4) simple total of the gap-filled main indicator divided by the simple total of the gap-filled secondary indicator; (5) simple total of the first gap-filled main indicator less the simple total of the second gap-filled main indicator, all divided by the simple total of the secondary indicator; (6) weighted total (by population); (7) median; (8) no aggregation; (9) simple arithmetic mean.

    b. Period averages: (1) arithmetic mean (using the same series as shown in the table, i.e., ratio if the rest of the table is shown as ratio, level if the rest of the table is shown as level, growth rate if the rest of the table is shown as growth rate); (2) least-squares growth rate (using main indicator); (3) least-squares growth rate (using main indicator in constant terms, with the rest of the table in current terms).

3

Prices and Exchange Rates

Information on prices and exchange rates is important in monitoring national economic performance. This chapter provides three sets of price deflators and six exchange rate indicators. The GDP deflator for national currency series shows changes in domestic prices only. The US dollar series GDP deflator includes the effects of both domestic price changes, as reflected in the national currency series GDP implicit deflator, and changes in the exchange rate between national currencies and U.S. dollars. The consumer price index measures the change in prices of a selected bundle of consumer goods, which differs among countries.

The US dollar exchange rate (units of national currency per US dollar) is reported because of extensive use of U.S. dollars to denominate international transactions; U.S. dollars are also widely used for statistical comparisons across countries. The SDR exchange rate index (based on SDRs per unit of national currency) is a broader measure of the changes in the

international value of domestic currencies because it is based on five major currencies. For Sub-Saharan Africa, it may be more representative of movements in non-dual exchange rates than that expressed in U.S. dollars alone because a large share of the region's foreign trade and debt is not denominated in U.S. dollars. A decrease in the index shows that the currency has depreciated, which indicates that foreign goods have become relatively more expensive than domestic goods. We have included information on the parallel market exchange rate and the ratio of the parallel to the official exchange rates to provide a measure of the premium on the official rate. It is tempting to view the divergence between the official and parallel rates as a measure of the disequilibrium in the official exchange rate. However, this is not necessarily true. Conversion factors are sometimes used in place of official exchange rates when the latter are considered to be especially unrepresentative of rates effectively applied to international transactions.

Prices and Exchange Rates.

3-1. GDP deflator (local currency series)

	Index 1995=100											Annual average		
	1980	1989	1990	1991	1992	1993	1994	1995	1996	1997	1998	75-84	85-89	90-MR
SUB-SAHARAN AFRICA	23.0	59.8	62.1	64.4	66.6	71.0	90.1	100.0	109.1	118.2	120.8	22.8	46.0	89.2
excluding South Africa	24.9	60.0	62.5	65.6	66.0	70.7	89.9	100.0	109.6	119.3	120.6	24.1	47.3	89.3
excl. S. Africa & Nigeria	26.8	60.2	63.0	66.7	66.6	71.0	90.1	100.0	109.1	118.2	120.3	26.4	49.9	89.4
Angola	..	0.0	0.0	0.0	0.0	0.2	5.0	100.0	5,527.1	10,549.0	16,550.0	..	0.0	3,636.8
Benin	47.5	60.7	61.7	62.1	64.2	64.9	86.7	100.0	106.7	111.7	116.3	45.9	59.6	86.0
Botswana	20.8	60.0	63.4	66.7	71.5	81.1	91.5	100.0	112.4	122.2	131.8	18.7	45.2	93.4
Burkina Faso	50.1	74.3	75.3	71.6	70.3	71.3	91.1	100.0	104.2	106.5	109.9	49.1	70.8	88.9
Burundi	46.0	65.8	69.7	72.6	76.9	85.4	86.8	100.0	119.4	147.2	177.5	38.6	59.1	103.9
Cameroon	43.0	72.6	73.8	76.4	75.4	77.0	85.4	100.0	105.4	108.2	109.5	42.9	74.0	90.1
Cape Verde	..	77.4	78.4	82.6	85.4	89.6	92.2	100.0	104.4	114.3	118.9	..	74.7	96.2
Central African Republic	35.0	74.3	75.9	74.7	76.5	73.9	90.7	100.0	101.9	103.5	105.4	35.1	71.6	89.2
Chad	55.6	73.4	81.8	78.5	67.3	60.7	91.9	100.0	112.3	120.5	122.3	54.9	75.9	92.8
Comoros	41.7	79.9	81.6	88.2	82.3	84.6	92.6	100.0	102.3	105.9	108.0	52.3	73.5	93.9
Congo, Democratic Rep. of	0.0	0.0	0.0	0.0	0.0	0.1	17.7	100.0	713.1	2,049.0	2,356.3	0.0	0.0	581.8
Congo, Republic of	55.8	74.4	73.7	72.6	71.5	70.7	96.7	100.0	115.1	122.1	101.0	56.6	73.7	91.5
Côte d'Ivoire	50.3	67.1	64.0	64.4	64.4	64.4	91.3	100.0	102.7	105.9	109.1	45.9	69.2	85.1
Djibouti	..	..	..	82.9	85.7	89.5	95.3	100.0	104.1	106.8	110.0	..	68.5	96.8
Equatorial Guinea	..	63.0	61.4	63.6	63.7	63.2	97.5	100.0	125.4	156.1	..	..	64.5	91.4
Eritrea	..	..	..	..	57.0	73.6	89.8	100.0	102.9	105.7	104.7	..	..	90.5
Ethiopia	..	57.1	59.1	68.6	76.5	86.6	88.7	100.0	101.0	104.2	114.4	41.8	56.4	88.8
Gabon	50.8	66.0	76.1	67.5	67.7	68.5	100.5	100.0	115.1	112.4	102.7	46.6	64.2	90.1
Gambia, The	18.0	67.9	76.0	82.3	88.2	92.7	96.2	100.0	102.9	106.2	108.1	17.6	52.1	94.7
Ghana	0.8	23.3	30.6	36.7	40.8	53.7	69.8	100.0	139.8	167.1	196.5	1.6	14.4	92.8
Guinea	..	51.8	64.5	76.8	96.0	97.3	96.2	100.0	104.4	107.6	112.7	..	39.3	95.1
Guinea-Bissau	0.2	10.4	13.6	22.8	37.6	56.1	69.1	100.0	148.6	200.4	215.8	0.3	4.2	96.0
Kenya	18.7	41.6	45.5	50.7	59.6	66.5	89.9	100.0	108.7	125.5	138.8	19.0	35.9	87.2
Lesotho	18.9	60.3	69.6	70.3	78.2	91.2	95.1	100.0	106.3	116.5	120.8	18.9	45.4	94.2
Liberia	..	..	..	..	..	..	..	..	..	..	..	..	..	..
Madagascar	6.6	30.1	33.6	38.3	43.1	48.6	68.9	100.0	117.8	126.6	137.7	7.7	22.6	79.4
Malawi	6.4	22.6	25.0	28.9	32.7	41.9	52.5	100.0	140.3	159.1	195.4	6.6	15.8	86.2
Mali	38.0	59.6	62.5	63.8	65.0	66.8	88.9	100.0	106.3	107.5	112.6	37.5	60.2	85.9
Mauritania	33.3	76.8	79.4	78.4	86.2	89.9	95.7	100.0	103.5	109.9	119.6	33.3	66.2	95.8
Mauritius	28.8	65.8	72.4	78.4	82.7	89.1	95.5	100.0	106.1	112.3	119.1	26.6	53.9	95.1
Mozambique	0.6	9.6	12.9	18.9	27.3	41.3	65.8	100.0	140.9	156.5	162.5	0.8	4.7	80.7
Namibia	19.8	61.2	66.3	67.6	74.7	81.3	93.3	100.0	110.1	119.3	132.9	23.5	46.5	93.9
Niger	57.9	75.8	74.6	70.8	71.5	71.5	94.9	100.0	104.8	107.9	111.1	55.8	77.7	89.7
Nigeria	3.2	13.9	14.9	17.9	32.9	50.2	64.1	100.0	136.9	151.3	167.3	3.2	8.4	81.7
Rwanda	24.9	35.5	40.2	46.3	49.6	56.5	64.9	100.0	109.6	129.9	136.7	25.0	34.0	81.5
São Tomé and Principe	..	9.4	12.0	18.9	23.8	33.0	57.3	100.0	150.8	301.9	413.9	..	6.5	123.5
Senegal	41.0	73.3	74.2	74.5	75.0	73.9	94.4	100.0	103.8	106.2	108.4	40.4	70.4	90.0
Seychelles	62.9	90.4	93.7	91.8	96.1	99.1	100.2	100.0	99.6	102.5	104.5	55.2	83.4	98.6
Sierra Leone	0.2	8.5	16.1	30.7	49.2	62.3	74.9	100.0	126.3	147.4	187.2	0.2	4.0	88.2
Somalia	..	..	..	..	..	..	..	..	..	..	..	..	..	..
South Africa	13.6	47.8	55.2	63.9	73.2	82.8	90.7	100.0	107.7	116.2	125.4	13.1	36.3	90.6
Sudan	0.2	3.6	5.8	10.5	20.3	39.2	70.9	100.0	207.4	342.1	441.1	0.2	1.8	137.5
Swaziland	21.2	51.2	55.1	58.7	66.0	74.6	84.2	100.0	109.8	122.0	132.4	20.1	40.8	89.2
Tanzania	..	25.1	30.6	38.3	53.9	60.5	77.6	100.0	122.6	147.1	169.6	..	17.5	88.9
Togo	40.6	65.5	67.4	69.2	71.5	66.7	89.2	100.0	105.1	117.1	120.2	41.8	62.9	89.6
Uganda	..	24.9	36.0	45.3	65.8	85.6	91.4	100.0	104.6	108.7	120.3	0.2	8.5	84.2
Zambia	0.1	1.8	3.7	7.2	19.1	46.7	73.0	100.0	124.3	156.5	192.8	0.1	0.9	80.4
Zimbabwe	11.0	31.3	35.9	46.9	59.9	73.0	90.3	100.0	127.9	145.8	201.3	11.5	24.2	97.9
NORTH AFRICA	26.2	60.7	66.8	73.6	82.4	88.2	92.0	100.0	106.9	112.3	116.0	25.5	49.6	93.1
Algeria	10.8	21.1	28.4	44.3	54.7	60.6	77.8	100.0	123.5	131.4	134.8	9.8	17.2	84.0
Egypt, Arab Republic	16.6	47.9	56.7	64.9	77.7	85.4	91.4	100.0	109.0	115.4	119.5	14.7	35.0	91.1
Libya	..	..	..	..	..	..	..	..	..	..	..	..	..	..
Morocco	40.2	74.9	79.1	84.3	88.0	91.2	92.6	100.0	101.2	103.2	108.9	39.4	68.2	94.3
Tunisia	35.7	73.6	76.9	82.3	87.0	91.1	95.1	100.0	104.7	109.1	112.6	36.5	64.3	95.4
ALL AFRICA	23.0	59.8	62.1	64.9	67.5	71.4	90.5	100.0	108.9	116.8	120.3	22.8	46.0	89.1

Note: 1998 data are preliminary (see page 3). Group data are medians of individual country values for each year. Some numbers for Angola and Dem. Rep. of Congo are shown in scientific notation.

3-2. GDP deflator (U.S. dollar series)

	Index 1995=100											Annual average		
	1980	*1989*	*1990*	*1991*	*1992*	*1993*	*1994*	*1995*	*1996*	*1997*	*1998*	*75-84*	*85-89*	*90-MR*
SUB-SAHARAN AFRICA	105.1	91.3	99.5	100.9	102.8	96.5	92.2	100.0	99.2	100.2	95.0	81.0	85.9	98.5
excluding South Africa	149.5	116.1	120.7	116.7	111.7	100.7	91.7	100.0	106.7	108.0	106.2	115.0	114.5	106.9
excl. S. Africa & Nigeria	113.6	118.4	121.9	119.1	109.5	105.7	92.8	100.0	103.9	103.3	100.7	93.2	114.2	106.3
Angola	..	150.6	166.8	196.9	98.3	118.0	89.3	100.0	135.0	123.2	113.8	..	131.1	126.8
Benin	112.1	95.0	113.0	109.9	91.4	114.5	77.9	100.0	104.1	95.5	98.4	83.7	88.8	100.5
Botswana	71.7	82.4	89.8	96.1	92.6	99.6	97.1	100.0	103.6	94.0	94.4	57.9	68.3	96.3
Burkina Faso	118.3	116.2	138.1	126.7	88.5	91.6	81.9	100.0	101.7	91.1	93.0	89.5	105.4	101.4
Burundi	127.7	103.5	101.7	99.8	92.2	87.8	85.8	100.0	98.5	104.3	99.0	104.0	113.4	96.6
Cameroon	106.7	119.3	127.2	147.5	139.5	150.4	101.9	100.0	108.9	103.7	94.6	83.4	110.7	119.3
Cape Verde		76.3	86.1	89.0	96.6	85.7	86.6	100.0	97.2	94.4	96.5	..	77.4	92.5
Central African Republic	82.6	116.2	139.2	132.2	144.2	130.2	81.5	100.0	99.5	88.7	89.2	62.5	106.6	111.6
Chad	131.3	114.9	150.0	138.9	126.9	106.9	82.7	100.0	109.6	103.1	103.5	100.3	112.1	113.5
Comoros	73.9	93.7	112.2	117.1	116.3	111.8	83.2	100.0	99.8	90.6	91.0	61.8	82.7	102.4
Congo, Democratic Rep. of	..	91.3	101.2	107.4	108.4	137.0	113.7	100.0	93.4	103.0	114.2	85.5	83.5	108.7
Congo, Republic of	131.8	116.5	135.2	128.5	134.9	89.1	87.0	100.0	112.3	104.4	85.4	101.1	108.2	108.5
Côte d'Ivoire	118.8	104.9	117.4	114.0	121.5	113.6	82.1	100.0	100.2	90.6	92.3	82.9	102.8	103.5
Djibouti	..	..	..	82.9	85.7	89.5	95.3	100.0	104.1	106.8	..	..	68.5	94.9
Equatorial Guinea	..	98.5	112.6	112.5	120.0	111.4	87.6	100.0	122.3	133.5	..	..	96.1	112.5
Eritrea	..	..	..	..	83.9	80.5	91.5	100.0	103.0	99.1	95.5	..	..	93.4
Ethiopia	..	159.4	133.3	108.7	120.1	118.9	89.9	100.0	93.8	94.0	97.4	118.4	159.2	106.2
Gabon	120.0	103.3	139.6	119.4	127.8	97.7	90.4	100.0	112.3	96.2	101.0	82.9	94.7	109.4
Gambia, The	99.9	85.4	92.1	89.2	94.7	96.9	95.9	100.0	100.4	99.4	98.8	75.8	77.4	96.4
Ghana	105.0	103.5	112.4	119.7	111.9	99.2	87.6	100.0	102.5	97.8	101.9	93.9	112.5	103.7
Guinea	? ..	86.8	96.9	101.0	105.5	100.9	97.7	100.0	103.1	97.4	85.9	..	84.0	98.7
Guinea-Bissau	82.8	104.1	112.3	112.6	98.0	100.5	96.9	100.0	101.8	95.5	101.7	85.3	87.1	102.1
Kenya	129.5	103.9	102.1	94.8	95.1	59.0	82.5	100.0	97.9	109.9	118.3	104.1	105.7	95.5
Lesotho	88.0	83.4	97.5	91.0	99.4	101.3	97.2	100.0	89.6	91.7	79.3	71.1	71.6	94.1
Liberia	..	..	..	..	..	..	..	..	..	..	..	..	..	..
Madagascar	132.6	80.2	95.9	89.0	98.5	108.4	95.8	100.0	123.8	106.1	107.9	108.3	93.2	102.8
Malawi	119.5	124.9	140.0	157.4	138.7	145.5	91.9	100.0	140.0	147.9	96.1	103.2	107.4	128.6
Mali	90.0	93.5	114.8	113.1	122.6	117.7	79.9	100.0	103.7	91.9	95.3	67.8	90.1	104.3
Mauritania	94.1	120.1	127.9	124.1	128.5	96.6	100.5	100.0	97.8	93.9	81.8	87.4	111.9	105.7
Mauritius	65.1	75.0	84.7	87.1	92.4	87.8	92.5	100.0	102.8	95.0	90.8	54.3	66.8	92.5
Mozambique	175.8	114.8	123.4	116.8	99.6	98.6	98.8	100.0	110.9	120.5	121.9	188.4	197.9	110.1
Namibia	92.1	84.6	92.9	88.8	95.0	90.3	95.3	100.0	92.9	93.9	87.6	81.8	73.8	93.0
Niger	136.8	118.7	136.8	125.2	134.9	91.1	85.3	100.0	102.3	92.3	94.0	100.7	115.4	106.9
Nigeria	287.2	103.8	114.5	104.9	122.0	77.9	86.3	100.0	120.4	131.2	133.7	210.6	116.3	110.1
Rwanda	70.3	116.2	127.7	96.9	97.6	102.7	77.4	100.0	93.6	113.0	114.8	69.8	105.8	102.6
São Tomé and Principe	..	106.6	118.5	132.7	105.4	109.1	111.1	100.0	97.2	94.2	85.4	..	131.1	106.0
Senegal	96.8	114.8	136.1	131.9	141.4	130.2	84.9	100.0	101.3	90.8	91.7	73.8	105.5	112.0
Seychelles	46.9	76.3	83.6	82.8	89.3	91.1	94.4	100.0	95.4	97.1	94.6	39.3	67.4	92.0
Sierra Leone	115.8	107.4	80.2	78.5	74.4	83.0	96.4	100.0	103.6	113.4	88.5	103.1	104.2	90.9
Somalia	..	..	..	..	..	..	..	..	..	..	..	..	..	..
South Africa	63.2	66.1	77.4	83.9	93.1	91.9	92.7	100.0	90.9	91.5	82.3	48.8	57.3	89.3
Sudan	178.4	329.8	276.4	226.0	120.8	142.9	142.1	100.0	96.3	126.1	123.7	177.1	344.5	150.5
Swaziland	98.5	70.9	77.2	77.2	84.0	82.8	86.1	100.0	93.2	96.1	86.9	75.8	64.6	87.1
Tanzania	..	112.8	94.5	101.8	115.4	95.4	87.2	100.0	113.1	131.6	142.6	..	108.4	109.1
Togo	95.8	102.5	123.6	122.5	134.8	117.5	80.2	100.0	102.5	100.1	101.7	76.6	94.2	109.2
Uganda	..	136.3	104.9	76.7	63.8	66.4	77.4	100.0	96.4	95.8	97.6	72.9	147.1	86.6
Zambia	122.9	113.4	93.8	96.4	92.5	89.0	94.3	100.0	88.9	102.9	89.5	98.8	81.3	94.1
Zimbabwe	148.7	128.3	127.1	118.5	101.8	97.7	96.0	100.0	111.6	106.2	73.6	130.8	117.2	103.6
NORTH AFRICA	117.8	96.0	104.2	88.6	94.5	96.4	93.9	100.0	105.5	105.9	106.8	93.4	101.0	99.5
Algeria	134.1	132.4	151.1	114.4	119.4	123.7	105.8	100.0	107.6	108.5	108.9	108.5	147.7	115.9
Egypt, Arab Republic	78.0	83.8	86.2	73.1	79.3	86.9	91.9	100.0	109.0	115.5	113.6	70.4	85.5	95.1
Libya	..	..	..	..	..	..	..	..	..	..	..	..	..	..
Morocco	87.2	75.4	82.0	82.6	88.0	83.8	86.0	100.0	99.2	92.5	..	66.2	66.6	89.3
Tunisia	83.5	73.4	82.7	84.6	93.5	86.2	89.0	100.0	101.7	93.3	103.3	68.3	71.2	92.7
ALL AFRICA	107.5	92.8	101.0	97.0	100.1	96.5	92.7	100.0	101.2	102.1	98.6	83.7	91.0	98.8

Note: 1998 data are preliminary (see page 3). Group data are obtained by dividing GDP in current US$ by GDP in constant US$ series for each group.

3-3. Consumer price index

	Index 1995=100											Average annual percentage growth		
	1980	*1989*	*1990*	*1991*	*1992*	*1993*	*1994*	*1995*	*1996*	*1997*	*1998*	*75-84*	*85-89*	*90-MR*
SUB-SAHARAN AFRICA	20.7	51.2	57.4	63.9	68.9	70.5	89.0	100.0	108.0	117.1	126.5	9.8	12.6	10.9
excluding South Africa	21.9	51.1	57.0	63.8	68.7	70.4	88.6	100.0	108.5	117.6	127.8	9.4	11.4	11.1
excl. S. Africa & Nigeria	23.0	51.3	57.4	63.9	68.9	70.5	89.0	100.0	108.0	116.7	126.5	9.8	10.6	10.9
Angola	..	0.0	0.0	0.0	0.0	0.2	2.7	100.0	1751.3	2872.2	5957.7	..	1.6	716.5
Benin	..	..	..	..	..	..	..	..	..	..	..	..	..	..
Botswana	20.7	50.8	56.6	63.3	73.5	81.8	90.5	100.0	110.1	120.6	131.3	12.1	9.5	11.3
Burkina Faso	59.6	74.2	73.6	75.4	73.9	74.4	92.8	100.0	106.1	108.5	111.3	..	-0.9	5.7
Burundi	28.9	56.0	60.0	65.4	66.5	73.0	83.8	100.0	126.4	165.8	186.6	13.4	5.4	14.7
Cameroon	33.6	72.4	73.2	73.3	73.2	70.5	79.5	100.0	106.6	112.1	115.3	11.5	6.4	6.3
Cape Verde	..	..	..	..	..	..	..	..	..	..	..	..	..	..
Central African Republic	..	72.1	72.0	69.9	69.4	67.4	83.9	100.0	104.4	106.1	104.1	..	-0.8	5.8
Chad	..	..	..	..	..	..	..	..	..	..	..	..	..	..
Comoros	..	81.0	75.5	77.7	95.4	96.1	98.2	100.0	103.7	108.0	112.8	..	3.9	4.4
Congo, Democratic Rep. of	..	..	..	..	..	..	..	..	..	..	..	..	..	..
Congo, Republic of	32.0	61.4	58.5	63.9	61.4	64.4	92.0	100.0	110.2	..	..	11.1	3.3	9.9
Côte d'Ivoire	40.2	65.1	64.7	65.7	68.5	70.2	92.9	100.0	103.5	106.6	109.8	13.3	5.3	7.5
Djibouti	..	72.0	77.6	82.9	85.7	89.5	95.3	100.0	104.2	106.3	..	..	7.1	5.0
Equatorial Guinea	..	..	..	..	..	..	..	..	..	..	..	..	..	..
Eritrea	..	..	..	..	..	..	..	..	..	..	..	..	..	..
Ethiopia	34.6	51.5	54.2	65.5	79.3	87.2	88.2	100.0	100.9	94.4	97.9	10.6	2.4	7.9
Gabon	41.0	67.0	72.2	76.1	72.4	65.9	96.7	100.0	106.2	108.3	116.0	12.5	1.0	6.8
Gambia, The	15.6	68.4	76.7	83.3	88.2	91.7	95.4	100.0	102.1	105.0	106.1	10.5	24.3	4.7
Ghana	0.8	20.6	28.3	33.4	36.8	45.9	57.4	100.0	146.6	187.5	223.7	67.9	27.7	31.6
Guinea	..	51.0	60.8	72.8	84.8	90.9	94.7	100.0	103.0	106.3	111.1	..	30.5	8.3
Guinea-Bissau	..	11.3	15.1	23.8	40.2	59.7	68.8	100.0	156.6	233.5	252.2	..	..	43.3
Kenya	..	29.7	34.4	41.2	52.4	76.5	98.5	100.0	109.0	121.2	134.1	..	10.0	19.5
Lesotho	15.5	48.5	54.2	63.8	74.7	84.6	91.5	100.0	109.3	118.7	129.1	14.2	13.7	11.5
Liberia	..	..	..	..	..	..	..	..	..	..	..	..	..	..
Madagascar	..	31.6	35.3	38.3	44.2	48.2	67.1	100.0	119.8	125.1	132.9	..	17.7	20.1
Malawi	5.5	21.9	24.5	27.6	33.9	40.5	54.5	100.0	137.6	150.1	183.3	..	20.4	30.1
Mali	..	74.8	75.2	76.6	71.8	71.3	89.0	100.0	106.5	105.8	110.1	..	1.3	5.4
Mauritania	..	66.6	70.9	74.9	82.5	90.2	93.9	100.0	104.7	109.4	118.2	..	6.8	6.6
Mauritius	32.3	62.6	71.0	76.0	79.5	87.9	94.3	100.0	106.5	113.8	119.4	14.9	5.3	7.3
Mozambique	0.4	10.0	14.4	19.2	27.9	39.7	64.8	100.0	144.6	153.8	154.7	..	68.4	40.1
Namibia	17.0	51.3	57.4	64.2	75.6	82.1	90.9	100.0	108.0	117.6	126.5	..	13.1	10.6
Niger	..	..	..	..	..	..	..	..	..	..	..	..	..	..
Nigeria	2.0	13.1	14.1	15.9	23.0	36.8	57.8	100.0	129.3	140.0	154.5	17.7	23.2	38.4
Rwanda	23.0	33.7	35.1	42.0	46.0	50.0	82.0	100.0	108.9	122.0	130.3	11.1	1.9	18.8
São Tomé and Principe	..	15.7	22.4	32.8	41.7	52.3	66.3	100.0	145.5	246.5	350.7	..	27.4	39.6
Senegal	40.7	71.6	71.8	70.6	70.6	69.9	92.2	100.0	102.7	104.6	106.7	9.7	1.7	5.9
Seychelles	68.5	88.8	92.3	94.2	97.2	98.5	100.3	100.0	98.9	99.5	97.0	10.6	1.5	1.0
Sierra Leone	..	7.0	13.4	26.9	53.4	71.7	84.6	100.0	133.5	146.4	154.9	..	92.4	39.3
Somalia	..	..	..	..	..	..	..	..	..	..	..	..	..	..
South Africa	14.9	51.2	58.6	67.6	77.0	84.5	92.1	100.0	107.4	116.6	124.7	12.8	15.7	10.2
Sudan	0.1	1.6	2.7	6.0	13.0	28.5	58.5	100.0	214.3	282.9	305.5	22.9	39.8	88.6
Swaziland	16.7	52.9	58.7	65.0	70.4	78.2	89.0	100.0	106.4	114.1	123.8	14.4	13.5	10.1
Tanzania	2.0	21.5	29.2	37.5	45.8	57.3	74.6	100.0	125.7	147.2	162.5	19.6	30.7	26.0
Togo	43.1	62.0	62.7	62.9	63.9	63.8	86.4	100.0	104.6	112.0	113.1	11.1	0.7	8.6
Uganda	..	26.8	38.9	48.5	68.9	88.5	94.3	100.0	107.5	115.9	122.6	..	158.9	17.4
Zambia	0.1	1.5	3.2	6.3	16.8	48.5	74.5	100.0	146.3	182.6	234.9	14.7	57.0	78.2
Zimbabwe	..	25.4	29.8	36.8	52.3	66.7	81.6	100.0	121.4	144.5	196.1	..	11.2	25.6
NORTH AFRICA	22.8	66.2	52.9	64.7	77.3	85.3	92.3	100.0	107.9	116.5	125.2	8.2	19.3	9.3
Algeria	12.1	26.2	30.6	37.6	49.5	59.7	77.1	100.0	118.7	125.4	131.7	10.9	8.9	21.8
Egypt, Arab Republic	..	66.2	52.9	64.7	77.3	85.3	92.3	100.0	107.9	116.5	125.2	..	19.3	9.3
Libya	..	..	..	..	..	..	..	..	..	..	..	..	..	..
Morocco	..	..	..	..	..	..	..	..	..	..	..	..	..	..
Tunisia	33.5	70.9	75.5	81.7	86.5	90.0	94.1	100.0	103.7	107.4	111.4	8.5	7.3	5.1
ALL AFRICA	20.7	51.3	57.0	64.1	69.2	70.9	89.0	100.0	108.0	116.6	125.9	9.8	12.7	10.9

Note: 1998 data are preliminary (see page 3). Group data are medians of individual country values for each year. Some numbers for Angola and Dem. Rep. of Congo are shown in scientific notation.

3-4. Official exchange rate

| | National currency per U.S. dollar | | | | | | | | | | | Annual average | | |
	1980	1989	1990	1991	1992	1993	1994	1995	1996	1997	1998	75-84	85-89	90-MR
SUB-SAHARAN AFRICA	..	..	..	..	..	..	..	..	..	..	..	..	..	..
excluding South Africa	..	..	..	..	..	..	..	..	..	..	..	..	..	..
excl. S. Africa & Nigeria	..	..	..	..	..	..	..	..	..	..	..	..	..	..
Angola	..	0.0	0.0	0.1	0.5	5.1	152.8	2,711.0	111,007.6	228,233.3	392,814.4	..	0.0	81,658.3
Benin	211.3	319.0	272.3	282.1	264.7	283.2	555.2	499.2	511.6	583.7	590.0	276.7	342.6	426.9
Botswana	0.8	2.0	1.9	2.0	2.1	2.4	2.7	2.8	3.3	3.5	3.7	0.9	1.9	2.7
Burkina Faso	211.3	319.0	272.3	282.1	264.7	283.2	555.2	499.2	511.6	583.7	590.0	325.9	342.6	426.9
Burundi	90.0	158.7	171.3	181.5	208.3	242.8	252.7	249.8	302.8	352.4	447.8	91.8	131.5	267.7
Cameroon	211.3	319.0	272.3	282.1	264.7	283.2	555.2	499.2	511.6	583.7	590.0	276.7	342.6	426.9
Cape Verde	..	78.0	70.0	71.4	68.0	80.4	81.9	76.9	82.6	93.2	94.7	84.9	78.9	79.9
Central African Republic	211.3	319.0	272.3	282.1	264.7	283.2	555.2	499.2	511.6	583.7	590.0	276.7	342.6	426.9
Chad	211.3	319.0	272.3	282.1	264.7	283.2	555.2	499.2	511.6	583.7	590.0	276.7	342.6	426.9
Comoros	211.3	319.0	272.3	282.1	264.7	283.2	416.4	374.4	383.7	437.8	444.5	276.7	342.6	351.0
Congo, Democratic Rep. of	..	..	..	0.0	0.2	2.5	1,194.1	7,024.4	49,566.3	131,377.6	129,100.8	..	..	39,783.2
Congo, Republic of	..	319.0	272.3	282.1	264.7	283.2	555.2	499.2	511.6	583.7	590.0	437.0	342.6	426.9
Côte d'Ivoire	..	319.0	272.3	282.1	264.7	283.2	555.2	499.2	511.6	583.7	590.0	437.0	342.6	426.9
Djibouti	177.7	177.7	177.7	177.7	177.7	177.7	177.7	177.7	177.7	177.7	177.7	177.7	177.7	177.7
Equatorial Guinea	..	319.0	272.3	282.1	264.7	283.2	0.0	0.0	0.0	0.0	0.0	437.0	342.6	122.5
Eritrea	..	..	..	..	4.6	6.2	6.6	6.8	6.7	7.2	7.4	..	..	6.5
Ethiopia	2.1	2.1	2.1	2.1	2.1	4.3	5.1	5.9	6.3	6.5	6.9	2.1	2.1	4.6
Gabon	211.3	319.0	272.3	282.1	264.7	283.2	555.2	499.2	511.6	583.7	590.0	276.7	342.6	426.9
Gambia, The	1.7	7.6	7.9	8.7	8.9	9.1	9.6	9.5	9.8	10.2	10.6	2.2	6.4	9.4
Ghana	2.8	270.0	326.3	367.8	437.1	649.1	956.7	1,200.4	1,637.2	2,050.2	2,314.0	6.1	153.9	1,104.3
Guinea	..	591.6	660.2	753.9	902.0	955.9	976.7	991.4	1,004.0	1,095.3	1,300.0	0.0	368.1	959.9
Guinea-Bissau	0.5	27.8	33.6	56.3	106.7	155.1	198.3	278.0	405.7	583.7	590.0	0.6	11.8	267.5
Kenya	7.4	20.6	22.9	27.5	32.2	58.0	56.1	51.4	57.1	58.7	60.4	9.4	17.5	47.1
Lesotho	6.7	2.6	2.6	2.8	2.8	3.3	3.5	3.6	4.3	4.6	5.9	4.8	0.5	3.7
Liberia	..	..	..	..	..	..	..	..	..	..	..	..	..	..
Madagascar	211.0	1,603.0	1,494.0	1,835.0	1,864.0	1,914.0	3,083.0	4,268.0	4,054.6	5,090.0	5,273.0	297.8	1,083.4	3,208.4
Malawi	0.8	2.8	2.7	2.8	3.6	4.4	8.7	15.3	15.3	16.4	31.1	1.0	2.2	11.2
Mali	211.3	319.0	272.3	282.1	264.7	283.2	555.2	499.1	511.6	583.7	590.0	276.7	342.6	426.9
Mauritania	45.9	83.1	80.6	81.9	87.0	120.8	123.6	129.8	137.2	151.9	189.0	49.0	76.7	122.4
Mauritius	7.7	15.3	14.9	15.7	15.6	17.6	18.0	17.4	17.9	20.6	22.7	8.5	14.1	17.8
Mozambique	32.4	744.9	929.1	1,434.5	2,432.7	3,722.7	5,918.1	8,889.8	11,293.8	11,545.6	11,850.3	34.3	328.8	6,446.3
Namibia	..	2.6	2.6	2.8	2.9	3.3	3.6	3.6	4.3	4.6	5.9	1.4	2.3	3.7
Niger	211.3	319.0	272.3	282.1	264.7	283.2	555.2	499.2	511.6	583.7	590.0	276.7	342.6	426.9
Nigeria	0.5	7.4	8.0	9.9	17.3	22.1	22.0	21.9	21.9	21.9	21.9	0.6	3.7	18.5
Rwanda	92.8	80.0	82.6	125.1	133.4	144.3	220.0	262.2	306.8	301.5	312.3	93.7	85.0	209.8
São Tomé and Principe	34.8	124.7	143.3	201.6	321.3	429.9	732.6	1,420.3	2,203.2	4,552.5	6,927.4	36.5	69.7	1,881.3
Senegal	211.3	319.0	272.3	282.1	264.7	283.2	555.2	499.2	511.6	583.7	590.0	276.7	342.6	426.9
Seychelles	6.4	5.6	5.3	5.3	5.1	5.2	5.1	4.8	5.0	5.0	5.3	6.7	6.0	5.1
Sierra Leone	..	46.2	96.7	199.0	424.0	539.2	576.2	618.3	900.2	929.1	982.0	2.5	23.0	585.0
Somalia	..	..	..	..	..	..	..	..	..	..	..	..	..	..
South Africa	0.8	2.6	2.6	2.8	2.9	3.3	3.5	3.6	4.3	4.6	5.8	1.0	2.3	3.7
Sudan	0.5	4.5	4.5	7.0	97.4	159.3	289.6	580.9	1,250.8	1,575.7	2,071.7	0.6	3.4	670.8
Swaziland	0.8	2.6	2.6	2.8	2.9	3.3	3.6	3.6	4.3	4.6	6.0	1.0	2.3	3.7
Tanzania	8.2	143.4	195.1	219.2	297.7	405.3	509.6	574.8	580.0	612.1	..	9.2	71.4	424.2
Togo	211.3	319.0	272.3	282.1	264.7	283.2	555.2	499.2	511.6	583.7	590.0	276.7	342.6	426.9
Uganda	..	170.4	319.6	550.9	960.8	1,201.8	1,101.0	932.5	1,012.8	1,058.1	1,149.7	2.3	53.2	920.8
Zambia	0.8	13.8	30.3	64.6	172.2	452.8	669.4	857.2	1,203.7	1,333.8	1,861.6	0.9	8.5	738.4
Zimbabwe	0.6	2.1	2.4	3.4	5.1	6.5	8.2	8.7	9.9	12.1	21.4	0.8	1.8	8.6
NORTH AFRICA	..	..	..	..	..	..	..	..	..	..	..	..	..	..
Algeria	3.8	7.6	9.0	18.5	21.8	23.3	35.1	47.7	54.7	57.7	60.4	4.3	5.6	36.5
Egypt, Arab Republic	..	2.5	2.6	3.0	3.3	3.3	3.4	3.4	3.4	3.4	3.4	..	1.9	3.2
Libya	..	..	..	..	..	..	..	..	..	..	..	..	..	..
Morocco	3.9	8.5	8.2	8.7	8.5	9.3	9.2	8.5	8.7	9.5	9.7	5.2	8.9	8.9
Tunisia	0.4	0.9	0.9	0.9	0.9	1.0	1.0	0.9	1.0	1.1	1.1	0.5	0.9	1.0
ALL AFRICA	..	..	..	..	..	..	..	..	..	..	..	..	..	..

Note: 1998 data are preliminary. Uganda changed currency in 1987, Congo Dem. Rep. in 1993. Angola and Congo Dem. Rep. again changed currency in 1998, but the changes are not reflected here. Guinea-Bissau joined WAMU in 1997.

3-5. SDR exchange rate index

	SDRs per unit of national currency, index 1995=100											Annual average		
	1980	*1989*	*1990*	*1991*	*1992*	*1993*	*1994*	*1995*	*1996*	*1997*	*1998*	*75-84*	*85-89*	*90-MR*
SUB-SAHARAN AFRICA	..	..	..	..	..	..	..	..	..	..	..	..	..	..
excluding South Africa	..	..	..	..	..	..	..	..	..	..	..	..	..	..
excl. S.Africa & Nigeria	..	..	..	..	..	..	..	..	..	..	..	..	..	..
Angola	4,972,386	5,049,470	4,772,656	2,736,650	773,107	77,622	6,952	100	4	1	0	5,637,729	5,353,748	929,677
Benin	275	185	205	197	203	192	95	100	102	94	95	245	185	143
Botswana	416	163	167	152	140	124	109	100	88	84	74	402	188	115
Burkina Faso	275	185	205	197	203	192	95	100	102	94	95	245	185	143
Burundi	323	186	163	153	129	112	105	100	86	78	63	354	244	110
Cameroon	275	185	205	197	203	192	95	100	102	94	95	245	185	143
Cape Verde	223	117	123	120	122	104	99	100	97	91	88	240	122	105
Central African Republic	275	185	205	197	203	192	95	100	102	94	95	245	185	143
Chad	275	185	205	197	203	192	95	100	102	94	95	245	185	143
Comoros	207	139	154	148	153	144	95	100	102	94	95	184	139	120
Congo, Democratic Rep. of	7.E+11	5.E+09	3.E+09	3.E+08	8.E+06	4.E+05	3.E+03	100	..	..	..	1.E+12	2.E+10	5.E+08
Congo, Republic of	275	185	205	197	203	192	95	100	102	94	95	245	185	143
Côte d'Ivoire	275	185	205	197	203	192	95	100	102	94	95	245	185	143
Djibouti	117	118	112	111	108	109	106	100	104	110	112	130	125	108
Equatorial Guinea	275	185	205	197	203	192	95	100	102	94	95	245	185	143
Eritrea	..	..	..	..	..	..	..	..	..	..	..	..	..	..
Ethiopia	347	352	333	330	274	134	120	100	101	101	97	386	373	177
Gabon	275	185	205	197	203	192	95	100	102	94	95	245	185	143
Gambia, The	647	150	136	121	115	114	106	100	102	103	100	568	204	111
Ghana	50,406	524	408	359	296	201	132	100	76	64	57	76,474	1,429	188
Guinea	6,092	199	168	146	119	113	108	100	103	171	..	6,082	1,435	128
Guinea-Bissau	61,655	1,173	909	551	281	193	148	100	73	52	52	62,731	7,181	262
Kenya	796	292	247	205	170	100	98	100	93	96	94	727	369	134
Lesotho	543	164	157	146	137	121	108	100	89	87	74	510	202	113
Liberia	117	118	112	111	108	109	106	100	104	110	112	130	125	108
Madagascar	2,349	314	318	258	246	241	160	100	110	92	87	2,029	587	179
Malawi	2,199	656	627	605	470	377	211	100	104	103	59	2,087	910	295
Mali	275	185	205	197	203	192	95	100	102	94	95	245	185	143
Mauritania	330	182	180	175	164	119	112	100	99	95	77	347	212	124
Mauritius	264	135	131	123	120	107	103	100	101	93	85	284	155	107
Mozambique	31,524	1,404	1,057	704	385	259	154	100	81	84	83	33,628	13,389	323
Namibia	543	164	157	146	137	121	108	100	89	87	74	510	202	113
Niger	275	185	205	197	203	192	95	100	102	94	95	245	185	143
Nigeria	4,669	352	305	246	145	108	106	100	105	110	112	4,415	1,462	148
Rwanda	302	356	324	213	195	181	115	100	82	88	86	333	356	154
São Tomé and Principe	4,681	1,337	1,090	824	477	355	210	100	67	36	23	5,055	3,204	354
Senegal	275	185	205	197	203	192	95	100	102	94	95	245	185	143
Seychelles	87	100	100	100	100	100	100	100	100	104	101	92	100	101
Sierra Leone	81,552	1,495	569	297	159	141	133	100	84	85	53	78,935	8,296	180
Somalia	..	..	..	..	..	..	..	..	..	..	..	..	..	..
South Africa	543	164	157	146	137	121	108	100	89	87	74	510	202	113
Sudan	129,985	14,664	13,854	11,388	865	392	214	100	49	39	31	142,261	23,432	2,992
Swaziland	543	164	157	146	137	121	108	100	89	87	74	510	202	113
Tanzania	8,149	477	329	291	210	156	119	100	103	103	96	8,361	1,975	168
Togo	275	185	205	197	203	192	95	100	102	94	95	245	185	143
Uganda	1,520,277	545	256	150	92	88	105	100	97	99	88	1,025,920	7,512	119
Zambia	126,813	7,855	3,302	1,535	590	210	121	100	75	72	52	127,103	18,640	673
Zimbabwe	1,570	485	395	280	183	145	113	100	91	80	45	1,556	622	159
NORTH AFRICA	..	..	..	..	..	..	..	..	..	..	..	..	..	..
Algeria	1,441	741	600	290	234	221	150	100	91	91	90	1,447	1,103	207
Egypt, Arab Republic	565	493	267	127	110	110	106	100	105	110	112	823	592	127
Libya	136	137	137	137	131	123	115	100	100	100	..	152	147	118
Morocco	253	119	116	109	108	100	98	100	102	99	99	225	121	104
Tunisia	272	118	120	114	115	102	99	100	101	94	93	254	140	104
ALL AFRICA	..	..	..	..	..	..	..	..	..	..	..	..	..	..

Note: 1998 data are preliminary (see page 3). Guinea-Bissau joined the Western African Monetary Union (W.A.M.U) in May, 1997.

3-6. Currency conversion factor

	Units of national currency per US dollar											Annual average		
	1980	*1989*	*1990*	*1991*	*1992*	*1993*	*1994*	*1995*	*1996*	*1997*	*1998*	*75-84*	*85-89*	*90-MR*
SUB-SAHARAN AFRICA	..	..	..	..	..	..	..	..	..	..	..	..	..	..
excluding South Africa	..	..	..	..	..	..	..	..	..	..	..	..	..	..
excl. S. Africa & Nigeria	..	..	..	..	..	..	..	..	..	..	..	..	..	..
Angola	..	0.0	0.0	0.1	0.5	5.1	152.8	2,711.0	111,007.6	232,185.0	394,399.4	..	0.0	82,273.5
Benin	211.3	319.0	272.3	282.1	350.6	283.2	555.2	499.2	511.6	583.7	590.0	276.7	342.6	436.4
Botswana	0.8	2.0	1.9	1.9	2.1	2.2	2.6	2.7	3.0	3.6	3.8	0.9	1.8	2.6
Burkina Faso	211.3	319.0	272.3	282.1	396.6	388.5	555.2	499.2	511.5	583.7	590.0	276.7	342.6	453.2
Burundi	90.0	158.7	171.3	181.5	208.3	242.8	252.7	249.8	302.8	352.4	447.8	91.8	131.5	267.7
Cameroon	209.2	315.4	300.7	268.6	280.4	265.4	435.0	518.5	501.8	541.1	599.8	265.6	356.7	412.4
Cape Verde	40.2	78.0	70.0	71.4	68.0	80.4	81.9	76.9	82.6	93.1	94.7	46.6	78.9	79.9
Central African Republic	211.3	319.0	272.3	282.1	264.7	283.2	555.2	499.2	511.6	582.4	590.0	276.7	342.6	426.7
Chad	211.3	319.0	272.3	282.1	264.7	283.2	555.2	499.2	511.6	583.7	590.0	276.7	342.6	426.9
Comoros	211.3	319.0	272.3	282.1	264.7	283.2	416.4	374.4	383.7	437.8	444.5	274.7	342.6	351.0
Congo, Democratic Rep. of	..	0.0	0.0	0.0	0.2	3.0	970.9	6,254.7	47,728.7	124,416.4	129,100.8	0.0	0.0	34,275.0
Congo, Republic of	211.3	319.0	272.3	282.1	264.7	396.1	555.2	499.2	511.6	583.7	590.0	276.7	342.6	439.4
Côte d'Ivoire	211.3	319.0	272.3	282.1	264.7	283.2	555.2	499.2	511.6	583.7	590.0	276.7	342.6	426.9
Djibouti	177.7	177.7	177.7	177.7	177.7	177.7	177.7	177.7	177.7	177.7	..	177.7	177.7	177.7
Equatorial Guinea	110.6	319.0	272.3	282.1	264.7	283.2	555.2	499.1	511.6	583.7	590.0	146.9	342.6	426.9
Eritrea	..	..	..	..	4.6	6.2	6.6	6.8	6.7	7.2	7.4	..	..	6.5
Ethiopia	..	2.1	2.6	3.7	3.7	4.3	5.8	5.9	6.3	6.5	6.9	2.1	2.1	5.1
Gabon	211.3	319.0	272.3	282.1	264.7	349.6	555.2	499.2	511.6	583.7	507.8	276.7	342.6	425.1
Gambia, The	1.7	7.6	7.9	8.8	8.9	9.1	9.6	9.5	9.8	10.2	10.4	2.3	6.4	9.4
Ghana	9.6	270.0	326.3	367.8	437.1	649.1	956.7	1,199.8	1,637.0	2,050.2	2,314.0	17.5	157.0	1,104.2
Guinea	19.0	591.6	660.2	753.9	902.0	955.5	976.6	991.4	1,004.0	1,095.3	1,300.0	21.1	373.0	959.9
Guinea-Bissau	0.8	27.8	33.6	56.3	106.7	155.1	198.3	278.0	405.7	583.7	590.0	0.8	12.3	267.5
Kenya	7.4	20.6	22.9	27.5	32.2	58.0	56.1	51.4	57.1	58.7	60.4	9.4	17.5	47.1
Lesotho	0.8	2.6	2.6	2.8	2.9	3.3	3.5	3.6	4.3	4.6	5.5	1.0	2.3	3.7
Liberia	1.0	1.0	1.0	1.0	..	..	..	..	..	..	..	1.0	1.0	1.0
Madagascar	211.3	1,603.4	1,494.2	1,835.4	1,864.0	1,913.8	3,067.3	4,265.6	4,061.3	5,090.9	5,441.4	297.7	1,083.7	3,226.0
Malawi	0.8	2.8	2.7	2.8	3.6	4.4	8.7	15.3	15.3	16.4	31.1	1.0	2.2	11.2
Mali	211.3	319.0	272.3	282.1	265.3	283.8	556.4	500.2	512.6	584.9	591.2	276.7	342.6	427.7
Mauritania	45.9	83.1	80.6	81.9	87.0	120.8	123.6	129.8	137.2	151.9	189.8	49.0	76.7	122.5
Mauritius	7.7	15.3	14.9	15.7	15.6	17.6	18.0	17.4	17.9	20.6	22.8	8.5	14.1	17.8
Mozambique	32.4	744.9	929.1	1,434.5	2,432.7	3,722.7	5,918.1	8,889.8	11,293.8	11,545.6	11,850.3	34.3	328.8	6,446.3
Namibia	0.8	2.6	2.6	2.8	2.9	3.3	3.6	3.6	4.3	4.6	5.5	0.9	2.3	3.7
Niger	211.3	319.0	272.3	282.1	264.7	391.4	555.2	499.2	511.6	583.7	590.0	276.7	342.6	438.9
Nigeria	0.8	9.4	9.2	12.0	19.0	45.3	52.3	70.4	80.0	81.1	88.0	1.1	5.3	50.8
Rwanda	92.8	80.0	82.6	125.1	133.4	144.3	220.0	262.2	306.8	301.5	312.3	93.7	85.0	209.8
São Tomé and Principe	34.8	124.7	143.3	201.8	320.0	430.0	732.6	1,420.3	2,203.2	4,552.5	6,882.9	36.5	69.7	1,876.3
Senegal	211.3	319.0	272.3	282.1	264.7	283.2	555.2	499.2	511.6	583.7	590.0	276.7	342.6	426.9
Seychelles	6.4	5.6	5.3	5.3	5.1	5.2	5.1	4.8	5.0	5.0	5.3	6.7	6.0	5.1
Sierra Leone	1.0	59.8	151.4	295.3	499.4	567.5	586.7	755.2	920.7	981.9	1,597.1	1.3	29.1	706.2
Somalia	28.8	512.2	1,896.1	..	..	..	..	..	..	..	..	28.1	236.3	1,896.1
South Africa	0.8	2.6	2.6	2.8	2.9	3.3	3.5	3.6	4.3	4.6	5.5	1.0	2.3	3.7
Sudan	0.6	6.3	12.2	27.0	97.4	159.3	289.6	580.9	1,250.8	1,575.7	2,071.7	0.7	3.1	673.9
Swaziland	0.8	2.6	2.6	2.8	2.8	3.3	3.5	3.6	4.3	4.6	5.5	1.0	2.3	3.7
Tanzania	..	119.4	173.5	201.8	250.5	340.1	477.6	536.4	581.4	599.5	637.8	9.8	57.9	422.1
Togo	211.3	319.0	272.3	282.1	264.7	283.2	555.2	499.2	511.6	583.7	590.0	276.7	342.6	426.9
Uganda	1.0	170.4	319.6	550.9	960.8	1,201.8	1,101.0	932.5	1,012.0	1,058.0	1,150.0	2.1	53.2	920.7
Zambia	0.8	13.8	34.5	64.6	179.0	452.8	669.4	864.1	1,207.9	1,314.5	1,862.1	0.9	8.5	738.8
Zimbabwe	0.6	2.1	2.4	3.4	5.1	6.5	8.2	8.7	9.9	11.9	23.7	0.8	1.8	8.9
NORTH AFRICA	..	..	..	..	..	..	..	..	..	..	..	..	..	..
Algeria	3.8	7.6	9.0	18.5	21.8	23.3	35.1	47.7	54.7	57.7	59.0	4.3	5.6	36.3
Egypt, Arab Republic	0.7	1.9	2.2	3.0	3.3	3.3	3.4	3.4	3.4	3.4	3.6	0.7	1.4	3.2
Libya	0.3	0.3	0.3	0.3	..	..	..	..	0.4	..	..	0.3	0.3	0.3
Morocco	3.9	8.5	8.2	8.7	8.5	9.3	9.2	8.5	8.7	9.5	..	5.2	8.8	8.8
Tunisia	0.4	0.9	0.9	0.9	0.9	1.0	1.0	0.9	1.0	1.1	1.0	0.5	0.9	1.0
ALL AFRICA	..	..	..	..	..	..	..	..	..	..	..	..	..	..

Note: Off. exch. rate adjusted for some countries to better reflect the rate at which intl. transactions are carried out. G. Bissau joined W.A.M.U. in 1997. Some values for Angola Congo D.R.are shown in scientific notation.

3-7. Parallel market exchange rate

	National currency per U.S. dollar										Annual average		
	1980	1989	1990	1991	1992	1993	1994	1995	1996	1997	75-84	85-89	90-MR
SUB-SAHARAN AFRICA	..	..	..	..	..	..	..	..	..	..	..	..	..
excluding South Africa	..	..	..	..	..	..	..	..	..	..	..	..	..
excl. S. Africa & Nigeria	..	..	..	..	..	..	..	..	..	..	..	..	..
Angola	..	..	..	1,266.7	1,087.5	31,740.0	203,137.5	569,573.8	163,370.0	283,138.8	900.0	1,837.5	179,044.9
Benin	209.5	324.8	281.8	289.0	270.1	288.0	586.4	499.3	516.4	593.3	304.2	343.9	415.5
Botswana	0.8	2.3	1.9	2.4	2.5	2.8	2.9	2.8	3.4	3.7	1.2	2.4	2.8
Burkina Faso	209.5	324.8	281.8	17.1	16.8	288.0	586.4	499.3	516.4	593.3	304.2	343.9	349.9
Burundi	106.0	214.0	186.1	269.3	310.9	370.7	409.4	340.8	369.6	459.2	122.3	161.7	339.5
Cameroon	209.5	324.8	281.8	289.0	270.1	288.0	586.4	499.3	516.4	593.3	304.2	343.9	415.5
Cape Verde	..	..	..	88.0	79.5	87.0	92.0	89.3	89.5	99.5	..	..	89.3
Central African Republic	209.5	324.8	281.8	289.0	270.1	288.0	586.4	499.3	516.4	593.3	304.2	343.9	415.5
Chad	209.5	324.8	281.8	289.0	270.1	288.0	586.4	499.3	516.4	593.3	304.2	343.9	415.5
Comoros	209.5	324.8	281.8	289.0	270.1	288.0	446.0	390.6	415.6	467.6	304.2	343.9	356.1
Congo, Democratic Rep. of	6.4	469.4	738.1	19,318.8	756,558.3	3,112,920.4	1,209.8	7,452.1	52,429.4	160,358.3	14.3	182.6	513,873.2
Congo, Republic of	209.5	324.8	281.8	289.0	270.1	288.0	586.4	499.3	516.4	593.3	304.2	343.9	415.5
Côte d'Ivoire	209.5	324.8	281.8	289.0	270.1	288.0	586.4	499.3	516.4	593.3	304.2	343.9	415.5
Djibouti	..	217.9	191.8	213.8	205.8	212.0	208.6	198.5	192.1	183.9	..	207.8	200.8
Equatorial Guinea	209.5	324.8	281.8	289.0	270.1	288.0	586.4	586.4	516.4	593.3	304.2	343.9	426.4
Eritrea	..	..	..	..	..	..	..	..	..	..	..	..	..
Ethiopia	2.8	5.9	6.0	6.7	9.5	13.3	12.0	10.7	10.2	7.5	3.5	5.1	9.5
Gabon	209.5	324.8	281.8	289.0	270.1	288.0	586.4	499.3	516.4	593.3	334.6	343.9	415.5
Gambia, The	1.7	7.4	8.3	8.8	11.5	9.1	9.0	10.4	10.8	10.8	2.5	7.1	9.8
Ghana	15.9	328.8	360.8	382.2	451.6	665.7	976.4	1,224.3	1,663.4	2,080.7	41.7	222.1	975.6
Guinea	41.7	580.1	693.3	793.0	1,608.1	1,156.9	1,074.1	1,017.9	1,025.9	1,125.3	102.9	453.8	1,061.8
Guinea-Bissau	..	..	..	4,172.5	6,075.0	9,883.3	14,012.5	19,166.7	26,855.0	..	..	1,800.0	13,360.8
Kenya	8.2	22.4	23.3	30.0	44.4	91.7	66.8	53.4	59.5	62.1	11.9	19.0	53.9
Lesotho	..	2.7	2.7	2.9	3.0	3.5	3.8	3.7	4.5	4.7	1.4	2.5	3.6
Liberia	..	..	..	..	..	40.0	45.0	42.3	45.8	48.5	..	1.5	44.3
Madagascar	265.0	1,639.1	1,589.2	2,071.3	2,239.2	2,217.9	3,122.9	4,397.5	4,551.7	5,582.1	521.1	1,133.5	3,221.5
Malawi	1.6	3.6	3.3	3.9	4.6	5.9	9.2	16.7	16.5	17.6	1.7	2.8	9.7
Mali	209.5	324.8	281.8	289.0	270.1	288.0	586.4	499.3	516.4	593.3	304.2	343.9	415.5
Mauritania	65.0	..	..	213.3	221.7	247.5	145.0	139.3	144.0	158.9	93.2	178.0	181.4
Mauritius	..	16.0	15.7	17.1	16.8	18.3	18.4	18.2	19.4	21.4	..	14.5	18.2
Mozambique	80.0	1,250.0	..	2,100.0	2,800.0	3,950.0	6,875.0	9,865.7	12,172.5	12,533.7	322.2	1,793.8	7,185.3
Namibia	..	..	..	..	..	..	..	..	..	4.9	..	..	4.9
Niger	209.5	324.8	281.8	289.0	270.1	288.0	586.4	499.3	516.4	593.3	304.2	343.9	415.5
Nigeria	0.9	10.7	9.3	6.7	21.9	56.8	71.7	78.3	81.8	84.7	1.4	6.4	51.4
Rwanda	115.0	109.8	104.2	209.1	238.9	297.4	286.5	268.1	331.8	360.5	135.4	111.4	262.1
São Tomé and Principe	..	..	..	222.5	360.0	432.5	810.0	1,503.3	2,407.5	7,300.0	..	..	1,862.3
Senegal	209.5	324.8	281.8	289.0	270.1	288.0	586.4	499.3	516.4	593.3	304.2	343.9	415.5
Seychelles	..	..	5.9	5.7	5.5	5.4	5.5	5.5	5.4	5.5	..	..	5.6
Sierra Leone	1.4	180.9	470.6	535.7	845.1	647.5	618.7	741.3	942.1	1,137.9	2.1	86.5	742.4
Somalia	9.9	398.8	1,982.1	4,675.0	6,095.0	7,456.3	6,961.3	6,549.2	7,789.8	5,919.3	14.7	224.0	5,928.5
South Africa	0.9	2.7	2.7	2.9	3.0	3.5	3.8	3.7	4.5	4.7	1.2	2.5	3.6
Sudan	1.0	15.9	43.6	105.3	62.4	31.6	45.3	77.5	147.2	171.2	1.3	8.4	85.5
Swaziland	..	3.0	2.7	3.1	3.3	3.8	3.9	3.9	4.7	4.9	..	2.5	3.8
Tanzania	21.0	263.5	292.4	348.5	405.9	443.5	523.2	587.3	604.7	656.9	30.5	175.4	482.8
Togo	209.5	324.8	281.8	289.0	270.1	288.0	586.4	499.3	516.4	593.3	304.2	343.9	415.5
Uganda	75.7	597.5	685.8	859.2	1,365.4	1,515.8	1,289.2	1,076.2	1,135.2	1,178.1	203.8	3,681.6	1,138.1
Zambia	1.3	107.8	121.2	133.3	104.2	531.0	805.4	935.6	1,281.8	1,583.0	1.7	33.5	686.9
Zimbabwe	1.1	3.5	3.3	5.3	6.7	7.7	9.4	8.9	10.8	13.9	1.7	2.8	8.3
NORTH AFRICA	..	..	..	..	..	..	..	..	..	..	..	..	..
Algeria	10.9	37.1	29.8	33.8	87.4	106.8	128.7	131.9	127.6	129.8	13.6	27.2	97.0
Egypt, Arab Republic	0.8	2.6	2.6	3.4	3.4	3.4	3.4	3.4	3.6	3.4	0.9	2.0	3.3
Libya	0.5	0.9	1.0	1.2	1.6	1.7	1.6	1.3	2.0	2.2	0.5	1.0	1.6
Morocco	4.1	9.2	9.3	9.2	8.9	9.4	9.4	8.6	8.8	9.7	6.0	9.1	9.2
Tunisia	0.4	1.0	0.9	1.0	1.0	1.0	1.1	0.9	1.0	1.1	0.6	0.9	1.0
ALL AFRICA	..	..	..	..	..	..	..	..	..	..	..	..	..

Note: Rates are annual avg. of month-end est., based on a sample of transactions. G. Bissau joined the WAMU in 97. New Ugandan shilling introduced in 1987. Some values for Angola Congo D.R. are shown in scientific notation.

3-8. Ratio of parallel market to official exchange rates

	Ratio of parallel market to official exchange rates										Annual average		
	1980	1989	1990	1991	1992	1993	1994	1995	1996	1997	75-84	85-89	90-MR
SUB-SAHARAN AFRICA	..	..	..	..	..	..	..	..	..	..	..	..	..
excluding South Africa	..	..	..	..	..	..	..	..	..	..	..	..	..
excl. S. Africa & Nigeria	..	..	..	..	..	..	..	..	..	..	..	..	..
Angola	..	..	..	19,192.42	2,377.57	6,227.80	1,329.58	210.10	1.47	1.24	..	61,454.85	4,191.46
Benin	0.99	1.02	1.04	1.02	1.02	1.02	1.06	1.00	1.01	1.02	1.03	1.01	1.02
Botswana	1.03	1.14	1.02	1.19	1.19	1.16	1.08	1.01	1.02	1.05	1.23	1.34	1.09
Burkina Faso	0.99	1.02	1.03	0.06	0.06	1.01	1.06	1.00	1.01	1.02	1.02	1.01	0.81
Burundi	1.18	1.35	1.09	1.48	1.49	1.53	1.62	1.36	1.22	1.30	1.28	1.27	1.38
Cameroon	0.99	1.02	0.94	1.08	0.96	1.09	1.35	0.96	1.03	1.10	1.03	1.01	1.06
Cape Verde	..	..	..	1.23	1.17	1.08	1.12	1.16	1.08	1.07	..	..	1.13
Central African Republic	0.99	1.02	1.04	1.02	1.02	1.02	1.06	1.00	1.01	1.02	1.03	1.01	1.02
Chad	0.99	1.02	1.03	1.02	1.02	1.02	1.06	1.00	1.01	1.02	1.03	1.01	1.02
Comoros	0.99	1.02	1.04	1.02	1.02	1.02	1.07	1.04	1.08	1.07	1.03	1.01	1.04
Congo, Democratic Rep. of	..	..	..	..	3,782,791.50	1,245,168.16	1.01	1.06	1.06	1.22	..	..	837,994.00
Congo, Republic of	..	1.02	1.03	1.02	1.02	1.02	1.06	1.00	1.01	1.02	1.04	1.01	1.02
Côte d'Ivoire	..	1.02	1.04	1.02	1.02	1.02	1.06	1.00	1.01	1.02	1.04	1.01	1.02
Djibouti	..	1.23	1.08	1.20	1.16	1.19	1.17	1.12	1.08	1.03	..	1.17	1.14
Equatorial Guinea	..	1.02	1.04	1.02	1.02	1.02	..	..	..	..	1.04	1.01	1.02
Eritrea	..	..	..	..	..	..	..	..	..	..	..	..	..
Ethiopia	1.35	2.85	2.90	3.24	4.59	3.12	2.36	1.82	1.61	1.15	1.70	2.39	2.63
Gabon	0.99	1.02	1.04	1.02	1.02	1.02	1.06	1.00	1.01	1.02	1.02	1.01	1.02
Gambia, The	0.99	0.98	1.05	1.01	1.29	1.00	0.94	1.09	1.10	1.06	1.05	1.14	1.06
Ghana	5.78	1.22	1.11	1.04	1.03	1.03	1.02	1.02	1.02	1.01	7.98	1.84	1.05
Guinea	..	0.98	1.05	1.05	1.78	1.21	1.10	1.03	1.02	1.03	..	1.07	1.14
Guinea-Bissau	..	..	..	74.13	56.95	63.72	70.65	68.93	66.19	..	..	105.43	66.76
Kenya	1.11	1.09	1.02	1.09	1.38	1.58	1.19	1.04	1.04	1.06	1.18	1.09	1.16
Lesotho	..	1.03	1.04	1.05	1.05	1.07	1.07	1.02	1.05	1.02	..	1.03	1.05
Liberia	..	..	..	..	..	..	..	..	..	..	..	..	..
Madagascar	1.26	1.02	1.06	1.13	1.20	1.16	1.01	1.03	1.12	1.10	1.53	1.13	1.09
Malawi	1.94	1.30	1.21	1.39	1.28	1.34	1.05	1.09	1.08	1.07	1.76	1.30	1.20
Mali	0.99	1.02	1.04	1.02	1.02	1.02	1.06	1.00	1.01	1.02	1.03	1.01	1.02
Mauritania	1.42	..	..	2.60	2.55	2.05	1.17	1.07	1.05	1.05	1.79	2.38	1.65
Mauritius	..	1.05	1.06	1.09	1.08	1.04	1.02	1.05	1.08	1.04	..	1.03	1.06
Mozambique	2.47	1.68	..	1.46	1.15	1.06	1.16	1.11	1.08	1.09	8.19	26.45	1.22
Namibia	..	..	..	..	..	..	..	..	..	1.06	..	..	1.06
Niger	0.99	1.02	1.04	1.02	1.02	0.74	1.06	1.00	1.01	1.02	1.03	1.01	0.99
Nigeria	1.65	1.45	1.16	0.68	1.27	2.57	3.26	3.58	3.74	3.87	2.09	2.56	2.40
Rwanda	1.24	1.37	1.26	1.67	1.79	2.06	1.30	1.02	1.08	1.20	1.44	1.38	1.42
São Tomé and Principe	..	..	..	1.10	1.12	1.01	1.11	1.06	1.09	1.60	..	..	1.16
Senegal	0.99	1.02	1.03	1.02	1.02	1.02	1.06	1.00	1.01	1.02	1.03	1.01	1.02
Seychelles	..	..	1.11	1.08	1.07	1.04	1.09	1.16	1.09	1.09	..	..	1.09
Sierra Leone	..	3.92	4.87	2.69	1.99	1.20	1.07	1.20	1.05	1.22	1.71	3.04	2.14
Somalia	..	..	..	..	..	..	..	..	..	..	..	..	..
South Africa	1.16	1.03	1.04	1.05	1.05	1.07	1.07	1.02	1.05	1.02	1.12	1.08	1.04
Sudan	2.00	3.53	9.69	15.14	0.64	0.20	0.16	0.13	0.12	0.11	1.63	2.28	3.30
Swaziland	..	1.14	1.04	1.12	1.16	1.16	1.10	1.08	1.09	1.06	..	1.11	1.11
Tanzania	2.56	1.84	1.50	1.59	1.36	1.09	1.03	1.02	1.04	1.07	3.02	3.19	1.28
Togo	0.99	1.02	1.04	1.02	1.02	1.02	1.06	1.00	1.01	1.02	1.03	1.01	1.02
Uganda	..	3.51	2.15	1.56	1.42	1.26	1.17	1.15	1.12	1.11	183.46	234.79	1.61
Zambia	1.65	7.80	4.00	2.06	0.61	1.17	1.20	1.09	1.06	1.19	1.69	2.85	2.24
Zimbabwe	1.71	1.66	1.35	1.55	1.32	1.19	1.15	1.03	1.09	1.15	2.10	1.67	1.27
NORTH AFRICA	..	..	..	..	..	..	..	..	..	..	..	..	..
Algeria	2.84	4.88	3.33	1.83	4.00	4.57	3.67	2.77	2.33	2.25	3.08	4.74	3.29
Egypt, Arab Republic	..	1.04	1.00	1.13	1.03	1.03	1.00	1.00	1.06	1.00	..	1.18	1.03
Libya	..	..	..	..	..	..	..	..	..	..	..	..	..
Morocco	1.05	1.08	1.13	1.06	1.05	1.01	1.02	1.01	1.01	1.02	1.07	1.03	1.04
Tunisia	0.99	1.05	1.03	1.08	1.13	1.00	1.09	0.95	1.03	0.99	1.02	1.05	1.04
ALL AFRICA	..	..	..	..	..	..	..	..	..	..	..	..	..

Note: 1998 data are preliminary (see page 3). Guinea-Bissau joined the W. A.M.U. in May, 1997. New Ugandan shilling = 100 old Ugandan shilling was introduced in 1987.

3-9. Real effective exchange rate index

	Index 1990=100											Annual average		
	1980	1989	1990	1991	1992	1993	1994	1995	1996	1997	1998	75-84	85-89	90-MR
SUB-SAHARAN AFRICA	111.5	100.6	100.0	97.6	93.9	92.1	75.8	78.4	82.3	86.9	86.1	69.4	106.9	88.1
excluding South Africa	110.6	100.9	100.0	97.1	93.3	91.0	71.8	78.0	82.3	85.6	84.6	68.1	107.4	87.1
excl. S. Africa & Nigeria	109.4	100.6	100.0	97.6	93.9	92.1	70.6	76.6	80.9	82.7	83.0	66.6	106.9	86.4
Angola	..	..	..	..	..	..	..	..	..	..	..	..	..	..
Benin	..	98.3	100.0	98.7	102.5	102.3	65.7	75.2	76.0	76.4	..	..	93.1	87.1
Botswana	..	..	..	..	..	..	..	..	..	..	..	..	..	..
Burkina Faso	..	..	..	..	..	..	..	..	..	..	..	..	..	..
Burundi	129.8	115.2	100.0	100.4	84.5	81.7	85.1	92.2	97.9	85.6	87.9	159.6	137.1	90.6
Cameroon	88.2	97.1	100.0	95.7	96.4	89.8	57.6	66.4	67.3	64.3	62.2	84.0	98.8	77.7
Cape Verde	..	..	..	..	..	..	..	..	..	..	..	..	..	..
Central African Republic	105.9	97.6	100.0	94.4	94.4	89.7	56.6	63.1	64.5	65.3	66.4	100.7	101.7	77.2
Chad	..	..	..	..	..	..	..	..	..	..	..	101.8	108.4	222.4
Comoros	..	97.2	100.0	101.1	344.3	344.3	..	..	..	..	..	..	..	..
Congo, Democratic Rep. of	..	..	..	..	..	..	..	..	..	..	..	102.2	102.1	84.6
Congo, Republic of	102.2	102.4	100.0	89.5	90.0	89.2	69.3	79.0	75.2	..	..	90.0	94.5	82.0
Côte d'Ivoire	106.1	98.5	100.0	96.5	100.7	99.2	60.8	70.1	70.4	70.0	70.3	..	..	..
Djibouti	..	..	..	..	..	..	..	..	..	..	..	..	..	..
Equatorial Guinea	..	..	..	..	..	..	..	..	..	..	..	..	..	..
Eritrea	..	..	..	..	..	..	..	..	..	..	..	..	..	..
Ethiopia	92.5	100.5	100.0	108.6	98.9	44.5	37.9	38.5	35.4	35.8	36.2	92.5	109.5	59.5
Gabon	113.4	92.0	100.0	87.1	87.2	84.1	56.5	62.5	63.9	62.4	67.8	102.5	98.7	74.6
Gambia, The	100.8	78.3	100.0	97.1	103.2	103.1	95.9	95.3	94.8	99.6	..	97.0	81.0	98.6
Ghana	..	94.1	100.0	101.7	92.1	77.5	63.9	73.4	82.3	88.3	95.4	312.6	128.9	86.1
Guinea	..	106.4	100.0	104.5	96.9	100.6	98.5	92.8	88.8	93.3	93.1	..	116.2	96.5
Guinea-Bissau	..	..	100.0	91.2	75.8	80.8	71.8	66.4	69.6	78.2	81.3	..	100.0	79.5
Kenya	142.5	108.8	100.0	98.1	102.5	87.2	113.1	117.8	113.4	124.4	129.5	141.2	120.5	109.6
Lesotho	112.4	102.0	100.0	106.8	115.4	114.6	109.1	109.1	99.5	102.7	93.9	110.9	104.3	105.7
Liberia	..	..	..	..	..	..	..	..	..	..	..	..	..	..
Madagascar	193.1	94.6	100.0	87.3	92.9	102.7	90.2	81.9	104.1	96.3	96.7	200.0	130.3	94.7
Malawi	110.6	100.6	100.0	103.5	95.2	97.0	68.6	59.6	82.3	91.8	62.3	108.1	97.5	84.5
Mali	222.9	100.0	100.0	100.0	100.0	100.0	100.0	100.0	100.0	100.0	..	208.6	100.0	100.0
Mauritania	120.7	103.9	100.0	101.8	102.6	93.8	86.3	78.9	79.6	79.9	..	139.8	115.1	90.4
Mauritius	..	..	..	..	..	..	..	..	..	..	..	..	..	..
Mozambique	127.0	100.5	100.0	83.6	63.5	61.9	59.8	57.2	65.7	71.5	71.7	159.1	210.6	70.6
Namibia	129.0	102.2	100.0	98.3	103.3	103.5	103.8	104.4	96.5	99.6	84.6	133.6	105.3	99.3
Niger	..	101.1	100.0	87.4	82.8	79.3	55.2	62.1	63.2	62.1	67.8	..	108.0	73.3
Nigeria	350.6	107.5	100.0	85.0	70.5	77.2	142.8	122.1	167.7	193.1	203.6	431.4	282.8	129.1
Rwanda	83.3	109.5	100.0	76.0	73.4	85.1	128.7	78.0	85.2	102.2	103.2	60.9	112.9	92.4
São Tomé and Principe	..	..	..	..	..	..	..	..	..	..	..	..	..	..
Senegal	108.2	97.9	100.0	93.7	93.3	91.0	58.8	63.7	64.2	59.9	62.2	98.2	106.9	76.3
Seychelles	90.6	104.1	100.0	99.2	99.5	106.0	104.5	102.1	97.3	101.1	101.1	103.8	109.4	101.2
Sierra Leone	100.0	137.3	100.0	100.4	91.8	103.7	..	..	..	..	..	149.6	167.0	99.0
Somalia	..	..	..	..	..	..	..	..	..	..	..	..	..	..
South Africa	133.9	97.4	100.0	104.2	107.7	105.5	100.8	97.8	90.3	96.6	87.6	134.6	97.3	98.9
Sudan	45.0	66.9	100.0	176.9	28.2	27.9	33.0	25.4	25.3	26.2	19.9	43.4	47.1	51.4
Swaziland	..	..	..	..	..	..	..	..	118.3	136.4	153.0	..	138.3	108.7
Tanzania	..	115.4	100.0	98.8	86.8	94.0	93.6	97.7	73.6	..	..	108.5	104.9	84.5
Togo	100.0	96.3	100.0	95.0	96.5	93.1	61.9	71.8	67.5	67.6	67.6	..	133.2	66.7
Uganda	..	114.8	100.0	62.9	51.6	51.8	63.6	68.0	67.5	..	..	..	133.2	66.7
Zambia	135.0	115.5	100.0	93.2	89.3	101.4	97.5	93.4	97.7	117.0	127.4	143.7	85.3	101.9
Zimbabwe	165.4	112.1	100.0	66.2	92.2	86.9	79.9	85.9	88.5	72.8	91.2	167.1	127.3	84.8
NORTH AFRICA	142.4	102.9	100.0	95.4	100.1	101.7	104.0	103.4	104.1	103.9	104.2	146.3	132.4	101.9
Algeria	133.2	110.6	100.0	62.2	60.7	72.3	61.7	51.7	52.1	54.3	54.3	147.2	152.2	63.3
Egypt, Arab Republic	..	88.8	100.0	95.4	100.1	107.6	111.9	116.8	121.8	129.5	131.5	..	103.3	112.7
Libya	..	..	..	..	..	..	..	..	..	..	..	..	..	..
Morocco	..	..	..	..	..	..	..	..	..	..	..	..	..	..
Tunisia	151.6	102.9	100.0	101.0	103.1	101.7	104.0	103.4	104.1	103.9	104.2	149.8	117.0	102.8
ALL AFRICA	112.9	100.9	100.0	97.1	94.4	93.1	79.9	78.9	82.3	88.3	87.6	85.5	107.5	89.1

Note: 1998 data are preliminary (see page 3).

Figure 3-1.   Real effective exchange rate, 1998

(index 1990=100)

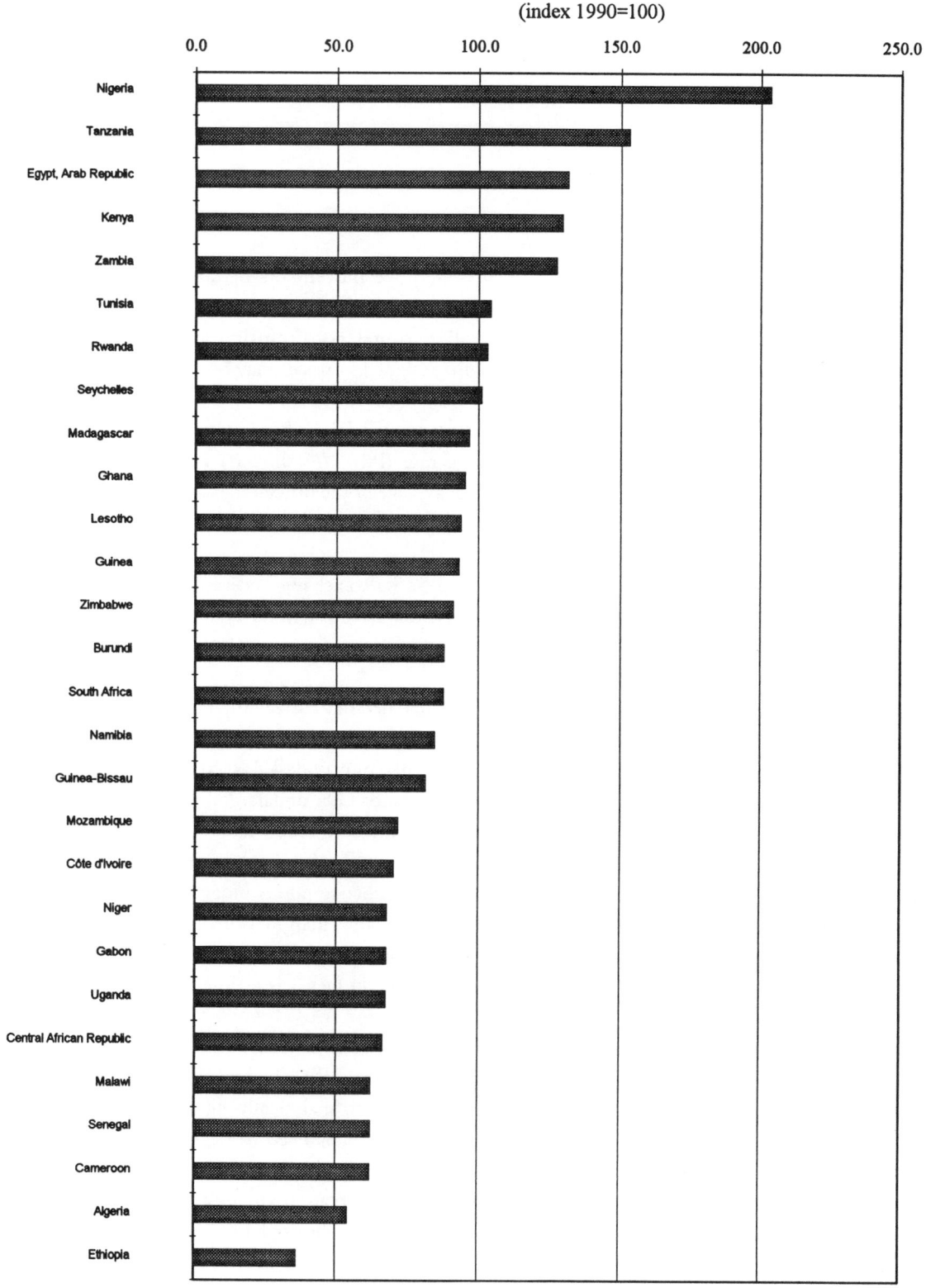

Technical Notes

Tables

Table 3-1. GDP deflator (local currency series). The implicit GDP deflator for national currency series is obtained by dividing, for each year of the time series, the value of GDP at current prices (World Bank country desks) by the value of GDP at constant 1995 prices (World Bank country desks), both in national currency.

Table 3-2. GDP deflator (US dollar series). The GDP deflator for US dollar series (with base year 1995 = 100) (World Bank country desks) is obtained by dividing, for each year of the time series, the value of GDP at current U.S. dollars (Table 2-5) by the value of GDP at constant 1995 dollars (Table 2-1). GDP at current U.S. dollars was obtained by converting current national series at single-year exchange rates, while GDP at constant 1995 dollars was obtained by converting constant national series at 1995 prices at a fixed (1995) exchange rate. As a result, the GDP deflator for US dollar series includes both the effects of domestic price changes and the effects of exchange rate variations.

Table 3-3. Consumer price index. Consumer price indexes (IMF, *IFS*, line 64) are generally compiled using the Laspeyres formula: goods in the consumption basket selected according to consumption patterns in the base year, derived from household expenditure surveys, are weighted by their relative prices in the base year. The data often relate only to selected representative income groups in capital cities or major urban areas. Thus, the consumer price indexes shown for some countries may not accurately

represent price movements because the underlying consumption basket may not be representative of overall national consumption patterns, and the weights assigned to prices may be outdated.

Table 3-4. Official exchange rate. The official exchange rate (IMF, *IFS*, line rf) is expressed as the annual average of the official market exchange rate in national currency per US dollar.

Table 3-5. SDR exchange rate index. This index is based on the average annual exchange rate for SDRs per unit of national currency (IMF, *IFS*, line rd-zf).

Table 3-6. Currency conversion factor. These are the annual exchange rates used by the World Bank (World Bank country desks) to convert national currency series into U.S. dollars. For most countries, in most years, the conversion factor is identical to the average annual official exchange rate. However, where the official exchange rate is judged to diverge by an exceptionally large margin from the rate effectively applied to international transactions, a more appropriate conversion factor is estimated. An alternative conversion factor is used when there are egregious differences between the official and effective transaction rates, when officially recognized multiple exchange rates have analytically significant spreads, or when exchange rates need to be adjusted to a fiscal year base. The objective in estimating alternative conversion factors is to approximate as closely as possible exchange rates actually used. For example, where multiple exchange rates are maintained, a transaction-weighted rate is calculated.

Note that national statistical compilers sometimes

use an official exchange rate to assign a national currency value to international transactions originally denominated in foreign currencies. In these cases, the official rate must be used to convert the same items back to dollars, regardless of whether it was the rate actually applied to the international transactions, even if an alternative conversion factor is used for other components of GDP.

Table 3-7. Parallel market exchange rate. Data reported here are from *Pick's Currency Yearbooks* and *Currency Alerts* (now discontinued) and *Global Currency Report*. They are averages of month-end rates for the period covered, based on a sample of transactions, usually in a capital city or a financial center of the country. They include the rates at the Bureaux de Change that have been established in some countries with auction markets as semi-official foreign exchange windows for small transactions. The current table corrects some errors contained in *ADI 1994-95*.

Table 3-8. Ratio of parallel market to official exchange rates. This ratio is obtained by dividing parallel market exchange rates (Table 3-7) by official exchange rates (Table 3-4), to measure the premium on the official exchange rate. The premium is usually

high in the presence of an overvalued exchange rate. The current table reflects the corrected series for Table 3-7.

Table 3-9. Real effective exchange rate index. This index (IMF, *IFS* Database) gives a measure of price competitiveness of the country's exports relative to its trading partners. A decline (increase) in the index indicates real depreciation (appreciation) of the exchange rate. The data have been rebased to 1990. The year 1987 coincided with the early period of massive devaluations in the process of adjustment by several Sub-Saharan African countries. As a result, the substantial devaluations that continued to take place after 1987 may not be very pronounced in the data. Relative movements in the inflation rates between a country and the trading partner(s) may diminish the real impact of a devaluation, particularly if inflationary tendencies are stronger domestically than abroad.

Figure

The following indicator has been used to derive the figure in this chapter.

Figure 3-1. Real effective exchange rate (Table 3-9).

Methodology used for regional aggregations and period averages in chapter 3

Table	Aggregations[a]			Period averages[b]	
	(4)	(7)	(8)	(1)	(2)
3-1		x		x	
3-2	x			x	
3-3		x			x
3-4			x	x	
3-5			x	x	
3-6			x	x	
3-7			x	x	
3-8			x	x	
3-9		x		x	

Note: Regional aggregations are shown in the rows for Sub-Saharan Africa, North Africa, and All Africa. Period averages are shown in the last three columns. This table shows only the methodologies used in this chapter.

a. Regional aggregations: (1) simple total; (2) simple total of the first indicator divided by the simple total of the second indicator (same country coverage); (3) simple total of the gap-filled indicator; (4) simple total of the gap-filled main indicator divided by the simple total of the gap-filled secondary indicator; (5) simple total of the first gap-filled main indicator less the simple total of the second gap-filled main indicator, all divided by the simple total of the secondary indicator; (6) weighted total (by population); (7) median; (8) no aggregation; (9) simple arithmetic mean.

b. Period averages: (1) arithmetic mean (using the same series as shown in the table, i.e., ratio if the rest of the table is shown as ratio, level if the rest of the table is shown as level, growth rate if the rest of the table is shown as growth rate); (2) least-squares growth rate (using main indicator); (3) least-squares growth rate (using main indicator in constant terms, with the rest of the table in current terms).

4

Money and Banking

Monetary variables directly affect prices and exchange rates and indirectly affect real economic performance. Money plays a vital role in any modern economy. Data in this chapter are concerned with the creation of the types of assets that transactors in the economy wish to hold from the types of liabilities that debtors are willing to incur. However, emphasis here is on the creation of the means of payment, that is, on the more liquid end of the liquidity spectrum for assets.

Money and the institutions that deal in money provide cover against credit risks, limit transactions costs, help mobilize savings, allocate credit, and facilitate investment and hence growth of the economy. Data on money and banking help to assess the pre-

vailing financial conditions of a country and to arrive at a proper evaluation of the financial policy options open to a country for achieving its macroeconomic objectives. The government usually intervenes in finance to control the supply of money and credit. The primary objective of such intervention is to maintain price stability. However, the government may also intervene to finance a budget deficit that in turn may threaten price stability. The government also ensures that financial institutions are properly supervised to ensure continued confidence in the financial system and to avoid destabilizing runs on the banking system. Time series are provided for nine indicators in this section.

4-1. Domestic Credit

	Level	Percentage annual change										Average annual percentage growth		
	1995	1980	1990	1991	1992	1993	1994	1995	1996	1997	1998	75-84	85-89	90-MR
SUB-SAHARAN AFRICA	..	19	11	10	11	5	21	12	10	13	9	10	10	..
excluding South Africa	..	19	11	10	12	6	21	12	10	14	9	14	10	..
excl. S. Africa & Nigeria	..	19	11	11	12	6	20	12	10	13	10	14	11	..
Angola	7,908,351	..	..	..	..	..	..	..	404	340	156	..	..	..
Benin	117,710	49	11	-30	-4	-26	74	21	4	-24	3	-4	1	..
Botswana	-4,747	-26	28	0	14	10	20	-3	16	146	19	..	..	..
Burkina Faso	66,293	3	1	-10	-16	-5	4	-14	30	116	9	5	6	..
Burundi	..	20	10	7	-6	4	16	..	..	20	..	6	5	..
Cameroon	791,344	28	-2	21	-34	-3	-1	-1	-4	6	9	5	-4	..
Cape Verde	21,027	39	15	27	17	19	23	19	11	21	6	15	17	..
Central African Republic	63,333	39	1	18	-18	0	31	-4	-4	-2	11	-2	2	..
Chad	71,717	-1	-22	35	12	-16	30	-9	28	0	2	1	6	..
Comoros	12,449	..	18	11	8	-20	9	0	-18	3	-2	6	-1	..
Congo, Democratic Rep. of	673,296	22	341	1,404	2,862	1,648	5,299	182	..	..	..	64	281	..
Congo, Republic of	183,036	17	-4	3	4	-32	3	10	8	14	11	1	0	..
Côte d'Ivoire	1,540,052	23	-5	0	2	-3	6	12	3	8	6	1	4	..
Djibouti	45,598	..	-2	3	8	-2	10	17	7	-3	..	4	5	..
Equatorial Guinea	20,830	..	-7	107	-10	-34	47	1	11	16	-15	0	7	..
Eritrea	..	..	..	..	..	..	..	..	..	..	..	..	..	..
Ethiopia	14,361	18	19	10	14	6	9	11	19	7	9	10	11	..
Gabon	453,735	11	-14	3	-7	1	25	15	-4	14	26	8	6	..
Gambia, The	281	23	-61	..	..	-17	-13	41	9	35	17	-18	12	..
Ghana	1,850,561	28	4	82	45	52	19	53	20	73	23	32	35	..
Guinea	282,748	..	..	..	35	9	22	29	15	-10	..	..	16	..
Guinea-Bissau	5,725	..	66	7	21	31	19	-19	42	..	..	60	17	..
Kenya	198,038	13	26	19	18	-2	50	36	19	21	9	14	20	..
Lesotho	-321	..	-12	-6	-51	-74	-294	217	81	91	7	25	-53	..
Liberia	1,692	19	..	..	14	11	6	14	..	..	..	15	..	..
Madagascar	2,506,189	50	6	12	28	16	29	-3	-2	2	..	10	12	..
Malawi	2,644	12	3	21	65	14	36	-3	16	12	-3	5	17	..
Mali	136,883	5	-17	-3	2	12	20	15	0	30	28	-2	9	..
Mauritania	32,877	13	11	10	0	7	-1	-37	-36	-38	-66	12	-21	..
Mauritius	46,369	14	16	25	19	25	23	13	6	26	21	10	18	..
Mozambique	892,400	..	25	38	-3	-38	130	29	-39	107	2	18	14	..
Namibia	5,595	..	..	10	91	29	28	31	22	-1	9	..	24	..
Niger	81,241	45	-4	-10	-4	-17	25	-17	10	23	3	-3	0	..
Nigeria	444,710	23	34	15	128	64	57	7	-23	-3	56	10	27	..
Rwanda	44,016	12	16	-15	33	23	-7	-7	-2	61	13	17	9	..
São Tomé and Principe	22,360	..	..	..	..	..	..	..	22	-110	-783	..	..	..
Senegal	538,122	16	-9	-2	-1	-2	7	2	7	1	6	2	1	..
Seychelles	1,615	12	11	10	11	25	20	15	16	23	31	15	16	..
Sierra Leone	54,413	35	204	24	-8	1	23	8	6	11	7	43	14	..
Somalia	..	31	..	..	..	..	..	..	..	..	..	49	..	..
South Africa	333,490	21	16	..	..	12	21	12	18	16	17	16	15	..
Sudan	462,385	22	39	56	153	65	48	47	114	18	24	34	49	..
Swaziland	328	0	38	-67	68	109	163	-36	-45	-15	-269	-3	10	..
Tanzania	693,880	24	72	13	23	40	11	11	-15	-1	17	29	14	..
Togo	169,769	13	14	10	-7	2	21	44	10	7	11	6	11	..
Uganda	203,530	64	..	..	..	-8	-14	-47	38	47	29	..	-1	..
Zambia	1,921,138	17	90	137	..	..	123	63	21	0	71	49	35	..
Zimbabwe	20,496	28	19	29	43	59	20	19	27	83	41	15	31	..
NORTH AFRICA	..	18	7	8	11	7	11	15	6	15	9	18	12	..
Algeria	968,930	17	13	17	32	17	4	25	10	10	9	10	14	..
Egypt, Arab Republic	157,300	42	26	8	4	7	13	17	14	16	19	18	12	..
Libya	9,845	-41	7	5	6	4	11	6	-7	-15	..	11	3	..
Morocco	166,721	18	-1	19	11	9	11	15	6	49	9	9	13	..
Tunisia	9,746	19	6	8	11	5	6	7	0	15	8	10	7	..
ALL AFRICA	..	19	11	10	11	7	20	12	10	14	9	9	11	..

Note: 1998 data are preliminary (see page 3). Levels for 1995 are expressed in millions of units of national currency. Group data are medians of individual country values in each year or period.

4-2. Credit to the private sector

	Level	Percentage annual change										Average annual percentage growth		
	1995	1980	1990	1991	1992	1993	1994	1995	1996	1997	1998	75-84	85-89	90-MR
SUB-SAHARAN AFRICA	..	15	14	12	6	10	15	17	13	15	15	16	28	9
excluding South Africa	..	16	14	13	6	11	16	17	13	15	16	16	27	10
excl. S. Africa & Nigeria	..	15	14	14	6	11	17	17	14	15	15	14	27	10
Angola	718,514	..	..	..	..	..	..	..	3,595	241	-1	..	..	..
Benin	80,447	34	-1	-16	-20	-2	11	7	27	-30	40	20	-2	-1
Botswana	1,560	10	52	43	36	12	12	-3	4	9	39	15	16	16
Burkina Faso	80,590	4	4	-23	-12	-9	-17	9	13	80	11	15	10	1
Burundi	..	14	37	20	7	35	8	..	..	7	..	20	18	18
Cameroon	371,390	29	1	0	-55	-8	0	1	4	-10	23	24	2	-11
Cape Verde	10,391	-14	20	15	20	59	1	37	17	20	12	19	11	21
Central African Republic	23,159	50	-4	-9	-37	-5	17	24	0	4	16	10	-2	-1
Chad	27,785	-2	-3	12	-1	-33	14	17	8	-3	17	8	-13	1
Comoros	9,525	..	43	7	3	-12	-3	10	-29	25	-17	..	6	-1
Congo, Democratic Rep. of	421,444	32	77	744	4,696	1,889	22,432	474	..	..	..	29	58	307
Congo, Republic of	85,683	23	6	3	-1	-46	15	13	14	9	5	21	-12	-2
Côte d'Ivoire	1,016,035	12	-3	-1	-11	-5	-5	19	2	12	4	15	1	1
Djibouti	37,901	..	-5	-3	-1	-6	2	13	3	-1	..	..	4	0
Equatorial Guinea	3,397	..	1	58	-36	-75	13	51	82	94	18	..	2	1
Eritrea	..	..	..	..	..	..	..	..	..	..	..	..	..	..
Ethiopia	5,336	-1	-5	-1	22	98	26	47	54	16	7	8	9	29
Gabon	196,080	16	1	7	-28	-3	0	25	-2	41	6	14	-7	3
Gambia, The	363	19	16	14	-24	59	7	-10	0	23	14	19	5	8
Ghana	393,289	18	14	-6	56	35	46	44	73	70	42	28	48	35
Guinea	181,518	..	..	..	34	22	11	26	4	-1	..	..	..	14
Guinea-Bissau	5,191	..	45	18	-2	63	73	5	20	..	..	..	66	26
Kenya	117,351	20	12	22	31	5	28	49	24	25	0	16	13	21
Lesotho	739	-10	22	31	16	59	39	6	-10	10	-2	22	18	18
Liberia	191	-39	..	..	53	-12	64	-20	..	..	..	-1	7	..
Madagascar	1,563,020	26	28	12	6	15	26	16	2	14	..	17	12	13
Malawi	1,264	8	35	28	34	-12	54	5	12	15	98	17	9	20
Mali	131,787	8	0	2	7	3	-9	52	31	15	27	8	1	12
Mauritania	31,417	13	13	11	2	3	3	-27	13	8	7	13	13	1
Mauritius	32,879	9	20	17	23	28	20	15	5	26	31	16	23	18
Mozambique	2,374,200	..	32	44	45	14	58	54	46	50	27	..	26	35
Namibia	4,743	..	..	17	30	30	31	34	19	16	9	..	..	22
Niger	42,004	20	-8	-9	-4	-10	10	-41	3	-18	39	19	-2	-9
Nigeria	172,628	38	16	26	79	17	77	50	24	25	25	24	15	33
Rwanda	28,538	46	-17	-17	26	17	-9	74	1	56	20	19	10	15
São Tomé and Principe	6,694	..	..	..	..	..	..	..	32	36	88	..	..	..
Senegal	357,834	16	-7	-4	6	2	-17	2	16	4	2	16	3	0
Seychelles	245	3	8	9	5	10	21	17	10	47	16	9	0	14
Sierra Leone	17,600	28	19	154	28	44	12	5	23	25	6	13	65	26
Somalia	..	-5	..	..	..	..	..	..	..	..	..	17	67	..
South Africa	327,114	26	14	..	..	11	18	16	17	14	16	16	16	15
Sudan	130,681	29	55	83	90	69	96	48	144	23	13	26	25	54
Swaziland	928	15	39	40	3	9	22	2	6	12	6	17	16	12
Tanzania	201,015	11	30	32	-12	40	20	-10	-42	43	44	12	72	7
Togo	131,241	13	3	12	0	-8	-1	28	7	10	5	14	7	6
Uganda	214,897	85	..	..	..	34	19	23	35	3	27	31	..	20
Zambia	253,971	10	61	57	..	..	98	81	47	10	3	10	43	36
Zimbabwe	15,276	18	28	70	42	44	29	28	21	49	37	..	24	32
NORTH AFRICA	..	13	12	9	14	11	25	9	10	17	16	26	7	24
Algeria	103,499	14	18	32	-77	1	25	7	33	-21	19	19	5	-8
Egypt, Arab Republic	66,777	-9	20	1	25	19	32	37	26	26	27	26	18	22
Libya	4,319	7	2	4	7	11	27	8	-10	17	..	16	3	8
Morocco	90,906	13	..	34	15	11	11	15	10	54	12	14	..	16
Tunisia	9,274	22	5	9	14	7	8	9	1	12	10	18	10	8
ALL AFRICA	..	14	14	12	7	11	18	16	13	16	16	21	21	15

Note: 1998 data are preliminary (see page 3). Data exclude credit to other financial institutions. 1995 levels are in millions of local currency. Group data are medians of individual country values for each year or period.

4-3. Credit to the government

	Level	Percentage annual change									Average annual percentage growth		
	1995	*1980*	*1990*	*1991*	*1992*	*1993*	*1994*	*1995*	*1996*	*1997*	*1998*	*75-84*	*85-89*	*90-MR*
SUB-SAHARAN AFRICA	..	23	8	7	19	10	35	3	6	5	14	27	8	20
excluding South Africa	..	23	8	7	19	11	34	3	6	8	17	29	8	21
excl. S. Africa & Nigeria	..	24	9	7	21	12	34	2	6	5	17	28	8	21
Angola	4,275,738	..	..	..	..	..	..	..	153	652	338	..	..	..
Benin	36,262	-9	-511	-178	-172	-308	-274	73	-45	8	-119	..	8	17
Botswana	-6,521	17	31	7	19	11	19	-3	12	111	24	..	..	..
Burkina Faso	-14,605	46	6	-51	4	-25	-115	-704	-63	-493	-3	..	..	58
Burundi	..	25	-25	2	-42	-55	176	..	..	80	..	38	-8	-21
Cameroon	368,878	40	73	-675	79	8	1	-4	-10	22	-5	..	..	6
Cape Verde	10,069	-54	29	84	33	27	120	5	6	25	0	70	27	30
Central African Republic	32,521	26	-21	112	15	2	39	-22	-6	-5	5	13	-11	8
Chad	36,277	1	-119	-962	399	15	45	-24	21	-9	-11	9	-2	26
Comoros	2,924	..	-24	25	23	-41	49	-23	17	-41	62	..	5	-3
Congo, Democratic Rep. of	109,484	19	396	1,399	2,945	1,629	3,724	-30	..	..	..	39	79	261
Congo, Republic of	82,754	7	-18	7	36	-6	-4	4	3	24	17	5	38	6
Côte d'Ivoire	510,099	-52	-11	6	70	2	35	1	6	1	11	50	1	13
Djibouti	7,233	..	-15	-48	-132	192	140	40	30	-16	..	..	..	47
Equatorial Guinea	16,716	..	-29	296	19	-10	52	-5	-5	-13	-44	..	-6	13
Eritrea	..	..	..	..	..	..	..	..	..	..	..	..	..	..
Ethiopia	8,286	18	26	14	15	-1	5	-4	-6	-1	11	27	11	4
Gabon	237,064	-3	-39	-9	75	7	54	9	-6	-13	61	-31	61	13
Gambia, The	-82	28	797	65	-113	-453	38	-60	-30	-43	-22	30	-92	..
Ghana	1,223,690	33	9	165	44	63	3	61	10	85	18	38	23	37
Guinea	96,782	..	..	..	37	-16	52	36	35	-24	..	..	..	18
Guinea-Bissau	-567	..	116	-2	45	18	-48	-144	-430	..	..	..	44	10
Kenya	64,657	8	57	14	0	-11	97	18	7	14	12	22	12	17
Lesotho	-1,060	329	-29	-40	-182	294	78	32	18	47	4	50	30	-43
Liberia	1,473	63	..	..	10	13	1	25	..	..	..	43	18	..
Madagascar	943,169	81	-20	11	68	16	33	-24	-7	-21	..	41	8	8
Malawi	1,070	31	-34	-22	300	31	43	-20	3	12	-120	28	-4	23
Mali	5,096	2	-77	-80	-374	-239	639	-84	-799	-41	19	7	-15	0
Mauritania	1,351	13	4	5	-6	25	-17	-85	-1,167	76	44	22	19	-19
Mauritius	13,358	18	4	49	10	20	32	11	9	26	-1	30	-6	17
Mozambique	-1,642,700	..	38	35	171	105	28	62	84	38	33	..	-54	..
Namibia	724	..	..	57	-255	29	4	17	54	-91	46	..	..	-22
Niger	39,237	-59	8	-13	-6	-39	102	50	17	62	-15	15	-6	13
Nigeria	270,389	6	54	3	201	88	53	-9	-54	-54	187	38	6	19
Rwanda	15,365	132	63	-13	41	28	-7	-50	-7	70	-1	9	43	2
São Tomé and Principe	7,829	..	..	..	..	..	..	..	137	-178	-68	..	..	..
Senegal	179,488	53	-15	2	-26	-23	174	3	-10	-6	18	40	-3	6
Seychelles	1,277	52	13	8	15	26	17	19	20	20	35	43	18	17
Sierra Leone	46,172	37	260	11	-16	-14	56	14	5	10	7	33	33	14
Somalia	..	38	..	..	..	..	..	..	..	..	..	29	12	..
South Africa	6,376	0	51	..	62	174	68	-60	81	79	50	0	-2	26
Sudan	315,067	13	40	62	174	68	34	49	105	16	30	23	41	49
Swaziland	-600	27	39	102	-3	-6	-28	50	34	19	50	..	..	..
Tanzania	492,865	25	121	1	55	40	7	23	-4	-12	6	23	17	17
Togo	38,278	14	-60	59	66	-57	-278	177	20	-3	33	13	-28	31
Uganda	-11,367	58	..	..	..	-20	-30	-105	-26	-1,469	34	37	..	-17
Zambia	1,630,301	23	99	154	..	..	147	61	17	-2	83	21	62	36
Zimbabwe	4,290	48	35	-32	117	103	17	-2	43	194	50	17	13	37
NORTH AFRICA	..	14	10	6	5	1	1	2	-4	12	8	20	20	5
Algeria	403,286	24	6	-5	43	133	-11	-14	-29	49	28	23	18	13
Egypt, Arab Republic	52,820	14	26	4	5	-7	7	2	-1	9	17	20	20	4
Libya	5,526	-93	10	6	5	1	1	5	-4	-38	..	15	25	-1
Morocco	74,178	21	-9	6	8	7	10	14	3	12	-1	18	8	7
Tunisia	473	2	13	6	-13	-14	-12	-16	-22	81	-17	18	6	-6
ALL AFRICA	..	20	9	6	15	7	30	2	3	9	17	26	8	20

Note: 1998 data are preliminary (see page 3). Data exclude credit to other financial institutions. 1995 levels are in millions of local currency. Group data are medians of individual country values for each year or period.

4-4. Net foreign assets

	Billions of units of national currency											Annual average		
	1980	1989	1990	1991	1992	1993	1994	1995	1996	1997	1998	75-84	85-89	90-MR
SUB-SAHARAN AFRICA	..	..	..	..	..	..	..	..	..	..	..	..	..	..
excluding South Africa	..	..	..	..	..	..	..	..	..	..	..	..	..	..
excl. S.Africa & Nigeria	..	..	..	..	..	..	..	..	..	..	..	..	..	..
Angola	..	..	..	..	..	..	..	-7,611	135,921	200,102	168,040		..	124,113
Benin	-23	-24	4	41	65	70	160	146	173	215	206	-17	-43	120
Botswana	0	5	6	8	9	11	11	12	19	22	28	0	3	14
Burkina Faso	0	67	66	76	90	106	164	236	220	204	183	6	58	149
Burundi	5	12	10	18	30	35	45	..	47	46	..	3	6	33
Cameroon	-14	-194	-185	-182	-182	-236	-318	-343	-302	-204	-195	13	-60	-239
Cape Verde	2	5	5	4	5	6	6	5	7	6	6	2	5	5
Central African Republic	3	20	19	14	13	21	85	92	101	90	66	1	14	56
Chad	-4	22	32	22	14	-1	14	48	55	56	43	0	12	31
Comoros	..	8	7	7	7	11	16	16	19	19	15	4	6	13
Congo, Democratic Rep. of	0	0	0	0	0	-18	-1,789	-8,806	..	..	..	0	0	-1,769
Congo, Republic of	8	-45	-8	-20	-19	-4	4	15	25	18	-44	-3	-22	-4
Côte d'Ivoire	-223	-487	-495	-474	-511	-515	-72	58	62	100	114	-211	-409	-192
Djibouti	..	36	42	45	35	37	36	34	28	26	..	21	32	35
Equatorial Guinea	..	-3	-6	-5	-6	-7	-14	-10	-7	-7	2	..	-4	-7
Eritrea	..	..	..	..	..	..	..	..	..	..	..	..	..	..
Ethiopia	..	..	..	..	1	2	5	5	4	5	6	1	..	4
Gabon	16	-66	2	18	-29	-33	52	9	86	69	-64	35	-20	12
Gambia, The	0	0	0	0	1	1	1	1	1	1	1	0	0	1
Ghana	0	-181	-152	-11	-126	-146	14	181	206	244	311	-2	-111	58
Guinea	..	..	..	81	113	162	121	109	86	155	..	..	..	118
Guinea-Bissau	..	-1	-1	-2	-4	-5	-6	-4	-3	..	..	..	-1	-3
Kenya	2	-2	-5	-8	-6	30	16	10	32	32	29	1	-2	14
Lesotho	0	0	0	0	1	1	1	2	2	3	4	0	0	2
Liberia	0	0	..	-1	-1	-1	-1	-1	..	..	..	0	0	-1
Madagascar	-110	-1,993	-2,202	-2,807	-133	-11	1	309	860	1,486	..	-150	-1,458	-312
Malawi	0	0	0	0	-1	0	-2	0	2	1	8	0	0	1
Mali	-8	14	27	65	69	74	107	120	184	205	172˙	-29	-33	114
Mauritania	-2	-12	-16	-24	-32	-30	-33	-25	-11	-2	4	-3	-11	-19
Mauritius	0	8	12	15	16	17	16	19	20	22	20	0	3	17
Mozambique	..	-731	-922	-2,002	-2,711	-5,685	-3,183	-3,556	-1,649	-886	-269	-26	-354	-2,318
Namibia	..	..	0	1	0	0	0	0	0	1	1	..	..	0
Niger	5	23	26	26	28	24	23	22	12	0	-9	5	16	17
Nigeria	6	18	41	54	36	63	56	109	149	222	209	3	8	104
Rwanda	15	6	3	12	10	5	3	28	38	46	46	9	10	21
São Tomé and Principe	..	..	..	..	..	..	..	9	19	101	139	..	..	67
Senegal	-97	-213	-188	-179	-172	-207	-130	-70	-46	36	78	-102	-233	-98
Seychelles	0	0	0	0	0	0	0	0	0	0	0	0	0	0
Sierra Leone	0	-21	-64	-145	-188	-204	-339	-396	-159	-169	-220	0	-11	-209
Somalia	0	-214	..	..	..	..	..	..	..	..	..	0	-63	..
South Africa	6	0	1	..	-11	-16	-21	-18	-31	-23	-32	2	1	-19
Sudan	0	-10	-12	-25	-367	-587	-1,217	-2,021	-4,444	-4,937	-6,868	-1	-7	-2,275
Swaziland	0	1	1	1	1	1	1	1	2	2	2	0	0	1
Tanzania	0	-105	-131	-159	-295	-384	-278	-207	-68	245	275	0	-79	-111
Togo	0	68	70	74	54	23	43	33	13	14	8	21	62	37
Uganda	0	..	..	..	-243	-193	-52	53	112	218	413	0	-3	44
Zambia	-1	-26	-51	-102	..	-496	-788	-1,022	-1,287	-1,228	-2,397	-1	-12	-921
Zimbabwe	0	0	0	-2	-3	-3	-2	-3	-3	-13	-30	0	0	-7
NORTH AFRICA	..	..	..	..	..	..	..	..	..	..	..	..	..	..
Algeria	17	7	7	24	23	20	60	26	134	350	281	12	10	103
Egypt, Arab Republic	-1	-1	-1	17	34	46	51	49	54	49	36	-1	1	37
Libya	5	1	2	1	2	1	2	2	3	2	..	2	2	2
Morocco	0	0	15	23	30	35	40	34	36	40	43	-1	-3	33
Tunisia	0	1	1	1	1	1	1	1	1	2	1	0	0	1
ALL AFRICA	..	..	..	..	..	..	..	..	..	..	..	..	..	..

Note: 1998 data are preliminary (see page 3).

4-5. Growth of money supply

	Level	Percentage annual change									Average annual percentage growth		
	1995	1980	1990	1991	1992	1993	1994	1995	1996	1997	1998	75-84	85-89	90-MR
SUB-SAHARAN AFRICA	..	19	10	14	11	12	34	15	14	15	8	14	13	19
excluding South Africa	..	20	11	15	11	12	33	15	14	16	9	15	12	18
excl. S. Africa & Nigeria	..	20	12	15	11	12	34	15	15	16	9	13	11	18
Angola	2,689,020	..	..	..	..	..	..	..	3,393	108	40	..	..	..
Benin	161,730	32	24	12	10	-13	67	-13	17	2	-4	17	-3	9
Botswana	829	10	16	5	-1	15	11	7	15	9	46	16	25	10
Burkina Faso	213,703	20	-2	6	1	12	39	25	7	17	-2	13	10	13
Burundi	..	11	9	11	10	12	28	..	..	10	..	16	7	12
Cameroon	319,242	13	-7	3	-28	-14	35	-12	-2	35	14	18	0	0
Cape Verde	11,867	26	8	9	31	7	8	3	11	22	-2	18	8	10
Central African Republic	111,237	32	-4	-3	-4	16	74	8	5	-8	-18	15	2	9
Chad	85,330	-16	0	4	-9	-28	32	43	33	-5	-9	12	-1	7
Comoros	12,040	..	6	-7	9	5	10	-5	8	-19	-6	..	9	1
Congo, Democratic Rep. of	1,889,470	73	176	2,387	4,114	2,461	5,635	407	..	..	..	47	57	308
Congo, Republic of	134,845	37	25	-7	6	-20	40	0	14	9	-14	16	-2	5
Côte d'Ivoire	944,519	1	3	-3	-4	1	62	18	2	12	14	11	-2	11
Djibouti	36,998	..	9	16	11	4	3	-2	-3	-10	..	..	6	4
Equatorial Guinea	9,504	..	-57	-16	35	-29	135	58	50	-4	10	..	-8	18
Eritrea	..	..	..	..	..	..	..	..	..	..	..	..	..	..
Ethiopia	9,280	0	22	18	15	4	21	3	0	9	-8	11	12	9
Gabon	219,087	10	6	8	-27	-3	42	12	26	8	-5	11	-1	7
Gambia, The	471	6	14	33	11	6	-12	16	-4	39	0	11	17	8
Ghana	925,287	30	11	14	53	28	50	33	31	45	17	35	39	29
Guinea	274,125	..	..	..	20	19	-3	9	0	21	..	..	..	8
Guinea-Bissau	7,219	..	61	34	83	27	58	47	51	..	..	..	52	41
Kenya	69,337	-8	27	15	47	27	13	4	14	15	3	12	11	17
Lesotho	521	..	8	18	12	23	12	7	22	20	27	..	17	15
Liberia	..	..	..	..	..	..	..	..	..	..	..	..	..	..
Madagascar	1,848,010	22	-4	31	22	12	57	15	17	23	..	14	19	21
Malawi	2,211	7	6	31	19	35	51	44	24	17	56	7	24	28
Mali	198,195	5	-11	9	1	9	48	14	21	7	4	12	0	13
Mauritania	18,202	12	3	10	4	4	-5	-8	-11	8	5	13	10	0
Mauritius	9,573	21	24	20	8	3	19	8	3	8	9	8	18	10
Mozambique	4,908,400	..	36	69	53	61	57	52	16	19	14	..	31	36
Namibia	1,822	..	..	34	22	46	15	8	54	4	27	..	..	22
Niger	100,238	13	-12	3	-10	11	15	9	-10	-19	-19	16	1	-1
Nigeria	204,415	50	30	41	59	55	46	16	14	18	17	19	16	29
Rwanda	40,658	7	5	8	25	11	16	41	12	23	-1	11	5	16
São Tomé and Principe	14,225	..	..	..	..	..	..	..	66	108	-3	..	..	..
Senegal	316,756	14	-12	4	2	-9	54	4	8	0	16	11	3	8
Seychelles	335	38	-1	23	10	14	-3	3	34	44	20	13	9	13
Sierra Leone	49,902	20	64	76	25	12	10	29	7	57	7	21	56	23
Somalia	..	19	..	..	..	..	..	..	..	..	..	22	62	..
South Africa	111,844	36	16	37	3	7	25	18	32	17	23	18	15	17
Sudan	404,636	31	46	60	101	76	55	67	86	32	29	26	37	50
Swaziland	363	22	14	10	20	14	7	17	16	16	2	13	19	13
Tanzania	428,284	28	35	23	34	33	33	30	5	10	10	19	29	22
Togo	131,199	5	19	4	-27	-18	105	38	-8	2	7	15	-7	9
Uganda	419,151	31	50	50	68	26	35	15	10	16	21	34	84	26
Zambia	227,058	0	61	78	..	..	45	61	19	31	17	11	45	29
Zimbabwe	11,270	37	28	23	6	95	18	52	23	54	24	12	16	30
NORTH AFRICA	..	21	17	8	9	5	11	7	7	13	8	22	12	10
Algeria	520,286	17	8	20	16	19	8	7	13	15	..	19	7	13
Egypt, Arab Republic	41,540	56	17	8	9	12	11	9	7	9	20	22	12	10
Libya	6,251	29	26	-4	16	4	13	6	1	11	..	15	3	8
Morocco	135,964	8	37	14	6	5	11	6	6	16	8	12	12	9
Tunisia	3,637	21	6	1	7	4	11	10	13	13	7	16	6	8
ALL AFRICA	..	20	14	13	10	12	25	11	13	15	9	15	11	18

Note: 1998 data are preliminary (see page 3). 1995 levels are in millions of local currency. Group data are medians of individual country values in each year or period.

4-6. Discount rate

	Percentage											Annual average		
	1980	*1989*	*1990*	*1991*	*1992*	*1993*	*1994*	*1995*	*1996*	*1997*	*1998*	*75-84*	*85-89*	*90-MR*
SUB-SAHARAN AFRICA	8.5	11.0	11.0	11.3	12.5	11.8	12.5	13.3	13.5	11.6	11.4	8.4	9.8	12.1
excluding South Africa	8.5	11.0	11.0	11.2	12.5	11.5	12.0	13.2	13.3	10.8	10.2	8.2	9.7	11.7
excl. S. Africa & Nigeria	8.5	11.0	11.0	11.0	12.5	11.5	12.0	13.0	13.0	10.6	9.1	8.4	9.7	11.5
Angola	..	..	..	..	..	..	..	160.0	2.0	48.0	58.0	..	..	67.0
Benin	10.5	11.0	11.0	11.0	12.5	10.5	10.0	7.5	6.5	6.0	6.3	9.5	9.6	9.0
Botswana	5.8	6.5	8.5	12.0	14.3	14.3	13.5	13.0	13.0	12.5	12.5	8.3	7.9	12.6
Burkina Faso	10.5	11.0	11.0	11.0	12.5	10.5	10.0	7.5	6.5	6.0	6.3	9.5	9.6	9.0
Burundi	7.0	7.0	8.0	10.7	9.8	9.8	9.4	9.9	..	..	..	6.4	6.6	9.6
Cameroon	8.5	10.0	11.0	10.8	12.0	.11.5	7.8	8.6	7.8	7.5	7.0	7.6	8.9	9.3
Cape Verde	..	..	..	..	..	..	..	..	..	..	..	..	..	...
Central African Republic	8.5	10.0	11.0	10.8	12.0	11.5	7.8	8.6	7.8	7.5	7.5	7.6	8.9	9.4
Chad	8.5	10.0	11.0	10.8	12.0	11.5	7.8	8.6	7.8	7.5	7.0	7.7	8.9	9.3
Comoros	..	..	..	..	..	..	..	..	..	..	..	10.0	9.3	..
Congo, Democratic Rep. of	12.0	50.0	45.0	55.0	55.0	95.0	145.0	125,0	238.0	..	..	14.7	33.6	108.3
Congo, Republic of	8.5	10.0	11.0	10.8	12.0	11.5	7.8	8.6	7.8	7.5	7.0	7.6	8.9	9.3
Côte d'Ivoire	10.5	11.0	11.0	11.0	12.5	10.5	10.0	7.5	6.5	6.0	6.3	9.5	9.6	9.0
Djibouti	..	..	..	..	..	..	..	..	..	..	..	..	..	..
Equatorial Guinea	..	10.0	11.0	10.8	12.0	11.5	7.8	8.6	7.8	7.5	7.0	..	8.9	9.3
Eritrea	..	..	..	..	..	..	..	..	..	..	..	..	..	..
Ethiopia	..	3.0	3.0	3.0	5.3	12.0	12.0	12.0	..	..	..	..	4.2	7.9
Gabon	8.5	10.0	11.0	10.8	12.0	11.5	7.8	8.6	7.8	7.5	7.0	7.6	8.9	9.3
Gambia, The	8.0	15.0	16.5	15.5	17.5	13.5	13.5	14.0	14.0	14.0	13.0	7.6	18.0	14.6
Ghana	13.5	26.0	33.0	20.0	30.0	35.0	33.0	45.0	45.0	45.0	37.0	12.7	22.9	35.9
Guinea	..	13.0	15.0	19.0	19.0	17.0	17.0	18.0	18.0	15.0	..	..	10.5	17.3
Guinea-Bissau	..	..	42.0	42.0	45.5	41.0	26.0	39.0	54.0	6.0	..	..	..	36.9
Kenya	8.0	16.5	19.4	20.3	20.5	45.5	21.5	24.5	26.9	32.3	17.1	9.9	14.0	25.3
Lesotho	8.0	17.0	15.8	18.0	15.0	13.5	13.5	15.5	17.0	15.6	19.5	11.8	12.6	15.9
Liberia	..	..	..	..	..	..	..	..	..	..	..	..	..	..
Madagascar	5.5	..	..	..	..	..	..	..	..	..	..	8.0	11.5	..
Malawi	10.0	11.0	14.0	13.0	20.0	25.0	40.0	50.0	27.0	23.0	43.0	8.5	11.6	28.3
Mali	10.5	11.0	11.0	11.0	12.5	10.5	10.0	7.5	6.5	6.0	6.3	9.5	9.6	9.0
Mauritania	6.0	7.0	7.0	7.0	7.0	..	..	..	..	..	..	5.5	6.6	7.0
Mauritius	10.5	12.0	12.0	11.3	8.3	8.3	13.8	11.4	11.8	10.5	17.2	9.5	10.8	11.6
Mozambique	..	..	..	..	..	..	..	..	..	..	..	..	..	..
Namibia	..	..	..	20.5	16.5	14.5	15.5	17.5	17.8	16.0	18.8	..	..	17.1
Niger	10.5	11.0	11.0	11.0	12.5	10.5	10.0	7.5	6.5	6.0	6.3	9.5	9.4	9.0
Nigeria	6.0	18.5	18.5	15.5	17.5	26.0	13.5	13.5	13.5	13.5	13.5	5.9	12.8	16.1
Rwanda	9.0	9.0	14.0	14.0	11.0	11.0	11.0	16.0	16.0	10.8	11.4	7.4	9.0	12.8
São Tomé and Principe	..	25.0	25.0	45.0	45.0	30.0	32.0	50.0	35.0	55.0	38.5	..	25.0	39.5
Senegal	10.5	11.0	11.0	11.0	12.5	10.5	10.0	7.5	6.5	6.0	6.3	9.5	9.6	9.0
Seychelles	..	6.0	1.0	1.0	1.0	1.0	1.0	1.0	1.0	1.0	1.0	6.0	6.0	1.0
Sierra Leone	12.0	16.0	55.0	..	..	..	..	..	..	..	..	10.2	15.6	55.0
Somalia	4.0	45.0	..	..	..	..	..	..	..	..	..	5.2	25.2	..
South Africa	6.5	18.0	18.0	17.0	14.0	12.0	13.0	15.0	17.0	16.0	19.3	11.1	12.9	15.7
Sudan	..	..	..	..	..	..	..	..	..	..	..	..	..	..
Swaziland	7.0	12.0	12.0	13.0	12.0	11.0	12.0	15.0	16.8	15.8	18.0	11.1	10.8	13.9
Tanzania	4.8	15.5	..	..	14.5	14.5	67.5	47.9	19.0	16.2	17.6	4.5	11.1	28.2
Togo	10.5	11.0	11.0	11.0	12.5	10.5	10.0	7.5	6.5	6.0	6.3	9.5	9.6	9.0
Uganda	8.0	55.0	50.0	46.0	41.0	24.0	15.0	13.3	15.9	14.1	9.1	13.7	38.2	25.4
Zambia	6.5	..	..	..	47.0	72.5	20.5	40.2	47.0	17.7	..	7.5	21.3	40.8
Zimbabwe	4.5	9.0	10.3	20.0	29.5	28.5	29.5	29.5	27.0	31.5	39.5	6.3	9.0	27.3
NORTH AFRICA	5.9	11.4	11.9	11.9	11.4	8.9	8.9	11.2	10.4	12.3	12.0	6.0	9.4	11.0
Algeria	..	..	..	..	..	..	..	..	..	..	..	..	..	..
Egypt, Arab Republic	11.0	14.0	14.0	20.0	18.4	16.5	14.0	13.5	13.0	12.3	12.0	9.7	13.2	14.9
Libya	5.0	5.0	5.0	5.0	5.0	5.0	..	..	..	..	..	5.0	5.0	5.0
Morocco	6.0	..	..	..	..	..	7.0	..	..	..	..	5.6	8.5	7.0
Tunisia	5.8	11.4	11.9	11.9	11.4	8.9	8.9	8.9	7.9	..	..	6.1	9.7	10.0
ALL AFRICA	8.5	11.0	11.0	11.6	12.5	11.5	12.0	13.3	13.0	12.3	11.7	8.1	9.8	12.1

Note: 1998 data are preliminary (see page 3). Group data are medians of individual country values in each year or period.

4-7. Real discount rate

	Percentage											Annual average		
	1980	1989	1990	1991	1992	1993	1994	1995	1996	1997	1998	75-84	85-89	90-MR
SUB-SAHARAN AFRICA	-4.1	2.3	3.1	1.6	1.7	2.6	-0.8	-0.1	2.4	4.8	4.2	-3.5	1.2	2.2
excluding South Africa	-3.6	2.0	3.1	1.6	2.1	3.1	-1.2	-0.2	2.1	4.5	4.2	-3.9	1.3	2.1
excl. S. Africa & Nigeria	-3.9	2.3	3.1	1.6	2.8	3.6	-0.8	-0.1	2.4	4.2	4.2	-3.4	1.3	2.3
Angola	..	..	..	..	..	..	..	-93.1	-94.2	-9.8	-23.8	..	..	-55.2
Benin	..	..	..	..	..	..	..	..	..	..	..	..	..	..
Botswana	-6.9	-4.6	-2.6	0.2	-1.6	2.6	2.6	2.3	2.6	2.7	3.3	-3.1	-1.5	1.3
Burkina Faso	..	11.4	11.9	8.3	14.8	9.8	-11.8	-0.3	0.4	3.6	3.7	3.9	10.6	4.5
Burundi	-2.3	-4.2	0.9	1.6	7.9	0.1	-4.7	-7.9	..	..	..	-5.6	0.9	-0.4
Cameroon	-1.0	11.9	9.8	10.6	12.1	15.8	-4.4	-13.7	1.1	2.2	4.1	-3.8	3.1	4.2
Cape Verde	..	..	..	..	..	..	..	..	..	..	..	..	..	..
Central African Republic	..	9.3	11.2	14.0	12.9	14.8	-13.5	-8.9	3.2	5.8	9.6	-1.3	8.7	5.5
Chad	..	..	..	..	..	..	..	..	..	..	..	..	..	..
Comoros	..	..	..	..	..	..	..	..	..	..	..	2.4	6.2	..
Congo, Democratic Rep. of	..	..	..	..	..	..	..	..	..	..	..	..	..	..
Congo, Republic of	1.2	5.7	16.5	1.5	16.5	6.3	-24.5	0.0	-2.2	..	..	-3.4	5.1	2.0
Côte d'Ivoire	-6.3	9.9	11.7	9.3	8.0	7.7	-16.8	-0.2	2.9	2.9	3.2	-2.3	4.8	3.2
Djibouti	..	..	..	..	..	..	..	..	..	..	..	..	..	..
Equatorial Guinea	..	..	..	..	..	..	..	..	..	..	..	..	..	..
Eritrea	..	..	..	..	..	..	..	..	..	..	..	..	..	..
Ethiopia	..	-6.0	-2.1	-14.8	-13.0	1.8	10.7	-1.2	..	..	..	..	0.5	-3.1
Gabon	-3.3	3.1	3.0	5.1	17.8	22.4	-26.6	5.0	1.5	5.4	0.0	-4.9	7.0	3.7
Gambia, The	1.1	6.2	3.8	6.4	11.0	9.1	9.1	8.8	11.7	10.9	11.8	-4.2	-3.1	9.2
Ghana	-24.4	0.6	-3.1	1.6	18.2	8.0	6.5	-16.8	-1.1	13.4	14.8	-30.2	-2.2	4.6
Guinea	..	-11.9	-3.6	-0.6	2.1	9.2	12.3	11.8	14.6	11.4	..	..	-15.1	7.1
Guinea-Bissau	..	..	6.8	-9.9	-14.1	-5.0	9.4	-4.4	-1.7	-28.9	..	..	..	-6.0
Kenya	..	2.6	3.2	0.6	-5.4	-0.3	-5.7	22.7	16.4	18.9	5.8	..	3.3	6.2
Lesotho	-6.6	2.0	3.7	0.3	-1.9	0.3	4.9	5.7	7.0	6.4	9.9	-1.6	-1.0	4.0
Liberia	..	..	..	..	..	..	..	..	..	..	..	..	..	..
Madagascar	..	..	..	..	..	..	..	..	..	..	..	..	-6.3	..
Malawi	..	-1.3	2.0	0.3	-2.2	4.5	4.0	-18.2	-7.7	12.7	17.1	-3.2	-5.9	1.4
Mali	..	11.1	10.3	9.0	20.0	11.2	-11.8	-4.3	0.0	6.7	2.1	..	8.4	4.8
Mauritania	..	-5.3	0.4	1.3	-2.8	..	..	..	..	..	..	..	-0.6	-0.4
Mauritius	-22.3	-0.6	-1.3	4.0	3.5	-2.0	6.0	5.1	5.0	3.4	11.7	-3.4	4.6	3.9
Mozambique	..	..	..	..	..	..	..	..	..	..	..	..	..	..
Namibia	..	..	..	7.7	-1.0	5.5	4.3	6.8	9.0	6.6	10.3	..	..	6.1
Niger	..	..	..	..	..	..	..	..	..	..	..	..	..	..
Nigeria	-3.6	-21.2	10.4	2.2	-18.7	-21.4	-27.7	-34.4	-12.2	4.8	2.9	-11.7	-8.1	-10.5
Rwanda	1.6	7.9	9.4	-4.7	1.3	2.2	-32.3	-4.9	6.5	-1.1	4.3	-3.6	7.2	-2.1
São Tomé and Principe	..	-14.4	-12.1	-1.0	13.9	3.6	4.3	-0.6	-7.2	-8.5	-2.7	..	-14.4	-1.1
Senegal	1.6	10.5	10.6	13.0	12.5	11.6	-16.7	-0.9	3.7	4.2	4.2	-1.2	7.1	4.7
Seychelles	..	4.4	-2.8	-1.0	-2.2	-0.3	-0.8	1.3	2.1	0.4	3.7	1.2	4.5	0.0
Sierra Leone	..	-20.3	-18.8	..	..	..	..	..	..	..	..	..	-37.0	-18.8
Somalia	..	..	..	..	..	..	..	..	..	..	..	..	..	..
South Africa	-6.4	2.9	3.1	1.5	0.1	2.1	3.7	5.9	8.9	6.8	11.6	-1.4	-2.4	4.9
Sudan	..	..	..	..	..	..	..	..	..	..	..	..	..	..
Swaziland	-9.6	3.4	0.9	2.0	3.5	-0.2	-1.6	2.4	9.7	8.0	8.8	-2.4	-2.4	3.7
Tanzania	-19.5	-8.2	..	..	-6.0	-8.6	28.6	10.4	-5.3	-0.8	6.5	-13.2	-14.8	3.5
Togo	-1.6	10.5	9.8	10.7	10.7	10.6	-18.7	-7.2	1.8	-1.0	5.2	-0.8	9.1	2.4
Uganda	..	-32.8	3.1	17.2	-0.7	-3.4	8.0	6.8	7.8	5.8	3.1	..	-44.4	5.3
Zambia	-4.6	..	..	..	-45.4	-40.1	-21.6	4.5	0.5	-5.7	..	-6.7	-17.2	-18.0
Zimbabwe	..	-3.4	-6.1	-2.7	-8.9	0.7	6.0	5.6	4.6	10.5	2.8	-7.4	-1.8	1.4
NORTH AFRICA	-2.1	-1.3	23.9	0.7	2.2	5.1	4.7	3.6	4.4	4.0	4.2	-2.3	-1.3	5.9
Algeria	..	..	..	..	..	..	..	..	..	..	..	..	..	..
Egypt, Arab Republic	..	-6.0	42.7	-2.0	-0.8	5.5	5.4	4.8	4.7	4.0	4.2	..	-4.7	7.6
Libya	..	..	..	..	..	..	..	..	..	..	..	..	..	..
Morocco	..	..	..	..	..	..	..	..	..	..	..	..	..	..
Tunisia	-2.1	3.4	5.0	3.4	5.3	4.7	4.1	2.5	4.0	..	..	-2.3	2.2	4.1
ALL AFRICA	-3.6	2.3	3.2	1.6	1.7	3.6	2.6	0.6	2.8	4.5	4.2	-3.4	1.2	2.7

Note: 1998 data are preliminary (see page 3). Real discount rate in each year is the nominal discount rate deflated by the annual change in the CPI.

4-8. Commercial bank lending rate

					Percentage								*Annual average*	
	1980	1989	1990	1991	1992	1993	1994	1995	1996	1997	1998	75-84	85-89	90-MR
SUB-SAHARAN AFRICA	12.0	15.1	18.5	18.1	17.8	17.5	17.5	19.3	22.0	22.0	22.0	12.1	14.0	19.4
excluding South Africa	12.0	15.1	18.5	18.1	17.8	17.5	17.5	20.2	22.0	22.0	22.0	12.0	14.0	19.5
excl. S. Africa & Nigeria	12.3	15.1	18.3	18.1	17.8	17.5	17.5	19.3	22.0	22.0	22.0	12.2	14.0	19.4
Angola	..	..	..	..	..	..	..	206.3	217.9	37.8	45.0	..	..	126.7
Benin	14.5	15.1	16.0	16.0	16.8	..	..	..	..	..	..	13.8	14.0	16.3
Botswana	8.5	7.7	7.9	11.8	14.0	14.9	13.9	14.3	14.5	14.1	13.5	13.5	9.6	13.2
Burkina Faso	14.5	15.1	16.0	16.0	16.8	..	..	..	..	..	..	13.8	14.0	16.3
Burundi	12.0	12.0	12.3	12.8	13.7	13.8	14.2	15.3	..	..	..	12.0	12.0	13.7
Cameroon	13.0	15.0	18.5	18.1	17.8	17.5	17.5	16.0	22.0	22.0	22.0	13.0	13.9	19.0
Cape Verde	6.5	10.0	10.0	10.0	10.0	10.0	10.7	12.0	12.0	12.1	12.5	6.5	10.0	11.0
Central African Republic	10.5	13.0	18.5	18.1	17.8	17.5	17.5	16.0	22.0	22.0	22.0	11.1	12.2	19.0
Chad	11.0	11.5	18.5	18.1	17.8	17.5	17.5	16.0	22.0	22.0	22.0	10.7	11.1	19.0
Comoros	..	..	..	..	..	..	..	..	..	..	..	15.0	14.0	..
Congo, Democratic Rep. of	..	..	..	..	..	..	..	..	..	..	..	..	..	..
Congo, Republic of	11.0	12.5	18.5	18.1	17.8	17.5	17.5	16.0	22.0	22.0	22.0	11.3	11.8	19.0
Côte d'Ivoire	14.5	15.1	16.0	16.0	16.8	..	..	..	..	..	..	13.8	14.0	16.3
Djibouti	..	..	..	..	..	..	..	..	..	..	..	..	..	..
Equatorial Guinea	..	15.5	18.5	18.1	17.8	17.5	17.5	16.0	22.0	22.0	22.0	..	14.8	19.0
Eritrea	..	..	..	..	..	..	..	..	..	..	..	..	..	..
Ethiopia	..	6.0	6.0	6.0	8.0	14.0	14.3	15.1	13.9	10.5	10.5	..	6.8	10.9
Gabon	12.5	12.5	18.5	18.1	17.8	17.5	17.5	16.0	22.0	22.0	22.0	11.8	11.9	19.0
Gambia, The	15.0	26.8	26.5	26.5	26.8	26.1	25.0	25.0	25.5	25.5	25.4	16.7	25.4	25.8
Ghana	19.0	..	..	..	..	..	..	..	..	..	..	19.3	23.1	..
Guinea	..	17.3	21.2	24.5	27.0	24.5	22.0	21.5	..	..	..	..	15.8	23.4
Guinea-Bissau	..	38.3	45.8	47.0	50.3	63.6	36.3	32.9	51.8	..	..	..	26.1	46.8
Kenya	10.6	17.3	18.8	19.0	21.1	30.0	36.2	28.8	33.8	30.2	29.5	11.8	14.9	27.5
Lesotho	11.0	18.8	20.4	20.0	18.3	15.8	14.3	16.4	17.7	18.0	20.1	15.2	15.3	17.9
Liberia	18.4	13.8	..	..	..	..	14.5	..	..	16.8	..	19.9	14.9	15.7
Madagascar	..	22.3	25.8	24.5	25.0	26.0	30.5	37.5	32.8	30.0	..	..	22.3	29.0
Malawi	16.7	23.0	21.0	20.0	22.0	29.5	31.0	47.3	45.3	28.3	37.7	17.7	20.4	31.3
Mali	14.5	15.1	16.0	16.0	16.8	..	..	..	..	..	..	13.8	14.0	16.3
Mauritania	12.0	10.0	10.0	10.0	10.0	..	..	..	..	..	..	12.0	11.6	10.0
Mauritius	..	16.1	18.0	17.8	17.1	16.6	18.9	20.8	20.8	18.9	19.9	13.5	14.7	18.8
Mozambique	..	..	..	..	..	..	..	..	..	..	..	..	..	..
Namibia	..	..	..	23.4	20.2	18.0	17.1	18.5	19.2	20.2	20.7	..	..	19.7
Niger	14.5	15.1	16.0	16.0	16.8	..	..	..	..	..	..	13.8	14.0	16.3
Nigeria	8.4	20.4	25.3	20.0	24.8	31.7	20.5	20.2	20.3	20.4	..	8.0	14.1	22.9
Rwanda	13.5	12.0	13.2	19.0	16.7	15.0	..	..	..	..	..	13.3	13.0	16.0
São Tomé and Principe	..	20.0	20.0	37.0	37.0	37.0	30.0	52.0	38.0	51.5	55.6	..	20.0	39.8
Senegal	14.5	15.1	16.0	16.0	16.8	..	..	..	..	..	..	13.8	14.0	16.3
Seychelles	..	15.5	15.6	15.6	15.6	15.7	15.7	15.8	16.2	14.9	14.4	..	15.5	15.5
Sierra Leone	11.0	29.7	52.5	56.3	62.8	50.5	27.3	28.8	32.1	23.9	23.8	12.7	24.1	39.8
Somalia	7.5	..	..	..	..	..	..	..	..	..	..	8.9	23.8	..
South Africa	9.5	19.8	21.0	20.3	18.9	16.2	15.6	17.9	19.5	20.0	21.8	14.1	16.7	19.0
Sudan	..	..	..	..	..	..	..	..	..	..	..	..	..	..
Swaziland	9.5	14.5	14.5	16.3	15.0	14.0	15.0	18.0	19.8	18.8	21.0	13.2	14.2	16.9
Tanzania	11.5	31.0	..	..	..	31.0	39.0	42.8	37.2	29.2	26.7	11.4	23.8	34.3
Togo	14.5	16.0	16.0	16.0	17.5	..	..	..	..	..	..	13.8	14.4	16.5
Uganda	10.8	40.0	38.7	34.4	..	..	..	20.2	20.3	21.4	20.9	15.2	33.4	26.0
Zambia	9.5	18.4	35.1	..	54.6	113.3	70.6	45.5	53.8	46.7	31.8	9.7	20.8	56.4
Zimbabwe	17.5	13.0	11.7	15.5	19.8	36.3	34.9	34.7	34.2	32.5	42.1	20.3	13.8	29.1
NORTH AFRICA	7.1	8.0	9.0	8.0	13.7	12.6	13.3	16.5	15.6	13.8	13.0	7.5	9.0	12.8
Algeria	..	..	..	..	..	..	..	..	..	..	..	..	..	..
Egypt, Arab Republic	13.3	18.3	19.0	..	20.3	18.3	16.5	16.5	15.6	13.8	13.0	12.5	16.3	16.6
Libya	7.0	7.0	7.0	7.0	7.0	7.0	..	..	..	..	..	7.0	7.0	7.0
Morocco	7.0	9.0	9.0	9.0	..	..	10.0	..	..	..	..	7.0	8.7	9.3
Tunisia	7.3	4.8	..	..	..	..	..	..	..	..	..	7.9	8.9	..
ALL AFRICA	11.8	15.1	18.5	18.1	17.8	17.5	17.5	18.5	22.0	22.0	22.0	11.6	14.0	19.3

Note: 1998 data are preliminary (see page 3). Group data are medians of individual country values in each year or period.

4-9. Commercial bank deposit rate

	Percentage											Annual average		
	1980	1989	1990	1991	1992	1993	1994	1995	1996	1997	1998	75-84	85-89	90-MR
SUB-SAHARAN AFRICA	6.2	8.8	7.5	9.6	9.0	10.6	10.7	12.4	12.5	9.5	7.6	6.6	7.9	9.9
excluding South Africa	6.2	8.8	7.5	9.2	8.4	9.6	10.4	12.2	12.5	9.4	7.5	6.6	7.8	9.6
excl. S. Africa & Nigeria	6.2	8.4	7.5	8.8	7.8	9.6	10.2	11.8	12.4	9.5	7.5	6.6	7.6	9.4
Angola	..	..	..	..	..	..	..	125.9	147.1	29.3	36.9	..	..	84.8
Benin	6.2	6.4	7.0	7.0	7.8	..	..	..	..	..	3.5	6.5	6.1	6.3
Botswana	5.0	5.6	6.1	11.4	12.5	13.5	10.4	10.0	10.4	9.3	8.7	9.3	7.2	10.3
Burkina Faso	6.2	6.4	7.0	7.0	7.8	..	..	..	..	..	3.5	6.5	6.1	6.3
Burundi	2.5	..	..	..	..	..	..	..	..	..	..	3.4	4.9	..
Cameroon	7.5	7.5	7.5	7.5	7.5	7.8	8.1	5.5	5.4	5.0	5.0	7.3	7.3	6.6
Cape Verde	..	4.0	4.0	4.0	4.0	4.0	4.0	5.0	5.0	5.0	5.3	..	4.0	4.5
Central African Republic	5.5	7.5	7.5	7.5	7.5	7.8	8.1	5.5	5.5	5.0	5.0	6.4	7.4	6.6
Chad	5.5	4.3	7.5	7.5	7.5	7.8	8.1	5.5	5.5	5.0	5.0	5.3	5.0	6.6
Comoros	..	..	..	..	..	..	..	..	..	..	..	7.5	7.0	..
Congo, Democratic Rep. of	..	..	..	..	..	..	..	..	..	..	..	..	..	..
Congo, Republic of	6.5	8.0	7.5	7.5	7.5	7.8	8.1	5.5	5.5	5.0	5.0	6.5	8.0	6.6
Côte d'Ivoire	6.2	6.4	7.0	7.0	7.8	..	..	..	..	..	3.5	6.5	6.1	6.3
Djibouti	..	..	..	..	3.0	2.6	..	..	..	..	..	..	..	2.8
Equatorial Guinea	..	6.5	7.5	7.5	7.5	7.8	8.1	5.5	5.5	5.0	5.0	..	7.3	6.6
Eritrea	..	..	..	..	..	..	..	..	..	..	..	..	..	..
Ethiopia	..	6.7	2.4	5.0	3.6	11.5	11.5	11.5	9.4	7.0	6.0	..	6.5	7.5
Gabon	7.5	8.8	7.5	7.5	7.5	7.8	8.1	5.5	5.5	5.0	5.0	7.4	8.1	6.6
Gambia, The	5.0	12.9	11.3	12.7	13.8	13.0	12.6	12.5	12.5	12.5	12.5	7.1	13.9	12.6
Ghana	11.5	..	..	21.3	16.3	23.6	23.1	28.7	34.5	35.8	32.0	12.0	16.7	26.9
Guinea	..	19.5	21.0	22.0	23.0	19.8	18.0	17.5	..	..	..	..	17.1	20.2
Guinea-Bissau	..	28.0	32.7	36.0	39.3	53.9	28.7	26.5	47.3	4.6	..	..	25.5	33.6
Kenya	5.8	12.0	13.7	..	..	..	..	13.6	17.6	16.7	18.4	7.7	11.0	16.0
Lesotho	..	12.8	13.0	13.0	10.6	8.1	8.4	13.3	12.7	11.8	10.7	10.2	10.0	11.3
Liberia	10.3	6.8	..	..	..	..	6.3	..	..	6.5	. .	10.4	6.9	6.4
Madagascar	..	17.8	20.5	20.5	20.5	19.5	19.5	18.5	19.0	14.4	..	..	17.8	19.0
Malawi	7.9	12.8	12.1	12.5	16.5	21.8	25.0	37.3	26.3	10.2	19.1	9.8	13.2	20.1
Mali	6.2	6.4	7.0	7.0	7.8	..	..	..	..	..	3.5	6.5	6.1	6.3
Mauritania	..	5.0	5.0	5.0	5.0	..	..	..	..	..	..	5.5	6.2	5.0
Mauritius	..	11.1	12.6	12.3	10.1	8.4	11.0	12.2	10.8	· 9.1	9.3	10.7	9.9	10.6
Mozambique	..	..	..	..	..	..	..	..	..	..	..	..	..	..
Namibia	..	..	..	12.8	11.4	9.6	9.2	10.8	12.6	12.7	12.9	..	..	11.5
Niger	6.2	6.4	7.0	7.0	7.8	..	..	..	..	..	3.5	6.5	6.1	6.3
Nigeria	5.3	14.7	19.8	14.9	18.0	23.2	13.1	13.5	13.0	7.3	..	5.1	11.8	15.4
Rwanda	6.3	6.3	6.9	8.8	7.7	5.0	..	..	10.9	9.5	8.5	5.1	6.3	8.2
São Tomé and Principe	..	16.0	16.0	35.0	35.0	35.0	35.0	35.0	31.0	36.8	38.3	..	16.0	33.0
Senegal	6.2	6.4	7.0	7.0	7.8	..	..	..	..	..	3.5	6.5	6.1	6.3
Seychelles	..	9.6	9.5	9.6	9.6	9.5	8.9	9.2	9.9	9.2	7.5	9.1	9.8	9.2
Sierra Leone	9.2	20.0	40.5	47.8	54.7	27.0	11.6	7.0	14.0	9.9	7.1	9.2	14.9	24.4
Somalia	4.5	25.0	..	..	..	..	..	..	..	..	..	5.5	18.2	..
South Africa	5.5	18.1	18.9	17.3	13.8	11.5	11.1	13.5	14.9	15.4	16.5	10.0	13.7	14.8
Sudan	6.0	..	..	..	..	..	..	..	..	..	..	9.2	..	..
Swaziland	4.5	8.9	8.9	10.9	9.0	7.4	8.0	10.3	12.3	11.3	13.4	9.0	7.8	10.1
Tanzania	4.0	17.0	..	..	..	..	. .	24.6	13.6	7.8	7.8	4.0	12.6	13.5
Togo	6.2	6.4	7.0	7.0	7.8	..	..	..	..	..	3.5	6.5	6.1	6.3
Uganda	6.8	32.2	31.3	31.2	35.8	16.3	10.0	7.6	10.6	11.8	11.4	9.9	23.4	18.4
Zambia	7.0	11.4	25.7	..	48.5	..	46.1	30.2	42.1	34.5	13.1	6.2	13.8	34.3
Zimbabwe	3.5	8.9	8.8	14.2	28.6	29.4	26.8	25.9	21.6	18.6	29.1	6.6	9.7	22.6
NORTH AFRICA	5.0	8.5	8.5	8.5	8.8	8.8	11.8	10.9	10.5	9.8	9.4	4.9	7.7	9.7
Algeria	..	..	..	..	..	..	..	..	..	..	..	..	..	..
Egypt, Arab Republic	8.3	11.7	12.0	12.0	12.0	12.0	11.8	10.9	10.5	9.8	9.4	8.0	11.1	11.2
Libya	5.1	5.5	5.5	5.5	5.5	5.5	..	..	..	..	..	4.7	5.5	5.5
Morocco	4.9	8.5	8.5	8.5	..	..	..	..	..	..	..	5.6	8.4	8.5
Tunisia	2.5	..	..	..	..	..	..	..	..	..	..	3.4	6.7	..
ALL AFRICA	6.2	8.8	8.0	9.2	9.0	10.6	11.0	12.2	12.5	9.6	7.8	6.4	7.9	10.0

Note: 1998 data are preliminary (see page 3).   Group data are medians of individual country values in each year or period.

Figure 4-1. Credit to private and public sectors as a share of GDP, 1998*

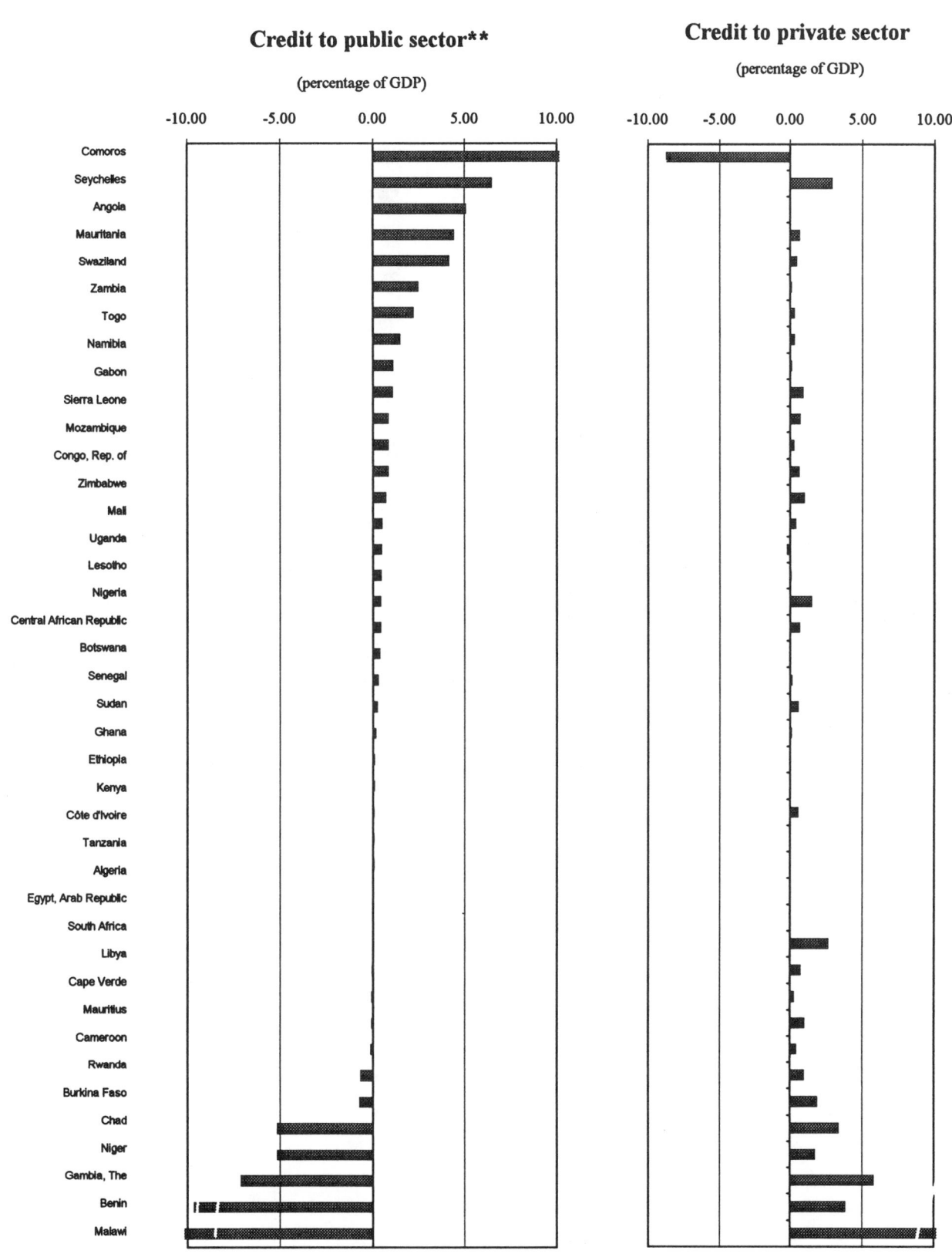

Credit to public sector**

(percentage of GDP)

Credit to private sector

(percentage of GDP)

* Or most recent year available.
** Sorted by credit to public sector.
Note: Nigeria's ratios are distorted because of official exchange rate over-valuation affecting oil exports and oil value added.

Figure 4-2. Real discount rate, average 1992-98*

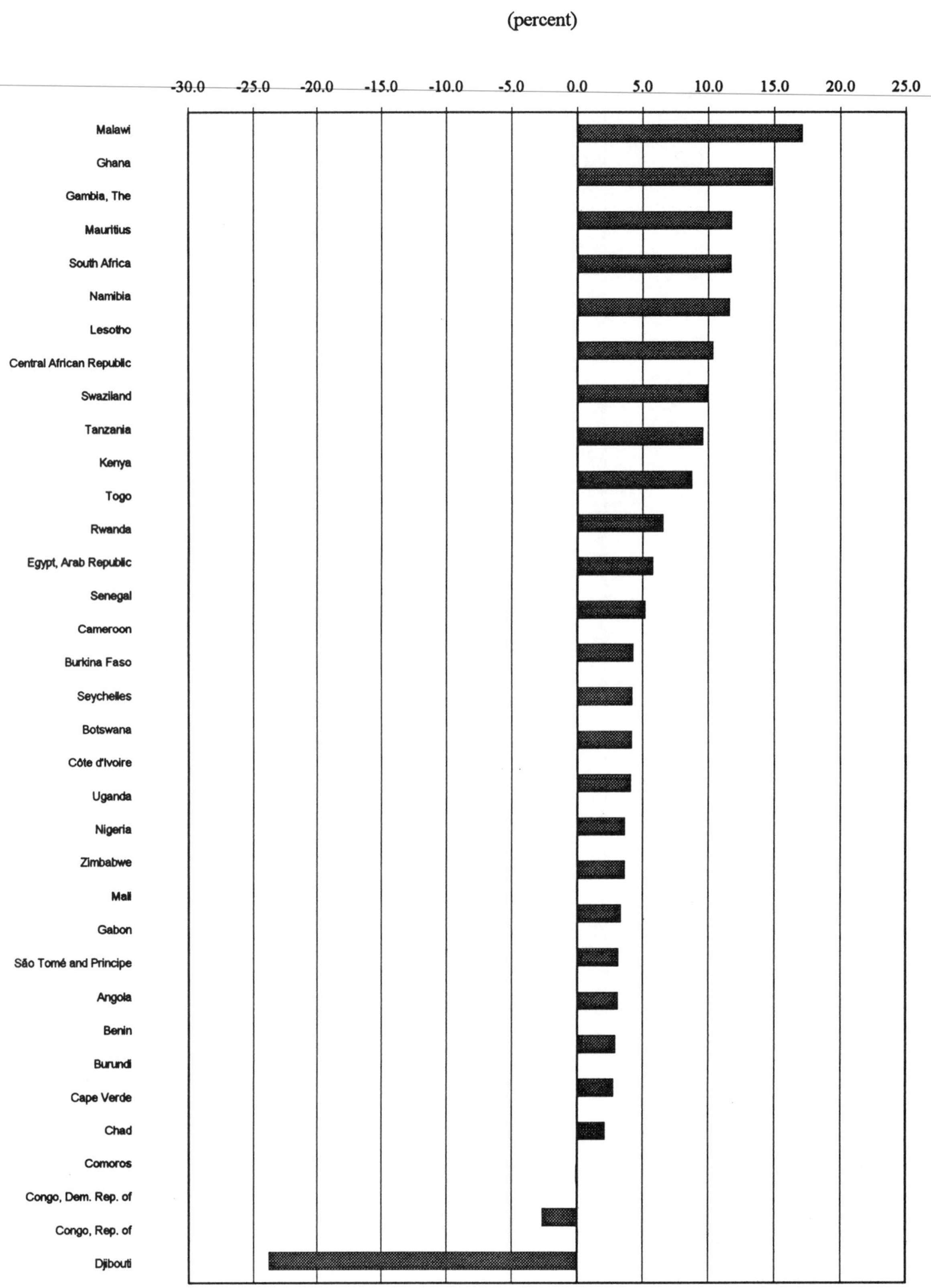

(percent)

	-30.0	-25.0	-20.0	-15.0	-10.0	-5.0	0.0	5.0	10.0	15.0	20.0	25.0

Malawi
Ghana
Gambia, The
Mauritius
South Africa
Namibia
Lesotho
Central African Republic
Swaziland
Tanzania
Kenya
Togo
Rwanda
Egypt, Arab Republic
Senegal
Cameroon
Burkina Faso
Seychelles
Botswana
Côte d'Ivoire
Uganda
Nigeria
Zimbabwe
Mali
Gabon
São Tomé and Principe
Angola
Benin
Burundi
Cape Verde
Chad
Comoros
Congo, Dem. Rep. of
Congo, Rep. of
Djibouti

* Or most recent year available.

Technical Notes

Tables

Table 4-1. Domestic credit. Domestic credit (IMF, *IFS*, line 32) includes all domestic assets of the banking system. It is the sum of the claims on the central government (net), on official entities, and on the private sector. Domestic credit is made up of credit to the private sector (Table 4-2) and credit to the government (Table 4-3).

Table 4-2. Credit to the private sector. Credit to the private sector is taken from IMF, *IFS*, line 32d.

Table 4-3. Credit to the government. Credit to the government sector is taken from IMF, *IFS*, line 32an. Negative numbers for net claims on the central government indicate that government is a net depositor to the banking system. The government's financial position with the monetary system is always presented on·a net basis because its recourse to the monetary system cannot always be analyzed meaningfully in terms of liquidity preferences or by considering debtor and creditor positions separately. Movements in net claims on the central government (that is, claims or credits less government deposits) indicate the impact of government operations on the liquidity of the rest of the economy.

Table 4-4. Net foreign assets. Data for net foreign assets are from the IMF, *IFS*, line 31n. As for credit to the government, the financial position of the foreign sector with the monetary system is presented on a net basis for the same reason as noted above. Movements in net foreign assets (that is, foreign assets less foreign liabilities) indicate the direct monetary impact of a country's transactions with the rest of the world.

Table 4-5. Growth of money supply. This table shows the annual percentage change in money (M1), defined as the sum of currency outside of banks and demand deposits other than those of the central government (IMF, *IFS*, line 34). The presentation of the money supply in the form of growth rates rather than levels reflects the importance from the point of view of macroeconomic stability of the rate of growth rather than the stock of money.

Table 4-6. Discount rate. The discount rate reported here is the nominal interest rate at which the monetary authorities lend to (or discount eligible paper from) deposit money banks (IMF, *IFS*, line 60).

Table 4-7. Real discount rate. The real discount rate in each year is the nominal discount rate (Table 4-6) deflated by the annual change in inflation as reflected by the consumer price index (CPI) (Table 3-3). It has been calculated using the formula:

$$\left\{ [l + (i/100)] \left/ [(\pi_t/\pi_{t-1})] -1 \right. \right\} \times 100$$

where i is nominal interest rate and π is inflation rate based on the CPI.

Table 4-8. Commercial bank lending rate. The commercial bank lending rate (IMF, *IFS*, line 60p) is the rate charged to borrowers by commercial banks for short- and medium-term use of funds.

Table 4-9. Commercial bank deposit rate. The deposit rate (IMF, *IFS*, line 60l) is the rate paid to depositors on time savings and demand deposits by deposit money banks and similar financial institutions.

Figure 4-1. Credit to the private sector (Table 4-2); credit to the public sector (Table 4-3); gross domestic product (Table 2-5).

Figure 4-2. Real discount rate (Table 4-7).

Figures

The following indicators have been used to derive the figures in this chapter.

Methodology used for regional aggregations and period averages in chapter 4

Table	Aggregations[a]		Period averages[b]	
	(7)	(8)	(1)	(2)
4-1	x			x
4-2	x			x
4-3	x			x
4-4		x	x	
4-5	x			x
4-6	x		x	
4-7	x		x	
4-8	x		x	
4-9	x		x	

Note: Regional aggregations are shown in the rows for Sub-Saharan Africa, North Africa, and All Africa. Period averages are shown in the last three columns. This table shows only the methodologies used in this chapter. The definitions of the methodologies used throughout the book are given below.

a. Regional aggregations: (1) simple total; (2) simple total of the first indicator divided by the simple total of the second indicator (same country coverage); (3) simple total of the gap-filled indicator; (4) simple total of the gap-filled main indicator divided by the simple total of the gap-filled secondary indicator; (5) simple total of the first gap-filled main indicator less the simple total of the second gap-filled main indicator, all divided by the simple total of the secondary indicator; (6) weighted total (by population); (7) median; (8) no aggregation; (9) simple arithmetic mean.

b. Period averages: (1) arithmetic mean (using the same series as shown in the table, i.e., ratio if the rest of the table is shown as ratio, level if the rest of the table is shown as level, growth rate if the rest of the table is shown as growth rate); (2) least-squares growth rate (using main indicator); (3) least-squares growth rate (using main indicator in constant terms, with the rest of the table in current terms).

5

External Sector

The external sector provides data on economic and financial relations between African countries and the rest of the world, with detailed accounting of commodity trade, one of the principal components of the current account within the balance of payments framework. Commodity trade and price data can also provide a partial basis for analyzing Africa's constraints and performance in the international marketplace, including its terms of trade. Commodity exports are a major source of foreign exchange. Other sources of foreign exchange include receipts from factor and nonfactor services, borrowing from abroad, incoming foreign investment, and foreign transfers and grants.

The balance of payments is a system of accounts, covering a given period, that is intended to record systematically: flows of real resources, including the services of the original factors of production, between the domestic economy of a country and the rest of the world; changes in the country's foreign assets and liabilities that arise from economic transactions; and transfer payments, which are the counterpart of real resources or financial claims provided to, or received

from, the rest of the world that carry no provision for repayment.

The tables provide gross entries for goods and services and net entries for unrequited transfers (official and private) and other financial flows; a table for current account balance as traditionally defined (with transfers above the line) is also shown. The information is presented for broad aggregates; fuller detail can be found in the IMF's *Balance of Payments Manual* (1993) and *Balance of Payments Yearbooks*.

Unit values for exports (f.o.b.) and imports (c.i.f.) measure changes in the aggregate price level of a country's exports and imports of goods and nonfactor services over time. Unit values reflect average price changes for broad groups of commodities, rather than for any single commodity. The terms of trade indicate relative movements in export and import unit values (here, they are based on goods and nonfactor services from the national accounts). If the prices of exports rise while the prices of imports rise more slowly, stay constant, or decline, the same quantity of exports "buys" a bigger quantity of imports. The effect of such price changes is equivalent to an increase in the real value of output (or increased productivity in value terms) of the export sector. Were import prices to rise more quickly than export prices, the reverse would be true. Export figures for specific commodities show physical quantities rather than value in either current or constant prices. Most of the key nonagricultural primary commodities are exported from a few countries with substantial mineral resources. Variations in export prices and earnings for the five major oil-exporting countries in Sub-Saharan Africa (which in the 1980s have accounted for about half of Sub-Saharan export earnings) have dominated trends in this region as a whole.

5-1. Merchandise exports, f.o.b.

	Millions of U.S. dollars (current prices)											Average annual percentage growth		
	1980	*1989*	*1990*	*1991*	*1992*	*1993*	*1994*	*1995*	*1996*	*1997*	*1998*	*75-84*	*85-89*	*90-MR*
SUB-SAHARAN AFRICA	78,822	61,088	69,343	66,374	66,282	62,688	65,767	77,985	86,685	87,145	75,323	6.9	2.9	3.3
excluding South Africa	53,221	38,709	45,822	42,594	41,814	37,944	39,428	47,913	56,439	55,901	45,894	5.3	0.5	2.9
excl. S. Africa & Nigeria	26,519	28,900	31,885	30,457	29,918	28,019	30,023	36,188	40,307	40,779	36,778	6.0	3.8	3.7
Angola	..	3,014	3,884	3,449	3,833	2,900	3,017	3,724	5,087	5,008	3,509	..	7.0	3.1
Benin	222	215	287	337	371	341	308	405	424	400	415	7.1	6.0	6.0
Botswana	545	1,820	1,795	1,871	1,744	1,722	1,874	2,160	2,233	2,311	2,426	20.0	24.5	3.7
Burkina Faso	161	205	283	269	238	260	188	237	233	229	307	8.1	11.1	0.7
Burundi	66	93	73	90	77	74	81	113	40	87	49	..	-1.0	-4.3
Cameroon	1,506	1,837	1,882	2,159	1,937	1,652	1,433	1,664	1,761	1,968	1,867	18.2	-5.5	-0.7
Cape Verde	9	8	6	4	4	4	5	8	13	13	16	15.5	2.9	12.6
Central African Republic	147	148	151	126	116	132	162	179	142	155	138	8.6	3.9	1.0
Chad	71	155	194	194	182	152	135	247	200	215	313	0.8	10.0	5.0
Comoros	11	18	18	24	21	22	11	11	6	6	6	..	15.7	-14.9
Congo, Democratic Rep. of	2,269	2,417	2,326	1,649	1,246	1,144	1,256	1,612	1,727	1,395	..	5.9	5.8	-5.1
Congo, Republic of	911	1,155	1,388	1,110	1,179	1,119	959	1,173	1,644	1,698	1,163	22.9	-3.2	2.0
Côte d'Ivoire	3,013	2,613	3,003	2,705	2,945	2,519	2,869	3,820	4,282	..	..	6.4	-0.4	5.7
Djibouti	..	..	..	72	53	71	56	38	40	43	..	..	..	-9.5
Equatorial Guinea	..	33	38	36	52	52	65	86	197	478	..	..	12.7	34.3
Eritrea	..	..	..	..	15	36	65	81	95	53	30	..	..	12.3
Ethiopia	459	444	366	276	154	222	280	454	410	599	602	6.3	-0.1	7.3
Gabon	2,531	1,629	2,490	2,230	2,257	2,326	2,365	2,643	3,190	3,043	2,322	8.9	-6.5	4.3
Gambia, The	51	85	108	132	151	141	124	121	115	108	132	3.2	7.9	1.5
Ghana	1,104	808	897	998	986	1,064	1,227	1,431	1,573	1,491	1,830	-3.8	8.5	9.2
Guinea	500	731	817	790	657	665	626	649	613	660	689	4.7	6.5	-2.0
Guinea-Bissau	..	14	19	20	6	16	33	24	22	48	27	..	1.3	10.9
Kenya	1,363	913	997	1,056	1,013	1,103	1,484	1,924	2,083	2,060	2,012	5.8	-2.1	11.4
Lesotho	58	66	60	67	109	134	144	154	181	195	183	10.4	25.7	15.3
Liberia	600	..	..	..	..	..	..	..	..	..	..	1.4	-5.6	..
Madagascar	437	318	318	334	324	332	447	523	524	505	536	2.0	-1.1	7.5
Malawi	281	269	412	476	397	321	327	404	483	567	509	8.8	-0.4	5.1
Mali	205	269	330	371	362	349	337	442	433	562	556	10.9	8.9	7.3
Mauritania	196	438	414	434	400	380	393	479	484	413	369	6.8	7.1	-0.3
Mauritius	434	995	1,201	1,213	1,303	1,334	1,386	1,592	1,841	1,624	1,643	2.9	24.5	5.8
Mozambique	281	105	126	162	139	132	164	174	226	230	248	..	4.5	9.2
Namibia	1,534	1,155	1,086	1,223	1,341	1,292	1,350	1,400	1,374	1,359	1,390	..	8.5	2.5
Niger	576	308	313	270	344	297	226	286	302	270	298	14.6	3.9	-1.0
Nigeria	25,956	9,812	13,914	12,127	11,886	9,924	9,415	11,734	16,117	15,208	9,727	3.8	-7.1	1.1
Rwanda	134	97	103	96	69	68	32	50	62	93	62	5.6	-6.0	-5.1
São Tomé and Principe	17	6	4	6	5	5	6	5	5	5	6	-3.0	-7.6	0.7
Senegal	480	759	912	904	828	719	791	968	986	932	956	2.1	6.0	2.0
Seychelles	6	15	57	49	48	49	52	53	78	115	84	-1.8	32.2	15.3
Sierra Leone	214	142	145	145	150	118	194	101	105	88	101	-1.0	0.0	-5.2
Somalia	133	61	58	..	..	..	..	..	..	..	..	3.6	-2.7	..
South Africa	25,698	22,399	23,560	23,805	24,487	24,750	26,342	30,084	30,285	31,213	29,116	10.3	7.4	3.8
Sudan	566	497	393	346	350	427	462	556	620	594	596	2.8	-4.4	5.6
Swaziland	368	494	550	594	639	685	791	868	896	961	914	6.3	22.6	7.9
Tanzania	508	423	389	394	414	411	486	593	696	794	645	-4.6	1.6	8.1
Togo	476	409	395	393	327	215	226	355	377	425	415	7.1	10.1	0.4
Uganda	319	282	210	176	172	157	254	595	590	671	466	1.3	-6.1	14.9
Zambia	1,457	1,410	1,264	1,085	1,111	949	1,067	1,186	993	1,119	874	-0.9	10.2	-3.2
Zimbabwe	281	1,692	1,753	1,785	1,530	1,610	1,947	2,216	2,496	2,424	2,047	0.0	9.3	4.3
NORTH AFRICA	40,721	23,404	32,082	33,212	32,680	31,153	30,607	37,627	41,511	42,800	42,366	9.7	-6.2	5.5
Algeria	13,652	9,569	12,889	12,387	11,439	10,410	8,899	10,260	13,210	13,820	13,298	14.3	-7.7	2.0
Egypt, Arab Republic	3,854	1,816	2,137	3,137	3,474	3,725	3,337	4,957	4,609	4,930	4,213	9.4	-19.0	10.4
Libya	21,919	7,274	11,352	..	..	..	..	..	..	..	..	6.7	-10.5	..
Morocco	2,415	3,851	4,955	5,094	5,010	4,936	5,538	6,872	7,066	7,039	7,505	5.3	14.2	7.0
Tunisia	2,395	2,913	3,517	3,708	4,014	3,746	4,643	5,470	5,519	5,559	6,013	12.0	10.7	8.1
ALL AFRICA	119,847	84,316	101,571	99,237	98,709	93,553	96,480	115,475	128,105	129,678	116,647	7.9	-0.2	4.0

Note: 1998 data are preliminary (see page 3).

5-2. Merchandise imports, f.o.b.

	1980	1989	1990	1991	1992	1993	1994	1995	1996	1997	1998	75-84	85-89	90-MR
	Millions of U.S. dollars (current prices)											*Average annual percentage growth*		
SUB-SAHARAN AFRICA	61,332	51,020	55,418	56,355	59,415	57,236	59,173	72,005	75,014	78,894	76,999	8.2	3.7	5.1
excluding South Africa	43,059	34,230	38,686	39,209	41,235	38,752	37,309	44,600	47,431	50,046	49,853	8.3	2.4	3.9
excl. S. Africa & Nigeria	28,289	28,346	31,640	31,319	32,336	30,452	30,848	36,424	39,227	40,751	39,912	6.4	5.9	3.9
Angola	..	1,338	1,578	1,347	1,988	1,463	1,454	1,852	2,040	2,477	1,976	..	-1.8	5.3
Benin	499	317	428	482	561	539	374	557	548	528	546	8.3	6.9	4.1
Botswana	603	1,185	1,611	1,604	1,557	1,455	1,350	1,579	1,436	1,554	1,651	17.4	18.4	1.3
Burkina Faso	368	442	542	490	516	534	349	485	563	510	607	8.1	10.3	1.5
Burundi	165	151	189	196	182	173	173	176	100	98	103	..	-1.8	-6.8
Cameroon	1,452	1,352	1,454	1,251	1,023	1,021	1,017	1,074	1,201	1,347	1,374	12.5	5.5	-0.3
Cape Verde	80	110	120	128	167	152	195	234	206	209	232	10.1	5.9	9.0
Central African Republic	185	186	242	179	189	158	151	179	126	145	150	8.7	4.6	-4.5
Chad	55	239	260	250	243	205	212	296	293	311	333	-1.8	12.5	3.5
Comoros	22	36	45	49	58	50	45	54	49	48	50	..	6.1	1.9
Congo, Democratic Rep. of	1,519	1,925	1,739	1,304	935	614	667	997	923	834	..	0.0	10.7	-9.7
Congo, Republic of	545	503	513	495	438	500	613	650	1,413	897	751	15.2	-5.0	9.0
Côte d'Ivoire	2,614	1,721	1,705	1,825	1,984	1,784	1,608	2,474	2,763	..	..	6.1	3.9	5.7
Djibouti	..	..	..	258	259	255	237	205	201	203	..	..	..	-5.0
Equatorial Guinea	..	45	52	90	62	52	67	97	248	367	..	..	10.7	24.9
Eritrea	..	..	..	..	278	275	396	404	514	490	494	..	..	11.9
Ethiopia	692	1,020	881	1,029	875	1,052	915	1,063	1,413	1,403	1,519	16.4	1.0	5.5
Gabon	829	812	805	861	887	845	777	898	969	1,018	809	4.6	0.0	1.3
Gambia, The	116	109	134	174	204	205	179	184	196	176	201	11.0	7.8	4.7
Ghana	908	1,011	1,200	1,313	1,457	1,728	1,580	1,685	1,937	2,128	2,213	-1.6	11.2	8.4
Guinea	339	587	723	735	740	732	688	758	584	573	624	5.0	9.1	-1.3
Guinea-Bissau	..	69	68	67	84	54	54	59	57	73	52	..	1.5	-2.3
Kenya	2,585	1,705	1,992	1,686	1,608	1,385	1,761	2,636	2,512	2,916	2,998	8.1	4.3	7.2
Lesotho	425	593	673	804	933	868	810	1,013	1,003	1,012	873	14.2	10.5	4.7
Liberia	478	..	..	..	..	..	..	..	..	..	..	1.8	-1.5	..
Madagascar	764	320	566	440	465	510	546	628	645	682	694	5.4	-3.1	7.0
Malawi	308	405	491	616	712	628	536	474	624	783	677	2.7	8.7	4.1
Mali	308	367	464	505	532	502	466	556	552	553	569	9.7	8.3	3.5
Mauritania	321	353	405	385	424	375	304	395	403	355	358	7.0	2.6	-0.6
Mauritius	516	1,206	1,470	1,419	1,473	1,576	1,784	1,828	2,124	2,083	1,961	4.6	27.6	6.0
Mozambique	720	723	780	791	745	830	881	727	783	760	868	..	11.4	0.9
Namibia	1,094	933	1,118	1,120	1,268	1,216	1,285	1,431	1,423	1,402	1,438	..	8.1	4.4
Niger	677	162	338	281	266	256	263	297	306	297	333	11.0	-14.5	3.9
Nigeria	14,735	5,912	7,070	7,892	8,891	8,293	6,470	8,183	8,216	9,256	9,822	12.7	-8.9	3.8
Rwanda	196	245	228	228	241	268	367	194	213	277	261	12.3	6.8	0.8
São Tomé and Principe	16	27	21	25	23	26	24	23	20	19	18	12.4	2.1	-3.2
Senegal	973	998	1,176	1,186	1,192	1,102	1,022	1,217	1,268	1,196	1,238	4.9	4.7	1.4
Seychelles	84	140	166	162	180	216	188	214	263	310	287	12.4	14.2	8.6
Sierra Leone	334	183	65	65	62	37	131	117	186	81	116	1.4	2.6	3.6
Somalia	402	352	211	..	..	..	..	..	..	..	..	15.0	-6.3	..
South Africa	18,268	16,810	16,778	17,190	18,224	18,518	21,875	27,412	27,599	?? 6	27,269	8.7	7.0	7.5
Sudan	1,440	960	1,092	1,201	1,002	975	957	1,036	1,315	??+3	1,636	5.6	-0.7	4.2
Swaziland	538	516	589	635	780	789	832	1,009	1,076	1,173	1,049	16.6	10.0	9.3
Tanzania	1,089	1,151	1,346	1,381	1,444	1,472	1,591	1,510	1,370	1,388	1,402	-4.9	9.0	1.3
Togo	524	465	511	453	409	251	212	350	418	455	447	9.4	13.8	-1.3
Uganda	318	562	584	545	451	531	672	1,086	1,218	1,246	1,393	4.5	9.9	13.1
Zambia	1,114	901	889	952	1,302	950	1,003	1,194	1,055	1,056	1,022	0.3	6.9	1.6
Zimbabwe	308	1,323	1,511	1,700	1,781	1,512	1,778	2,128	2,247	2,654	1,968	1.4	6.5	0.6
NORTH AFRICA	30,710	29,482	34,376	32,550	34,990	34,258	36,728	43,253	42,919	42,668	46,237	8.1	-2.2	4.7
Algeria	9,596	9,362	9,659	7,747	8,541	7,990	9,158	10,100	9,090	8,130	9,100	5.6	-3.1	0.0
Egypt, Arab Republic	6,814	7,052	8,817	9,390	8,959	9,656	9,583	11,531	12,698	13,248	14,560	10.2	-8.8	7.3
Libya	10,368	6,509	7,575	..	..	..	..	..	..	..	..	12.0	-3.1	..
Morocco	3,770	5,345	6,815	6,834	7,451	6,977	7,619	9,268	8,996	8,913	9,308	8.3	8.7	5.6
Tunisia	3,453	4,372	5,193	4,895	6,079	5,757	6,210	7,458	7,277	7,548	8,035	13.2	7.2	6.7
ALL AFRICA	91,212	80,127	89,545	88,813	94,261	91,315	95,621	115,023	117,843	121,589	123,091	7.8	1.3	5.0

Note: 1998 data are preliminary (see page 3).

5-3. Exports of total services

	Millions of U.S. dollars (current prices)											Average annual percentage growth		
	1980	1989	1990	1991	1992	1993	1994	1995	1996	1997	1998	75-84	85-89	90-MR
SUB-SAHARAN AFRICA	12,213	11,784	13,715	13,753	14,050	13,646	13,698	16,670	17,533	17,995	18,995	6.3	6.3	4.9
excluding South Africa	8,679	8,249	9,338	9,704	9,780	9,683	8,985	10,922	11,435	11,425	12,729	7.7	7.1	4.0
excl. S. Africa & Nigeria	6,228	7,955	8,974	9,247	9,546	9,538	8,821	10,712	11,036	10,956	11,834	8.8	8.6	3.8
Angola	..	150	119	186	159	117	163	129	311	251	325	..	3.5	9.2
Benin	84	88	115	123	143	137	108	145	142	140	150	11.3	8.9	4.2
Botswana	203	355	626	693	731	746	417	744	669	707	724	14.8	16.5	4.1
Burkina Faso	65	39	86	85	83	80	66	80	71	55	67	9.2	5.8	0.3
Burundi	26	24	25	35	31	25	23	27	17	13	12	..	7.3	-8.9
Cameroon	395	490	378	334	436	394	310	405	458	492	482	21.7	-1.7	1.7
Cape Verde	14	45	58	49	52	49	60	79	92	99	128	43.1	11.6	11.3
Central African Republic	58	66	70	56	56	54	45	53	47	43	30	7.0	10.9	-6.9
Chad	0	44	44	40	44	47	60	68	72	66	71	-13.0	10.2	7.4
Comoros	3	22	21	28	33	35	30	38	38	26	28	..	48.5	3.6
Congo, Democratic Rep. of	135	231	258	226	135	151	66	159	66	63	..	3.1	13.3	-16.3
Congo, Republic of	119	7	114	118	79	68	159	82	85	77	74	7.6	-29.0	11.5
Côte d'Ivoire	588	645	596	675	810	773	536	813	774	..	..	9.4	1.6	2.5
Djibouti	..	..	..	194	178	192	182	188	184	188	..	..	..	-0.1
Equatorial Guinea	..	8	8	10	7	8	7	5	5	5	..	..	137.6	-8.3
Eritrea	..	..	..	..	73	103	80	99	113	158	111	..	..	9.3
Ethiopia	131	314	311	271	305	291	283	354	413	442	451	5.0	11.5	5.1
Gabon	350	308	270	352	369	344	231	286	298	263	235	12.2	10.1	-2.8
Gambia, The	21	47	43	58	70	77	62	55	71	80	84	10.0	19.7	6.0
Ghana	110	72	87	103	137	156	169	164	181	192	200	-5.8	14.7	11.7
Guinea	54	27	56	60	64	51	53	54	115	121	135	..	53.2	14.8
Guinea-Bissau	..	5	5	5	5	5	6	6	7	8	4	..	-13.6	2.2
Kenya	835	1,008	1,230	1,177	1,144	1,152	1,184	1,050	958	952	879	7.1	9.9	-2.6
Lesotho	305	413	496	518	538	481	407	476	456	511	449	14.8	6.8	-0.1
Liberia	13		..	..	..	..	..	..	..	..	..	18.0	17.0	..
Madagascar	82	161	209	151	177	187	208	246	306	276	299	2.6	24.1	7.6
Malawi	34	40	45	45	27	19	29	22	42	61	48	-7.4	5.5	2.0
Mali	58	72	108	96	106	99	78	88	103	90	92	10.7	14.1	0.3
Mauritania	74	57	55	66	53	34	40	48	33	23	42	9.6	9.8	-7.2
Mauritius	150	453	589	643	691	632	677	817	953	968	1,001	8.1	31.6	8.3
Mozambique	171	167	173	203	223	240	246	292	314	342	333	..	9.0	8.9
Namibia	206	304	320	395	375	461	488	699	657	626	670	..	8.8	10.4
Niger	68	71	71	59	56	49	37	41	40	35	39	7.4	10.5	-7.9
Nigeria	2,164	319	379	478	259	171	187	239	427	405	389	2.7	-11.0	0.9
Rwanda	49	60	47	47	50	37	22	38	27	60	57	27.2	8.4	-1.6
São Tomé and Principe	6	5	4	5	5	5	6	4	6	7	7	20.1	7.8	5.5
Senegal	416	516	602	598	616	577	504	604	630	582	599	9.0	10.8	0.7
Seychelles	97	190	176	173	198	211	201	224	245	256	291	15.4	14.2	5.3
Sierra Leone	1	0	70	69	66	75	19	61	56	27	40	-28.7	0.0	31.1
Somalia	71	27	33	..	..	..	..	..	..	..	..	13.9	-15.9	..
South Africa	3,560	3,544	4,391	4,062	4,281	3,975	4,720	5,756	6,106	6,640	6,581	8.5	4.5	7.3
Sudan	228	207	139	54	74	111	96	134	57	47	29	12.6	-3.4	-13.1
Swaziland	82	238	269	356	296	248	265	324	276	296	206	15.4	18.4	-0.9
Tanzania	179	122	134	141	141	206	369	511	472	520	525	-5.9	1.8	22.2
Togo	95	152	180	172	161	115	81	103	117	103	102	17.7	10.9	-6.5
Uganda	11	22	36	27	27	85	90	87	157	192	218	9.2	1.4	31.3
Zambia	168	103	79	87	94	107	123	152	143	188	184	3.7	1.7	9.8
Zimbabwe	34	279	287	297	330	401	443	542	646	692	600	5.2	8.4	11.9
NORTH AFRICA	10,619	10,620	12,975	14,351	18,489	19,819	20,286	23,054	25,549	27,257	25,555	12.4	3.0	10.6
Algeria	978	689	587	504	729	746	808	800	960	1,330	1,449	7.4	3.1	10.2
Egypt, Arab Republic	2,662	4,101	5,156	6,678	8,262	9,215	9,313	11,182	12,465	13,293	11,741	19.9	0.3	13.0
Libya	1,446	565	783	..	..	..	..	..	..	..	..	12.8	1.9	..
Morocco	896	1,590	1,977	1,821	2,444	2,412	2,374	2,248	2,556	2,617	2,611	8.6	15.1	4.9
Tunisia	1,214	1,715	1,783	1,507	2,107	2,143	2,364	2,657	2,732	2,723	2,915	11.2	14.5	7.2
ALL AFRICA	21,089	21,599	25,410	26,566	30,220	30,848	31,281	36,755	39,704	41,549	41,055	11.6	5.6	7.4

Note: 1998 data are preliminary (see page 3).

5-4. Imports of total services

| | Millions of U.S. dollars (current prices) | | | | | | | | | | | Average annual percentage growth | | |
	1980	1989	1990	1991	1992	1993	1994	1995	1996	1997	1998	75-84	85-89	90-MR
SUB-SAHARAN AFRICA	32,074	33,102	38,409	37,248	38,059	36,063	35,506	40,554	42,311	43,074	41,118	7.7	5.4	2.2
excluding South Africa	24,420	25,385	29,286	29,406	29,888	28,040	27,069	30,619	32,433	32,603	31,297	8.7	5.9	1.9
excl. S. Africa & Nigeria	15,738	20,801	23,507	23,659	24,566	23,242	21,820	25,206	27,194	26,662	26,271	9.9	7.7	2.3
Angola	..	1,963	2,584	2,967	2,980	2,568	2,534	3,149	3,914	3,754	3,581	..	20.3	6.0
Benin	112	150	174	170	219	192	171	225	234	221	226	11.2	4.1	4.3
Botswana	351	712	898	803	790	587	777	960	893	988	1,064	18.6	18.7	3.5
Burkina Faso	228	158	192	279	238	230	162	204	198	180	193	9.1	5.1	-0.7
Burundi	58	131	149	158	158	134	110	120	57	53	54	..	14.1	-12.1
Cameroon	1,026	1,083	964	1,350	1,741	1,626	1,071	1,114	1,270	1,320	1,287	19.0	-12.1	1.0
Cape Verde	8	33	35	24	31	36	40	66	77	74	88	29.3	20.3	14.6
Central African Republic	144	171	192	157	179	155	126	157	124	123	134	7.0	12.4	-4.2
Chad	28	222	260	219	239	240	232	279	290	291	307	-7.6	16.6	3.4
Comoros	12	43	51	48	55	52	45	52	48	30	32	..	2.8	-3.9
Congo, Democratic Rep. of	1,160	1,547	1,556	1,552	1,223	1,092	1,186	1,266	1,192	1,315	..	8.5	11.3	-3.1
Congo, Republic of	650	700	1,244	1,232	1,115	1,219	1,253	1,177	1,605	1,148	979	16.3	6.0	2.4
Côte d'Ivoire	2,110	2,563	2,940	2,519	2,726	2,484	1,638	2,359	2,383	..	..	11.2	11.6	-3.5
Djibouti	..	..	..	..	131	118	97	96	91	93	..	..	..	-6.9
Equatorial Guinea	..	40	49	36	41	51	82	95	224	335	..	..	69.2	29.8
Eritrea	..	..	..	..	0	1	7	44	69	107	101	..	..	151.6
Ethiopia	105	270	260	274	292	314	273	293	318	352	403	-1.9	16.5	3.9
Gabon	1,414	1,167	1,668	1,519	1,781	1,688	1,336	1,679	1,985	1,833	1,614	10.8	-3.3	2.8
Gambia, The	44	59	66	72	80	80	70	70	73	72	79	14.3	15.0	1.7
Ghana	355	386	417	461	513	568	543	588	627	677	687	0.4	8.9	6.6
Guinea	238	345	355	320	285	270	261	329	418	406	420	..	9.0	2.7
Guinea-Bissau	..	42	39	47	43	39	41	48	48	48	34	..	10.7	0.1
Kenya	872	971	1,057	999	906	930	1,041	1,222	1,101	1,033	883	4.9	4.3	0.3
Lesotho	58	91	103	104	115	93	104	144	137	189	161	12.9	14.1	7.2
Liberia	97	..	..	..	..	..	..	..	..	..	..	28.2	7.5	..
Madagascar	368	437	436	440	421	457	480	539	555	492	523	10.1	8.7	2.7
Malawi	330	103	100	121	96	84	111	125	149	143	150	11.5	-0.9	5.0
Mali	221	315	391	360	440	356	322	395	446	409	407	7.9	8.8	2.0
Mauritania	172	270	277	270	267	258	221	295	298	233	222	13.2	4.1	-1.4
Mauritius	207	429	519	542	619	592	609	708	752	749	834	8.7	22.1	6.7
Mozambique	155	312	286	312	355	367	393	416	404	424	511	..	7.0	5.6
Namibia	787	639	515	638	700	647	639	800	820	711	591	..	5.2	2.0
Niger	339	195	258	197	189	177	193	215	193	173	176	10.7	3.6	-2.0
Nigeria	8,498	4,587	5,770	5,743	5,328	4,806	5,250	5,420	5,252	5,991	5,155	5.3	-0.8	0.6
Rwanda	139	190	152	131	147	154	132	156	169	221	222	13.4	8.8	3.3
São Tomé and Principe	7	18	26	26	23	22	22	28	27	27	18	14.9	10.8	0.6
Senegal	475	741	808	803	832	787	657	763	743	683	701	12.0	9.6	-1.5
Seychelles	43	72	96	84	91	104	94	116	131	144	165	14.6	19.7	8.3
Sierra Leone	31	49	187	146	161	165	167	165	147	69	104	6.2	12.9	0.0
Somalia	139	200	..	..	..	..	..	..	..	..	..	9.9	6.1	..
South Africa	7,720	7,755	9,168	7,904	8,231	8,077	8,485	9,987	9,937	10,518	9,794	10.5	4.0	3.0
Sudan	416	1,203	1,145	1,097	1,091	1,146	1,183	1,236	1,271	1,390	1,492	19.8	5.6	2.7
Swaziland	121	233	247	344	282	364	347	291	268	283	121	9.8	18.1	-3.7
Tanzania	160	600	402	379	635	723	805	659	759	793	918	2.9	19.5	7.7
Togo	227	259	288	273	262	200	183	208	225	194	194	14.0	9.9	-4.2
Uganda	132	217	169	187	222	221	241	371	450	460	504	6.2	11.9	13.3
Zambia	872	806	799	693	623	559	566	588	490	672	528	3.0	7.5	-4.1
Zimbabwe	330	706	784	931	961	836	1,016	1,120	1,224	1,415	1,152	8.8	7.5	6.6
NORTH AFRICA	7,882	12,399	10,338	18,136	17,964	18,092	17,933	19,788	18,947	17,968	..	4.9	3.8	6.0
Algeria	4,956	2,400	2,789	2,896	4,065	3,507	3,769	4,329	4,710	4,620	..	2.1	-8.2	8.5
Egypt, Arab Republic	2,931	5,530	2,943	8,971	7,121	7,450	6,916	7,538	6,496	6,217	..	20.4	7.5	4.2
Libya	..	..	..	..	..	..	..	..	..	..	..	..	..	..
Morocco	2,037	2,078	2,038	2,766	2,941	3,049	3,153	3,544	3,364	3,062	..	2.7	7.9	6.2
Tunisia	666	1,000	1,398	1,451	1,803	2,038	2,065	2,136	2,232	2,035	..	13.4	7.8	9.0
ALL AFRICA	41,545	46,211	49,505	55,571	56,254	54,296	53,569	60,540	61,588	61,532	..	6.3	5.6	3.3

Note: 1998 data are preliminary (see page 3).

5-5. Net private transfers

	Millions of U.S. dollars (current prices)											Annual average		
	1980	1989	1990	1991	1992	1993	1994	1995	1996	1997	1998	75-84	85-89	90-MR
SUB-SAHARAN AFRICA	267	1,386	868	1,044	2,302	2,182	2,548	2,709	3,163	4,212	4,839	661	1,315	2,652
excluding South Africa	173	1,272	912	1,051	2,299	2,189	2,560	2,726	3,186	4,209	4,829	542	1,224	2,662
excl. S.Africa & Nigeria	173	1,282	886	1,023	1,515	1,396	2,011	1,928	2,241	2,671	3,037	542	1,231	1,856
Angola	..	-68	-122	-12	26	-5	-4	-34	11	38	54	26	-19	-5
Benin	107	78	86	84	95	94	50	68	67	72	75	60	77	77
Botswana	-11	-31	-41	-39	-19	-65	-85	103	-23	20	20	-5	-9	-14
Burkina Faso	112	140	105	98	169	153	97	106	84	74	68	75	164	106
Burundi	3	9	10	13	13	17	18	16	11	9	11	6	9	13
Cameroon	19	-17	-67	-59	-72	-95	-41	-23	7	87	70	11	-69	-21
Cape Verde	40	43	55	58	70	˚71	81	100	96	93	101	30	32	80
Central African Republic	0	-25	-31	-30	-27	-31	-10	-11	-10	-10	-9	0	-14	-19
Chad	-4	-10	-1	-9	-15	-23	2	-14	-6	-6	-5	-6	-5	-8
Comoros	2	8	10	10	16	16	7	9	12	11	12	2	6	11
Congo, Democratic Rep. of	-79	-109	-81	-82	-97	-123	-98	-124	-138	-35	..	-47	-72	-97
Congo, Republic of	-1	-73	-16	-15	-19	-9	60	-19	-27	-29	-19	-44	-64	-10
Côte d'Ivoire	..	..	..	..	..	..	..	..	..	..	..	-319	..	..
Djibouti	..	..	..	-8	-9	-10	-11	-11	-10	-9	..	..	..	-10
Equatorial Guinea	..	-2	-2	-2	-4	-3	0	-3	-3	-3	..	0	-1	-2
Eritrea	..	..	..	..	128	165	276	215	244	348	233	..	..	230
Ethiopia	20	188	171	203	316	248	247	311	313	258	317	37	162	265
Gabon	-124	-135	-158	-126	-190	-209	-163	-192	-216	-218	-154	-81	-143	-181
Gambia, The	2	15	9	10	12	13	15	16	17	17	16	2	3	14
Ghana	-3	202	202	220	255	261	271	263	276	360	378	7	136	276
Guinea	-3	-43	-51	-42	-63	-54	-41	-35	-66	-47	-39	-3	-34	-49
Guinea-Bissau	..	1	1	1	1	1	1	3	2	2	16	-10	-1	3
Kenya	27	79	167	144	68	147	148	408	433	497	475	41	76	276
Lesotho	2	9	19	14	16	13	13	3	2	2	1	29	21	9
Liberia	-29	..	..	..	..	..	..	..	..	..	..	-32	-25	..
Madagascar	-21	72	77	67	109	114	46	75	88	116	86	-14	54	86
Malawi	..	..	˙..	13	55	46	36	12	8	-19	-20	..	..	16
Mali	41	64	102	70	74	93	85	96	90	72	68	24	53	83
Mauritania	-28	-10	6	1	77	28	14	30	40	54	56	-25	69	34
Mauritius	0	68	74	71	79	92	94	95	110	87	93	4	47	88
Mozambique	..	..	..	..	..	0	0	0	0	0	0	0	0	0
Namibia	0	0	0	0	0	0	0	˙0	0	0	0	0	0	0
Niger	-57	0	-50	-38	-40	-34	-41	-23	-25	-22	-22	-40	-26	-33
Nigeria	..	-10	26	28	784	792	549	799	945	1,537	1,792	-137	-18	806
Rwanda	0	8	6	21	20	22	45	16	27	25	18	1	7	22
São Tomé and Principe	1	0	0	1	1	2	3	1	1	1	1	1	0	1
Senegal	0	6	29	28	26	40	39	40	40	36	37	-1	7	35
Seychelles	..	9	-3	-2	-3	-6	-7	-5	-6	-6	-6	..	9	-5
Sierra Leone	0	0	0	0	0	0	0	0	0	0	0	1	1	0
Somalia	57	..	..	..	..	..	..	..	..	..	..	43	..	..
South Africa	94	114	-44	-7	3	-7	-12	-17	-23	3	10	79	91	-10
Sudan	257	243	134	124	138	81	68	60	321	429	490	267	330	205
Swaziland	0	2	4	9	4	27	40	37	32	21	50	1	3	25
Tanzania	22	467	196	173	194	197	465	18	20	26	30	26	364	147
Togo	1	9	10	14	9	10	9	11	14	12	13	-1	8	11
Uganda	-2	114	78	81	136	129	304	330	421	322	521	7	95	258
Zambia	-176	-28	-43	-40	-33	-19	-19	-20	-17	-16	-17	-86	-34	-25
Zimbabwe	..	..	..	..	..	..	..	..	..	..	..	..	..	..
NORTH AFRICA	..	..	..	..	..	..	..	..	..	..	..	..	..	..
Algeria	..	..	..	..	..	..	..	..	..	..	..	..	..	..
Egypt, Arab Republic	2,791	3,323	3,748	3,723	5,466	3,835	3,232	3,279	2,798	3,256	3,478	2,091	3,191	3,646
Libya	-1,089	-472	-446	..	..	..	..	..	..	..	..	-1,075	-571	-446
Morocco	1,070	1,461	2,146	2,152	..	..	..	..	..	..	..	812	1,419	2,149
Tunisia	348	503	613	563	570	597	688	753	820	790	863	255	435	695
ALL AFRICA	3,387	6,201	6,929	7,482	8,338	6,614	6,468	6,741	6,781	8,258	9,180	3,369	5,788	7,421

Note: 1998 data are preliminary (see page 3). Nigeria's series shows a data break between 1991 and 1992.

5-6. Net official current transfers

	Millions of U.S. dollars (current prices)										Annual average		
	1980	*1989*	*1990*	*1991*	*1992*	*1993*	*1994*	*1995*	*1996*	*1997*	*1998*	*75-84*	*85-89*	*90-MR*
SUB-SAHARAN AFRICA	..	2,448	2,759	2,122	2,195	1,686	1,890	1,546	1,532	1,084	1,045	..	1,894	1,762
excluding South Africa	..	2,376	2,655	2,627	2,564	2,320	2,486	2,174	2,255	1,809	1,793	..	1,861	2,298
excl. S.Africa & Nigeria	..	2,248	2,607	2,605	2,572	2,266	2,535	2,240	2,324	1,835	1,752	..	1,847	2,304
Angola	..	64	45	40	77	171	249	190	213	68	80	..	67	126
Benin	0	58	74	56	73	64	39	36	48	28	19	0	12	49
Botswana	65	244	171	218	135	142	160	-131	113	129	129	31	135	118
Burkina Faso	0	0	158	128	79	108	127	133	121	89	106	0	0	117
Burundi	42	88	105	120	102	111	126	112	30	39	39	45	65	87
Cameroon	64	102	28	118	248	76	61	80	28	0	25	40	115	74
Cape Verde	0	29	31	35	60	37	42	52	50	50	44	0	10	44
Central African Republic	0	..	..	..	50	50	32	33	8	6	22	0	0	29
Chad	0	89	105	102	109	49	97	86	75	43	50	0	95	79
Comoros	11	44	36	33	24	38	21	24	21	11	11	20	38	24
Congo, Democratic Rep. of	267	69	54	25	8	7	99	153	112	68	..	137	113	66
Congo, Republic of	0	14	10	5	0	0	19	21	8	2	6	0	3	8
Côte d'Ivoire	-1	197	226	74	-20	46	-31	-27	-28	-23	-19	23	92	22
Djibouti	..	..	..	34	26	49	42	50	48	41	..	..	..	41
Equatorial Guinea	..	5	8	2	1	1	2	4	2	1	..	0	6	3
Eritrea	..	..	..	..	43	17	44	22	27	15	4	..	..	25
Ethiopia	60	50	49	26	57	108	87	148	133	1	32	40	57	71
Gabon	..	9	21	14	6	14	15	0	0	0	17	..	16	10
Gambia, The	..	..	..	..	..	0	0	0	0	0	3	..	..	0
Ghana	..	..	..	..	..	..	..	..	..	..	..	..	..	..
Guinea	0	0	0	0	0	0	0	0	0	0	0	0	0	0
Guinea-Bissau	..	24	40	25	29	21	26	30	30	38	9	..	24	28
Kenya	0	0	0	0	0	0	0	0	0	0	0	0	0	0
Lesotho	-90	-159	-161	-45	-33	-39	139	242	225	225	165	-174	-166	80
Liberia	36	..	..	..	..	..	..	..	..	..	..	57	78	..
Madagascar	0	131	161	113	54	70	44	17	33	80	16	37	106	65
Malawi	..	..	..	..	..	..	..	..	0	0	0	..	..	0
Mali	-6	97	124	179	214	132	143	97	106	55	50	2	98	122
Mauritania	118	264	72	65	86	102	56	46	125	110	89	119	112	83
Mauritius	0	17	14	17	14	6	7	14	11	38	0	3	19	13
Mozambique	..	..	..	..	..	..	..	..	..	..	..	..	..	..
Namibia	101	253	249	275	338	240	219	286	311	322	267	360	294	279
Niger	154	11	25	18	34	61	0	0	0	0	0	127	104	15
Nigeria	-167	128	48	22	-9	54	-49	-66	-68	-26	41	-44	8	-6
Rwanda	104	12	138	162	92	78	347	231	196	176	173	92	74	177
São Tomé and Principe	0	7	12	9	3	2	3	5	2	10	9	0	6	6
Senegal	28	10	3	3	8	-26	95	70	18	5	19	-10	-4	22
Seychelles	..	..	21	19	20	22	15	13	22	21	21	..	..	19
Sierra Leone	26	8	21	21	20	10	25	33	64	17	80	21	13	32
Somalia	143	357	265	..	..	..	..	..	..	..	..	111	291	265
South Africa	145	72	104	-505	-369	-634	-596	-628	-723	-725	-748	96	55	-536
Sudan	84	321	274	237	177	77	55	44	41	23	17	124	335	105
Swaziland	79	92	98	100	124	128	116	102	110	128	79	46	60	109
Tanzania	0	0	264	235	262	266	0	0	0	0	0	0	0	114
Togo	86	59	77	68	56	28	16	26	24	21	22	55	56	37
Uganda	0	0	0	0	0	0	0	0	0	0	0	6	0	0
Zambia	..	..	..	..	..	..	..	..	..	..	..	..	..	..
Zimbabwe	0	0	0	0	0	0	0	0	0	0	0	0	0	0
NORTH AFRICA	..	..	1,109	..	..	..	..	..	..	..	..	..	..	1,109
Algeria	0	0	0	0	0	0	0	0	0	0	0	0	0	0
Egypt, Arab Republic	..	668	970	1,349	1,123	1,902	814	919	724	890	908	..	614	1,066
Libya	-46	-16	-35	..	..	..	..	..	..	..	..	-85	-39	-35
Morocco	144	142	174	118	77	30	55	70	32	48	49	90	95	72
Tunisia	42	0	0	0	0	0	0	0	0	0	0	36	7	0
ALL AFRICA	..	3,242	3,868	3,588	3,395	3,618	2,758	2,535	2,289	2,022	2,002	..	2,740	2,897

Note: 1998 data are preliminary (see page 3).

5-7. Current account balance, excluding net capital grants

	Millions of U.S. dollars (current prices)											Annual average		
	1980	*1989*	*1990*	*1991*	*1992*	*1993*	*1994*	*1995*	*1996*	*1997*	*1998*	*75-84*	*85-89*	*90-MR*
SUB-SAHARAN AFRICA	-673	-7,635	-7,374	-10,435	-12,928	-13,287	-10,922	-13,869	-8,746	-11,770	-18,025	-8,535	-7,311	-11,928
excluding South Africa	-4,182	-9,199	-9,439	-12,696	-14,875	-14,776	-11,016	-11,665	-6,855	-9,507	-15,921	-8,194	-9,608	-11,861
excl. S.Africa & Nigeria	-8,492	-8,949	-10,966	-11,716	-13,577	-12,619	-9,398	-10,768	-10,808	-11,385	-12,893	-6,427	-7,768	-11,570
Angola	..	-141	-236	-651	-874	-848	-563	-993	-331	-866	-1,589	..	-49	-772
Benin	-197	-27	-40	-52	-97	-95	-40	-128	-101	-110	-113	-174	-75	-86
Botswana	-152	492	42	337	244	503	239	338	663	626	584	-101	301	397
Burkina Faso	-259	-215	-101	-188	-186	-163	-34	-133	-251	-242	-251	-203	-227	-172
Burundi	-86	-68	-126	-95	-117	-79	-37	-29	-59	-3	-45	-98	-90	-66
Cameroon	-495	-22	-197	-50	-216	-620	-324	-62	-217	-121	-218	-389	-356	-225
Cape Verde	-25	-17	-5	-5	-13	-27	-47	-61	-34	-27	-30	-38	-30	-28
Central African Republic	-43	-123	-189	-111	-173	-108	-48	-81	-63	-73	-102	-31	-96	-105
Chad	-16	-184	-178	-143	-162	-219	-150	-188	-242	-283	-210	-80	-150	-197
Comoros	-9	6	-22	-12	-35	-7	-22	-24	-20	-24	-25	-14	-9	-21
Congo, Democratic Rep. of	-88	-863	-738	-1,037	-866	-528	-530	-465	-348	-658	-583	-366	-514	-639
Congo, Republic of	-167	-100	-261	-508	-315	-541	-670	-569	-1,308	-296	-507	-258	-230	-553
Côte d'Ivoire	..	-1,211	-1,321	-1,257	-1,353	-1,235	-131	-668	-588	-529	-517	-411	-1,211	-844
Djibouti	..	..	..	-77	-130	-71	-65	-28	-30	-32	..	..	..	-62
Equatorial Guinea	..	-40	-49	-81	-47	-45	-76	-99	-270	-221	..	-15	-35	-111
Eritrea	..	..	..	..	-19	46	62	-31	-104	-21	-216	..	..	-41
Ethiopia	-126	-294	-244	-528	-335	-497	-291	-90	-461	-456	-520	-176	-376	-380
Gabon	514	-168	150	91	-226	-58	336	159	317	237	-3	157	-490	111
Gambia, The	-86	-22	-41	-46	-51	-54	-48	-62	-65	-43	-46	-47	-33	-51
Ghana	-54	-315	-432	-454	-592	-815	-456	-414	-534	-763	-492	-154	-254	-550
Guinea	-26	-216	-257	-248	-367	-341	-311	-418	-339	-246	-259	-62	-202	-310
Guinea-Bissau	..	-67	-42	-62	-86	-50	-29	-45	-44	-25	-30	..	-49	-46
Kenya	-1,233	-676	-655	-309	-290	88	14	-475	-140	-441	-515	-493	-572	-303
Lesotho	-207	-355	-363	-354	-418	-372	-212	-283	-276	-269	-235	-222	-270	-309
Liberia	46	..	..	..	..	..	..	..	..	..	..	15	-15	..
Madagascar	-635	-75	-238	-216	-222	-263	-280	-307	-249	-198	-281	-264	-142	-250
Malawi	-310	-213	-145	-250	-371	-342	-271	-177	-273	-318	-289	-163	-110	-271
Mali	-232	-179	-191	-150	-216	-185	-146	-228	-265	-184	-209	-168	-216	-197
Mauritania	-133	118	-152	-105	-125	-114	-117	-143	-144	-99	-128	-133	-111	-125
Mauritius	-139	-102	-111	-17	-6	-103	-229	-18	38	-115	-58	-81	-6	-69
Mozambique	-423	-763	-766	-738	-738	-825	-864	-677	-647	-612	-799	-489	-635	-741
Namibia	-40	139	23	135	87	130	133	154	98	194	299	20	112	139
Niger	-429	32	-236	-169	-61	-60	-234	-208	-183	-187	-195	-247	-74	-170
Nigeria	4,310	-249	1,527	-980	-1,298	-2,158	-1,618	-897	3,953	1,878	-3,028	-1,767	-1,841	-291
Rwanda	-48	-259	-86	-33	-157	-218	-53	-15	-70	-144	-173	-24	-157	-105
São Tomé and Principe	1	-27	-27	-30	-31	-33	-28	-37	-34	-23	-12	-6	-20	-28
Senegal	-524	-448	-438	-455	-546	-578	-251	-298	-336	-322	-327	-392	-488	-394
Seychelles	-23	2	-11	-8	-8	-42	-21	-44	-55	-68	-63	-17	7	-36
Sierra Leone	-124	-81	-15	24	12	0	-60	-87	-108	-18	2	-100	-56	-28
Somalia	-136	-153	-81	..	..	..	..	..	..	..	..	-117	-121	-81
South Africa	3,508	1,564	2,065	2,261	1,947	1,489	94	-2,204	-1,891	-2,263	-2,104	-341	2,297	-67
Sudan	-721	-897	-1,299	-1,538	-1,354	-1,426	-1,459	-1,479	-1,548	-1,639	-1,996	-555	-603	-1,526
Swaziland	-130	77	85	80	1	-64	34	30	-30	-49	14	-61	42	11
Tanzania	-540	-740	-767	-818	-1,068	-1,115	-1,076	-1,047	-942	-842	-1,120	-558	-586	-977
Togo	-95	-95	-137	-79	-119	-84	-64	-63	-112	-88	-89	-101	-90	-93
Uganda	-121	-361	-429	-449	-338	-381	-265	-444	-500	-521	-692	-57	-221	-447
Zambia	-538	-222	-388	-513	-753	-472	-398	-464	-426	-438	-513	-377	-306	-485
Zimbabwe	-444	-78	-257	-547	-842	-311	-318	-370	-180	-827	-343	-353	-46	-444
NORTH AFRICA	6,368	-5,815	2,961	-2,229	1,595	549	-3,003	-3,322	1,710	5,574	-1,192	-3,538	-5,292	294
Algeria	242	-1,030	1,352	2,223	1,020	802	-1,820	-2,240	1,250	3,460	1,699	-1,008	-1,123	861
Egypt, Arab Republic	-438	-2,674	252	-3,474	2,244	1,571	196	1,267	1,402	2,906	-2,198	-1,765	-3,226	463
Libya	8,259	-1,010	2,236	..	..	..	..	..	..	..	..	1,034	-408	2,236
Morocco	-1,323	-789	-200	-400	-580	-542	-726	-1,520	-418	-123	-201	-1,291	-220	-523
Tunisia	-373	-312	-679	-577	-1,089	-1,283	-654	-830	-524	-669	-492	-508	-314	-755
ALL AFRICA	5,694	-13,450	-4,413	-12,664	-11,333	-12,739	-13,925	-17,191	-7,037	-6,196	-19,216	-12,074	-12,603	-11,635

Note: 1998 data are preliminary (see page 3).

5-8. Current account balance, excluding net capital grants/GDP

	Percentage											Annual average		
	1980	*1989*	*1990*	*1991*	*1992*	*1993*	*1994*	*1995*	*1996*	*1997*	*1998*	*75-84*	*85-89*	*90-MR*
SUB-SAHARAN AFRICA	0.1	-2.9	-2.5	-3.5	-4.3	-4.7	-3.9	-4.4	-2.7	-3.4	-5.5	-4.4	-3.0	-3.9
excluding South Africa	-2.4	-5.4	-5.2	-7.1	-8.7	-9.5	-7.7	-7.1	-3.7	-4.9	-8.1	-6.6	-6.3	-6.9
excl. S. Africa & Nigeria	-9.9	-6.0	-7.1	-7.7	-9.8	-9.4	-7.9	-7.9	-7.3	-7.4	-8.3	-8.4	-6.0	-8.1
Angola	..	-1.5	-2.3	-5.3	-15.1	-16.0	-13.9	-19.6	-4.3	-11.6	-23.9	..	-0.6	-12.5
Benin	-14.0	-1.8	-2.2	-2.8	-6.0	-4.5	-2.6	-6.4	-4.6	-5.2	-4.9	-16.6	-5.2	-4.3
Botswana	-13.7	15.8	1.2	8.1	5.9	11.1	5.2	6.8	12.0	11.7	10.3	-10.9	13.6	8.0
Burkina Faso	-15.2	-9.1	-3.7	-6.8	-9.3	-7.9	-1.8	-5.7	-9.9	-10.2	-9.7	-15.6	-11.4	-7.2
Burundi	-9.3	-6.1	-11.1	-8.2	-10.8	-8.1	-4.0	-2.9	-6.6	-0.3	-4.8	-9.8	-8.0	-6.3
Cameroon	-7.3	-0.2	-1.8	-0.4	-1.9	-5.2	-4.1	-0.8	-2.4	-1.3	-2.5	-7.5	-3.2	-2.3
Cape Verde	..	-6.4	-1.5	-1.6	-3.5	-8.2	-13.4	-14.5	-7.9	-6.4	-6.6	..	-9.2	-7.1
Central African Republic	-5.4	-9.7	-12.7	-7.9	-12.1	-8.3	-5.6	-7.2	-5.9	-7.3	-9.6	-4.3	-8.2	-8.5
Chad	-1.5	-13.7	-11.1	-8.0	-9.1	-15.8	-12.7	-13.0	-14.8	-17.7	-12.1	-8.6	-13.0	-12.7
Comoros	-7.2	2.8	-8.7	-5.0	-13.3	-2.5	-11.7	-11.1	-9.2	-12.1	-12.8	-13.0	-6.0	-9.6
Congo, Democratic Rep. of	..	-9.6	-7.9	-11.4	-10.6	-5.9	-7.4	-7.3	-5.9	-10.8	-8.4	-1.8	-6.2	-8.4
Congo, Republic of	-9.8	-4.2	-9.3	-18.7	-10.7	-28.2	-37.8	-26.9	-51.8	-12.9	-25.8	-21.5	-11.1	-24.7
Côte d'Ivoire	..	-12.4	-12.2	-12.0	-12.1	-11.9	-1.7	-6.7	-5.5	-5.2	-4.7	-7.1	-12.4	-8.0
Djibouti	..	..	..	-16.8	-27.6	-15.1	-13.2	-5.7	-6.1	-6.4	..	..	..	-13.0
Equatorial Guinea	..	-36.0	-37.1	-61.8	-30.6	-29.7	-60.6	-60.2	-104.4	-44.3	..	..	-30.6	-53.6
Eritrea	..	..	..	..	-4.4	11.2	12.1	-5.4	-16.4	-3.2	-33.3	..	..	-5.6
Ethiopia	..	-3.7	-3.6	-9.9	-6.0	-8.0	-5.9	-1.6	-7.7	-7.1	-8.0	-5.8	-5.1	-6.4
Gabon	12.0	-4.0	2.5	1.7	-4.0	-1.3	8.0	3.2	5.5	4.6	-0.1	4.2	-13.9	2.2
Gambia, The	-35.7	-7.7	-12.8	-14.4	-14.7	-14.6	-13.3	-16.3	-16.6	-10.6	-10.7	-22.5	-15.1	-13.8
Ghana	-1.2	-6.0	-7.3	-6.9	-9.2	-13.7	-8.4	-6.4	-7.7	-11.1	-6.6	-3.9	-5.0	-8.6
Guinea	..	-8.9	-9.1	-8.2	-11.2	-10.4	-9.1	-11.4	-8.6	-6.3	-7.2	..	-8.9	-9.0
Guinea-Bissau	..	-31.3	-17.2	-24.2	-37.8	-21.0	-12.4	-17.6	-16.4	-9.3	-14.8	..	-26.4	-19.0
Kenya	-17.0	-8.1	-7.7	-3.8	-3.6	1.8	0.2	-5.3	-1.5	-4.2	-4.5	-8.4	-7.4	-3.2
Lesotho	-56.1	-69.3	-58.3	-60.5	-63.2	-53.0	-27.9	-33.3	-32.1	-28.3	-29.7	-78.2	-69.0	-42.9
Liberia	4.1	..	..	..	..	..	..	..	..	..	..	1.9	-1.2	..
Madagascar	-15.7	-3.0	-7.7	-8.1	-7.4	-7.8	-9.4	-9.7	-6.2	-5.6	-7.5	-7.6	-5.3	-7.7
Malawi	-25.0	-14.0	-8.0	-11.3	-20.6	-16.5	-23.1	-12.1	-12.0	-12.6	-17.1	-15.6	-8.4	-14.8
Mali	-13.0	-8.9	-7.9	-6.2	-7.6	-6.9	-7.8	-9.2	-10.0	-7.3	-7.8	-12.9	-12.6	-7.9
Mauritania	-16.4	10.9	-13.4	-9.3	-10.5	-12.1	-11.4	-13.4	-13.1	-9.0	-12.9	-17.4	-12.2	-11.7
Mauritius	-12.3	-4.7	-4.2	-0.6	-0.2	-3.2	-6.5	-0.4	0.9	-2.8	-1.4	-7.6	0.0	-2.0
Mozambique	-12.0	-33.0	-30.5	-29.6	-37.8	-39.2	-38.1	-28.3	-22.8	-17.8	-20.5	-14.2	-23.1	-29.4
Namibia	-1.8	6.2	0.9	5.2	3.0	4.8	4.3	4.6	3.1	5.9	9.6	1.2	6.6	4.6
Niger	-17.1	1.4	-9.5	-7.3	-2.6	-3.7	-14.9	-11.1	-9.2	-10.1	-9.5	-13.6	-5.2	-8.7
Nigeria	6.7	-1.0	5.4	-3.6	-0.4	-10.1	-6.8	-3.2	11.2	4.7	-7.3	-4.5	-8.5	-1.5
Rwanda	-4.1	-10.8	-3.3	-1.7	-7.7	-11.0	-7.1	-1.1	-5.1	-7.7	-8.3	-1.6	-7.0	-5.9
São Tomé and Principe	2.3	-59.1	-53.4	-53.3	-67.9	-70.2	-57.3	-80.2	-75.3	-53.3	-29.9	-18.5	-41.8	-60.1
Senegal	-17.5	-9.7	-7.7	-8.3	-9.1	-10.6	-6.9	-6.6	-7.0	-7.1	-6.8	-16.1	-12.4	-7.8
Seychelles	-15.9	0.6	-2.9	-2.1	-1.7	-9.0	-4.4	-8.7	-10.8	-12.7	-11.7	-15.8	3.4	-7.1
Sierra Leone	-10.3	-6.9	-1.7	2.9	1.7	0.0	-6.5	-10.1	-11.4	-2.2	0.2	-7.8	-5.0	-3.0
Somalia	-22.6	-14.0	-8.8	..	..	..	..	..	..	..	..	-17.3	-12.2	-8.8
South Africa	4.4	1.6	1.8	1.9	1.5	1.1	0.1	-1.5	-1.3	-1.5	-1.6	-0.5	3.2	0.1
Sudan	-9.5	-5.7	-9.9	-13.5	-21.1	-18.1	-17.9	-20.6	-21.5	-16.3	-19.3	-7.0	-3.8	-17.6
Swaziland	-22.3	10.6	9.8	9.1	0.1	-6.4	3.2	2.4	-2.5	-3.7	1.2	-11.0	5.4	1.5
Tanzania	..	-15.5	-18.2	-17.2	-21.8	-24.5	-25.5	-21.1	-16.1	-11.9	-14.1	..	-14.3	-18.9
Togo	-8.4	-7.0	-8.4	-4.9	-7.0	-6.8	-6.5	-4.8	-7.6	-5.8	-5.9	-12.2	-7.8	-6.4
Uganda	-9.7	-6.9	-10.0	-13.5	-11.8	-11.8	-6.6	-7.7	-8.3	-8.3	-10.2	-6.1	-4.0	-9.8
Zambia	-13.8	-5.6	-11.8	-15.2	-23.7	-14.4	-11.9	-13.4	-13.0	-11.1	-15.2	-11.9	-13.0	-14.4
Zimbabwe	-6.6	-0.9	-2.9	-6.3	-12.5	-4.7	-4.6	-5.2	-2.1	-9.9	-5.8	-5.0	-0.8	-6.0
NORTH AFRICA	5.0	-3.9	0.5	-1.8	1.2	0.4	-2.1	-2.2	1.0	3.2	-0.7	-3.9	-3.6	-0.1
Algeria	0.6	-1.9	2.2	4.8	2.1	1.6	-4.3	-5.4	2.7	7.4	3.4	-4.5	-1.9	1.6
Egypt, Arab Republic	-1.9	-6.7	0.6	-9.4	5.4	3.3	0.4	2.1	2.1	3.8	-2.8	-9.6	-8.7	0.6
Libya	23.2	-4.6	..	..	..	..	..	..	..	..	..	4.8	-2.2	..
Morocco	-7.0	-3.5	-0.8	-1.4	-2.0	-2.0	-2.4	-4.6	-1.1	-0.4	..	-9.8	-1.5	-1.8
Tunisia	-4.3	-3.1	-5.5	-4.4	-7.0	-8.7	-4.2	-4.6	-2.7	-3.5	-2.2	-7.4	-3.5	-4.8
ALL AFRICA	1.9	-3.2	-1.5	-3.0	-2.6	-3.0	-3.3	-3.7	-1.4	-1.2	-4.0	-4.2	-3.3	-2.6

Note: 1998 data are preliminary (see page 3). Since 1994, Nigeria's ratios are distorted because the official exchange rate used by the Government for oil exports and oil value added is significantly over-valued.

5-9. Net capital grants

	Millions of U.S. dollars (current prices)											Annual average		
	1980	*1989*	*1990*	*1991*	*1992*	*1993*	*1994*	*1995*	*1996*	*1997*	*1998*	*75-84*	*85-89*	*90-MR*
SUB-SAHARAN AFRICA	1,150	3,453	3,578	4,042	5,076	4,367	3,940	4,120	3,755	3,468	3,724	1,059	2,684	4,008
excluding South Africa	1,150	3,438	3,566	4,078	5,118	4,425	3,874	4,160	3,802	3,662	3,780	1,074	2,680	4,052
excl. S.Africa & Nigeria	1,150	3,438	3,566	4,078	5,118	4,425	3,874	4,160	3,802	3,662	3,780	1,074	2,680	4,052
Angola	0	0	0	0	0	0	0	0	0	0	0	0	0	0
Benin	63	108	59	45	59	63	54	70	56	84	53	63	63	60
Botswana	8	6	3	4	7	9	6	3	-5	45	45	6	4	13
Burkina Faso	211	223	68	98	142	98	64	103	159	139	144	151	193	113
Burundi	34	44	59	66	63	·53	18	24	20	12	12	38	37	36
Cameroon	0	0	0	0	0	0	0	0	0	0	0	0	0	0
Cape Verde	29	0	1	4	8	17	18	17	8	11	16	20	28	11
Central African Republic	0	0	0	0	0	0	0	0	0	0	0	0	0	0
Chad	28	138	88	77	76	95	87	96	91	89	100	76	107	89
Comoros	0	0	14	11	21	14	0	0	6	12	13	0	0	10
Congo, Democratic Rep. of	0	207	163	76	24	19	41	204	110	1	..	0	108	80
Congo, Republic of	0	0	0	0	0	0	0	0	0	0	0	0	0	0
Côte d'Ivoire	..	0	0	53	57	95	53	70	79	69	68	..	0	61
Djibouti	0	0	0	56	58	42	24	10	9	13	..	0	0	26
Equatorial Guinea	..	22	35	35	26	29	5	3	2	3	..	7	20	17
Eritrea	..	..	..	..	125	52	36	49	53	26	35	..	..	54
Ethiopia	0	159	113	266	375	293	199	280	259	225	229	26	183	249
Gabon	0	0	0	0	0	0	0	0	0	0	0	0	0	0
Gambia, The	..	43	44	38	36	40	35	28	26	28	28	17	41	34
Ghana	83	219	214	202	216	256	201	260	206	160	231	69	144	216
Guinea	..	98	101	110	136	118	120	148	125	132	124	..	77	124
Guinea-Bissau	..	43	30	33	29	37	44	56	41	32	0	16	26	33
Kenya	118	195	205	204	214	94	87	90	125	82	83	84	174	132
Lesotho	..	53	69	58	50	42	40	44	45	43	20	6	25	46
Liberia	..	..	..	..	..	..	..	..	..	..	..	..	..	..
Madagascar	0	0	0	0	72	87	72	85	99	113	114	16	0	71
Malawi	50	75	81	59	147	120	111	152	97	83	157	33	50	112
Mali	116	109	106	138	144	106	99	126	136	109	119	61	109	120
Mauritania	0	25	21	22	21	20	26	27	10	11	39	0	42	22
Mauritius	11	18	25	15	19	2	1	13	13	13	13	5	18	13
Mozambique	56	388	448	502	499	503	565	339	225	313	313	90	293	412
Namibia	0	0	43	29	32	27	43	40	42	24	25	0	0	34
Niger	0	126	159	140	95	94	134	120	117	113	113	0	55	121
Nigeria	0	0	0	0	0	0	0	0	0	0	0	0	0	0
Rwanda	0	0	0	0	79	87	7	69	68	87	71	10	0	52
São Tomé and Principe	0	9	8	7	4	8	8	18	20	22	9	0	3	12
Senegal	92	250	262	262	328	266	256	272	273	251	207	138	226	264
Seychelles	15	32	21	19	20	22	15	13	22	21	20	10	23	19
Sierra Leone	11	4	0	0	0	0	0	0	3	0	2	5	5	1
Somalia	0	0	0	0	0	0	0	0	0	0	..	0	0	0
South Africa	0	15	12	-36	-42	-58	66	-40	-47	-194	-56	-16	4	-44
Sudan	0	0	0	0	20	29	15	11	8	4	0	4	0	10
Swaziland	-2	1	2	0	0	0	0	0	0	0	0	-1	0	0
Tanzania	108	517	530	549	809	759	634	525	581	690	669	165	378	638
Togo	..	47	37	24	26	4	7	8	7	13	15	24	34	16
Uganda	38	131	153	262	206	269	228	303	277	307	380	47	72	265
Zambia	23	72	296	521	636	384	338	318	304	198	240	13	91	359
Zimbabwe	58	79	108	95	242	173	181	167	85	85	77	50	68	135
NORTH AFRICA	141	206	970	695	81	133	157	132	142	119	127	529	618	284
Algeria	0	0	0	0	0	0	0	0	0	0	0	0	0	0
Egypt, Arab Republic	2	0	0	0	0	0	0	0	0	0	0	182	461	0
Libya	0	0	0	0	0	0	0	0	0	0	..	0	0	0
Morocco	98	0	760	573	0	30	55	62	72	0	0	139	81	172
Tunisia	42	206	210	122	81	104	103	70	70	119	127	27	75	112
ALL AFRICA	1,291	3,659	4,547	4,737	5,157	4,500	4,097	4,252	3,896	3,588	3,851	1,323	3,302	4,292

Note: 1998 data are preliminary (see page 3).

5-10. Net foreign direct investment

| | Millions of U.S. dollars (current prices) | | | | | | | | | | | Annual average | | |
	1980	1989	1990	1991	1992	1993	1994	1995	1996	1997	1998	75-84	85-89	90-MR
SUB-SAHARAN AFRICA	-729	3,556	756	1,696	-362	1,023	1,065	1,427	3,642	5,483	3,643	690	1,800	2,041
excluding South Africa	37	3,546	760	1,656	1,571	1,311	1,921	2,683	3,868	4,017	4,814	878	1,934	2,511
excl. S.Africa & Nigeria	776	1,103	158	1,068	857	730	1,333	2,006	3,109	2,871	3,462	796	1,077	1,733
Angola	..	200	-336	665	288	302	327	303	588	492	898	346	192	392
Benin	4	1	2	4	26	-7	8	4	-6	19	25	2	1	8
Botswana	109	42	89	-17	-12	-296	-24	30	89	50	50	46	64	-5
Burkina Faso	0	1	-11	22	9	9	24	20	16	11	-14	1	0	10
Burundi	1	1	1	1	1	0	0	1	0	0	0	1	1	0
Cameroon	105	436	110	147	206	134	105	101	93	111	105	58	322	123
Cape Verde	..	-1	0	1	-1	3	2	26	28	20	42	..	1	14
Central African Republic	5	1	1	-8	4	-15	-13	4	12	-8	-13	6	4	-4
Chad	0	15	25	5	3	21	14	10	15	16	16	11	21	14
Comoros	0	3	-1	3	-1	0	0	1	1	0	0	0	3	0
Congo, Democratic Rep. of	0	12	13	0	0	0	0	0	0	0	..	91	9	2
Congo, Republic of	40	0	-60	-65	49	254	285	297	823	224	102	24	18	212
Côte d'Ivoire	83	22	26	45	35	24	-25	234	223	314	247	51	53	125
Djibouti	..	..	..	2	2	1	1	3	3	2	..	..	..	2
Equatorial Guinea	..	1	12	43	-3	-10	65	94	264	216	..	0	1	85
Eritrea	..	..	..	..	0	0	0	0	37	38	30	..	..	15
Ethiopia	..	..	..	..	..	..	..	..	..	..	..	10	..	..
Gabon	24	85	80	-150	-87	-114	-100	-109	-146	-63	-60	59	219	-83
Gambia, The	..	7	6	10	11	9	6	6	8	9	8	..	5	8
Ghana	16	15	15	20	22	106	206	259	70	55	-11	13	7	83
Guinea	34	26	41	55	96	79	51	66	58	49	36	12	28	59
Guinea-Bissau	..	0	0	0	0	0	0	0	0	0	0	..	0	0
Kenya	78	52	23	19	6	2	4	33	13	40	40	25	27	20
Lesotho	5	13	17	8	3	15	19	32	26	18	193	2	9	37
Liberia	..	..	..	..	..	..	..	..	..	..	..	47	2	..
Madagascar	0	13	22	14	21	15	6	10	10	14	29	-1	3	16
Malawi	10	0	0	0	0	0	0	0	30	25	35	4	0	10
Mali	2	15	-14	-8	-9	-7	38	30	60	-14	-50	0	1	3
Mauritania	27	3	6	4	5	12	3	7	0	-3	0	1	2	4
Mauritius	1	36	35	14	-16	-18	10	27	18	30	25	2	19	14
Mozambique	0	3	9	23	25	32	35	45	73	64	213	0	3	58
Namibia	..	..	28	114	117	49	60	118	151	125	113	..	..	97
Niger	44	1	-12	0	0	0	0	0	0	0	0	17	-5	-1
Nigeria	-739	2,443	602	588	714	581	588	677	760	1,147	1,351	206	857	779
Rwanda	16	22	7	5	6	6	0	2	2	3	7	11	19	4
São Tomé and Principe	..	4	1	3	1	4	2	2	2	0	4	..	1	2
Senegal	61	-15	-13	-4	-53	-48	48	-10	-5	92	5	34	-25	1
Seychelles	6	15	9	8	-3	6	17	27	17	45	28	5	11	17
Sierra Leone	10	2	3	3	5	18	17	18	24	17	18	4	1	14
Somalia	..	..	..	..	..	..	..	..	..	..	..	-1	..	..
South Africa	-765	10	-5	40	-1,933	-288	-856	-1,256	-226	1,466	-1,171	-178	-134	-470
Sudan	..	..	..	..	..	..	..	0	70	180	670	..	..	230
Swaziland	18	52	23	58	50	44	-1	10	23	34	10	15	35	28
Tanzania	..	..	0	10	15	62	63	104	134	150	165	..	..	78
Togo	42	17	8	12	19	2	6	5	24	19	1	23	13	11
Uganda	0	13	6	1	2	4	5	2	110	160	190	1	22	53
Zambia	62	0	0	0	0	0	40	97	117	207	219	8	0	76
Zimbabwe	-26	-10	-12	3	15	32	30	98	35	110	88	-18	-5	44
NORTH AFRICA	65	560	563	648	1,352	1,586	2,281	1,308	1,397	2,697	2,700	145	321	1,615
Algeria	281	-25	-39	-34	3	-2	0	0	270	260	350	-2	-67	90
Egypt, Arab Republic	541	124	136	141	359	453	1,285	735	612	723	1,100	456	171	616
Libya	-1,136	90	54	..	..	..	..	..	..	..	..	-564	-33	54
Morocco	143	226	227	376	503	590	555	278	258	1,294	821	73	122	545
Tunisia	236	144	185	166	487	545	442	295	256	420	429	182	128	358
ALL AFRICA	-664	4,116	1,319	2,343	990	2,609	3,347	2,735	5,039	8,180	6,342	816	2,121	3,656

Note: 1998 data are preliminary (see page 3).

5-11. Net long-term borrowing

	Millions of U.S. dollars (current prices)											Annual average		
	1980	1989	1990	1991	1992	1993	1994	1995	1996	1997	1998	75-84	85-89	90-MR
SUB-SAHARAN AFRICA	7,742	6,720	5,139	4,362	3,872	5,003	4,354	3,880	-43	1,769	-1,192	5,954	5,678	3,016
excluding South Africa	7,742	6,720	5,139	4,362	3,872	5,003	2,831	2,402	435	1,278	-1,192	5,954	5,678	2,681
excl. S.Africa & Nigeria	6,231	5,739	5,392	4,437	5,216	5,038	2,979	2,888	1,545	1,803	594	4,938	5,475	3,321
Angola	..	458	679	95	503	624	264	219	-463	-401	-673	..	758	94
Benin	56	126	102	84	65	63	84	77	83	23	..	77	57	72
Botswana	21	34	-37	49	22	45	-10	1	-45	-52	..	28	37	-3
Burkina Faso	55	82	61	121	128	119	80	83	73	39	..	48	73	88
Burundi	35	85	69	60	86	58	31	27	23	7	65	37	85	47
Cameroon	500	664	449	220	520	264	249	-103	-41	-11	..	313	237	193
Cape Verde	3	7	8	-1	10	7	24	18	20	16	48	10	8	17
Central African Republic	24	56	105	94	41	48	36	30	25	4	..	17	68	48
Chad	3	78	100	88	139	52	61	56	89	68	118	21	41	86
Comoros	13	4	5	-3	15	4	6	9	6	4	..	11	14	6
Congo, Democratic Rep. of	271	353	267	263	54	53	1	0	3	0	..	281	239	80
Congo, Republic of	488	-15	-42	-167	33	383	30	-67	-136	-30	-279	222	141	-30
Côte d'Ivoire	1,017	340	521	389	351	278	524	204	64	-580	-10	636	141	193
Djibouti	8	3	18	46	36	19	17	9	15	7	1	8	17	19
Equatorial Guinea	18	19	9	7	13	9	4	2	0	1	..	8	17	6
Eritrea	..	..	..	..	..	..	27	7	7	33	40	..	..	23
Ethiopia	93	332	225	357	263	314	170	140	1	128	-149	425	448	161
Gabon	-109	131	170	68	8	58	38	57	-42	-23	85	52	207	46
Gambia, The	51	17	3	13	37	7	5	5	48	13	15	18	21	16
Ghana	143	243	293	388	353	324	302	338	493	336	251	69	243	342
Guinea	47	186	100	145	149	245	122	49	85	141	0	44	132	115
Guinea-Bissau	72	35	34	38	37	22	25	13	23	25	5	22	40	25
Kenya	424	548	317	545	179	103	-301	138	-66	-165	-111	250	335	71
Lesotho	10	40	43	47	59	50	44	44	33	34	179	15	32	59
Liberia	61	-1	-1	-13	0	20	-14	0	0	0	..	61	22	-1
Madagascar	329	113	144	150	77	89	51	66	93	216	..	170	153	111
Malawi	120	102	69	120	106	151	74	149	117	106	90	75	72	109
Mali	88	148	141	127	130	58	69	138	110	71	67	78	123	101
Mauritania	108	33	54	23	81	91	82	42	83	23	-17	100	77	51
Mauritius	79	50	102	77	-1	22	83	255	32	691	223	37	58	165
Mozambique	..	179	190	73	168	135	176	196	222	221	57	..	281	160
Namibia	..	..	..	..	..	..	..	..	..	..	5	..	..	5
Niger	223	91	92	-32	56	44	35	-3	8	54	..	107	105	32
Nigeria	1,510	981	-253	-76	-1,343	-35	-148	-486	-1,110	-525	-1,786	1,015	203	-640
Rwanda	25	51	53	77	71	50	20	43	53	62	195	27	71	69
São Tomé and Principe	9	15	15	19	24	14	14	14	10	1	5	6	11	13
Senegal	171	244	81	33	225	100	7	4	67	141	91	166	215	83
Seychelles	12	-5	-4	9	13	6	8	-7	2	2	5	7	7	4
Sierra Leone	50	12	17	14	41	95	47	40	34	34	6	25	14	36
Somalia	106	64	43	13	0	0	0	0	0	0	..	136	83	7
South Africa	..	..	..	..	..	..	1,524	1,478	-478	492	..	..	..	754
Sudan	658	191	171	116	94	91	9	36	17	5	..	495	164	67
Swaziland	21	-4	-21	-6	-10	-9	-4	3	8	8	195	22	0	18
Tanzania	318	123	215	162	220	151	164	136	65	171	174	290	184	162
Togo	78	36	56	47	35	11	34	19	77	27	..	88	30	38
Uganda	51	240	234	118	204	298	182	162	168	196	..	62	197	195
Zambia	391	100	64	127	146	148	57	93	62	76	42	210	175	90
Zimbabwe	93	131	177	239	437	325	55	144	20	82	-130	164	44	150
NORTH AFRICA	4,953	2,205	1,567	385	1,228	200	1,408	1,499	891	-799	2,591	5,087	3,328	997
Algeria	869	446	156	-692	474	-453	1,446	1,496	922	-436	3,831	1,435	808	749
Egypt, Arab Republic	2,337	656	301	299	-89	180	123	-382	-438	-161	..	2,162	1,483	-21
Libya	..	..	..	..	..	..	..	..	..	..	..	..	..	..
Morocco	1,394	916	965	427	491	196	-293	-180	-66	-894	-1,240	1,118	825	-66
Tunisia	352	187	145	352	352	277	131	565	473	691	..	373	212	373
ALL AFRICA	12,695	8,925	6,706	4,747	5,100	5,203	5,762	5,380	848	971	1,399	11,041	9,006	4,013

5-12. Other capital flows

	Millions of U.S. dollars (current prices)											Annual average		
	1980	1989	1990	1991	1992	1993	1994	1995	1996	1997	1998	75-84	85-89	90-MR
SUB-SAHARAN AFRICA	..	-2,126	1,563	2,957	1,767	2,528	2,445	3,116	7,852	2,050	..	245	524	3,035
excluding South Africa	..	-2,126	1,563	2,957	1,767	2,528	4,218	3,461	4,022	3,907	..	245	524	3,053
excl. S.Africa & Nigeria	..	-224	1,341	2,203	1,855	1,641	3,041	2,356	5,271	3,345	..	-1,210	-399	2,632
Angola	..	-523	-145	-108	198	-977	-64	-154	1,854	593	1,275	..	-862	275
Benin	54	-104	-12	33	38	6	-32	-41	26	1	..	22	-41	2
Botswana	104	3	211	1	143	137	-76	-158	-153	292	..	76	10	50
Burkina Faso	5	-133	-14	-10	-33	9	-17	71	-2	19	..	15	-26	3
Burundi	8	-12	-5	-5	-20	-32	36	-12	-41	-31	-41	-10	4	-17
Cameroon	51	-1,059	-306	-287	-441	513	281	54	247	163	..	57	-119	28
Cape Verde	..	-5	-6	0	5	-12	-16	14	-25	19	-61	..	-4	-9
Central African Republic	24	72	79	16	133	102	97	58	46	59	..	4	22	74
Chad	-19	-9	-32	-35	-90	19	38	84	43	84	12	-25	-10	14
Comoros	-8	-15	0	-3	1	3	12	10	16	..	..	-2	-5	6
Congo, Democratic Rep. of	-149	492	294	654	790	441	472	222	250	636	..	-81	218	470
Congo, Republic of	-302	120	362	694	206	-102	411	345	638	82	643	11	70	365
Côte d'Ivoire	..	831	625	820	675	926	373	380	261	808	155	..	831	558
Djibouti	..	..	..	-21	17	1	25	-1	4	-2	..	..	..	3
Equatorial Guinea	..	-4	-6	-1	4	16	3	8	9	2	..	14	-7	4
Eritrea	..	..	..	..	..	..	-46	-91	-68	-27	4	..	..	-46
Ethiopia	-7	-207	-141	58	-257	2	179	-78	284	-88	570	-305	-257	59
Gabon	-337	417	-348	57	84	35	-137	-148	-45	-112	-45	-259	245	-73
Gambia, The	..	-41	-22	-20	-34	3	-3	27	-4	1	2	..	-29	-5
Ghana	-284	-36	28	15	-124	169	-89	-232	-249	236	121	-22	-96	-14
Guinea	..	-73	66	-44	-10	-51	-15	168	44	-28	95	..	-42	25
Guinea-Bissau	..	-17	-7	-18	25	-18	-46	-25	-10	-7	24	..	-18	-9
Kenya	483	-59	-5	-549	-33	44	301	81	485	584	545	127	231	161
Lesotho	..	240	251	285	356	144	230	273	284	317	-150	111	205	221
Liberia	..	..	..	..	..	..	..	..	..	..	..	..	..	..
Madagascar	389	-17	-66	69	70	92	143	192	164	-121	..	72	31	68
Malawi	113	-4	23	82	25	78	57	-37	138	50	119	27	-11	59
Mali	36	38	43	72	40	56	27	1	87	16	6	34	22	39
Mauritania	-4	-315	39	85	16	16	-5	198	118	122	139	22	-44	81
Mauritius	74	35	-8	-68	4	106	91	-168	-54	-577	-33	14	-61	-79
Mozambique	..	190	125	154	85	108	141	156	286	128	278	..	75	162
Namibia	..	..	..	..	..	..	..	..	..	..	-389	..	..	-389
Niger	109	-266	19	65	-99	-73	59	91	42	-1	..	117	-121	13
Nigeria	-536	-1,903	222	755	-87	887	1,177	1,105	-1,250	562	3,461	109	922	759
Rwanda	-26	83	-33	17	-40	44	30	-65	-44	29	-77	-44	-23	-15
São Tomé and Principe	..	-1	3	1	2	7	4	8	1	4	-5	..	5	3
Senegal	65	64	172	180	66	149	180	114	56	-29	36	-3	77	103
Seychelles	-1	-40	-12	-18	-18	12	-25	11	11	6	3	-4	-45	-3
Sierra Leone	20	63	-3	-30	-37	-100	7	24	39	-29	-45	33	39	-19
Somalia	..	..	..	..	..	..	..	..	..	..	..	-8	..	..
South Africa	..	..	..	..	..	..	-1,773	-344	3,830	-1,857	..	..	..	-36
Sudan	..	..	..	..	..	..	..	322	276	175	..	..	..	258
Swaziland	127	-74	-77	-118	51	-35	-42	-13	15	32	-199	33	-59	-43
Tanzania	..	..	78	160	126	20	322	328	242	104	113	..	..	166
Togo	..	64	40	11	-46	-57	5	42	-8	63	..	55	34	6
Uganda	-23	-41	27	32	-73	-162	-60	124	18	-10	..	-78	-85	-13
Zambia	-100	315	140	-106	73	14	118	-42	-5	-12	-154	18	28	3
Zimbabwe	194	-195	-35	84	-23	-12	70	216	-3	-205	327	26	-9	47
NORTH AFRICA	-3,511	1,020	-3,865	5,639	1,763	1,986	2,621	-37	-947	-934	..	-2,520	448	778
Algeria	-50	-33	-1,554	-970	-1,430	-396	863	214	-322	546	-4,917	-385	145	-885
Egypt, Arab Republic	-2,611	1,461	-2,411	6,794	2,557	1,818	502	-867	-1,006	-1,556	..	-1,455	949	729
Libya	..	..	..	..	..	..	..	..	..	..	..	..	..	..
Morocco	-658	-280	45	-22	386	168	923	613	202	278	931	-396	-603	391
Tunisia	-192	-128	56	-164	251	396	333	2	179	-202	..	-26	-44	106
ALL AFRICA	..	-1,107	-2,302	8,596	3,530	4,514	5,066	3,079	6,904	1,117	..	-1,898	971	3,813

Note: Includes all capital account flows, except changes in reserves, that are not included in the tables on foreign investment or long-term borrowing.

5-13. Use of reserves

	Millions of U.S. dollars (current prices)											Annual average		
	1980	1989	1990	1991	1992	1993	1994	1995	1996	1997	1998	75-84	85-89	90-MR
SUB-SAHARAN AFRICA	-4,661	-2,963	-4,200	-12	1,796	-2,401	-2,171	1,613	-6,191	-734	-144	1,271	-1,272	-1,383
excluding South Africa	-3,846	-3,049	-2,784	-1,511	1,597	328	-3,116	-753	-5,003	-3,090	583	1,083	-1,296	-1,528
excl. S.Africa & Nigeria	699	-1,777	-686	-1,224	-418	-397	-3,117	-354	-2,650	-29	582	647	-1,155	-921
Angola	0	6	37	0	-115	900	35	624	-1,649	183	89	33	-40	12
Benin	19	-103	-110	-113	-92	-30	-75	18	-58	-16	-34	10	-5	-57
Botswana	-91	-577	-307	-374	-405	-397	-135	-213	-548	-960	-559	-55	-416	-433
Burkina Faso	-11	41	-2	-43	-61	-72	-117	-143	4	35	33	-13	-14	-41
Burundi	8	-50	2	-26	-13	0	-48	-12	58	16	9	10	-37	-2
Cameroon	-162	-20	-58	-29	-70	-291	-311	10	-81	-143	39	-38	-85	-104
Cape Verde	0	16	1	1	-9	12	18	-14	2	-39	-15	-1	-3	-5
Central African Republic	-11	-7	4	10	-4	-27	-72	-11	-20	18	41	-4	3	-7
Chad	5	-37	-3	8	34	32	-50	-59	4	27	-35	-3	-9	-5
Comoros	4	2	3	4	0	-14	4	4	-9	..	..	0	-3	-1
Congo, Democratic Rep. of	-35	-202	1	43	-1	14	17	39	-15	21	..	76	-60	15
Congo, Republic of	-59	-6	0	45	27	5	-56	-6	-17	20	40	1	2	6
Côte d'Ivoire	112	18	150	-50	235	-88	-794	-222	-39	-82	56	92	-75	-93
Djibouti	..	..	..	-6	17	8	-4	7	-1	12	..	..	..	5
Equatorial Guinea	13	3	-2	-4	8	2	-1	-8	-4	-3	..	2	3	-1
Eritrea	..	..	..	..	-91	-109	-78	66	75	-50	108	..	..	-11
Ethiopia	40	10	46	-154	-46	-112	-256	-253	-83	191	-129	27	2	-88
Gabon	-93	-466	-51	-67	222	79	-137	42	-83	-39	23	-9	-180	-1
Gambia, The	..	-4	8	5	1	-6	5	-4	-13	-7	-8	5	-4	-2
Ghana	96	-127	-118	-171	124	-41	-164	-212	14	-25	-99	25	-44	-77
Guinea	-30	-22	-51	-18	-3	-49	34	-13	27	-47	4	-2	-8	-13
Guinea-Bissau	0	6	-15	9	-5	9	6	1	-9	-25	1	5	-6	-3
Kenya	131	-60	115	91	-76	-331	-104	133	-417	-100	-42	7	-194	-81
Lesotho	-41	8	-17	-42	-50	120	-121	-108	-112	-143	-6	-8	-1	-53
Liberia	41	-10	-1	..	0	-1	-3	..	..	..	..	27	-3	-1
Madagascar	-83	-33	137	-17	-17	-20	8	-46	-118	-24	115	6	-44	2
Malawi	17	40	-29	-11	94	-7	29	-87	-109	53	-111	16	-1	-20
Mali	-9	-130	-84	-178	-89	-28	-87	-68	-128	3	67	-6	-38	-66
Mauritania	2	135	32	-28	3	-26	11	-131	-67	-53	-32	9	32	-32
Mauritius	-25	-38	-42	-22	0	-8	43	-109	-48	-43	-170	24	-28	-44
Mozambique	32	3	-6	-13	-40	46	-52	-60	-159	-115	-62	46	-17	-51
Namibia	..	..	-37	12	7	-91	-75	-24	-23	-68	-54	..	..	-39
Niger	53	16	-22	-4	10	-6	5	0	16	21	16	6	5	4
Nigeria	-4,545	-1,272	-2,098	-287	2,015	725	1	-399	-2,353	-3,061	1	436	-142	-606
Rwanda	33	105	58	-66	41	31	-4	-34	-9	-37	-23	19	91	-5
São Tomé and Principe	12	1	0	0	0	0	0	-5	0	-4	-2	0	0	-1
Senegal	135	-95	-66	-16	-20	112	-240	-82	-55	-132	-11	56	-5	-57
Seychelles	-8	-4	-3	-10	-4	-3	6	1	4	-5	8	-1	-1	-1
Sierra Leone	32	1	-1	-10	-21	-13	-11	6	8	-5	18	19	-4	-3
Somalia	18	-24	-51	..	..	..	..	..	..	..	..	5	-12	-51
South Africa	-815	86	-1,416	1,499	199	-2,729	945	2,366	-1,188	2,356	-726	188	25	145
Sudan	177	53	-52	-23	35	2	1	1,110	1,176	1,275	1,301	85	135	536
Swaziland	-34	-51	-11	-14	-92	64	13	-30	-15	-25	-20	-8	-17	-15
Tanzania	66	65	-57	-63	-102	123	-107	-46	-81	-272	-1	9	-2	-67
Togo	2	-68	-3	-15	86	125	11	-12	12	-35	19	-18	-21	21
Uganda	55	18	10	37	-2	-29	-90	-146	-73	-132	-134	25	-10	-62
Zambia	162	-265	-111	-29	-101	-75	-155	-2	-52	-32	161	152	12	-44
Zimbabwe	125	73	19	126	171	-207	-17	-255	43	755	-19	46	-52	68
NORTH AFRICA	-7,299	613	-1,064	-4,987	-6,539	-4,489	-3,464	420	-3,192	-6,658	-1,618	560	55	-3,510
Algeria	-1,341	642	85	-527	-67	48	-489	530	-2,120	-3,830	-963	-39	237	-815
Egypt, Arab Republic	168	433	1,723	-3,760	-5,070	-4,022	-2,106	-754	-570	-1,912	-107	421	161	-1,842
Libya	-6,407	-292	-1,158	150	-520	-35	..	..	..	..	..	73	-81	-391
Morocco	346	-74	-1,797	-953	-800	-441	-513	747	-48	-556	-311	126	-206	-519
Tunisia	-65	-97	83	103	-82	-39	-355	-103	-454	-360	-238	-20	-57	-161
ALL AFRICA	-11,959	-2,350	-5,264	-4,999	-4,743	-6,890	-5,635	2,034	-9,383	-7,392	-1,762	1,831	-1,217	-4,893

Note: Excludes IMF credit transactions, which appear in the table on long-term borrowing.

5-14. Import coverage ratio of reserves

| | Reserves in months of imports of goods and services | | | | | | | | | | | Annual average | | |
	1980	1989	1990	1991	1992	1993	1994	1995	1996	1997	1998	75-84	85-89	90-MR
SUB-SAHARAN AFRICA	4	6	6	6	7	8	8	7	8	9	9	3	5	8
excluding South Africa	5	7	7	8	9	10	10	9	9	12	12	3	6	9
excl. S.Africa & Nigeria	3	9	8	9	10	11	11	10	10	12	12	3	7	10
Angola	..	..	..	..	..	..	..	1	1	1	0	..	..	1
Benin	0	0	1	4	4	4	6	3	4	4	4	1	0	4
Botswana	4	18	16	19	20	24	25	23	26	27	27	4	15	23
Burkina Faso	2	5	5	5	5	6	6	6	5	6	6	2	5	6
Burundi	6	5	4	5	6	7	9	9	11	9	5	3	3	7
Cameroon	1	0	0	0	0	0	0	0	0	0	0	1	1	0
Cape Verde	6	6	6	5	5	4	2	2	2	2	1	6	7	3
Central African Republic	2	4	3	4	3	4	9	9	11	8	6	2	3	7
Chad	2	3	3	3	2	1	2	3	3	3	2	1	2	3
Comoros	2	5	4	4	3	5	6	5	6	6	6	2	3	5
Congo, Democratic Rep. of	2	1	1	1	1	0	1	1	0	..	..	1	2	1
Congo, Republic of	1	0	0	0	0	0	0	0	0	0	0	0	0	0
Côte d'Ivoire	0	0	0	0	0	0	1	1	1	2	2	0	0	1
Djibouti	..	..	..	..	3	2	3	3	3	3	..	..	..	3
Equatorial Guinea	..	0	0	1	2	0	0	0	0	0	..	0	0	0
Eritrea	..	..	..	..	..	..	..	..	..	..	..	..	..	..
Ethiopia	4	1	1	1	3	4	6	7	5	3	3	5	2	4
Gabon	1	0	1	2	0	0	1	1	1	1	0	1	1	1
Gambia, The	0	1	3	3	4	..	5	5	5	5	5	2	2	4
Ghana	3	4	2	4	3	3	4	4	4	..	2	3	5	3
Guinea	..	..	..	1	1	2	1	1	1	1	..	..	..	1
Guinea-Bissau	..	2	2	2	2	2	2	2	1	..	..	..	1	2
Kenya	2	1	1	1	0	2	3	1	3	2	2	2	2	2
Lesotho	1	1	1	2	2	3	5	5	5	6	7	1	1	4
Liberia	0	..	..	..	..	..	..	..	..	..	..	0	0	..
Madagascar	0	4	1	1	..	..	1	1	2	3	2	1	3	2
Malawi	1	2	3	3	1	1	1	2	4	2	4	1	2	2
Mali	1	2	3	5	4	5	3	4	5	5	5	1	1	4
Mauritania	4	2	1	1	1	1	1	2	2	4	4	3	1	2
Mauritius	2	4	5	6	5	4	4	4	4	3	3	2	3	4
Mozambique	..	2	3	3	3	2	2	2	3	5	5	1	2	3
Namibia	..	..	..	..	0	1	1	1	1	1	2	..	..	1
Niger	2	7	5	5	6	5	3	2	2	1	1	2	6	3
Nigeria	5	2	4	4	1	2	2	2	4	..	..	3	2	3
Rwanda	7	2	1	4	2	1	1	3	3	4	4	5	4	3
São Tomé and Principe	..	..	..	..	..	..	..	1	1	3	3	..	..	2
Senegal	0	0	0	0	0	0	1	2	2	3	3	0	0	1
Seychelles	2	1	1	1	1	1	1	1	1	1	1	1	1	1
Sierra Leone	1	0	0	1	1	2	2	1	1	3	2	1	1	1
Somalia	1	1	..	..	..	..	..	..	..	..	..	2	0	..
South Africa	3	1	1	2	2	2	2	2	1	2	2	2	2	2
Sudan	0	1	0	0	0	0	..	..	..	..	..	0	0	0
Swaziland	3	3	3	2	3	3	3	3	2	2	4	3	3	3
Tanzania	0	0	1	1	2	1	2	1	2	3	3	0	0	2
Togo	1	5	5	6	5	4	3	3	2	2	2	3	6	4
Uganda	0	0	1	1	2	2	4	4	4	4	5	1	1	3
Zambia	1	1	1	1	..	2	2	1	2	2	1	1	1	1
Zimbabwe	8	2	2	1	2	3	3	3	3	1	1	3	2	2
NORTH AFRICA	..	..	..	..	7	8	8	8	9	10	..	..	..	8
Algeria	6	3	3	4	3	4	4	3	5	9	..	4	4	4
Egypt, Arab Republic	3	2	4	4	9	10	10	11	11	12	..	2	2	9
Libya	..	..	..	..	..	..	..	..	..	..	..	..	..	..
Morocco	2	1	3	4	4	5	5	4	4	4	..	1	1	4
Tunisia	2	2	2	2	1	1	2	2	2	3	..	2	2	2
ALL AFRICA	4	5	5	5	7	8	8	8	8	9	..	3	4	7

Note: 1998 data are preliminary (see page 3).　Based on total reserves, excluding gold, at year-end and on imports of all goods and services at current prices and exchange rates.

5-15. Export unit values

	Index 1995=100											Average annual percentage growth		
	1980	1989	1990	1991	1992	1993	1994	1995	1996	1997	1998	75-84	85-89	90-MR
SUB-SAHARAN AFRICA	122.3	90.6	102.0	97.1	99.1	90.6	91.7	100.0	101.6	97.6	86.2	6.2	3.7	-0.3
excluding South Africa	125.3	90.2	104.7	97.5	100.5	89.1	89.3	100.0	106.9	101.6	87.5	4.3	3.0	0.0
excl. S. Africa & Nigeria	112.0	90.6	98.5	96.5	91.7	85.9	88.5	100.0	102.4	97.6	91.1	2.8	1.6	0.4
Angola	..	137.8	152.2	180.2	89.8	107.8	89.3	100.0	135.0	126.1	101.3	..	4.1	-3.2
Benin	44.2	57.1	83.0	76.3	53.5	65.3	71.0	100.0	87.6	81.6	83.2	5.9	5.7	3.7
Botswana	..	82.0	89.4	95.7	92.0	99.5	96.9	100.0	103.6	82.8	80.7	..	9.5	0.0
Burkina Faso	51.6	90.2	93.9	87.2	60.5	59.6	85.0	100.0	88.9	75.1	90.7	5.1	12.3	0.3
Burundi	149.5	121.0	93.7	100.7	69.7	77.5	98.9	100.0	76.8	72.2	47.1	6.3	-0.9	-6.1
Cameroon	130.4	78.4	83.9	96.6	86.4	89.8	86.1	100.0	101.3	100.7	92.3	4.8	-3.4	2.1
Cape Verde	..	76.3	86.1	89.0	96.6	85.7	86.6	100.0	97.2	119.0	98.0	..	..	3.1
Central African Republic	139.5	170.2	176.8	143.7	153.5	144.1	85.7	100.0	87.8	66.8	57.0	8.4	6.4	-11.9
Chad	92.3	67.9	91.9	91.2	88.2	77.1	74.7	100.0	94.9	84.0	90.3	-0.7	3.2	1.5
Comoros	138.0	127.8	152.3	137.4	146.8	122.8	96.9	100.0	88.1	60.9	65.1	..	12.8	-9.3
Congo, Democratic Rep. of	..	61.8	74.9	60.6	76.9	62.7	108.0	100.0	79.2	79.8	..	..	1.7	4.3
Congo, Republic of	142.5	95.4	115.0	117.4	112.9	76.0	91.6	100.0	121.0	112.1	73.1	9.7	-6.1	-1.6
Côte d'Ivoire	115.9	84.0	83.1	83.0	94.0	88.3	80.4	100.0	99.7	90.8	91.8	-1.1	-1.1	1.5
Djibouti	..	..	..	..	..	..	..	..	..	..	..	..	..	..
Equatorial Guinea	..	150.8	184.0	169.6	191.3	141.6	79.4	100.0	109.5	85.2	..	..	17.8	-9.2
Eritrea	..	..	..	..	83.9	80.5	91.5	100.0	103.0	99.1	95.5	..	..	3.3
Ethiopia	..	88.5	65.9	49.1	76.3	86.1	69.1	100.0	95.3	81.3	91.7	..	2.0	3.5
Gabon	170.0	89.2	114.2	103.4	101.7	74.9	86.8	100.0	109.9	100.6	88.6	8.8	-4.5	-0.3
Gambia, The	91.0	84.0	91.8	94.4	100.3	99.8	98.2	100.0	102.2	100.8	112.1	3.4	13.0	2.2
Ghana	42.6	89.8	95.5	98.5	94.6	78.2	85.8	100.0	88.4	85.1	90.0	0.9	8.5	-0.6
Guinea	..	121.5	133.6	103.4	101.8	91.4	91.3	100.0	96.1	106.3	99.7	..	0.6	-2.3
Guinea-Bissau	57.6	127.3	124.0	102.6	88.6	109.8	102.2	100.0	102.1	102.3	86.4	14.1	0.9	-2.7
Kenya	129.2	93.4	88.6	88.3	87.2	71.6	82.3	100.0	97.3	111.0	112.8	5.5	-1.7	2.6
Lesotho	61.0	51.5	61.9	58.3	90.7	92.0	93.2	100.0	91.6	108.5	80.4	4.7	4.1	6.6
Liberia	..	..	..	..	..	..	..	..	..	..	..	..	..	..
Madagascar	68.8	85.0	82.5	74.3	79.5	78.5	90.7	100.0	104.9	119.9	122.0	6.5	3.4	5.2
Malawi	87.0	93.7	112.4	122.3	102.6	86.5	82.2	100.0	104.3	109.9	97.0	3.8	1.4	-0.5
Mali	108.5	96.3	112.8	106.5	99.2	92.6	82.7	100.0	97.8	83.2	81.7	3.5	6.5	-2.5
Mauritania	71.4	97.8	104.5	110.1	120.5	127.8	94.6	100.0	98.7	100.4	86.4	1.7	7.5	-1.7
Mauritius	72.2	81.9	93.1	92.2	95.8	88.1	90.9	100.0	105.4	95.1	90.8	0.5	8.9	1.2
Mozambique	142.6	137.3	140.9	149.2	116.5	86.4	82.6	100.0	99.3	103.8	101.3	..	4.8	-4.4
Namibia	123.2	96.0	114.2	89.6	93.5	85.9	100.0	100.0	93.0	91.6	102.0	..	6.0	-0.3
Niger	162.4	115.7	117.9	107.9	136.6	91.2	85.2	100.0	102.3	92.0	93.9	12.0	6.0	-2.9
Nigeria	145.5	88.6	129.2	101.6	133.7	101.2	92.7	100.0	122.2	115.6	75.2	3.1	10.3	-1.4
Rwanda	109.5	75.8	77.1	80.4	71.3	73.8	86.6	100.0	89.9	136.8	118.2	8.0	-8.3	6.1
São Tomé and Principe	..	129.8	148.1	147.4	128.1	127.8	112.3	100.0	89.4	73.1	73.2	..	-11.4	-7.8
Senegal	86.1	88.7	100.2	93.3	103.9	91.3	88.4	100.0	100.7	92.9	92.6	2.5	6.8	0.1
Seychelles	..	68.6	77.0	68.9	81.0	80.9	73.8	100.0	93.1	99.2	96.2	..	-5.3	4.2
Sierra Leone	143.0	143.8	86.3	82.0	85.4	96.7	97.6	100.0	127.6	121.4	81.1	18.9	-11.8	0.0
Somalia	..	..	..	..	..	..	..	..	..	..	..	..	..	..
South Africa	116.8	91.3	97.4	96.3	96.8	93.0	95.7	100.0	93.1	91.4	84.0	9.1	5.0	-0.7
Sudan	..	..	..	..	..	..	..	..	..	..	..	..	..	..
Swaziland	86.4	70.0	65.4	69.6	78.3	84.0	81.8	100.0	90.5	94.3	104.6	3.8	4.5	5.1
Tanzania	..	95.9	88.7	93.7	102.5	92.6	90.0	100.0	99.4	110.9	127.5	..	..	2.7
Togo	96.2	98.8	109.0	106.2	105.1	93.2	84.1	100.0	103.5	103.9	101.9	-1.9	5.9	-0.3
Uganda	..	114.0	81.0	68.2	59.6	56.7	66.2	100.0	83.8	73.9	73.3	..	-2.1	-1.1
Zambia	96.6	86.7	107.2	96.8	66.3	72.4	86.3	100.0	81.1	79.6	67.8	2.4	9.3	-2.3
Zimbabwe	156.5	128.3	127.1	118.5	101.8	97.7	96.0	100.0	111.6	106.2	83.7	0.3	3.9	-3.3
NORTH AFRICA	162.7	84.9	102.1	102.5	100.3	94.2	92.2	100.0	104.2	102.3	..	6.6	-5.9	1.1
Algeria	200.9	96.8	132.1	123.3	108.5	98.6	93.5	100.0	116.1	111.3	103.8	11.3	-10.2	-0.7
Egypt, Arab Republic	106.9	72.5	82.5	95.0	99.4	99.7	95.4	100.0	99.5	108.5	85.7	9.8	-7.5	2.2
Libya	..	..	..	..	..	..	..	..	..	..	..	..	..	..
Morocco	92.1	95.5	100.4	98.2	97.7	87.1	88.9	100.0	96.6	89.4	..	2.6	6.2	-0.7
Tunisia	91.3	74.1	84.8	84.4	91.1	84.9	88.9	100.0	103.3	94.2	98.8	5.3	1.6	2.9
ALL AFRICA	129.5	88.9	102.0	98.8	99.5	91.8	91.9	100.0	102.4	99.1	88.0	6.8	0.7	-0.1

Note: 1998 data are preliminary (see page 3).

5-16. Import unit values

					Index 1995=100							Average annual percentage growth		
	1980	1989	1990	1991	1992	1993	1994	1995	1996	1997	1998	75-84	85-89	90-MR
SUB-SAHARAN AFRICA	76.3	83.5	92.3	91.6	97.8	91.0	91.7	100.0	95.3	95.3	90.3	5.8	8.1	0.7
excluding South Africa	69.8	80.5	89.8	89.4	97.1	89.4	90.3	100.0	97.1	97.4	93.9	3.6	9.7	1.5
excl. S. Africa & Nigeria	87.4	83.6	92.0	92.9	93.0	88.4	90.2	100.0	102.5	97.4	95.9	..	4.4	1.4
Angola	..	104.9	105.4	197.1	98.3	117.9	89.3	100.0	135.0	126.1	144.8	..	1.2	1.2
Benin	54.3	92.2	83.0	86.2	66.7	84.4	93.6	100.0	99.3	90.4	87.1	6.3	13.3	1.3
Botswana	..	69.1	81.0	92.7	90.1	97.7	96.3	100.0	102.9	90.6	88.4	..	5.0	2.3
Burkina Faso	103.1	99.2	103.2	100.4	68.5	70.8	89.5	100.0	99.1	89.3	99.5	5.8	4.3	0.2
Burundi	111.3	117.0	125.6	126.9	122.8	110.7	96.3	100.0	104.3	80.2	63.6	8.9	7.4	-6.1
Cameroon	143.8	109.3	95.8	87.3	124.2	112.4	87.8	100.0	100.2	91.7	90.6	6.9	-1.1	-1.3
Cape Verde	..	78.5	86.1	89.0	96.6	85.7	86.6	100.0	97.2	101.8	101.3	..	..	2.5
Central African Republic	102.6	111.1	143.1	102.8	105.1	101.4	83.0	100.0	101.7	85.8	88.6	4.4	4.1	-3.6
Chad	78.5	66.7	78.9	77.3	80.0	76.7	87.6	100.0	96.0	87.8	87.6	2.2	5.8	3.1
Comoros	62.8	73.4	89.6	89.1	91.9	86.3	89.3	100.0	96.1	79.9	84.0	..	11.9	0.7
Congo, Democratic Rep. of	..	42.8	69.1	59.6	63.4	55.5	129.3	100.0	90.1	97.4	..	..	-4.9	10.2
Congo, Republic of	82.4	69.4	95.2	92.9	95.7	62.2	90.9	100.0	97.2	89.5	88.7	5.8	7.4	1.5
Côte d'Ivoire	100.7	89.3	101.8	94.0	101.5	94.9	82.5	100.0	106.7	97.4	95.1	4.4	6.3	0.4
Djibouti	..	..	..	..	..	..	..	100.0	..	..	..	..	..	..
Equatorial Guinea	..	110.1	169.8	173.4	177.4	156.2	80.0	100.0	97.3	80.3	..	..	12.9	-7.7
Eritrea	..	..	..	..	89.5	89.2	92.4	100.0	95.6	90.8	87.2	..	..	0.0
Ethiopia	..	82.1	73.5	54.9	54.7	79.5	82.5	100.0	106.9	106.9	103.0	..	-0.9	6.2
Gabon	64.7	75.5	84.4	84.3	87.6	67.1	84.6	100.0	91.6	82.5	91.5	1.3	10.7	1.6
Gambia, The	45.5	82.7	90.3	90.0	96.0	100.7	99.0	100.0	101.5	100.1	110.7	7.6	10.0	2.5
Ghana	20.9	84.7	95.8	96.4	99.0	91.9	84.5	100.0	99.9	96.1	91.8	2.0	11.9	0.5
Guinea	..	88.4	96.0	77.2	95.5	92.4	98.2	100.0	103.0	96.0	99.8	..	5.8	1.7
Guinea-Bissau	47.0	80.4	86.7	82.8	87.0	79.3	84.2	100.0	102.5	102.6	97.0	8.1	13.0	2.7
Kenya	134.5	128.4	131.0	117.9	115.0	80.4	81.2	100.0	95.8	102.8	106.9	9.6	0.1	-2.9
Lesotho	58.4	61.2	73.6	78.4	89.8	91.5	93.1	100.0	91.9	99.6	79.7	7.5	6.3	3.5
Liberia	..	..	..	..	..	..	..	..	..	..	..	..	..	..
Madagascar	63.5	71.8	83.5	83.0	87.1	85.1	90.6	100.0	99.6	95.6	97.3	9.1	6.5	3.1
Malawi	68.8	87.5	97.3	100.4	103.3	97.8	96.5	100.0	98.6	98.7	89.1	6.4	8.7	0.0
Mali	103.1	81.0	92.7	92.7	96.5	93.4	90.5	100.0	97.2	85.7	82.5	1.7	4.9	0.0
Mauritania	100.4	102.8	109.1	108.1	112.0	109.0	99.4	100.0	105.7	99.6	87.6	5.6	4.9	-1.6
Mauritius	73.0	78.1	86.0	86.2	89.5	86.8	91.5	100.0	104.6	95.0	89.8	6.1	5.5	2.0
Mozambique	64.3	80.8	87.5	90.7	80.1	73.2	95.3	100.0	103.9	105.6	97.2	..	8.4	2.8
Namibia	82.7	68.6	84.9	87.7	93.4	90.0	89.8	100.0	92.5	97.0	95.8	..	3.9	2.7
Niger	128.8	116.0	131.0	129.1	132.8	91.2	85.3	100.0	102.2	92.3	94.0	1.8	9.3	-3.8
Nigeria	44.1	65.0	80.0	75.2	113.9	93.6	90.7	100.0	74.8	97.4	86.7	-3.4	31.6	2.2
Rwanda	153.8	148.8	153.6	79.1	83.0	77.9	73.4	100.0	102.2	93.4	88.0	5.9	6.4	-3.8
São Tomé and Principe	..	83.0	87.0	87.8	91.1	90.3	94.4	100.0	101.9	95.6	86.0	..	4.5	1.2
Senegal	81.2	76.7	86.6	92.0	94.0	88.7	88.5	100.0	98.9	89.7	85.5	3.8	5.6	1.1
Seychelles	..	98.0	107.7	105.0	103.8	94.1	96.5	100.0	96.6	97.8	90.0	..	1.8	-1.2
Sierra Leone	117.3	148.9	72.2	83.1	96.2	85.3	97.6	100.0	127.6	119.2	81.5	16.5	-14.4	0.3
Somalia	..	..	..	..	..	..	..	..	..	..	..	..	..	..
South Africa	97.5	90.8	98.8	97.3	99.3	94.5	94.5	100.0	91.9	91.2	83.8	10.3	4.2	-0.9
Sudan	..	..	..	..	..	..	..	..	..	..	..	..	..	..
Swaziland	75.8	69.0	56.3	61.6	67.3	63.3	82.6	100.0	97.8	103.7	127.3	4.6	8.4	8.6
Tanzania	..	85.3	84.6	92.2	112.5	98.9	91.6	100.0	101.6	117.6	139.9	..	..	4.2
Togo	84.2	78.6	85.5	84.9	88.9	84.8	87.0	100.0	99.0	84.3	81.3	0.2	7.0	0.8
Uganda	..	122.8	109.2	100.2	96.9	98.6	98.9	100.0	104.5	96.6	93.7	..	10.9	-1.8
Zambia	71.0	85.4	81.7	86.5	78.7	84.8	93.2	100.0	90.3	84.0	80.9	11.9	3.7	0.4
Zimbabwe	179.1	129.7	127.1	116.9	98.1	97.0	95.4	100.0	111.5	96.8	79.9	5.7	3.7	-3.8
NORTH AFRICA	70.8	76.4	97.0	88.9	90.9	92.5	92.9	100.0	101.9	99.2	97.2	5.3	6.5	2.0
Algeria	69.1	61.1	104.8	88.2	86.8	97.3	94.7	100.0	100.0	89.4	88.8	4.7	4.2	2.0
Egypt, Arab Republic	58.2	90.0	95.5	88.5	93.5	94.2	93.2	100.0	104.5	109.9	102.5	8.6	9.7	1.9
Libya	..	..	..	..	..	..	..	..	..	..	..	4.9	1.3	0.7
Morocco	97.6	89.8	99.6	95.8	92.7	89.6	94.4	100.0	100.7	96.9	..	5.1	4.4	3.3
Tunisia	75.0	70.3	82.0	82.8	90.5	85.6	88.1	100.0	100.7	94.8	97.8	5.7	7.7	1.1
ALL AFRICA	73.2	80.9	94.1	90.7	95.3	91.5	92.1	100.0	97.4	96.5	92.1	5.7	7.7	1.1

Note: 1998 data are preliminary (see page 3).

5-17. Terms of trade

	Index 1995=100											Average annual percentage growth		
	1980	1989	1990	1991	1992	1993	1994	1995	1996	1997	1998	75-84	85-89	90-MR
SUB-SAHARAN AFRICA	160.2	108.5	110.5	106.0	101.4	99.6	100.0	100.0	106.7	102.5	95.4	0.4	-4.1	-1.0
excluding South Africa	179.4	112.1	116.6	109.2	103.4	99.6	98.9	100.0	110.1	104.3	93.2	0.7	-6.2	-1.5
excl. S. Africa & Nigeria	128.1	108.4	107.1	103.9	98.6	97.3	98.0	100.0	99.9	100.2	95.0	..	-2.7	-1.1
Angola	..	131.3	144.5	91.4	91.3	91.4	100.1	100.0	100.0	100.0	70.0	..	2.8	-4.4
Benin	81.4	61.9	100.0	88.5	80.1	77.3	75.9	100.0	88.2	90.3	95.4	-0.3	-6.7	2.3
Botswana	..	118.6	110.4	103.2	102.1	101.9	100.6	100.0	100.7	91.4	91.4	..	4.3	-2.3
Burkina Faso	50.0	90.9	91.0	86.8	88.4	84.2	95.0	100.0	89.7	84.1	91.2	-0.7	7.7	0.1
Burundi	134.4	103.3	74.6	79.3	56.8	70.0	102.8	100.0	73.6	90.1	74.0	-2.4	-7.8	0.0
Cameroon	90.6	71.7	87.6	110.7	69.6	79.9	98.1	100.0	101.1	109.8	101.8	-1.9	-2.4	3.4
Cape Verde	..	97.2	100.0	100.0	100.0	100.0	100.0	100.0	100.0	116.9	96.7	..	..	0.6
Central African Republic	136.0	153.2	123.6	139.8	146.0	142.1	103.3	100.0	86.4	77.8	64.4	3.9	2.1	-8.6
Chad	117.5	101.8	116.5	118.0	110.3	100.5	85.2	100.0	98.9	95.6	103.1	-2.8	-2.4	-1.6
Comoros	219.7	174.0	170.0	154.3	159.7	142.3	108.4	100.0	91.7	76.3	77.5	..	0.8	-9.9
Congo, Democratic Rep. of	..	144.2	108.3	101.7	121.5	113.0	83.5	100.0	87.9	81.9	..	..	7.0	-5.3
Congo, Republic of	173.0	137.5	120.8	126.4	117.9	122.2	100.8	100.0	124.4	125.2	82.4	3.7	-12.6	-3.1
Côte d'Ivoire	115.1	94.1	81.7	88.3	92.6	93.1	97.5	100.0	93.4	93.2	96.5	-5.2	-7.0	1.0
Djibouti	..	..	..	..	..	..	..	..	..	..	..	..	..	..
Equatorial Guinea	..	137.0	108.4	97.8	107.8	90.7	99.3	100.0	112.5	106.1	..	..	4.3	-1.6
Eritrea	..	..	..	..	93.8	90.3	98.9	100.0	107.7	109.2	109.5	..	..	3.4
Ethiopia	..	107.8	89.7	89.5	139.4	108.3	83.8	100.0	89.1	76.0	89.1	..	2.9	-2.5
Gabon	262.6	118.1	135.2	122.7	116.0	111.6	102.6	100.0	120.0	121.9	96.8	7.5	-13.7	-1.9
Gambia, The	199.9	101.5	101.7	104.9	104.4	99.1	99.3	100.0	100.7	100.7	101.3	-3.9	2.7	-0.3
Ghana	203.9	106.0	99.7	102.2	95.6	85.1	101.5	100.0	88.5	88.5	98.1	-1.1	-3.0	-1.2
Guinea	..	137.5	139.2	134.0	106.6	98.9	93.0	100.0	93.3	110.7	99.9	..	-5.0	-3.9
Guinea-Bissau	122.7	158.5	143.0	123.9	101.8	138.4	121.3	100.0	99.6	99.6	89.0	5.4	-10.7	-5.3
Kenya	96.1	72.7	67.6	74.9	75.8	89.0	101.4	100.0	101.6	107.9	105.5	-3.8	-1.8	5.7
Lesotho	104.6	84.2	84.1	74.4	101.0	100.5	100.1	100.0	99.7	109.0	100.8	-2.5	-2.1	3.0
Liberia	..	..	..	..	..	..	..	..	..	..	..	..	..	..
Madagascar	108.3	118.3	98.9	89.5	91.3	92.3	100.2	100.0	105.4	125.3	125.3	-2.4	-2.9	2.0
Malawi	126.4	107.1	115.5	121.8	99.3	88.4	85.2	100.0	105.8	111.4	108.9	-2.4	-6.7	-0.5
Mali	105.2	119.0	121.7	114.9	102.8	99.1	91.4	100.0	100.6	97.1	99.1	1.8	1.5	-2.4
Mauritania	71.1	95.1	95.8	101.8	107.6	117.2	95.1	100.0	93.4	100.8	98.6	-3.6	2.5	-0.1
Mauritius	98.9	104.9	108.2	107.0	107.0	101.5	99.4	100.0	100.8	100.1	101.1	-5.3	3.2	-0.8
Mozambique	221.8	170.0	161.1	164.5	145.4	118.1	86.7	100.0	95.6	98.3	104.2	..	-3.4	-7.0
Namibia	149.1	139.9	134.5	102.2	100.1	95.5	111.3	100.0	100.5	94.4	106.5	..	2.0	-2.9
Niger	126.1	99.8	90.0	83.6	102.9	100.0	99.9	100.0	100.0	99.7	100.0	10.1	-3.0	0.9
Nigeria	329.7	136.3	161.5	135.1	117.3	108.2	102.3	100.0	163.2	118.7	86.8	6.7	-16.2	-3.5
Rwanda	71.4	51.0	50.2	101.6	85.8	94.8	118.0	100.0	88.0	146.4	134.4	2.0	-13.8	10.3
São Tomé and Principe	..	156.4	170.2	167.7	140.6	141.5	119.0	100.0	87.7	76.5	85.1	..	-15.2	-9.0
Senegal	106.1	115.7	115.7	101.4	110.5	102.9	99.9	100.0	101.8	103.5	108.3	-1.2	1.1	-1.0
Seychelles	..	70.0	71.5	65.6	78.0	86.0	76.5	100.0	96.3	101.4	106.9	..	-7.0	5.5
Sierra Leone	121.9	96.6	119.5	98.7	88.8	113.3	100.0	100.0	100.0	101.8	99.5	2.1	3.0	-0.3
Somalia	..	..	..	..	..	..	..	..	..	..	..	..	..	..
South Africa	119.8	100.6	98.6	99.0	97.6	98.5	101.3	100.0	101.4	100.1	100.2	-1.2	0.8	0.2
Sudan	..	..	..	..	..	..	..	..	..	..	..	..	..	..
Swaziland	113.9	101.5	116.1	113.1	116.3	132.8	99.1	100.0	92.6	90.9	82.2	-0.7	-3.5	-3.2
Tanzania	..	112.5	104.9	101.6	91.1	93.6	98.2	100.0	97.8	94.4	91.1	..	..	-1.5
Togo	114.3	125.6	127.5	125.2	118.2	109.9	96.7	100.0	104.6	123.3	125.3	-2.1	-1.0	-1.1
Uganda	..	92.8	74.2	68.1	61.5	57.5	66.9	100.0	80.2	76.5	78.2	..	-11.7	0.7
Zambia	136.1	101.6	131.1	112.0	84.3	85.3	92.6	100.0	89.8	94.8	83.8	-8.5	5.4	-2.7
Zimbabwe	87.4	98.9	100.0	101.4	103.7	100.7	100.6	100.0	100.1	109.7	104.7	-5.1	0.1	0.6
NORTH AFRICA	230.0	111.1	105.3	115.3	110.4	101.8	99.2	100.0	102.2	103.1	..	1.3	-11.6	-1.3
Algeria	290.6	158.5	126.1	139.8	125.0	101.4	98.7	100.0	116.1	124.4	116.9	6.2	-13.8	-2.7
Egypt, Arab Republic	183.9	80.6	86.4	107.3	106.3	105.9	102.4	100.0	95.2	98.7	83.6	1.0	-15.6	0.3
Libya	..	..	..	..	..	..	..	..	..	..	..	..	..	..
Morocco	94.4	106.4	100.8	102.5	105.4	97.2	94.2	100.0	96.0	92.3	..	-2.2	4.8	-1.5
Tunisia	121.7	105.5	103.4	101.9	100.7	99.2	100.9	100.0	102.5	99.4	101.0	0.2	-2.7	-0.4
ALL AFRICA	176.9	109.8	108.5	109.0	104.4	100.3	99.7	100.0	105.2	102.7	95.6	1.0	-6.5	-1.2

Note: 1998 data are preliminary (see page 3).

5-18. Forest products exports

	Thousands of cubic meters											Average annual percentage growth		
	1980	*1987*	*1988*	*1989*	*1990*	*1991*	*1992*	*1993*	*1994*	*1995*	*1996*	*75-84*	*85-89*	*90-MR*
SUB-SAHARAN AFRICA	8,169	6,803	8,821	7,032	6,931	6,824	7,170	4,764	4,364	3,788	4,289	-2.6	2.4	-9.3
excluding South Africa	7,413	5,283	6,044	5,855	5,794	5,632	5,478	4,339	3,960	3,300	3,748	-2.6	-1.3	-8.2
excl. S. Africa & Nigeria	7,402	5,266	6,028	5,844	5,757	5,583	5,444	3,908	3,672	3,030	3,499	-2.5	-1.1	-9.5
Angola	..	0	0	3	0	..	2	..	..	..	..	..	56.3	..
Benin	..	..	..	..	..	0	0	..	..	..	..	..	..	..
Botswana	..	..	..	..	..	..	..	..	..	..	..	..	..	..
Burkina Faso	..	..	..	..	..	..	..	..	..	..	..	..	..	..
Burundi	..	..	..	..	..	..	..	..	..	..	..	..	..	..
Cameroon	934	521	652	539	837	1,049	816	..	..	..	..	-1.9	-4.7	..
Cape Verde	..	..	..	..	..	..	..	..	..	..	..	..	..	..
Central African Republic	177	74	80	113	67	37	36	..	..	..	..	-2.3	-5.5	..
Chad	..	..	..	..	..	..	..	..	..	..	..	..	..	..
Comoros	..	..	..	..	1	..	0	..	..	..	..	..	..	..
Congo, Democratic Rep. of	116	147	163	143	142	172	136	113	101	74	91	5.7	0.4	-9.3
Congo, Republic of	385	643	941	937	816	609	530	..	..	..	..	2.8	28.3	..
Côte d'Ivoire	3,394	1,175	1,138	1,084	1,127	967	878	..	..	..	..	-2.4	-16.9	..
Djibouti	..	..	..	..	..	..	..	..	..	..	..	..	..	..
Equatorial Guinea	16	133	133	142	129	126	143	400	380	..	5	24.0	12.4	-24.1
Eritrea	..	..	..	..	..	..	..	..	..	..	..	..	..	..
Ethiopia														
Gabon	1,150	1,353	1,343	1,460	1,244	1,392	1,447	1,685	1,729	1,359	1,632	-0.6	0.8	2.4
Gambia, The	..	..	..	..	..	0	0	..	..	..	..	..	..	..
Ghana	183	514	531	371	361	390	426	936	735	754	1,018	-19.0	26.0	17.3
Guinea	..	8	8	8	13	15	17	45	45	45	45	-14.9	-7.6	31.0
Guinea-Bissau	6	5	4	4	6	12	9	5	5	6	8	-15.1	22.1	1.3
Kenya	33	4	4	3	4	3	0	82	94	95	27	-7.0	-26.5	78.3
Lesotho	..	..	..	..	..	..	..	..	..	..	..	..	..	..
Liberia	524	255	701	729	663	429	642	149	145	206	225	-3.6	30.0	-20.0
Madagascar	0	2	1	2	3	26	6	6	10	8	4	-17.5	21.2	10.2
Malawi	..	..	1	0	0	0	1	1	1	1	1	1.8	..	20.3
Mali	..	..	..	..	..	0	..	..	..	..	..	..	..	..
Mauritania	..	..	..	..	1	..	..	..	..	..	..	..	..	..
Mauritius	..	..	..	..	..	..	2	..	..	..	..	..	..	..
Mozambique	31	5	10	2	5	4	1	149	137	140	158	-34.2	-3.8	115.9
Namibia	..	..	..	..	..	..	..	..	..	..	..	..	..	..
Niger	..	..	..	..	..	..	..	..	..	..	..	..	..	..
Nigeria	11	17	16	11	37	49	34	431	288	269	248	-5.0	-32.2	59.9
Rwanda	..	..	..	..	..	0	..	..	..	..	..	..	..	..
São Tomé and Principe	..	..	..	..	0	..	..	0	..	..	..	..	..	..
Senegal	..	..	..	..	..	..	..	..	..	..	..	..	..	..
Seychelles	..	..	..	..	0	..	..	..	..	..	..	..	..	..
Sierra Leone	..	1	1	0	0	0	0	..	..	..	..	..	-8.8	..
Somalia	..	..	..	..	..	..	..	48	..	..	..	..	..	..
South Africa	756	1,520	2,777	1,177	1,137	1,191	1,692	425	405	488	541	-2.2	24.9	-15.6
Sudan	..	..	..	..	..	0	..	..	..	..	..	..	..	..
Swaziland	421	355	293	285	254	254	254	241	239	299	270	2.8	-13.1	0.2
Tanzania	5	5	6	3	25	14	8	40	40	37	9	-15.9	3.0	16.4
Togo	..	..	..	..	0	..	..	0	0	1	0	..	..	14.9
Uganda	0	..	..	..	..	..	..	9	11	7	7	-30.6	..	..
Zambia	..	..	..	..	0	0	..	..	..	..	..	..	..	..
Zimbabwe	26	65	17	17	56	83	89	..	..	..	..	-0.6	-14.1	..
NORTH AFRICA	88	94	117	95	95	77	105	78	84	71	60	1.3	6.1	-5.4
Algeria	..	..	..	..	1	..	..	..	..	..	..	..	..	..
Egypt, Arab Republic	..	..	..	..	0	0	..	3	6	0	..	..	..	63.4
Libya	..	..	..	..	..	0	0	..	..	..	..	..	..	..
Morocco	74	85	102	88	84	70	98	43	48	50	39	4.9	6.3	-11.4
Tunisia	14	10	16	7	10	8	7	32	29	20	21	-8.4	3.4	22.6
ALL AFRICA	8,258	6,897	8,938	7,127	7,026	6,901	7,275	4,842	4,448	3,859	4,349	-2.5	2.5	-9.3

5-19. Petroleum exports

| | *Thousands of metric tons* | | | | | | | | | | | *Average annual percentage growth* | | |
	1980	1988	1989	1990	1991	1992	1993	1994	1995	1996	1997	75-84	85-89	90-MR
SUB-SAHARAN AFRICA	116,952	105,341	121,307	128,181	134,063	135,261	147,227	135,454	141,429	153,851	..	-4.6	4.9	2.7
excluding South Africa	116,952	105,341	121,307	128,181	134,063	135,261	146,925	135,257	141,345	153,851	..	-4.6	4.9	2.7
excl. S. Africa & Nigeria	20,221	43,082	45,358	51,038	53,895	52,255	54,730	54,997	56,347	67,117	..	3.2	9.9	4.1
Angola	6,334	21,177	21,520	22,462	23,738	22,605	23,057	22,960	24,322	33,718	..	0.3	21.7	4.2
Benin	..	148	148	296	300	273	307	315	232	196	..	..	50.5	1.2
Botswana	..	..	..	..	..	..	..	..	..	..	..	..	..	..
Burkina Faso	..	..	..	..	..	..	..	..	..	..	..	..	..	..
Burundi	..	..	..	..	..	..	..	..	..	..	..	..	..	..
Cameroon	1,886	7,222	6,819	7,388	7,166	6,456	6,097	6,091	5,278	5,014	..	73.9	5.3	-5.1
Cape Verde	..	..	..	..	..	..	..	..	..	..	..	..	..	..
Central African Republic	..	..	..	..	..	..	..	..	..	..	..	..	..	..
Chad	..	..	..	..	..	..	..	..	..	..	..	..	..	..
Comoros	..	..	..	..	..	..	..	..	..	..	..	..	..	..
Congo, Democratic Rep. of	859	1,239	1,264	1,158	1,125	995	1,019	1,085	1,087	1,087	..	0.3	-0.8	-1.7
Congo, Republic of	3,383	5,893	6,869	7,611	7,498	8,136	9,227	8,837	8,001	9,221	..	12.3	3.5	3.6
Côte d'Ivoire	122	49	..	..	..	..	..	..	..	..	..	..	-34.8	..
Djibouti	..	..	..	..	..	..	..	..	..	..	..	..	..	..
Equatorial Guinea	..	..	..	..	..	..	..	..	..	..	..	..	..	..
Eritrea	..	..	..	..	..	..	..	..	..	..	..	..	..	..
Ethiopia	..	..	..	..	..	..	..	..	..	..	..	..	..	..
Gabon	7,637	7,355	8,739	12,123	14,068	13,790	15,023	15,710	17,427	17,881	..	-4.5	1.9	9.0
Gambia, The	..	..	..	..	..	..	..	..	..	..	..	..	..	..
Ghana	..	..	..	..	..	..	..	..	..	..	..	..	..	..
Guinea	..	..	..	..	..	..	..	..	..	..	..	..	..	..
Guinea-Bissau	..	..	..	..	..	..	..	..	..	..	..	..	..	..
Kenya	..	..	..	..	..	..	..	..	..	..	..	..	..	..
Lesotho	..	..	..	..	..	..	..	..	..	..	..	..	..	..
Liberia	..	..	..	..	..	..	..	..	..	..	..	..	..	..
Madagascar	..	..	..	..	..	..	..	..	..	..	..	..	..	..
Malawi	..	..	..	..	..	..	..	..	..	..	..	..	..	..
Mali	..	..	..	..	..	..	..	..	..	..	..	..	..	..
Mauritania	..	..	..	..	..	..	..	..	..	..	..	..	..	..
Mauritius	..	..	..	..	..	..	..	..	..	..	..	..	..	..
Mozambique	..	..	..	..	..	..	..	..	..	..	..	..	..	..
Namibia	..	..	..	..	..	..	..	..	..	..	..	..	..	..
Niger	..	..	..	..	..	..	..	..	..	..	..	..	..	..
Nigeria	96,731	62,259	75,949	77,143	80,168	83,006	92,194	80,260	84,998	86,734	..	-6.8	2.2	1.8
Rwanda	..	..	..	..	..	..	..	..	..	..	..	..	..	..
São Tomé and Principe	..	..	..	..	..	..	..	..	..	..	..	..	..	..
Senegal	..	..	..	..	..	..	..	..	..	..	..	..	..	..
Seychelles	..	..	..	..	..	..	..	..	..	..	..	..	..	..
Sierra Leone	..	..	..	..	..	..	..	..	..	..	..	..	..	..
Somalia	..	..	..	..	..	..	..	..	..	..	..	..	..	..
South Africa	..	..	..	..	..	..	303	196	84	..	..	..	..	..
Sudan	..	..	..	..	..	..	..	..	..	..	..	..	..	..
Swaziland	..	..	..	..	..	..	..	..	..	..	..	..	..	..
Tanzania	..	..	..	..	..	..	..	..	..	..	..	..	..	..
Togo	..	..	..	..	..	..	..	..	..	..	..	..	..	..
Uganda	..	..	..	..	..	..	..	..	..	..	..	..	..	..
Zambia	..	..	..	..	..	..	..	..	..	..	..	..	..	..
Zimbabwe	..	..	..	..	..	..	..	..	..	..	..	..	..	..
NORTH AFRICA	145,865	91,415	101,229	111,594	114,246	114,092	110,404	109,192	108,025	109,287	..	-3.7	-0.6	0.2
Algeria	38,918	28,114	30,430	32,526	31,870	31,108	32,138	32,125	32,323	35,823	..	-5.7	1.1	1.4
Egypt, Arab Republic	17,146	20,962	20,261	19,929	18,461	20,412	19,924	18,134	17,564	14,703	..	20.7	-2.8	-3.5
Libya	85,054	38,971	47,242	55,766	60,403	58,463	54,893	55,661	54,573	55,365	..	-6.4	-0.4	0.8
Morocco	..	..	..	..	..	..	..	..	..	..	..	..	..	..
Tunisia	4,747	3,368	3,296	3,373	3,512	4,109	3,449	3,271	3,566	3,397	..	-0.5	-3.9	0.1
ALL AFRICA	262,817	196,756	222,536	239,774	248,308	249,353	257,632	244,645	249,454	263,138	..	-4.1	2.1	1.6

5-20. Copper exports

	Thousands of metric tons											Average annual percentage growth		
	1980	1988	1989	1990	1991	1992	1993	1994	1995	1996	1997	75-84	85-89	90-MR
SUB-SAHARAN AFRICA	1,286	1,062	1,074	973	792	714	598	495	419	409	438	5.2	-3.1	-12.2
excluding South Africa	1,164	960	958	883	688	581	517	421	339	335	322	4.6	-3.4	-13.9
excl. S. Africa & Nigeria	1,164	960	958	883	688	581	517	421	339	335	322	4.6	-3.4	-13.9
Angola	0	0	0	0	0	0	0	0	0	0	0	..	..	..
Benin	0	0	0	0	0	0	0	0	0	0	0	..	..	..
Botswana	20	25	19	19	20	19	22	20	18	23	18	..	1.0	0.3
Burkina Faso	0	0	0	0	0	0	0	0	0	0	0	..	..	..
Burundi	0	0	0	0	0	0	0	0	0	0	0	..	..	..
Cameroon	0	0	0	0	0	0	0	0	0	0	0	..	..	..
Cape Verde	0	0	0	0	0	0	0	0	0	0	0	..	..	..
Central African Republic	0	0	0	0	0	0	0	0	0	0	0	..	..	..
Chad	0	0	0	0	0	0	0	0	0	0	0	..	..	..
Comoros	0	0	0	0	0	0	0	0	0	0	0	..	..	..
Congo, Democratic Rep. of	461	461	439	374	252	116	28	14	5	17	..	16.8	-2.7	-48.0
Congo, Republic of	1	0	0	0	0	0	0	0	0	0	0	..	..	..
Côte d'Ivoire	0	0	0	0	0	0	0	0	0	0	0	..	..	..
Djibouti	0	0	0	0	0	0	0	0	0	0	0	..	..	..
Equatorial Guinea	0	0	0	0	0	0	0	0	0	0	0	..	..	..
Eritrea	0	0	0	0	0	0	0	0	0	0	0	..	..	..
Ethiopia	0	0	0	0	0	0	0	0	0	0	0	..	..	..
Gabon	0	0	0	0	0	0	0	0	0	0	0	..	..	..
Gambia, The	0	0	0	0	0	0	0	0	0	0	0	..	..	..
Ghana	0	0	0	0	0	0	0	0	0	0	0	..	..	..
Guinea	0	0	0	0	0	0	0	0	0	0	0	..	..	..
Guinea-Bissau	0	0	0	0	0	0	0	0	0	0	0	..	..	..
Kenya	0	0	0	0	0	0	0	0	0	0	0	..	..	..
Lesotho	0	0	0	0	0	0	0	0	0	0	0	..	..	..
Liberia	0	0	0	0	0	0	0	0	0	0	0	..	..	..
Madagascar	0	0	0	0	0	0	0	0	0	0	0	..	..	..
Malawi	0	0	0	0	0	0	0	0	0	0	0	..	..	..
Mali	0	0	0	0	0	0	0	0	0	0	0	..	..	..
Mauritania	1	0	0	0	0	0	0	0	0	0	0	..	..	..
Mauritius	0	0	0	0	0	0	0	0	0	0	0	..	..	..
Mozambique	0	0	0	0	0	0	0	0	0	0	0	..	..	..
Namibia	41	38	33	30	34	35	30	26	25	18	..	1.9	-7.0	-6.8
Niger	0	0	0	0	0	0	0	0	0	0	0	..	..	..
Nigeria	0	0	0	0	0	0	0	0	0	0	0	..	..	..
Rwanda	0	0	0	0	0	0	0	0	0	0	0	..	..	..
São Tomé and Principe	0	0	0	0	0	0	0	0	0	0	0	..	..	..
Senegal	0	0	0	0	0	0	0	0	0	0	0	..	..	..
Seychelles	0	0	0	0	0	0	0	0	0	0	0	..	..	..
Sierra Leone	0	0	0	0	0	0	0	0	0	0	0	..	..	..
Somalia	0	0	0	0	0	0	0	0	0	0	0	..	..	..
South Africa	121	103	115	90	104	132	81	74	79	74	116	13.2	-0.8	-2.7
Sudan	0	0	0	0	0	0	0	0	0	0	0	..	..	..
Swaziland	0	0	0	0	0	0	0	0	0	0	0	..	..	..
Tanzania	0	0	0	0	0	0	0	0	0	0	0	..	..	..
Togo	0	0	0	0	0	0	0	0	0	0	0	..	..	..
Uganda	0	0	0	0	0	0	0	0	0	0	0	..	..	..
Zambia	617	424	456	460	382	412	437	361	292	276	304	-1.8	-3.4	-6.2
Zimbabwe	23	12	10	0	0	0	0	0	0	0	0	3.8	-16.6	..
NORTH AFRICA	6	13	12	16	16	17	13	19	16	16	0	..	-13.1	2.5
Algeria	0	0	0	0	0	0	0	0	0	0	0	..	..	..
Egypt, Arab Republic	0	0	0	0	0	0	0	0	0	0	0	..	..	..
Libya	0	0	0	0	0	0	0	0	0	0	0	..	..	..
Morocco	6	13	12	16	16	17	13	19	16	16	..	..	-12.9	2.5
Tunisia	0	0	0	0	0	0	0	0	0	0	0	..	..	..
ALL AFRICA	1,292	1,075	1,086	989	807	730	611	514	435	425	438	5.4	-3.3	-12.1

5-21. Iron exports

	Thousands of metric tons										Average annual percentage growth		
	1980	*1988*	*1989*	*1990*	*1991*	*1992*	*1993*	*1994*	*1995*	*1996*	*75-84*	*85-89*	*90-MR*
SUB-SAHARAN AFRICA	28,215	22,981	24,956	21,057	17,509	15,778	18,986	19,465	21,397	19,545	..	-0.4	-1.3
excluding South Africa	17,482	15,734	15,780	9,988	7,474	6,114	6,276	6,722	7,196	7,000	..	-2.3	-8.7
excl. S. Africa & Nigeria	17,482	15,734	15,780	9,988	7,474	6,114	6,276	6,722	7,196	7,000	..	-2.3	-8.7
Angola	0	0	0	0	0	0	0	0	0	0	..	..	..
Benin	0	0	0	0	0	0	0	0	0	0	..	..	..
Botswana	0	0	0	0	0	0	0	0	0	0	..	..	..
Burkina Faso	0	0	0	0	0	0	0	0	0	0	..	..	..
Burundi	0	0	0	0	0	0	0	0	0	0	..	..	..
Cameroon	0	0	0	0	0	0	0	0	0	0	..	..	..
Cape Verde	0	0	0	0	0	0	0	0	0	0	..	..	..
Central African Republic	0	0	0	0	0	0	0	0	0	0	..	..	..
Chad	0	0	0	0	0	0	0	0	0	0	..	..	..
Comoros	0	0	0	0	0	0	0	0	0	0	..	..	..
Congo, Democratic Rep. of	0	0	0	0	0	0	0	0	0	0	..	..	..
Congo, Republic of	0	0	0	0	0	0	0	0	0	0	..	..	..
Côte d'Ivoire	0	0	0	0	0	0	0	0	0	0	..	..	..
Djibouti	0	0	0	0	0	0	0	0	0	0	..	..	..
Equatorial Guinea	0	0	0	0	0	0	0	0	0	0	..	..	..
Eritrea	0	0	0	0	0	0	0	0	0	0	..	..	..
Ethiopia	0	0	0	0	0	0	0	0	0	0	..	..	..
Gabon	0	0	0	0	0	0	0	0	0	0	..	..	..
Gambia, The	0	0	0	0	0	0	0	0	0	0	..	..	..
Ghana	0	0	0	0	0	0	0	0	0	0	..	..	..
Guinea	0	0	0	0	0	0	0	0	0	0	..	..	..
Guinea-Bissau	0	0	0	0	0	0	0	0	0	0	..	..	..
Kenya	0	0	0	0	0	0	0	0	0	0	..	..	..
Lesotho	0	0	0	0	0	0	0	0	0	0	..	..	..
Liberia	11,695	9,231	8,540	2,607	670	853	0	0	0	0	..	-5.4	..
Madagascar	0	0	0	0	0	0	0	0	0	0	..	..	..
Malawi	0	0	0	0	0	0	0	0	0	0	..	..	..
Mali	0	0	0	0	0	0	0	0	0	0	..	..	..
Mauritania	5,673	6,503	7,240	7,381	6,804	5,261	6,276	6,722	7,196	7,000	..	3.0	-0.3
Mauritius	0	0	0	0	0	0	0	0	0	0	..	..	..
Mozambique	0	0	0	0	0	0	0	0	0	0	..	..	..
Namibia	0	0	0	0	0	0	0	0	0	0	..	..	..
Niger	0	0	0	0	0	0	0	0	0	0	..	..	..
Nigeria	0	0	0	0	0	0	0	0	0	0	..	..	..
Rwanda	0	0	0	0	0	0	0	0	0	0	..	..	..
São Tomé and Principe	0	0	0	0	0	0	0	0	0	0	..	..	..
Senegal	0	0	0	0	0	0	0	0	0	0	..	..	..
Seychelles	0	0	0	0	0	0	0	0	0	0	..	..	..
Sierra Leone	0	0	0	0	0	0	0	0	0	0	..	..	..
Somalia	0	0	0	0	0	0	0	0	0	0	..	..	..
South Africa	10,733	7,247	9,176	11,069	10,035	9,664	12,710	12,743	14,201	12,545	..	4.0	5.4
Sudan	0	0	0	0	0	0	0	0	0	0	..	..	..
Swaziland	114	0	0	0	0	0	0	0	0	0	..	..	..
Tanzania	0	0	0	0	0	0	0	0	0	0	..	..	..
Togo	0	0	0	0	0	0	0	0	0	0	..	..	..
Uganda	0	0	0	0	0	0	0	0	0	0	..	..	..
Zambia	0	0	0	0	0	0	0	0	0	0	..	..	..
Zimbabwe	0	0	0	0	0	0	0	0	0	0	..	..	..
NORTH AFRICA	784	48	62	47	50	55	58	42	21	4	..	-11.3	-24.3
Algeria	699	0	10	9	10	20	25	25	5	4	..	-41.9	-6.9
Egypt, Arab Republic	0	0	0	0	0	0	0	0	0	0	..	..	..
Libya	0	0	0	0	0	0	0	0	0	0	..	..	..
Morocco	85	48	52	38	40	35	33	17	16	0	..	..	-17.4
Tunisia	0	0	0	0	0	0	0	0	0	0	..	..	..
ALL AFRICA	28,999	23,029	25,018	21,104	17,559	15,833	19,044	19,507	21,418	19,549	..	-0.6	-1.4

5-22. Phosphates exports

	1980	1988	1989	1990	1991	1992	1993	1994	1995	1996	1997	75-84	85-89	90-MR
				Thousands of metric tons								*Average annual percentage growth*		
SUB-SAHARAN AFRICA	4,277	5,983	5,877	4,995	5,544	4,617	3,940	4,484	4,077	4,580	4,290	0.4	6.9	-3.5
excluding South Africa	4,274	4,715	4,783	3,778	4,378	3,272	2,840	3,184	2,712	3,230	2,990	-0.6	4.6	-5.4
excl. S. Africa & Nigeria	4,274	4,715	4,783	3,778	4,378	3,272	2,840	3,184	2,712	3,230	2,990	-0.6	4.6	-5.4
Angola	0	0	0	0	0	0	0	0	0	0	0	..	..	..
Benin	0	0	0	0	0	0	0	0	0	0	0	..	..	..
Botswana	0	0	0	0	0	0	0	0	0	0	0	..	..	..
Burkina Faso	0	0	0	0	0	0	0	0	0	0	0	..	..	..
Burundi	0	0	0	0	0	0	0	0	0	0	0	..	..	..
Cameroon	0	0	0	0	0	0	0	0	0	0	0	..	..	..
Cape Verde	0	0	0	0	0	0	0	0	0	0	0	..	..	..
Central African Republic	0	0	0	0	0	0	0	0	0	0	0	..	..	..
Chad	0	0	0	0	0	0	0	0	0	0	0	..	..	..
Comoros	0	0	0	0	0	0	0	0	0	0	0	..	..	..
Congo, Democratic Rep. of	0	0	0	0	0	0	0	0	0	0	0	..	..	..
Congo, Republic of	0	0	0	0	0	0	0	0	0	0	0	..	..	..
Côte d'Ivoire	0	0	0	0	0	0	0	0	0	0	0	..	..	..
Djibouti	0	0	0	0	0	0	0	0	0	0	0	..	..	..
Equatorial Guinea	0	0	0	0	0	0	0	0	0	0	0	..	..	..
Eritrea	0	0	0	0	0	0	0	0	0	0	0	..	..	..
Ethiopia	0	0	0	0	0	0	0	0	0	0	0	..	..	..
Gabon	0	0	0	0	0	0	0	0	0	0	0	..	..	..
Gambia, The	0	0	0	0	0	0	0	0	0	0	0	..	..	..
Ghana	0	0	0	0	0	0	0	0	0	0	0	..	..	..
Guinea	0	0	0	0	0	0	0	0	0	0	0	..	..	..
Guinea-Bissau	0	0	0	0	0	0	0	0	0	0	0	..	..	..
Kenya	0	0	0	0	0	0	0	0	0	0	0	..	..	..
Lesotho	0	0	0	0	0	0	0	0	0	0	0	..	..	..
Liberia	0	0	0	0	0	0	0	0	0	0	0	..	..	..
Madagascar	0	0	0	0	0	0	0	0	0	0	0	..	..	..
Malawi	0	0	0	0	0	0	0	0	0	0	0	..	..	..
Mali	0	0	0	0	0	0	0	0	0	0	0	..	..	..
Mauritania	0	0	0	0	0	0	0	0	0	0	0	..	..	..
Mauritius	0	0	0	0	0	0	0	0	0	0	0	..	..	..
Mozambique	0	0	0	0	0	0	0	0	0	0	0	..	..	..
Namibia	0	0	0	0	0	0	0	0	0	0	0	..	..	..
Niger	0	0	0	0	0	0	0	0	0	0	0	..	..	..
Nigeria	0	0	0	0	0	0	0	0	0	0	0	..	..	..
Rwanda	0	0	0	0	0	0	0	0	0	0	0	..	..	..
São Tomé and Principe	0	0	0	0	0	0	0	0	0	0	0	..	..	..
Senegal	1,378	1,847	1,435	1,356	1,304	1,187	1,100	950	862	830	598	-3.9	4.4	-9.6
Seychelles	0	0	0	0	0	0	0	0	0	0	0	..	..	..
Sierra Leone	0	0	0	0	0	0	0	0	0	0	0	..	..	..
Somalia	0	0	0	0	0	0	0	0	0	0	0	..	..	..
South Africa	4	1,268	1,094	1,217	1,166	1,344	1,100	1,300	1,365	1,350	1,300	39.6	20.6	2.2
Sudan	0	0	0	0	0	0	0	0	0	0	0	..	..	..
Swaziland	0	0	0	0	0	0	0	0	0	0	0	..	..	..
Tanzania	0	0	0	0	0	0	0	0	0	0	0	..	..	..
Togo	2,896	2,868	3,347	2,422	3,074	2,086	1,740	2,234	1,850	2,400	2,392	1.9	4.5	-3.8
Uganda	0	0	0	0	0	0	0	0	0	0	0	..	..	..
Zambia	0	0	0	0	0	0	0	0	0	0	0	..	..	..
Zimbabwe	0	0	0	0	0	0	0	0	0	0	0	..	..	..
NORTH AFRICA	18,932	16,560	14,700	13,297	10,537	10,912	10,338	11,392	11,377	11,792	13,398	-1.1	-2.3	-0.9
Algeria	768	877	970	735	804	678	718	536	648	445	474	5.6	8.5	-8.0
Egypt, Arab Republic	258	268	246	297	164	180	100	33	0	1	8	12.4	3.8	-46.2
Libya	0	0	0	0	0	0	0	0	0	0	0	..	..	..
Morocco	16,457	14,260	12,407	11,672	9,143	9,130	8,398	9,527	9,420	10,140	11,669	-0.8	-3.1	-0.9
Tunisia	1,449	1,156	1,077	593	426	926	1,122	1,296	1,308	1,206	1,247	-6.9	-0.8	9.2
ALL AFRICA	23,210	22,543	20,576	18,292	16,080	15,529	14,278	15,876	15,454	16,372	17,688	-0.8	-0.2	-1.6

5-23. Cocoa exports

	Thousands of metric tons											Average annual percentage growth		
	1980	1988	1989	1990	1991	1992	1993	1994	1995	1996	1997	75-84	85-89	90-MR
SUB-SAHARAN AFRICA	869	1,089	1,363	1,352	1,371	1,190	1,469	1,268	1,341	1,887	1,325	0.4	5.3	1.5
excluding South Africa	869	1,087	1,360	1,349	1,365	1,180	1,456	1,257	1,333	1,877	1,315	0.4	5.3	1.5
excl. S. Africa & Nigeria	718	866	1,211	1,196	1,204	1,069	1,296	1,109	1,194	1,695	1,165	1.1	5.2	1.5
Angola	0	0	0	0	0	0	0	0	0	0	0	-20.0	..	..
Benin	5	0	0	0	0	0	0	0	0	0	0	6.2	-63.8	..
Botswana	0	0	0	0	0	0	0	0	0	0	0	..	128.8	-6.8
Burkina Faso	..	..	..	..	..	..	..	..	..	..	..	..	..	..
Burundi	..	..	..	..	..	..	..	..	..	..	..	..	..	..
Cameroon	105	135	107	119	98	68	112	82	120	142	107	0.1	3.8	1.9
Cape Verde	0	0	0	0	0	0	0	0	0	0	0	..	..	..
Central African Republic	0	0	0	0	0	0	0	0	0	0	0	-21.8	..	..
Chad	..	..	..	..	..	..	..	..	..	..	..	..	..	..
Comoros	0	0	0	0	0	0	0	0	0	0	0	-14.3	..	..
Congo, Democratic Rep. of	4	5	5	5	5	3	3	3	4	3	3	-0.2	2.8	-6.5
Congo, Republic of	2	1	1	1	0	0	0	0	0	1	1	-5.1	-18.7	-1.3
Côte d'Ivoire	332	457	795	767	793	724	872	744	795	1,138	708	9.1	5.4	1.3
Djibouti	..	..	..	..	..	..	..	..	..	..	..	..	..	..
Equatorial Guinea	7	8	7	6	6	5	3	3	3	6	4	-0.2	0.4	-6.6
Eritrea	..	..	..	..	..	..	..	..	..	..	..			
Ethiopia	..	..	..	..	..	..	..	..	..	..	..	..	..	..
Gabon	4	2	2	2	1	2	1	1	1	1	1	-4.2	2.6	-10.5
Gambia, The	..	..	..	..	..	..	..	..	..	..	..	..	..	..
Ghana	218	223	266	270	265	243	278	252	253	372	304	-7.7	9.0	2.4
Guinea	4	3	3	2	2	2	4	4	3	6	7	4.3	-6.2	12.8
Guinea-Bissau	..	..	..	..	..	..	..	..	..	..	..			
Kenya	0	0	0	0	0	1	1	1	0	0	0	-8.2	46.3	37.9
Lesotho	..	..	..	..	..	..	..	..	..	..	..			
Liberia	4	3	3	3	2	0	0	0	0	0	0	9.1	-15.1	-46.9
Madagascar	2	4	2	3	4	3	4	3	2	2	1	5.8	7.6	-10.7
Malawi	0	0	0	0	0	0	0	0	0	0	0	-21.2	..	..
Mali	..	..	..	..	..	..	..	..	..	..	..	..	..	..
Mauritania	..	..	..	..	..	..	..	..	..	..	..	..	..	..
Mauritius	0	0	0	0	0	0	0	0	0	0	0	..	..	-34.6
Mozambique	0	0	0	0	0	0	0	0	0	0	0	..	..	..
Namibia	..	..	..	..	..	..	..	..	..	..	..	..	..	..
Niger	0	0	0	0	0	0	0	0	0	0	0	..	..	..
Nigeria	151	220	149	154	161	111	161	148	139	182	151	-2.6	4.2	0.9
Rwanda	..	..	..	..	..	..	..	..	..	..	..	..	..	..
São Tomé and Principe	7	4	3	3	5	4	4	3	3	4	4	-4.3	0.4	0.7
Senegal	0	0	0	0	0	0	0	0	0	0	0	65.7	-28.8	54.1
Seychelles	0	0	0	0	0	0	0	0	0	0	0	..	..	..
Sierra Leone	8	9	8	5	13	5	4	3	2	3	3	6.0	-4.6	-15.1
Somalia	..	..	..	..	..	..	..	..	..	..	..	..	..	..
South Africa	0	3	2	3	6	10	13	11	8	10	10	-8.5	34.0	18.8
Sudan	..	..	..	..	..	..	..	..	..	..	..	..	..	..
Swaziland	0	0	0	0	0	0	0	0	0	0	0	..	..	..
Tanzania	1	2	2	3	2	2	2	2	3	3	3	9.0	9.7	3.5
Togo	15	11	7	8	6	6	5	6	4	11	18	-1.7	-11.9	7.6
Uganda	0	0	0	0	1	1	1	1	1	1	1	2.5	5.5	16.4
Zambia	0	0	0	0	0	0	0	0	0	0	0	..	..	..
Zimbabwe	0	0	0	0	0	0	0	0	0	0	0	-14.6	-4.1	24.2
NORTH AFRICA	0	0	1	1	2	1	0	0	1	1	1	6.1	25.6	-4.8
Algeria	0	0	0	0	0	0	0	0	0	0	0	..	..	..
Egypt, Arab Republic	0	0	0	1	2	0	0	0	0	1	1	-22.9	81.9	-0.2
Libya	0	0	0	0	0	0	0	0	0	0	0	..	..	..
Morocco	0	0	0	0	0	0	0	0	0	0	0	..	-17.2	-10.7
Tunisia	0	0	1	0	0	0	0	0	0	0	0	..	17.4	-14.3
ALL AFRICA	869	1,090	1,364	1,353	1,373	1,191	1,469	1,268	1,342	1,888	1,326	0.4	5.3	1.5

5-24. Coffee exports

	Thousands of metric tons											Average annual percentage growth		
	1980	1988	1989	1990	1991	1992	1993	1994	1995	1996	1997	75-84	85-89	90-MR
SUB-SAHARAN AFRICA	819	818	906	1,032	828	847	831	751	788	953	973	-2.3	0.0	-0.3
excluding South Africa	818	817	906	1,030	827	846	831	750	787	951	971	-2.4	-0.1	-0.3
excl. S. Africa & Nigeria	816	816	905	1,030	827	846	830	750	786	951	970	-2.4	-0.1	-0.3
Angola	47	11	8	5	5	5	2	0	2	3	3	-17.7	-19.0	-14.3
Benin	0	0	1	0	0	0	0	0	0	0	0	18.1	-21.6	..
Botswana	0	0	0	0	0	0	0	0	0	0	0	3.8	56.4	-30.2
Burkina Faso	..	..	..	..	..	..	..	..	..	..	..	..	..	..
Burundi	19	37	29	34	41	40	23	29	29	13	32	3.0	-0.2	-5.6
Cameroon	92	95	152	158	113	104	67	54	63	74	82	0.0	4.4	-10.3
Cape Verde	0	0	0	0	0	0	0	0	0	0	0	..	..	..
Central African Republic	11	15	25	13	9	6	8	8	14	5	12	2.2	10.4	-7.7
Chad	..	..	..	..	..	..	..	..	..	..	..	..	..	..
Comoros	0	0	0	0	0	0	0	0	0	0	0	-17.4	..	..
Congo, Democratic Rep. of	74	68	98	104	84	104	56	63	61	49	35	0.3	2.7	-11.8
Congo, Republic of	2	0	0	0	0	0	0	0	2	1	0	8.4	-28.7	14.1
Côte d'Ivoire	207	204	130	232	199	203	226	122	135	145	265	-2.6	-7.4	0.3
Djibouti	..	..	..	..	..	..	..	..	..	..	..	..	..	..
Equatorial Guinea	0	0	0	0	0	0	0	0	0	0	0	-10.7	-18.2	-19.1
Eritrea	..	..	..	..	..	..	..	..	..	..	..			
Ethiopia	..	..	..	..	..	..	70	89	77	110	119	..	..	13.7
Gabon	1	2	2	0	0	0	0	0	0	0	0	26.9	12.9	-20.3
Gambia, The	0	0	0	0	0	0	0	0	0	0	0	..	..	..
Ghana	0	1	1	1	1	2	3	1	2	1	1	-21.1	12.5	11.1
Guinea	3	6	10	7	4	5	6	12	19	8	18	0.4	105.1	12.3
Guinea-Bissau	..	..	..	..	..	..	..	..	..	..	..	..	..	..
Kenya	80	88	94	112	83	78	88	80	89	114	68	2.9	-2.7	-1.8
Lesotho	..	..	..	..	..	..	..	..	..	..	..	..	..	..
Liberia	13	4	5	2	0	0	0	0	0	0	0	6.3	-10.9	..
Madagascar	69	43	60	48	41	50	51	37	35	40	26	-2.5	2.6	-7.2
Malawi	0	4	4	7	6	9	6	5	5	5	4	25.2	12.9	-3.3
Mali	0	0	0	0	0	0	0	0	0	0	0	..	..	..
Mauritania	..	..	..	..	..	..	..	..	..	..	..	..	..	..
Mauritius	0	0	0	0	0	0	0	0	0	0	0	..	..	..
Mozambique	0	0	0	0	0	0	0	0	0	0	0	..	..	..
Namibia	..	..	..	..	..	..	..	..	..	..	..	..	..	..
Niger	0	0	0	0	0	0	0	0	0	0	0	..	..	..
Nigeria	2	1	0	0	0	0	1	0	1	1	1	-1.8	41.6	27.2
Rwanda	22	31	36	46	38	34	30	2	8	16	12	1.4	1.4	-20.2
São Tomé and Principe	0	0	0	0	0	0	0	0	0	0	0	-6.1	-41.0	..
Senegal	1	0	0	0	0	0	0	0	0	0	0	0.9	-2.6	..
Seychelles	0	0	0	0	0	0	0	0	0	0	0	..	..	..
Sierra Leone	10	8	5	8	6	4	3	4	5	5	3	-0.7	12.2	-7.6
Somalia	..	..	..	..	..	..	..	..	..	..	..	..	..	..
South Africa	0	1	0	1	1	1	0	0	1	1	2	24.9	26.1	6.6
Sudan	..	..	..	..	..	..	..	..	..	..	..	..	..	..
Swaziland	..	..	..	..	..	..	..	..	..	..	..	..	..	..
Tanzania	43	39	50	61	52	51	59	37	48	64	47	0.8	-2.2	-1.0
Togo	9	11	13	14	9	19	13	9	13	5	19	-6.2	28.6	-2.9
Uganda	110	144	176	141	127	119	114	194	169	279	210	-2.8	3.8	6.5
Zambia	0	0	1	1	0	1	1	0	1	2	2	..	59.2	14.2
Zimbabwe	3	6	7	35	9	10	4	4	10	11	12	13.2	-9.3	-3.3
NORTH AFRICA	0	0	2	2	0	0	0	0	0	0	0	-34.0	..	-40.2
Algeria	0	0	0	1	0	0	0	0	0	0	0	..	..	..
Egypt, Arab Republic	0	0	2	1	0	0	0	0	0	0	0	..	..	-68.2
Libya	..	..	..	..	..	..	..	..	..	..	..	..	..	..
Morocco	0	0	0	0	0	0	0	0	0	0	0	..	..	-40.5
Tunisia	0	0	0	0	0	0	0	0	0	0	0	..	..	11.4
ALL AFRICA	819	818	908	1,033	828	847	831	751	788	953	973	-2.4	0.0	-0.3

5-25. Cotton exports

	Thousands of metric tons											Average annual percentage growth		
	1980	*1988*	*1989*	*1990*	*1991*	*1992*	*1993*	*1994*	*1995*	*1996*	*1997*	*75-84*	*85-89*	*90-MR*
SUB-SAHARAN AFRICA	459	661	812	700	661	693	695	735	783	819	834	1.2	7.6	1.6
excluding South Africa	459	656	803	694	658	689	695	734	783	819	831	1.3	7.4	1.8
excl. S. Africa & Nigeria	459	656	802	691	657	688	691	732	781	817	829	1.3	7.4	1.7
Angola	0	1	2	0	0	0	0	0	0	0	0	-27.7	10.4	..
Benin	8	19	56	41	43	58	60	74	99	89	102	-0.6	13.3	11.6
Botswana	0	0	0	0	0	0	1	1	1	1	1	..	..	24.3
Burkina Faso	28	55	43	59	55	55	60	40	55	42	44	10.8	14.3	-2.0
Burundi	1	1	0	0	0	0	2	2	1	0	0	-0.4	2.0	61.7
Cameroon	26	22	85	38	23	42	51	59	54	66	66	15.1	19.5	4.5
Cape Verde	0	0	0	0	0	0	0	0	0	..	..	..	..	..
Central African Republic	14	6	8	9	13	6	8	5	12	15	9	-4.0	-12.8	3.5
Chad	35	43	48	57	65	85	40	32	62	50	62	-2.4	-0.4	-0.7
Comoros	0	0	0	0	0	0	0	0	0	0	0	..	..	..
Congo, Democratic Rep. of	2	0	0	0	0	0	0	1	1	1	1	..	..	..
Congo, Republic of	0	0	0	0	0	0	0	0	0	0	0	..	..	..
Côte d'Ivoire	39	96	89	89	97	67	96	100	88	75	65	14.7	15.3	-2.6
Djibouti	0	0	0	0	0	0	0	0	0	0	0	..	..	..
Equatorial Guinea	0	0	0	0	0	0	0	0	0	0	0	..	..	..
Eritrea	0	0	0	0	0	0	0	0	0	0	0	..	..	..
Ethiopia	0	0	0	0	0	0	0	0	8	8	8	..	..	227.2
Gabon	0	0	0	0	0	0	0	0	0	0	0	..	..	..
Gambia, The	0	0	1	1	2	1	1	1	1	1	1	..	10.6	-9.5
Ghana	0	0	0	0	0	0	2	7	1	0	0	..	..	..
Guinea	0	1	1	2	1	4	10	6	7	5	4	..	..	22.6
Guinea-Bissau	0	1	1	0	1	0	1	1	1	1	1	..	25.4	2.5
Kenya	4	0	0	0	1	6	8	7	1	0	0	-18.6	-73.2	-37.5
Lesotho	0	0	0	0	0	0	0	0	0	0	0	..	..	..
Liberia	0	0	0	0	0	0	0	0	0	0	0	..	..	..
Madagascar	1	0	1	0	3	0	0	1	1	1	0	22.2	-16.8	-6.7
Malawi	3	0	4	3	6	3	0	0	0	0	0	-20.5	-0.6	-75.6
Mali	53	70	99	93	114	113	133	126	105	130	118	9.9	14.2	2.8
Mauritania	0	0	0	0	0	0	0	0	0	0	0	..	..	..
Mauritius	0	0	0	0	0	0	0	0	0	0	0	..	..	..
Mozambique	6	4	5	6	6	11	13	16	13	15	13	-8.0	1.1	15.3
Namibia	0	0	0	0	0	0	0	0	0	0	0	..	..	..
Niger	0	1	3	1	0	1	1	1	0	0	0	-12.4	80.4	-19.0
Nigeria	0	0	1	3	1	0	3	3	2	2	2	..	..	9.4
Rwanda	0	0	0	0	0	0	0	0	0	0	0	..	..	..
São Tomé and Principe	0	0	0	0	0	0	0	0	0	0	0	..	..	..
Senegal	6	8	8	5	12	16	20	15	9	11	10	2.1	-6.4	4.3
Seychelles	0	0	0	0	0	0	0	0	0	0	0	..	..	..
Sierra Leone	0	0	0	0	0	0	0	0	0	0	0	..	..	..
Somalia	0	0	0	0	0	0	0	0	0	0	0	..	..	..
South Africa	0	5	9	6	3	5	0	0	0	0	3	-30.6	269.4	-38.6
Sudan	132	177	176	126	87	76	48	78	96	104	94	0.0	1.2	-4.6
Swaziland	4	6	9	19	10	6	7	4	3	4	4	4.8	40.8	-15.8
Tanzania	31	52	54	46	39	73	61	60	71	90	77	-3.9	17.8	7.7
Togo	5	29	34	33	36	39	42	43	61	56	48	27.3	22.1	7.1
Uganda	2	2	2	4	8	8	8	4	6	10	10	-21.5	-25.3	12.8
Zambia	5	2	8	3	2	2	1	1	0	0	0	15.9	12.7	-36.6
Zimbabwe	54	59	65	54	34	16	18	47	27	44	91	4.2	-0.2	2.3
NORTH AFRICA	167	86	66	41	16	16	20	114	68	23	42	0.1	-17.0	2.3
Algeria	0	0	0	0	0	0	0	0	0	0	0	..	..	..
Egypt, Arab Republic	164	80	58	39	13	16	18	113	67	23	42	0.2	-18.9	4.0
Libya	0	0	0	0	0	0	0	0	0	0	0	..	..	..
Morocco	3	6	7	1	3	1	2	1	0	0	0	3.4	..	-41.6
Tunisia	0	0	0	0	0	0	0	0	0	0	0	..	..	..
ALL AFRICA	627	746	877	740	677	710	715	849	851	843	876	0.9	3.6	1.7

5-26. Groundnut exports

| | \multicolumn{11}{c}{Thousands of metric tons} | | | | | | | | | | Average annual percentage growth | | |
	1980	1988	1989	1990	1991	1992	1993	1994	1995	1996	1997	75-84	85-89	90-MR
SUB-SAHARAN AFRICA	605	687	580	574	341	336	276	397	280	388	385	-8.9	15.7	-4.9
excluding South Africa	560	661	502	535	309	312	249	337	244	350	327	-8.7	15.2	-5.5
excl. S. Africa & Nigeria	559	661	502	535	309	310	249	330	243	345	306	-8.2	15.1	-6.0
Angola	1	0	0	0	0	0	0	0	0	0	0	-4.9	..	..
Benin	2	2	0	0	0	0	0	0	0	0	0	-27.0	..	..
Botswana	0	0	0	0	0	0	0	0	0	0	0	-10.2	29.0	-24.7
Burkina Faso	1	4	1	1	1	1	0	0	0	0	0	-43.9	152.2	-12.6
Burundi	..	..	..	..	..	..	..	..	..	..	..	..	..	..
Cameroon	1	0	0	0	0	0	0	0	0	0	0	-39.5	15.8	20.6
Cape Verde	0	0	0	0	0	0	0	0	0	0	0	..	..	..
Central African Republic	0	0	0	0	0	0	0	1	1	0	0	..	..	..
Chad	0	3	0	0	0	0	1	2	0	0	0	..	..	..
Comoros	..	..	..	..	..	..	..	..	..	..	..	..	..	..
Congo, Democratic Rep. of	0	0	0	0	0	0	0	0	0	0	0	..	..	..
Congo, Republic of	0	0	0	0	0	0	0	0	0	0	0	-10.6	..	..
Côte d'Ivoire	0	1	0	0	0	0	0	0	1	0	1	-8.4	..	..
Djibouti	..	..	..	..	..	..	..	..	..	..	..	..	..	..
Equatorial Guinea	..	..	..	..	..	..	..	..	..	..	..	..	..	..
Eritrea	..	..	..	..	..	..	..	..	..	..	..	..	..	..
Ethiopia	..	..	..	..	..	..	0	0	0	0	0	..	..	..
Gabon	0	0	0	0	0	0	0	0	0	0	0	..	..	..
Gambia, The	67	30	24	24	17	18	28	26	38	32	21	-7.7	-11.7	3.8
Ghana	2	0	0	0	0	0	0	0	0	0	0	..	..	..
Guinea	0	0	0	0	0	0	0	0	0	0	0	..	..	..
Guinea-Bissau	8	4	2	2	0	0	0	0	0	0	0	-4.4	-17.9	-22.6
Kenya	0	0	0	0	0	0	1	0	0	0	0	-24.6	23.1	1.6
Lesotho	..	..	..	..	..	..	..	..	..	..	..	..	..	..
Liberia	..	..	..	..	..	..	..	..	..	..	..	..	..	..
Madagascar	4	0	0	0	1	0	0	0	0	0	1	-44.9	..	1.4
Malawi	28	36	3	0	1	0	0	1	1	1	1	-17.8	23.7	10.8
Mali	15	11	11	12	10	11	12	17	16	15	17	-11.7	9.3	6.5
Mauritania	0	0	0	0	0	0	0	0	0	0	0	..	..	..
Mauritius	0	0	0	0	0	0	0	0	0	0	0	..	..	..
Mozambique	10	2	3	2	0	0	0	0	0	0	0	-8.5	22.4	-22.2
Namibia	..	..	..	..	..	..	..	..	..	..	..	..	..	..
Niger	1	2	6	1	1	1	0	0	0	0	0	-38.0	182.2	-27.4
Nigeria	1	1	0	0	0	1	0	7	1	4	21	-37.9	..	93.0
Rwanda	0	0	0	0	0	0	0	0	0	0	0	..	..	..
São Tomé and Principe	..	..	..	..	..	..	..	..	..	..	..	..	..	..
Senegal	175	396	348	360	215	219	119	164	98	207	102	-9.1	21.2	-13.1
Seychelles	..	..	..	..	..	..	..	..	..	..	..	..	..	..
Sierra Leone	..	..	..	..	..	..	..	..	..	..	..	..	..	..
Somalia	0	0	0	0	0	0	0	0	0	0	0	..	..	..
South Africa	45	26	78	39	32	24	27	59	36	38	58	-12.5	23.7	-0.2
Sudan	238	164	98	109	39	51	84	110	82	84	156	-6.0	15.7	5.8
Swaziland	..	..	..	..	..	..	..	..	..	..	..	..	..	..
Tanzania	1	0	1	7	16	7	0	0	0	0	0	..	181.1	-38.1
Togo	0	0	0	0	0	0	0	0	0	2	0	-36.2	296.1	68.2
Uganda	0	0	0	0	0	0	1	0	0	0	0	..	..	-6.6
Zambia	0	0	0	0	5	1	0	0	0	0	0	-26.0	..	-31.4
Zimbabwe	3	6	4	16	3	1	3	7	3	1	5	-19.6	107.4	-10.7
NORTH AFRICA	13	1	3	7	5	5	21	16	15	9	18	-7.3	-19.9	21.4
Algeria	0	0	0	0	0	0	0	0	0	0	0	..	..	..
Egypt, Arab Republic	13	1	3	4	2	4	12	9	10	6	11	-7.3	-19.9	19.6
Libya	0	0	0	3	4	1	8	4	5	4	7	..	..	14.0
Morocco	0	0	0	0	0	0	0	0	0	0	0	..	..	-9.5
Tunisia	0	0	0	0	0	0	0	3	0	0	0	..	..	..
ALL AFRICA	618	688	583	581	347	341	296	413	295	398	403	-8.9	15.5	-4.5

5-27. Oil palm products exports

	Thousands of metric tons											Average annual percentage growth		
	1980	1988	1989	1990	1991	1992	1993	1994	1995	1996	1997	75-84	85-89	90-MR
SUB-SAHARAN AFRICA	280	277	211	233	194	269	319	250	175	216	170	-12.2	9.6	-2.3
excluding South Africa	280	274	211	232	194	267	317	247	174	215	170	-12.2	9.5	-2.3
excl. S. Africa & Nigeria	184	173	147	223	186	264	315	237	174	198	165	-9.3	6.3	-0.2
Angola	0	0	0	0	0	0	0	0	0	0	0	..	..	..
Benin	13	8	3	6	1	2	3	7	9	8	8	-12.5	8.9	17.7
Botswana	0	0	0	0	0	0	0	0	0	0	0	..	..	108.5
Burkina Faso	..	..	..	..	..	..	..	..	..	..	..	..	..	..
Burundi	0	0	0	0	0	0	0	0	0	0	0	..	..	..
Cameroon	21	21	31	28	10	27	27	30	8	41	23	-7.7	12.3	-0.4
Cape Verde	..	..	..	..	..	..	..	..	..	..	..	..	..	..
Central African Republic	0	0	0	0	0	0	0	0	0	0	0	..	..	..
Chad	..	..	..	..	..	..	..	..	..	..	..	..	..	..
Comoros	..	..	..	..	..	..	..	..	..	..	..	..	..	..
Congo, Democratic Rep. of	10	2	4	4	1	1	1	3	1	1	1	-23.7	-21.9	-18.6
Congo, Republic of	0	0	0	0	0	0	0	0	0	0	0	-17.6	..	..
Côte d'Ivoire	99	122	78	166	158	186	207	153	121	103	74	-7.9	9.5	-3.9
Djibouti	0	0	0	0	0	0	0	0	0	0	0	..	..	..
Equatorial Guinea	0	0	0	0	0	0	0	0	0	0	0	..	..	..
Eritrea	..	..	..	..	..	..	..	..	..	..	..	..	..	..
Ethiopia	..	..	..	..	..	..	..	..	..	..	..	..	..	..
Gabon	0	1	8	4	2	5	1	0	3	6	8	..	9.6	3.4
Gambia, The	1	0	0	0	0	0	0	0	0	0	0	-19.8	..	..
Ghana	0	2	8	7	3	8	9	11	12	21	18	..	39.0	17.6
Guinea	15	2	1	1	1	1	7	1	0	1	1	-3.6	1.5	-7.3
Guinea-Bissau	6	8	5	2	5	3	2	3	1	3	1	2.0	5.1	-14.3
Kenya	0	0	0	0	1	25	53	14	13	10	26	-52.7	..	68.8
Lesotho	..	..	..	..	..	..	..	..	..	..	..	..	..	..
Liberia	6	6	8	5	4	5	5	5	5	5	5	24.9	12.7	-2.3
Madagascar	0	0	0	0	0	0	0	0	0	0	0	..	..	18.7
Malawi	..	..	..	..	..	..	..	..	..	..	..	..	..	..
Mali	..	..	..	..	..	..	..	..	..	..	..	..	..	..
Mauritania	..	..	..	..	..	..	..	..	..	..	..	..	..	..
Mauritius	0	0	0	0	0	0	0	0	0	0	0	..	..	41.8
Mozambique	..	..	..	..	..	..	..	..	..	..	..	..	..	..
Namibia	..	..	..	..	..	..	..	..	..	..	..	..	..	..
Niger	..	..	..	..	..	..	..	..	..	..	..	..	..	..
Nigeria	96	102	64	9	8	3	2	10	0	17	5	-16.9	17.9	-11.8
Rwanda	..	..	..	..	..	..	..	..	..	..	..	..	..	..
São Tomé and Principe	0	0	0	0	0	0	0	0	0	0	0	-19.1	..	..
Senegal	0	0	0	0	0	0	0	0	0	0	0	-55.4	18.6	16.0
Seychelles	0	0	0	0	0	0	0	0	0	0	0	..	..	..
Sierra Leone	1	1	0	0	0	0	0	11	0	0	0	-11.4	-48.9	-21.7
Somalia	..	..	..	..	..	..	..	..	..	..	..	..	..	..
South Africa	0	3	0	0	1	2	2	3	0	1	0	..	..	30.5
Sudan	..	..	..	..	..	..	..	..	..	..	..	..	..	..
Swaziland	..	..	..	..	..	..	..	..	..	..	..	..	..	..
Tanzania	1	0	0	0	0	0	0	0	0	0	0	..	..	..
Togo	10	0	0	0	0	2	0	0	0	0	0	-13.6	-15.9	65.0
Uganda	0	0	0	0	0	0	0	0	0	0	0	..	..	..
Zambia	0	0	0	0	0	0	0	0	0	0	0	..	..	..
Zimbabwe	0	0	0	0	0	0	0	0	0	0	0	..	..	..
NORTH AFRICA	0	0	0	0	0	0	0	0	0	0	0	..	..	5.7
Algeria	..	..	..	..	..	..	..	..	..	..	..	..	..	..
Egypt, Arab Republic	0	0	0	0	0	0	0	0	0	0	0	..	..	6.4
Libya	..	..	..	..	..	..	..	..	..	..	..	..	..	..
Morocco	0	0	0	0	0	0	0	0	0	0	0	..	..	..
Tunisia	0	0	0	0	0	0	0	0	0	0	0	..	..	..
ALL AFRICA	280	277	211	233	195	269	319	250	175	216	171	-12.2	9.6	-2.3

5-28. Sisal exports

	Thousands of metric tons											Average annual percentage growth		
	1980	1988	1989	1990	1991	1992	1993	1994	1995	1996	1997	75-84	85-89	90-MR
SUB-SAHARAN AFRICA	109	51	50	50	42	44	42	41	47	35	37	-9.6	-8.7	-3.5
excluding South Africa	109	50	50	50	42	43	42	41	47	35	37	-9.7	-8.7	-3.5
excl. S. Africa & Nigeria	109	50	50	50	42	43	42	41	47	35	37	-9.7	-8.7	-3.5
Angola	3	0	0	0	0	0	0	0	0	0	0	-30.8	..	..
Benin	0	0	0	0	0	0	0	0	0	0	0	..	..	..
Botswana	0	0	0	0	0	0	0	0	0	0	0	..	..	..
Burkina Faso	0	0	0	0	0	0	0	0	0	0	0	..	..	..
Burundi	0	0	0	0	0	0	0	0	0	0	0	..	..	..
Cameroon	0	0	0	0	0	0	0	0	0	0	0	..	..	..
Cape Verde	0	0	0	0	0	0	0	0	0	0	0	..	..	..
Central African Republic	0	0	0	0	0	0	0	0	0	0	0	..	..	..
Chad	0	0	0	0	0	0	0	0	0	0	0	..	..	..
Comoros	0	0	0	0	0	0	0	0	0	0	0	..	..	..
Congo, Democratic Rep. of	0	0	0	0	0	0	0	0	0	0	0	..	..	..
Congo, Republic of	0	0	0	0	0	0	0	0	0	0	0	..	..	..
Côte d'Ivoire	0	0	0	0	0	0	0	0	0	0	0	..	..	..
Djibouti	0	0	0	0	0	0	0	0	0	0	0	..	..	..
Equatorial Guinea	0	0	0	0	0	0	0	0	0	0	0	..	..	..
Eritrea	0	0	0	0	0	0	0	0	0	0	0	..	..	..
Ethiopia	0	0	0	0	0	0	0	0	0	0	0	..	..	..
Gabon	0	0	0	0	0	0	0	0	0	0	0	..	..	..
Gambia, The	0	0	0	0	0	0	0	0	0	0	0	..	..	..
Ghana	0	0	0	0	0	0	0	0	0	0	0	..	..	..
Guinea	0	0	0	0	0	0	0	0	0	0	0	..	..	..
Guinea-Bissau	0	0	0	0	0	0	0	0	0	0	0	..	..	..
Kenya	40	31	33	30	28	32	27	26	25	17	19	-1.3	-4.8	-7.0
Lesotho	0	0	0	0	0	0	0	0	0	0	0	..	..	..
Liberia	0	0	0	0	0	0	0	0	0	0	0	..	..	..
Madagascar	10	9	7	12	10	7	9	8	10	10	4	-5.9	-8.1	-4.7
Malawi	0	0	0	0	0	0	0	0	0	0	0	..	..	..
Mali	0	0	0	0	0	0	0	0	0	0	0	..	..	..
Mauritania	0	0	0	0	0	0	0	0	0	0	0	..	..	..
Mauritius	0	0	0	0	0	0	0	0	0	0	0	..	..	..
Mozambique	7	1	1	0	0	0	0	0	0	0	0	-14.5	1.7	-6.1
Namibia	0	0	0	0	0	0	0	0	0	0	0	..	..	..
Niger	0	0	0	0	0	0	0	0	0	0	0	..	..	..
Nigeria	0	0	0	0	0	0	0	0	0	0	0	..	..	..
Rwanda	0	0	0	0	0	0	0	0	0	0	0	..	..	..
São Tomé and Principe	0	0	0	0	0	0	0	0	0	0	0	..	..	..
Senegal	0	0	0	0	0	0	0	0	0	0	0	38.6	..	..
Seychelles	0	0	0	0	0	0	0	0	0	0	0	..	..	..
Sierra Leone	0	0	0	0	0	0	0	0	0	0	0	..	..	..
Somalia	0	0	0	0	0	0	0	0	0	0	0	..	..	..
South Africa	0	1	0	0	0	0	0	0	0	0	0	-4.4	-7.3	-33.6
Sudan	0	0	0	0	0	0	0	0	0	0	0	..	..	..
Swaziland	0	0	0	0	0	0	0	0	0	0	0	..	..	..
Tanzania	48	10	9	8	5	4	5	7	11	8	14	-12.1	-16.9	7.3
Togo	0	0	0	0	0	0	0	0	0	0	0	..	..	..
Uganda	0	0	0	0	0	0	0	0	0	0	0	..	..	..
Zambia	0	0	0	0	0	0	0	0	0	0	0	..	..	..
Zimbabwe	0	0	0	0	0	0	0	0	0	0	0	..	..	..
NORTH AFRICA	0	0	0	0	0	0	0	0	0	0	0	..	..	17.5
Algeria	0	0	0	0	0	0	0	0	0	0	0	..	..	..
Egypt, Arab Republic	0	0	0	0	0	0	0	0	0	0	0	..	..	..
Libya	0	0	0	0	0	0	0	0	0	0	0	..	..	..
Morocco	0	0	0	0	0	0	0	0	0	0	0	..	..	58.9
Tunisia	0	0	0	0	0	0	0	0	0	0	0	..	..	-14.9
ALL AFRICA	109	51	50	50	42	44	42	41	47	35	37	-9.6	-8.7	-3.5

5-29. Tea exports

	Thousands of metric tons											Average annual percentage growth		
	1980	*1988*	*1989*	*1990*	*1991*	*1992*	*1993*	*1994*	*1995*	*1996*	*1997*	*75-84*	*85-89*	*90-MR*
SUB-SAHARAN AFRICA	182	245	258	267	277	271	298	273	351	363	272	3.8	4.9	2.7
excluding South Africa	180	245	257	266	275	270	297	272	350	362	271	3.7	4.8	2.7
excl. S. Africa & Nigeria	180	245	257	266	275	270	297	272	350	362	271	3.7	4.8	2.7
Angola	0	0	0	0	0	0	0	0	0	0	0	..	..	..
Benin	0	0	0	0	0	0	0	0	0	0	0			
Botswana	0	0	0	0	0	0	0	0	0	0	0	21.8	-48.8	17.5
Burkina Faso	0	0	0	0	0	0	0	0	0	0	0	-6.7	..	..
Burundi	1	4	4	4	5	6	5	7	7	4	4	12.3	2.6	0.6
Cameroon	1	0	0	3	0	0	0	0	0	0	0	23.2	-32.4	-18.9
Cape Verde	0	0	0	0	0	0	0	0	0	0	0	..	..	..
Central African Republic	0	0	0	0	0	0	0	0	0	0	0			
Chad	0	0	0	0	0	0	0	0	0	0	0			
Comoros	0	0	0	0	0	0	0	0	0	0	0	..	..	..
Congo, Democratic Rep. of	1	2	3	3	2	1	2	2	2	2	2	-8.5	-4.9	-5.0
Congo, Republic of	0	0	0	0	0	0	0	0	0	0	0	..	..	..
Côte d'Ivoire	0	0	0	0	0	0	0	0	0	0	0			
Djibouti	0	0	0	0	0	0	0	0	0	0	0			
Equatorial Guinea	0	0	0	0	0	0	0	0	0	0	0	..	..	..
Eritrea	0	0	0	0	0	0	0	0	0	0	0	..	..	..
Ethiopia	0	0	0	0	0	0	0	0	0	0	0			
Gabon	0	0	0	0	0	0	0	0	0	0	0	..	..	..
Gambia, The	0	0	0	0	0	0	0	0	0	0	0	..	..	..
Ghana	0	0	0	0	0	0	0	0	0	0	0	..	..	..
Guinea	0	0	0	0	0	0	0	0	0	0	0			
Guinea-Bissau	0	0	0	0	0	0	0	0	0	0	0	..	..	..
Kenya	84	155	165	166	176	172	199	177	259	261	199	6.7	8.4	5.0
Lesotho	0	0	0	0	0	0	0	0	0	0	0	..	..	..
Liberia	0	0	0	0	0	0	0	0	0	0	0	..	..	..
Madagascar	0	0	0	0	0	0	0	0	0	0	0	..	-54.8	59.5
Malawi	31	37	38	41	37	37	35	35	32	37	14	3.8	-0.2	-7.5
Mali	0	0	0	0	0	0	0	0	0	0	0	..	..	..
Mauritania	0	0	0	0	0	0	0	0	0	0	0	..	..	..
Mauritius	4	5	5	4	4	5	4	4	3	1	0	8.2	-7.0	-21.1
Mozambique	30	1	0	1	1	1	0	0	0	0	0	-0.2	-48.5	-5.7
Namibia	0	0	0	0	0	0	0	0	0	0	0	..	..	..
Niger	0	0	0	0	0	0	0	0	0	0	0			
Nigeria	0	0	0	0	0	0	0	0	0	0	0	..	..	18.2
Rwanda	7	12	13	12	13	13	12	5	5	5	4	8.5	8.0	-16.4
São Tomé and Principe	0	0	0	0	0	0	0	0	0	0	0	..	..	..
Senegal	0	0	1	1	0	0	0	0	0	0	0	-8.6	281.6	..
Seychelles	0	0	0	0	0	0	0	0	0	0	0	-7.6	..	-7.6
Sierra Leone	0	0	0	0	0	0	0	0	0	0	0	..	..	..
Somalia	0	0	0	0	0	0	0	0	0	0	0			
South Africa	2	1	1	1	1	1	1	1	1	1	1	44.8	13.6	-0.6
Sudan	0	0	0	0	0	0	0	0	0	0	0	..	..	..
Swaziland	0	0	0	0	0	0	0	0	0	0	0	..	..	..
Tanzania	13	11	12	15	18	20	20	22	22	25	20	2.6	1.2	7.1
Togo	0	0	0	0	0	0	0	0	0	0	0	..	..	..
Uganda	1	3	3	5	7	8	10	11	11	15	15	-28.0	11.3	19.4
Zambia	0	0	0	0	0	0	0	0	0	0	0	..	..	23.4
Zimbabwe	6	13	13	12	11	6	8	10	9	12	13	10.5	5.4	0.2
NORTH AFRICA	0	0	0	0	0	0	0	0	0	0	0	..	87.0	20.3
Algeria	0	0	0	0	0	0	0	0	0	0	0	..	..	..
Egypt, Arab Republic	0	0	0	0	0	0	0	0	0	0	0	..	..	38.0
Libya	0	0	0	0	0	0	0	0	0	0	0	..	..	..
Morocco	0	0	0	0	0	0	0	0	0	0	0	..	..	58.4
Tunisia	0	0	0	0	0	0	0	0	0	0	0	..	..	-26.3
ALL AFRICA	182	245	259	267	277	271	298	274	351	363	273	3.8	4.9	2.7

5-30. Sugar exports

	Thousands of metric tons											Average annual percentage growth		
	1980	1988	1989	1990	1991	1992	1993	1994	1995	1996	1997	75-84	85-89	90-MR
SUB-SAHARAN AFRICA	2,148	2,299	2,505	2,441	2,068	1,627	1,260	1,741	1,604	2,365	2,365	0.8	2.6	-1.3
excluding South Africa	1,362	1,389	1,415	1,469	1,356	1,343	1,118	1,422	1,215	1,532	1,381	3.1	0.5	-0.2
excl. S. Africa & Nigeria	1,362	1,368	1,415	1,469	1,356	1,343	1,118	1,422	1,215	1,532	1,381	3.1	0.3	-0.2
Angola	0	0	0	0	0	0	0	0	0	0	0	..	..	..
Benin	0	0	0	0	0	0	0	0	0	0	0			
Botswana	0	0	0	0	0	0	0	0	0	1	1	-14.0	65.9	30.6
Burkina Faso	2	0	0	0	0	0	0	0	0	0	0	91.6	..	..
Burundi	0	0	0	0	0	10	0	0	0	0	0	..	..	-19.1
Cameroon	9	1	1	0	2	0	1	0	1	7	7	42.1	-24.4	20.8
Cape Verde	0	0	0	0	0	0	0	0	0	0	0	..	..	..
Central African Republic	0	0	0	0	0	0	0	0	0	0	0	..	..	-10.4
Chad	0	0	0	0	0	0	0	0	0	0	0	..	..	..
Comoros	0	0	0	0	0	0	0	0	0	0	0	..	..	..
Congo, Democratic Rep. of	0	0	0	0	0	0	0	0	0	0	0	..	..	..
Congo, Republic of	0	18	14	26	23	29	18	11	14	20	20	-1.3	-14.0	-2.2
Côte d'Ivoire	11	7	18	23	40	23	39	33	12	29	31	142.4	-18.9	1.3
Djibouti	0	0	0	0	0	0	0	0	0	0	0	..	..	..
Equatorial Guinea	0	0	0	0	0	0	0	0	0	0	0	..	..	..
Eritrea	0	0	0	0	0	0	0	0	0	0	0			
Ethiopia	0	0	0	0	0	0	15	5	0	0	0	..	..	..
Gabon	2	0	0	0	8	7	0	0	0	0	0	9.3	..	..
Gambia, The	0	0	0	0	0	0	0	0	0	0	0	..	..	..
Ghana	0	0	0	0	0	0	0	0	0	1	1	..	..	..
Guinea	0	0	0	0	0	0	0	0	0	0	0			
Guinea-Bissau	0	0	0	0	0	0	0	0	0	0	0	..	..	..
Kenya	56	0	0	0	0	104	50	112	13	52	31	19.0	-15.5	158.2
Lesotho	0	0	0	0	0	0	0	0	0	0	0	..	..	..
Liberia	0	0	0	0	0	0	0	0	0	0	0	8.1	..	..
Madagascar	26	19	72	47	21	17	11	24	15	7	1	-1.1	19.9	-30.5
Malawi	92	99	54	62	51	22	26	34	66	54	45	13.9	-5.4	-0.3
Mali	0	0	0	0	0	0	0	0	0	0	0	..	..	..
Mauritania	0	0	0	0	0	0	0	0	0	0	0	..	..	..
Mauritius	618	653	637	578	551	598	535	519	524	773	575	-0.7	4.4	0.4
Mozambique	64	12	13	18	25	52	0	52	54	25	59	-12.8	-8.1	15.4
Namibia	0	0	0	0	0	0	0	0	0	0	0	..	..	..
Niger	0	0	1	1	0	0	0	0	0	0	0	..	..	4.4
Nigeria	0	22	0	0	0	0	0	0	0	0	0	..	..	4.4
Rwanda	0	0	0	0	0	0	0	0	0	0	0*	..	..	..
São Tomé and Principe	0	0	0	0	0	0	0	0	0	0	0	..	..	..
Senegal	0	8	7	3	0	0	0	0	0	0	0	-34.3	244.7	-25.3
Seychelles	0	0	0	0	0	0	0	0	0	0	0	..	..	..
Sierra Leone	0	0	0	0	0	0	0	0	0	0	0	..	..	..
Somalia	0	0	0	0	0	0	0	0	0	0	0	..	..	..
South Africa	786	910	1,089	971	712	284	141	318	390	833	983	-2.7	6.2	-3.2
Sudan	0	0	0	65	49	54	39	136	20	49	80	..	..	-0.3
Swaziland	300	375	414	425	492	379	363	279	275	241	229	9.2	1.5	-8.8
Tanzania	13	11	12	22	0	11	11	11	11	12	12	33.4	0.9	-4.0
Togo	0	0	0	0	0	0	0	0	0	0	0	..	..	-0.7
Uganda	0	0	0	0	0	0	0	0	0	0	0	..	..	..
Zambia	0	4	2	2	4	26	11	7	50	69	69	60.8	-21.0	60.4
Zimbabwe	169	159	171	197	89	12	0	201	160	192	219	3.9	-7.3	8.5
NORTH AFRICA	23	3	14	6	25	1	1	7	6	4	1	-29.0	53.1	-22.3
Algeria	0	0	0	0	13	0	0	0	0	0	0	..	..	..
Egypt, Arab Republic	10	0	14	2	8	1	1	7	6	4	0	-12.4	134.0	-17.6
Libya	0	0	0	0	0	0	0	0	0	0	0	..	..	..
Morocco	0	1	0	0	0	0	0	0	0	0	0	..	-17.5	34.4
Tunisia	13	2	0	3	4	0	0	0	0	0	0	-28.6	-44.5	-40.9
ALL AFRICA	2,171	2,302	2,518	2,446	2,093	1,628	1,261	1,748	1,610	2,369	2,365	0.4	2.7	-1.3

5-31. Tobacco exports

	Hundreds of metric tons											Average annual percentage growth		
	1980	1988	1989	1990	1991	1992	1993	1994	1995	1996	1997	75-84	85-89	90-MR
SUB-SAHARAN AFRICA	1,777	1,832	1,817	2,259	2,494	2,817	3,164	4,414	3,123	3,607	2,865	3.0	0.4	7.1
excluding South Africa	1,705	1,753	1,722	2,179	2,404	2,736	3,070	4,244	3,011	3,519	2,789	3.2	0.2	7.4
excl. S. Africa & Nigeria	1,705	1,752	1,722	2,178	2,403	2,731	3,068	4,241	3,010	3,510	2,786	3.2	0.2	7.3
Angola	16	0	0	0	0	0	0	0	0	0	0	-4.7	..	..
Benin	0	0	0	0	0	0	0	0	0	0	0	-36.9	..	..
Botswana	1	0	1	0	0	0	0	0	0	1	1	32.5	-1.9	18.7
Burkina Faso	0	0	0	0	0	0.	0	0	0	0	0	..	..	..
Burundi	0	9	8	7	11	11	10	4	0	2	2	..	89.6	-20.5
Cameroon	21	5	9	8	7	7	6	1	3	0	0	-7.9	-11.6	-23.9
Cape Verde	0	0	0	0	0	0	0	0	0	0	0	..	..	..
Central African Republic	8	4	2	0	1	1	1	1	2	1	1	-8.6	-2.0	1.8
Chad	0	0	0	0	0	0	0	0	0	0	0	..	..	..
Comoros	0	0	0	0	0	0	0	0	0	0	0	..	..	..
Congo, Democratic Rep. of	0	0	0	0	0	0	0	0	0	0	0	..	..	..
Congo, Republic of	1	0	0	0	0	0	0	0	0	0	0	-23.6	-46.4	..
Côte d'Ivoire	0	0	0	1	0	0	0	0	2	2	1	-2.6	..	19.8
Djibouti	0	0	0	0	0	0	0	0	0	0	0	..	..	..
Equatorial Guinea	0	0	0	0	0	0	0	0	0	0	0	..	..	..
Eritrea	0	0	0	0	0	0	0	0	0	0	0	..	..	..
Ethiopia	0	0	0	0	0	0	0	0	0	0	0	..	..	..
Gabon	0	0	0	0	0	0	0	0	0	0	0	..	..	..
Gambia, The	0	0	0	0	0	0	0	0	1	1	1	..	..	..
Ghana	0	1	1	3	3	2	3	5	2	7	7	-33.6	-12.6	19.2
Guinea	0	0	0	0	0	0	0	0	0	0	0	..	..	..
Guinea-Bissau	0	0	0	0	0	0	0	0	0	0	0	..	..	..
Kenya	0	7	9	0	19	48	56	29	30	76	51	9.8	31.8	51.5
Lesotho	0	0	0	0	0	0	0	0	0	0	0	..	..	..
Liberia	0	0	0	0	0	0	0	0	0	0	0	3.3	..	..
Madagascar	1	5	5	0	0	0	0	0	4	4	1	-11.2	-6.9	8.1
Malawi	611	596	546	874	982	973	957	983	980	1,067	940	8.4	-3.3	4.7
Mali	0	0	0	0	0	0	0	0	0	0	0	-53.9	..	..
Mauritania	0	0	0	0	0	0	0	0	0	0	0	..	..	..
Mauritius	0	0	0	0	0	0	0	0	0	0	0	..	..	..
Mozambique	0	0	0	0	0	0	0	0	0	0	0	..	..	..
Namibia	0	0	0	0	0	0	0	0	0	0	0	..	..	..
Niger	3	8	8	9	0	0	0	0	0	0	0	39.9	..	..
Nigeria	0	1	0	1	1	5	2	4	2	9	3	..	..	30.4
Rwanda	0	0	0	0	0	0	0	0	0	0	0	..	..	..
São Tomé and Principe	0	0	0	0	0	0	0	0	0	0	0	..	..	..
Senegal	0	0	2	3	0	0	1	1	1	1	1	..	..	-6.2
Seychelles	0	0	0	0	0	0	0	0	0	0	0	..	..	..
Sierra Leone	0	1	2	1	2	7	2	2	2	2	2	..	23.3	2.9
Somalia	0	0	0	0	0	0	0	0	0	0	0	..	..	..
South Africa	72	79	95	80	90	81	94	169	112	88	76	-1.8	7.0	0.9
Sudan	0	0	0	0	0	0	0	0	0	0	0	..	..	..
Swaziland	2	0	0	0	0	0	1	1	1	1	1	-17.4	-22.6	8.1
Tanzania	83	82	71	71	80	127	106	154	178	240	63	-7.4	6.4	8.6
Togo	0	0	0	0	0	0	0	0	0	0	0	4.7	..	..
Uganda	3	0	5	23	25	23	41	41	35	31	36	-8.6	-20.7	18.5
Zambia	26	26	10	20	13	25	41	30	9	34	31	-13.6	0.0	9.5
Zimbabwe	930	1,007	1,041	1,158	1,261	1,505	1,843	2,989	1,760	2,042	1,650	3.9	2.3	8.5
NORTH AFRICA	15	10	7	10	11	7	7	9	12	4	6	6.5	-7.2	-4.3
Algeria	0	0	0	0	0	0	0	0	0	0	0	..	..	..
Egypt, Arab Republic	0	0	2	1	0	0	0	0	0	0	0	..	..	-48.4
Libya	0	0	0	0	0	0	0	0	0	0	0	..	..	..
Morocco	0	0	0	0	0	3	3	1	0	0	0	..	..	..
Tunisia	15	10	5	9	11	4	4	8	12	4	6	26.9	-5.4	-1.1
ALL AFRICA	1,792	1,842	1,824	2,269	2,505	2,825	3,171	4,423	3,135	3,611	2,871	3.0	0.4	7.1

5-32. Meat exports

	Hundreds of metric tons											Average annual percentage growth		
	1980	1988	1989	1990	1991	1992	1993	1994	1995	1996	1997	75-84	85-89	90-MR
SUB-SAHARAN AFRICA	1,022	509	537	543	578	652	897	734	937	936	931	-9.1	-6.3	8.5
excluding South Africa	651	448	484	471	530	592	798	669	706	665	663	-9.2	-7.0	5.1
excl. S. Africa & Nigeria	651	448	484	471	530	592	798	669	706	665	663	-9.2	-7.0	5.1
Angola	0	0	0	0	0	0	0	0	0	0	0	..	..	..
Benin	0	0	0	0	0	0	0	0	0	0	0	..	..	..
Botswana	165	174	189	158	199	193	222	191	181	142	138	-1.9	-7.3	-2.9
Burkina Faso	3	0	0	0	0	0	0	0	0	0	0	-3.9	-51.0	..
Burundi	0	0	0	0	0	0	0	0	0	0	0	..	..	..
Cameroon	0	0	0	0	0	0	0	0	0	0	0	-56.8	-59.9	..
Cape Verde	0	0	0	0	0	0	0	0	0	0	0	..	..	..
Central African Republic	20	0	0	0	0	0	0	0	0	0	0	-19.8	..	..
Chad	0	1	2	4	2	2	2	2	2	2	2	-50.2	88.8	-2.2
Comoros	0	0	0	0	0	0	0	0	0	0	0	..	..	..
Congo, Democratic Rep. of	0	0	0	0	0	0	0	0	0	0	0	..	..	..
Congo, Republic of	0	0	0	0	0	0	0	0	0	0	0	..	..	37.4
Côte d'Ivoire	0	0	0	0	0	0	0	0	0	0	0	9.1	..	..
Djibouti	0	0	0	0	0	0	0	0	0	0	0	..	..	..
Equatorial Guinea	0	0	0	0	0	0	0	0	0	0	0	..	..	..
Eritrea	0	0	0	0	0	0	0	0	0	0	0	..	..	..
Ethiopia	0	0	0	0	0	0	0	2	6	5	5	..	..	88.8
Gabon	0	0	0	0	0	0	0	0	0	0	0	..	..	..
Gambia, The	0	0	0	0	0	0	0	0	0	0	0	..	..	..
Ghana	0	0	0	0	0	0	0	0	0	0	0	..	..	..
Guinea	0	0	0	0	0	0	0	0	0	0	0	..	..	..
Guinea-Bissau	0	0	0	0	0	0	0	0	0	0	0	..	..	..
Kenya	2	1	1	3	3	3	6	5	4	5	7	-24.4	-26.2	21.7
Lesotho	0	0	0	0	0	0	0	0	0	0	0	..	..	..
Liberia	0	0	0	0	0	0	0	0	0	0	0	..	..	..
Madagascar	65	0	0	1	4	13	17	23	38	19	6	-11.2	-59.7	52.2
Malawi	0	0	0	0	0	0	0	0	0	0	0	..	-51.9	..
Mali	0	0	0	0	0	0	0	0	0	0	0	-25.5	..	..
Mauritania	0	0	0	0	0	0	0	0	0	0	0	..	..	..
Mauritius	0	0	0	4	2	2	0	0	0	0	0	15.5	-42.9	-36.5
Mozambique	0	0	0	0	0	0	0	0	0	0	0	15.4	..	..
Namibia	230	181	247	208	258	262	313	281	251	251	251	4.6	8.7	1.1
Niger	0	0	0	0	0	0	0	0	0	0	0	-30.9	..	..
Nigeria	0	0	0	0	0	0	0	0	0	0	0	..	..	..
Rwanda	0	0	0	0	0	0	0	0	0	0	0	..	..	..
São Tomé and Principe	0	0	0	0	0	0	0	0	0	0	0	..	..	..
Senegal	1	0	3	1	0	1	1	1	0	0	0	-5.1	-1.9	-11.9
Seychelles	0	0	0	0	0	0	0	0	0	0	0	..	..	..
Sierra Leone	0	0	0	0	0	0	0	0	0	0	0	..	..	..
Somalia	0	0	0	0	0	0	0	0	0	0	0	-23.7	..	..
South Africa	371	61	54	71	49	60	100	65	231	271	268	-10.3	0.2	25.5
Sudan	0	0	0	0	0	7	61	40	65	134	157	-12.0	..	70.7
Swaziland	27	1	1	10	15	4	10	10	9	10	10	-3.0	-52.8	20.7
Tanzania	0	0	0	43	0	0	0	0	0	0	0	-41.8	..	..
Togo	0	0	0	0	0	0	0	0	0	0	0	..	..	-1.7
Uganda	0	0	0	0	0	0	0	0	0	0	0	..	..	..
Zambia	0	0	0	0	2	0	1	1	1	1	1	-11.8	49.7	3.1
Zimbabwe	134	88	42	40	45	105	164	112	150	95	84	-22.1	-21.2	14.2
NORTH AFRICA	34	2	17	58	11	42	37	23	16	11	17	-2.5	19.2	-7.5
Algeria	0	0	0	0	0	0	0	0	0	0	0	-58.2	..	..
Egypt, Arab Republic	1	1	16	55	10	40	36	20	14	9	13	1.9	55.0	-9.8
Libya	0	0	0	2	0	0	0	0	0	0	0	..	..	..
Morocco	33	0	0	0	0	0	0	1	1	1	2	-3.0	-21.6	27.0
Tunisia	1	1	1	1	1	2	1	2	1	1	2	-6.5	-3.2	6.1
ALL AFRICA	1,056	511	554	600	589	694	935	757	953	948	948	-8.9	-6.0	7.9

5-33. Manufactured goods exports

| | \multicolumn{11}{c|}{*Millions of U.S. dollars (current prices)*} | \multicolumn{3}{c}{*Annual average*} |
	1980	1988	1989	1990	1991	1992	1993	1994	1995	1996	1997	75-84	85-89	90-MR
SUB-SAHARAN AFRICA	..	7,408	9,048	10,245	10,272	9,781	10,162	11,410	14,033	14,017	14,903	..	8,228	11,853
excluding South Africa	..	..	..	..	..	..	..	..	..	5,812	..	..	..	5,812
excl. S.Africa & Nigeria	..	..	..	..	..	..	..	..	..	5,765	..	..	..	5,765
Angola	..	91	70	56	56	66	63	72	78	105	101	..	89	75
Benin	..	0	0	0	0	0	0	0	0	0	0	0	0	0
Botswana	..	..	..	..	..	..	..	..	..	..	0	..	..	0
Burkina Faso	..	..	..	..	..	..	..	..	..	..	..	..	..	..
Burundi	1	7	4	4	4	11	9	5	7	4	1	3	8	6
Cameroon	96	171	300	359	268	241	227	204	259	302	291	81	232	269
Cape Verde	..	0	0	1	1	1	1	2	6	0	0	..	1	2
Central African Republic	..	0	0	0	0	0	0	0	0	0	0	0	0	0
Chad	..	3	3	2	0	1	0	0	1	2	1	5	4	1
Comoros	..	0	0	0	0	0	0	0	0	0	0	0	0	0
Congo, Democratic Rep. of	..	..	..	..	297	163	93	140	225	305	..	..	..	204
Congo, Republic of	..	36	45	35	26	25	20	13	23	17	16	56	40	22
Côte d'Ivoire	..	904	849	1,149	988	1,037	956	1,012	1,294	1,330	1,210	672	841	1,122
Djibouti	..	..	..	..	..	..	..	..	..	..	..	..	..	..
Equatorial Guinea	..	0	0	0	0	0	0	0	0	0	0	0	0	0
Eritrea	..	..	..	..	..	1	16	21	31	41	21	..	..	22
Ethiopia	..	..	..	..	..	..	..	..	..	..	..	..	..	..
Gabon	..	0	0	0	0	0	0	0	0	0	0	0	0	0
Gambia, The	..	..	..	..	..	..	..	..	..	..	..	..	..	..
Ghana	..	..	..	..	..	..	..	..	..	..	..	..	..	..
Guinea	..	0	0	0	0	0	0	0	0	0	0	..	0	0
Guinea-Bissau	..	..	..	..	..	..	..	..	..	..	..	..	..	..
Kenya	..	139	137	140	171	144	230	224	298	290	283	128	127	223
Lesotho	..	..	..	..	..	..	..	..	..	5	..	..	..	5
Liberia	..	..	..	..	..	..	..	..	..	..	..	..	..	..
Madagascar	..	75	109	146	159	180	183	237	335	356	342	44	72	242
Malawi	..	0	0	0	0	0	0	0	0	0	0	..	0	0
Mali	..	..	..	..	..	..	..	..	..	..	..	..	..	..
Mauritania	..	..	..	..	..	..	..	..	..	..	..	0	..	..
Mauritius	..	0	485	645	645	703	753	756	852	983	964	156	97	788
Mozambique	..	5	8	20	14	..	..	..	..	..	..	0	3	17
Namibia	158	197	193	292	401	492	472	530	514	434	475	169	161	451
Niger	..	0	0	0	0	0	0	0	0	0	0	0	0	0
Nigeria	..	28	39	70	85	36	40	47	70	47	40	..	34	54
Rwanda	..	0	4	2	2	2	7	2	4	5	18	5	4	5
São Tomé and Principe	..	..	..	..	..	..	..	..	..	..	..	..	..	..
Senegal	136	164	167	181	213	129	164	201	255	250	254	145	157	206
Seychelles	..	11	9	10	12	13	11	17	19	34	57	0	5	22
Sierra Leone	0	0	0	0	0	0	0	0	0	0	0	0	0	0
Somalia	..	..	..	..	..	..	..	..	..	..	..	..	..	..
South Africa	3,548	4,622	5,694	6,100	6,021	5,653	5,972	6,794	8,504	8,205	9,455	2,600	4,358	7,088
Sudan	..	53	33	11	..	..	..	..	..	..	..	31	30	11
Swaziland	..	27	23	25	42	54	103	117	120	94	115	..	20	84
Tanzania	90	68	89	104	87	67	59	76	69	117	102	55	55	85
Togo	..	115	100	150	145	128	75	60	86	78	76	66	92	100
Uganda	..	..	..	..	..	..	..	..	..	..	..	..	..	..
Zambia	..	51	36	67	46	62	58	129	155	168	180	101	47	108
Zimbabwe	..	642	652	675	590	573	652	750	829	846	900	319	495	727
NORTH AFRICA	..	3,941	4,441	5,705	5,837	6,327	5,730	5,641	7,020	6,619	6,493	..	3,797	6,172
Algeria	..	216	234	258	226	213	68	28	30	32	40	7	105	112
Egypt, Arab Republic	..	961	978	1,302	1,163	1,461	1,167	1,127	1,655	1,314	1,304	..	868	1,312
Libya	..	..	..	..	..	..	..	..	..	..	..	..	..	..
Morocco	..	979	1,130	1,525	1,568	1,551	1,482	1,474	1,586	1,531	1,469	434	823	1,523
Tunisia	905	1,785	2,099	2,621	2,880	3,102	3,012	3,012	3,749	3,742	3,680	718	1,473	3,225
ALL AFRICA	..	11,349	13,489	15,949	16,109	16,108	15,892	17,052	21,053	20,635	21,396	..	12,419	18,024

5-34. Manufactured goods exports, growth

	1980	1988	1989	1990	1991	1992	1993	1994	1995	1996	1997	Average annual percentage growth		
					Percent							75-84	85-89	90-MR
SUB-SAHARAN AFRICA	..	21.7	-0.9	13.1	-0.8	0.7	1.9	7.5	8.1	11.8	-2.5	40.3	29.3	4.8
excluding South Africa	..	21.7	-0.9	13.1	-0.8	0.7	1.9	7.5	8.1	11.8	-2.5	40.3	29.3	4.8
excl. S.Africa & Nigeria	..	20.7	-1.2	12.5	-1.2	2.0	1.8	7.5	7.8	12.3	-2.5	40.3	29.0	4.9
Angola	..	40.4	-2.6	-55.0	13.4	-6.6	28.2	12.1	-4.9	5.2	-1.0	..	9.2	0.9
Benin	..	..	..	..	..	..	..	..	..	..	..	..	..	..
Botswana	..	..	..	..	..	..	..	..	..	..	..	..	..	..
Burkina Faso	..	..	..	..	..	..	..	..	..	..	..	..	..	..
Burundi	..	-47.2	-42.3	-5.6	-15.2	185.3	-19.1	-39.1	19.1	-36.5	-87.7	..	0.3	-13.9
Cameroon	21.3	-15.2	84.3	4.2	-16.0	1.1	-0.4	-4.6	-5.5	21.1	5.6	13.0	0.7	-0.7
Cape Verde	..	..	..	..	..	..	..	..	..	..	..	..	..	..
Central African Republic	..	..	..	..	..	..	..	..	..	..	..	..	..	..
Chad	..	30.4	8.6	9.9	1.1	-2.9	-4.5	-0.8	22.6	14.0	0.0			4.1
Comoros	..	..	..	..	..	..	..	..	..	..	..	..	..	..
Congo, Democratic Rep. of	..	..	..	..	..	..	..	..	..	..	..	..	..	..
Congo, Republic of	..	0.0	0.0	0.0	0.0	0.0	-32.3	0.0	0.0	0.0	0.0	..	..	-6.3
Côte d'Ivoire	..	-0.8	-5.9	15.1	-7.4	5.5	-7.3	19.7	1.2	11.5	2.0	..	0.7	4.2
Djibouti	..	..	..	..	..	..	..	..	..	..	..	..	..	..
Equatorial Guinea	..	..	..	..	..	..	..	..	..	..	..	..	..	..
Eritrea	..	..	..	..	..	..	..	..	..	..	..	..	..	..
Ethiopia	..	..	..	..	..	..	..	..	..	..	..	..	..	..
Gabon	..	..	..	..	..	..	..	..	..	..	..	..	..	..
Gambia, The	..	..	..	..	..	..	..	..	..	..	..	..	..	..
Ghana	..	..	..	..	..	..	..	..	..	..	..	..	..	..
Guinea	..	..	..	..	..	..	..	..	..	..	..	..	..	..
Guinea-Bissau	..	..	..	..	..	..	..	..	..	..	..	..	..	..
Kenya	..	-14.4	-3.6	27.9	10.3	-8.3	7.0	10.2	9.4	18.8	5.2	..	-9.1	8.2
Lesotho	..	..	..	..	..	..	..	..	..	..	..	..	..	..
Liberia	..	..	..	..	..	..	..	..	..	..	..	..	..	..
Madagascar	..	7.2	35.1	25.0	5.6	12.1	5.4	4.5	68.1	12.8	11.3	..	11.3	16.6
Malawi	..	..	..	..	..	..	..	..	..	..	..	..	..	..
Mali	..	..	..	..	..	..	..	..	..	..	..	..	..	..
Mauritania	..	..	..	..	..	..	..	..	..	..	..	..	..	..
Mauritius	..	..	-12.5	23.2	6.1	7.4	9.5	1.0	5.0	5.0	5.0	..	14.9	6.7
Mozambique	..	..	60.6	149.1	-31.1	..	..	..	..	..	..	..	..	..
Namibia	..	-4.1	1.0	49.8	31.3	37.1	2.3	-1.1	-10.5	4.7	3.4	..	3.0	10.4
Niger	..	..	..	..	..	..	..	..	..	..	..	..	..	..
Nigeria	..	..	42.3	67.6	19.4	-59.5	10.0	15.2	36.8	-30.8	-8.3	..	..	-4.2
Rwanda	..	0.0	-12.5	-28.6	-20.0	12.5	-22.2	-42.9	175.0	-18.2	11.1	..	-21.8	-3.0
São Tomé and Principe	..	..	..	..	..	..	..	..	..	..	..	..	..	..
Senegal	..	5.4	-5.0	27.5	13.1	-35.4	18.5	-37.2	41.0	-4.5	-10.8	..	8.8	-4.4
Seychelles	..	78.4	12.1	-35.1	18.8	47.4	27.4	-60.7	33.3	-55.4	..	..	..	-8.5
Sierra Leone	..	..	..	..	..	..	..	..	..	..	..	..	..	..
Somalia	..	..	..	..	..	..	..	..	..	..	..	..	..	..
South Africa	..	..	..	..	..	..	..	..	..	..	..	..	..	..
Sudan	..	..	..	..	..	..	..	..	..	..	..	..	..	..
Swaziland	..	..	..	..	..	..	..	..	..	..	..	..	..	..
Tanzania	..	..	..	..	..	..	..	..	..	26.9	..	..	..	..
Togo	..	-15.9	-49.4	10.6	-1.9	-164.5	192.4	-22.7	88.5	-94.3	1063.5	..	..	..
Uganda	..	..	..	..	..	..	..	..	..	..	..	..	..	..
Zambia	..	14.3	-29.2	73.5	-32.2	30.0	-5.8	114.3	13.3	11.8	11.3	..	-11.3	20.5
Zimbabwe	..	6.9	2.1	-3.9	-14.5	-6.9	14.2	10.9	2.0	4.7	9.1	..	..	2.2
NORTH AFRICA	..	40.4	-3.2	17.2	-1.0	2.7	-5.3	-13.4	22.1	-11.0	-2.8	..	27.3	-0.5
Algeria	..	2359.7	-76.4	-9.6	-34.1	8.7	-23.5	-57.7	-1.6	7.7	27.2	..	99.8	-18.8
Egypt, Arab Republic	..	33.2	-1.4	30.0	-14.0	21.6	-21.6	-5.0	38.5	-22.7	-0.4	..	..	-0.1
Libya	..	..	..	..	..	..	..	..	..	..	..	..	..	..
Morocco	..	4.2	17.8	24.4	2.0	-8.4	-0.1	-4.1	15.5	-11.6	-1.0	..	15.1	0.3
Tunisia	..	13.9	19.1	10.5	6.8	0.0	1.7	-19.3	18.3	-4.5	-5.4	..	16.5	-0.3
ALL AFRICA	394.7	32.5	-2.3	15.6	-0.9	1.9	-2.6	-5.0	15.7	-1.3	-2.7	62.5	28.0	1.7

5-35. Food imports

	Millions of U.S. dollars (current prices)											Annual average		
	1980	1988	1989	1990	1991	1992	1993	1994	1995	1996	1997	75-84	85-89	90-MR
SUB-SAHARAN AFRICA	..	4,770	4,619	5,131	5,223	5,164	5,074	5,693	7,757	7,633	8,018	..	4,908	6,212
excluding South Africa	..	3,762	3,653	4,186	4,258	4,216	4,124	4,277	5,801	5,791	6,368	..	3,823	4,878
excl. S.Africa & Nigeria	..	3,257	3,228	3,542	3,498	3,409	3,353	3,539	4,741	4,862	5,149	..	3,077	4,012
Angola	..	248	242	286	57	244	203	215	205	275	365	..	263	231
Benin	..	191	58	78	99	116	111	80	118	116	112	..	141	104
Botswana	109	171	150	227	265	347	316	289	305	293	318	121	140	295
Burkina Faso	..	..	..	97	104	90	0	0	70	86	71	..	..	65
Burundi	18	15	10	12	15	11	19	30	29	11	11	19	14	17
Cameroon	82	177	155	190	199	189	161	189	124	138	155	70	134	168
Cape Verde	0	29	36	38	42	75	53	65	85	45	47	0	25	56
Central African Republic	..	25	27	34	28	30	25	23	29	22	20	20	26	26
Chad	..	15	15	18	7	0	4	5	4	4	4	..	16	6
Comoros	..	11	11	10	12	13	10	9	18	12	20	8	8	13
Congo, Democratic Rep. of	..	..	..	..	..	..	..	..	..	..	..	..	..	..
Congo, Republic of	..	18	25	30	31	34	36	·15	16	18	19	104	23	25
Côte d'Ivoire	435	502	483	471	490	377	431	317	523	563	538	389	441	464
Djibouti	..	..	..	..	..	..	..	..	..	..	..	..	..	..
Equatorial Guinea	..	..	..	..	..	..	..	..	..	..	..	..	..	..
Eritrea	..	..	..	..	..	25	35	76	69	92	94	..	..	65
Ethiopia	..	137	186	73	152	131	167	126	181	215	110	126	219	144
Gabon	..	137	126	143	157	174	166	166	181	191	189	142	151	171
Gambia, The	..	7	7	10	13	14	13	7	8	8	8	..	7	10
Ghana	..	43	42	39	39	38	..	..	..	..	..	39	48	39
Guinea	..	12	12	12	8	49	53	76	77	76	77	..	12	54
Guinea-Bissau	..	15	16	15	21	32	25	17	26	25	31	16	14	24
Kenya	..	138	114	125	149	156	145	173	277	199	996	111	123	277
Lesotho	..	..	..	..	..	..	..	..	..	..	..	..	..	..
Liberia	..	..	..	..	..	..	..	..	..	..	..	..	..	..
Madagascar	89	17	38	49	35	58	51	79	67	60	49	87	42	56
Malawi	..	3	4	5	14	63	6	68	92	51	33	..	3	42
Mali	..	83	68	114	117	97	97	86	111	113	111	131	88	106
Mauritania	..	118	115	127	121	137	105	107	95	105	92	76	107	111
Mauritius	..	130	173	197	195	214	237	270	307	368	375	93	118	270
Mozambique	..	44	29	30	32	..	..	..	..	..	..	..	37	31
Namibia	..	..	..	..	..	..	..	..	396	413	..	..	..	405
Niger	..	44	27	40	31	22	22	16	18	19	27	..	30	24
Nigeria	3,161	505	425	644	760	807	771	738	1,060	929	1,219	1,906	902	866
Rwanda	..	23	29	32	35	29	59	218	56	51	54	27	31	67
São Tomé and Principe	..	9	8	8	6	6	7	7	7	6	5	8	7	6
Senegal	210	283	334	361	362	..	349	310	394	395	329	237	243	357
Seychelles	..	33	30	34	33	40	46	42	47	63	88	17	25	49
Sierra Leone	0	50	54	45	32	33	43	52	20	75	32	4	49	41
Somalia	..	..	..	..	..	..	..	..	..	..	..	..	..	..
South Africa	933	1,008	966	945	965	948	950	1,416	1,956	1,842	1,650	835	972	1,334
Sudan	..	172	245	231	275	..	..	..	215	232	238	219	189	238
Swaziland	42	66	68	98	97	110	134	136	202	172	169	32	49	140
Tanzania	..	91	81	59	32	25	58	97	97	54	57	96	86	60
Togo	..	159	163	160	156	131	82	75	96	149	209	118	137	132
Uganda	..	..	..	..	..	..	..	..	..	..	..	..	..	..
Zambia	..	14	14	9	..	258	50	55	98	25	12	24	16	72
Zimbabwe	..	28	32	36	41	43	36	43	78	119	84	77	28	60
NORTH AFRICA	..	4,125	6,495	5,550	4,623	5,428	5,359	5,522	7,457	6,878	6,667	..	5,164	5,935
Algeria	..	1,808	2,925	2,134	1,894	2,127	2,092	2,206	2,520	1,923	1,720	1,757	2,102	2,077
Egypt, Arab Republic	..	1,254	2,404	2,328	1,802	1,979	1,878	1,982	2,760	2,955	3,194	..	1,999	2,360
Libya	..	..	..	..	..	..	..	..	..	..	..	..	..	..
Morocco	..	509	588	583	591	892	972	799	1,362	1,287	1,065	660	511	944
Tunisia	388	554	578	506	336	430	417	536	815	712	688	333	428	555
ALL AFRICA	..	8,894	11,113	10,680	9,846	10,592	10,433	11,216	15,213	14,511	14,685	..	9,330	12,147

5-36. Food imports, growth

					Percent							*Average annual percentage growth*		
	1980	1988	1989	1990	1991	1992	1993	1994	1995	1996	1997	75-84	85-89	90-MR
SUB-SAHARAN AFRICA	80.7	-12.5	-5.1	11.2	-8.5	8.3	-0.5	0.8	10.8	0.3	8.8	25.7	-2.0	3.1
excluding South Africa	80.7	-12.5	-5.1	11.2	-8.5	8.3	-0.5	0.8	10.8	0.3	8.8	25.7	-2.0	3.1
excl. S.Africa & Nigeria	556.5	-4.3	-3.0	3.1	-15.4	9.4	0.4	4.8	5.2	6.3	0.6	51.8	10.6	2.0
Angola	..	12.3	1.9	25.2	-79.9	340.7	-12.6	2.4	-13.1	34.1	47.2	..	-12.7	7.3
Benin	..	..	..	..	..	..	..	..	..	..	..	..	..	..
Botswana	..	..	..	..	..	..	..	..	..	..	..	..	..	..
Burkina Faso	..	..	..	..	..	..	..	..	..	..	..	..	..	..
Burundi	..	-0.1	-0.3	0.2	0.2	-0.2	75.4	61.3	-4.0	-62.1	2.8	..	3.3	5.7
Cameroon	0.9	13.0	-18.0	11.8	35.3	-6.8	-17.2	9.5	-27.6	-3.8	20.6	-0.9	20.2	-2.4
Cape Verde	..	-30.9	24.1	13.8	9.6	78.8	-27.7	12.1	19.8	-16.0	-0.4	..	..	8.1
Central African Republic	..	-16.1	7.2	19.4	-19.3	1.6	-17.0	-11.2	19.2	-26.7	-7.5	..	..	-7.4
Chad	..	3.0	3.0	3.0	2.0	-89.5	500.0	25.0	-12.8	-0.3	-1.9	..	..	-2.0
Comoros	..	83.3	9.1	-25.0	22.2	0.0	-9.1	30.0	76.9	-30.4	0.0	..	5.8	7.8
Congo, Democratic Rep. of	..	..	..	..	..	..	..	..	62.8	50.1	..	..	..	..
Congo, Republic of	..	-5.3	-9.2	-7.8	-2.5	-16.4	32.0	10.9	-0.7	-0.7	9.3	..	-6.4	3.3
Côte d'Ivoire	..	-10.2	-0.7	-13.3	2.5	-25.8	13.0	-27.5	52.7	1.5	7.1	..	..	-1.5
Djibouti	..	..	..	..	..	..	..	..	..	..	..	..	..	..
Equatorial Guinea	..	..	..	..	..	..	..	..	..	..	..	..	..	..
Eritrea	..	..	..	..	..	..	..	..	..	..	..	..	..	..
Ethiopia	..	..	..	..	..	..	..	..	..	..	..	..	-11.2	..
Gabon	..	..	..	..	..	..	..	..	..	..	..	..	..	..
Gambia, The	..	-10.0	15.9	28.8	23.4	7.8	-12.0	-41.8	3.1	-1.5	-1.5	..	..	-5.6
Ghana	..	-42.8	2.7	1.6	2.5	4.3	5.6	4.1	5.3	7.8	-0.7	..	8.4	4.3
Guinea	..	-22.8	-1.7	-9.7	-34.3	511.9	12.9	38.7	-7.3	0.0	-2.0	..	8.1	32.0
Guinea-Bissau	..	64.0	1.6	-14.1	37.7	43.8	-21.6	-15.4	60.8	-7.7	20.0	..		9.1
Kenya	..	73.5	-41.7	1.7	-37.6	112.6	-41.6	186.6	-59.6	66.3	97.6	..	22.4	12.1
Lesotho	..	..	..	..	..	..	..	..	..	..	..	..	..	..
Liberia	..	..	..	..	..	..	..	..	..	..	..	..	..	..
Madagascar	..	-69.2	162.5	28.6	-40.7	62.5	-17.3	51.2	-26.2	-18.8	-10.3	..	-16.7	-1.1
Malawi	..	0.0	50.0	66.7	140.0	341.7	-90.6	980.0	24.1	-47.8	-31.4	..		34.1
Mali	..	20.2	-18.3	45.5	11.1	-21.0	1.9	-8.6	13.3	11.3	7.5	..	-17.6	2.6
Mauritania	..	-11.3	-3.1	19.6	-4.5	12.4	-22.5	-5.1	-19.4	4.6	-6.2	..	-3.0	-5.7
Mauritius	..	-11.8	15.2	9.3	5.8	6.9	8.0	6.0	2.5	8.0	7.5	..	-11.1	6.5
Mozambique	..	..	-39.4	4.3	..	..	..	..	..	..	..	..	..	..
Namibia	..	..	..	..	..	..	..	..	..	..	..	..	..	..
Niger	..	..	..	..	..	..	..	..	..	..	..	..	..	..
Nigeria	59.2	-40.7	-16.3	63.4	19.1	5.2	-3.1	-11.8	31.4	-17.1	39.7	20.0	-27.0	7.9
Rwanda	..	-32.5	28.7	5.2	5.4	1.7	0.8	5.0	8.3	12.1	-10.8	..	-11.6	4.0
São Tomé and Principe	..	61.5	-12.0	-3.0	-22.1	-1.9	23.5	-14.2	3.0	-24.9	-14.7	..	20.0	-6.2
Senegal	..	37.4	10.2	26.7	-3.1	..	..	-54.6	41.0	-1.9	-27.0	..	17.0	-9.0
Seychelles	..	27.2	-19.1	9.3	-1.5	14.3	27.4	-16.3	10.2	38.8	40.5	..	6.2	11.7
Sierra Leone	..	6.3	16.8	11.2	1.1	2.0	31.1	13.0	-65.3	255.7	-55.3	..	2.7	1.3
Somalia	..	..	..	..	..	..	..	..	..	..	..	..	..	..
South Africa	..	..	..	..	..	..	..	..	..	..	..	..	..	..
Sudan	..	-22.2	5.8	..	..	..	..	..	..	..	..	..	10.1	..
Swaziland	..	..	..	..	..	..	..	..	..	..	..	..	..	..
Tanzania	..	..	..	..	..	..	..	..	..	-64.1	..	..	..	..
Togo	..	-5.3	-5.9	-2.2	..	..	..	..	..	..	..	..	2.6	..
Uganda	..	..	..	..	..	..	..	..	..	..	..	..	..	..
Zambia	..	18.2	7.7	-35.7	..	..	-80.4	1.9	61.8	-75.3	-50.0	..	-11.9	3.6
Zimbabwe	..	-14.4	12.8	23.2	13.4	3.9	-13.9	8.6	82.6	43.6	-33.2	..	-12.7	13.7
NORTH AFRICA	..	-10.8	24.7	-14.8	-7.4	15.8	-0.5	-1.2	10.8	-2.1	2.2	..	17.8	1.4
Algeria	..	48.0	19.9	-29.4	3.5	8.6	-10.5	7.5	-12.0	-7.0	-10.5	..	10.0	-4.7
Egypt, Arab Republic	..	-55.0	70.7	0.2	-19.2	9.8	-4.8	2.0	27.8	-0.9	7.9	..	..	2.6
Libya	..	..	..	..	..	..	..	..	..	..	..	..	..	..
Morocco	..	-15.5	-6.2	7.9	16.6	46.8	26.5	-24.1	19.2	16.2	11.8	..	-4.5	13.3
Tunisia	..	50.1	-12.7	-19.0	-35.6	22.1	2.3	21.1	35.1	-28.5	-6.9	..	6.6	0.1
ALL AFRICA	80.7	-11.4	14.9	-7.7	-7.8	13.3	-0.5	-0.6	10.8	-1.3	4.3	30.6	9.9	1.9

5-37. Nonfood consumer goods imports

	1980	1988	1989	1990	1991	1992	1993	1994	1995	1996	1997	75-84	85-89	90-MR
					Millions of U.S. dollars (current prices)								*Annual average*	
SUB-SAHARAN AFRICA	..	11,514	11,772	12,184	12,369	12,779	11,817	14,177	18,009	17,726	16,139	..	10,215	14,400
excluding South Africa	..	5,034	4,782	5,343	5,385	5,920	4,945	5,122	6,679	6,842	6,408	..	4,428	5,830
excl. S.Africa & Nigeria	..	5,034	4,782	5,343	5,385	5,920	4,945	5,122	6,679	6,842	6,408	..	4,428	5,830
Angola	..	478	467	551	676	1,009	778	712	1,069	1,119	1,263	..	328	897
Benin	. ..	129	82	102	107	124	119	85	127	125	121	..	97	114
Botswana	146	238	304	406	426	394	355	363	367	350	380	158	197	380
Burkina Faso	..	..	..	214	168	215	0	0	170	192	176	..	..	142
Burundi	53	39	39	44	36	45	33	28	28	8	19	43	38	30
Cameroon	136	238	193	109	131	68	89	76	64	74	179	222	262	99
Cape Verde	..	42	43	46	57	60	57	65	90	48	47	0	43	59
Central African Republic	..	36	35	62	20	27	26	30	12	32	51	30	45	32
Chad	..	98	104	120	117	102	88	57	69	73	78	..	108	88
Comoros	..	33	27	36	40	49	41	36	35	41	25	25	29	38
Congo, Democratic Rep. of	..	..	..	..	..	..	..	..	..	..	..	..	..	..
Congo, Republic of	..	234	3	3	2	3	3	5	5	7	9	261	212	5
Côte d'Ivoire	630	472	492	438	398	534	491	454	743	793	771	466	475	578
Djibouti	..	..	..	..	..	..	..	..	..	..	..	..	..	..
Equatorial Guinea	..	38	25	25	28	33	25	22	29	50	73	21	27	36
Eritrea	0	0	0	0	0	198	109	95	28	59	64	0	0	69
Ethiopia	..	156	136	176	168	174	189	183	176	241	245	116	140	194
Gabon	..	176	174	202	224	252	241	71	77	78	79	330	236	153
Gambia, The	..	1	0	0	1	0	0	0	0	0	0	..	0	0
Ghana	..	163	137	160	228	306	..	..	..	..	..	80	125	231
Guinea	..	314	309	339	334	313	318	320	389	313	355	..	259	335
Guinea-Bissau	..	6	14	12	10	7	5	6	7	7	9	11	9	8
Kenya	..	728	729	727	550	537	376	689	818	894	364	394	599	619
Lesotho	..	..	..	..	..	..	..	..	..	..	..	..	..	..
Liberia	..	..	..	..	..	..	..	..	..	..	..	..	..	..
Madagascar	..	74	88	159	155	188	209	236	299	309	353	89	90	239
Malawi	..	42	54	65	51	57	53	37	26	42	58	..	43	49
Mali	..	87	127	118	151	182	188	176	159	182	169	40	95	166
Mauritania	..	33	28	38	27	29	16	-24	-4	20	18	23	32	15
Mauritius	..	118	110	126	138	152	163	173	187	182	173	49	91	162
Mozambique	..	140	137	137	164	..	..	..	..	..	..	..	139	151
Namibia	..	..	..	..	..	..	..	..	318	326	..	..	..	322
Niger	..	103	89	93	87	94	92	117	112	154	130	..	113	110
Nigeria	..	..	..	..	..	..	..	..	..	..	..	..	..	..
Rwanda	..	33	64	83	46	92	88	158	69	71	125	31	46	91
São Tomé and Principe	..	11	7	4	9	10	11	9	7	8	8	15	9	8
Senegal	152	198	203	223	216	..	193	170	199	203	191	139	166	199
Seychelles	..	21	23	26	23	29	39	33	33	40	51	8	16	34
Sierra Leone	0	23	24	23	23	22	13	4	4	5	6	1	21	12
Somalia	..	..	..	..	..	..	..	..	..	..	..	..	..	..
South Africa	8,206	6,480	6,990	6,841	6,984	6,859	6,872	9,055	11,330	10,884	9,731	6,185	5,787	8,570
Sudan	..	115	108	98	126	..	..	..	17	15	32	120	88	58
Swaziland	127	53	49	64	85	143	81	136	163	101	109	86	75	110
Tanzania	..	143	153	144	179	274	293	237	355	268	323	71	117	259
Togo	..	113	79	22	19	27	16	22	27	29	28	61	89	24
Uganda	..	..	..	..	..	..	..	..	..	..	..	..	..	..
Zambia	..	..	..	..	..	..	..	167	199	200	125	..	..	173
Zimbabwe	..	113	129	147	165	173	147	173	205	183	203	303	198	175
NORTH AFRICA	..	4,137	3,607	4,866	4,678	5,052	5,498	7,241	7,264	7,405	7,540	..	4,321	6,193
Algeria	..	1,841	2,051	2,224	1,501	1,631	1,386	2,041	2,180	2,269	2,030	2,087	2,034	1,908
Egypt, Arab Republic	..	836	-159	267	799	813	1,448	2,159	1,531	1,357	1,662	..	948	1,254
Libya	..	..	..	..	..	..	..	..	..	..	..	..	..	..
Morocco	..	526	591	804	855	714	725	787	934	1,097	1,122	237	453	880
Tunisia	595	933	1,123	1,570	1,523	1,895	1,939	2,255	2,619	2,682	2,726	462	799	2,151
ALL AFRICA	..	15,651	15,379	17,050	17,047	17,831	17,315	21,418	25,273	25,131	23,679	..	14,069	20,593

5-38. Nonfood consumer goods imports, growth

					Percent							Average annual percentage growth		
	1980	1988	1989	1990	1991	1992	1993	1994	1995	1996	1997	75-84	85-89	90-MR
SUB-SAHARAN AFRICA	2.5	0.8	9.2	12.7	-7.5	14.9	-4.0	11.2	11.7	9.9	6.7	19.1	19.0	6.4
excluding South Africa	2.5	0.8	9.2	12.7	-7.5	14.9	-4.0	11.2	11.7	9.9	6.7	19.1	19.0	6.4
excl. S.Africa & Nigeria	2.5	0.8	9.2	12.7	-7.5	14.9	-4.0	11.2	11.7	9.9	6.7	19.1	19.0	6.4
Angola	..	-16.7	2.2	24.9	23.4	54.2	-18.9	-11.5	36.5	4.8	25.0	..	52.2	12.3
Benin	..	..	..	..	..	..	..	..	..	..	..	..	..	..
Botswana	..	..	..	..	..	..	..	..	..	..	..	..	..	..
Burkina Faso	..	..	..	..	..	..	..	..	..	..	..	..	..	..
Burundi	..	-3.1	-6.1	14.2	-18.4	9.2	-33.2	-46.2	-0.5	..	..	..	-9.7	-16.4
Cameroon	-40.2	-21.5	16.4	-10.6	28.4	58.8	-25.5	69.5	-22.2	40.4	21.7	-3.7	-3.0	15.6
Cape Verde	..	-11.9	6.1	16.0	30.2	8.1	-4.5	-6.4	27.9	-3.3	-3.6	..	..	6.6
Central African Republic	..	-19.6	-4.4	69.2	-68.9	29.8	-1.4	8.2	-64.1	165.9	67.3	..	..	-5.5
Chad	..	-5.7	-4.1	-8.7	-23.3	9.5	-20.4	-96.4	-313.0	183.6	-5.4	..	..	-43.9
Comoros	..	-3.0	-12.5	17.9	12.1	16.2	-9.3	25.6	-10.2	20.5	0.0	..	-7.0	7.7
Congo, Democratic Rep. of	..	..	..	..	..	..	..	..	..	..	..	..	..	..
Congo, Republic of	..	-3.8	32.6	-7.9	-1.9	-16.5	32.2	10.9	-1.1	140.8	-22.9	..	2.9	11.9
Côte d'Ivoire	..	-10.2	-0.7	-13.3	2.6	22.8	-8.1	-8.4	48.7	5.0	4.7	..	..	6.6
Djibouti	..	..	..	..	..	..	..	..	..	..	..	..	..	..
Equatorial Guinea	..	-1.2	-14.7	6.0	38.1	-6.6	13.5	-8.5	18.6	71.3	87.3	..	1.5	18.3
Eritrea	..	..	..	..	..	..	..	..	..	..	..	..	..	..
Ethiopia	..	..	..	..	..	..	..	..	..	..	..	..	..	..
Gabon	..	..	..	..	..	..	..	..	..	..	..	..	..	..
Gambia, The	..	-20.0	0.0	0.0	125.0	-55.6	0.0	-25.0	0.0	0.0	0.0	..	..	-7.2
Ghana	..	14.7	-15.6	10.0	40.0	28.6	69.6	-30.7	4.8	10.3	0.9	..	11.8	13.8
Guinea	..	33.9	-0.6	4.0	-3.7	-9.4	6.3	-3.0	10.6	-20.2	18.6	..	12.1	-1.1
Guinea-Bissau	..	-9.6	180.9	12.1	-25.7	-32.7	-36.5	17.0	12.7	11.3	11.6	..	..	-9.3
Kenya	..	-5.6	7.4	67.3	-23.5	20.9	-25.3	70.4	-0.9	-19.5	7.1	..	9.0	5.1
Lesotho	..	..	..	..	..	..	..	..	..	..	..	..	..	..
Liberia	..	..	..	..	..	..	..	..	..	..	..	..	..	..
Madagascar	..	-28.6	20.0	65.5	-0.7	15.2	17.6	8.0	16.3	6.4	23.6	..	-9.2	14.8
Malawi	..	14.7	28.2	12.0	-23.2	7.0	-4.3	-31.8	-36.7	68.4	43.8	..	..	-6.6
Mali	..	-10.1	55.4	-21.2	29.3	9.5	7.7	-9.6	-19.0	17.8	10.4	..	9.9	1.8
Mauritania	..	0.0	-17.6	31.5	-31.3	2.8	-47.0	-12.4	23.5	7.6	-7.1	..	-10.9	-10.8
Mauritius	..	86.7	37.9	-7.8	17.3	-3.3	-1.7	6.0	-1.8	5.0	4.0	..	33.0	2.1
Mozambique	..	..	-1.5	4.3	..	..	..	..	..	..	..	..	..	..
Namibia	..	..	..	..	..	..	..	..	..	..	..	..	..	..
Niger	..	..	..	..	..	..	..	..	..	..	..	..	..	..
Nigeria	..	..	..	..	..	..	..	..	..	..	..	..	..	..
Rwanda	..	-41.5	99.1	21.7	11.6	3.8	-6.2	3.2	11.8	12.5	177.8	..	0.1	13.3
São Tomé and Principe	..	8.7	-28.3	-47.3	111.1	7.8	13.2	-20.2	-31.9	17.5	1.1	..	-9.4	0.1
Senegal	..	6.3	-3.9	28.2	-6.4	..	..	-55.1	30.5	-0.3	-17.5	..	26.6	-10.7
Seychelles	..	19.1	21.4	14.8	-10.1	18.2	46.9	-25.4	-1.5	34.7	23.9	..	21.2	8.7
Sierra Leone	..	9.8	2.1	-5.4	1.4	-2.1	-43.2	-158.2	-182.6	5.3	-20.0	..	-6.0	-19.9
Somalia	..	..	..	..	..	..	..	..	..	..	..	..	..	..
South Africa	..	..	..	..	..	..	..	..	..	..	..	..	..	..
Sudan	..	..	..	..	..	..	..	..	..	..	..	..	..	..
Swaziland	..	..	..	..	..	..	..	..	..	..	..	..	..	..
Tanzania	..	..	..	..	..	..	..	..	..	13.1	..	..	..	..
Togo	..	27.7	22.5	-14.9	..	..	..	..	..	..	..	..	10.7	..
Uganda	..	..	..	..	..	..	..	..	..	..	..	..	..	..
Zambia	..	..	..	..	..	..	..	..	10.4	4.7	-33.5	..	..	..
Zimbabwe	..	1.3	14.3	5.9	10.1	0.4	-14.9	13.5	9.6	-8.4	13.8	..	-19.5	2.2
NORTH AFRICA	..	-26.4	-35.2	27.7	13.4	-8.8	22.2	19.4	-10.4	-5.5	4.9	..	-3.2	6.2
Algeria	..	3.1	-36.0	-8.5	-1.4	-21.9	-9.3	-4.5	16.7	-10.5	-10.5	..	-16.0	-6.4
Egypt, Arab Republic	..	-64.4	-118.4	-264.0	187.8	-1.5	74.7	46.6	-33.1	-13.7	23.0	..	..	20.1
Libya	..	..	..	..	..	..	..	..	..	..	..	..	..	..
Morocco	..	0.0	12.5	28.6	4.5	-20.0	-4.8	4.7	-9.5	49.0	-18.6	..	12.2	0.6
Tunisia	..	14.6	22.7	21.0	-5.0	0.9	19.9	11.6	3.1	-9.4	7.5	..	9.7	5.6
ALL AFRICA	2.5	-15.6	-14.2	18.6	1.4	3.6	7.0	15.1	0.7	3.1	6.0	40.7	6.2	6.3

5-39. Fuel imports

	Millions of U.S. dollars (current prices)											Annual average		
	1980	1988	1989	1990	1991	1992	1993	1994	1995	1996	1997	75-84	85-89	90-MR
SUB-SAHARAN AFRICA	..	8,773	9,263	10,055	10,117	9,451	9,506	11,223	13,318	14,739	15,958	9,313	8,202	11,796
excluding South Africa	..	2,524	2,752	3,682	3,611	3,061	3,105	3,075	3,858	4,742	4,908	..	2,724	3,755
excl. S.Africa & Nigeria	..	2,460	2,706	3,628	3,567	3,012	3,059	2,989	3,740	4,653	4,765	..	2,667	3,677
Angola	..	0	0	0	0	0	0	0	0	0	0	..	0	0
Benin	..	34	31	54	63	74	71	51	76	74	72	..	38	67
Botswana	90	73	70	100	123	102	113	98	98	111	121	91	68	108
Burkina Faso	..	..	..	83	80	53	0	0	52	73	69	..	..	51
Burundi	25	27	20	30	29	26	24	29	27	18	14	30	27	25
Cameroon	187	13	11	16	9	8	7	7	139	151	136	96	13	59
Cape Verde	0	6	6	10	8	8	6	5	11	10	10	0	3	8
Central African Republic	..	14	20	23	16	16	15	11	17	14	15	17	18	16
Chad	..	31	32	37	11	4	3	8	8	10	12	20	28	12
Comoros	..	4	2	6	6	7	6	6	8	4	8	5	4	6
Congo, Democratic Rep. of	..	..	..	..	..	..	..	..	..	..	..	..	..	..
Congo, Republic of	..	7	3	129	196	104	162	367	187	215	225	23	9	198
Côte d'Ivoire	557	288	449	569	530	511	460	396	470	589	624	433	355	518
Djibouti	..	..	..	..	..	..	..	..	..	..	..	..	..	..
Equatorial Guinea	..	6	6	7	3	4	3	3	3	5	12	5	5	5
Eritrea	..	..	..	..	..	1	1	2	7	6	7	..	..	4
Ethiopia	..	104	103	109	102	120	198	222	169	215	232	183	125	171
Gabon	..	7	7	11	10	12	11	161	173	221	217	44	33	102
Gambia, The	..	7	13	19	1	16	15	9	9	10	10	..	9	11
Ghana	..	148	161	205	175	162	158	176	194	266	240	161	156	197
Guinea	..	55	54	65	68	69	73	69	82	87	90	..	55	75
Guinea-Bissau	..	4	9	8	10	5	3	6	8	9	10	9	7	8
Kenya	..	288	315	466	385	412	407	333	401	448	519	476	343	421
Lesotho	..	..	..	..	..	..	..	..	..	..	..	..	..	..
Liberia	..	..	..	..	..	..	..	..	..	..	..	..	..	..
Madagascar	159	66	35	113	71	72	85	72	81	106	117	123	60	90
Malawi	..	43	42	50	54	47	40	25	49	59	79	..	38	50
Mali	..	66	45	69	79	84	74	53	85	102	105	62	67	81
Mauritania	..	27	37	46	39	36	37	34	95	117	103	43	34	63
Mauritius	..	75	99	131	131	125	120	119	138	179	172	78	75	139
Mozambique	..	68	78	78	84	..	..	..	..	..	..	..	73	81
Namibia	..	..	..	..	..	..	..	..	116	122	..	..	..	119
Niger	..	19	18	27	19	22	23	20	35	32	28	..	19	26
Nigeria	340	64	46	54	44	49	46	86	118	89	143	270	58	79
Rwanda	..	52	48	45	39	37	35	24	22	27	32	49	52	33
São Tomé and Principe	..	0	0	3	2	3	2	2	3	4	5	..	0	3
Senegal	276	166	155	159	148	..	124	142	138	176	191	235	170	154
Seychelles	..	22	30	36	38	33	34	32	30	43	50	26	23	37
Sierra Leone	0	26	28	30	26	22	27	29	24	23	11	4	25	24
Somalia	..	..	..	..	..	..	..	..	..	..	..	..	..	..
South Africa	7,555	6,249	6,511	6,373	6,506	6,390	6,401	8,148	9,460	9,997	11,050	5,461	5,478	8,041
Sudan	..	212	204	244	356	225	249	..	225	355	324	351	230	283
Swaziland	99	70	85	79	95	108	91	42	17	135	184	57	71	94
Tanzania	..	158	150	174	189	142	101	124	186	189	194	247	175	162
Togo	..	26	28	48	35	37	26	22	41	34	42	33	25	36
Uganda	..	69	76	78	83	72	58	55	64	90	92	91	69	74
Zambia	..	62	103	119	83	53	47	56	41	51	87	144	85	67
Zimbabwe	..	118	134	153	172	180	153	180	213	275	309	213	143	204
NORTH AFRICA	..	..	..	..	..	..	..	..	..	..	..	..	..	..
Algeria	..	169	127	141	130	147	141	150	200	131	117	211	183	145
Egypt, Arab Republic	..	..	..	..	..	..	..	..	..	..	..	..	..	..
Libya	..	..	..	..	..	..	..	..	..	..	..	..	..	..
Morocco	..	628	843	1,171	991	1,124	957	1,113	1,177	1,294	1,296	1,021	776	1,140
Tunisia	799	243	380	487	396	449	455	466	496	607	578	387	313	492
ALL AFRICA	..	9,814	10,613	11,854	11,635	11,171	11,058	12,952	15,191	16,770	17,949	..	9,473	13,573

5-40. Fuel imports, growth

					Percent							Average annual percentage growth		
	1980	1988	1989	1990	1991	1992	1993	1994	1995	1996	1997	75-84	85-89	90-MR
SUB-SAHARAN AFRICA	93.0	6.5	-1.5	-7.0	4.7	-12.3	22.5	-20.3	19.7	8.3	8.0	14.8	1.4	1.9
excluding South Africa	93.0	6.5	-1.5	-7.0	4.7	-12.3	22.5	-20.3	19.7	8.3	8.0	14.8	1.4	1.9
excl. S.Africa & Nigeria	438.0	4.1	-0.1	-7.0	4.9	-12.8	23.0	-22.9	19.3	10.9	5.8	42.8	1.7	1.4
Angola	..	..	..	..	..	..	..	..	..	..	..	..	..	..
Benin	..	..	..	..	..	..	..	..	..	..	..	..	..	..
Botswana	..	..	..	..	..	..	..	..	..	..	..	..	..	..
Burkina Faso	..	..	..	..	..	..	..	..	..	..	..	..	..	..
Burundi	..	15.9	-35.9	15.6	15.3	-8.5	2.4	29.0	-15.1	-42.3	-19.9	..	-0.3	-4.3
Cameroon	9.7	3.8	-32.7	16.2	-14.0	-63.1	373.2	-38.1	40.0	-12.5	101.4	-42.6	10.2	10.9
Cape Verde	..	30.2	-18.8	44.6	-8.6	-1.4	-9.6	-15.2	103.6	-14.9	0.0	..	..	5.7
Central African Republic	..	37.8	37.8	9.1	-33.5	-3.7	-6.2	-27.9	46.6	-25.6	18.8	..	..	-7.5
Chad	..	-4.6	-3.1	-7.0	-19.2	-61.0	-21.0	190.0	35.4	20.5	9.3	..	..	4.1
Comoros	..	-50.0	-25.0	100.0	0.0	0.0	0.0	33.3	25.0	-50.0	0.0	..	-11.9	4.8
Congo, Democratic Rep. of	..	..	..	..	..	..	..	..	..	..	..	..	..	..
Congo, Republic of	..	-53.2	79.3	-7.7	-2.1	-17.0	33.3	11.5	-1.7	-3.5	12.7	..	-2.6	3.2
Côte d'Ivoire	..	-10.2	-0.7	-13.3	2.5	-3.1	1.8	-8.8	9.8	26.7	6.2	..	..	2.2
Djibouti	..	..	..	..	..	..	..	..	..	..	..	..	..	..
Equatorial Guinea	..	20.4	-14.7	-14.0	-50.3	24.3	-2.4	-4.5	15.8	23.9	153.4	..	22.7	3.9
Eritrea	..	..	..	..	..	..	..	..	..	..	..	..	..	..
Ethiopia	..	35.3	-26.2	5.0	46.5	20.0	119.8	..	..	..	..	..	-10.4	40.0
Gabon	..	..	..	..	..	..	..	..	..	..	..	..	..	..
Gambia, The	..	-13.9	111.3	38.9	-95.1	1522.2	-11.6	-40.3	1.3	-2.6	-1.3	..	..	-1.9
Ghana	..	2.8	17.8	-13.3	4.2	-7.1	3.3	18.9	3.9	9.9	17.9	..	9.3	4.7
Guinea	..	13.3	-18.2	-3.7	26.0	1.5	14.1	0.0	10.2	11.1	1.5	..	-3.4	8.0
Guinea-Bissau	..	-5.6	94.1	-11.1	17.0	-49.5	-38.5	134.4	45.3	14.7	4.0	..	..	4.5
Kenya	..	-15.5	15.7	6.5	29.8	-9.5	2.8	-18.7	12.8	11.7	16.0	..	-10.2	3.1
Lesotho	..	..	..	..	..	..	..	..	..	..	..	..	..	..
Liberia	..	..	..	..	..	..	..	..	..	..	..	..	..	..
Madagascar	..	50.9	-55.4	124.3	-25.3	1.6	33.3	-14.3	4.2	12.0	16.7	..	-4.5	7.7
Malawi	..	32.5	-20.8	-4.8	27.5	-11.8	-4.4	-32.6	75.9	3.9	41.5	..	..	4.6
Mali	..	13.9	9.6	28.1	-9.4	2.5	-14.0	12.9	28.2	14.8	20.2	..	2.7	7.2
Mauritania	..	-1.7	14.3	-12.3	1.3	-7.2	17.1	-2.7	158.9	3.3	-6.0	..	6.2	15.7
Mauritius	..	-23.7	28.4	25.6	9.1	-7.9	1.7	4.8	2.3	5.1	5.0	..	-16.9	3.7
Mozambique	..	..	5.4	-62.4	..	..	..	..	..	..	..	..	..	..
Namibia	..	..	..	..	..	..	..	..	..	..	..	..	..	..
Niger	..	..	..	..	..	..	..	..	..	..	..	..	..	..
Nigeria	-35.1	192.6	-40.5	-8.5	-4.7	14.6	4.3	100.0	26.5	-36.3	72.2	-10.6	-9.8	16.2
Rwanda	..	-27.8	-7.2	-12.0	-14.3	0.0	-8.0	-5.4	7.9	18.6	-5.5	..	-6.9	-2.2
São Tomé and Principe	..	..	..	..	-25.9	16.7	-21.8	-1.8	36.7	6.1	40.7	..	..	4.3
Senegal	..	-5.6	-12.5	19.8	-9.9	..	..	-41.6	8.1	24.7	-5.0	..	0.8	-7.9
Seychelles	..	43.8	35.8	-6.1	6.5	0.9	8.1	-3.3	-14.4	45.0	17.6	..	3.1	4.4
Sierra Leone	..	-1.8	-4.0	-14.2	-7.8	0.4	37.2	13.8	-24.5	-6.5	-49.7	..	11.6	-4.0
Somalia	..	..	..	..	..	..	..	..	..	..	..	..	..	..
South Africa	..	..	..	..	..	..	..	..	..	..	..	..	..	..
Sudan	..	14.2	-3.4	..	..	..	..	..	..	..	..	..	-15.0	..
Swaziland	..	..	..	..	..	..	..	..	..	..	..	..	..	..
Tanzania	..	..	..	..	..	..	..	..	..	-5.2	..	..	..	..
Togo	..	2.3	-3.9	57.7	-22.8	..	..	..	..	..	..	..	5.3	..
Uganda	..	..	..	..	..	..	..	..	..	..	..	..	..	..
Zambia	..	-13.4	65.5	9.4	-31.4	-38.9	-11.4	15.4	-33.3	33.3	77.5	..	-5.9	-9.3
Zimbabwe	..	34.0	-6.5	-10.9	32.8	6.8	-4.1	24.7	9.2	8.5	-5.4	..	-0.9	8.8
NORTH AFRICA	..	-0.7	13.9	7.4	-3.7	11.0	-0.1	19.5	2.3	-15.9	5.8	..	5.8	3.3
Algeria	..	-2.1	-43.4	87.7	-9.9	8.0	-13.6	6.0	1.3	-12.8	-9.9	..	-8.7	0.6
Egypt, Arab Republic	..	..	..	..	..	..	..	..	..	..	..	..	..	..
Libya	..	..	..	..	..	..	..	..	..	..	..	..	..	..
Morocco	..	2.5	14.7	5.4	-0.5	10.4	-3.1	23.3	1.1	-16.6	8.2	..	6.4	3.4
Tunisia	..	-11.3	35.4	-0.6	-13.1	14.9	16.5	9.9	7.1	-14.0	1.2	..	9.4	3.9
ALL AFRICA	93.0	3.0	5.7	0.2	0.2	-0.2	9.5	0.6	8.9	-5.9	6.9	17.8	3.4	2.7

5-41. Primary intermediate goods imports

	1980	1988	1989	1990	1991	1992	1993	1994	1995	1996	1997	75-84	85-89	90-MR
				Millions of U.S. dollars (current prices)									*Annual average*	
SUB-SAHARAN AFRICA	..	..	..	..	..	..	..	..	..	..	..	..	..	..
excluding South Africa	..	..	..	..	..	..	..	..	..	..	..	..	..	..
excl. S.Africa & Nigeria	..	..	..	..	..	..	..	..	..	..	..	..	..	..
Angola	..	310	303	357	254	223	89	129	157	0	0	..	292	151
Benin	..	..	..	..	..	..	..	..	..	..	..	..	..	..
Botswana	22	53	63	102	103	106	97	95	145	127	134	25	41	114
Burkina Faso	..	..	..	19	28	28	0	0	42	42	40	..	..	25
Burundi	0	0	0	0	0	0	0	0	0	0	0	0	0	0
Cameroon	55	74	67	85	65	72	61	60	69	77	94	61	76	73
Cape Verde	..	..	..	..	..	..	..	..	..	16	16	..	..	16
Central African Republic	..	50	53	63	55	53	40	45	58	44	39	..	53	50
Chad	..	0	0	0	0	0	0	0	0	0	0	..	0	0
Comoros	..	2	1	4	3	3	4	4	4	2	0	2	2	3
Congo, Democratic Rep. of	..	..	..	..	..	..	..	..	..	..	..	..	..	..
Congo, Republic of	..	..	32	32	23	28	28	72	78	98	89	..	32	56
Côte d'Ivoire	..	..	..	..	..	..	..	..	..	..	..	..	..	..
Djibouti	..	..	..	..	..	..	..	..	..	..	..	..	..	..
Equatorial Guinea	..	..	..	..	..	..	..	..	..	..	..	..	..	..
Eritrea	0	0	0	0	0	1	5	7	10	17	9	0	0	6
Ethiopia	..	26	26	28	28	17	21	15	21	29	31	35	28	24
Gabon	..	10	11	9	10	10	10	10	10	10	11	..	10	10
Gambia, The	..	..	42	51	79	86	88	79	76	82	73	..	42	77
Ghana	..	..	..	..	..	..	..	..	..	..	..	..	..	..
Guinea	..	0	0	0	0	0	0	0	0	0	0	..	0	0
Guinea-Bissau	..	..	..	..	..	..	..	..	..	12	15	..	..	13
Kenya	..	56	52	56	57	59	47	51	71	75	67	42	47	60
Lesotho	..	..	..	..	..	..	..	..	..	..	..	..	..	..
Liberia	..	..	..	..	..	..	..	..	..	..	..	..	..	..
Madagascar	..	..	..	..	..	..	..	..	..	..	46	..	..	46
Malawi	..	146	152	184	76	85	80	56	39	62	86	..	119	84
Mali	..	..	..	..	..	..	..	..	..	..	..	..	..	..
Mauritania	..	0	0	0	0	0	0	0	0	0	0	..	0	0
Mauritius	..	30	136	169	162	170	180	192	224	265	263	16	49	203
Mozambique	..	124	140	140	167	..	..	..	..	..	..	..	132	153
Namibia	..	..	..	..	..	..	..	..	159	163	..	..	..	161
Niger	..	..	..	..	..	..	..	..	..	..	..	..	..	..
Nigeria	..	..	..	..	..	..	..	..	..	..	..	..	..	..
Rwanda	..	1	0	0	0	0	0	0	0	0	0	0	0	0
São Tomé and Principe	..	0	0	0	0	0	0	0	0	0	0	..	0	0
Senegal	..	..	..	..	..	..	..	..	..	..	..	..	..	..
Seychelles	..	0	0	0	0	0	0	0	0	0	0	..	0	0
Sierra Leone	0	0	0	0	0	0	0	14	28	30	44	0	0	15
Somalia	..	..	..	..	..	..	..	..	..	..	..	..	..	..
South Africa	4,184	2,224	2,276	2,227	2,274	2,233	2,237	2,653	2,886	2,487	3,507	2,678	1,970	2,563
Sudan	..	247	167	81	154	..	..	..	134	234	190	172	195	158
Swaziland	64	61	43	64	66	67	87	110	152	172	209	41	34	116
Tanzania	..	265	379	371	236	132	116	113	255	381	284	134	232	236
Togo	..	..	..	..	..	..	..	..	..	..	..	..	..	..
Uganda	..	..	..	..	..	..	..	..	..	..	..	..	..	..
Zambia	..	47	72	49	34	48	20	72	80	80	50	..	45	54
Zimbabwe	..	229	259	296	333	349	297	349	367	371	463	39	163	353
NORTH AFRICA	..	..	..	..	..	..	..	..	..	..	..	..	..	..
Algeria	..	626	851	939	870	981	942	999	1,000	872	780	638	652	923
Egypt, Arab Republic	..	..	..	..	..	..	..	..	..	..	..	..	..	..
Libya	..	..	..	..	..	..	..	..	..	..	..	..	..	..
Morocco	..	781	628	835	807	930	657	815	1,062	886	860	515	656	856
Tunisia	..	0	0	0	0	0	0	0	0	491	470	..	0	120
ALL AFRICA	..	..	..	..	..	..	..	..	..	..	..	..	..	..

5-42. Primary intermediate goods imports, growth

					Percent								Average annual percentage growth	
	1980	1988	1989	1990	1991	1992	1993	1994	1995	1996	1997	75-84	85-89	90-MR
SUB-SAHARAN AFRICA	17.1	8.3	12.7	11.4	-23.7	0.5	-24.6	12.8	20.4	-7.8	-11.0	35.9	34.4	-3.9
excluding South Africa	17.1	8.3	12.7	11.4	-23.7	0.5	-24.6	12.8	20.4	-7.8	-11.0	35.9	34.4	-3.9
excl. S.Africa & Nigeria	17.1	8.3	12.7	11.4	-23.7	0.5	-24.6	12.8	20.4	-7.8	-11.0	35.9	34.4	-3.9
Angola	..	-4.0	2.3	24.5	-28.4	-9.6	-58.1	40.7	10.9	..	..	..	-3.2	-15.8
Benin	..	..	..	..	..	..	..	..	..	..	..	..	..	..
Botswana	..	..	..	..	..	..	..	..	..	..	..	..	..	..
Burkina Faso	..	..	..	..	..	..	..	..	..	..	..	..	..	..
Burundi	..	..	..	..	..	..	..	..	..	..	..	..	..	..
Cameroon	17.1	-32.7	-5.6	39.4	-21.1	16.1	-16.5	-19.4	2.7	-8.8	12.6	15.3	0.6	-4.7
Cape Verde	..	..	..	..	..	..	..	..	..	..	..	..	..	..
Central African Republic	..	-17.5	5.5	12.7	-14.3	-8.4	-25.1	8.5	19.3	-26.5	-7.7	..	..	-7.0
Chad	..	..	..	..	..	..	..	..	..	..	..	..	..	..
Comoros	..	0.0	-50.0	200.0	0.0	0.0	0.0	100.0	-16.7	-40.0	..	..	-14.5	15.8
Congo, Democratic Rep. of	..	..	..	..	..	..	..	..	..	..	..	..	..	..
Congo, Republic of	..	..	..	..	..	..	..	..	..	..	..	..	..	..
Côte d'Ivoire	..	..	..	..	..	..	..	..	..	..	..	..	..	..
Djibouti	..	..	..	..	..	..	..	..	..	..	..	..	..	..
Equatorial Guinea	..	..	..	..	..	..	..	..	..	..	..	..	..	..
Eritrea	..	..	..	..	..	..	..	..	..	..	..	..	..	..
Ethiopia	..	..	..	..	..	..	..	..	..	..	..	..	..	..
Gabon	..	..	..	..	..	..	..	..	..	..	..	..	..	..
Gambia, The	..	..	..	16.0	51.3	4.6	0.5	-10.9	-8.0	4.3	-13.8	..	..	3.0
Ghana	..	..	..	..	..	..	..	..	..	..	..	..	..	..
Guinea	..	..	..	..	..	..	..	..	..	..	..	..	..	..
Guinea-Bissau	..	..	..	..	..	..	..	..	..	..	..	..	..	..
Kenya	..	3.6	16.2	-11.1	9.4	1.6	-17.6	5.1	50.3	-10.8	14.7	..	0.8	3.9
Lesotho	..	..	..	..	..	..	..	..	..	..	..	..	..	..
Liberia	..	..	..	..	..	..	..	..	..	..	..	..	..	..
Madagascar	..	..	..	..	..	..	..	..	..	..	..	..	..	..
Malawi	..	23.6	4.4	12.7	-59.4	6.2	-4.3	-33.3	-34.1	65.5	45.8	..	..	-13.2
Mali	..	..	..	..	..	..	..	..	..	..	..	..	..	..
Mauritania	..	..	..	..	..	..	..	..	..	..	..	..	..	..
Mauritius	..	-17.3	9.8	40.3	5.2	2.4	10.8	5.1	2.4	4.1	4.5	..	-8.4	7.1
Mozambique	..	..	3.8	4.3	..	..	..	..	..	..	..	..	..	..
Namibia	..	..	..	..	..	..	..	..	..	..	..	..	..	..
Niger	..	..	..	..	..	..	..	..	..	..	..	..	..	..
Nigeria	..	..	..	..	..	..	..	..	..	..	..	..	..	..
Rwanda	..	..	..	..	..	..	..	..	..	..	..	..	..	..
São Tomé and Principe	..	..	..	..	..	..	..	..	..	..	..	..	..	..
Senegal	..	..	..	..	..	..	..	..	..	..	..	..	..	..
Seychelles	..	..	..	..	..	..	..	..	..	..	..	..	..	..
Sierra Leone	..	..	..	..	..	..	..	..	88.9	10.6	53.2	..	..	..
Somalia	..	..	..	..	..	..	..	..	..	..	..	..	..	..
South Africa	..	..	..	..	..	..	..	..	..	..	..	..	..	..
Sudan	..	..	..	..	..	..	..	..	..	..	..	..	..	..
Swaziland	..	..	..	..	..	..	..	..	..	..	..	..	..	..
Tanzania	..	..	..	..	..	..	..	..	..	43.8	..	..	..	..
Togo	..	..	..	..	..	..	..	..	..	..	..	..	..	..
Uganda	..	..	..	..	..	..	..	..	..	..	..	..	..	..
Zambia	..	-2.2	54.5	-35.3	-34.1	37.9	-57.5	241.2	1.7	5.1	-33.9	..	54.0	1.3
Zimbabwe	..	1.3	14.3	5.9	10.1	0.4	-14.9	13.5	-2.9	3.8	28.1	..	42.1	2.7
NORTH AFRICA	..	15.1	-6.9	1.6	-5.4	15.2	-6.7	2.6	5.3	21.4	5.5	..	1.9	4.3
Algeria	..	7.0	21.3	-23.3	-10.0	8.0	-13.5	10.1	1.3	-10.8	-10.6	..	-2.7	-4.4
Egypt, Arab Republic	..	..	..	..	..	..	..	..	..	..	..	..	..	..
Libya	..	..	..	..	..	..	..	..	..	..	..	..	..	..
Morocco	..	20.3	-23.3	24.7	-2.8	19.0	-3.5	-0.6	7.2	-0.3	14.5	..	6.0	5.1
Tunisia	..	..	..	..	..	..	..	..	..	..	-1.3	..	..	..
ALL AFRICA	17.1	12.3	0.8	5.9	-13.8	9.2	-13.5	5.9	10.6	10.3	0.3	79.7	10.3	1.2

5-43. Manufactured goods imports

	Millions of U.S. dollars (current prices)											Annual average		
	1980	1988	1989	1990	1991	1992	1993	1994	1995	1996	1997	75-84	85-89	90-MR
SUB-SAHARAN AFRICA	..	..	..	..	..	..	..	..	..	..	..	..	..	..
excluding South Africa														
excl. S.Africa & Nigeria	..	..	..	..	..	..	..	..	..	..	..	..	..	..
Angola	..	133	128	151	91	135	72	71	94	343	400	..	154	170
Benin	..	..	..	..	..	..	..	..	..	..	..	..	..	..
Botswana	54	102	125	1,588	174	175	163	159	177	178	193	59	86	351
Burkina Faso	..	..	..	..	..	..	..	..	..	..	..	..	..	..
Burundi	40	49	48	60	68	55	57	55	62	38	33	46	49	54
Cameroon	605	617	504	603	455	367	378	370	363	398	385	511	569	415
Cape Verde	..	..	..	..	..	..	..	..	..	10	10	..	..	10
Central African Republic	..	..	..	..	..	..	..	..	..	..	..	..	..	..
Chad	..	79	84	96	108	127	105	91	62	73	73	..	87	92
Comoros	..	3	1	1	2	2	2	2	2	2	3	0	2	2
Congo, Democratic Rep. of	..	..	..	..	..	60	61	45	52	82	..	..	..	60
Congo, Republic of	..	135	115	149	116	142	141	86	94	118	141	141	128	123
Côte d'Ivoire	..	..	..	..	..	..	..	..	..	..	..	..	..	..
Djibouti	..	..	..	..	..	..	..	..	..	..	..	..	..	..
Equatorial Guinea	..	..	..	..	..	..	..	..	..	..	..	..	..	..
Eritrea	..	..	..	..	..	41	63	102	117	177	153	..	..	109
Ethiopia	..	158	172	156	115	113	95	129	183	253	270	117	140	164
Gabon	..	91	78	85	100	103	89	30	32	286	289	..	85	127
Gambia, The	..	..	42	51	79	86	88	79	76	82	73	..	42	77
Ghana	..	..	..	..	..	..	..	..	..	..	..	..	..	..
Guinea	..	..	..	..	..	..	..	..	..	..	..	..	..	..
Guinea-Bissau	..	..	..	..	..	..	..	..	..	5	6	..	..	6
Kenya	..	320	270	265	289	291	307	293	487	443	465	186	268	355
Lesotho	..	..	..	..	..	..	..	..	..	..	..	..	..	..
Liberia	..	..	..	..	..	..	..	..	..	..	..	..	..	..
Madagascar	..	..	..	..	..	..	..	..	..	..	92	..	..	92
Malawi	..	35	36	43	126	170	163	138	86	133	187	..	29	131
Mali	..	109	102	131	148	156	136	122	150	150	148	..	93	142
Mauritania	..	103	125	139	151	137	133	129	111	103	98	..	101	125
Mauritius	..	548	497	554	551	587	626	659	724	764	732	181	412	650
Mozambique	..	185	229	221	307	..	..	..	..	..	..	..	207	264
Namibia	..	..	..	..	..	..	..	..	159	164	..	..	..	162
Niger	..	..	..	..	..	..	..	..	..	..	..	..	..	..
Nigeria	..	..	..	..	..	..	..	..	..	..	..	..	..	..
Rwanda	..	118	104	97	128	92	91	23	41	55	71	82	100	75
São Tomé and Principe	..	0	0	0	0	0	0	0	0	0	0	..	0	0
Senegal	..	..	..	..	..	..	..	..	..	..	..	..	..	..
Seychelles	..	0	0	0	0	0	0	0	0	0	0	..	0	0
Sierra Leone	0	0	0	0	0	0	0	15	27	43	44	0	0	16
Somalia	..	..	..	..	..	..	..	..	..	..	..	..	..	..
South Africa	959	665	900	880	899	883	884	1,156	1,377	1,536	2,136	708	650	1,219
Sudan	..	163	145	77	175	..	..	..	307	324	353	160	122	247
Swaziland	165	147	140	176	174	241	249	271	322	275	282	91	104	249
Tanzania	..	5	4	7	17	21	12	10	15	17	27	6	7	16
Togo	..	92	80	120	116	102	60	48	80	72	63	67	74	83
Uganda	..	..	..	..	..	..	..	..	..	..	..	..	..	..
Zambia	..	..	..	..	..	..	..	40	54	55	116	..	..	66
Zimbabwe	..	190	216	247	277	291	247	290	364	369	447	166	184	316
NORTH AFRICA	..	..	..	..	..	..	..	..	..	..	..	..	..	..
Algeria	..	1,905	2,011	2,225	2,045	2,306	2,213	2,348	2,100	2,047	1,830	3,053	2,073	2,139
Egypt, Arab Republic	..	..	..	..	..	..	..	..	..	..	..	..	..	..
Libya	..	..	..	..	..	..	..	..	..	..	..	..	..	..
Morocco	..	1,539	1,783	2,193	2,342	2,488	2,433	2,908	3,589	3,383	3,518	738	1,247	2,857
Tunisia	..	0	0	0	0	0	0	0	0	1,738	1,716	0	0	432
ALL AFRICA	..	..	..	..	..	..	..	..	..	..	..	..	..	..

5-44. Manufactured goods imports, growth

					Percent							Average annual percentage growth		
	1980	*1988*	*1989*	*1990*	*1991*	*1992*	*1993*	*1994*	*1995*	*1996*	*1997*	*75-84*	*85-89*	*90-MR*
SUB-SAHARAN AFRICA	21.8	2.6	0.8	-0.3	-12.7	-0.1	5.4	-1.6	19.5	8.8	7.0	12.1	9.6	3.1
excluding South Africa	21.8	2.6	0.8	-0.3	-12.7	-0.1	5.4	-1.6	19.5	8.8	7.0	12.1	9.6	3.1
excl. S.Africa & Nigeria	21.8	2.6	0.8	-0.3	-12.7	-0.1	5.4	-1.6	19.5	8.8	7.0	12.1	9.6	3.1
Angola	..	0.9	0.0	25.7	-39.4	53.5	-43.9	-5.4	21.4	263.5	29.4	..	-15.5	11.9
Benin	..	..	..	..	..	..	..	..	..	..	..	..	..	..
Botswana	..	..	..	..	..	..	..	..	..	..	..	..	..	..
Burkina Faso	..	..	..	..	..	..	..	..	..	..	..	..	..	..
Burundi	..	-1.3	-1.3	17.2	9.7	-21.6	1.9	-6.4	4.3	-36.2	-7.9	..	-4.2	-7.2
Cameroon	16.5	-15.7	6.3	-4.1	-5.0	-17.1	31.5	-12.3	10.6	2.4	0.8	-3.9	3.5	0.5
Cape Verde	..	..	..	..	..	..	..	..	..	..	..	..	..	..
Central African Republic	..	..	..	..	..	..	..	..	..	..	..	..	..	..
Chad	..	-4.6	-3.1	-7.0	-19.2	19.2	-13.0	27.0	21.5	18.3	-0.6	..	..	6.4
Comoros	..	0.0	-66.7	0.0	100.0	0.0	0.0	50.0	0.0	0.0	0.0	..	6.9	16.0
Congo, Democratic Rep. of	..	..	..	..	..	..	..	..	..	..	..	..	..	..
Congo, Republic of	..	0.2	-5.3	..	..	..	..	..	..	..	..	..	4.7	..
Côte d'Ivoire	..	..	..	..	..	..	..	..	..	..	..	..	..	..
Djibouti	..	..	..	..	..	..	..	..	..	..	..	..	..	..
Equatorial Guinea	..	..	..	..	..	..	..	..	..	..	..	..	..	..
Eritrea	..	..	..	..	..	..	..	..	..	..	..	..	..	..
Ethiopia	..	..	..	..	..	..	..	..	..	..	..	..	..	..
Gabon	..	..	..	..	..	..	..	..	..	..	..	..	..	..
Gambia, The	..	..	..	16.0	51.3	4.6	0.5	-10.9	-8.0	4.3	-13.8	..	..	3.0
Ghana	..	..	..	..	..	..	..	..	..	..	..	..	..	..
Guinea	..	..	..	..	..	..	..	..	..	..	..	..	..	..
Guinea-Bissau	..	..	..	..	..	..	..	..	..	..	..	..	..	..
Kenya	..	6.7	-1.8	-20.6	17.1	-1.5	9.6	-7.7	86.9	-12.3	0.5	..	1.3	8.5
Lesotho	..	..	..	..	..	..	..	..	..	..	..	..	..	..
Liberia	..	..	..	..	..	..	..	..	..	..	..	..	..	..
Madagascar	..	..	..	..	..	..	..	..	..	..	..	..	..	..
Malawi	..	39.1	3.1	12.1	191.9	28.7	-3.6	-18.7	-42.2	60.3	48.5	..	..	13.8
Mali	..	14.3	-4.2	13.6	18.6	4.7	-4.9	-13.6	10.2	3.5	4.8	..	0.0	2.5
Mauritania	..	16.6	23.0	5.1	6.4	-13.4	-2.3	-6.3	-20.4	-3.7	0.8	..	-2.7	-6.2
Mauritius	..	-10.5	7.3	8.3	6.1	3.7	13.1	5.0	2.5	5.6	4.5	..	3.3	6.1
Mozambique	..	..	13.5	-3.3	..	..	..	..	..	..	..	..	..	..
Namibia	..	..	..	..	..	..	..	..	..	..	..	..	..	..
Niger	..	..	..	..	..	..	..	..	..	..	..	..	..	..
Nigeria	..	..	..	..	..	..	..	..	..	..	..	..	..	..
Rwanda	..	-15.3	-11.2	-12.1	-19.7	3.9	-6.3	3.3	11.2	-3.0	-8.1	..	-0.3	-2.7
São Tomé and Principe	..	..	..	..	..	..	..	..	..	..	..	..	..	..
Senegal	..	..	..	..	..	..	..	..	..	..	..	..	..	..
Seychelles	..	..	..	..	..	..	..	..	..	..	..	..	..	..
Sierra Leone	..	..	..	..	..	..	..	..	76.0	52.1	0.3	..	..	..
Somalia	..	..	..	..	..	..	..	..	..	..	..	..	..	..
South Africa	..	..	..	..	..	..	..	..	..	..	..	..	..	..
Sudan	..	..	..	..	..	..	..	..	..	..	..	..	..	..
Swaziland	..	..	..	..	..	..	..	..	..	..	..	..	..	..
Tanzania	..	..	..	..	..	..	..	..	..	-29.2	..	..	..	..
Togo	..	..	..	..	..	..	..	..	..	..	..	..	..	..
Uganda	..	..	..	..	..	..	..	..	..	..	..	..	..	..
Zambia	..	15.9	-39.2	51.1	..	..	..	..	25.0	7.5	120.9	..	..	-18.0
Zimbabwe	..	1.3	14.3	5.9	10.1	0.4	-14.9	13.5	15.9	3.9	24.3	..	-2.9	5.2
NORTH AFRICA	..	0.2	29.9	-4.6	1.5	6.2	-6.9	12.3	4.8	28.3	-0.9	..	-1.8	5.2
Algeria	..	-25.0	51.3	-19.9	-10.0	8.1	-13.6	6.7	1.3	-11.1	-10.6	..	-12.3	-4.7
Egypt, Arab Republic	..	..	..	..	..	..	..	..	..	..	..	..	..	..
Libya	..	..	..	..	..	..	..	..	..	..	..	..	..	..
Morocco	..	33.8	13.8	10.6	9.7	5.1	-2.8	15.3	6.5	4.7	1.4	..	18.4	6.2
Tunisia	..	..	..	..	..	..	..	..	..	..	3.0	..	..	..
ALL AFRICA	21.8	1.3	16.8	-2.9	-4.2	3.9	-2.6	7.1	9.9	21.0	1.8	34.4	2.2	4.4

5-45. Capital goods imports

	Millions of U.S. dollars (current prices)											Annual average		
	1980	1988	1989	1990	1991	1992	1993	1994	1995	1996	1997	75-84	85-89	90-MR
SUB-SAHARAN AFRICA	..	7,393	7,409	8,039	8,163	8,054	7,300	7,341	10,363	11,546	10,300	..	6,250	8,888
excluding South Africa	..	7,393	7,409	8,039	8,163	8,054	7,300	7,341	10,363	11,546	10,300	..	6,250	8,888
excl. S.Africa & Nigeria	..	7,393	7,409	8,039	8,163	8,054	7,300	7,341	10,363	11,546	10,300	..	6,250	8,888
Angola	..	203	198	233	269	378	322	327	327	303	354	..	263	314
Benin	..	168	123	157	182	212	203	146	217	213	206	..	120	192
Botswana	195	448	579	674	642	536	542	485	657	523	580	197	348	580
Burkina Faso	..	..	..	129	111	131	0	0	151	169	155	..	..	106
Burundi	33	70	65	80	91	78	78	81	88	49	45	45	67	74
Cameroon	388	512	424	452	392	319	325	314	315	362	399	359	480	360
Cape Verde	0	46	52	52	65	98	71	98	129	119	79	0	29	89
Central African Republic	..	53	51	59	60	64	53	43	63	14	20	73	67	47
Chad	..	73	77	88	100	97	84	83	85	100	106	52	67	93
Comoros	..	..	..	..	..	..	..	..	..	..	13	..	..	13
Congo, Democratic Rep. of	..	..	..	..	..	683	464	553	788	862	..	..	..	670
Congo, Republic of	..	244	434	237	180	188	203	113	336	1,105	510	199	249	359
Côte d'Ivoire	1,102	542	449	397	404	481	417	410	584	734	740	663	512	521
Djibouti	..	..	..	..	..	..	..	..	..	..	..	..	..	..
Equatorial Guinea	..	21	14	20	60	26	24	42	64	192	282	10	15	89
Eritrea	0	0	0	0	0	12	62	114	173	162	161	0	0	85
Ethiopia	..	518	397	340	466	320	382	239	334	460	515	449	396	382
Gabon	..	371	356	354	360	335	320	320	339	355	388	188	245	346
Gambia, The	..	2	5	2	1	3	3	3	15	13	12	..	4	6
Ghana	..	182	190	226	248	277	..	..	..	..	..	200	171	250
Guinea	..	..	..	..	..	..	..	..	..	..	..	..	..	..
Guinea-Bissau	..	11	20	22	15	24	14	15	16	10	19	12	13	17
Kenya	..	571	497	673	527	411	328	503	995	869	844	384	455	644
Lesotho	..	..	..	..	..	..	..	..	..	..	..	..	..	..
Liberia	..	..	..	..	..	..	..	..	..	..	..	..	..	..
Madagascar	333	131	120	186	165	129	140	143	141	164	146	160	109	152
Malawi	..	103	118	143	294	291	285	210	181	277	340	..	91	253
Mali	..	169	155	194	188	201	183	193	246	226	221	80	146	206
Mauritania	..	108	77	88	78	121	114	82	130	91	73	85	115	97
Mauritius	..	398	310	440	380	377	394	511	397	520	508	54	224	441
Mozambique	..	166	170	154	211	..	..	..	..	..	..	..	168	183
Namibia	..	..	..	..	..	..	..	..	318	322	..	..	..	320
Niger	..	106	118	148	102	85	80	67	87	56	68	..	107	87
Nigeria	..	..	..	..	..	..	..	..	..	..	..	..	..	..
Rwanda	..	100	86	58	54	69	72	36	50	54	62	50	84	57
São Tomé and Principe	..	7	18	12	13	9	11	12	12	7	7	1	10	11
Senegal	158	144	173	195	197	..	159	154	180	186	184	136	141	179
Seychelles	..	49	45	49	40	40	60	48	67	166	75	16	35	68
Sierra Leone	0	44	52	44	33	30	29	18	10	21	10	5	40	24
Somalia	..	..	..	..	..	..	..	..	..	..	..	..	..	..
South Africa	..	..	..	..	..	..	..	..	..	..	..	..	..	..
Sudan	..	314	355	304	348	..	..	..	322	387	443	348	266	361
Swaziland	126	118	196	181	200	196	231	232	249	312	321	95	107	240
Tanzania	..	508	443	540	579	639	628	597	602	461	503	458	472	569
Togo	..	111	117	132	113	102	58	41	75	105	101	51	95	91
Uganda	..	..	..	..	..	..	..	..	..	..	..	..	..	..
Zambia	..	292	372	346	285	349	328	365	722	644	665	118	243	463
Zimbabwe	..	487	553	632	711	745	632	743	901	930	1,148	345	440	805
NORTH AFRICA	..	5,840	6,891	9,335	8,398	8,047	7,782	7,746	8,611	9,292	9,108	..	5,929	8,540
Algeria	..	1,967	2,335	3,092	1,888	1,894	1,835	2,118	2,100	1,848	1,613	3,129	2,444	2,048
Egypt, Arab Republic	..	2,188	2,311	3,151	3,340	2,610	2,545	2,349	3,108	4,102	4,030	..	2,088	3,154
Libya	..	..	..	..	..	..	..	..	..	..	..	..	..	..
Morocco	..	1,066	1,409	1,856	1,867	1,965	1,833	1,845	1,887	1,781	1,660	733	982	1,837
Tunisia	742	618	836	1,235	1,304	1,578	1,569	1,433	1,516	1,561	1,805	719	643	1,500
ALL AFRICA	..	13,232	14,300	17,373	16,561	16,101	15,082	15,087	18,974	20,837	19,408	..	12,190	17,428

5-46. Capital goods imports, growth

					Percent							Average annual percentage growth		
	1980	1988	1989	1990	1991	1992	1993	1994	1995	1996	1997	75-84	85-89	90-MR
SUB-SAHARAN AFRICA	69.0	6.3	1.2	-3.2	-3.7	0.4	-1.3	1.1	27.0	11.1	1.3	29.8	14.4	4.3
excluding South Africa	69.0	6.3	1.2	-3.2	-3.7	0.4	-1.3	1.1	27.0	11.1	1.3	29.8	14.4	4.3
excl. S.Africa & Nigeria	69.0	6.3	1.2	-3.2	-3.7	0.4	-1.3	1.1	27.0	11.1	1.3	29.8	14.4	4.3
Angola	..	-15.3	2.3	24.4	16.0	44.9	-10.3	-1.8	-9.0	-7.1	29.2	..	-19.2	6.3
Benin	..													
Botswana	..													
Burkina Faso	..													
Burundi	..	-9.0	-5.7	16.1	8.8	-16.8	6.9	0.2	-3.3	-42.7	2.8		-3.0	-6.2
Cameroon	-7.5	-24.9	-13.0	3.9	12.2	-1.9	2.3	-15.3	13.2	21.9	6.3	-5.6	8.2	3.6
Cape Verde		-7.1	12.0	0.0	24.4	49.3	-27.7	36.0	29.4	-27.2	4.8	..		9.2
Central African Republic	..	-18.3	-2.8	8.9	-1.0	2.9	-17.2	-21.3	34.2	-79.0	46.9	..	..	-16.0
Chad		-4.6	-3.1	-7.0	-19.2	-7.0	-8.0	-2.0	29.6	18.9	5.9	..	..	0.5
Comoros	..													
Congo, Democratic Rep. of	..													
Congo, Republic of		22.0	-39.7	-7.9	-1.9	-16.5	32.2	10.9	-1.1	199.4	-58.4		7.6	10.2
Côte d'Ivoire	..	-10.2	-0.7	-13.3	2.5	52.6	-13.5	-2.5	29.4	23.7	8.5			10.2
Djibouti	..					..		..					..	
Equatorial Guinea	..	11.2	-35.1	35.3	194.2	-58.9	-4.3	67.5	39.0	189.2	52.6	..	3.3	34.0
Eritrea	..													
Ethiopia	..													
Gabon	..													
Gambia, The	..	26.7	173.7	-69.2	-43.8	188.9	-11.5	26.1	317.2	-12.4	-12.3			24.8
Ghana	..	5.9	4.3	12.2	7.4	7.3	14.7	6.0	9.1	24.8	-17.1	..	-3.1	8.9
Guinea	..													
Guinea-Bissau	..	84.7	71.4	3.5	-36.0	58.9	-40.8	26.1	13.4	-37.4	74.0			-2.8
Kenya	..	0.3	-16.4	72.9	-19.2	-23.4	-15.9	50.3	102.4	-12.6	-2.9		-3.7	10.4
Lesotho	..													
Liberia	..					..							..	
Madagascar	..	21.6	-8.1	41.2	-9.3	-25.3	13.8	-2.4	-9.9	20.2	-3.1		3.5	-1.1
Malawi	..	17.1	15.6	12.6	100.8	-5.6	-1.7	-28.8	-20.5	59.8	29.9	..		6.1
Mali	..	2.5	-7.2	11.1	0.7	3.0	-5.0	2.2	15.5	-8.0	8.9	..	3.2	2.5
Mauritania	..	-22.5	-28.6	8.6	-13.7	48.8	-4.9	-31.1	46.9	-26.3	-15.8	..	-14.3	-1.2
Mauritius	..	37.7	-25.7	33.1	-4.5	-4.0	6.7	4.0	-20.0	7.0	7.0	..	19.8	0.4
Mozambique	..	..	-14.1	-9.6										
Namibia	..													
Niger	..													
Nigeria	..													
Rwanda	..	-25.0	-12.8	7.0	-10.3	4.0	-6.4	3.4	11.1	-3.0	-8.1	..	6.4	-0.1
São Tomé and Principe	..	1.9	162.6	-39.5	12.5	-32.4	20.8	3.8	-6.3	-37.9	0.2	..	18.8	-10.1
Senegal	..	-12.2	11.7	32.1	-2.1	..	..	-50.7	30.3	0.8	-13.4	..	22.7	-9.7
Seychelles	..	64.7	11.0	-4.0	-9.4	8.8	52.1	-12.6	32.7	125.4	-46.4		23.4	15.2
Sierra Leone	..	25.4	14.6	-19.0	-17.1	-1.2	9.0	-34.6	-24.7	-37.4	..		5.0	-16.9
Somalia	..													
South Africa	..	..	..									..	..	
Sudan	..	119.2	51.2		..								20.1	
Swaziland	..							..		..				
Tanzania	..									-22.7				
Togo	..	4.3	-0.9	15.6								..	6.7	..
Uganda	..											..		
Zambia	..	9.6	27.0	-12.1	-19.3	17.4	-5.9	7.3	82.9	-6.7	8.8	..	16.6	8.4
Zimbabwe	..	1.3	14.3	5.9	10.1	0.4	-14.9	13.5	11.8	6.0	26.5		3.4	5.0
NORTH AFRICA	..	5.8	18.0	39.6	-11.9	-10.3	-2.9	-7.4	7.3	12.9	2.4	..	-2.3	0.0
Algeria	..	-9.2	25.6	60.1	-35.2	-13.1	-10.5	7.6	7.0	8.9	-1.0	..	-20.6	-2.7
Egypt, Arab Republic	..	14.3	2.4	33.1	2.0	-24.3	-4.4	-9.2	24.7	28.5	-1.3	..		1.8
Libya	..												..	
Morocco	..	13.1	32.3	24.5	-1.2	0.5	-2.5	-2.9	-12.3	6.5	1.3	..	5.8	-0.7
Tunisia	..	13.5	38.1	27.7	3.4	21.2	8.7	-23.8	-4.1	-10.7	22.4	..	-9.2	1.2
ALL AFRICA	69.0	6.0	10.4	21.9	-9.2	-6.6	-2.3	-4.2	15.1	12.1	1.9	58.2	3.2	1.6

5-47. Direction of trade matrix, imports, 1986

Exporters		DZA	AGO	BEN	BFA	BDI	CMR	CPV	CAF	TCD	COM	ZAR	COG	CIV	DJI	EGY	GNQ
		Importers										*Percentage of total imports*					
Algeria	DZA	**	..	0.26	1.89	..	0.00	..	..	..	..	..	0.01	0.08	..	0.00	..
Angola	AGO	..	**	..	..	..	..	..	..	..	..	..	..	..	..	..	..
Benin	BEN	..	..	**	..	..	..	..	..	..	..	..	..	..	..	..	..
Burkina Faso	BFA	..	..	..	**	..	..	..	..	..	..	..	..	..	..	..	..
Burundi	BDI	..	..	..	..	**	..	..	..	..	..	..	..	..	..	..	..
Cameroon	CMR	0.12	0.07	0.08	0.01	..	**	..	10.89	16.15	..	0.00	3.07	0.62	0.01	0.00	17.01
Cape Verde	CPV	..	..	..	..	..	..	**	..	..	..	..	..	..	..	..	..
Central African Republic	CAF	..	..	..	..	..	..	..	**	..	..	..	..	..	..	..	..
Chad	TCD	..	..	..	..	..	..	..	..	**	..	..	..	..	..	..	..
Comoros	COM	..	..	..	..	..	..	..	..	..	**	..	..	..	..	..	..
Congo, Democratic Rep. of	ZAR	..	..	..	..	..	..	..	..	..	..	**	..	..	..	..	..
Congo, Republic of	COG	0.02	0.19	0.04	..	..	0.00	..	0.04	0.52	..	0.07	**	0.02	..	..	..
Côte d'Ivoire	CIV	..	..	..	..	..	..	..	..	..	..	..	..	**	..	..	..
Djibouti	DJI	0.00	..	..	..	..	..	..	..	0.01	0.08	0.00	..	..	**	0.00	..
Egypt, Arab Rep.	EGY	0.07	..	..	..	0.00	0.00	..	..	0.00	..	0.02	..	0.00	0.02	**	..
Equatorial Guinea	GNQ	..	..	..	..	..	..	..	..	..	..	..	..	..	..	..	**
Ethiopia	ETH	0.00	..	..	0.00	0.00	..	..	..	..	..	..	0.00	..	9.22	..	..
Gabon	GAB	..	..	..	..	..	..	..	..	..	..	..	..	..	..	..	..
Gambia, The	GMB	..	..	..	..	..	..	..	..	..	..	..	..	..	..	..	..
Ghana	GHA	..	..	..	..	..	..	..	..	..	..	..	..	..	..	..	..
Guinea	GIN	..	..	..	..	..	..	..	..	..	..	..	..	..	..	..	..
Guinea-Bissau	GNB	..	..	..	..	..	..	..	..	..	..	..	..	..	..	..	..
Kenya	KEN	0.00	0.16	0.00	0.02	8.64	0.00	0.57	0.16	..	2.32	1.19	0.00	0.04	1.45	0.07	..
Liberia	LBR	..	..	..	..	..	..	..	..	..	..	..	..	..	..	..	..
Libya	LBY	0.00	..	..	..	..	..	..	..	..	..	..	..	..	..	..	..
Madagascar	MDG	0.00	..	..	..	..	0.01	..	..	0.01	0.40	0.00	..	..	0.04	0.00	0.61
Malawi	MWI	..	..	..	..	0.41	0.02	..	..	..	..	0.41	..	0.00	..	0.04	..
Mali	MLI	..	..	..	..	..	..	..	..	..	..	..	..	..	..	..	..
Mauritania	MRT	..	..	..	..	..	..	..	..	..	..	..	..	..	..	..	..
Mauritius	MUS	0.00	..	0.02	..	..	0.00	..	..	..	0.63	..	0.00	0.00	0.00	0.02	..
Morocco	MAR	0.00	0.09	0.35	0.03	0.00	0.54	..	0.33	..	0.22	0.48	0.96	0.60	0.01	0.02	0.10
Mozambique	MOZ	..	..	..	..	..	..	..	..	..	..	..	..	..	..	..	..
Niger	NER	..	..	..	..	..	..	..	..	..	..	..	..	..	..	..	..
Nigeria	NGA	0.00	0.07	0.29	0.00	..	0.09	..	..	0.27	0.16	0.87	0.00	6.41	..	0.00	..
Reunion	REU	..	..	0.00	0.01	..	0.00	..	..	..	7.88	..	0.00	..	0.01	..	..
Rwanda	RWA	..	..	..	..	..	..	..	..	..	..	..	..	..	..	..	..
South Africa	ZAF	..	..	..	..	..	..	..	..	..	..	..	..	..	..	..	..
São Tomé and Principe	STP	..	..	..	..	..	..	..	..	..	..	..	..	..	..	..	..
Senegal	SEN	0.00	..	1.05	1.74	0.00	0.92	1.24	0.21	0.27	0.00	0.06	0.75	1.61	..	0.00	0.01
Seychelles	SYC	..	..	..	..	..	0.00	..	..	..	..	..	..	..	..	..	..
Sierra Leone	SLE	..	..	..	..	..	..	..	..	..	..	..	..	..	..	..	..
Somalia	SOM	..	..	..	..	..	..	..	..	..	..	..	..	..	..	..	..
Sudan	SDN	..	..	..	..	..	..	..	..	..	..	..	..	..	..	..	..
Tanzania	TZA	..	..	..	..	..	..	..	..	..	..	..	..	..	..	..	..
Togo	TGO	..	..	0.35	2.37	..	0.00	0.11	0.00	0.01	..	..	0.01	0.02	..	0.00	0.09
Tunisia	TUN	1.21	0.01	0.14	0.03	..	0.50	..	0.04	..	..	0.00	0.02	0.11	0.01	0.05	..
Uganda	UGA	..	..	..	..	..	..	..	..	..	..	..	..	..	..	..	..
Zambia	ZMB	..	..	..	..	..	..	..	..	..	..	..	..	..	..	..	..
Zimbabwe	ZWE	0.01	0.16	0.00	..	0.49	0.00	0.99	0.07	..	0.00	1.42	0.06	0.04	0.00	0.03	..
Sub-Saharan Africa	SSA	0.16	0.65	1.84	4.13	9.54	1.04	2.91	11.37	17.23	3.59	4.02	3.89	8.77	10.73	0.16	17.71
European Community	EEC	72.88	48.46	63.60	80.37	76.52	76.84	75.44	71.11	75.49	58.44	67.31	74.33	70.12	53.72	53.33	74.12
North America	NNA	7.87	7.44	4.98	3.89	1.36	2.84	..	1.14	4.60	26.94	9.89	1.93	4.21	1.80	19.26	0.12
Rest Of World	ROW	19.08	43.45	29.59	11.60	12.58	19.27	21.65	16.38	2.67	11.04	18.78	19.85	16.91	33.76	27.25	8.05
World	WLD	100.00	100.00	100.00	100.00	100.00	100.00	100.00	100.00	100.00	100.00	100.00	100.00	100.00	100.00	100.00	100.00

Note: ** means "not applicable."

(Table continues on the following page)

5-47. (continued)

Percentage of total imports

ETH	GAB	GMB	GHA	GIN	GNB	KEN	LBR	LBY	MDG	MWI	MLI	MRT	MUS	MAR	MOZ	NER	NGA	REU	RWA
..	..	..	..	..	..	..	0.09	0.01	..	..	0.03	0.04	0.00	..	..	0.03	..	..	..
..	..	..	..	..	..	..	..	..	..	..	..	..	..	..	..	..	..	..	..
..	..	..	..	..	..	..	..	..	..	..	..	..	..	..	..	..	..	..	..
..	..	..	..	..	..	..	..	..	..	..	..	..	..	..	..	..	..	..	..
0.00	4.42	..	0.20	0.45	..	0.00	0.00	0.00	0.00	0.00	0.01	0.00	0.00	0.01	..	..	0.85	0.00	0.01
..	..	..	..	..	..	..	..	..	..	..	..	..	..	..	..	..	..	..	..
..	..	..	..	..	..	..	..	..	..	..	..	..	..	..	..	..	..	..	..
..	..	..	..	..	..	..	..	..	..	..	..	..	..	..	..	..	..	..	..
..	..	..	..	..	..	..	..	..	..	..	..	..	..	..	..	..	..	..	..
..	..	..	..	..	..	..	..	..	..	..	..	..	..	..	..	..	..	..	..
..	0.01	..	..	0.03	..	..	..	..	..	..	0.00	0.00	0.01	0.33	..	..	0.00	0.25	..
0.06	0.00	..	..	..	..	0.00	0.00	0.00	0.02	..	0.00	..	0.00	0.00	0.00	..	0.00	0.05	..
0.25	..	..	..	..	..	0.00	..	0.00	..	0.00	0.00	0.00	..	0.11	0.05	0.00	0.00	..	..
**	..	..	..	..	..	0.04	..	..	..	0.00	0.00	..	..	..	0.00	..	0.00	..	..
..	**	..	..	..	..	..	..	..	..	..	..	..	..	..	..	..	..	..	..
..	..	**	..	..	..	..	..	..	..	..	..	..	..	..	..	..	..	..	..
..	..	..	**	..	..	..	..	..	..	..	..	..	..	..	..	..	..	..	..
..	..	..	..	**	..	..	..	..	..	..	..	..	..	..	..	..	..	..	..
..	..	..	..	..	**	..	..	..	..	..	..	..	..	..	..	..	..	..	..
0.87	0.00	..	0.01	0.00	..	**	0.00	0.01	0.07	0.39	0.00	0.01	0.68	0.02	0.63	0.00	0.01	0.44	17.27
..	..	..	..	..	..	..	**	..	..	..	..	..	..	..	..	..	..	..	..
..	..	..	..	..	..	..	..	**	..	..	..	..	..	1.68	..	..	..	..	..
0.00	0.00	..	..	..	..	0.02	0.00	..	**	0.03	0.00	..	0.37	..	0.02	..	..	0.99	0.00
0.00	0.05	0.24	0.01	..	..	0.00	0.01	0.02	..	**	..	..	0.05	..	2.50	..	0.00	..	0.03
..	..	..	..	..	..	..	..	..	..	..	**	..	..	..	..	..	..	..	..
..	..	..	..	..	..	..	..	..	..	..	..	**	..	..	..	..	..	..	..
..	0.00	..	..	0.01	..	0.01	..	..	0.14	0.01	0.03	..	**	0.10	0.00	..	..	1.55	..
..	0.74	0.04	..	0.76	0.03	..	0.19	1.01	..	..	0.60	0.26	0.19	**	..	0.15	0.01	0.30	0.03
..	..	..	..	..	..	..	..	..	..	..	..	..	..	..	**	..	..	..	..
..	..	..	..	..	..	..	..	..	..	..	..	..	..	..	..	**	..	..	..
..	0.00	0.01	11.88	0.01	0.00	..	0.05	..	..	..	..	..	..	0.12	0.00	1.95	**	..	..
..	..	..	..	..	..	..	..	..	1.49	..	..	..	0.24	..	..	..	..	**	..
..	..	..	..	..	..	..	..	..	..	..	..	..	..	..	..	..	..	..	**
..	..	..	..	..	..	..	..	..	..	..	..	..	..	..	..	..	..	..	..
0.00	0.15	2.22	0.02	1.96	3.71	0.02	0.01	..	0.00	..	6.01	6.13	..	0.02	0.01	0.88	0.05	0.00	0.00
..	..	..	..	..	0.00	..	..	..	..	..	..	..	0.00	..	..	..	..	0.06	..
..	..	..	..	..	..	..	..	..	..	..	..	..	..	..	..	..	..	..	..
..	..	..	..	..	..	..	..	..	..	..	..	..	..	..	..	..	..	..	..
..	0.01	..	0.41	0.08	0.00	..	0.00	0.00	..	..	0.17	0.00	..	0.07	..	0.34	0.05	..	..
0.00	0.21	0.00	0.00	0.30	..	0.11	0.00	0.12	0.01	..	0.04	0.06	..	0.22	0.38	0.19	0.00	..	..
..	..	..	..	..	..	..	..	..	..	..	..	..	..	..	..	..	..	..	..
0.56	0.01	..	0.07	..	..	0.56	0.00	0.06	..	9.90	..	0.00	0.06	0.15	8.59	0.01	0.01	0.59	1.07
1.49	4.65	2.47	12.58	2.54	3.72	0.65	0.07	0.09	0.23	10.33	6.22	6.14	1.17	0.82	11.75	3.17	0.97	3.92	18.38
60.95	79.11	62.92	54.49	74.72	45.54	61.69	23.22	64.95	64.98	71.25	79.17	80.77	50.38	70.99	49.90	84.81	65.15	90.06	59.77
13.81	4.33	10.49	14.22	8.25	35.27	7.79	3.29	2.36	9.10	2.67	6.13	4.45	2.31	15.46	7.40	1.05	9.23	0.10	2.46
23.75	11.90	24.12	18.70	14.49	15.47	29.86	73.42	32.60	25.70	15.75	8.47	8.64	46.13	12.74	30.95	10.96	24.66	5.93	19.39
100.00	100.00	100.00	100.00	100.00	100.00	100.00	100.00	100.00	100.00	100.00	100.00	100.00	100.00	100.00	100.00	100.00	100.00	100.00	100.00

Note: ** means "not applicable."

(Table continues on the following page)

5-47. (continued)

Percentage of total imports

ZAF	STP	SEN	SYC	SLE	SOM	SDN	TZA	TGO	TUN	UGA	ZMB	ZWE	SSA	EEC	NNA	ROW	WLD
..	..	0.01	..	1.06	..	..	..	..	1.58	..	..	..	0.04	0.77	0.34	0.10	0.43
..	..	..	..	..	..	..	..	..	..	..	..	..	..	..	..	..	..
..	..	..	..	..	..	..	..	..	..	..	..	..	..	..	..	..	..
..	..	..	..	..	..	..	..	..	..	..	..	..	..	..	..	..	..
..	..	..	..	..	..	..	..	..	..	..	..	..	..	..	..	..	..
..	..	0.15	..	0.05	..	0.01	..	0.39	0.04	..	0.01	0.00	0.56	0.07	0.01	0.01	0.04
..	..	..	..	..	..	..	..	..	..	..	..	..	..	..	..	..	..
..	..	..	..	..	..	..	..	..	..	..	..	..	..	..	..	..	..
..	..	..	..	..	..	..	..	..	..	..	..	..	..	..	..	..	..
..	..	..	..	..	..	..	..	..	..	..	..	..	..	..	..	..	..
0.00	0.12	0.00	..	..	..	..	..	0.00	0.11	..	..	0.03	0.02	0.04	0.11	0.00	0.04
..	..	0.00	..	..	0.42	0.00	0.00	0.00	0.00	..	0.01	..	0.01	0.00	0.00	0.00	0.00
0.02	..	0.00	..	..	0.01	4.17	0.04	0.00	0.19	0.07	..	..	0.17	0.11	0.02	0.20	0.12
..	..	0.00	..	..	..	0.01	0.00	..	..	0.00	0.00	..	0.08	0.03	0.02	0.02	0.03
..	..	..	..	..	..	..	..	..	..	..	..	..	..	..	..	..	..
..	..	..	..	..	..	..	..	..	..	..	..	..	..	..	..	..	..
..	..	..	..	..	..	..	..	..	..	..	..	..	..	..	..	..	..
0.02	0.46	0.03	3.66	0.04	2.60	2.51	4.06	0.00	0.03	29.26	0.34	0.63	0.92	0.07	0.03	0.04	0.06
..	..	..	..	..	..	2.93	..	..	0.05	..	..	..	0.11	0.79	..	0.27	0.42
0.00	..	0.00	0.09	..	0.00	0.00	0.05	0.00	..	0.00	0.02	..	0.01	0.02	0.01	0.01	0.02
0.23	..	0.03	0.09	0.04	0.24	..	0.16	..	..	..	1.33	1.01	0.12	0.02	0.01	0.01	0.01
..	..	..	..	..	..	..	..	..	..	..	..	..	..	..	..	..	..
0.01	..	0.00	0.81	..	0.00	..	0.02	..	0.00	0.00	0.00	0.01	0.01	0.07	0.03	0.01	0.04
0.00	..	1.22	..	0.01	..	0.00	0.07	0.26	0.54	0.00	..	0.01	0.23	0.19	0.01	0.14	0.13
..	..	..	..	..	..	..	..	..	..	..	..	..	..	..	..	..	..
0.06	..	2.96	..	7.61	..	..	..	0.03	..	..	0.01	..	0.95	0.41	0.55	0.05	0.32
0.00	..	..	0.06	..	..	..	..	..	..	..	0.00	0.00	0.04	0.02	0.00	0.00	0.01
..	..	..	..	..	..	..	..	..	..	..	..	..	..	..	..	..	..
**	..	..	..	..	..	..	..	..	..	..	..	..	..	..	..	..	..
..	**	..	..	..	..	..	..	..	..	..	..	..	..	..	..	..	..
0.00	..	**	..	0.26	..	..	0.00	0.88	0.00	0.01	0.01	0.00	0.45	0.04	0.00	0.04	0.03
0.00	..	..	**	..	..	..	..	..	..	..	..	..	0.00	0.00	0.00	0.00	0.00
..	..	..	..	**	..	..	..	..	..	..	..	..	..	..	..	..	..
..	..	..	..	..	**	..	..	..	..	..	..	..	..	..	..	..	..
..	..	..	..	..	..	**	..	..	..	..	..	..	..	..	..	..	..
..	..	..	..	..	..	..	**	..	..	..	..	..	..	..	..	..	..
..	..	0.00	..	0.01	..	..	..	**	0.04	..	..	..	0.06	0.02	0.01	0.01	0.01
..	..	0.17	..	0.00	..	0.00	0.01	0.06	**	0.01	..	..	0.07	0.17	0.00	0.06	0.10
..	..	..	..	..	..	..	..	..	..	**	..	..	..	..	..	..	..
..	..	..	..	..	..	..	..	..	..	..	**	..	..	..	..	..	..
1.96	..	0.01	0.11	0.01	0.11	0.15	0.35	0.01	0.04	0.37	6.70	**	0.47	0.06	0.02	0.06	0.06
2.28	0.58	3.18	4.76	8.01	3.38	2.69	4.64	1.32	0.27	29.63	8.40	1.69	3.65	0.85	0.78	0.26	0.66
55.56	69.01	75.07	67.23	55.49	58.15	53.42	50.15	65.79	80.28	42.10	59.95	67.20	61.33	70.75	22.46	34.08	47.15
14.93	..	7.98	1.33	15.33	18.41	11.36	7.02	4.47	8.00	1.79	10.08	12.68	7.32	7.67	26.85	18.79	15.77
27.23	30.40	13.77	26.68	21.17	20.06	32.54	38.18	28.42	11.45	26.48	21.57	18.43	27.69	20.73	49.90	46.87	36.42
100.00	100.00	100.00	100.00	100.00	100.00	100.00	100.00	100.00	100.00	100.00	100.00	100.00	100.00	100.00	100.00	100.00	100.00

Note: ** means "not applicable."

5-48. Direction of trade matrix, imports, 1990

Exporters		DZA	AGO	BEN	BFA	BDI	CMR	CPV	CAF	TCD	COM	ZAR	COG	CIV	DJI	EGY	GNQ
Algeria	DZA	**	..	..	0.01	..	..	..	..	..	..	..	0.01	0.00	1.09	0.18	..
Angola	AGO	..	**	..	..	..	..	..	..	..	..	..	0.00	0.04	..	..	..
Benin	BEN	..	..	**	..	..	..	..	..	..	..	..	..	..	..	..	..
Burkina Faso	BFA	..	..	..	**	..	..	..	..	..	..	..	..	..	..	..	..
Burundi	BDI	..	..	..	..	**	..	..	..	..	..	..	..	..	..	..	..
Cameroon	CMR	0.06	0.00	0.03	0.20	0.00	**	..	18.88	8.66	..	..	0.22	2.51	0.24	..	0.01	34.47
Cape Verde	CPV	..	..	..	..	..	..	**	..	..	..	..	..	..	..	..	..
Central African Republic	CAF	..	..	..	..	..	..	..	**	..	..	..	..	..	..	..	..
Chad	TCD	..	..	..	..	..	..	..	..	**	..	..	..	..	..	..	..
Comoros	COM	..	..	..	..	..	..	..	..	..	**	..	..	..	..	..	..
Congo, Democratic Rep. of	ZAR	..	..	..	..	..	..	..	..	..	..	**	..	..	..	..	..
Congo, Republic of	COG	..	..	..	..	..	..	..	..	..	..	..	**	..	..	..	..
Côte d'Ivoire	CIV	..	..	..	..	..	..	..	..	..	..	..	..	**	..	..	..
Djibouti	DJI	..	0.00	..	0.00	..	0.00	..	0.01	..	0.10	..	..	0.00	**	0.00	..
Egypt, Arab Rep.	EGY	0.05	0.00	0.04	..	0.03	0.00	..	..	0.02	..	0.00	0.00	0.04	0.17	**	0.00
Equatorial Guinea	GNQ	..	..	..	..	..	..	..	..	..	..	..	..	..	..	..	**
Ethiopia	ETH	..	0.00	..	..	0.00	..	..	0.55	0.00	..	..	0.00	0.00	12.52	0.00	..
Gabon	GAB	..	..	..	..	..	..	..	..	..	..	..	..	..	..	..	..
Gambia, The	GMB	..	..	..	..	..	..	..	..	..	..	..	..	..	..	..	..
Ghana	GHA	..	..	..	..	..	..	..	..	..	..	..	..	..	..	..	..
Guinea	GIN	..	..	..	..	..	..	..	..	..	..	..	..	..	..	..	..
Guinea-Bissau	GNB	..	..	..	..	..	..	..	..	..	..	..	..	..	..	..	..
Kenya	KEN	0.00	0.36	0.00	0.00	12.37	0.01	0.01	0.00	0.00	0.71	1.97	0.00	0.03	8.09	0.14	0.00
Liberia	LBR	..	..	..	..	..	..	..	..	..	..	..	..	..	..	..	..
Libya	LBY	0.06	..	..	0.18	..	..	..	..	..	..	..	..	0.00	..	0.71	..
Madagascar	MDG	0.00	..	0.00	..	0.02	0.00	..	..	..	2.54	..	0.01	0.00	0.01	0.00	0.00
Malawi	MWI	..	0.00	..	..	0.34	0.00	..	..	..	..	0.16	..	0.00	..	0.05	..
Mali	MLI	0.01	..	..	0.44	..	..	..	..	..	..	..	..	11.31	..	..	..
Mauritania	MRT	..	..	..	..	..	..	..	..	..	..	..	..	..	..	..	..
Mauritius	MUS	0.00	..	0.00	0.00	0.01	0.00	..	..	..	1.75	0.01	0.00	0.00	0.01	0.00	..
Morocco	MAR	0.62	0.34	0.41	0.19	..	0.50	..	0.58	..	0.28	0.53	0.86	0.46	0.01	0.03	0.60
Mozambique	MOZ	..	..	..	..	..	..	..	..	..	..	..	..	..	..	..	..
Niger	NER	..	..	..	..	..	..	..	..	..	..	..	..	..	..	..	..
Nigeria	NGA	..	..	..	..	..	..	..	..	..	..	..	..	..	..	..	..
Reunion	REU	..	..	..	..	..	..	..	..	..	..	8.60	0.01	..	0.00	0.10	..
Rwanda	RWA	..	..	..	..	..	..	..	..	..	..	..	..	..	..	..	..
South Africa	ZAF	..	..	..	..	..	..	..	..	..	..	..	..	..	..	..	..
São Tomé and Principe	STP	..	..	..	..	..	..	..	..	..	..	..	..	..	..	..	..
Senegal	SEN	..	..	1.14	1.05	0.05	1.64	0.12	0.19	0.12	..	..	0.04	0.95	1.41	..	0.00
Seychelles	SYC	..	..	..	..	..	..	..	..	..	..	..	..	..	..	..	..
Sierra Leone	SLE	..	..	..	..	..	..	..	..	..	..	..	..	..	..	..	..
Somalia	SOM	..	..	..	..	..	..	..	..	..	..	..	..	..	..	..	..
Sudan	SDN	..	..	..	..	..	..	..	..	..	..	..	..	..	..	..	..
Tanzania	TZA	..	..	..	..	..	..	..	..	..	..	..	..	..	..	..	..
Togo	TGO	0.00	..	1.55	2.95	..	0.01	0.61	0.03	0.01	..	0.00	0.04	0.06	0.01	..	0.17
Tunisia	TUN	0.88	..	0.17	0.16	0.00	0.81	..	..	0.00	..	..	0.10	0.49	0.19	0.03	..
Uganda	UGA	..	..	..	..	..	..	..	..	..	..	..	..	..	..	..	..
Zambia	ZMB	..	..	..	..	..	..	..	..	..	..	..	..	..	..	..	..
Zimbabwe	ZWE	0.00	0.74	0.00	..	1.81	0.00	0.02	..	..	..	..	1.14	0.04	0.01	0.00	0.04
Sub-Saharan Africa	SSA	0.08	1.11	2.72	4.64	14.61	1.68	0.75	19.66	8.79	5.10	3.54	3.55	13.10	20.64	0.23	34.64
European Community	EEC	70.76	70.45	60.03	79.35	70.28	78.51	88.65	69.00	76.59	76.73	70.93	70.82	68.45	45.89	49.88	59.90
North America	NNA	13.00	10.70	6.92	5.38	0.70	5.99	4.35	0.70	6.05	0.13	11.62	14.55	5.47	2.72	20.67	0.33
Rest Of World	ROW	16.17	17.74	30.33	10.63	14.41	13.83	6.24	10.64	8.56	18.04	13.90	11.09	12.98	30.75	29.22	5.13
World	WLD	100.00	100.00	100.00	100.00	100.00	100.00	100.00	100.00	100.00	100.00	100.00	100.00	100.00	100.00	100.00	100.00

Note: ** means "not applicable."

(Table continues on the following page.)

5-48. (continued)

Percentage of total imports

ETH	GAB	GMB	GHA	GIN	GNB	KEN	LBR	LBY	MDG	MWI	MLI	MRT	MUS	MAR	MOZ	NER	NGA	REU	RWA
..	0.01	..	..	..	..	..	..	0.07	..	..	0.05	7.79	..	0.67	..	0.09	..	..	..
..	..	..	..	..	..	..	0.87	..	..	..	..	..	..	..	..	..	..	..	..
..	..	..	..	..	..	..	..	..	..	..	..	..	..	..	..	..	..	..	..
..	..	..	..	..	..	..	..	..	..	..	..	..	..	..	..	..	..	..	..
..	..	..	..	..	..	..	..	..	..	..	..	..	..	..	..	..	..	..	..
..	4.28	0.01	0.05	0.44	..	0.00	0.00	..	0.00	..	0.01	0.05	0.00	0.03	..	0.06	0.67	0.05	0.00
..	..	..	..	..	..	..	..	..	..	..	..	..	..	..	..	..	..	..	..
..	..	..	..	..	..	..	..	..	..	..	..	..	..	..	..	..	..	..	..
..	..	..	..	..	..	..	..	..	..	..	..	..	..	..	..	..	..	..	..
..	..	..	..	..	..	..	..	..	..	..	..	..	..	..	..	..	..	..	..
..	..	..	..	..	..	..	..	..	..	..	..	..	..	..	..	..	..	..	..
..	..	..	..	..	..	..	..	..	..	..	..	..	..	..	..	..	..	..	..
0.04	0.00	0.00	..	0.00	..	0.00	..	0.00	0.04	..	0.00	..	..	0.00	..	0.00	..	0.02	..
0.01	..	..	0.00	0.00	..	0.00	0.00	0.88	..	0.00	0.00	0.00	..	0.10	0.02	0.03	0.01	..	0.00
**	0.00	0.00	0.00	0.00	..	0.05	..	..	0.00	0.00	..	..	0.00	0.00	0.00	0.00	0.00	..	..
..	**	..	..	..	..	..	..	..	..	..	..	..	..	..	..	..	..	..	..
..	..	**	..	..	..	..	..	..	..	..	..	..	..	..	..	..	..	..	..
..	..	..	**	..	..	..	..	..	..	..	..	..	..	..	..	..	..	..	..
..	..	..	..	**	..	..	..	..	..	..	..	..	..	..	..	..	..	..	..
..	..	..	..	..	**	..	..	..	..	..	..	..	..	..	..	..	..	..	..
0.91	0.00	..	0.01	0.01	..	**	0.00	0.00	0.05	0.42	..	0.00	0.29	0.01	0.14	..	0.03	0.23	33.62
..	..	..	..	..	..	..	**	..	..	..	..	..	..	..	..	..	..	..	..
..	..	..	0.00	0.08	..	..	..	**	..	..	0.00	0.08	..	1.85	..	0.05	0.00	..	..
0.00	0.00	..	..	0.01	..	0.04	..	..	**	0.00	0.02	0.11	0.69	0.01	0.81	0.00	0.00	0.92	0.00
0.00	0.05	1.68	0.00	0.15	..	0.01	..	..	..	**	..	..	0.01	..	0.12	..	0.00	..	0.34
..	0.00	..	0.01	0.25	..	..	..	..	..	..	**	0.00	..	..	..	0.08	0.00	..	..
..	..	..	..	..	..	..	..	..	..	..	..	**	..	..	..	..	..	..	..
0.00	0.01	..	0.00	0.00	..	0.06	0.00	..	2.08	0.05	0.00	0.00	**	0.05	0.00	..	0.00	1.35	0.01
..	1.12	0.10	0.32	1.19	0.00	..	0.01	2.41	0.11	0.03	1.53	0.93	0.16	**	..	0.27	0.23	0.13	..
..	..	..	..	..	..	..	..	..	..	..	..	..	..	..	**	..	..	..	..
..	..	..	..	..	..	..	..	..	..	..	..	..	..	..	..	..	..	..	..
..	..	..	..	..	..	..	..	..	..	..	..	..	..	..	..	**	..	..	..
..	..	..	..	..	..	..	..	..	..	..	..	..	..	..	..	..	**	..	..
..	..	..	..	..	0.00	..	..	..	1.27	..	..	..	0.29	..	..	..	..	**	..
..	..	..	..	..	..	..	..	..	..	..	..	..	..	..	..	..	..	..	**
..	..	..	..	..	..	..	..	..	..	..	..	..	..	..	..	..	..	..	..
0.00	0.37	3.91	0.09	3.28	4.52	0.00	0.02	..	0.04	0.00	14.75	0.05	..	0.02	..	0.12	0.07	..	..
..	..	..	..	..	0.00	..	..	..	..	..	..	..	0.01	..	..	..	..	0.20	..
..	..	..	..	..	..	..	..	..	..	..	..	..	..	..	..	..	..	..	..
..	..	..	..	..	..	..	..	..	..	..	..	..	..	..	..	..	..	..	..
..	..	..	..	..	..	..	..	..	..	..	..	..	..	..	..	..	..	..	..
..	0.09	0.01	0.37	0.80	0.01	0.01	0.00	0.00	..	..	0.19	..	..	0.04	0.00	1.56	0.17	0.00	..
..	0.02	..	0.76	0.09	0.84	..	0.00	3.27	..	..	0.00	0.44	..	0.38	..	0.04	0.01	..	0.00
..	..	..	..	..	..	..	..	..	..	..	..	..	..	..	..	..	..	..	..
0.14	0.01	..	0.09	0.01	..	1.00	0.00	0.01	0.03	25.06	0.01	..	0.10	0.00	7.57	0.15	0.01	0.00	0.52
1.09	4.81	5.62	0.62	4.95	4.53	1.16	0.89	0.01	2.24	25.53	14.98	0.21	1.11	0.14	8.65	1.98	0.96	2.77	34.50
61.13	75.63	58.31	58.10	69.75	70.96	61.61	32.93	69.13	70.68	53.97	72.41	73.38	49.68	73.52	50.59	79.68	61.21	91.44	49.28
18.73	7.45	5.03	13.22	10.28	1.19	9.00	1.16	0.92	2.74	5.61	3.45	3.45	1.22	11.01	10.26	5.89	10.92	0.32	0.75
19.05	12.11	31.04	28.06	15.01	23.33	28.22	65.02	29.94	24.33	14.89	9.16	22.96	47.99	15.33	30.49	12.45	26.91	5.47	15.47
100.00	100.00	100.00	100.00	100.00	100.00	100.00	100.00	100.00	100.00	100.00	100.00	100.00	100.00	100.00	100.00	100.00	100.00	100.00	100.00

Note: ** means "not applicable."

(Table continues on the following page.)

5-48. (continued)

Percentage of total imports

ZAF	STP	SEN	SYC	SLE	SOM	SDN	TZA	TGO	TUN	UGA	ZMB	ZWE	SSA	EEC	NNA	ROW	WLD
..	..	0.00	..	..	..	..	..	0.00	3.64	0.22	..	..	0.12	0.55	0.38	0.10	0.35
0.00	4.19	..	..	..	..	..	..	0.34	..	..	..	..	0.12	0.11	0.37	0.03	0.12
..	..	..	..	..	..	..	..	..	..	..	..	..	..	..	..	..	..
..	..	..	..	..	..	..	..	..	..	..	..	..	..	..	..	..	..
0.00	0.40	0.38	..	0.03	..	..	0.05	0.16	0.07	..	..	..	0.52	0.12	0.03	0.01	0.07
..	..	..	..	..	..	..	..	..	..	..	..	..	..	..	..	..	..
..	..	..	..	..	..	..	..	..	..	..	..	..	..	..	..	..	..
..	..	..	..	..	..	..	..	..	..	..	..	..	..	..	..	..	..
..	..	0.00	..	..	0.17	0.00	0.00	..	0.00	0.00	..	..	0.00	0.00	0.00	0.00	0.00
0.00	..	0.00	..	0.04	0.04	2.29	0.00	..	0.38	0.03	0.05	0.01	0.07	0.07	0.04	0.11	0.08
..	..	..	..	..	..	..	..	..	..	..	..	..	..	..	..	..	..
0.00	..	0.00	..	..	..	0.03	0.00	..	..	0.00	0.00	0.00	0.12	0.01	0.01	0.01	0.01
..	..	..	..	..	..	..	..	..	..	..	..	..	..	..	..	..	..
..	..	..	..	..	..	..	..	..	..	..	..	..	..	..	..	..	..
..	..	..	..	..	..	..	..	..	..	..	..	..	..	..	..	..	..
..	..	..	..	..	..	..	..	..	..	..	..	..	..	..	..	..	..
0.01	0.03	..	0.69	0.00	6.16	1.61	2.18	0.04	0.01	37.60	0.27	0.94	1.29	0.02	0.01	0.02	0.03
..	..	0.22	..	..	..	16.65	3.29	..	1.48	..	..	..	0.58	0.85	0.00	0.17	0.44
0.00	..	0.00	0.13	..	0.38	0.00	0.17	0.00	0.00	..	..	..	0.06	0.01	0.01	0.01	0.01
0.25	..	0.01	..	0.20	0.01	0.00	0.09	0.01	..	0.00	0.83	0.80	0.07	0.01	0.01	0.01	0.01
..	..	5.65	..	..	..	..	..	0.00	..	..	..	..	0.75	0.01	0.00	0.00	0.01
..	..	..	..	..	..	..	..	..	..	..	..	..	..	..	..	..	..
0.05	..	0.00	2.64	..	0.00	0.00	0.01	0.01	0.00	0.01	0.04	0.39	0.06	0.07	0.03	0.01	0.04
0.00	..	0.46	..	0.20	..	0.01	0.00	0.66	1.27	..	..	..	0.27	0.20	0.02	0.11	0.13
..	..	..	..	..	..	..	..	..	..	..	..	..	..	..	..	..	..
..	..	..	..	..	..	..	..	..	..	..	..	..	..	..	..	..	..
0.00	..	..	0.51	..	..	..	..	..	..	..	0.00	..	0.05	0.01	0.00	0.00	0.01
**	..	..	..	..	..	..	..	..	..	..	..	..	..	..	..	1.73	0.64
..	**	..	..	..	..	..	..	..	..	..	..	..	..	..	..	..	..
..	..	**	..	0.10	..	..	..	0.88	0.06	..	0.01	0.00	0.47	0.03	0.00	0.02	0.02
0.00	..	..	**	..	..	..	..	..	..	..	..	..	0.00	0.00	0.00	0.00	0.00
..	..	..	..	**	..	..	..	..	..	..	..	..	..	..	..	..	..
..	..	..	..	..	**	..	..	..	..	..	..	..	..	..	..	..	..
..	..	..	..	..	..	**	..	..	..	..	..	..	..	..	..	..	..
..	..	..	..	..	..	..	**	..	..	..	..	..	..	..	..	..	..
0.00	..	0.02	..	..	..	..	..	**	0.03	..	..	..	0.12	0.01	0.01	0.01	0.01
..	..	0.12	..	0.03	..	0.11	0.01	0.31	**	..	0.22	0.00	0.12	0.20	0.01	0.06	0.11
..	..	..	..	..	..	..	..	..	..	**	..	..	..	..	..	..	..
..	..	..	..	..	..	..	..	..	..	..	**	..	..	..	..	..	..
1.80	0.02	0.01	0.16	0.02	0.02	0.06	1.26	0.00	0.00	1.13	7.70	**	0.77	0.04	0.02	0.04	0.05
2.12	4.64	6.08	3.62	0.35	6.73	1.70	3.75	1.44	0.18	38.75	8.86	2.13	4.35	0.44	0.48	0.16	0.38
60.86	56.09	73.16	59.32	65.25	72.62	46.98	59.56	61.22	79.11	40.29	55.45	56.64	59.81	70.42	20.54	30.94	46.63
15.37	27.80	5.67	2.11	15.62	5.41	5.30	6.91	5.62	4.59	5.68	13.34	18.50	7.85	7.77	30.28	18.14	15.69
21.65	11.47	15.10	34.95	18.78	15.24	46.01	29.78	31.72	16.13	15.28	22.36	22.73	27.99	21.37	48.70	50.76	37.30
100.00	100.00	100.00	100.00	100.00	100.00	100.00	100.00	100.00	100.00	100.00	100.00	100.00	100.00	100.00	100.00	100.00	100.00

Note: ** means "not applicable."

5-49. Direction of trade matrix, imports, 1995

Exporters		DZA	AGO	BEN	BFA	BDI	CMR	CPV	CAF	TCD	COM	ZAR	COG	CIV	DJI	EGY	GNQ
		Importers								*Percentage of total imports*							
Algeria	DZA	**	..	..	0.00	..	..	0.00	..	2.15	..	..	0.00	..	..	0.04	..
Angola	AGO	..	**	..	..	..	..	..	..	..	..	..	..	..	..	..	..
Benin	BEN	..	..	**	..	..	..	..	..	..	..	..	..	..	..	..	..
Burkina Faso	BFA	..	..	..	**	..	..	..	..	..	..	..	..	..	..	..	..
Burundi	BDI	..	..	..	..	**	..	..	..	..	..	..	..	..	..	..	..
Cameroon	CMR	0.00	0.11	0.30	0.19	0.00	**	..	8.93	4.59	..	0.30	2.31	0.41	..	0.00	30.06
Cape Verde	CPV	..	..	..	..	..	..	**	..	..	..	..	..	..	..	..	..
Central African Republic	CAF	0.00	0.00	0.00	0.00	..	0.19	..	**	0.40	..	0.18	0.18	0.00	..	..	0.03
Chad	TCD	..	..	.	..	..	..	..	..	**	..	..	..	..	..	..	..
Comoros	COM	..	..	..	..	..	..	..	..	..	**	..	..	..	..	..	..
Congo, Democratic Rep. of	ZAR	..	..	..	..	..	..	..	..	..	..	**	..	..	..	..	..
Congo, Republic of	COG	0.01	0.39	0.00	..	..	0.01	..	0.01	..	..	0.65	**	0.00	..	0.01	0.00
Côte d'Ivoire	CIV	..	..	..	..	..	..	..	..	..	..	..	..	**	..	..	..
Djibouti	DJI	..	..	..	..	..	..	..	..	..	..	..	..	..	**	..	..
Egypt, Arab Rep.	EGY	0.35	0.03	0.01	0.05	0.10	0.04	..	..	0.03	..	0.03	0.47	0.33	0.17	**	0.00
Equatorial Guinea	GNQ	..	..	..	..	..	..	..	..	..	..	..	..	..	..	..	**
Ethiopia	ETH	0.00	..	..	..	..	..	..	..	..	..	0.00	..	0.00	10.61	0.02	..
Gabon	GAB	..	..	..	..	..	..	..	..	..	..	..	..	..	..	..	..
Gambia, The	GMB	..	..	..	..	..	..	..	..	..	..	..	..	..	..	..	..
Ghana	GHA	..	..	..	..	..	..	..	..	..	..	..	..	..	..	..	..
Guinea	GIN	..	..	..	..	..	..	..	..	..	..	..	..	..	..	..	..
Guinea-Bissau	GNB	..	..	..	..	..	..	..	..	..	..	..	..	..	..	..	..
Kenya	KEN	0.00	0.02	0.00	0.01	4.77	0.04	0.01	0.00	0.00	1.35	3.89	0.03	0.02	0.39	0.40	0.22
Liberia	LBR	..	..	..	..	..	..	..	..	..	..	..	..	..	..	..	..
Libya	LBY	..	..	..	..	..	..	..	..	..	..	..	..	..	..	..	..
Madagascar	MDG	0.06	..	0.00	0.01	0.00	0.00	0.09	0.01	0.01	2.81	0.00	0.00	0.01	0.02	0.00	..
Malawi	MWI	..	..	0.01	..	0.31	..	..	..	..	..	0.05	..	..	..	0.02	..
Mali	MLI	..	..	..	..	..	..	..	..	..	..	..	..	..	..	..	..
Mauritania	MRT	..	..	..	..	..	..	..	..	..	..	..	..	..	..	..	..
Mauritius	MUS	..	..	..	..	0.24	0.00	..	0.02	..	1.47	0.00	0.00	0.00	0.00	0.00	..
Morocco	MAR	0.63	0.15	0.35	0.38	..	0.44	0.15	0.23	0.03	0.14	0.83	0.40	0.87	0.01	0.03	1.15
Mozambique	MOZ	..	0.01	..	..	..	..	..	..	..	..	0.00	..	..	..	..	..
Niger	NER	..	..	..	..	..	..	..	..	..	..	..	..	..	..	..	..
Nigeria	NGA	..	..	..	..	..	..	..	..	..	..	..	..	..	..	..	..
Reunion	REU	..	..	..	..	..	..	..	..	..	6.15	..	..	0.00	0.00	..	..
Rwanda	RWA	..	..	..	..	..	..	..	..	..	..	..	..	..	..	..	..
South Africa	ZAF	0.01	7.42	0.13	0.36	2.40	1.04	0.16	1.03	0.12	12.25	18.45	1.52	1.36	0.25	0.17	1.78
São Tomé and Principe	STP	.	..	..	..	..	..	..	..	..	..	..	..	..	..	..	..
Senegal	SEN	0.01	0.01	1.95	1.78	..	0.89	1.18	0.67	1.05	..	0.00	0.25	0.37	..	0.00	0.01
Seychelles	SYC	..	..	..	..	..	..	..	..	..	..	..	..	..	..	..	..
Sierra Leone	SLE	..	..	..	..	..	..	..	..	..	..	..	..	..	..	..	..
Somalia	SOM	..	..	..	..	..	..	..	..	..	..	..	..	..	..	..	..
Sudan	SDN	..	..	..	..	..	..	..	..	..	..	0.00	..	..	0.42	0.14	..
Tanzania	TZA	..	..	..	..	..	..	..	..	..	..	..	..	..	..	..	..
Togo	TGO	..	..	..	..	..	..	..	..	..	..	..	..	..	..	..	..
Tunisia	TUN	2.09	0.02	0.07	0.37	..	0.82	..	0.05	0.02	..	0.02	0.01	0.26	0.00	0.17	0.09
Uganda	UGA	..	..	..	..	..	..	..	..	..	..	..	..	..	..	..	..
Zambia	ZMB	..	0.02	0.00	..	2.26	..	..	0.01	..	..	2.53	..	..	..	0.00	..
Zimbabwe	ZWE	0.01	0.70	0.00	0.00	0.93	0.05	..	0.01	..	0.01	0.80	0.00	0.03	..	0.06	..
Sub-Saharan Africa	SSA	0.08	1.27	2.26	2.00	8.53	1.18	1.28	9.67	6.05	5.65	8.41	2.78	0.84	11.44	0.64	30.33
European Community	EEC	68.10	62.69	58.22	79.09	62.94	75.79	86.24	57.39	73.41	67.13	43.24	81.63	69.83	35.89	43.61	51.99
North America	NNA	12.78	15.78	5.63	6.32	2.57	5.99	3.07	4.39	9.18	0.43	9.88	7.24	8.28	2.72	21.07	6.68
Rest Of World	ROW	19.04	20.26	33.89	12.60	25.96	17.04	9.41	28.55	11.36	26.80	38.47	8.36	21.05	49.94	34.68	11.00
World	WLD	100.00	100.00	100.00	100.00	100.00	100.00	100.00	100.00	100.00	100.00	100.00	100.00	100.00	100.00	100.00	100.00

Note: ** means "not applicable."

(Table continues on the following page.)

5-49. (continued)

Percentage of total imports

ETH	GAB	GMB	GHA	GIN	GNB	KEN	LBR	LBY	MDG	MWI	MLI	MRT	MUS	MAR	MOZ	NER	NGA	REU	RWA
..	..	..	..	0.04	..	..	0.27	0.05	0.00	..	0.00	3.76	..	1.00	..	0.01	0.00	..	..
..	..	..	..	..	..	..	..	..	..	..	..	..	..	..	..	..	..	..	..
..	..	..	..	..	..	..	..	..	..	..	..	..	..	..	..	..	..	..	..
..	..	..	..	..	..	..	..	..	..	..	..	..	..	..	..	..	..	..	..
..	3.25	..	0.03	0.20	0.00	0.02	..	0.03	0.05	..	0.11	0.00	0.30	0.06	0.05	0.05	0.17	0.09	..
..	0.00	..	..	..	..	..	..	..	0.00	..	..	0.00	..	0.00	..	0.00	0.00	..	..
..	..	..	..	..	..	..	..	..	..	..	..	..	..	..	..	..	..	..	..
..	..	..	..	..	..	..	..	..	..	..	..	..	..	..	..	..	..	..	..
..	0.02	..	0.00	0.00	..	..	..	..	..	..	0.01	0.01	0.01	0.11	..	0.00	0.00	0.16	..
..	..	..	..	..	..	..	..	..	..	..	..	..	..	..	..	..	..	..	..
0.11	0.02	0.00	0.05	0.02	0.02	0.13	0.00	1.17	0.01	0.01	0.04	0.00	0.01	0.19	0.01	0.01	0.03	..	0.01
**	..	0.00	0.00	..	..	0.00	0.00	..	..	..	..	..	..	..	0.00	..	..	..	0.00
..	**	..	..	..	..	..	..	..	..	..	..	..	..	..	..	..	..	..	..
..	..	**	..	..	..	..	..	..	..	..	..	..	..	..	..	..	..	..	..
..	..	..	**	..	..	..	..	..	..	..	..	..	..	..	..	..	..	..	..
..	..	..	..	**	..	..	..	..	..	..	..	..	..	..	..	..	..	..	..
..	..	..	..	..	**	..	..	..	..	..	..	..	..	..	..	..	..	..	..
4.56	0.01	0.00	0.02	0.00	..	**	..	0.00	0.08	0.69	..	0.02	0.54	0.00	0.13	..	0.06	..	19.87
..	..	..	..	..	..	..	**	..	..	..	..	..	..	..	..	..	..	..	..
..	0.00	..	..	0.00	..	0.00	0.00	0.00	**	0.02	0.01	..	0.58	0.00	0.07	0.01	0.00	0.92	0.01
0.00	0.00	0.47	..	0.05	0.04	0.02	..	..	0.00	**	..	..	0.04	0.00	0.51	..	0.00	0.00	0.01
..	..	..	..	..	..	..	..	..	..	..	**	..	..	..	..	..	..	..	..
..	..	..	..	..	..	..	..	..	..	..	..	**	..	..	..	..	..	..	..
..	0.01	..	..	..	..	0.07	..	0.00	7.10	0.13	..	0.00	**	0.00	0.02	0.00	0.00	1.29	0.53
..	0.93	0.32	0.28	1.95	0.04	0.03	0.00	3.57	0.09	..	1.35	1.47	0.12	**	0.01	0.27	0.16	0.04	0.00
0.01	..	..	..	..	..	0.00	..	..	0.01	0.62	..	..	0.01	..	**	..	..	..	0.08
..	..	..	..	..	..	..	..	..	..	..	..	..	..	..	..	**	..	..	..
..	..	..	..	..	..	..	..	..	..	..	..	..	..	..	..	..	**	..	..
0.03	0.02	..	..	..	..	0.00	..	..	1.18	0.00	..	0.00	0.25	0.00	0.00	..	..	**	..
..	..	..	..	..	..	..	..	..	..	..	..	..	..	..	..	..	..	..	**
0.36	0.78	0.73	2.72	0.32	0.06	9.84	0.06	0.01	8.06	45.82	3.62	0.03	11.73	0.21	58.00	0.74	1.06	2.34	1.67
..	0.11	4.13	0.04	1.16	3.43	0.00	0.00	..	0.05	..	9.12	2.20	..	0.01	..	0.35	0.24	..	..
..	..	..	..	..	..	0.00	..	..	..	..	..	..	0.01	..	..	..	..	0.07	..
..	..	..	..	..	..	..	..	..	..	..	..	..	..	..	..	..	..	..	..
..	..	..	..	..	..	..	..	..	..	..	..	..	..	..	..	..	..	..	..
0.03	0.00	..	..	..	..	0.01	..	0.01	..	..	0.00	..	..	..	..	0.00	0.00	..	..
..	..	..	..	..	..	..	..	..	..	..	..	..	..	..	..	..	..	..	..
..	0.08	0.01	0.12	0.18	0.04	..	0.00	4.25	0.01	..	0.11	0.20	0.00	0.33	0.01	0.08	0.01	0.04	..
0.06	..	..	..	..	..	0.09	..	..	..	2.05	0.00	..	..	..	0.01	..	..	0.01	0.11
0.02	..	0.02	0.15	..	..	0.13	..	0.06	0.00	11.90	..	0.00	0.37	0.01	4.84	0.00	0.03	0.01	0.16
4.67	3.41	4.62	0.24	1.42	3.47	0.36	0.00	0.10	7.28	15.41	9.25	2.23	1.86	0.20	5.64	0.41	0.53	2.54	20.76
54.52	73.70	43.02	55.82	63.16	50.59	43.18	31.46	65.76	58.42	21.14	62.28	62.78	42.13	75.15	17.50	71.43	53.17	88.66	41.66
13.24	7.36	2.85	10.75	12.01	0.77	4.78	0.81	1.08	1.86	5.40	6.14	8.48	1.36	8.04	5.81	8.24	12.59	0.18	24.00
27.58	15.53	49.51	33.18	23.42	45.17	51.68	67.73	33.05	32.43	58.05	22.33	26.50	54.65	16.61	71.06	19.92	33.71	8.62	13.58
100.00	100.00	100.00	100.00	100.00	100.00	100.00	100.00	100.00	100.00	100.00	100.00	100.00	100.00	100.00	100.00	100.00	100.00	100.00	100.00

Note: ** means "not applicable."

(Table continues on the following page.)

5-49. (continued)

Percentage of total imports

ZAF	STP	SEN	SYC	SLE	SOM	SDN	TZA	TGO	TUN	UGA	ZMB	ZWE	SSA	EEC	NNA	ROW	WLD
0.00	..	0.01	..	..	..	..	..	..	1.64	..	..	..	0.09	0.34	0.21	0.08	0.20
..	..	..	..	..	..	..	..	..	..	..	..	..	..	..	..	..	..
..	..	..	..	..	..	..	..	..	..	..	..	..	..	..	..	..	..
..	..	..	..	..	..	..	..	..	..	..	..	..	..	..	..	..	..
0.02	4.80	0.62	..	..	..	..	0.01	0.23	0.02	..	0.04	0.00	0.33	0.07	0.00	0.01	0.03
0.00	..	0.00	..	..	..	0.06	..	0.00	..	..	..	..	0.02	0.01	0.00	0.00	0.00
..	..	..	..	..	..	..	..	..	..	..	..	..	..	..	..	..	..
..	..	..	..	..	..	..	..	..	..	..	..	..	..	..	..	..	..
..	..	0.00	..	..	..	..	..	0.00	0.00	..	..	0.01	0.04	0.03	0.04	0.02	0.02
..	..	..	..	..	..	..	..	..	..	..	..	..	..	..	..	..	..
0.02	..	0.04	..	0.09	0.20	3.03	0.03	0.01	0.42	0.07	0.02	0.01	0.12	0.09	0.06	0.07	0.07
0.00	..	0.00	..	..	..	0.14	0.01	..	0.06	0.00	0.00	0.00	0.10	0.01	0.00	0.01	0.01
..	..	..	..	..	..	..	..	..	..	..	..	..	..	..	..	..	..
..	..	..	..	..	..	..	..	..	..	..	..	..	..	..	..	..	..
..	..	..	..	..	..	..	..	..	..	..	..	..	..	..	..	..	..
..	..	..	..	..	..	..	..	..	..	..	..	..	..	..	..	..	..
0.21	..	0.04	1.35	0.11	22.37	2.66	14.90	0.02	0.04	37.48	0.36	0.12	1.80	0.04	0.01	0.02	0.04
..	..	..	..	..	..	..	..	..	..	..	..	..	..	..	..	..	..
0.01	..	0.00	0.22	..	..	0.00	0.00	0.00	0.02	0.01	0.00	0.06	0.04	0.01	0.00	0.00	0.01
0.18	..	0.00	0.03	0.10	..	0.00	0.34	0.01	0.00	0.13	0.47	0.27	0.06	0.01	0.01	0.01	0.01
..	..	..	..	..	..	..	..	..	..	..	..	..	..	..	..	..	..
0.03	..	0.01	1.34	..	..	..	0.06	..	0.00	0.21	0.03	0.30	0.15	0.06	0.03	0.01	0.03
0.01	..	0.44	0.02	0.47	..	0.01	0.02	0.39	0.80	0.00	..	..	0.26	0.16	0.02	0.08	0.10
0.17	..	..	..	..	0.00	..	0.01	..	..	..	0.01	0.27	0.02	0.00	0.00	0.00	0.00
..	..	..	..	..	..	..	..	..	..	..	..	..	..	..	..	..	..
0.00	..	0.00	0.60	..	..	..	..	0.00	..	..	..	..	0.06	0.01	0.00	0.00	0.00
..	..	..	..	..	..	..	..	..	..	..	..	..	..	..	..	..	..
**	4.21	0.65	17.37	1.73	1.85	0.65	11.92	0.93	0.01	3.48	40.86	57.07	9.41	0.42	0.27	0.74	0.61
..	**	..	..	..	..	..	..	..	..	..	..	..	..	..	..	..	..
0.01	..	**	..	0.76	..	..	..	0.90	0.00	..	..	..	0.35	0.01	0.00	0.01	0.01
0.00	..	..	**	..	..	..	..	..	..	..	..	..	0.00	0.00	0.00	0.00	0.00
..	..	..	..	**	..	..	..	..	..	..	..	..	..	..	..	..	..
..	..	..	..	..	**	..	..	..	..	..	..	..	..	..	..	..	..
0.00	..	..	..	..	..	**	..	..	0.04	0.24	..	0.00	0.01	0.01	0.01	0.02	0.01
..	..	..	..	..	..	..	**	..	..	..	..	..	..	..	..	..	..
..	..	..	..	..	..	..	..	**	..	..	..	..	..	..	..	..	..
0.02	..	0.19	..	..	..	..	0.00	0.48	**	0.04	0.02	..	0.07	0.24	0.01	0.05	0.12
..	..	..	..	..	..	..	..	..	..	**	..	..	..	..	..	..	..
0.10	..	..	..	..	..	..	1.52	..	..	0.12	**	1.45	0.25	0.01	0.01	0.04	0.02
1.45	0.06	..	0.48	0.00	..	0.05	0.67	..	0.01	0.51	10.05	**	0.62	0.04	0.01	0.04	0.04
2.19	4.86	0.68	3.41	0.97	22.37	2.91	17.52	1.17	0.20	38.71	10.96	2.47	3.79	0.30	0.12	0.19	0.25
49.22	75.89	67.76	34.46	57.85	18.06	44.93	28.56	47.28	81.99	32.47	21.02	22.13	47.81	69.26	17.40	30.37	43.20
12.78	4.38	6.14	3.55	9.81	6.49	5.52	5.22	3.30	4.39	4.08	6.12	6.06	6.90	7.07	31.20	17.33	15.81
35.81	14.88	25.42	58.57	31.37	53.07	46.64	48.70	48.26	13.42	24.74	61.90	69.34	41.50	23.36	51.28	52.11	40.74
100.00	100.00	100.00	100.00	100.00	100.00	100.00	100.00	100.00	100.00	100.00	100.00	100.00	100.00	100.00	100.00	100.00	100.00

Note: ** means "not applicable."

5-50. Direction of trade matrix, exports, 1986

		Importers DZA	AGO	BEN	BFA	BDI	CMR	CPV	CAF	TCD	COM	ZAR	COG	CIV	DJI	*Percentage of total exports* EGY	GNQ
Exporters																	
Algeria	DZA	**	..	0.01	0.06	..	0.00	..	..	..	..	..	..	0.00	0.02	..	0.00	..
Angola	AGO	..	**	..	..	..	..	..	..	..	..	..	..	..	..	..	..
Benin	BEN	..	..	**	..	..	..	..	..	..	..	..	..	..	..	..	..
Burkina Faso	BFA	..	..	..	**	..	..	..	..	..	..	..	..	..	..	..	..
Burundi	BDI	..	..	..	..	**	..	..	..	..	..	..	..	..	..	..	..
Cameroon	CMR	1.17	0.11	0.04	0.00	..	**	..	1.58	1.97	..	0.00	2.06	1.22	0.00	0.00	0.65
Cape Verde	CPV	..	..	..	..	..	..	**	..	..	..	..	..	..	..	..	..
Central African Republic	CAF	..	..	..	..	..	..	..	**	..	..	..	..	..	..	..	..
Chad	TCD	..	..	..	..	..	..	..	..	**	..	..	..	..	..	..	..
Comoros	COM	..	..	..	..	..	..	..	..	..	**	..	..	..	..	..	..
Congo, Democratic Rep. o	ZAR	..	..	..	..	..	..	..	..	..	..	**	..	..	..	..	..
Congo, Republic of	COG	0.20	0.28	0.02	..	..	0.01	..	0.01	0.06	..	0.10	**	0.05	..	..	..
Côte d'Ivoire	CIV	..	..	..	..	..	..	..	..	..	..	..	..	**	..	..	..
Djibouti	DJI	0.02	..	..	..	..	..	..	..	0.06	0.23	0.01	..	..	**	..	0.05
Egypt, Arab Rep.	EGY	0.24	..	..	..	0.00	0.00	..	..	0.00	..	0.01	..	0.00	0.00	**	..
Equatorial Guinea	GNQ	..	..	..	..	..	..	..	..	..	..	..	..	..	..	..	**
Ethiopia	ETH	0.00	..	..	0.00	0.00	..	..	..	..	..	..	0.00	..	4.22	..	
Gabon	GAB	..	..	..	..	..	..	..	..	..	..	..	..	..	..	..	
Gambia, The	GMB	..	..	..	..	..	..	..	..	..	..	..	..	..	..	..	
Ghana	GHA	..	..	..	..	..	..	..	..	..	..	..	..	..	..	..	
Guinea	GIN	..	..	..	..	..	..	..	..	..	..	..	..	..	..	..	
Guinea-Bissau	GNB	..	..	..	..	..	..	..	..	..	..	..	..	..	..	..	
Kenya	KEN	0.02	0.16	0.00	0.00	0.92	0.00	0.05	0.02	..	0.13	1.19	0.00	0.06	0.26	0.53	
Liberia	LBR	..	..	..	..	..	..	..	..	..	..	..	..	..	..	..	
Libya	LBY	0.00	..	..	..	..	..	..	..	..	..	..	..	..	..	..	
Madagascar	MDG	0.05	..	..	..	..	0.03	..	..	0.00	0.08	0.00	..	..	0.03	0.00	0.06
Malawi	MWI	..	..	..	..	0.21	0.12	..	..	..	..	2.02	..	0.02	..	1.70	
Mali	MLI	..	..	..	..	..	..	..	..	..	..	..	..	..	..	..	
Mauritania	MRT	..	..	..	..	..	..	..	..	..	..	..	..	..	..	..	
Mauritius	MUS	0.00	..	0.01	..	..	0.01	..	..	..	0.06	..	0.00	0.00	0.00	0.27	..
Morocco	MAR	0.00	0.04	0.05	0.00	0.00	0.34	..	0.02	..	0.01	0.23	0.21	0.38	0.00	0.06	0.00
Mozambique	MOZ	..	..	..	..	..	..	..	..	..	..	..	..	..	..	..	
Niger	NER	..	..	..	..	..	..	..	..	..	..	..	..	..	..	..	
Nigeria	NGA	0.00	0.01	0.02	0.00	..	0.02	..	..	0.00	0.00	0.17	0.00	1.67	..	0.00	
Reunion	REU	..	..	0.00	0.02	..	0.01	..	..	..	3.83	..	0.00	..	0.01	..	
Rwanda	RWA	..	..	..	..	..	..	..	..	..	..	..	..	..	..	..	
South Africa	ZAF	..	..	..	..	..	..	..	..	..	..	..	..	..	..	..	
São Tomé and Principe	STP	..	..	..	..	..	..	..	..	..	..	..	..	..	..	..	
Senegal	SEN	0.03	..	0.63	0.69	0.00	2.24	0.21	0.04	0.04	0.00	0.11	0.63	3.96	..	0.00	0.00
Seychelles	SYC	..	..	..	..	..	0.02	..	..	..	..	..	..	..	..	..	
Sierra Leone	SLE	..	..	..	..	..	..	..	..	..	..	..	..	..	..	..	
Somalia	SOM	..	..	..	..	..	..	..	..	..	..	..	..	..	..	..	
Sudan	SDN	..	..	..	..	..	..	..	..	..	..	..	..	..	..	..	
Tanzania	TZA	..	..	..	..	..	..	..	..	..	..	..	..	..	..	..	
Togo	TGO	..	..	0.64	2.90	..	0.01	0.06	0.00	0.00	..	..	0.01	0.13	..	0.01	0.01
Tunisia	TUN	5.10	0.00	0.03	0.00	..	0.44	..	0.00	..	..	0.00	0.01	0.09	0.00	0.24	
Uganda	UGA	..	..	..	..	..	..	..	..	..	..	..	..	..	..	..	
Zambia	ZMB	..	..	..	..	..	..	..	..	..	..	..	..	..	..	..	
Zimbabwe	ZWE	0.10	0.19	0.00	..	0.06	0.00	0.11	0.01	..	0.00	1.63	0.03	0.06	0.00	0.28	
Sub-Saharan Africa	SSA	0.10	0.06	0.06	0.08	0.10	0.13	0.03	0.11	0.14	0.02	0.39	0.17	1.11	0.19	0.12	0.04
European Community	EEC	0.63	0.07	0.03	0.02	0.01	0.14	0.01	0.01	0.01	0.00	0.09	0.05	0.12	0.01	0.56	0.00
North America	NNA	0.20	0.03	0.01	0.00	0.00	0.02	..	0.00	0.00	0.01	0.03	0.02	0.02	0.00	0.60	0.00
Rest Of World	ROW	0.21	0.08	0.02	0.00	0.00	0.04	0.00	0.00	0.00	0.00	0.03	0.02	0.04	0.01	0.37	0.00
World	WLD	0.41	0.06	0.02	0.01	0.01	0.08	0.01	0.01	0.01	0.00	0.06	0.03	0.08	0.01	0.49	0.00

Note: ** means "not applicable."

(Table continues on the following page.)

5-50. (continued)

Percentage of total exports

ETH	GAB	GMB	GHA	GIN	GNB	KEN	LBR	LBY	MDG	MWI	MLI	MRT	MUS	MAR	MOZ	NER	NGA	REU	RWA
..	..	..	..	..	..	..	0.02	0.00	..	..	0.00	0.00	0.00	..	..	0.00	..	..	..
..	..	..	..	..	..	..	..	..	..	..	..	..	..	..	..	..	..	..	..
..	..	..	..	..	..	..	..	..	..	..	..	..	..	..	..	..	..	..	..
..	..	..	..	..	..	..	..	..	..	..	..	..	..	..	..	..	..	..	..
0.00	4.46	..	0.18	0.18	..	0.00	0.00	0.01	0.00	0.00	0.00	0.00	0.00	0.03	..	..	4.96	0.00	0.00
..	..	..	..	..	..	..	..	..	..	..	..	..	..	..	..	..	..	..	..
..	..	..	..	..	..	..	..	..	..	..	..	..	..	..	..	..	..	..	..
..	..	..	..	..	..	..	..	..	..	..	..	..	..	..	..	..	..	..	..
..	..	..	..	..	..	..	..	..	..	..	..	..	..	..	..	..	..	..	..
..	..	..	..	..	..	..	..	..	..	..	..	..	..	..	..	..	..	..	..
..	0.01	..	..	0.01	..	..	..	..	..	..	..	0.00	0.00	0.01	1.40	..	..	0.00	0.27
2.49	0.02	..	..	..	..	0.33	0.02	0.01	0.28	..	0.05	..	0.06	0.04	0.00	..	0.00	1.90	..
0.10	..	..	..	..	..	0.00	..	0.01	..	0.00	0.00	0.00	..	0.16	0.01	0.00	0.01	..	..
..	..	..	..	..	..	..	..	..	..	..	..	..	..	..	..	..	..	..	..
**	..	..	..	..	..	0.10	..	..	..	0.00	0.00	..	..	..	0.00	..	0.00	..	..
..	**	..	..	..	..	..	..	..	..	..	..	..	..	..	..	..	..	..	..
..	..	**	..	..	..	..	..	..	..	..	..	..	..	..	..	..	..	..	..
..	..	..	**	..	..	..	..	..	..	..	..	..	..	..	..	..	..	..	..
..	..	..	..	**	..	..	..	..	..	..	..	..	..	..	..	..	..	..	..
..	..	..	..	..	**	..	..	..	..	..	..	..	..	..	..	..	..	..	..
0.68	0.00	..	0.01	0.00	..	**	0.00	0.02	0.02	0.04	0.00	0.00	0.27	0.06	0.21	0.00	0.02	0.32	2.58
..	..	..	..	..	..	..	**	..	..	..	..	..	..	..	..	..	..	..	..
..	..	..	..	..	..	..	..	**	..	..	..	..	..	0.71	..	..	..	..	..
0.00	0.00	..	..	..	..	0.08	0.00	..	**	0.01	0.00	..	0.54	..	0.02	..	..	2.61	0.00
0.00	0.15	0.13	0.02	..	..	0.02	0.08	0.30	..	**	..	..	0.09	..	3.98	..	0.04	..	0.02
..	..	..	..	..	..	..	..	..	..	..	**	..	..	..	..	..	..	..	..
..	..	..	..	..	..	..	..	..	..	..	..	**	..	..	..	..	..	..	..
..	0.00	..	..	0.00	..	0.03	..	..	0.06	0.00	0.01	..	**	0.49	0.00	..	..	1.95	..
..	0.24	0.00	..	0.10	0.00	..	0.16	1.71	..	..	0.07	0.04	0.04	**	..	0.01	0.01	0.10	0.00
..	..	..	..	..	..	..	..	..	..	..	..	..	..	..	**	..	..	..	..
..	..	..	..	..	..	..	..	..	..	..	..	..	..	..	..	**	..	..	..
..	0.00	0.00	1.49	0.00	0.00	..	0.02	..	..	..	..	..	..	0.06	0.00	0.07	**	..	..
..	..	..	..	..	..	..	..	..	3.25	..	..	..	0.86	..	..	..	..	**	..
..	..	..	..	..	..	..	..	..	..	..	..	..	..	..	..	..	..	..	**
..	..	..	..	..	..	..	..	..	..	..	..	..	..	..	..	..	..	..	..
0.00	0.19	0.47	0.02	1.00	0.43	0.04	0.02	..	0.00	..	2.73	3.45	..	0.10	0.00	0.28	0.35	0.00	0.00
..	..	..	..	..	..	0.23	..	..	..	..	..	..	0.56	..	..	..	..	21.44	..
..	..	..	..	..	..	..	..	..	..	..	..	..	..	..	..	..	..	..	..
..	..	..	..	..	..	..	..	..	..	..	..	..	..	..	..	..	..	..	..
..	..	..	..	..	..	..	..	..	..	..	..	..	..	..	..	..	..	..	..
..	0.03	..	1.49	0.12	0.00	..	0.00	0.00	..	..	0.24	0.01	..	1.10	..	0.33	1.02	..	..
0.00	0.09	0.00	0.00	0.05	..	0.08	0.00	0.28	0.00	..	0.01	0.01	..	0.42	0.08	0.02	0.00	..	..
..	..	..	..	..	..	..	..	..	..	..	..	..	..	..	..	..	..	..	..
0.51	0.01	..	0.05	..	..	0.75	0.00	0.24	..	1.23	..	0.00	0.03	0.48	3.20	0.00	0.04	0.49	0.18
0.11	0.30	0.03	0.76	0.07	0.02	0.07	0.01	0.03	0.01	0.11	0.14	0.18	0.04	0.22	0.37	0.05	0.36	0.27	0.26
0.06	0.07	0.01	0.05	0.03	0.00	0.10	0.05	0.31	0.02	0.01	0.03	0.03	0.03	0.27	0.02	0.02	0.34	0.09	0.01
0.04	0.01	0.00	0.04	0.01	0.01	0.04	0.02	0.03	0.01	0.00	0.01	0.01	0.00	0.18	0.01	0.00	0.14	0.00	0.00
0.03	0.01	0.00	0.02	0.01	0.00	0.06	0.22	0.20	0.01	0.00	0.00	0.00	0.03	0.06	0.02	0.00	0.17	0.01	0.01
0.05	0.04	0.01	0.04	0.02	0.00	0.07	0.11	0.22	0.02	0.01	0.02	0.02	0.03	0.18	0.02	0.01	0.25	0.05	0.01

Note: ** means "not applicable."

(Table continues on the following page.)

5-50. (continued)

Percentage of total exports

ZAF	STP	SEN	SYC	SLE	SOM	SDN	TZA	TGO	TUN	UGA	ZMB	ZWE	SSA	EEC	NNA	ROW	WLD
..	..	0.00	..	0.02	..	..	..	..	0.50	..	..	..	0.14	74.53	17.41	7.92	100.00
..	..	..	..	..	..	..	..	..	..	..	..	..	..	..	..	..	..
..	..	..	..	..	..	..	..	..	..	..	..	..	..	..	..	..	..
..	..	..	..	..	..	..	..	..	..	..	..	..	..	..	..	..	..
..	..	..	..	..	..	..	..	..	..	..	..	..	..	..	..	..	..
..	..	0.14	..	0.01	..	0.01	..	0.23	0.13	..	0.00	0.00	17.83	71.66	2.93	7.57	100.00
..	..	..	..	..	..	..	..	..	..	..	..	..	..	..	..	..	..
..	..	..	..	..	..	..	..	..	..	..	..	..	..	..	..	..	..
..	..	..	..	..	..	..	..	..	..	..	..	..	..	..	..	..	..
..	..	..	..	..	..	..	..	..	..	..	..	..	..	..	..	..	..
0.01	0.00	0.00	..	..	..	..	..	0.00	0.35	..	..	0.02	0.58	41.65	54.19	3.58	100.00
..	..	0.04	..	..	6.53	0.04	0.02	0.00	0.40	..	0.12	..	10.30	51.65	0.73	37.32	100.00
0.08	..	0.00	..	..	0.00	1.75	0.01	0.00	0.22	0.01	..	..	1.90	36.20	3.12	58.77	100.00
..	..	0.00	..	..	..	0.03	0.01	..	..	0.00	0.00	..	4.37	54.54	16.32	24.77	100.00
..	..	..	..	..	..	..	..	..	..	..	..	..	..	..	..	..	..
..	..	..	..	..	..	..	..	..	..	..	..	..	..	..	..	..	..
..	..	..	..	..	..	..	..	..	..	..	..	..	..	..	..	..	..
..	..	..	..	..	..	..	..	..	..	..	..	..	..	..	..	..	..
0.18	0.00	0.02	0.23	0.00	0.70	1.99	2.57	0.00	0.07	7.25	0.12	0.25	19.77	48.72	9.56	21.95	100.00
..	..	..	..	..	..	..	..	..	..	..	..	..	..	..	..	..	..
..	..	..	..	..	..	0.35	..	..	0.02	..	..	..	0.35	77.19	..	22.46	100.00
0.00	..	0.00	0.02	..	0.00	0.00	0.13	0.00	..	0.00	0.02	..	1.04	58.26	15.36	25.33	100.00
8.36	..	0.10	0.03	0.02	0.32	..	0.49	..	..	..	2.42	1.97	12.26	55.79	9.06	22.88	100.00
..	..	..	..	..	..	..	..	..	..	..	..	..	..	..	..	..	..
0.19	..	0.00	0.09	..	0.00	..	0.02	..	0.00	0.00	0.00	0.01	0.31	76.41	18.09	5.19	100.00
0.00	..	0.38	..	0.00	..	0.00	0.02	0.05	0.55	0.00	..	0.00	2.40	59.33	1.90	36.37	100.00
..	..	..	..	..	..	..	..	..	..	..	..	..	..	..	..	..	..
..	..	..	..	..	..	..	..	..	..	..	..	..	..	..	..	..	..
0.09	..	0.38	..	0.20	..	..	..	0.00	..	..	0.00	..	4.05	52.83	37.35	5.77	100.00
0.11	..	..	0.03	..	..	..	..	..	..	..	0.00	0.00	8.01	88.25	0.18	3.56	100.00
..	..	..	..	..	..	..	..	..	..	..	..	..	..	..	..	..	..
**	..	..	..	..	..	..	..	..	..	..	..	..	..	..	..	..	..
..	**	..	..	..	..	..	..	..	..	..	..	..	..	..	..	..	..
0.00	..	**	..	0.06	..	..	0.00	0.65	0.02	0.00	0.01	0.00	18.25	43.42	0.26	38.07	100.00
0.40	..	..	**	..	..	..	..	..	..	..	..	..	0.82	33.07	0.57	65.54	100.00
..	..	..	..	**	..	..	..	..	..	..	..	..	..	..	..	..	..
..	..	..	..	..	**	..	..	..	..	..	..	..	..	..	..	..	..
..	..	..	..	..	..	**	..	..	..	..	..	..	..	..	..	..	..
..	..	..	..	..	..	..	**	..	..	..	..	..	..	..	..	..	..
..	..	0.01	..	0.00	..	..	..	**	0.45	..	..	..	7.01	56.14	13.00	23.85	100.00
..	..	0.07	..	0.00	..	0.00	0.00	0.02	**	0.00	..	..	1.03	74.28	0.79	23.90	100.00
..	..	..	..	..	..	..	..	..	..	**	..	..	..	..	..	..	..
..	..	..	..	..	..	..	..	..	..	..	**	..	..	..	..	..	..
16.84	..	0.00	0.01	0.00	0.03	0.14	0.25	0.00	0.10	0.10	2.85	**	11.48	43.65	6.23	38.64	100.00
1.64	0.00	0.20	0.03	0.10	0.09	0.20	0.28	0.05	0.06	0.70	0.30	0.06	7.52	53.28	25.59	13.61	100.00
0.56	0.00	0.07	0.01	0.01	0.02	0.06	0.04	0.03	0.23	0.01	0.03	0.04	1.78	62.28	10.34	25.60	100.00
0.45	..	0.02	0.00	0.01	0.02	0.04	0.02	0.01	0.07	0.00	0.02	0.02	0.64	20.18	36.96	42.22	100.00
0.36	0.00	0.02	0.00	0.00	0.01	0.05	0.04	0.02	0.04	0.01	0.01	0.01	1.04	23.63	29.75	45.59	100.00
0.48	0.00	0.04	0.00	0.01	0.02	0.05	0.04	0.02	0.14	0.02	0.02	0.03	1.37	41.50	21.71	35.42	100.00

Note: ** means "not applicable."

5-51. Direction of trade matrix, exports, 1990

Exporters		DZA	AGO	BEN	BFA	BDI	CMR	CPV	CAF	TCD	COM	ZAR	COG	CIV	DJI	EGY	GNQ
														Percentage of total exports			
Algeria	DZA	**	..	..	0.00	..	..	..	..	..	..	..	0.00	0.00	0.03	0.18	..
Angola	AGO	..	**	..	..	..	..	..	..	..	..	..	0.00	0.02	..	..	..
Benin	BEN	..	..	**	..	..	..	..	..	..	..	..	..	..	..	..	..
Burkina Faso	BFA	..	..	..	**	..	..	..	..	..	..	..	..	..	..	..	..
Burundi	BDI	..	..	..	..	**	..	..	..	..	..	..	..	..	..	..	..
Cameroon	CMR	0.29	0.00	0.01	0.03	0.00	**	..	1.41	0.55	..	0.13	0.75	0.18	..	0.03	1.45
Cape Verde	CPV	..	..	..	..	..	..	**	..	..	..	..	..	..	..	..	..
Central African Republic	CAF	..	..	..	..	..	..	..	**	..	..	..	..	..	..	..	..
Chad	TCD	..	..	..	..	..	..	..	..	**	..	..	..	..	..	..	..
Comoros	COM	..	..	..	..	..	•	..	..	..	**	..	..	..	..	..	..
Congo, Democratic Rep. of	ZAR	..	..	..	..	'	..	..	..	..	..	**	..	..	..	..	..
Congo, Republic of	COG	..	..	..	..	..	..	..	..	..	..	..	**	..	..	..	..
Côte d'Ivoire	CIV	..	..	..	..	..	..	..	..	..	..	..	..	**	..	..	..
Djibouti	DJI	..	0.07	..	0.04	..	0.05	..	0.03	..	0.38	..	..	0.00	**	0.31	..
Egypt, Arab Rep.	EGY	0.18	0.00	0.01	..	0.00	0.00	..	..	0.00	..	0.00	0.00	0.02	0.02	**	0.00
Equatorial Guinea	GNQ	..	..	..	..	..	..	..	..	..	..	..	..	..	..	..	**
Ethiopia	ETH	..	0.00	..	..	0.00	..	..	0.29	0.00	..	..	0.00	0.00	12.00	0.00	..
Gabon	GAB	..	..	..	..	..	..	..	..	..	..	..	..	..	..	..	..
Gambia, The	GMB	..	..	..	..	..	..	..	..	..	..	..	..	..	..	..	..
Ghana	GHA	..	..	..	..	..	..	..	..	..	..	..	..	..	..	..	..
Guinea	GIN	..	..	..	..	..	..	..	..	..	..	..	..	..	..	..	..
Guinea-Bissau	GNB	..	..	..	..	..	..	..	..	..	..	..	..	..	..	..	..
Kenya	KEN	0.03	0.56	0.00	0.00	1.98	0.01	0.00	0.00	0.00	0.06	2.41	0.00	0.04	2.23	1.49	0.00
Liberia	LBR	..	..	..	..	..	..	..	..	..	..	..	..	..	..	..	..
Libya	LBY	0.04	..	..	0.00	..	..	'	..	..	..	..	..	..	..	0.57	..
Madagascar	MDG	0.00	..	0.00	..	0.01	0.00	..	..	..	0.80	..	0.01	0.00	0.01	0.00	0.00
Malawi	MWI	..	0.01	..	..	0.14	0.01	..	..	..	..	..	0.49	..	0.01	..	1.33	..
Mali	MLI	0.18	..	..	0.40	..	..	..	..	..	..	..	..	53.18	..	..	..
Mauritania	MRT	..	..	..	..	..	..	..	..	..	..	..	..	..	..	..	..
Mauritius	MUS	0.00	..	0.00	0.00	0.00	0.00	..	..	..	0.13	0.01	0.00	0.00	0.00	0.00	..
Morocco	MAR	1.36	0.13	0.04	0.01	..	0.14	..	0.02	..	0.01	0.16	0.13	0.17	0.00	0.09	0.01
Mozambique	MOZ	..	..	..	..	..	..	..	..	..	..	..	..	..	..	..	..
Niger	NER	..	..	..	..	..	..	..	..	..	..	..	..	..	..	..	..
Nigeria	NGA	..	..	..	..	..	..	..	..	..	..	..	..	..	..	..	..
Reunion	REU	..	..	..	..	..	..	..	..	..	4.24	0.04	..	0.00	0.15	..	..
Rwanda	RWA	..	..	..	..	..	..	..	..	..	..	..	..	..	..	..	..
South Africa	ZAF	..	..	..	..	..	..	..	..	..	..	..	..	..	..	..	..
São Tomé and Principe	STP	..	..	..	..	..	..	..	..	..	..	..	..	..	..	..	..
Senegal	SEN	..	..	0.53	0.40	0.01	2.53	0.02	0.04	0.02	..	0.07	0.75	2.79	..	0.05	..
Seychelles	SYC	..	..	..	..	..	..	..	..	..	..	..	..	..	..	..	..
Sierra Leone	SLE	..	..	..	..	..	..	..	..	..	..	..	..	..	..	..	..
Somalia	SOM	..	..	..	..	..	..	..	..	..	..	..	..	..	..	..	..
Sudan	SDN	..	..	..	..	..	..	..	..	..	..	..	..	..	..	..	..
Tanzania	TZA	..	..	..	..	..	..	..	..	..	..	..	..	..	..	..	..
Togo	TGO	0.01	..	2.12	3.30	..	0.06	0.30	0.01	0.00	..	0.01	0.10	0.35	0.01	..	0.05
Tunisia	TUN	2.32	..	0.02	0.01	0.00	0.28	..	..	0.00	..	..	0.02	0.22	0.02	0.10	..
Uganda	UGA	..	..	..	..	..	..	..	..	..	..	..	..	..	..	..	..
Zambia	ZMB	..	..	..	..	..	..	..	..	..	..	..	..	..	..	..	..
Zimbabwe	ZWE	0.00	0.79	0.00	..	0.20	0.00	0.00	..	..	..	..	0.97	0.02	0.01	0.00	0.28	..
Sub-Saharan Africa	SSA	0.06	0.14	0.08	0.12	0.20	0.17	0.01	0.25	0.10	0.04	0.36	0.18	1.68	0.48	0.21	0.25
European Community	EEC	0.44	0.07	0.01	0.02	0.01	0.06	0.01	0.01	0.01	0.00	0.06	0.03	0.07	0.01	0.37	0.00
North America	NNA	0.24	0.03	0.01	0.00	0.00	0.01	0.00	0.00	0.00	0.00	0.03	0.02	0.02	0.00	0.46	0.00
Rest Of World	ROW	0.13	0.02	0.01	0.00	0.00	0.01	0.00	0.00	0.00	0.00	0.01	0.01	0.02	0.01	0.27	0.00
World	WLD	0.29	0.05	0.01	0.01	0.01	0.04	0.00	0.00	0.00	0.00	0.04	0.02	0.05	0.01	0.35	0.00

Note: ** means "not applicable."

(Table continues on the following page.)

5-51. (continued)

Percentage of total exports

ETH	GAB	GMB	GHA	GIN	GNB	KEN	LBR	LBY	MDG	MWI	MLI	MRT	MUS	MAR	MOZ	NER	NGA	REU	RWA
..	0.00	..	..	..	..	..	..	0.03	..	..	0.00	0.32	..	0.38	..	0.00	..	..	..
..	..	..	..	..	..	..	0.87	..	..	..	..	..	..	..	..	..	..	..	..
..	..	..	..	..	..	..	..	..	..	..	..	..	..	..	..	..	..	..	..
..	..	..	..	..	..	..	..	..	..	..	..	..	..	..	..	..	..	..	..
..	1.47	0.00	0.03	0.10	..	0.00	0.00	..	0.00	..	0.00	0.01	0.00	0.08	..	0.01	1.68	0.04	0.00
..	..	..	..	..	..	..	..	..	..	..	..	..	..	..	..	..	..	..	..
..	..	..	..	..	..	..	..	..	..	..	..	..	..	..	..	..	..	..	..
..	..	..	..	..	..	..	..	..	..	..	..	..	..	..	..	..	..	..	..
..	..	..	..	..	..	..	..	..	..	..	..	..	..	..	..	..	..	..	..
1.57	0.06	0.00	..	0.02	..	0.02	..	0.06	0.82	..	0.02	..	..	0.00	..	0.02	..	1.06	..
0.00	..	..	0.00	0.00	..	0.00	0.00	1.69	..	0.00	0.00	0.00	..	0.23	0.00	0.00	0.03	..	0.00
..	..	..	..	..	..	..	..	..	..	..	..	..	..	..	..	..	..	..	..
**	0.00	0.00	0.00	0.00	..	0.30	..	..	0.00	0.00	..	..	0.00	0.00	0.00	0.00	0.00	..	..
..	**	..	..	..	..	..	..	..	..	..	..	..	..	..	..	..	..	..	..
..	..	**	..	..	..	..	..	..	..	..	..	..	..	..	..	..	..	..	..
..	..	..	**	..	..	..	..	..	..	..	..	..	..	..	..	..	..	..	..
..	..	..	..	**	..	..	..	..	..	..	..	..	..	..	..	..	..	..	..
..	..	..	..	..	**	..	..	..	..	..	..	..	..	..	..	..	..	..	..
0.83	0.00	..	0.01	0.01	..	**	0.00	0.00	0.02	0.12	..	0.00	0.29	0.03	0.10	..	0.15	0.37	7.34
..	..	..	..	..	..	..	**	..	..	..	..	..	..	..	..	..	..	..	..
..	..	..	0.00	0.00	..	..	..	**	..	..	0.00	0.00	..	0.83	..	0.00	0.00	..	..
0.00	0.00	..	..	0.02	..	0.24	..	..	**	0.00	0.02	0.17	2.40	0.11	1.97	0.00	0.00	5.16	0.00
0.00	0.08	0.74	0.00	0.18	..	0.05	..	..	..	**	..	..	0.04	..	0.22	..	0.02	..	0.19
..	0.01	..	0.02	0.36	..	..	..	..	..	..	**	0.00	..	..	..	0.06	0.00	..	..
..	..	..	..	..	..	..	..	..	..	..	..	**	..	..	..	..	..	..	..
0.00	0.01	..	0.00	0.00	..	0.09	0.00	..	0.79	0.01	0.00	0.00	**	0.24	0.00	..	0.00	1.80	0.00
..	0.19	0.00	0.09	0.13	0.00	..	0.01	2.80	0.01	0.00	0.14	0.10	0.04	**	..	0.01	0.28	0.05	..
..	..	..	..	..	..	..	..	..	..	..	..	..	..	..	**	..	..	..	..
..	..	..	..	..	..	..	..	..	..	..	..	..	..	..	..	**	..	..	..
..	..	..	..	..	..	..	..	..	..	..	..	..	..	..	..	..	**	..	..
..	..	..	..	..	..	0.00	..	..	3.19	..	..	..	1.56	..	..	..	..	**	..
..	..	..	..	..	..	..	..	..	..	..	..	..	..	..	..	..	..	..	**
..	..	..	..	..	..	..	..	..	..	..	..	..	..	..	..	..	..	..	..
..	..	..	..	..	..	..	..	..	..	..	..	..	..	..	..	..	..	..	..
0.00	0.34	0.88	0.13	1.95	0.57	0.00	0.08	..	0.02	0.00	7.11	0.03	..	0.12	..	0.04	0.49	..	..
..	..	..	..	..	..	0.01	..	..	..	..	..	..	0.74	..	..	..	..	23.68	..
..	..	..	..	..	..	..	..	..	..	..	..	..	..	..	..	..	..	..	..
..	..	..	..	..	..	..	..	..	..	..	..	..	..	..	..	..	..	..	..
..	0.25	0.01	1.54	1.39	0.00	0.03	0.01	0.02	..	..	0.27	..	..	0.94	0.01	1.36	3.27	0.00	..
..	0.00	..	0.24	0.01	0.02	..	0.00	4.60	..	..	0.00	0.06	..	0.67	..	0.00	0.01	..	0.00
..	..	..	..	..	..	..	..	..	..	..	..	..	..	..	..	..	..	..	..
0.09	0.00	..	0.07	0.00	..	1.23	0.00	0.03	0.01	4.82	0.00	..	0.07	0.00	3.68	0.02	0.05	0.00	0.08
0.08	0.28	0.08	0.06	0.19	0.04	0.17	0.29	0.00	0.09	0.60	0.47	0.01	0.09	0.07	0.51	0.04	0.41	0.37	0.63
0.04	0.04	0.01	0.04	0.02	0.00	0.08	0.09	0.23	0.02	0.01	0.02	0.02	0.03	0.31	0.02	0.01	0.22	0.10	0.01
0.04	0.01	0.00	0.03	0.01	0.00	0.03	0.01	0.01	0.00	0.00	0.00	0.00	0.00	0.14	0.01	0.00	0.11	0.00	0.00
0.02	0.01	0.00	0.03	0.01	0.00	0.04	0.22	0.12	0.01	0.00	0.00	0.01	0.04	0.08	0.02	0.00	0.12	0.01	0.00
0.03	0.02	0.01	0.04	0.01	0.00	0.06	0.12	0.16	0.01	0.01	0.01	0.01	0.03	0.20	0.02	0.01	0.16	0.05	0.01

Note: ** means "not applicable."

(Table continues on the following page.)

5-51. (continued)

Percentage of total exports

ZAF	STP	SEN	SYC	SLE	SOM	SDN	TZA	TGO	TUN	UGA	ZMB	ZWE	SSA	EEC	NNA	ROW	WLD
..	..	0.00	..	..	..	..	..	0.00	1.61	0.01	..	..	0.37	69.69	19.56	10.38	100.00
0.01	0.05	..	..	..	..	..	..	0.05	..	..	..	..	0.99	37.75	53.59	7.67	100.00
..	..	..	..	..	..	..	..	..	..	..	..	..	..	..	..	..	..
..	..	..	..	..	..	..	..	..	..	..	..	..	..	..	..	..	..
0.00	0.01	0.20	..	0.00	..	..	0.02	0.04	0.16	..	..	..	8.07	76.61	7.61	7.71	100.00
..	..	..	..	..	..	..	..	..	..	..	..	..	..	..	..	..	..
..	..	..	..	..	..	..	..	..	..	..	..	..	..	..	..	..	..
..	..	..	..	..	..	..	..	..	..	..	..	..	..	..	..	..	..
..	..	..	..	..	..	..	..	..	..	..	..	..	..	..	..	..	..
..	..	..	..	..	..	..	..	..	..	..	..	..	..	..	..	..	..
..	..	0.03	..	..	1.74	0.03	0.00	..	0.15	0.09	..	..	4.97	54.45	0.24	40.33	100.00
0.00	..	0.00	..	0.00	0.00	0.80	0.00	..	0.71	0.01	0.01	0.00	0.93	38.89	8.83	51.35	100.00
..	..	..	..	..	..	..	..	..	..	..	..	..	..	..	..	..	..
0.00	..	0.01	..	..	..	0.09	0.00	..	..	0.00	0.00	0.00	12.71	40.22	11.15	35.92	100.00
..	..	..	..	..	..	..	..	..	..	..	..	..	..	..	..	..	..
..	..	..	..	..	..	..	..	..	..	..	..	..	..	..	..	..	..
..	..	..	..	..	..	..	..	..	..	..	..	..	..	..	..	..	..
..	..	..	..	..	..	..	..	..	..	..	..	..	..	..	..	..	..
0.09	0.00	..	0.08	0.00	1.58	1.43	2.02	0.02	0.05	18.49	0.18	0.75	40.75	33.84	2.96	22.46	100.00
..	..	0.02	..	..	..	1.09	0.22	..	0.52	..	..	..	1.34	84.39	0.00	14.27	100.00
0.14	..	0.00	0.05	..	0.34	0.00	0.53	0.00	0.02	..	..	..	6.60	52.19	17.91	23.30	100.00
7.62	..	0.03	..	0.09	0.00	0.00	0.22	0.02	..	0.00	1.37	1.63	5.53	50.72	12.11	31.64	100.00
..	..	18.88	..	..	..	..	..	0.00	..	..	..	..	72.90	26.02	0.00	1.08	100.00
0.55	..	0.00	0.26	..	0.00	0.00	0.01	0.00	0.02	0.00	0.02	0.26	1.62	77.00	13.19	8.19	100.00
0.00	..	0.12	..	0.01	..	0.00	0.00	0.09	1.46	..	..	..	2.04	65.90	2.26	29.81	100.00
..	..	..	..	..	..	..	..	..	..	..	..	..	..	..	..	..	..
..	..	..	..	..	..	..	..	..	..	..	..	..	..	..	..	..	..
0.28	..	..	0.34	..	..	..	..	..	..	..	0.00	..	9.54	85.72	0.02	4.73	100.00
**	..	..	..	..	..	..	..	..	..	..	..	..	..	..	..	100.00	100.00
..	**	..	..	..	..	..	..	..	..	..	..	..	..	..	..	..	..
..	..	**	..	0.02	..	..	..	0.65	0.40	..	0.01	0.00	19.50	53.35	0.23	26.92	100.00
0.78	..	..	**	..	..	..	..	..	..	..	..	..	0.76	67.80	0.14	31.30	100.00
..	..	..	..	**	..	..	..	..	..	..	..	..	..	..	..	..	..
..	..	..	..	..	**	..	..	..	..	..	..	..	..	..	..	..	..
..	..	..	..	..	..	**	..	..	..	..	..	..	..	..	..	..	..
..	..	..	..	..	..	..	**	..	..	..	..	..	..	..	..	..	..
0.01	..	0.09	..	..	..	..	..	**	0.51	..	..	..	14.57	40.89	13.58	30.95	100.00
..	..	0.04	..	0.00	..	0.03	0.00	0.05	**	..	0.04	0.00	1.08	78.12	0.93	19.87	100.00
..	..	..	..	..	..	..	..	..	..	**	..	..	..	..	..	..	..
..	..	..	..	..	..	..	..	..	..	..	**	..	..	..	..	..	..
15.15	0.00	0.01	0.01	0.00	0.00	0.04	0.81	0.00	0.00	0.39	3.50	**	16.87	42.09	7.28	33.76	100.00
2.16	0.02	0.55	0.04	0.01	0.15	0.13	0.29	0.07	0.07	1.61	0.49	0.14	11.59	50.24	22.50	15.67	100.00
0.51	0.00	0.05	0.00	0.01	0.01	0.03	0.04	0.02	0.26	0.01	0.03	0.03	1.31	66.04	7.93	24.72	100.00
0.38	0.00	0.01	0.00	0.01	0.00	0.01	0.01	0.01	0.05	0.01	0.02	0.03	0.51	21.66	34.73	43.10	100.00
0.23	0.00	0.01	0.00	0.00	0.00	0.04	0.02	0.02	0.07	0.01	0.01	0.02	0.76	25.06	23.49	50.69	100.00
0.39	0.00	0.03	0.00	0.01	0.01	0.03	0.03	0.02	0.15	0.02	0.02	0.03	1.02	43.73	17.99	37.26	100.00

Note: ** means "not applicable."

5-52. Direction of trade matrix, exports, 1995

Exporters		*Importers* DZA	AGO	BEN	BFA	BDI	CMR	CPV	CAF	TCD	COM	ZAR	COG	CIV	DJI	*Percentage of total exports* EGY	GNQ
Algeria	DZA	**	..	..	0.00	..	..	0.00	..	0.03	..	..	0.00	..	..	0.06	..
Angola	AGO	..	**	..	..	..	..	..	..	..	..	..	..	..	..	..	..
Benin	BEN	..	..	**	..	..	..	..	..	..	..	..	..	..	..	..	..
Burkina Faso	BFA	..	..	..	**	..	..	..	..	..	..	..	..	..	..	..	..
Burundi	BDI	..	..	..	..	**	..	..	..	..	..	..	..	..	..	..	..
Cameroon	CMR	0.01	0.12	0.13	0.03	0.00	**	..	0.83	0.37	..	0.21	1.14	0.59	..	0.00	1.60
Cape Verde	CPV	..	..	..	..	..	..	**	..	..	..	..	..	..	..	..	..
Central African Republic	CAF	0.01	0.04	0.00	0.00	..	1.54	..	**	0.42	..	1.61	1.16	0.00	..	..	0.02
Chad	TCD	..	..	..	..	..	..	..	..	**	..	..	..	..	..	..	..
Comoros	COM	..	..	..	..	..	..	..	..	..	**	..	..	..	..	..	..
Congo, Democratic Rep. of	ZAR	..	..	..	..	..	..	..	..	..	..	**	..	..	..	..	..
Congo, Republic of	COG	0.05	0.60	0.00	..	..	0.01	..	0.00	..	..	0.63	**	0.00	..	0.08	0.00
Côte d'Ivoire	CIV	..	..	..	..	..	..	..	..	..	..	..	..	**	..	..	..
Djibouti	DJI	..	..	..	..	..	..	..	..	..	..	..	..	..	**	..	..
Egypt, Arab Rep.	EGY	0.91	0.02	0.00	0.00	0.00	0.01	..	..	..	0.00	0.01	0.10	0.21	0.02	**	0.00
Equatorial Guinea	GNQ	..	..	..	..	..	..	..	..	..	..	..	..	..	..	..	**
Ethiopia	ETH	0.02	..	..	..	..	..	..	..	..	..	0.01	..	0.00	9.13	0.71	..
Gabon	GAB	..	..	..	..	..	..	..	..	..	..	..	..	..	..	..	..
Gambia, The	GMB	..	..	..	..	..	..	..	..	..	..	..	..	..	..	..	..
Ghana	GHA	..	..	..	..	..	..	..	..	..	..	..	..	..	..	..	..
Guinea	GIN	..	..	..	..	..	..	..	..	..	..	..	..	..	..	..	..
Guinea-Bissau	GNB	..	..	..	..	..	..	..	..	..	..	..	..	..	..	..	..
Kenya	KEN	0.01	0.02	0.00	0.00	0.42	0.02	0.00	0.00	0.00	0.12	2.25	0.01	0.02	0.08	3.18	0.01
Liberia	LBR	..	..	..	..	..	..	..	..	..	..	..	..	..	..	..	..
Libya	LBY	..	..	..	..	..	..	..	..	..	..	..	..	..	..	..	..
Madagascar	MDG	1.43	..	0.01	0.00	0.00	0.00	0.06	0.01	0.00	1.29	0.01	0.01	0.04	0.02	0.02	..
Malawi	MWI	..	..	0.01	..	0.12	..	..	..	..	..	0.12	..	..	..	0.58	..
Mali	MLI	..	..	..	..	..	..	..	..	..	..	..	..	..	..	..	..
Mauritania	MRT	..	..	..	..	..	..	..	..	..	..	..	..	..	..	..	..
Mauritius	MUS	..	..	..	..	0.03	0.00	..	0.00	..	0.15	0.00	0.00	0.01	0.00	0.03	..
Morocco	MAR	1.19	0.05	0.05	0.02	..	0.09	0.01	0.01	0.00	0.00	0.18	0.07	0.41	0.00	0.08	0.02
Mozambique	MOZ	..	0.08	..	..	..	..	..	..	..	..	0.00	..	..	..	..	..
Niger	NER	..	..	..	..	..	..	..	..	..	..	..	..	..	..	..	..
Nigeria	NGA	..	..	..	..	..	..	..	..	..	..	..	..	..	..	..	..
Reunion	REU	..	..	..	..	..	..	..	..	..	..	4.72	..	0.02	0.00	..	..
Rwanda	RWA	..	..	..	..	..	..	..	..	..	..	..	..	..	..	..	..
South Africa	ZAF	0.00	0.44	0.00	0.00	0.01	0.04	0.00	0.01	0.00	0.07	0.69	0.04	0.11	0.00	0.09	0.01
São Tomé and Principe	STP	..	..	..	..	..	..	..	..	..	..	..	..	..	..	..	..
Senegal	SEN	0.13	0.03	2.55	0.89	..	1.64	0.50	0.18	0.25	..	0.00	0.36	1.54	..	0.03	0.00
Seychelles	SYC	..	..	..	..	..	..	..	..	..	..	..	..	..	..	..	..
Sierra Leone	SLE	..	..	..	..	..	..	..	..	..	..	..	..	..	..	..	..
Somalia	SOM	..	..	..	..	..	..	..	..	..	..	..	..	..	..	..	..
Sudan	SDN	..	..	..	..	..	..	..	..	..	..	0.00	..	..	0.23	3.04	..
Tanzania	TZA	..	..	..	..	..	..	..	..	..	..	..	..	..	..	..	..
Togo	TGO	..	..	..	..	..	..	..	..	..	..	..	..	..	..	..	..
Tunisia	TUN	3.39	0.01	0.01	0.02	..	0.15	..	0.00	0.00	..	0.00	0.00	0.10	0.00	0.45	0.00
Uganda	UGA	..	..	..	..	..	..	..	..	..	..	..	..	..	..	..	..
Zambia	ZMB	..	0.03	0.00	..	0.35	..	..	0.00	..	..	2.53	..	..	..	0.00	..
Zimbabwe	ZWE	0.03	0.63	0.00	0.00	0.08	0.03	..	0.00	..	0.00	0.46	0.00	0.03	..	0.49	..
Sub-Saharan Africa	SSA	0.06	0.18	0.13	0.05	0.12	0.10	0.02	0.12	0.07	0.08	0.77	0.18	0.16	0.36	0.81	0.21
European Community	EEC	0.30	0.05	0.02	0.01	0.01	0.04	0.01	0.00	0.00	0.01	0.02	0.03	0.08	0.01	0.32	0.00
North America	NNA	0.16	0.04	0.01	0.00	0.00	0.01	0.00	0.00	0.00	0.00	0.01	0.01	0.02	0.00	0.42	0.00
Rest Of World	ROW	0.09	0.02	0.01	0.00	0.00	0.01	0.00	0.00	0.00	0.00	0.02	0.00	0.02	0.01	0.27	0.00
World	WLD	0.19	0.04	0.01	0.01	0.00	0.02	0.00	0.00	0.00	0.00	0.02	0.02	0.05	0.01	0.32	0.00

Note: ** means "not applicable."

(Table continues on the following page.)

5-52. (continued)

Percentage of total exports

ETH	GAB	GMB	GHA	GIN	GNB	KEN	LBR	LBY	MDG	MWI	MLI	MRT	MUS	MAR	MOZ	NER	NGA	REU	RWA
..	..	..	..	0.00	..	..	0.15	0.02	0.00	..	0.00	0.21	..	0.87	..	0.00	0.00	..	..
..	..	..	..	..	..	..	..	..	..	..	..	..	..	..	..	..	..	..	..
..	..	..	..	..	..	..	..	..	..	..	..	..	..	..	..	..	..	..	..
..	..	..	..	..	..	..	..	..	..	..	..	..	..	..	..	..	..	..	..
..	1.59	..	0.03	0.08	0.00	0.03	..	0.10	0.02	..	0.04	0.00	0.32	0.33	0.03	0.01	0.55	0.13	..
..	0.00	..	..	..	..	..	..	..	0.00	..	..	0.01	..	0.01	..	0.01	0.18	..	..
..	..	..	..	..	..	..	..	..	..	..	..	..	..	..	..	..	..	..	..
..	0.02	..	0.00	0.00	..	..	..	..	..	..	0.01	0.00	0.01	0.83	..	0.00	0.01	0.33	..
..	..	..	..	..	..	..	..	..	..	..	..	..	..	..	..	..	..	..	..
0.04	0.00	0.00	0.03	0.00	0.00	0.10	0.00	1.54	0.00	0.00	0.01	0.00	0.00	0.44	0.00	0.00	0.05	..	0.00
**	..	0.00	0.00	..	..	0.02	0.03	..	..	..	..	..	..	..	0.00	..	..	..	0.00
..	**	..	..	..	..	..	..	..	..	..	..	..	..	..	..	..	..	..	..
..	..	**	..	..	..	..	..	..	..	..	..	..	..	..	..	..	..	..	..
..	..	..	**	..	..	..	..	..	..	..	..	..	..	..	..	..	..	..	..
..	..	..	..	**	..	..	..	..	..	..	..	..	..	..	..	..	..	..	..
..	..	..	..	..	**	..	..	..	..	..	..	..	..	..	..	..	..	..	..
2.92	0.00	0.00	0.02	0.00	..	**	..	0.00	0.02	0.16	..	0.01	0.49	0.01	0.07	..	0.17	..	1.87
..	..	..	..	..	..	..	**	..	..	..	..	..	..	..	..	..	..	..	..
..	..	..	..	..	..	..	..	**	..	..	..	..	..	..	..	..	..	..	..
..	0.00	..	..	0.00	..	0.03	0.00	0.00	**	0.02	0.01	..	2.69	0.12	0.21	0.00	0.03	5.74	0.00
0.00	0.00	0.24	..	0.07	0.01	0.15	..	..	0.00	**	..	..	0.14	0.10	1.30	..	0.02	0.00	0.00
..	..	..	..	..	..	..	..	..	..	..	**	..	..	..	..	..	..	..	..
..	..	..	..	..	..	..	..	..	..	..	..	**	..	..	..	..	..	..	..
..	0.00	..	..	..	..	0.11	..	0.00	2.59	0.03	..	0.00	**	0.00	0.01	0.00	0.01	1.83	0.06
..	0.15	0.01	0.10	0.24	0.00	0.01	0.00	3.42	0.01	..	0.14	0.16	0.04	**	0.00	0.01	0.17	0.02	0.00
0.06	..	..	..	..	..	0.06	..	..	0.03	1.51	..	..	0.07	..	**	..	..	..	0.07
..	..	..	..	..	..	..	..	..	..	..	..	..	..	..	..	**	..	..	..
..	..	..	..	..	..	..	..	..	..	..	..	..	..	..	..	..	**	..	..
0.15	0.07	..	..	..	..	0.00	..	..	3.18	0.01	..	0.00	1.95	0.00	0.00	..	..	**	..
..	..	..	..	..	..	..	..	..	..	..	..	..	..	..	..	..	..	..	**
0.02	0.02	0.01	0.17	0.01	0.00	0.93	0.01	0.00	0.16	0.68	0.06	0.00	0.68	0.06	2.20	0.01	0.18	0.18	0.01
..	0.16	1.67	0.14	1.27	0.78	0.00	0.01	..	0.05	..	8.53	2.20	..	0.13	..	0.14	2.24	..	..
..	..	..	..	..	..	0.03	..	..	..	..	..	..	0.99	..	..	..	..	6.72	..
..	..	..	..	..	..	..	..	..	..	..	..	..	..	..	..	..	..	..	..
0.04	0.00	..	..	..	..	0.06	..	0.04	..	..	0.00	..	..	..	..	0.00	0.00	..	..
..	..	..	..	..	..	..	..	..	..	..	..	..	..	..	..	..	..	..	..
..	0.01	0.00	0.04	0.02	0.00	..	0.00	3.51	0.00	..	0.01	0.02	0.00	0.49	0.00	0.00	0.01	0.02	..
..	..	..	..	..	..	..	..	..	..	..	..	..	..	..	..	..	..	..	..
0.07	..	..	..	..	..	0.23	..	..	..	0.81	0.00	..	..	..	0.01	..	..	..	0.02
0.01	..	0.00	0.15	..	..	0.18	..	0.15	0.00	2.70	..	0.00	0.32	0.04	2.80	0.00	0.09	0.01	0.01
0.47	0.22	0.09	0.04	0.07	0.04	0.08	0.00	0.04	0.35	0.56	0.39	0.10	0.26	0.14	0.52	0.01	0.22	0.48	0.31
0.03	0.03	0.00	0.05	0.02	0.00	0.06	0.08	0.15	0.02	0.00	0.02	0.02	0.03	0.30	0.01	0.01	0.13	0.10	0.00
0.02	0.01	0.00	0.03	0.01	0.00	0.02	0.01	0.01	0.00	0.00	0.00	0.01	0.00	0.09	0.01	0.00	0.08	0.00	0.01
0.02	0.01	0.01	0.03	0.01	0.00	0.07	0.19	0.08	0.01	0.01	0.01	0.01	0.05	0.07	0.04	0.00	0.09	0.01	0.00
0.03	0.02	0.00	0.04	0.01	0.00	0.06	0.11	0.10	0.01	0.01	0.01	0.01	0.04	0.17	0.02	0.00	0.10	0.05	0.00

Note: ** means "not applicable."

(Table continues on the following page.)

5-52. (continued)

Percentage of total exports

ZAF	STP	SEN	SYC	SLE	SOM	SDN	TZA	TGO	TUN	UGA	ZMB	ZWE	SSA	EEC	NNA	ROW	WLD
0.00	..	0.00	..	..	..	..	..	..	1.16	..	..	..	0.39	64.84	19.06	15.70	100.00
..	..	..	..	..	..	..	..	..	..	..	..	..	..	..	..	..	..
..	..	..	..	..	..	..	..	..	..	..	..	..	..	..	..	..	..
..	..	..	..	..	..	..	..	..	..	..	..	..	..	..	..	..	..
0.24	0.13	0.49	..	..	..	..	0.01	0.09	0.10	..	0.02	0.00	8.46	77.06	2.36	12.12	100.00
..	..	..	..	..	..	..	..	..	..	..	..	..	..	..	..	..	..
0.23	..	0.01	..	..	..	0.38	..	0.01	..	..	..	..	5.38	90.77	0.49	3.37	100.00
..	..	..	..	..	..	..	..	..	..	..	..	..	..	..	..	..	..
..	..	..	..	..	..	..	..	..	..	..	..	..	..	..	..	..	..
..	..	0.00	..	..	..	..	..	0.00	0.01	..	..	0.01	1.30	41.28	28.55	28.87	100.00
..	..	..	..	..	..	..	..	..	..	..	..	..	..	..	..	..	..
0.13	..	0.01	..	0.00	0.01	0.71	0.01	0.00	0.80	0.01	0.01	0.00	1.39	45.80	15.39	37.41	100.00
0.22	..	0.00	..	..	..	0.28	0.04	..	1.00	0.00	0.00	0.00	9.51	51.69	7.01	31.80	100.00
..	..	..	..	..	..	..	..	..	..	..	..	..	..	..	..	..	..
..	..	..	..	..	..	..	..	..	..	..	..	..	..	..	..	..	..
2.77	..	0.03	0.15	0.01	1.73	1.18	11.84	0.01	0.14	15.19	0.18	0.14	39.15	35.58	3.38	21.89	100.00
0.78	..	0.01	0.13	..	0.00	0.00	0.00	0.00	0.39	0.03	0.00	0.35	4.97	61.56	6.83	26.64	100.00
10.21	..	0.01	0.01	0.04	..	0.01	1.17	0.01	0.04	0.22	1.04	1.40	6.09	48.82	13.71	31.39	100.00
0.44	..	0.00	0.17	..	..	..	0.06	..	0.00	0.10	0.02	0.43	3.80	72.45	15.75	8.00	100.00
0.04	..	0.11	0.00	0.02	..	0.00	0.00	0.05	1.12	0.00	..	..	2.17	62.06	4.02	31.76	100.00
23.91	..	..	..	..	0.00	..	0.07	..	..	..	0.03	3.40	5.39	41.45	7.35	45.81	100.00
..	..	..	..	..	..	..	..	..	..	..	..	..	..	..	..	..	..
0.21	..	0.00	0.57	..	..	..	..	..	0.00	..	..	..	10.67	79.93	0.61	8.79	100.00
**	0.01	0.03	0.12	0.01	0.01	0.02	0.62	0.02	0.00	0.09	1.35	4.47	13.32	26.81	8.27	51.60	100.00
..	**	..	..	..	..	..	..	..	..	..	..	..	..	..	..	..	..
0.24	..	**	..	0.27	..	..	..	1.01	0.00	..	..	..	26.41	23.99	0.62	48.98	100.00
0.88	..	..	**	..	..	..	..	..	..	..	..	..	1.02	81.90	0.33	16.75	100.00
..	..	..	..	**	..	..	..	..	..	..	..	..	..	..	..	..	..
..	..	..	..	..	**	..	..	..	..	..	..	..	..	..	..	..	..
0.01	..	..	..	..	..	**	..	..	0.39	0.26	..	0.00	0.60	32.56	8.43	58.41	100.00
..	..	..	..	..	..	..	**	..	..	..	..	..	..	..	..	..	..
..	..	..	..	..	..	..	..	**	..	..	..	..	..	..	..	..	..
0.09	..	0.04	..	..	..	..	0.00	0.05	**	0.01	0.00	..	0.51	78.98	1.30	19.20	100.00
..	..	..	..	..	..	..	..	..	..	**	..	..	..	..	..	..	..
2.23	..	..	..	..	..	..	2.08	..	..	0.08	**	3.02	9.25	13.16	6.11	71.48	100.00
18.47	0.00	..	0.05	0.00	..	0.02	0.53	..	0.03	0.21	5.03	**	13.35	40.27	4.95	41.43	100.00
4.44	0.02	0.07	0.06	0.02	0.27	0.20	2.19	0.06	0.11	2.47	0.87	0.47	12.97	47.12	8.55	31.37	100.00
0.58	0.00	0.04	0.00	0.01	0.00	0.02	0.02	0.01	0.27	0.01	0.01	0.02	0.95	62.06	7.37	29.61	100.00
0.41	0.00	0.01	0.00	0.00	0.00	0.01	0.01	0.00	0.04	0.00	0.01	0.02	0.37	17.31	36.14	46.18	100.00
0.45	0.00	0.02	0.01	0.00	0.00	0.02	0.04	0.02	0.05	0.01	0.03	0.08	0.87	22.20	23.05	53.88	100.00
0.51	0.00	0.03	0.00	0.00	0.00	0.02	0.03	0.01	0.14	0.02	0.02	0.05	0.86	38.71	18.31	42.12	100.00

Note: ** means "not applicable."

5-53. Direction of trade matrix, current U.S. dollars, 1986

Importers — *Millions of current US dollars*

Exporters		DZA	AGO	BEN	BFA	BDI	CMR	CPV	CAF	TCD	COM	ZAR	COG	CIV	DJI	EGY	GNQ
Algeria	DZA	**	..	1	5	..	0	..	..	..	..	..	0	1	..	0	..
Angola	AGO	..	**	..	..	..	..	..	..	..	..	..	..	..	..	..	..
Benin	BEN	..	..	**	..	..	..	..	..	..	..	..	..	..	..	..	..
Burkina Faso	BFA	..	..	..	**	..	..	..	..	..	..	..	..	..	..	..	..
Burundi	BDI	..	..	..	..	**	..	..	..	..	..	..	..	..	..	..	..
Cameroon	CMR	9	1	0	0	..	**	..	12	15	..	0	16	9	0	0	5
Cape Verde	CPV	..	..	..	..	..	..	**	..	..	..	..	..	..	..	..	..
Central African Republic	CAF	..	..	..	..	..	..	..	**	..	..	..	..	..	..	..	..
Chad	TCD	..	..	..	..	..	..	..	..	**	..	..	..	..	..	..	..
Comoros	COM	..	..	..	..	..	..	..	..	..	**	..	..	..	..	..	..
Congo, Democratic Rep. of	ZAR	..	..	..	..	..	..	..	..	..	..	**	..	..	..	..	..
Congo, Republic of	COG	2	2	0	..	..	0	..	..	0	0	1	**	0	..	..	..
Côte d'Ivoire	CIV	..	..	..	..	..	..	..	..	..	..	..	..	**	..	..	..
Djibouti	DJI	0	..	..	..	..	..	..	..	0	0	0	..	..	**	0	..
Egypt, Arab Rep.	EGY	5	..	..	..	0	0	..	..	0	..	..	0	..	0	**	..
Equatorial Guinea	GNQ	..	..	..	..	..	..	..	..	..	..	..	..	..	..	..	**
Ethiopia	ETH	0	..	..	0	0	..	..	..	..	..	..	0	..	..	20	..
Gabon	GAB	..	..	..	..	..	..	..	..	..	..	..	..	..	..	..	..
Gambia, The	GMB	..	..	..	..	..	..	..	..	..	..	..	..	..	..	..	..
Ghana	GHA	..	..	..	..	..	..	..	..	..	..	..	..	..	..	..	..
Guinea	GIN	..	..	..	..	..	..	..	..	..	..	..	..	..	..	..	..
Guinea-Bissau	GNB	..	..	..	..	..	..	..	..	..	..	..	..	..	..	..	..
Kenya	KEN	0	2	0	0	11	0	1	0	..	1	14	0	1	3	6	..
Liberia	LBR	..	..	..	..	..	..	..	..	..	..	..	..	..	..	..	..
Libya	LBY	0	..	..	..	..	..	..	..	..	..	..	..	..	..	..	..
Madagascar	MDG	0	..	..	..	..	0	..	..	0	0	0	..	..	0	0	0
Malawi	MWI	..	..	..	..	1	0	..	..	..	..	5	..	0	..	4	..
Mali	MLI	..	..	..	..	..	..	..	..	..	..	..	..	..	..	..	..
Mauritania	MRT	..	..	..	..	..	..	..	..	..	..	..	..	..	..	..	..
Mauritius	MUS	0	..	0	..	..	0	..	..	..	0	..	0	0	0	2	..
Morocco	MAR	0	1	1	0	0	8	..	0	..	0	6	5	9	0	1	0
Mozambique	MOZ	..	..	..	..	..	..	..	..	..	..	..	..	..	..	..	..
Niger	NER	..	..	..	..	..	..	..	..	..	..	..	..	..	..	..	..
Nigeria	NGA	0	1	1	0	..	1	..	..	0	0	10	0	98	..	0	..
Reunion	REU	..	..	0	0	..	0	..	..	..	5	..	0	..	0	..	..
Rwanda	RWA	..	..	..	..	..	..	..	..	..	..	..	..	..	..	..	..
South Africa	ZAF	..	..	..	..	..	..	..	..	..	..	..	..	..	..	..	..
São Tomé and Principe	STP	..	..	..	..	..	..	..	..	..	..	..	..	..	..	..	..
Senegal	SEN	0	..	4	4	0	14	1	0	0	0	1	4	25	..	0	0
Seychelles	SYC	..	..	..	..	..	0	..	..	..	..	..	..	..	..	..	..
Sierra Leone	SLE	..	..	..	..	..	..	..	..	..	..	..	..	..	..	..	..
Somalia	SOM	..	..	..	..	..	..	..	..	..	..	..	..	..	..	..	..
Sudan	SDN	..	..	..	..	..	..	..	..	..	..	..	..	..	..	..	..
Tanzania	TZA	..	..	..	..	..	..	..	..	..	..	..	..	..	..	..	..
Togo	TGO	..	..	1	6	..	0	0	0	0	..	..	0	0	..	0	0
Tunisia	TUN	90	0	1	0	..	8	..	0	..	..	0	0	2	0	4	..
Uganda	UGA	..	..	..	..	..	..	..	..	..	..	..	..	..	..	..	..
Zambia	ZMB	..	..	..	..	..	..	..	..	..	..	..	..	..	..	..	..
Zimbabwe	ZWE	1	2	0	..	1	0	1	0	..	0	17	0	1	0	3	..
Sub-Saharan Africa	SSA	12	8	7	10	12	16	3	13	16	2	47	20	135	23	15	5
European Community	EEC	5412	567	238	201	95	1174	82	81	72	37	787	389	1077	114	4832	22
North America	NNA	584	87	19	10	2	43	..	1	4	17	116	10	65	4	1745	0
Rest Of World	ROW	1417	509	111	29	16	295	24	19	3	7	220	104	260	72	2469	2
World	WLD	7426	1170	374	250	124	1528	109	113	96	63	1169	524	1536	213	9061	30

Note: ** means "not applicable."

(Table continues on the following page.)

5-53. (continued)

Millions of current US dollars

ETH	GAB	GMB	GHA	GIN	GNB	KEN	LBR	LBY	MDG	MWI	MLI	MRT	MUS	MAR	MOZ	NER	NGA	REU	RWA
..	..	..	..	..	..	..	2	0	..	..	0	0	0	..	..	0	..	..	..
..	..	..	..	..	..	..	..	..	..	..	..	..	..	..	..	..	..	..	..
..	..	..	..	..	..	..	..	..	..	..	..	..	..	..	..	..	..	..	..
..	..	..	..	..	..	..	..	..	..	..	..	..	..	..	..	..	..	..	..
0	35	..	1	1	..	0	0	0	0	0	0	0	0	0	..	..	39	0	0
..	..	..	..	..	..	..	..	..	..	..	..	..	..	..	..	..	..	..	..
..	..	..	..	..	..	..	..	..	..	..	..	..	..	..	..	..	..	..	..
..	..	..	..	..	..	..	..	..	..	..	..	..	..	..	..	..	..	..	..
..	..	..	..	..	..	..	..	..	..	..	..	..	..	..	..	..	..	..	..
..	0	..	..	0	..	..	..	..	..	..	0	0	0	11	..	..	0	2	..
..	..	..	..	..	..	..	..	..	..	..	..	..	..	..	..	..	..	..	..
1	0	..	..	..	..	0	0	0	0	..	0	..	0	0	0	..	0	0	..
2	..	..	..	..	..	0	..	0	..	0	0	0	..	4	0	0	0	..	..
..	..	..	..	..	..	..	..	..	..	..	..	..	..	..	..	..	..	..	..
**	..	..	..	..	..	0	..	..	..	0	0	..	..	..	0	..	0	..	..
..	**	..	..	..	..	..	..	..	..	..	..	..	..	..	..	..	..	..	..
..	..	**	..	..	..	..	..	..	..	..	..	..	..	..	..	..	..	..	..
..	..	..	**	..	..	..	..	..	..	..	..	..	..	..	..	..	..	..	..
..	..	..	..	**	..	..	..	..	..	..	..	..	..	..	..	..	..	..	..
..	..	..	..	..	**	..	..	..	..	..	..	..	..	..	..	..	..	..	..
8	0	..	0	0	..	**	0	0	0	0	0	0	3	1	2	0	0	4	30
..	..	..	..	..	..	..	**	..	..	..	..	..	..	..	..	..	..	..	..
..	..	..	..	..	..	..	..	**	..	..	..	..	..	55	..	..	..	..	..
0	0	..	..	..	..	0	0	..	**	0	0	..	2	..	0	..	..	8	0
0	0	0	0	..	..	0	0	1	..	**	..	..	0	..	9	..	0	..	0
..	..	..	..	..	..	..	..	..	..	..	**	..	..	..	..	..	..	..	..
..	..	..	..	..	..	..	..	..	..	..	..	**	..	..	..	..	..	..	..
..	0	..	..	0	..	0	..	..	0	0	0	..	**	3	0	..	..	13	..
..	6	0	..	2	0	..	4	42	..	..	2	1	1	**	..	0	0	3	0
..	..	..	..	..	..	..	..	..	..	..	..	..	..	**	..	..	..	..	..
..	..	..	..	..	..	..	..	..	..	..	..	..	..	..	..	**	..	..	..
..	0	0	88	0	0	..	1	..	..	..	..	..	..	4	0	4	**	..	..
..	..	..	..	..	..	..	..	..	4	..	..	..	1	..	..	..	..	**	..
..	..	..	..	..	..	..	..	..	..	..	..	..	..	..	..	..	..	..	**
..	..	..	..	..	..	..	..	..	..	..	..	..	..	..	..	..	..	..	..
0	1	3	0	6	3	0	0	..	0	..	17	22	..	1	0	2	2	0	0
..	..	..	..	..	..	..	0	..	..	..	..	..	0	..	..	..	..	0	..
..	..	..	..	..	..	..	..	..	..	..	..	..	..	..	..	..	..	..	..
..	..	..	..	..	..	..	..	..	..	..	..	..	..	..	..	..	..	..	..
..	..	..	..	..	..	..	..	..	..	..	..	..	..	..	..	..	..	..	..
..	0	..	3	0	0	..	0	0	..	..	0	0	..	2	..	1	2	..	..
0	2	0	0	1	..	1	0	5	0	..	0	0	..	7	1	0	0	..	..
..	..	..	..	..	..	..	..	..	..	..	..	..	..	..	..	..	..	..	..
..	..	..	..	..	..	..	..	..	..	13	..	..	..	..	..	..	..	..	..
5	0	..	1	..	..	8	0	2	..	13	..	0	0	5	33	0	0	5	2
14	37	3	93	8	3	9	1	4	1	13	18	22	5	27	45	6	44	33	32
557	624	82	402	237	33	844	469	2669	185	90	224	284	232	2326	189	168	2956	755	104
126	34	14	105	26	25	107	66	97	26	3	17	16	11	507	28	2	419	1	4
217	94	32	138	46	11	409	1482	1340	73	20	24	30	212	417	117	22	1119	50	34
914	788	131	738	317	72	1369	2019	4110	285	126	283	351	460	3277	380	198	4538	838	175

Note: ** means "not applicable."

(Table continues on the following page.)

5-53. (continued)

Millions of current US dollars

ZAF	STP	SEN	SYC	SLE	SOM	SDN	TZA	TGO	TUN	UGA	ZMB	ZWE	SSA	EEC	NNA	ROW	WLD
..	..	0	..	2	..	..	..	..	39	..	..	..	11	5836	1363	620	7831
..	..	..	..	..	..	..	..	..	..	..	..	..	..	..	..	..	..
..	..	..	..	..	..	..	..	..	..	..	..	..	..	..	..	..	..
..	..	..	..	..	..	..	..	..	..	..	..	..	..	..	..	..	..
..	..	1	..	0	..	0	..	2	1	..	0	0	139	560	23	59	781
..	..	..	..	..	..	..	..	..	..	..	..	..	..	..	..	..	..
..	..	..	..	..	..	..	..	..	..	..	..	..	..	..	..	..	..
..	..	..	..	..	..	..	..	..	..	..	..	..	..	..	..	..	..
0	0	0	..	..	..	..	..	0	3	..	..	0	5	324	421	28	777
..	..	0	..	..	1	0	0	0	0	..	0	..	2	11	0	8	20
2	..	0	..	..	0	39	0	0	5	0	..	..	42	802	69	1301	2214
..	..	0	..	..	..	0	0	..	..	0	0	..	20	253	76	115	464
..	..	..	..	..	..	..	..	..	..	..	..	..	..	..	..	..	..
..	..	..	..	..	..	..	..	..	..	..	..	..	..	..	..	..	..
..	..	..	..	..	..	..	..	..	..	..	..	..	..	..	..	..	..
2	0	0	3	0	8	23	30	0	1	85	1	3	231	569	112	256	1168
..	..	..	..	..	..	27	..	..	1	..	..	..	27	5979	..	1740	7746
0	..	0	0	..	0	0	0	0	..	0	0	..	3	184	49	80	317
20	..	0	0	0	1	..	1	..	..	..	6	5	29	133	22	55	238
..	..	..	..	..	..	..	..	..	..	..	..	..	..	..	..	..	..
1	..	0	1	..	0	..	0	..	0	0	0	0	2	508	120	35	664
0	..	9	..	0	..	0	0	1	13	0	..	0	58	1440	46	883	2428
..	..	..	..	..	..	..	..	..	..	..	..	..	..	..	..	..	..
5	..	22	..	12	..	..	..	0	..	..	0	..	239	3117	2203	341	5900
0	..	..	0	..	..	..	..	..	..	..	0	0	10	115	0	5	130
..	..	..	..	..	..	..	..	..	..	..	..	..	..	..	..	..	..
**	..	..	..	..	..	..	..	..	..	..	..	..	..	..	..	..	..
..	**	..	..	..	..	..	..	..	..	..	..	..	..	..	..	..	..
0	..	**	..	0	..	..	0	4	0	0	0	0	114	271	2	238	625
0	..	..	**	..	..	..	..	..	..	..	..	..	0	1	0	1	2
..	..	..	..	**	..	..	..	..	..	..	..	..	..	..	..	..	..
..	..	..	..	..	**	..	..	..	..	..	..	..	..	..	..	..	..
..	..	..	..	..	..	**	..	..	..	..	..	..	..	..	..	..	..
..	..	..	..	..	..	..	**	..	..	..	..	..	..	..	..	..	..
..	..	0	..	0	..	..	..	**	1	..	..	..	14	114	26	49	204
..	..	1	..	0	..	0	0	0	**	0	..	..	18	1307	14	421	1760
..	..	..	..	..	..	..	..	..	..	**	..	..	..	..	..	..	..
..	..	..	..	..	..	..	..	..	..	..	**	..	..	..	..	..	..
172	..	0	0	0	0	1	3	0	1	1	29	**	117	445	63	394	1019
200	0	24	3	12	11	25	34	6	7	86	36	8	916	6489	3117	1657	12179
4875	8	568	48	85	184	495	372	301	2000	122	260	312	15374	538270	89375	221294	864314
1310	..	60	1	24	58	105	52	20	199	5	44	59	1836	58327	106841	122032	289035
2390	4	104	19	33	63	302	283	130	285	77	94	86	6941	157706	198569	304320	667537
8774	12	757	72	154	316	927	741	458	2492	289	434	465	25068	760792	397902	649304	1833066

Note: ** means "not applicable."

5-54. Direction of trade matrix, current U.S. dollars, 1990

Exporters		*Importers* DZA	AGO	BEN	BFA	BDI	CMR	CPV	CAF	TCD	COM	ZAR	COG	*Millions of current US dollars* CIV	DJI	EGY	GNQ
Algeria	DZA	**	..	..	0	..	..	..	..	..	..	..	0	0	3	20	..
Angola	AGO	..	**	..	..	..	..	..	..	..	..	..	0	1	..	..	..
Benin	BEN	..	..	**	..	..	..	..	..	..	..	..	..	..	..	..	..
Burkina Faso	BFA	..	..	..	**	..	..	..	..	..	..	..	..	..	..	..	..
Burundi	BDI	..	..	..	..	**	..	..	..	..	..	..	..	..	..	..	..
Cameroon	CMR	6	0	0	1	0	**	..	29	11	..	3	16	4	..	1	30
Cape Verde	CPV	..	..	..	..	..	..	**	..	..	..	..	..	..	..	..	..
Central African Republic	CAF	..	..	..	..	..	..	..	**	..	..	..	..	..	..	..	..
Chad	TCD	..	..	..	..	..	..	..	..	**	..	..	..	..	..	..	..
Comoros	COM	..	..	..	..	..	..	..	..	..	**	..	..	..	..	..	..
Congo, Democratic Rep. of	ZAR	..	..	..	..	..	..	..	..	..	..	**	..	..	..	..	..
Congo, Republic of	COG	..	..	..	..	..	..	..	..	..	..	..	**	..	..	..	..
Côte d'Ivoire	CIV	..	..	..	..	..	..	..	..	..	..	..	..	**	..	..	..
Djibouti	DJI	..	0	..	0	..	0	..	0	..	0	..	..	0	**	0	..
Egypt, Arab Rep.	EGY	5	0	0	..	0	0	..	..	0	..	0	0	1	0	**	0
Equatorial Guinea	GNQ	..	..	..	..	..	..	..	..	..	..	..	..	..	..	..	**
Ethiopia	ETH	..	0	..	..	0	..	..	1	0	..	..	0	0	35	0	..
Gabon	GAB	..	..	..	..	..	..	..	..	..	..	..	..	..	..	..	..
Gambia, The	GMB	..	..	..	..	..	..	..	..	..	..	..	..	..	..	..	..
Ghana	GHA	..	..	..	..	..	..	..	..	..	..	..	..	..	..	..	..
Guinea	GIN	..	..	..	..	..	..	..	..	..	..	..	..	..	..	..	..
Guinea-Bissau	GNB	..	..	..	..	..	..	..	..	..	..	..	..	..	..	..	..
Kenya	KEN	0	6	0	0	20	0	0	0	0	1	25	0	0	23	15	0
Liberia	LBR	..	..	..	..	..	..	..	..	..	..	..	..	..	..	..	..
Libya	LBY	6	..	..	1	..	..	..	..	..	..	..	..	..	..	79	..
Madagascar	MDG	0	..	0	..	0	0	..	..	..	2	..	0	0	0	0	0
Malawi	MWI	..	0	..	..	1	0	..	..	..	..	2	..	0	..	5	..
Mali	MLI	1	..	..	1	..	..	..	..	..	..	..	..	176	..	..	..
Mauritania	MRT	..	..	..	..	..	..	..	..	..	..	..	..	..	..	..	..
Mauritius	MUS	0	..	0	0	0	0	..	..	..	2	0	0	0	0	0	..
Morocco	MAR	57	5	2	1	..	6	..	1	..	0	7	5	7	0	4	1
Mozambique	MOZ	..	..	..	..	..	..	..	..	..	..	..	..	..	..	..	..
Niger	NER	..	..	..	..	..	..	..	..	..	..	..	..	..	..	..	..
Nigeria	NGA	..	..	..	..	..	..	..	..	..	..	..	..	..	..	..	..
Reunion	REU	..	..	..	..	..	..	..	..	..	8	0	..	0	0	..	..
Rwanda	RWA	..	..	..	..	..	..	..	..	..	..	..	..	..	..	..	..
South Africa	ZAF	..	..	..	..	..	..	..	..	..	..	..	..	..	..	..	..
São Tomé and Principe	STP	..	..	..	..	..	..	..	..	..	..	..	..	..	..	..	..
Senegal	SEN	..	..	4	3	0	20	0	0	0	..	1	6	22	..	0	..
Seychelles	SYC	..	..	..	..	..	..	..	..	..	..	..	..	..	..	..	..
Sierra Leone	SLE	..	..	..	..	..	..	..	..	..	..	..	..	..	..	..	..
Somalia	SOM	..	..	..	..	..	..	..	..	..	..	..	..	..	..	..	..
Sudan	SDN	..	..	..	..	..	..	..	..	..	..	..	..	..	..	..	..
Tanzania	TZA	..	..	..	..	..	..	..	..	..	..	..	..	..	..	..	..
Togo	TGO	0	..	6	9	..	0	1	0	0	..	0	0	1	0	..	0
Tunisia	TUN	81	..	1	0	0	10	..	..	0	..	..	1	8	1	4	..
Uganda	UGA	..	..	..	..	..	..	..	..	..	..	..	..	..	..	..	..
Zambia	ZMB	..	..	..	..	..	..	..	..	..	..	..	..	..	..	..	..
Zimbabwe	ZWE	0	12	0	..	3	0	0	..	..	..	14	0	0	0	4	..
Sub-Saharan Africa	SSA	7	17	10	14	24	20	1	31	12	5	44	22	203	58	26	30
European Community	EEC	6511	1100	220	238	115	948	116	107	101	70	884	439	1063	129	5509	52
North America	NNA	1196	167	25	16	1	72	6	1	8	0	145	90	85	8	2283	0
Rest Of World	ROW	1488	277	111	32	24	167	8	17	11	17	173	69	202	87	3227	4
World	WLD	9202	1562	366	300	164	1208	130	155	132	92	1246	620	1553	282	11046	88

Note: ** means "not applicable."   (Table continues on the following page.)

5-54. (continued)

Millions of current US dollars

ETH	GAB	GMB	GHA	GIN	GNB	KEN	LBR	LBY	MDG	MWI	MLI	MRT	MUS	MAR	MOZ	NER	NGA	REU	RWA
..	0	..	..	..	..	..	..	3	..	..	0	35	..	42	..	0	..	..	..
..	..	..	..	..	..	..	34	..	..	..	..	..	..	..	..	..	..	..	..
..	..	..	..	..	..	..	..	..	..	..	..	..	..	..	..	..	..	..	..
..	31	0	1	2	..	0	0	..	0	..	0	0	0	2	..	0	35	1	0
..	..	..	..	..	..	..	..	..	..	..	..	..	..	..	..	..	..	..	..
..	..	..	..	..	..	..	..	..	..	..	..	..	..	..	..	..	..	..	..
..	..	..	..	..	..	..	..	..	..	..	..	..	..	..	..	..	..	..	..
..	..	..	..	..	..	..	..	..	..	..	..	..	..	..	..	..	..	..	..
0	0	0	..	0	..	0	..	0	0	..	0	..	..	0	..	0	..	0	..
0	..	..	0	0	..	0	0	44	..	0	0	0	..	6	0	0	1	..	0
..	..	..	..	..	..	..	..	..	..	..	..	..	..	..	..	..	..	..	..
**	0	0	0	0	..	1	..	..	0	0	..	..	0	0	0	0	0	..	..
..	**	..	..	..	..	..	..	..	..	..	..	..	..	..	..	..	..	..	..
..	..	**	..	..	..	..	..	..	..	..	..	..	..	..	..	..	..	..	..
..	..	..	**	..	..	..	..	..	..	..	..	..	..	..	..	..	..	..	..
..	..	..	..	**	..	..	..	..	..	..	..	..	..	..	..	..	..	..	..
..	..	..	..	..	**	..	..	..	..	..	..	..	..	..	..	..	..	..	..
8	0	..	0	0	..	**	0	0	0	1	..	0	3	0	1	..	2	4	75
..	..	..	..	..	..	..	**	..	..	..	..	..	..	..	..	..	..	..	..
..	..	..	0	0	..	..	..	**	..	..	0	0	..	115	..	0	0	..	..
0	0	..	..	0	..	1	..	..	**	0	0	0	7	0	6	0	0	15	0
0	0	3	0	1	..	0	..	..	..	**	..	..	0	..	1	..	0	..	1
..	0	..	0	1	..	..	..	..	..	..	**	0	..	..	..	0	0	..	..
..	..	..	..	..	..	..	..	..	..	..	..	**	..	..	..	..	..	..	..
0	0	..	0	0	..	1	0	..	10	0	0	0	**	3	0	..	0	22	0
..	8	0	4	6	0	..	1	119	1	0	6	4	2	**	..	1	12	2	..
..	..	..	..	..	..	..	..	..	..	..	..	..	..	..	**	..	..	..	..
..	..	..	..	..	..	..	..	..	..	..	..	..	..	..	..	**	..	..	..
..	..	..	..	..	..	..	..	..	..	..	..	..	..	..	..	..	**	..	..
..	..	..	..	..	..	0	..	..	6	..	..	3	..	..	..	..	..	**	..
..	..	..	..	..	..	..	..	..	..	..	..	..	..	..	..	..	..	..	**
..	..	..	..	..	..	..	..	..	..	..	..	..	..	..	..	..	..	..	..
0	3	7	1	15	4	0	1	..	0	0	56	0	..	1	..	0	4	..	..
..	..	..	..	..	..	0	..	..	..	..	..	..	0	..	..	..	..	3	..
..	..	..	..	..	..	..	..	..	..	..	..	..	..	..	..	..	..	..	..
..	..	..	..	..	..	..	..	..	..	..	..	..	..	..	..	..	..	..	..
..	1	0	4	4	0	0	0	0	..	..	1	..	..	3	0	4	9	0	..
..	0	..	9	0	1	..	0	161	..	..	0	2	..	24	..	0	0	..	0
..	..	..	..	..	..	..	..	..	..	..	..	..	..	..	..	..	..	..	..
1	0	..	1	0	..	18	0	0	0	71	0	..	1	0	54	0	1	0	1
10	34	10	7	23	4	21	35	1	10	72	57	1	11	9	62	5	50	45	77
572	540	103	653	325	70	1116	1286	3403	329	152	273	334	503	4577	361	186	3184	1493	110
175	53	9	148	48	1	163	45	45	13	16	13	16	12	685	73	14	568	5	2
178	87	55	315	70	23	511	2540	1474	113	42	35	105	486	954	218	29	1400	89	34
936	714	177	1124	466	99	1811	3907	4923	466	282	377	456	1012	6225	713	234	5201	1633	223

Note: ** means "not applicable."

(Table continues on the following page.)

5-54. (continued)

Millions of current US dollars

ZAF	STP	SEN	SYC	SLE	SOM	SDN	TZA	TGO	TUN	UGA	ZMB	ZWE	SSA	EEC	NNA	ROW	WLD
..	..	0	..	..	..	..	..	0	177	1	..	..	40	7674	2154	1143	11011
0	2	..	..	..	..	..	..	2	..	..	..	..	39	1476	2096	300	3910
..	..	..	..	..	..	..	..	..	..	..	..	..	..	..	..	..	..
..	..	..	..	..	..	..	..	..	..	..	..	..	..	..	..	..	..
0	0	4	..	0	..	..	0	1	3	..	..	..	168	1594	158	160	2081
..	..	..	..	..	..	..	..	..	..	..	..	..	..	..	..	..	..
..	..	..	..	..	..	..	..	..	..	..	..	..	..	..	..	..	..
..	..	..	..	..	..	..	..	..	..	..	..	..	..	..	..	..	..
..	..	..	..	..	..	..	..	..	..	..	..	..	..	..	..	..	..
..	..	0	..	..	0	0	0	..	0	0	..	..	1	14	0	10	25
0	..	0	..	0	0	21	0	..	18	0	0	0	24	1004	228	1326	2582
..	..	..	..	..	..	..	..	..	..	..	..	..	..	..	..	..	..
0	..	0	..	..	..	0	0	..	..	0	0	0	37	118	33	106	294
..	..	..	..	..	..	..	..	..	..	..	..	..	..	..	..	..	..
..	..	..	..	..	..	..	..	..	..	..	..	..	..	..	..	..	..
..	..	..	..	..	..	..	..	..	..	..	..	..	..	..	..	..	..
1	0	..	..	0	16	15	21	0	1	189	2	8	416	345	30	229	1020
..	..	..	..	..	..	..	..	..	..	..	..	..	..	..	..	..	..
..	..	2	..	..	..	151	31	..	72	..	..	..	186	11711	0	1980	13877
0	..	0	0	..	1	0	2	0	0	..	..	..	19	153	52	68	292
31	..	0	..	0	0	0	1	0	..	0	6	7	22	204	49	127	402
..	..	62	..	..	..	..	..	0	..	..	..	..	241	86	0	4	330
..	..	..	..	..	..	..	..	..	..	..	..	..	..	..	..	..	..
7	..	0	3	..	0	0	0	0	0	0	0	3	20	940	161	100	1221
0	..	5	..	0	..	0	0	4	62	..	..	..	86	2788	96	1261	4231
..	..	..	..	..	..	..	..	..	..	..	..	..	..	..	..	..	..
..	..	..	..	..	..	..	..	..	..	..	..	..	..	..	..	..	..
1	..	..	1	..	..	..	..	..	..	..	0	..	18	159	0	9	186
..	..	..	..	..	..	..	..	..	..	..	..	..	..	..	..	..	..
**	..	..	..	..	..	..	..	..	..	..	..	..	..	..	..	20397	20397
..	**	..	..	..	..	..	..	..	..	..	..	..	..	..	..	..	..
..	..	**	..	0	..	..	..	5	3	..	0	0	153	418	2	211	783
0	..	..	**	..	..	..	..	..	..	..	..	..	0	9	0	4	14
..	..	..	..	**	..	..	..	..	..	..	..	..	..	..	..	..	..
..	..	..	..	..	**	..	..	..	..	..	..	..	..	..	..	..	..
..	..	..	..	..	..	**	..	..	..	..	..	..	..	..	..	..	..
..	..	..	..	..	..	..	**	..	..	..	..	..	..	..	..	..	..
0	..	0	..	..	..	..	..	**	1	..	..	..	39	110	36	83	268
..	..	1	..	0	..	1	0	2	**	..	1	0	38	2733	33	695	3498
..	..	..	..	..	..	..	..	..	..	**	..	..	..	..	..	..	..
..	..	..	..	..	..	..	..	..	..	..	**	..	..	..	..	..	..
222	0	0	0	0	0	1	12	0	0	6	51	**	248	618	107	495	1468
261	2	67	4	1	18	15	35	8	9	194	59	17	1403	6084	2724	1897	12108
7498	27	808	72	118	190	425	563	355	3860	202	370	465	19277	974784	117003	364889	1475953
1893	14	63	3	28	14	48	65	33	224	29	89	152	2531	107561	172446	213986	496524
2667	6	167	43	34	40	416	281	184	787	77	149	186	9021	295884	277348	598589	1180842
12319	49	1104	122	180	262	905	945	580	4879	502	667	820	32233	1384313	569521	1179362	3165428

Note: ** means "not applicable."

5-55. Direction of trade matrix, current U.S. dollars, 1995

Exporters		Importers DZA	AGO	BEN	BFA	BDI	CMR	CPV	CAF	TCD	COM	ZAR	COG	CIV	DJI	Millions of current US dollars EGY	GNQ
Algeria	DZA	**	..	..	0	..	..	0	..	3	..	..	0	..	..	5	..
Angola	AGO	..	**	..	..	..	..	..	..	..	..	..	..	..	..	..	..
Benin	BEN	..	..	**	..	..	..	..	..	..	..	..	..	..	..	..	..
Burkina Faso	BFA	..	..	..	**	..	..	..	..	..	..	..	..	..	..	..	..
Burundi	BDI	..	..	..	..	**	..	..	..	..	..	..	..	..	..	..	..
Cameroon	CMR	0	2	2	0	0	**	..	13	6	..	..	3	18	9	..	0	25
Cape Verde	CPV	..	..	..	..	..	..	**	..	..	..	..	..	..	..	..	..
Central African Republic	CAF	0	0	0	0	..	2	..	**	0	..	2	1	0	..	..	0
Chad	TCD	..	..	..	..	..	..	•	..	**	..	..	..	..	..	..	..
Comoros	COM	..	..	..	..	..	.	..	..	..	**	..	..	..	..	..	..
Congo, Democratic Rep. of	ZAR	..	..	..	..	..	..	..	..	..	..	**	..	..	..	..	..
Congo, Republic of	COG	1	6	0	..	..	0	..	0	..	..	7	**	0	..	1	0
Côte d'Ivoire	CIV	..	..	..	..	..	..	..	..	..	..	..	..	**	..	..	..
Djibouti	DJI	..	..	..	..	..	..	..	..	..	..	..	..	..	**	..	..
Egypt, Arab Rep.	EGY	31	1	0	0	0	0	..	..	0	..	0	4	7	1	**	0
Equatorial Guinea	GNQ	..	..	..	..	..	..	..	..	..	..	..	..	..	..	..	**
Ethiopia	ETH	0	..	..	..	..	..	..	..	..	..	0	..	0	39	3	..
Gabon	GAB	..	..	..	..	..	..	..	..	..	..	..	..	..	..	..	..
Gambia, The	GMB	..	..	..	..	..	..	..	..	..	..	..	..	..	..	..	..
Ghana	GHA	..	..	..	..	..	..	..	..	..	..	..	..	..	..	..	..
Guinea	GIN	..	..	..	..	..	..	..	..	..	..	..	..	..	..	..	..
Guinea-Bissau	GNB	..	..	..	..	..	..	..	..	..	..	..	..	..	..	..	..
Kenya	KEN	0	0	0	0	8	0	0	0	0	2	41	0	0	1	58	..
Liberia	LBR	..	..	..	..	..	..	..	..	..	..	..	..	..	..	..	..
Libya	LBY	..	..	..	..	..	..	..	..	..	..	..	..	..	..	..	..
Madagascar	MDG	5	..	0	0	0	0	0	0	0	5	0	0	0	0	0	..
Malawi	MWI	..	..	0	..	1	..	..	..	..	..	0	..	..	..	2	..
Mali	MLI	..	..	..	..	..	..	..	..	..	..	..	..	..	..	..	..
Mauritania	MRT	..	..	..	..	..	..	..	..	..	..	..	..	..	..	..	..
Mauritius	MUS	..	..	..	..	0	0	..	0	..	2	0	0	0	0	0	..
Morocco	MAR	56	3	2	1	..	4	0	0	0	0	9	3	19	0	4	1
Mozambique	MOZ	..	0	..	..	..	..	..	..	..	..	0	..	..	..	..	..
Niger	NER	..	..	..	..	..	..	..	..	:	..	..	..	..	..	..	..
Nigeria	NGA	..	..	..	..	..	..	..	..	..	..	..	..	..	..	..	..
Reunion	REU	..	..	..	..	..	..	..	..	..	10	..	..	0	0	..	..
Rwanda	RWA	..	..	..	..	..	..	..	..	..	..	..	..	..	..	..	..
South Africa	ZAF	1	123	1	1	4	10	0	1	0	20	195	12	30	1	25	1
São Tomé and Principe	STP	..	..	..	..	..	..	..	..	..	..	..	..	..	..	..	..
Senegal	SEN	1	0	13	5	..	9	3	1	1	..	0	2	8	..	0	0
Seychelles	SYC	..	..	..	..	..	..	..	..	..	..	..	..	..	..	..	..
Sierra Leone	SLE	..	..	..	..	..	..	..	..	..	..	..	..	..	..	..	..
Somalia	SOM	..	..	..	..	..	..	..	..	..	..	..	..	..	..	..	..
Sudan	SDN	..	..	..	..	..	..	..	..	..	..	0	..	..	..	2	20
Tanzania	TZA	..	..	..	..	..	..	..	..	..	..	..	..	..	..	..	..
Togo	TGO	..	..	..	..	..	..	..	..	..	..	..	..	..	..	..	..
Tunisia	TUN	185	0	0	1	..	8	..	0	0	..	0	0	6	0	25	0
Uganda	UGA	..	..	..	..	..	..	..	..	..	..	..	..	..	..	..	..
Zambia	ZMB	..	0	0	..	4	..	..	0	..	..	27	..	..	..	0	..
Zimbabwe	ZWE	1	12	0	0	2	1	..	0	..	0	8	0	1	..	9	..
Sub-Saharan Africa	SSA	7	21	16	5	14	11	3	14	8	9	89	21	19	42	94	25
European Community	EEC	6057	1040	401	208	102	735	192	82	92	108	456	620	1538	130	6394	43
North America	NNA	1137	262	39	17	4	58	7	6	11	1	104	55	182	10	3089	5
Rest Of World	ROW	1694	336	234	33	42	165	21	41	14	43	406	64	464	181	5085	9
World	WLD	8894	1659	689	263	161	970	222	143	125	160	1055	760	2202	363	14662	82

Note: ** means "not applicable."

(Table continues on the following page.)

5-55. (continued)

Millions of current US dollars

ETH	GAB	GMB	GHA	GIN	GNB	KEN	LBR	LBY	MDG	MWI	MLI	MRT	MUS	MAR	MOZ	NER	NGA	REU	RWA
..	..	..	..	0	..	..	14	2	0	..	0	20	..	81	..	0	0	..	..
..	..	..	..	..	..	..	..	..	..	..	..	..	..	..	..	..	..	..	..
..	..	..	..	..	..	..	..	..	..	..	..	..	..	..	..	..	..	..	..
..	..	..	..	..	..	..	..	..	..	..	..	..	..	..	..	..	..	..	..
..	24	..	0	1	0	0	..	2	0	..	1	0	5	5	1	0	8	2	..
..	..	..	..	..	..	..	..	..	..	..	..	..	..	..	..	..	..	..	..
..	0	..	..	..	..	..	..	..	0	..	..	0	..	0	..	0	0	..	..
..	..	..	..	..	..	..	..	..	..	..	..	..	..	..	..	..	..	..	..
..	..	..	..	..	..	..	..	..	..	..	..	..	..	..	..	..	..	..	..
..	0	..	0	0	..	..	..	..	..	..	0	0	0	..	9	0	0	4	..
..	..	..	..	..	..	..	..	..	..	..	..	..	..	..	..	..	..	..	..
1	0	0	1	0	0	3	0	53	0	0	0	0	0	15	0	0	2	..	0
**	..	0	0	..	..	0	0	..	..	..	..	..	..	..	0	..	..	..	0
..	**	..	..	..	..	..	..	..	..	..	..	..	..	..	..	..	..	..	..
..	..	**	..	..	..	..	..	..	..	..	..	..	..	..	..	..	..	..	..
..	..	..	**	..	..	..	..	..	..	..	..	..	..	..	..	..	..	..	..
..	..	..	..	**	..	..	..	..	..	..	..	..	..	..	..	..	..	..	..
..	..	..	..	..	**	..	..	..	..	..	..	..	..	..	..	..	..	..	..
53	0	0	0	0	..	**	..	0	0	3	..	0	9	0	1	..	3	..	34
..	..	..	..	..	..	..	**	..	..	..	..	..	..	..	..	..	..	..	..
..	0	..	..	0	..	0	0	0	**	0	0	..	9	0	1	0	0	20	0
0	0	1	..	0	0	1	..	..	0	**	..	..	1	0	5	..	0	0	0
..	..	..	..	..	..	..	..	..	..	..	**	..	..	..	..	..	..	..	..
..	..	..	..	..	..	..	..	..	..	..	..	**	..	..	..	..	..	..	..
..	0	..	..	..	..	2	..	0	40	1	..	0	**	0	0	0	0	28	1
..	7	1	5	11	0	1	0	161	1	..	7	8	2	**	0	1	8	1	0
0	..	..	..	..	..	0	..	..	0	3	..	..	0	..	**	..	..	..	0
..	..	..	..	..	..	..	..	..	..	..	..	..	..	..	..	**	..	..	..
..	..	..	..	..	..	..	..	..	..	..	..	..	..	..	..	..	**	..	..
0	0	..	..	..	..	0	..	..	7	0	..	0	4	0	0	..	..	**	..
..	..	..	..	..	..	..	..	..	..	..	..	..	..	..	..	..	..	..	**
4	6	2	48	2	0	260	3	0	45	192	18	0	191	17	618	2	51	51	3
..	..	..	..	..	..	..	..	..	..	..	..	..	..	..	..	..	..	..	..
..	1	9	1	7	4	0	0	..	0	..	45	12	..	1	..	1	12	..	..
..	..	..	..	..	..	0	..	..	..	..	..	..	0	..	..	..	..	2	..
..	..	..	..	..	..	..	..	..	..	..	..	..	..	..	..	..	..	..	..
0	0	..	..	..	..	0	..	0	..	..	0	..	..	..	..	0	0	..	..
..	..	..	..	..	..	..	..	..	..	..	..	..	..	..	..	..	..	..	..
..	..	..	..	..	..	..	..	..	..	..	..	..	..	..	..	..	..	..	..
..	1	0	2	1	0	..	0	192	0	..	1	1	0	27	0	0	0	1	..
..	..	..	..	..	..	..	..	..	..	..	..	..	..	..	..	..	..	..	..
1	..	..	..	..	..	2	..	..	..	9	0	..	..	..	0	..	..	..	..
0	..	0	3	..	..	3	..	3	0	50	..	0	6	1	52	0	2	0	0
55	26	10	4	8	4	9	0	5	41	65	46	12	30	16	60	1	26	56	36
637	554	92	990	365	60	1141	1627	2975	328	89	307	330	686	6074	186	156	2572	1944	72
155	55	6	191	69	1	126	42	49	10	23	30	45	22	650	62	18	609	4	41
322	117	106	589	135	54	1365	3502	1496	182	243	110	139	890	1343	757	44	1631	189	23
1169	752	213	1774	579	119	2642	5171	4524	561	419	493	526	1628	8083	1065	219	4837	2193	172

Note: ** means "not applicable."

(Table continues on the following page.)

5-55. (continued)

Millions of current US dollars

ZAF	STP	SEN	SYC	SLE	SOM	SDN	TZA	TGO	TUN	UGA	ZMB	ZWE	SSA	EEC	NNA	ROW	WLD
0	..	0	..	..	..	..	..	..	108	..	..	..	37	6067	1784	1469	9357
..	..	..	..	..	..	..	..	..	..	..	..	..	..	..	..	..	..
..	..	..	..	..	..	..	..	..	..	..	..	..	..	..	..	..	..
..	..	..	..	..	..	..	..	..	..	..	..	..	..	..	..	..	..
4	2	8	..	..	..	..	0	1	2	..	0	0	130	1186	36	187	1539
..	..	..	..	..	..	..	..	..	..	..	..	..	..	..	..	..	..
0	..	0	..	..	..	0	..	0	..	..	..	..	6	108	1	4	119
..	..	..	..	..	..	..	..	..	..	..	..	..	..	..	..	..	..
..	..	..	..	..	..	..	..	..	..	..	..	..	..	..	..	..	..
..	..	0	..	..	..	..	..	0	0	..	..	0	14	450	311	315	1090
..	..	..	..	..	..	..	..	..	..	..	..	..	..	..	..	..	..
..	..	..	..	..	..	..	..	..	..	..	..	..	..	..	..	..	..
5	..	0	..	0	0	24	0	0	27	1	0	0	48	1577	530	1289	3444
..	..	..	..	..	..	..	..	..	..	..	..	..	..	..	..	..	..
1	..	0	..	..	..	1	0	..	4	0	0	0	40	218	30	134	422
..	..	..	..	..	..	..	..	..	..	..	..	..	..	..	..	..	..
..	..	..	..	..	..	..	..	..	..	..	..	..	..	..	..	..	..
..	..	..	..	..	..	..	..	..	..	..	..	..	..	..	..	..	..
..	..	..	..	..	..	..	..	..	..	..	..	..	..	..	..	..	..
51	..	1	3	0	32	21	216	0	3	277	3	3	714	649	62	399	1825
..	..	..	..	..	..	..	..	..	..	..	..	..	..	..	..	..	..
..	..	..	..	..	..	..	..	..	..	..	..	..	..	..	..	..	..
3	..	0	0	..	..	0	0	0	1	0	0	1	17	216	24	93	350
43	..	0	0	0	..	0	5	0	0	1	4	6	26	206	58	132	421
..	..	..	..	..	..	..	..	..	..	..	..	..	..	..	..	..	..
7	..	0	3	..	..	..	1	..	0	2	0	7	58	1114	242	123	1538
2	..	5	0	1	..	0	0	2	53	0	..	..	102	2929	189	1499	4719
41	..	..	..	..	0	..	0	..	..	..	0	6	9	71	13	79	172
..	..	..	..	..	..	..	..	..	..	..	..	..	..	..	..	..	..
..	..	..	..	..	..	..	..	..	..	..	..	..	..	..	..	..	..
0	..	0	1	..	..	..	..	..	0	..	..	..	22	167	1	18	209
..	..	..	..	..	..	..	..	..	..	..	..	..	..	..	..	..	..
**	2	8	34	3	3	5	173	5	1	26	378	1254	3734	7518	2318	14468	28039
..	**	..	..	..	..	..	..	..	..	..	..	..	..	..	..	..	..
1	..	**	..	1	..	..	..	5	0	..	..	..	139	126	3	258	527
0	..	..	**	..	..	..	..	..	..	..	..	..	0	20	0	4	24
..	..	..	..	**	..	..	..	..	..	..	..	..	..	..	..	..	..
..	..	..	..	..	**	..	..	..	..	..	..	..	..	..	..	..	..
0	..	..	..	..	..	**	..	..	3	2	..	0	4	217	56	389	666
..	..	..	..	..	..	..	**	..	..	..	..	..	..	..	..	..	..
..	..	..	..	..	..	..	..	**	..	..	..	..	..	..	..	..	..
5	..	2	..	..	..	..	0	3	**	0	0	..	28	4324	71	1051	5475
..	..	..	..	..	..	..	..	..	..	**	..	..	..	..	..	..	..
24	..	..	..	..	..	..	22	..	..	1	**	32	98	139	65	754	1055
341	0	..	1	0	..	0	10	..	1	4	93	**	246	743	91	764	1845
515	2	8	7	2	32	23	254	7	13	286	101	54	1503	5462	991	3636	11592
11598	32	826	68	108	26	363	414	277	5413	240	194	486	18973	1240684	147413	591992	1999062
3011	2	75	7	18	9	45	76	19	290	30	57	133	2738	126605	264341	337767	731451
8438	6	310	115	59	75	377	706	283	886	183	572	1524	16471	418506	434498	1015836	1885310
23562	42	1220	197	187	141	808	1450	587	6602	739	924	2198	39685	1791257	847244	1949231	4627416

Note: ** means "not applicable."

Figure 5-1. Terms of trade gains and losses, average 1992-98*

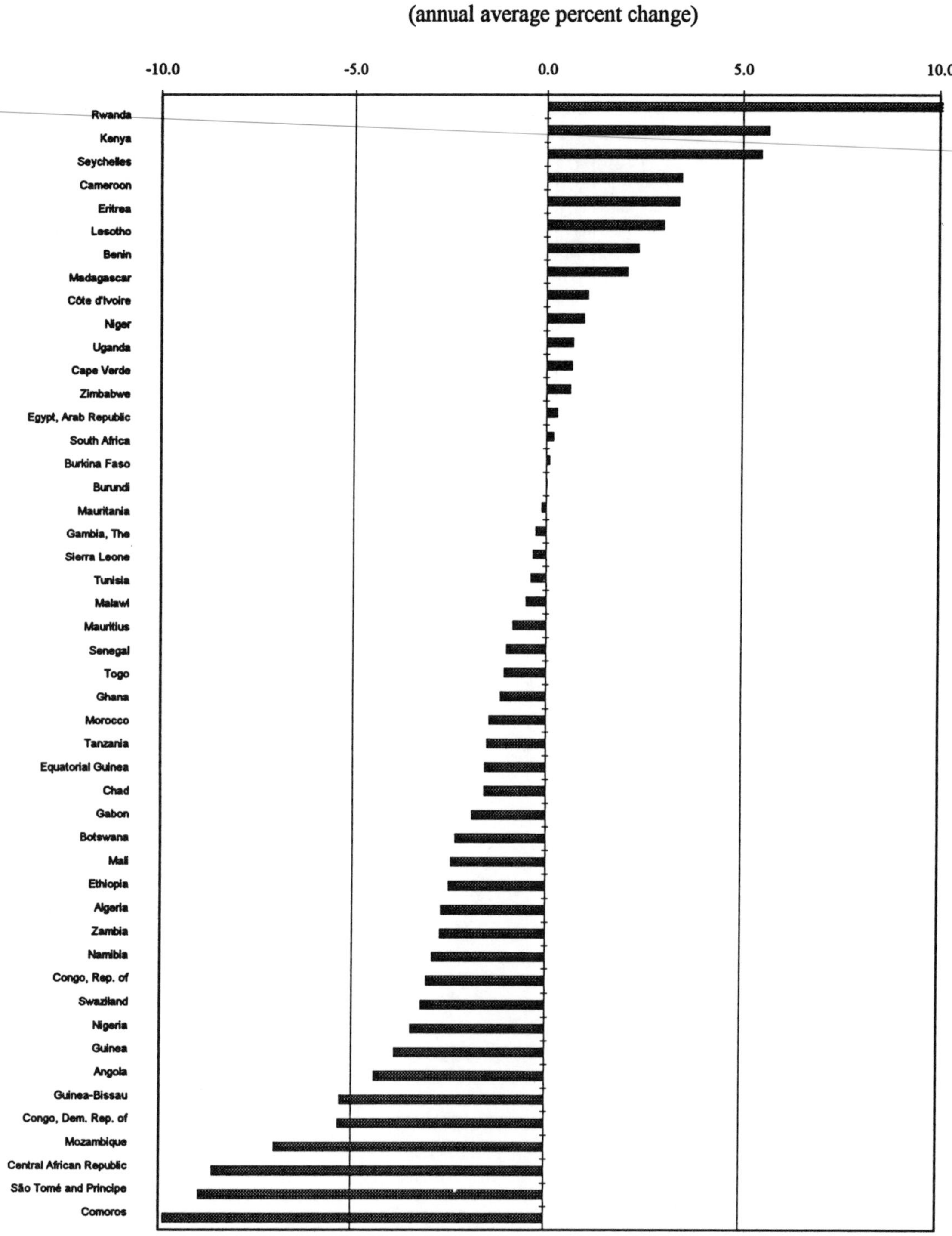

(annual average percent change)

	-10.0	-5.0	0.0	5.0	10.0

Rwanda
Kenya
Seychelles
Cameroon
Eritrea
Lesotho
Benin
Madagascar
Côte d'Ivoire
Niger
Uganda
Cape Verde
Zimbabwe
Egypt, Arab Republic
South Africa
Burkina Faso
Burundi
Mauritania
Gambia, The
Sierra Leone
Tunisia
Malawi
Mauritius
Senegal
Togo
Ghana
Morocco
Tanzania
Equatorial Guinea
Chad
Gabon
Botswana
Mali
Ethiopia
Algeria
Zambia
Namibia
Congo, Rep. of
Swaziland
Nigeria
Guinea
Angola
Guinea-Bissau
Congo, Dem. Rep. of
Mozambique
Central African Republic
São Tomé and Principe
Comoros

* Or most recent year available.

Technical Notes

Tables

Tables 5-1 and 5-2. Merchandise exports and merchandise imports, f.o.b. Merchandise exports and imports (World Bank country desks) are both valued f.o.b. and comprise all transactions involving a change of ownership of goods, including nonmonetary gold, between residents of a country and the rest of the world. These transactions include those in which ownership changes even though goods do not cross customs borders. The few types of goods not covered by the merchandise account include travelers' purchases abroad, which are included in travel, and purchases of goods by diplomatic and military personnel, which are classified under other official goods, services, and income.

Tables 5-3 and 5-4. Exports and imports of total services. Service exports and imports (World Bank country desks) include total nonfactor and factor services, based on transactions involving ownership changes as explained above for goods. Nonfactor services comprise shipment, passenger and other transport services, and travel, as well as current account transactions not separately reported (that is, not classified as merchandise, nonfactor services, or transfers). These include transactions with nonresidents by government agencies and their personnel abroad, as well as transactions by private residents with foreign governments and government personnel stationed in the reporting country. Factor services comprise services of labor and capital, thus covering income from direct investment abroad, interest, dividends, and property and labor income. Net interest is recorded on an accrual basis; that is, interest obligations are included whether payments are made or not.

Table 5-5. Net private transfers. Net private transfers (World Bank country desks) are inflows (from private sources to either private or public recipients) less outflows from private sources to either private or public recipients that carry no provisions for repayments. They include workers' remittances; transfers by migrants; gifts, dowries, and inheritances; and alimony and other support remittances.

Table 5-6. Net current official transfers. Net official transfers (World Bank country desks) are the official sources counterpart of Table 5-5. They include transfers on both current and capital accounts, including government grants of real resources and financial items such as subsidies to current budgets, grants of technical assistance, and government contributions to international organizations for administrative expenses.

Table 5-7. Current account balance, excluding net capital grants. Current account balance (World Bank country desks), as presented here, is the difference between exports of goods and all services plus inflows of unrequited current transfers (official and private) and imports of goods and all services plus outflows of unrequited transfers to the rest of the world. Other common presentations exclude or include both current and capital official transfers. Data in previous volumes included both.

Table 5-8. Current account balance, excluding net capital grants, as a percentage of GDP. It is defined as the ratio of figures presented in Table 5-7 to GDP in current prices (Table 2-5).

Table 5-9. Net capital grants. These grants (World Bank country desks) are unrequited transfers, often used to finance balance of payments deficits.

Table 5-10. Net foreign direct investment. Net foreign direct investment (World Bank country desks) is the net amount invested or reinvested by nonresidents to acquire a lasting interest in enterprises in which they exercise significant managerial control. Investment includes equity capital, reinvested earnings, and other capital. The net figures subtract the value of direct investment abroad by residents of the reporting country.

Table 5-11. Net long-term borrowing. Net long-term borrowing is calculated as disbursements less the repayment of principal (amortization) of public, publicly guaranteed, and private nonguaranteed borrowings that have an original or extended maturity of more than one year and that are repayable in foreign currencies, goods, or services. These data are as reported in the World Bank's Debtor Reporting System (DRS) and are in accord with the data on external debt discussed in Chapter 6.

Table 5-12. Other capital flows. Other capital flows comprise the net balance of inflows and outflows of capital not elsewhere included. It covers, for example, changes in the stock of short-term debt, arrears, and other liabilities (all adjusted for valuation changes resulting from exchange rate changes and other factors), and errors and omissions. This table incorporates corrections to data in *ADI 1992*.

Table 5-13. Use of reserves. This table (World Bank country desks) shows the variation from year to year of the net balance of international reserve assets and is valued throughout at year-end London prices (for example, US$37.37 an ounce in 1970 and US$484.10 an ounce in 1987). Positive numbers represent a decrease or use of reserves; negative numbers represent an increase in reserves. This table incorporates corrections to data in *ADI 1996*.

Table 5-14. Import coverage ratio of reserves. This ratio gives the number of months, at current import levels, that can adequately be covered by available foreign exchange reserves (World Bank country desks). It is obtained by dividing the stock of reserves by imports divided by 12.

Tables 5-15 and 5-16. Export and import unit values. The indexes for total export and import unit values (World Bank country desks) are based on exports and imports of goods and nonfactor services from the national accounts. These indexes are calculated by dividing the values of exports and imports expressed in current U.S. dollars (Tables 2-14 and 2-15) by the volume of exports (f.o.b.) and imports (c.i.f.) expressed in constant 1995 U.S. dollars (Tables 2-16 and 2-17). Because of the way these trade unit value indexes are calculated (Paasche indexes, with changing weights), they reflect the composition of exports and imports in each year and may not give a reliable trend in unit values when trade composition changes dramatically. By contrast, this index reflects more accurately shifts in a country's actual composition of trade than would an index using weights based on trade shares in a single year. Data may differ from those in *ADI 1992* and *ADI 1994–95* because a different source was used for this volume.

Table 5-17. Terms of trade. Terms of trade measure the relative movement of export and import prices. This series is calculated as the ratio of a country's export unit values or prices (Table 5-15) to its import unit values or prices (Table 5-16). It shows changes over a base year (1995) in the level of export unit values as a percentage of import unit values. Data may differ from those in *ADI 1992* and *ADI 1994–95* because a different source was used for this volume.

Table 5-18. Forest products exports. Exports of forest production (FAO data) is given as an aggregate including all wood from trees and forests (coniferous and nonconiferous), whether in natural form or partially processed (SITC 245, 246, and 247); sawwood and sleepers (SITC 248); and wood-based panels and fiberwood, compressed or noncompressed (SITC 634 and 641).

Table 5-19. Petroleum exports. This table contains the volumes of crude petroleum exported (World Bank, IEABAL). Data may differ from *ADI 1992* and *ADI 1994–95* because a different source was used for this volume.

Table 5-20. Copper exports. The table presents the unweighted sum of the metal content weights of copper ore and concentrate and of unrefined plus refined copper, metal, and alloys, unwrought (World Bank, METMIN). Data may differ from *ADI 1992* and *ADI 1994–95* because a different source was used for this volume.

Table 5-21. Iron exports. These are exports measured in metal content weight of iron ore (World Bank, METMIN).

Table 5-22. Phosphates exports. These are the volume of phosphates exports, expressed as the weight of mineral content in phosphate rock (World Bank, METMIN).

Table 5-23. Cocoa exports. Cocoa exports include cocoa beans, cocoa powder and cake, cocoa paste, cocoa butter, and chocolate products not elsewhere specified (FAO data).

Table 5-24. Coffee exports. Coffee exports are shown for green and roasted beans (FAO data).

Table 5-25. Cotton exports. Cotton exports refer to cotton lint only (FAO data).

Table 5-26. Groundnut exports. Groundnut exports include the weight of groundnuts in shelled equivalent (using a conversion factor of 70 percent), groundnut oil, and groundnut cake (FAO data).

Table 5-27. Oil palm products exports. Exports of oil palm products consist of palm oil and palm kernels (FAO data).

Table 5-28. Sisal exports. Only sisal fiber exports are included (FAO data).

Table 5-29. Tea exports. Tea exports figures are for processed tea (FAO data).

Table 5-30. Sugar exports. Sugar exports are shown in terms of raw sugar equivalent. The conversion factor to express refined sugar in raw sugar equivalent is 1.087 for all countries (FAO data).

Table 5-31. Tobacco exports. Only tobacco leaves are included (FAO data).

Table 5-32. Meat exports. Meat exports are defined as fresh, chilled, or frozen meat (SITC category 011) (FAO data).

Tables 5-33 and 5-34. Manufactured goods exports. Data reported in these tables follow the classification of manufacturing industries as reported in the UN *International Standard Industrial Classification of All Economic Activities* (ISIC), Revision 2 (World Bank country desks). First table is expressed in current prices; second table shows growth.

Tables 5-35 and 5-36. Food imports. Data refer to the sum of food, beverages, tobacco, oilseeds and oleaginous fruits, animal and vegetable oils, and fats (SITC sections 0, 1, and 4 and division 22) (World Bank country desks). First table is expressed in current prices; second table shows growth.

Tables 5-37 and 5-38. Nonfood consumer goods imports. Data reported in these tables show consumer goods imports other than food. Data are calculated as total merchandise imports less food, fuel, intermediate goods, and capital goods imports (World Bank country desks). First table is expressed in current prices; second table shows growth.

Tables 5-39 and 5-40. Fuel imports. Figures are defined as SITC section 3 (sum of Canada, Mexico, and United States) (World Bank country desks). First table presents data in current prices; second table shows growth.

Tables 5-41 and 5-42. Primary intermediate goods imports. Data on these tables comprise minerals, ores, and metals imports (the sum of SITC divisions 27, 28, and 68 and item 522.56) and agricultural raw materials imports (the sum of SITC section 2, less divisions 22, 27, and 28 and groups 233, 244, 266, and 267). Synthetics are excluded (World Bank country desks). First table presents data in current prices; second table shows growth.

Tables 5-43 and 5-44. Manufactured goods imports. Data reported on these tables follow the classification of manufacturing industries as reported in the UN *International Standard Industrial Classification of All Economic Activities* (ISIC), Revision 2 (World Bank country desks). First table presents data in current prices; second table shows growth.

Tables 5-45 and 5-46. Capital goods imports. Data shown here are for machinery and transport equipment (SITC section 7) (World Bank country desks). First table presents data in current prices; second table shows growth.

Tables 5-47, 5-48, and 5-49. Direction of trade matrix, imports. These tables show, for each importing country, the percentage of the value of its total imports that originates from each of the exporting countries for 1986, 1990, and 1995, respectively. They are calculated from Tables 5-53 to 5-55, below.

In these tables data posted under South Africa are for South Africa Customs Union, which comprises Botswana, Lesotho, Namibia, South Africa, and Swaziland.

Tables 5-50, 5-51, and 5-52. Direction of trade matrix, exports. As with the foregoing, for each exporter, these tables show the percentage of the value of total exports, f.o.b., that goes to each of its trade partners for 1986, 1990, and 1995, respectively. These are calculated from Tables 5-53 to 5-55, below.

In these tables data posted under South Africa are for South Africa Customs Union, which comprises Botswana, Lesotho, Namibia, South Africa, and Swaziland.

Tables 5-53, 5-54, and 5-55. Direction of trade matrix, current U.S. dollars. These are the value of trade in goods and services to or from the countries indicated. Matrices are shown for 1986, 1990, and 1995. They form the basis for the calculations in the previous six tables (UNSTAT, COMTRADE). Data for South Africa are for the South Africa Customs Union, which comprises Botswana, Lesotho, Namibia, South Africa, and Swaziland.

Figure

The following indicator has been used to derive the figures in this chapter.

Figure 5-1. Terms of trade gains or losses (Table 5-17).

Methodology used for regional aggregations and period averages in chapter 5

Table	Aggregations[a] (1)	(3)	(4)	(6)	Period averages[b] (1)	(2)
5-1		x				x
5-2		x				x
5-3		x				x
5-4		x				x
5-5	x				x	
5-6	x				x	
5-7	x				x	
5-8				x	x	
5-9	x				x	
5-10	x				x	
5-11	x				x	
5-12	x				x	
5-13	x				x	
5-14				x	x	
5-15			x		x	
5-16			x		x	
5-17			x/x		x	
5-18	x					x
5-19	x					x
5-20	x					x
5-21	x					x
5-22	x					x
5-23	x					x
5-24	x					x
5-25	x					x
5-26	x					x
5-27	x					x
5-28	x					x
5-29	x					x
5-30	x					x
5-31	x					x
5-32	x				x	
5-33	x				x	
5-34	x					x
5-35	x				x	
5-36	x					x
5-37	x				x	
5-38	x					x
5-39	x				x	
5-40	x					x
5-41	x				x	
5-42	x					x
5-43	x				x	
5-44	x					x
5-45	x				x	
5-46	x					x
5-47	x					
5-48	x					
5-49	x					
5-50	x					
5-51	x					
5-52	x					
5-53	x					
5-54	x					
5-55	x					

Note: Regional aggregations are shown in the rows for Sub-Saharan Africa, North Africa, and All Africa. Period averages are shown in the last three columns. This table shows only the methodologies used in this chapter.

a. Regional aggregations: (1) simple total; (2) simple total of the first indicator divided by the simple total of the second indicator (same country coverage); (3) simple total of the gap-filled indicator; (4) simple total of the gap-filled main indicator divided by the simple total of the gap-filled secondary indicator; (5) simple total of the first gap-filled main indicator less the simple total of the second gap-filled main indicator, all divided by the simple total of the secondary indicator; (6) weighted total; (7) median; (8) no aggregation; (9) simple arithmetic mean.

b. Period averages: (1) arithmetic mean (using the same series as shown in the table, i.e., ratio if the rest of the table is shown as ratio, level if the rest of the table is shown as level, growth rate if the rest of the table is shown as growth rate); (2) least-squares growth rate (using main indicator); (3) least-squares growth rate (using main indicator in constant terms, with the rest of the table in current terms).

6

External Debt and Related Flows

The tables in this chapter provide a consistent presentation of the structure and terms of external debt and debt servicing. No data are presented on debt owed to domestic lenders. The aggregates and ratios provide various measures of a country's external debt situation. These measures include the size of debt and its servicing requirements, the amount of debt relative to GDP, the ratio of debt-servicing payments to exports, and the interest rate and terms of the stock of debt (including grace period, maturity, and grant element).

Unlike the presentation in the *ADI 1992*, these tables follow the presentation in the *World Debt Tables* and therefore show IMF purchases, repurchases, charges, and net purchases separately from long- and short-term lending, repayments, interests, or net lending. While IMF purchases and repurchases are not strictly lending (they are swaps of currency), they do add to, or subtract from, the resources available for consumption or investment and do impose a liability against future income streams. For this reason, IMF transactions are included here.

Data on debt and related flows are drawn largely from the World Bank's Debtor Reporting System

(DRS), to which member countries submit detailed accounts on the annual status, transactions, and terms of debt and related flows. World Bank and IMF staff estimates based on other sources of data supplement DRS data, especially for recent years, on debt not guaranteed by debtor governments and on short-term debt. The figures in this chapter are based mostly on data supplied by debtor countries. Other data series on debt, on which the World Bank may base some of its estimates, are maintained by the Organization for Economic Cooperation and Development (OECD) and the Bank for International Settlements (BIS) from data provided by creditor governments and agencies. No figures are given for Libya and Namibia, which do not report debt information to the DRS. However, totals do include estimates for these countries.

The following definitions apply throughout the chapter. Long-term loans have an original or extended maturity of more than one year, while the maturity on short-term loans is one year or less. Official and private refer to the source of the foreign loans. Official loans are from multilateral organizations (excluding the IMF) and from foreign governments; these loans are either made directly to the government of the borrowing country or guaranteed by it, or its agencies, when made to a third party. Private loans are from the private sector, including foreign parent companies and their affiliates, suppliers, financial markets (such as commercial banks), and other sources. These private loans may or may not be guaranteed by creditor or debtor governments and agencies. "Public and publicly guaranteed" loans, as defined by the DRS, refer to loans from both official and private foreign sources that are made to, or guaranteed by, the debtor government or its agencies. Almost all loans from foreign official sources are public or publicly guaranteed. Some loans from foreign private sources are made to, or guaranteed by, the debtor government or

its agencies (these are labeled *private guaranteed* by the DRS). Some loans from foreign private sources are not public or publicly guaranteed (these are labeled *private nonguaranteed* by DRS).

Concessional loans carry a grant element of 25 percent or more (based on a standard 10 percent discount rate), which is consistent with the Development Assistance Committee of the OECD (DAC) definition of ODA (see Chapter 12). Nonconcessional loans carry a grant element of less than 25 percent. In this chapter, private loans are shown separately from official nonconcessional loans.

Additional information, definitions, and methodology are available in the World Bank, *Global Development Finance 1999* (formerly *World Debt Tables*).

6-1. Gross disbursements: official concessional long-term loans

	Millions of U.S. dollars (current prices)											Annual average		
	1980	1988	1989	1990	1991	1992	1993	1994	1995	1996	1997	75-84	85-89	90-MR
SUB-SAHARAN AFRICA	2,557	4,707	4,822	4,920	4,508	4,836	4,869	4,830	4,646	4,186	3,970	2,657	4,433	4,596
excluding South Africa	2,557	4,707	4,822	4,920	4,508	4,836	4,869	4,830	4,646	4,186	3,970	2,657	4,433	4,596
excl. S.Africa & Nigeria	2,509	4,698	4,731	4,813	4,464	4,800	4,802	4,753	4,547	4,092	3,873	2,632	4,411	4,518
Angola	4	27	25	61	78	40	31	73	63	43	34	4	38	53
Benin	35	51	121	111	94	76	79	101	96	104	49	33	66	89
Botswana	9	22	37	18	47	21	40	33	57	15	13	11	18	30
Burkina Faso	41	71	83	68	137	133	131	105	110	102	70	36	75	107
Burundi	38	90	103	91	84	105	76	52	45	34	19	32	95	63
Cameroon	143	102	193	108	91	380	311	372	64	155	220	118	115	213
Cape Verde	3	10	11	7	5	14	6	28	16	17	21	5	11	14
Central African Republic	19	79	63	110	95	45	50	44	32	27	5	15	65	51
Chad	5	59	78	95	91	69	58	69	60	99	80	16	43	77
Comoros	13	8	4	5	3	18	6	8	10	7	5	11	13	8
Congo, Democratic Rep. of	131	287	293	214	116	66	58	1	0	3	0	125	234	57
Congo, Republic of	49	65	32	116	29	17	8	194	14	2	3	61	71	48
Côte d'Ivoire	42	40	185	304	231	366	466	766	546	395	150	62	91	403
Djibouti	1	22	12	27	54	43	26	26	18	24	12	7	23	29
Equatorial Guinea	4	19	15	9	7	15	10	4	2	2	3	3	17	6
Eritrea	..	..	..	..	..	..	2	27	7	5	32	..	..	15
Ethiopia	70	401	342	259	155	184	348	213	199	224	96	395	438	210
Gabon	16	41	16	67	71	10	19	54	64	27	96	11	36	51
Gambia, The	27	22	28	22	26	48	22	24	19	63	26	13	26	31
Ghana	114	324	298	309	362	318	342	324	389	353	374	66	251	346
Guinea	56	230	242	190	185	156	228	125	123	84	177	57	176	158
Guinea-Bissau	49	47	39	37	40	40	23	26	21	28	30	16	32	30
Kenya	160	292	374	398	389	229	299	169	523	285	151	117	222	305
Lesotho	8	28	41	44	45	54	28	43	28	21	28	11	27	36
Liberia	39	3	0	0	2	0	33	0	0	0	0	34	20	4
Madagascar	153	202	162	197	186	102	104	72	88	116	214	97	169	135
Malawi	45	90	95	119	172	137	187	107	211	157	138	44	86	154
Mali	75	127	160	163	142	162	79	120	188	153	118	73	139	141
Mauritania	96	103	67	89	58	73	142	111	101	114	77	82	106	96
Mauritius	16	45	34	72	64	48	42	25	22	13	30	14	34	39
Mozambique	1	153	158	180	98	187	155	221	219	272	239	79	255	197
Namibia	..	..	..	..	..	..	..	..	..	..	..	..	..	..
Niger	59	147	95	90	30	81	67	68	28	40	85	39	108	61
Nigeria	49	9	91	107	44	36	67	77	99	94	97	25	21	78
Rwanda	27	85	64	62	89	80	61	22	54	62	70	27	80	62
São Tomé and Principe	8	12	17	15	19	25	15	15	14	11	5	4	11	15
Senegal	113	253	347	198	135	241	84	98	150	183	212	88	279	163
Seychelles	6	2	4	5	9	4	3	1	1	4	6	4	6	4
Sierra Leone	33	32	5	20	16	42	96	61	94	76	44	18	19	56
Somalia	74	63	71	46	13	0	0	0	0	0	0	101	82	7
South Africa	0	0	0	0	0	0	0	0	0	0	0	0	0	0
Sudan	270	294	219	180	129	93	95	10	27	2	0	313	203	67
Swaziland	9	8	13	10	7	6	2	16	15	6	6	9	10	8
Tanzania	159	307	156	239	255	336	187	230	201	198	245	186	196	236
Togo	35	105	59	82	61	43	15	40	26	95	54	35	70	52
Uganda	13	116	239	246	175	229	327	267	221	212	275	33	148	244
Zambia	243	123	69	50	282	223	254	211	296	211	220	100	122	218
Zimbabwe	1	95	64	83	89	243	190	183	85	49	141	29	85	133
NORTH AFRICA	2,079	1,379	952	1,561	1,661	1,480	1,625	1,545	1,703	1,386	1,044	1,742	1,087	1,500
Algeria	79	56	85	292	164	222	352	392	683	344	148	78	69	324
Egypt, Arab Republic	1,064	883	443	721	963	524	534	437	337	408	373	1,085	566	537
Libya	0	0	0	0	0	0	0	0	0	0	0	0	0	0
Morocco	731	220	206	326	296	433	497	439	405	471	360	406	265	403
Tunisia	205	220	219	222	239	301	242	277	278	164	163	173	186	236
ALL AFRICA	4,636	6,086	5,774	6,481	6,169	6,316	6,494	6,375	6,349	5,572	5,014	4,398	5,519	6,096

6-2. Gross disbursements: official nonconcessional long-term loans

	Millions of U.S. dollars (current prices)											Annual average		
	1980	1988	1989	1990	1991	1992	1993	1994	1995	1996	1997	75-84	85-89	90-MR
SUB-SAHARAN AFRICA	1,689	1,895	2,316	2,326	2,176	2,076	1,698	1,442	1,169	920	901	1,358	2,036	1,589
excluding South Africa	1,689	1,895	2,316	2,326	2,176	2,076	1,698	1,442	1,169	920	901	1,358	2,036	1,589
excl. S.Africa & Nigeria	1,616	1,491	1,649	1,791	1,626	1,581	1,222	921	835	706	684	1,179	1,496	1,171
Angola	-4	42	169	108	60	66	21	0	62	1	0	-4	103	40
Benin	24	5	12	10	5	5	2	4	5	5	1	8	7	5
Botswana	16	33	33	12	56	63	32	19	9	13	9	16	46	27
Burkina Faso	18	23	11	11	9	10	7	2	2	1	1	11	14	5
Burundi	1	7	5	3	2	3	1	1	0	1	0	4	8	1
Cameroon	108	107	201	450	228	148	84	68	44	21	25	71	142	133
Cape Verde	0	0	0	5	0	4	5	1	1	1	0	5	0	2
Central African Republic	6	11	1	3	2	1	0	0	1	0	1	3	9	1
Chad	0	1	3	8	1	75	1	0	0	0	0	2	2	11
Comoros	0	0	0	0	0	0	0	0	0	0	0	1	1	0
Congo, Democratic Rep. of	70	117	99	99	188	17	0	0	0	0	0	64	82	38
Congo, Republic of	60	106	26	12	3	0	0	137	1	2	21	38	54	22
Côte d'Ivoire	189	249	211	454	436	285	157	152	122	70	34	178	234	214
Djibouti	4	0	0	0	0	0	0	0	0	0	0	1	0	0
Equatorial Guinea	11	3	4	1	1	0	0	0	0	0	0	3	2	0
Eritrea	0	0	0	0	0	0	-2	0	0	2	1	0	0	0
Ethiopia	7	55	150	68	28	29	21	21	33	49	53	11	62	38
Gabon	19	99	106	91	71	99	71	79	157	62	30	36	71	82
Gambia, The	2	0	1	1	3	7	3	1	0	0	0	2	2	2
Ghana	106	31	55	69	56	66	26	21	19	17	20	38	38	36
Guinea	8	7	13	6	44	43	47	44	47	42	39	12	11	39
Guinea-Bissau	6	1	1	0	15	1	0	3	0	1	0	3	6	2
Kenya	73	95	165	32	72	99	19	59	39	58	15	100	134	49
Lesotho	1	10	6	8	11	23	41	18	24	18	14	3	9	20
Liberia	26	12	0	0	0	0	0	0	0	0	0	23	11	0
Madagascar	59	22	19	16	13	15	19	10	1	21	102	49	50	25
Malawi	60	14	26	9	9	7	6	4	4	1	2	26	21	5
Mali	8	10	13	4	2	0	5	1	5	3	0	4	5	3
Mauritania	16	44	19	47	13	60	25	28	11	16	9	24	26	26
Mauritius	20	72	22	25	33	15	23	11	17	37	45	18	37	26
Mozambique	-1	16	24	7	10	10	9	8	11	10	20	-79	19	11
Namibia	0	0	0	0	0	0	0	0	0	0	0	0	0	0
Niger	33	6	3	1	1	1	34	5	0	1	0	27	10	5
Nigeria	73	404	667	535	549	495	477	522	334	214	218	180	540	418
Rwanda	0	0	0	1	0	0	0	0	0	0	2	0	0	0
São Tomé and Principe	2	0	1	1	1	0	0	0	0	0	0	2	1	0
Senegal	74	13	21	9	29	73	68	34	7	1	3	63	28	28
Seychelles	6	3	3	2	2	6	7	8	7	8	5	2	3	5
Sierra Leone	9	0	7	0	0	10	3	3	1	2	0	4	1	2
Somalia	13	1	0	0	0	0	0	0	0	0	0	19	2	0
South Africa	0	0	0	0	0	0	0	0	0	0	0	0	0	0
Sudan	297	89	17	5	0	15	6	2	24	15	5	138	23	9
Swaziland	20	5	3	6	8	1	7	1	4	23	18	15	7	8
Tanzania	87	13	38	49	22	14	18	18	20	5	7	82	26	19
Togo	12	8	2	1	6	1	2	0	0	2	0	15	4	2
Uganda	5	18	31	16	6	21	62	3	11	14	9	15	42	18
Zambia	71	81	52	67	56	38	25	29	14	6	6	93	77	30
Zimbabwe	77	65	78	75	126	252	369	129	133	180	186	31	64	181
NORTH AFRICA	1,580	2,108	2,931	3,335	3,371	2,957	2,612	2,668	2,467	2,712	2,233	1,555	2,405	2,794
Algeria	487	690	1,019	1,461	1,540	1,196	786	1,136	938	1,188	1,014	489	644	1,157
Egypt, Arab Republic	840	520	603	503	309	437	442	347	141	143	205	702	826	316
Libya	0	0	0	0	0	0	0	0	0	0	0	0	0	0
Morocco	135	577	875	894	859	882	785	602	954	860	490	229	616	791
Tunisia	119	321	433	477	663	442	599	583	433	521	524	135	319	530
ALL AFRICA	3,269	4,003	5,247	5,661	5,547	5,033	4,310	4,110	3,636	3,632	3,134	2,913	4,441	4,383

6-3. Gross disbursements: private long-term loans

	Millions of U.S. dollars (current prices)											Annual average		
	1980	1988	1989	1990	1991	1992	1993	1994	1995	1996	1997	75-84	85-89	90-MR
SUB-SAHARAN AFRICA	6,290	3,432	3,136	2,533	1,975	1,904	1,901	4,636	5,129	3,541	4,849	4,353	3,511	3,308
excluding South Africa	6,290	3,432	3,136	2,533	1,975	1,904	1,901	1,118	1,580	1,250	1,377	4,353	3,511	1,705
excl. S.Africa & Nigeria	4,659	2,930	2,306	2,248	1,782	1,900	1,901	1,118	1,580	1,250	1,377	2,954	2,729	1,644
Angola	..	649	404	693	189	540	634	344	424	3	48	..	712	359
Benin	4	1	0	0	0	0	0	0	0	0	0	44	1	0
Botswana	3	3	1	0	0	0	30	0	0	0	0	6	4	4
Burkina Faso	6	0	4	0	0	0	0	0	0	0	0	8	1	0
Burundi	0	6	1	2	0	0	0	0	0	0	0	5	2	0
Cameroon	364	414	474	160	103	141	104	8	0	25	14	230	354	69
Cape Verde	0	0	0	0	0	0	0	0	4	5	2	0	0	1
Central African Republic	0	1	0	0	0	0	0	0	0	0	0	2	1	0
Chad	0	1	0	0	0	0	0	0	0	0	0	5	1	0
Comoros	0	0	0	0	0	0	0	0	0	0	0	0	0	0
Congo, Democratic Rep. of	263	6	59	3	0	0	0	0	0	0	0	176	16	0
Congo, Republic of	412	439	127	185	6	114	451	1	0	0	0	207	272	95
Côte d'Ivoire	1,508	238	279	261	236	202	190	317	75	411	52	791	219	218
Djibouti	5	0	0	0	0	0	0	0	0	0	0	1	0	0
Equatorial Guinea	5	0	0	0	0	0	0	0	0	0	0	3	0	0
Eritrea	..	..	..	..	..	..	..	0	0	0	0	..	..	0
Ethiopia	33	147	36	51	261	113	10	4	0	22	30	45	98	61
Gabon	135	133	31	37	16	0	3	2	0	0	20	174	174	10
Gambia, The	22	0	0	0	0	0	0	0	0	0	0	5	0	0
Ghana	0	67	44	59	82	103	77	123	132	327	138	12	64	130
Guinea	57	38	0	0	0	0	11	0	0	17	20	29	13	6
Guinea-Bissau	21	0	0	0	0	0	0	0	0	0	0	5	5	0
Kenya	387	334	302	236	440	175	87	6	132	94	36	224	279	151
Lesotho	5	15	8	7	6	2	0	0	13	12	15	4	8	7
Liberia	11	0	0	0	0	0	0	0	0	0	0	23	0	0
Madagascar	163	14	0	1	0	0	0	0	1	0	0	64	10	0
Malawi	48	15	11	7	1	14	1	10	0	0	0	29	7	4
Mali	10	0	0	0	0	0	0	0	0	0	0	6	1	0
Mauritania	14	2	2	0	0	0	0	0	0	25	0	24	4	3
Mauritius	61	120	48	65	76	63	39	150	369	91	752	28	45	201
Mozambique	..	14	32	44	6	4	8	4	36	0	6	..	46	13
Namibia	..	..	..	..	..	..	..	..	..	..	..	..	..	..
Niger	190	28	49	48	0	0	0	0	0	0	0	91	45	6
Nigeria	1,631	501	830	285	193	4	0	0	0	0	0	1,399	782	60
Rwanda	0	0	0	0	0	0	0	0	0	0	0	3	1	0
São Tomé and Principe	0	0	0	0	0	0	0	0	0	0	0	1	0	0
Senegal	141	14	8	15	11	8	1	1	1	0	21	74	29	7
Seychelles	0	4	2	2	10	15	8	9	0	1	0	1	6	6
Sierra Leone	42	0	4	4	0	0	0	0	0	0	0	24	1	1
Somalia	27	0	0	0	0	0	0	0	0	0	0	25	1	0
South Africa	..	..	..	..	..	..	..	3,518	3,549	2,291	3,472	..	..	3,208
Sudan	145	0	0	0	0	0	0	0	0	0	0	100	0	0
Swaziland	0	0	0	0	0	0	0	0	0	0	0	3	3	0
Tanzania	122	37	36	17	4	38	45	17	42	6	0	62	48	21
Togo	50	0	0	0	0	0	0	0	0	0	0	63	0	0
Uganda	65	33	41	38	5	6	18	0	0	0	0	36	60	8
Zambia	289	42	92	48	46	33	11	9	19	5	44	157	66	27
Zimbabwe	55	116	214	266	284	329	172	115	330	207	178	167	128	235
NORTH AFRICA	5,015	7,615	6,178	6,700	6,061	7,541	6,567	4,491	3,644	2,430	1,717	4,733	6,362	4,894
Algeria	2,832	5,421	4,455	5,182	4,824	6,118	5,363	3,268	2,092	1,321	399	2,743	4,206	3,571
Egypt, Arab Republic	776	1,382	1,082	773	666	387	169	263	41	32	188	778	1,316	315
Libya	..	..	..	..	..	..	..	..	..	..	..	..	..	..
Morocco	1,119	459	433	426	327	569	755	762	734	428	301	906	519	538
Tunisia	288	353	208	319	244	467	281	199	777	649	829	306	322	471
ALL AFRICA	11,304	11,047	9,315	9,233	8,037	9,445	8,468	9,127	8,773	5,971	6,566	9,086	9,873	8,202

6-4. Disbursements: long-term loans and IMF purchases

| | Millions of U.S. dollars (current prices) | | | | | | | | | | | Annual average | | |
	1980	1988	1989	1990	1991	1992	1993	1994	1995	1996	1997	75-84	85-89	90-MR
SUB-SAHARAN AFRICA	11,709	10,994	11,205	10,762	9,602	9,535	9,690	8,383	10,425	7,019	6,829	9,317	10,816	9,031
excluding South Africa	11,709	10,994	11,205	10,762	9,602	9,535	8,832	8,383	10,425	7,019	6,829	9,317	10,816	8,923
excl. S.Africa & Nigeria	9,956	10,080	9,617	9,835	8,815	9,000	8,289	7,785	9,992	6,711	6,515	7,714	9,473	8,368
Angola	0	718	598	862	327	647	685	417	550	47	82	0	853	452
Benin	71	57	141	120	112	81	103	130	115	128	57	86	76	106
Botswana	28	58	71	30	103	84	102	52	66	28	22	34	69	61
Burkina Faso	70	94	98	79	155	143	151	132	139	112	132	56	90	130
Burundi	45	121	120	96	91	126	77	53	45	35	19	44	112	68
Cameroon	626	716	887	718	433	669	499	478	121	230	296	427	634	430
Cape Verde	3	10	11	12	5	18	10	29	21	24	24	10	12	18
Central African Republic	40	103	64	121	98	46	50	59	33	27	6	27	82	55
Chad	5	61	93	112	92	143	58	83	72	123	92	26	51	97
Comoros	13	8	4	5	4	18	6	10	10	7	5	12	14	8
Congo, Democratic Rep. of	603	410	659	316	304	83	58	1	0	3	0	482	461	96
Congo, Republic of	526	610	185	319	38	132	459	350	15	24	24	310	399	170
Côte d'Ivoire	1,777	648	712	1,172	948	853	813	1,405	924	1,014	236	1,114	599	921
Djibouti	10	22	12	27	54	43	26	26	18	28	14	9	24	29
Equatorial Guinea	38	26	19	10	16	15	14	7	2	2	3	12	21	8
Eritrea	..	..	..	..	..	..	..	27	7	7	33	..	..	19
Ethiopia	119	603	528	378	443	346	409	258	232	315	179	470	606	320
Gabon	171	349	158	204	162	108	93	198	279	121	168	222	308	167
Gambia, The	56	27	38	33	31	55	26	24	19	63	26	26	35	35
Ghana	249	639	574	502	659	487	509	468	581	737	533	184	494	559
Guinea	129	290	278	196	241	210	286	182	200	143	269	103	212	216
Guinea-Bissau	75	48	43	37	55	41	23	28	24	31	36	24	44	34
Kenya	713	898	944	802	949	502	436	266	694	474	201	515	716	540
Lesotho	15	57	60	62	66	86	80	66	66	51	57	19	47	67
Liberia	109	15	0	0	2	0	33	0	0	0	0	113	31	4
Madagascar	444	248	214	231	217	117	123	82	90	156	335	236	264	169
Malawi	190	143	155	161	203	158	194	147	227	180	151	120	129	178
Mali	108	154	179	194	144	176	98	164	238	186	147	94	155	168
Mauritania	155	154	99	148	71	145	179	163	133	176	105	141	150	140
Mauritius	143	237	103	162	173	127	105	186	409	140	827	87	128	266
Mozambique	0	207	229	243	156	265	194	254	267	300	300	0	331	247
Namibia	..	..	..	..	..	..	..	..	..	..	..	..	..	..
Niger	290	193	158	148	31	83	100	89	28	55	111	164	180	81
Nigeria	1,753	914	1,588	927	787	535	544	599	433	308	314	1,603	1,344	556
Rwanda	34	85	64	62	101	81	61	22	68	62	92	31	81	69
São Tomé and Principe	10	12	19	17	20	25	15	15	15	11	5	7	13	15
Senegal	395	337	441	252	233	322	153	200	241	219	286	261	399	238
Seychelles	12	9	8	9	20	25	18	18	8	12	11	7	16	15
Sierra Leone	104	32	16	24	16	52	100	200	115	92	51	62	26	81
Somalia	135	64	71	46	13	0	0	0	0	0	0	158	101	7
South Africa	0	0	0	0	0	0	858	0	0	0	0	0	0	107
Sudan	877	309	304	506	492	299	176	87	86	29	19	637	253	212
Swaziland	31	13	17	15	15	7	8	16	19	29	25	29	21	17
Tanzania	433	400	230	334	309	478	250	265	262	246	336	353	295	310
Togo	119	137	84	104	67	55	17	55	59	97	69	122	89	65
Uganda	161	241	362	382	264	311	408	322	288	289	344	135	287	326
Zambia	693	246	213	165	384	293	290	249	2,582	222	285	487	290	559
Zimbabwe	132	276	357	424	499	1,045	797	502	628	435	505	257	277	604
NORTH AFRICA	9,014	11,271	10,844	11,661	11,696	12,199	10,804	9,545	8,288	7,271	5,457	8,255	10,213	9,615
Algeria	3,398	6,168	6,163	6,935	6,835	7,536	6,501	5,638	4,187	3,596	2,025	3,310	5,040	5,407
Egypt, Arab Republic	2,743	2,784	2,128	1,997	2,020	1,470	1,145	1,046	519	582	766	2,624	2,738	1,193
Libya	..	..	..	..	..	..	..	..	..	..	..	..	..	..
Morocco	2,262	1,404	1,693	1,711	1,482	1,910	2,037	1,802	2,093	1,759	1,151	1,704	1,557	1,743
Tunisia	611	915	860	1,018	1,358	1,283	1,122	1,059	1,488	1,334	1,516	616	877	1,272
ALL AFRICA	20,723	22,264	22,049	22,423	21,297	21,734	20,494	17,929	18,713	14,290	12,286	17,572	21,029	18,646

Note: In 1995, Zambia was able to clear its arrears to the IMF after completing a 3 year Rights Arrangement Program.

6-5. Amortization: official concessional long-term loans

	Millions of U.S. dollars (current prices)											Annual average		
	1980	*1988*	*1989*	*1990*	*1991*	*1992*	*1993*	*1994*	*1995*	*1996*	*1997*	*75-84*	*85-89*	*90-MR*
SUB-SAHARAN AFRICA	247	618	591	586	618	589	764	717	882	891	1,108	234	533	769
excluding South Africa	247	618	591	586	618	589	764	717	882	891	1,108	234	533	769
excl. S.Africa & Nigeria	233	611	590	580	615	587	602	716	880	890	1,036	221	523	738
Angola	0	1	7	1	5	3	2	9	3	8	14	0	2	6
Benin	1	5	3	7	9	8	12	12	15	14	18	2	4	12
Botswana	0	6	5	6	7	9	13	14	11	15	30	1	5	13
Burkina Faso	4	13	10	13	14	9	11	18	20	23	25	2	8	16
Burundi	1	13	13	14	17	14	15	16	14	6	8	1	10	13
Cameroon	13	24	6	24	23	20	37	12	12	14	49	12	23	24
Cape Verde	0	2	2	1	3	5	2	2	2	1	4	0	1	2
Central African Republic	0	2	2	3	2	2	1	5	2	2	2	1	2	2
Chad	3	2	3	2	2	3	1	6	2	7	6	1	3	4
Comoros	0	0	0	0	1	2	2	2	0	1	1	0	0	1
Congo, Democratic Rep. of	3	9	7	8	4	5	4	0	0	0	0	4	9	3
Congo, Republic of	11	2	2	2	0	0	1	8	7	22	0	10	4	5
Côte d'Ivoire	18	56	56	75	77	88	75	56	64	80	67	15	35	73
Djibouti	2	8	8	8	8	7	6	9	9	8	5	1	5	8
Equatorial Guinea	0	0	0	1	1	0	0	0	0	1	1	0	0	0
Eritrea	0	0	0	0	0	0	0	0	0	0	0	0	0	0
Ethiopia	7	74	58	19	21	14	16	19	25	35	26	9	53	22
Gabon	4	5	3	1	7	23	7	8	12	9	39	5	4	13
Gambia, The	0	6	10	11	9	8	8	9	7	9	11	1	5	9
Ghana	14	36	26	40	29	33	32	56	55	56	47	20	33	43
Guinea	44	42	39	53	51	19	16	26	86	44	30	36	42	41
Guinea-Bissau	0	1	4	1	15	1	1	2	4	3	5	0	2	4
Kenya	6	28	32	34	41	33	39	67	70	68	58	8	24	51
Lesotho	0	3	4	4	4	5	9	6	11	11	13	1	3	8
Liberia	1	4	1	0	11	0	1	1	0	0	0	4	2	2
Madagascar	21	20	17	17	12	20	12	13	10	21	55	21	13	20
Malawi	2	3	4	7	14	10	9	10	16	19	21	2	4	13
Mali	4	26	19	22	13	22	23	39	45	41	43	4	17	31
Mauritania	3	37	26	26	20	26	40	33	37	37	39	3	28	32
Mauritius	2	12	16	14	19	31	23	22	24	27	47	2	10	26
Mozambique	0	6	8	9	10	13	12	17	24	29	27	2	17	18
Namibia	..	..	..	..	..	..	..	..	..	..	..	..	..	..
Niger	16	10	7	5	5	4	12	7	6	7	14	5	8	7
Nigeria	14	7	1	7	2	1	162	1	2	1	72	13	10	31
Rwanda	0	6	11	7	10	8	11	2	11	8	9	1	7	8
São Tomé and Principe	0	1	2	0	1	1	0	0	1	1	3	0	1	1
Senegal	7	35	40	54	44	32	31	68	72	66	50	5	28	52
Seychelles	0	2	3	2	3	4	4	3	4	2	2	0	1	3
Sierra Leone	2	3	3	3	2	5	3	9	7	6	10	3	3	5
Somalia	2	1	2	2	0	0	0	0	0	0	0	2	2	0
South Africa	0	0	0	0	0	0	0	0	0	0	0	0	0	0
Sudan	14	42	35	4	6	8	5	3	9	0	0	16	48	4
Swaziland	1	4	4	6	8	7	7	7	8	11	8	1	3	7
Tanzania	19	29	63	36	41	36	38	40	38	54	34	14	32	40
Togo	2	8	6	6	8	5	4	4	7	15	12	2	6	8
Uganda	2	7	6	8	12	10	16	23	22	25	67	2	5	23
Zambia	3	6	2	2	4	4	10	21	52	36	80	2	3	26
Zimbabwe	2	14	17	21	25	31	33	35	61	50	58	1	9	39
NORTH AFRICA	294	402	424	561	426	504	569	733	694	756	973	264	374	652
Algeria	73	100	91	103	85	86	84	62	54	97	124	72	97	87
Egypt, Arab Republic	119	124	160	271	149	100	56	69	152	224	283	111	121	163
Libya	..	..	..	..	..	..	..	..	..	..	..	..	..	..
Morocco	62	50	37	47	55	169	281	343	289	227	361	41	48	221
Tunisia	41	128	135	141	138	150	147	260	199	209	205	39	108	181
ALL AFRICA	541	1,020	1,015	1,147	1,044	1,093	1,333	1,450	1,575	1,647	2,081	498	907	1,421

6-6. Amortization: official nonconcessional long-term loans

	Millions of U.S. dollars (current prices)											Annual average		
	1980	*1988*	*1989*	*1990*	*1991*	*1992*	*1993*	*1994*	*1995*	*1996*	*1997*	*75-84*	*85-89*	*90-MR*
SUB-SAHARAN AFRICA	424	1,361	1,230	1,975	1,845	1,455	1,434	1,925	2,117	2,444	1,929	338	1,129	1,891
excluding South Africa	424	1,361	1,230	1,975	1,845	1,455	1,434	1,925	2,117	2,444	1,929	338	1,129	1,891
excl. S.Africa & Nigeria	393	1,027	933	1,208	1,298	1,123	1,106	1,496	1,649	1,717	1,419	304	860	1,377
Angola	0	38	64	60	69	41	22	35	26	30	47	0	31	41
Benin	1	5	4	11	7	7	6	9	10	11	10	2	5	9
Botswana	6	30	29	43	45	50	43	46	47	49	40	3	22	45
Burkina Faso	4	6	5	5	11	6	9	9	10	7	7	2	4	8
Burundi	1	4	4	6	6	6	3	5	3	6	4	0	4	5
Cameroon	16	64	50	74	86	61	101	119	134	180	177	18	60	117
Cape Verde	0	2	3	3	3	3	2	3	2	2	3	0	2	2
Central African Republic	0	2	5	4	1	2	1	2	0	0	0	1	4	1
Chad	0	1	0	0	1	1	4	2	1	3	7	0	1	2
Comoros	0	0	0	0	5	1	0	0	0	0	0	0	0	1
Congo, Democratic Rep. of	100	48	56	26	24	19	0	0	0	0	0	37	53	9
Congo, Republic of	10	20	23	68	4	1	0	137	25	104	53	11	16	49
Côte d'Ivoire	37	151	128	172	196	202	218	299	415	430	262	30	103	274
Djibouti	1	0	0	0	0	0	0	0	0	0	0	0	0	0
Equatorial Guinea	1	0	0	0	1	2	1	0	0	2	0	1	2	1
Eritrea	0	0	0	0	0	0	0	0	0	0	0	0	0	0
Ethiopia	4	43	33	26	17	15	12	13	19	26	18	6	30	18
Gabon	15	13	14	16	34	61	24	55	78	71	105	14	16	55
Gambia, The	0	2	1	2	4	6	6	6	7	5	3	0	1	5
Ghana	22	22	23	25	35	44	36	45	61	44	39	15	22	41
Guinea	20	27	17	24	22	23	17	12	20	14	21	9	18	19
Guinea-Bissau	0	1	1	1	2	2	0	1	4	3	1	0	1	2
Kenya	25	121	121	146	148	141	139	183	199	181	155	22	96	161
Lesotho	0	8	4	4	7	8	6	6	7	5	8	1	4	6
Liberia	2	6	1	1	5	10	12	13	0	0	0	6	6	4
Madagascar	1	38	35	36	27	12	14	14	9	18	43	9	36	22
Malawi	4	23	22	54	37	26	21	23	27	18	13	5	20	27
Mali	0	1	4	2	4	7	3	13	11	5	4	0	2	6
Mauritania	1	41	23	55	26	25	36	24	32	35	22	6	25	32
Mauritius	4	25	25	25	31	53	34	37	36	31	31	4	19	35
Mozambique	0	9	9	14	10	13	15	35	34	25	12	0	7	20
Namibia	..	..	..	..	..	..	..	..	..	..	..	..	..	..
Niger	2	11	11	4	3	3	20	8	1	2	2	5	12	5
Nigeria	31	334	296	767	547	331	328	429	468	727	510	35	269	514
Rwanda	0	0	0	0	1	0	0	0	0	1	1	0	0	0
São Tomé and Principe	1	0	1	1	0	1	1	1	0	1	1	1	1	1
Senegal	12	67	33	57	54	27	19	47	55	40	39	8	44	42
Seychelles	0	1	3	3	3	4	3	3	3	3	5	0	2	3
Sierra Leone	2	5	0	5	1	7	2	8	20	38	0	2	2	10
Somalia	5	0	5	0	0	0	0	0	0	0	0	3	1	0
South Africa	0	0	0	0	0	0	0	0	0	0	0	0	0	0
Sudan	32	16	10	11	6	6	4	0	6	0	0	24	14	4
Swaziland	4	15	14	28	12	9	9	12	8	10	8	3	13	12
Tanzania	7	38	34	41	65	51	50	45	62	71	32	8	47	52
Togo	8	16	16	21	11	4	2	2	0	6	9	8	28	7
Uganda	9	37	30	36	26	27	61	49	38	25	20	6	21	35
Zambia	34	31	28	43	200	98	81	97	128	95	80	28	37	103
Zimbabwe	3	38	47	57	50	50	71	81	109	121	140	5	30	85
NORTH AFRICA	288	1,733	1,938	2,284	2,531	2,493	2,510	2,373	2,772	2,236	2,882	312	1,655	2,510
Algeria	171	864	906	1,069	1,162	1,092	1,054	591	586	529	916	157	760	875
Egypt, Arab Republic	32	374	489	617	609	412	334	307	394	344	347	54	358	420
Libya	..	..	..	..	..	..	..	..	..	..	..	..	..	..
Morocco	52	291	355	384	517	677	806	1,128	1,353	980	1,242	57	353	886
Tunisia	32	205	188	215	243	313	317	347	438	382	377	44	185	329
ALL AFRICA	712	3,093	3,168	4,260	4,376	3,948	3,944	4,298	4,888	4,680	4,811	650	2,784	4,400

6-7. Amortization: private long-term loans

| | Millions of U.S. dollars (current prices) | | | | | | | | | | | Annual average | | |
	1980	1988	1989	1990	1991	1992	1993	1994	1995	1996	1997	75-84	85-89	90-MR
SUB-SAHARAN AFRICA	2,123	2,164	1,734	2,079	1,835	2,900	1,267	3,911	4,065	5,355	4,915	1,845	2,641	3,291
excluding South Africa	2,123	2,164	1,734	2,079	1,835	2,900	1,267	1,917	1,994	2,585	1,934	1,845	2,641	2,064
excl. S.Africa & Nigeria	1,926	1,813	1,425	1,673	1,522	1,355	1,178	1,601	1,546	1,895	1,676	1,305	1,778	1,556
Angola	..	58	69	121	158	100	38	109	302	472	422	..	62	215
Benin	3	0	0	0	0	0	0	0	0	0	0	4	8	0
Botswana	0	5	4	19	3	3	1	2	6	9	5	2	6	6
Burkina Faso	2	2	1	0	1	0	0	0	0	0	0	2	5	0
Burundi	3	7	7	8	3	2	1	1	1	1	0	2	6	2
Cameroon	85	292	147	171	93	67	98	67	65	49	43	76	292	81
Cape Verde	0	0	0	0	0	0	0	0	0	0	1	0	0	0
Central African Republic	1	1	2	1	0	1	0	0	0	0	0	1	1	0
Chad	0	0	1	1	1	0	1	0	0	0	0	1	1	0
Comoros	0	0	0	0	0	0	0	0	0	0	0	0	0	0
Congo, Democratic Rep. of	90	23	35	15	13	5	0	0	0	0	0	42	32	4
Congo, Republic of	12	270	174	285	200	97	75	157	50	15	0	62	236	110
Côte d'Ivoire	667	194	150	251	240	212	242	356	60	302	487	350	264	269
Djibouti	0	2	1	1	0	0	0	0	0	0	0	1	2	0
Equatorial Guinea	0	1	0	0	0	0	0	0	0	0	0	1	0	0
Eritrea	..	..	..	..	..	..	..	0	0	0	0	..	..	0
Ethiopia	7	80	106	107	49	33	37	36	48	231	7	10	68	69
Gabon	260	15	5	8	48	17	4	33	75	51	25	149	55	32
Gambia, The	0	1	1	8	5	5	4	4	0	0	0	1	1	3
Ghana	42	84	105	79	48	58	52	66	85	104	112	11	56	75
Guinea	11	18	13	19	10	8	8	9	15	0	44	8	9	14
Guinea-Bissau	3	0	0	0	0	0	0	0	0	0	0	1	0	0
Kenya	165	173	139	169	167	151	123	284	288	254	154	161	180	199
Lesotho	3	5	6	7	5	7	6	5	4	2	2	2	5	5
Liberia	12	0	0	0	0	0	0	0	0	0	0	9	0	0
Madagascar	23	28	17	16	11	8	8	5	5	5	2	10	28	7
Malawi	28	9	3	6	11	16	13	14	23	4	1	17	19	11
Mali	2	2	1	1	1	3	1	1	0	0	0	1	3	1
Mauritania	13	1	6	1	2	2	0	0	0	0	2	21	5	1
Mauritius	14	68	13	21	46	43	26	45	93	50	58	17	28	48
Mozambique	..	19	18	18	21	7	10	5	13	6	5	..	14	11
Namibia	..	..	..	..	..	..	..	..	..	..	..	..	..	..
Niger	40	35	38	39	55	20	24	24	24	24	14	40	38	28
Nigeria	197	351	310	406	313	1,546	89	316	448	690	258	540	863	508
Rwanda	2	3	3	2	1	1	0	0	0	0	0	1	4	0
São Tomé and Principe	0	0	0	0	0	0	0	0	0	0	0	0	0	0
Senegal	137	64	59	30	45	39	4	10	27	11	7	46	49	22
Seychelles	0	7	8	8	5	4	5	4	9	5	3	0	5	5
Sierra Leone	29	1	1	0	0	0	0	0	28	0	0	16	2	4
Somalia	0	0	0	0	0	0	0	0	0	0	0	3	0	0
South Africa	..	..	..	..	..	..	..	1,995	2,070	2,770	2,980	..	..	2,454
Sudan	7	0	0	0	0	0	0	0	0	0	0	16	1	0
Swaziland	3	2	2	2	2	2	2	2	0	0	0	2	5	1
Tanzania	23	9	10	12	12	80	11	16	27	18	15	18	7	24
Togo	9	2	2	0	0	0	0	0	0	0	6	16	10	1
Uganda	21	34	36	22	30	14	32	16	10	7	1	15	27	17
Zambia	175	75	82	57	54	46	51	75	55	30	35	111	51	50
Zimbabwe	34	226	162	169	185	305	301	256	234	245	226	58	195	240
NORTH AFRICA	3,139	4,803	5,494	7,183	7,751	7,752	7,525	4,191	2,849	2,645	1,937	2,367	4,496	5,229
Algeria	2,284	3,623	4,116	5,606	5,972	5,883	5,816	2,698	1,577	1,305	957	1,646	3,255	3,727
Egypt, Arab Republic	192	693	824	809	882	925	575	547	355	452	297	238	746	605
Libya	..	..	..	..	..	..	..	..	..	..	..	..	..	..
Morocco	477	171	205	250	484	548	754	624	631	618	441	325	174	544
Tunisia	186	317	350	517	413	395	380	321	287	270	242	157	321	353
ALL AFRICA	5,262	6,967	7,228	9,261	9,586	10,652	8,791	8,102	6,913	8,000	6,851	4,212	7,137	8,520

6-8. Amortization: long-term loans and IMF repurchases

| | Millions of U.S. dollars (current prices) | | | | | | | | | | | Annual average | | |
	1980	1988	1989	1990	1991	1992	1993	1994	1995	1996	1997	75-84	85-89	90-MR
SUB-SAHARAN AFRICA	3,178	5,358	4,859	5,592	4,911	5,473	3,920	7,020	9,436	9,286	9,016	2,699	5,446	6,832
excluding South Africa	3,178	5,358	4,859	5,592	4,911	5,473	3,920	5,026	7,365	6,517	5,613	2,699	5,446	5,552
excl. S.Africa & Nigeria	2,935	4,666	4,252	4,412	4,048	3,595	3,341	4,279	6,447	5,099	4,774	2,112	4,305	4,499
Angola	0	97	140	183	233	144	62	152	331	510	483	0	95	262
Benin	6	13	9	21	16	15	18	21	26	27	32	7	20	22
Botswana	6	40	38	67	54	62	57	62	65	73	75	6	32	64
Burkina Faso	11	24	18	19	25	15	20	27	29	31	34	7	20	25
Burundi	4	28	26	28	25	24	23	28	27	21	20	5	24	25
Cameroon	131	388	208	270	214	203	282	204	217	248	281	112	381	240
Cape Verde	0	4	4	4	6	8	4	5	3	3	8	0	3	5
Central African Republic	7	16	22	17	7	7	3	13	10	8	9	6	17	9
Chad	5	5	8	7	4	4	8	10	10	16	24	4	7	10
Comoros	0	0	0	0	6	3	2	2	0	1	2	0	0	2
Congo, Democratic Rep. of	277	211	441	200	91	29	4	5	1	37	0	123	279	46
Congo, Republic of	41	294	203	362	209	98	77	305	84	140	56	86	259	166
Côte d'Ivoire	722	586	496	621	618	594	585	787	625	860	838	405	550	691
Djibouti	2	10	9	9	8	8	6	9	9	9	5	2	7	8
Equatorial Guinea	2	3	5	4	2	2	1	1	1	3	4	2	6	2
Eritrea	..	..	..	..	..	..	..	0	0	0	0	..	..	0
Ethiopia	17	214	219	177	92	62	66	68	91	292	52	30	177	113
Gabon	279	33	22	40	114	137	71	119	216	137	172	169	75	126
Gambia, The	0	15	17	26	23	22	21	23	21	22	20	4	15	22
Ghana	106	418	337	260	189	198	186	248	309	330	363	57	248	260
Guinea	76	92	78	110	93	51	44	54	129	67	106	56	77	82
Guinea-Bissau	3	4	6	2	16	3	1	4	9	7	6	2	4	6
Kenya	205	423	424	454	396	407	363	548	595	564	434	217	410	470
Lesotho	3	17	15	15	16	20	20	18	25	22	27	4	13	20
Liberia	18	12	5	2	15	0	13	15	0	0	0	23	10	6
Madagascar	48	133	121	121	84	56	48	43	38	60	118	47	123	71
Malawi	35	65	56	86	83	72	49	53	76	56	51	30	70	66
Mali	9	53	47	44	27	38	35	63	62	54	54	8	43	47
Mauritania	26	88	66	99	62	61	82	63	79	82	70	35	72	75
Mauritius	19	146	90	104	117	128	83	103	154	108	136	30	99	116
Mozambique	0	34	35	41	41	34	44	67	85	92	59	0	39	58
Namibia	..	..	..	..	..	..	..	..	..	..	..	..	..	..
Niger	58	89	74	63	74	36	66	48	41	44	45	50	74	52
Nigeria	242	692	607	1,180	862	1,878	579	746	918	1,418	840	588	1,141	1,053
Rwanda	3	12	17	10	12	10	11	2	11	10	.13	3	13	10
São Tomé and Principe	1	1	3	1	1	1	1	1	1	2	4	1	2	2
Senegal	165	229	193	197	190	142	81	154	195	161	158	67	183	160
Seychelles	0	10	14	13	11	12	12	10	16	10	10	1	8	12
Sierra Leone	50	11	6	12	10	16	13	98	59	47	10	28	16	33
Somalia	11	2	18	5	0	0	0	0	0	0	0	9	20	1
South Africa	0	0	0	0	0	0	0	1,995	2,070	2,770	3,403	0	0	1,280
Sudan	131	58	45	16	12	14	9	3	54	36	42	90	63	23
Swaziland	8	25	21	36	21	17	17	20	16	21	16	6	24	21
Tanzania	81	86	116	118	145	172	104	116	146	165	112	59	101	135
Togo	19	52	49	43	27	19	14	13	18	32	39	27	61	26
Uganda	45	158	141	111	102	80	119	112	98	107	146	35	129	109
Zambia	269	112	130	126	292	184	212	213	2,061	161	195	193	130	430
Zimbabwe	40	356	264	270	266	387	406	372	404	424	449	67	306	372
NORTH AFRICA	3,942	7,250	8,142	10,414	11,096	11,128	11,093	7,665	6,696	5,952	6,210	3,022	6,850	8,782
Algeria	2,529	4,587	5,113	6,779	7,220	7,227	7,282	3,546	2,387	2,067	2,347	1,875	4,112	4,857
Egypt, Arab Republic	446	1,249	1,496	1,743	1,720	1,478	965	945	996	1,105	941	449	1,274	1,236
Libya	..	..	..	..	..	..	..	..	..	..	..	..	..	..
Morocco	678	764	860	908	1,227	1,535	1,998	2,246	2,374	1,872	2,047	454	849	1,776
Tunisia	290	650	673	984	929	888	850	928	939	908	875	243	615	913
ALL AFRICA	7,120	12,607	13,001	16,006	16,006	16,601	15,013	14,685	16,132	15,238	15,227	5,722	12,297	15,613

Note: In 1995, Zambia was able to clear its arrears to the IMF after completing a 3 year Rights Arrangement Program.

6-9. Interest payments: official concessional long-term loans

	Millions of U.S. dollars (current prices)											Annual average		
	1980	1988	1989	1990	1991	1992	1993	1994	1995	1996	1997	75-84	85-89	90-MR
SUB-SAHARAN AFRICA	238	409	395	726	524	804	762	603	616	794	761	173	353	699
excluding South Africa	238	409	395	726	524	804	762	603	616	794	761	173	353	699
excl. S.Africa & Nigeria	230	409	391	414	490	443	506	601	614	792	693	165	349	569
Angola	0	3	1	1	4	3	3	7	7	3	7	0	1	4
Benin	1	5	4	7	9	7	9	9	10	9	.11	1	5	9
Botswana	1	2	3	4	5	5	6	3	3	8	7	1	2	5
Burkina Faso	2	7	8	7	6	6	6	7	8	11	13	2	6	8
Burundi	1	10	9	7	8	9	9	10	9	6	7	1	8	8
Cameroon	15	18	10	32	29	16	24	19	54	37	61	13	24	34
Cape Verde	0	1	1	1	1	1	1	1	1	1	2	0	1	1
Central African Republic	0	5	3	5	3	6	2	6	3	3	2	0	4	4
Chad	0	3	1	3	4	4	4	5	3	7	5	0	2	4
Comoros	0	0	1	1	2	1	1	1	1	1	1	0	1	1
Congo, Democratic Rep. of	47	14	15	17	14	10	7	0	0	0	0	11	12	6
Congo, Republic of	12	12	6	30	8	5	4	93	9	35	1	6	7	23
Côte d'Ivoire	14	5	7	5	52	29	30	32	47	76	75	13	12	43
Djibouti	1	3	2	2	2	2	2	2	2	3	2	1	2	2
Equatorial Guinea	0	1	0	1	1	1	0	1	0	1	1	0	0	1
Eritrea	0	0	0	0	0	0	0	0	0	0	1	0	0	0
Ethiopia	7	40	30	16	13	10	12	16	19	19	21	7	26	16
Gabon	3	2	3	2	9	20	4	15	40	39	51	2	2	23
Gambia, The	0	3	3	4	3	3	4	4	3	4	5	0	2	4
Ghana	11	25	21	23	25	32	38	39	28	51	45	13	19	35
Guinea	12	13	16	29	26	20	23	27	29	22	23	10	12	25
Guinea-Bissau	0	1	3	2	4	1	2	2	3	3	3	0	2	3
Kenya	9	30	21	23	54	28	39	47	59	57	47	9	22	44
Lesotho	0	2	2	3	4	6	5	4	5	5	5	0	2	4
Liberia	2	3	0	0	1	0	1	0	0	0	0	2	2	0
Madagascar	5	15	14	19	18	19	14	11	11	12	42	8	11	18
Malawi	4	6	7	9	12	11	13	13	19	17	16	4	6	14
Mali	2	13	12	14	10	14	38	19	19	57	18	3	11	24
Mauritania	8	11	12	13	12	11	20	22	18	18	19	8	13	17
Mauritius	1	9	8	10	11	16	15	16	18	17	15	1	6	15
Mozambique	0	11	12	9	15	22	31	16	19	25	27	0	14	20
Namibia	..	..	..	..	..	..	..	..	..	..	..	..	..	..
Niger	2	10	6	5	5	4	7	6	7	5	8	2	7	6
Nigeria	9	0	5	312	34	361	256	2	2	3	68	8	4	130
Rwanda	1	8	7	6	6	5	4	2	8	6	7	1	6	6
São Tomé and Principe	0	1	0	0	1	1	1	1	1	1	2	0	0	1
Senegal	7	31	75	29	31	19	7	25	22	79	30	4	30	30
Seychelles	0	2	2	1	2	2	1	1	2	1	1	0	1	1
Sierra Leone	0	1	0	2	1	7	3	4	5	4	7	1	1	4
Somalia	2	3	4	4	0	0	0	0	0	0	0	2	3	1
South Africa	0	0	0	0	0	0	0	0	0	0	0	0	0	0
Sudan	28	16	9	7	8	10	6	0	1	0	0	13	17	4
Swaziland	1	2	2	2	2	2	2	2	2	3	2	14	2	2
Tanzania	15	18	17	20	23	22	49	28	28	55	27	14	15	32
Togo	1	10	6	8	8	7	6	5	5	13	8	1	6	7
Uganda	1	6	6	7	10	10	13	18	23	25	27	1	6	17
Zambia	14	13	8	12	14	19	23	40	37	30	23	5	8	24
Zimbabwe	1	16	15	17	16	18	19	24	26	23	22	2	12	21
NORTH AFRICA	289	256	365	370	245	575	668	783	908	941	798	237	256	661
Algeria	36	21	19	22	23	26	26	56	90	144	125	32	20	64
Egypt, Arab Republic	153	128	205	212	82	394	421	470	571	548	410	121	132	389
Libya	..	..	..	..	..	..	..	..	..	..	..	..	..	..
Morocco	70	37	69	64	69	81	145	153	161	167	186	55	44	128
Tunisia	30	69	73	72	71	74	75	104	87	82	77	29	60	80
ALL AFRICA	527	665	761	1,096	769	1,379	1,430	1,386	1,524	1,735	1,558	410	609	1,360

6-10. Interest payments: official nonconcessional long-term loans

	Millions of U.S. dollars (current prices)											Annual average		
	1980	1988	1989	1990	1991	1992	1993	1994	1995	1996	1997	75-84	85-89	90-MR
SUB-SAHARAN AFRICA	454	1,751	1,524	1,988	2,367	1,428	1,189	1,421	1,398	1,872	1,314	385	1,316	1,622
excluding South Africa	454	1,751	1,524	1,988	2,367	1,428	1,189	1,421	1,398	1,872	1,314	385	1,316	1,622
excl. S.Africa & Nigeria	400	1,034	946	1,000	1,151	961	875	1,086	1,076	1,360	1,017	326	915	1,066
Angola	0	30	22	18	24	12	5	4	6	24	14	0	17	13
Benin	1	2	2	7	4	4	4	10	11	7	7	1	3	7
Botswana	6	31	29	32	28	28	26	26	22	61	18	6	26	30
Burkina Faso	2	6	8	3	9	9	10	8	9	4	3	2	6	7
Burundi	0	5	4	4	4	4	3	3	2	3	2	1	4	3
Cameroon	27	67	61	93	100	71	106	116	99	185	113	22	59	110
Cape Verde	0	3	2	1	2	2	1	1	1	1	1	1	2	1
Central African Republic	0	2	5	3	2	1	1	2	0	0	0	1	4	1
Chad	0	0	0	0	1	2	4	2	1	6	4	0	0	2
Comoros	0	0	0	0	1	1	0	0	0	0	0	0	0	0
Congo, Democratic Rep. of	59	70	45	60	36	17	1	0	0	0	0	33	75	14
Congo, Republic of	13	22	32	39	6	1	0	89	11	141	40	8	25	41
Côte d'Ivoire	64	178	160	182	220	210	188	236	206	252	194	48	160	211
Djibouti	0	0	0	0	0	0	0	0	0	0	0	0	0	0
Equatorial Guinea	0	1	0	0	1	1	0	0	0	0	0	0	1	0
Eritrea	0	0	0	0	0	0	0	0	0	0	0	0	0	0
Ethiopia	8	10	12	8	9	10	9	15	13	19	21	6	10	13
Gabon	17	42	52	66	76	182	25	59	134	181	177	11	28	112
Gambia, The	0	2	1	1	2	3	2	2	2	1	1	0	1	2
Ghana	13	23	24	22	27	30	30	24	23	26	23	10	19	26
Guinea	9	13	13	18	12	13	13	12	14	21	19	7	13	15
Guinea-Bissau	0	2	1	1	1	2	0	1	2	1	0	0	1	1
Kenya	45	118	103	111	100	83	87	113	107	106	65	37	99	96
Lesotho	0	3	4	3	5	6	6	7	8	7	8	1	3	6
Liberia	5	6	1	1	1	0	8	0	0	0	0	6	7	1
Madagascar	3	40	71	53	41	11	10	7	4	5	51	6	50	23
Malawi	6	18	16	22	18	15	12	10	16	9	6	8	17	14
Mali	1	1	2	2	2	2	2	4	3	2	2	0	2	2
Mauritania	1	20	12	22	13	8	22	16	14	11	14	4	15	15
Mauritius	6	23	22	23	25	24	19	18	18	16	14	5	18	20
Mozambique	0	10	15	8	13	17	40	36	52	21	14	0	8	25
Namibia	..	..	..	..	..	..	..	..	..	..	..	..	..	..
Niger	5	26	8	2	6	1	7	3	0	1	2	5	19	3
Nigeria	54	717	577	988	1,216	466	314	335	322	512	297	59	401	556
Rwanda	0	0	0	0	0	0	0	0	0	0	0	0	0	0
São Tomé and Principe	0	0	2	1	0	0	0	0	0	0	0	0	1	0
Senegal	15	63	52	42	44	20	14	36	43	36	44	13	57	35
Seychelles	0	2	2	2	2	2	2	2	3	2	3	0	2	2
Sierra Leone	2	2	0	2	1	4	10	16	14	6	2	2	1	7
Somalia	0	0	7	1	0	0	0	0	0	3	0	0	2	0
South Africa	0	0	0	0	0	0	0	0	0	0	0	0	0	0
Sudan	16	5	3	2	2	1	2	0	2	0	0	13	9	1
Swaziland	6	10	9	7	5	5	4	4	3	9	5	4	9	5
Tanzania	19	28	28	25	27	30	49	33	49	37	13	15	24	33
Togo	11	53	21	21	11	3	1	1	2	11	5	8	30	7
Uganda	1	14	15	11	17	11	17	15	9	13	12	2	13	13
Zambia	40	29	37	31	205	60	55	66	80	39	29	32	37	70
Zimbabwe	0	53	45	50	49	58	79	90	95	95	92	6	40	76
NORTH AFRICA	301	1,395	1,572	1,500	1,488	1,715	1,805	2,012	2,297	2,497	2,180	369	1,244	1,937
Algeria	124	308	285	290	321	345	339	342	714	1,090	1,024	104	284	558
Egypt, Arab Republic	68	528	601	519	315	455	452	546	541	397	244	162	480	434
Libya	..	..	..	..	..	..	..	..	..	..	..	..	..	..
Morocco	66	407	537	517	661	700	780	865	762	723	650	66	352	707
Tunisia	44	153	149	175	191	214	234	258	281	287	261	37	128	238
ALL AFRICA	755	3,146	3,096	3,488	3,854	3,143	2,993	3,433	3,695	4,369	3,494	754	2,560	3,559

6-11. Interest payments: private long-term loans

	Millions of U.S. dollars (current prices)											*Annual average*		
	1980	*1988*	*1989*	*1990*	*1991*	*1992*	*1993*	*1994*	*1995*	*1996*	*1997*	*75-84*	*85-89*	*90-MR*
SUB-SAHARAN AFRICA	1,685	1,616	1,726	1,647	1,537	1,620	747	1,936	1,976	2,135	1,720	1,254	1,639	1,665
excluding South Africa	1,685	1,616	1,726	1,647	1,537	1,620	747	1,319	1,121	1,212	938	1,254	1,639	1,268
excl. S.Africa & Nigeria	1,219	855	828	824	733	616	455	580	586	684	760	845	973	655
Angola	..	72	79	81	76	32	18	40	66	246	291	..	51	106
Benin	1	0	6	0	0	0	0	0	0	0	0	3	7	0
Botswana	1	4	4	3	3	2	1	1	3	9	2	1	3	3
Burkina Faso	3	0	0	0	0	0	0	0	0	0	0	1	1	0
Burundi	1	2	2	1	1	0	0	0	0	0	0	1	2	0
Cameroon	78	128	62	73	41	65	26	21	21	14	16	56	93	35
Cape Verde	0	0	0	0	0	0	0	0	0	0	1	0	0	0
Central African Republic	0	0	0	1	1	0	0	0	0	0	0	1	0	0
Chad	0	0	0	0	0	0	0	0	0	0	0	0	0	0
Comoros	0	0	0	0	0	0	0	0	0	0	0	0	0	0
Congo, Democratic Rep. of	99	14	34	12	7	1	0	0	0	0	0	61	40	2
Congo, Republic of	13	48	54	52	36	22	17	50	40	3	0	36	64	27
Côte d'Ivoire	513	184	233	256	220	171	163	159	138	145	145	343	341	174
Djibouti	0	0	0	0	0	0	0	0	0	0	0	0	0	0
Equatorial Guinea	0	0	0	0	0	0	0	0	0	0	0	0	0	0
Eritrea	..	..	..	..	..	..	..	0	0	0	0	..	..	0
Ethiopia	2	33	31	24	16	22	3	9	29	15	4	4	24	15
Gabon	100	20	15	11	51	36	6	29	44	12	10	52	26	25
Gambia, The	0	0	0	5	2	1	0	0	0	0	0	0	1	1
Ghana	7	23	19	14	14	19	17	21	8	28	41	4	16	20
Guinea	2	5	3	6	1	0	1	2	1	0	4	2	2	2
Guinea-Bissau	1	0	0	0	0	0	0	0	0	0	0	0	0	0
Kenya	110	90	75	95	92	88	81	128	96	82	71	69	81	91
Lesotho	1	2	2	2	1	1	1	1	3	3	5	1	1	2
Liberia	16	0	0	0	0	0	0	0	0	0	0	5	0	0
Madagascar	19	18	16	13	7	3	1	1	1	2	0	12	12	3
Malawi	25	4	5	6	7	4	2	2	4	2	1	13	7	4
Mali	1	0	0	1	0	0	0	0	0	0	0	1	1	0
Mauritania	4	1	1	1	1	0	0	0	0	0	2	3	2	0
Mauritius	15	12	13	10	13	13	8	11	21	38	94	11	11	26
Mozambique	..	7	6	6	5	5	4	2	4	1	1	..	6	4
Namibia	..	..	..	..	..	..	..	..	..	..	..	..	..	..
Niger	58	31	21	16	10	8	7	6	6	5	3	30	26	8
Nigeria	466	761	897	823	805	1,004	292	739	535	528	178	409	667	613
Rwanda	0	1	0	0	0	0	0	0	0	0	0	0	1	0
São Tomé and Principe	0	0	0	0	0	0	0	0	0	0	0	0	0	0
Senegal	46	25	22	13	18	8	2	2	4	2	1	22	22	6
Seychelles	0	3	2	2	1	1	2	3	2	1	1	0	2	2
Sierra Leone	5	0	0	0	0	0	0	0	0	0	0	4	0	0
Somalia	0	0	0	0	0	0	0	0	0	0	0	1	0	0
South Africa	..	..	..	..	..	..	..	617	855	923	782	..	..	794
Sudan	5	0	0	0	0	0	0	0	0	0	0	15	9	0
Swaziland	2	1	1	1	1	1	0	0	0	0	0	1	1	0
Tanzania	13	4	5	3	4	6	5	1	5	5	2	9	3	4
Togo	8	6	5	5	0	0	0	0	0	0	0	7	6	1
Uganda	1	4	4	1	7	5	3	1	2	0	0	2	4	2
Zambia	63	35	31	29	20	20	15	11	16	5	6	43	23	15
Zimbabwe	9	78	77	83	81	81	72	80	75	67	59	30	83	75
NORTH AFRICA	2,078	2,152	2,382	2,113	2,176	3,260	1,970	1,680	1,605	1,453	1,221	1,372	2,062	1,935
Algeria	1,280	1,353	1,435	1,472	1,445	1,443	1,338	1,098	918	771	819	837	1,283	1,163
Egypt, Arab Republic	129	247	295	281	257	191	167	138	131	97	69	128	267	166
Libya	..	..	..	..	..	..	..	..	..	..	..	..	..	..
Morocco	515	400	496	213	352	1,516	354	345	437	447	192	319	370	482
Tunisia	154	153	156	147	123	110	110	100	118	138	140	88	142	123
ALL AFRICA	3,763	3,768	4,108	3,760	3,713	4,880	2,717	3,617	3,581	3,588	2,941	2,625	3,701	3,600

6-12. Interest payments: long-term loans and IMF charges

	Millions of U.S. dollars (current prices)											Annual average		
	1980	1988	1989	1990	1991	1992	1993	1994	1995	1996	1997	75-84	85-89	90-MR
SUB-SAHARAN AFRICA	2,481	4,056	3,936	4,599	4,656	4,038	2,836	4,130	4,548	4,925	3,896	1,939	3,663	4,204
excluding South Africa	2,481	4,056	3,936	4,599	4,656	4,038	2,836	3,474	3,643	3,962	3,081	1,939	3,663	3,786
excl. S.Africa & Nigeria	1,951	2,578	2,456	2,476	2,601	2,207	1,974	2,399	2,784	2,919	2,537	1,463	2,591	2,487
Angola	0	105	102	100	103	47	25	51	79	274	312	0	69	124
Benin	3	8	12	14	13	11	13	19	22	17	18	5	14	16
Botswana	8	37	36	39	35	36	33	31	28	78	28	8	31	38
Burkina Faso	6	14	16	10	15	14	16	15	18	16	16	5	13	15
Burundi	3	17	15	12	13	14	12	13	11	9	9	2	14	12
Cameroon	121	213	141	209	180	160	159	157	176	238	192	92	177	184
Cape Verde	0	4	2	2	3	3	2	2	2	2	4	1	3	2
Central African Republic	1	9	10	10	7	7	4	9	5	4	3	3	10	6
Chad	1	4	2	4	5	6	8	8	5	14	11	1	3	8
Comoros	0	0	1	1	2	3	1	1	1	1	1	0	1	1
Congo, Democratic Rep. of	220	147	141	127	67	35	10	2	16	5	0	118	179	33
Congo, Republic of	38	82	92	121	51	29	21	232	62	181	41	50	97	92
Côte d'Ivoire	590	410	439	474	524	436	399	437	398	478	416	417	560	445
Djibouti	1	4	2	2	2	2	2	2	2	3	2	1	3	2
Equatorial Guinea	0	2	1	1	2	1	1	1	1	1	1	0	2	1
Eritrea	..	..	..	..	..	..	..	0	0	0	1	..	..	0
Ethiopia	19	88	77	51	38	42	24	40	61	54	46	20	65	45
Gabon	120	68	79	91	148	246	41	106	223	236	244	66	60	167
Gambia, The	1	7	6	12	7	7	6	6	5	5	6	2	6	7
Ghana	35	119	106	96	96	102	100	95	69	112	114	30	100	98
Guinea	24	32	35	55	40	33	37	41	44	44	46	20	29	42
Guinea-Bissau	1	4	4	3	5	3	2	4	6	4	3	1	3	4
Kenya	171	266	229	254	264	210	211	290	264	246	184	125	236	240
Lesotho	2	7	7	8	10	13	12	11	15	15	18	2	6	13
Liberia	24	9	1	1	2	1	9	0	2	2	0	17	10	2
Madagascar	28	85	112	95	72	37	27	20	17	19	93	30	85	47
Malawi	37	36	35	42	42	33	28	26	40	29	24	28	39	33
Mali	4	20	18	20	15	17	41	24	22	60	21	5	19	28
Mauritania	15	36	29	38	27	20	43	38	33	30	36	16	33	33
Mauritius	26	53	50	48	51	53	42	45	56	71	123	24	47	61
Mozambique	0	27	32	23	34	43	76	55	76	48	42	0	27	50
Namibia	..	..	..	..	..	..	..	..	..	..	..	..	..	..
Niger	65	73	40	27	24	15	23	16	14	11	14	37	57	18
Nigeria	529	1,478	1,480	2,124	2,054	1,831	862	1,075	859	1,043	544	476	1,072	1,299
Rwanda	2	8	8	6	6	6	5	2	8	7	8	1	7	6
São Tomé and Principe	0	1	3	1	1	1	1	1	1	1	2	0	1	1
Senegal	70	137	165	99	103	53	26	66	72	121	78	45	126	77
Seychelles	0	7	6	6	4	5	5	6	7	5	5	0	5	5
Sierra Leone	10	3	1	4	2	14	14	58	19	11	9	8	5	16
Somalia	2	3	14	5	0	0	0	0	1	3	0	5	11	1
South Africa	0	0	0	0	0	0	0	656	905	963	816	0	0	417
Sudan	63	21	25	9	10	13	11	1	15	12	15	57	52	11
Swaziland	9	13	11	10	8	8	7	6	5	12	7	5	12	8
Tanzania	54	54	54	53	57	59	104	62	83	98	44	41	46	70
Togo	19	73	37	37	22	12	9	6	8	24	14	17	47	17
Uganda	7	41	42	32	41	29	34	36	36	40	42	14	44	36
Zambia	142	79	76	74	304	167	152	158	551	85	63	102	88	194
Zimbabwe	10	156	142	152	147	163	179	203	209	196	184	41	150	179
NORTH AFRICA	2,698	3,898	4,445	4,155	4,059	5,696	4,544	4,544	4,913	4,983	4,302	2,015	3,663	4,649
Algeria	1,440	1,682	1,762	1,846	1,848	1,883	1,746	1,527	1,791	2,081	2,061	972	1,591	1,848
Egypt, Arab Republic	367	913	1,114	1,027	665	1,054	1,053	1,165	1,252	1,044	724	422	886	998
Libya	..	..	..	..	..	..	..	..	..	..	..	..	..	..
Morocco	663	913	1,169	866	1,145	2,341	1,311	1,375	1,367	1,338	1,028	466	844	1,346
Tunisia	229	391	401	418	402	417	436	477	503	519	488	155	341	457
ALL AFRICA	5,179	7,955	8,381	8,755	8,715	9,734	7,380	8,674	9,461	9,907	8,198	3,954	7,325	8,853

6-13. Total external debt service payments: long-term loans & IMF credit

	Millions of U.S. dollars (current prices)											Annual average		
	1980	1988	1989	1990	1991	1992	1993	1994	1995	1996	1997	75-84	85-89	90-MR
SUB-SAHARAN AFRICA	5,658	9,414	8,795	10,192	9,566	9,512	6,757	11,150	13,984	14,212	12,912	4,638	9,109	11,036
excluding South Africa	5,658	9,414	8,795	10,192	9,566	9,512	6,757	8,500	11,009	10,480	8,693	4,638	9,109	9,339
excl. S.Africa & Nigeria	4,887	7,243	6,709	6,888	6,650	5,803	5,316	6,678	9,232	8,019	7,310	3,575	6,896	6,987
Angola	0	202	241	283	336	191	87	203	410	783	795	0	164	386
Benin	9	21	21	35	29	26	31	40	48	44	51	13	34	38
Botswana	14	77	73	106	89	98	90	93	92	151	102	13	64	103
Burkina Faso	17	38	33	29	40	29	36	42	47	47	49	11	33	40
Burundi	7	45	42	41	38	38	35	41	38	30	29	8	38	36
Cameroon	252	602	349	479	394	363	441	361	393	486	473	203	559	424
Cape Verde	0	8	7	6	9	11	5	6	5	6	12	1	6	7
Central African Republic	8	25	32	28	14	14	7	21	15	12	12	9	27	15
Chad	6	9	10	10	9	10	16	18	15	30	35	5	10	18
Comoros	0	1	1	1	8	6	2	3	1	1	2	1	1	3
Congo, Democratic Rep. of	497	358	583	327	158	64	15	6	18	42	0	241	458	79
Congo, Republic of	78	376	295	483	260	127	98	538	146	321	96	136	355	259
Côte d'Ivoire	1,312	996	934	1,095	1,142	1,030	984	1,224	1,023	1,338	1,254	822	1,110	1,136
Djibouti	3	14	12	11	10	10	9	11	11	12	7	3	10	10
Equatorial Guinea	2	5	6	5	4	3	1	2	2	5	5	3	7	3
Eritrea	..	..	..	..	..	..	..	0	0	0	1	..	..	0
Ethiopia	36	301	296	228	131	104	90	107	153	346	98	51	242	157
Gabon	399	101	101	131	261	383	112	225	439	373	415	235	134	292
Gambia, The	1	21	23	37	30	29	27	30	26	27	26	5	21	29
Ghana	141	536	444	356	285	300	286	343	378	442	476	87	348	358
Guinea	100	124	113	165	133	84	81	94	173	110	151	76	105	124
Guinea-Bissau	4	8	10	6	22	6	3	7	15	11	9	2	8	10
Kenya	376	689	653	708	660	616	574	839	859	810	618	343	646	710
Lesotho	5	24	22	23	26	34	33	29	40	37	45	6	19	33
Liberia	43	21	6	3	17	1	22	15	2	2	0	41	21	8
Madagascar	76	217	234	215	156	93	75	63	55	79	211	76	208	118
Malawi	71	101	91	128	126	105	78	79	116	84	75	57	109	99
Mali	13	73	65	64	42	55	76	87	84	114	75	13	62	75
Mauritania	40	124	95	137	89	81	124	102	112	112	106	51	104	108
Mauritius	44	199	141	151	168	180	125	148	210	179	259	54	146	178
Mozambique	0	61	67	64	75	78	119	122	161	140	101	0	66	108
Namibia	..	..	..	..	..	..	..	..	..	..	..	..	..	..
Niger	122	162	114	90	98	51	88	64	55	56	59	87	130	70
Nigeria	772	2,170	2,087	3,304	2,917	3,709	1,441	1,822	1,777	2,461	1,383	1,064	2,213	2,352
Rwanda	4	20	24	16	18	15	16	3	20	17	20	4	20	16
São Tomé and Principe	1	2	5	2	2	2	2	2	2	3	6	1	3	3
Senegal	235	366	358	296	293	196	108	220	267	282	236	112	309	237
Seychelles	0	17	20	18	15	17	17	16	23	15	14	1	13	17
Sierra Leone	60	14	6	16	12	30	27	155	78	58	19	36	21	49
Somalia	13	5	32	10	0	0	0	0	1	3	0	14	31	2
South Africa	0	0	0	0	0	0	0	2,650	2,976	3,732	4,219	0	0	1,697
Sudan	194	79	71	25	22	27	20	3	69	48	58	147	115	34
Swaziland	17	38	33	46	29	25	24	26	21	33	24	12	36	28
Tanzania	135	140	170	171	202	231	208	179	228	264	155	100	147	205
Togo	38	126	86	80	50	32	23	19	26	56	52	44	108	42
Uganda	52	199	182	143	143	109	154	148	135	147	187	49	172	146
Zambia	411	191	206	200	596	352	363	371	2,611	245	258	296	219	624
Zimbabwe	50	511	406	422	413	550	585	575	613	620	633	107	456	551
NORTH AFRICA	6,640	11,148	12,587	14,569	15,155	16,824	15,638	12,210	11,609	10,934	10,512	5,037	10,513	13,431
Algeria	3,968	6,269	6,874	8,624	9,067	9,110	9,027	5,073	4,179	4,148	4,408	2,848	5,703	6,705
Egypt, Arab Republic	813	2,163	2,610	2,770	2,385	2,532	2,017	2,109	2,248	2,149	1,665	871	2,160	2,234
Libya	..	..	..	..	..	..	..	..	..	..	..	..	..	..
Morocco	1,341	1,677	2,029	1,774	2,372	3,876	3,308	3,622	3,741	3,210	3,075	921	1,693	3,122
Tunisia	518	1,040	1,074	1,402	1,331	1,305	1,285	1,405	1,442	1,427	1,363	398	956	1,370
ALL AFRICA	12,298	20,562	21,383	24,761	24,721	26,335	22,394	23,359	25,593	25,146	23,424	9,676	19,622	24,467

Note: In 1995, Zambia was able to clear its arrears to the IMF after completing a 3 year Rights Arrangement Program.

6-14. Interest payments: short-term loans

	Millions of U.S. dollars (current prices)											Annual average		
	1980	1988	1989	1990	1991	1992	1993	1994	1995	1996	1997	75-84	85-89	90-MR
SUB-SAHARAN AFRICA	1,031	656	624	715	603	558	527	635	819	885	1,041	541	692	723
excluding South Africa	1,031	656	624	715	603	558	527	384	404	381	487	541	692	507
excl. S.Africa & Nigeria	652	616	593	683	575	518	477	334	348	333	454	304	523	465
Angola	..	31	25	43	53	54	66	55	53	49	46	..	35	52
Benin	11	7	5	4	3	2	1	1	2	2	4	5	7	2
Botswana	2	0	0	0	0	0	0	0	0	0	1	0	0	0
Burkina Faso	5	5	5	6	6	5	2	2	2	2	3	2	4	3
Burundi	2	2	1	2	1	1	1	1	1	0	0	1	2	1
Cameroon	28	74	57	43	33	31	30	24	39	24	40	17	54	33
Cape Verde	0	0	0	0	0	0	0	0	1	0	0	0	0	0
Central African Republic	2	2	2	2	2	2	2	2	1	1	1	1	2	2
Chad	0	0	2	2	2	1	1	0	1	0	1	0	0	1
Comoros	0	1	1	0	0	0	0	0	0	0	0	0	0	0
Congo, Democratic Rep. of	45	34	26	21	20	13	13	9	8	7	12	18	27	13
Congo, Republic of	31	46	46	48	40	35	30	20	35	18	16	12	45	30
Côte d'Ivoire	95	79	142	167	138	130	110	20	23	37	105	47	80	91
Djibouti	1	2	3	4	4	2	2	1	1	0	1	1	2	2
Equatorial Guinea	1	0	0	0	0	0	0	1	0	0	1	1	0	0
Eritrea	..	..	..	..	..	..	..	0	0	0	0	..	..	0
Ethiopia	9	8	8	8	7	5	5	4	1	1	1	4	7	4
Gabon	33	32	45	45	48	50	45	43	17	11	18	13	31	35
Gambia, The	3	2	1	1	1	1	1	2	1	1	1	1	2	1
Ghana	18	9	10	12	17	19	22	26	28	36	29	12	12	24
Guinea	9	4	4	4	4	4	3	3	5	3	10	4	5	4
Guinea-Bissau	1	2	2	3	1	0	0	0	0	1	1	1	2	1
Kenya	58	46	51	78	55	49	53	38	36	30	30	24	39	46
Lesotho	1	0	0	0	0	0	0	0	0	0	0	0	0	0
Liberia	11	4	0	0	0	0	0	0	0	0	0	4	3	0
Madagascar	29	1	4	7	5	3	3	2	3	4	1	9	4	4
Malawi	16	5	5	4	4	4	1	1	3	4	3	5	5	3
Mali	3	4	4	3	3	2	2	1	2	2	3	2	4	2
Mauritania	7	9	8	9	10	6	4	4	5	4	8	5	7	6
Mauritius	8	3	4	5	5	3	4	10	16	19	23	3	3	11
Mozambique	..	9	12	15	7	5	3	1	1	1	3	..	8	5
Namibia	..	..	..	..	..	..	..	..	..	..	..	..	..	..
Niger	19	7	9	9	10	2	2	2	1	1	2	7	7	4
Nigeria	379	40	31	32	28	40	50	50	56	48	33	236	169	42
Rwanda	3	3	5	5	6	6	6	1	1	1	2	1	3	3
São Tomé and Principe	0	0	1	1	0	0	1	0	0	1	1	0	0	1
Senegal	24	23	24	29	21	15	15	14	14	7	11	13	21	16
Seychelles	37	1	4	4	3	2	1	1	1	1	1	5	2	1
Sierra Leone	6	5	1	5	4	5	4	5	1	1	1	3	4	3
Somalia	0	1	0	0	0	0	0	0	0	0	0	0	0	0
South Africa	..	..	..	..	..	..	..	251	415	504	555	..	..	431
Sudan	70	100	25	25	0	0	0	0	0	0	0	39	38	3
Swaziland	2	1	2	0	0	0	0	0	0	0	8	1	1	1
Tanzania	26	22	7	9	5	5	4	5	4	6	6	12	19	5
Togo	14	6	6	6	5	5	4	4	3	2	2	6	6	4
Uganda	5	3	4	5	5	5	3	3	2	3	4	2	3	4
Zambia	0	0	0	3	3	1	1	2	1	9	10	0	0	4
Zimbabwe	15	22	33	49	48	45	33	28	35	44	44	22	25	41
NORTH AFRICA	869	851	726	750	527	570	385	333	316	289	428	589	736	450
Algeria	116	272	126	179	100	200	36	33	22	13	13	150	125	74
Egypt, Arab Republic	422	305	300	301	220	168	164	130	132	133	262	246	351	189
Libya	..	..	..	..	..	..	..	..	..	..	..	..	..	..
Morocco	105	73	13	20	18	15	18	18	24	9	6	57	71	16
Tunisia	26	18	27	30	39	37	67	52	38	39	49	9	21	44
ALL AFRICA	1,901	1,506	1,350	1,466	1,130	1,128	912	968	1,135	1,175	1,470	1,129	1,428	1,173

6-15. Net flows: long-and short-term loans, including IMF

	Millions of U.S. dollars (current prices)											Annual average		
	1980	1988	1989	1990	1991	1992	1993	1994	1995	1996	1997	75-84	85-89	90-MR
SUB-SAHARAN AFRICA	7,742	7,290	7,483	7,445	3,904	5,053	5,256	9,783	6,658	2,353	5,027	5,954	7,568	5,685
excluding South Africa	7,742	7,290	7,483	7,445	3,904	5,053	5,256	521	3,246	1,672	4,440	5,954	7,568	3,942
excl. S.Africa & Nigeria	6,231	5,653	6,917	7,479	4,066	5,761	4,784	1,181	3,804	3,007	5,102	4,938	6,343	4,398
Angola	..	800	880	977	226	907	295	306	-89	-512	-357	..	1,029	219
Benin	56	-18	110	94	94	39	65	87	93	83	112	77	53	83
Botswana	21	18	33	-37	49	22	45	-10	2	-43	-18	28	37	1
Burkina Faso	55	65	76	70	122	105	96	92	97	72	39	48	78	87
Burundi	35	55	89	66	60	85	49	31	35	13	11	37	86	44
Cameroon	500	244	506	686	72	434	181	279	57	-210	647	313	267	268
Cape Verde	3	0	4	11	-1	12	7	26	37	-3	18	10	8	13
Central African Republic	24	89	50	108	97	41	56	21	32	20	6	17	69	48
Chad	3	60	88	103	97	120	53	59	57	91	77	21	45	82
Comoros	13	1	4	2	-3	15	5	5	11	4	9	11	14	6
Congo, Democratic Rep. of	271	362	364	240	175	-28	0	-136	63	-55	242	281	291	63
Congo, Republic of	488	-93	32	97	-261	-35	310	64	169	-471	98	222	189	-4
Côte d'Ivoire	1,017	292	1,048	1,159	621	719	775	-1,096	840	2,026	435	636	443	685
Djibouti	8	10	23	21	17	30	36	-10	13	14	10	8	22	16
Equatorial Guinea	18	19	19	13	1	13	9	15	-7	1	22	8	14	8
Eritrea	..	..	..	..	..	..	..	27	7	7	33	..	..	19
Ethiopia	93	444	296	232	365	213	285	170	133	-1	130	425	453	191
Gabon	-109	238	291	170	106	-156	55	-59	8	-111	240	52	269	32
Gambia, The	51	13	13	12	18	38	28	-14	-4	57	3	18	17	17
Ghana	143	237	353	391	480	369	371	406	409	542	357	69	238	416
Guinea	47	187	206	100	119	131	231	113	76	80	379	44	145	154
Guinea-Bissau	72	45	29	46	34	23	19	28	12	28	22	22	33	26
Kenya	424	330	600	611	272	200	176	-366	145	-150	86	250	371	122
Lesotho	10	39	36	43	48	60	50	44	44	33	34	15	32	44
Liberia	61	9	-1	0	-15	-1	10	-13	0	11	-21	61	25	-4
Madagascar	329	96	114	227	136	66	79	34	74	57	207	170	140	110
Malawi	120	39	97	82	96	125	113	75	181	170	31	75	71	109
Mali	88	101	143	149	124	110	77	60	162	112	65	78	120	107
Mauritania	108	107	27	106	73	-52	80	78	56	92	142	100	85	72
Mauritius	79	147	34	120	77	55	22	260	312	110	768	37	57	216
Mozambique	..	157	213	162	16	172	66	178	208	211	321	..	298	167
Namibia	..	..	..	..	..	..	..	..	..	..	..	..	..	..
Niger	223	153	73	130	-117	57	35	21	1	10	91	107	110	29
Nigeria	1,510	1,637	566	-34	-162	-708	472	-660	-559	-1,334	-663	1,015	1,225	-456
Rwanda	25	78	53	55	79	73	50	-11	39	53	95	27	72	54
São Tomé and Principe	9	11	25	10	18	26	15	9	15	30	3	6	13	16
Senegal	171	74	216	249	-80	222	97	-69	31	-3	172	166	213	77
Seychelles	12	-1	-6	7	10	-1	-3	6	-17	-2	9	7	10	1
Sierra Leone	50	17	25	16	27	117	170	34	-152	32	18	25	45	33
Somalia	106	49	65	61	13	0	0	0	0	0	-7	136	75	8
South Africa	..	..	..	..	..	..	..	9,263	3,412	681	588	..	..	3,486
Sudan	658	346	214	171	116	272	91	9	39	-83	-115	495	74	63
Swaziland	21	-17	10	-38	-7	-9	-8	-3	7	-1	164	22	2	13
Tanzania	318	331	-126	231	129	223	127	184	114	133	182	290	150	165
Togo	78	98	114	5	52	27	-51	47	17	79	7	88	50	23
Uganda	51	98	250	241	123	212	253	196	158	191	207	62	202	198
Zambia	391	287	-15	-75	182	129	148	57	-10	151	-129	210	270	56
Zimbabwe	93	39	241	359	209	583	219	-49	331	138	258	164	57	256
NORTH AFRICA	4,953	4,650	2,518	-639	829	559	-530	1,502	1,741	1,227	-370	5,087	3,265	540
Algeria	869	1,886	665	-892	-244	28	-545	1,382	1,118	992	-602	1,435	824	155
Egypt, Arab Republic	2,337	1,525	770	-1,201	385	-672	-333	51	57	-462	483	2,162	1,430	-212
Libya	..	..	..	..	..	..	..	..	..	..	..	..	..	..
Morocco	1,394	915	855	1,051	311	671	122	-380	-202	-42	-906	1,118	757	78
Tunisia	352	325	228	404	377	532	226	448	769	739	654	373	253	519
ALL AFRICA	12,695	11,940	10,001	6,806	4,732	5,612	4,725	11,285	8,399	3,580	4,658	11,041	10,833	6,225

6-16. Net flows: long-term loans, including IMF

| | *Millions of U.S. dollars (current prices)* | | | | | | | | | | | *Annual average* | | |
	1980	*1988*	*1989*	*1990*	*1991*	*1992*	*1993*	*1994*	*1995*	*1996*	*1997*	*75-84*	*85-89*	*90-MR*
SUB-SAHARAN AFRICA	7,889	5,916	6,738	5,151	4,411	3,935	5,878	4,380	3,831	-76	1,321	6,027	5,689	3,604
excluding South Africa	7,889	5,916	6,738	5,151	4,411	3,935	5,020	2,856	2,353	402	1,252	6,027	5,689	3,172
excl. S.Africa & Nigeria	6,379	5,694	5,757	5,404	4,486	5,278	5,055	3,004	2,838	1,512	1,778	5,011	5,486	3,669
Angola	..	620	458	679	95	503	624	264	219	-463	-401	..	758	190
Benin	56	46	126	102	84	65	63	84	77	83	23	77	57	72
Botswana	21	18	34	-37	49	22	45	-10	1	-45	-52	28	37	-3
Burkina Faso	55	73	82	61	121	128	119	80	83	73	39	48	73	88
Burundi	35	80	85	69	60	86	58	31	27	23	7	37	85	45
Cameroon	500	243	664	449	220	520	264	249	-103	-41	-11	313	237	193
Cape Verde	3	6	7	8	-1	10	7	24	18	20	16	10	8	13
Central African Republic	24	85	56	105	94	41	48	36	30	25	4	17	68	48
Chad	0	56	85	105	88	139	50	74	62	107	68	22	43	87
Comoros	13	8	4	5	-3	15	4	6	9	6	4	11	14	6
Congo, Democratic Rep. of	271	330	353	267	263	54	53	1	0	3	0	281	239	80
Congo, Republic of	488	319	-15	-42	-167	33	383	30	-67	-136	-30	222	141	1
Côte d'Ivoire	1,017	126	340	521	389	351	278	524	204	64	-580	636	141	219
Djibouti	8	12	3	18	46	36	19	17	9	15	7	8	17	21
Equatorial Guinea	36	24	14	6	14	13	13	6	1	-1	-2	10	15	6
Eritrea	..	..	..	..	..	..	..	27	7	7	33	..	..	19
Ethiopia	93	406	332	225	357	263	314	170	140	1	128	425	448	200
Gabon	-109	241	131	170	68	8	58	38	57	-42	-23	52	207	42
Gambia, The	51	13	17	3	13	37	7	5	5	48	13	18	21	16
Ghana	143	281	243	293	388	353	324	302	338	493	336	69	243	353
Guinea	47	187	186	100	145	149	245	122	49	85	141	44	132	129
Guinea-Bissau	72	45	35	34	38	37	22	25	13	23	25	22	40	27
Kenya	424	400	548	317	545	179	103	-301	138	-66	-165	250	335	94
Lesotho	10	37	40	43	47	59	50	44	44	33	34	15	32	44
Liberia	61	4	-1	-1	-13	0	20	-14	0	0	0	61	22	-1
Madagascar	329	151	113	144	150	77	89	51	66	93	216	170	153	111
Malawi	120	84	102	69	120	106	151	74	149	117	106	75	72	112
Mali	88	107	148	141	127	130	58	69	138	110	71	78	123	105
Mauritania	108	69	33	54	23	81	91	82	42	83	23	100	77	60
Mauritius	79	132	50	102	77	-1	22	83	255	32	691	37	58	158
Mozambique	0	173	194	202	115	231	150	187	182	208	241	0	292	190
Namibia	..	..	..	..	..	..	..	..	..	..	..	..	..	..
Niger	223	125	91	92	-32	56	44	35	-3	8	54	107	105	32
Nigeria	1,510	222	981	-253	-76	-1,343	-35	-148	-486	-1,110	-525	1,015	203	-497
Rwanda	25	76	51	53	77	71	50	20	43	53	62	27	71	54
São Tomé and Principe	9	11	15	15	19	24	14	14	14	10	1	6	11	14
Senegal	171	115	244	81	33	225	100	7	4	67	141	166	215	82
Seychelles	12	-1	-5	-4	9	13	6	8	-7	2	2	7	7	4
Sierra Leone	50	22	12	17	14	41	95	47	40	34	34	25	14	40
Somalia	106	63	64	43	13	0	0	0	0	0	0	136	83	7
South Africa	0	0	0	0	0	0	858	1,524	1,478	-478	69	0	0	431
Sudan	790	324	191	169	116	94	91	9	-3	-18	-38	565	163	53
Swaziland	21	-8	-4	-21	-6	-10	-9	-4	3	8	8	22	0	-4
Tanzania	318	281	123	215	162	220	151	164	136	65	171	290	184	161
Togo	78	88	36	56	47	35	11	34	19	77	27	88	30	38
Uganda	51	90	240	234	118	204	298	182	162	168	196	62	197	195
Zambia	391	134	100	64	127	146	148	57	93	62	76	210	175	97
Zimbabwe	93	-2	131	177	239	437	325	55	144	20	82	164	44	185
NORTH AFRICA	4,953	4,164	2,205	1,567	385	1,228	200	1,408	1,499	891	-799	5,087	3,328	797
Algeria	869	1,581	446	156	-692	474	-453	1,446	1,496	922	-436	1,435	808	364
Egypt, Arab Republic	2,337	1,594	656	301	299	-89	180	123	-382	-438	-161	2,162	1,483	-21
Libya	..	..	..	..	..	..	..	..	..	..	..	..	..	..
Morocco	1,394	745	916	965	427	491	196	-293	-180	-66	-894	1,118	825	81
Tunisia	352	245	187	145	352	352	277	131	565	473	691	373	212	373
ALL AFRICA	12,842	10,080	8,943	6,718	4,795	5,163	6,079	5,788	5,330	815	523	11,114	9,017	4,401

6-17. Net transfers: long- and short-term loans, including IMF

| | Millions of U.S. dollars (current prices) | | | | | | | | | | | Annual average | | |
	1980	1988	1989	1990	1991	1992	1993	1994	1995	1996	1997	75-84	85-89	90-MR
SUB-SAHARAN AFRICA	5,190	2,398	2,471	1,842	-1,148	2,042	3,358	692	2,793	-2,111	6,222	4,216	2,905	1,711
excluding South Africa	5,190	2,398	2,471	1,842	-1,389	306	1,760	-2,744	148	-2,393	888	4,216	2,905	-198
excl. S.Africa & Nigeria	4,588	2,280	3,416	4,031	855	2,885	2,201	-958	1,621	32	2,127	3,913	2,921	1,599
Angola	0	664	754	834	70	805	203	201	-220	-835	-715	0	926	43
Benin	51	-36	99	74	91	26	73	92	81	82	91	69	31	76
Botswana	12	-19	-2	-77	13	-14	12	-41	-26	-122	-48	20	5	-38
Burkina Faso	48	44	53	54	110	86	91	100	104	64	38	43	59	81
Burundi	37	49	81	51	52	85	32	12	15	-5	-6	35	74	29
Cameroon	346	42	323	433	-143	189	-55	124	-150	-449	440	207	51	49
Cape Verde	3	-4	2	9	-3	9	5	24	34	-6	14	9	5	11
Central African Republic	30	79	24	95	85	31	48	21	19	9	-5	17	55	38
Chad	-1	53	91	102	91	113	42	63	57	95	65	21	44	78
Comoros	13	0	3	1	-4	12	4	6	11	4	8	11	13	5
Congo, Democratic Rep. of	61	50	61	-59	38	-76	-23	-151	38	-103	229	223	28	-13
Congo, Republic of	417	-224	-109	-74	-357	-99	258	-174	69	-650	39	162	47	-123
Côte d'Ivoire	370	-262	344	548	-100	61	217	-1,459	514	1,602	-109	245	-290	159
Djibouti	6	3	18	15	11	26	31	-12	11	15	9	6	16	13
Equatorial Guinea	35	20	13	9	6	11	12	15	-9	-1	17	9	10	8
Eritrea	..	..	..	..	..	..	..	27	7	7	33	..	..	18
Ethiopia	75	332	188	148	313	186	285	146	70	-35	83	415	363	150
Gabon	-262	213	172	28	-109	-489	-67	-167	-226	-331	-2	-26	205	-170
Gambia, The	52	4	10	3	5	27	19	-26	-17	43	-10	19	8	5
Ghana	90	50	230	232	450	185	249	203	246	308	48	85	129	240
Guinea	20	162	182	27	79	106	188	76	49	25	346	23	116	112
Guinea-Bissau	70	38	26	40	27	20	17	23	7	26	23	21	28	23
Kenya	280	93	291	310	-38	-141	-118	-676	-194	-451	-195	148	66	-188
Lesotho	10	34	34	39	40	54	47	36	25	14	11	13	27	33
Liberia	56	-4	-5	-2	-17	-1	1	-14	-2	10	-21	67	9	-6
Madagascar	340	-25	-22	92	42	10	35	0	39	37	114	151	38	46
Malawi	103	-8	54	41	49	69	78	69	141	145	-2	58	14	74
Mali	91	71	105	135	97	98	40	67	176	73	62	79	86	94
Mauritania	107	58	-11	55	24	-74	39	54	30	69	111	86	47	38
Mauritius	90	50	-57	24	0	-1	-24	204	241	21	621	30	-23	136
Mozambique	0	145	185	136	16	187	3	133	116	148	295	0	274	129
Namibia	0	0	0	0	0	0	0	0	0	0	0	0	0	0
Niger	149	52	18	88	-162	31	1	9	-24	1	87	69	46	4
Nigeria	602	118	-945	-2,190	-2,244	-2,579	-440	-1,785	-1,474	-2,425	-1,239	303	-16	-1,797
Rwanda	26	64	38	43	79	61	39	-14	44	45	104	25	60	50
São Tomé and Principe	9	10	23	8	17	25	13	7	13	28	0	6	12	14
Senegal	135	-93	31	94	-193	109	28	-110	-13	-141	69	136	67	-20
Seychelles	-25	-9	-16	-2	3	-7	-10	-2	-25	-7	4	1	3	-6
Sierra Leone	39	8	22	2	14	94	143	28	-156	31	16	23	31	21
Somalia	122	45	39	53	13	0	0	0	-1	-3	-7	144	62	7
South Africa	0	0	0	0	241	1,736	1,598	3,436	2,645	282	5,334	0	0	1,909
Sudan	782	226	152	136	106	110	115	150	312	91	-41	529	8	122
Swaziland	13	-35	-4	-49	-15	-17	-15	-9	2	-13	149	16	-14	4
Tanzania	272	288	-197	170	70	244	14	102	8	45	186	241	96	105
Togo	67	16	70	-33	17	11	-72	46	27	42	-6	72	-5	4
Uganda	104	48	186	241	121	204	206	186	147	162	164	85	117	179
Zambia	282	208	-109	-177	-160	-77	-75	-124	-134	58	-188	191	166	-110
Zimbabwe	67	-217	27	135	8	596	74	-205	166	-111	5	128	-191	83
NORTH AFRICA	1,704	-59	-1,895	-5,645	-3,393	-5,714	-5,849	-2,803	-3,295	-3,521	-4,956	2,756	-932	-4,397
Algeria	-686	-68	-619	-2,917	-1,884	-2,221	-2,655	467	-392	-495	-2,561	313	-772	-1,582
Egypt, Arab Republic	1,508	248	-668	-2,576	-499	-1,813	-1,549	-1,265	-1,422	-1,724	-518	1,507	174	-1,421
Libya	..	..	..	..	..	..	..	..	..	..	..	..	..	..
Morocco	817	-176	-409	3	-1,024	-1,801	-1,363	-1,925	-1,693	-1,436	-1,943	727	-275	-1,398
Tunisia	66	-63	-199	-155	14	122	-282	-81	213	134	66	209	-59	4
ALL AFRICA	6,894	2,339	576	-3,803	-4,540	-3,672	-2,491	-2,111	-502	-5,632	1,266	6,972	1,973	-2,686

6-18. Net transfers: long-term loans, including IMF

	Millions of U.S. dollars (current prices)											Annual average		
	1980	1988	1989	1990	1991	1992	1993	1994	1995	1996	1997	75-84	85-89	90-MR
SUB-SAHARAN AFRICA	5,409	1,859	2,802	551	-245	-103	3,042	251	-717	-5,001	-2,575	4,088	2,026	-600
excluding South Africa	5,409	1,859	2,802	551	-245	-103	2,184	-618	-1,291	-3,560	-1,828	4,088	2,026	-614
excl. S.Africa & Nigeria	4,428	3,116	3,300	2,928	1,885	3,071	3,081	606	54	-1,407	-759	3,548	2,895	1,182
Angola	0	516	357	579	-9	456	598	214	140	-736	-713	0	689	66
Benin	53	39	114	88	71	54	50	66	55	66	4	72	42	57
Botswana	14	-19	-2	-77	14	-13	12	-41	-26	-123	-80	20	6	-42
Burkina Faso	48	59	66	51	106	114	103	65	65	57	24	44	60	73
Burundi	32	63	70	56	47	71	46	18	16	14	-2	34	71	33
Cameroon	379	29	523	240	40	360	105	92	-279	-279	-203	221	60	10
Cape Verde	3	2	5	6	-3	7	5	22	16	18	12	9	6	11
Central African Republic	23	76	46	95	87	34	44	28	26	21	1	14	58	42
Chad	-1	52	83	101	83	134	42	66	57	93	57	21	40	79
Comoros	13	8	3	5	-5	12	3	5	9	6	4	11	13	5
Congo, Democratic Rep. of	52	182	212	140	196	18	43	-1	-16	-2	0	163	59	47
Congo, Republic of	450	237	-107	-162	-218	4	362	-203	-129	-317	-71	172	45	-92
Côte d'Ivoire	427	-284	-99	47	-135	-85	-121	87	-194	-414	-996	219	-419	-226
Djibouti	7	8	0	16	44	33	17	15	7	12	5	7	14	19
Equatorial Guinea	36	22	13	5	12	11	12	5	0	-3	-3	9	13	5
Eritrea	..	..	..	..	..	..	..	27	7	7	33	..	..	18
Ethiopia	74	318	254	175	319	221	289	130	79	-53	81	405	382	155
Gabon	-228	173	52	79	-80	-239	17	-68	-166	-279	-267	-14	147	-125
Gambia, The	50	7	11	-8	5	30	1	-1	-1	44	7	17	15	10
Ghana	108	163	137	197	292	251	224	208	270	380	222	38	143	256
Guinea	23	156	152	45	105	116	208	81	5	41	95	24	103	87
Guinea-Bissau	71	42	31	31	33	35	20	22	7	19	22	22	36	24
Kenya	253	134	319	63	281	-31	-108	-592	-125	-312	-350	125	99	-147
Lesotho	8	30	33	35	37	45	38	33	28	18	16	13	27	31
Liberia	36	-4	-3	-2	-15	-1	11	-14	-2	-2	0	44	12	-3
Madagascar	301	67	0	49	78	40	62	31	50	74	122	140	68	63
Malawi	84	48	66	27	78	73	123	48	109	88	83	47	33	78
Mali	83	87	130	121	112	113	17	45	116	50	50	73	104	78
Mauritania	94	34	4	16	-4	61	49	43	9	52	-12	84	45	27
Mauritius	53	79	0	54	26	-54	-21	37	199	-39	568	13	11	96
Mozambique	0	146	162	179	81	188	75	132	106	160	199	0	265	140
Namibia	..	..	..	..	..	..	..	..	..	..	..	..	..	..
Niger	158	52	52	65	-55	41	22	19	-16	-3	41	70	49	14
Nigeria	981	-1,257	-499	-2,377	-2,130	-3,174	-897	-1,223	-1,344	-2,153	-1,069	540	-869	-1,796
Rwanda	23	68	43	47	71	65	45	19	34	47	54	26	64	48
São Tomé and Principe	9	10	12	14	18	23	13	13	13	9	-1	6	9	13
Senegal	100	-22	78	-18	-70	171	73	-59	-68	-54	63	121	89	5
Seychelles	12	-8	-11	-9	5	8	0	2	-14	-3	-3	6	3	-2
Sierra Leone	41	19	11	13	12	28	81	-11	21	23	25	16	9	24
Somalia	104	60	51	38	13	0	0	0	-1	-3	0	131	71	6
South Africa	0	0	0	0	0	0	858	868	573	-1,441	-747	0	0	14
Sudan	727	303	166	161	106	81	81	9	-18	-31	-53	509	111	42
Swaziland	12	-21	-15	-31	-14	-17	-16	-10	-2	-4	1	16	-13	-12
Tanzania	264	226	69	162	105	162	48	102	53	-33	127	249	138	91
Togo	59	15	-1	19	25	22	3	27	11	53	13	70	-17	22
Uganda	44	49	198	202	76	175	264	147	126	128	154	48	153	159
Zambia	249	55	24	-10	-177	-22	-3	-101	-458	-23	13	107	87	-98
Zimbabwe	82	-157	-11	26	92	274	146	-149	-65	-176	-102	123	-106	6
NORTH AFRICA	2,255	266	-2,240	-2,588	-3,675	-4,468	-4,344	-3,137	-3,414	-4,092	-5,100	3,072	-335	-3,852
Algeria	-570	-101	-1,316	-1,689	-2,540	-1,409	-2,198	-81	-296	-1,159	-2,497	463	-784	-1,484
Egypt, Arab Republic	1,970	681	-458	-726	-367	-1,144	-873	-1,042	-1,633	-1,482	-885	1,740	597	-1,019
Libya	..	..	..	..	..	..	..	..	..	..	..	..	..	..
Morocco	732	-168	-253	100	-718	-1,850	-1,115	-1,668	-1,547	-1,404	-1,922	651	-19	-1,265
Tunisia	124	-145	-214	-272	-50	-65	-158	-346	62	-46	203	218	-129	-84
ALL AFRICA	7,663	2,125	562	-2,037	-3,920	-4,571	-1,302	-2,886	-4,131	-9,093	-7,675	7,160	1,691	-4,452

6-19. Long-term debt: official concessional

	Millions of U.S. dollars (current prices)											Annual average		
	1980	1988	1989	1990	1991	1992	1993	1994	1995	1996	1997	75-84	85-89	90-MR
SUB-SAHARAN AFRICA	16,325	48,287	50,589	58,839	63,433	66,340	69,996	76,163	81,231	83,324	83,420	16,306	42,869	72,843
excluding South Africa	16,325	48,287	50,589	58,839	63,433	66,340	69,996	76,163	81,231	83,324	83,420	16,306	42,869	72,843
excl. S.Africa & Nigeria	15,887	47,848	50,147	58,318	62,471	65,368	68,903	74,873	79,855	81,971	82,098	15,939	42,451	71,732
Angola	..	630	886	1,199	1,282	1,304	1,317	1,407	1,492	2,166	2,230	..	423	1,550
Benin	166	531	919	1,009	1,036	1,105	1,165	1,270	1,253	1,293	1,265	166	539	1,175
Botswana	59	134	164	185	229	233	264	293	340	322	290	86	126	269
Burkina Faso	221	599	512	597	724	820	914	906	1,001	1,085	1,077	177	493	891
Burundi	104	675	757	780	836	891	946	1,012	1,047	1,041	989	107	570	943
Cameroon	873	1,343	1,604	1,829	1,864	2,339	2,484	3,507	4,105	4,156	3,955	690	1,335	3,030
Cape Verde	20	88	95	95	98	105	108	136	152	161	172	21	80	128
Central African Republic	59	442	494	511	609	629	674	723	765	768	726	64	354	676
Chad	171	273	301	402	495	538	592	674	694	763	804	141	218	620
Comoros	43	173	148	159	158	168	163	172	183	184	173	44	152	170
Congo, Democratic Rep. of	862	2,006	2,609	3,115	3,242	3,181	3,192	3,376	3,483	3,334	3,102	819	1,928	3,253
Congo, Republic of	404	1,004	1,036	1,741	1,816	1,756	1,690	1,884	1,984	2,003	1,854	373	885	1,841
Côte d'Ivoire	438	1,958	2,159	3,096	3,402	3,510	3,698	3,886	4,565	4,809	4,507	411	1,770	3,934
Djibouti	15	151	128	152	202	217	229	253	267	278	252	19	123	231
Equatorial Guinea	32	102	122	117	124	131	139	141	147	144	138	31	83	135
Eritrea	..	..	..	..	..	..	..	29	37	42	73	..	..	45
Ethiopia	562	6,639	6,789	7,538	7,677	7,858	8,185	8,485	8,717	8,695	8,633	1,352	5,913	8,223
Gabon	113	279	300	422	488	448	408	574	790	824	971	87	230	616
Gambia, The	68	212	225	250	269	298	311	338	360	398	394	59	185	327
Ghana	772	1,626	1,827	2,120	2,383	2,574	2,895	3,343	3,724	3,919	3,976	682	1,447	3,117
Guinea	678	1,490	1,398	1,675	1,804	1,977	2,157	2,329	2,457	2,426	2,484	734	1,256	2,164
Guinea-Bissau	87	287	324	393	415	439	475	534	564	675	666	63	238	520
Kenya	680	2,032	1,980	2,406	2,739	2,814	3,110	3,390	3,870	3,923	3,727	647	1,738	3,247
Lesotho	44	203	239	292	335	371	382	440	469	465	456	48	183	401
Liberia	211	568	568	594	585	573	599	622	635	610	585	221	540	600
Madagascar	469	1,497	1,493	1,723	1,944	1,958	1,952	2,118	2,242	2,132	2,679	520	1,249	2,093
Malawi	258	865	920	1,051	1,227	1,311	1,502	1,681	1,897	1,942	1,946	275	743	1,570
Mali	613	1,816	1,940	2,247	2,379	2,690	2,692	2,464	2,660	2,687	2,621	592	1,652	2,555
Mauritania	526	1,285	1,237	1,280	1,328	1,327	1,521	1,598	1,688	1,739	1,698	507	1,174	1,522
Mauritius	65	244	260	349	393	383	383	416	439	402	345	65	207	389
Mozambique	..	2,174	2,231	2,085	2,394	2,634	2,848	3,228	2,925	3,216	3,385	..	1,910	2,839
Namibia	..	..	..	..	..	..	..	..	..	..	..	..	..	..
Niger	155	783	699	827	834	881	933	979	1,018	1,032	1,057	173	611	945
Nigeria	438	439	442	521	961	972	1,094	1,290	1,377	1,354	1,322	367	417	1,111
Rwanda	141	600	571	659	743	787	835	903	961	977	985	126	487	856
São Tomé and Principe	20	76	89	109	129	149	163	183	228	225	223	16	65	176
Senegal	400	2,026	1,731	1,968	1,947	2,080	2,111	2,103	2,239	2,286	2,394	412	1,598	2,141
Seychelles	19	61	61	71	76	70	66	67	68	67	67	13	55	69
Sierra Leone	175	303	298	312	329	384	492	590	700	738	733	156	266	535
Somalia	546	1,420	1,456	1,557	1,577	1,540	1,546	1,576	1,596	1,557	1,503	564	1,304	1,557
South Africa	..	..	..	..	..	..	..	0	0	0	0	..	..	0
Sudan	1,730	3,921	4,193	4,452	4,599	4,597	4,671	4,775	4,838	4,750	4,636	1,697	3,727	4,665
Swaziland	86	132	141	160	157	146	135	153	167	154	141	63	122	151
Tanzania	2,693	3,190	3,175	3,469	3,577	3,848	4,016	4,372	4,454	4,482	5,091	2,556	3,034	4,164
Togo	245	575	544	699	760	788	795	880	901	962	955	186	456	842
Uganda	254	893	1,152	1,451	1,625	1,806	2,130	2,456	2,768	2,878	2,949	222	792	2,258
Zambia	797	1,801	1,585	2,267	2,688	2,611	2,796	3,156	3,446	3,824	3,797	672	1,561	3,073
Zimbabwe	15	744	788	906	955	1,100	1,221	1,455	1,522	1,441	1,398	81	628	1,250
NORTH AFRICA	13,487	23,901	24,755	24,061	25,763	26,520	27,725	30,652	32,883	36,551	34,169	11,989	22,005	29,790
Algeria	1,269	628	618	860	955	1,056	1,313	2,053	3,110	3,283	3,099	1,031	599	1,966
Egypt, Arab Republic	8,115	14,486	14,717	12,520	16,621	17,151	17,996	19,531	20,285	24,021	22,573	7,116	13,200	18,837
Libya	..	..	..	..	..	..	..	..	..	..	..	..	..	..
Morocco	2,717	6,421	6,964	7,984	5,374	5,467	5,532	6,013	6,371	6,334	5,876	2,597	5,982	6,119
Tunisia	1,386	2,365	2,455	2,698	2,813	2,846	2,884	3,056	3,117	2,914	2,622	1,245	2,224	2,869
ALL AFRICA	29,812	72,188	75,343	82,900	89,195	92,860	97,721	106,815	114,114	119,875	117,589	28,295	64,873	102,634

6-20. Long-term debt: official nonconcessional

| | \multicolumn{11}{c|}{*Millions of U.S. dollars (current prices)*} | \multicolumn{3}{c}{*Annual average*} |
	1980	*1988*	*1989*	*1990*	*1991*	*1992*	*1993*	*1994*	*1995*	*1996*	*1997*	*75-84*	*85-89*	*90-MR*
SUB-SAHARAN AFRICA	9,328	38,748	44,085	50,395	52,656	51,765	50,461	54,655	56,269	52,184	47,166	8,369	34,401	51,944
excluding South Africa	9,328	38,748	44,085	50,395	52,656	51,765	50,461	54,655	56,269	52,184	47,166	8,369	34,401	51,944
excl. S.Africa & Nigeria	8,774	28,416	29,851	33,908	34,465	34,410	33,308	36,133	37,153	34,894	31,477	7,635	25,324	34,469
Angola	14	549	605	666	655	656	648	712	762	726	661	18	409	686
Benin	50	65	181	193	196	215	203	213	226	152	125	30	85	190
Botswana	76	352	345	345	360	351	340	334	306	249	205	76	309	311
Burkina Faso	39	138	102	115	152	154	148	130	130	70	58	34	111	120
Burundi	6	62	62	63	59	52	49	48	47	40	33	9	55	49
Cameroon	364	988	1,435	2,056	2,201	2,658	2,555	2,785	3,007	3,026	3,154	299	961	2,680
Cape Verde	1	31	28	33	30	30	31	31	32	30	26	12	32	30
Central African Republic	40	115	106	92	87	81	78	62	71	68	64	37	106	75
Chad	34	26	38	53	57	126	116	78	137	134	118	24	28	102
Comoros	0	14	13	14	9	7	7	8	8	9	8	2	13	9
Congo, Democratic Rep. of	1,747	4,088	4,479	5,003	5,157	4,915	4,741	5,044	5,261	5,067	4,681	1,336	3,793	4,984
Congo, Republic of	200	1,051	1,053	1,318	1,332	1,236	1,192	1,949	2,059	1,797	1,598	158	815	1,560
Côte d'Ivoire	809	3,652	3,907	4,590	5,031	5,086	4,904	4,756	4,652	3,978	3,399	694	3,117	4,549
Djibouti	7	6	3	3	3	3	2	2	2	1	1	4	5	2
Equatorial Guinea	14	64	68	74	75	67	61	63	66	62	56	13	62	65
Eritrea	0	0	0	0	0	0	0	0	0	2	3	0	0	1
Ethiopia	76	196	314	368	381	380	399	432	462	435	440	82	208	412
Gabon	204	1,143	1,542	2,013	2,060	1,976	1,929	2,853	2,988	3,004	2,569	173	807	2,424
Gambia, The	5	39	38	40	39	39	35	32	24	18	13	5	34	30
Ghana	259	332	359	431	442	439	426	417	387	320	279	181	307	393
Guinea	183	410	449	469	497	382	398	460	448	458	453	149	378	445
Guinea-Bissau	10	191	190	205	230	224	212	200	201	180	172	15	146	203
Kenya	522	1,416	1,340	1,330	1,261	1,167	1,055	1,436	1,351	1,151	918	490	1,311	1,209
Lesotho	2	44	45	52	56	66	97	115	133	129	125	5	38	97
Liberia	148	316	309	330	326	314	303	306	318	301	285	131	299	310
Madagascar	105	1,618	1,484	1,472	1,451	1,399	1,277	1,333	1,380	1,344	1,148	253	1,408	1,350
Malawi	184	275	271	253	225	193	177	170	157	126	106	132	256	176
Mali	15	53	66	73	71	81	89	79	77	75	66	13	44	76
Mauritania	57	390	394	411	398	410	363	383	385	361	316	73	343	378
Mauritius	89	296	278	300	304	254	242	234	224	213	210	74	244	248
Mozambique	0	914	922	1,478	1,469	1,857	1,832	1,888	2,227	2,132	2,027	61	796	1,864
Namibia	0	0	0	0	0	0	0	0	0	0	0	0	0	0
Niger	101	337	247	288	302	285	277	289	312	298	274	90	302	291
Nigeria	554	10,332	14,234	16,487	18,191	17,355	17,153	18,521	19,115	17,291	15,689	733	9,077	17,475
Rwanda	2	1	1	2	1	1	1	1	7	6	7	1	2	3
São Tomé and Principe	4	23	23	24	24	23	23	23	11	5	·4	5	21	17
Senegal	253	990	729	791	789	800	829	840	868	817	705	272	916	805
Seychelles	6	27	26	27	26	28	31	38	42	41	39	6	24	34
Sierra Leone	71	162	170	193	189	257	245	233	198	159	154	52	152	204
Somalia	21	325	323	333	332	322	316	323	329	325	315	60	299	324
South Africa	0	0	0	0	0	0	0	0	0	0	0	0	0	0
Sudan	1,564	2,651	2,884	3,048	3,038	2,911	2,870	2,990	3,083	3,026	2,886	1,201	2,537	2,981
Swaziland	79	112	99	83	79	66	63	57	56	66	70	57	113	67
Tanzania	349	1,584	1,613	1,837	1,766	1,618	1,417	1,391	1,376	1,257	715	343	1,385	1,422
Togo	236	431	343	324	319	283	267	287	322	289	253	180	423	293
Uganda	39	353	360	375	357	367	354	320	212	196	177	65	311	295
Zambia	705	2,060	2,068	2,139	1,945	1,782	1,564	1,518	1,475	1,430	1,294	635	1,854	1,643
Zimbabwe	86	525	541	602	689	852	1,142	1,271	1,338	1,322	1,272	86	464	1,061
NORTH AFRICA	8,111	30,312	29,251	24,941	25,793	25,910	25,705	30,746	35,345	32,201	30,667	8,070	26,647	28,914
Algeria	2,226	4,047	4,067	4,735	5,313	5,212	4,946	8,610	12,314	14,657	15,165	1,739	3,838	8,869
Egypt, Arab Republic	4,507	17,861	15,903	8,669	7,848	7,525	7,448	8,201	8,509	3,486	3,142	4,824	15,536	6,854
Libya	0	0	0	0	0	0	0	0	0	0	0	0	0	0
Morocco	802	6,500	7,177	9,007	9,608	10,121	9,955	10,114	10,149	9,408	7,908	983	5,535	9,534
Tunisia	575	1,904	2,104	2,531	3,023	3,052	3,356	3,821	4,373	4,650	4,452	524	1,738	3,657
ALL AFRICA	17,439	69,060	73,336	75,336	78,450	77,675	76,166	85,401	91,613	84,385	77,833	16,439	61,048	80,857

6-21. Long-term debt: private

	Millions of U.S. dollars (current prices)											*Annual average*		
	1980	*1988*	*1989*	*1990*	*1991*	*1992*	*1993*	*1994*	*1995*	*1996*	*1997*	*75-84*	*85-89*	*90-MR*
SUB-SAHARAN AFRICA	20,778	41,788	39,803	40,620	38,929	32,646	32,621	44,750	46,645	42,685	40,425	17,295	37,438	39,915
excluding South Africa	20,778	41,788	39,803	40,620	38,929	32,646	32,621	31,715	31,873	28,351	26,546	17,295	37,438	32,912
excl. S.Africa & Nigeria	16,402	24,485	24,822	25,692	25,413	24,164	24,125	23,260	23,924	21,264	20,631	12,799	23,459	23,559
Angola	..	4,722	5,187	5,740	5,768	6,173	6,729	7,007	7,299	6,474	5,994	..	3,834	6,398
Benin	118	362	61	17	8	5	4	4	4	4	3	142	295	6
Botswana	8	48	42	27	25	21	48	50	47	36	28	15	43	35
Burkina Faso	20	30	34	38	6	5	4	4	5	4	4	18	34	9
Burundi	8	19	14	9	6	4	3	2	2	1	1	10	22	4
Cameroon	1,014	1,525	1,680	1,714	1,716	1,525	1,467	1,245	1,147	1,028	777	727	1,386	1,327
Cape Verde	0	3	3	3	2	2	2	2	6	12	13	0	3	5
Central African Republic	48	23	21	22	21	20	21	18	18	14	14	40	23	19
Chad	54	39	8	9	8	7	6	6	2	17	17	42	31	9
Comoros	0	0	0	0	0	0	0	0	0	0	0	0	0	0
Congo, Democratic Rep. of	1,462	847	878	889	872	852	836	860	878	861	834	1,393	877	860
Congo, Republic of	653	1,430	1,414	1,147	893	883	1,232	941	913	866	832	546	1,408	963
Côte d'Ivoire	5,091	5,338	5,489	5,537	5,436	5,263	5,126	5,210	5,345	4,429	4,592	3,507	5,570	5,117
Djibouti	5	1	1	0	0	0	0	0	0	0	0	3	3	0
Equatorial Guinea	7	18	16	18	17	16	15	16	17	16	14	9	18	16
Eritrea	..	..	..	..	..	..	..	0	0	0	0	..	..	0
Ethiopia	49	680	597	577	786	765	704	654	596	354	354	103	565	599
Gabon	955	878	768	716	676	626	596	268	199	143	131	767	851	419
Gambia, The	24	26	25	18	14	9	5	1	0	0	0	16	25	6
Ghana	131	329	269	257	319	332	345	419	477	701	704	132	291	444
Guinea	159	142	121	108	98	103	104	98	82	98	72	133	133	95
Guinea-Bissau	36	46	36	33	32	30	25	28	32	1	1	17	45	23
Kenya	1,286	1,344	1,518	1,904	2,254	1,756	1,687	1,258	1,148	960	788	898	1,218	1,469
Lesotho	11	29	32	34	35	28	21	17	28	34	44	9	19	30
Liberia	156	193	188	192	196	195	200	208	208	199	192	115	186	199
Madagascar	346	219	166	140	125	112	87	86	84	77	45	256	272	94
Malawi	192	63	71	80	69	64	50	49	28	24	21	128	72	48
Mali	36	25	19	16	12	6	4	2	2	0	0	30	37	5
Mauritania	131	122	93	97	94	88	19	9	8	25	24	118	125	45
Mauritius	165	183	214	262	292	306	275	448	751	783	1,421	94	148	567
Mozambique	..	701	718	671	491	227	162	105	93	70	64	..	768	235
Namibia	..	..	..	..	..	..	..	..	..	..	..	..	..	..
Niger	432	352	358	372	226	206	182	157	133	110	96	267	368	185
Nigeria	4,376	17,303	14,981	14,928	13,516	8,482	8,496	8,455	7,949	7,086	5,915	4,496	13,979	9,353
Rwanda	8	7	5	4	3	2	1	2	2	2	1	7	9	2
São Tomé and Principe	0	2	1	1	1	1	1	1	0	0	0	1	2	1
Senegal	461	270	235	241	202	162	156	153	127	53	66	301	303	145
Seychelles	0	30	23	19	23	33	35	43	36	30	25	2	27	31
Sierra Leone	111	82	86	99	98	36	26	26	8	8	6	91	84	38
Somalia	28	35	35	37	36	35	34	36	37	36	34	86	58	36
South Africa	..	..	..	..	..	..	..	13,035	14,772	14,335	13,879	..	..	14,005
Sudan	854	1,804	1,888	2,151	2,079	1,972	1,949	2,131	2,355	2,090	1,973	872	1,730	2,087
Swaziland	24	10	9	7	5	4	2	1	0	0	0	14	15	2
Tanzania	339	482	496	484	468	406	409	407	452	428	289	259	473	418
Togo	415	52	50	52	52	51	50	51	52	50	0	247	64	45
Uganda	244	347	335	335	301	260	115	93	84	77	76	149	301	168
Zambia	726	599	599	476	418	377	333	207	174	147	155	675	612	286
Zimbabwe	595	1,029	1,022	1,141	1,233	1,196	1,054	938	1,046	1,003	930	561	1,113	1,068
NORTH AFRICA	21,549	34,864	35,246	35,968	32,043	30,049	28,198	26,957	25,366	22,302	19,463	16,616	31,613	27,543
Algeria	13,545	19,731	19,928	20,822	19,701	19,221	18,588	17,514	15,647	13,129	10,477	9,882	17,164	16,888
Egypt, Arab Republic	2,070	6,676	6,946	7,184	4,847	3,671	2,859	2,457	1,998	1,430	1,143	2,131	6,539	3,199
Libya	..	..	..	..	..	..	..	..	..	..	..	..	..	..
Morocco	4,505	6,538	6,604	6,310	6,010	5,646	5,373	5,661	5,900	5,654	5,306	3,534	6,064	5,733
Tunisia	1,429	1,919	1,768	1,652	1,486	1,511	1,379	1,324	1,821	2,089	2,537	1,069	1,846	1,725
ALL AFRICA	42,327	76,652	75,049	76,588	70,973	62,695	60,819	71,707	72,011	64,987	59,888	33,912	69,051	67,458

6-22. Total external debt

	Millions of U.S. dollars (current prices)											Annual average		
	1980	*1988*	*1989*	*1990*	*1991*	*1992*	*1993*	*1994*	*1995*	*1996*	*1997*	*75-84*	*85-89*	*90-MR*
SUB-SAHARAN AFRICA	60,641	150,535	157,351	177,400	183,595	182,555	188,707	219,670	233,687	229,462	219,322	54,451	136,848	204,300
excluding South Africa	60,641	150,535	157,351	177,400	183,595	182,555	188,707	197,999	208,329	203,412	194,100	54,451	136,848	192,012
excl. S.Africa & Nigeria	51,720	120,914	127,229	143,960	150,068	153,536	158,008	164,907	174,236	172,005	165,645	45,935	110,924	160,296
Angola	..	6,290	7,291	8,594	9,002	10,061	10,575	11,296	11,515	10,541	10,160	..	5,137	10,218
Benin	424	1,113	1,242	1,292	1,324	1,373	1,447	1,589	1,614	1,594	1,624	408	1,078	1,482
Botswana	147	539	555	563	620	612	660	689	703	614	562	182	481	628
Burkina Faso	330	845	717	834	967	1,040	1,117	1,129	1,267	1,294	1,297	269	708	1,118
Burundi	166	801	889	907	964	1,022	1,061	1,123	1,158	1,127	1,066	153	697	1,054
Cameroon	2,588	4,778	5,440	6,679	6,898	7,415	7,456	8,326	9,346	9,542	9,293	1,976	4,445	8,119
Cape Verde	21	127	128	135	135	142	149	180	220	211	220	33	120	174
Central African Republic	195	669	694	699	794	814	875	888	946	933	885	181	557	854
Chad	284	392	399	524	629	723	768	828	902	997	1,027	227	323	800
Comoros	44	199	174	185	180	188	185	192	204	206	197	48	175	192
Congo, Democratic Rep. of	4,770	8,562	9,239	10,270	10,826	10,964	11,270	12,322	13,241	12,826	12,330	4,319	7,984	11,756
Congo, Republic of	1,526	4,090	4,279	4,953	4,832	4,770	5,081	5,414	6,004	5,241	5,071	1,227	3,849	5,171
Côte d'Ivoire	7,462	13,342	14,821	17,251	18,174	18,547	19,071	17,395	18,898	19,524	15,609	5,644	12,570	18,059
Djibouti	32	185	179	205	226	235	264	263	282	296	284	33	163	257
Equatorial Guinea	76	211	229	241	254	255	264	288	292	282	283	71	185	270
Eritrea	..	..	..	..	..	..	..	29	37	44	76	..	..	46
Ethiopia	824	7,704	7,842	8,634	9,119	9,341	9,703	10,067	10,309	10,078	10,079	1,656	6,850	9,666
Gabon	1,514	2,845	3,351	3,984	4,223	3,850	3,861	4,171	4,360	4,310	4,285	1,231	2,393	4,131
Gambia, The	137	325	338	369	383	403	426	425	425	456	430	116	301	415
Ghana	1,398	3,128	3,397	3,873	4,371	4,499	4,878	5,459	5,857	6,136	5,982	1,311	2,972	5,132
Guinea	1,134	2,266	2,175	2,476	2,622	2,648	2,848	3,110	3,242	3,240	3,520	1,119	1,948	2,963
Guinea-Bissau	140	564	593	692	745	761	787	852	897	937	921	110	465	824
Kenya	3,383	5,781	5,863	7,056	7,455	6,907	7,118	7,168	7,376	6,904	6,486	2,643	5,233	7,059
Lesotho	72	287	328	396	448	495	541	620	677	670	660	69	249	563
Liberia	686	1,656	1,685	1,849	1,954	1,923	1,957	2,056	2,154	2,107	2,012	620	1,545	2,001
Madagascar	1,250	3,684	3,431	3,701	3,908	3,911	3,805	4,097	4,322	4,145	4,105	1,210	3,267	3,999
Malawi	830	1,359	1,410	1,558	1,665	1,709	1,826	2,025	2,242	2,312	2,206	659	1,263	1,943
Mali	727	2,020	2,127	2,467	2,596	2,898	2,902	2,694	2,957	3,006	2,945	699	1,879	2,808
Mauritania	840	2,044	1,957	2,096	2,188	2,088	2,141	2,223	2,350	2,412	2,453	805	1,844	2,244
Mauritius	467	874	847	985	1,043	1,051	1,008	1,382	1,756	1,818	2,472	359	768	1,439
Mozambique	..	4,163	4,363	4,653	4,718	5,130	5,195	5,622	5,726	5,782	5,991	..	3,803	5,352
Namibia	..	..	..	..	..	..	..	..	..	..	..	..	..	..
Niger	863	1,672	1,496	1,726	1,494	1,517	1,542	1,525	1,586	1,536	1,579	640	1,481	1,563
Nigeria	8,921	29,621	30,122	33,440	33,527	29,019	30,699	33,092	34,093	31,407	28,455	8,515	25,924	31,716
Rwanda	190	654	623	712	810	857	909	952	1,029	1,043	1,111	158	540	928
São Tomé and Principe	24	109	135	151	171	194	214	228	252	261	261	22	97	217
Senegal	1,473	3,886	3,271	3,732	3,570	3,666	3,803	3,658	3,841	3,664	3,671	1,269	3,396	3,701
Seychelles	84	153	144	163	173	164	157	171	159	148	149	127	140	160
Sierra Leone	469	1,032	1,066	1,151	1,206	1,245	1,396	1,493	1,178	1,181	1,149	442	942	1,250
Somalia	660	2,086	2,159	2,370	2,449	2,447	2,501	2,616	2,678	2,643	2,561	785	1,939	2,533
South Africa	..	..	..	..	..	..	..	21,671	25,358	26,050	25,222	..	..	24,575
Sudan	5,177	11,531	13,359	14,762	15,227	15,450	15,837	16,918	17,603	16,972	16,326	4,807	10,945	16,137
Swaziland	210	264	270	254	245	222	208	220	235	222	368	149	272	247
Tanzania	5,322	6,012	5,854	6,447	6,568	6,690	6,807	7,270	7,447	7,412	7,177	4,881	6,277	6,977
Togo	1,049	1,222	1,176	1,275	1,342	1,339	1,278	1,444	1,464	1,479	1,339	714	1,127	1,370
Uganda	689	1,923	2,177	2,583	2,777	2,928	3,029	3,372	3,573	3,674	3,708	611	1,733	3,205
Zambia	3,261	6,863	6,729	7,265	7,336	6,972	6,791	6,583	6,859	7,182	6,758	2,971	6,112	6,968
Zimbabwe	786	2,668	2,791	3,247	3,437	4,071	4,299	4,537	5,053	5,005	4,961	982	2,671	4,326
NORTH AFRICA	51,281	99,695	101,530	92,973	90,862	88,746	86,680	94,054	99,659	97,859	91,413	43,825	91,654	92,781
Algeria	19,365	26,027	27,072	27,877	28,204	27,078	26,020	29,973	32,810	33,428	30,921	14,323	23,682	29,539
Egypt, Arab Republic	19,131	46,084	45,611	32,947	32,543	31,067	30,509	32,314	33,266	31,299	29,849	18,165	42,350	31,724
Libya	..	..	..	..	..	..	..	..	..	..	..	..	..	..
Morocco	9,258	20,785	21,874	24,458	21,866	22,061	21,459	22,158	22,669	21,667	19,321	8,335	19,338	21,957
Tunisia	3,527	6,799	6,974	7,691	8,250	8,541	8,692	9,609	10,914	11,465	11,323	3,002	6,284	9,561
ALL AFRICA	111,922	250,229	258,881	270,373	274,457	271,301	275,387	313,724	333,346	327,321	310,735	98,276	228,501	297,080

6-23. Structure of external debt

	Bilateral				Multilateral				Private		Short-term		IMF	
Millions of U.S. dollars (current prices)	Concessional		Nonconcessional		Concessional		Nonconcessional							
	1980	1997	1980	1997	1980	1997	1980	1997	1980	1997	1980	1997	1980	1997
SUB-SAHARAN AFRICA	12,375	42,088	5,711	34,820	3,950	41,332	3,618	12,346	20,778	40,425	11,212	40,981	3,033	7,393
excluding South Africa	12,375	42,088	5,711	34,820	3,950	41,332	3,618	12,346	20,778	26,546	11,212	30,053	3,033	6,979
excluding South Africa & Nigeria	11,974	41,262	5,689	22,648	3,912	40,836	3,084	8,829	16,402	20,631	7,659	24,524	3,033	6,979
Angola	..	2,062	1	596	..	168	13	65	..	5,994	..	1,275	0	0
Benin	82	413	31	106	84	852	20	19	118	3	73	136	16	95
Botswana	28	98	23	14	32	192	53	190	8	28	4	40	0	0
Burkina Faso	89	124	30	8	133	953	9	50	20	4	35	66	15	92
Burundi	49	149	1	0	55	840	5	33	8	1	12	16	36	28
Cameroon	663	3,220	142	2,424	210	735	222	730	1,014	777	278	1,314	59	93
Cape Verde	3	29	1	10	17	143	0	16	0	13	0	9	0	0
Central African Republic	17	134	28	50	42	593	12	14	48	14	25	63	24	19
Chad	97	94	34	79	75	710	0	39	54	17	12	26	14	61
Comoros	21	30	0	0	21	143	0	8	0	0	1	13	0	3
Congo, Democratic Rep. of	667	1,566	1,620	4,039	194	1,537	127	643	1,462	834	326	3,306	373	407
Congo, Republic of	355	1,615	132	1,217	49	239	69	380	653	832	247	754	22	34
Côte d'Ivoire	369	3,076	355	1,529	69	1,431	454	1,870	5,091	4,592	1,059	2,661	65	450
Djibouti	14	117	5	0	1	135	1	1	5	0	6	25	0	5
Equatorial Guinea	30	55	13	46	2	84	1	10	7	14	7	61	16	13
Eritrea	..	34	0	0	..	39	0	3	..	0	..	0	..	0
Ethiopia	281	6,400	18	214	282	2,233	58	227	49	354	57	565	79	87
Gabon	103	941	173	2,072	10	30	30	498	955	131	228	482	15	131
Gambia, The	33	81	0	0	36	313	5	13	24	0	23	13	16	10
Ghana	633	1,015	119	60	139	2,960	140	219	131	704	131	677	105	347
Guinea	615	1,183	116	197	63	1,301	67	256	159	72	80	413	35	99
Guinea-Bissau	58	294	5	157	29	372	5	15	36	1	5	71	1	12
Kenya	414	1,345	159	515	267	2,382	364	403	1,286	788	640	803	254	250
Lesotho	4	82	2	31	40	374	0	94	11	44	8	8	6	28
Liberia	179	388	50	77	33	197	98	208	156	192	81	646	89	305
Madagascar	321	1,119	71	1,047	148	1,560	34	101	346	45	244	164	87	69
Malawi	111	245	112	16	147	1,702	72	90	192	21	116	27	80	106
Mali	451	1,197	6	36	163	1,424	9	29	36	0	24	83	39	176
Mauritania	420	924	38	151	106	774	18	164	131	24	65	304	62	113
Mauritius	39	284	37	25	25	60	53	184	165	1,421	47	496	102	0
Mozambique	..	1,852	0	1,934	..	1,533	0	92	..	64	..	327	0	189
Namibia	..	..	..	..	..	..	..	..	..	..	..	..	..	..
Niger	42	214	70	236	112	843	30	38	432	96	159	92	16	61
Nigeria	401	826	21	12,172	38	496	533	3,517	4,376	5,915	3,553	5,529	0	0
Rwanda	51	136	1	7	91	850	0	0	8	1	26	77	14	40
São Tomé and Principe	9	68	4	3	11	155	0	1	0	0	0	34	0	0
Senegal	221	791	169	506	179	1,604	84	199	461	66	219	213	140	292
Seychelles	16	47	4	6	3	21	2	33	0	25	59	18	0	0
Sierra Leone	136	258	47	135	39	475	23	19	111	6	53	89	59	167
Somalia	400	797	9	298	147	706	13	17	28	34	47	558	18	151
South Africa	..	0	0	0	..	0	0	0	..	13,879	..	10,928	0	415
Sudan	1,361	2,838	1,298	2,683	368	1,798	266	203	854	1,973	599	6,035	431	797
Swaziland	69	76	34	1	17	65	45	69	24	0	15	158	6	0
Tanzania	2,388	2,278	88	588	305	2,813	261	126	339	289	1,770	837	171	246
Togo	155	252	210	239	90	703	26	14	415	0	120	44	33	88
Uganda	191	619	23	108	63	2,331	16	69	244	76	63	112	89	394
Zambia	778	1,808	327	1,056	19	1,989	378	238	726	155	586	374	447	1,138
Zimbabwe	15	920	83	134	0	478	3	1,138	595	930	90	977	0	385
NORTH AFRICA	11,435	30,710	6,098	16,916	2,053	3,459	2,012	13,752	21,549	19,463	8,063	5,647	868	2,191
Algeria	1,255	2,742	1,956	11,642	14	356	270	3,523	13,545	10,477	2,325	162	0	2,018
Egypt, Arab Republic	6,231	20,603	3,767	1,221	1,885	1,970	741	1,922	2,070	1,143	4,027	2,991	411	0
Libya	..	..	..	..	..	..	..	..	..	..	..	..	..	..
Morocco	2,638	5,092	158	2,650	79	783	644	5,258	4,505	5,306	778	231	457	0
Tunisia	1,311	2,273	218	1,403	75	350	357	3,049	1,429	2,537	136	1,539	0	173
ALL AFRICA	23,810	72,798	11,809	51,735	6,002	44,791	5,630	26,098	42,327	59,888	19,275	46,627	3,901	9,584

6-24. Structure of external debt service payments

	Millions of U.S. dollars (current prices)													
	Bilateral				Multilateral				Private		Short-term		IMF	
	Concessional		Nonconcessional		Concessional		Nonconcessional							
	1980	1997	1980	1997	1980	1997	1980	1997	1980	1997	1980	1997	1980	1997
SUB-SAHARAN AFRICA	426	1,096	453	825	59	772	425	2,418	3,809	6,635	1,029	1,039	487	1,166
excluding South Africa	426	1,096	453	825	59	772	425	2,418	3,809	2,872	1,029	485	487	710
excluding South Africa & Nigeria	404	961	438	760	58	768	354	1,675	3,145	2,436	650	452	487	710
Angola	..	20	0	61	..	1	0	1	..	713	0	46	0	0
Benin	1	7	1	11	1	23	1	6	4	0	11	4	0	5
Botswana	1	22	2	6	0	15	10	53	1	7	2	1	0	0
Burkina Faso	3	8	4	1	3	30	2	8	5	0	5	3	0	2
Burundi	1	0	0	0	0	15	1	6	4	0	2	0	1	8
Cameroon	25	70	18	76	4	40	24	214	163	58	28	40	19	15
Cape Verde	0	1	0	1	0	4	0	3	0	2	0	0	0	0
Central African Republic	0	0	0	0	0	4	0	0	1	0	2	1	7	8
Chad	1	0	0	6	2	11	0	5	0	0	0	1	3	12
Comoros	0	0	0	0	0	2	0	0	0	0	0	0	0	0
Congo, Democratic Rep. of	48	0	136	0	2	0	22	0	189	0	45	12	101	0
Congo, Republic of	22	0	13	19	1	1	11	74	25	0	31	16	8	3
Côte d'Ivoire	29	89	55	80	3	53	46	376	1,180	632	95	105	0	25
Djibouti	2	4	1	0	0	3	0	0	0	0	1	1	0	0
Equatorial Guinea	0	0	1	0	0	1	0	1	0	0	1	1	0	3
Eritrea	..	0	0	0	..	0	0	0	..	0	0	0	..	0
Ethiopia	11	7	1	5	2	41	10	34	9	12	9	1	2	6
Gabon	6	86	28	199	0	4	4	82	359	35	33	18	1	9
Gambia, The	0	9	0	0	0	7	0	3	0	0	3	1	1	6
Ghana	24	49	22	12	1	42	13	50	48	153	18	29	33	171
Guinea	55	26	7	7	0	27	21	32	14	48	9	10	2	11
Guinea-Bissau	0	2	0	0	0	6	0	1	4	0	1	1	0	1
Kenya	13	68	22	81	2	37	47	139	274	225	58	30	17	69
Lesotho	0	7	0	5	0	11	0	11	4	7	1	0	0	4
Liberia	3	0	0	0	0	0	7	0	27	0	11	0	5	0
Madagascar	24	56	2	28	1	41	3	66	42	2	29	1	3	18
Malawi	4	13	7	1	2	24	3	18	53	1	16	3	3	18
Mali	4	24	0	3	1	37	0	4	3	0	3	3	4	8
Mauritania	8	29	0	7	3	29	2	29	17	3	7	8	11	8
Mauritius	2	57	4	6	0	4	6	39	29	152	8	23	3	0
Mozambique	..	35	0	13	..	20	0	12	..	6	0	3	0	16
Namibia	..	..	0	0	..	..	0	0	..	..	..	..	..	..
Niger	3	2	5	3	16	20	2	2	98	17	19	2	0	16
Nigeria	22	135	15	65	1	4	70	743	663	436	379	33	0	0
Rwanda	0	1	0	1	1	15	0	0	3	0	3	2	0	3
São Tomé and Principe	0	2	1	0	0	3	0	0	0	0	0	1	0	0
Senegal	13	38	19	50	1	41	8	33	183	8	24	11	12	66
Seychelles	0	2	0	2	0	1	0	6	0	4	37	1	0	0
Sierra Leone	2	11	2	1	0	5	2	1	35	0	6	1	19	1
Somalia	3	0	0	0	1	0	5	0	0	0	0	0	4	0
South Africa	..	0	0	0	..	0	0	0	..	3,762	0	555	0	456
Sudan	37	0	30	0	5	0	18	0	12	0	70	0	92	57
Swaziland	2	8	6	0	0	2	4	13	5	0	2	8	0	0
Tanzania	32	6	2	1	2	56	23	44	36	17	26	6	39	32
Togo	2	5	17	6	1	15	2	8	16	6	14	2	0	12
Uganda	3	58	8	18	1	36	2	14	22	2	5	4	16	60
Zambia	16	71	22	20	0	32	51	88	238	41	0	10	84	6
Zimbabwe	3	70	0	33	0	10	3	200	43	285	15	44	0	36
NORTH AFRICA	571	1,592	328	2,106	11	179	261	2,955	5,216	3,157	669	330	253	522
Algeria	107	224	226	1,004	2	25	69	936	3,564	1,776	116	13	0	443
Egypt, Arab Republic	265	628	50	134	7	65	51	457	320	366	422	262	121	15
Libya	..	..	0	0	..	..	0	0	..	..	..	..	..	..
Morocco	130	489	24	879	1	58	94	1,013	992	633	105	6	100	3
Tunisia	70	251	28	89	1	31	47	550	340	382	26	49	33	60
ALL AFRICA	997	2,688	782	2,931	70	951	685	5,373	9,025	9,792	1,699	1,370	739	1,688

Note: In 1995, Zambia was able to clear its arrears to the IMF after completing a 3 year Rights Arrangement Program.

6-25. Terms of long-term external financing, 1997

	Concessional terms				Nonconcessional terms				Structure of financing (percentage of total)		
	Interest (percent)	Grace period (years)	Maturity (years)	Grant element (percent)	Interest (percent)	Grace period (years)	Maturity (years)	Grant element (percent)	Grants	Conces-sional loans	Noncon-cessional loans
SUB-SAHARAN AFRICA	1.0	9.6	39.4	76.2	7.2	6.2	23.2	17.4	66.2	31.7	2.0
excluding South Africa	1.0	9.6	39.4	76.2	7.2	6.2	23.2	17.4	65.6	32.3	2.1
excl. S. Africa & Nigeria	1.0	9.6	39.4	76.2	7.2	6.3	23.2	17.4	65.6	32.4	2.1
Angola	..	..	..	..	..	..	..	..	100.0	0.0	0.0
Benin	1.4	7.9	33.3	66.6	..	..	..	..	67.0	33.0	0.0
Botswana	..	..	..	..	..	..	..	..	100.0	0.0	0.0
Burkina Faso	0.6	10.3	43.0	83.0	..	..	..	..	61.1	38.9	0.0
Burundi	..	..	..	..	..	..	..	..	100.0	0.0	0.0
Cameroon	0.5	9.3	38.7	81.6	..	..	..	..	84.4	15.6	0.0
Cape Verde	0.8	10.6	50.0	83.5	..	..	..	..	85.5	14.5	0.0
Central African Republic	..	..	..	..	..	..	..	..	100.0	0.0	0.0
Chad	0.7	10.2	46.7	83.1	..	..	..	..	57.2	42.8	0.0
Comoros	0.5	10.3	39.8	82.8	..	..	..	..	35.8	64.2	0.0
Congo, Democratic Rep. of	..	..	..	..	..	..	..	..	100.0	0.0	0.0
Congo, Republic of	..	..	..	..	..	..	..	..	100.0	0.0	0.0
Côte d'Ivoire	1.6	8.6	30.9	67.3	..	..	..	..	56.0	44.0	0.0
Djibouti	0.8	4.1	30.3	66.9	..	..	..	..	75.9	24.1	0.0
Equatorial Guinea	..	..	..	..	..	..	..	..	100.0	0.0	0.0
Eritrea	1.1	10.7	36.2	74.6	..	..	..	..	26.1	73.9	0.0
Ethiopia	1.0	9.0	44.0	77.3	..	..	..	..	81.0	19.0	0.0
Gabon	5.0	5.2	10.7	25.6	5.3	0.3	15.3	22.2	37.6	56.0	6.5
Gambia, The	1.0	9.8	46.7	79.5	..	..	..	..	42.9	57.1	0.0
Ghana	1.3	9.9	38.9	74.5	6.4	0.9	7.4	11.0	40.1	57.8	2.2
Guinea	1.3	10.3	41.2	75.7	7.2	7.8	30.7	20.5	40.6	54.0	5.5
Guinea-Bissau	0.7	10.3	46.3	83.1	..	..	..	..	55.9	44.1	0.0
Kenya	0.5	10.3	39.8	82.6	..	..	..	..	68.3	31.7	0.0
Lesotho	2.7	5.0	22.3	48.9	10.0	1.9	19.4	-1.4	83.2	16.6	0.1
Liberia	..	..	..	..	..	..	..	..	100.0	0.0	0.0
Madagascar	0.8	10.3	42.0	81.2	7.0	7.3	23.8	21.1	63.3	25.2	11.5
Malawi	0.7	10.1	47.8	83.0	..	..	..	..	59.9	40.1	0.0
Mali	0.9	9.9	43.8	79.7	..	..	..	..	63.6	36.4	0.0
Mauritania	1.8	7.8	33.6	66.8	..	..	..	..	71.0	29.0	0.0
Mauritius	4.0	3.4	13.9	31.8	5.7	3.2	11.7	20.3	48.2	40.4	11.4
Mozambique	0.7	9.9	43.1	80.6	8.8	7.7	32.3	9.2	62.6	33.8	3.5
Namibia	..	..	..	..	..	..	..	..	..	..	..
Niger	1.1	8.1	35.3	72.9	..	..	..	..	74.3	25.7	0.0
Nigeria	..	..	..	..	..	..	..	..	100.0	0.0	0.0
Rwanda	0.5	10.3	39.8	82.9	..	..	..	..	89.9	10.1	0.0
São Tomé and Principe	0.8	10.4	49.9	83.4	..	..	..	..	73.7	26.3	0.0
Senegal	0.8	10.2	40.8	80.2	7.5	10.1	39.6	20.2	54.6	41.9	3.5
Seychelles	5.0	4.0	17.0	29.6	7.3	6.4	20.4	17.6	22.0	26.3	51.7
Sierra Leone	0.8	10.6	50.1	83.5	..	..	..	..	82.6	17.4	0.0
Somalia	..	..	..	..	..	..	..	..	100.0	0.0	0.0
South Africa	..	..	..	..	..	..	..	..	100.0	0.0	0.0
Sudan	..	..	..	..	..	..	..	..	100.0	0.0	0.0
Swaziland	..	..	..	..	..	..	..	..	100.0	0.0	0.0
Tanzania	0.8	10.0	43.4	80.3	14.0	3.4	10.9	-21.0	57.4	42.6	0.0
Togo	1.0	9.6	38.8	76.8	..	..	..	..	35.9	64.1	0.0
Uganda	0.6	10.2	43.1	82.8	..	..	..	..	64.8	35.2	0.0
Zambia	0.5	8.9	37.9	76.8	9.8	0.8	5.3	0.0	54.2	45.3	0.5
Zimbabwe	0.8	7.8	34.4	69.9	7.1	1.6	8.1	9.9	59.4	29.4	11.3
NORTH AFRICA	3.4	6.4	21.1	46.1	6.1	3.7	13.8	17.2	29.0	27.6	43.4
Algeria	2.7	5.6	19.3	48.6	5.6	3.5	11.5	16.5	2.5	0.7	96.9
Egypt, Arab Republic	0.7	9.9	33.0	77.6	7.5	3.8	13.8	12.8	87.7	7.9	4.4
Libya	..	..	..	..	..	..	..	..	..	..	..
Morocco	2.9	7.0	21.0	49.8	6.1	2.9	15.8	20.1	19.3	43.7	37.1
Tunisia	4.2	5.4	19.7	38.2	7.4	5.8	18.6	16.1	12.0	57.1	30.8
ALL AFRICA	1.7	8.7	34.3	67.8	6.2	4.0	14.7	17.2	48.7	29.8	21.6

6-26. External debt and debt service ratios, 1997

	Debt-GDP ratio		Total external debt per capita (US dollars)	Percentage of debt disbursed	Debt-export ratio		Present value of debt-export ratio	Debt service-export ratio (Ex post)
	Concessional	Non-concessional			Concessional	Non-concessional		
SUB-SAHARAN AFRICA	24	39	359	88	80	131	176	13
excluding South Africa	43	57	340	88	126	168	241	14
excl. S. Africa & Nigeria	53	54	366	87	163	166	262	15
Angola	30	9	871	91	41	148	163	16
Benin	59	6	280	80	208	59	159	9
Botswana	5	4	367	91	10	9	15	3
Burkina Faso	45	2	124	74	290	59	190	14
Burundi	103	3	166	88	990	77	548	29
Cameroon	43	35	667	90	157	212	315	20
Cape Verde	40	6	548	65	85	24	68	6
Central African Republic	72	6	259	92	367	80	266	7
Chad	50	7	144	77	286	79	195	13
Comoros	89	4	381	86	395	56	289	5
Congo, Democratic Rep. of	51	77	264	95	213	633	783	1
Congo, Republic of	80	69	1,873	95	104	181	253	6
Côte d'Ivoire	44	33	1,098	92	93	230	276	28
Djibouti	50	0	446	84	109	14	76	3
Equatorial Guinea	28	11	674	88	29	30	46	1
Eritrea	11	0	20	21	18	1	9	0
Ethiopia	135	7	169	91	829	139	795	10
Gabon	19	50	3,717	90	29	100	128	13
Gambia, The	97	3	364	86	189	18	109	13
Ghana	58	4	333	78	235	118	231	30
Guinea	63	12	509	85	315	131	314	20
Guinea-Bissau	248	64	810	91	1,203	462	1,150	18
Kenya	35	9	227	84	124	92	162	22
Lesotho	48	13	328	76	65	29	62	6
Liberia	..	..	697	99	..	..	..	..
Madagascar	76	32	290	89	299	159	325	24
Malawi	77	4	215	80	310	41	182	12
Mali	104	3	286	82	362	45	247	11
Mauritania	155	29	997	88	339	151	353	23
Mauritius	8	5	2,153	80	12	77	86	10
Mozambique	98	59	360	86	591	455	770	18
Namibia	..	0	..	..	..	..	..	..
Niger	57	15	161	82	341	169	329	20
Nigeria	3	39	241	94	8	174	173	9
Rwanda	53	0	141	80	643	82	402	14
São Tomé and Principe	507	9	1,882	84	1,688	287	1,125	50
Senegal	53	16	418	81	148	79	152	15
Seychelles	12	7	1,920	73	18	22	35	4
Sierra Leone	89	19	242	84	635	360	628	17
Somalia	..	..	292	89	..	..	..	..
South Africa	0	0	621	87	0	67	63	13
Sudan	46	29	589	94	723	1,822	2,366	9
Swaziland	11	5	384	67	11	18	25	3
Tanzania	72	10	229	83	388	159	405	12
Togo	64	17	308	85	177	71	162	10
Uganda	47	3	183	82	342	88	239	22
Zambia	97	33	716	92	291	227	386	20
Zimbabwe	17	15	433	75	45	114	134	22
NORTH AFRICA	20	33	724	84	59	98	135	19
Algeria	7	32	1,055	82	19	171	181	27
Egypt, Arab Republic	30	4	495	94	105	34	99	9
Libya	..	..	..	..	..	..	..	..
Morocco	18	24	707	81	51	116	149	27
Tunisia	14	24	1,229	73	29	97	117	16
ALL AFRICA	22	37	422	87	73	119	161	15

Figure 6-1.   Debt service ratio (ex post), 1997

(percent of exports of goods and services)

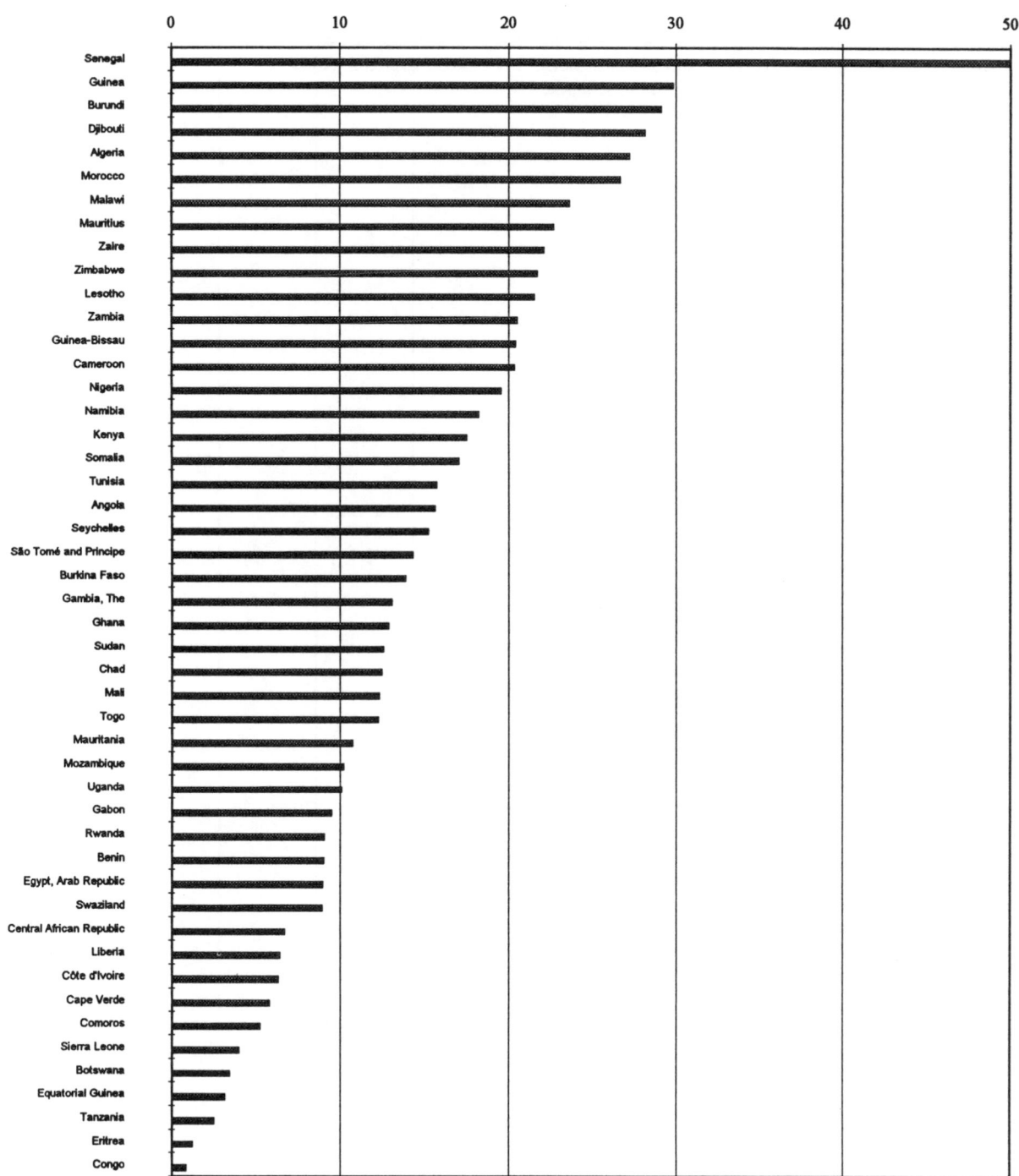

Figure 6-2.   Debt to GDP ratio, 1997

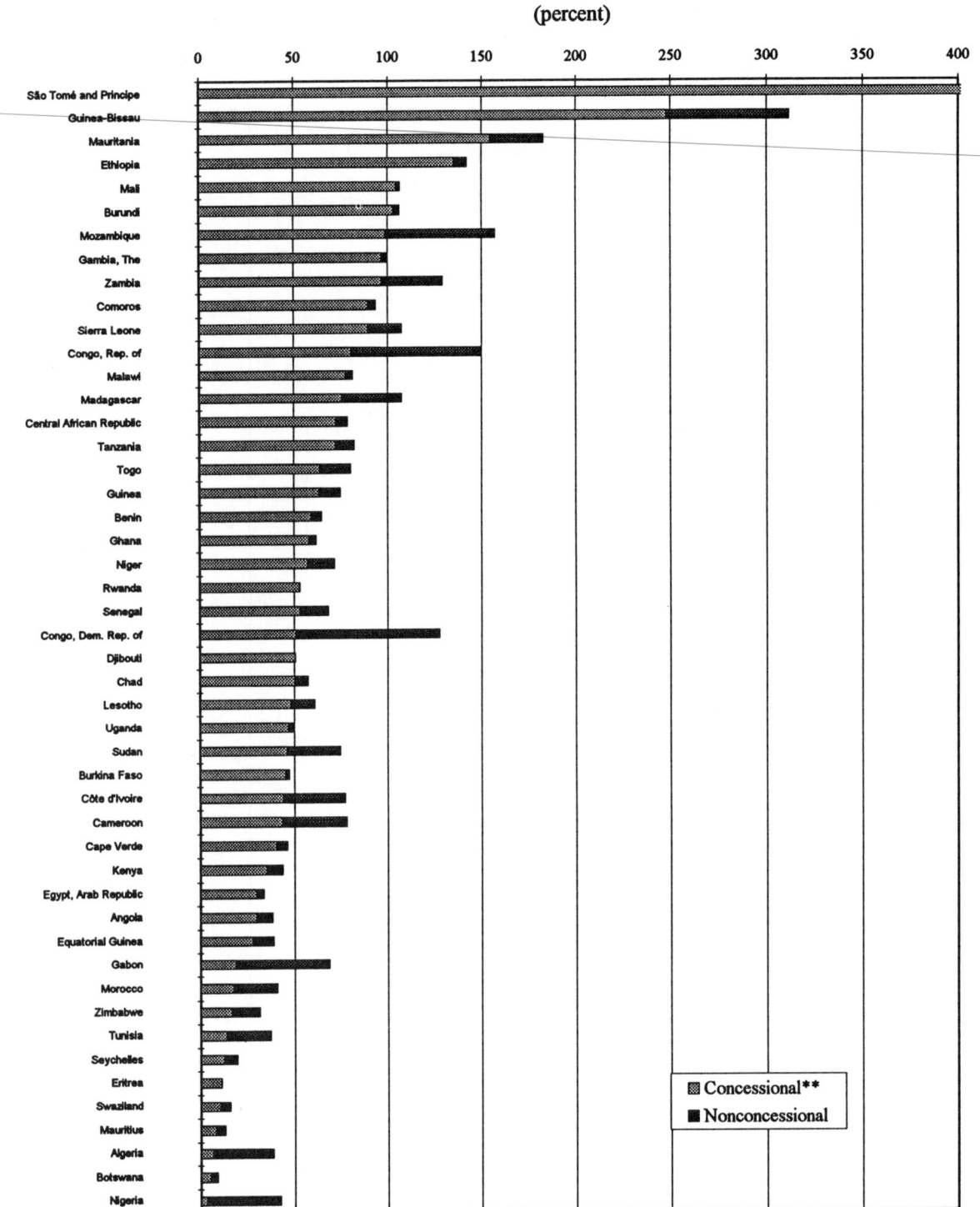

(percent)

* Debt to GDP ratio is greater than 400.
** Sorted by concessional debt.

Technical Notes

Tables

Tables 6-1, 6-2, and 6-3. Gross disbursements: official concessional, official nonconcessional, and private long-term loans. Gross disbursements are from commitments of long-term external loans by official concessional, official nonconcessional, and private sources, respectively (World Bank, DRS).

Table 6-4. Disbursements: long-term loans and IMF purchases. This is the sum of tables 6-1 through 6-3, plus IMF purchases.

Tables 6-5, 6-6, and 6-7. Amortization: official concessional, official nonconcessional, and private long-term loans. Amortization is the actual repayment of principal made in foreign currencies, goods, or services on outstanding long-term official concessional, official nonconcessional, and private long-term loans as described above (World Bank, DRS).

Table 6-8. Amortization: long-term loans and IMF repurchases. This is the sum of Tables 6-5 to 6-7, plus repurchases of drawings from the IMF.

Tables 6-9, 6-10, and 6-11. Interest payments: official concessional, official nonconcessional, and private long-term loans. These are actual payments made in foreign currencies, goods, and services to various lenders described above on interest obligations, including IMF charges on drawings due on disbursed debt and on commitment charges due on undisbursed debt (where information is available), that is, on long-term official concessional, official nonconcessional, and private loans (World Bank, DRS).

Table 6-12. Interest payments: long-term loans and IMF charges. This is the sum of Tables 6-9 through 6-11, plus IMF charges on drawings.

Table 6-13. Total external debt service payments: long-term loans and IMF credit. Total external debt service payments include the sum of amortization on long-term loans and IMF credit and interest payments on long-term loans and IMF credit (World Bank, DRS).

Table 6-14. Interest payments: short-term loans. These are estimated for the respective year based on the estimated year-end stock of short-term debt (which may include interest arrears on long-term debt) and the annual average six-month London interbank offered rate (LIBOR) on notes denominated in U.S. dollars as reported in the *IFS* (with no adjustment for spreads). Actual payments may be different because the LIBOR only approximates actual interest rates on short-term loans, and because not all interest due on short-term loans is actually paid (World Bank, DRS).

Table 6-15. Net flows: long- and short-term loans, including IMF. These flows represent all disbursements of long- and short-term loans net of all repayments of principal on long- and short-term loans and IMF credit (World Bank, DRS).

Table 6-16. Net flows: long-term loans, including IMF. Net flows of long-term loans are as defined above for Table 6-15, but excluding short-term loans (World Bank, DRS).

Table 6-17. Net transfers: long- and short-term loans, including IMF. Net transfers are net flows (Table 6-15) less interest payments (Tables 6-12 and 6-14).

Table 6-18. Net transfers: long-term loans, including IMF. Net transfers include long-term loans and IMF credit only (Table 6-16 less Table 6-12).

Tables 6-19, 6-20, and 6-21. Long-term debt: official concessional, official nonconcessional, and private. This series reflects the total debt outstanding and disbursed of official concessional, official nonconcessional, and private loans (World Bank, DRS). The time series reflects changes in the valuation of year-end debt stocks (because of US dollar exchange rate fluctuation) and debt cancellation, as well as net disbursements. Therefore changes in debt stocks from year to year cannot be used as a measure of net borrowing or vice versa.

Table 6-22. Total external debt. When Tables 6-19 to 6-21 are supplemented with IMF credit and estimates of total short-term debt (which includes interest in arrears on public and publicly guaranteed long-term loans), they sum up to total external debt (World Bank, DRS).

Table 6-23. Structure of external debt. This table summarizes debt structure for 1980 and 1997 (World Bank, DRS). The columns cover the type of creditor and concessionality. The private debt shown includes both the private guaranteed (by an entity of the debtor government) and the private nonguaranteed debt. For each year, all components shown add to the total in Table 6-22.

Table 6-24. Structure of external debt service payments. This summary table compares debt service payments for all types of creditors in 1980 and 1997 (World Bank, DRS). Debt service payments on short-term loans are excluded, to be consistent with Table 6-13. Debt service payments are actual repayments of principal (amortization) and actual payments of interest. The column headings have the same definitions as given above for Table 6-23.

Table 6-25. Terms of long-term external financing, 1997. This table presents the average interest rates, grace periods, maturities, and grant elements shown separately for concessional and nonconcessional long-term loans (official and private); short-term loans are excluded (World Bank, DRS). Grant elements are calculated using a standard 10 percent discount rate. The indicators are weighted averages (based on amount of commitments) across all loans in each category. For the column on structure of financing (that is, total flows), grants are based on sources for Chapter 12 (Aid Flows) and are not comparable with net official transfers shown in Chapter 5.

Table 6-26. External debt and debt service ratios, 1997. This table includes the ratio of debt outstanding and disbursed to GDP; per capita debt; the ratio of debt outstanding and disbursed to debt outstanding, including undisbursed; the ratio of debt outstanding and disbursed and the ratio of the present value of debt to exports of goods and all services, including receipts of workers' remittances; and the ratio of total debt service paid to exports of goods and all services, more commonly called the debt service ratio (World Bank, DRS). Ratios are shown separately for concessional debt and for all nonconcessional (including private) debt. Both the stock of external debt and debt service payments include short- and long-term loans and IMF credit, except for the ratio of debt outstanding to debt outstanding including undisbursed, which is calculated for public and publicly guaranteed debt only. The data for exports of goods and all services, plus receipts of workers' remittances, are taken from balance of payments data in Chapter 5. The present value of debt is the sum of all future payments discounted to the present (usually with a commercial discount rate similar to LIBOR. The debt service ratio is shown for the ex post category, depicting the amount actually paid after debt relief and/or arrears.

Figures

The following indicators have been used to derive the figures in this chapter.

Figure 6-1. Debt service ratio (Table 6-26).

Figure 6-2. Debt to GDP ratio (Table 6-26).

Methodology used for regional aggregations and period averages in chapter 6

| Table | Aggregations[a] | | | Period averages[b] |
	(1)	(2)	(6)	(1)
6-1	x			x
6-2	x			x
6-3	x			x
6-4	x			x
6-5	x			x
6-6	x			x
6-7	x			x
6-8	x			x
6-9	x			x
6-10	x			x
6-11	x			x
6-12	x			x
6-13	x			x
6-14	x			x
6-15	x			x
6-16	x			x
6-17	x			x
6-18	x			x
6-19	x			x
6-20	x			x
6-21	x			x
6-22	x			
6-23	x			
6-24	x			
6-25			x	
6-26		x		

Note: Regional aggregations are shown in the rows for Sub-Saharan Africa, North Africa, and All Africa. Period averages are shown in the last three columns. This table shows only the methodologies used in this chapter.

a. Regional aggregations: (1) simple total; (2) simple total of the first indicator divided by the simple total of the second indicator (same country coverage); (3) simple total of the gap-filled indicator; (4) simple total of the gap-filled main indicator divided by the simple total of the gap-filled secondary indicator; (5) simple total of the first gap-filled main indicator less the simple total of the second gap-filled main indicator, all divided by the simple total of the secondary indicator; (6) weighted total; (7) median; (8) no aggregation; (9) simple arithmetic mean.

b. Period averages: (1) arithmetic mean (using the same series as shown in the table, i.e., ratio if the rest of the table is shown as ratio, level if the rest of the table is shown as level, growth rate if the rest of the table is shown as growth rate); (2) least-squares growth rate (using main indicator); (3) least-squares growth rate (using main indicator in constant terms, with the rest of the table in current terms).

7

Government Finance

The data in this chapter pertain to consolidated government (except when not available) instead of to central government operations, which were reported in previous volumes.

Definitions have been taken from the IMF's *Government Finance Statistics* (*GFS*). For this volume, data are taken from country desks. When not available from country desks, data are taken from the *GFS* and supplemented with data from IMF, World Bank, or staff reports, or from other national government sources. Data from various sources have been harmonized to produce a consistent and comparable time series.

The focus of this chapter is on the principal financial transactions of government—taxing, borrowing, spending, and lending—rather than on the production and consumption of goods and services, the use of labor, or other government activities. Spending covers both current and capital transactions.

The data cover major government finance indicators—fiscal deficit or surplus, expenditure and lending minus repayments, revenue, grants, and domestic and foreign financing—expressed as a percentage of GDP. The chapter also includes information on the major components of revenue and expenditure by economic category, shown as percentages of total revenue and as a percentage of expenditure and lending minus repayments, respectively.

Measures of fiscal deficit or surplus are among the single most important indicators of government fiscal performance. The measure is usually calculated as the difference between total revenue (including grants) and total expenditure (including lending minus repayments). As such, it measures government net financing requirements. *GFS* methodology recommends grouping grants receipts with revenue because they can be spent without incurring an obligation for future payments but lists them separately. because grants can sometimes be treated as financing items. Financing includes all government borrowing from others (at home and abroad) minus amortization (government repayment of its borrowing from others and changes in cash balances). Other measures of fiscal balance include the fiscal deficit or surplus without capital grants, which measures the government's ability to operate without foreign capital transfers, and the fiscal deficit or surplus, excluding interest payments from expenditure, referred to as the primary deficit or surplus.

Revenue is divided between taxes—unrequited compulsory payments to government—and nontax revenue. It includes only non-repayable receipts other than grants. Tax revenue is also classified according to the base upon which the tax is levied (for example, income and profits).

Expenditure is classified by economic category (such as wages, purchases, and interest payments). Lending minus repayments—government lending less repayment of past government lending—is grouped with expenditure, except in certain cases (see Technical Notes).

The economic classification of expenditures (for example, on wages) is presented as a percentage of total expenditure and lending minus repayments, because lending minus repayments is itself a separate economic classification.

No attempt was made to reconcile *GFS* data in this chapter with the System of National Accounts (SNA). The fundamental difference between the two systems is that *GFS* focuses on government financial transactions, whereas the SNA considers government transactions as part of total demand and value added. (For further discussion, see World Bank 1988b, box 2.1, p. 45.) Indicators calculated as ratios to GDP use GDP at purchaser values or market prices (see Technical Notes to Chapter 1). Because GDP at purchaser values includes import duties (and GDP at market prices includes indirect taxes), ratios for revenues tend to understate tax burdens, especially where such taxes are an important source of government revenue.

Fiscal year data are compared with the calendar year GDP data that correspond either to the second half of the fiscal year or to the calendar year in which most of the fiscal year falls. Fiscal years do not correspond to calendar years in Botswana, Cameroon, Egypt, Ethiopia, the Gambia, Ghana (before 1982), Kenya, Lesotho, Liberia, Malawi, Mauritius, Niger, Nigeria, Senegal, Sierra Leone, Sudan, Swaziland, Tanzania, Uganda, and Zimbabwe (after 1985).

Tables in this volume contain corrections to mislabeled subtitles in *ADI 1992*. Thus subtitles in tables 7-1 through 7-8 are now correctly labeled percentage of total GDP (instead of revenues).

7-1. Government deficit/surplus (including grants)

	Percentage of GDP											Annual average		
	1980	1989	1990	1991	1992	1993	1994	1995	1996	1997	1998	75-84	85-89	90-MR
SUB-SAHARAN AFRICA	-12.1	-3.8	-4.2	-4.9	-6.3	-6.9	-5.9	-3.9	-3.5	-3.2	-4.3	-6.6	-5.0	-4.8
excluding South Africa	..	-6.1	-5.2	-5.7	-5.3	-5.1	-5.6	-2.8	-1.9	-1.9	-3.8	-4.3	-5.5	-4.1
excl. S. Africa & Nigeria	..	-5.8	-5.5	-5.4	-7.0	-5.6	-5.7	-4.2	-3.3	-2.5	-2.9	-4.3	-5.2	-4.7
Angola	..	-25.2	-26.7	-22.0	-56.9	-21.7	-20.0	-27.3	-10.4	-18.8	-14.6	..	-11.1	-24.3
Benin	..	-2.3	-4.9	-5.2	-4.8	-0.8	-2.4	-3.2	-0.4	0.3	2.0	0.0	11.5	-2.1
Botswana	..	9.6	10.5	9.1	9.5	8.7	3.1	1.8	6.4	4.8	-3.3	9.7	14.5	5.6
Burkina Faso	-9.4	-16.8	-4.6	-3.6	-2.9	-4.6	-3.2	-3.6	-0.6	-3.2	-2.9	-22.6	-17.4	-3.3
Burundi	9.8	-4.3	-2.7	-0.2	-2.7	-3.6	-4.3	-4.9	-10.1	-5.4	-4.3	9.5	-4.4	-4.2
Cameroon	0.4	-4.5	-7.6	-8.2	-6.3	-6.3	-9.2	-3.2	-1.7	-0.7	-1.6	0.5	-5.2	-5.0
Cape Verde	..	-15.1	-12.2	-6.3	-8.7	-10.2	-16.6	-15.1	-16.8	-13.1	-12.1	..	-7.4	-12.3
Central African Republic	..	-4.9	-7.4	-9.2	-9.0	-8.2	-10.0	-5.1	-3.5	-2.3	-0.9	0.9	-4.5	-6.2
Chad	..	-7.6	-8.3	-4.3	-8.6	-9.1	-4.7	-4.4	-5.0	-3.8	-4.9	-1.1	-4.2	-5.9
Comoros	..	-3.4	-0.5	-2.2	-2.5	2.6	-7.7	-7.9	-5.8	-2.8	-3.0	19.1	11.2	-3.3
Congo, Democratic Rep. of	..	..	..	..	..	..	..	..	..	..	..	..	..	..
Congo, Republic of	..	-1.6	-6.6	-13.1	-14.1	-12.6	-13.2	-8.2	-5.0	-8.6	-12.1	-2.7	-9.0	-10.4
Côte d'Ivoire	-8.5	-16.6	-12.0	-12.9	-11.3	-11.9	-6.5	-3.7	-2.1	-2.1	-1.8	-11.0	-8.6	-7.1
Djibouti	..	..	-20.6	-3.0	-11.7	-13.0	-8.4	-8.1	-4.0	-5.6	-2.3	..	..	-8.5
Equatorial Guinea	..	-16.5	-5.3	-5.9	-8.9	-15.1	-5.7	-5.6	-6.3	-0.4	8.9	..	-11.2	-4.9
Eritrea	..	..	..	..	-3.2	-6.4	-12.7	-22.4	-19.8	-7.0	-32.4	..	..	-14.9
Ethiopia	..	-6.2	-9.8	-8.5	-7.0	-5.9	-7.7	-3.9	-5.6	-1.5	-3.9	-6.6	-5.7	-6.0
Gabon	..	-6.1	-4.1	-2.2	-5.2	-5.7	-1.6	3.2	2.7	6.0	-4.1	..	-7.1	-1.2
Gambia, The	-3.9	3.2	-0.1	1.1	1.3	1.3	-1.1	-6.7	-9.8	-6.5	-2.5	0.3	3.8	-2.6
Ghana	..	-2.1	-3.1	-1.4	-9.4	-9.9	-8.9	-6.4	-9.5	-9.2	-6.3	-2.3	-2.7	-7.1
Guinea	..	-5.0	-5.2	-4.5	-3.1	-3.7	-3.6	-2.7	-3.0	-2.9	-3.2	..	-5.4	-3.5
Guinea-Bissau	0.0	-12.5	-6.5	-17.7	-21.4	-12.9	-8.5	-1.5	-12.1	-18.2	-16.2	-10.7	-6.1	-12.8
Kenya	-7.1	-4.7	-6.2	-5.2	-5.1	-8.7	-5.2	-2.5	-2.3	-1.9	-1.2	-4.8	-5.2	-4.3
Lesotho	..	-9.2	-2.4	-0.7	3.1	5.7	5.9	4.4	4.6	-0.1	-6.7	-5.4	-6.4	1.5
Liberia	..	..	..	..	..	..	..	..	..	..	..	..	..	..
Madagascar	-12.8	-4.1	-0.7	-5.5	-6.6	-7.2	-8.4	-6.2	-4.9	-2.4	-4.1	-7.4	-3.6	-5.1
Malawi	-11.6	-2.2	-5.0	-3.0	-13.6	-6.0	-27.9	-6.5	-3.1	-6.9	-6.3	-8.3	-6.0	-8.7
Mali	..	-2.7	-2.7	-4.1	-3.9	-4.1	-4.3	-3.1	-0.9	-2.1	-2.4	2.7	-5.4	-3.1
Mauritania	..	-3.7	-1.5	-7.6	-0.5	-7.5	-0.5	3.3	8.1	5.2	4.8	0.0	0.6	0.4
Mauritius	..	-2.6	-1.9	-2.2	-2.3	-2.2	-3.1	-5.3	-6.7	-5.1	-2.5	-6.6	-2.5	-3.5
Mozambique	-2.0	-4.3	-6.2	-3.1	-2.7	-3.6	-5.3	-3.2	-2.9	-2.6	-2.4	-8.5	-8.1	-3.6
Namibia	0.0	-1.5	-2.5	-1.5	-3.1	-3.8	-1.2	-2.4	-5.5	-3.6	-4.8	-10.0	-7.6	-3.2
Niger	-13.5	-5.9	-7.0	-3.6	-4.7	-3.8	-6.7	-3.9	-0.2	-2.7	-1.9	-14.2	-4.8	-3.8
Nigeria	-0.3	-7.2	-3.4	-7.1	3.3	-2.7	-5.1	4.4	5.2	1.1	-8.6	-5.8	-7.0	-1.4
Rwanda	-2.0	-4.4	-5.0	-5.4	-8.1	-8.2	-11.5	-2.3	-5.7	-2.5	-2.8	-4.9	-6.2	-5.7
São Tomé and Principe	..	-32.3	-28.7	-24.1	-32.7	-24.2	-43.0	-37.6	-32.3	-26.7	-24.9	..	-15.4	-30.5
Senegal	-4.6	-2.1	-3.0	2.0	-1.8	-3.1	-1.9	-0.2	-0.2	0.0	0.0	-5.7	-2.0	-0.9
Seychelles	..	-8.0	0.2	-4.9	-5.8	-9.3	-9.0	-11.4	-11.4	-12.7	-3.8	4.7	-7.7	-7.6
Sierra Leone	-22.6	-9.9	-10.1	-9.6	-8.4	-7.4	-7.1	-9.8	-6.5	-7.2	-10.0	-9.3	-13.0	-8.4
Somalia	..	..	..	..	..	..	..	..	..	..	..	..	..	..
South Africa	-18.0	-1.2	-3.1	-3.9	-7.4	-8.9	-6.2	-5.2	-5.4	-4.6	-5.0	-6.5	-4.3	-5.5
Sudan	..	-11.7	-9.2	-15.3	-20.1	-1.7	..	-3.2	-3.8	-0.7	-0.6	-12.2	-12.1	-6.9
Swaziland	..	..	..	5.5	-0.1	-3.4	-3.0	-2.0	-1.0	-1.1	-1.0	..	..	-0.8
Tanzania	..	-0.2	3.2	2.8	3.6	-1.6	1.9	-3.9	-2.2	2.0	0.2	..	-2.1	0.7
Togo	..	-3.5	-2.9	-6.1	-4.2	-15.6	-11.7	-6.4	-5.8	-2.1	-5.1	-2.1	-3.7	-6.7
Uganda	0.0	-3.2	-4.4	-3.7	-7.3	-3.2	-3.8	-2.9	-1.9	-1.8	-0.6	-0.4	-3.6	-3.3
Zambia	..	-4.3	-8.3	-7.0	-2.5	-5.6	-6.5	-4.3	-2.6	-1.1	-3.1	..	-10.8	-4.5
Zimbabwe	7.6	-7.6	-6.5	-5.2	-6.8	-6.1	-6.7	-10.1	-7.8	-7.7	-2.9	8.0	-7.9	-6.6
NORTH AFRICA	..	-7.7	-4.3	-5.1	-2.3	-4.6	-2.2	-1.5	0.6	1.1	-1.8	..	-9.7	-2.2
Algeria	..	-1.8	3.6	1.7	-1.1	-8.7	-2.9	-0.3	3.0	2.3	-3.2	-8.1	-8.0	-0.6
Egypt, Arab Republic	..	-13.2	-12.5	-12.5	-3.1	-2.3	-0.9	-0.3	-0.7	-0.3	-0.4	..	-14.0	-3.7
Libya	..	..	..	..	..	..	..	..	..	..	..	..	..	..
Morocco	-9.5	-6.0	-0.6	-1.0	-2.2	-3.0	-3.7	-5.5	-0.5	2.2	-2.7	-10.5	-6.3	-1.9
Tunisia	..	..	..	..	..	..	..	..	..	..	..	..	..	..
ALL AFRICA	..	-5.0	-4.2	-4.9	-5.0	-6.2	-4.7	-3.1	-2.2	-1.8	-3.6	-5.5	-6.2	-4.0

Note: 1998 data are preliminary. Nigeria: from 1992 accounts are for consolidated budget; since 1994, ratios are distorted as off. exch. rate used by the Gov. for oil exports oil value added is significantly over-valued.

7-2. Government deficit/surplus (excluding grants)

	Percentage of GDP										Annual average		
	1980	1989	1990	1991	1992	1993	1994	1995	1996	1997	1998	75-84	85-89	90-MR
SUB-SAHARAN AFRICA	-12.2	-4.9	-5.2	-6.1	-7.7	-8.2	-7.3	-5.1	-4.5	-4.1	-5.3	-6.9	-5.8	-5.9
excluding South Africa	..	-8.1	-7.0	-7.7	-7.6	-7.5	-8.3	-4.9	-3.7	-3.8	-5.5	-5.4	-7.2	-6.2
excl. S. Africa & Nigeria	..	-8.3	-7.7	-7.8	-9.8	-8.4	-9.0	-6.8	-5.5	-4.7	-4.9	-5.7	-7.2	-7.2
Angola	..	-25.2	-26.7	-22.0	-56.9	-21.7	-20.0	-27.3	-10.4	-19.7	-15.7	..	-11.1	-24.5
Benin	..	-12.0	-10.8	-8.6	-8.9	-4.7	-7.0	-7.3	-4.3	-4.2	-1.3	..	-12.0	-6.3
Botswana	..	8.7	9.1	8.1	8.5	7.1	2.2	1.5	6.0	4.7	-3.4	7.3	12.6	4.9
Burkina Faso	..	-27.7	-7.3	-8.2	-9.1	-10.1	-10.6	-10.3	-9.0	-10.2	-9.7	-17.1	-22.8	-9.4
Burundi	6.1	-7.5	-10.8	-8.8	-11.3	-12.3	-6.8	-8.5	-12.4	-8.4	-7.0	5.4	-6.0	-9.6
Cameroon	0.4	-4.5	-7.6	-8.2	-6.3	-6.3	-9.4	-3.3	-1.7	-0.7	-1.6	0.9	-5.2	-5.0
Cape Verde	..	-15.1	-12.7	-19.8	-28.0	-27.0	-34.6	-32.5	-31.5	-27.7	-23.1	..	-19.0	-26.3
Central African Republic	..	-9.7	-11.6	-13.8	-14.7	-13.5	-14.9	-11.4	-5.0	-6.3	-8.6	-4.3	-9.6	-11.1
Chad	..	-17.8	-16.9	-9.6	-13.8	-13.9	-14.2	-11.9	-11.0	-9.9	-8.7	..	-17.1	-12.2
Comoros	..	-19.8	-15.5	-18.5	-17.6	-11.9	-24.0	-19.7	-14.7	-12.5	-11.9	-19.1	-24.0	-16.2
Congo, Democratic Rep. of	..	..	..	..	..	..	..	..	..	..	..	..	..	..
Congo, Republic of	..	-1.6	-7.0	-13.3	-14.1	-12.6	-14.3	-9.2	-5.3	-8.7	-12.4	..	-1.6	-10.8
Côte d'Ivoire	..	-16.6	-12.0	-13.4	-11.8	-12.4	-7.2	-4.4	-2.8	-2.8	-2.5	-1.6	-8.6	-7.7
Djibouti	..	..	-20.6	-15.2	-24.1	-21.8	-13.4	-10.1	-5.8	-8.1	-4.4	..	..	-13.7
Equatorial Guinea	..	-38.2	-35.6	-33.6	-26.0	-34.4	-9.9	-8.2	-7.2	-1.1	8.3	..	-19.2	-16.4
Eritrea	..	..	..	..	-12.3	-26.5	-31.2	-35.1	-31.7	-13.2	-38.4	..	..	-26.9
Ethiopia	..	-10.9	-12.0	-10.9	-9.6	-7.6	-11.1	-7.3	-8.5	-5.2	-6.8	-8.7	-9.4	-8.8
Gabon	..	-6.5	-4.4	-2.4	-5.3	-6.0	-2.0	3.2	2.7	6.0	-4.1	..	-7.6	-1.4
Gambia, The	..	-5.7	-6.0	-4.3	-3.3	-2.4	-4.2	-9.1	-12.0	-7.8	-4.5	..	-10.5	-6.0
Ghana	..	-5.3	-5.7	-4.5	-12.7	-14.1	-12.4	-10.0	-12.1	-11.0	-9.0	-3.1	-5.1	-10.2
Guinea	..	-8.7	-8.8	-8.2	-7.1	-7.3	-7.1	-6.7	-6.1	-6.0	-5.9	..	-8.5	-7.0
Guinea-Bissau	0.0	-39.8	-24.5	-33.2	-37.2	-29.8	-23.2	-17.8	-21.1	-30.9	-19.5	-12.6	-36.6	-26.4
Kenya	-7.9	-7.1	-8.4	-7.2	-7.7	-11.8	-7.9	-4.5	-3.6	-2.9	-2.0	-5.7	-6.9	-6.2
Lesotho	..	-19.4	-13.5	-10.4	-4.5	-0.3	0.6	-0.8	-0.6	-4.6	-9.3	-8.9	-12.5	-4.8
Liberia	..	..	..	..	..	..	..	..	..	..	..	..	..	..
Madagascar	-12.8	-8.2	-5.1	-7.7	-10.1	-10.7	-11.4	-9.1	-9.1	-7.7	-7.5	-7.7	-4.9	-8.7
Malawi	-15.9	-7.2	-7.3	-6.4	-16.2	-9.1	-42.7	-15.3	-8.0	-10.6	-14.8	-12.6	-10.0	-14.5
Mali	..	-7.9	-8.7	-12.3	-11.0	-9.6	-13.8	-10.6	-8.0	-7.8	-8.0	..	-10.5	-10.0
Mauritania	..	-6.3	-3.9	-9.9	-3.4	-11.3	-4.5	-0.8	5.3	4.2	2.1	..	-3.9	-2.5
Mauritius	..	-2.9	-2.1	-2.3	-2.4	-2.4	-3.4	-5.7	-6.9	-5.2	-2.8	-7.0	-3.3	-3.7
Mozambique	-3.9	-13.6	-15.9	-14.2	-16.5	-15.5	-19.2	-13.0	-10.1	-11.9	-10.7	-10.4	-13.4	-14.1
Namibia	..	-1.5	-3.7	-2.6	-3.9	-4.5	-1.6	-2.8	..	..	..	-16.7	-7.6	-3.2
Niger	..	-10.6	-12.4	-8.4	-8.6	-9.4	-12.5	-8.0	-5.1	-7.2	-6.6	-8.3	-9.4	-8.7
Nigeria	-0.3	-7.2	-3.4	-7.1	3.3	-2.7	-5.1	4.4	5.1	1.0	-8.6	-5.8	-7.0	-1.5
Rwanda	..	-8.7	-9.6	-12.8	-14.2	-14.6	-12.4	-13.3	-13.1	-9.2	-7.9	-9.5	-9.7	-11.9
São Tomé and Principe	..	-50.8	-43.9	-36.0	-41.7	-40.9	-60.5	-60.9	-55.8	-54.5	-34.6	..	-22.2	-47.7
Senegal	-5.3	-4.0	-4.3	0.3	-3.1	-4.2	-6.1	-3.5	-2.2	-1.7	-1.7	-6.6	-3.4	-2.9
Seychelles	..	-9.5	-1.7	-6.4	-7.1	-10.8	-9.8	-11.9	-12.0	-13.1	-5.7	11.0	-9.9	-8.7
Sierra Leone	-23.6	-10.2	-10.1	-9.6	-8.4	-7.4	-7.1	-9.8	-8.5	-7.8	-12.3	-9.7	-13.6	-9.0
Somalia	..	..	..	..	..	..	..	..	..	..	..	..	..	..
South Africa	..	-1.4	-3.3	-4.3	-7.8	-9.0	-6.2	-5.2	-5.4	-4.6	-5.0	-4.9	-4.4	-5.6
Sudan	..	..	..	..	..	..	..	-3.2	-3.8	-0.7	-0.6	..	..	-2.1
Swaziland	..	..	..	4.7	-1.5	-4.6	-3.9	-2.8	-1.7	-1.8	-1.8	..	..	-1.7
Tanzania	..	-3.9	-0.5	0.4	0.9	-5.3	-2.0	-5.9	-4.3	-1.6	-2.2	..	-6.8	-2.3
Togo	..	-6.1	-6.2	-8.0	-5.8	-15.9	-13.1	-7.8	-6.3	-3.5	-6.8	-7.1	-6.9	-8.1
Uganda	..	-4.8	-5.9	-7.6	-14.4	-11.3	-10.3	-7.5	-5.9	-6.2	-5.7	-3.6	-4.7	-8.3
Zambia	..	-6.6	-12.7	-16.0	-12.6	-13.6	-11.8	-9.5	-8.7	-6.2	-9.5	..	-12.0	-11.2
Zimbabwe	6.9	-8.3	-7.3	-6.3	-8.4	-8.1	-8.6	-11.9	-9.1	-8.8	-4.3	7.0	-9.0	-8.1
NORTH AFRICA	..	-8.9	-6.3	-6.9	-3.4	-5.4	-2.9	-2.0	0.3	0.9	-2.1	..	-10.8	-3.1
Algeria	..	..	..	..	..	..	..	..	..	2.3	-3.2	..	..	-0.4
Egypt, Arab Republic	..	-15.4	-15.1	-15.2	-5.5	-3.5	-2.1	-1.3	-1.3	-0.9	-1.0	..	-16.0	-5.1
Libya	..	..	..	..	..	..	..	..	..	..	..	..	..	..
Morocco	-10.6	-6.8	-4.4	-3.7	-2.6	-4.1	-4.3	-5.9	-0.7	2.2	-2.7	-12.5	-7.6	-2.9
Tunisia	..	..	..	..	..	..	..	..	..	..	..	..	..	..
ALL AFRICA	..	-6.2	-5.6	-6.3	-6.3	-7.3	-5.8	-4.1	-3.0	-2.5	-4.3	-6.0	-7.1	-5.0

Note: 1998 data are preliminary. Nigeria: from 1992 accounts are for consolidated budget; since 1994, ratios are distorted as off. exch. rate used by the Gov. for oil exports oil value added is significantly overvalued.

7-3. Government primary deficit/surplus (-/+)

	1980	1989	1990	1991	1992	1993	1994	1995	1996	1997	1998	75-84	85-89	90-MR
						Percentage of GDP							*Annual average*		
SUB-SAHARAN AFRICA	..	..	..	..	..	..	..	..	..	..	-9.5	..	..	-9.5
excluding South Africa	..	-11.5	-11.3	-11.6	-10.8	-11.7	-11.4	-7.5	-5.8	-5.0	-7.1	..	-12.3	-9.1
excl. S. Africa & Nigeria	..	-9.9	-10.5	-10.2	-11.9	-11.8	-11.6	-9.4	-7.9	-6.0	-6.4	..	-9.9	-9.5
Angola	..	-19.8	-21.5	-15.9	-48.6	-12.2	-8.1	-16.5	1.1	..	..	..	-14.7	-17.4
Benin	..	0.9	-1.8	-2.6	-1.1	1.9	0.8	-0.4	2.1	2.0	3.3	..	13.5	0.4
Botswana	..	..	..	..	..	..	..	..	..	4.7	-3.9	..	..	0.4
Burkina Faso	..	-15.7	-3.5	-2.2	-1.5	-3.1	-1.8	-2.2	0.3	-2.3	-2.1	-9.0	-16.2	-2.0
Burundi	10.1	-2.1	-0.9	1.4	-0.9	-2.2	-2.8	-3.1	-8.3	-3.4	-2.7	10.1	-1.7	-2.5
Cameroon	..	-2.8	-5.5	-4.1	-1.2	-1.5	-2.2	3.2	5.0	5.4	4.1	..	-4.7	0.4
Cape Verde	..	-13.7	-10.6	-5.0	-7.5	-8.9	-15.4	-11.4	-12.6	-9.0	-7.5	..	-5.9	-9.8
Central African Republic	..	-3.5	-6.1	-7.8	-7.0	-6.1	-7.6	-2.8	-1.5	-0.9	0.5	..	-3.5	-4.4
Chad	..	-7.4	-7.8	..	-7.8	-7.8	-3.5	-3.4	-4.0	-2.9	-4.1	..	-7.4	-5.2
Comoros	..	..	..	..	..	..	..	..	..	..	..	..	..	..
Congo, Democratic Rep. of	..	..	..	..	..	..	..	..	..	..	..	..	..	..
Congo, Republic of	..	..	3.6	-4.4	-6.2	-5.2	-1.1	5.9	7.0	4.4	2.2	..	-5.3	0.7
Côte d'Ivoire	..	-7.2	-2.2	-2.0	-0.9	-3.2	1.4	3.2	3.8	3.0	2.6	7.2	0.0	0.6
Djibouti	..	..	-19.9	..	-11.1	-12.5	-8.1	-7.5	-3.4	-5.1	..	..	..	-9.7
Equatorial Guinea	..	..	1.3	1.1	-0.9	-7.4	1.4	0.3	-2.4	2.6	11.2	..	..	0.8
Eritrea	..	..	..	..	..	..	..	..	..	..	-27.3	..	..	-27.3
Ethiopia	..	-4.7	-8.5	-7.2	-5.5	-3.9	-4.3	-1.4	-3.2	0.7	-2.1	-5.7	-4.2	-3.9
Gabon	..	-0.3	1.5	3.9	1.1	1.3	5.1	11.3	8.5	11.9	3.2	-34.5	-2.4	5.3
Gambia, The	..	7.4	3.9	4.7	4.7	5.1	2.6	-2.9	-5.3	-1.4	2.9	..	8.0	1.6
Ghana	..	-0.8	-1.6	0.4	-7.3	-6.4	-4.4	-2.1	-4.4	-2.7	0.1	-1.1	-1.2	-3.2
Guinea	..	..	..	..	..	-2.4	-2.0	-1.3	-1.7	-1.3	-1.8	..	..	-1.7
Guinea-Bissau	..	..	..	..	..	..	..	..	..	..	..	..	..	..
Kenya	..	..	2.7	4.2	5.1	8.8	8.3	7.3	6.2	6.2	5.8	..	..	6.1
Lesotho	..	..	..	..	..	..	8.1	6.3	6.5	2.1	-4.4	..	..	3.7
Liberia	..	..	..	..	..	..	..	..	..	..	..	..	..	..
Madagascar	..	-2.4	0.8	-3.5	-3.2	-3.2	-3.0	-1.1	-0.2	0.7	-1.8	-5.0	-1.9	-1.6
Malawi	-8.4	3.5	-1.4	-0.3	-8.6	-2.4	-16.2	1.0	2.3	-5.1	6.9	-5.1	0.2	-2.6
Mali	..	-0.7	-0.3	-2.3	-2.2	-2.5	-2.0	-1.7	0.2	-1.1	-1.6	..	-2.4	-1.5
Mauritania	..	..	..	..	..	..	2.4	6.5	11.4	8.1	8.4	..	..	7.4
Mauritius	..	1.6	2.5	1.9	1.1	0.6	-0.2	-2.2	-3.3	-1.4	0.8	-0.6	2.3	0.0
Mozambique	..	-2.5	-4.3	-1.8	-0.4	-1.1	-4.2	-1.6	-1.5	-1.3	-1.4	..	-4.6	-1.9
Namibia	..	..	..	..	..	..	..	..	..	..	..	..	..	..
Niger	..	-3.1	-4.7	-1.7	-3.1	-2.1	-4.4	-1.5	1.4	-1.1	-0.4	-2.8	-2.0	-2.0
Nigeria	1.1	2.8	7.9	3.0	13.1	5.5	0.5	8.1	7.5	3.3	-6.9	-4.1	1.0	4.7
Rwanda	-1.8	-3.4	-4.0	-3.6	-6.2	-6.1	-7.0	0.0	-4.1	-1.3	-1.9	-2.6	-5.3	-3.8
São Tomé and Principe	..	..	..	..	..	..	..	..	-0.3	11.3	-2.8	..	..	2.7
Senegal	-2.5	1.1	-0.3	4.5	0.2	-0.8	1.6	2.7	2.1	2.2	1.7	-4.3	1.2	1.5
Seychelles	..	-0.1	8.2	3.0	2.1	-1.3	-0.6	-1.8	-2.8	-3.3	5.2	16.5	-1.1	1.0
Sierra Leone	-20.8	-3.9	-4.4	-3.3	-2.6	-3.4	-4.5	-7.8	-4.4	-5.0	-5.1	-16.7	-8.3	-4.5
Somalia	..	..	..	..	..	..	..	..	..	..	..	..	..	..
South Africa	..	..	..	..	..	..	..	..	..	..	1.9	..	..	1.9
Sudan	..	..	..	..	..	..	..	..	..	..	..	..	..	..
Swaziland	..	..	..	..	..	..	..	..	..	..	-0.7	..	..	-0.7
Tanzania	..	2.4	1.7	2.5	2.9	-2.8	0.6	-0.5	1.2	4.6	2.2	..	0.8	1.4
Togo	..	0.7	0.3	-2.9	-1.4	-11.4	-6.2	-3.0	-3.0	0.2	-3.0	4.0	1.0	-3.4
Uganda	..	-2.5	-3.8	-2.4	-4.0	-1.4	-2.3	-1.9	-0.9	-0.9	0.4	..	-2.5	-1.9
Zambia	..	1.3	-0.5	1.5	6.1	6.7	5.2	3.8	2.1	3.5	0.1	..	-1.3	3.2
Zimbabwe	-2.2	-2.7	-1.7	-0.7	-1.1	0.1	0.0	-0.7	0.7	-0.4	8.0	-3.2	-3.2	0.5
NORTH AFRICA	..	-11.1	-8.1	-9.6	-7.1	-10.0	-8.7	-7.7	-6.0	-5.7	-6.5	..	-13.9	-7.7
Algeria	..	0.0	5.3	3.5	1.0	-6.3	-1.6	1.7	6.5	6.4	0.3	-7.0	-6.4	1.9
Egypt, Arab Republic	..	-9.3	-8.7	-6.1	3.7	6.1	8.6	7.0	6.2	5.7	5.4	..	-12.4	3.1
Libya	..	..	..	..	..	..	..	..	..	..	..	..	..	..
Morocco	-7.0	0.2	5.6	4.5	3.4	2.9	2.0	0.4	1.7	2.2	2.6	-7.6	-0.2	2.8
Tunisia	..	-2.2	-3.2	-3.0	0.1	0.3	1.0	-1.3	-1.6	0.2	2.5	-4.5	-1.9	-0.5
ALL AFRICA	..	..	..	..	..	..	..	..	..	..	-8.4	..	..	-8.4

Note: 1998 data are preliminary. Corrected for error in last vol. Nigeria: from 1992 data are for consolidated budget; since 1994 ratios are distorted as off. ex. rt. used by Gov. for oil sector is significantly over valued.

7-4. Government expenditure and lending minus repayments

	Percentage of GDP											Annual average		
	1980	*1989*	*1990*	*1991*	*1992*	*1993*	*1994*	*1995*	*1996*	*1997*	*1998*	*75-84*	*85-89*	*90-MR*
SUB-SAHARAN AFRICA	23.6	27.2	27.8	27.3	29.7	30.8	30.1	28.4	27.8	27.7	28.4	24.6	27.7	28.7
excluding South Africa	..	26.0	26.3	25.7	28.4	26.8	26.6	24.4	22.9	23.2	23.2	23.5	26.2	25.3
excl. S. Africa & Nigeria	..	27.0	26.6	25.8	27.7	26.5	27.2	25.6	24.4	24.2	23.1	25.2	27.4	25.7
Angola	..	51.8	52.4	40.2	92.5	60.7	62.1	57.3	54.8	56.4	41.6	..	43.3	57.6
Benin	..	20.0	19.9	19.0	20.8	17.8	19.8	22.1	19.5	18.8	16.8	17.7	5.4	19.4
Botswana	..	34.1	39.4	41.2	42.0	42.5	36.6	36.6	36.0	40.3	41.1	33.6	33.4	39.5
Burkina Faso	40.9	36.9	19.6	21.5	20.9	22.6	21.6	21.1	21.3	23.3	22.8	74.7	33.4	21.6
Burundi	11.9	27.5	25.9	25.8	28.4	29.0	24.8	26.2	27.9	22.2	19.4	12.6	23.9	25.5
Cameroon	16.0	20.6	21.8	23.4	22.1	20.0	19.3	16.2	16.0	15.8	17.8	10.6	23.9	19.1
Cape Verde	..	32.7	31.4	37.5	48.6	52.7	62.2	60.4	56.5	53.4	49.8	..	36.2	50.3
Central African Republic	..	19.7	22.2	23.0	23.6	21.2	22.4	20.6	11.1	14.0	17.6	12.1	19.1	19.5
Chad	..	24.5	24.1	16.0	20.4	21.4	19.1	18.1	18.1	17.2	17.7	10.1	20.3	19.1
Comoros	..	33.9	32.5	32.4	33.4	26.4	38.3	34.0	28.5	27.6	27.8	36.8	36.9	31.2
Congo, Democratic Rep. of	..	..	..	6.1	3.6	4.5	5.4	11.7	9.5	10.2	-12.2	..	..	4.8
Congo, Republic of	..	23.5	34.3	38.6	36.6	36.7	36.7	32.8	33.0	38.4	35.7	38.3	34.9	35.9
Côte d'Ivoire	37.4	38.5	33.4	32.9	31.9	30.0	27.1	26.5	25.3	25.0	23.8	37.0	35.8	28.4
Djibouti	..	..	48.1	41.0	51.0	50.1	43.0	39.2	35.3	35.6	31.1	..	..	41.6
Equatorial Guinea	..	54.5	56.8	54.5	47.6	55.9	27.1	24.6	24.9	17.8	13.8	..	35.2	35.9
Eritrea	..	..	..	..	36.7	61.8	59.3	69.2	64.0	54.9	72.2	..	..	59.7
Ethiopia	..	34.2	29.7	24.6	20.2	19.6	25.0	24.7	26.9	24.2	25.4	26.1	29.5	24.5
Gabon	..	25.4	24.1	26.7	28.3	28.6	25.5	26.3	22.9	25.1	31.9	36.9	37.6	26.6
Gambia, The	68.7	27.9	26.9	25.7	26.4	25.4	25.1	27.6	30.7	27.1	23.2	71.2	31.8	26.5
Ghana	18.7	18.9	18.2	19.1	24.6	29.0	31.2	30.4	29.7	28.4	27.7	13.1	18.3	26.5
Guinea	..	24.1	24.6	22.7	19.3	18.5	17.3	17.8	16.1	17.1	16.4	..	23.0	18.9
Guinea-Bissau	0.0	50.5	42.7	45.6	48.0	40.3	35.5	30.4	33.6	46.3	25.0	14.6	49.5	38.6
Kenya	32.5	30.2	32.0	31.6	32.6	41.7	36.4	33.6	31.4	29.4	28.8	25.2	29.6	33.1
Lesotho	..	55.7	50.9	57.6	55.3	53.0	51.2	53.3	53.2	52.3	57.1	37.6	50.4	53.8
Liberia	..	..	..	..	..	..	..	..	..	..	..	..	..	..
Madagascar	27.9	19.7	17.0	16.4	20.0	20.6	19.8	17.6	17.8	17.4	18.1	20.6	17.8	18.3
Malawi	35.7	30.9	28.5	25.5	38.0	27.0	64.4	35.2	25.1	26.7	37.3	29.2	32.9	34.2
Mali	..	25.0	26.3	28.4	24.4	23.4	25.8	23.5	23.1	23.6	24.1	12.4	25.6	24.7
Mauritania	..	36.0	35.3	41.8	24.8	36.8	27.7	24.8	24.5	22.7	25.1	0.0	35.2	29.3
Mauritius	..	26.3	24.9	25.0	24.5	23.8	23.8	24.1	25.7	25.5	23.6	29.4	26.1	24.6
Mozambique	17.3	26.7	28.7	26.7	30.3	29.5	30.9	24.4	20.9	23.6	22.2	26.5	24.5	26.4
Namibia	0.0	33.2	34.2	36.0	36.9	38.1	33.4	35.2	38.4	39.3	39.7	23.5	36.6	36.8
Niger	36.7	20.9	22.7	16.9	16.8	16.7	18.5	15.2	12.9	15.6	15.6	38.1	20.1	16.8
Nigeria	24.3	21.0	24.9	24.7	31.8	28.2	23.6	18.2	15.1	17.8	24.0	23.6	20.6	23.2
Rwanda	14.3	18.6	19.7	23.2	24.4	23.7	16.1	20.0	22.3	19.5	18.1	17.4	20.1	20.8
São Tomé and Principe	..	50.8	43.9	36.0	62.0	58.9	73.8	77.5	69.3	70.1	59.6	..	22.2	61.2
Senegal	27.4	20.7	21.0	19.1	21.5	20.8	21.0	19.8	18.2	18.0	17.8	25.6	20.6	19.7
Seychelles	..	57.7	49.4	50.7	51.6	62.8	62.5	59.1	56.6	59.2	45.4	28.0	57.0	55.2
Sierra Leone	23.6	18.6	19.8	20.9	21.4	21.3	19.0	19.3	16.9	13.4	17.4	9.7	20.5	18.8
Somalia	..	..	..	..	..	..	..	..	..	..	..	..	..	..
South Africa	24.1	28.5	29.3	29.2	31.1	35.5	34.0	33.0	33.5	32.9	34.5	26.4	29.3	32.6
Sudan	..	19.0	15.5	22.5	29.0	10.0	..	12.0	10.8	7.6	7.9	23.1	20.8	14.4
Swaziland	..	..	..	27.6	31.6	46.4	44.0	39.7	37.5	35.3	33.8	..	..	37.0
Tanzania	..	16.5	17.2	15.8	15.9	19.7	17.8	18.3	17.6	15.1	14.5	..	20.6	16.9
Togo	40.5	28.8	28.8	25.4	22.0	26.6	25.1	22.5	20.9	18.2	21.1	34.9	32.4	23.4
Uganda	0.0	10.2	12.7	15.0	21.2	18.6	18.6	17.3	16.2	17.2	15.9	1.4	11.0	17.0
Zambia	38.1	25.2	32.9	34.7	31.0	29.4	31.9	29.4	29.3	26.0	27.6	35.1	32.1	30.2
Zimbabwe	4.2	33.9	34.3	33.0	36.1	34.8	33.1	38.5	34.8	38.2	34.8	11.4	35.6	35.3
NORTH AFRICA	..	34.0	31.2	33.9	32.8	33.5	31.8	30.1	28.3	28.6	29.4	..	36.4	31.1
Algeria	..	30.7	25.2	30.2	30.7	36.2	33.9	32.0	29.7	31.8	33.6	46.3	39.3	31.5
Egypt, Arab Republic	..	39.3	37.9	40.9	36.6	33.2	32.2	29.1	27.8	26.1	26.0	..	41.3	32.2
Libya	..	..	..	..	..	..	..	..	..	..	..	..	..	..
Morocco	30.5	28.6	27.5	26.0	28.4	29.9	28.1	29.1	27.0	28.7	29.7	34.3	28.1	28.3
Tunisia	..	..	..	..	..	..	..	..	..	..	..	..	..	..
ALL AFRICA	..	29.4	28.9	29.4	30.6	31.7	30.7	28.9	27.9	28.0	28.7	28.8	30.3	29.4

Note: 1998 data are preliminary. Nigeria: from 1992 accounts are for consolidated budget; since 1994, ratios are distorted as off. exch. rate used by the Gov. for oil exports oil value added is significantly over-valued.

7-5. Government interest payments

						Percentage of GDP						*Annual average*		
	1980	1989	1990	1991	1992	1993	1994	1995	1996	1997	1998	75-84	85-89	90-MR
SUB-SAHARAN AFRICA	..	..	..	..	..	..	..	..	..	..	5.1	..	..	5.1
excluding South Africa	..	5.0	5.6	5.7	5.8	5.7	5.5	4.8	4.1	3.6	3.4	..	5.2	4.9
excl. S. Africa & Nigeria	..	3.6	4.1	4.5	4.7	5.1	5.4	5.1	4.6	3.9	3.8	..	3.6	4.6
Angola	..	5.4	5.2	6.1	8.2	9.4	12.1	10.8	11.5	..	..	..	5.0	9.1
Benin	..	3.1	3.0	2.6	3.7	2.7	3.2	2.8	2.4	1.7	1.3	..	2.0	2.6
Botswana	..	..	..	..	..	..	..	..	..	-0.1	-0.6	..	..	-0.3
Burkina Faso	..	1.0	1.1	1.4	1.4	1.6	1.5	1.4	0.9	0.8	0.8	0.7	1.2	1.2
Burundi	0.2	2.3	1.8	1.6	1.8	1.4	1.5	1.8	1.9	2.0	1.6	0.7	2.0	1.7
Cameroon	..	1.7	2.1	4.1	5.2	4.8	7.0	6.4	6.7	6.1	5.7	..	1.4	5.3
Cape Verde	..	1.4	1.5	1.3	1.2	1.3	1.2	3.7	4.2	4.2	4.5	..	1.5	2.6
Central African Republic	..	1.4	1.2	1.4	1.9	2.1	2.4	2.3	1.9	1.4	1.4	..	1.5	1.8
Chad	..	0.2	0.4	..	0.8	1.2	1.2	1.0	1.0	0.9	0.8	..	0.2	0.9
Comoros	..	..	..	..	..	..	..	..	..	..	..	..	..	..
Congo, Democratic Rep. of	..	..	..	..	..	..	..	..	..	..	..	..	..	..
Congo, Republic of	..	..	10.2	8.7	7.9	7.4	12.1	14.1	12.1	13.1	14.3	..	7.7	11.1
Côte d'Ivoire	..	9.4	9.8	10.9	10.4	8.7	7.9	6.9	5.9	5.1	4.4	8.1	8.1	7.8
Djibouti	..	..	0.7	..	0.6	0.4	0.3	0.6	0.6	0.5	..	..	..	0.5
Equatorial Guinea	..	..	6.6	6.9	8.0	7.6	7.1	5.9	3.9	3.0	2.2	..	..	5.7
Eritrea	..	..	..	..	..	..	..	..	..	..	5.1	..	..	5.1
Ethiopia	..	1.5	1.3	1.3	1.5	2.0	3.4	2.5	2.4	2.2	1.9	0.9	1.5	2.0
Gabon	..	5.7	5.6	6.0	6.4	7.0	6.7	8.1	5.9	5.9	7.2	2.4	4.8	6.5
Gambia, The	..	4.2	4.0	3.5	3.4	3.8	3.7	3.8	4.4	5.2	5.4	..	4.2	4.1
Ghana	..	1.3	1.4	1.8	2.2	3.5	4.4	4.2	5.1	6.5	6.4	1.3	1.5	3.9
Guinea	..	..	..	..	..	1.3	1.6	1.4	1.3	1.6	1.4	..	..	1.4
Guinea-Bissau	..	..	..	..	..	..	..	..	..	..	..	..	..	..
Kenya	..	..	8.9	9.1	8.4	14.3	11.2	8.1	7.0	5.9	5.7	..	..	8.7
Lesotho	..	..	..	..	..	..	2.2	1.9	1.9	2.1	2.3	..	..	2.1
Liberia	..	..	..	..	..	..	..	..	..	..	..	..	..	..
Madagascar	..	1.6	1.5	2.0	3.4	4.0	5.4	5.1	4.7	3.0	2.3	1.0	1.8	3.5
Malawi	3.2	5.7	3.6	2.7	3.5	3.3	7.0	7.4	5.4	3.4	4.7	4.2	6.1	4.6
Mali	..	2.0	2.4	1.8	1.8	1.6	2.3	1.4	1.1	1.0	0.7	..	1.9	1.6
Mauritania	..	..	..	..	..	..	2.9	3.2	3.3	3.0	3.5	..	..	3.2
Mauritius	..	4.1	4.4	4.1	3.4	2.8	2.9	3.2	3.4	3.7	3.3	6.0	4.8	3.5
Mozambique	..	1.8	1.9	1.3	2.4	2.5	1.1	1.6	1.5	1.3	1.0	..	1.5	1.6
Namibia	..	..	..	..	..	..	..	..	..	..	..	..	..	..
Niger	..	2.7	2.3	1.9	1.6	1.7	2.3	2.4	1.7	1.5	1.6	2.1	2.8	1.9
Nigeria	1.4	10.0	11.3	10.1	9.8	8.2	5.6	3.7	2.3	2.2	1.7	1.7	8.0	6.1
Rwanda	0.2	1.1	1.0	1.8	1.9	2.1	4.5	2.2	1.6	1.2	0.9	0.4	1.0	1.9
São Tomé and Principe	..	..	..	..	..	..	..	..	10.0	11.3	12.4	..	..	11.2
Senegal	2.0	3.2	2.7	2.5	2.0	2.3	3.5	2.9	2.3	2.2	1.7	2.5	3.2	2.4
Seychelles	1.8	7.9	8.0	7.9	7.9	8.0	8.4	9.7	8.6	9.4	9.0	1.9	6.6	8.5
Sierra Leone	1.8	6.0	5.7	6.3	5.8	4.0	2.6	2.0	2.1	2.2	4.8	2.0	4.7	3.9
Somalia	..	..	..	..	..	..	..	..	..	..	..	..	..	..
South Africa	..	..	..	..	..	..	..	..	..	..	6.9	..	..	6.9
Sudan	..	..	..	..	..	..	..	..	..	..	..	..	..	..
Swaziland	..	..	..	..	..	..	..	..	..	..	0.3	..	..	0.3
Tanzania	..	2.6	2.3	2.1	1.9	2.5	2.6	3.4	3.3	2.6	2.0	..	2.9	2.5
Togo	..	4.2	3.2	3.2	2.8	4.2	5.5	3.5	2.7	2.3	2.1	7.2	4.8	3.3
Uganda	..	0.6	0.6	1.3	3.3	1.8	1.4	1.0	1.0	0.9	1.0	..	0.6	1.4
Zambia	4.1	5.6	7.8	8.5	8.5	12.3	11.6	8.1	4.7	4.7	3.2	4.2	9.5	7.7
Zimbabwe	1.2	4.9	4.8	4.6	5.7	6.2	6.7	9.3	8.5	7.3	9.6	2.6	4.8	7.0
NORTH AFRICA	..	3.6	3.5	4.4	4.8	5.6	6.0	5.5	5.3	5.1	4.7	..	3.5	5.0
Algeria	..	1.7	1.6	1.8	2.2	2.3	2.8	3.2	3.5	4.0	3.5	1.2	1.6	2.8
Egypt, Arab Republic	..	3.9	3.8	6.3	6.8	8.5	9.4	7.4	7.0	6.0	5.8	..	3.8	6.8
Libya	..	..	..	..	..	..	..	..	..	..	..	..	..	..
Morocco	2.5	6.2	6.2	5.5	5.6	5.9	5.7	6.0	5.1	5.9	5.3	2.9	6.1	5.7
Tunisia	1.6	3.1	3.0	2.9	3.2	3.5	3.6	4.1	4.3	3.8	3.4	1.8	2.8	3.5
ALL AFRICA	..	..	..	..	..	..	..	..	..	..	5.0	..	..	5.0

Note: 1998 data are preliminary. Nigeria: from 1992 accounts are for consolidated budget; since 1994, ratios are distorted as off. exch. rate used by the Gov. for oil exports oil value added is significantly over-valued.

7-6. Government revenue (excluding grants)

	Percentage of GDP											*Annual average*		
	1980	*1989*	*1990*	*1991*	*1992*	*1993*	*1994*	*1995*	*1996*	*1997*	*1998*	*75-84*	*85-89*	*90-MR*
SUB-SAHARAN AFRICA	11.3	22.3	22.5	21.7	22.5	23.2	23.0	23.7	23.7	23.9	23.2	18.1	21.9	23.0
excluding South Africa	..	17.8	19.4	18.7	21.8	20.3	18.6	20.0	19.7	20.0	17.7	17.7	19.0	19.6
excl. S. Africa & Nigeria	..	18.7	18.9	19.0	19.1	19.2	18.7	19.5	19.6	20.2	18.1	19.2	20.2	19.1
Angola	..	26.6	25.7	18.3	35.6	39.1	42.1	30.0	44.5	36.7	25.9	..	32.3	33.1
Benin	..	8.0	9.2	10.4	11.9	13.1	12.8	14.9	15.2	14.6	15.5	14.2	11.9	13.1
Botswana	..	42.7	48.5	49.3	50.4	49.6	38.8	38.1	41.9	45.0	37.7	40.8	46.0	44.4
Burkina Faso	31.5	9.2	12.3	13.3	11.7	12.6	11.0	10.8	12.3	13.0	13.1	51.2	10.6	12.3
Burundi	18.1	20.0	15.1	16.9	17.1	16.7	18.0	17.7	15.5	13.7	12.5	18.0	17.9	15.9
Cameroon	16.3	16.0	14.3	15.2	15.7	13.7	9.9	12.9	14.3	15.1	16.2	11.1	18.6	14.1
Cape Verde	..	17.6	18.7	17.7	20.6	25.7	27.7	28.0	25.0	25.7	26.7	..	17.2	24.0
Central African Republic	..	10.1	10.7	9.2	8.9	7.7	7.5	9.2	6.1	7.7	9.0	7.8	9.5	8.4
Chad	..	6.7	7.2	6.4	6.7	7.4	4.9	6.2	7.1	7.3	9.0	3.8	5.7	6.9
Comoros	..	14.1	17.0	13.9	15.8	14.5	14.3	14.3	13.8	15.1	15.9	17.6	12.9	15.0
Congo, Democratic Rep. of	..	..	..	..	..	..	..	..	..	..	..	..	..	..
Congo, Republic of	..	21.9	27.4	25.3	22.5	24.1	22.4	23.6	27.7	29.6	23.3	34.6	25.9	25.1
Côte d'Ivoire	28.9	21.8	21.5	19.5	20.1	17.6	19.9	22.1	22.5	22.2	21.3	26.0	27.2	20.7
Djibouti	..	..	27.5	25.8	26.9	28.4	29.5	29.1	29.5	27.5	26.7	..	..	27.9
Equatorial Guinea	..	16.4	21.1	20.9	21.6	21.4	17.3	16.4	17.7	16.7	22.1	..	19.4	19.5
Eritrea	..	..	..	..	24.4	35.3	28.1	34.1	32.2	41.7	33.8	..	..	32.8
Ethiopia	..	23.2	17.7	13.7	10.6	12.0	13.9	17.4	18.4	19.0	18.7	17.4	20.0	15.7
Gabon	..	18.9	19.6	24.3	22.9	22.6	23.5	29.5	25.5	31.1	27.8	..	30.0	25.2
Gambia, The	64.7	22.2	20.9	21.5	23.2	23.0	20.9	18.5	18.8	19.3	18.8	65.7	21.3	20.5
Ghana	..	13.6	12.5	14.6	11.9	14.9	18.7	20.4	17.6	17.3	18.7	8.0	13.2	16.3
Guinea	..	15.5	15.8	14.5	12.2	11.2	10.2	11.0	10.0	11.1	10.6	..	14.4	11.9
Guinea-Bissau	0.0	10.8	18.2	12.4	10.9	10.5	12.3	12.7	12.5	15.3	5.5	1.9	12.9	12.2
Kenya	24.6	23.1	23.6	24.4	24.9	29.9	28.5	29.1	27.8	26.5	26.8	19.5	22.7	26.8
Lesotho	..	36.2	37.4	47.2	50.8	52.6	51.8	52.6	52.6	47.7	47.7	34.4	38.0	48.9
Liberia	..	..	..	..	..	..	..	..	..	..	..	..	..	..
Madagascar	15.1	11.5	12.0	8.7	10.0	9.9	8.3	8.5	8.7	9.7	10.6	12.9	12.8	9.6
Malawi	19.8	23.7	21.2	19.1	21.8	17.9	21.8	19.8	17.1	16.1	22.5	18.1	22.9	19.7
Mali	..	17.1	17.6	16.0	13.3	13.8	12.0	12.8	15.2	15.8	16.1	10.8	15.1	14.7
Mauritania	..	29.6	31.4	31.9	21.4	25.4	23.2	24.0	29.8	26.9	27.2	0.0	31.2	26.8
Mauritius	..	23.4	22.8	22.7	22.1	21.4	20.4	18.5	18.8	20.3	20.8	22.4	22.8	20.9
Mozambique	13.5	13.1	12.8	12.5	13.9	14.0	11.8	11.3	10.8	11.6	11.5	16.1	11.1	12.2
Namibia	0.0	31.7	30.5	33.4	33.0	33.6	31.8	32.4	32.6	35.4	34.9	13.5	28.8	33.1
Niger	23.2	10.3	10.2	8.5	7.3	7.3	6.0	7.2	7.8	8.4	9.0	23.5	10.7	8.1
Nigeria	24.0	13.8	21.5	17.7	35.1	25.5	18.5	22.6	20.2	18.8	15.4	17.8	13.6	21.7
Rwanda	12.3	9.9	10.1	10.4	10.1	9.1	3.7	6.7	9.2	10.3	10.2	9.4	10.5	8.9
São Tomé and Principe	..	0.0	0.0	0.0	20.2	18.0	13.3	16.5	13.4	15.6	25.0	..	0.0	13.6
Senegal	22.1	16.6	16.8	19.4	18.4	16.6	14.9	16.3	16.0	16.3	16.1	18.7	17.2	16.8
Seychelles	..	48.1	47.7	44.2	44.5	51.9	52.7	47.1	44.6	46.1	39.7	22.4	47.0	46.5
Sierra Leone	0.0	8.4	9.7	11.3	13.0	13.9	11.9	9.5	8.4	5.6	5.1	0.0	7.0	9.8
Somalia	..	..	..	..	..	..	..	..	..	..	..	..	..	..
South Africa	6.0	27.1	26.1	24.9	23.4	26.5	27.8	27.8	28.1	28.3	29.6	19.9	24.9	26.9
Sudan	..	7.3	6.3	7.2	8.8	8.3	8.8	8.7	7.0	6.8	7.3	10.9	8.7	7.7
Swaziland	..	..	..	32.3	30.1	41.8	40.0	36.9	35.8	33.5	31.9	..	..	35.3
Tanzania	..	12.6	16.7	16.3	16.8	14.4	15.9	12.5	13.2	13.5	12.3	..	13.8	14.6
Togo	..	22.6	22.6	17.5	16.2	10.7	12.1	14.7	14.6	14.7	14.3	28.1	25.5	15.3
Uganda	0.0	5.5	6.8	7.5	6.8	7.3	8.3	9.8	10.2	11.0	10.2	1.1	6.3	8.7
Zambia	..	18.6	20.3	18.7	18.4	15.9	20.1	19.9	20.6	19.8	18.1	..	20.1	19.1
Zimbabwe	11.1	25.7	27.0	26.6	27.7	26.8	24.5	26.7	25.7	29.4	30.5	18.5	26.6	27.2
NORTH AFRICA	..	25.5	25.2	27.0	29.2	28.1	28.9	27.8	28.1	28.9	27.2	..	26.0	27.8
Algeria	..	28.9	28.9	31.8	29.5	27.6	31.0	31.7	32.7	34.1	30.4	38.2	31.3	30.9
Egypt, Arab Republic	..	23.8	22.8	25.7	31.2	29.7	30.0	27.8	26.5	25.2	25.0	..	25.3	27.1
Libya	..	..	..	..	..	..	..	..	..	..	..	..	..	..
Morocco	20.0	21.8	23.1	22.3	25.8	25.8	23.8	23.2	26.3	30.8	27.0	21.8	20.4	25.3
Tunisia	..	28.6	27.1	26.7	27.2	27.8	28.0	25.5	24.7	24.2	26.2	32.8	29.5	26.4
ALL AFRICA	..	23.4	23.5	23.5	24.8	24.9	25.0	25.1	25.2	25.6	24.5	23.3	23.5	24.7

Note: 1998 data are preliminary. Nigeria: from 1992 accounts are for consolidated budget; since 1994, ratios are distorted as off. exch. rate used by the Gov. for oil exports oil value added is significantly over-valued.

7-7. Grants to government

	Percentage of GDP											Annual average		
	1980	1989	1990	1991	1992	1993	1994	1995	1996	1997	1998	75-84	85-89	90-MR
SUB-SAHARAN AFRICA	0.1	1.1	1.0	1.2	1.4	1.3	1.3	1.1	1.0	1.0	0.9	0.2	0.9	1.1
excluding South Africa	0.3	1.9	1.7	1.9	2.3	2.3	2.5	2.1	1.8	1.8	1.7	0.3	1.5	2.0
excl. S. Africa & Nigeria	0.3	2.3	2.0	2.3	2.7	2.8	2.9	2.5	2.1	2.1	2.0	0.4	1.8	2.4
Angola	..	0.0	0.0	0.0	0.0	0.0	0.0	0.0	0.0	0.8	1.1	..	0.0	0.2
Benin	0.0	9.7	5.9	3.4	4.1	3.9	4.6	4.0	3.9	4.5	3.3	1.1	5.0	4.2
Botswana	0.0	0.9	1.4	1.0	1.1	1.6	0.9	0.3	0.4	0.1	0.1	0.2	2.0	0.8
Burkina Faso	0.0	10.9	2.7	4.6	6.2	5.4	7.3	6.7	8.4	7.0	6.8	0.7	5.5	6.1
Burundi	3.7	3.2	8.1	8.7	8.6	8.7	2.4	3.6	2.2	3.1	2.7	2.0	1.6	5.3
Cameroon	0.0	0.0	0.0	0.0	0.0	0.0	0.1	0.0	0.0	0.0	0.0	0.0	0.0	0.0
Cape Verde	..	0.0	0.5	13.5	19.3	16.8	18.0	17.3	14.7	14.6	11.1	..	11.6	14.0
Central African Republic	4.4	4.8	4.2	4.6	5.7	5.3	4.9	6.3	1.5	4.0	7.7	1.6	5.1	4.9
Chad	0.0	10.2	8.7	5.2	5.2	4.9	9.5	7.5	6.0	6.0	3.8	0.8	10.4	6.3
Comoros	0.0	16.4	15.1	16.3	15.0	14.4	16.3	11.8	8.9	9.7	8.9	7.7	35.2	12.9
Congo, Democratic Rep. of	0.0	0.0	0.0	0.0	1.9	1.2	0.6	0.3	0.5	0.5	0.0	0.0	0.0	0.5
Congo, Republic of	0.0	0.0	0.3	0.2	0.0	0.0	1.1	1.0	0.3	0.1	0.3	0.2	0.1	0.4
Côte d'Ivoire	0.0	0.0	0.0	0.5	0.5	0.5	0.7	0.7	0.7	0.7	0.7	0.0	0.0	0.6
Djibouti	..	0.0	0.0	12.2	12.4	8.8	5.0	2.0	1.9	2.6	2.2	..	0.0	5.2
Equatorial Guinea	..	21.7	30.4	27.7	17.1	19.3	4.2	2.6	0.9	0.7	0.7	0.0	4.6	11.5
Eritrea	..	..	..	..	9.1	20.1	18.5	12.7	12.0	6.2	5.9	..	..	12.1
Ethiopia	..	4.8	2.3	2.4	2.6	1.7	3.5	3.3	2.9	3.6	2.8	2.1	3.7	2.8
Gabon	0.0	0.4	0.4	0.3	0.1	0.3	0.4	0.0	0.0	0.0	0.0	0.0	0.5	0.1
Gambia, The	0.0	8.8	5.9	5.4	4.5	3.7	3.1	2.4	2.2	1.3	2.0	0.0	14.2	3.4
Ghana	0.1	3.2	2.7	3.1	3.3	4.3	3.5	3.6	2.6	1.9	2.7	0.1	2.3	3.1
Guinea	..	3.6	3.7	3.6	4.0	3.6	3.5	4.0	3.1	3.2	2.7	..	3.1	3.5
Guinea-Bissau	0.0	27.3	18.0	15.5	15.8	16.9	14.7	16.3	9.0	12.8	3.3	1.9	30.5	13.6
Kenya	0.8	2.4	2.2	2.0	2.6	3.1	2.7	2.0	1.3	1.0	0.8	0.6	1.7	2.0
Lesotho	0.0	10.3	11.1	9.7	7.6	6.1	5.3	5.1	5.2	4.6	2.6	1.0	6.1	6.4
Liberia	0.0	0.0	..	..	..	..	..	..	..	..	..	0.0	0.0	..
Madagascar	0.0	4.1	4.4	2.1	3.5	3.5	3.0	2.9	4.2	5.3	3.4	0.2	1.3	3.6
Malawi	4.3	5.0	2.3	3.4	2.6	3.1	14.8	8.9	4.9	3.7	8.5	2.2	4.0	5.8
Mali	0.0	5.2	6.0	8.2	7.1	5.5	9.5	7.5	7.1	5.7	5.6	1.7	5.1	6.9
Mauritania	0.0	2.6	2.3	2.3	2.9	3.8	4.0	4.1	2.8	1.0	2.7	0.0	4.5	2.9
Mauritius	0.0	0.3	0.2	0.1	0.1	0.2	0.3	0.3	0.2	0.1	0.3	0.0	0.8	0.2
Mozambique	1.8	9.3	9.7	11.1	13.7	11.9	13.8	9.8	7.1	9.3	8.3	1.9	5.4	10.5
Namibia	0.0	0.0	1.2	1.1	0.9	0.7	0.4	0.4	0.4	0.4	0.0	0.0	0.0	0.6
Niger	0.0	4.7	5.4	4.8	3.9	5.6	5.8	4.1	4.9	4.5	4.6	0.3	4.6	4.9
Nigeria	0.0	0.0	0.0	0.0	0.0	0.0	0.0	0.0	0.1	0.1	0.0	0.0	0.0	0.0
Rwanda	0.0	4.3	4.6	7.4	6.2	6.4	0.9	11.0	7.4	6.7	5.1	1.6	3.5	6.2
São Tomé and Principe	0.0	18.6	15.2	11.9	9.0	16.6	17.5	23.4	23.5	27.8	9.7	0.0	5.5	17.2
Senegal	0.7	1.9	1.3	1.7	1.3	1.1	4.2	3.3	2.0	1.7	1.7	0.6	1.4	2.0
Seychelles	0.0	1.5	1.9	1.5	1.3	1.6	0.8	0.5	0.6	0.4	1.9	1.0	2.2	1.2
Sierra Leone	1.0	0.3	0.0	0.0	0.0	0.0	0.0	0.0	2.0	0.6	2.4	0.4	0.5	0.5
Somalia	0.0	0.0	0.0	..	..	..	..	..	..	..	..	0.0	0.0	0.0
South Africa	0.0	0.1	0.2	0.4	0.3	0.1	0.0	0.0	0.0	0.0	0.0	0.0	0.1	0.1
Sudan	0.0	0.0	0.0	0.0	0.0	0.0	0.0	0.0	0.0	0.0	0.0	0.0	0.0	0.0
Swaziland	0.0	0.0	0.0	0.7	1.4	1.2	0.9	0.8	0.7	0.8	0.9	0.0	0.0	0.8
Tanzania	..	3.7	3.8	2.4	2.7	3.8	3.8	2.0	2.2	3.6	2.4	..	4.7	3.0
Togo	1.5	2.6	3.2	1.9	1.6	0.3	1.4	1.4	0.5	1.4	1.7	1.4	3.1	1.5
Uganda	0.0	1.6	1.5	3.8	7.1	8.1	6.5	4.6	4.1	4.4	5.1	0.0	1.1	5.0
Zambia	0.0	2.3	4.3	9.0	10.2	8.0	5.3	5.2	6.1	5.0	6.4	0.0	1.2	6.6
Zimbabwe	0.7	0.7	0.9	1.1	1.7	2.0	1.9	1.8	1.3	1.1	1.3	0.5	1.0	1.4
NORTH AFRICA	0.2	0.9	1.8	1.6	1.0	0.7	0.6	0.5	0.3	0.3	0.2	0.4	0.6	0.8
Algeria	0.0	0.0	0.0	0.0	0.0	0.0	0.0	0.0	0.0	0.0	0.0	0.0	0.0	0.0
Egypt, Arab Republic	0.0	2.2	2.6	2.8	2.3	1.2	1.3	0.9	0.6	0.6	0.6	0.0	1.2	1.4
Libya	0.0	0.0	..	..	..	..	..	..	..	..	..	0.0	0.0	..
Morocco	1.1	0.8	3.8	2.7	0.4	1.1	0.6	0.4	0.2	0.0	0.0	2.1	1.3	1.0
Tunisia	0.0	0.0	0.0	0.0	0.0	0.0	0.0	0.3	0.2	0.3	0.0	0.0	0.0	0.1
ALL AFRICA	0.2	1.0	1.3	1.3	1.2	1.1	1.1	0.9	0.7	0.7	0.7	0.2	0.8	1.0

Note: 1998 data are preliminary. Nigeria: from 1992 accounts are for consolidated budget; since 1994, ratios are distorted as off. exch. rate used by the Gov. for oil exports oil value added is significantly over-valued.

7-8. Foreign financing

	Percentage of GDP											Annual average		
	1980	1989	1990	1991	1992	1993	1994	1995	1996	1997	1998	75-84	85-89	90-MR
SUB-SAHARAN AFRICA	0.9	1.9	1.6	1.3	0.1	0.8	2.0	0.7	1.6	0.6	0.7	1.0	1.4	1.0
excluding South Africa	..	3.8	3.4	2.3	0.0	1.4	3.4	1.0	2.8	0.8	1.2	..	3.0	1.8
excl. S. Africa & Nigeria	..	3.9	4.2	2.9	3.4	2.7	4.9	1.8	3.8	1.2	1.7	..	3.3	2.9
Angola	..	2.9	3.9	1.6	1.2	-8.7	7.4	-2.7	20.6	9.1	2.3	..	0.5	3.9
Benin	..	27.9	9.3	11.3	7.9	6.9	10.3	8.3	7.6	5.1	6.9	..	27.9	8.2
Botswana	..	..	..	0.3	0.8	0.5	0.0	-0.3	-0.3	-0.7	-0.4	..	..	0.0
Burkina Faso	..	-7.1	3.5	8.4	9.4	10.0	10.0	12.1	10.9	9.3	9.8	3.0	1.1	9.3
Burundi	3.3	6.5	8.1	10.6	14.2	10.2	4.7	3.8	3.0	1.6	2.1	5.6	7.5	6.5
Cameroon	2.2	4.8	5.3	1.9	8.4	0.1	20.5	0.1	8.2	-3.5	9.3	1.6	3.0	5.6
Cape Verde	..	1.8	1.8	0.7	2.5	3.6	4.4	2.4	3.9	7.1	13.8	..	1.8	4.4
Central African Republic	0.4	0.4	1.2	1.6	0.8	0.3	2.3	0.6	-1.6	-1.6	-1.6	1.0	1.9	0.2
Chad	..	8.4	6.7	2.8	2.1	2.9	2.6	2.8	5.8	5.1	3.9	0.5	4.3	3.9
Comoros	..	3.3	2.0	3.2	-2.5	2.4	4.8	4.5	3.8	2.5	0.2	18.9	6.9	2.3
Congo, Democratic Rep. of	..	..	..	..	..	..	..	..	..	..	..	..	..	..
Congo, Republic of	11.2	-8.6	24.8	8.3	7.0	8.1	5.4	-14.1	75.8	-2.2	-1.7	5.7	6.9	12.4
Côte d'Ivoire	7.9	10.5	11.5	10.9	9.8	7.5	11.0	4.2	3.0	1.0	0.7	6.8	6.1	6.6
Djibouti	..	..	..	0.4	0.1	3.0	2.4	1.6	3.4	1.7	..	..	..	1.8
Equatorial Guinea	..	6.1	0.1	-7.0	0.4	0.6	-8.5	-8.0	-0.4	-0.7	-0.9	..	-0.8	-2.7
Eritrea	..	..	..	..	..	0.1	4.6	1.2	1.3	4.3	6.2	..	..	2.9
Ethiopia	..	3.6	2.8	2.1	1.4	2.7	6.0	3.7	3.7	1.8	1.7	2.6	3.1	2.9
Gabon	..	7.6	-3.1	-2.8	-4.2	-5.1	-3.2	-5.7	-3.0	-5.2	-4.5	..	6.8	-4.1
Gambia, The	..	3.0	4.2	4.6	4.1	2.0	0.7	2.9	6.6	4.1	1.2	4.7	5.6	3.4
Ghana	0.9	3.2	4.5	3.5	3.5	6.2	4.5	4.3	3.7	3.6	2.3	0.7	2.7	4.0
Guinea	..	3.5	2.0	1.3	1.5	3.1	-0.3	1.7	1.1	4.1	4.1	..	4.7	2.1
Guinea-Bissau	..	5.9	4.9	2.1	18.9	14.0	9.8	3.3	9.0	20.8	8.7	..	15.9	10.2
Kenya	3.9	2.9	2.6	1.0	1.3	1.2	-0.5	-0.5	-0.6	-1.0	-0.9	2.0	1.0	0.3
Lesotho	..	-2.7	-3.4	-2.0	0.9	0.8	-1.0	0.7	3.2	-0.2	0.0	-0.5	-5.6	-0.1
Liberia	..	..	..	..	..	..	..	..	..	..	..	..	..	..
Madagascar	5.6	4.6	2.1	3.9	2.7	2.9	1.7	1.9	5.0	3.8	1.0	4.1	3.4	2.8
Malawi	4.0	3.2	5.4	3.3	5.5	7.2	10.2	2.3	5.1	3.3	5.5	4.8	3.5	5.3
Mali	..	11.8	5.4	6.2	4.3	3.4	7.4	7.4	6.0	3.3	3.6	4.7	8.1	5.2
Mauritania	..	0.4	-6.1	-8.1	-5.8	15.4	0.3	-4.8	-5.1	-6.9	-14.2	..	-0.6	-3.9
Mauritius	..	-0.9	-0.7	-0.8	-0.7	-0.4	-0.4	1.5	1.7	-0.1	0.5	-1.0	0.6	0.1
Mozambique	2.1	4.7	6.1	3.6	2.1	2.6	5.9	3.8	4.3	5.9	4.7	3.7	4.1	4.3
Namibia	..	..	..	..	0.3	0.6	0.4	0.7	0.8	0.7	0.1	..	..	0.5
Niger	..	3.3	6.8	0.6	1.5	-0.1	12.5	-0.6	4.0	3.5	4.4	5.4	4.2	3.6
Nigeria	0.5	3.7	-0.1	-0.1	-15.1	-4.7	-3.7	-2.9	-2.1	-1.3	-1.4	0.6	1.9	-3.5
Rwanda	-0.3	2.1	3.0	4.0	4.2	3.0	-1.5	2.1	2.5	2.2	6.4	0.9	3.4	2.9
São Tomé and Principe	..	19.8	18.8	19.1	40.7	23.4	26.3	29.4	24.5	26.5	5.3	..	8.1	23.8
Senegal	2.7	3.2	3.5	0.5	0.8	0.6	9.2	3.6	1.5	1.6	0.8	3.3	3.2	2.4
Seychelles	..	1.9	-1.8	3.1	-1.5	0.9	-1.4	-2.0	-1.2	-0.7	1.9	6.6	3.2	-0.3
Sierra Leone	0.8	0.6	..	0.7	10.7	6.7	7.4	7.4	4.7	2.9	2.8	0.5	0.6	5.4
Somalia	..	..	..	..	..	..	..	..	..	..	..	..	..	..
South Africa	-0.1	0.0	-0.1	0.2	0.2	0.0	0.4	0.4	0.2	0.5	0.2	0.1	-0.1	0.2
Sudan	..	..	..	..	..	2.0	1.1	1.0	0.2	0.2	0.2	..	..	0.8
Swaziland	..	..	..	-0.5	-0.4	..	..	..	..	..	4.0	..	..	1.0
Tanzania	..	-0.6	0.2	0.9	1.8	1.9	2.4	0.9	-1.2	-0.5	1.3	..	0.8	0.9
Togo	..	7.7	4.9	4.0	2.4	0.8	4.9	11.7	5.9	5.4	4.4	..	7.3	4.9
Uganda	..	2.2	6.7	3.9	5.2	5.2	5.5	4.7	3.4	3.2	2.7	..	1.2	4.5
Zambia	..	1.1	6.3	2.2	2.3	6.4	4.1	4.1	2.3	3.9	3.0	..	4.5	3.8
Zimbabwe	0.4	0.9	1.1	2.1	3.5	2.0	0.5	0.2	0.2	0.5	-2.5	1.8	1.9	0.8
NORTH AFRICA	..	0.7	0.0	4.0	-0.3	-0.4	1.8	2.0	0.5	0.0	-0.5	1.4	1.2	0.8
Algeria	..	0.6	0.6	0.6	-0.3	0.1	7.9	7.6	2.9	2.6	-0.7	0.0	0.6	2.4
Egypt, Arab Republic	..	1.7	0.6	10.2	-0.2	-1.0	-1.0	-1.1	-1.2	-1.2	-0.4	3.7	4.0	0.5
Libya	..	..	..	..	..	..	..	..	..	..	..	..	..	..
Morocco	4.7	-2.0	-3.1	-1.8	-1.3	-0.7	-1.8	-0.8	-1.1	-2.6	-1.0	4.0	-4.0	-1.6
Tunisia	..	2.8	2.1	2.4	1.0	1.2	1.4	2.9	2.8	2.3	0.5	2.4	2.8	1.8
ALL AFRICA	..	1.5	1.0	2.3	0.0	0.4	1.9	1.1	1.2	0.4	0.3	1.1	1.3	1.0

Note: 1998 data are preliminary. Nigeria: from 1992 accounts are for consolidated budget; since 1994, ratios are distorted as off. exch. rate used by the Gov. for oil exports oil value added is significantly over-valued.

7-9. Taxes on income and profits

	1980	1989	1990	1991	1992	1993	1994	1995	1996	1997	1998	75-84	85-89	90-MR
					Percentage of total revenue								*Annual average*	
SUB-SAHARAN AFRICA	..	35.5	36.7	36.9	37.5	33.6	32.9	32.7	33.9	34.6	33.8	40.5	37.3	34.7
excluding South Africa	..	21.2	21.2	19.2	20.0	19.6	20.0	20.4	21.0	20.8	20.7	19.5	20.8	20.3
excl. S. Africa & Nigeria	..	26.0	26.0	23.4	24.4	23.8	24.3	24.5	25.4	25.1	25.0	..	25.6	24.6
Angola	..	54.1	64.6	46.3	65.6	66.4	72.8	71.2	92.9	89.0	79.7	..	47.8	72.0
Benin	..	19.2	19.8	19.7	22.5	24.8	30.5	28.4	26.9	23.5	23.6	..	19.2	24.4
Botswana	..	8.4	8.2	8.7	8.3	8.1	8.6	7.0	5.5	4.0	4.0	12.1	8.1	6.9
Burkina Faso	..	23.5	21.5	20.4	22.0	18.9	18.7	23.4	24.7	21.9	21.8	19.7	19.1	21.5
Burundi	18.9	14.1	23.1	23.7	23.1	26.9	20.0	21.2	25.1	25.7	22.6	21.0	17.7	23.5
Cameroon	21.7	44.4	44.3	17.3	18.0	10.9	12.6	10.9	10.0	13.6	15.4	26.9	49.7	17.0
Cape Verde	..	20.4	20.9	21.1	20.4	22.2	23.1	22.6	26.3	27.8	27.9	..	23.4	23.6
Central African Republic	..	22.1	24.1	24.0	22.8	22.9	24.3	20.6	24.4	19.3	14.0	..	25.2	21.8
Chad	..	21.8	18.7	26.7	27.6	23.5	28.7	38.9	37.6	32.7	27.5	..	19.1	29.1
Comoros	..	13.8	19.8	13.5	11.1	9.0	12.6	12.2	12.8	11.2	11.4	6.6	15.4	12.6
Congo, Democratic Rep. of	..	..	..	..	..	..	..	..	..	..	..	..	..	..
Congo, Republic of	..	34.1	51.6	62.6	51.9	51.3	67.8	53.4	62.2	79.7	56.7	..	34.1	59.7
Côte d'Ivoire	..	20.5	22.5	20.9	20.3	19.4	14.9	18.3	20.5	22.9	23.6	16.1	18.5	20.4
Djibouti	..	..	30.9	32.6	38.9	38.7	38.5	37.2	41.0	39.2	..	..	..	37.1
Equatorial Guinea	..	5.8	11.1	5.0	11.0	15.4	19.6	19.6	52.9	61.9	68.5	..	5.0	29.4
Eritrea	..	..	..	..	13.1	20.1	33.2	25.7	27.7	22.8	34.3	..	..	25.3
Ethiopia	..	27.2	29.4	30.7	30.1	23.1	24.0	22.2	25.2	24.2	22.2	28.6	28.9	25.7
Gabon	..	21.9	14.2	13.0	13.4	12.8	10.7	10.5	10.6	10.7	14.4	..	23.7	12.3
Gambia, The	..	13.2	13.2	13.2	14.8	16.2	17.7	19.4	20.0	21.1	22.3	..	13.8	17.5
Ghana	..	23.8	23.0	17.6	18.6	19.1	17.5	17.4	21.7	24.8	22.9	18.7	22.9	20.3
Guinea	..	2.2	2.1	4.2	6.8	6.9	8.8	9.1	10.9	9.7	9.7	..	1.6	7.6
Guinea-Bissau	..	15.6	6.7	5.6	7.6	7.8	6.9	7.8	8.0	8.3	15.0	..	15.6	8.2
Kenya	28.0	29.3	29.3	29.0	28.8	32.9	35.2	33.8	33.0	31.6	30.4	27.1	29.2	31.6
Lesotho	..	11.6	11.4	15.8	16.7	13.8	15.2	16.3	15.1	15.4	16.2	16.5	11.7	15.1
Liberia	..	..	..	..	..	..	..	..	..	..	..	..	..	..
Madagascar	79.6	10.1	12.7	15.0	12.9	16.2	19.8	14.6	18.3	18.8	15.7	29.4	12.2	16.0
Malawi	83.9	53.0	52.4	51.2	48.0	56.2	52.6	45.4	55.7	53.0	38.1	83.5	70.3	50.3
Mali	..	12.1	13.2	12.8	14.3	13.1	15.2	18.4	18.5	18.0	18.8	..	12.7	15.8
Mauritania	..	21.4	20.0	18.5	27.7	26.5	26.0	25.3	17.3	19.3	18.5	..	19.0	22.1
Mauritius	..	19.6	20.6	20.5	19.7	18.4	19.0	21.5	21.1	19.5	25.5	13.2	16.3	20.7
Mozambique	12.3	20.0	17.8	17.7	15.6	14.3	17.3	16.6	18.2	19.0	17.9	15.5	21.4	17.1
Namibia	..	38.1	35.8	24.6	26.4	29.8	29.0	27.4	..	..	..	19.2	34.3	28.8
Niger	..	27.3	23.6	28.8	33.8	33.7	30.0	30.5	25.3	21.1	22.1	22.0	25.9	27.7
Nigeria	..	..	..	..	..	..	..	..	..	..	..	..	..	..
Rwanda	..	27.4	25.3	21.2	23.4	24.8	25.8	12.5	26.2	25.1	27.7	31.6	25.3	23.6
São Tomé and Principe	..	..	..	..	6.7	8.9	10.7	14.1	21.2	29.3	16.4	..	..	15.3
Senegal	26.2	24.4	24.6	23.0	24.2	23.4	21.1	21.9	21.6	21.8	23.5	26.2	23.7	22.8
Seychelles	..	17.3	22.9	21.0	17.0	26.8	30.0	35.3	26.8	28.0	21.3	16.4	18.4	25.5
Sierra Leone	..	23.4	23.3	22.6	22.7	21.9	18.3	15.8	19.8	13.1	18.2	..	24.2	19.5
Somalia	..	..	..	..	..	..	..	..	..	..	..	..	..	..
South Africa	..	50.2	52.7	55.4	56.0	48.3	46.6	46.5	48.0	49.8	48.2	57.8	53.8	50.2
Sudan	..	..	..	..	..	..	..	28.7	28.3	20.0	19.9	..	..	24.2
Swaziland	..	..	..	32.1	34.9	..	..	..	..	..	31.1	..	..	32.7
Tanzania	..	30.1	22.0	26.8	27.5	30.9	31.2	41.1	37.4	37.3	39.6	33.6	31.5	32.6
Togo	..	37.7	31.8	30.4	30.6	31.5	40.6	41.7	30.9	26.8	23.6	36.6	34.3	32.0
Uganda	..	9.8	10.1	10.2	12.7	14.5	14.6	14.7	13.2	14.0	15.7	11.1	8.3	13.3
Zambia	..	24.2	23.1	27.0	33.0	28.6	28.7	28.9	30.0	32.0	35.2	..	27.5	29.6
Zimbabwe	..	46.5	47.0	44.1	46.0	48.7	47.7	45.9	45.7	47.6	48.0	43.1	45.4	46.7
NORTH AFRICA	..	..	..	..	..	..	..	..	..	17.5	25.2	..	..	21.3
Algeria	..	..	..	..	..	..	..	..	..	8.8	31.5	..	..	20.1
Egypt, Arab Republic	..	18.7	19.4	22.4	23.0	23.8	22.9	21.8	22.5	22.6	22.2	..	18.0	22.3
Libya	..	..	..	..	..	..	..	..	..	..	..	..	..	..
Morocco	23.9	24.6	24.0	24.9	27.0	23.7	22.5	24.4	24.4	19.6	25.4	22.5	23.7	24.0
Tunisia	..	..	..	..	..	..	..	..	..	19.2	18.4	..	..	18.8
ALL AFRICA	..	31.8	32.8	33.5	34.3	31.2	30.5	30.3	31.3	28.6	30.8	..	32.7	31.5

Note: 1998 data are preliminary (see page 3). Total revenue does not include grants. Nigeria's fiscal data are for consolidated government starting from 1992.

7-10. Taxes on international trade and transactions

	Percentage of total revenue											Annual average		
	1980	1989	1990	1991	1992	1993	1994	1995	1996	1997	1998	75-84	85-89	90-MR
SUB-SAHARAN AFRICA	10.1	12.2	10.7	10.6	10.2	10.5	11.6	12.8	13.0	12.8	12.6	7.2	9.6	11.6
excluding South Africa	..	15.8	16.0	16.7	17.0	17.3	19.2	21.4	21.5	21.1	20.3	9.3	14.0	18.9
excl. S. Africa & Nigeria	..	19.0	19.2	20.1	20.4	20.8	23.1	25.7	25.8	25.4	24.2	11.5	16.9	22.8
Angola	..	2.7	1.3	1.4	13.8	6.5	4.6	4.9	4.3	5.3	8.1	..	2.8	5.6
Benin	..	45.5	46.5	46.9	41.9	42.4	39.7	40.4	40.9	45.5	43.3	..	45.5	43.1
Botswana	..	12.8	13.2	17.7	21.3	17.3	16.1	15.5	12.9	10.6	9.9	22.3	13.3	14.9
Burkina Faso	..	46.2	38.3	36.8	33.3	36.4	54.0	48.4	28.2	27.6	26.0	35.3	45.7	36.6
Burundi	30.5	28.1	21.0	23.7	21.9	21.1	29.7	28.9	17.7	19.2	28.7	22.5	28.3	23.5
Cameroon	..	14.9	15.4	13.1	18.0	16.6	18.3	19.5	19.3	17.1	16.8	..	17.7	17.1
Cape Verde	..	41.6	43.7	48.4	49.1	41.3	40.5	41.6	44.7	40.7	40.6	..	40.4	43.4
Central African Republic	..	31.4	39.8	37.5	34.7	33.1	32.5	42.5	38.9	38.0	44.8	..	31.9	38.0
Chad	..	24.0	24.4	15.3	15.6	13.6	19.4	27.1	31.2	30.3	29.8	..	26.1	23.0
Comoros	..	48.4	41.8	38.6	32.2	36.6	36.6	32.3	33.9	43.1	41.8	..	48.4	37.4
Congo, Democratic Rep. of	..	..	..	..	..	..	..	..	..	..	..	..	..	..
Congo, Republic of	..	21.5	16.0	17.4	21.2	20.0	13.9	19.2	16.3	8.8	12.9	..	21.5	16.2
Côte d'Ivoire	..	34.0	26.2	31.0	25.3	26.3	39.0	38.9	39.6	36.5	34.3	..	34.9	33.0
Djibouti	..	..	..	..	13.9	16.8	19.3	19.2	17.2	17.2	..	..	..	17.3
Equatorial Guinea	..	36.7	32.2	29.1	27.2	28.7	26.9	29.5	19.0	19.8	14.7	..	42.0	25.2
Eritrea	..	..	..	..	25.5	21.9	20.9	17.0	19.7	15.2	14.1	..	..	19.2
Ethiopia	..	13.5	15.1	17.2	19.0	22.6	32.9	27.4	26.0	27.5	26.4	24.3	17.9	23.8
Gabon	..	..	19.2	21.1	19.4	21.1	16.0	17.6	19.6	18.8	21.8	..	..	19.4
Gambia, The	..	51.3	54.0	53.9	50.4	44.3	37.6	49.4	61.9	59.4	60.2	..	55.2	52.4
Ghana	..	39.6	38.8	23.8	22.6	21.0	28.2	22.7	27.3	25.8	28.4	..	39.1	26.5
Guinea	..	6.4	8.7	11.6	12.8	14.6	15.7	14.4	14.1	15.5	14.5	..	6.4	13.6
Guinea-Bissau	..	18.8	26.2	28.5	18.3	29.3	35.9	27.4	32.8	23.8	34.6	..	33.3	28.5
Kenya	..	..	..	4.6	9.5	12.7	14.6	14.7	15.0	14.3	..	..	..	12.2
Lesotho	..	50.8	55.3	52.8	54.0	58.0	58.6	54.8	50.4	54.2	51.1	51.3	57.3	54.4
Liberia	..	..	..	..	..	..	..	..	..	..	..	..	..	..
Madagascar	..	43.8	46.2	43.4	44.7	42.2	44.0	55.1	53.3	54.0	54.4	32.4	40.5	48.6
Malawi	..	31.9	32.7	35.3	31.6	30.2	38.4	41.4	39.4	39.3	13.0	..	29.4	33.5
Mali	..	26.4	26.4	41.1	42.9	45.3	44.4	46.1	45.8	48.7	50.0	..	27.2	43.4
Mauritania	..	22.2	20.2	23.0	35.6	36.0	34.4	22.5	16.6	12.0	10.9	..	23.2	23.5
Mauritius	..	50.1	49.4	46.5	44.6	45.2	41.8	38.8	36.1	34.0	34.6	49.8	52.9	41.2
Mozambique	18.2	19.5	21.9	24.4	25.5	25.5	21.8	24.0	19.9	17.6	17.9	11.6	12.5	22.1
Namibia	..	27.0	26.5	38.0	31.9	29.3	26.0	27.9	..	..	..	47.3	33.5	29.9
Niger	..	34.3	39.5	39.0	35.4	41.3	41.5	43.2	46.7	47.7	52.4	36.9	34.7	43.0
Nigeria	..	..	..	..	..	..	..	..	..	..	..	..	..	..
Rwanda	..	36.1	27.5	30.9	31.0	27.8	35.8	38.5	29.2	31.8	23.9	51.0	45.0	30.7
São Tomé and Principe	..	..	..	..	29.0	28.2	30.8	24.1	25.5	21.0	18.6	..	..	25.3
Senegal	..	..	..	..	..	27.6	31.5	31.1	33.7	30.0	26.7	38.1	..	30.1
Seychelles	..	..	51.7	50.7	54.2	37.7	31.0	26.6	23.9	25.8	47.0	..	..	38.7
Sierra Leone	..	41.7	38.5	36.2	35.5	38.0	40.9	49.5	..	..	..	..	44.2	39.8
Somalia	..	..	..	..	..	..	..	..	..	..	..	..	..	..
South Africa	..	8.2	4.9	3.7	2.7	2.9	3.0	3.2	3.6	3.4	3.7	5.0	4.8	3.5
Sudan	..	..	..	..	..	..	..	31.2	44.0	47.6	44.2	..	..	41.7
Swaziland	..	..	..	46.0	43.3	..	..	..	..	..	36.7	..	..	42.0
Tanzania	..	22.7	18.8	20.2	18.7	14.2	15.7	27.6	27.0	28.2	29.2	17.3	19.9	22.2
Togo	..	34.7	37.8	40.9	34.8	36.0	41.3	37.7	41.2	44.3	45.0	33.3	34.4	39.9
Uganda	..	..	..	..	..	..	..	..	..	..	..	..	..	..
Zambia	..	32.5	36.1	32.4	32.9	33.3	30.8	27.4	29.7	28.2	25.2	..	29.8	30.7
Zimbabwe	..	..	..	..	..	..	..	..	..	..	16.7	..	..	16.7
NORTH AFRICA	..	19.5	19.0	19.4	17.1	16.8	17.3	18.4	16.6	14.4	13.8	..	16.8	17.0
Algeria	..	..	..	..	..	..	..	..	..	12.6	14.8	..	..	13.7
Egypt, Arab Republic	..	15.6	13.3	11.4	10.6	10.7	11.6	12.6	13.0	12.6	13.4	..	14.9	12.1
Libya	..	..	..	..	..	..	..	..	..	..	..	..	..	..
Morocco	35.6	34.4	34.7	35.8	32.9	31.5	32.3	31.8	25.9	20.5	13.8	36.5	32.0	28.8
Tunisia	..	..	..	..	..	..	..	..	..	14.6	12.2	..	..	13.4
ALL AFRICA	..	14.7	13.6	13.7	12.6	12.7	13.6	14.7	14.3	13.3	13.0	8.8	11.6	13.5

Note: 1998 data are preliminary (see page 3). Total revenue does not include grants. Nigeria's fiscal data are for consolidated government starting from 1992.

7-11. Indirect taxes

	1980	1989	1990	1991	1992	1993	1994	1995	1996	1997	1998	75-84	85-89	90-MR
				Percentage of total revenue									*Annual average*	
SUB-SAHARAN AFRICA	75.8	45.9	43.6	43.6	40.8	41.6	42.6	43.6	43.1	42.6	42.5	43.4	42.4	42.7
excluding South Africa	..	49.4	47.2	48.3	44.5	44.3	45.3	47.5	47.6	47.2	46.3	44.4	46.4	46.5
excl. S. Africa & Nigeria	..	59.6	57.0	58.2	53.5	53.3	54.5	57.2	57.2	56.8	55.2	54.7	56.0	55.9
Angola	..	24.3	22.8	34.7	32.7	31.9	25.7	27.8	6.6	9.6	16.7	..	19.4	23.2
Benin	..	53.4	57.6	60.9	59.3	60.1	55.7	54.1	56.0	63.8	63.1	..	53.4	59.0
Botswana	..	73.7	71.1	68.6	66.5	63.6	70.8	68.8	66.1	63.8	66.9	70.8	72.4	67.4
Burkina Faso	..	73.0	57.7	53.1	49.8	51.2	71.2	66.8	65.6	67.4	67.0	61.9	68.6	61.1
Burundi	53.8	58.0	62.5	63.4	60.3	59.9	71.9	71.9	57.6	66.7	72.1	50.3	58.7	65.1
Cameroon	61.6	50.3	52.0	46.0	46.5	52.7	59.5	61.0	58.9	51.7	52.7	40.4	39.9	53.4
Cape Verde	..	49.2	51.3	56.1	55.3	47.4	47.9	48.4	52.9	47.3	44.7	..	47.4	50.1
Central African Republic	..	67.1	73.8	68.0	69.4	70.4	66.4	75.1	74.7	74.9	75.3	86.2	69.2	72.0
Chad	..	71.4	77.2	53.2	53.6	54.0	67.5	49.7	51.4	57.0	62.6	..	74.6	58.5
Comoros	..	58.7	50.9	65.0	71.5	78.5	75.9	74.0	75.4	82.1	83.1	62.7	71.2	72.9
Congo, Democratic Rep. of	..	..	..	..	..	..	..	..	..	..	..	..	..	..
Congo, Republic of	..	64.5	44.9	35.6	46.2	45.7	30.7	41.7	35.7	19.5	41.8	..	64.5	38.0
Côte d'Ivoire	..	62.4	59.3	65.7	63.8	64.6	65.2	63.0	64.0	60.9	58.6	49.6	56.8	62.8
Djibouti	..	..	54.3	61.1	49.8	50.7	51.2	50.1	46.5	46.4	..	..	..	51.3
Equatorial Guinea	..	77.1	64.7	61.0	65.2	65.0	61.2	59.8	35.1	30.9	24.8	..	73.8	52.0
Eritrea	..	..	..	47.9	38.0	35.9	28.5	32.8	26.0	24.9	..	..	33.4
Ethiopia	..	33.6	39.3	45.2	43.2	46.0	54.1	43.4	42.6	43.8	40.4	46.7	38.8	44.2
Gabon	..	73.6	35.5	35.9	35.1	37.0	26.7	26.1	25.3	25.6	30.6	..	73.4	30.9
Gambia, The	..	77.3	80.8	80.7	76.5	74.0	70.7	70.6	71.4	68.3	68.1	..	77.9	73.4
Ghana	..	66.6	68.7	72.5	71.9	69.0	68.7	54.5	63.9	59.8	65.9	63.8	66.0	65.9
Guinea	..	91.2	90.2	89.9	85.9	86.3	84.1	84.6	82.6	83.5	83.7	..	92.1	85.6
Guinea-Bissau	..	28.1	34.9	42.5	28.5	40.9	48.6	46.7	46.8	43.8	52.6	20.0	51.4	42.8
Kenya	56.6	56.3	55.1	55.7	57.7	57.3	53.4	51.4	52.4	51.3	49.9	58.1	58.6	53.8
Lesotho	..	73.8	76.5	70.3	70.6	73.0	72.6	68.6	62.9	68.1	63.9	54.4	77.1	69.6
Liberia	..	..	..	..	..	..	..	..	..	..	..	..	..	..
Madagascar	..	66.8	66.2	63.3	73.9	66.2	72.4	82.9	79.3	77.9	79.9	60.6	65.2	73.5
Malawi	..	31.9	32.7	35.3	31.6	30.2	38.4	41.4	39.4	39.3	46.5	..	29.4	37.2
Mali	..	46.5	43.6	62.4	63.3	66.9	68.0	64.6	65.3	66.9	68.3	..	50.0	63.2
Mauritania	..	61.5	61.9	63.5	49.2	48.4	51.1	45.6	41.4	38.7	39.2	..	64.6	48.8
Mauritius	..	72.1	72.3	70.5	69.6	71.1	68.3	66.9	66.6	66.0	63.4	73.8	73.3	68.3
Mozambique	65.6	68.3	71.6	67.3	71.3	76.7	71.3	74.7	73.6	72.6	75.2	53.7	58.2	72.7
Namibia	..	49.5	51.6	62.1	59.7	60.0	58.8	61.6	..	..	..	70.0	53.4	59.0
Niger	..	51.9	53.6	54.1	47.9	56.1	59.1	60.8	61.4	64.9	67.8	65.3	54.9	58.4
Nigeria	..	..	..	..	..	..	..	..	..	..	..	..	..	..
Rwanda	..	81.7	61.7	66.0	64.3	67.5	73.5	81.4	65.8	69.5	67.1	83.9	83.5	68.5
São Tomé and Principe	..	..	..	..	59.3	63.4	64.5	45.1	46.0	38.6	35.7	..	..	50.4
Senegal	67.7	55.5	59.7	57.2	60.0	73.0	76.7	74.3	77.2	72.7	72.7	66.8	59.8	69.3
Seychelles	..	53.6	57.4	56.5	60.6	56.7	49.5	46.8	48.6	49.8	54.6	34.7	52.0	53.4
Sierra Leone	..	71.7	72.1	73.1	72.5	73.4	77.9	79.3	86.9	72.9	103.9	..	70.0	79.1
Somalia	..	..	..	..	..	..	..	..	..	..	..	..	..	..
South Africa	..	41.9	39.5	38.4	36.6	38.6	39.5	39.1	38.1	37.4	38.1	30.9	38.1	38.4
Sudan	..	..	..	..	..	..	..	50.3	56.4	64.8	60.7	..	..	58.0
Swaziland	..	..	..	58.5	56.4	..	..	..	..	..	54.5	..	..	56.5
Tanzania	..	57.7	44.6	49.0	46.8	35.0	37.8	49.5	48.2	51.1	51.9	59.6	61.1	46.0
Togo	..	48.2	50.4	56.8	45.0	50.7	51.1	50.5	58.0	63.3	66.8	41.2	46.1	54.7
Uganda	..	75.0	81.5	83.6	80.2	77.5	78.5	77.7	80.7	80.1	78.4	88.9	83.1	79.8
Zambia	..	71.6	75.1	70.9	62.5	68.0	64.4	62.7	62.1	62.6	61.5	..	63.9	65.5
Zimbabwe	..	42.3	41.4	46.1	44.0	39.1	40.3	42.7	44.6	44.2	44.6	45.9	42.6	43.0
NORTH AFRICA	..	57.3	58.1	59.9	59.4	59.2	58.9	62.0	60.5	57.7	53.6	..	54.4	58.8
Algeria	..	..	..	..	..	..	..	..	..	85.2	65.3	..	..	75.3
Egypt, Arab Republic	..	35.3	34.3	31.8	32.9	34.7	36.8	39.7	40.3	40.2	40.8	..	34.0	36.8
Libya	..	..	..	..	..	..	..	..	..	..	..	..	..	..
Morocco	70.0	71.2	66.2	68.2	65.5	66.4	66.7	68.9	55.6	46.6	59.7	69.1	71.4	62.6
Tunisia	..	..	..	..	..	..	..	..	..	64.1	55.3	..	..	59.7
ALL AFRICA	..	49.9	48.6	49.3	47.2	47.7	48.2	50.0	49.1	47.8	46.3	46.8	47.1	48.3

Note: 1998 data are preliminary (see page 3). Total revenue does not include grants. Nigeria's fiscal data are for consolidated government starting from 1992.

7-12. Nontax revenue, excluding grants

	Percentage of total revenue											Annual average		
	1980	1989	1990	1991	1992	1993	1994	1995	1996	1997	1998	75-84	85-89	90-MR
SUB-SAHARAN AFRICA	31.4	8.1	8.1	8.0	8.6	10.7	10.0	11.4	11.1	10.8	11.9	15.8	9.3	10.1
excluding South Africa	..	9.6	9.5	11.0	11.0	9.0	6.9	9.1	8.8	9.2	10.8	16.2	10.9	9.5
excl. S. Africa & Nigeria	..	11.6	11.4	13.2	13.3	10.8	8.3	10.9	10.7	11.2	10.4	19.9	13.2	11.1
Angola	..	..	..	..	8.0	6.3	1.5	1.0	0.5	1.4	3.6	..	..	3.2
Benin	..	71.0	60.6	35.8	39.0	31.6	29.8	26.8	29.0	20.5	17.3	..	71.0	32.2
Botswana	..	20.0	23.6	24.8	27.3	31.5	22.9	25.1	29.4	32.4	29.4	23.0	23.8	27.4
Burkina Faso	..	12.1	22.4	34.1	40.6	44.5	45.4	31.4	26.7	16.2	20.8	19.9	14.3	31.3
Burundi	6.7	33.4	33.6	31.0	31.3	34.1	11.1	13.7	17.6	21.1	17.5	8.5	13.9	23.5
Cameroon	16.7	5.3	3.8	36.7	35.5	36.3	29.4	28.4	31.2	34.8	31.9	32.7	10.4	29.8
Cape Verde	..	22.3	20.6	78.7	98.0	58.8	60.6	63.1	64.4	67.8	67.9	..	25.5	64.4
Central African Republic	..	10.8	2.1	8.0	7.7	6.7	9.3	4.3	0.9	5.8	10.7	..	10.7	6.2
Chad	..	6.8	4.1	67.2	44.6	35.2	59.4	43.7	38.1	20.0	9.9	..	6.3	35.8
Comoros	..	..	..	..	62.9	79.6	81.2	68.6	62.7	43.7	39.1	..	..	62.5
Congo, Democratic Rep. of	..	..	..	..	..	..	..	..	..	..	..	..	..	..
Congo, Republic of	..	1.1	3.5	2.5	1.9	3.0	6.3	9.2	3.2	1.2	2.8	..	1.1	3.7
Côte d'Ivoire	..	17.1	18.2	13.4	15.9	16.0	19.9	18.7	15.5	16.2	17.8	34.3	24.7	16.8
Djibouti	..	..	14.9	6.3	11.4	10.6	10.3	12.7	12.6	14.4	..	..	..	11.7
Equatorial Guinea	..	29.9	41.6	37.8	23.9	22.1	19.2	24.7	12.0	7.3	6.7	..	24.4	21.7
Eritrea	..	..	..	..	39.1	41.9	30.8	45.8	39.5	51.2	40.8	..	..	41.3
Ethiopia	..	39.2	31.3	24.1	26.7	30.9	21.9	34.4	32.2	27.6	33.7	24.7	32.4	29.2
Gabon	..	6.9	52.1	52.1	51.9	51.3	64.2	63.4	64.1	63.6	54.9	..	5.2	57.5
Gambia, The	..	27.3	13.1	16.9	21.1	18.6	16.4	9.8	8.7	10.6	12.7	..	41.0	14.2
Ghana	..	9.7	8.3	20.1	19.3	23.5	18.9	34.1	18.3	18.0	16.5	17.5	11.0	19.7
Guinea	..	6.5	7.7	5.9	7.3	6.8	7.1	6.3	6.5	6.8	6.6	..	6.3	6.8
Guinea-Bissau	..	..	92.6	74.9	93.2	65.3	50.3	98.5	53.6	85.8	91.7	..	..	78.4
Kenya	18.5	24.6	24.9	23.5	24.0	20.3	20.7	21.4	18.6	20.4	22.3	19.5	19.8	21.8
Lesotho	..	14.3	12.0	13.8	12.7	13.2	12.2	15.2	22.0	16.4	19.9	29.2	11.9	15.3
Liberia	..	..	..	..	..	..	..	..	..	..	..	..	..	..
Madagascar	..	33.3	32.1	27.9	22.3	25.1	12.3	5.1	10.4	24.9	7.0	25.6	28.4	18.6
Malawi	..	15.1	14.9	13.5	20.4	13.6	9.0	13.1	4.9	7.7	15.4	..	15.6	12.5
Mali	..	49.6	52.5	45.7	44.9	31.5	49.9	34.7	29.0	23.5	20.2	..	42.5	36.9
Mauritania	..	18.1	19.5	19.0	28.6	31.6	29.1	34.4	47.6	42.3	43.7	..	16.6	32.9
Mauritius	..	8.4	7.1	9.0	10.7	10.4	12.6	11.5	12.3	14.5	9.6	13.0	10.5	10.9
Mozambique	24.7	39.6	44.0	47.7	59.5	41.3	62.4	41.3	35.4	46.1	43.1	33.1	36.7	46.8
Namibia	..	12.2	12.3	13.1	13.9	10.2	12.2	11.0	..	..	..	10.8	12.2	12.1
Niger	..	25.5	32.7	26.3	29.3	47.8	46.3	22.2	41.3	33.9	36.0	12.7	21.2	35.1
Nigeria	..	..	..	..	..	..	..	..	..	..	..	..	..	..
Rwanda	..	18.5	40.2	57.2	73.0	77.8	25.7	..	87.7	70.4	55.2	17.8	15.3	60.9
São Tomé and Principe	..	..	..	..	34.0	27.7	31.2	63.9	43.7	38.6	25.4	..	..	37.8
Senegal	6.0	26.9	18.3	24.0	18.3	4.3	20.2	15.7	5.7	8.2	7.9	8.7	20.8	13.6
Seychelles	..	29.1	7.7	9.0	13.5	8.6	14.8	8.9	11.6	12.3	19.4	19.7	29.6	11.8
Sierra Leone	..	4.8	4.7	4.3	4.7	4.7	3.8	4.9	..	..	..	..	5.7	4.5
Somalia	..	..	..	..	..	..	..	..	..	..	..	..	..	..
South Africa	..	7.3	8.1	7.5	8.7	13.1	13.6	13.9	13.6	12.6	13.4	11.0	7.9	11.6
Sudan	..	..	..	..	..	..	..	21.0	15.4	15.2	19.4	..	..	17.7
Swaziland	..	..	..	11.8	13.5	..	..	..	..	..	8.7	..	..	11.3
Tanzania	..	12.1	10.8	9.6	9.8	8.0	6.9	9.5	14.4	11.7	8.6	6.8	7.4	9.9
Togo	..	17.2	21.2	15.3	25.1	17.9	13.8	12.8	11.3	13.2	14.3	26.5	23.5	16.1
Uganda	..	15.2	8.4	6.3	7.2	8.0	6.9	7.7	6.1	5.9	5.9	0.0	8.6	6.9
Zambia	..	4.2	1.8	2.1	4.5	3.4	6.8	8.4	8.0	5.5	3.4	..	8.6	4.9
Zimbabwe	..	11.1	11.6	9.8	10.0	12.2	12.0	11.4	9.7	8.2	7.4	11.0	11.9	10.2
NORTH AFRICA	..	15.2	14.7	18.1	16.8	19.1	19.0	16.7	16.5	17.1	18.2	..	17.2	17.4
Algeria	..	..	..	..	..	..	..	..	..	2.2	1.9	..	..	2.0
Egypt, Arab Republic	..	26.8	24.2	35.4	31.2	35.0	34.3	33.5	32.0	31.4	31.1	..	26.7	32.0
Libya	..	..	..	..	..	..	..	..	..	..	..	..	..	..
Morocco	8.8	8.0	13.4	9.8	9.1	10.9	12.3	8.2	12.6	18.8	14.8	11.0	8.2	12.2
Tunisia	..	..	..	..	..	..	..	..	..	15.4	25.3	..	..	20.3
ALL AFRICA	..	10.5	10.4	11.5	11.4	13.6	13.2	13.2	13.0	13.0	14.1	12.5	11.4	12.6

Note: 1998 data are preliminary (see page 3). Total revenue does not include grants. Nigeria's fiscal data are for consolidated government starting from 1992.

7-13. Government expenditure: wages and salaries

	Percentage of total expenditure and lending minus repayments											Annual average		
	1980	*1989*	*1990*	*1991*	*1992*	*1993*	*1994*	*1995*	*1996*	*1997*	*1998*	*75-84*	*85-89*	*90-MR*
SUB-SAHARAN AFRICA	12.9	19.9	20.9	21.2	27.4	27.1	26.6	26.3	26.4	26.8	29.9	14.7	12.2	25.8
excluding South Africa	..	17.5	19.1	19.2	19.8	21.8	20.1	19.8	20.6	21.1	24.1	13.5	15.6	20.6
excl. S. Africa & Nigeria	..	19.6	21.4	21.5	23.0	24.7	22.7	22.0	22.7	23.7	25.3	16.5	17.9	23.0
Angola		42.4	46.0	52.8	24.4	21.5	8.8	13.0	15.7	17.2	23.6	..	45.7	24.8
Benin	..	38.5	36.3	37.1	33.0	35.5	27.8	24.3	26.4	26.5	28.3	33.5	38.5	30.6
Botswana	..	..	..	..	..	22.8	25.0	24.1	22.8	20.2	21.3	..	..	22.7
Burkina Faso	..	19.8	38.8	31.9	30.8	29.0	26.2	24.9	23.4	20.9	20.7	22.0	19.2	27.4
Burundi	49.1	23.2	24.6	26.1	23.0	23.7	30.0	27.7	28.2	32.2	31.0	49.0	27.7	27.4
Cameroon	31.4	40.1	39.2	38.4	42.0	43.6	31.4	29.1	25.8	27.3	27.8	24.7	29.0	33.8
Cape Verde	..	23.8	26.2	25.1	19.9	22.1	19.2	20.2	21.6	21.6	22.2	..	21.7	22.0
Central African Republic	..	31.3	26.4	27.7	27.3	29.5	24.2	22.5	41.7	32.5	24.2	..	31.6	28.4
Chad	..	16.6	19.4	25.1	21.1	27.1	28.0	28.6	27.3	24.4	22.3	..	15.0	24.8
Comoros	..	28.9	30.8	32.0	27.7	30.8	23.2	28.3	35.5	36.6	33.4	..	28.9	30.9
Congo, Democratic Rep. of	..	..	..	..	..	..	..	..	..	..	..	..	..	..
Congo, Republic of	..	43.7	30.4	43.8	47.5	48.8	36.3	32.1	24.8	20.2	24.8	..	32.7	34.3
Côte d'Ivoire	..	29.6	34.6	34.4	35.5	35.6	28.5	26.2	28.1	27.3	26.7	27.2	28.2	30.8
Djibouti	..	..	41.6	46.0	46.6	48.0	56.4	61.6	60.3	62.2	..	..	..	52.8
Equatorial Guinea	..	10.6	10.5	11.6	12.7	10.8	16.4	17.9	17.3	13.7	19.4	..	15.4	14.5
Eritrea	..	..	..	..	18.6	15.0	23.0	24.3	29.3	27.3	20.8	..	..	22.6
Ethiopia	..	20.6	27.5	33.8	28.0	28.3	24.8	22.6	20.6	21.7	23.2	25.1	22.5	25.6
Gabon	..	30.7	32.2	32.4	34.4	34.0	27.9	27.4	27.3	25.0	21.4	16.2	25.1	29.1
Gambia, The	..	19.5	20.7	21.0	19.5	21.1	23.3	21.5	20.5	24.0	27.5	..	17.6	22.1
Ghana	..	23.4	23.5	22.8	24.8	20.2	18.3	18.3	18.2	18.8	19.5	17.6	25.6	20.5
Guinea	..	17.5	17.1	20.0	23.1	24.2	25.1	23.9	27.1	23.4	23.5	..	14.3	23.0
Guinea-Bissau	..	9.0	9.4	10.3	7.9	8.1	7.5	9.2	9.5	6.8	18.8	15.0	14.2	9.7
Kenya	..	..	..	..	28.8	24.3	25.5	28.3	28.5	30.6	31.2	..	..	28.2
Lesotho	..	23.2	21.9	27.2	29.1	29.2	31.3	30.5	29.6	31.6	32.5	32.1	32.7	29.2
Liberia	..	..	..	..	..	..	..	..	..	..	..	..	..	..
Madagascar	..	21.3	23.1	26.5	19.7	18.0	17.0	18.1	17.7	20.3	20.3	32.5	27.0	20.1
Malawi	14.2	17.3	17.0	18.4	18.2	23.4	15.4	21.1	20.3	22.8	20.3	16.4	16.3	19.7
Mali	..	24.0	22.0	21.9	22.6	23.0	16.7	16.6	16.1	16.4	15.8	46.8	25.0	19.0
Mauritania	..	15.2	16.0	14.0	23.2	15.4	19.0	20.3	20.3	21.1	19.3	..	16.4	18.7
Mauritius	..	31.1	29.6	28.1	28.3	30.4	32.0	30.8	27.9	28.1	28.5	29.2	29.7	29.3
Mozambique	25.8	9.3	9.7	10.6	9.9	10.4	7.9	9.6	10.8	10.1	12.7	19.3	12.2	10.2
Namibia	..	23.6	37.4	45.6	47.1	47.0	47.2	47.1	47.6	46.9	44.8	19.6	22.6	45.6
Niger	..	23.7	24.0	34.9	37.4	38.3	29.4	34.8	25.5	26.2	23.9	18.8	21.2	30.5
Nigeria	..	7.2	7.9	7.0	3.6	6.7	7.6	8.5	9.6	8.0	17.7	..	5.6	8.5
Rwanda	..	30.6	27.8	23.9	22.1	24.1	25.0	19.5	20.1	26.1	24.6	30.6	28.0	23.7
São Tomé and Principe	..	..	..	..	11.6	9.1	7.0	4.3	6.0	8.4	11.3	..	..	8.2
Senegal	39.7	41.0	39.7	46.8	40.4	41.4	35.0	35.4	36.3	33.7	32.1	39.2	41.9	37.9
Seychelles	..	..	25.1	25.6	27.2	21.6	22.0	25.3	27.7	26.5	20.6	..	..	24.6
Sierra Leone	..	6.9	7.3	8.2	10.1	12.9	16.1	15.6	20.2	25.4	20.8	30.3	8.6	15.2
Somalia	..	..	..	..	..	..	..	..	..	..	..	..	..	..
South Africa	17.2	22.5	22.8	23.5	36.3	33.4	33.7	33.8	33.1	33.4	36.8	17.7	21.2	31.8
Sudan	..	..	..	..	..	17.1	..	12.0	22.6	31.2	33.6	..	..	23.3
Swaziland	..	..	..	..	30.9	40.0	40.5	39.4	39.5	38.7	37.9	..	..	38.1
Tanzania	..	21.4	21.3	20.0	19.3	19.0	21.7	22.8	26.2	31.2	30.0	20.9	21.3	23.5
Togo	..	27.6	28.6	36.5	39.1	41.4	36.1	35.6	34.0	35.8	31.4	27.1	25.7	35.4
Uganda	..	10.7	7.4	8.8	8.2	8.7	10.3	14.6	16.9	19.8	20.6	8.3	11.5	12.8
Zambia	..	..	23.3	21.3	25.4	17.7	16.1	20.2	19.0	24.1	19.0	..	..	20.7
Zimbabwe	..	..	..	..	..	..	..	..	..	..	35.6	..	..	35.6
NORTH AFRICA	..	27.5	28.1	25.0	26.2	26.3	27.2	28.1	28.4	26.7	27.7	..	26.3	27.1
Algeria	..	35.2	36.7	27.5	31.8	28.9	30.2	29.7	29.7	28.4	27.7	19.1	27.8	30.1
Egypt, Arab Republic	..	17.3	16.7	15.6	15.8	18.8	19.7	21.5	22.0	23.0	22.3	..	17.2	19.5
Libya	..	..	..	..	..	..	..	..	..	..	..	..	..	..
Morocco	35.0	35.5	37.1	39.5	38.1	37.0	37.3	38.4	39.0	31.2	38.3	31.1	34.5	37.3
Tunisia	..	..	..	..	..	..	..	..	..	..	..	..	..	..
ALL AFRICA	..	22.3	23.2	22.4	27.1	26.9	26.8	26.8	27.0	26.7	29.2	18.9	16.1	26.2

Note: 1998 data are preliminary (see page 3). Nigeria's fiscal data are for consolidated government starting from 1992.

7-14. Government expenditure: trends in real wages and salaries

	Index 1987=100											Annual average		
	1980	1989	1990	1991	1992	1993	1994	1995	1996	1997	1998	75-84	85-89	90-MR
SUB-SAHARAN AFRICA	95	105	108	116	118	120	105	99	100	105	110	91	99	109
excluding South Africa	95	105	108	116	118	120	105	99	100	105	110	91	99	109
excl. S.Africa & Nigeria	95	105	107	114	117	119	103	96	97	104	109	91	99	107
Angola	..	107	125	104	61	19	17	13	55	77	57	..	89	59
Benin	..	..	..	..	..	..	..	..	..	..	..	..	..	..
Botswana	..	..	..	..	..	..	..	..	..	..	..	..	..	..
Burkina Faso	..	125	132	121	117	119	106	104	103	106	110	73	100	113
Burundi	95	114	116	124	125	126	117	102	96	82	78	96	102	107
Cameroon	54	103	101	106	105	101	67	50	46	49	58	68	97	76
Cape Verde	..	..	..	..	..	..	..	..	..	..	..	..	..	..
Central African Republic	..	102	97	106	103	100	90	76	71	74	75	..	99	88
Chad	..	..	..	..	..	..	..	..	..	..	..	..	..	..
Comoros	..	..	..	..	..	..	..	..	..	..	..	..	..	..
Congo, Democratic Rep. of	..	..	..	..	..	..	..	..	..	..	..	..	..	..
Congo, Republic of	..	87	92	138	149	144	97	76	65	..	..	..	95	109
Côte d'Ivoire	..	97	94	91	87	80	63	62	67	68	67	87	93	75
Djibouti	..	..	..	..	..	..	..	..	..	..	..	..	..	..
Equatorial Guinea	..	..	..	..	..	..	..	..	..	..	..	..	..	..
Eritrea	..	..	..	..	..	..	..	..	..	..	..	..	..	..
Ethiopia	..	105	123	114	68	77	91	86	95	105	124	100	97	98
Gabon	..	102	114	113	130	148	111	116	114	114	108	97	106	119
Gambia, The	..	..	..	..	..	..	..	..	..	..	..	..	..	..
Ghana	..	106	101	110	162	173	181	150	146	140	147	28	97	146
Guinea	..	174	189	207	228	226	225	227	246	236	239	..	140	225
Guinea-Bissau	..	116	107	140	112	98	88	96	109	103	111	..	106	107
Kenya	..	..	..	..	..	..	..	..	..	..	..	..	..	..
Lesotho	..	..	..	..	..	..	..	..	..	..	..	..	..	..
Liberia	..	..	..	..	..	..	..	..	..	..	..	..	..	..
Madagascar	..	93	89	97	87	87	80	75	74	89	99	..	98	86
Malawi	89	98	93	101	127	136	179	159	123	160	208	93	94	143
Mali	..	91	90	98	102	102	89	85	84	95	98	..	93	94
Mauritania	..	101	99	99	99	97	97	95	97	100	105	..	101	99
Mauritius	..	126	119	119	126	135	148	149	151	157	157	77	101	140
Mozambique	337	127	134	156	152	179	151	147	149	182	249	318	132	167
Namibia	..	98	153	198	209	211	206	218	252	258	261	76	96	218
Niger	..	..	..	..	..	..	..	..	..	..	..	..	..	..
Nigeria	..	152	213	209	180	289	224	180	185	192	585	..	121	251
Rwanda	..	105	107	101	102	104	26	43	56	75	71	85	99	76
São Tomé and Principe	..	..	..	..	..	..	..	..	..	..	..	..	..	..
Senegal	102	106	109	119	119	115	98	95	96	93	92	96	98	104
Seychelles	..	..	..	..	..	..	..	..	..	..	..	..	..	..
Sierra Leone	..	92	105	109	100	120	141	141	158	134	173	343	131	131
Somalia	..	..	..	..	..	..	..	..	..	..	..	..	..	..
South Africa	..	..	..	..	..	..	..	..	..	..	..	..	..	..
Sudan	..	..	..	..	..	..	..	..	..	..	..	..	..	..
Swaziland	..	..	..	..	..	..	..	..	..	..	..	..	..	..
Tanzania	..	135	133	117	119	146	151	161	180	196	195	148	116	155
Togo	..	100	105	121	109	109	103	95	93	92	94	83	94	102
Uganda	..	132	121	179	250	256	323	489	563	708	754	134	148	405
Zambia	..	..	..	..	..	..	..	..	..	..	..	..	..	..
Zimbabwe	..	..	..	..	..	..	..	..	..	..	..	..	..	..
NORTH AFRICA	75	106	111	117	130	130	139	127	135	143	162	86	99	133
Algeria	..	106	103	116	130	125	121	115	115	120	127	85	97	119
Egypt, Arab Republic	..	99	144	138	131	144	151	157	164	166	162	..	101	151
Libya	..	..	..	..	..	..	..	..	..	..	..	..	..	..
Morocco	..	..	..	..	..	..	..	..	..	..	..	..	..	..
Tunisia	75	109	111	117	125	130	139	127	135	143	178	87	102	134
ALL AFRICA	92	105	109	117	119	125	111	104	109	110	117	89	99	114

Note: 1998 data are preliminary (see page 3). Nigeria's fiscal data are for consolidated government starting from 1992.

7-15. Government expenditure: other goods and services

	Percentage of total expenditure and lending minus repayments											Annual average		
	1980	1989	1990	1991	1992	1993	1994	1995	1996	1997	1998	75-84	85-89	90-MR
SUB-SAHARAN AFRICA	..	..	..	..	..	..	23.4	24.9	25.7	26.6	27.6	..	..	25.6
excluding South Africa	..	18.7	19.2	19.2	20.0	21.6	21.7	24.1	23.1	24.5	29.5	..	20.2	22.5
excl. S. Africa & Nigeria	..	20.2	20.1	19.3	19.3	20.6	19.5	22.2	21.4	23.0	22.4	..	20.2	20.9
Angola	..	12.5	19.9	17.0	10.9	43.1	41.0	47.2	48.4	56.5	49.5	..	26.3	37.0
Benin	..	7.4	7.1	8.2	7.6	8.4	6.3	5.2	7.7	6.9	7.4	9.7	7.4	7.2
Botswana	..	..	..	..	..	36.0	41.0	42.3	42.3	37.3	39.3	..	..	39.7
Burkina Faso	..	3.4	7.1	7.7	8.6	10.7	12.0	10.8	9.8	8.7	9.9	3.5	3.5	9.5
Burundi	28.0	13.9	17.2	15.6	12.4	20.4	21.3	23.7	20.6	33.3	25.9	22.6	16.9	21.1
Cameroon	22.9	16.6	17.4	12.5	10.5	10.7	7.5	15.8	16.0	16.7	14.6	20.3	13.7	13.5
Cape Verde	..	3.9	4.0	3.3	2.5	1.8	1.6	1.4	1.5	16.1	16.1	..	3.7	5.4
Central African Republic	..	11.5	12.7	11.6	11.6	11.5	13.8	9.9	12.5	15.6	10.1	..	9.9	12.2
Chad	..	19.6	21.0	34.4	26.4	26.3	14.4	11.7	15.4	13.3	12.2	..	18.5	19.5
Comoros	..	20.3	20.0	22.2	19.7	26.4	20.3	22.4	17.8	14.1	16.9	..	20.3	20.0
Congo, Democratic Rep. of	..	..	..	..	..	..	..	..	..	..	..	..	..	..
Congo, Republic of	..	8.6	8.3	10.7	10.4	9.1	8.1	7.7	7.2	29.9	15.2	..	10.0	11.9
Côte d'Ivoire	..	24.9	24.9	23.3	22.4	22.2	21.9	22.8	23.7	24.0	22.1	33.6	31.7	23.0
Djibouti	..	..	26.7	31.5	29.2	29.2	24.2	22.4	19.9	16.2	..	..	..	24.9
Equatorial Guinea	..	9.4	9.7	10.1	14.6	10.1	20.3	25.2	23.8	20.5	28.3	..	18.8	18.1
Eritrea	..	..	..	..	71.0	44.1	49.8	43.2	41.0	32.0	45.7	..	..	46.7
Ethiopia	..	34.0	34.9	29.1	22.1	25.7	25.0	25.3	23.1	25.5	33.0	30.5	32.0	27.1
Gabon	..	25.0	23.5	21.0	20.5	19.4	19.2	17.3	21.1	19.9	18.3	13.8	20.4	20.0
Gambia, The	..	20.3	19.0	21.1	23.5	25.5	25.1	20.1	21.4	17.9	15.2	..	19.5	21.0
Ghana	..	13.3	12.9	13.1	10.0	12.6	10.5	8.1	7.2	7.1	7.9	34.5	15.4	9.9
Guinea	..	19.4	18.9	18.7	15.6	13.9	13.2	11.3	11.7	11.4	11.6	..	24.7	14.0
Guinea-Bissau	..	13.3	14.6	13.0	10.8	9.4	12.6	11.9	10.0	8.4	18.5	..	13.5	12.1
Kenya	..	..	..	..	19.2	16.7	16.8	20.4	26.8	27.0	30.2	..	..	22.4
Lesotho	..	17.2	17.0	19.0	23.7	7.9	26.4	31.1	25.8	30.3	38.9	19.9	23.6	24.4
Liberia	..	..	..	..	..	..	..	..	..	..	..	..	..	..
Madagascar	..	12.2	11.8	10.3	15.9	11.5	12.9	10.0	7.2	15.8	11.8	18.9	15.0	11.9
Malawi	0.0	0.0	0.0	0.0	0.0	0.0	0.0	0.0	0.0	0.0	18.0	0.0	0.0	2.0
Mali	..	3.1	2.1	8.3	9.8	10.2	10.6	12.2	11.7	13.0	12.4	42.5	4.7	10.0
Mauritania	..	10.1	12.3	12.0	18.9	14.4	17.6	20.2	20.0	21.7	20.8	..	8.8	17.6
Mauritius	..	8.4	8.3	9.5	10.1	9.7	9.5	9.3	8.7	8.6	9.3	7.2	8.1	9.2
Mozambique	44.4	33.0	30.7	29.0	31.5	29.3	33.8	22.4	23.7	21.4	29.3	36.0	34.2	27.9
Namibia	..	21.9	24.6	28.4	26.3	22.5	25.3	24.8	21.5	20.9	19.4	16.2	21.9	23.8
Niger	..	14.8	17.4	12.5	21.3	15.3	18.8	17.0	21.4	23.0	24.3	13.8	14.9	19.0
Nigeria	..	13.2	15.8	18.9	23.3	26.2	31.0	32.7	30.9	31.3	64.3	..	16.5	30.5
Rwanda	..	21.3	23.7	28.0	30.9	24.8	26.4	25.1	26.3	19.5	24.0	16.8	19.6	25.4
São Tomé and Principe	..	..	..	..	5.4	4.3	5.0	4.6	5.0	5.0	5.5	..	..	5.0
Senegal	22.9	16.5	15.2	9.8	21.1	11.9	11.8	11.4	12.2	11.0	14.1	19.6	15.5	13.2
Seychelles	..	..	30.3	30.9	31.6	26.0	24.9	19.5	19.2	20.7	38.4	..	..	26.8
Sierra Leone	..	43.1	42.7	36.8	37.8	39.7	42.9	57.0	45.0	47.0	29.2	45.3	35.5	42.0
Somalia	..	..	..	..	..	..	..	..	..	..	..	..	..	..
South Africa	..	..	..	..	..	..	25.1	25.7	28.5	28.9	25.6	..	..	26.8
Sudan	..	..	..	..	..	37.4	..	47.5	36.0	48.7	43.4	..	..	42.6
Swaziland	..	..	..	..	15.3	28.3	27.8	27.7	26.1	25.0	21.3	..	..	24.5
Tanzania	..	32.3	28.6	40.2	36.2	30.7	30.4	28.9	24.2	23.7	21.2	30.5	31.5	29.3
Togo	..	20.2	20.8	19.2	17.0	19.0	16.4	18.2	21.7	20.2	22.4	20.7	21.3	19.4
Uganda	..	49.5	43.9	31.9	31.8	26.6	29.7	32.7	33.1	32.9	32.0	33.3	45.9	32.7
Zambia	..	..	15.4	19.1	24.5	20.3	22.3	22.5	19.7	19.2	20.3	..	..	20.4
Zimbabwe	..	..	..	..	..	..	..	..	..	..	13.3	..	..	13.3
NORTH AFRICA	..	9.5	9.4	9.0	9.1	10.9	10.9	11.4	11.5	14.3	12.2	..	9.8	11.0
Algeria	..	2.6	2.7	3.1	2.3	4.0	3.6	4.7	4.6	5.0	4.9	2.3	2.3	3.9
Egypt, Arab Republic	..	14.8	14.1	12.4	13.0	15.3	15.5	16.1	15.9	16.3	15.9	..	15.1	14.9
Libya	..	..	..	..	..	..	..	..	..	..	..	..	..	..
Morocco	11.5	9.4	10.4	11.3	11.7	12.6	13.0	12.2	13.4	24.2	16.0	11.7	10.4	13.9
Tunisia	..	..	..	..	..	..	..	..	..	..	..	..	..	..
ALL AFRICA	..	..	..	..	..	..	19.2	20.5	21.1	22.6	22.7	..	..	21.2

Note: 1998 data are preliminary (see page 3). Nigeria's fiscal data are for consolidated government starting from 1992.

7-16. Government expenditure: interest payments

	Percentage of total expenditure and lending minus repayments											*Annual average*		
	1980	*1989*	*1990*	*1991*	*1992*	*1993*	*1994*	*1995*	*1996*	*1997*	*1998*	*75-84*	*85-89*	*90-MR*
SUB-SAHARAN AFRICA	2.4	9.6	9.8	10.0	8.5	8.8	9.6	9.0	8.4	7.5	16.3	4.0	9.2	9.8
excluding South Africa	..	18.4	18.6	18.6	15.9	16.4	18.3	16.8	15.6	14.0	13.3	14.3	17.6	16.4
excl. S. Africa & Nigeria	..	12.3	13.1	14.3	12.9	14.0	17.1	16.1	15.6	14.3	14.4	11.8	13.3	14.7
Angola	..	10.4	9.9	15.1	8.9	15.5	19.5	18.9	21.0	..	..	..	10.3	15.5
Benin	..	15.6	15.3	13.8	17.5	15.0	15.9	12.6	12.4	9.0	7.6	..	83.1	13.2
Botswana	..	..	..	..	..	..	..	..	..	-0.2	-1.5	..	..	-0.8
Burkina Faso	..	2.8	5.7	6.5	6.9	6.9	6.9	6.6	4.2	3.6	3.7	2.6	3.6	5.7
Burundi	2.0	8.2	7.1	6.1	6.4	5.0	6.0	6.9	6.6	8.9	8.1	5.3	8.9	6.8
Cameroon	..	8.2	9.7	17.6	23.4	24.1	36.5	39.5	41.8	38.4	32.1	..	6.3	29.2
Cape Verde	..	4.4	4.9	3.4	2.5	2.5	1.9	6.2	7.5	7.8	9.1	..	3.9	5.1
Central African Republic	..	7.1	5.6	6.3	8.3	9.9	10.7	11.2	17.5	9.8	7.9	..	7.2	9.7
Chad	..	0.8	1.8	..	3.8	5.8	6.1	5.6	5.6	5.3	4.4	..	0.8	4.8
Comoros	..	..	..	..	..	..	..	..	..	..	..	..	..	..
Congo, Democratic Rep. of	..	..	..	..	..	..	..	..	..	..	..	..	..	..
Congo, Republic of	..	..	29.7	22.5	21.6	20.1	33.0	43.0	36.5	34.1	39.9	..	20.5	31.1
Côte d'Ivoire	..	24.6	29.3	33.2	32.7	29.0	29.0	25.9	23.3	20.2	18.4	26.3	22.7	26.8
Djibouti	..	..	1.4	..	1.1	0.8	0.8	1.5	1.6	1.4	..	..	..	1.2
Equatorial Guinea	..	..	11.6	12.7	16.7	13.7	26.0	24.0	15.6	16.7	16.3	..	..	17.0
Eritrea	..	..	..	..	..	..	..	..	..	..	7.1	..	..	7.1
Ethiopia	..	4.3	4.3	5.4	7.3	10.2	13.5	10.0	9.0	9.2	7.3	3.4	5.1	8.5
Gabon	..	22.6	23.2	22.6	22.5	24.4	26.4	30.9	25.6	23.5	22.7	6.6	14.1	24.6
Gambia, The	..	15.0	14.9	13.8	12.9	14.8	14.8	13.9	14.3	19.1	23.0	..	13.4	15.7
Ghana	..	7.0	7.8	9.2	8.9	12.0	14.2	13.9	17.2	22.9	22.9	11.4	8.3	14.3
Guinea	..	..	..	..	..	7.2	9.0	8.1	8.1	9.2	8.3	..	..	8.3
Guinea-Bissau	..	..	..	..	..	..	..	..	..	..	..	..	..	..
Kenya	..	..	27.8	28.9	25.9	34.3	30.9	24.1	22.3	20.1	19.7	..	..	26.0
Lesotho	..	..	..	..	..	..	4.2	3.6	3.5	4.1	4.0	..	..	3.9
Liberia	..	..	..	..	..	..	..	..	..	..	..	..	..	..
Madagascar	..	8.3	8.9	12.3	17.1	19.4	27.3	29.0	26.3	17.5	12.6	5.6	9.9	18.9
Malawi	8.9	18.5	12.7	10.5	9.1	12.2	10.8	21.0	21.6	12.9	12.6	12.9	18.6	13.7
Mali	..	8.1	9.1	6.3	7.3	6.9	9.0	6.1	4.8	4.1	3.1	..	7.6	6.3
Mauritania	..	..	..	..	..	..	10.4	13.0	13.4	13.0	14.0	..	..	12.8
Mauritius	..	15.7	17.7	16.4	13.7	11.9	12.4	13.1	13.1	14.4	13.9	20.4	18.3	14.1
Mozambique	..	6.7	6.7	4.8	7.9	8.6	3.6	6.6	7.0	5.7	4.5	..	5.7	6.2
Namibia	..	..	..	..	..	..	..	..	..	..	..	..	..	..
Niger	..	13.1	10.1	11.5	9.8	10.2	12.3	15.5	12.8	9.8	10.1	11.1	13.7	11.3
Nigeria	5.7	47.6	45.3	40.8	31.0	29.1	23.8	20.2	15.3	12.5	7.2	7.9	37.9	25.0
Rwanda	1.7	5.7	5.1	7.7	7.8	9.1	27.9	11.2	7.2	6.2	5.2	2.5	4.7	9.7
São Tomé and Principe	..	..	..	..	..	..	..	..	14.4	16.1	20.8	..	..	17.1
Senegal	7.5	15.6	12.6	12.9	9.3	10.9	16.8	14.5	12.5	12.3	9.6	9.4	15.7	12.4
Seychelles	..	13.7	16.2	15.7	15.3	12.7	13.4	16.3	15.2	15.9	19.8	3.4	11.6	15.6
Sierra Leone	7.7	32.2	28.7	30.0	26.9	18.8	13.6	10.5	12.5	16.3	27.8	10.5	23.7	20.6
Somalia	..	..	..	..	..	..	..	..	..	..	..	..	..	..
South Africa	..	..	..	..	..	..	..	..	..	..	19.8	..	..	19.8
Sudan	..	..	..	..	..	..	..	..	..	..	..	..	..	..
Swaziland	..	..	..	..	..	..	..	..	..	..	0.8	..	..	0.8
Tanzania	..	15.6	13.2	13.2	12.2	12.9	14.4	18.4	18.9	17.4	13.9	8.0	12.3	14.9
Togo	..	14.7	11.3	12.6	12.9	15.9	21.9	15.4	13.0	12.8	10.2	20.9	14.8	14.0
Uganda	..	6.3	4.9	8.9	15.5	9.7	7.8	5.7	6.0	5.5	6.1	..	6.3	7.8
Zambia	10.9	22.0	23.7	24.4	27.5	41.8	36.5	27.7	16.2	18.0	11.7	12.2	28.6	25.3
Zimbabwe	27.7	14.4	14.1	13.9	15.6	17.9	20.4	24.2	24.5	19.1	27.7	24.8	13.5	19.7
NORTH AFRICA	..	11.2	11.6	13.6	14.9	17.7	20.1	19.0	19.2	19.0	17.3	..	10.7	17.0
Algeria	..	5.6	6.4	6.0	7.0	6.4	8.2	9.9	11.9	12.7	10.4	2.5	4.2	8.8
Egypt, Arab Republic	..	10.0	10.0	15.5	18.7	25.5	29.3	25.4	25.1	23.1	22.4	..	9.1	21.7
Libya	..	..	..	..	..	..	..	..	..	..	..	..	..	..
Morocco	8.3	21.7	22.6	21.1	19.6	19.7	20.2	20.5	19.0	20.5	17.9	8.5	21.8	20.1
Tunisia	..	..	..	..	..	..	..	..	..	..	..	..	..	..
ALL AFRICA	..	10.1	10.4	11.1	10.6	11.7	13.0	12.2	11.8	11.2	16.6	7.7	9.5	12.1

Note: 1998 data are preliminary (see page 3). Nigeria's fiscal data are for consolidated government starting from 1992.

7-17. Government expenditure: subsidies and other current transfers

| | \multicolumn{11}{c}{*Percentage of total expenditure and lending minus repayments*} | | | \multicolumn{3}{c}{*Annual average*} |
	1980	1989	1990	1991	1992	1993	1994	1995	1996	1997	1998	75-84	85-89	90-MR
SUB-SAHARAN AFRICA	2.4	1.6	1.3	1.1	1.5	1.3	3.4	2.7	2.5	2.4	2.1	2.1	1.5	2.0
excluding South Africa	..	3.0	2.5	2.1	2.8	2.4	2.3	1.9	1.8	1.9	1.4	2.6	2.9	2.1
excl. S. Africa & Nigeria	..	3.6	3.0	2.5	3.4	2.9	2.8	2.3	2.2	2.2	1.7	3.2	3.3	2.5
Angola	..	2.8	6.2	4.9	8.1	9.1	0.0	0.0	0.0	0.0	0.0	..	5.4	3.2
Benin	..	..	..	..	..	..	..	..	..	..	..	..	0.0	..
Botswana	..	..	..	..	..	..	..	..	..	0.0	0.0	..	..	0.0
Burkina Faso	..	0.0	..	..	..	..	..	..	..	..	..	0.0	0.0	..
Burundi	10.9	7.0	6.7	6.0	8.0	5.7	7.5	6.7	5.8	6.1	7.5	10.1	5.7	6.7
Cameroon	11.2	0.0	0.0	0.0	0.0	0.0	0.0	0.0	0.0	0.0	0.0	8.6	0.0	0.0
Cape Verde	..	0.7	0.6	0.5	0.3	0.1	0.0	0.1	0.0	0.0	0.0	1.2	0.7	0.2
Central African Republic	..	..	..	..	..	..	..	..	..	..	..	..	..	..
Chad	..	0.0	0.0	0.0	0.0	0.0	0.0	0.0	0.0	0.0	0.0	..	0.0	0.0
Comoros	..	0.0	0.0	0.0	0.0	0.0	0.0	0.0	0.0	0.0	0.0	0.0	0.0	0.0
Congo, Democratic Rep. of	..	..	..	..	21.6	9.1	13.3	4.8	6.1	3.9	..	..	..	9.8
Congo, Republic of	..	3.2	1.9	0.0	0.0	0.0	0.0	0.0	0.0	0.0	0.0	..	2.4	0.2
Côte d'Ivoire	..	13.2	3.6	0.2	0.0	3.0	3.7	3.9	2.9	3.7	3.6	0.0	5.4	2.7
Djibouti	..	..	..	..	0.6	0.6	0.3	0.4	0.5	1.3	..	..	..	0.6
Equatorial Guinea	..	3.6	6.0	4.9	4.1	3.5	4.4	4.4	4.0	3.9	5.6	..	7.2	4.5
Eritrea	..	..	..	..	0.0	0.0	0.0	0.0	0.0	0.0	0.0	..	..	0.0
Ethiopia	..	1.9	1.7	1.3	1.4	0.1	1.2	1.8	1.7	1.3	0.0	3.5	1.4	1.2
Gabon	..	0.0	0.0	0.0	0.0	0.0	0.0	0.0	0.0	0.0	0.0	..	0.0	0.0
Gambia, The	..	4.6	3.0	0.0	0.5	0.6	0.1	0.0	0.0	0.0	0.0	..	10.4	0.5
Ghana	17.9	0.0	0.0	0.0	0.0	0.0	0.0	0.0	0.0	0.0	0.0	16.0	0.0	0.0
Guinea	..	7.0	3.8	3.5	4.0	3.6	4.3	6.2	6.0	5.8	5.6	..	6.8	4.7
Guinea-Bissau	..	0.0	0.0	0.0	0.0	0.0	0.0	0.0	0.0	..	..	0.0	0.0	0.0
Kenya	0.1	1.5	1.7	0.9	0.0	0.0	0.0	0.0	0.0	0.0	0.0	0.2	1.4	0.3
Lesotho	..	4.0	4.0	4.9	4.9	..	..	10.8	11.5	10.5	33.7	..	3.8	11.5
Liberia	..	..	..	..	..	..	..	..	..	..	..	..	..	..
Madagascar	..	..	..	..	..	..	..	..	..	..	..	0.0	..	..
Malawi	0.0	0.0	0.0	0.0	0.0	0.0	0.0	0.0	0.0	0.0	0.0	0.0	0.0	0.0
Mali	..	2.0	1.8	2.3	2.7	2.7	1.6	1.3	1.4	1.2	5.7	..	1.6	2.3
Mauritania	..	..	..	..	..	..	..	..	..	..	..	..	..	..
Mauritius	..	18.2	19.1	20.2	21.0	21.3	21.8	23.0	23.9	25.2	6.2	19.9	18.3	20.2
Mozambique	1.5	4.4	3.6	2.2	2.2	1.2	0.9	1.3	1.2	1.0	1.0	7.1	14.3	1.6
Namibia	..	2.3	2.7	2.7	4.0	3.4	2.5	1.4	0.2	0.0	0.0	5.0	4.2	1.9
Niger	..	5.2	7.4	6.7	6.9	12.9	6.6	4.2	6.0	7.6	7.2	9.4	6.6	7.3
Nigeria	0.0	0.0	0.0	..	..	..	..	..	..	..	0.0	0.0	1.2	0.0
Rwanda	0.0	5.8	17.2	8.3	8.1	5.0	3.8	4.8	3.3	5.6	5.7	0.6	3.9	6.9
São Tomé and Principe	..	..	..	..	..	..	..	..	..	..	..	..	..	..
Senegal	13.9	8.2	10.5	8.9	8.2	13.9	11.4	9.9	8.8	9.7	8.1	12.1	10.1	9.9
Seychelles	..	9.4	7.4	5.8	5.4	4.8	5.1	10.4	-3.7	1.3	4.8	3.8	7.2	4.6
Sierra Leone	0.0	0.2	1.9	2.6	2.4	2.3	2.4	2.0	0.0	0.0	0.0	0.0	0.5	1.5
Somalia	..	..	..	..	..	..	..	..	..	..	..	..	..	..
South Africa	..	..	..	..	..	..	4.5	3.5	3.2	3.0	2.9	..	..	3.4
Sudan	..	..	..	..	..	..	..	..	..	..	..	..	..	..
Swaziland	..	..	..	..	..	..	..	..	..	..	0.0	..	..	0.0
Tanzania	..	0.0	0.0	0.0	0.0	0.0	0.0	0.0	0.0	0.0	0.0	0.0	0.0	0.0
Togo	..	4.2	4.4	5.1	5.9	4.6	9.0	6.7	5.1	6.9	6.4	2.3	0.7	6.0
Uganda	..	0.0	0.0	0.0	0.0	0.0	0.0	0.0	0.0	0.0	0.0	0.0	0.0	0.0
Zambia	13.7	13.5	10.9	11.6	2.5	0.6	0.0	0.0	0.0	0.2	0.9	9.9	11.9	3.0
Zimbabwe	29.3	5.6	5.9	7.7	8.3	4.9	1.4	0.5	0.3	0.1	0.0	23.2	8.5	3.2
NORTH AFRICA	..	4.9	6.5	7.3	11.6	8.3	7.3	6.4	7.3	5.0	5.3	..	5.0	7.2
Algeria	..	0.0	0.4	1.0	10.4	9.1	7.8	5.3	4.9	3.9	4.2	..	0.0	5.2
Egypt, Arab Republic	..	9.7	11.4	12.2	14.2	7.7	5.8	6.6	6.8	6.2	5.9	..	10.2	8.5
Libya	..	..	..	..	..	..	..	..	..	..	..	..	..	..
Morocco	7.4	3.1	6.4	7.2	8.5	8.4	9.5	7.8	11.7	4.2	6.1	6.6	3.9	7.8
Tunisia	..	..	..	..	..	..	..	..	..	..	..	..	..	..
ALL AFRICA	..	2.6	3.0	3.1	4.7	3.5	4.6	3.9	4.0	3.2	3.1	1.8	2.3	3.7

Note: 1998 data are preliminary (see page 3). Nigeria's fiscal data are for consolidated government starting from 1992.

7-18. Government expenditure: capital and net lending

	Percentage of total expenditure and lending minus repayments											Annual average		
	1980	1989	1990	1991	1992	1993	1994	1995	1996	1997	1998	75-84	85-89	90-MR
SUB-SAHARAN AFRICA	30.9	17.8	19.2	17.7	18.6	20.1	18.9	18.7	18.9	19.0	15.6	27.5	20.3	18.5
excluding South Africa	..	27.2	26.7	25.3	26.4	26.7	27.3	26.8	28.0	28.7	23.5	30.6	29.5	26.6
excl. S. Africa & Nigeria	..	27.1	26.4	24.1	23.3	24.6	25.2	24.6	24.8	24.9	25.9	28.9	28.1	24.9
Angola	..	32.6	18.0	10.2	6.4	10.7	5.7	12.1	8.8	8.5	6.0	..	17.1	9.6
Benin	..	27.0	26.9	28.1	21.1	26.8	32.9	36.6	32.9	35.4	34.7	40.5	27.0	30.6
Botswana	..	48.2	50.5	47.3	42.4	39.5	32.0	31.8	33.4	34.4	33.3	43.3	45.1	38.3
Burkina Faso	27.8	70.2	27.8	44.5	43.4	34.4	40.8	45.9	51.3	56.5	54.6	45.6	68.9	44.4
Burundi	..	45.8	41.9	43.7	47.9	43.4	32.6	31.1	36.8	18.0	25.8	89.5	47.7	35.7
Cameroon	32.5	23.8	26.2	23.2	15.5	13.8	17.3	7.1	5.9	9.5	16.4	40.3	43.0	15.0
Cape Verde	..	45.3	38.9	48.0	59.2	58.4	61.0	52.3	52.4	51.9	49.6	68.1	57.5	52.4
Central African Republic	..	41.9	41.4	42.4	40.2	41.0	46.0	50.2	21.8	37.5	54.1	100.0	55.6	41.6
Chad	..	59.8	54.9	32.3	45.1	38.0	47.5	50.4	49.1	53.2	53.0	37.0	61.0	47.1
Comoros	..	20.0	16.4	14.2	32.3	15.6	32.1	21.4	21.9	23.8	22.0	54.8	60.0	22.2
Congo, Democratic Rep. of	..	..	..	..	..	..	0.0	0.0	0.0	0.0	..	..	..	0.0
Congo, Republic of	..	25.0	7.9	2.3	2.1	4.6	7.6	9.1	24.4	10.9	12.3	45.8	25.9	9.0
Côte d'Ivoire	38.3	7.8	7.6	8.9	9.5	10.3	16.9	21.2	21.9	24.9	29.1	31.8	12.0	16.7
Djibouti	..	..	27.5	22.5	18.3	16.4	12.9	9.4	11.3	12.1	13.9	..	..	16.0
Equatorial Guinea	..	64.4	62.2	60.7	51.9	61.9	32.9	28.5	39.4	45.1	30.4	..	39.2	45.9
Eritrea	..	..	..	..	12.4	29.2	22.6	20.5	30.8	44.2	29.9	..	..	27.1
Ethiopia	..	33.8	27.3	25.0	22.6	34.2	38.0	37.7	45.2	42.9	38.1	27.2	32.9	34.6
Gabon	..	16.7	16.1	19.6	18.9	17.7	22.1	20.9	22.8	28.5	33.6	58.1	35.4	22.2
Gambia, The	0.0	33.3	34.0	34.4	34.6	29.9	27.4	34.8	35.9	29.3	22.2	12.2	31.2	31.4
Ghana	17.8	41.0	41.0	41.1	41.9	38.3	42.7	46.1	44.8	40.9	39.4	14.5	38.0	41.8
Guinea	..	46.0	49.8	45.6	47.0	49.4	46.3	48.5	45.2	47.6	46.9	..	42.5	47.4
Guinea-Bissau	..	65.0	64.0	61.2	66.9	64.5	59.1	49.5	53.0	66.9	24.4	25.0	65.0	56.6
Kenya	29.8	24.0	23.2	20.7	18.9	17.8	19.0	19.3	17.3	17.0	13.8	23.8	21.7	18.5
Lesotho	..	43.4	45.0	38.4	35.5	34.7	31.7	34.8	41.1	34.0	24.6	37.9	24.1	35.5
Liberia	..	..	..	..	..	..	..	..	..	..	..	..	..	..
Madagascar	40.4	45.1	42.7	36.4	37.6	38.2	33.3	34.8	39.7	35.4	40.8	35.9	34.4	37.7
Malawi	48.7	22.8	22.3	20.0	24.0	20.1	23.5	20.8	19.9	20.8	29.6	38.0	27.4	22.3
Mali	..	57.8	61.7	57.7	53.3	50.4	50.4	53.5	56.2	51.4	56.2	2.8	59.1	54.5
Mauritania	..	..	..	..	..	..	..	..	..	..	..	..	..	..
Mauritius	..	19.5	18.3	18.7	19.6	19.2	17.0	16.9	19.8	16.6	16.3	13.9	19.4	18.0
Mozambique	43.9	49.2	51.9	52.4	50.3	49.3	51.1	57.3	55.1	55.8	48.3	40.0	35.6	52.4
Namibia	..	13.5	20.0	14.0	13.8	17.1	12.7	13.6	13.1	12.9	12.3	21.7	17.1	14.4
Niger	..	38.5	39.0	30.4	21.9	21.5	28.6	26.1	29.7	30.6	30.8	31.0	40.8	28.7
Nigeria	57.1	27.6	28.1	31.3	42.2	38.0	37.5	38.6	44.2	48.2	10.9	61.0	36.2	35.5
Rwanda	0.0	34.1	30.1	30.2	30.3	32.1	16.6	39.3	41.3	42.0	35.9	32.6	34.1	33.1
São Tomé and Principe	..	88.7	94.5	96.4	65.8	60.6	57.9	69.1	60.7	60.3	51.8	..	92.9	68.6
Senegal	17.6	13.4	12.2	15.0	24.1	20.3	23.6	26.5	28.5	31.7	34.4	16.3	13.5	24.0
Seychelles	..	29.4	23.4	22.5	19.7	23.6	25.6	24.4	17.9	20.3	16.1	23.5	24.1	21.5
Sierra Leone	0.0	16.7	17.8	21.2	21.8	25.0	23.3	13.5	19.6	11.3	24.0	3.6	24.0	19.7
Somalia	..	..	..	..	..	..	..	..	..	..	..	..	..	..
South Africa	25.8	7.4	10.9	9.0	9.6	12.3	9.6	9.2	8.4	7.8	6.5	23.6	10.3	9.3
Sudan	..	11.8	12.0	13.6	16.2	28.7	..	13.4	5.7	7.7	9.1	16.9	14.0	13.3
Swaziland	..	..	..	25.5	23.5	21.6	20.0	19.1	17.7	16.4	16.3	..	..	20.0
Tanzania	..	16.9	17.7	10.9	16.7	21.2	20.8	17.6	20.4	17.3	25.5	26.2	22.1	18.7
Togo	49.9	25.9	25.7	17.7	16.0	8.8	9.1	15.6	13.2	11.1	19.4	34.5	32.1	15.2
Uganda	..	33.5	43.8	50.4	44.5	55.0	52.2	46.9	44.1	41.8	41.2	41.7	34.8	46.6
Zambia	10.5	8.7	18.9	15.5	12.1	10.7	12.5	17.5	29.7	29.1	39.5	11.6	2.2	20.6
Zimbabwe	43.1	18.7	18.2	20.2	18.0	16.8	17.6	14.5	12.7	12.3	6.7	42.7	15.7	15.2
NORTH AFRICA	..	34.5	32.4	29.1	27.2	24.8	22.9	22.7	20.9	21.9	22.0	..	36.5	24.9
Algeria	..	35.3	30.8	27.3	28.2	31.3	31.0	29.4	26.6	25.6	21.2	56.9	46.5	27.9
Egypt, Arab Republic	..	38.4	38.3	34.8	29.0	20.9	18.1	18.2	18.7	20.0	22.7	..	39.0	24.5
Libya	..	..	..	..	..	..	..	..	..	..	..	..	..	..
Morocco	30.5	25.8	23.4	20.9	22.2	22.3	20.1	21.1	16.8	20.0	21.8	37.4	24.3	21.0
Tunisia	..	..	..	..	..	..	..	..	..	..	..	..	..	..
ALL AFRICA	..	23.2	23.4	21.3	21.3	21.6	20.2	19.9	19.6	19.9	17.6	27.4	25.4	20.6

Note: 1998 data are preliminary (see page 3). Nigeria's fiscal data are for consolidated government starting from 1992.

7-19. Government expenditure: trends in real defense spending

	Index 1980=100											Annual average		
	1980	1989	1990	1991	1992	1993	1994	1995	1996	1997	1998	75-84	85-89	90-MR
SUB-SAHARAN AFRICA	100.0	..	110.0	..	..	..	102.8	..	..	..	..	100.0	95.9	106.4
excluding South Africa	100.0	..	109.8	..	..	..	113.4	..	..	..	..	100.0	94.7	111.6
excl. S. Africa & Nigeria	100.0	..	110.0	..	..	..	124.0	..	..	..	..	100.0	95.9	117.0
Angola	..	..	..	..	..	..	..	..	..	..	..	..	..	..
Benin	..	..	..	..	..	..	..	..	..	..	..	..	..	..
Botswana	100.0	..	298.0	..	..	..	347.8	..	..	..	..	100.0	98.9	322.9
Burkina Faso	100.0	..	188.2	..	..	..	339.2	..	..	..	..	100.0	140.5	263.7
Burundi	100.0	..	..	..	..	..	66.7	..	..	..	..	100.0	95.9	66.7
Cameroon	100.0	..	..	..	..	..	124.0	..	..	..	..	100.0	190.6	124.0
Cape Verde	..	..	..	..	..	..	..	..	..	..	..	..	..	..
Central African Republic	..	..	..	..	..	..	..	..	..	..	..	..	..	..
Chad	..	..	..	..	..	..	..	..	..	..	..	..	..	..
Comoros	..	..	..	..	..	..	..	..	..	..	..	..	..	..
Congo, Democratic Rep. of	..	..	..	..	..	..	..	..	..	..	..	..	..	..
Congo, Republic of	100.0	..	89.4	..	..	..	41.5	..	..	..	..	100.0	125.3	65.5
Côte d'Ivoire	100.0	..	91.6	..	..	..	62.7	..	..	..	..	100.0	83.3	77.2
Djibouti	..	..	..	..	..	..	..	..	..	..	..	..	..	..
Equatorial Guinea	..	..	..	..	..	..	..	..	..	..	..	..	..	..
Eritrea	..	..	..	..	..	..	..	..	..	..	..	..	..	..
Ethiopia	..	..	..	..	..	..	..	..	..	..	..	..	..	..
Gabon	100.0	..	116.9	..	..	..	140.4	..	..	..	..	100.0	162.2	128.7
Gambia, The	..	..	..	..	..	..	..	..	..	..	..	..	..	..
Ghana	..	..	..	..	..	..	..	..	..	..	..	..	..	..
Guinea	..	..	..	..	..	..	..	..	..	..	..	..	..	..
Guinea-Bissau	..	..	..	..	..	..	..	..	..	..	..	..	..	..
Kenya	..	..	..	..	..	..	..	..	..	..	..	..	..	..
Lesotho	..	..	..	..	..	..	..	..	..	..	..	..	..	..
Liberia	100.0	..	..	..	..	..	..	..	..	..	..	100.0	69.3	..
Madagascar	..	..	..	..	..	..	..	..	..	..	..	..	..	..
Malawi	100.0	..	23.4	..	..	..	21.3	..	..	..	..	100.0	59.2	22.3
Mali	..	..	..	..	..	..	..	..	..	..	..	..	..	..
Mauritania	..	..	..	..	..	..	..	..	..	..	..	..	..	..
Mauritius	100.0	..	110.3	..	..	..	149.0	..	..	..	..	100.0	55.9	129.6
Mozambique	100.0	..	78.9	..	..	..	79.0	..	..	..	..	100.0	55.6	78.9
Namibia	..	..	..	..	..	..	..	..	..	..	..	..	..	..
Niger	..	..	..	..	..	..	..	..	..	..	..	..	..	..
Nigeria	100.0	..	21.0	..	..	..	16.5	..	..	..	..	100.0	40.1	18.8
Rwanda	100.0	..	94.2	..	..	..	234.0	..	..	..	..	100.0	98.2	164.1
São Tomé and Principe	..	..	..	..	..	..	..	..	..	..	..	..	..	..
Senegal	100.0	..	109.8	..	..	..	102.8	..	..	..	..	100.0	93.6	106.3
Seychelles	..	..	..	..	..	..	..	..	..	..	..	..	..	..
Sierra Leone	..	..	..	..	..	..	..	..	..	..	..	..	..	..
Somalia	..	..	..	..	..	..	..	..	..	..	..	..	..	..
South Africa	100.0	..	128.4	..	..	..	94.1	..	..	..	..	100.0	143.0	111.3
Sudan	100.0	..	238.7	..	..	..	..	..	..	..	..	100.0	141.4	238.7
Swaziland	100.0	..	110.2	..	..	..	137.2	..	..	..	..	100.0	59.0	123.7
Tanzania	..	..	..	..	..	..	..	..	..	..	..	..	..	..
Togo	100.0	..	153.9	..	..	..	137.1	..	..	..	..	100.0	124.1	145.5
Uganda	..	..	..	..	..	..	..	..	..	..	..	..	..	..
Zambia	100.0	..	9.8	..	..	..	6.2	..	..	..	..	100.0	31.9	8.0
Zimbabwe	..	..	..	..	..	..	..	..	..	..	..	..	..	..
NORTH AFRICA	100.0	..	105.1	..	..	..	166.8	..	..	..	..	100.0	144.0	135.9
Algeria	100.0	..	148.0	..	..	..	273.1	..	..	..	..	100.0	111.1	210.6
Egypt, Arab Republic	..	..	..	..	..	..	..	..	..	..	..	..	..	..
Libya	..	..	..	..	..	..	..	..	..	..	..	..	..	..
Morocco	..	..	..	..	..	..	..	..	..	..	..	..	..	..
Tunisia	100.0	..	62.1	..	..	..	60.4	..	..	..	..	100.0	176.9	61.3
ALL AFRICA	100.0	..	110.0	..	..	..	102.8	..	..	..	..	100.0	98.2	106.4

Note: Nigeria's fiscal data are for federal level only. Nigeria's fiscal data are for consolidated government starting from 1992.

7-20. Government expenditure: real per capita education spending

	Constant 1995 U.S. dollars											Annual average		
	1980	1989	1990	1991	1992	1993	1994	1995	1996	1997	1998	75-84	85-89	90-MR
SUB-SAHARAN AFRICA	..	..	..	..	..	..	..	..	..	..	..	..	..	..
excluding South Africa	..	..	..	..	..	..	..	..	..	..	..	..	..	..
excl. S. Africa & Nigeria	..	..	..	..	..	..	..	..	..	..	..	..	..	..
Angola	..	..	..	..	..	..	..	..	..	..	..	..	..	..
Benin	..	..	..	..	..	..	..	..	..	..	..	11.7	..	..
Botswana	112.6	184.8	219.8	235.7	247.4	263.0	262.9	292.4	330.4	..	..	97.3	154.8	264.5
Burkina Faso	3.9	6.1	6.2	6.8	7.2	7.0	..	..	..	..	..	3.8	5.2	6.8
Burundi	..	..	..	7.5	9.4	7.9	7.8	7.0	6.1	4.7	..	6.8	..	7.2
Cameroon	14.2	20.2	25.2	24.5	23.5	18.1	16.4	11.2	..	..	..	17.7	27.1	19.8
Cape Verde	..	..	..	..	..	..	..	..	..	..	..	..	..	..
Central African Republic	..	..	..	..	..	..	..	..	..	..	..	15.5	..	..
Chad	..	..	..	..	..	..	..	..	..	..	..	..	..	..
Comoros	..	..	..	..	..	..	..	..	..	..	..	55.5	47.9	..
Congo, Democratic Rep. of	7.3	..	..	..	1.5	0.0	0.0	0.1	..	..	..	7.3	..	0.4
Congo, Republic of	..	..	..	..	..	..	..	..	..	..	..	45.5	..	..
Côte d'Ivoire	..	..	..	..	..	..	..	..	..	..	..	..	..	..
Djibouti	..	..	..	..	..	..	..	..	..	..	..	..	..	..
Equatorial Guinea	..	..	..	..	..	..	..	..	..	..	..	..	..	..
Eritrea	..	..	..	..	..	..	..	..	..	..	..	..	..	..
Ethiopia	..	2.9	2.7	2.2	2.2	2.8	3.5	3.4	..	..	..	2.8	2.7	2.8
Gabon	..	..	..	..	..	..	..	..	..	..	..	..	..	..
Gambia, The	14.7	..	10.1	..	..	..	..	..	..	..	..	12.4	..	10.1
Ghana	..	..	..	..	..	..	14.9	14.5	15.7	14.2	15.3	..	..	14.9
Guinea	..	..	..	..	..	..	..	..	..	..	..	..	..	..
Guinea-Bissau	..	2.8	..	..	..	..	..	..	..	..	..	12.0	6.8	..
Kenya	16.7	21.0	19.4	20.3	18.2	18.5	16.9	19.5	19.8	..	..	15.9	19.2	18.9
Lesotho	..	30.8	33.2	47.3	42.7	..	..	..	..	..	..	20.8	27.2	41.1
Liberia	..	..	..	..	..	..	..	..	..	..	..	..	..	..
Madagascar	..	6.4	6.6	6.6	6.5	7.0	4.9	4.7	3.7	..	..	..	6.3	5.7
Malawi	5.2	3.9	4.2	..	..	..	..	..	..	..	..	5.1	5.1	4.2
Mali	9.2	..	..	..	..	..	..	..	..	..	..	8.2	6.6	..
Mauritania	..	..	..	..	..	..	..	..	..	..	..	19.1	..	..
Mauritius	86.4	95.4	95.2	99.3	108.4	106.9	125.0	141.6	137.6	160.6	..	79.7	78.5	121.8
Mozambique	..	..	..	..	..	..	..	..	..	..	..	..	..	..
Namibia	..	..	..	..	..	..	..	..	..	..	..	..	..	..
Niger	11.0	..	..	..	..	..	..	..	..	..	..	8.4	..	..
Nigeria	..	..	..	..	..	..	..	..	..	..	..	6.8	2.2	..
Rwanda	..	..	..	..	..	..	..	..	..	..	..	..	..	..
São Tomé and Principe	..	..	..	..	..	..	..	..	..	..	..	..	..	..
Senegal	29.9	..	..	..	..	..	..	..	..	..	..	26.9	..	..
Seychelles	..	..	..	..	..	548.6	545.6	434.2	..	..	..	..	..	509.5
Sierra Leone	..	..	2.2	..	..	..	..	..	..	..	..	8.7	..	2.2
Somalia	..	..	..	..	..	..	..	..	..	..	..	..	..	..
South Africa	..	..	..	..	..	..	..	..	..	..	..	..	..	..
Sudan	3.9	..	..	..	..	..	..	..	..	..	..	2.9	..	..
Swaziland	66.5	75.5	103.5	117.5	..	..	..	..	..	..	..	59.7	72.3	110.5
Tanzania	..	..	..	..	..	..	..	..	..	..	..	..	..	..
Togo	..	..	..	..	..	..	..	..	..	..	..	20.8	19.6	..
Uganda	..	..	..	..	..	..	..	..	..	..	..	2.6	3.7	..
Zambia	23.2	11.8	11.0	13.9	10.3	10.0	13.0	16.0	15.2	..	..	29.3	14.4	12.8
Zimbabwe	27.7	45.3	..	..	..	..	..	..	..	..	..	29.0	43.8	..
NORTH AFRICA	45.0	52.7	52.9	54.2	54.6	57.9	60.7	61.0	..	..	..	46.1	51.7	56.9
Algeria	..	..	..	..	..	..	..	..	..	..	..	..	..	..
Egypt, Arab Republic	29.4	38.5	37.1	40.4	39.1	42.7	47.3	48.2	..	..	..	31.9	40.5	42.5
Libya	..	..	..	..	..	..	..	..	..	..	..	..	..	..
Morocco	63.8	67.3	68.7	67.8	69.5	72.7	72.0	69.0	..	..	..	60.7	61.4	69.9
Tunisia	88.3	101.0	107.4	102.6	109.9	112.2	113.9	121.0	129.1	..	..	92.8	94.4	113.7
ALL AFRICA	..	..	..	..	..	..	..	..	..	..	..	..	..	..

Note: Nigeria's fiscal data are for consolidated government starting from 1992.

Figure 7-1. Government deficit/surplus as percentage of GDP, 1992-98*

(percent)

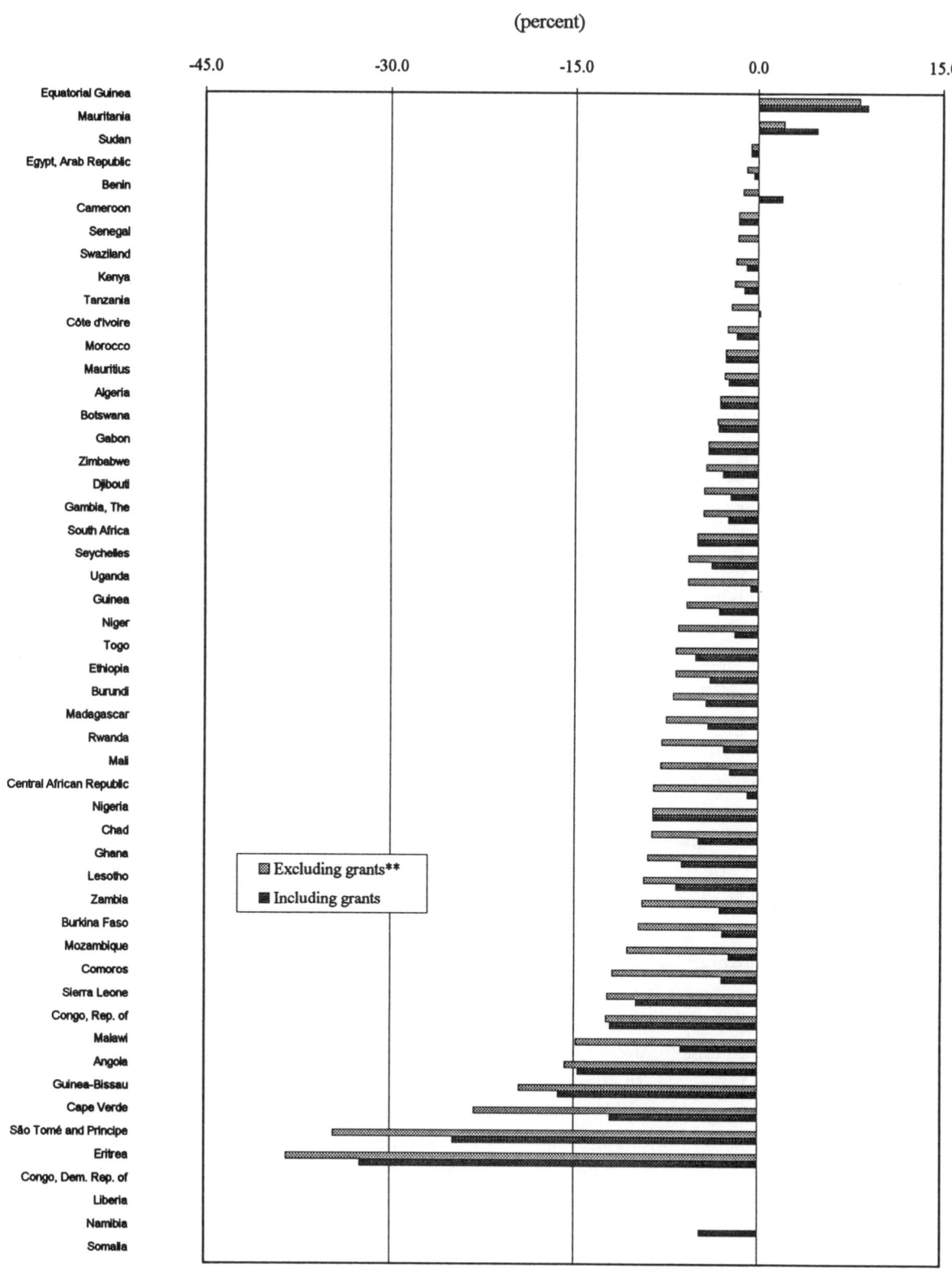

* Or most recent year available.
** Sorted by deficit excluding grants.
Note: Nigeria's ratios are distorted because of official exchange rate over-valuation affecting oil exports and oil value added.

Technical Notes

Tables

Table 7-1. Government deficit/surplus (including grants). Overall surplus/deficit is the difference between total revenue plus grants (as defined in *GFS* line A-I) and total expenditures and lending minus repayments (as defined in *GFS* line C-I). It represents the net financing requirement of the consolidated government. This indicator is shown as a percentage of current GDP in national currency (World Bank country desks).

Table 7-2. Government deficit/surplus (excluding grants). This is calculated as above, except that capital grants are excluded from receipts (as defined in *GFS* line A-II, less line C-I). It is a measure of the ability of a government to fund its activities from its own resources. Because some budgetary grants may be tied to certain expenditures that would not otherwise be incurred, excluding grants may overstate the deficit or understate the surplus if no account is taken of the expenditures dependent on these grants. This indicator is shown as a percentage of current GDP in national currency (World Bank country desks).

Table 7-3. Government primary deficit/surplus (–/+). The primary deficit or surplus is the government deficit or surplus including grants (as presented in Table 7-1) excluding interest expenditures on both domestic and foreign debt (Table 7-5). In countries with large government interest payments, this ratio may provide a more reliable indicator for monitoring fiscal stabilization efforts. This indicator is shown as a percentage of current GDP in national currency (World Bank country desks).

Table 7-4. Government expenditure and lending minus repayments. Total expenditure and lending minus repayments (as defined in *GFS* line C-I) represents the government's total outlays for current or capital purposes. Expenditure includes all nonrepayable payments by the government. Lending minus repayments comprises government transactions in debt and equity claims upon others, acquired for purposes of public policy rather than for managing government liquidity or earning a return. It consists of gross lending and acquisition of financial equity minus repayments of past government lending and government sales of equities. (This definition differs from the concept of lending minus repayments adopted in the SNA, which is gross government lending minus repayments of past government lending minus net government borrowing.) In determining a government's deficit or surplus, lending minus repayments is grouped with expenditures rather than with financing. This indicator is shown as a percentage of current GDP in national currency (World Bank country desks).

Table 7-5. Government interest payments. Government interest payments (as defined in *GFS* line C2) include interest on all borrowings, both domestic and foreign, but exclude commission charges paid for assistance in placement of debt (which would be classified as expenditure for the payment of goods and services). This indicator is shown as a percentage of current GDP in national currency (World Bank country desks).

Table 7-6. Government revenue (excluding grants). Government revenue less grants (as defined in *GFS* line A-II) refers to current revenues (tax and nontax) and capital revenues, such as proceeds from the sale of real assets, including land. They do not include grant receipts from other governments or international organizations. This indicator is shown as a percentage of current GDP in national currency (World Bank country desks).

Table 7-7. Grants to government. These are unrequited, nonrepayable, noncompulsory government receipts from other governments or international institutions (as defined in *GFS* line A-II). Grants of goods and services in kind are excluded. This indicator is shown as a percentage of current GDP in national currency (World Bank country desks).

Table 7-8. Foreign financing. Includes all government financing transactions except grants (as defined in *GFS* line D-III) with nonresident individuals, enterprises, governments, international organizations, and other entities. It may be affected by trading in outstanding government securities between residents and nonresidents. The data also reflect changes, resulting from transactions but not revaluations, in government holdings of foreign exchange, deposits in nonresident financial institutions, and securities issued by nonresident entities held by government for liquidity purposes (reserves). This indicator is shown as a percentage of current GDP in national currency (World Bank country desks).

Table 7-9. Taxes on income and profits. These taxes (as defined in *GFS* line A1) are levied on the actual or presumptive net income of individuals and profits of enterprises. Also included are taxes levied on capital gains that are realized on land sales, securities, and other assets. This indicator is shown as a percentage of total revenue (as defined in *GFS* line A-II) (World Bank country desks).

Table 7-10. Taxes on international trade and transactions. Include import duties, export duties, profits of export or import monopolies remitted to government, and monopoly profits of monetary authorities made in foreign exchange transactions as well as taxes levied on the sale of foreign exchange (as defined in *GFS* line A6). This indicator is shown as a percentage of total revenue (as defined in *GFS* line A-II) (World Bank country desks).

Table 7-11. Indirect taxes. These are sales and excise taxes and duties (as defined in *GFS* line A-IV less A1). This indicator is shown as a percentage of total revenue (as defined in *GFS* line A-II) (World Bank country desks).

Table 7-12. Nontax revenue, excluding grants. This is all nonrepayable government receipts, other than compulsory unrequited receipts (taxes) and revenue from capital sales or government grants, plus all fines and penalties other than for noncompliance with taxes (as defined in *GFS* line A-V). For some mineral-exporting countries in Africa, this category is quite large, since royalties on the extraction of minerals, such as petroleum in Egypt and Nigeria and bauxite in Guinea, make up significant portions of total government revenues. This indicator is shown as a percentage of total revenue (as defined in *GFS* line A-II) (World Bank country desks).

Table 7-13. Government expenditure: wages and salaries. Are payments in cash, but not in kind, to employees in return for services, before withholding taxes and employee contributions to social security and pension funds are deducted (as defined in *GFS* line C1.1). Included are basic wages and salaries; pay for overtime, weekends, and nights; cost of living allowances; local allowances and expatriation allowances; and similar compensation. Reimbursement to employees for expenses incurred as part of their employment are excluded. This indicator is shown as a percentage of total expenditure and lending minus repayments (as defined in *GFS* line C-I) (World Bank country desks).

Table 7-14. Government expenditure: trends in real wages and salaries. Includes expenditure on wages and salaries as discussed above (as defined in *GFS* line C1.1), deflated by the CPI. For most countries the trend is shown in index numbers beginning with 100 in 1987 (World Bank country desks).

Table 7-15. Government expenditure: other goods and services. Includes expenditures for all goods and services (except fixed capital assets and wages and salaries) bought on the market, goods and services to be used to produce fixed capital assets, strategic or emergency stocks, stocks held by market regulatory organizations, and land and intangible assets. This category encompasses purchases of materials, office supplies, fuel and lighting, travel services, and payment of rent, as well as payments in kind to certain civil servants (as defined in *GFS* line C1.3). This indicator is presented as a percentage of total expenditure and lending minus repayments (as defined in *GFS* lines C-I) (World Bank country desks).

Table 7-16. Government expenditure: interest payments. Are payments for the use of all borrowed money, excluding commission charges paid for assistance in placing debt, which would be classified as expenditures for payment of other goods and services (as defined in *GFS* line C2). This indicator is presented as a percentage of total expenditure and lending minus repayments (as defined in *GFS* lines C-I) (World Bank country desks).

Table 7-17. Government expenditure: subsidies and current transfers. Are all unrequited, nonrepayable government payments for current purposes (as defined in *GFS* line C3). Transfers for capital purposes (that is, to permit the recipient to acquire capital assets) and transfers in kind are excluded. This indicator is presented as a percentage of total expenditure

and lending minus repayments (as defined in *GFS* line C-I) (World Bank country desks).

Table 7-18. Government expenditure: capital and net lending. Represents payments for acquiring land, buildings, and other nonfinancial assets to be used for more than one year in the process of production, including transfers for capital assets as well as net lending (as defined in *GFS* lines C-IV plus C-V). This indicator is presented as a percentage of total expenditure and lending minus repayments (as defined in *GFS* line C-I) (World Bank country desks).

Table 7-19. Government expenditure: trends in real defense spending. Real defense spending has been calculated by deflating defense spending in current prices national currency (IMF, as defined in *GFS* line B2) by the national GDP deflator (Table 3-1). The results are presented in the form of 1980 base indexes.

Table 7-20. Government expenditure: real per capita education spending. Presents education spending (IMF, as defined in *GFS* line B4) deflated by the national GDP deflator (Table 3-1) and divided by total population (Table 2-1). The result is converted into 1995 U.S. dollars by using the 1995 local currency/US dollar conversion factor (Table 3-6).

Figure

The following indicators have been used to derive the figure in this chapter.

Figure 7-1. Government deficit/surplus (Tables 7-1 and 7-2).

Methodology used for regional aggregations and period averages in chapter 7

Table	Aggregations[a] (6)	(7)	Period averages[b] (1)
7-1	x		x
7-2	x		x
7-3	x		x
7-4	x		x
7-5	x		x
7-6	x		x
7-7	x		x
7-8	x		x
7-9	x		x
7-10	x		x
7-11	x		x
7-12	x		x
7-13	x		x
7-14		x	x
7-15	x		x
7-16	x		x
7-17	x		x
7-18	x		x
7-19		x	x
7-20	x		x

Note: Regional aggregations are shown in the rows for Sub-Saharan Africa, North Africa, and All Africa. Period averages are shown in the last three columns. This table shows only the methodologies used in this chapter. **For aggregation purposes, all data used in this chapter were converted to U.S. dollars, using the conversion factors shown in Table 3-6.**

a. Regional aggregations: (1) simple total; (2) simple total of the first indicator divided by the simple total of the second indicator (same country coverage); (3) simple total of the gap-filled indicator; (4) simple total of the gap-filled main indicator divided by the simple total of the gap-filled secondary indicator; (5) simple total of the first gap-filled main indicator less the simple total of the second gap-filled main indicator, all divided by the simple total of the secondary indicator; (6) weighted total; (7) median; (8) no aggregation; (9) simple arithmetic mean.

b. Period averages: (1) arithmetic mean (using the same series as shown in the table, i.e., ratio if the rest of the table is shown as ratio, level if the rest of the table is shown as level, growth rate if the rest of the table is shown as growth rate); (2) least-squares growth rate (using main indicator); (3) least-squares growth rate (using main indicator in constant terms, with the rest of the table in current terms).

8

Agriculture

Agriculture is one of Africa's important sectors. African agriculture has two major components: food production and export commodities. Food production, including meat, is the livelihood for most Africans. Export crops provide many African countries with their main source of foreign exchange and thus the capacity to import, invest, and develop. The information in this chapter provides a basis for assessing recent trends in producer prices, aggregate agricultural production and trade, cereal imports, and food aid in Africa.

The data in this chapter are estimates based on a variety of sources whose quality and reliability vary from country to country and year to year. Furthermore, production and export data are probably underestimated for two reasons. It is difficult to estimate production levels of staple food crops, especially roots and tubers, when much of the output is consumed directly by farmers, rather than marketed. Moreover, parallel market activity, including trade, may not be fully accounted for.

8-1. Nominal producer prices

	Category	*1980*	*1986*	*1987*	*1988*	*1989*	*1990*	*1991*	*1992*	*1993*	*1994*	*1995*
					Local currency per kilogram							
ALGERIA												
Wheat (hard)	F1	1.2	2.2	2.2	2.7	3.7	4.6	5.4	10.3	10.3	10.3	19.0
Citrus (oranges)	F2	..	..	..	..	..	..	..	..	..	..	..
Dates	F3	4.5	11.3	11.5	..	..	..	..	..	..	..	..
Barley	NT1	0.8	1.4	1.7	1.7	2.3	2.3	2.3	4.7	4.7	6.0	14.0
Potatoes	NT2	1.3	2.6	2.8	2.7	3.0	3.3	3.3	6.5	6.5	6.5	10.0
ANGOLA												
Coffee	X1	..	67.0	67.0	67.0	67.0	135.0	158.0	..	..	..	..
Maize	F1	..	10.0	10.0	11.5	11.5	11.5	100.0	..	..	..	..
Millet	F2	4.0	10.0	10.0	10.0	10.0	10.0	100.0	..	..	..	..
Wheat	F3	4.5	17.5	17.5	17.5	17.5	17.5	200.0	..	..	..	..
Cassava	NT1	..	5.0	5.0	7.7	7.7	7.7	150.0	..	..	..	..
Sweet potatoes	NT2	2.5	7.5	7.5	14.0	14.0	14.0	200.0	..	..	..	..
BENIN												
Cotton (seed cotton)	X1	65.0	110.0	100.0	105.0	95.0	100.0	100.0	100.0	94.8	..	..
Palm kernels	X2	35.0	20.0	20.0	30.0	30.0	30.0	35.0	35.0	..	..	..
Maize	F1	40.0	65.0	68.0	64.0	55.0	85.0	58.0	62.0	53.0	..	..
Sorghum	F2	46.0	65.0	72.0	67.0	60.0	60.0	63.0	65.0	55.0	..	..
Cassava	NT1	30.0	15.0	20.0	16.0	16.0	16.0	17.0	17.5	18.2	..	..
Yams	NT2	32.0	50.0	58.0	49.0	49.0	49.0	49.0	50.0	52.0	..	..
BOTSWANA												
Groundnuts (in shell)	X1	0.2	0.7	0.7	0.7	0.7	0.7	1.1	1.0	1.4	..	..
Sorghum	F1	0.1	0.3	0.3	0.3	0.3	0.3	0.3	0.4	0.4	..	..
Maize	F2	0.1	0.3	0.3	0.3	0.3	0.3	0.3	0.3	0.4	..	..
BURKINA FASO												
Cotton (seed cotton)	X1	55.0	97.2	89.7	94.4	94.6	95.0	..	..	..	..	..
Groundnuts (in shell)	X2	54.0	50.0	60.0	55.0	60.0	60.0	..	..	..	..	..
Sesame seed	X3	70.0	80.0	55.0	65.0	85.0	80.0	..	..	..	..	..
Sorghum	F1	45.0	40.0	45.0	40.0	45.0	60.0	..	..	..	..	..
Millet	F2	45.0	40.0	45.0	40.0	45.0	60.0	..	..	..	..	..
Maize	F3	45.0	45.0	55.0	45.0	50.0	65.0	..	..	..	..	..
BURUNDI												
Coffee (green)	X1	..	..	..	..	..	..	..	..	..	..	..
Tea	X2	..	..	..	..	..	..	..	..	..	..	..
Cotton (seed)	X3	36.1	51.9	52.6	55.3	57.8	60.2	62.4	64.4	..	..	..
Maize	F1	25.0	..	..	..	..	..	..	..	..	..	..
Sorghum	F2	20.0	..	..	..	..	..	..	..	..	..	..
Rice	F3	25.0	..	..	..	..	..	..	..	..	..	..
Millet	F4	20.0	..	..	..	..	..	..	..	..	..	..
Bananas	NT1	..	..	..	..	..	..	..	..	..	..	..
Cassava	NT1	10.9	..	..	..	..	..	..	..	..	..	..
CAMEROON												
Coffee (Arabica)	X1	320.0	475.0	475.0	475.0	458.0	186.0	165.0	..	..	..	..
Cocoa (grade 1, superior)	X2	300.0	420.0	420.0	42.0	250.0	220.0	200.0	200.0	200.0	..	..
Cotton (seed cotton, nonselected)	X3	70.0	130.0	130.0	140.0	95.0	95.0	95.0	85.0	..	..	..
Maize	F1	60.0	83.2	76.8	82.4	57.0	51.7	..	..	..	..	..
Sorghum	F2	40.0	38.9	60.6	47.2	43.0	77.9	..	..	..	..	..
Millet	F3	40.0	38.9	60.6	47.2	43.0	77.9	..	..	..	..	..
Rice (paddy)	F4	105.0	91.0	64.7	77.5	82.7	53.5	..	..	..	..	..
Cassava	NT1	19.0	48.0	46.6	41.7	..	..	..	..	..	..	..
Plantains	NT2	25.0	45.3	46.7	47.3	..	54.0	..	..	..	..	..
CENTRAL AFRICAN REPUBLIC												
Coffee (Robusta, cherries)	X1	120.0	135.0	135.0	190.0	110.0	80.0	40.0	40.0	120.0	120.0	240.0
Cotton (seed cotton)	X2	60.0	100.0	100.0	100.0	100.0	..	68.5	60.0	60.0	87.0	117.0
Sorghum	F1	..	103.5	128.3	107.7	92.5	..	..	..	..	136.7	168.9
Maize	F2	40.0	65.3	67.7	104.3	111.6	..	..	..	..	136.0	271.0
Groundnuts (unshelled)	F3	70.0	..	..	171.7	..	..	..	..	..	217.6	526.3
Cassava	NT1	30.0	76.2	89.5	57.5	103.7	..	..	..	..	119.2	176.6
Yams	NT2	25.0	107.1	91.0	124.5	86.6	..	..	..	..	..	222.5
CHAD												
Cotton (seed cotton, avg. white/yellow)	X1	..	99.0	99.0	97.0	88.0	88.0	88.0	77.0	89.0	..	..
Millet	F2	..	31.0	31.0	48.0	47.0	52.0	62.0	41.0	41.0	..	..
Groundnuts	F3	..	57.0	46.0	44.0	46.0	48.0	70.0	67.0	77.0	..	..

8-1. Nominal producer prices (continued)

| | | | | | | Local currency per kilogram | | | | | |
	Category	1980	1986	1987	1988	1989	1990	1991	1992	1993	1994	1995
COMOROS												
Vanilla	X1	1150.0	..	..	..	..	..	..	..	..	..	..
Cloves	X2	1250.0	..	..	..	..	..	..	..	..	..	..
Ylang Ylang (flower)	X3	45.0	90.0	65.0	65.0	..	..	..	..	..	..	..
Copra	X4	40.0	..	..	..	..	..	..	..	..	..	..
Bananas	F1	50.0	..	..	..	..	..	..	..	..	..	..
Cassava	NT1	40.0	..	..	..	..	..	..	..	..	..	..
CONGO, DEMOCRATIC REPUBLIC OF												
Coffee (Arabica, green beans)	X1	4.0	42.6	69.3	107.5	166.9	440.5	13837.3	..	..	..	..
Palm oil	X2	2.1	23.0	37.6	59.4	93.8	247.7	7778.7	..	..	..	..
Rubber (natural)	X3	..	..	..	..	..	..	..	..	..	..	..
Cocoa (beans)	X4	..	30.0	50.0	..	..	..	..	..	..	..	..
Maize	F1	1.2	7.5	10.1	25.8	40.3	106.4	..	..	..	..	..
Rice (paddy)	F2	2.0	11.5	17.0	28.7	45.2	119.4	..	..	..	..	..
Cassava	NT1	1.3	3.0	3.9	8.4	13.2	34.7	1090.8	..	..	..	..
Plantains	NT2	2.9	..	..	..	..	..	..	..	..	..	..
CONGO, REPUBLIC OF												
Coffee	X1	146.0	215.0	215.0	115.0	115.0	115.0	115.0	115.0	115.0	..	..
Cocoa	X2	134.8	190.0	240.0	108.0	108.0	88.0	88.0	88.0	88.0	88.0	88.0
Maize	F1	43.0	73.0	85.0	60.0	60.0	60.0	60.0	100.0	100.0	100.0	100.0
Cassava	NT1	..	..	..	..	..	..	..	..	..	..	..
Plantains	NT2	..	..	..	..	..	..	..	..	..	..	..
COTE D'IVOIRE												
Coffee (Robusta, green)	X1	310.6	399.5	400.0	400.0	404.0	419.0	390.0	232.0	200.0	530.0	700.0
Cocoa (beans)	X2	300.0	400.0	400.0	400.0	400.0	200.0	200.0	200.0	200.0	315.0	320.0
Palm oil	X3	..	..	..	..	213.8	213.8	213.8	190.0	190.0	190.0	225.0	225.0
Rice (paddy)	F1	50.0	84.0	84.0	60.0	60.0	60.0	60.0	60.0	75.0	75.0	110.0
Maize	F2	68.0	76.0	45.0	45.0	45.0	45.0	45.0	..	..	..	..
Cassava	NT1	49.0	46.0	..	..	..	..	..	..	..	..	..
Yams	NT2	59.0	99.9	..	..	..	..	..	..	..	..	..
EGYPT												
Cotton	X1	0.3	0.6	0.7	0.9	1.3	1.7	2.0	2.4	2.4	2.1	..
Rice (96% humidity)	X2	0.1	0.2	0.2	0.3	0.4	0.4	0.4	0.5	0.5	0.6	..
Wheat (94% humidity)	F1	0.1	0.2	0.2	0.2	0.4	0.5	0.5	0.5	0.5	0.5	..
Sugarcane	F2	0.0	0.0	0.0	0.0	0.1	0.1	0.1	0.1	0.1	0.1	0.1
Broadbeans	NT1	0.2	0.5	0.6	0.6	0.6	0.7	0.9	1.1	1.0	1.0	..
EQUATORIAL GUINEA												
Cocoa (first grade dried beans)	X1	..	..	..	..	..	..	..	..	..	..	..
Coffee (Robusta, cherry)	X2	..	..	..	..	..	..	..	..	..	..	..
Cassava	NT1	..	..	..	..	..	..	..	..	..	..	..
Plantains	NT2	..	..	..	..	..	..	..	..	..	..	..
ETHIOPIA												
Coffee (Arabica, beans)	X1	2.6	3.7	4.1	4.2	4.2	4.2	3.1	3.1	..	..	..
Sesame seed	X2	..	1.1	1.1	1.3	1.3	1.4	1.7	..	..	..	..
Sorghum (mixed)	F1	..	0.5	0.4	0.5	0.5	0.5	0.8	0.8	..	..	..
Maize	F2	..	0.5	0.4	0.4	0.5	0.4	0.6	0.7	..	..	..
Barley (non-white mixed)	NT1	..	0.5	0.4	0.5	0.5	0.5	0.7	0.9	..	..	..
GABON												
Cocoa (first quality)	X1	320.0	430.0	430.0	370.0	210.0	224.0	224.0	269.0	260.0	..	..
Coffee (merchant, processed)	X2	180.0	0.0	260.0	260.0	130.0	130.0	..	150.0	147.0	..	..
Maize	F1	..	..	..	..	..	..	..	..	..	..	..
Cassava	NT1	139.5	..	..	..	..	..	..	..	..	..	..
Yams	NT3	124.5	..	..	..	..	..	..	..	..	..	..
GAMBIA, THE												
Groundnuts (unshelled)	X1	0.5	1.8	1.5	1.1	1.5	1.8	..	..	..	..	..
Cotton (seed cotton)	X2	0.5	1.3	1.5	1.6	1.8	1.9	1.9	2.0	2.0	2.2	2.2
Palm kernels	X3	0.3	0.3	..	..	..	..	..	..	..	..	..
Millet	F1	0.5	1.1	1.2	1.2	1.5	1.9	1.9	..	..	..	..
Rice (paddy)	F2	..	..	2.1	2.1	3.4	2.8	2.7	..	..	..	..
Maize	F3	..	0.0	1.2	1.2	1.4	2.1	1.9	..	..	..	..
Sorghum	F4	0.3	0.9	0.0	0.0	1.2	0.0	1.9	..	..	..	..

8-1. Nominal producer prices (continued)

	Category	Local currency per kilogram										
		1980	1986	1987	1988	1989	1990	1991	1992	1993	1994	1995
GHANA												
Cocoa	X1	4.0	80.3	101.3	153.8	..	..	..	..	..	..	..
Maize	F1	4.1	25.0	42.0	48.0	35.8	86.9	69.5	83.5	93.7	..	..
Millet	F2	5.3	24.2	36.0	83.3	89.7	77.9	113.5	141.4	149.9	..	..
Groundnuts	F3	8.4	..	..	..	..	..	..	..	..	..	..
Cassava	NT1	1.5	8.8	10.8	12.9	10.0	10.0	15.8	22.5	25.3	..	..
Plantains	NT2	1.9	15.0	18.6	43.0	45.9	27.8	26.8	35.5	91.4	..	..
GUINEA												
Coffee (Robusta)	X1	49.0	400.0	400.0	..	..	..	..	..	..	..	..
Palm kernels	X2	6.0	60.0	60.0	..	..	..	..	..	..	..	..
Rice (paddy)	F1	9.0	..	..	..	..	168.0	166.0	..	..	..	..
Maize	F2	7.0	..	..	..	..	130.0	144.0	..	..	..	..
Groundnuts (unshelled)	F3	11.0	..	..	..	250.0	213.0	..	..	..	..	..
Cassava	NT1	5.0	..	..	..	..	..	81.0	..	..	..	..
Plantains	NT2	4.5	..	..	..	..	..	..	..	..	..	..
GUINEA-BISSAU												
Cashew nuts	X1	..	38.5	125.0	230.0	350.0	450.0	550.0	1000.0	3500.0	..	..
Groundnuts (unshelled, grade 1)	X2	..	32.5	40.0	80.0	140.0	225.0	275.0	500.0	1000.0	..	..
Palm kernels	X3	..	..	..	..	..	..	..	..	..	..	..
Rice (paddy, grade 1)	F1	8.5	37.5	50.0	85.0	180.0	225.0	400.0	650.0	1100.0	..	..
Sorghum	F2	..	..	..	..	..	..	..	..	..	..	..
Maize (grade 1)	F3	..	..	..	..	..	..	..	..	740.0	..	..
KENYA												
Coffee (Arabica, washed bean, grade 1-6)	X1	26.4	54.8	34.1	43.0	43.1	36.4	46.5	49.4	98.9	..	..
Tea	X2	15.9	33.8	25.0	26.8	27.2	35.2	38.5	47.5	92.4	..	..
Sugar (cane)	X3	0.1	0.3	0.3	0.4	0.4	0.5	0.5	0.6	0.8	..	..
Sisal	X4	4.2	7.4	7.1	7.4	8.9	9.2	9.4	9.8	9.9	..	..
Maize	F1	1.0	2.1	2.1	2.2	2.7	2.6	3.1	4.7	8.1	..	..
Wheat	F2	1.6	2.9	3.0	3.2	3.4	4.5	5.0	5.6	5.7	..	..
LESOTHO												
Wheat	X1	0.2	0.4	0.5	0.5	0.6	..	..	0.8	..	..	..
Beans	X2	0.5	1.1	1.3	1.3	1.4	..	..	..	..	..	..
Peas	X3	0.4	0.9	0.9	1.1	1.2	1.2	..	..	..	..	..
Maize	X4	0.1	0.3	0.3	0.4	0.4	0.4	0.5	0.6	0.6	0.6	..
Sorghum	F1	0.2	0.2	0.3	0.3	0.3	0.3	..	0.5	0.6	..	..
LIBERIA												
Rubber (nonspec. coagul.)	X1	0.8	1.0	1.0	..	..	..	..	..	..	..	..
Coffee (Robusta)	X2	2.1	1.6	1.6	..	..	..	..	..	..	..	..
Cocoa (fair average quality)	X3	2.1	2.3	2.3	..	..	..	..	..	..	..	..
Rice	F1	0.3	0.3	0.3	0.3	..	..	..	..	..	..	..
Cassava	NT1	0.0	0.1	0.1	0.1	..	..	..	..	..	..	..
LIBYA												
Wheat	F1	0.0	..	..	..	..	..	..	..	..	..	..
Olives	F2	..	..	..	..	..	..	..	..	..	..	..
Oranges	F3	..	..	..	..	..	..	..	..	..	..	..
Barley	NT1	..	..	..	..	..	..	..	..	..	..	..
MADAGASCAR												
Coffee (Robusta)	X1	215.0	600.0	800.0	950.0	950.0	950.0	..	..	..	..	..
Vanilla (green)	X2	600.0	1100.0	1200.0	1700.0	2000.0	2000.0	2000.0	..	..	..	..
Cloves	X3	395.0	525.0	600.0	600.0	600.0	600.0	..	..	..	..	..
Rice (paddy)	F1	42.5	100.0	127.5	180.0	250.0	250.0	274.0	..	..	..	..
Cassava	NT1	7.0	55.0	55.0	..	..	..	124.0	..	..	..	..
Sweet potatoes	NT2	..	50.0	60.0	60.0	60.0	..	116.0	..	..	..	..
MALAWI												
Tobacco (flue-cured)	X1	..	..	..	..	..	..	..	..	..	..	..
Tobacco (Northen division dark-fired, G2)	X1	0.4	1.0	1.0	1.1	1.7	2.5	2.8	2.8	2.8	3.5	6.0
Tea (dry leaves)	X2	0.7	1.0	1.0	1.5	1.6	2.0	2.0	2.5	2.5	3.0	5.0
Groundnuts (in shell)	X3	0.3	0.5	0.6	0.6	0.6	0.8	0.7	0.9	1.1	1.6	2.5
Cotton (seed cotton)	X4	..	0.5	0.5	0.7	0.8	0.8	0.8	0.9	0.9	1.0	2.5
Maize	F1	0.1	0.1	0.1	0.2	0.2	0.3	0.3	0.3	0.4	0.5	0.7
Sorghum	F2	0.1	0.2	0.1	0.1	0.2	0.2	0.0	0.0	0.7	0.8	1.1
Rice (paddy, grade 1)	F3	0.1	0.2	0.2	0.3	0.3	0.4	0.4	0.5	0.9	1.5	1.8
Cassava	NT1	0.0	..	..	0.1	0.1	0.1	..	..	..	..	..

8-1. Nominal producer prices (continued)

		Local currency per kilogram										
	Category	1980	1986	1987	1988	1989	1990	1991	1992	1993	1994	1995
MALI												
Cotton (seed cotton)	X1	55.0	85.0	85.0	85.0	85.0	85.0	85.0	85.0	..	..	..
Groundnuts (unshelled)	X2	40.0	..	..	..	..	..	..	..			
Millet	F1	35.0	55.0	55.0	0.0	0.0	77.0	41.5	42.0	..	..	..
Rice (paddy)	F2	37.5	70.0	70.0	70.0	70.0	70.0	70.0	68.0	..	..	..
Sorghum	F3	35.0	55.0	55.0	58.0	60.0	61.0	..	..	..	..	..
Maize	F4	35.0	55.0	55.0	..	..	54.0	35.0	35.0	..	..	..
MAURITANIA												
Sorghum	F1	11.0	15.4	15.4	16.0	16.0	16.0	16.5	16.5	16.8	17.0	17.2
Millet	F2	11.0	..	..	..	..	..	..	..	..	..	..
Rice (paddy)	F3	10.0	..	..	..	..	..	..	·	..	..	..
Maize	F4	15.0	..	..	..	..	..	..	..	..	..	..
MAURITIUS												
Sugarcane	X1	..	..	..	..	..	..	..	..	..		
Tea	X2	..	9.2	7.4	10.3	10.4	13.5	13.4	16.8	16.4	..	..
Maize (12% moisture)	F1	2.0	4.3	4.3	4.8	4.8	4.8	4.8	5.0	5.0	..	..
Rice (paddy, 14% moisture)	F2	1.4	4.9	4.9	5.0	7.0	..	..	..	..	..	..
Potatoes	NT1	2.2	1.9	2.5	2.5	2.8	3.1	3.7	4.1	4.7	..	..
Onions	NT2	4.2	4.2	4.8	5.8	5.7	7.1	7.8	7.7	7.6	..	..
MOROCCO												
Citrus (oranges)	X1	1.3	1.6	1.6	1.7	1.8	1.9	2.0	2.1	2.2	2.3	2.4
Cotton	X3	3.2	6.0	6.0	6.0	6.7	0.0	6.7	5.7	5.7	..	..
Wheat (hard)	F1	1.5	2.2	2.2	2.1	2.3	2.5	2.5	2.9	2.9	2.5	..
Sugarbeet (16.5% sugar)	F2	0.1	0.2	0.2	0.2	0.2	0.2	0.3	0.3	0.3	..	..
Barley	NT1	1.3	1.3	1.3	1.2	1.3	1.5	1.5	2.0	2.0	2.1	..
MOZAMBIQUE												
Cashew nuts	X1	7.5	13.2	86.0	..	..	..	..	..	..	..	..
Cotton (seed, prime grade)	X2	11.0	16.0	65.0	..	..	..	..	..	..	..	..
Tea	X3	25.6	..	..	..	..	..	..	..	..	..	..
Maize	F1	..	..	..	..	..	..	..	..	..	..	..
Rice	F2	6.2	16.0	48.0	..	..	..	..	..	..	..	..
Cassava	NT1	2.0	..	..	..	..	..	..	..	..	..	..
NAMIBIA												
Wheat	F1	..	0.4	0.4	0.4	0.5	0.6	0.6	0.7	0.7	0.7	..
Maize (white)	F2	..	0.3	0.3	0.4	0.4	0.4	0.5	0.5	0.6	0.7	..
NIGER												
Cowpeas	X1	45.0	80.0	80.0	..	..	..	..	..	..	..	..
Cotton (unginned, top grade)	X2	62.0	120.0	120.0	120.0	130.0	110.0	70.0	70.0	77.0	..	..
Groundnuts (in shell)	X3	50.0	130.0	130.0	130.0	132.0	133.0	134.0	135.0	140.0	143.8	146.4
Millet	F1	50.0	..	..	..	..	..	..	..	..	..	..
Sorghum (red)	F2	50.0	..	..	..	..	..	..	..	..	..	..
NIGERIA												
Cocoa (bean)	X1	1.3	3.5	7.5	11.0	10.1	8.5	10.2	12.7	..	..	..
Palm kernels	X2	0.2	0.4	0.9	1.0	1.3	1.2	..	..	..	..	..
Cotton (seed cotton)	X3	0.4	1.0	4.0	4.5	2.4	2.6	4.2	3.8	..	..	..
Groundnuts (in shell)	X4	0.4	1.0	2.3	2.3	4.8	4.3	6.3	6.8	19.7	10.6	..
Sorghum	F1	0.2	0.6	0.8	1.6	2.0	1.7	3.6	4.7	7.0	5.3	..
Millet	F2	0.2	0.6	0.6	1.3	2.1	1.7	3.4	5.7	6.6	6.2	..
Maize	F3	0.2	0.5	0.6	1.6	2.7	2.1	3.3	5.5	7.5	5.6	..
Rice (paddy)	F4	0.3	1.0	2.3	3.8	6.3	6.3	7.5	12.6	18.8	12.3	..
Yams	NT1	..	1.0	0.9	2.0	2.4	2.3	2.6	5.9	11.7	14.4	..
Cassava (gari)	NT2	..	0.3	0.4	0.8	1.2	2.2	2.1	2.3	4.6	4.5	..
RWANDA												
Coffee	X1	120.0	122.5	125.0	125.0	125.0	99.7	107.4	115.0	..	..	427.0
Tea	X2	75.0	75.0	75.0	..	..	..	..	..	..	..	..
Beans (dry)	F1	20.3	22.3	28.6	30.5	38.4	37.9	40.8	40.2	..	..	90.0
Sorghum	F2	12.7	20.2	20.2	19.3	23.3	24.5	29.3	33.6	..	..	141.0
Maize	F3	11.9	15.6	15.4	13.6	24.7	26.9	32.4	29.0	..	..	45.0
Bananas	NT1	..	..	..	10.6	10.7	12.7	15.9	14.9	..	..	..
Sweet potatoes	NT2	5.7	6.1	6.2	5.5	9.4	9.8	9.9	6.8	..	..	24.0
SAO TOME & PRINCIPE												
Cocoa	X1	16.5	24.0	25.0	26.0	27.0	28.0	29.0	30.0	..	..	..
Maize	F1	1.9	2.5	2.6	2.6	2.7	2.7	2.8	2.8	..	..	..
Cassava	NT1	2.1	2.7	2.7	2.8	2.8	2.9	2.9	3.0	..	..	..

8-1. Nominal producer prices (continued)

	Category	Local currency per kilogram										
		1980	1986	1987	1988	1989	1990	1991	1992	1993	1994	1995
SENEGAL												
Groundnuts (in shell)	X1	50.0	90.0	90.0	70.0	70.0	70.0	70.0	70.0	100.0	120.0	125.0
Cotton (seed cotton, first quality)	X2	60.0	100.0	100.0	100.0	100.0	100.0	100.0	100.0	115.0	150.0	170.0
Millet	F1	40.0	70.0	70.0	70.0	70.0	70.0	70.0	70.0	70.0	70.0	70.0
Rice (paddy)	F2	41.5	85.0	85.0	85.0	85.0	85.0	85.0	85.0	90.0	..	..
Maize	F3	37.0	70.0	70.0	70.0	70.0	70.0	70.0	70.0	70.0	70.0	70.0
Sorghum	F4	40.0	70.0	70.0	70.0	70.0	70.0	70.0	70.0	70.0	70.0	70.0
SIERRA LEONE												
Cocoa	X1	2.1	17.8	30.2	30.2	..	..	..	..	..	..	..
Coffee (Robusta)	X2	2.0	25.0	40.3	..	..	..	..	..	..	..	..
Palm kernels	X3	0.2	1.1	1.3	..	..	..	..	..	..	..	..
Rice (paddy)	F1	0.4	2.8	7.4	22.2	29.0	37.0	44.4	..	..	..	..
Cassava	NT1	0.3	4.9	..	..	..	..	..	..	..	..	..
SOMALIA												
Bananas	X1	..	..	..	..	..	..	..	..	..	..	..
Maize	F1	5.5	21.4	34.5	..	..	..	..	..	..	..	..
Sorghum	F2	5.8	18.9	22.7	..	..	..	..	..	..	..	..
Sesame (seed)	NT1	25.2	61.6	76.4	..	..	..	..	..	..	..	..
SOUTH AFRICA												
Maize	X1	0.1	0.2	0.3	0.3	0.3	0.3	0.4	0.5	0.4	0.4	0.6
Wheat	X2	0.2	0.4	0.4	0.4	0.5	0.5	0.6	0.7	0.8	0.8	0.8
Sugar cane	X3	0.0	0.0	0.0	0.0	..	0.1	0.1	0.1	0.1	0.1	0.0
Sorghum	F1	0.1	0.2	0.2	0.2	0.2	0.2	0.3	0.5	0.5	0.4	0.4
Barley	F2	0.2	0.3	0.3	0.3	0.4	0.5	0.5	0.6	0.7	0.7	0.7
SUDAN												
Cotton (seed cotton, long-staple, grade 1)	X1	0.4	1.8	2.5	4.3	4.8	6.7	14.1	37.2	..	..	..
Groundnuts (El-Obeid, in shell)	X2	0.2	1.1	1.2	1.8	4.4	23.5	21.1	22.6	..	..	..
Sesame (El-Obeid, mixed)	X3	0.3	1.3	1.6	5.0	6.5	12.7	30.9	41.6	..	..	..
Gum arabic (El-Obeid)	X4	0.0	6.8	9.0	9.4	10.2	10.3	18.9	17.8	..	..	..
Sorghum	F1	0.1	0.2	0.8	0.9	1.9	11.4	6.6	11.8	..	..	..
Wheat	F2	0.2	0.7	1.0	2.3	2.9	5.7	8.3	11.4	33.3	..	..
SWAZILAND												
Sugarcane (sucrose)	X1	0.0	0.0	0.0	0.0	0.0	..	..	..	..	..	..
Citrus	X2	0.2	0.4	0.2	0.4	0.4	..	..	..	..	..	..
Pineapple	X3	0.0	0.3	0.2	0.2	0.3	0.4	0.5	0.5	0.5	0.6	0.6
Cotton (seed cotton)	X4	0.5	0.9	0.9	1.1	1.1	..	..	..	..	..	..
Maize	F1	0.1	0.3	0.3	0.3	0.4	..	..	..	..	..	..
TANZANIA												
Coffee (Arabica) (parchment)	X1	9.0	50.8	66.0	90.0	..	..	..	..	..	..	..
Cotton (seed cotton, AR)	X2	3.2	16.9	19.5	22.4	28.0	..	..	..	..	..	..
Tea (green leaves)	X3	1.5	7.6	9.9	13.4	..	..	..	..	..	..	..
Maize	F1	1.0	6.3	8.2	9.0	11.0	..	..	..	..	..	..
Sorghum	F2	1.0	4.8	6.0	0.0	0.0	..	..	..	..	..	..
Rice (paddy)	F3	1.8	9.6	14.4	17.3	19.0	..	..	..	..	..	..
Millet	F4	1.5	4.8	6.0	6.6	7.3	..	..	..	..	..	..
Cassava (grade 1, Makopa)	NT1	0.7	3.6	4.5	5.0	5.5	..	..	..	..	..	..
TOGO												
Coffee (Robusta)	X1	200.0	365.0	400.0	350.0	175.0	175.0	185.0	140.0	350.0	650.0	..
Cocoa	X2	220.0	330.0	360.0	300.0	225.0	250.0	250.0	225.0	300.0	550.0	..
Cotton (seed cotton)	X3	52.0	105.0	105.0	95.0	95.0	100.0	100.0	90.0	110.0	145.0	..
Maize	F1	68.4	73.0	72.0	79.0	60.0	61.0	58.0	73.0	43.0	62.0	..
Sorghum	F2	68.0	76.0	66.0	98.0	69.0	68.0	67.0	92.0	64.0	68.0	..
Millet	F3	66.7	59.0	61.0	87.0	72.0	58.0	75.0	87.0	61.0	52.0	..
Cassava	NT1	20.3	30.0	32.0	26.0	30.0	23.0	28.0	29.0	30.0	31.0	..
Yams	NT2	48.5	61.0	63.0	63.0	68.0	68.0	66.0	66.0	63.0	59.0	..
TUNISIA												
Olives	X1	0.1	0.1	0.2	0.2	0.2	0.2	0.3	0.3	0.3	0.3	0.3
Citrus (oranges)	X2	0.1	0.1	0.2	0.2	0.2	0.3	0.3	..	..	..	..
Wheat	F1	0.1	0.2	0.2	0.2	0.2	0.2	0.2	0.3	0.3	0.3	0.3
Barley	NT1	0.1	0.1	0.1	0.1	0.1	0.2	0.2	0.2	0.2	0.2	0.2

8-1. Nominal producer prices (continued)

| | Category | *Local currency per kilogram* | | | | | | | | | | |
		1980	1986	1987	1988	1989	1990	1991	1992	1993	1994	1995
UGANDA												
Coffee	X1	0.1	8.5	24.0	44.5	60.0	97.5	210.0	190.0	..	..	..
Cotton (seed cotton)	X2	0.2	4.0	19.0	56.0	105.0	175.0	286.7	340.0	..	..	..
Tea (greenleaf)	X3	0.0	5.0	10.0	20.0	35.0	38.3	45.0	70.0	..	..	..
Millet	F1	0.2	7.4	17.6	30.7	109.6	134.8	142.6	294.3	..	..	..
Maize	F2	0.1	4.6	11.3	26.0	82.9	72.0	80.0	225.0	..	..	..
Sorghum	F3	0.1	5.4	18.3	30.5	84.6	104.0	115.3	237.3	..	..	..
Cassava	NT1	0.1	2.3	9.3	22.5	35.5	39.5	76.0	163.0	..	..	..
Plantains	NT2	0.1	3.9	7.5	13.6	46.9	51.2	64.5	156.7	..	..	..
ZAMBIA												
Cotton (seed cotton)	X1	0.5	1.0	1.6	3.0	3.6	9.7	..	..	..	..	..
Tobacco (Virginia)	X2	1.6	5.1	6.3	14.0	14.4	60.0	94.5	..	..	..	..
Sunflower (seeds)	X3	0.3	0.8	1.4	1.8	3.2	6.4	11.4	..	..	..	..
Maize	F1	0.1	0.6	0.9	0.9	1.2	3.2	5.6	..	..	..	..
Wheat	F2	0.2	1.0	1.2	2.1	..	5.4	8.6	..	..	..	..
Cassava	NT1	..	0.6	0.7	1.0	1.4	3.2	5.4	..	..	..	..
ZIMBABWE												
Tobacco	X1	0.8	3.1	2.2	3.9	4.0	6.5	11.6	8.1	6.5	..	..
Cotton (seed cotton)	X2	0.4	0.8	0.8	0.9	1.1	1.4	1.6	1.4	2.6	..	..
Sugarcane	X3	0.0	..	..	..	..	..	..	..	..	..	..
Maize	X4	0.1	0.2	0.2	0.2	0.2	0.2	0.3	0.6	0.9	..	..
Wheat	F1	0.2	0.3	0.3	0.4	0.4	0.5	0.5	1.0	1.5	..	..

Notes: The categories of crops are defined in the technical notes.

Categories are mutually exclusive, and ordering is intended to reflect relative importance of these crops as of 1986-88. In many cases official markets operat simultaneously with parallel or open market activites. Where a large majority of marketed production is believed to pass through the official channels, th official price is also reported as the farmgate price. In most cases, only very rough estimates of the share of marketed production passing through each channel is available.

The CPI is based in 1987 rescaled from price index based in 1980.

For each country one to four export crops (X1,...,X4) are presented in order of importance, in terms of value of total production

Similarly, up to three traded food crops (F1,...,F3) and two nontraded staples (NT1,NT2) are included

8-2. Food price index

	Index (average 1995 = 100)											Average annual percentage growth		
	1980	1988	1989	1990	1991	1992	1993	1994	1995	1996	1997	75-84	85-89	90-MR
SUB-SAHARAN AFRICA	12	42	48	52	61	69	71	90	100	108	124	..	13.2	12.9
excluding South Africa	11	44	48	53	61	68	70	89	100	109	125	..	13.1	12.8
excl. S. Africa & Nigeria	14	45	49	55	62	69	71	89	100	108	125	..	11.3	12.4
Angola	..	..	..	..	0	0	0	4	100	..	..	..	..	1,085.8
Benin	..	..	..	..	..	..	..	..	..	..	..	..	..	..
Botswana	18	45	49	55	61	72	83	90	100	113	125	..	9.6	12.6
Burkina Faso	..	84	81	80	87	81	76	89	100	115	..	..	-2.6	4.4
Burundi	35	54	64	69	74	73	72	85	100	..	..	..	3.3	6.3
Cameroon	..	..	..	..	..	..	..	..	..	..	..	..	..	..
Cape Verde	..	..	..	..	..	..	..	..	..	..	..	..	..	..
Central African Republic	..	70	71	71	69	68	65	81	100	106	107	..	-2.1	6.4
Chad	..	..	..	..	..	..	..	..	..	..	..	..	..	..
Comoros	..	..	..	..	..	..	..	..	..	..	..	..	..	..
Congo, Democratic Rep. of	..	..	..	..	..	..	..	..	..	..	..	..	..	..
Congo, Republic of	42	66	66	67	65	59	63	94	100	107	..	..	-1.0	8.0
Côte d'Ivoire	..	..	..	..	..	..	..	..	..	..	..	..	..	..
Djibouti	..	..	..	..	..	..	..	..	..	..	..	..	..	..
Equatorial Guinea	..	..	..	..	..	..	..	..	..	..	..	..	..	..
Eritrea	..	..	..	..	..	..	..	..	..	..	..	..	..	..
Ethiopia	34	45	48	51	71	80	81	89	100	..	..	..	0.4	13.2
Gabon	..	69	75	84	83	69	70	93	100	107	..	..	0.1	4.5
Gambia, The	14	60	64	73	79	86	93	92	100	101	103	..	24.8	5.9
Ghana	1	19	23	33	36	39	49	62	100	136	..	..	23.1	26.6
Guinea	..	40	46	60	70	81	88	93	100	101	..	..	..	11.2
Guinea-Bissau	..	..	..	..	..	..	..	..	..	..	..	..	..	..
Kenya	..	..	..	32	40	54	78	102	100	108	125	..	..	21.8
Lesotho	15	42	46	52	61	76	84	89	100	111	..	..	12.9	13.4
Liberia	..	..	..	..	..	..	..	..	..	..	..	..	..	..
Madagascar	7	28	30	34	38	44	47	66	100	119	124	..	13.8	21.6
Malawi	5	16	18	20	23	30	37	52	100	145	..	..	21.1	34.9
Mali	..	..	..	..	..	..	..	..	..	..	..	..	..	..
Mauritania	..	..	..	..	..	..	..	..	..	..	..	..	..	..
Mauritius	..	56	64	71	74	76	87	95	100	105	..	..	6.7	7.5
Mozambique	..	..	..	..	..	..	..	..	..	..	..	..	..	..
Namibia	..	42	51	59	62	74	79	90	100	107	..	..	14.3	11.4
Niger	..	..	-	..	..	..	..	..	..	..	..	..	..	..
Nigeria	4	17	25	26	29	43	68	100	100	224	..	..	23.1	36.4
Rwanda	..	..	..	..	..	..	..	..	..	..	..	..	..	..
São Tomé and Principe	..	..	..	..	..	..	..	..	..	..	..	..	..	..
Senegal	43	69	69	70	68	67	66	91	100	102	..	..	0.6	6.6
Seychelles	..	..	..	..	..	..	..	..	..	..	..	..	..	..
Sierra Leone	..	..	..	..	..	..	..	..	..	..	..	..	..	..
Somalia	..	..	..	..	..	..	..	..	..	..	..	..	..	..
South Africa	12	39	44	51	60	76	81	92	100	106	116	..	17.3	13.0
Sudan	..	..	..	..	..	..	..	..	..	..	..	..	..	..
Swaziland	..	..	..	..	..	..	..	..	..	..	..	..	..	..
Tanzania	3	23	28	31	38	46	57	75	100	120	141	..	31.3	24.0
Togo	..	..	..	..	..	..	..	..	..	..	..	..	..	..
Uganda	..	..	..	47	58	96	92	96	100	107	..	..	..	13.4
Zambia	0	1	1	3	5	17	50	75	100	146	..	..	57.7	103.6
Zimbabwe	6	17	20	23	29	45	62	78	100	127	149	..	11.8	31.0
NORTH AFRICA	23	51	57	63	71	75	85	92	100	106	110	..	10.1	8.9
Algeria	13	22	24	29	35	43	54	76	100	120	127	..	9.7	25.6
Egypt, Arab Republic	11	42	53	61	71	77	83	91	100	108	112	..	21.6	9.7
Libya	..	..	..	..	..	..	..	..	..	..	..	..	..	..
Morocco	32	59	60	65	70	74	87	93	100	101	100	..	3.7	7.4
Tunisia	34	66	71	76	83	86	89	92	100	104	108	..	7.4	5.2
ALL AFRICA	13	42	49	55	62	71	74	90	100	108	120	..	13.6	12.1

8-3. Food production index

	Index (average 1989-91 = 100)										Average annual percentage growth		
	1980	*1988*	*1989*	*1990*	*1991*	*1992*	*1993*	*1994*	*1995*	*1996*	*1997*	*75-84*	*85-89*	*90-MR*
SUB-SAHARAN AFRICA	78	95	98	99	104	104	108	112	113	118	118	1.0	3.9	2.6
excluding South Africa	77	95	97	99	104	105	109	113	115	119	119	1.0	3.9	2.8
excl. S. Africa & Nigeria	81	97	99	99	103	102	104	107	110	114	114	1.1	3.2	2.0
Angola	93	101	99	98	103	108	105	121	124	134	133	-0.7	1.0	4.4
Benin	62	91	95	99	106	109	111	116	130	131	127	3.1	3.6	4.2
Botswana	73	90	93	100	107	103	103	87	103	108	102	0.7	-1.9	0.6
Burkina Faso	59	103	98	92	110	115	121	120	120	124	123	2.4	6.7	3.4
Burundi	79	100	93	103	105	108	106	89	97	97	96	0.3	3.3	-0.6
Cameroon	83	95	97	100	103	102	107	109	115	122	119	0.6	1.5	2.9
Cape Verde	62	121	107	100	93	83	137	96	126	96	96	1.8	19.7	0.4
Central African Republic	80	98	100	100	100	106	108	112	114	130	124	2.0	4.8	3.3
Chad	93	97	97	91	112	113	98	118	119	114	119	0.9	4.2	2.8
Comoros	86	97	99	99	102	102	107	108	114	112	118	0.6	4.0	2.2
Congo, Democratic Rep. of	73	93	97	101	103	105	104	106	106	105	104	2.3	3.4	0.8
Congo, Republic of	80	102	101	101	99	101	104	107	112	116	116	2.4	2.3	2.2
Côte d'Ivoire	70	98	97	101	102	106	109	110	117	126	115	4.1	3.7	2.8
Djibouti	54	94	115	108	78	82	75	79	82	83	83	10.9	9.2	-3.3
Equatorial Guinea	88	106	99	101	100	99	101	93	87	98	98	0.0	2.1	-0.8
Eritrea	..	..	..	..	..	..	88	117	101	100	107	..	..	2.2
Ethiopia	90	93	96	102	102	106	..	..	..	..	..	1.8	2.8	..
Gabon	81	95	97	98	105	103	100	102	104	105	107	3.0	3.0	0.9
Gambia, The	72	101	121	84	95	73	87	91	89	72	84	-1.1	3.6	-3.0
Ghana	74	94	106	88	106	110	117	130	146	149	148	-1.6	4.1	6.4
Guinea	98	85	93	100	108	115	117	121	126	129	133	0.9	-1.9	4.4
Guinea-Bissau	67	91	99	103	98	104	106	112	113	108	112	3.3	2.3	1.7
Kenya	67	98	100	100	100	98	93	101	102	102	105	2.2	7.3	0.5
Lesotho	88	107	106	112	82	84	101	109	93	120	101	1.0	3.3	0.8
Liberia	..	..	..	..	..	..	..	..	..	..	..	..	..	..
Madagascar	84	95	99	100	101	102	105	102	104	105	107	1.3	1.2	0.9
Malawi	89	102	98	97	105	79	112	90	105	111	100	1.8	1.2	1.1
Mali	77	93	100	99	102	101	107	114	115	114	127	3.3	5.0	3.0
Mauritania	87	92	98	101	102	95	92	95	99	106	105	2.8	3.5	0.6
Mauritius	78	98	96	101	102	107	105	99	103	106	109	0.0	1.6	1.0
Mozambique	100	95	98	106	96	81	93	91	103	123	133	-1.4	1.1	3.3
Namibia	109	94	101	97	102	106	113	115	111	120	126	-2.6	5.4	3.0
Niger	104	106	96	89	115	115	103	125	110	124	121	2.7	6.7	3.2
Nigeria	59	85	92	98	110	118	125	129	132	135	136	0.5	6.8	5.1
Rwanda	88	94	103	100	97	93	83	66	73	77	81	4.1	0.3	-4.3
São Tomé and Principe	113	115	105	97	98	120	121	117	123	122	122	-2.5	0.6	2.9
Senegal	60	92	105	95	100	92	103	104	115	101	112	-3.6	8.3	1.4
Seychelles	131	95	102	96	102	100	93	118	146	142	141	-0.3	..	-0.3
Sierra Leone	85	97	100	100	100	93	92	98	91	96	97	0.8	2.1	-0.6
Somalia	..	..	..	..	..	..	..	..	..	..	..	..	..	..
South Africa	91	97	102	98	100	85	97	101	88	105	100	0.6	4.0	0.0
Sudan	103	114	96	93	111	125	114	132	129	145	146	1.4	1.3	5.7
Swaziland	82	95	98	97	105	98	94	102	89	98	93	3.3	1.3	-0.8
Tanzania	74	93	101	100	100	94	96	96	100	98	94	3.5	2.2	-0.5
Togo	76	92	99	103	98	101	120	99	120	132	138	1.2	3.6	4.2
Uganda	67	88	96	101	103	104	109	109	111	102	110	-1.6	3.6	1.3
Zambia	75	109	109	94	97	82	117	98	88	105	94	-1.4	8.3	-0.5
Zimbabwe	76	110	101	104	96	64	88	98	74	105	106	-1.6	4.1	0.2
NORTH AFRICA	68	88	94	98	108	106	106	107	109	126	116	1.7	4.8	2.8
Algeria	72	87	93	94	114	117	111	100	117	129	108	0.3	3.4	2.5
Egypt, Arab Republic	69	91	94	101	105	111	114	114	125	132	133	2.1	4.4	4.3
Libya	85	87	96	100	104	100	93	90	90	101	101	4.8	0.1	-0.2
Morocco	58	92	100	93	107	83	83	109	77	113	95	2.0	10.3	0.0
Tunisia	74	62	79	97	124	105	115	84	84	136	105	0.5	-1.0	1.9
ALL AFRICA	76	93	97	98	105	104	108	111	112	120	118	1.1	4.0	2.6

8-4. Nonfood production index

	Index (average 1989-91 = 100)											Average annual percentage growth		
	1980	1988	1989	1990	1991	1992	1993	1994	1995	1996	1997	75-84	85-89	90-MR
SUB-SAHARAN AFRICA	83	98	100	98	101	100	96	100	100	105	108	2.0	1.0	0.9
excluding South Africa	82	98	100	99	101	100	97	100	100	110	111	2.2	1.3	1.2
excl. S. Africa & Nigeria	83	99	100	98	101	100	96	100	100	105	111	2.1	1.1	1.0
Angola	209	121	112	93	95	89	95	84	91	96	99	-19.4	-0.8	-0.9
Benin	12	78	73	100	126	117	195	174	253	279	295	8.1	3.9	19.0
Botswana	100	100	100	100	100	100	100	100	100	100	81	0.0	0.0	-1.4
Burkina Faso	35	84	90	111	100	100	92	96	92	125	206	8.9	10.5	6.0
Burundi	59	104	96	97	107	113	87	112	79	72	59	5.3	3.4	-5.6
Cameroon	86	115	100	95	105	91	74	81	87	100	117	3.5	0.9	0.5
Cape Verde	94	95	170	95	36	21	21	21	21	21	21	-3.0	6.1	-20.9
Central African Republic	89	119	107	102	91	78	61	94	85	131	137	-0.5	..	3.0
Chad	51	85	94	97	109	76	65	73	99	138	138	-4.4	11.2	4.0
Comoros	64	107	114	114	72	79	65	79	86	79	69	-5.0	4.6	-4.5
Congo, Democratic Rep. of	105	108	100	103	97	94	92	92	90	70	61	0.6	-3.5	-5.4
Congo, Republic of	155	108	114	92	94	97	99	102	99	99	93	0.0	-5.1	-0.7
Côte d'Ivoire	77	85	102	107	91	67	76	81	84	81	113	0.2	12.5	-0.6
Djibouti	..	..	..	..	..	..	..	..	..	..	..	..	..	..
Equatorial Guinea	86	100	100	100	100	100	100	100	100	100	93	2.2	0.4	-0.5
Eritrea	..	..	..	..	..	..	96	99	98	100	100	..	..	0.7
Ethiopia	..	..	..	..	..	..	92	101	111	111	111	..	..	4.8
Gabon	36	134	153	69	78	67	93	124	142	148	149	19.5	21.2	6.9
Gambia, The	55	79	132	73	95	123	157	180	168	213	51	22.5	3.9	1.5
Ghana	86	57	73	90	137	178	242	175	192	251	275	-6.0	4.4	16.2
Guinea	48	66	89	100	111	120	121	117	112	94	90	0.9	11.1	-0.2
Guinea-Bissau	111	152	88	109	103	66	83	75	100	100	100	25.0	-7.5	0.6
Kenya	62	94	99	101	101	94	99	98	114	117	104	6.1	4.5	1.7
Lesotho	87	59	85	111	105	176	176	176	183	113	113	2.0	-9.1	3.9
Liberia	..	..	..	..	..	..	..	..	..	..	..	..	..	..
Madagascar	90	97	107	101	93	86	91	89	83	84	73	-1.0	0.9	-3.7
Malawi	59	81	90	99	110	109	117	95	120	132	142	6.4	2.0	4.6
Mali	55	73	94	96	111	127	97	106	135	162	181	7.6	11.9	7.6
Mauritania	..	..	..	..	..	..	..	..	..	..	..	..	..	..
Mauritius	84	118	99	99	102	104	105	92	73	51	39	5.0	-5.6	-10.3
Mozambique	251	72	87	90	122	116	117	124	126	127	159	-6.7	-4.3	6.1
Namibia	279	123	117	110	74	87	93	120	106	93	106	-6.7	-1.0	0.2
Niger	84	128	127	84	89	131	89	86	86	86	86	-5.3	4.4	-3.3
Nigeria	43	62	86	106	108	116	116	107	119	111	93	-8.0	21.9	0.9
Rwanda	61	119	100	107	93	116	85	27	62	50	58	6.4	3.6	-10.6
São Tomé and Principe	321	166	43	198	59	70	107	118	134	134	134	1.1	-20.6	9.7
Senegal	51	100	79	91	131	124	129	129	97	129	174	2.1	-2.4	6.3
Seychelles	21	52	74	108	119	110	121	121	111	110	111	7.6	..	7.6
Sierra Leone	44	98	99	100	101	101	96	106	97	97	114	11.2	5.0	0.7
Somalia	..	..	..	..	..	..	..	..	..	..	..	..	..	..
South Africa	107	98	103	98	99	90	72	68	61	70	68	0.7	0.0	-6.3
Sudan	102	119	119	85	97	75	74	104	117	119	112	-1.6	-7.4	2.5
Swaziland	85	95	115	92	93	21	36	27	25	55	43	-3.4	12.1	-12.3
Tanzania	97	96	97	93	110	118	121	93	96	125	115	-2.2	4.3	1.8
Togo	34	87	87	90	123	126	124	121	105	129	145	5.1	20.5	4.7
Uganda	82	97	108	88	104	84	107	141	131	195	161	-5.8	0.7	8.6
Zambia	49	119	109	78	113	60	134	68	101	86	96	5.1	7.4	-0.5
Zimbabwe	77	102	100	90	110	101	117	106	103	129	137	2.1	1.8	3.8
NORTH AFRICA	73	93	98	102	101	98	94	89	87	95	101	3.8	1.1	-0.9
Algeria	46	93	98	98	104	106	111	107	106	107	107	10.1	1.1	1.1
Egypt, Arab Republic	171	108	99	100	101	121	135	86	85	115	114	0.6	-6.5	0.4
Libya	105	89	98	102	100	98	94	89	87	86	88	0.2	-1.6	-2.2
Morocco	46	98	99	102	99	94	89	92	91	95	101	0.9	6.2	-0.6
Tunisia	73	92	95	103	102	92	87	74	75	74	74	3.8	3.8	-4.6
ALL AFRICA	82	98	99	99	101	100	96	99	99	100	106	2.2	1.2	0.4

8-5. Food production per capita index

	Index (average 1989-91 = 100)											Average annual percentage growth		
	1980	*1988*	*1989*	*1990*	*1991*	*1992*	*1993*	*1994*	*1995*	*1996*	*1997*	*75-84*	*85-89*	*90-MR*
SUB-SAHARAN AFRICA	105	101	101	100	99	96	96	95	97	95	94	-1.5	0.4	-0.8
excluding South Africa	105	101	101	100	99	97	97	95	97	96	94	-1.5	0.3	-0.8
excl. S. Africa & Nigeria	105	101	101	100	99	96	96	95	97	95	94	-1.6	0.3	-0.8
Angola	122	107	102	98	100	101	96	107	106	111	106	-3.3	-1.8	1.1
Benin	85	97	98	99	103	103	102	103	113	110	104	0.3	0.5	1.3
Botswana	103	96	96	100	104	97	95	78	90	92	86	-2.8	-5.2	-2.0
Burkina Faso	78	109	101	92	107	108	111	107	104	105	101	-0.1	3.8	0.5
Burundi	105	106	95	103	103	103	100	82	87	85	82	-2.1	0.2	-2.7
Cameroon	110	101	100	100	100	97	99	98	100	104	98	-2.2	-1.3	0.1
Cape Verde	73	126	109	100	91	79	127	87	111	83	81	0.8	17.6	-2.1
Central African Republic	..	..	..	..	..	..	..	..	..	..	..			
Chad	116	102	99	91	110	108	91	106	104	98	99	-1.3	2.1	0.2
Comoros	117	103	102	99	99	95	97	95	97	92	94	-2.9	0.8	-0.9
Congo, Democratic Rep. of	101	100	100	101	99	97	93	91	87	84	81	-0.8	0.1	-2.8
Congo, Republic of	106	108	104	101	96	95	95	95	97	97	94	-0.5	-0.7	-0.8
Côte d'Ivoire	100	105	101	101	98	99	98	97	100	105	94	0.2	0.3	-0.3
Djibouti	98	103	119	107	74	76	68	69	70	69	67	4.0	2.8	-6.2
Equatorial Guinea	142	110	101	101	98	95	94	84	77	84	82	-2.2	-1.0	-3.3
Eritrea	..	..	..	..	..	..	84	109	91	88	90	..	..	-0.8
Ethiopia	..	..	..	..	..	..	98	95	101	106	103	..	..	2.2
Gabon	109	101	100	98	102	97	92	91	90	89	88	-0.1	-0.1	-1.9
Gambia, The	102	110	125	84	91	67	77	77	73	58	66	-4.1	-0.5	-6.4
Ghana	103	100	110	88	103	104	107	116	127	125	121	-4.0	0.8	3.4
Guinea	128	92	97	100	103	104	100	99	99	99	101	-0.8	-4.3	0.0
Guinea-Bissau	82	95	101	103	96	100	100	103	102	96	97	-0.5	0.4	-0.3
Kenya	94	105	103	100	97	92	·85	89	88	86	87	-1.6	3.7	-2.3
Lesotho	115	112	109	111	80	79	93	98	82	103	84	-1.8	0.6	-1.7
Liberia	..	..	..	..	..	..	..	..	..	..	..	..	..	..
Madagascar	117	102	102	100	98	95	96	89	89	86	85	-1.8	-2.1	-2.3
Malawi	134	111	101	97	103	77	108	87	101	104	92	-1.3	-4.1	0.0
Mali	104	99	103	99	99	95	97	101	98	95	102	0.9	1.9	-0.2
Mauritania	112	97	100	101	99	91	85	86	87	91	88	0.3	1.0	-1.9
Mauritius	85	99	97	101	101	105	102	95	98	99	101	-1.4	0.8	-0.1
Mozambique	118	98	100	106	93	75	83	78	85	98	104	-4.1	0.4	-0.4
Namibia	143	99	104	97	100	100	104	103	98	103	105	-5.2	2.5	0.4
Niger	144	113	100	89	111	108	93	109	94	101	96	-0.6	3.4	-0.2
Nigeria	79	91	95	98	107	111	114	115	114	113	110	-2.2	3.8	2.0
Rwanda	117	95	101	99	100	103	100	86	97	98	95	0.8	-3.4	-0.9
São Tomé and Principe	143	120	107	97	96	114	113	107	110	107	105	-5.1	-1.7	0.7
Senegal	79	97	108	95	97	87	95	94	·101	87	93	-6.3	5.3	-1.2
Seychelles	..	..	..	..	..	..	..	..	..	..	..	..	..	..
Sierra Leone	105	101	102	99	99	91	90	94	86	90	87	-1.2	-0.3	-1.9
Somalia	..	..	..	..	..	..	..	..	..	..	..			
South Africa	116	101	105	98	97	81	91	93	79	92	85	-1.9	1.6	-2.2
Sudan	133	119	99	93	108	120	107	122	116	128	126	-1.6	-1.0	3.5
Swaziland	108	101	101	97	102	93	87	91	78	83	76	0.3	-1.5	-3.5
Tanzania	102	100	104	100	96	88	87	84	85	81	76	0.3	-0.9	-3.6
Togo	103	97	102	103	95	95	109	87	104	111	112	-1.5	0.5	1.2
Uganda	85	93	99	101	100	97	99	95	94	84	88	-4.5	1.3	-1.9
Zambia	94	114	112	94	94	79	109	89	78	92	80	-4.3	5.7	-2.7
Zimbabwe	106	116	104	104	93	61	81	89	65	90	89	-4.6	0.7	-2.2
NORTH AFRICA	94	93	96	97	105	101	104	91	76	112	92	-1.4	1.4	-0.8
Algeria	96	91	95	94	111	112	104	91	104	112	92	-2.8	0.7	0.1
Egypt, Arab Republic	88	96	96	102	103	107	107	105	113	117	116	-0.3	1.8	2.3
Libya	127	93	99	100	101	93	84	78	75	82	80	0.3	-3.6	-3.6
Morocco	72	96	102	93	105	79	78	101	70	101	83	-0.3	8.0	-1.9
Tunisia	94	64	81	97	122	101	109	78	76	122	92	-2.1	-3.2	0.0
ALL AFRICA	105	101	101	99	100	97	97	94	97	97	92	-1.4	0.5	-0.9

8-6. Volume of food output, by major food crop

	1980	1989	1990	1991	1992	1993	1994	1995	1996	1997	1998	Average annual percentage growth		
				Thousands of metric tons								75-84	85-89	90-MR
ALGERIA														
Wheat	1511	1,152	750	1,869	1,837	1,017	714	1,500	2,983	662	2,280	-4.3	-3.8	5.1
Citrus	422	268	281	324	362	361	376	323	334	351	408	-6.9	1.5	2.0
Dates	201	210	206	209	261	262	317	285	361	303	387	2.5	2.4	4.6
Barley	794	790	833	1,810	1,398	408	234	585	1,800	191	700	1.4	-4.7	-2.0
Potatoes	591	1,001	809	1,077	1,158	1,065	716	1,200	1,150	948	1,115	0.6	11.0	1.1
ANGOLA														
Maize	360	204	180	299	320	275	201	211	398	370	505	-5.9	-2.6	4.5
Millet	57	63	63	67	75	40	60	61	102	62	89	-4.7	5.3	2.2
Cassava	1150	1,600	1,600	1,640	1,861	1,861	2,379	2,500	2,600	2,326	3,211	-1.7	4.2	5.0
Sweet potatoes	165	165	165	170	180	185	180	190	195	190	195	0.5	-0.4	1.3
BENIN														
Palm oil	34	20	20	14	14	14	9	11	13	13	13	0.0	-9.9	-3.5
Maize	271	424	410	431	460	483	492	597	504	714	714	4.5	0.5	3.2
Sorghum	56	106	99	115	110	106	113	108	112	120	120	-0.5	5.2	0.7
Cassava	583	977	937	1,046	1,041	1,147	1,146	1,343	1,452	1,926	1,926	0.5	6.6	4.3
Yam	694	1,010	1,046	1,178	1,125	1,185	1,250	1,259	1,346	1,408	1,408	5.0	4.7	2.1
BOTSWANA														
Livestock (1,000 heads)	149	286	317	349	300	250	238	250	240	240	250	-6.6	10.5	-2.0
Onions ,dry	1	1	1	1	1	1	1	1	1	1	1	-60.8	0.0	-1.0
Sorghum	29	53	38	33	11	38	37	38	55	17	7	-22.3	61.6	-4.9
Maize	12	20	12	15	3	6	11	5	23	12	1	-25.3	95.2	-9.3
Millet	2	2	2	1	1	2	2	2	4	2	1	-20.1	16.1	2.2
BURKINA FASO														
Groundnuts	54	131	134	99	143	206	203	213	230	152	152	-0.3	8.4	3.8
Sorghum	547	991	751	1,238	1,292	1,310	1,232	1,266	1,254	943	943	-0.7	9.2	1.2
Millet	351	649	449	849	784	899	831	734	811	604	604	1.5	11.2	1.1
Maize	105	257	258	315	341	271	350	212	294	366	366	2.2	23.0	1.0
Rice	40	42	48	39	47	54	61	84	95	90	90	0.9	-3.4	6.5
BURUNDI														
Maize	9	13	13	13	14	13	11	14	11	17	14	2.1	4.2	-0.2
Sorghum	52	66	64	65	67	65	45	66	66	68	66	13.9	5.0	-0.2
Rice	10	40	40	40	40	40	38	27	42	65	64	8.0	18.6	1.0
Millet	9	13	13	13	14	13	11	14	11	17	14	2.1	4.2	-0.2
Bananas	1100	1,524	1,547	1,586	1,626	1,586	1,487	1,421	1,545	1,543	1,573	-0.7	4.4	-0.2
Cassava	400	569	569	584	598	584	527	501	549	603	610	2.2	2.9	-0.2
CAMEROON														
Maize	414	387	369	450	380	430	450	654	750	600	600	-2.3	1.9	4.5
Sorghum	331	343	329	400	380	390	350	460	439	400	500	-1.1	7.2	2.4
Millets	100	65	63	63	55	60	50	66	71	71	71	-8.0	16.9	0.6
Rice	46	62	55	90	52	79	80	62	54	55	55	9.8	-6.4	-0.8
Cassava	980	1,210	1,588	1,500	1,500	1,550	1,500	1,400	1,700	1,700	1,500	4.7	-4.1	0.8
Plantains	1020	1,136	870	870	900	930	950	970	1,000	1,030	1,030	1.9	-2.1	0.3
CENTRAL AFRICAN REP														
Sorghum	36	37	20	18	21	20	21	33	35	38	38	1.9	2.5	2.7
Maize	41	62	57	58	59	58	63	71	76	82	82	0.5	8.5	2.3
Groundnuts	123	103	80	63	71	72	84	86	91	97	100	-1.1	7.2	1.0
Cassava	920	516	547	586	580	575	518	492	526	579	579	-1.7	-4.8	-0.1
Yam	150	200	230	230	260	260	280	320	340	340	340	1.6	1.1	3.7
CHAD														
Sorghum	250	237	280	286	387	306	379	437	453	427	450	-6.2	0.1	4.5
Millet	200	179	168	226	293	212	307	228	258	248	270	-8.0	8.7	2.8
Groundnuts	99	152	108	230	224	190	207	293	200	250	250	-1.1	9.3	3.9
COMOROS														
Bananas	32	50	50	54	54	55	57	56	57	58	57	2.8	7.4	1.0
Cassava	33	45	45	45	47	48	48	49	50	50	50	-3.8	14.0	0.8
CONGO, DEM. REP. OF														
Palm oil	168	178	179	180	181	182	183	186	184	180	175	-2.1	3.3	0.1
Maize	594	960	1,008	1,023	1,053	1,130	1,184	1,225	1,100	1,000	900	4.3	6.2	0.4
Rice	234	370	392	394	403	430	426	441	430	347	340	3.4	4.9	0.2
Cassava	13087	18,000	18,715	19,366	19,780	18,890	19,102	19,378	16,800	16,800	16,500	2.8	3.6	-0.6
Plantains	1563	1,950	2,097	2,090	2,117	2,186	2,262	2,424	2,400	2,300	2,250	2.7	1.7	1.2
CONGO, REP. OF														
Maize	9	21	21	21	20	20	20	21	20	20	20	-4.7	8.8	-0.2
Cassava	628	699	700	585	600	632	740	790	791	780	790	3.1	0.9	1.5
Plantains	56	62	68	70	73	75	76	75	76	76	76	6.9	2.9	1.2

8-6. Volume of food output, by major food crop (continued)

					Thousands of metric tons							*Average annual percentage growth*		
	1980	1989	1990	1991	1992	1993	1994	1995	1996	1997	1998	75-84	85-89	90-MR
COTE D'IVOIRE														
Palm oil	189	193	250	264	290	283	285	249	267	229	274	1.8	3.6	1.3
Rice	420	635	660	687	714	890	988	1,045	833	1,287	1,223	-0.7	4.3	4.2
Maize	380	484	497	515	517	529	517	552	569	576	547	8.1	-1.3	0.9
Cassava	1010	1349	1393	1465	1502	1,509	1,564	1,641	1,653	1,699	1,700	4	2	2
Yams	2040	2474	2528	2690	2758	2,771	2,824	1,701	2,924	2,986	2,800	2	0	0
EGYPT														
Rice	2382	2,679	3,167	3,448	3,910	4,161	4,583	4,788	4,895	5,580	5,585	0.2	1.9	4.7
Wheat	1736	3,182	4,268	4,483	4,618	4,833	4,437	5,722	5,735	5,849	6,093	0.0	13.4	3.6
Sugarcane	8618	11,213	11,095	11,624	11,708	12,412	13,822	14,105	13,958	13,726	13,850	1.7	3.2	1.9
Dry Broadbeans	213	460	451	466	382	438	357	392	442	476	523	1.0	10.0	0.0
EQUATORIAL GUINEA														
Cassava	32	44	45	46	47	47	47	47	49	49	49	1.7	1.6	0.7
Sweet Potatoes	21	30	30	35	35	35	35	35	37	36	35	2.0	2.8	1.2
ETHIOPIA														
Sorghum	0	0	0	0	0	1,079	1,125	1,600	1,980	1,226	1,500	..	..	..
Maize	0	0	0	0	0	1,644	2,011	2,500	3,088	2,137	2,500	..	..	..
Barley	0	0	0	0	0	996	1,284	1,417	1,608	1,413	1,450	..	..	..
Sugarcane	0	0	0	0	0	1,700	1,200	1,200	1,600	980	1,650	..	..	..
GABON														
Oil palm	2	5	5	5	4	3	3	3	3	3	4	2.9	9.3	-2.7
Maize	10	20	23	24	25	27	28	29	30	31	31	5.5	12.9	2.9
Cassava	250	212	210	222	230	207	211	215	210	215	215	1.2	4.7	-0.1
Yam	79	100	110	110	120	110	125	130	140	140	140	5.7	3.6	2.2
Plantains	175	235	220	291	253	238	243	248	260	260	260	6.1	1.0	0.5
GAMBIA, THE														
Groundnuts	60	130	75	84	55	77	81	75	46	78	78	-2.6	5.7	-3.0
Palm oil	3	3	3	3	3	3	3	3	3	3	3	-0.6	0.0	0.0
Millet	15	51	47	58	46	52	53	54	61	66	66	11.1	2.8	1.7
Rice	43	21	21	21	19	12	20	19	20	17	17	3.7	-1.9	-1.2
Maize	6	14	14	20	18	24	13	14	10	8	8	11.3	-3.0	-3.7
Sorghum	5	11	8	12	12	9	9	12	14	13	13	4.2	-1.3	1.8
GHANA														
Maize	382	715	553	932	731	961	940	1,034	1,008	1,093	1,093	0.7	2.8	3.7
Millet	82	180	75	112	133	198	168	201	193	154	154	-1.4	7.1	3.3
Groundnuts	142	200	113	67	100	100	176	168	133	135	135	0.8	6.1	1.2
Cassava	1858	3,327	2,717	3,600	4,000	4,500	6,025	6,612	7,111	7,127	7,127	1.6	7.7	7.1
Plantains	734	1,036	799	1,178	1,082	1,322	1,475	1,638	1,823	1,878	1,878	-2.6	-3.9	5.4
GUINEA														
Palm oil	40	40	40	40	40	40	50	50	55	55	50	0.8	0.0	2.3
Rice	480	358	424	501	512	531	544	631	663	697	700	0.5	-3.8	4.2
Maize	90	68	74	80	88	85	83	79	79	81	81	4.3	-9.8	0.8
Groundnuts	84	59	78	104	139	128	126	132	139	146	146	0.4	-9.2	5.4
Cassava	480	317	372	437	512	550	525	601	646	694	745	-2.9	-11.5	5.4
Plantains	350	380	400	410	420	429	429	429	429	429	429	3.1	1.2	0.7
GUINEA-BISSAU														
Groundnuts	30	16	18	15	16	18	18	18	17	18	18	-3.3	-14.4	0.7
Palm kernels	9	10	7	10	8	7	8	8	8	8	8	0.3	3.7	-0.8
Rice	42	110	123	123	124	126	131	133	120	125	125	7.4	0.0	0.6
Sorghum	18	9	11	13	11	14	14	16	22	19	19	17.6	-13.0	5.0
Maize	12	10	14	13	10	13	14	15	9	9	9	11.9	-0.7	-1.0
KENYA														
Sugarcane	4532	4,825	4,750	4,600	4,180	4,370	3,800	4,550	4,650	4,450	4,900	8.8	3.0	-0.1
Maize	1620	2,631	2,290	2,340	2,430	2,089	3,060	2,699	2,160	2,214	2,600	-1.5	9.8	0.3
Wheat	216	244	190	195	126	150	297	313	320	252	250	2.0	7.5	3.2
LESOTHO														
Wheat	28	30	33	7	12	8	12	11	30	34	14	-14.4	10.2	-2.2
Dry Beans	4	10	8	2	1	2	3	5	6	14	8	-19.2	45.3	0.3
Dry Peas	5	1	3	1	2	1	1	1	4	3	3	-6.9	-14.0	3.6
Maize	106	137	172	49	61	92	149	63	188	142	94	-0.8	13.6	0.1
Sorghum	59	31	36	10	19	52	61	7	36	29	20	-5.4	-1.6	-1.2
LIBERIA														
Rice	243	294	185	130	110	65	50	56	94	168	210	2.2	0.2	-5.2
Cassava	300	446	360	270	280	245	250	175	213	283	313	-0.1	15.9	-3.5

8-6. Volume of food output, by major food crop (continued)

	Thousands of metric tons											Average annual percentage growth		
	1980	1989	1990	1991	1992	1993	1994	1995	1996	1997	1998	75-84	85-89	90-MR
LIBYA														
Wheat	141	185	129	150	160	175	155	167	168	169	169	14.8	0.5	0.6
Olives	161	65	68	70	68	55	60	52	55	58	58	3.3	-15.8	-1.6
MADAGASCAR														
Rice Paddy	2109	2,380	2,420	2,342	2,450	2,550	2,357	2,450	2,500	2,558	2,447	0.5	1.4	0.2
Cassava	1683	2,277	2,292	2,307	2,280	2,350	2,360	2,400	2,353	2,418	2,404	5.0	1.4	0.4
Sweet potatoes	373	483	486	488	452	500	560	450	500	510	510	3.8	0.9	0.3
MALAWI														
Groundnuts	177	62	37	58	26	55	31	32	40	69	108	-3.6	-5.7	1.3
Maize	1186	1,510	1,343	1,589	612	2,034	1,040	1,661	1,793	1,226	1,725	2.0	1.3	1.9
Sorghum	20	20	15	19	4	22	17	45	55	40	48	-23.2	3.8	10.0
Cassava	292	155	145	168	129	216	190	190	190	200	200	-1.6	-11.2	2.3
MALI														
Groundnuts	144	157	180	184	127	149	215	166	157	134	134	-8.7	19.0	-0.6
Millet	407	842	758	663	582	708	858	815	765	739	739	1.8	9.2	0.3
Rice	132	338	304	454	410	428	469	427	463	614	614	-5.6	20.7	3.4
Sorghum	356	605	531	478	602	777	746	807	710	540	540	2.3	6.7	1.5
Maize	45	225	207	257	236	283	322	286	248	290	290	0.8	15.7	1.9
MAURITANIA														
Sorghum	28	111	45	58	50	92	147	157	145	46	57	-4.0	28.3	3.6
Millet	3	14	3	2	2	4	7	8	8	3	1	-4.3	23.1	-4.1
Rice	11	55	52	42	51	65	53	54	64	67	81	25.9	24.5	2.5
Maize	5	3	2	2	3	7	6	1	14	6	12	2.2	13.2	10.1
MAURITIUS														
Sugarcane	4564	5,436	5,548	5,621	5,781	5,402	4,813	5,159	5,260	5,797	5,800	-0.5	1.2	-0.2
Potatoes	12	20	18	16	19	14	18	16	11	18	18	6.5	-5.2	-1.9
Dry Onions	2	3	3	3	3	4	5	6	6	5	5	8.5	-1.1	5.9
MOROCCO														
Citrus	1084	1,441	1,039	1,462	1,111	1,230	1,324	997	1,393	1,200	1,620	3.1	6.2	0.7
Wheat	1811	3,927	3,614	4,939	1,562	1,573	5,523	1,091	5,916	2,316	4,109	0.4	13.9	-0.1
Sugarbeet	2241	2,877	2,984	3,036	2,754	3,162	3,144	2,717	2,750	2,613	2,600	3.1	4.6	-0.7
Barley	2210	2,999	2,138	3,253	1,081	1,027	3,720	608	3,831	1,324	2,039	-4.3	11.7	-1.7
MOZAMBIQUE														
Cashew nuts	71	50	23	31	54	24	23	33	65	43	60	-17.3	20.2	2.9
Maize	380	330	453	327	132	533	489	734	947	1,042	1,124	-1.2	-4.1	9.6
Rice	75	95	96	56	33	66	101	113	139	180	192	-0.2	2.4	6.0
Cassava	3600	3,700	4,590	3,690	3,239	3,511	3,352	4,178	4,734	5,337	5,639	1.6	0.1	1.9
NAMIBIA														
Wheat	2	4	4	6	3	6	6	3	4	6	6	18.4	4.0	0.1
Maize	32	24	29	50	13	26	44	13	18	49	14	2.9	-3.4	-4.5
NIGER														
Cowpeas	266	319	217	433	402	168	525	184	450	420	420	2.9	16.1	1.7
Groundnuts	126	26	18	46	57	26	67	111	100	100	100	-3.6	-4.1	12.2
Sorghum	368	422	281	463	387	421	393	266	425	435	430	2.1	13.7	0.2
Millet	1364	1,333	1,111	1,833	1,788	1,658	1,968	1,769	1,832	1,713	1,713	3.5	9.0	2.3
NIGERIA														
Groundnuts	471	895	992	1,361	1,297	1,323	1,453	1,579	2,278	2,531	2,531	-5.3	9.0	6.6
Palm oil	650	700	730	760	792	825	837	860	776	810	810	0.2	6.2	1.0
Sorghum	3690	4,831	4,185	5,367	5,909	6,051	6,197	6,184	7,084	7,297	7,516	1.8	1.2	3.4
Millet	2450	4,770	5,136	4,109	4,501	4,602	4,757	4,952	5,681	5,902	5,926	-2.3	5.7	1.5
Maize	612	5,008	5,768	5,810	5,840	6,290	6,902	7,048	5,667	5,354	5,858	2.0	35.4	1.0
Rice	1090	3,303	2,500	3,226	3,260	3,065	2,427	2,920	3,122	3,268	3,268	16.2	18.8	0.1
Yam	5248	9,609	13,624	16,956	19,781	21,632	23,153	22,818	23,201	19,566	19,566	-4.9	17.3	4.8
Cassava	11500	17,404	19,043	26,004	29,185	30,128	31,005	31,404	31,418	30,409	30,409	0.9	8.3	3.9
RWANDA														
Sorghum	179	147	183	205	154	109	85	72	104	130	130	4.1	-7.0	-4.3
Maize	85	95	101	104	109	74	60	71	67	78	78	5.0	1.7	-3.0
Plantains	2063	3,020	2,747	2,120	2,316	2,136	1,489	2,002	2,105	2,248	2,248	3.3	5.6	-2.3
Sweet potatoes	871	772	857	1,000	1,063	1,100	800	950	950	1,000	1,000	4.2	-1.9	0.9
SENEGAL														
Groundnuts	523	844	703	724	578	628	678	791	588	506	506	-6.6	9.8	-2.0
Millet	451	639	505	593	446	654	548	667	601	426	426	-3.1	4.4	-0.6
Rice	65	168	181	170	177	193	162	155	149	174	174	1.1	2.9	-0.7
Maize	57	131	133	103	115	138	108	107	89	60	60	6.7	2.8	-3.9
Sorghum	102	127	157	78	117	99	123	127	133	118	118	-2.8	0.1	0.2

8-6. Volume of food output, by major food crop (continued)

	Thousands of metric tons											Average annual percentage growth		
	1980	1989	1990	1991	1992	1993	1994	1995	1996	1997	1998	75-84	85-89	90-MR
SIERRA LEONE														
Palm oil	47	49	50	51	48	47	50	45	46	51	51	1.7	0.2	-0.3
Palm kernels	30	33	29	30	31	33	32	29	30	29	29	-2.5	-3.1	-0.4
Rice	513	518	504	504	479	486	405	356	392	411	411	-1.7	1.2	-2.3
Cassava	95	118	123	123	117	106	244	219	281	310	310	2.5	2.8	7.8
SOMALIA														
Bananas	60	105	110	70	70	55	43	50	55	55	53	-5.7	14.3	-5.3
Maize	110	299	315	100	101	79	150	146	142	128	121	9.9	3.0	-4.3
Sorghum	140	334	250	145	92	80	252	136	145	153	108	5.8	6.7	-4.7
Sesame	38	50	45	35	20	22	22	25	25	24	21	3.2	1.6	-5.2
SOUTH AFRICA														
Maize	10896	12,035	8,709	8,614	3,277	9,997	13,275	4,866	10,171	10,106	7,544	-5.3	12.3	-1.0
Wheat	1470	2,026	1,709	2,142	1,324	1,984	1,840	1,977	2,712	2,294	1,500	2.2	5.3	0.3
Sugarcane	14062	18,587	18,084	20,078	12,955	11,244	15,683	16,714	20,951	22,155	24,640	0.3	-1.8	1.3
Sorghum	701	470	341	302	118	515	520	291	536	427	319	-4.0	0.9	1.1
Barley	60	291	262	170	100	230	275	300	176	193	170	11.6	2.4	-1.1
SUDAN														
Groundnuts	712	218	123	180	380	428	714	738	815	1,051	1,051	-8.2	-1.3	15.0
Sesame	221	140	80	97	266	175	170	313	416	339	339	-4.4	4.5	9.9
Sorghum	2084	1,536	1,180	3,581	4,042	2,386	3,648	2,450	4,179	3,369	3,700	-2.6	4.2	6.0
Wheat	231	247	409	686	895	453	475	448	527	642	637	-5.7	13.8	2.8
SWAZILAND														
Sugarcane	2782	3,797	3,842	3,941	3,885	3,647	3,786	3,440	3,846	3,694	3,886	8.6	1.4	-0.2
Citrus (oranges)	45	30	35	37	40	30	48	29	33	33	31	-0.1	-7.6	-0.3
Maize	97	133	94	139	54	73	99	76	151	108	107	-4.2	-6.3	0.0
TANZANIA														
Maize	1726	3,125	2,445	2,332	2,226	2,282	2,159	2,567	2,663	2,107	2,822	5.8	8.3	0.0
Sorghum	510	537	368	550	587	719	478	839	609	498	427	8.8	-1.0	1.1
Rice	291	718	740	625	392	641	614	723	734	533	1,013	1.8	14.6	1.9
Millet	340	300	200	200	263	210	218	411	338	347	148	8.4	-6.2	0.0
Cassava	4828	6,896	7,792	7,460	7,112	6,833	7,209	5,969	5,992	5,704	6,193	5.2	-3.2	-1.5
TOGO														
Maize	138	287	285	231	278	393	348	290	388	452	358	4.6	9.2	2.3
Sorghum	95	153	115	141	112	126	110	172	156	152	156	..	4.8	1.3
Millet	43	97	58	50	75	75	57	51	55	58	49	-7.8	0.7	-2.8
Cassava	408	409	593	511	452	389	412	602	548	596	556	-0.1	-2.8	1.1
Yam	484	405	392	376	368	530	364	531	605	662	693	-0.1	2.4	3.8
TUNISIA														
Olive oil	115	130	165	265	120	210	75	60	310	90	170	-3.6	-1.3	-0.4
Citrus	160	261	237	226	186	298	208	194	224	206	227	3.9	4.3	-0.8
Wheat	869	420	1,122	1,786	1,584	1,413	503	531	2,018	885	1,354	-0.9	-18.3	2.6
Barley	296	200	478	721	570	478	145	80	835	160	303	4.6	-20.4	-2.2
UGANDA														
Millet	459	610	560	576	634	610	610	632	440	502	580	-4.8	11.4	-0.7
Maize	286	624	602	567	657	804	850	913	759	740	750	-5.2	11.5	2.4
Sorghum	299	347	360	363	375	383	390	399	298	294	350	-3.2	6.3	-0.3
Cassava	2072	3,568	3,420	3,229	2,896	3,139	2,080	2,224	2,245	2,291	2,285	1.7	4.6	-3.7
Plantains	5699	7,469	7,842	8,080	7,806	8,222	8,500	9,012	9,144	9,303	9,250	-4.4	3.8	1.5
ZAMBIA														
Sunflower seeds	28	15	20	11	1	21	10	22	27	8	7	15.8	-21.2	1.1
Maize	937	1,845	1,093	1,096	483	1,598	1,021	738	1,409	960	650	-6.1	16.2	-3.1
Wheat	10	47	55	65	58	71	43	50	60	60	70	22.4	29.5	1.0
Cassava	290	480	520	530	540	540	530	520	550	750	817	6.7	7.1	2.1
ZIMBABWE														
Sugarcane	2528	3,671	3,093	3,236	125	538	3,420	3,773	2,826	4,651	4,808	4.6	-0.5	4.1
Maize	1511	2,019	1,972	1,586	362	2,012	2,326	840	2,609	2,192	1,466	-4.2	4.4	0.1
Wheat	191	284	326	259	58	276	239	83	280	250	275	1.2	17.9	-1.3

Notes: Crops shown represent same major food crops as in Table 8-1, Nominal producer prices, excluding beverages (coffee, tea, cocoa), cotton, and tobacco.
The following commodities are in their least-processed form unless otherwise indicated

    Groundnuts, unshelled
    Rice, paddy
    Sunflower, seeds
    Citrus, total for country
    Sesame, seeds
    Livestock = combined total head of cattle, sheep, goats, pigs, horses, asses, and mules
    Chickens/rabbits = combined total

For South Africa, barley production is for white areas only
Countries excluded from listing: Cape Verde, Djibouti, Eritrea, São Tomé and Principe, and Seychelles

8-7. Value of agricultural exports

| | Millions of U.S. dollars (current prices) | | | | | | | | | | | Average annual percentage growth | | |
	1980	1988	1989	1990	1991	1992	1993	1994	1995	1996	1997	75-84	85-89	90-MR
SUB-SAHARAN AFRICA	12,212	10,099	10,711	10,358	9,563	9,258	9,317	11,506	13,108	14,312	13,368	1.8	2.0	4.6
excluding South Africa	9,695	8,582	8,699	8,440	7,725	7,467	7,738	9,389	10,823	11,823	10,904	2.0	0.6	4.8
excl. S. Africa & Nigeria	9,249	8,141	8,444	8,210	7,511	7,277	7,462	9,062	10,420	11,281	10,383	2.4	0.6	4.5
Angola	172	22	16	6	5	5	3	1	5	6	6	-12.8	-30.5	-7.6
Benin	55	44	79	84	86	93	83	115	201	188	198	3.0	-4.2	14.2
Botswana	51	74	79	79	90	91	96	97	132	115	115	5.2	2.7	5.9
Burkina Faso	80	87	66	116	94	86	93	80	141	123	119	5.3	5.1	5.6
Burundi	64	127	73	69	88	67	53	113	96	32	82	8.8	-4.0	-1.9
Cameroon	699	510	661	563	341	364	245	393	565	624	504	2.6	5.1	0.5
Cape Verde	0	0	0	0	0	0	0	0	0	0	0	18.6	36.1	-29.6
Central African Republic	60	54	69	45	46	33	36	37	51	28	33	6.8	3.3	-6.4
Chad	115	112	114	134	136	127	84	118	145	127	135	13.2	-7.4	0.9
Comoros	7	18	13	11	20	16	18	8	7	4	4	8.6	13.4	-16.4
Congo, Democratic Rep. of	235	165	182	141	78	83	53	93	135	102	95	-1.7	-8.5	-3.9
Congo, Republic of	13	10	7	15	14	17	9	7	11	16	15	-1.7	-15.1	2.8
Côte d'Ivoire	2,009	1,735	1,807	1,615	1,532	1,434	1,605	1,557	2,216	2,421	2,001	7.0	-2.7	4.2
Djibouti	0	0	0	0	0	0	0	0	0	0	0	7.9	18.8	-7.9
Equatorial Guinea	12	12	8	8	6	6	3	4	4	7	4	-4.0	-10.3	-6.5
Eritrea	..	..	..	..	..	..	4	4	2	2	2	..	..	-14.3
Ethiopia	..	..	..	..	..	..	193	362	409	426	526		..	24.2
Gabon	14	8	7	3	6	7	4	5	8	10	10	13.3	-1.1	8.4
Gambia, The	28	13	10	14	12	11	15	15	16	16	12	-5.0	-22.1	2.9
Ghana	744	482	426	413	369	319	302	358	393	638	616	-5.1	3.2	5.2
Guinea	33	32	31	27	23	31	43	45	61	43	48	5.3	10.7	9.4
Guinea-Bissau	6	13	10	13	16	4	14	32	21	22	22	9.0	2.8	12.4
Kenya	693	735	669	687	641	812	975	1,044	1,153	1,165	1,157	6.5	-1.8	9.1
Lesotho	16	25	21	13	12	13	12	13	12	9	9	7.0	7.7	-7.7
Liberia	151	119	135	23	27	23	32	24	13	13	20	5.7	0.6	-16.5
Madagascar	334	180	206	176	157	143	133	237	200	138	92	2.6	-4.9	-4.8
Malawi	251	274	249	376	462	371	286	288	389	383	359	9.2	-0.6	1.5
Mali	192	208	240	251	267	266	251	239	270	312	271	12.3	3.8	1.8
Mauritania	39	33	34	44	47	48	49	31	38	40	40	7.3	-0.6	-0.6
Mauritius	302	356	346	379	365	402	367	367	420	501	405	-1.1	13.2	2.8
Mozambique	157	47	44	41	45	53	26	64	67	50	50	-8.0	1.4	3.4
Namibia	188	161	170	147	180	200	185	201	199	202	201	-8.0	18.9	3.1
Niger	86	50	54	62	65	55	48	48	45	45	45	8.4	-7.5	-4.1
Nigeria	446	440	255	230	214	189	275	327	403	542	522	-4.4	-2.5	12.9
Rwanda	66	99	113	95	85	60	52	14	42	39	38	5.5	8.6	-15.1
São Tomé and Principe	19	6	5	4	4	4	4	5	2	3	3	0.1	-9.9	-5.5
Senegal	115	153	204	219	135	126	91	126	115	87	58	-5.6	7.7	-12.7
Seychelles	3	1	1	1	1	1	1	1	2	2	2	-1.8	..	-1.8
Sierra Leone	59	31	21	18	24	11	9	21	15	16	14	-0.3	-11.6	-3.9
Somalia	125	76	75	74	41	62	60	68	75	76	76	4.9	3.6	2.4
South Africa	2,517	1,517	2,012	1,918	1,838	1,792	1,580	2,118	2,284	2,489	2,464	0.6	10.6	3.7
Sudan	553	507	662	550	381	367	455	471	501	565	556	1.9	5.8	0.3
Swaziland	211	272	253	347	339	306	265	283	291	311	300	6.7	20.8	0.0
Tanzania	406	289	299	279	243	281	303	379	431	496	400	-0.2	-0.6	7.5
Togo	77	100	92	120	101	125	75	76	127	133	128	5.4	4.8	2.7
Uganda	344	284	280	173	167	134	180	425	469	491	405	1.1	-7.4	13.9
Zambia	13	13	20	24	29	36	27	16	32	46	50	-8.1	10.3	8.7
Zimbabwe	453	608	592	750	731	584	617	1,177	895	1,207	1,157	4.4	5.0	9.1
NORTH AFRICA	1,544	1,310	1,296	1,406	1,591	1,396	1,313	1,708	1,892	1,876	1,895	-2.1	1.0	5.0
Algeria	120	30	35	50	54	76	97	35	108	137	91	-12.7	-9.2	13.2
Egypt, Arab Republic	677	514	532	427	391	401	360	553	536	521	442	-1.9	-6.9	1.4
Libya	0	0	0	0	0	0	0	0	0	0	0	-43.0	4.9	26.2
Morocco	606	572	520	647	670	581	509	598	780	896	832	0.4	11.9	5.5
Tunisia	140	193	208	282	477	338	347	523	468	322	530	-2.7	8.0	7.8
ALL AFRICA	13,756	11,408	12,007	11,764	11,154	10,654	10,630	13,214	15,000	16,188	15,263	1.2	1.9	4.6

8-8. Cereal production

	Thousands of metric tons											Average annual percentage growth		
	1980	1988	1989	1990	1991	1992	1993	1994	1995	1996	1997	75-84	85-89	90-MR
SUB-SAHARAN AFRICA	49,682	68,327	71,095	62,764	69,042	60,414	80,218	86,431	78,471	91,685	85,631	-0.7	7.8	4.2
excluding South Africa	36,465	56,980	56,211	51,682	57,752	55,534	67,425	70,464	70,979	78,035	72,555	0.0	7.2	5.0
excl. S. Africa & Nigeria	28,581	40,420	38,204	34,004	39,137	35,937	47,334	50,091	49,773	56,382	50,610	-0.3	5.6	5.9
Angola	435	334	272	249	372	402	322	285	300	530	461	-6.0	-1.4	6.2
Benin	346	557	565	546	587	609	627	646	747	668	891	3.0	2.0	5.1
Botswana	44	106	76	53	50	15	46	51	46	83	31	-20.5	60.0	-1.8
Burkina Faso	1,048	2,101	1,952	1,518	2,455	2,477	2,552	2,492	2,308	2,470	2,015	0.3	10.9	2.5
Burundi	217	292	296	293	300	306	300	225	269	273	310	3.9	5.4	-0.9
Cameroon	892	900	858	816	1,003	867	959	930	1,242	1,314	1,126	-1.6	3.5	5.2
Cape Verde	9	17	10	11	8	10	12	8	8	10	10	2.1	52.9	-0.8
Central African Republic	100	143	124	95	92	94	94	101	122	138	149	1.4	4.0	4.3
Chad	573	768	617	601	812	976	683	1,059	907	975	979	-5.1	8.2	6.2
Comoros	18	17	19	19	20	20	21	21	21	21	21	1.4	1.4	1.6
Congo, Democratic Rep. of	889	1,332	1,415	1,491	1,507	1,553	1,655	1,708	1,766	1,628	1,443	3.9	5.8	1.3
Congo, Republic of	12	21	22	22	22	21	22	22	22	21	20	-6.2	8.1	-0.9
Côte d'Ivoire	860	1,144	1,197	1,239	1,286	1,319	1,511	1,599	1,690	1,494	1,963	2.6	1.7	5.6
Djibouti	0	0	0	0	0	0	0	0	0	0	0	..	-5.1	10.4
Equatorial Guinea	..	..	..	..	..	..	..	..	..	..	..	..	..	..
Eritrea	..	..	..	..	..	..	87	259	153	124	130	..	..	0.7
Ethiopia	..	..	..	..	..	..	6,906	7,276	9,167	11,060	8,381			8.4
Gabon	11	25	21	24	25	26	27	29	30	31	32	5.7	12.4	5.1
Gambia, The	70	100	97	90	111	96	97	95	98	105	104	7.0	0.1	0.8
Ghana	674	1,146	1,184	844	1,436	1,254	1,645	1,594	1,797	1,770	1,791	-0.6	3.9	7.9
Guinea	725	547	583	627	686	683	711	718	825	866	908	1.2	-4.6	5.4
Guinea-Bissau	93	150	148	167	179	169	181	190	201	174	193	8.3	-1.6	2.6
Kenya	2,233	3,285	3,178	2,729	2,773	2,849	2,530	3,663	3,275	2,773	2,768	-2.3	9.8	0.1
Lesotho	194	234	199	242	67	94	153	223	81	256	206	-4.8	9.5	2.6
Liberia	243	298	294	185	130	110	65	50	56	94	95	2.2	0.2	-13.9
Madagascar	2,238	2,308	2,545	2,581	2,497	2,591	2,724	2,517	2,642	2,685	2,742	0.5	1.5	0.8
Malawi	1,252	1,492	1,588	1,413	1,680	644	2,137	1,110	1,778	1,943	1,349	0.6	1.4	1.6
Mali	968	1,610	2,031	1,824	1,896	1,853	2,228	2,417	2,363	2,205	2,202	0.6	10.2	2.7
Mauritania	47	174	184	103	105	107	169	215	220	231	122	1.8	25.5	5.1
Mauritius	1	4	2	2	2	2	2	1	0	0	0	-0.9	-9.5	-27.3
Mozambique	663	562	607	734	546	242	765	791	1,127	1,379	1,531	-1.0	-4.7	14.7
Namibia	74	83	97	99	114	33	76	119	57	87	172	3.7	3.5	3.1
Niger	1,775	2,389	1,842	1,480	2,384	2,253	2,155	2,430	2,112	2,344	2,225	3.2	9.7	3.3
Nigeria	7,884	16,560	18,007	17,678	18,615	19,597	20,091	20,373	21,206	21,653	21,945	1.3	11.3	2.9
Rwanda	273	292	262	306	329	292	195	157	152	183	220	4.4	-3.0	-7.1
São Tomé and Principe	0	2	2	3	4	4	4	4	3	4	4	1.5	24.6	5.0
Senegal	676	867	1,067	977	946	856	1,086	943	1,059	976	783	-1.6	3.2	-1.5
Seychelles	..	..	..	..	..	..	..	..	..	..	..	..	..	..
Sierra Leone	551	547	574	562	560	534	542	466	411	445	467	-1.0	1.0	-3.7
Somalia	267	601	654	581	256	209	165	405	285	290	284	8.2	5.2	-7.3
South Africa	13,217	11,347	14,884	11,082	11,290	4,880	12,793	15,967	7,492	13,651	13,076	-3.5	10.1	0.8
Sudan	2,701	5,132	1,975	1,702	4,637	5,438	3,102	5,146	3,305	5,202	4,706	-3.5	4.1	10.7
Swaziland	105	118	138	99	142	58	77	103	79	153	110	-4.2	-6.3	-0.4
Tanzania	2,961	3,685	4,791	3,842	3,792	3,538	3,936	3,532	4,597	4,431	3,533	5.8	6.5	-0.7
Togo	296	504	566	484	465	495	634	559	550	660	709	4.1	6.4	3.9
Uganda	1,078	1,398	1,636	1,580	1,576	1,743	1,880	1,986	2,030	1,588	1,625	-4.5	10.3	1.0
Zambia	984	2,055	1,967	1,210	1,225	613	1,757	1,168	881	1,574	1,125	-6.3	16.3	-2.4
Zimbabwe	1,989	3,080	2,553	2,560	2,060	481	2,498	2,780	987	3,127	2,673	-4.1	5.6	1.8
NORTH AFRICA	16,445	19,339	21,528	22,835	29,195	23,405	21,479	26,585	20,965	34,741	23,842	-0.3	5.1	1.9
Algeria	2,419	1,038	2,006	1,627	3,810	3,330	1,454	965	2,140	4,902	870	-2.5	-4.7	-4.0
Egypt, Arab Republic	8,100	9,764	11,131	13,022	13,864	14,611	14,961	15,012	16,097	16,542	17,492	1.0	5.4	4.9
Libya	215	283	322	273	298	313	328	307	318	321	322	4.2	3.8	1.0
Morocco	4,515	7,959	7,429	6,276	8,668	2,952	2,820	9,642	1,787	10,107	4,102	-2.2	12.2	-4.8
Tunisia	1,197	295	641	1,638	2,556	2,199	1,917	660	623	2,869	1,056	0.5	-18.7	-0.6
ALL AFRICA	66,127	87,666	92,623	85,600	98,238	83,820	101,698	113,017	99,436	126,427	109,473	-0.6	7.1	3.7

8-9. Crop production index

	Index (average 1989-91 = 100)											Average annual percentage growth		
	1980	1988	1989	1990	1991	1992	1993	1994	1995	1996	1997	75-84	85-89	90-MR
SUB-SAHARAN AFRICA	79	98	100	99	106	106	110	116	117	125	124	-0.1	4.7	3.1
excluding South Africa	78	99	100	100	108	109	112	117	120	126	126	-0.1	4.6	3.2
excl. S. Africa & Nigeria	83	101	100	99	104	103	103	110	112	119	119	0.1	3.5	2.5
Angola	107	101	100	96	104	111	107	136	140	154	147	-6.6	0.9	6.5
Benin	53	88	91	99	110	111	127	128	154	159	155	3.2	4.2	7.5
Botswana	94	121	107	97	97	63	87	94	80	110	75	-6.4	13.1	-1.6
Burkina Faso	55	106	99	91	110	116	121	120	116	126	124	2.2	8.1	3.4
Burundi	77	101	92	102	106	108	105	90	95	95	94	0.8	3.3	-0.9
Cameroon	91	99	98	99	104	100	101	105	112	124	123	0.4	0.0	3.1
Cape Verde	93	132	118	98	84	79	92	74	72	75	75	3.0	20.1	-4.8
Central African Republic	103	104	103	100	96	99	97	108	111	125	128	0.0	1.7	3.2
Chad	70	95	95	89	117	110	90	109	122	121	127	-1.2	7.0	3.7
Comoros	82	95	98	99	103	102	108	108	115	112	119	1.1	4.7	2.5
Congo, Democratic Rep. of	73	93	96	101	103	105	104	106	104	104	103	2.4	3.0	0.6
Congo, Republic of	82	102	102	100	98	99	102	105	112	115	115	2.0	2.0	2.0
Côte d'Ivoire	71	96	99	102	99	97	101	104	109	116	107	3.3	4.8	1.6
Djibouti	71	92	105	97	98	99	99	100	100	102	102	29.6	2.4	0.1
Equatorial Guinea	88	104	99	101	100	99	100	95	91	98	98	0.6	1.5	-0.6
Eritrea	..	..	..	..	..	..	91	157	115	113	130	..	..	3.8
Ethiopia	91	94	95	102	103	108	..	..	..	..	..	2.1	4.3	..
Gabon	79	96	98	96	106	103	99	102	105	107	109	4.6	4.0	1.2
Gambia, The	66	102	125	81	94	69	85	90	86	66	80	-1.0	4.0	-3.8
Ghana	73	93	107	86	107	113	121	136	157	159	159	-2.5	4.7	7.6
Guinea	92	82	92	100	109	117	118	121	125	126	130	0.9	-1.1	4.1
Guinea-Bissau	64	90	99	104	97	102	104	112	114	107	112	3.6	2.1	1.7
Kenya	72	100	104	98	99	98	95	108	111	109	109	1.6	6.3	1.5
Lesotho	92	118	113	127	60	71	90	122	78	142	88	-3.8	9.5	0.7
Liberia	..	..	..	..	..	..	..	..	..	..	..	..	..	..
Madagascar	85	94	100	100	101	100	106	100	102	102	104	0.3	1.1	0.4
Malawi	82	97	96	97	107	85	114	91	111	118	113	2.2	1.3	2.3
Mali	59	87	99	97	103	101	100	116	120	123	150	0.6	10.4	4.8
Mauritania	59	116	125	86	89	90	104	137	136	138	129	2.4	17.8	4.8
Mauritius	80	100	98	101	102	105	101	91	96	96	100	0.1	0.3	-0.5
Mozambique	111	94	98	108	94	79	93	92	105	130	144	-2.3	0.5	4.2
Namibia	80	93	98	99	103	75	90	107	90	101	124	1.9	2.2	1.8
Niger	98	115	96	83	120	119	97	132	108	129	124	2.1	9.7	3.8
Nigeria	52	83	92	97	111	120	126	130	134	136	136	-1.0	9.8	5.2
Rwanda	86	96	103	101	96	94	81	60	70	73	78	4.3	0.4	-5.1
São Tomé and Principe	118	118	106	98	96	118	120	116	122	120	120	-2.7	0.4	2.7
Senegal	58	93	109	94	97	84	95	95	108	88	103	-5.1	8.6	-0.2
Seychelles	189	104	99	94	107	86	87	104	118	124	114	-2.8	..	-2.8
Sierra Leone	81	97	101	99	100	92	91	97	89	95	95	1.0	2.2	-0.9
Somalia	..	..	..	..	..	..	..	..	..	..	..	..	..	..
South Africa	94	97	108	96	97	69	96	108	84	112	103	-0.4	6.3	0.8
Sudan	118	148	98	85	117	144	110	151	142	170	169	-2.1	-0.3	8.1
Swaziland	77	98	103	97	100	82	77	85	73	89	77	3.6	2.0	-3.3
Tanzania	79	94	102	99	100	93	95	91	95	96	88	2.9	1.7	-1.3
Togo	71	92	98	100	102	104	121	100	116	132	137	1.8	5.2	4.1
Uganda	65	92	98	100	102	100	108	111	112	108	113	-3.2	4.4	1.8
Zambia	66	119	117	89	94	64	117	89	82	107	90	-2.5	10.4	-0.7
Zimbabwe	76	112	102	98	100	59	100	105	76	119	121	-0.6	4.0	2.2
NORTH AFRICA	79	92	100	102	117	113	112	109	110	141	119	0.9	3.7	2.5
Algeria	82	82	98	85	118	127	110	92	112	145	100	-1.7	2.3	2.2
Egypt, Arab Republic	77	91	93	102	104	112	115	111	122	134	133	2.1	3.2	4.3
Libya	80	93	98	99	103	99	94	90	89	88	88	4.0	1.7	-1.9
Morocco	59	94	100	91	109	73	74	112	67	121	87	0.6	9.7	-0.4
Tunisia	76	54	74	98	129	103	115	74	71	136	91	0.5	-2.5	0.5
ALL AFRICA	79	97	100	100	108	107	110	115	115	128	123	0.1	4.5	3.0

8-10. Fertilizer use

	Thousands of metric tons											Average annual percentage growth		
	1980	1988	1989	1990	1991	1992	1993	1994	1995	1996	1997	75-84	85-89	90-MR
SUB-SAHARAN AFRICA	1,973	1,926	1,914	1,972	1,931	1,995	2,225	1,994	1,817	1,965	..	4.4	-0.6	0.0
excluding South Africa	909	1,090	1,138	1,181	1,192	1,262	1,382	1,242	1,069	1,185	..	5.3	2.2	0.0
excl. S. Africa & Nigeria	735	778	760	781	762	764	876	946	886	1,050	..	2.4	0.8	4.5
Angola	17	16	24	10	7	9	8	10	10	10	..	-0.5	16.0	-5.5
Benin	1	7	3	11	12	15	17	21	36	35	..	7.5	-15.0	33.5
Botswana	1	1	1	1	1	1	1	1	2	3	..	-5.7	2.7	18.5
Burkina Faso	4	15	21	21	20	21	21	23	24	24	..	23.4	11.1	2.6
Burundi	1	3	5	2	1	˙5	4	3	5	6	..	11.4	15.1	14.3
Cameroon	32	34	29	17	18	19	22	30	30	34	..	12.9	-9.8	7.2
Cape Verde	0	..	0	..	0	..	0	..	0	..	..	-0.6	22.3	..
Central African Republic	1	1	1	1	1	1	1	1	1	1	..	-11.1	-17.6	6.8
Chad	1	5	5	6	9	10	5	7	9	10	..	-4.9	-7.3	7.4
Comoros	..	..	0	..	0	0	0	0	0	0	..	..	..	0.0
Congo, Democratic Rep. of	8	3	8	6	8	2	4	10	12	10	..	0.1	-9.8	7.7
Congo, Republic of	1	1	1	2	1	2	2	˙2	2	3	..	4.0	-33.9	18.3
Côte d'Ivoire	53	41	39	36	44	56	54	65	64	70	..	1.4	-0.6	10.2
Djibouti	1	..	0	..	0	..	0	..	0	..	..	-44.2	..	..
Equatorial Guinea	0	..	0	..	0	..	0	..	0	..	..	0.0	..	..
Eritrea	..	..	..	..	..	..	0	..	2	5	..	..	..	..
Ethiopia	..	..	..	..	..	..	72	128	135	154	..	..	..	..
Gabon	0	1	1	1	1	1	0	0	0	0	..	28.9	-18.8	-15.6
Gambia, The	2	1	2	1	1	1	1	1	1	1	..	7.9	-13.3	-5.1
Ghana	12	13	8	13	8	10	8	12	12	13	..	-0.9	1.3	4.3
Guinea	0	1	1	1	2	1	2	1	4	3	..	-15.8	29.7	18.9
Guinea-Bissau	0	0	1	1	1	0	0	1	3	1	..	9.8	..	9.0
Kenya	62	125	117	116	95	100	103	138	75	120	..	6.1	6.4	-1.0
Lesotho	5	5	5	5	6	6	6	6	7	7	..	18.1	2.3	6.3
Liberia	3	3	3	0	0	..	0	..	0	..	..	-11.1	24.9	..
Madagascar	9	11	6	11	9	8	11	11	13	13	..	3.1	-1.5	8.5
Malawi	33	51	55	48	70	74	74	27	34	41	..	12.4	7.4	-7.6
Mali	14	13	18	15	15	23	25	25	29	32	..	14.3	-16.4	11.1
Mauritania	1	3	2	4	5	7	5	4	4	5	..	-9.6	28.4	5.3
Mauritius	27	28	32	28	28	27	26	29	32	35	..	0.7	3.3	1.5
Mozambique	28	2	2	3	5	5	3	7	9	11	..	6.5	-13.1	23.0
Namibia	..	..	..	..	..	..	..	..	..	..	..	..	..	..
Niger	3	2	3	2	1	1	2	6	10	11	..	23.0	-2.8	33.8
Nigeria	174	312	378	400	429	498	506	296	183	135	..	23.8	5.5	-13.5
Rwanda	0	1	1	3	2	1	3	..	0	0	..	11.8	-18.3	-25.9
São Tomé and Principe	..	..	..	..	..	..	..	..	..	..	..	..	..	..
Senegal	19	26	13	12	15	17	25	20	16	15	..	-8.9	-3.3	4.7
Seychelles	..	..	0	..	0	..	0	..	0	..	..	..	..	..
Sierra Leone	2	1	2	1	1	1	3	3	3	3	..	-3.5	-17.8	18.6
Somalia	1	2	3	3	0	..	0	..	0	1	..	7.3	-7.4	..
South Africa	1,064	836	776	792	740	733	844	752	748	780	..	3.6	-3.9	-0.1
Sudan	81	47	49	89	93	74	52	58	52	92	..	-1.5	-3.8	-0.1
Swaziland	20	14	14	13	12	12	12	13	6	6	..	4.0	11.8	-10.5
Tanzania	36	41	49	51	50	48	50	38	28	38	..	-1.0	5.7	-6.4
Togo	3	12	12	12	12	12	10	11	16	18	..	8.6	10.2	5.0
Uganda	1	0	0	0	1	1	2	2	3	3	..	-16.2	-5.2	47.2
Zambia	79	85	79	60	63	85	86	59	51	41	..	2.2	6.1	-6.4
Zimbabwe	173	166	149	177	148	108	157	171	146	174	..	2.0	-0.3	1.2
NORTH AFRICA	1,221	1,708	1,585	1,589	1,555	1,457	1,642	1,423	1,659	1,708	..	6.5	1.3	0.7
Algeria	236	170	117	139	96	97	131	118	48	59	..	1.6	-11.9	-10.3
Egypt, Arab Republic	664	1,034	965	965	963	875	973	852	1,134	1,194	..	7.5	3.5	2.4
Libya	53	88	79	78	85	89	106	70	104	71	..	14.2	0.3	0.4
Morocco	207	315	321	326	312	290	336	295	282	298	..	5.4	3.0	-1.5
Tunisia	62	101	104	83	99	106	96	89	90	86	..	6.3	3.2	-1.5
ALL AFRICA	3,194	3,634	3,500	3,562	3,486	3,453	3,867	3,417	3,475	3,673	..	5.3	0.3	0.3

8-11. Fertilizer imports

| | Thousands of metric tons | | | | | | | | | | | Average annual percentage growth | | |
	1980	1988	1989	1990	1991	1992	1993	1994	1995	1996	1997	75-84	85-89	90-MR
SUB-SAHARAN AFRICA	970	1,025	1,117	1,003	1,050	1,161	1,402	1,341	1,018	1,257	..	6.0	-0.3	2.2
excluding South Africa	740	895	936	870	889	962	1,231	1,156	838	1,052	..	6.9	0.2	2.0
excl. S. Africa & Nigeria	564	730	716	673	681	711	846	862	786	1,013	..	3.7	3.9	5.0
Angola	17	22	24	7	7	9	8	10	10	10	..	-0.2	19.3	-3.4
Benin	1	7	3	11	12	16	18	21	21	35	..	6.7	-16.1	29.2
Botswana	1	1	1	1	1	1	1	1	1	4	..	-5.7	2.7	13.4
Burkina Faso	5	19	23	19	20	21	21	23	24	31	..	23.7	14.8	4.7
Burundi	1	3	5	2	1	6	5	4	4	6	..	11.9	13.6	14.2
Cameroon	32	40	29	17	18	20	22	30	30	34	..	13.2	-9.4	7.1
Cape Verde	0	..	..	..	..	..	..	..	..	..	..	-0.6	22.3	..
Central African Republic	..	..	..	..	..	..	..	..	..	1	..	..	..	..
Chad	1	5	5	6	9	10	5	8	8	10	..	-4.9	-7.3	7.0
Comoros	..	..	..	..	0	0	0	0	0	0	..	..	..	0.0
Congo, Democratic Rep. of	8	3	11	6	8	2	4	10	12	10	..	0.1	-5.6	4.9
Congo, Republic of	1	1	1	2	1	2	2	3	3	3	..	34.9	-38.7	23.0
Côte d'Ivoire	45	43	41	35	42	60	55	96	91	78	..	6.4	-6.9	14.7
Djibouti	1	..	..	..	..	..	..	..	..	..	..	-44.2	..	..
Equatorial Guinea	0	..	..	..	..	..	..	..	..	..	..	0.0	..	..
Eritrea	..	..	..	..	..	..	..	..	..	6	..	..	..	..
Ethiopia	..	..	..	..	..	..	140	140	153	215	..	..	..	..
Gabon	0	1	1	1	1	1	0	0	0	0	..	28.0	-18.8	-15.6
Gambia, The	2	1	2	1	1	1	1	1	1	1	..	7.9	-15.0	-5.3
Ghana	12	13	23	7	8	11	7	12	12	13	..	-2.3	15.5	-0.7
Guinea	0	1	1	1	2	1	2	1	1	3	..	-16.0	29.7	9.6
Guinea-Bissau	0	0	1	1	1	0	0	0	0	1	..	9.8	..	-10.3
Kenya	62	139	120	116	95	100	108	138	75	120	..	5.2	7.7	-1.1
Lesotho	5	5	5	5	6	6	6	6	6	7	..	18.1	2.3	5.8
Liberia	3	3	3	0	..	..	..	..	..	..	..	-11.1	24.9	..
Madagascar	9	11	6	11	9	8	11	11	8	13	..	3.1	-1.5	5.9
Malawi	33	51	55	48	76	68	74	31	29	41	..	13.9	4.8	-8.2
Mali	14	13	18	19	13	30	25	25	29	32	..	14.3	-16.4	10.0
Mauritania	1	3	2	5	7	9	7	4	4	5	..	-9.6	28.4	3.2
Mauritius	17	25	30	52	37	28	24	24	29	33	..	0.0	5.5	-4.2
Mozambique	20	2	2	3	5	5	3	7	10	12	..	24.2	-23.1	25.0
Namibia	..	..	..	..	..	..	..	..	..	..	..	..	..	..
Niger	3	2	3	2	1	1	2	5	8	10	..	23.0	-2.8	29.8
Nigeria	177	165	220	197	208	251	385	294	52	39	..	23.0	-9.1	-18.6
Rwanda	0	1	2	1	2	1	3	..	..	0	..	11.8	1.3	-27.8
São Tomé and Principe	..	..	..	..	..	..	..	..	..	..	..	..	..	..
Senegal	16	23	24	29	31	27	37	23	19	16	..	-7.7	6.8	-6.4
Seychelles	..	..	..	..	..	..	..	..	..	..	..	..	..	..
Sierra Leone	2	1	2	1	1	2	2	3	3	3	..	-4.1	-17.7	17.6
Somalia	2	2	3	3	..	..	..	..	..	1	..	0.9	20.5	..
South Africa	229	130	181	132	162	199	171	185	180	205	..	2.9	-3.2	3.2
Sudan	81	47	49	89	93	74	53	60	50	97	..	0.0	-6.8	0.2
Swaziland	18	14	15	13	12	12	12	13	15	6	..	1.2	13.1	-5.6
Tanzania	20	52	56	38	53	40	50	38	22	38	..	4.0	14.1	-7.1
Togo	3	14	13	12	6	12	13	13	14	22	..	7.6	9.6	8.9
Uganda	1	0	0	0	1	1	2	2	3	3	..	-13.1	-5.2	47.2
Zambia	69	85	101	67	63	86	83	56	48	39	..	-1.1	42.7	-9.9
Zimbabwe	56	78	40	44	41	41	40	42	41	54	..	5.9	5.3	2.2
NORTH AFRICA	588	449	474	491	426	370	373	374	444	400	..	-2.2	-0.1	-2.4
Algeria	189	30	51	40	31	28	29	54	40	48	..	-1.8	-18.3	1.5
Egypt, Arab Republic	182	150	182	184	102	96	60	41	133	66	..	-10.2	3.6	-13.3
Libya	53	80	74	68	83	87	108	73	100	56	..	11.5	4.2	-0.2
Morocco	133	166	159	172	196	147	172	198	161	226	..	3.3	3.0	2.8
Tunisia	30	23	8	28	15	12	5	10	10	4	..	-0.7	5.2	-13.6
ALL AFRICA	1,557	1,474	1,591	1,494	1,476	1,530	1,775	1,716	1,462	1,657	..	3.0	-0.3	0.9

8-12. Area under major crops

	Thousands of hectares											Average annual percentage growth		
	1980	1988	1989	1990	1991	1992	1993	1994	1995	1996	1997	75-84	85-89	90-MR
SUB-SAHARAN AFRICA	15,999	17,392	17,550	17,715	17,803	17,938	18,725	18,383	18,707	18,938	..	1.3	1.2	1.1
excluding South Africa	15,185	16,570	16,725	16,887	16,973	17,106	17,891	17,546	17,867	18,098	..	1.3	1.2	1.2
excl. S. Africa & Nigeria	12,650	14,035	14,190	14,352	14,438	14,571	15,356	15,011	15,329	15,560	..	1.6	1.4	1.4
Angola	500	500	500	500	500	500	500	500	500	500	..	0.0	0.0	0.0
Benin	445	450	450	450	450	450	450	450	450	450	..	0.2	0.1	0.0
Botswana	..	..	0	..	0	..	0	..	0	..	..	..	..	..
Burkina Faso	40	60	60	55	50	45	40	40	40	40	..	8.5	0.0	-6.0
Burundi	260	335	335	340	340	330	330	330	330	330	..	1.6	4.0	-0.4
Cameroon	1,020	1,068	1,068	1,068	1,070	1,080	1,080	1,080	1,080	1,080	..	2.6	0.3	0.2
Cape Verde	2	2	2	2	2	2	2	2	2	2	..	0.0	0.0	0.0
Central African Republic	75	86	86	86	86	90	90	90	90	90	..	2.5	1.0	0.8
Chad	10	15	15	15	15	15	15	15	15	15	..	18.8	0.0	0.0
Comoros	20	35	35	35	40	40	40	40	40	40	..	5.7	3.6	1.9
Congo, Democratic Rep. of	790	915	930	950	960	970	970	970	970	970	..	2.0	1.1	0.5
Congo, Republic of	26	30	30	30	35	35	35	35	35	35	..	0.7	1.5	2.2
Côte d'Ivoire	2,300	3,300	3,400	3,500	3,500	3,600	3,600	3,800	4,100	4,300	..	3.4	5.5	3.2
Djibouti	..	..	..	..	..	..	..	..	..	..	..	..	..	..
Equatorial Guinea	100	100	100	100	100	100	100	100	100	100	..	0.0	0.0	0.0
Eritrea	..	..	..	..	..	..	80	80	80	80	..	..	..	..
Ethiopia	..	..	..	..	..	..	650	..	..	..	..	..	..	..
Gabon	162	162	162	162	162	165	165	165	170	170	..	2.0	0.0	0.8
Gambia, The	..	..	..	..	..	..	..	..	..	..	..	..	..	..
Ghana	1,700	1,500	1,500	1,500	1,520	1,520	1,600	1,700	1,700	1,700	..	0.4	-1.6	2.3
Guinea	220	265	265	265	275	285	285	290	290	290	..	1.5	2.2	1.5
Guinea-Bissau	30	35	35	40	40	40	40	40	40	40	..	0.0	3.6	1.1
Kenya	480	495	498	500	510	520	520	520	520	520	..	0.3	0.5	0.7
Lesotho	..	..	..	..	..	..	..	..	..	..	..	..	..	..
Liberia	245	245	245	230	220	210	210	200	200	200	..	0.2	0.0	-2.8
Madagascar	500	560	580	600	590	580	550	540	540	540	..	3.0	1.3	-1.6
Malawi	82	98	100	100	103	103	103	103	103	103	..	2.9	1.4	0.4
Mali	40	40	40	40	40	40	40	40	40	44	..	2.8	0.0	0.8
Mauritania	4	5	5	6	6	7	8	9	10	12	..	1.0	0.0	12.7
Mauritius	7	6	6	6	6	6	6	6	6	6	..	0.7	-3.5	0.0
Mozambique	230	230	230	230	230	230	230	230	230	230	..	0.0	0.0	0.0
Namibia	2	2	2	2	2	2	2	3	4	4	..	9.9	0.0	12.0
Niger	3	4	4	5	5	5	5	6	6	6	..	0.0	6.8	5.2
Nigeria	2,535	2,535	2,535	2,535	2,535	2,535	2,535	2,535	2,538	2,538	..	0.2	0.0	0.0
Rwanda	255	304	304	304	300	300	300	300	300	300	..	2.9	1.2	-0.2
São Tomé and Principe	35	35	39	40	37	38	39	39	39	39	..	0.0	1.6	0.1
Senegal	9	15	15	15	15	16	20	20	20	20	..	13.5	3.3	5.6
Seychelles	4	5	5	5	6	6	6	6	6	6	..	2.5	..	2.5
Sierra Leone	49	54	54	54	54	54	54	54	54	54	..	1.3	0.4	0.0
Somalia	16	17	17	17	17	18	20	20	20	20	..	0.7	1.6	3.1
South Africa	814	822	825	828	830	832	834	837	840	840	..	-0.1	0.3	0.3
Sudan	57	60	70	70	70	75	75	75	80	80	..	2.8	3.0	2.2
Swaziland	4	13	12	12	12	12	12	12	11	11	..	5.3	12.4	-1.2
Tanzania	860	800	800	820	850	860	860	870	870	885	..	-1.6	0.6	1.3
Togo	360	360	360	360	360	360	360	355	360	360	..	0.0	0.0	0.0
Uganda	1,600	1,705	1,705	1,710	1,730	1,730	1,730	1,740	1,740	1,750	..	2.5	0.1	0.3
Zambia	8	8	8	8	8	8	8	8	8	8	..	1.1	0.0	0.0
Zimbabwe	100	116	118	120	122	124	126	128	130	130	..	0.7	1.8	1.5
NORTH AFRICA	3,130	3,692	3,793	3,896	3,917	3,968	4,000	4,041	4,144	4,176	..	1.9	1.0	1.3
Algeria	634	541	544	554	546	532	531	529	510	519	..	-0.4	-2.2	-1.0
Egypt, Arab Republic	159	271	275	364	376	381	399	390	466	466	..	3.2	9.3	6.2
Libya	327	320	300	300	300	300	300	300	300	300	..	0.6	-2.2	0.0
Morocco	500	670	707	736	738	782	805	839	832	855	..	3.2	2.9	2.8
Tunisia	1,510	1,890	1,967	1,942	1,957	1,973	1,965	1,983	2,036	2,036	..	2.5	0.8	0.6
ALL AFRICA	19,129	21,084	21,343	21,611	21,720	21,906	22,725	22,424	22,851	23,114	..	1.4	1.1	1.2

8-13. Agricultural yields by major crop

	Category	Thousands of hectograms per hectare										Average annual percentage growth		
		1980	1990	1991	1992	1993	1994	1995	1996	1997	1998	75-84	85-89	90-MR
ALGERIA														
Wheat	F1	7.3	6.3	10.8	9.9	8.1	8.0	8.9	13.1	8.0	8.9	-0.2	1.0	7.7
Citrus	F2	262.9	74.5	87.2	92.5	87.1	91.4	80.2	86.1	87.2	90.5	-4.4	-11.9	4.2
Dates	F3	30.0	26.2	25.5	31.2	31.0	37.2	32.8	37.3	31.4	38.7	0.5	-0.9	12.1
Barley	NT1	8.4	7.6	11.6	9.0	6.3	6.5	7.1	14.0	7.2	6.9	0.1	0.9	0.6
Potatoes	NT2	77.7	78.9	90.7	107.9	111.2	95.1	136.8	134.6	141.0	139.4	-0.9	5.0	14.5
ANGOLA														
Coffee(green)	X1	2.2	0.3	0.5	0.5	0.5	0.2	0.4	0.4	0.5	0.5	-17.2	-7.7	-4.4
Maize	F1	6.0	2.7	4.0	3.8	2.6	2.5	3.5	7.0	6.0	7.4	-5.9	-10.8	27.0
Millet	F2	7.1	5.7	4.8	4.8	2.7	5.4	5.1	4.8	3.8	5.0	-2.8	-3.0	-3.0
Wheat	F3	5.8	8.0	8.0	8.0	8.6	10.0	16.7	16.7	16.7	17.1	-6.5	5.8	28.1
Cassava	NT1	33.8	40.0	40.3	42.3	42.3	58.6	50.0	49.1	44.2	55.7	-0.8	3.0	10.1
Sweet potatoes	NT2	91.7	86.8	89.5	90.0	88.1	85.7	86.4	84.8	86.4	84.8	0.3	-0.4	-1.0
BENIN														
Seed Cotton	X1	6.6	11.9	11.7	12.0	17.9	13.9	14.0	12.4	10.3	10.3	6.5	-4.6	0.7
Maize	F1	7.4	9.0	9.3	9.8	9.8	10.2	11.3	11.0	12.2	12.2	-0.6	0.6	8.7
Sorghum	F2	6.3	7.3	7.8	7.7	7.6	7.8	7.5	7.7	8.1	8.1	-2.3	0.2	1.0
Cassava	NT1	65.9	79.8	83.0	83.8	84.9	81.5	85.0	87.2	103.7	103.7	-0.5	2.6	4.8
Yams	NT2	97.2	111.5	114.0	106.0	107.7	108.4	107.4	103.0	107.9	107.9	-1.5	1.9	-1.9
BOTSWANA														
Sorghum	F1	2.2	2.5	3.7	2.0	3.8	2.5	2.5	2.8	1.7	1.4	-16.0	19.9	-9.4
Maize	F2	2.5	2.9	4.0	1.9	2.4	5.4	3.3	9.2	7.7	1.3	-8.9	18.0	-0.9
Millet	F3	1.6	1.8	1.8	1.1	1.8	2.0	2.2	4.0	2.5	1.4	-16.2	13.4	9.8
BURKINA FASO														
Seed Cotton	X1	8.3	11.4	9.3	10.0	9.6	8.9	8.5	9.4	12.4	12.4	6.9	-5.9	0.8
Groundnuts	X2	5.1	7.1	5.6	6.3	9.5	8.4	8.2	8.2	6.5	6.5	2.3	1.8	3.6
Sorghum	F1	5.7	5.8	9.1	9.1	8.9	8.0	8.0	7.8	6.8	6.8	0.6	2.7	0.8
Millet	F2	4.9	4.4	7.0	6.5	7.0	6.3	6.4	6.2	5.2	5.2	1.9	0.1	3.4
Maize	F3	9.0	14.6	16.9	13.5	13.7	16.0	13.3	14.0	15.2	15.2	0.4	6.4	2.3
BURUNDI														
Coffee	X1	6.3	8.4	9.0	9.3	8.2	9.4	7.3	7.2	6.7	5.9	2.6	-0.8	-7.3
Tea	X2	4.0	7.7	8.8	10.7	9.0	10.4	9.8	7.5	5.6	7.5	0.5	1.5	-0.7
Maize	F1	10.8	13.5	13.9	14.2	14.3	12.3	12.8	13.1	13.2	12.7	0.1	3.9	-2.4
Sorghum	F2	10.0	11.0	11.2	11.5	11.3	9.9	12.2	12.2	12.4	12.2	0.3	0.1	2.4
Rice, paddy	F3	23.5	33.3	30.9	31.1	30.9	29.4	26.8	27.9	32.6	32.0	3.3	-1.3	-3.6
Millet	F4	10.0	10.9	11.2	11.0	10.3	11.1	11.1	10.3	12.9	11.7	1.5	1.5	0.5
Bananas	NT1	..	..	..	..	..	..	..	..	..	..	..	..	..
Cassava	NT2	90.9	89.0	89.8	92.0	89.9	87.9	83.5	85.8	86.2	87.1	0.1	-1.5	-0.5
CAMEROON														
Coffee	X1	3.0	3.4	4.0	2.6	1.5	1.0	1.2	2.0	3.1	3.4	0.9	0.4	-17.7
Cocoa	X2	2.6	3.2	3.0	2.7	3.0	3.1	3.8	3.5	3.5	3.5	-0.3	1.5	5.3
Seed Cotton	X3	12.9	12.1	12.7	12.7	12.3	11.8	12.3	13.7	7.3	8.1	7.6	2.7	-4.6
Maize	F1	8.3	18.5	18.0	18.1	18.7	20.2	21.8	21.4	20.0	20.0	3.4	1.8	4.4
Sorghum	F2	8.7	8.5	7.7	7.6	7.6	7.3	8.7	8.3	7.3	8.3	-3.6	2.4	2.9
Millet	F3	7.6	10.5	10.5	10.0	10.3	10.0	10.2	10.1	10.1	10.1	-2.8	6.7	-1.6
Rice	F4	23.4	50.0	60.0	34.7	52.4	50.0	38.8	47.0	45.8	45.8	12.3	7.2	-4.9
Cassava	NT1	59.0	164.4	187.5	187.5	193.8	187.5	175.0	170.0	188.9	166.7	7.2	-1.0	0.7
Plantains	NT2	..	..	..	..	..	..	..	..	..	..	..	..	..
CENTRAL AFRICAN REPUBLIC														
Coffee	X1	3.6	5.9	6.9	6.2	4.1	8.2	4.7	7.2	6.0	5.4	4.5	2.3	-1.1
Seed Cotton	X2	3.4	7.9	5.1	6.0	6.6	6.5	7.6	6.9	7.7	7.0	7.9	-2.0	2.6
Sorghum	F1	6.5	7.8	10.1	12.6	11.6	8.0	11.0	10.7	11.9	12.7	4.6	3.9	2.6
Maize	F2	3.8	8.2	8.1	9.0	9.0	8.5	8.5	8.5	9.1	9.1	1.4	8.7	0.0
Groundnuts	F3	10.1	9.2	8.6	9.8	9.8	10.0	9.4	9.3	9.7	10.0	-0.7	5.1	-1.3
Cassava	NT1	30.7	28.4	33.6	34.5	34.5	31.0	28.9	29.2	30.5	30.5	2.5	-4.5	-1.4
Yams	NT2	60.0	65.7	65.7	68.4	65.0	66.7	66.7	68.0	68.0	68.0	1.5	0.1	0.7
CHAD														
Seed Cotton	X1	5.1	7.7	6.2	5.7	6.3	6.8	7.6	7.5	7.5	7.5	5.6	3.1	0.7
Sorghum	F1	5.1	6.4	5.7	7.4	5.9	6.6	6.5	6.7	6.6	6.9	-0.5	3.4	4.5
Millet	F2	4.7	3.4	4.0	5.2	3.7	4.9	3.6	4.2	4.0	4.4	-0.8	-2.4	4.9
Groundnuts	F3	5.7	5.9	8.5	8.3	6.9	7.0	9.2	6.7	7.9	7.9	1.5	10.1	-7.2
COMOROS														
Bananas	F1	..	..	..	..	..	..	..	..	..	..	..	..	..
Cassava	NT1	48.5	50.5	50.2	52.0	52.8	53.6	54.4	55.2	55.6	55.6	-1.3	5.3	3.2

8-13. Agricultural yields by major crop (continued)

CONGO, DEM. REP. OF.													
Coffee(green)	X1	3.7	3.5	3.3	3.2	3.6	3.5	3.4	2.7	2.2	2.5	-1.1	0.9	-6.2
Palm oil	X2	..	..	..	..	..	..	..	..	..	..			
Maize	F1	8.0	8.2	8.1	8.1	8.3	8.3	8.8	8.1	7.7	7.5	1.9	-0.3	-0.5
Rice	F2	8.0	8.1	8.0	7.3	7.2	7.3	7.5	7.2	6.9	6.8	1.2	-1.2	-4.0
Cassava	NT1	70.0	80.7	80.0	80.0	78.1	77.2	77.5	76.4	76.4	75.0	0.4	1.7	-2.0
Plantains	NT2	..	..	..	..	..	..	..	..	..	..			..
CONGO, REP. OF												•		
Coffee	X1	8.0	4.2	4.0	4.2	4.3	4.6	4.3	4.3	4.2	4.4	5.4	-8.5	-0.3
Cocoa beans	X2	5.6	4.1	3.8	3.9	3.9	4.0	3.8	3.3	3.2	3.0	-3.9	-6.5	-5.1
Maize	F1	8.1	8.4	8.4	8.0	8.0	8.0	8.4	8.0	8.0	8.0	2.4	3.4	-0.9
Cassava	NT1	68.8	65.0	73.7	73.9	65.6	67.3	71.8	71.9	70.9	71.8	3.5	-1.7	2.3
Plantains	NT2	..	..	..	..	..	..	..	..	..	..			..
COTE D'IVOIRE														
Coffee	X1	2.4	2.2	1.6	1.0	1.1	1.1	1.4	1.2	1.6	1.8	-6.6	12.1	-10.2
Cocoa	X2	5.0	5.2	5.4	5.6	5.5	5.4	5.7	5.8	5.6	5.6	0.1	1.0	1.4
Oil Palm, fruit	X3	..	..	..	..	..	..	..	..	..	..	..	..	..
Rice	F1	11.7	11.5	11.0	11.0	17.6	15.8	16.1	12.8	16.1	15.3	-0.9	-1.1	9.4
Maize	F2	8.1	7.2	7.5	7.9	8.0	7.7	8.1	8.2	8.2	8.2	5.8	-5.0	3.8
Cassava	NT1	52.3	55.1	52.0	50.1	49.5	50.5	52.9	50.9	50.7	50.7	1.8	0.7	-1.8
Yams	NT2	90.7	95.0	89.7	89.0	88.0	89.6	91.9	108.3	108.6	101.8	1.8	-0.5	2.6
EGYPT														
Seed Cotton	X1	26.9	20.1	22.8	27.6	29.2	22.4	21.4	24.8	26.3	21.0	4.0	-5.9	2.3
Rice, paddy	X2	58.3	72.7	74.6	76.5	77.2	79.1	81.4	82.9	85.6	85.3	1.0	2.8	6.3
Wheat	F1	31.2	52.0	48.2	52.5	53.0	50.0	54.2	56.4	56.0	58.0	0.7	7.1	3.9
Sugarcane	F3	812.5	1,003.3	1,036.4	1,029.1	1,061.7	1,093.4	1,095.3	1,107.4	1,089.3	1,108.0	..	0.5	3.6
Dry Broadbeans	NT1	20.7	31.1	34.0	21.4	35.1	22.7	31.7	32.0	31.9	32.7	-0.7	6.4	1.3
EQUATORIAL GUINEA														
Cocoa	X1	1.1	1.0	1.0	0.8	0.9	0.8	0.7	0.8	0.7	0.8	-3.0	1.9	-7.9
Coffee(green)	X2	3.4	3.8	3.8	3.8	3.8	3.8	3.8	3.8	3.6	3.5	0.4	0.0	-1.1
Cassava	NT1	24.6	25.0	25.6	26.1	26.1	26.1	26.1	25.8	25.8	25.8	0.9	0.6	-1.3
ETHIOPIA														
Coffee(green)	X1	..	..	..	..	..	..	..	..	..	..	..	..	..
Sorghum	F1	..	..	..	..	..	..	..	..	..	..	..	..	..
Maize	F2	..	..	..	..	..	..	..	..	..	..	..	..	..
Barley	NT1	..	..	..	..	..	..	..	..	..	..	..	..	..
GABON														
Coffee(green)	X2	2.4	3.6	4.1	3.9	4.3	4.3	2.7	3.7	3.7	4.3	8.6	7.9	-4.8
Sugarcane	X3	497.5	520.8	517.0	488.9	542.0	568.6	573.3	576.7	583.3	576.7	15.4	0.5	4.0
Maize	F1	16.6	16.3	16.9	17.6	17.9	17.7	17.6	17.6	17.2	17.2	2.8	-2.3	3.9
Cassava	NT1	50.0	50.0	51.6	51.1	49.3	49.1	50.1	50.0	50.0	50.0	0.0	0.0	-0.5
Taro (cocoyam)	NT2	58.8	56.8	57.8	57.6	60.4	61.7	59.6	60.0	61.1	61.1	0.5	-0.5	2.0
Yams	NT3	56.4	64.7	64.7	66.7	64.7	69.4	68.4	70.0	70.0	70.0	1.1	1.5	3.1
GAMBIA, THE														
Groundnuts	X1	8.7	8.3	10.5	8.5	12.1	10.8	9.6	7.1	11.1	11.1	-1.0	1.8	-5.7
Seed Cotton	X2	6.9	5.3	8.5	8.0	9.3	8.8	9.2	9.0	4.3	4.3	..	1.7	-1.3
Oil Palm, fruit	X3	..	..	..	..	..	..	..	..	..	..	..	..	..
Millet	F1	8.7	9.3	10.3	11.2	10.3	10.6	9.8	11.0	9.0	9.0	2.8	-2.8	0.4
Rice, paddy	F2	19.7	14.7	15.3	17.3	14.6	15.4	12.3	11.6	10.7	10.7	7.9	-9.6	-9.0
Maize	F3	10.7	12.0	11.8	15.1	16.3	12.6	12.9	12.2	11.7	11.7	3.1	-3.0	-1.9
Sorghum	F4	8.0	6.3	9.6	9.5	11.0	10.6	8.5	10.8	9.6	9.6	4.6	-1.6	3.3
GHANA														
Cocoa	X1	2.3	4.2	3.4	4.3	3.6	4.2	4.3	4.2	4.2	4.2	-2.8	15.1	1.5
Maize	F1	8.7	11.9	15.3	12.0	15.1	14.9	15.1	15.2	16.5	16.5	-4.6	6.6	7.4
Millet	F2	5.9	6.0	5.4	6.4	9.7	8.8	9.8	10.2	8.2	8.2	0.4	3.1	13.5
Groundnuts	F3	17.0	8.9	6.7	7.7	7.7	9.4	9.3	8.2	8.4	8.4	-1.6	4.5	-3.5
Cassava	NT1	80.8	84.2	67.3	72.5	84.6	115.8	119.9	120.4	120.2	120.2	2.7	-1.5	16.7
Plantains	NT2	..	..	..	..	..	..	..	..	..	..			..
GUINEA														
Coffee(green)	X1	3.2	5.0	5.2	5.3	5.2	5.5	5.1	4.1	4.0	4.2	-1.2	7.9	-4.6
Oil Palm, fruit	X2	..	..	..	..	..	..	..	..	..	..	..	..	..
Rice, paddy	F1	9.0	9.7	13.8	13.3	13.8	13.8	14.4	14.5	14.5	14.4	-1.8	8.6	9.2
Maize	F2	10.0	10.1	10.4	10.7	10.4	10.3	9.7	9.5	9.5	9.5	-1.5	-2.7	-1.6
Groundnuts	F3	6.6	7.6	8.8	10.1	8.8	9.2	9.1	9.2	9.2	9.2	-0.6	0.7	6.8
Cassava	NT1	70.0	78.2	74.9	71.7	75.5	71.9	63.0	66.4	66.4	66.5	0.0	3.0	-5.7
GUINEA-BISSAU														
Groundnuts	X1	3.5	10.1	7.8	10.1	10.0	11.7	11.3	11.0	11.3	11.3	-3.3	21.1	7.5
Rice, paddy	F1	7.0	20.5	20.1	19.0	19.7	20.1	19.1	18.4	18.9	18.9	0.8	11.3	-2.2
Sorghum	F2	6.4	8.8	10.3	8.6	9.0	9.2	9.3	9.1	9.5	9.5	0.0	11.0	1.9
Millet	F3	7.2	8.7	12.2	8.6	8.6	7.7	9.1	8.6	9.1	9.1	4.3	7.0	-3.0
Maize	F4	10.0	10.7	11.4	9.5	9.3	9.3	10.0	9.4	10.0	10.0	-0.1	13.8	-2.0

8-13. Agricultural yields by major crop (continued)

KENYA														
Coffee(green)	X1	8.9	6.8	5.6	5.5	4.7	5.0	5.9	6.0	4.9	3.6	0.8	1.8	-11.3
Tea	X2	11.7	20.3	20.4	18.2	20.1	19.8	22.0	22.6	19.4	24.3	4.0	6.7	4.4
Sugarcane	X3	1,211.8	1,173.0	960.7	877.7	841.3	662.1	810.4	815.8	794.6	844.8	5.4	4.0	-10.3
Sisal	X4	9.9	12.0	11.4	11.4	11.7	11.3	13.2	13.4	13.4	13.8	1.8	-4.4	6.1
Maize	F1	12.0	15.8	15.9	17.3	16.0	20.4	19.6	16.6	14.7	17.2	1.9	4.0	1.6
Wheat	F2	21.6	18.6	18.6	12.6	9.7	19.2	19.6	20.0	16.1	18.5	2.0	-0.6	4.9
LESOTHO														
Wheat	X1	9.7	8.1	2.0	8.6	7.3	4.2	6.2	13.3	11.8	7.0	-4.8	4.8	12.0
Dry Peas	X2	7.8	2.4	0.7	5.6	5.4	3.1	2.9	9.2	3.5	3.1	-4.6	11.6	5.8
Dry Beans	X3	5.2	18.8	3.4	2.9	10.7	3.2	12.4	6.3	10.4	8.0	-6.8	18.5	3.6
Maize	X4	9.6	11.0	5.4	5.8	8.9	8.6	8.1	12.5	9.9	9.4	-1.9	7.7	4.2
Sorghum	F1	9.7	10.1	5.4	6.1	13.0	8.8	8.0	8.6	8.1	8.0	-3.8	1.8	3.0
LIBERIA														
Rubber	X1	7.6	10.0	9.5	10.7	10.0	10.0	9.3	10.0	10.0	10.0	0.7	2.9	-1.2
Coffee(green)	X2	4.6	1.1	1.0	1.9	2.0	2.0	2.0	2.0	2.0	2.0	6.1	-17.7	8.1
Cocoa	X3	2.3	1.4	1.0	0.9	0.8	0.9	1.3	1.1	0.9	0.9	-2.1	-8.1	-11.2
Rice, paddy	F1	12.3	9.3	9.3	9.2	10.8	11.1	11.2	12.5	12.4	12.9	0.6	-1.2	7.0
Cassava	NT1	66.7	69.2	64.3	66.7	61.3	62.5	60.3	65.0	65.1	65.3	0.1	9.6	-3.3
LIBYA														
Wheat	F1	5.2	12.3	11.5	10.7	10.6	9.7	10.6	10.5	10.4	10.4	-0.5	4.6	0.9
MADAGASCAR														
Coffee	X1	3.7	3.5	3.8	3.7	3.7	4.2	3.5	3.5	2.9	3.1	-0.9	1.1	-3.0
Vanilla	X2	0.4	0.9	0.6	0.4	0.7	0.6	0.6	0.6	0.6	0.6	-12.4	3.7	-9.3
Cloves	X3	1.7	1.2	1.8	1.4	2.1	1.8	1.7	1.9	1.9	1.9	-8.4	-15.4	17.0
Rice	F1	17.6	20.8	20.5	20.9	20.8	20.7	21.3	21.9	21.7	20.9	-0.7	2.5	0.9
Cassava	NT1	60.8	66.5	66.5	67.1	67.7	67.4	68.9	67.4	67.5	67.2	-1.0	2.0	0.6
Sweet potatoes	NT2	48.6	53.4	50.3	53.1	51.1	53.8	59.1	58.1	56.0	56.0	-0.8	2.0	2.9
MALAWI														
Tobacco leaves	X1	8.6	10.1	9.7	9.7	10.0	12.5	12.2	12.4	13.8	11.9	3.5	3.4	8.1
Tea	X2	17.1	21.0	21.9	15.4	21.3	18.7	18.2	19.8	22.0	22.0	3.1	-0.6	-0.9
Groundnuts	X3	7.1	7.7	8.2	4.0	9.0	5.6	4.6	5.6	6.9	9.0	0.3	-7.8	3.9
Seed Cotton	X4	6.9	5.3	8.5	8.0	9.3	8.8	9.2	9.0	4.3	4.3	..	1.7	-1.3
Maize	F1	12.2	10.0	11.4	4.5	15.2	9.2	13.5	14.4	9.9	13.9	0.6	-0.3	10.4
Sorghum	F2	6.7	5.0	6.0	1.4	4.9	3.1	6.1	7.2	4.7	5.6	-5.8	-0.2	4.4
Cassava	NT1	58.4	23.5	23.4	20.1	28.8	27.1	27.1	27.1	27.8	27.8	-7.0	-7.4	7.8
MALI														
Seed Cotton	X1	11.3	14.0	12.7	13.0	12.7	10.9	10.9	12.1	10.8	10.7	3.5	2.6	-5.0
Groundnuts	X2	8.9	7.3	10.9	7.5	7.8	8.4	8.7	9.4	9.8	9.8	-1.4	3.2	0.4
Millet	F1	6.2	6.2	6.7	5.9	5.4	6.1	6.0	6.0	7.9	7.9	-0.2	3.5	-0.9
Rice, paddy	F2	9.7	15.5	18.1	15.9	16.6	16.5	15.2	15.3	18.9	18.9	-3.8	15.0	1.7
Sorghum	F3	8.0	6.6	6.9	6.8	7.5	7.6	8.1	8.3	10.0	10.0	2.3	-7.6	7.9
Maize	F4	11.1	12.2	13.8	12.3	11.0	11.3	12.1	12.1	16.0	16.0	1.5	2.9	1.7
MAURITANIA														
Sorghum	F1	3.2	5.2	4.5	5.0	5.9	5.8	6.4	6.9	3.2	3.8	-4.9	19.2	-3.7
Rice	F2	32.0	33.3	28.1	39.9	29.1	27.7	27.0	38.5	38.3	36.8	6.0	-2.9	-1.3
Millet	F3	2.3	2.8	2.7	2.6	2.6	2.9	3.6	3.4	1.4	0.6	13.7	-8.0	-23.3
Maize	F4	6.5	6.8	6.0	7.7	12.3	5.0	10.0	5.9	4.3	8.9	4.1	9.2	4.8
MAURITIUS														
Sugarcane	X1	576.8	727.1	740.0	770.0	729.7	659.2	716.5	720.6	795.8	794.5	-0.2	1.5	0.8
Potatoes	NT1	165.6	181.1	197.4	192.1	200.9	175.7	198.5	141.9	226.5	230.8	4.6	-5.5	-1.7
Onions	NT2	107.6	122.0	137.7	151.4	164.6	176.0	184.4	177.9	179.5	179.3	1.7	0.1	11.8
MOROCCO														
Wheat	F1	10.6	13.3	18.7	7.0	6.8	18.1	5.5	18.4	9.3	13.3	0.8	6.4	-3.4
Sugarbeet	F2	353.5	464.0	438.7	528.6	506.8	499.8	467.7	487.1	466.6	522.1	3.3	0.9	2.7
Barley	NT1	10.3	8.9	13.8	4.8	4.8	14.4	3.9	15.8	6.6	8.4	-4.7	9.6	-4.6
MOZAMBIQUE														
Seed Cotton	X2	4.9	3.7	5.3	5.8	6.1	6.6	6.0	6.8	4.4	4.6	-4.4	0.6	17.6
Tea	X3	10.3	6.9	7.7	5.1	5.6	6.3	6.2	6.3	5.6	6.2	-0.5	-14.9	1.2
Maize	F1	5.4	4.5	3.2	1.6	6.3	5.2	6.8	9.4	9.0	9.3	-4.1	-8.0	38.0
Rice, paddy	F2	8.3	8.7	5.3	3.0	6.2	8.3	8.7	9.7	10.9	10.9	-3.5	0.4	12.3
Cassava	NT1	41.4	48.6	38.0	33.3	41.7	36.9	42.4	47.7	53.8	55.6	0.1	0.1	5.4
NAMIBIA														
Wheat	F1	25.0	42.9	57.5	51.9	43.8	52.5	45.0	45.6	47.5	47.7	5.4	7.3	-1.4
Maize	F2	12.3	14.9	12.5	3.2	8.9	13.4	7.2	6.8	16.2	6.9	0.0	1.5	-14.7
NIGER														
Cowpeas	X1	2.4	0.8	1.7	1.0	0.5	1.8	0.5	1.7	1.6	1.6	-3.9	7.7	3.2
Groundnuts	X3	6.7	2.8	3.4	3.3	2.3	4.5	4.1	3.7	3.7	3.7	0.9	6.9	3.5
Millet	F1	4.4	2.4	4.2	3.6	3.5	4.0	3.4	3.5	3.3	3.3	-1.0	5.7	1.1
Sorghum	F2	4.8	1.3	2.1	1.5	1.9	2.0	1.4	2.8	3.1	3.1	-4.4	4.7	9.2

8-13. Agricultural yields by major crop (continued)

NIGERIA													
Cocoa	X1	3.9	4.0	2.8	3.6	3.4	3.6	3.7	3.8	3.6	3.6	-3.1	3.7	0.1
Oil Palm, fruit	X2	..	..	..	..	..	..	..	..	..	..	..	..	..
Seed Cotton	X3	1.8	6.7	7.0	6.8	7.9	8.0	8.0	7.5	8.1	7.3	-8.1	42.6	7.5
Groundnuts	X4	8.4	14.0	12.1	12.4	11.8	9.2	8.9	10.1	11.2	11.2	3.7	0.5	-4.5
Sorghum	F1	11.2	10.0	9.7	10.8	10.8	10.8	10.7	11.4	11.1	11.0	8.0	-6.5	4.0
Millet	F2	8.7	10.7	9.0	10.3	9.5	9.5	9.8	10.6	10.8	10.8	8.3	-7.0	-1.0
Maize	F3	13.2	11.3	11.3	11.2	11.8	12.7	12.9	13.3	12.7	13.8	1.0	6.1	3.0
Rice, paddy	F4	19.8	20.7	19.5	19.6	19.6	14.2	16.3	17.5	16.0	16.0	2.2	-0.1	-7.2
Yams	NT1	105.4	106.8	103.5	113.5	113.5	114.0	107.7	110.5	90.2	90.2	-7.9	14.9	-1.4
Cassava	NT2	95.8	116.5	101.9	105.9	105.9	105.9	106.8	106.5	112.7	112.7	-0.9	1.8	0.2
RWANDA														
Coffee(green)	X1	6.9	6.3	5.2	6.8	4.9	2.9	5.0	3.1	2.8	3.3	5.0	-10.1	-17.1
Tea	X2	7.4	10.5	11.1	10.9	10.5	7.1	8.2	8.6	10.0	10.0	-5.1	7.7	-6.8
Sorghum	F1	12.4	12.2	11.4	10.3	10.9	10.6	10.8	13.9	13.7	13.7	0.6	-1.0	4.2
Maize	F2	11.8	13.5	13.0	13.6	14.8	15.0	38.6	11.2	10.4	10.4	1.9	5.5	1.3
Plantains	NT1	..	..	..	..	..	..	..	..	..	..	..	..	..
Sweet potatoes	NT2	76.3	53.6	62.5	66.4	66.7	59.3	63.3	63.3	66.7	66.7	-0.4	-5.3	6.5
SENEGAL														
Groundnuts	X1	4.9	7.7	8.3	6.0	8.5	7.6	9.4	6.9	6.3	6.3	-4.2	7.6	-6.9
Seed Cotton	X2	6.9	10.0	11.8	10.7	11.4	11.0	8.2	7.6	9.5	9.5	1.7	6.7	-8.3
Millet	F1	4.7	5.8	6.7	5.8	6.7	5.9	7.5	6.2	5.2	5.2	-2.7	5.6	-2.2
Rice, paddy	F2	9.6	24.8	23.5	24.1	24.8	20.9	22.5	20.2	22.3	22.3	4.6	0.1	-2.3
Maize	F3	7.3	11.4	11.3	10.9	12.7	10.1	10.9	10.4	10.0	10.0	1.0	0.2	-6.2
Sorghum	F4	7.7	9.1	7.8	8.9	7.8	8.7	8.6	8.9	8.2	8.2	-0.4	-0.4	-2.0
SIERRA LEONE														
Cocoa	X1	14.2	41.7	38.4	27.0	27.0	33.5	33.3	33.3	43.3	43.3	11.4	10.8	-2.8
Coffee(green)	X2	12.7	23.0	22.6	23.0	23.0	18.5	17.9	17.9	21.9	21.9	12.3	5.2	-6.9
Palm oil	X3	..	..	..	..	..	..	..	..	..	..	..	..	..
Rice, paddy	F1	12.5	12.8	13.5	13.5	12.7	12.3	13.0	13.5	13.0	13.0	-0.8	-3.4	0.1
Cassava	NT1	38.0	59.9	54.0	53.3	45.8	58.7	58.5	58.6	49.9	49.9	-4.3	5.0	-1.9
SOMALIA														
Bananas	X1	..	..	..	..	..	..	..	..	..	..	..	..	..
Maize	F1	10.1	11.5	10.0	10.1	9.9	4.1	7.3	7.1	6.4	6.1	1.0	-1.4	-17.7
Sorghum	F2	3.1	5.6	4.1	3.1	2.9	4.1	3.4	3.2	3.1	2.7	3.0	3.4	-16.3
Sesame	NT1	4.6	4.5	4.1	3.3	3.1	3.0	3.4	3.4	3.3	3.0	-4.8	-1.7	-10.0
SOUTH AFRICA														
Maize	X1	25.2	25.1	22.6	7.9	22.8	28.5	13.8	27.0	25.1	25.5	-4.3	14.0	-1.3
Wheat	X2	9.1	10.9	14.9	17.7	18.5	17.6	14.5	21.0	16.6	12.5	0.9	5.9	8.9
Sugarcane	X3	661.4	487.4	534.0	341.8	295.1	400.1	423.1	509.8	528.8	575.7	-5.0	0.1	1.6
Sorghum	F1	28.8	17.4	18.2	6.2	21.6	22.9	16.1	30.8	26.6	24.3	-1.2	1.0	16.5
Barley	F2	8.8	23.8	12.6	12.5	19.8	22.9	24.0	13.9	14.6	13.6	9.3	-1.8	-5.9
SUDAN														
Seed Cotton	X1	8.2	12.6	14.6	11.4	12.1	14.1	12.4	10.3	13.8	12.3	0.7	-2.5	-4.1
Groundnuts	X2	8.0	5.5	7.8	7.0	5.5	8.0	6.8	8.6	7.6	7.6	-6.4	-2.0	14.4
Sesame	X3	2.6	1.7	1.8	2.0	1.4	1.3	2.1	2.2	1.9	1.9	-1.6	-1.7	8.3
Sorghum	F1	7.1	4.3	7.0	6.5	5.1	5.7	4.9	6.4	6.0	6.7	-6.3	3.4	8.8
Wheat	F2	12.1	15.9	14.8	23.2	13.8	13.3	16.1	17.7	19.5	21.2	1.6	2.0	4.9
SWAZILAND														
Sugarcane	X1	1,077.2	1,052.5	985.3	971.2	911.8	946.5	908.4	986.0	953.9	996.3	-0.5	0.0	-2.1
Seed Cotton	X3	10.2	9.5	9.8	2.9	6.3	5.9	7.7	11.7	11.0	12.9	-3.5	-3.7	8.6
Maize	F1	13.6	10.3	17.3	9.4	12.2	17.6	12.7	24.5	17.8	17.9	-3.1	-7.4	14.1
TANZANIA														
Coffee	X1	4.2	4.3	3.9	4.2	4.3	3.9	3.6	4.2	3.7	3.1	-0.1	-3.9	-4.2
Seed Cotton	X2	4.5	4.6	5.1	5.7	5.3	4.5	3.7	5.8	5.8	4.7	-5.6	17.0	-3.7
Tea	X3	10.9	14.4	10.4	11.8	12.0	13.3	13.2	10.1	11.8	13.8	6.8	-3.7	-3.7
Maize	F1	12.3	15.0	12.6	11.7	12.5	13.3	15.5	16.2	12.9	13.9	4.2	2.1	1.0
Rice	F2	11.9	19.2	16.9	12.8	18.1	17.4	15.1	15.3	14.5	20.6	-1.3	4.8	-0.7
Sorghum	F3	6.9	9.7	9.2	8.6	11.2	7.2	12.2	8.8	8.0	8.7	8.2	-2.3	-2.9
Millet	F4	7.6	11.2	7.8	8.5	6.5	6.4	10.9	9.0	9.8	7.3	5.7	-5.1	-5.4
Cassava	NT1	107.3	132.0	123.5	104.0	104.0	103.9	102.1	103.5	101.2	89.3	6.3	-3.3	-4.3
TOGO														
Coffee(green)	X1	4.9	6.2	6.8	6.8	7.0	6.6	6.7	6.5	5.3	6.9	-6.2	29.8	3.0
Cocoa	X2	4.5	2.0	1.9	1.8	2.1	2.0	1.9	2.8	2.9	2.0	-3.6	-8.2	3.1
Seed Cotton	X3	7.7	12.5	12.4	11.6	11.2	13.5	10.6	13.3	13.9	13.6	14.6	2.8	3.7
Maize	F1	9.2	9.7	9.1	10.1	11.6	9.3	8.6	9.4	10.7	9.4	-3.4	4.4	-2.8
Sorghum	F2	7.5	6.2	7.4	7.8	6.4	7.1	8.7	6.3	7.4	6.2	..	0.4	-2.4
Millet	F3	2.6	4.1	3.7	5.6	5.0	4.8	4.6	4.7	6.2	4.5	2.6	-14.4	-5.1
Cassava	NT1	103.3	76.9	77.9	69.0	68.6	53.8	59.2	56.9	60.3	55.6	-16.6	3.0	-9.5
Yams	NT2	86.6	90.7	90.3	83.3	103.4	82.2	85.8	87.2	91.9	88.8	-2.1	-1.1	-3.2

8-13. Agricultural yields by major crop (continued)

TUNISIA														
Wheat	F1	10.2	12.7	17.0	17.0	13.7	10.7	12.8	16.2	10.9	14.0	0.8	-4.1	8.0
Barley	F2	7.7	9.4	13.1	12.0	9.3	5.9	6.6	11.9	5.2	11.6	-0.3	-6.7	8.0
UGANDA														
Coffee(green)	X1	6.0	4.8	5.5	4.2	5.5	7.5	6.9	10.3	8.1	6.8	-2.8	1.8	12.0
Seed Cotton	X2	0.4	2.8	2.0	1.3	3.0	3.3	3.3	3.3	3.3	3.4	-3.6	-9.7	23.1
Millet	F1	16.5	15.0	15.0	16.0	15.1	14.8	16.0	11.0	12.7	14.5	1.0	7.4	-4.4
Maize	F2	11.1	15.0	13.5	15.0	16.0	15.1	16.0	13.0	12.4	12.5	0.0	6.7	-2.4
Sorghum	F3	17.9	15.0	14.8	15.0	15.0	15.0	15.0	11.0	10.7	12.5	3.6	2.8	-5.7
Cassava	NT1	68.6	83.0	83.0	80.0	85.1	65.0	67.0	67.0	67.0	66.8	7.3	3.4	-8.6
Plantains	NT2	..	..	..	..	..	..	..	..	..	..	..	..	..
ZAMBIA														
Seed Cotton	X1	5.0	4.8	6.6	4.3	7.3	7.8	6.7	5.6	5.3	5.0	0.3	-4.3	1.5
Tobacco leaves	X2	10.4	8.7	17.8	4.4	5.1	6.7	8.3	10.5	10.8	12.1	2.2	-7.9	5.8
Sunflower	X3	9.2	4.5	2.9	0.5	5.4	6.6	6.8	5.6	4.0	3.7	1.6	-14.5	21.3
Maize	F1	16.9	14.3	17.1	7.3	25.2	15.0	14.2	20.9	16.0	14.4	3.6	3.1	2.1
Wheat	F2	40.7	43.9	43.8	43.3	40.1	23.9	27.8	33.7	33.3	36.8	1.2	4.2	-11.1
Cassava	NT1	50.0	50.4	50.5	49.1	49.1	50.5	49.5	50.0	62.5	62.8	0.7	-0.1	3.3
ZIMBABWE														
Tobacco leaves	X1	19.5	21.7	24.9	24.3	21.9	24.6	24.2	24.2	21.7	21.7	5.8	-0.5	0.3
Seed Cotton	X2	17.5	8.2	7.8	2.7	8.6	7.8	4.6	9.2	8.9	9.9	0.8	-5.5	0.3
Sugarcane	X3	1,031.2	955.2	1,027.2	89.3	597.8	1,072.5	1,109.7	905.1	1,107.4	1,118.1	0.0	-0.7	9.7
Maize	F1	13.4	17.2	14.4	4.1	16.3	16.6	6.0	17.0	13.4	12.0	-8.1	6.8	-6.3
Wheat	F2	49.7	58.2	56.4	48.3	70.3	56.1	20.8	54.9	43.1	52.9	4.8	-0.1	-7.9

Notes: The following commodities are in their least-processed form unless otherwise indicated

Cotton, seed cotton

Groundnuts, unshelled

Coffee, green or roasted

Rice, paddy

Cloves, whole

Cocoa, beans

Tobacco, leaves

Sunflower, seeds

1 hectogram = 100 grams = 3.527 oz.

Countries excluded from listing: Cape Verde, Djibouti, Sao Tome and Principe, and Seychelles.

For livestock "yield", see Table 8.6. Food Output by Major Crops.

8-14. Incidence of drought

	1986	1987	1988	1989	1990	1991	1992	1993	1994	1995	1996	1997	1998
							D=Significant shortage of rain						
SUB-SAHARAN AFRICA	..	..	..	..	..	..	..	..	..	..	..	..	..
excluding South Africa	..	..	..	..	..	..	..	..	..	..	..	..	..
excluding South Africa & Nigeria	..	..	..	..	..	..	..	..	..	..	..	..	..
Angola	..	..	..	..	..	..	..	..	..	..	..	..	..
Benin	..	..	..	..	..	..	..	..	..	..	..	..	..
Botswana	D	D	..	..	..	..	D	..	..	D	..	..	..
Burkina Faso	..	..	..	..	..	..	..	..	..	..	..	D	..
Burundi	..	..	..	..	..	..	..	..	..	..	..	..	D
Cameroon	..	..	..	..	..	..	..	..	..	..	D	D	..
Cape Verde	..	..	..	..	..	..	..	D	D	..	..	D	D
Central African Republic	..	..	..	..	..	..	..	..	..	..	..	..	..
Chad	..	..	..	..	..	..	..	D	..	D	D	D	..
Comoros	..	..	..	..	..	..	..	..	..	..	..	..	..
Congo, Democratic Rep. of	..	..	..	..	..	..	..	..	..	..	..	..	..
Congo, Republic of	..	..	..	..	..	..	..	..	..	..	..	..	..
Côte d'Ivoire	..	..	..	..	..	..	..	..	..	..	..	D	..
Djibouti	..	..	..	..	..	..	..	..	..	..	..	..	..
Equatorial Guinea	..	..	..	..	..	..	..	..	..	..	..	..	..
Eritrea	..	..	..	..	..	..	..	..	..	..	D	D	..
Ethiopia	..	D	D	..	..	D	D	..	D	..	..	D	..
Gabon	..	..	..	..	..	..	..	..	..	..	..	..	..
Gambia, The	..	..	..	..	..	..	..	..	..	..	..	..	..
Ghana	..	..	..	..	..	..	..	..	..	..	..	..	D
Guinea	..	..	..	..	..	..	..	..	..	..	..	..	..
Guinea-Bissau	..	..	..	..	..	..	..	..	..	..	..	..	..
Kenya	..	..	..	..	..	..	D	D	..	..	..	D	D
Lesotho	..	..	..	..	..	..	D	..	..	D	..	..	..
Liberia	..	..	..	..	..	..	..	..	..	..	..	..	..
Madagascar	..	..	..	..	..	..	..	..	..	..	..	..	..
Malawi	..	..	..	..	..	..	D	..	D	D	..	D	D
Mali	..	..	..	..	..	..	..	..	..	..	..	..	..
Mauritania	..	..	..	..	..	..	..	..	..	..	..	..	..
Mauritius	..	..	..	..	..	..	..	..	..	..	..	..	..
Mozambique	..	..	..	..	..	..	D	..	..	D	..	..	D
Namibia	..	..	..	..	..	..	D	..	..	D	..	..	..
Niger	..	D	..	..	D	..	..	..	..	D	D	D	..
Nigeria	..	..	..	..	..	..	..	..	..	..	..	..	..
Rwanda	..	..	..	..	..	..	..	..	..	D	D	..	D
São Tomé and Principe	..	..	..	..	..	..	..	..	..	..	..	..	..
Senegal	..	..	..	..	..	..	..	..	..	..	..	..	..
Seychelles	..	..	..	..	..	..	..	..	..	..	..	..	..
Sierra Leone	..	..	..	..	..	..	..	..	..	..	..	..	..
Somalia	..	..	..	..	..	..	..	..	..	..	..	..	D
South Africa	..	..	..	..	..	..	D	..	..	D	..	D	..
Sudan	..	D	..	D	D	..	..	..	..	D	..	D	..
Swaziland	..	D	..	..	..	..	D	..	..	D	..	..	..
Tanzania	..	..	..	..	..	..	D	..	..	..	..	D	D
Togo	..	..	..	..	..	..	..	..	..	..	..	D	..
Uganda	..	..	..	..	..	..	..	..	..	..	..	D	..
Zambia	..	..	..	..	..	..	D	..	D	D	..	D	D
Zimbabwe	..	..	..	..	..	..	D	..	D	D	..	..	..
NORTH AFRICA	..	..	..	..	..	..	..	..	..	..	..	..	
Algeria	..	..	D	D	..	..	..	D	D	D	..	D	..
Egypt, Arab Republic	..	..	..	..	..	..	..	..	..	..	..	..	..
Libya	..	..	..	..	..	..	..	..	..	..	..	..	..
Morocco	..	..	..	..	..	..	..	..	..	D	..	D	..
Tunisia	D	..	D	D	..	..	..	..	..	D	..	..	..
ALL AFRICA	..	..	..	..	..	..	..	..	..	..	..	..	

Figure 8-1.   Food price index, 1997*

(Index, average 1995 = 100)

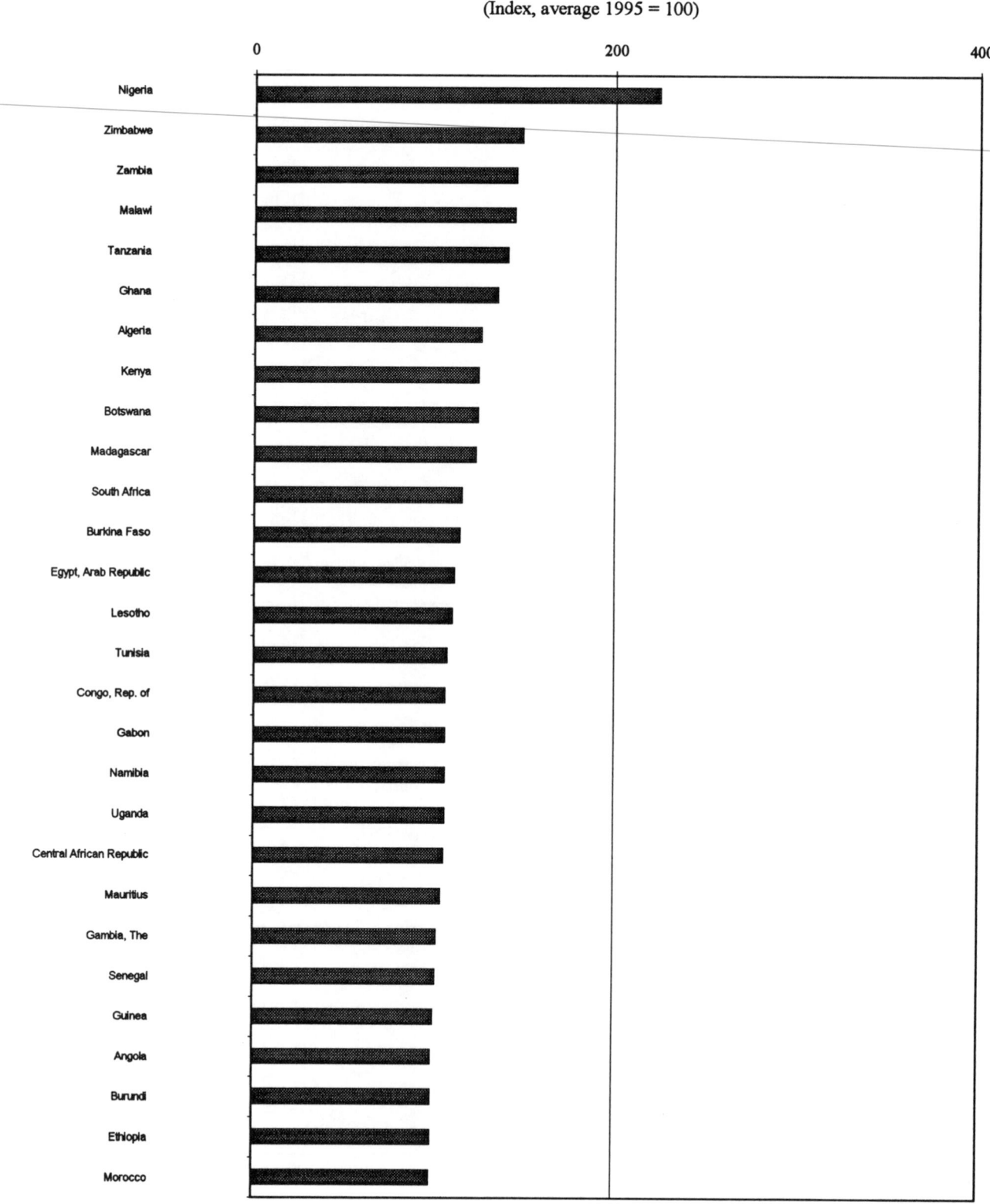

* Or most recent year available.
** Food price index is greater than 1400.

Figure 8-2. Food production per capita index, 1997*

(index, average 1989-91 = 100)

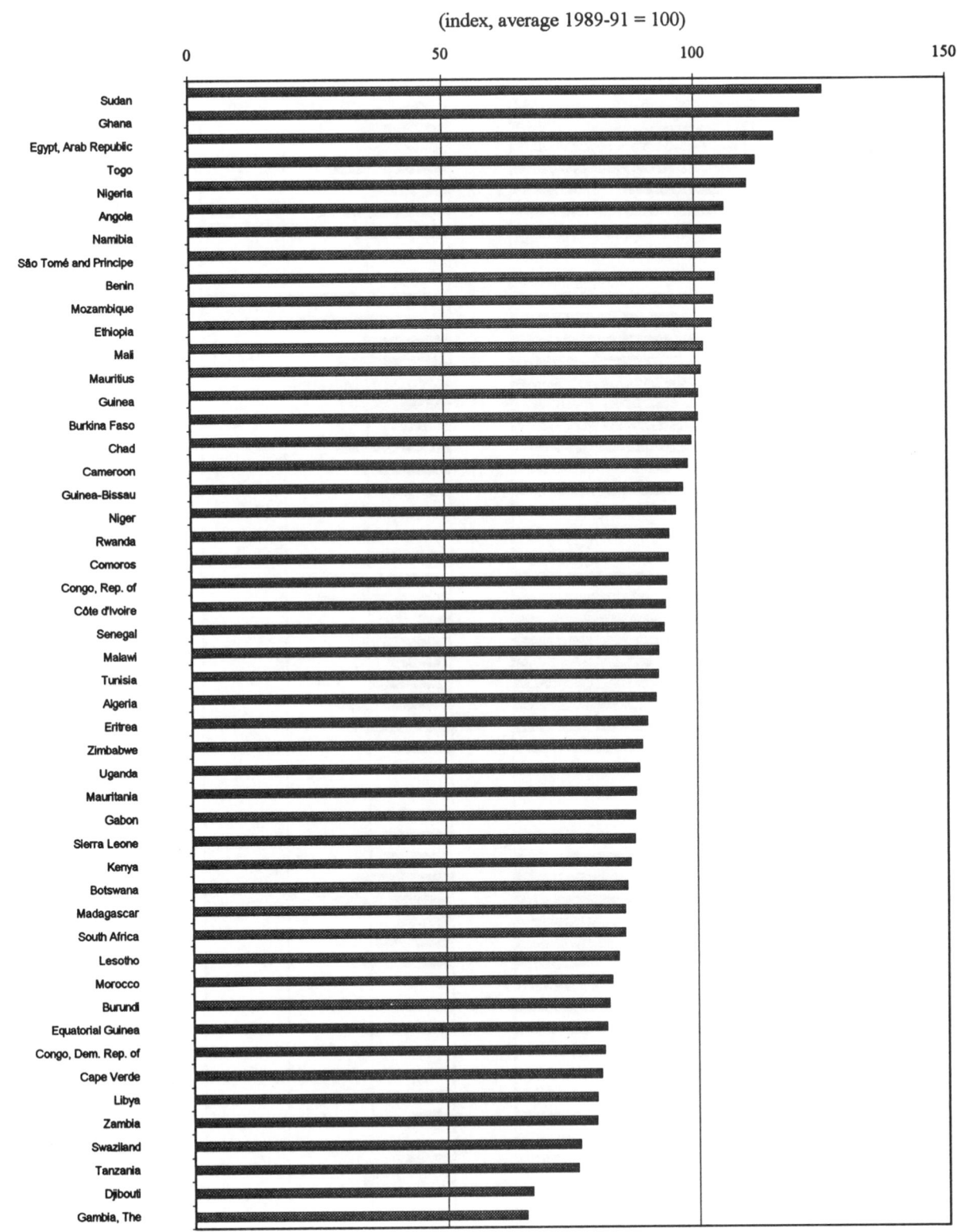

* Or most recent year available.

Figure 8-3. Food and nonfood production index, 1997*

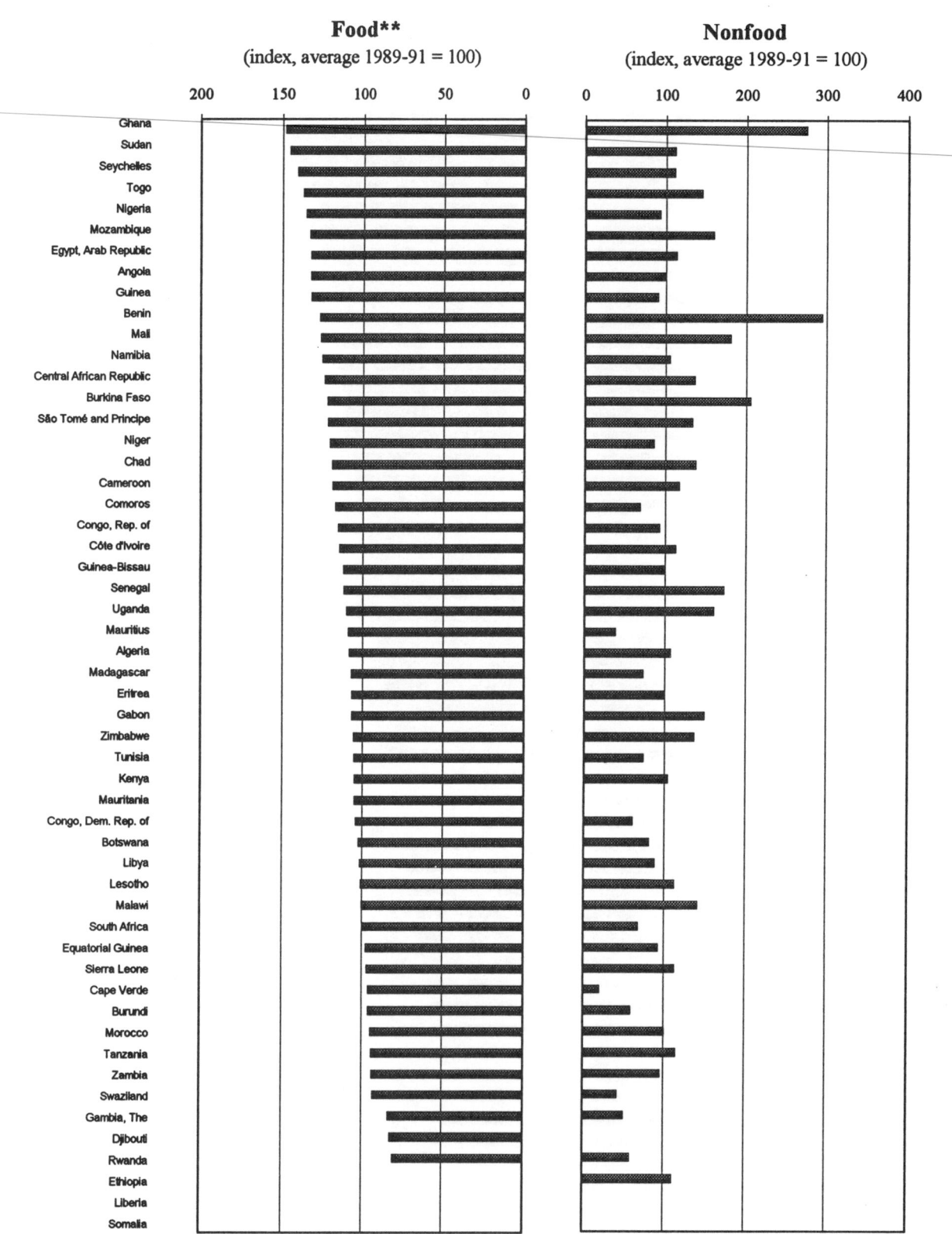

| **Food**** | **Nonfood** |
| (index, average 1989-91 = 100) | (index, average 1989-91 = 100) |

* Or most recent year available.

** Sorted by food production.

Figure 8-4.   Agricultural exports, 1997*

(millions of U.S. dollars)

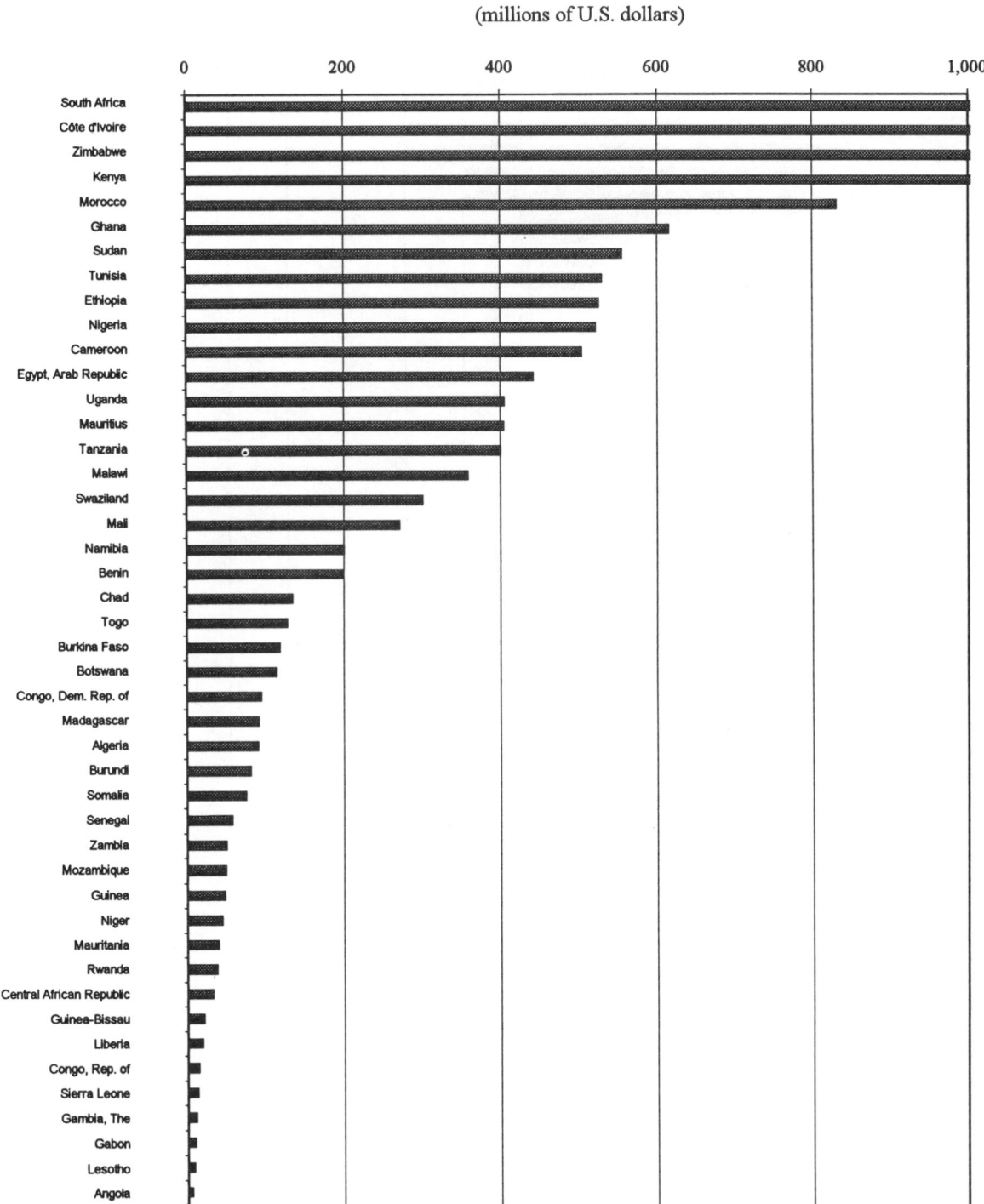

* Or most recent year available.
** Agricultural exports are greater than 1,000.

Figure 8-5.   Drought, 1980-98

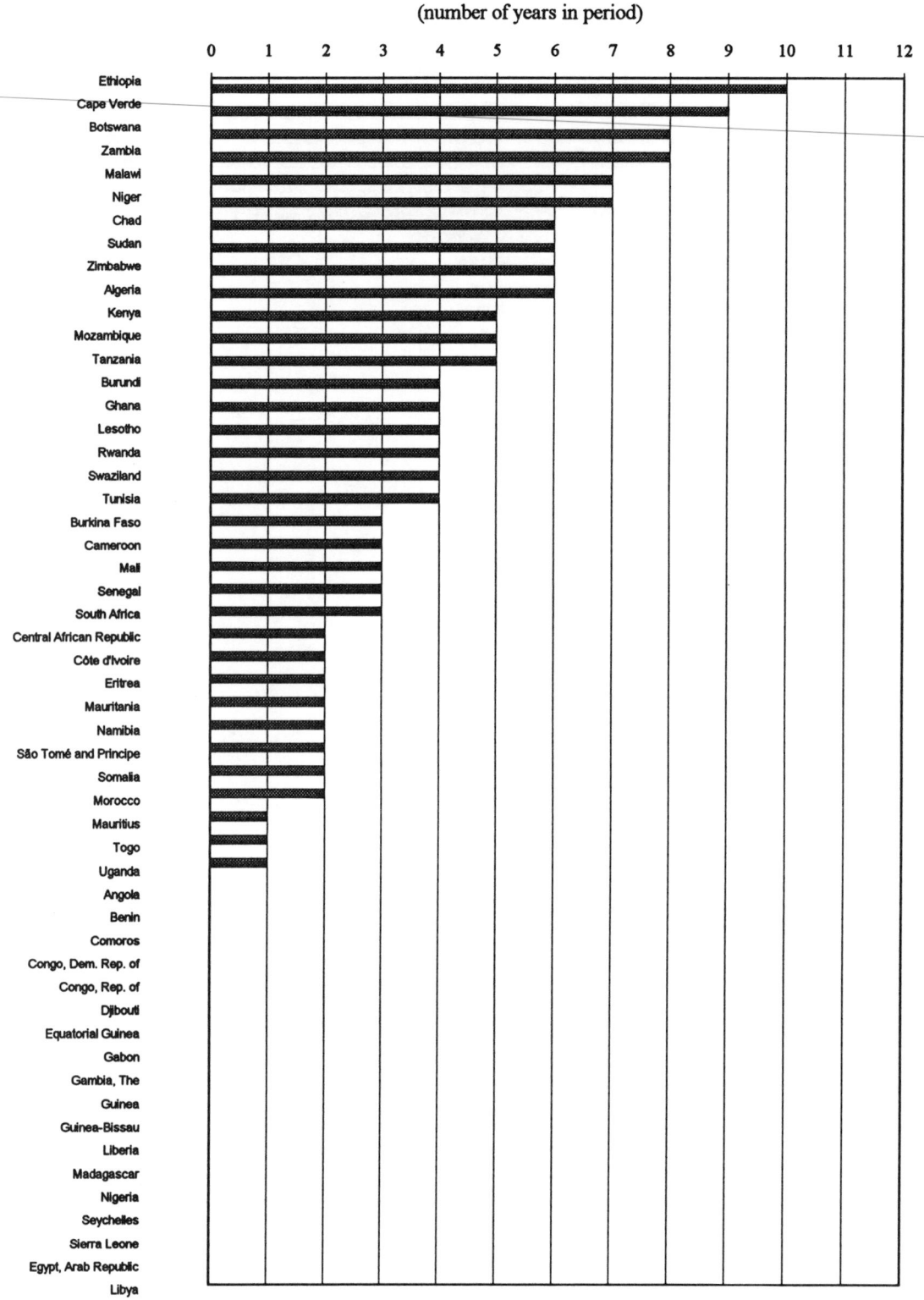

(number of years in period)

Technical Notes

Tables

Table 8-1. Nominal producer prices. Data on nominal producer prices are compiled from the FAO. In general, the figures reflect the average annual price received by farmers in the most important producing regions. But given the wide regional and seasonal variation and the lack of precision in recording specifics about prices quoted, the data should be interpreted only as a rough indication of price levels for an entire country during an entire year.

Unlike *ADI 1992*, because of lack of recent information, this volume does not differentiate between official producer prices and farmgate prices. In most cases they happen to be the same.

Crop years for most countries span parts of two calendar years; planting takes place in the first calendar year, while harvest and marketing take place at the end of the first and beginning of the second year. For consistency, producer prices are listed corresponding to the calendar year during which planting decisions are made. For example, producer prices for the crop year 1987/88 are listed as 1987.

For each country, up to four export crops and five food crops are included, which represent the most important commodities for that country in terms of value of total production during the early 1980s. The food crops include up to three cereals of "traded" grains (those commonly imported or exported) and up to two "nontraded" staples, generally roots and tubers, which are not normally imported or exported by African countries. In the table, these categories of crops are designated by the following symbols: X1 through X4 for export crops; F1 through F3 for traded food crops; and NT1 and NT2 for nontraded staple food crops.

The categorization is consistent across countries, but the numbering of crops within categories in each country depends on which crops are most important.

Where commodities may be marketed in several different forms, the form is generally specified (for instance, shelled or unshelled groundnuts). When not specified, the form of the commodity is the most common (for instance, shelled and dried maize). Where commodities are graded, an average grade has been used unless otherwise specified.

Table 8-2. Food price index. This is a subindex of the consumer price index. It reflects the cost to the average consumer of acquiring a fixed basket of food (*IMF, IFS*).

Table 8-3. Food production index. These indexes are based on 169 commodities that provide calories when consumed (FAO data). Some of these (such as cottonseed, cocoa, and vanilla) are not, however, a significant part of African diets, but are produced primarily for export.

Table 8-4. Nonfood production index. Data in this table are derived from 29 products that are not considered nutritious, including coffee, rubber, cotton lint, and tobacco leaves (FAO data).

Table 8-5. Food production per capita index. These are derived as the ratio of the food production index (Table 8-3) and estimated total midyear population figures (Table 1-2).

Table 8-6. Volume of food output, by major food crop. The table covers, with only a few differences, the same major food crops as presented in Table 8-1, excluding beverages (coffee, tea, cocoa), cotton, and tobacco. Included also are figures for livestock, which represent the combined total head of cattle, sheep, goats, pigs, horses, asses, and mules, and figures for the total head of rabbits (FAO data).

Table 8-7. Value of agricultural exports. Value of agricultural exports is expressed in current U.S. dollars at f.o.b. prices (FAO data).

Table 8-8. Cereal production. This refers to crops harvested for dry grain only. Cereal crops harvested for hay or harvested green for food, feed, or silage and those used for grazing are excluded (FAO data).

Table 8-9. Crop production index. Shows agricultural production for each year relative to the base period 1989–91. It includes all crops except fodder crops (FAO data).

Tables 8-10 and 8-11. Fertilizer use and imports. Figures are in metric tons and represent the aggregate of nitrogenous, phosphate, and potash fertilizers (FAO database for *Fertilizer Yearbook*).

Table 8-12. Area under major crops. Reflects arable land and land under permanent crops as defined and reported by the FAO.

Table 8-13. Agricultural yields, by major crop. This table follows closely the selection of commodities of Table 8-1. Units are in thousands of hectograms (which are equivalent to hundreds of kilograms) per hectare. Most of the data come from the database for the FAO *Production Yearbook*, with additional information taken from World Bank agricultural sector reports.

Table 8-14. Incidence of drought. This is the only indicator in this chapter based on subjective consid-

erations. Data on rainfall levels from other sources are usually presented to suit different purposes, without considering seasonal and regional characteristics of the producing regions. A low rainfall level might not harm agricultural production, if it did not adversely affect the regions where the main crops are produced, whereas an average rainfall level might be associated with difficulties in the producing regions, due to delay, for example. Therefore, simply presenting the annual rainfall levels would not necessarily enrich the agricultural data.

For each country, a binary classification was thus created. A "D" was assigned to a country if a significant shortage of rain unfavorably affected its agricultural production. For normal or average rainfall, the standard sign was given, as in the cases of insufficient information or "not applicable." (Specialists who work on the relevant countries were surveyed, as well as World Bank agricultural and environmental experts. In addition, the Federal Early Warning System project of the U.S. Agency for International Development provided information for 1993–94 for about half of the countries listed.)

Figures

The following indicators have been used to derive the figures in this chapter.

Figure 8-1. Food price index (Table 8-2).

Figure 8-2. Food production per capita index (Table 8-5).

Figure 8-3. Food production index (Table 8-3); non-food production index (Table 8-4).

Figure 8-4. Agricultural exports (Table 8-7).

Figure 8-5. Drought (Table 8-14).

Methodology used for regional aggregations and period averages in chapter 8

Table	Aggregations[a]				Period averages[b]
	(1)	(6)	(7)	(8)	(2)
8-1				x	
8-2			x		x
8-3		x			x
8-4			x		
8-5			x		x
8-6				x	x
8-7	x				x
8-8	x				x
8-9		x			x
8-10	x				x
8-11	x				x
8-12	x				x
8-13				x	x
8-14				x	

Note: Regional aggregations are shown in the rows for Sub-Saharan Africa, North Africa, and All Africa. Period averages are shown in the last three columns. This table shows only the methodologies used in this chapter.

a. Regional aggregations: (1) simple total; (2) simple total of the first indicator divided by the simple total of the second indicator (same country coverage); (3) simple total of the gap-filled indicator; (4) simple total of the gap-filled main indicator divided by the simple total of the gap-filled secondary indicator; (5) simple total of the first gap-filled main indicator less the simple total of the second gap-filled main indicator, all divided by the simple total of the secondary indicator; (6) weighted total; (7) median; (8) no aggregation; (9) simple arithmetic mean.

b. Period averages: (1) arithmetic mean (using the same series as shown in the table, i.e., ratio if the rest of the table is shown as ratio, level if the rest of the table is shown as level, growth rate if the rest of the table is shown as growth rate); (2) least-squares growth rate (using main indicator); (3) least-squares growth rate (using main indicator in constant terms, with the rest of the table in current terms).

9

Power, Communications, and Transportation

This chapter provides data on the power, communications, and transportation sectors of the economy.

An adequate and reliable supply of power is a vital ingredient for the economic development of African countries. This chapter presents information on electric power production and distribution losses. Data are from the International Energy Agency's (IEA's) *Energy Statistics and Balances of Non-OECD Countries, 1993–94* (1997).

Telecommunications are also an essential ingredient of a modern economy. In this chapter telephone main lines represent the supply side of the system, which in Africa is well short of demand. In fact, waiting time for telephone lines is the highest of any other geographical region. Data on telecommunications are from the International Telecommunications Union's (ITU) *World Telecommunications Development Report* (1996).

In addition to power and communication, countries must have a solid transportation sector to underpin expansion of their economies and ensure support to the activities of households, producers, and government. This chapter presents data on vehicle use, roads, and railway traffic. Data are from the World Bank databases and from the International World Road Federation's *World Road Statistics* (1996).

9-1. Electric power consumption per capita

	KWH										Annual average		
	1980	1988	1989	1990	1991	1992	1993	1994	1995	1996	75-84	85-89	90-MR
SUB-SAHARAN AFRICA	443.7	455.8	457.7	448.2	445.4	437.7	442.4	430.3	436.8	439.1	412.1	450.8	440.0
excluding South Africa	150.6	135.0	132.3	125.4	130.9	132.0	133.6	127.4	124.0	123.4	133.0	133.7	128.1
excl. S. Africa & Nigeria	181.6	153.3	146.5	143.6	149.5	149.4	148.2	142.1	139.0	137.9	158.8	152.2	144.2
Angola	67.2	65.6	64.1	60.3	65.3	64.1	62.1	60.4	58.8	61.0	74.9	67.1	61.7
Benin	35.8	44.7	42.9	44.7	44.0	43.7	45.2	44.5	43.3	47.9	41.4	48.4	44.8
Botswana	..	..	..	..	..	..	..	..	..	..	..	..	..
Burkina Faso	..	..	..	..	..	..	..	..	..	..	..	..	..
Burundi	..	..	..	..	..	..	..	..	..	..	..	..	..
Cameroon	166.6	236.3	240.1	224.9	219.3	213.8	208.4	203.1	198.0	170.8	189.3	239.4	205.5
Cape Verde	..	..	..	..	..	..	..	..	..	..	..	..	..
Central African Republic	..	..	..	..	..	..	..	..	..	..	..	..	..
Chad	..	..	..	..	..	..	..	..	..	..	..	..	..
Comoros	..	..	..	..	..	..	..	..	..	..	..	..	..
Congo, Democratic Rep. of	147.3	134.8	130.3	121.8	131.7	130.4	147.4	144.9	132.0	129.6	138.8	136.1	134.0
Congo, Republic of	94.1	205.2	212.4	254.0	236.3	224.6	220.3	216.1	212.4	206.9	100.0	202.1	224.4
Côte d'Ivoire	191.6	187.7	185.9	187.0	179.5	174.3	167.4	168.9	164.6	174.3	166.4	179.6	173.7
Djibouti	..	..	..	..	..	..	..	..	..	..	..	..	..
Equatorial Guinea	..	..	..	..	..	..	..	..	..	..	..	..	..
Eritrea	..	..	..	..	..	..	..	..	..	..	..	..	..
Ethiopia	16.2	17.9	17.4	17.2	17.8	21.8	22.9	22.2	21.8	17.9	16.3	18.0	20.2
Gabon	617.9	956.2	784.9	806.2	784.8	762.5	747.4	754.5	736.8	742.2	603.3	942.4	762.1
Gambia, The	..	..	..	..	..	..	..	..	..	..	..	..	..
Ghana	426.2	311.4	328.7	346.8	357.0	369.7	345.7	322.3	318.2	274.9	340.3	292.9	333.5
Guinea	..	..	..	..	..	..	..	..	..	..	..	..	..
Guinea-Bissau	..	..	..	..	..	..	..	..	..	..	..	..	..
Kenya	92.5	105.9	109.2	114.7	116.1	116.3	119.2	120.9	120.4	125.5	90.1	106.4	119.0
Lesotho	..	..	..	..	..	..	..	..	..	..	..	..	..
Liberia	..	..	..	..	..	..	..	..	..	..	..	..	..
Madagascar	..	..	..	..	..	..	..	..	..	..	..	..	..
Malawi	..	..	..	..	..	..	..	..	..	..	..	..	..
Mali	..	..	..	..	..	..	..	..	..	..	..	..	..
Mauritania	..	..	..	..	..	..	..	..	..	..	..	..	..
Mauritius	..	..	..	..	..	..	..	..	..	..	..	..	..
Mozambique	369.7	57.4	57.7	42.5	48.2	48.5	54.2	52.9	73.6	76.1	109.5	50.0	56.6
Namibia	..	..	..	..	..	..	..	..	..	..	..	..	..
Niger	..	..	..	..	..	..	..	..	..	..	..	..	..
Nigeria	68.2	86.5	94.7	77.1	81.6	85.5	95.3	88.8	84.8	85.3	64.6	84.9	85.5
Rwanda	..	..	..	..	..	..	..	..	..	..	..	..	..
São Tomé and Principe	..	..	..	..	..	..	..	..	..	..	..	..	..
Senegal	96.6	105.7	103.5	98.7	98.3	105.1	101.6	99.4	90.6	103.3	93.1	101.3	99.6
Seychelles	..	..	..	..	..	..	..	..	..	..	..	..	..
Sierra Leone	..	..	..	..	..	..	..	..	..	..	..	..	..
Somalia	..	..	..	..	..	..	..	..	..	..	..	..	..
South Africa	3,212.9	3,611.5	3,681.5	3,676.0	3,618.2	3,548.1	3,581.3	3,530.7	3,659.8	3,718.7	3,037.2	3,555.5	3,619.0
Sudan	42.2	46.0	44.7	42.1	40.7	39.9	39.0	38.3	37.5	51.4	43.1	46.8	41.3
Swaziland	..	..	..	..	..	..	..	..	..	..	..	..	..
Tanzania	50.3	42.8	49.6	52.6	57.8	58.1	59.2	50.8	52.4	58.8	43.4	42.5	55.7
Togo	..	..	..	..	..	..	..	..	..	..	..	..	..
Uganda	..	..	..	..	..	..	..	..	..	..	..	..	..
Zambia	1,015.7	803.7	580.6	502.8	651.8	623.4	606.2	589.5	574.3	560.0	1,058.2	807.9	586.9
Zimbabwe	990.4	925.8	910.8	920.9	897.5	901.7	817.3	753.9	738.1	765.3	960.3	939.3	827.8
NORTH AFRICA	362.8	635.7	655.6	675.9	738.3	740.8	759.9	783.6	800.5	814.6	352.0	601.0	759.1
Algeria	265.3	395.9	439.1	449.2	467.6	464.2	505.4	506.7	513.7	524.3	259.8	399.9	490.2
Egypt, Arab Republic	379.9	641.4	667.5	697.1	822.2	817.2	840.6	865.8	896.3	923.6	377.8	606.0	837.0
Libya	1,588.2	3,964.2	3,886.6	3,804.4	3,707.0	3,649.7	3,576.2	3,661.9	3,623.9	3,578.6	1,505.7	3,643.7	3,657.4
Morocco	222.8	322.3	316.7	339.8	355.4	380.9	377.1	402.8	408.7	408.4	212.1	299.2	381.9
Tunisia	379.2	476.0	501.0	531.5	543.2	572.0	608.1	646.9	664.7	674.4	323.6	459.5	605.8
ALL AFRICA	424.7	497.1	502.9	500.0	511.8	506.0	513.9	509.4	517.7	522.1	397.9	485.4	511.5

9-2. Energy production and use

	Energy production (KT oil equivalent)		Commercial energy use (KT oil equivalent)		Electric power transmission and distribution losses (% of output)	
	1980	1996	1980	1996	1980	1996
SUB-SAHARAN AFRICA	322,273	478,251	207,332	304,286	..	..
excluding South Africa	249,205	350,392	141,978	205,207	..	..
excl. S. Africa & Nigeria	100,726	179,939	89,132	122,537	..	..
Angola	11,301	40,485	4,538	6,017	25	28
Benin	1,212	1,951	1,363	1,920	220	87
Botswana	..	..	..	..	..	..
Burkina Faso	..	..	..	..	..	..
Burundi	..	..	..	..	..	..
Cameroon	5,824	10,016	3,687	5,000	7	20
Cape Verde	..	..	..	..	..	..
Central African Republic	..	..	..	..	..	..
Chad	..	..	..	..	..	..
Comoros	..	..	..	..	..	..
Congo, Democratic Rep. of	8,697	13,689	8,706	13,799	8	3
Congo, Republic of	3,970	11,493	845	1,205	1	0
Côte d'Ivoire	2,419	4,762	3,662	5,301	7	16
Djibouti	..	..	..	..	..	..
Equatorial Guinea	..	..	..	..	..	..
Eritrea	..	..	..	..	..	..
Ethiopia	10,588	15,536	11,157	16,566	8	1
Gabon	9,441	19,706	1,493	1,578	1	10
Gambia, The	..	..	..	..	..	..
Ghana	3,305	5,604	4,071	6,657	0	0
Guinea	..	..	..	..	..	..
Guinea-Bissau	..	..	..	..	..	..
Kenya	7,891	11,245	9,791	13,279	16	16
Lesotho	..	..	..	..	..	..
Liberia	..	..	..	..	..	..
Madagascar	..	..	..	..	..	..
Malawi	..	..	..	..	..	..
Mali	..	..	..	..	..	..
Mauritania	..	..	..	..	..	..
Mauritius	..	..	..	..	..	..
Mozambique	8,556	7,249	8,386	7,813	..	0
Namibia	..	..	..	..	..	..
Niger	..	..	..	..	..	..
Nigeria	148,479	170,453	52,846	82,669	36	32
Rwanda	..	..	..	..	..	..
São Tomé and Principe	..	..	..	..	..	..
Senegal	1,046	1,566	1,921	2,588	11	16
Seychelles	..	..	..	..	..	..
Sierra Leone	..	..	..	..	..	..
Somalia	..	..	..	..	..	..
South Africa	73,068	127,859	65,355	99,079	8	8
Sudan	7,089	9,486	8,169	10,787	14	32
Swaziland	..	..	..	..	..	..
Tanzania	9,502	13,073	10,280	13,798	14	12
Togo	..	..	..	..	..	..
Uganda	..	..	..	..	..	..
Zambia	4,198	5,357	4,551	5,790	7	11
Zimbabwe	5,688	8,721	6,511	10,442	14	7
NORTH AFRICA	205,735	260,865	44,231	92,350	..	..
Algeria	67,061	116,207	12,410	24,150	11	18
Egypt, Arab Republic	34,168	59,759	15,970	37,790	13	0
Libya	96,662	77,742	7,173	14,911	..	0
Morocco	877	868	4,778	8,822	10	4
Tunisia	6,966	6,289	3,900	6,676	12	11
ALL AFRICA	528,008	739,116	251,563	396,636	..	..

Power, Communications, and Transportation

9-3. Telephone, radio and television availability, 1994-97

	Telephones				Radios	Television
	Mainlines	*Waiting list*	*Average cost of call*	*Mobile phones*		sets
	(per 1,000 persons)	*(Thousands)*	*US$ per three minutes*	*(per 1,000 persons)*	*(per 1,000 persons)*	*(per 1,000 persons)*
SUB-SAHARAN AFRICA	11	1,440	..	4	172	44
excluding South Africa	5	1,303	..	0	162	39
excl. S. Africa & Nigeria	5	1,213	..	0	153	33
Angola	5	..	0.09	1	54	91
Benin	5	3	0.13	1	108	91
Botswana	41	12	0.03	0	155	27
Burkina Faso	3	..	0.10	0	32	6
Burundi	3	5	0.04	0	68	10
Cameroon	5	45	0.07	0	162	81
Cape Verde	56	10	0.05	0	179	45
Central African Republic	2	0	0.20	0	84	5
Chad	1	1	0.17	0	249	2
Comoros	9	..	0.20	0	138	4
Congo, Democratic Rep. of	1	6	..	0	98	43
Congo, Republic of	8	1	0.12	0	124	8
Côte d'Ivoire	9	82	0.11	2	157	61
Djibouti	13	0	0.19	0	81	71
Equatorial Guinea	6	..	..	0	427	107
Eritrea	5	42	0.03	0	101	11
Ethiopia	3	207	0.03	0	194	5
Gabon	29	10	0.15	8	182	135
Gambia, The	18	22	0.34	4	164	4
Ghana	4	28	0.08	1	238	109
Guinea	2	2	0.11	0	47	41
Guinea-Bissau	9	1	0.09	0	43	..
Kenya	9	77	0.06	0	108	19
Lesotho	9	9	0.04	1	48	24
Liberia	..	2	..	0	318	21
Madagascar	2	10	0.10	0	192	45
Malawi	3	31	0.03	0	256	2
Mali	2	..	0.17	0	49	10
Mauritania	4	1	0.13	0	150	89
Mauritius	132	23	0.05	32	368	228
Mozambique	4	17	0.04	0	39	4
Namibia	51	7	0.04	8	143	32
Niger	1	1	0.15	0	69	26
Nigeria	4	98	0.26	0	197	61
Rwanda	2	..	..	0	102	..
São Tomé and Principe	19	1	0.01	0	272	185
Senegal	10	17	0.09	1	141	41
Seychelles	176	2	0.16	15	541	191
Sierra Leone	4	14	0.07	0	251	20
Somalia	2	..	..	0	46	13
South Africa	100	116	0.07	37	316	125
Sudan	3	320	0.03	0	270	143
Swaziland	22	15	0.14	0	170	107
Tanzania	3	37	0.10	1	278	21
Togo	5	13	0.10	1	217	19
Uganda	2	6	0.19	0	123	26
Zambia	9	12	0.09	0	121	80
Zimbabwe	14	109	0.03	1	96	29
NORTH AFRICA	47	2,187	..	1	273	124
Algeria	42	732	0.02	1	239	67
Egypt, Arab Republic	47	1,310	0.01	0	316	127
Libya	64	..	0.03	0	232	143
Morocco	44	29	0.08	3	241	160
Tunisia	58	78	0.06	1	218	182
ALL AFRICA	18	2,338	..	3	190	59

9-4. Vehicle ownership

	Units per 1000 persons											Annual average		
	1980	*1988*	*1989*	*1990*	*1991*	*1992*	*1993*	*1994*	*1995*	*1996*	*1997*	*75-84*	*85-89*	*90-MR*
SUB-SAHARAN AFRICA	..	..	..	21	22	22	23	21	21	21	..	..	..	21
excluding South Africa	..	..	..	9	10	11	11	12	12	12	..	..	..	11
excl. S.Africa & Nigeria	..	..	..	9	10	11	11	12	12	12	..	..	..	11
Angola	..	..	..	19	19	20	20	20	20	20	..	..	..	20
Benin	..	..	..	3	4	5	6	6	7	8	..	..	..	5
Botswana	27	..	..	18	23	28	32	36	41	44	..	27	..	32
Burkina Faso	..	..	..	4	4	5	5	5	5	6		..	..	5
Burundi	..	..	..	0	..	..	..	..	..	..	..	..	..	0
Cameroon	8	..	..	10	10	11	11	11	12	12	..	8	..	11
Cape Verde	..	..	..	9	9	9	9	10	10	10	..	..	..	9
Central African Republic	8	..	..	1	1	0	1	1	0	0	..	8	..	0
Chad	..	..	..	2	3	3	3	3	4	4	..	..	..	3
Comoros	..	..	..	13	15	17	18	23	24	28	..	..	..	20
Congo, Democratic Rep. of	..	..	..	22	25	28	28	29	30	31	..	..	..	27
Congo, Republic of	..	..	..	18	19	20	20	19	20	20	..	..	..	19
Côte d'Ivoire	24	..	..	24	24	26	28	30	31	33	..	24	..	28
Djibouti	..	..	..	14	15	15	16	17	17	18	..	..	..	16
Equatorial Guinea	..	..	..	3	4	4	4	5	5	5	..	..	..	4
Eritrea	..	..	..	1	1	1	1	1	2	2	..	..	..	1
Ethiopia	2	..	1	1	1	1	1	1	1	1	2	2	1	1
Gabon	..	..	..	31	32	34	35	35	36	36	..	..	..	34
Gambia, The	..	..	..	13	13	13	13	15	15	15	..	..	..	14
Ghana	..	..	..	..	..	..	..	8	8	8	..	..	..	8
Guinea	..	..	..	4	4	5	5	5	5	5	..	..	..	5
Guinea-Bissau	..	..	..	7	7	7	8	10	10	11	..	..	..	9
Kenya	8	..	12	12	12	13	13	13	13	13	..	8	12	13
Lesotho	10	..	..	10	11	13	14	16	17	19	..	10	..	14
Liberia	1	..	..	14	14	14	14	15	14	15	..	1	..	14
Madagascar	..	..	..	6	5	5	5	5	6	6	..	..	..	5
Malawi	5	..	..	4	5	5	5	5	6	6	..	5	..	5
Mali	..	..	..	3	4	4	4	4	4	4	..	..	..	4
Mauritania	..	..	..	9	10	10	10	11	11	12	..	..	..	11
Mauritius	44	..	54	59	63	68	71	75	79	83	84	44	54	73
Mozambique	..	..	..	4	5	5	5	3	2	1	..	..	..	3
Namibia	..	..	..	72	86	76	81	84	84	85	..	..	..	81
Niger	6	..	5	6	6	6	6	6	6	6	..	6	5	6
Nigeria	4	..	..	..	..	..	..	13	12	12	..	4	..	12
Rwanda	2	..	1	2	3	3	3	4	4	4	..	2	1	3
São Tomé and Principe	..	..	..	36	37	37	38	40	40	41	..	..	..	38
Senegal	19	..	..	11	11	12	13	13	13	14	..	19	..	13
Seychelles	..	..	..	104	104	105	107	116	114	119	..	..	..	110
Sierra Leone	..	..	10	10	10	11	10	11	9	6	..	..	10	10
Somalia	..	..	..	2	2	2	1	1	1	1	..	..	..	1
South Africa	133	..	160	139	140	139	136	141	139	142	..	133	160	140
Sudan	..	..	..	9	10	10	10	12	12	12	..	..	..	11
Swaziland	52	..	63	66	71	68	65	62	66	68	..	52	63	67
Tanzania	3	..	..	5	4	5	5	5	5	5	..	3	..	5
Togo	..	..	1	23	24	25	25	25	26	27	..	..	1	25
Uganda	1	..	..	2	3	3	3	3	4	4	..	1	..	3
Zambia	..	..	..	14	16	18	20	22	24	26	..	..	..	20
Zimbabwe	..	..	..	..	..	33	34	33	32	32	..	..	..	33
NORTH AFRICA	..	..	38	33	34	34	34	46	49	49	..	..	38	40
Algeria	..	..	54	..	..	..	33	55	54	52	..	..	54	48
Egypt, Arab Republic	..	..	26	29	29	29	28	29	29	30	..	..	26	29
Libya	..	..	..	..	..	..	..	158	229	230	..	..	..	206
Morocco	..	..	..	37	38	41	43	47	48	48	..	..	..	43
Tunisia	38	..	62	48	49	50	52	59	59	64	..	38	62	54
ALL AFRICA	..	..	..	23	24	24	25	25	26	26	..	..	..	25

9-5. Road-to-population ratio

	Road 1000 km/1 million persons											Annual average		
	1980	*1988*	*1989*	*1990*	*1991*	*1992*	*1993*	*1994*	*1995*	*1996*	*1997*	*75-84*	*85-89*	*90-MR*
SUB-SAHARAN AFRICA	3.3	..	..	2.5	..	..	2.5	2.4	2.9	2.4	..	3.3	3.1	2.5
excluding South Africa	3.1	..	..	2.2	..	..	2.5	2.4	2.5	2.4	..	3.1	2.8	2.4
excl. S. Africa & Nigeria	3.5	..	..	2.6	..	..	2.8	2.6	2.7	2.6	..	3.5	3.3	2.6
Angola	10.3	..	..	7.9	..	7.3	7.1	6.8	6.6	6.4	6.2	11.1	9.0	6.9
Benin	2.1	..	1.3	1.8	1.2	1.2	1.3	1.3	1.2	1.2	..	2.1	1.6	1.3
Botswana	9.1	..	..	7.0	..	..	13.2	12.9	12.5	12.4	..	11.7	9.8	11.6
Burkina Faso	1.1	..	..	..	..	1.4	1.1	1.1	1.3	1.2	..	1.7	1.2	1.2
Burundi	1.2	..	..	1.2	..	2.5	2.5	2.4	2.4	2.3	..	1.8	0.6	2.2
Cameroon	7.2	..	..	6.1	..	..	2.7	2.7	2.6	..	..	6.6	5.5	3.5
Cape Verde	..	..	..	..	..	..	3.0	3.0	2.9	2.8	..	..	..	2.9
Central African Republic	9.8	..	8.3	8.0	7.9	7.7	7.5	7.4	7.3	7.2	..	9.8	7.9	7.6
Chad	6.0	..	..	4.7	..	..	5.0	5.0	4.9	4.8	..	6.6	5.3	4.9
Comoros	..	..	..	..	..	..	1.8	1.8	1.8	1.8	..	2.3	..	1.8
Congo, Democratic Rep. of	5.4	..	..	..	3.8	3.6	3.6	3.6	3.5	3.5	..	5.4	4.6	3.6
Congo, Republic of	5.0	..	..	..	5.6	5.4	5.3	5.1	5.0	4.9	..	5.5	4.5	5.2
Côte d'Ivoire	5.0	..	..	4.2	..	..	3.9	3.8	3.7	3.6	..	5.6	4.8	3.9
Djibouti	..	..	5.8	5.6	5.4	..	5.1	5.0	4.8	4.7	..	7.6	6.7	5.1
Equatorial Guinea	..	..	..	..	..	..	7.2	7.1	7.1	7.0	..	5.2	..	7.1
Eritrea	..	..	..	..	..	..	1.1	1.1	1.1	1.1	..	..	..	1.1
Ethiopia	1.0	..	0.4	0.5	0.5	..	0.5	0.5	0.5	0.5	..	0.9	0.7	0.5
Gabon	10.2	..	..	..	7.6	7.4	7.2	7.1	7.0	6.8	..	10.9	9.3	7.2
Gambia, The	3.4	..	..	2.6	..	..	2.4	2.4	2.4	2.4	..	3.0	4.2	2.4
Ghana	3.0	..	2.6	2.6	..	..	2.3	2.2	2.2	2.2	..	2.8	2.7	2.3
Guinea	5.4	..	..	..	..	2.6	0.0	4.7	4.6	4.5	..	4.2	5.8	3.3
Guinea-Bissau	..	..	..	..	..	..	4.1	4.1	4.0	4.0	..	4.7	..	4.0
Kenya	3.1	..	2.7	2.6	2.6	..	2.5	2.4	2.3	2.3	..	3.2	3.0	2.4
Lesotho	3.0	..	..	..	..	2.9	2.9	2.8	2.6	2.5	..	2.7	2.7	2.7
Liberia	2.9	..	..	2.4	..	..	3.8	3.8	3.8	3.8	..	3.9	3.2	3.5
Madagascar	5.7	4.5	1.3	..	2.9	2.8	4.0	3.9	3.7	3.6	..	4.8	4.0	3.5
Malawi	1.7	..	1.4	3.2	..	..	1.5	1.5	1.5	1.5	1.6	1.9	1.5	1.8
Mali	2.0	1.8	1.7	1.7	1.7	..	1.6	1.5	1.5	1.5	..	2.1	1.8	1.6
Mauritania	4.7	..	..	3.6	..	..	3.4	3.3	3.3	3.2	..	4.7	4.1	3.4
Mauritius	1.8	1.7	1.7	1.7	1.7	..	1.8	1.7	1.7	1.7	1.7	2.2	1.7	1.7
Mozambique	2.9	1.9	1.9	2.5	..	..	1.9	1.9	1.9	1.9	..	3.3	2.0	2.0
Namibia	..	..	..	28.7	..	..	42.8	42.2	41.0	39.9	39.0	..	..	38.9
Niger	2.8	..	..	1.5	..	..	1.6	1.1	1.1	1.1	..	2.4	2.7	1.3
Nigeria	1.5	..	..	1.2	..	..	1.6	1.6	1.7	1.7	..	1.5	1.3	1.5
Rwanda	2.1	..	1.8	1.9	..	..	1.9	2.3	2.3	2.2	..	1.7	1.9	2.1
São Tomé and Principe	..	..	..	..	..	..	2.4	2.3	2.3	2.4	..	..	..	2.4
Senegal	2.5	..	..	2.0	..	..	1.8	1.8	1.8	1.7	..	2.4	2.2	1.8
Seychelles	..	..	..	..	..	..	3.6	3.5	3.6	3.7	..	..	..	3.6
Sierra Leone	2.4	..	..	..	..	2.8	2.7	2.7	2.5	2.4	2.4	2.5	2.3	2.6
Somalia	2.9	..	..	2.8	..	..	2.6	2.6	2.7	2.6	..	3.5	3.3	2.7
South Africa	6.7	5.3	5.3	5.3	5.1	..	..	..	8.5	..	..	7.1	5.5	6.3
Sudan	0.5	..	..	0.4	..	..	0.4	0.4	0.4	0.4	..	0.7	0.4	0.4
Swaziland	5.8	..	3.8	3.6	3.5	3.6	3.3	3.3	4.1	4.1	..	5.1	4.4	3.7
Tanzania	2.5	..	..	..	2.1	2.1	3.1	3.1	3.0	2.9	..	2.5	3.8	2.7
Togo	2.7	2.3	..	2.1	2.1	2.0	1.9	1.9	1.8	1.8	..	2.8	2.3	2.0
Uganda	2.1	..	..	1.8	..	1.7	..	..	..	..	..	2.1	2.0	1.7
Zambia	6.3	..	5.0	4.8	4.7	4.5	4.4	4.4	7.4	7.2	7.1	6.4	5.3	5.6
Zimbabwe	12.0	..	..	..	..	8.9	8.7	1.8	1.7	1.6	..	12.0	9.4	4.5
NORTH AFRICA	2.1	1.5	1.6	..	1.9	1.6	2.5	..	..	..	..	2.1	1.6	2.0
Algeria	3.9	..	..	..	3.5	3.6	3.7	3.6	3.7	3.6	..	4.1	3.6	3.6
Egypt, Arab Republic	0.7	0.7	0.9	0.9	0.9	0.9	0.8	..	..	..	..	0.7	0.7	0.9
Libya	..	..	..	..	..	..	16.5	16.5	16.4	4.8	..	..	..	13.6
Morocco	3.0	2.6	2.5	..	2.4	1.1	2.4	2.3	2.3	2.3	2.1	2.9	2.6	2.1
Tunisia	3.7	3.5	3.7	..	..	..	2.4	2.5	2.5	2.5	..	3.4	3.6	2.5
ALL AFRICA	3.1	..	..	2.3	..	..	2.5	2.6	3.0	2.5	..	3.1	2.9	2.6

9-6. Paved primary roads

	Percentage of roads							Percent in good condition
	1991	*1992*	*1993*	*1994*	*1995*	*1996*	*1997*	*1989*
SUB-SAHARAN AFRICA	17.0	16.5	16.4	16.1	16.2	16.5	..	39
excluding South Africa	17.0	16.5	16.4	16.1	16.0	16.5	..	39
excl. S. Africa & Nigeria	17.0	16.0	15.8	15.6	15.5	15.8	..	41
Angola	..	25.0	25.0	25.0	25.0	25.0	25.0	..
Benin	20.0	20.0	20.0	20.0	20.0	20.0	..	13
Botswana	34.0	19.9	21.1	22.2	23.3	23.5	..	94
Burkina Faso	17.1	17.6	18.2	18.7	16.0	..	..	70
Burundi	17.5	7.1	7.1	7.1	7.1	..	..	75
Cameroon	10.9	11.3	11.7	·12.1	12.5	..	..	25
Cape Verde	78.0	78.0	78.0	78.0	78.0	..	..	14
Central African Republic	..	..	..	..	..	..	..	30
Chad	0.8	0.8	0.8	0.8	0.8	..	..	..
Comoros	70.7	72.1	73.5	75.0	76.5	..	..	43
Congo, Democratic Rep. of	..	..	..	..	..	..	..	20
Congo, Republic of	9.7	9.7	9.7	9.7	9.7	9.7	..	50
Côte d'Ivoire	8.9	9.1	9.2	9.4	9.6	9.7	..	75
Djibouti	12.6	12.6	12.6	12.6	12.6	12.6	..	51
Equatorial Guinea	..	..	..	..	..	..	..	27
Eritrea	19.8	20.2	20.6	21.0	21.4	21.8	..	..
Ethiopia	15.0	15.0	15.0	15.0	15.0	15.0	..	47
Gabon	8.2	8.2	8.2	8.2	8.2	8.2	..	30
Gambia, The	32.6	33.3	34.0	34.6	35.3	35.4	..	22
Ghana	23.0	23.5	23.9	24.4	24.9	24.1	..	28
Guinea	15.2	15.5	15.8	16.1	16.4	16.5	..	50
Guinea-Bissau	8.7	9.1	9.4	9.8	10.2	10.3	..	39
Kenya	13.3	13.8	14.3	13.6	13.8	13.9	..	32
Lesotho	17.0	16.0	15.0	15.0	17.9	17.9	..	53
Liberia	5.6	5.7	5.9	6.0	6.1	6.2	..	85
Madagascar	15.4	15.4	11.5	11.5	11.5	11.6	..	56
Malawi	17.0	17.0	18.0	18.0	20.0	20.0	19.0	56
Mali	11.1	11.3	11.5	11.8	12.0	12.1	..	70
Mauritania	11.0	11.1	11.1	11.1	11.2	11.3	..	58
Mauritius	93.0	93.0	93.0	93.0	93.0	93.0	93.0	95
Mozambique	17.2	17.5	17.8	18.2	18.6	18.7	..	19
Namibia	10.9	10.9	7.3	7.9	7.9	8.2	8.3	..
Niger	..	..	..	7.9	7.9	7.9	..	67
Nigeria	30.0	30.0	30.0	21.3	18.8	18.8	..	34
Rwanda	9.2	9.4	9.6	9.7	9.9	9.1	..	41
São Tomé and Principe	62.8	64.1	65.4	66.7	68.0	68.1	..	..
Senegal	27.8	28.3	28.3	28.4	28.5	29.3	..	28
Seychelles	58.0	59.1	60.3	61.5	62.8	62.9	..	..
Sierra Leone	10.8	11.0	11.0	11.0	8.0	8.0	8.0	62
Somalia	11.3	11.5	11.8	11.8	11.8	11.8	..	52
South Africa	..	..	..	..	41.5	..	..	..
Sudan	33.7	33.7	34.5	35.4	36.2	36.3	..	27
Swaziland	54.7	58.6	59.8	28.2	..	..	..	35
Tanzania	37.0	37.0	4.2	4.2	4.2	4.2	..	39
Togo	21.6	31.0	31.6	31.6	31.6	31.6	..	75
Uganda	..	..	..	..	..	..	..	10
Zambia	16.9	17.3	17.6	18.0	..	..	..	40
Zimbabwe	15.0	16.0	17.0	54.9	48.0	47.4	..	70
NORTH AFRICA	70.0	66.0	66.7	68.0	68.9	78.1	..	..
Algeria	70.0	66.0	66.7	68.0	68.9	..	..	..
Egypt, Arab Republic	72.0	73.0	72.0	75.0	78.0	78.1	..	..
Libya	52.7	53.8	54.9	56.0	57.1	..	..	..
Morocco	49.5	49.5	49.6	50.2	50.2	50.2	51.8	..
Tunisia	75.5	74.6	76.0	77.4	78.8	78.9	..	..
ALL AFRICA	17.2	17.5	17.8	18.1	18.6	18.3	..	39

9-7. Rail goods traffic-to-$PPP GDP ratio

	Ton-km per million of $PPP GDP										Annual average		
	1980	*1987*	*1988*	*1989*	*1990*	*1991*	*1992*	*1993*	*1994*	*1995*	*75-84*	*85-89*	*90-MR*
SUB-SAHARAN AFRICA	..	..	..	..	..	..	..	..	..	..	..	..	..
excluding South Africa	..	..	..	..	..	..	..	..	..	..	..	..	..
excl. S. Africa & Nigeria	..	..	..	..	..	..	..	..	..	..	..	..	..
Angola	..	..	..	..	..	..	..	..	..	..	..	..	..
Benin	..	..	..	..	..	..	..	..	..	..	..	..	..
Botswana	..	..	..	..	..	..	..	..	..	..	..	..	..
Burkina Faso	..	..	..	..	..	..	..	..	..	..	..	..	..
Burundi	..	..	..	..	..	..	..	..	..	..	..	..	..
Cameroon	53,079	27,014	24,351	30,449	33,209	28,563	30,278	26,212	33,686	34,023	51,036	35,728	30,917
Cape Verde	..	..	..	..	..	..	..	..	..	..	..	..	..
Central African Republic	..	..	..	..	..	..	..	..	..	..	..	..	..
Chad	..	..	..	..	..	..	..	..	..	..	..	..	..
Comoros	..	..	..	..	..	..	..	..	..	..	..	..	..
Congo, Democratic Rep. of	52,895	31,173	32,300	..	32,198	..	..	..	4,284	..	48,838	37,881	18,241
Congo, Republic of	..	141,444	..	..	..	144,851	83,764	63,230	56,202	..	172,300	169,479	87,012
Côte d'Ivoire	53,319	30,147	..	..	15,791	14,554	13,559	8,392	8,400	13,486	46,229	31,763	12,363
Djibouti	..	..	..	..	..	..	..	..	..	..	..	..	..
Equatorial Guinea	..	..	..	..	..	..	..	..	..	..	..	..	..
Eritrea	..	..	..	..	..	..	..	..	..	..	..	..	..
Ethiopia	..	..	..	6,446	..	2,467	..	..	..	..	9,901	8,173	4,456
Gabon	7,537	42,067	47,741	33,211	..	..	44,163	49,058	47,013	61,973	15,530	33,979	47,084
Gambia, The	..	..	..	..	..	..	..	..	..	..	..	..	..
Ghana	11,733	7,068	7,303	..	6,811	..	..	..	..	..	9,220	7,338	6,811
Guinea	..	..	..	..	..	..	..	..	..	..	..	..	..
Guinea-Bissau	..	..	..	..	..	..	..	..	..	..	..	..	..
Kenya	201,741	83,240	79,408	82,928	75,496	67,289	52,415	45,482	43,424	..	170,744	102,229	61,172
Lesotho	..	..	..	..	..	..	..	..	..	..	..	..	..
Liberia	..	..	..	..	..	..	..	..	..	..	..	..	..
Madagascar	..	..	..	..	..	..	..	..	..	..	..	..	..
Malawi	93,702	24,101	16,363	15,916	14,881	14,530	11,131	9,144	9,311	10,003	70,675	25,684	12,131
Mali	41,774	46,956	49,656	54,729	53,882	51,326	46,168	..	..	..	44,405	56,552	51,526
Mauritania	..	..	..	..	..	..	..	..	..	..	..	..	..
Mauritius	..	..	..	..	..	..	..	..	..	..	..	..	..
Mozambique	..	..	..	..	..	..	..	..	..	..	..	..	..
Namibia	..	..	..	..	308,833	199,432	183,736	165,858	147,659	139,137	..	..	190,776
Niger	..	..	..	..	..	..	..	..	..	..	..	..	..
Nigeria	17,643	5,351	3,107	2,389	3,009	..	552	..	..	..	24,752	9,417	1,984
Rwanda	..	..	..	..	..	..	..	..	..	..	..	..	..
São Tomé and Principe	..	..	..	..	..	..	..	..	..	..	..	..	..
Senegal	57,116	55,610	50,412	46,200	51,209	42,987	39,395	32,641	30,531	..	51,551	54,738	40,494
Seychelles	..	..	..	..	..	..	..	..	..	..	..	..	..
Sierra Leone	..	..	..	..	..	..	..	..	..	..	..	..	..
Somalia	..	..	..	..	..	..	..	..	..	..	..	..	..
South Africa	733,358	435,582	381,113	401,199	430,594	389,895	363,229	359,057	350,403	337,153	625,505	460,494	375,933
Sudan	143,912	..	..	..	..	25,726	..	..	..	38,360	92,226	43,816	32,043
Swaziland	..	..	..	..	..	..	..	..	..	..	..	..	..
Tanzania	..	..	..	63,187	..	77,466	79,374	93,254	79,068	91,623	..	63,187	80,662
Togo	..	..	..	..	..	..	..	..	..	..	..	..	..
Uganda	..	8,130	7,509	7,540	12,582	10,061	8,031	8,227	11,679	11,567	11,342	8,406	9,955
Zambia	323,197	209,379	188,532	188,289	73,728	146,520	135,367	129,881	80,128	56,426	292,245	231,610	115,763
Zimbabwe	783,391	379,018	312,175	281,331	274,759	244,338	269,047	251,520	182,610	196,429	624,074	413,243	242,862
NORTH AFRICA	..	..	..	..	..	..	..	..	..	..	..	..	..
Algeria	45,159	29,910	27,566	25,140	25,161	24,989	21,960	19,995	19,678	..	41,533	31,057	22,820
Egypt, Arab Republic	46,395	..	..	..	23,310	25,465	21,606	25,026	26,905	..	42,399	37,227	24,462
Libya	..	..	..	..	..	..	..	..	..	..	..	..	..
Morocco	122,619	84,281	87,396	66,031	72,108	57,694	65,061	56,735	53,338	55,523	116,475	89,772	60,927
Tunisia	117,471	81,729	73,398	72,332	58,795	54,810	53,665	51,211	53,870	53,343	101,162	81,950	56,861
ALL AFRICA	..	..	..	..	..	..	..	..	..	..	..	..	..

9-8. Rail load-to-locomotive ratio

	Million rail ton-km/locomotive											Annual average		
	1980	1988	1989	1990	1991	1992	1993	1994	1995	1996	1997	75-84	85-89	90-MR
SUB-SAHARAN AFRICA	..	..	..	20.5	18.5	16.8	..	19.1	..	..	..	14.9	15.2	18.7
excluding South Africa	..	..	..	..	..	..	..	..	..	..	..	..	..	..
excl. S. Africa & Nigeria	..	..	..	..	..	..	..	..	..	..	..	..	..	..
Angola	..	..	..	..	..	..	..	..	..	..	..	..	..	..
Benin	..	..	..	..	..	..	..	..	..	..	..	..	..	..
Botswana	..	..	..	..	..	..	..	..	..	..	19.9	..	..	19.9
Burkina Faso	..	..	..	..	..	..	..	..	..	18.0	24.9	..	..	21.5
Burundi	..	..	..	..	..	..	..	..	..	..	..	..	..	..
Cameroon	10.9	6.5	9.0	10.1	8.9	9.6	8.6	12.4	13.3	10.0	14.2	9.8	8.4	10.9
Cape Verde	..	..	..	..	..	..	..	..	..	..	..	..	..	..
Central African Republic	..	..	..	..	..	..	..	..	..	..	..	..	..	..
Chad	..	..	..	..	..	..	..	..	..	..	..	..	..	..
Comoros	..	..	..	..	..	..	..	..	..	..	..	..	..	..
Congo, Democratic Rep. of	11.7	10.9	..	11.2	..	..	..	1.0	..	..	1.7	12.0	11.5	4.6
Congo, Republic of	..	..	..	..	14.8	9.4	..	5.8	..	..	3.0	11.3	9.4	8.3
Côte d'Ivoire	12.8	..	..	8.0	6.7	6.8	4.5	4.5	5.7	..	17.4	12.3	12.3	7.7
Djibouti	..	..	..	..	..	..	..	..	..	..	..	..	..	..
Equatorial Guinea	..	..	..	..	..	..	..	..	..	..	..	..	..	..
Eritrea	..	..	..	..	..	..	..	..	..	..	..	..	..	..
Ethiopia	..	..	6.1	..	2.3	..	..	..	..	..	..	..	6.1	2.3
Gabon	2.1	7.4	6.1	..	..	4.8	5.2	5.3	7.6	..	30.8	4.2	6.6	10.7
Gambia, The	..	..	..	..	..	..	..	..	..	..	..	..	..	..
Ghana	..	..	..	3.3	..	..	..	..	..	..	..	..	1.6	3.3
Guinea	..	..	..	..	..	..	..	..	..	..	..	..	..	..
Guinea-Bissau	..	..	..	..	..	..	..	..	..	..	..	..	..	..
Kenya	6.9	..	9.2	8.8	9.0	..	..	..	..	..	..	9.2	8.7	8.9
Lesotho	..	..	..	..	..	..	..	..	..	..	..	..	..	..
Liberia	..	..	..	..	..	..	..	..	..	..	..	..	..	..
Madagascar	..	..	..	..	..	..	..	..	..	..	..	..	..	..
Malawi	..	1.4	1.4	1.4	1.5	1.1	1.0	0.9	1.1	..	..	3.5	1.9	1.2
Mali	..	6.7	7.8	7.8	7.8	7.9	..	..	..	..	11.2	6.6	9.0	8.7
Mauritania	..	..	..	..	..	..	..	..	..	..	..	..	..	..
Mauritius	..	..	..	..	..	..	..	..	..	..	..	..	..	..
Mozambique	..	..	..	..	..	..	..	..	..	..	5.9	..	..	5.9
Namibia	..	..	..	27.7	21.4	22.3	19.9	20.3	21.6	..	..	..	..	22.2
Niger	..	..	..	..	..	..	..	..	..	..	..	..	..	..
Nigeria	3.8	..	..	..	0.3	..	0.0	..	..	..	..	5.0	2.5	0.2
Rwanda	..	..	..	..	..	..	..	..	..	..	..	..	..	..
São Tomé and Principe	..	..	..	..	..	..	..	..	..	..	..	..	..	..
Senegal	13.3	18.4	16.7	20.9	18.0	16.4	14.6	16.1	..	..	..	14.3	18.0	17.2
Seychelles	..	..	..	..	..	..	..	..	..	..	..	..	..	..
Sierra Leone	..	..	..	..	..	..	..	..	..	10.8	15.4	..	..	13.1
Somalia	..	..	..	..	..	..	..	..	..	..	..	..	..	..
South Africa	..	19.9	23.2	25.4	23.6	22.6	25.8	26.4	26.9	..	..	18.2	20.5	25.1
Sudan	8.0	..	..	..	4.5	..	..	..	11.1	14.2	12.3	7.1	4.8	10.5
Swaziland	..	..	..	..	..	..	..	..	..	..	..	..	..	..
Tanzania	..	..	8.4	..	11.7	11.4	13.9	12.2	14.9	..	17.4	7.8	8.2	13.6
Togo	..	..	..	..	..	..	..	..	..	..	..	..	..	..
Uganda	..	2.1	1.9	3.1	2.7	2.0	2.3	3.5	4.1	..	8.3	..	1.5	3.7
Zambia	16.1	23.0	22.7	7.5	15.4	14.6	15.1	9.9	6.8	..	7.2	17.2	21.1	10.9
Zimbabwe	21.7	19.3	..	13.6	14.0	16.0	17.5	27.9	27.5	..	..	20.7	20.0	19.4
NORTH AFRICA	9.9	..	..	10.2	10.6	9.7	10.3	10.4	..	..	10.3	9.9	10.3	10.2
Algeria	9.8	15.6	13.3	12.2	12.5	10.7	11.1	10.8	..	..	7.7	10.9	13.6	10.8
Egypt, Arab Republic	3.9	..	..	3.7	6.1	3.6	4.9	4.9	..	..	5.1	3.7	3.8	4.7
Libya	..	..	..	..	..	..	..	..	..	..	..	..	..	..
Morocco	19.5	24.2	18.7	20.4	17.3	19.6	17.4	19.2	19.8	..	22.3	19.1	20.3	19.4
Tunisia	13.9	10.8	10.5	9.3	9.3	10.3	14.0	12.7	13.4	..	13.5	12.7	10.4	11.8
ALL AFRICA	..	..	..	16.0	15.2	13.9	16.4	15.5	..	..	..	12.9	13.9	15.4

•

Technical Notes

Tables

Table 9-1. Electric power consumption per capita. This table refers to per capita electricity consumption, which means the production of power plants and combined heat and power plants, less distribution losses, and own use by heat and power plants (IEA and UN *Energy Statistics Yearbook*).

Table 9-2. Energy production and use, 1980 and 1996. This table presents three indicators. *Energy production* refers to commercial forms of primary energy—petroleum (crude oil, natural gas liquids, and oil from nonconventional sources), natural gas, solid fuels, and primary electricity—all converted into oil equivalent (IEA and UN *Energy Statistics Yearbook*). *Commercial energy use* is indigenous production plus imports and stock changes, minus exports and international marine bunkers (IEA and UN *Energy Statistics Yearbook*). *Electric power transmission* includes losses in transmission between sources of supply and points of distribution and in the distribution to consumers, including pilferage. Production less transmission and distribution losses, own-use, and transformation losses is equal to end-use electricity consumption (IEA and UN *Energy Statistics Yearbook*).

Table 9-3. Telephone, radio, and television availability, 1994–97. This table presents data for six communication indicators. Telephone mainlines (ITU) refer to telephone lines connecting a customer's equipment to the public switched telephone network, where mainline is normally identified by a unique number. Mainlines are presented for every 1,000 people (Table 1.2). *Waiting list* shows the number of applications (in thousands) for a connection to a mainline that have been held up by a lack of technical capacity (ITU). *Cost of local call* is the cost of a three-minute call within the same exchange area using the subscriber's equipment (that is, not from a public phone) (ITU). *Mobile phones* refer to users of portable telephones who subscribe to an automatic public mobile telephone service using cellular technology that provides access to the public switched-telephone network, per 1,000 people (Table 1.2) (ITU). *Radios* are the estimated number of radio receivers in use for broadcast to the general public, per 1,000 people (Table 1.2) (*UNESCO Statistical Yearbook*). *Television sets* are the estimated number of television sets in use, per 1,000 people (Table 1.2) (ITU).

Table 9-4. Vehicle ownership. Vehicles (International Road Federation) include all forms of road transportation, except buses. They are expressed as a ratio of 1,000 people (Table 1.2).

Table 9-5. Road-to-population ratio. This table presents the ratio of 1,000 kilometers of paved or unpaved road (International Road Federation) per 1 million people (Table 1.2).

Table 9-6. Paved primary roads. This table presents paved primary roads, that is, those that have been sealed with asphalt or similar road-bonding material (International Road Federation) as a ratio to total roads and then shows the percentage that is in good condition (World Bank data).

Table 9-7. Rail goods traffic-to-$ PPP GDP ratio.
This measures the tonnage of goods per million dollars of GDP measured in PPP terms (World Bank data).

Table 9-8. Rail load-to-locomotive ratio. This is the volume of rail transported goods (measured in millions of metric tons times kilometers traveled) per single locomotive (World Bank data).

Methodology used for regional aggregations and period averages in chapter 9

Table	Aggregations[a] (1)	(6)	(7)	(8)	Period averages[b] (1)
9-1		x			x
9-2					
Columns 1-4	x				
Columns 5-6				x	
9-3					
Column 1-2, 4-6		x			
Column 3				x	
9-4		x	x		
9-5		x	x		
9-6,					
Columns 1-8				x	
Column 9		x			
9-7				x	x
9-8		x	x		

Note: Regional aggregations are shown in the rows for Sub-Saharan Africa, North Africa, and All Africa. Period averages are shown in the last three columns. This table shows only the methodologies used in this chapter.

a. Regional aggregations: (1) simple total; (2) simple total of the first indicator divided by the simple total of the second indicator (same country coverage); (3) simple total of the gap-filled indicator; (4) simple total of the gap-filled main indicator divided by the simple total of the gap-filled secondary indicator; (5) simple total of the first gap-filled main indicator less the simple total of the second gap-filled main indicator, all divided by the simple total of the secondary indicator; (6) weighted total; (7) median; (8) no aggregation; (9) simple arithmetic mean.

b. Period averages: (1) arithmetic mean (using the same series as shown in the table, i.e., ratio if the rest of the table is shown as ratio, level if the rest of the table is shown as level, growth rate if the rest of the table is shown as growth rate); (2) least-squares growth rate (using main indicator); (3) least-squares growth rate (using main indicator in constant terms, with the rest of the table in current terms).

10

Privatization of Public Enterprises

In the past, the dominance of the public enterprise sector in most African economies warranted the collection and publication of the sector's performance. With its diminishing size and importance due to privatization, it is no longer informative to produce such data. Instead, as privatization programs advance to maturity, it will become important to track the performance of private sector businesses. In the meantime, measurement of the level of privatization activity is a useful gauge of the decreasing role of governments in commercial business; conversely, it indicates how much of state-owned commercial activity has been transferred to the private sector. To the extent that data is available, it is also possible to measure how privatization has, over time, contributed to government revenues and mobilized savings and investment. However, this measurement is by no means easy or precise, partly because of incomplete and inconsistent data but also because of redefinitions of the public enterprise sector. For example, some enterprises, notably those formerly in a monopolistic position, are being split in order to separate their commercial, social, developmental, and regulatory activities. In some cases, separate operating divisions

or geographically distinct assets are sold separately. And in yet other cases, commercial and semi-commercial activities are being separated out from government ministries and other agencies to become redefined as "commercial enterprises". These include, for example, business centers, media, and some training institutes. So, the public enterprise sector, as defined several years ago, has changed. Nevertheless, the well over 3,000 privatization transactions that were reported across Africa up to the end of 1998 have brought about fundamental changes:

- The fiscal burden of public enterprises has been reduced or eliminated.
- Privatization receipts have contributed to a reduction in fiscal deficits.
- Privatization has attracted foreign direct investment both to acquire enterprises and for post-privatization investment in those businesses.
- The process has stimulated private sector development by making investment opportunities available, spurring capital market development, and contributing to a more competitive business environment.
- Being a politically sensitive subject, the process

has highlighted the need for transparency and public accountability.

The tables presented in this chapter summarizes data contained in the World Bank's Africa Privatization Database which is accessible through the internet at:

http://www4.worldbank.org/afr/database/afrpriv/p1query.cfm

10-1. Summary of privatization activity

	Total no. of trans-actions	Total sales value (US$m)	Transactions completed						Transactions by sector					
			Before 1994	1994	1995	1996	1997	1998	Agric. prod. & process	Financial	Manu-facturing	Services	Trade	Other
SUB-SAHARAN AFRIC	3,165	6,426	1,582	352	485	422	240	53	655	120	826	636	299	182
excluding South Africa	3,158	4,102	1,579	352	485	421	238	52	655	120	823	633	299	181
excl. S. Africa & Nigeri	3,077	3,895	1,498	352	485	422	240	53	655	120	804	621	299	178
Angola	331	25	275	..	..	56	..	..	9	..	29	9	9	..
Benin	46	63	36	3	5	..	..	..	7	1	14	17	5	2
Botswana	..	..	..	..	..	..	..	..	..	..	..	..	..	..
Burkina Faso	16	10	8	5	3	..	..	..	1	4	7	2	1	1
Burundi	42	11	25	1	..	13	3	..	21	4	4	8	2	3
Cameroon	48	72	8	5	3	23	5	4	24	4	2	12	1	5
Cape Verde	40	25	1	11	9	10	9	..	8	4	11	13	4	4
Central African Republi	35	0	35	..	..	..	..	..	8	..	5	11	..	7
Chad	31	6	1	11	13	6	14	5	9	5	2	7	3	5
Comoros	4	0	4	..	..	..	..	..	..	..	..	..	..	..
Congo, Dem. Rep. of	61	50	2	..	44	15	..	..	20	5	13	21	1	2
Congo, Rep. of	21	0	16	..	2	3	..	..	3	1	5	10	..	1
Côte d'Ivoire	84	622	12	10	24	19	..	..	29	2	12	18	..	17
Djibouti	..	..	..	..	..	..	..	..	..	..	..	..	..	..
Equatorial Guinea	3	0	3	..	..	..	..	..	..	..	..	..	..	..
Eritrea	..	..	..	..	..	..	..	..	..	..	..	..	..	..
Ethiopia	125	203	115	..	9	..	..	1	..	..	5	3	1	1
Gabon	26	0	25	..	..	..	1	..	..	..	..	..	..	1
Gambia, The	30	10	27	3	..	..	..	..	7	3	6	8	5	1
Ghana	217	642	78	69	23	20	25	2	41	5	86	32	29	24
Guinea	117	9	110	2	4	..	1	..	11	7	50	13	29	7
Guinea-Bissau	29	1	15	3	11	..	..	..	4	..	5	14	4	2
Kenya	189	248	49	17	69	23	27	4	71	11	57	41	7	2
Lesotho	9	7	..	..	8	..	1	..	..	2	2	2	3	..
Liberia	..	..	..	..	..	..	..	..	..	..	..	..	..	..
Madagascar	85	29	57	3	24	..	..	..	31	3	31	14	4	2
Malawi	45	57	35	..	..	9	..	1	28	3	12	2	..	..
Mali	64	32	59	..	..	..	..	..	11	2	19	21	8	3
Mauritania	47	1	29	..	3	..	..	..	19	3	5	16	2	2
Mauritius	..	..	..	..	..	..	..	..	..	..	..	..	..	..
Mozambique	579	217	262	136	112	38	31	..	74	2	243	132	122	6
Namibia	..	..	..	..	..	..	..	..	..	..	..	..	..	..
Niger	34	3	29	3	2	..	..	..	2	2	5	4	3	..
Nigeria	81	207	81	..	..	..	..	..	23	24	19	12	..	3
Rwanda	2	0	2	..	..	..	..	..	1	..	1	..	..	..
São Tomé and Principe	9	0	8	..	1	..	..	..	..	..	3	2	3	1
Senegal	60	328	37	..	1	11	3	4	7	10	9	26	2	6
Seychelles	..	..	..	..	..	..	..	..	..	..	..	..	..	..
Sierra Leone	9	0	6	1	1	..	..	..	..	..	1	6	..	2
Somalia	..	..	..	..	..	..	..	..	..	..	..	..	..	..
South Africa	7	2,324	3	..	..	1	2	1	..	..	3	3	..	1
Sudan	32	0	29	3	..	..	..	..	11	1	7	10	1	2
Swaziland	..	..	..	..	..	..	..	..	..	..	..	..	..	..
Tanzania	198	236	48	16	30	47	40	15	77	1	69	24	17	10
Togo	63	36	22	3	1	19	18	..	8	1	20	30	1	3
Uganda	87	141	17	27	23	18	2	..	17	3	22	27	12	6
Zambia	253	700	13	17	60	91	55	16	69	6	41	66	20	50
Zimbabwe	6	111	..	3	..	..	3	..	4	1	1	..	..	..
NORTH AFRICA	142	595	27	17	27	30	40	1	13	0	58	53	2	16
Algeria	..	..	..	..	..	..	..	..	..	..	..	..	..	..
Egypt	54	307	..	5	10	8	31	..	5	..	34	8	1	6
Libya	..	..	..	..	..	..	..	..	..	..	..	..	..	..
Morocco	52	259	..	12	17	16	6	1	4	..	10	28	..	10
Tunisia	36	29	27	..	..	6	3	..	4	..	14	17	1	..
ALL AFRICA	3,307	7,020	1,609	369	512	452	280	54	668	120	884	689	301	198

10-2. Privatization Methods Employed (to end 1998)

| | Sales of shares | | | | Sale of Assets | | | Other methods | | | | | | | |
	Competitive sale	Direct Sale	Pre-emption rights	Public flotation	Liqui-dation	Competitive sale	Direct sale	Debt/ Equity swaps	Leases	Joint ventures	Mgmt./ employee buyouts	Mgmt. con-tracts	Trustees	Restit-ution	Other
SUB-SAHARAN AFRICA	910	85	157	91	571	501	38	11	127	39	36	53	31	48	467
excluding South Africa	904	85	157	91	571	501	38	11	127	39	36	53	31	48	467
excl. S. Africa & Nigeria	899	85	157	91	571	501	38	11	127	39	36	53	31	48	467
Angola	..	..	..	..	..	57	..	..	..	..	..	..	..	..	274
Benin	1	2	..	..	23	12	3	..	2	..	..	2	..	1	..
Botswana	..	..	..	..	..	..	..	..	..	..	..	..	..	..	..
Burkina Faso	9	3	..	..	2	..	..	..	..	..	..	1	1	..	..
Burundi	11	3	..	..	13	5	..	..	..	..	1	9	..	..	..
Cameroon	20	..	..	..	18	..	..	..	..	..	..	..	..	..	10
Cape Verde	15	2	5	..	10	1	1	..	..	..	6	..	..	..	..
Central African Republic	..	..	..	..	26	..	..	..	1	1	..	1	..	..	6
Chad	12	2	..	..	11	..	..	..	..	..	..	5	..	..	1
Comoros	..	..	..	..	..	..	..	..	..	..	..	..	..	..	4
Congo, Dem. Rep. of	1	..	..	..	53	..	..	..	..	..	..	2	5	..	..
Congo, Rep. of	1	..	..	..	15	..	..	..	..	..	..	5	..	..	..
Côte d'Ivoire	18	9	10	14	2	16	7	..	2	2	..	..	1	..	3
Djibouti	..	..	..	..	..	..	..	..	..	..	..	..	..	..	..
Equatorial Guinea	..	..	..	..	..	..	..	..	..	..	..	..	..	..	3
Eritrea	..	..	..	..	..	..	..	..	..	..	..	..	..	..	..
Ethiopia	..	..	..	..	..	10	..	..	..	..	..	..	..	..	115
Gabon	..	..	..	..	..	..	..	..	..	..	..	..	..	..	26
Gambia, The	13	7	..	..	3	1	..	..	5	..	1	..	..	..	..
Ghana	5	11	19	13	52	73	12	2	5	14	..	1	..	10	..
Guinea	42	1	..	..	67	1	..	..	4	..	..	2	..	..	..
Guinea-Bissau	7	2	..	..	8	2	..	..	2	1	..	7	..	..	..
Kenya	13	..	96	16	36	18	4	1	..	..	1	1	..	..	3
Lesotho	4	1	..	..	3	..	..	..	..	..	1	..	..	..	..
Liberia	..	..	..	..	..	..	..	..	..	..	..	..	..	..	..
Madagascar	6	13	..	..	29	15	6	..	1	1	1	3	..	8	2
Malawi	22	5	..	2	..	13	..	..	..	..	..	..	3	..	..
Mali	14	1	..	..	30	10	..	..	1	..	..	1	3	..	4
Mauritania	21	..	..	..	15	5	..	..	..	..	..	2	3	..	1
Mauritius	..	..	..	..	..	..	..	..	..	..	..	..	..	..	..
Mozambique	509	..	..	..	..	22	..	..	37	10	..	1	..	..	..
Namibia	..	..	..	..	..	..	..	..	..	..	..	..	..	..	..
Niger	13	..	..	..	17	..	..	..	..	..	..	2	..	..	2
Nigeria	5	5	..	37	2	29	..	..	..	..	1	..	2	..	..
Rwanda	..	..	..	..	..	..	..	..	..	..	..	..	..	..	2
São Tomé and Principe	..	1	..	..	6	..	..	..	..	..	1	1	..	..	..
Senegal	26	1	1	1	23	1	..	1	3	1	..	1	..	..	1
Seychelles	..	..	..	..	..	..	..	..	..	..	..	..	..	..	..
Sierra Leone	..	..	..	..	1	..	..	..	5	..	..	3	..	..	..
Somalia	..	..	..	..	..	..	..	..	..	..	..	..	..	..	..
South Africa	6	..	..	..	..	1	..	..	..	..	..	..	..	..	..
Sudan	7	..	..	..	..	15	..	5	1	..	..	..	4	..	..
Swaziland	..	..	..	..	..	..	..	..	..	..	..	..	..	..	..
Tanzania	56	2	7	1	49	42	3	..	21	4	5	1	3	2	2
Togo	8	7	..	..	17	25	1	..	3	..	..	2	..	..	..
Uganda	8	0	5	..	18	24	..	2	1	4	1	..	5	11	8
Zambia	35	6	14	4	22	103	1	..	33	1	17	..	1	16	..
Zimbabwe	2	1	..	3	..	..	..	..	..	..	..	..	..	..	..
NORTH AFRICA	..	..	..	..	..	..	..	..	..	..	..	..	..	..	..
Algeria	..	..	..	..	..	..	..	..	..	..	..	..	..	..	..
Egypt	..	..	..	..	..	..	..	..	..	..	..	..	..	..	..
Libya	..	..	..	..	..	..	..	..	..	..	..	..	..	..	..
Morocco	..	..	..	..	..	..	..	..	..	..	..	..	..	..	..
Tunisia	..	..	..	..	..	..	..	..	..	..	..	..	..	..	..
ALL AFRICA	910	85	157	91	571	501	38	11	127	39	36	53	31	48	467

10-3. Enterprise ownership and control changes through privatization (to end 1998)

	Transfer of Government majority owner-ship to private shareholders	Government retention of majority ownership	Government retention of minority interest	Sales of minority government interest	Total share transactions	Total asset sales and liquidation	Other transactions	Total trans-actions
SUB-SAHARAN AFRICA	2,235	195	341	702	1,243	1,110	812	3,165
excluding South Africa	2,230	193	341	702	1,237	1,109	812	3,158
excl. S. Africa & Nigeria	2,175	192	341	702	1,190	1,078	809	3,077
Angola	56	..	..	275	0	57	274	331
Benin	42	3	1	1	3	38	5	46
Botswana	..	..	..	..	0	0	0	0
Burkina Faso	10	..	11	2	12	2	2	16
Burundi	31	..	1	11	14	18	10	42
Cameroon	47	1	1	..	20	18	10	48
Cape Verde	29	2	3	9	22	12	6	40
Central African Republic	29	2	1	4	0	26	9	35
Chad	19	5	6	5	14	11	6	31
Comoros	..	..	..	4	0	0	4	4
Congo, Dem. Rep. of	60	1	1	..	1	53	7	61
Congo, Rep. of	16	5	..	..	1	15	5	21
Côte d'Ivoire	44	3	26	25	51	25	8	84
Djibouti	..	..	..	..	0	0	0	0
Equatorial Guinea	..	..	..	3	0	0	3	3
Eritrea	..	..	..	..	0	0	0	0
Ethiopia	10	..	..	115	0	10	115	125
Gabon	..	1	..	25	0	0	26	26
Gambia, The	19	5	..	6	20	4	6	30
Ghana	173	12	26	27	48	137	32	217
Guinea	108	9	18	..	43	68	6	117
Guinea-Bissau	20	9	..	..	9	10	10	29
Kenya	79	3	53	104	125	58	6	189
Lesotho	8	1	1	..	5	3	1	9
Liberia	..	..	..	..	0	0	0	0
Madagascar	80	5	15	..	19	50	16	85
Malawi	39	1	7	5	29	13	3	45
Mali	55	..	4	8	15	40	9	64
Mauritania	30	2	4	14	21	20	6	47
Mauritius	..	..	..	..	0	0	0	0
Mozambique	536	43	75	..	509	22	48	579
Namibia	..	..	..	..	0	0	0	0
Niger	29	2	3	3	13	17	4	34
Nigeria	55	1	8	24	47	31	3	81
Rwanda	..	..	..	2	0	0	2	2
São Tomé and Principe	8	1	..	..	1	6	2	9
Senegal	43	8	11	6	29	24	7	60
Seychelles	..	..	..	..	0	0	0	0
Sierra Leone	..	9	..	..	0	1	8	9
Somalia	..	..	..	..	0	0	0	0
South Africa	5	2	..	..	6	1	0	7
Sudan	31	1	3	..	7	15	10	32
Swaziland	..	..	..	..	0	0	0	0
Tanzania	170	22	31	6	66	94	38	198
Togo	50	4	1	9	15	43	5	63
Uganda	83	1	6	3	13	42	32	87
Zambia	217	30	21	5	59	126	68	253
Zimbabwe	4	1	3	1	6	0	0	6
NORTH AFRICA	..	..	..	..	..	..	..	..
Algeria	..	..	..	..	..	..	..	..
Egypt	..	..	..	..	..	..	..	..
Libya	..	..	..	..	..	..	..	..
Morocco	..	..	..	..	..	..	..	..
Tunisia	..	..	..	..	..	..	..	..
ALL AFRICA	..	..	..	..	..	..	..	..

Technical Notes

Tables

Table 10-1. Summary of privatization activity. For purposes of monitoring and reporting on privatization activity, all reported transactions involving a sale of assets or shares (however small) or the formal yielding of management control (as through a management contract) are included in the World Bank's Africa Privatization Database. Hence, in the table, "privatization" is used generically to include: the sale or disposal of some or all of the assets of public enterprises, the sale of government-owned shares in enterprises, the reduction in equity percentage held by a government through share dilutions or through transfer of enterprise assets to a new joint venture, liquidations, leases, and management contracts. Sometimes, the process of privatizing an enterprise involves several consecutive transactions (for example, a sale of a block of shares to a core investor and a subsequent initial public offering). The table summarizes the data contained in the Africa Privatization Database which originate from national privatization agencies and other sources. The data are frequently updated and changes to previous entries occur as more information becomes available. There are a few instances where previously reported privatizations are removed from the database because a transaction has been nullified due to non-fulfillment of contractual conditions on the part of one of the parties. For financial data, the term "sale value" is preferred since the use of the term "proceeds" might imply the value of amounts actually paid. In practice, some deals are structured so that new investors may acquire assets or shares on deferred terms. Also, it should be noted that:

(i) in the cases of some subsidiary companies, the cash proceeds are not paid to government but instead go to the parent company; and (ii) for official liquidations, the proceeds are paid to the liquidator who first applies them toward settling enterprise debts.

Table 10-2. Privatization methods employed (to end 1988). The table shows the various privatization methods employed in each country. The methods employed could not be confirmed for all transactions. "Direct sales" refers to transactions which were negotiated directly with one party and which were not the outcome of a competitive bidding process. However, in some cases a direct sale was concluded (on a noncompetitive basis) as a result of a failure of an earlier competitive bidding process. "Preemptive rights" refers to transactions whereby a government has sold shares to an existing private shareholder (or shareholders) who exercised preemptive rights to acquire those shares in accordance with specific provisions of the company's charter (Articles of Association). In some cases, the charter specified the amount to be paid per share or the formula for calculating that amount; otherwise it has been the subject of negotiation. "Joint ventures" refer to the type of transaction whereby a government concluded a deal (usually with a foreign investor) involving the formation of a new company in which the government's equity contribution was in the form of the major or all assets of a public enterprise. The remaining shell company would then be maintained only as a book company or be liquidated; if it were liquidated it is not included as a liquidation since this would be double counting. Transactions described as "Trustees" refer to privatizations achieved by transference of shares of a public enterprise to a trustee for onward sale, at a later date or over a period, to the public or to selected segments of the public. "Restitutions" are those transactions whereby a company has been handed back to a previous owner from whom the company had been expropriated. "Other sales" includes sundry methods, such as enterprises donated by governments to local communities, but principally comprises transactions where the method of privatization was not reported.

Table 10-3. Enterprise ownership and control changes through privatization (to end 1998). This table presents the inferred outcome of privatization transactions on the ownership and control of enterprises or their assets. Ownership changes are important in indicating the effect that privatization transactions may or may not have on the enterprises concerned and in indicating the extent of a government's willingness and/or ability to exit from equity participation in commercial activity. Although a government's influence is not necessarily restricted by its equity participation, it is generally assumed that once a government owns less than 50 percent of the voting shares of a company, that company is "private" and the private shareholders (except in the instance of exercise of golden share rights) have management control of the company. Ownership control is usually unaffected when government continues to be a majority shareholder or sells a minority interest. Concessions, leases, and management contracts are assumed not to have affected ownership rights but to have transferred management control to the private sector for a defined period. The table shows the number of reported transactions where governments have: fully sold wholly- or majority-owned enterprises, sold shares and transferred ownership control but retained a minority equity interest, sold shares but retained ownership control, sold a proportion of a minority stake, and other transactions where management control has been ceded.

Methodology used for regional aggregations and period averages in chapter 10

Table	Aggregations[a]			Period averages[b]
	(1)	*(2)*	*(8)*	*(1)*
10-1	x			
10-2	x			
10-3	x			

Note: Regional aggregations are shown in the rows for Sub-Saharan Africa, North Africa, and All Africa. Period averages are shown in the last three columns. This table shows only the methodologies used in this chapter.

a. Regional aggregations: (1) simple total; (2) simple total of the first indicator divided by the simple total of the second indicator (same country coverage); (3) simple total of the gap-filled indicator; (4) simple total of the gap-filled main indicator divided by the simple total of the gap-filled secondary indicator; (5) simple total of the first gap-filled main indicator less the simple total of the second gap-filled main indicator, all divided by the simple total of the secondary indicator; (6) weighted total; (7) median; (8) no aggregation; (9) simple arithmetic mean.

b. Period averages: (1) arithmetic mean (using the same series as shown in the table, i.e., ratio if the rest of the table is shown as ratio, level if the rest of the table is shown as level, growth rate if the rest of the table is shown as growth rate); (2) least-squares growth rate (using main indicator); (3) least-squares growth rate (using main indicator in constant terms, with the rest of the table in current terms).

11

Labor Force and Employment

This chapter presents data on the level and structure of the labor force. The distribution of the labor force into various industrial activities is also given, as well as the participation rates of the population in economic activities. Information is also presented on average wages in different sectors.

The treatment of statistics on public sector employment is not consistent among countries. The scope covered often varies. While some countries include education and health sectors, others leave them out. Staff of local, regional, and state or provincial governments are likewise treated differently.

The stipulations on wages take different forms among the countries where such practice exists. While some countries have a minimum wage per hour worked, others stipulate a minimum monthly wage for a worker. To permit some measure of comparability, we have computed and reported the monthly average earnings per wage earner. These earnings are further converted to U.S. dollars at the *Atlas* exchange rate. These data should be used with caution since some countries have more than one minimum wage rate based on the industry and the occupation within the industry as well as on the region of the country concerned.

The definition of labor force or economically active population is that used by the International Labour Organization (ILO), which follows the UN system of national accounts (SNA). The labor force is measured by dividing economically active persons into two categories: employed and unemployed. Caution in the use of the data is necessary because, as pointed out in the ILO's *World Labor Report 1* (1987), there are many persons who do not clearly come within one of these categories or the other. Many are visibly underemployed in that they work less than full time. Others work full time but earn less than a subsistence income. Some of the unemployed may even be voluntarily idle.

The comparability of the data is further hampered by the fact that practices vary among countries as regards the treatment of such groups as armed forces, inmates of institutions, persons living on reservations, persons seeking their first job, seasonal workers, and persons engaged in part-time economic activities. In some countries, all or part of these groups are included among the economically active, while in others they are treated as inactive. In addition, the extent to which family workers who assist in family enterprises are included among the enumerated economically active population, particularly females, varies considerably from country to country. Further, in some countries the statistics of the economically active relate only to employed and unemployed persons above a specified age, while in others there is no such age provision.

The reference period is also an important factor of difference, especially when it comes to the classification of the labor force according to industry. In some countries, such classification refers to the ac-

tual position of each individual on the day of the census or survey date, while in others the data recorded refer to the usual position of each person, generally without reference to any given period of time.

The sources for the tables in this chapter are various issues of the ILO's *Yearbook of Labor Statistics*, and electronic ILO files kept in World Bank SIMA.

11-1. Number and gender structure of the labor force

	Total labor force (thousands)			Percentage of total labor force that are females		
	1970	*1980*	*1997*	*1970*	*1980*	*1997*
SUB-SAHARAN AFRICA	132,558	169,972	268,267	41.6	41.5	41.5
excluding South Africa	124,385	159,493	252,432	42.4	42.1	41.9
excl. S. Africa & Nigeria	102,035	130,322	205,273	43.9	43.6	43.4
Angola	2,906	3,439	5,363	47.4	47.0	46.4
Benin	1,355	1,663	2,608	48.4	47.0	48.3
Botswana	287	399	675	53.5	50.1	45.7
Burkina Faso	3,267	3,829	5,237	48.9	47.6	46.6
Burundi	1,968	2,272	3,475	50.5	50.2	48.9
Cameroon	3,042	3,635	5,714	37.3	36.8	37.7
Cape Verde	85	92	160	29.1	34.0	39.0
Central African Republic						
Chad	1,826	2,239	3,433	42.5	43.4	44.5
Comoros	..	151	233	..	43.1	42.4
Congo, Democratic Rep. of	9,527	11,884	19,618	45.2	44.5	43.5
Congo, Republic of	543	701	1,110	41.2	42.4	43.4
Côte d'Ivoire	2,316	3,278	5,684	33.0	32.2	33.0
Djibouti	..	..	..	..	..	..
Equatorial Guinea	134	95	177	36.3	35.1	35.4
Eritrea	952	1,215	1,887	47.5	47.4	47.4
Ethiopia	13,311	16,973	25,693	42.4	42.3	40.8
Gabon	282	359	542	45.7	45.0	44.5
Gambia, The	246	327	602	44.9	44.8	44.9
Ghana	4,048	5,048	8,453	50.6	51.0	50.6
Guinea	2,067	2,275	3,321	47.7	47.1	47.3
Guinea-Bissau	273	398	.534	39.7	39.9	40.4
Kenya	5,634	7,817	14,592	45.2	46.0	46.1
Lesotho	468	565	826	39.4	37.9	36.8
Liberia	609	788	1,183	38.0	38.4	39.5
Madagascar	3,430	4,348	6,650	45.5	45.2	44.8
Malawi	2,349	3,092	4,933	50.6	50.6	48.9
Mali	2,828	3,361	5,042	46.5	46.7	46.3
Mauritania	623	744	1,132	46.7	45.0	43.8
Mauritius	248	348	494	19.9	25.7	31.9
Mozambique	5,261	6,652	8,648	49.2	49.0	48.4
Namibia	356	443	665	39.7	40.1	40.8
Niger	2,124	2,793	4,605	45.1	44.6	44.2
Nigeria	22,350	29,171	47,159	36.8	36.2	36.1
Rwanda	1,976	2,633	4,184	49.4	49.1	48.9
São Tomé and Principe	..	..	..	..	..	..
Senegal	1,996	2,547	3,956	41.6	42.2	42.5
Seychelles	..	..	..	..	..	..
Sierra Leone	1,062	1,262	1,757	35.6	35.5	36.4
Somalia	1,728	2,692	3,773	43.9	43.4	43.4
South Africa	8,172	10,479	15,835	32.7	35.1	37.6
Sudan	5,128	6,912	10,817	26.7	26.9	28.8
Swaziland	159	203	345	33.5	33.5	37.6
Tanzania	7,258	9,476	15,971	50.6	49.8	49.3
Togo	909	1,151	1,781	39.0	39.3	39.9
Uganda	5,200	6,660	10,159	48.2	47.9	47.7
Zambia	1,885	2,410	3,966	44.6	45.4	45.2
Zimbabwe	2,367	3,154	5,275	44.4	44.4	44.4
NORTH AFRICA	22,349	29,252	47,371	25.6	27.0	29.6
Algeria	3,574	4,854	9,382	20.3	21.4	25.7
Egypt, Arab Republic	11,569	14,306	22,329	25.9	26.5	29.4
Libya	616	943	1,508	16.3	18.6	21.7
Morocco	5,052	6,978	10,651	31.4	33.5	34.6
Tunisia	1,538	2,171	3,502	23.7	28.9	30.9
ALL AFRICA	154,906	199,223	315,638	38.6	38.7	39.2

11-2. Children under 14 working in the labor force

	As percentage of population aged 10 to 14			
	1970	*1980*	*1990*	*1997*
SUB-SAHARAN AFRICA	36.3	34.7	32.2	29.8
excluding South Africa	39.1	37.2	34.5	31.7
excl. S.Africa & Nigeria	41.1	39.3	36.2	33.5
Angola	31.4	29.7	28.1	26.7
Benin	34.5	30.4	28.6	27.1
Botswana	32.3	25.9	19.4	15.9
Burkina Faso	75.1	70.9	58.7	48.0
Burundi	50.8	50.0	49.4	48.8
Cameroon	38.9	33.9	27.5	24.3
Cape Verde	17.4	16.0	14.7	13.9
Central African Republic	45.1	39.4	33.8	30.1
Chad	41.9	41.6	40.0	37.6
Comoros	45.8	44.8	41.0	38.6
Congo, Democratic Rep. of	36.5	33.2	30.5	29.2
Congo, Republic of	28.3	27.5	26.6	25.8
Côte d'Ivoire	34.6	28.4	22.3	19.7
Djibouti	..	..	..	..
Equatorial Guinea	42.9	40.5	35.8	33.2
Eritrea	46.1	43.8	40.8	39.1
Ethiopia	48.5	46.3	43.5	41.8
Gabon	35.6	29.1	22.7	16.7
Gambia, The	45.9	44.4	40.2	35.7
Ghana	16.3	16.2	14.6	12.8
Guinea	43.3	41.2	37.0	32.9
Guinea-Bissau	45.2	43.3	40.4	37.8
Kenya	45.0	45.1	43.4	40.4
Lesotho	30.9	27.6	23.5	21.5
Liberia	31.1	25.7	21.9	17.3
Madagascar	41.7	40.2	37.6	35.1
Malawi	50.7	45.2	38.9	33.7
Mali	62.5	61.2	57.9	53.2
Mauritania	33.3	29.6	25.8	23.2
Mauritius	5.7	4.8	4.0	2.6
Mozambique	40.7	39.5	35.2	33.2
Namibia	40.1	33.6	26.0	20.0
Niger	48.8	47.8	46.8	44.5
Nigeria	30.8	29.2	27.6	25.0
Rwanda	43.3	42.5	42.1	41.6
São Tomé and Principe	..	..	..	..
Senegal	46.9	42.9	35.4	29.7
Seychelles	..	..	..	..
Sierra Leone	21.7	19.4	17.1	14.9
Somalia	39.9	37.7	34.5	32.3
South Africa	2.7	0.9	0.0	0.0
Sudan	27.0	33.3	31.4	28.6
Swaziland	19.1	17.2	15.3	13.2
Tanzania	45.6	42.8	42.1	38.4
Togo	40.4	36.1	30.4	27.9
Uganda	50.4	48.9	46.8	44.7
Zambia	21.1	19.0	16.9	16.0
Zimbabwe	41.1	36.7	31.8	28.5
NORTH AFRICA	12.7	15.1	8.8	5.8
Algeria	7.4	7.1	3.3	1.0
Egypt, Arab Republic	15.0	18.3	13.2	10.4
Libya	10.8	8.7	0.5	0.2
Morocco	13.3	20.9	10.6	3.6
Tunisia	11.7	5.8	0.0	0.0
ALL AFRICA	31.4	30.9	28.0	25.8

11-3. Unpaid family workers as share of active workers

| | *Percentage of unpaid family workers in economically active workers* | | |
| | *(most recent year available between 1980-96)* | | |
	Female	*Male*	*Total*
SUB-SAHARAN AFRICA	..	..	..
excluding South Africa	..	..	..
excl. S.Africa & Nigeria	..	..	..
Angola	..	..	..
Benin	..	..	..
Botswana	41.8	36.0	77.7
Burkina Faso	..	..	..
Burundi	..	..	..
Cameroon	32.7	9.2	41.9
Cape Verde	..	..	..
Central African Republic	..	..	..
Chad	..	..	..
Comoros	..	..	..
Congo, Democratic Rep. of	..	..	..
Congo, Republic of	..	..	..
Côte d'Ivoire	..	..	..
Djibouti	..	..	..
Equatorial Guinea	..	..	..
Eritrea	..	..	..
Ethiopia	..	..	..
Gabon	..	..	..
Gambia, The	..	..	..
Ghana	..	0.0	0.0
Guinea	..	..	..
Guinea-Bissau	..	..	..
Kenya	..	..	..
Lesotho	..	..	..
Liberia	..	..	..
Madagascar	..	..	..
Malawi	..	..	..
Mali	..	..	..
Mauritania	..	..	..
Mauritius	..	..	..
Mozambique	..	..	..
Namibia	..	..	..
Niger	..	..	..
Nigeria	14.9	8.6	23.5
Rwanda	..	..	..
São Tomé and Principe	..	..	..
Senegal	..	..	..
Seychelles	0.5	0.2	0.6
Sierra Leone	..	..	..
Somalia	..	..	..
South Africa	..	..	..
Sudan	..	..	..
Swaziland	..	..	..
Tanzania	..	..	..
Togo	..	..	..
Uganda	..	..	..
Zambia	..	..	..
Zimbabwe	..	..	..
NORTH AFRICA	..	6.9	13.5
Algeria	..	5.6	6.2
Egypt, Arab Republic	1.9	15.0	16.9
Libya	..	..	..
Morocco	..	..	..
Tunisia	18.5	5.1	23.6
ALL AFRICA	..	..	..

11-4. Industrial structure of the labor force

	Percentage of labor force working in								
	Agriculture			*Industry*			*Services*		
	1970	*1980*	*1990*	*1970*	*1980*	*1990*	*1970*	*1980*	*1990*
SUB-SAHARAN AFRICA	78	72	68	8	9	9	14	20	24
excluding South Africa	82	76	71	6	7	7	12	18	22
excl. S.Africa & Nigeria	84	80	77	6	7	7	11	13	16
Angola	78	76	75	7	8	8	15	16	17
Benin	81	67	64	5	7	8	14	26	28
Botswana	82	64	46	5	10	20	13	26	33
Burkina Faso	92	92	92	3	3	2	5	5	6
Burundi	94	93	92	2	2	3	4	5	6
Cameroon	85	73	70	5	8	9	10	19	21
Cape Verde	47	37	31	27	31	30	27	33	40
Central African Republic	89	85	80	2	3	3	8	12	16
Chad	92	88	83	2	3	4	5	9	13
Comoros	83	81	77	7	8	9	10	11	13
Congo, Democratic Rep. of	75	72	68	11	12	13	14	16	19
Congo, Republic of	66	58	49	11	13	15	23	29	37
Côte d'Ivoire	76	65	60	6	8	10	19	27	30
Djibouti	..	..	..	..	..	..	..	..	..
Equatorial Guinea	82	78	75	5	5	5	14	17	20
Eritrea	86	83	80	4	5	5	10	12	15
Ethiopia	91	89	86	2	2	2	7	9	12
Gabon	79	65	52	9	12	16	12	22	33
Gambia, The	87	84	82	5	7	8	8	9	11
Ghana	60	61	59	15	13	13	25	25	28
Guinea	92	91	87	1	1	2	7	8	11
Guinea-Bissau	89	87	85	1	2	2	9	11	13
Kenya	86	82	80	5	6	7	9	11	13
Lesotho	43	40	40	36	34	28	21	26	32
Liberia	81	76	72	7	6	6	12	17	22
Madagascar	84	82	78	5	6	7	11	13	15
Malawi	91	87	87	4	5	5	5	7	8
Mali	93	89	86	1	2	2	6	9	12
Mauritania	84	72	55	3	7	10	12	22	34
Mauritius	34	27	17	25	28	43	41	45	40
Mozambique	86	84	83	6	7	8	8	8	9
Namibia	64	56	49	15	15	15	21	29	36
Niger	93	91	90	2	3	4	5	5	6
Nigeria	71	54	43	11	8	7	19	38	50
Rwanda	94	93	92	3	3	3	4	4	5
São Tomé and Principe	..	..	..	..	..	..	..	..	..
Senegal	83	81	77	6	6	8	12	13	16
Seychelles	..	..	..	..	..	..	..	..	..
Sierra Leone	76	70	67	12	14	15	12	16	17
Somalia	81	78	75	6	7	8	13	14	16
South Africa	31	17	14	30	35	32	39	48	54
Sudan	77	72	69	6	8	8	17	20	22
Swaziland	65	50	39	13	19	22	22	31	38
Tanzania	90	86	84	3	4	5	7	10	11
Togo	74	69	66	9	10	10	17	22	24
Uganda	90	87	85	3	4	5	7	9	11
Zambia	79	76	75	7	8	8	14	16	17
Zimbabwe	77	72	68	11	12	8	12	15	24
NORTH AFRICA	51	51	37	18	20	25	31	29	38
Algeria	47	36	26	21	27	31	31	37	43
Egypt, Arab Republic	52	57	40	16	16	22	32	27	38
Libya	29	25	11	25	24	23	46	51	66
Morocco	58	56	45	17	20	25	25	24	31
Tunisia	42	39	28	26	30	33	33	31	39
ALL AFRICA	75	69	63	9	10	11	16	21	26

Note: Figures may not add up to 100 because of rounding.

11-5. Industrial structure of economically active population

	Agriculture				Industry				Services			
	Male		Female		Male		Female		Male		Female	
	1980	1990	1980	1990	1980	1990	1980	1990	1980	1990	1980	1990
SUB-SAHARAN AFRICA	66	62	79	75	12	12	4	4	22	26	17	21
excluding South Africa	70	66	83	79	10	10	3	3	20	25	14	18
excl. S.Africa & Nigeria	75	72	88	85	10	10	3	3	16	18	10	12
Angola	67	65	87	86	13	14	1	2	20	21	11	13
Benin	66	62	69	65	10	12	4	4	24	27	27	30
Botswana	53	39	74	55	18	30	2	9	28	31	24	36
Burkina Faso	92	91	93	94	3	2	2	2	5	7	5	5
Burundi	88	86	98	98	4	4	1	1	9	10	1	1
Cameroon	65	62	87	83	11	12	2	3	24	26	11	14
Cape Verde	35	30	40	32	37	38	19	17	28	33	41	51
Central African Republic	79	74	90	87	5	6	1	0	16	20	9	13
Chad	82	77	95	91	6	7	0	1	12	16	4	8
Comoros	71	68	93	91	12	13	3	4	18	20	3	5
Congo, Democratic Rep. of	62	58	84	81	18	20	4	5	20	23	12	14
Congo, Republic of	42	33	81	69	20	23	2	4	38	44	17	27
Côte d'Ivoire	60	54	75	72	10	12	5	6	30	34	20	22
Djibouti	..	..	..	..	..	..	..	..	..	..	..	..
Equatorial Guinea	71	66	92	91	7	8	1	1	22	26	7	8
Eritrea	79	77	88	85	7	8	2	2	14	16	11	13
Ethiopia	90	86	89	86	2	2	2	2	8	11	10	12
Gabon	59	46	74	59	18	21	5	10	24	33	21	32
Gambia, The	78	74	93	92	10	12	2	3	13	15	5	6
Ghana	66	64	57	55	12	12	14	14	22	25	29	31
Guinea	86	83	96	92	2	3	1	1	12	15	3	7
Guinea-Bissau	81	78	98	96	3	3	0	0	17	19	2	3
Kenya	77	75	88	85	10	11	2	3	13	15	10	12
Lesotho	26	29	64	59	52	41	5	5	22	30	31	36
Liberia	69	65	89	84	10	9	1	1	22	26	10	16
Madagascar	73	70	93	88	9	10	2	3	19	20	5	9
Malawi	78	78	96	96	10	9	1	1	12	13	3	3
Mali	86	83	92	89	2	2	1	2	12	15	7	9
Mauritania	65	49	79	63	11	16	2	4	25	35	19	34
Mauritius	27	18	27	14	28	40	27	50	45	42	46	36
Mozambique	72	70	97	96	14	15	1	1	14	15	2	3
Namibia	52	46	64	54	22	21	5	8	27	33	31	39
Niger	86	84	98	97	5	6	1	1	9	10	1	1
Nigeria	52	43	57	44	10	9	5	3	38	49	38	53
Rwanda	88	86	98	98	5	6	1	1	7	8	1	2
São Tomé and Principe	..	..	..	..	..	..	..	..	..	..	..	..
Senegal	74	70	90	86	9	10	2	4	17	20	8	11
Seychelles	..	..	..	..	..	..	..	..	..	..	..	..
Sierra Leone	63	60	82	81	20	22	4	4	17	18	14	16
Somalia	69	66	90	88	12	13	2	2	19	21	8	11
South Africa	18	16	16	10	45	42	16	15	37	42	68	76
Sudan	66	64	88	84	9	10	4	5	24	26	8	11
Swaziland	43	31	63	54	25	31	6	8	32	38	31	39
Tanzania	80	78	92	91	7	8	2	2	13	14	7	7
Togo	70	66	67	65	12	12	7	7	19	22	26	29
Uganda	84	81	91	88	6	7	2	2	10	12	8	10
Zambia	69	68	85	83	13	13	3	3	19	19	13	14
Zimbabwe	63	58	85	81	19	13	4	2	18	29	12	17
NORTH AFRICA	40	29	39	50	24	28	12	13	34	41	36	28
Algeria	27	18	69	57	33	38	6	7	40	45	25	36
Egypt, Arab Republic	43	33	8	43	20	23	10	8	32	39	56	31
Libya	16	7	63	28	29	27	3	5	55	66	34	68
Morocco	48	35	72	63	23	28	14	19	29	37	14	18
Tunisia	33	23	53	42	30	33	32	32	37	44	16	27
ALL AFRICA	62	56	75	72	14	15	5	5	24	28	19	22

Percentage of population economically active

11-6. Wages in agriculture

	Monthly earnings in current US dollars											
	1980	1987	1988	1989	1990	1991	1992	1993	1994	1995	1996	1997
SUB-SAHARAN AFRICA	..	..	..	..	..	..	..	..	..	..	..	..
excluding South Africa	..	..	..	..	..	..	..	..	..	..	..	..
excl. S. Africa & Nigeria	..	..	..	..	..	..	..	..	..	..	..	..
Angola	..	..	..	..	..	..	..	..	..	..	..	..
Benin	..	..	..	..	..	..	..	..	..	..	..	..
Botswana	..	55	54	71	80	97	97	90	90	90	80	80
Burkina Faso	..	..	..	..	..	..	..	..	..	..	..	..
Burundi	..	..	..	..	..	..	..	..	..	..	..	..
Cameroon	..	..	..	..	..	..	..	..	..	..	..	..
Cape Verde	..	..	..	..	..	..	..	..	..	..	..	..
Central African Republic	..	..	..	..	..	..	..	..	..	..	..	..
Chad	..	..	..	..	..	..	..	..	..	..	..	..
Comoros	..	..	..	..	..	..	..	..	..	..	..	..
Congo, Democratic Rep. of	..	..	..	..	..	..	..	..	..	..	..	..
Congo, Republic of	..	..	..	..	..	..	..	..	..	..	..	..
Côte d'Ivoire	..	..	..	..	..	..	..	..	..	..	..	..
Djibouti	..	..	..	..	..	..	..	..	..	..	..	..
Equatorial Guinea	..	..	..	..	..	..	..	..	..	..	..	..
Eritrea	..	..	..	..	..	..	..	..	..	..	..	..
Ethiopia	..	..	..	..	..	..	..	..	..	..	..	..
Gabon	..	..	..	..	..	..	..	..	..	..	..	..
Gambia, The	..	..	..	..	..	..	..	..	..	..	..	..
Ghana	34	52	52	73	64	104	..	..	..	..	..	..
Guinea	..	..	..	..	..	..	..	..	..	..	..	..
Guinea-Bissau	..	..	..	..	..	..	..	..	..	..	..	..
Kenya	59	48	53	48	47	45	..	..	..	..	..	39
Lesotho	..	..	..	..	..	..	..	..	..	..	..	..
Liberia	..	..	..	..	..	..	..	..	..	..	..	..
Madagascar	..	..	..	..	..	..	..	..	..	..	..	..
Malawi	20	13	12	13	15	16	..	..	..	..	..	..
Mali	..	..	..	..	..	..	..	..	..	..	..	..
Mauritania	..	..	..	..	..	..	..	..	..	..	..	..
Mauritius	..	..	..	..	..	..	..	..	..	..	..	..
Mozambique	..	..	..	..	..	..	..	..	..	..	..	..
Namibia	..	..	..	..	..	..	..	..	..	..	..	..
Niger	..	..	..	..	..	..	..	..	..	..	..	..
Nigeria	..	..	..	..	..	..	..	..	..	..	..	..
Rwanda	..	..	..	..	..	..	..	..	..	..	..	..
São Tomé and Principe	..	..	..	..	..	..	..	..	..	..	..	..
Senegal	..	..	..	..	..	..	..	..	..	..	..	..
Seychelles	139	305	304	305	348	366	434	442	456	513	..	..
Sierra Leone	..	..	..	..	..	..	..	..	..	..	..	..
Somalia	..	..	..	..	..	..	..	..	..	..	..	..
South Africa	..	..	..	..	..	..	..	..	..	..	..	..
Sudan	..	..	..	..	..	..	..	..	..	..	..	..
Swaziland	..	310	..	437	423	496	533	512	550	483	..	..
Tanzania	..	..	..	..	..	..	..	..	..	..	..	..
Togo	..	..	..	..	..	..	..	..	..	..	..	..
Uganda	..	..	..	..	..	..	..	..	..	..	..	..
Zambia	112	..	..	..	..	..	..	..	..	..	..	..
Zimbabwe	..	74	76	71	75	56	34	38	35	34	..	..
NORTH AFRICA	..	..	..	..	..	..	..	..	..	..	..	..
Algeria	..	..	..	..	..	..	..	..	..	..	..	..
Egypt, Arab Republic	..	154	154	144	94	53	53	65	69	75	..	..
Libya	..	..	..	..	..	..	..	..	..	..	..	..
Morocco	..	..	..	..	..	..	..	..	..	..	..	..
Tunisia	..	80	82	77	92	89	101	..	..	..	..	..
ALL AFRICA	..	..	..	..	..	..	..	..	..	..	..	..

11-7. Wages in manufacturing

					Monthly earnings in current US dollars						
	1980	*1987*	*1988*	*1989*	*1990*	*1991*	*1992*	*1993*	*1994*	*1995*	*1996*	*1997*
SUB-SAHARAN AFRICA	..	..	..	..	..	..	..	..	..	..	..	..
excluding South Africa	..	..	..	..	..	..	..	..	..	..	..	..
excl. S. Africa & Nigeria	..	..	..	..	..	..	..	..	..	..	..	..
Angola	..	..	..	..	..	..	..	..	..	..	..	..
Benin	..	..	..	..	..	..	..	..	..	..	..	..
Botswana	..	166	181	171	206	199	242	250	200	210	186	173
Burkina Faso	..	..	..	..	..	..	..	..	..	..	..	..
Burundi	..	..	..	..	..	..	..	..	..	..	..	..
Cameroon	..	..	..	..	..	..	..	..	..	..	..	..
Cape Verde	..	..	..	..	..	..	..	..	..	..	..	..
Central African Republic	..	..	..	..	..	..	..	..	..	..	..	..
Chad	..	..	..	..	..	..	..	..	..	..	..	..
Comoros	..	..	..	..	..	..	..	..	..	..	..	..
Congo, Democratic Rep. of	..	..	..	..	..	..	..	..	..	..	..	..
Congo, Republic of	..	..	..	..	..	..	..	..	..	..	..	..
Côte d'Ivoire	..	..	..	..	..	..	..	..	..	..	..	..
Djibouti	..	..	..	..	..	..	..	..	..	..	..	..
Equatorial Guinea	..	..	..	..	..	..	..	..	..	..	..	..
Eritrea	..	..	..	..	..	..	..	..	..	..	..	..
Ethiopia	..	..	..	..	..	..	..	..	..	..	..	..
Gabon	..	..	..	..	..	..	..	..	..	..	..	..
Gambia, The	..	..	..	..	..	..	..	..	..	..	..	..
Ghana	57	99	106	136	138	93	..	..	..	..	..	..
Guinea	..	58	..	..	121	113	122	115	133	131	152	..
Guinea-Bissau	..	..	..	..	..	..	..	..	..	..	..	..
Kenya	169	139	139	136	134	121	..	..	..	..	..	94
Lesotho	..	..	..	..	..	..	..	..	..	..	..	..
Liberia	..	..	..	..	..	..	..	..	..	..	..	..
Madagascar	..	..	..	..	..	..	..	..	..	..	..	..
Malawi	75	57	53	53	65	55	47	40	21	13	..	..
Mali	..	..	..	..	..	..	..	..	..	..	..	..
Mauritania	..	..	..	..	..	..	..	..	..	..	..	..
Mauritius	..	160	181	184	209	235	258	250	287	326	333	306
Mozambique	..	..	..	..	..	..	..	..	..	..	..	..
Namibia	..	..	..	..	..	..	..	..	..	..	..	..
Niger	..	..	..	..	..	..	..	..	..	..	..	..
Nigeria	..	..	..	..	..	..	..	..	..	..	..	..
Rwanda	..	..	..	..	..	..	..	..	..	..	..	..
São Tomé and Principe	..	..	..	..	..	..	..	..	..	..	..	..
Senegal	..	..	..	..	..	..	..	..	..	..	..	..
Seychelles	212	371	346	350	410	427	459	474	479	528	..	..
Sierra Leone	..	..	..	..	..	..	..	..	..	..	..	..
Somalia	..	..	..	..	..	..	..	..	..	..	..	..
South Africa	475	513	535	548	642	685	770	749	..	..	..	..
Sudan	..	..	55	..	83	..	12	..	..	..	..	..
Swaziland	571	507	414	397	533	513	521	351	524	588	556	..
Tanzania	..	..	..	..	..	..	..	..	..	..	..	..
Togo	..	..	..	..	..	..	..	..	..	..	..	..
Uganda	..	..	..	..	..	..	..	..	..	..	..	..
Zambia	..	..	..	..	..	..	..	..	..	..	..	..
Zimbabwe	..	318	327	314	325	256	220	192	191	221	230	..
NORTH AFRICA	..	..	..	..	..	..	..	..	..	..	..	..
Algeria	..	..	..	..	..	..	..	..	..	..	..	..
Egypt, Arab Republic	..	233	252	228	150	75	80	90	98	107	..	..
Libya	..	..	..	..	..	..	..	..	..	..	..	..
Morocco	..	..	..	..	..	..	..	..	..	..	..	..
Tunisia	..	..	..	..	..	..	..	..	..	..	..	..
ALL AFRICA	..	..	..	..	..	..	..	..	..	..	..	..

11-8. Wages in mining and quarrying

						Monthly earnings in current US dollars						
	1980	1987	1988	1989	1990	1991	1992	1993	1994	1995	1996	1997
SUB-SAHARAN AFRICA	..	..	..	..	..	..	..	..	..	..	..	..
excluding South Africa	..	..	..	..	..	..	..	..	..	..	..	..
excl. S. Africa & Nigeria	..	..	..	..	..	..	..	..	..	..	..	..
Angola	..	..	..	..	..	..	..	..	..	..	..	..
Benin	..	..	..	..	..	..	..	..	..	..	..	..
Botswana	..	291	287	319	450	424	436	496	430	428	372	371
Burkina Faso	..	..	..	..	..	..	..	..	..	..	..	..
Burundi	..	..	..	..	..	..	..	..	..	..	..	..
Cameroon	..	..	..	..	..	..	..	..	..	..	..	..
Cape Verde	..	..	..	..	..	..	..	..	..	..	..	..
Central African Republic	..	..	..	..	..	..	..	..	..	..	..	..
Chad	..	..	..	..	..	..	..	..	..	..	..	..
Comoros	..	..	..	..	..	..	..	..	..	..	..	..
Congo, Democratic Rep. of	..	..	..	..	..	..	..	..	..	..	..	..
Congo, Republic of	..	..	..	..	..	..	..	..	..	..	..	..
Côte d'Ivoire	..	..	..	..	..	..	..	..	..	..	..	..
Djibouti	..	..	..	..	..	..	..	..	..	..	..	..
Equatorial Guinea	..	..	..	..	..	..	..	..	..	..	..	..
Eritrea	..	..	..	..	..	..	..	..	..	..	..	..
Ethiopia	..	..	..	..	..	..	..	..	..	..	..	..
Gabon	..	..	..	..	..	..	..	..	..	..	..	..
Gambia, The	..	..	..	..	..	..	..	..	..	..	..	..
Ghana	64	111	57	64	117	75	..	..	..	..	..	..
Guinea	..	..	..	..	..	..	..	..	..	..	..	..
Guinea-Bissau	..	..	..	..	..	..	..	..	..	..	..	..
Kenya	157	110	104	106	101	93	..	..	..	..	..	96
Lesotho	..	..	..	..	..	..	..	..	..	..	..	..
Liberia	..	..	..	..	..	..	..	..	..	..	..	..
Madagascar	..	..	..	..	..	..	..	..	..	..	..	..
Malawi	36	20	17	17	20	30	23	59	30	18	..	..
Mali	..	..	..	..	..	..	..	..	..	..	..	..
Mauritania	..	..	..	..	..	..	..	..	..	..	..	..
Mauritius	..	202	245	231	256	272	302	280	374	436	457	415
Mozambique	..	..	..	..	..	..	..	..	..	..	..	..
Namibia	..	..	..	..	..	..	..	..	..	..	..	..
Niger	..	..	..	..	..	..	..	..	..	..	..	..
Nigeria	..	..	..	..	..	..	..	..	..	..	..	..
Rwanda	..	..	..	..	..	..	..	..	..	..	..	..
São Tomé and Principe	..	..	..	..	..	..	..	..	..	..	..	..
Senegal	..	..	..	..	..	..	..	..	..	..	..	..
Seychelles	212	327	334	317	348	378	444	455	477	523	..	..
Sierra Leone	..	..	..	..	..	..	..	..	..	..	..	..
Somalia	..	..	..	..	..	..	..	..	..	..	..	..
South Africa	330	371	397	403	477	514	561	541	..	..	..	..
Sudan	..	..	53	..	99	..	..	..	..	..	..	..
Swaziland	822	560	483	309	395	367	395	379	387	523	485	..
Tanzania	..	..	..	..	..	..	..	..	..	..	..	..
Togo	..	..	..	..	..	..	..	..	..	..	..	..
Uganda	..	..	..	..	..	..	..	..	..	..	..	..
Zambia	358		..	..	..	..	..	..	..	..	..	..
Zimbabwe	..	240	254	242	254	204	180	153	153	187	204	..
NORTH AFRICA	..	..	..	..	..	..	..	..	..	..	..	..
Algeria	..	..	..	..	..	..	..	..	..	..	..	..
Egypt, Arab Republic	..	362	375	427	316	174	167	208	210	203	..	..
Libya	..	..	..	..	..	..	..	..	..	..	..	..
Morocco	..	..	..	..	..	..	..	..	..	..	..	..
Tunisia	..	..	..	..	..	..	..	..	..	..	..	..
ALL AFRICA	..	..	..	..	..	..	..	..	..	..	..	..

11-9. Wages in construction

	1980	1987	1988	1989	1990	1991	1992	1993	1994	1995	1996	1997
	Monthly earnings in current US dollars											
SUB-SAHARAN AFRICA	..	..	..	..	..	..	..	..	..	..	..	..
excluding South Africa	..	..	..	..	..	..	..	..	..	..	..	..
excl. S. Africa & Nigeria	..	..	..	..	..	..	..	..	..	..	..	..
Angola	..	..	..	..	..	..	..	..	..	..	..	..
Benin	..	..	..	..	..	..	..	..	..	..	..	..
Botswana	..	149	148	159	182	196	211	220	214	228	197	218
Burkina Faso	..	..	..	..	..	..	..	..	..	..	..	..
Burundi	..	..	..	..	..	..	..	..	..	..	..	..
Cameroon	..	..	..	..	..	..	..	..	..	..	..	..
Cape Verde	..	..	..	..	..	..	..	..	..	..	..	..
Central African Republic	..	..	..	..	..	..	..	..	..	..	..	..
Chad	..	..	..	..	..	..	..	..	..	..	..	..
Comoros	..	..	..	..	..	..	..	..	..	..	..	..
Congo, Democratic Rep. of	..	..	..	..	..	..	..	..	..	..	..	..
Congo, Republic of	..	..	..	..	..	..	..	..	..	..	..	..
Côte d'Ivoire	..	..	..	..	..	..	..	..	..	..	..	..
Djibouti	..	..	..	..	..	..	..	..	..	..	..	..
Equatorial Guinea	..	..	..	..	..	..	..	..	..	..	..	..
Eritrea	..	..	..	..	..	..	..	..	..	..	..	..
Ethiopia	..	..	..	..	..	..	..	..	..	..	..	..
Gabon	..	..	..	..	..	..	..	..	..	..	..	..
Gambia, The	..	..	..	..	..	..	..	..	..	..	..	..
Ghana	37	45	43	51	59	71	..	..	..	..	..	..
Guinea	..	..	84	115	173	159	..	135	132	177	174	..
Guinea-Bissau	..	..	..	..	..	..	..	..	..	..	..	..
Kenya	133	97	98	96	99	95	..	..	..	..	..	80
Lesotho	..	..	..	..	..	..	..	..	..	..	..	..
Liberia	..	..	..	..	..	..	..	..	..	..	..	..
Madagascar	..	..	..	..	..	..	..	..	..	..	..	..
Malawi	60	29	29	29	30	31	34	33	22	17	..	..
Mali	..	..	..	..	..	..	..	..	..	..	..	..
Mauritania	..	..	..	..	..	..	..	..	..	..	..	..
Mauritius	..	170	220	245	255	297	364	324	368	481	507	488
Mozambique	..	..	..	..	..	..	..	..	..	..	..	..
Namibia	..	..	..	..	..	..	..	..	..	..	..	..
Niger	..	..	..	..	..	..	..	..	..	..	..	..
Nigeria	..	..	..	..	..	..	..	..	..	..	..	..
Rwanda	..	..	..	..	..	..	..	..	..	..	..	..
São Tomé and Principe	..	..	..	..	..	..	..	..	..	..	..	..
Senegal	..	..	..	..	..	..	..	..	..	..	..	..
Seychelles	..	..	..	..	..	..	..	..	..	..	..	..
Sierra Leone	..	..	..	..	..	..	..	..	..	..	..	..
Somalia	..	..	..	..	..	..	..	..	..	..	..	..
South Africa	371	347	367	348	394	437	475	424	..	..	..	..
Sudan	..	..	56	..	180	..	13	..	..	..	..	..
Swaziland	525	335	267	192	247	283	470	211	333	227	246	..
Tanzania	..	..	..	..	..	..	..	..	..	..	..	..
Togo	..	..	..	..	..	..	..	..	..	..	..	..
Uganda	..	..	..	..	..	..	..	..	..	..	..	..
Zambia	172											
Zimbabwe	..	209	200	182	179	144	110	102	88	114	124	..
NORTH AFRICA	..	..	..	..	..	..	..	..	..	..	..	..
Algeria	..	..	..	..	..	..	..	..	..	..	..	..
Egypt, Arab Republic	..	246	276	253	153	84	80	96	112	115	..	..
Libya	..	..	..	..	..	..	..	..	..	..	..	..
Morocco	..	..	..	..	..	..	..	..	..	..	..	..
Tunisia	..	..	..	..	..	..	..	..	..	..	..	..
ALL AFRICA	..	..	..	..	..	..	..	..	..	..	..	..

11-10. Wages in transport, storage, and communication

Monthly earnings in current US dollars

	1980	1987	1988	1989	1990	1991	1992	1993	1994	1995	1996	1997
SUB-SAHARAN AFRICA	..	..	..	..	..	..	..	..	..	..	..	..
excluding South Africa	..	..	..	..	..	..	..	..	..	..	..	..
excl. S. Africa & Nigeria	..	..	..	..	..	..	..	..	..	..	..	..
Angola	..	..	..	..	..	..	..	..	..	..	..	..
Benin	..	..	..	..	..	..	..	..	..	..	..	..
Botswana	..	192	239	296	346	417	457	434	468	435	376	344
Burkina Faso	..	..	..	..	..	..	..	..	..	..	..	..
Burundi	..	..	..	..	..	..	..	..	..	..	..	..
Cameroon	..	..	..	..	..	..	..	..	..	..	..	..
Cape Verde	..	..	..	..	..	..	..	..	..	..	..	..
Central African Republic	..	..	..	..	..	..	..	..	..	..	..	..
Chad	..	..	..	..	..	..	..	..	..	..	..	..
Comoros	..	..	..	..	..	..	..	..	..	..	..	..
Congo, Democratic Rep. of	..	..	..	..	..	..	..	..	..	..	..	..
Congo, Republic of	..	..	..	..	..	..	..	..	..	..	..	..
Côte d'Ivoire	..	..	..	..	..	..	..	..	..	..	..	..
Djibouti	..	..	..	..	..	..	..	..	..	..	..	..
Equatorial Guinea	..	..	..	..	..	..	..	..	..	..	..	..
Eritrea	..	..	..	..	..	..	..	..	..	..	..	..
Ethiopia	..	..	..	..	..	..	..	..	..	..	..	..
Gabon	..	..	..	..	..	..	..	..	..	..	..	..
Gambia, The	..	..	..	..	..	..	..	..	..	..	..	..
Ghana	55	36	89	96	100	106	..	..	..	..	..	..
Guinea	..	..	..	..	..	..	..	..	119	121	125	..
Guinea-Bissau	..	..	..	..	..	..	..	..	..	..	..	..
Kenya	237	195	207	193	187	171	..	..	..	..	..	131
Lesotho	..	..	..	..	..	..	..	..	..	..	..	..
Liberia	..	..	..	..	..	..	..	..	..	..	..	..
Madagascar	..	..	..	..	..	..	..	..	..	..	..	..
Malawi	99	47	49	62	63	70	66	63	37	25	..	..
Mali	..	..	..	..	..	..	..	..	..	..	..	..
Mauritania	..	..	..	..	..	..	..	..	..	..	..	..
Mauritius	..	231	290	289	307	339	380	353	376	422	453	426
Mozambique	..	..	..	..	..	..	..	..	..	..	..	..
Namibia	..	..	..	..	..	..	..	..	..	..	..	..
Niger	..	..	..	..	..	..	..	..	..	..	..	..
Nigeria	..	..	..	..	..	..	..	..	..	..	..	..
Rwanda	..	..	..	..	..	..	..	..	..	..	..	..
São Tomé and Principe	..	..	..	..	..	..	..	..	..	..	..	..
Senegal	..	..	..	..	..	..	..	..	..	..	..	..
Seychelles	299	..	..	..	..	..	..	..	..	..	..	..
Sierra Leone	..	..	..	..	..	..	..	..	..	..	..	..
Somalia	..	..	..	..	..	..	..	..	..	..	..	..
South Africa	..	571	583	577	702	794	1,110	1,075	..	..	..	..
Sudan	..	..	48	..	79	..	14	..	..	..	..	..
Swaziland	520	243	242	192	364	442	357	393	480	539	455	..
Tanzania	..	..	..	..	..	..	..	..	..	..	..	..
Togo	..	..	..	..	..	..	..	..	..	..	..	..
Uganda	..	..	..	..	..	..	..	..	..	..	..	..
Zambia	153	..	..	..	..	..	..	..	..	..	..	..
Zimbabwe	..	400	425	429	465	334	289	284	258	275	289	..
NORTH AFRICA	..	..	..	..	..	..	..	..	..	..	..	..
Algeria	..	..	..	..	..	..	..	..	..	..	..	..
Egypt, Arab Republic	..	221	283	248	147	78	84	121	112	117	..	..
Libya	..	..	..	..	..	..	..	..	..	..	..	..
Morocco	..	..	..	..	..	..	..	..	..	..	..	..
Tunisia	..	..	..	..	..	..	..	..	..	..	..	..
ALL AFRICA	..	..	..	..	..	..	..	..	..	..	..	..

11-11. Wages in community, social, and personal services

| | *Monthly earnings in current US dollars* | | | | | | | | | | |
	1980	*1987*	*1988*	*1989*	*1990*	*1991*	*1992*	*1993*	*1994*	*1995*	*1996*	*1997*
SUB-SAHARAN AFRICA	..	..	..	..	..	..	..	..	..	..	..	..
excluding South Africa	..	..	..	..	..	..	..	..	..	..	..	..
excl. S. Africa & Nigeria	..	..	..	..	..	..	..	..	..	.. ·	..	..
Angola	..	..	..	..	..	..	..	..	..	..	..	..
Benin	..	..	..	..	..	..	..	..	..	..	..	..
Botswana	..	186	195	189	231	239	249	265	254	280	243	250
Burkina Faso	..	..	..	..	..	..	..	..	..	..	..	..
Burundi	..	..	..	..	..	..	..	..	..	..	..	..
Cameroon	..	..	..	..	..	..	..	..	..	..	..	..
Cape Verde	..	..	..	..	..	..	..	..	..	..	..	..
Central African Republic	..	..	..	..	..	..	..	..	..	..	..	..
Chad	..	..	..	..	..	..	..	..	..	..	..	..
Comoros	..	..	..	..	..	..	..	..	..	..	..	..
Congo, Democratic Rep. of	..	..	..	..	..	..	..	..	..	..	..	..
Congo, Republic of	..	..	..	..	..	..	..	..	..	..	..	..
Côte d'Ivoire	..	..	..	..	..	..	..	..	..	..	..	..
Djibouti	..	..	..	..	..	..	..	..	..	..	..	..
Equatorial Guinea	..	..	..	..	..	..	..	..	..	..	..	..
Eritrea	..	..	..	..	..	..	..	..	..	..	..	..
Ethiopia	..	..	..	..	..	..	..	..	..	..	..	..
Gabon	..	..	..	..	..	..	..	..	..	..	..	..
Gambia, The	..	..	..	..	..	..	..	..	..	..	..	..
Ghana	..	55	59	81	68	98	..	..	..	..	..	..
Guinea	..	..	..	..	..	..	..	..	..	..	..	..
Guinea-Bissau	..	..	..	..	..	..	..	..	..	..	..	..
Kenya	..	121	128	118	114	104	..	..	..	..	..	75
Lesotho	..	..	..	..	..	..	..	..	..	..	..	..
Liberia	..	..	..	..	..	..	..	..	..	..	..	..
Madagascar	..	..	..	..	..	..	..	..	..	..	..	..
Malawi	..	..	..	..	..	59	50	43	24	12	..	..
Mali	..	..	..	..	..	..	..	..	..	..	..	..
Mauritania	..	..	..	..	..	..	..	..	..	..	..	..
Mauritius	..	183	235	245	262	278	307	278	357	392	394	404
Mozambique	..	..	..	..	..	..	..	..	..	..	..	..
Namibia	..	..	..	..	..	..	..	..	..	..	..	..
Niger	..	..	..	..	..	..	..	..	..	..	..	..
Nigeria	..	..	..	..	..	..	..	..	..	..	..	..
Rwanda	..	..	..	..	..	..	..	..	..	..	..	..
São Tomé and Principe	..	..	..	..	..	..	..	..	..	..	..	..
Senegal	..	..	..	..	..	..	..	..	..	..	..	..
Seychelles	..	..	..	..	..	..	..	..	..	..	..	..
Sierra Leone	..	..	..	..	..	..	..	..	..	..	..	..
Somalia	..	..	..	..	..	..	..	..	..	..	..	..
South Africa	..	537	532	563	679	735	937	..	..	..	..	..
Sudan	..	..	..	..	..	..	..	..	..	..	..	..
Swaziland	..	..	..	223	446	276	412	238	455	352	352	..
Tanzania	..	..	..	..	..	..	..	..	..	..	..	..
Togo	..	..	..	..	..	..	..	..	..	..	..	..
Uganda	..	..	..	..	..	..	..	..	..	..	..	..
Zambia	..	..	..	..	..	..	..	..	..	..	..	..
Zimbabwe	..	246	255	240	259	206	161	139	128	143	192	..
NORTH AFRICA	..	..	..	..	..	..	..	..	..	..	..	..
Algeria	..	..	..	..	..	..	..	..	..	..	..	..
Egypt, Arab Republic	..	203	203	179	128	64	65	67	80	112	..	..
Libya	..	..	..	..	..	..	..	..	..	..	..	..
Morocco	..	..	..	..	..	..	..	..	..	..	..	..
Tunisia	..	..	..	..	..	..	..	..	..	..	..	..
ALL AFRICA	..	..	..	..	..	..	..	..	..	..	..	..

Technical Notes

Tables

Table 11-1. Number and gender structure of the labor force. This table (ILO data) provides the total number of persons in the labor force and the percentage that is female. Labor force refers to "economically active" persons, including the armed forces and the unemployed but excluding housewives and students. The "economically active" population comprises all persons of either gender who furnish the labor to produce economic goods and services, as defined by the SNA, during a specified period. The production of economic goods and services should include all production and processing of primary products, whether for the market, for barter, or for own consumption; the production of all other goods and services for the market; and, for households that produce such goods and services for the markets, the corresponding production for own consumption.

Table 11-2. Children under 14 working in the labor force. This table (ILO data) shows the percentage of children between the ages of 10 to 14 that participate in the labor force.

Table 11-3. Unpaid family workers as share of active workers. This table (ILO data) shows the percentage of family members—male and female—that are active workers but receive no compensation for their services.

Table 11-4. Industrial structure of the labor force. The industrial structure of the labor force can often indicate the relative level of development of the econ-omy. This table (ILO data) shows the distribution of the labor force among the various sectors of economic activities. The agriculture sector includes farming, animal husbandry, hunting, forestry, and fishing. The industry sector includes mining and quarrying, manu-facturing, construction and public works, electricity, water, and gas. All other branches of activity are included in services.

Table 11-5. Industrial structure of economically active population. This is the percentage of the eco-nomically active population working in agriculture, industry, or services. Data are shown for males and females (ILO data).

Table 11-6. Wages in agriculture. Data are from ILO, *Yearbook of Labor Statistics* (1988, 1993, 1994, 1995, and 1998) and show the monthly earnings at the average wage converted to U.S. dollars at the *Atlas* exchange rates in the countries concerned. Earnings here are limited to wages and salaries of employees only unless otherwise specified. They include remu-neration for time not worked, such as for annual vacation, other paid leave or holidays, bonuses and gratuities, and housing and family allowances paid by the employer to the employee. They exclude employ-ers' contributions to social security and pension schemes and the benefits received by employees under these schemes, as well as severance and termination pay.

It should be remembered that these earnings do not reflect worker's disposable or net earnings since they include gross wages before deductions, such as taxes or social security contributions.

International comparisons of wages in agriculture should be interpreted with caution because they entail wide coverage variations mainly as a result of the form of remuneration, the nature of the work, and the length of the working day.

For the following countries wages are paid entirely in cash: Botswana, Burundi, Egypt, Malawi, Mauritius, Seychelles, Swaziland, Tanzania, Tunisia, and Zambia.

For the following countries, wages shown are cash portion only, although the workers receive other payments in kind in addition: Ghana, Kenya, and Zimbabwe. Wages for these three countries include the value of food and lodging allowances.

Data for Burundi include family allowances. Data for Egypt are for establishments with 10 or more persons employed. Data for Ghana include forestry and fishing. Data for Kenya include the value of payments in kind. Data for Malawi include forestry and fishing. Data for Mauritius include sugar and tea factories. Data for Seychelles exclude hunting. Data for Swaziland include forestry and refer to skilled male workers only. Data for Zimbabwe include forestry and refer to all persons engaged.

Figures for Egypt were converted from weekly to monthly earnings using a rate of 4.3 weeks per month. Figures for Mauritius and Tunisia were converted from daily to monthly earnings using a rate of 22 days per month.

Table 11-7. Wages in manufacturing. Data are from ILO, *Yearbook of Labor Statistics* (1988, 1993, 1994, 1995, and 1998). Refer to the definitions in Table 11-6.

Data for Burundi include family allowances. Data for Egypt are for establishments with 10 or more persons employed. Data for The Gambia are for establishments with five or more persons employed. Data for Mauritius exclude sugar and tea factories. Data for Seychelles include electricity and water before 1992, and beginning in 1988 earnings are exempted from income tax. Data for Swaziland refer to skilled male workers only. Data for Zimbabwe include the value of payments in kind and refer to all persons engaged.

Figures for Egypt and Sierra Leone were converted from weekly to monthly earnings using a rate of 4.3 weeks per month. Figures for The Gambia were converted from daily to monthly earnings using a rate of 22 days per month.

Table 11-8. Wages in mining and quarrying. Data are from ILO, *Yearbook of Labor Statistics* (1988, 1993, 1994, 1995, and 1998). Refer to the definitions in Table 11-6.

Data for Burundi include family allowances. Data for Egypt are for establishments with 10 or more persons employed. Data for Kenya include the value of payments in kind. Data for Swaziland refer to skilled male workers only. Data for Seychelles include construction, and beginning in 1988 earnings are exempted from income tax. Data for South Africa exclude salt and iron works. Data for Swaziland refer to skilled male workers only. Data for Zimbabwe include the value of payments in kind and refer to all persons engaged.

Figures for Egypt and Sierra Leone were converted from weekly to monthly earnings using a rate of 4.3 weeks per month.

Table 11-9. Wages in construction. Data are from ILO, *Yearbook of Labor Statistics* (1988, 1993, 1994, 1995, and 1998). Refer to the definitions in Table 11-6.

Data for Burundi include family allowances. Data for Egypt are for establishments with 10 or more persons employed. Data for The Gambia are for establishments with five or more persons employed. Data for Kenya include the value of payments in kind. Data for Swaziland refer to skilled male workers only. Data for South Africa include private construction. Data for Swaziland refer to skilled male workers only. Data for Zimbabwe include the value of payments in kind and refer to all persons engaged.

Figures for Egypt and Sierra Leone were converted from weekly to monthly earnings using a rate of 4.3 weeks per month. Figures for The Gambia were converted from daily to monthly earnings using a rate of 22 days per month.

Table 11-10. Wages in transport, storage, and communications. Data are from ILO, *Yearbook of Labor Statistics* (1988, 1993, 1994, 1995, and 1998). Refer to the definitions in Table 11-6.

Data for Burundi include family allowances. Data for Egypt are for establishments with 10 or more persons employed. Data for The Gambia are for establishments with five or more persons employed. Data for Kenya include the value of payments in kind. Data for Swaziland refer to skilled male workers only. Data for Zimbabwe include the value of payments in kind and refer to all persons engaged.

Figures for Egypt and Sierra Leone were converted from weekly to monthly earnings using a rate of 4.3 weeks per month. Figures for The Gambia were converted from daily to monthly earnings using a rate of 22 days per month.

Table 11-11. Wages in community, social, and personal services. Data are from ILO Yearbook of Labor Statistics (1998). Refer to the definitions in Table 11-6. This sector comprises public administration and defense; sanitary and similar services; educational services; research and scientific institutes; medical, dental, and other health services; welfare institutions; business, professional, and labour associations; and other social and community services. Data for Egypt refer to wage earners. Figures for Egypt were converted from weekly to monthly earnings using a rate of 4.3 weeks per month.

Methodology used for regional aggregations and period averages in chapter 11

Table	Aggregations[a]		
	(1)	*(6)*	*(8)*
11-1			
Col. 1-3	x		
Col. 4-6		x	
11-2		x	
11-3			x
11-4		x	
11-5		x	
11-6			x
11-7			x
11-8			x
11-9			x
11-10			x
11-11			x

Note: Regional aggregations are shown in the rows for Sub-Saharan Africa, North Africa, and All Africa. Period averages are shown in the last three columns. This table shows only the methodologies used in this chapter.

a. Regional aggregations: (1) simple total; (2) simple total of the first indicator divided by the simple total of the second indicator (same country coverage); (3) simple total of the gap-filled indicator; (4) simple total of the gap-filled main indicator divided by the simple total of the gap-filled secondary indicator; (5) simple total of the first gap-filled main indicator less the simple total of the second gap-filled main indicator, all divided by the simple total of the secondary indicator; (6) weighted total; (7) median; (8) no aggregation; (9) simple arithmetic mean.

12

Aid Flows

Official development assistance (ODA) consists of concessional financial flows that aim to promote economic development and welfare. ODA disbursements from bilateral and multilateral sources became increasingly important to Africa in the second half of the 1980s. For many countries, the foreign savings made available to them through ODA flows are equivalent to a sizable share of GDP and to the bulk of their domestic investment. Thus, monitoring aid flows is of special importance because of their significance for the economic performance of the region.

The tables in this chapter show data on net ODA flows and their relative importance to key economic and demographic indicators in recipient countries, real growth in net ODA flows to Sub-Saharan Africa in the 1980s and early 1990s from major donors or donor groups, and the share of each donor's worldwide aid portfolio allocated to Sub-Saharan Africa.

These flows are concessional in character and contain a grant element of at least 25 percent (based on a standard 10 percent discount rate). Net ODA disbursements equal gross ODA disbursements less principal repayments (amortization) of previous ODA loans.

ODA includes both grants (inflows of unrequited transfers from official sources) for current and capital expenditures and disbursements of concessional loans. However, because of different sources and definitions of data, the ODA flows shown in this chapter will not necessarily equal those that could be calculated by adding net disbursements of official concessional long-term loans (Table 6-1 less Table 6-4) and net official transfers (Tables 5-6 and 5-9). For example, one of the reasons for differences is that the flows shown here include "off-shore" disbursements of grants, primarily for technical cooperation, which are generally excluded from transfers as recorded in the balance of payments (Tables 5-6 and 5-9). Other reasons include possible differences in the timing of the recording of disbursements and in the recording of multilateral ODA.

The data on net ODA disbursements are taken from the most recent electronic version of OECD, *Geographical Distribution of Financial Flows to Developing Countries*. The tables include only those flows for which the recipient is specified in creditor reports.

Growth rates (based on constant price series) presented in this chapter may differ from those presented in *ADI 1992* because import price deflators (from World Bank) have been used to deflate the current price series, regardless of the type of donor, to indicate the volume of imports that aid can finance over time. In *ADI 1992*, donor country GNP deflators were used to deflate each DAC donor's aid flows (with the GNP deflators for DAC countries taken from the 1988 DAC chairman's report) thereby indicating the real resource transfer from individual donors, and the ODA flows from multilateral agencies and non-DAC donors were deflated by the average import price deflator for Sub-Saharan countries.

12-1. Net ODA from all donors, nominal

	Millions of U.S. dollars (current prices)											Annual average		
	1980	1988	1989	1990	1991	1992	1993	1994	1995	1996	1997	75-84	85-89	90-MR
SUB-SAHARAN AFRICA	7,395	13,725	14,519	17,276	16,988	18,270	16,818	18,155	17,923	15,686	14,212	5,836	11,868	16,916
excluding South Africa	7,395	13,725	14,519	17,276	16,988	18,270	16,543	17,860	17,537	15,325	13,714	5,836	11,868	16,689
excl. S.Africa & Nigeria	7,360	13,605	14,173	17,026	16,726	18,012	16,264	17,670	17,325	15,133	13,513	5,792	11,742	16,458
Angola	53	159	171	269	280	351	294	451	418	544	436	51	138	380
Benin	90	159	269	269	268	270	289	257	282	293	225	72	158	269
Botswana	106	151	160	148	136	114	133	89	92	81	125	83	133	115
Burkina Faso	212	294	270	335	424	439	470	436	487	418	370	165	264	422
Burundi	117	202	207	265	259	312	218	313	288	204	119	96	188	247
Cameroon	265	276	453	447	519	716	545	731	444	413	501	187	261	540
Cape Verde	64	88	88	110	106	122	118	121	112	120	110	42	89	115
Central African Republic	111	205	189	251	175	178	173	166	168	167	92	80	163	171
Chad	35	263	256	316	266	241	228	215	239	305	225	79	214	254
Comoros	43	52	45	46	65	49	50	40	43	40	28	30	49	45
Congo, Democratic Rep. of	428	553	731	898	476	269	178	245	195	167	168	317	537	325
Congo, Republic of	92	87	91	218	134	114	123	362	125	430	268	82	101	222
Côte d'Ivoire	210	425	396	689	633	758	765	1,594	1,212	968	445	136	271	883
Djibouti	73	93	75	195	108	113	134	129	106	97	87	60	94	121
Equatorial Guinea	9	48	57	62	63	62	53	30	34	31	24	7	39	45
Eritrea	..	..	..	..	..	..	68	158	150	157	123	..	..	131
Ethiopia	212	963	749	1,020	1,097	1,182	1,094	1,074	888	849	637	208	736	980
Gabon	56	106	133	132	143	69	102	182	145	127	40	50	92	118
Gambia, The	55	85	100	100	103	113	87	71	48	38	41	38	88	75
Ghana	192	577	718	563	882	613	618	546	653	654	498	137	453	628
Guinea	90	257	365	296	382	450	410	360	416	295	382	68	226	374
Guinea-Bissau	59	103	117	130	115	105	96	175	116	180	126	49	92	130
Kenya	397	836	1,064	1,187	921	886	911	677	732	606	459	319	667	797
Lesotho	94	111	137	143	126	145	143	117	115	107	94	72	107	124
Liberia	98	65	59	112	158	119	123	63	123	207	96	77	78	125
Madagascar	230	298	349	399	456	363	363	289	303	364	838	148	295	422
Malawi	143	375	433	505	525	573	498	470	434	501	348	115	279	482
Mali	267	436	451	487	458	435	366	443	545	505	455	194	398	462
Mauritania	176	185	253	240	220	202	328	269	231	274	250	177	214	252
Mauritius	33	57	60	89	68	46	26	14	22	20	42	36	52	41
Mozambique	169	918	820	1,007	1,070	1,468	1,183	1,231	1,101	923	963	141	625	1,118
Namibia	0	23	59	123	184	143	155	138	189	189	166	0	24	161
Niger	170	379	305	398	377	370	347	377	270	259	341	165	333	342
Nigeria	36	120	345	250	263	259	279	190	212	192	202	44	125	231
Rwanda	155	249	230	293	364	354	358	715	711	674	592	131	222	508
São Tomé and Principe	4	25	45	55	52	57	47	50	84	47	34	7	22	53
Senegal	263	601	710	823	639	676	504	645	669	582	427	254	569	621
Seychelles	22	21	20	36	23	19	19	13	13	19	15	16	23	20
Sierra Leone	91	102	100	63	105	135	209	277	207	195	130	51	85	165
Somalia	433	433	427	494	186	654	890	538	191	91	104	283	462	394
South Africa	0	0	0	0	0	0	275	295	386	361	498	0	0	227
Sudan	625	938	773	827	881	550	458	413	236	230	188	541	936	473
Swaziland	50	37	28	55	54	54	53	56	56	31	28	33	34	48
Tanzania	679	1,016	918	1,174	1,081	1,343	953	969	882	894	964	513	797	1,032
Togo	91	206	200	261	202	224	98	126	193	166	124	81	162	174
Uganda	114	397	452	671	667	728	612	753	830	684	840	85	304	723
Zambia	318	478	374	481	883	1,036	872	719	2,035	614	618	204	411	907
Zimbabwe	164	273	265	340	393	792	500	562	493	374	327	114	259	473
NORTH AFRICA	2,709	2,450	2,453	7,166	6,981	5,354	3,696	3,859	2,910	3,308	2,863	2,680	2,572	4,517
Algeria	176	172	159	263	340	406	349	420	312	309	248	137	177	331
Egypt, Arab Republic	1,387	1,498	1,545	5,438	5,025	3,604	2,401	2,695	2,022	2,212	1,949	1,775	1,640	3,168
Libya	17	6	17	20	26	6	6	7	8	10	9	9	9	12
Morocco	898	457	450	1,051	1,232	947	713	631	496	651	462	536	494	773
Tunisia	232	318	283	393	357	390	228	107	71	126	194	223	252	233
ALL AFRICA	10,105	16,175	16,971	24,442	23,969	23,624	20,514	22,014	20,832	18,994	17,075	8,516	14,440	21,433

Note: In 1995, Zambia completed a 3 year Rights Arrangement Program permitting disbursement of 833.4 M SDR under a new SAF/ESAF arrangement.

12-2. Net ODA from DAC donors, nominal

	Millions of U.S. dollars (current prices)											Annual average		
	1980	1988	1989	1990	1991	1992	1993	1994	1995	1996	1997	75-84	85-89	90-MR
SUB-SAHARAN AFRICA	4,351	8,971	9,059	10,815	10,264	10,769	10,158	10,326	9,882	9,080	8,120	3,429	7,516	9,927
excluding South Africa	4,351	8,971	9,059	10,815	10,264	10,769	9,975	10,112	9,564	8,768	7,705	3,429	7,516	9,746
excl. S.Africa & Nigeria	4,334	8,874	8,749	10,642	10,092	10,632	9,904	10,065	9,492	8,720	7,653	3,402	7,414	9,650
Angola	36	106	110	164	159	194	151	224	241	294	227	30	94	207
Benin	36	93	149	126	160	171	148	142	177	165	148	36	88	155
Botswana	83	125	120	121	104	93	80	57	54	68	56	63	102	79
Burkina Faso	151	219	199	239	270	268	255	265	251	269	218	112	182	254
Burundi	60	83	90	158	123	149	126	108	107	68	38	50	85	110
Cameroon	171	240	301	339	377	579	528	397	345	280	330	130	205	397
Cape Verde	39	61	61	76	79	80	81	82	72	77	68	28	61	77
Central African Republic	75	107	99	100	98	107	117	94	122	121	61	52	92	103
Chad	20	146	131	183	138	148	146	104	127	122	96	44	119	133
Comoros	13	34	32	31	31	23	29	18	22	22	15	11	28	24
Congo, Democratic Rep. of	317	403	434	633	343	163	99	97	117	106	105	221	336	208
Congo, Republic of	55	78	81	202	118	102	116	253	105	395	260	49	88	194
Côte d'Ivoire	152	226	260	531	435	527	708	820	726	449	233	105	191	554
Djibouti	32	71	64	88	83	92	94	94	80	71	62	35	61	83
Equatorial Guinea	1	25	36	44	35	36	28	17	22	23	18	2	22	28
Eritrea	0	0	0	0	0	0	48	96	94	125	81	0	0	56
Ethiopia	91	560	379	510	464	457	417	567	525	445	373	86	413	470
Gabon	49	99	121	127	140	65	97	161	136	113	30	42	80	109
Gambia, The	17	55	56	57	55	50	50	38	25	17	17	16	50	39
Ghana	107	236	352	265	449	333	312	332	359	349	292	75	187	336
Guinea	33	160	192	139	173	233	185	186	220	135	126	20	126	175
Guinea-Bissau	34	52	66	75	62	57	56	124	77	125	59	29	46	79
Kenya	277	610	621	735	608	520	426	401	459	346	301	244	477	474
Lesotho	64	70	74	85	74	69	74	45	62	49	45	44	63	63
Liberia	60	48	39	42	57	26	25	35	31	112	31	53	54	45
Madagascar	91	214	175	268	274	216	228	190	195	230	549	77	169	269
Malawi	76	181	182	216	209	208	159	251	221	264	174	63	134	213
Mali	131	260	301	312	280	239	221	243	284	298	257	104	248	267
Mauritania	54	114	162	106	110	116	196	128	126	99	96	45	116	122
Mauritius	25	45	52	76	62	35	27	8	10	-1	3	23	43	27
Mozambique	115	732	578	750	769	1,007	813	733	698	552	622	104	476	743
Namibia	0	17	36	39	95	98	123	113	144	136	123	0	16	109
Niger	105	242	200	255	264	262	254	261	190	163	181	97	209	229
Nigeria	17	97	310	173	172	138	71	47	72	47	52	27	103	97
Rwanda	97	137	132	183	233	187	201	487	338	252	179	83	127	258
São Tomé and Principe	1	9	22	31	24	26	28	26	61	29	21	2	9	31
Senegal	182	369	536	589	421	454	364	475	397	392	292	157	355	423
Seychelles	18	18	15	33	17	15	7	7	11	8	6	14	17	13
Sierra Leone	57	52	72	40	68	74	106	54	60	67	41	28	50	64
Somalia	139	311	267	270	116	497	688	438	119	40	46	93	299	277
South Africa	0	0	0	0	0	0	183	214	318	312	415	0	0	180
Sudan	272	502	435	420	369	188	164	174	130	118	86	211	499	206
Swaziland	33	23	12	36	31	27	33	27	38	21	16	22	21	29
Tanzania	524	786	692	844	764	816	650	570	587	605	569	383	617	676
Togo	52	128	108	155	124	135	77	63	118	97	76	46	93	106
Uganda	42	188	164	244	285	255	348	344	422	370	439	31	112	338
Zambia	234	407	314	409	583	699	511	434	439	354	367	156	326	474
Zimbabwe	112	233	228	296	359	536	310	280	348	281	222	86	226	329
NORTH AFRICA	1,660	2,199	2,095	4,221	5,342	4,405	2,640	3,077	2,381	2,631	1,975	1,427	2,192	3,334
Algeria	118	121	96	232	307	376	265	373	290	263	193	116	123	287
Egypt, Arab Republic	1,187	1,435	1,409	3,172	4,157	2,996	1,824	2,311	1,689	1,933	1,496	959	1,533	2,447
Libya	10	2	7	8	3	1	2	2	3	2	2	4	5	3
Morocco	188	404	403	595	611	734	422	318	347	391	215	189	354	454
Tunisia	158	237	180	214	264	298	127	73	51	41	69	160	178	142
ALL AFRICA	6,011	11,170	11,153	15,036	15,605	15,174	12,797	13,403	12,264	11,711	10,095	4,856	9,709	13,261

12-3. Net ODA from non-DAC bilateral donors, nominal

| | Millions of U.S. dollars (current prices) | | | | | | | | | | | Annual average | | |
	1980	1988	1989	1990	1991	1992	1993	1994	1995	1996	1997	75-84	85-89	90-MR
SUB-SAHARAN AFRICA	685	197	99	456	131	42	36	14	11	37	120	560	317	106
excluding South Africa	685	197	99	456	131	42	36	14	11	37	120	560	317	106
excl. S.Africa & Nigeria	685	197	99	456	131	42	36	14	11	37	121	560	317	106
Angola	1	3	3	2	2	1	3	0	0	0	0	0	1	1
Benin	2	1	5	0	-2	0	0	3	7	6	2	1	2	2
Botswana	0	1	-2	-2	2	-2	7	1	0	-2	-3	2	0	0
Burkina Faso	0	2	0	11	10	2	0	0	6	2	20	2	5	7
Burundi	4	4	4	0	-3	*-2	-2	-3	-3	-1	-8	4	7	-3
Cameroon	23	-4	0	-3	-2	-1	0	0	1	-2	35	7	0	4
Cape Verde	2	1	0	0	0	0	1	0	0	3	0	1	1	0
Central African Republic	2	2	-1	2	3	0	0	-1	0	1	-4	1	3	0
Chad	0	0	0	2	2	0	3	1	1	3	10	3	0	3
Comoros	16	0	0	0	0	0	0	0	0	0	0	6	1	0
Congo, Democratic Rep. of	5	0	0	77	0	2	0	0	0	2	9	3	0	11
Congo, Republic of	15	0	0	0	0	0	0	0	0	0	0	10	0	0
Côte d'Ivoire	0	0	0	0	0	0	0	0	0	0	1	0	0	0
Djibouti	33	3	1	88	3	-1	10	12	3	5	5	17	14	16
Equatorial Guinea	0	0	0	0	6	0	0	0	0	0	-2	0	0	0
Eritrea	0	0	0	0	0	0	1	12	5	3	13	0	0	4
Ethiopia	0	-1	-2	68	1	0	1	0	0	0	1	11	1	9
Gabon	0	-2	-1	0	0	0	0	0	-1	-2	-3	3	3	-1
Gambia, The	7	-2	-1	0	2	-2	-2	-2	-2	-2	-8	5	-1	-2
Ghana	25	13	2	1	9	-4	-4	-6	-6	-2	-105	7	2	-15
Guinea	0	14	18	4	-1	-2	-4	-2	6	20	56	11	10	10
Guinea-Bissau	1	6	2	0	1	3	1	0	0	1	5	3	5	1
Kenya	0	3	0	5	3	-4	-4	-5	2	-3	-66	4	7	-9
Lesotho	0	-1	0	0	-1	1	1	0	0	4	3	1	0	1
Liberia	9	0	0	0	0	0	0	0	0	·0	1	3	0	0
Madagascar	48	-1	-2	-1	0	0	0	0	0	0	1	12	-2	0
Malawi	0	0	0	0	0	0	0	0	0	1	-8	0	0	-1
Mali	33	5	3	15	4	4	-4	-11	-14	-8	18	17	16	1
Mauritania	86	-4	-5	25	1	-7	-6	-10	-16	-12	2	83	26	-3
Mauritius	0	3	-1	1	-2	-1	0	*1	-2	-2	10	1	2	1
Mozambique	20	3	3	0	0	2	3	2	2	3	18	3	4	4
Namibia	0	0	0	0	0	0	0	0	0	0	0	0	0	0
Niger	2	6	2	4	4	0	2	5	0	0	28	17	5	5
Nigeria	0	0	0	0	0	0	0	0	0	0	-1	0	0	0
Rwanda	1	3	6	10	3	0	2	1	0	1	-2	2	5	2
São Tomé and Principe	0	0	0	0	0	0	0	0	0	0	0	0	0	0
Senegal	2	24	12	2	22	16	14	1	12	10	13	19	27	11
Seychelles	0	0	0	0	0	0	1	0	-1	3	3	0	1	1
Sierra Leone	4	10	0	0	0	0	0	0	1	4	8	2	4	2
Somalia	128	4	1	82	0	10	9	0	0	0	1	81	7	13
South Africa	0	0	0	0	0	0	0	0	0	0	0	0	0	0
Sudan	160	103	25	8	16	20	2	0	1	0	-7	183	148	5
Swaziland	0	0	0	0	0	0	0	0	0	0	1	0	0	0
Tanzania	27	0	1	3	-2	-3	-1	6	4	-3	56	12	3	8
Togo	0	-1	-1	-1	-1	-2	0	0	0	-2	2	1	3	0
Uganda	1	0	28	43	51	15	1	11	7	8	5	6	7	18
Zambia	23	0	0	0	0	0	0	0	0	0	14	11	0	2
Zimbabwe	5	-3	-2	9	-1	-3	-1	-3	-4	-3	-3	6	-2	-1
NORTH AFRICA	739	35	47	2,655	985	455	389	110	101	47	71	794	176	602
Algeria	41	27	22	8	2	4	1	2	-12	7	12	7	28	3
Egypt, Arab Republic	4	-16	-14	2,186	510	409	379	94	117	53	51	453	14	475
Libya	0	0	0	0	0	0	0	0	0	0	0	0	0	0
Morocco	644	20	-2	361	470	52	18	29	19	26	26	299	111	125
Tunisia	49	3	42	100	3	-10	-9	-15	-23	-38	-18	35	23	-1
ALL AFRICA	1,424	231	146	3,111	1,116	498	425	124	113	84	191	1,354	493	708

12-4. Net ODA from multilateral donors, nominal

	Millions of U.S. dollars (current prices)											Annual average		
	1980	1988	1989	1990	1991	1992	1993	1994	1995	1996	1997	75-84	85-89	90-MR
SUB-SAHARAN AFRICA	2,359	4,557	5,361	6,005	6,593	7,459	6,624	7,815	8,029	6,569	5,971	1,847	4,035	6,883
excluding South Africa	2,359	4,557	5,361	6,005	6,593	7,459	6,532	7,735	7,961	6,520	5,889	1,847	4,035	6,837
excl. S.Africa & Nigeria	2,340	4,534	5,325	5,928	6,502	7,338	6,324	7,592	7,822	6,376	5,739	1,830	4,012	6,702
Angola	16	50	58	103	119	156	139	227	177	250	209	20	42	172
Benin	53	64	115	144	111	99	142	112	98	122	76	34	68	113
Botswana	23	25	42	29	30	23	47	31	37	15	72	17	31	36
Burkina Faso	61	73	70	85	143	169	215	171	230	147	133	52	77	162
Burundi	54	115	113	108	139	165	95	208	183	137	89	42	95	140
Cameroon	71	40	153	111	143	138	17	334	97	136	136	51	56	139
Cape Verde	23	26	27	34	26	43	36	40	40	40	42	13	27	38
Central African Republic	34	96	91	149	74	71	57	73	45	44	34	27	68	68
Chad	15	117	125	131	126	92	79	110	112	180	118	33	95	119
Comoros	13	17	13	16	34	26	21	22	22	18	13	12	20	21
Congo, Democratic Rep. of	106	150	297	188	134	105	79	148	78	59	55	93	201	106
Congo, Republic of	22	9	10	16	16	12	7	109	20	35	8	23	13	28
Côte d'Ivoire	58	199	135	159	198	230	56	774	486	518	211	31	80	329
Djibouti	9	18	10	18	23	22	30	23	23	22	20	8	19	23
Equatorial Guinea	8	23	21	18	22	26	25	14	12	8	9	4	17	17
Eritrea	0	0	0	0	0	0	19	50	50	29	29	0	0	22
Ethiopia	120	404	372	442	632	725	675	507	362	404	264	111	322	501
Gabon	7	9	13	6	3	5	4	20	10	15	12	5	9	9
Gambia, The	31	32	45	43	46	65	39	35	24	24	32	17	39	38
Ghana	59	328	363	297	425	285	310	220	301	307	311	55	264	307
Guinea	57	83	155	152	210	219	229	175	190	140	200	36	90	190
Guinea-Bissau	24	45	49	54	52	46	38	52	40	54	62	18	41	50
Kenya	120	223	444	448	310	370	488	281	271	263	224	71	183	332
Lesotho	31	41	64	58	53	74	68	71	53	54	46	27	44	60
Liberia	29	16	20	70	101	93	98	28	92	94	64	21	24	80
Madagascar	91	86	176	132	182	147	135	99	108	135	288	59	128	153
Malawi	68	194	252	289	316	365	339	219	213	236	183	52	144	270
Mali	103	170	147	160	174	192	149	210	274	215	181	73	134	194
Mauritania	36	74	96	109	109	93	138	151	121	186	152	49	72	132
Mauritius	8	9	9	13	8	11	-1	7	14	22	29	12	7	13
Mozambique	34	183	238	256	301	459	367	496	401	368	324	34	145	371
Namibia	0	5	23	84	89	46	32	25	45	52	43	0	8	52
Niger	64	132	103	140	108	108	91	111	80	96	132	50	118	108
Nigeria	18	23	36	78	91	121	208	143	140	144	150	17	23	134
Rwanda	57	109	92	100	127	166	154	226	373	421	415	46	90	248
São Tomé and Principe	3	16	23	24	28	31	19	24	23	18	13	5	13	22
Senegal	79	209	162	231	196	205	126	168	259	180	122	78	187	186
Seychelles	3	3	5	3	6	4	12	6	3	8	6	2	5	6
Sierra Leone	30	40	27	23	37	61	103	223	147	125	81	21	31	100
Somalia	166	118	159	143	70	146	193	100	72	51	57	109	157	104
South Africa	0	0	0	0	0	0	92	80	67	49	82	0	0	46
Sudan	192	333	312	399	496	342	292	238	105	112	109	147	289	262
Swaziland	17	14	17	19	23	27	20	29	18	10	11	12	12	19
Tanzania	128	230	225	327	319	530	304	392	291	291	339	118	177	349
Togo	39	79	93	107	78	91	20	62	75	71	46	34	65	69
Uganda	70	210	261	384	331	459	264	398	400	306	396	49	186	367
Zambia	62	71	60	72	301	337	361	285	1,595	260	238	37	85	431
Zimbabwe	47	43	39	36	35	259	191	284	149	96	108	22	34	145
NORTH AFRICA	311	216	311	290	654	493	667	673	427	629	817	459	204	581
Algeria	17	24	41	23	31	27	83	44	35	39	44	15	26	41
Egypt, Arab Republic	196	79	150	81	358	199	198	290	216	225	402	363	93	246
Libya	7	4	10	13	23	5	4	5	5	8	7	6	4	9
Morocco	66	32	49	94	151	161	273	285	129	234	221	48	30	194
Tunisia	25	77	61	79	91	102	110	49	43	123	143	28	51	92
ALL AFRICA	2,669	4,773	5,672	6,295	7,247	7,952	7,291	8,487	8,456	7,199	6,788	2,306	4,239	7,464

Note: In 1995, Zambia completed a 3 year Rights Arrangement Program permitting disbursement of 833.4 M SDR under a new SAF/ESAF arrangement.

12-5. Net ODA from all donors, real

	Millions of U.S. dollars (constant 1995 prices)											Average annual percentage growth		
	1980	1988	1989	1990	1991	1992	1993	1994	1995	1996	1997	75-84	85-89	90-MR
SUB-SAHARAN AFRICA	9,685	16,584	17,186	18,996	18,975	19,559	18,565	19,850	17,923	15,628	14,930	6.7	10.0	-2.1
excluding South Africa	9,685	16,584	17,186	18,996	18,975	19,559	18,261	19,528	17,537	15,268	14,407	6.7	10.0	-2.5
excl. S. Africa & Nigeria	9,638	16,439	16,777	18,720	18,682	19,282	17,953	19,320	17,325	15,077	14,195	6.9	9.7	-2.4
Angola	69	192	202	296	312	375	325	493	418	542	458	39.7	9.4	10.4
Benin	118	192	318	296	300	289	320	281	282	292	237	2.3	19.9	-2.3
Botswana	139	182	189	163	152	122	147	97	92	81	131	5.4	7.4	-7.7
Burkina Faso	278	356	319	368	473	470	519	477	487	417	389	4.0	4.5	2.1
Burundi	154	244	245	292	289	334	241	342	288	203	125	9.5	4.7	-6.1
Cameroon	347	334	537	492	579	766	602	799	444	412	527	1.5	14.5	-1.8
Cape Verde	84	106	105	121	118	131	130	133	112	120	115	13.4	1.8	0.4
Central African Republic	145	248	224	276	195	190	191	182	168	166	97	6.5	7.8	-8.4
Chad	46	318	303	348	297	258	251	235	239	304	236	-4.4	11.8	-3.2
Comoros	57	63	53	51	72	52	55	44	43	40	30	2.9	-1.8	-6.9
Congo, Democratic Rep. of	560	668	866	987	532	288	197	268	195	167	177	0.8	15.9	-20.5
Congo, Republic of	121	105	108	240	149	122	136	396	125	428	282	2.6	-2.1	11.3
Côte d'Ivoire	275	514	468	758	707	811	845	1,743	1,212	964	467	-0.6	27.6	4.4
Djibouti	96	112	89	214	121	121	148	141	106	97	91	4.8	-7.4	-3.9
Equatorial Guinea	12	58	67	68	70	67	59	33	34	31	26	17.9	30.0	-13.1
Eritrea	0	0	0	0	0	0	75	173	150	157	129	..	..	10.3
Ethiopia	277	1,163	887	1,121	1,226	1,266	1,207	1,175	888	846	669	5.5	9.2	-4.4
Gabon	73	128	157	146	160	74	113	199	145	126	42	2.3	9.1	-7.9
Gambia, The	71	103	118	110	115	121	95	77	48	38	43	15.3	10.0	-14.5
Ghana	251	698	849	620	985	656	682	597	653	651	523	5.5	25.4	-4.4
Guinea	117	310	432	325	427	482	452	394	416	294	401	16.8	21.1	-1.4
Guinea-Bissau	78	124	138	143	129	113	106	192	116	179	132	16.5	13.6	1.4
Kenya	519	1,010	1,260	1,305	1,029	949	1,005	740	732	604	482	9.8	17.2	-11.1
Lesotho	124	134	162	157	141	155	158	127	115	107	98	12.1	2.3	-6.1
Liberia	128	78	69	123	176	128	136	69	123	206	101	18.3	-17.4	2.9
Madagascar	301	360	414	439	509	388	401	316	303	363	880	8.4	12.7	2.0
Malawi	188	453	513	556	586	614	549	514	434	499	366	6.5	21.5	-4.0
Mali	350	527	534	536	511	466	404	484	545	503	478	4.5	1.9	-0.8
Mauritania	230	223	299	264	246	216	362	294	231	273	263	0.4	-0.3	-0.4
Mauritius	43	69	72	98	75	49	29	16	22	20	44	1.1	11.7	-15.9
Mozambique	222	1,110	970	1,107	1,195	1,572	1,306	1,346	1,101	920	1,012	40.7	26.0	-1.2
Namibia	0	27	70	135	206	154	171	151	189	188	174	..	55.3	7.7
Niger	223	458	361	438	421	396	383	413	270	258	358	-1.0	7.6	-4.0
Nigeria	47	145	409	275	293	277	308	208	212	191	212	-11.8	50.7	-7.5
Rwanda	204	301	272	322	406	379	395	781	711	672	621	4.8	3.8	13.0
São Tomé and Principe	5	30	53	60	58	61	52	55	84	47	35	14.0	24.9	-2.9
Senegal	344	727	841	905	714	723	557	705	669	579	449	6.6	12.7	-6.5
Seychelles	28	25	23	40	26	21	21	14	13	19	16	3.2	..	3.2
Sierra Leone	119	124	118	69	117	144	230	302	207	195	137	14.6	6.6	9.7
Somalia	567	523	505	544	208	700	983	588	191	91	109	10.4	0.8	-17.9
South Africa	0	0	0	0	0	0	304	322	386	360	523	..	..	12.7
Sudan	818	1,133	915	909	984	588	505	452	236	229	197	10.4	-2.8	-20.0
Swaziland	66	45	33	61	60	58	58	61	56	30	30	2.0	-0.7	-4.3
Tanzania	889	1,228	1,087	1,291	1,207	1,438	1,052	1,059	882	890	1,013	6.9	10.7	-3.8
Togo	119	249	237	287	226	240	108	138	193	165	130	4.1	9.2	-7.9
Uganda	149	480	535	738	745	780	676	824	830	681	883	19.6	20.2	3.4
Zambia	417	578	443	529	987	1,109	962	786	2,035	612	650	11.0	5.5	5.3
Zimbabwe	215	330	314	374	439	848	552	614	493	373	344	66.6	-3.9	0.4
NORTH AFRICA	3,548	2,960	2,903	7,879	7,797	5,731	4,079	4,220	2,910	3,296	3,008	-5.3	-5.0	-7.6
Algeria	230	208	188	289	380	435	385	459	312	308	261	-6.8	0.2	2.0
Egypt, Arab Republic	1,816	1,810	1,829	5,980	5,612	3,858	2,650	2,947	2,022	2,204	2,048	-7.8	-7.2	-7.8
Libya	22	7	20	22	29	7	7	7	8	10	10	-8.4	12.8	-12.2
Morocco	1,175	552	532	1,155	1,376	1,014	787	690	496	648	485	6.6	-4.3	-7.3
Tunisia	304	384	335	433	399	418	251	117	71	126	204	-5.2	9.1	-15.9
ALL AFRICA	13,233	19,544	20,089	26,874	26,772	25,290	22,644	24,070	20,832	18,924	17,938	2.4	6.9	-3.4

Note: In 1995, Zambia completed a 3 year Rights Arrangement Program permitting disbursement of 833.4 M SDR under a new SAF/ESAF arrangement.

12-6. Net ODA from DAC donors, real

	Millions of U.S. dollars (constant 1995 prices)											Average annual percentage growth		
	1980	1988	1989	1990	1991	1992	1993	1994	1995	1996	1997	75-84	85-89	90-MR
SUB-SAHARAN AFRICA	5,698	10,840	10,723	11,891	11,464	11,529	11,213	11,291	9,882	9,046	8,531	7.2	10.7	-3.4
excluding South Africa	5,698	10,840	10,723	11,891	11,464	11,529	11,011	11,056	9,564	8,735	8,095	7.2	10.7	-4.0
excl. S. Africa & Nigeria	5,676	10,723	10,356	11,701	11,272	11,382	10,932	11,004	9,492	8,688	8,040	7.6	10.1	-3.7
Angola	47	128	131	181	177	208	167	245	241	293	238	41.1	10.1	8.0
Benin	47	113	177	138	179	183	163	155	177	164	155	1.2	22.9	-0.3
Botswana	109	151	142	133	116	100	88	62	54	68	59	3.9	12.9	-11.9
Burkina Faso	198	264	236	262	302	287	281	289	251	268	229	6.0	8.4	-0.7
Burundi	78	101	106	173	137	159	139	119	107	68	40	9.0	-0.2	-11.7
Cameroon	224	290	356	373	421	620	583	434	345	279	347	3.7	11.4	-2.8
Cape Verde	51	73	72	83	88	86	90	89	72	77	71	25.2	5.1	-1.1
Central African Republic	98	130	118	110	110	114	129	103	122	121	64	8.1	6.8	-3.3
Chad	26	176	155	202	154	159	161	113	127	121	101	-4.0	11.9	-6.4
Comoros	18	42	38	34	34	25	32	19	22	22	16	-0.6	11.2	-9.3
Congo, Democratic Rep. of	415	487	514	696	383	174	109	106	117	106	110	-0.7	12.9	-21.7
Congo, Republic of	73	94	96	222	131	109	128	277	105	393	273	2.3	3.6	11.2
Côte d'Ivoire	199	273	308	583	486	565	782	897	726	448	245	2.1	16.2	-0.7
Djibouti	42	86	76	97	93	98	104	103	80	71	65	-1.0	3.2	-3.0
Equatorial Guinea	2	30	42	48	39	38	31	18	22	23	19	118.6	36.9	-11.6
Eritrea	0	0	0	0	0	0	53	105	94	124	85	..	..	11.7
Ethiopia	120	676	448	560	519	489	460	620	525	444	391	0.1	8.0	-1.6
Gabon	64	119	143	139	157	69	108	176	136	113	32	3.6	10.7	-9.5
Gambia, The	22	66	66	63	61	54	55	42	25	17	18	16.8	8.4	-16.9
Ghana	140	285	417	291	501	356	345	363	359	348	307	1.6	25.1	-2.2
Guinea	43	193	227	153	194	250	204	204	220	134	132	19.4	30.2	-4.1
Guinea-Bissau	45	62	78	83	70	61	62	135	77	124	61	37.9	14.7	2.1
Kenya	363	737	735	808	679	556	471	438	459	344	316	8.6	12.9	-10.9
Lesotho	83	85	87	94	83	74	81	50	62	49	47	13.9	0.3	-8.6
Liberia	79	58	46	46	63	28	27	39	31	112	33	23.9	-19.9	0.3
Madagascar	119	258	208	295	306	231	251	208	195	229	577	11.9	11.4	3.9
Malawi	99	219	215	238	233	223	175	275	221	263	183	-0.7	30.0	-0.4
Mali	172	314	356	344	312	256	244	266	284	296	270	5.8	0.5	-2.8
Mauritania	70	138	192	117	123	125	216	140	126	98	100	11.1	9.3	-4.8
Mauritius	33	54	62	83	69	37	30	8	10	-1	3	4.0	13.6	-35.0
Mozambique	150	884	685	825	859	1,078	897	801	698	550	653	42.9	26.6	-3.5
Namibia	0	21	43	43	106	105	136	123	144	136	129	..	73.9	15.5
Niger	137	292	236	280	295	280	280	286	190	163	190	-0.9	7.4	-5.5
Nigeria	23	117	367	190	192	147	78	52	72	47	55	-17.2	74.4	-21.8
Rwanda	127	166	156	201	260	201	222	533	338	251	188	4.1	3.1	5.0
São Tomé and Principe	2	11	26	34	27	28	31	29	61	29	22	33.3	32.2	0.9
Senegal	238	445	635	648	471	486	402	519	397	391	307	8.5	13.5	-7.5
Seychelles	24	21	18	36	19	17	8	8	11	8	7	1.5	..	1.5
Sierra Leone	74	63	85	44	76	79	117	59	60	67	44	16.2	18.1	-3.6
Somalia	182	376	316	296	130	532	759	478	119	39	48	28.9	6.5	-20.6
South Africa	0	0	0	0	0	0	202	234	318	311	436	..	..	19.9
Sudan	356	606	515	462	412	201	181	191	130	118	90	22.9	-1.7	-20.1
Swaziland	43	27	14	40	35	29	37	30	38	21	17	1.5	-7.5	-1.5
Tanzania	686	950	819	928	853	874	718	624	587	603	598	5.3	11.2	-5.9
Togo	68	155	128	170	139	144	85	69	118	97	80	2.8	14.2	-7.5
Uganda	55	227	194	269	319	273	384	377	422	368	461	25.8	30.5	9.2
Zambia	307	492	372	450	651	748	564	475	439	353	386	8.7	9.4	-3.0
Zimbabwe	147	282	269	325	401	574	342	306	348	280	234	61.0	-3.5	-3.2
NORTH AFRICA	2,174	2,657	2,480	4,641	5,966	4,716	2,914	3,364	2,381	2,621	2,075	8.4	-4.6	-7.4
Algeria	154	146	113	255	343	402	293	408	290	262	202	-5.3	-7.2	3.5
Egypt, Arab Republic	1,554	1,734	1,668	3,487	4,643	3,208	2,013	2,526	1,689	1,926	1,572	18.4	-7.5	-6.9
Libya	13	2	8	8	3	2	2	2	3	2	2	-10.3	4.0	-15.3
Morocco	246	489	477	655	682	785	466	348	347	390	226	1.5	5.4	-10.6
Tunisia	207	286	214	236	295	319	140	79	51	41	73	-4.3	6.1	-21.4
ALL AFRICA	7,872	13,497	13,202	16,532	17,430	16,245	14,127	14,654	12,264	11,668	10,605	7.5	6.7	-4.4

12-7. Net ODA from non-DAC bilateral donors, real

	Millions of U.S. dollars (constant 1995 prices)											Average annual percentage growth		
	1980	1988	1989	1990	1991	1992	1993	1994	1995	1996	1997	75-84	85-89	90-MR
SUB-SAHARAN AFRICA	898	238	117	502	147	45	40	15	11	37	126	2.0	-28.4	-20.5
excluding South Africa	898	238	117	502	147	45	40	15	11	37	126	2.0	-28.4	-20.5
excl. S. Africa & Nigeria	898	238	117	502	147	45	40	15	11	37	127	2.0	-28.4	-20.5
Angola	1	3	3	2	2	1	4	0	0	0	0	..	17.6	-30.8
Benin	2	1	6	0	-3	0	0	4	7	6	2	1.9	-3.4	0.7
Botswana	0	1	-3	-2	2	-2	8	1	0	-2	-4	..	..	..
Burkina Faso	0	3	0	12	12	3	0	1	6	2	21	8.9	-52.2	20.6
Burundi	5	4	5	0	-3	-2	-3	-3	-3	-1	-9	28.0	-21.4	..
Cameroon	30	-5	0	-3	-2	-1	0	0	1	-2	37	4.6	-72.8	..
Cape Verde	3	1	1	0	0	0	1	0	0	3	0	-3.2	-21.2	10.4
Central African Republic	3	3	-1	3	3	0	0	-1	0	1	-4	-17.0	106.7	..
Chad	0	0	0	2	3	0	3	1	1	3	11	-27.6	..	30.3
Comoros	22	0	0	0	0	0	0	0	0	0	0	6.9	-62.7	-30.1
Congo, Democratic Rep. of	7	0	0	85	0	2	0	0	0	2	9	-63.9	..	16.6
Congo, Republic of	20	0	0	0	0	0	0	0	0	0	0	11.0	..	..
Côte d'Ivoire	0	0	0	0	0	0	0	0	0	0	1	..	..	..
Djibouti	43	4	1	97	3	-1	11	13	3	5	5	-13.1	-47.8	-4.8
Equatorial Guinea	0	0	0	0	7	0	0	0	0	0	-3	..	43.8	..
Eritrea	0	0	0	0	0	0	1	13	5	3	13	..	..	53.2
Ethiopia	0	-2	-2	74	1	0	1	0	0	0	1	7.3	..	-44.7
Gabon	0	-2	-1	0	0	0	0	0	-1	-2	-3	-21.6	..	..
Gambia, The	9	-2	-2	1	2	-2	-2	-2	-2	-2	-8	-2.9	..	..
Ghana	33	16	3	1	10	-5	-5	-6	-6	-2	-111	117.9	..	..
Guinea	0	16	21	5	-1	-2	-4	-2	6	20	59	10.4	7.8	13.4
Guinea-Bissau	2	7	3	0	1	3	1	0	0	1	6	-6.7	4.6	-7.7
Kenya	0	4	0	5	3	-4	-4	-6	2	-3	-70	166.1	-47.8	..
Lesotho	0	-1	0	0	-1	1	1	0	0	4	3	81.9	..	29.9
Liberia	12	0	0	0	0	0	0	0	0	0	1	-69.9	-10.1	..
Madagascar	63	-2	-3	-1	0	0	0	0	0	0	1	54.7	..	..
Malawi	0	0	0	0	0	0	0	0	0	1	-9	..	..	..
Mali	43	7	3	17	5	4	-5	-12	-14	-8	19	3.5	-33.1	16.4
Mauritania	113	-4	-5	27	1	-8	-6	-11	-16	-12	2	-5.9	-33.2	..
Mauritius	0	4	-1	1	-2	-1	0	-1	-2	-2	11	..	1.5	..
Mozambique	27	4	4	0	0	2	4	3	2	3	19	51.0	-10.6	37.6
Namibia	0	0	0	0	0	0	0	0	0	0	0	..	..	..
Niger	2	7	3	4	5	0	2	5	0	0	29	16.3	-8.5	8.4
Nigeria	0	0	0	0	0	0	0	0	0	0	-1	..	-13.5	..
Rwanda	2	3	7	11	4	0	3	1	0	1	-2	-3.9	-9.3	-26.5
São Tomé and Principe	0	0	0	0	0	0	0	0	0	0	0	..	..	..
Senegal	3	29	14	3	24	18	16	2	12	10	13	18.1	-27.0	0.3
Seychelles	0	1	0	0	0	0	1	0	-1	3	3	..	..	..
Sierra Leone	6	12	0	0	0	0	0	0	1	4	8	3.5	-24.0	62.4
Somalia	167	5	1	90	0	11	10	0	0	0	1	-12.3	-44.0	-44.6
South Africa	0	0	0	0	0	0	0	0	0	0	0	..	..	..
Sudan	210	125	30	8	18	21	2	0	1	0	-7	0.7	-27.5	-52.9
Swaziland	0	0	0	0	0	0	0	0	0	0	1	..	..	..
Tanzania	36	0	1	4	-3	-3	-1	6	4	-3	59	45.4	-48.3	43.5
Togo	0	-2	-1	-1	-1	-2	0	0	0	-2	2	-7.2	2.2	..
Uganda	2	0	33	47	57	16	1	12	7	8	6	-19.5	205.0	-24.3
Zambia	29	0	0	0	0	0	0	0	0	0	14	19.3	..	..
Zimbabwe	7	-4	-2	10	-1	-3	-1	-3	-4	-3	-3	15.6	..	..
NORTH AFRICA	967	42	56	2,919	1,100	487	429	120	101	47	75	-28.4	-24.0	-25.2
Algeria	54	33	26	9	2	5	1	3	-12	7	13	..	222.3	-4.7
Egypt, Arab Republic	5	-19	-17	2,403	570	437	419	103	117	53	54	-58.6	..	-40.6
Libya	0	0	0	0	0	0	0	0	0	0	0	..	..	..
Morocco	843	24	-3	397	525	56	19	31	19	26	27	16.7	-38.7	-35.4
Tunisia	64	4	49	110	3	-11	-10	-17	-23	-38	-19	-9.3	14.7	..
ALL AFRICA	1,865	280	173	3,420	1,247	533	470	135	113	84	201	-14.1	-28.2	-24.3

12-8. Net ODA from multilateral donors, real

	Millions of U.S. dollars (constant 1995 prices)											Average annual percentage growth		
	1980	1988	1989	1990	1991	1992	1993	1994	1995	1996	1997	75-84	85-89	90-MR
SUB-SAHARAN AFRICA	3,089	5,506	6,346	6,603	7,364	7,985	7,312	8,544	8,029	6,545	6,273	7.0	12.4	0.3
excluding South Africa	3,089	5,506	6,346	6,603	7,364	7,985	7,210	8,457	7,961	6,496	6,187	7.0	12.4	0.1
excl. S. Africa & Nigeria	3,065	5,479	6,303	6,517	7,262	7,855	6,981	8,300	7,822	6,352	6,029	7.1	12.4	-0.1
Angola	21	61	68	114	133	167	154	248	177	249	219	42.6	7.3	14.2
Benin	69	78	136	158	124	106	156	122	98	122	79	3.2	16.2	-5.3
Botswana	30	30	50	32	34	24	51	34	37	15	76	6.1	0.1	-0.2
Burkina Faso	80	89	83	94	160	181	237	187	230	146	139	0.6	-0.4	7.2
Burundi	71	139	134	118	155	176	105	227	183	137	94	9.2	12.8	-0.7
Cameroon	93	49	181	122	160	147	19	365	97	135	143	-4.0	31.2	-1.2
Cape Verde	31	31	32	37	30	46	40	44	40	40	44	2.8	-3.3	3.5
Central African Republic	44	116	107	164	83	76	62	80	45	44	36	3.9	9.1	-14.6
Chad	20	142	148	144	141	99	87	121	112	180	124	-2.6	11.9	-0.5
Comoros	18	21	15	17	38	27	23	24	22	18	14	23.5	-12.2	-2.4
Congo, Democratic Rep. of	138	181	352	206	149	112	87	162	78	58	58	5.2	20.8	-18.1
Congo, Republic of	28	11	12	18	18	13	8	119	20	35	8	-2.2	-16.9	5.3
Côte d'Ivoire	77	241	160	174	221	247	62	846	486	516	222	-11.4	84.0	13.1
Djibouti	11	22	12	20	25	24	33	25	23	22	21	37.3	-14.5	4.0
Equatorial Guinea	11	28	25	20	24	28	28	15	12	8	9	28.5	22.5	-13.5
Eritrea	0	0	0	0	0	0	21	55	50	29	31	..	..	1.2
Ethiopia	158	488	440	486	706	776	746	555	362	403	277	9.0	11.1	-6.6
Gabon	9	11	15	6	3	5	5	22	10	15	13	3.7	7.2	10.1
Gambia, The	40	39	54	47	51	69	43	38	24	24	33	13.9	14.3	-9.6
Ghana	78	397	430	327	474	305	342	241	301	306	327	12.4	23.8	-4.0
Guinea	75	101	184	168	234	234	253	192	190	140	210	29.0	18.3	-1.0
Guinea-Bissau	31	54	57	60	58	49	42	56	40	53	65	19.4	13.1	-0.8
Kenya	157	269	525	492	346	397	539	307	271	262	236	11.5	36.1	-9.3
Lesotho	40	50	75	63	59	80	75	77	53	54	48	9.0	7.9	-4.1
Liberia	38	20	24	77	113	100	108	31	92	94	68	7.6	-9.9	5.4
Madagascar	120	104	208	146	203	158	149	109	108	134	302	3.6	11.2	-0.6
Malawi	89	234	298	318	353	391	374	239	213	235	192	16.4	16.3	-6.7
Mali	135	206	174	175	194	206	165	230	274	215	190	2.2	8.7	3.0
Mauritania	47	89	113	120	121	100	152	166	121	186	160	1.8	8.7	5.5
Mauritius	10	11	11	14	8	12	-1	8	14	22	30	-6.8	16.3	10.6
Mozambique	45	222	282	282	336	492	405	542	401	367	340	37.7	25.1	3.4
Namibia	0	6	27	92	100	49	35	28	45	52	45	..	33.4	-3.0
Niger	83	159	122	154	121	116	101	122	80	95	139	-4.9	9.4	-2.8
Nigeria	24	28	42	85	102	129	230	156	140	144	158	-1.0	8.3	13.6
Rwanda	75	132	109	110	142	178	171	247	373	420	436	6.7	5.7	21.8
São Tomé and Principe	4	19	27	26	31	33	20	26	23	18	13	11.6	20.8	-7.8
Senegal	104	252	192	254	219	220	139	184	259	179	128	1.8	24.4	-4.1
Seychelles	4	3	6	4	7	4	13	6	3	8	6	24.9	..	24.9
Sierra Leone	39	48	32	25	41	65	114	244	147	124	85	10.1	-1.8	23.1
Somalia	218	142	188	157	78	156	213	109	72	51	60	12.2	-5.1	-13.2
South Africa	0	0	0	0	0	0	102	88	67	49	86	..	..	-8.7
Sudan	252	402	370	439	554	366	322	261	105	112	114	8.4	4.2	-18.8
Swaziland	23	17	20	21	25	29	22	31	18	10	11	3.7	9.0	-8.2
Tanzania	167	277	266	360	357	567	335	429	291	290	356	11.6	11.0	-0.3
Togo	51	96	110	118	87	97	22	68	75	71	48	6.1	5.7	-8.8
Uganda	92	253	309	422	369	491	291	435	400	304	416	24.3	13.3	0.4
Zambia	81	86	71	79	336	361	399	311	1,595	259	250	18.8	-7.5	21.2
Zimbabwe	61	52	46	39	39	278	210	311	149	96	113	127.5	-4.8	16.3
NORTH AFRICA	407	261	368	319	731	528	736	735	427	627	858	-4.4	2.4	8.1
Algeria	22	29	48	25	35	29	91	48	35	39	46	-11.3	19.8	2.7
Egypt, Arab Republic	256	96	178	89	399	213	218	317	216	224	422	-3.2	-5.3	9.4
Libya	9	4	12	14	26	5	4	6	5	8	8	-4.0	22.2	-10.5
Morocco	86	39	58	103	169	172	301	311	129	233	233	6.7	4.0	14.3
Tunisia	33	93	72	87	101	109	121	54	43	123	150	-4.5	14.6	2.6
ALL AFRICA	3,496	5,767	6,714	6,921	8,095	8,513	8,048	9,280	8,456	7,172	7,131	4.6	11.7	0.9

Note: In 1995, Zambia completed a 3 year Rights Arrangement Program permitting disbursement of 833.4 M SDR under a new SAF/ESAF arrangement.

12-9. Net ODA from all donors as share of recipient GDP

	Percentage of GDP											*Annual average*		
	1980	*1988*	*1989*	*1990*	*1991*	*1992*	*1993*	*1994*	*1995*	*1996*	*1997*	*75-84*	*85-89*	*90-MR*
SUB-SAHARAN AFRICA	2.5	5.2	5.4	5.8	5.6	5.8	5.5	6.3	5.6	4.7	4.1	2.6	4.8	5.4
excluding South Africa	3.8	8.0	8.4	9.4	9.3	10.2	10.0	12.1	10.5	8.2	7.0	3.9	7.2	9.6
excl. S. Africa & Nigeria	6.5	9.1	9.5	11.0	10.8	12.5	11.4	14.3	12.5	10.0	8.6	6.1	8.4	11.4
Angola	..	2.0	1.8	2.6	2.3	6.1	5.6	11.1	8.3	7.1	5.8	..	1.8	6.1
Benin	6.4	9.8	17.9	14.6	14.3	16.6	13.7	17.2	14.0	13.3	10.5	7.0	11.1	14.3
Botswana	9.6	5.2	5.1	4.1	3.3	2.7	2.9	1.9	1.9	1.5	2.3	9.8	6.4	2.6
Burkina Faso	12.4	12.4	11.4	12.1	15.2	22.0	22.9	23.5	20.7	16.5	15.6	12.4	13.1	18.6
Burundi	12.8	18.6	18.6	23.4	22.2	28.7	22.4	33.9	28.8	22.6	12.5	11.9	16.6	24.3
Cameroon	3.9	2.2	4.1	4.0	4.2	6.3	4.6	9.3	5.6	4.5	5.5	3.6	2.4	5.5
Cape Verde	..	33.1	32.9	36.2	33.1	34.1	35.6	35.0	26.8	28.3	25.8	..	34.6	31.9
Central African Republic	13.9	16.0	14.9	16.9	12.4	12.4	13.3	19.5	14.9	15.6	9.1	12.8	14.0	14.3
Chad	3.4	18.9	19.1	19.7	15.0	13.5	16.4	18.2	16.6	18.6	14.0	8.7	18.2	16.5
Comoros	35.1	25.0	22.5	18.5	26.3	18.3	19.0	21.5	20.2	18.8	14.5	36.9	29.0	19.6
Congo, Democratic Rep. of	..	6.2	8.1	9.6	5.2	3.3	2.0	3.4	3.1	2.9	2.8	3.8	6.5	4.0
Congo, Republic of	5.4	3.9	3.8	7.8	4.9	3.9	6.4	20.5	5.9	17.0	11.6	6.4	4.6	9.8
Côte d'Ivoire	2.1	4.1	4.1	6.4	6.0	6.8	7.4	20.8	12.1	9.0	4.3	1.9	2.8	9.1
Djibouti	..	23.3	18.8	45.8	23.8	24.1	28.4	26.5	21.6	20.1	17.3	..	25.1	26.0
Equatorial Guinea	..	37.8	50.8	46.8	48.3	40.3	34.9	24.1	20.6	12.0	4.9	1.1	35.1	29.0
Eritrea	..	..	..	..	..	0.0	16.7	31.0	26.1	24.9	18.8	..	..	19.6
Ethiopia	..	12.5	9.4	14.9	20.6	21.2	17.5	22.0	15.4	14.1	10.0	5.1	10.0	17.0
Gabon	1.3	2.8	3.2	2.2	2.7	1.2	2.3	4.3	2.9	2.2	0.8	1.6	2.5	2.3
Gambia, The	22.6	31.9	35.2	31.6	32.4	32.5	23.6	19.5	12.5	9.8	10.2	19.6	38.4	21.5
Ghana	4.3	11.1	13.7	9.6	13.4	9.6	10.4	10.0	10.1	9.4	7.2	3.6	8.7	10.0
Guinea	..	10.8	15.0	10.5	12.7	13.7	12.5	10.5	11.3	7.5	9.7	..	11.2	11.0
Guinea-Bissau	53.7	62.4	54.9	53.2	44.9	46.5	40.4	74.5	45.9	66.5	46.7	37.3	55.4	52.3
Kenya	5.5	9.8	12.8	13.9	11.5	11.1	18.3	9.5	8.1	6.6	4.3	5.5	8.6	10.4
Lesotho	25.6	24.8	26.8	22.9	21.6	21.9	20.4	15.4	13.5	12.5	9.8	24.7	29.9	17.2
Liberia	8.8	5.4	4.9	..	..	..	..	..	..	..	..	7.4	6.9	..
Madagascar	5.7	12.2	14.0	13.0	17.0	12.1	10.8	9.7	9.6	9.1	23.6	4.6	11.0	13.1
Malawi	11.6	28.1	28.5	28.0	23.8	31.9	24.0	40.0	29.6	22.1	13.8	11.1	21.4	26.7
Mali	15.0	22.4	22.4	20.1	18.9	15.3	13.7	23.9	22.1	19.0	18.2	15.0	22.8	19.4
Mauritania	21.6	17.3	23.3	21.1	19.5	17.0	34.8	26.2	21.6	25.0	22.8	24.2	22.3	23.5
Mauritius	2.9	2.7	2.8	3.4	2.4	1.4	0.8	0.4	0.6	0.5	1.0	3.6	3.0	1.3
Mozambique	4.8	43.9	35.4	40.1	42.9	75.1	56.3	54.3	46.0	32.5	28.0	5.8	24.5	46.9
Namibia	0.0	1.0	2.6	5.0	7.2	4.9	5.7	4.5	5.7	5.9	5.1	0.0	1.2	5.5
Niger	6.8	16.6	14.0	16.1	16.2	15.8	21.6	24.1	14.4	13.0	18.4	9.9	16.9	17.4
Nigeria	0.1	0.5	1.4	0.9	1.0	0.8	1.3	0.8	0.8	0.5	0.5	0.1	0.5	0.8
Rwanda	13.4	10.4	9.5	11.3	19.0	17.4	18.2	95.2	53.6	48.5	31.8	12.5	10.5	36.9
São Tomé and Principe	9.1	50.6	97.8	109.8	90.8	125.2	98.5	101.1	185.2	104.7	76.3	20.7	46.9	111.4
Senegal	8.8	12.1	15.4	14.4	11.6	11.2	9.3	17.7	14.9	12.1	9.4	10.5	13.7	12.6
Seychelles	14.7	7.3	6.4	9.8	6.1	4.4	4.1	2.7	2.6	3.7	2.8	14.5	10.1	4.5
Sierra Leone	7.6	8.0	8.5	7.0	13.0	19.5	27.1	29.8	23.9	20.8	15.8	4.6	8.0	19.6
Somalia	71.8	41.7	39.1	53.9	..	..	..	..	..	..	..	42.1	46.8	53.9
South Africa	0.0	0.0	0.0	0.0	0.0	0.0	0.2	0.2	0.3	0.3	0.3	0.0	0.0	0.2
Sudan	8.2	6.2	4.9	6.3	7.7	8.6	5.8	5.1	3.3	3.2	1.9	6.6	6.1	5.2
Swaziland	8.6	5.3	3.9	6.4	6.1	5.5	5.4	5.3	4.4	2.5	2.2	7.9	6.2	4.7
Tanzania	..	20.0	19.2	27.8	22.8	27.4	20.9	23.0	17.8	15.3	13.6	..	21.8	21.1
Togo	8.0	14.9	14.8	16.0	12.6	13.2	7.9	12.8	14.7	11.3	8.3	10.0	14.0	12.1
Uganda	9.1	6.1	8.6	15.6	20.1	25.5	19.0	18.8	14.4	11.3	13.3	7.2	5.9	17.3
Zambia	8.2	12.8	9.4	14.6	26.2	32.5	26.6	21.5	58.6	18.7	15.7	6.3	16.5	26.8
Zimbabwe	2.5	3.5	3.2	3.9	4.6	11.7	7.6	8.2	6.9	4.4	3.9	1.6	3.8	6.4
NORTH AFRICA	2.1	1.7	1.6	5.0	5.6	4.0	2.7	2.8	1.9	1.9	1.6	3.0	1.7	3.2
Algeria	0.4	0.3	0.3	0.4	0.7	0.8	0.7	1.0	0.8	0.7	0.5	0.5	0.3	0.7
Egypt, Arab Republic	6.1	4.3	3.9	12.6	13.6	8.6	5.1	5.2	3.4	3.3	2.6	10.3	4.4	6.8
Libya	0.0	0.0	0.1	..	..	..	..	..	..	..	..	0.0	0.0	..
Morocco	4.8	2.1	2.0	4.1	4.4	3.3	2.7	2.1	1.5	1.8	1.4	3.8	2.9	2.7
Tunisia	2.7	3.1	2.8	3.2	2.7	2.5	1.6	0.7	0.4	0.6	1.0	3.5	2.6	1.6
ALL AFRICA	2.4	3.9	4.1	5.5	5.6	5.2	4.6	5.1	4.4	3.8	3.3	2.7	3.6	4.7

Note: Nigeria's ratios are distorted for 1994-95 because of official exchange rate over-valuation affecting oil exports and oil value added (see chapter 3).

12-10. Net ODA from DAC donors as share of recipient GDP

	Percentage of GDP											Annual average		
	1980	*1988*	*1989*	*1990*	*1991*	*1992*	*1993*	*1994*	*1995*	*1996*	*1997*	*75-84*	*85-89*	*90-MR*
SUB-SAHARAN AFRICA	1.4	3.4	3.4	3.7	3.4	3.4	3.3	3.5	3.1	2.7	2.4	1.5	3.0	3.2
excluding South Africa	2.2	5.2	5.2	5.9	5.6	6.0	6.0	6.7	5.7	4.7	3.9	2.2	4.5	5.6
excl. S. Africa & Nigeria	3.7	6.0	5.8	6.9	6.5	7.3	6.9	8.0	6.9	5.8	4.9	3.4	5.3	6.6
Angola	..	1.3	1.2	1.6	1.3	3.4	2.9	5.5	4.8	3.9	3.0	..	1.2	3.3
Benin	2.5	5.8	9.9	6.8	8.5	10.5	7.0	9.5	8.8	7.5	6.9	3.6	6.1	8.2
Botswana	7.6	4.3	3.9	3.3	2.5	2.3	1.8	1.2	1.1	1.2	1.0	7.6	4.9	1.8
Burkina Faso	8.8	9.2	8.4	8.6	9.7	13.4	12.4	14.3	10.7	10.6	9.2	8.3	8.9	11.1
Burundi	6.5	7.7	8.0	13.9	10.5	13.7	12.9	11.7	10.7	7.5	4.0	6.3	7.5	10.6
Cameroon	2.5	1.9	2.7	3.0	3.0	5.1	4.4	5.1	4.3	3.1	3.6	2.5	1.9	4.0
Cape Verde	..	22.9	22.8	24.9	24.8	22.3	24.6	23.5	17.2	18.2	16.0	..	24.2	21.4
Central African Republic	9.4	8.4	7.8	6.7	7.0	7.4	9.0	11.0	10.9	11.3	6.1	8.2	8.0	8.7
Chad	2.0	10.5	9.7	11.4	7.8	8.3	10.5	8.8	8.8	7.4	6.0	4.8	10.2	8.6
Comoros	10.9	16.6	16.0	12.2	12.4	8.7	10.9	9.6	10.0	10.3	7.9	14.0	15.6	10.3
Congo, Democratic Rep. of	..	4.5	4.8	6.8	3.8	2.0	1.1	1.4	1.8	1.8	1.7	2.7	4.1	2.5
Congo, Republic of	3.2	3.5	3.4	7.2	4.3	3.5	6.1	14.3	5.0	15.6	11.3	3.8	4.0	8.4
Côte d'Ivoire	1.5	2.2	2.7	4.9	4.1	4.7	6.8	10.7	7.3	4.2	2.3	1.5	2.0	5.6
Djibouti	..	17.9	16.0	20.8	18.2	19.6	19.9	19.3	16.2	14.6	12.4	..	16.2	17.6
Equatorial Guinea	..	19.5	31.9	33.0	27.0	23.3	18.2	13.1	13.2	9.0	3.6	0.0	19.7	17.5
Eritrea	..	..	..	..	..	0.0	11.8	18.8	16.5	19.8	12.4	..	..	13.2
Ethiopia	..	7.3	4.7	7.5	8.7	8.2	6.7	11.6	9.1	7.4	5.8	1.9	5.6	8.1
Gabon	1.1	2.6	2.9	2.1	2.6	1.2	2.2	3.8	2.7	2.0	0.6	1.3	2.2	2.2
Gambia, The	6.8	20.5	19.7	18.0	17.4	14.5	13.6	10.5	6.6	4.4	4.3	8.7	21.8	11.2
Ghana	2.4	4.5	6.7	4.5	6.8	5.2	5.2	6.1	5.5	5.0	4.2	2.0	3.6	5.3
Guinea	..	6.7	7.9	4.9	5.7	7.1	5.6	5.4	6.0	3.4	3.2	..	6.3	5.2
Guinea-Bissau	31.1	31.3	31.0	30.9	24.2	25.1	23.8	52.4	30.2	46.1	21.8	21.9	27.6	31.8
Kenya	3.8	7.2	7.4	8.6	7.6	6.5	8.6	5.6	5.1	3.7	2.8	4.3	6.2	6.1
Lesotho	17.3	15.7	14.4	13.7	12.7	10.4	10.5	6.0	7.2	5.7	4.7	15.1	17.6	8.9
Liberia	5.4	4.0	3.2	..	..	..	..	..	..	..	..	5.1	4.8	..
Madagascar	2.2	8.7	7.0	8.7	10.2	7.2	6.8	6.4	6.2	5.8	15.5	2.4	6.3	8.3
Malawi	6.1	13.6	11.9	12.0	9.5	11.6	7.7	21.4	15.1	11.6	6.9	6.3	10.4	12.0
Mali	7.4	13.3	15.0	12.9	11.5	8.4	8.3	13.1	11.5	11.2	10.2	8.0	14.2	10.9
Mauritania	6.6	10.7	14.9	9.4	9.8	9.8	20.8	12.5	11.8	9.0	8.7	5.8	11.9	11.5
Mauritius	2.2	2.1	2.4	2.9	2.2	1.1	0.8	0.2	0.2	0.0	0.1	2.3	2.5	0.9
Mozambique	3.3	35.0	25.0	29.9	30.8	51.5	38.7	32.3	29.2	19.4	18.1	4.3	18.7	31.2
Namibia	0.0	0.8	1.6	1.6	3.7	3.3	4.5	3.7	4.3	4.3	3.7	0.0	0.8	3.6
Niger	4.2	10.6	9.2	10.3	11.4	11.2	15.8	16.7	10.1	8.2	9.8	5.9	10.7	11.7
Nigeria	0.0	0.4	1.3	0.6	0.6	0.4	0.3	0.2	0.3	0.1	0.1	0.1	0.4	0.3
Rwanda	8.3	5.7	5.5	7.1	12.2	9.2	10.2	65.0	25.5	18.1	9.6	7.9	6.0	19.6
São Tomé and Principe	2.8	17.8	48.1	62.0	42.4	57.3	59.5	53.2	135.2	64.3	48.2	6.1	18.7	65.2
Senegal	6.1	7.4	11.6	10.3	7.7	7.5	6.7	13.0	8.8	8.2	6.4	6.5	8.6	8.6
Seychelles	12.4	6.3	4.9	8.9	4.5	3.6	1.4	1.5	2.2	1.5	1.2	13.0	7.2	3.1
Sierra Leone	4.7	4.1	6.1	4.4	8.4	10.7	13.7	5.8	6.9	7.1	5.0	2.5	4.7	7.8
Somalia	23.1	30.0	24.4	29.4	..	..	..	..	..	..	..	13.4	30.1	29.4
South Africa	0.0	0.0	0.0	0.0	0.0	0.0	0.1	0.2	0.2	0.2	0.3	0.0	0.0	0.1
Sudan	3.6	3.3	2.8	3.2	3.2	2.9	2.1	2.1	1.8	1.6	0.9	2.5	3.3	2.2
Swaziland	5.6	3.2	1.6	4.2	3.5	2.7	3.4	2.6	3.0	1.7	1.2	5.1	4.1	2.8
Tanzania	..	15.5	14.5	20.0	16.1	16.6	14.3	13.5	11.8	10.4	8.1	..	17.0	13.9
Togo	4.6	9.3	8.0	9.5	7.8	8.0	6.3	6.5	9.0	6.6	5.0	5.7	8.0	7.3
Uganda	3.4	2.9	3.1	5.7	8.6	8.9	10.8	8.6	7.3	6.1	7.0	3.0	2.1	7.9
Zambia	6.0	10.9	7.9	12.4	17.3	22.0	15.6	13.0	12.7	10.8	9.3	4.8	12.9	14.1
Zimbabwe	1.7	3.0	2.7	3.4	4.2	7.9	4.7	4.1	4.9	3.3	2.7	1.2	3.3	4.4
NORTH AFRICA	1.3	1.5	1.4	2.9	4.3	3.3	1.9	2.2	1.6	1.5	1.1	1.4	1.5	2.4
Algeria	0.3	0.2	0.2	0.4	0.7	0.8	0.5	0.9	0.7	0.6	0.4	0.4	0.2	0.6
Egypt, Arab Republic	5.2	4.1	3.6	7.4	11.2	7.2	3.9	4.5	2.9	2.9	2.0	4.6	4.1	5.2
Libya	0.0	0.0	0.0	..	..	..	..	..	..	..	..	0.0	0.0	..
Morocco	1.0	1.8	1.8	2.3	2.2	2.6	1.6	1.0	1.1	1.1	0.6	1.5	1.9	1.6
Tunisia	1.8	2.3	1.8	1.7	2.0	1.9	0.9	0.5	0.3	0.2	0.4	2.5	1.9	1.0
ALL AFRICA	1.4	2.7	2.7	3.4	3.6	3.4	2.9	3.1	2.6	2.3	1.9	1.4	2.4	2.9

Note: Nigeria's ratios are distorted for 1994-95 because of official exchange rate over-valuation affecting oil exports and oil value added (see chapter 3).

12-11. Net ODA from multilateral donors as share of recipient GDP

	Percentage of GDP											Annual average		
	1980	1988	1989	1990	1991	1992	1993	1994	1995	1996	1997	75-84	85-89	90-MR
SUB-SAHARAN AFRICA	0.8	1.7	2.0	2.0	2.1	2.4	2.2	2.8	2.5	2.0	1.7	0.8	1.6	2.2
excluding South Africa	1.2	2.7	3.1	3.2	3.6	4.2	4.0	5.3	4.8	3.5	3.0	1.3	2.5	3.9
excl. S. Africa & Nigeria	2.1	3.0	3.6	3.8	4.2	5.1	4.5	6.2	5.6	4.2	3.6	2.0	2.9	4.7
Angola	..	0.6	0.6	1.0	1.0	2.7	2.6	5.6	3.5	3.3	2.8	..	0.6	2.8
Benin	3.8	4.0	7.6	7.8	5.9	6.1	6.7	7.5	4.9	5.5	3.5	3.3	4.8	6.0
Botswana	2.0	0.8	1.4	0.8	0.7	0.5	1.0	0.7	0.8	0.3	1.4	2.0	1.5	0.8
Burkina Faso	3.6	3.1	3.0	3.1	5.1	8.5	10.5	9.2	9.8	5.8	5.6	3.9	3.9	7.2
Burundi	5.9	10.6	10.2	9.5	11.9	15.2	9.7	22.5	18.3	15.2	9.3	5.2	8.4	14.0
Cameroon	1.1	0.3	1.4	1.0	1.2	1.2	0.1	4.3	1.2	1.5	1.5	1.0	0.5	1.5
Cape Verde	..	9.8	10.0	11.2	8.3	11.9	10.9	11.5	9.5	9.4	9.9	..	10.0	10.3
Central African Republic	4.2	7.5	7.2	10.0	5.3	5.0	4.4	8.6	4.0	4.1	3.4	4.4	5.8	5.6
Chad	1.5	8.4	9.3	8.1	7.1	5.2	5.7	9.3	7.8	11.0	7.4	3.6	8.0	7.7
Comoros	10.8	8.3	6.4	6.2	13.9	9.6	8.1	12.0	10.1	8.4	6.8	14.1	12.4	9.4
Congo, Democratic Rep. of	..	1.7	3.3	2.0	1.5	1.3	0.9	2.1	1.2	1.0	0.9	1.2	2.5	1.4
Congo, Republic of	1.3	0.4	0.4	0.6	0.6	0.4	0.4	6.2	1.0	1.4	0.3	1.9	0.6	1.4
Côte d'Ivoire	0.6	1.9	1.4	1.5	1.9	2.1	0.5	10.1	4.9	4.8	2.1	0.5	0.8	3.5
Djibouti	..	4.6	2.6	4.3	5.0	4.7	6.4	4.8	4.8	4.5	4.0	..	5.1	4.8
Equatorial Guinea	..	18.3	18.7	13.7	16.5	17.0	16.7	11.0	7.4	3.0	1.8	0.7	15.3	10.9
Eritrea	..	..	..	..	..	0.0	4.7	9.9	8.8	4.7	4.5	..	..	5.4
Ethiopia	..	5.3	4.7	6.5	11.9	13.0	10.8	10.4	6.3	6.7	4.1	2.8	4.4	8.7
Gabon	0.2	0.2	0.3	0.1	0.1	0.1	0.1	0.5	0.2	0.3	0.2	0.2	0.2	0.2
Gambia, The	12.8	12.2	15.9	13.5	14.4	18.6	10.6	9.6	6.3	6.1	7.8	8.5	16.9	10.8
Ghana	1.3	6.3	6.9	5.1	6.4	4.4	5.2	4.1	4.7	4.4	4.5	1.4	5.1	4.8
Guinea	..	3.5	6.4	5.4	7.0	6.7	7.0	5.1	5.2	3.5	5.1	..	4.4	5.6
Guinea-Bissau	21.4	27.4	22.8	22.3	20.3	20.2	16.1	21.9	15.6	19.8	23.0	13.1	24.8	19.9
Kenya	1.6	2.6	5.3	5.2	3.9	4.6	-9.8	3.9	3.0	2.9	2.1	1.2	2.3	4.4
Lesotho	8.3	9.3	12.5	9.3	9.0	11.2	9.7	9.3	6.3	6.3	4.8	9.4	12.1	8.2
Liberia	2.6	1.4	1.7	..	..	..	..	..	..	..	..	2.1	2.1	..
Madagascar	2.3	3.5	7.1	4.3	6.8	4.9	4.0	3.3	3.4	3.4	8.1	1.9	4.8	4.8
Malawi	5.5	14.5	16.5	16.0	14.3	20.3	16.4	18.6	14.6	10.4	7.2	4.8	11.0	14.7
Mali	5.8	8.7	7.3	6.6	7.2	6.8	5.6	11.4	11.1	8.1	7.2	5.6	7.5	8.0
Mauritania	4.4	6.9	8.8	9.6	9.6	7.8	14.6	14.7	11.3	17.0	13.9	6.6	7.3	12.3
Mauritius	0.7	0.4	0.4	0.5	0.3	1.0	0.0	0.2	0.4	0.5	0.7	1.2	0.4	0.4
Mozambique	1.0	8.8	10.3	10.2	12.1	23.5	17.4	21.9	16.8	13.0	9.4	1.3	5.6	15.5
Namibia	0.0	0.2	1.0	3.4	3.5	1.6	1.2	0.8	1.3	1.6	1.3	0.0	0.4	1.8
Niger	2.5	5.8	4.7	5.7	4.7	4.6	5.7	7.1	4.3	4.8	7.1	3.1	6.0	5.5
Nigeria	0.0	0.1	0.1	0.3	0.3	0.4	1.0	0.6	0.5	0.4	0.4	0.0	0.1	0.5
Rwanda	4.9	4.6	3.8	3.9	6.7	8.2	7.8	30.1	28.1	30.3	22.3	4.3	4.2	17.2
São Tomé and Principe	6.3	32.8	49.6	47.9	48.5	67.9	39.0	47.9	50.0	40.4	28.6	14.6	28.3	46.3
Senegal	2.6	4.2	3.5	4.1	3.6	3.4	2.3	4.6	5.8	3.7	2.7	3.2	4.4	3.8
Seychelles	2.3	0.9	1.6	0.9	1.6	1.0	2.5	1.2	0.5	1.6	1.1	1.3	2.5	1.3
Sierra Leone	2.5	3.1	2.3	2.5	4.6	8.8	13.4	24.0	16.9	13.3	9.8	2.0	2.9	11.7
Somalia	27.5	11.4	14.6	15.6	..	..	..	..	..	..	..	15.9	16.0	15.6
South Africa	0.0	0.0	0.0	0.0	0.0	0.0	0.1	0.1	0.0	0.0	0.1	0.0	0.0	0.0
Sudan	2.5	2.2	2.0	3.0	4.4	5.3	3.7	2.9	1.5	1.6	1.1	1.8	1.9	2.9
Swaziland	3.0	2.1	2.3	2.2	2.6	2.8	2.0	2.7	1.4	0.8	0.8	2.7	2.1	1.9
Tanzania	..	4.5	4.7	7.8	6.7	10.8	6.7	9.3	5.9	5.0	4.8	..	4.8	7.1
Togo	3.4	5.8	6.9	6.6	4.9	5.4	1.6	6.3	5.7	4.8	3.1	4.2	5.7	4.8
Uganda	5.6	3.2	5.0	8.9	10.0	16.1	8.2	10.0	7.0	5.1	6.3	4.2	3.7	8.9
Zambia	1.6	1.9	1.5	2.2	8.9	10.6	11.0	8.5	46.0	7.9	6.0	1.1	3.6	12.6
Zimbabwe	0.7	0.5	0.5	0.4	0.4	3.8	2.9	4.1	2.1	1.1	1.3	0.3	0.5	2.0
NORTH AFRICA	0.2	0.1	0.2	0.2	0.5	0.4	0.5	0.5	0.3	0.4	0.5	0.5	0.1	0.4
Algeria	0.0	0.0	0.1	0.0	0.1	0.1	0.2	0.1	0.1	0.1	0.1	0.1	0.0	0.1
Egypt, Arab Republic	0.9	0.2	0.4	0.2	1.0	0.5	0.4	0.6	0.4	0.3	0.5	2.2	0.2	0.5
Libya	0.0	0.0	0.0	..	..	..	..	..	..	..	..	0.0	0.0	..
Morocco	0.4	0.1	0.2	0.4	0.5	0.6	1.0	0.9	0.4	0.6	0.7	0.3	0.2	0.6
Tunisia	0.3	0.8	0.6	0.6	0.7	0.7	0.7	0.3	0.2	0.6	0.8	0.4	0.5	0.6
ALL AFRICA	0.6	1.2	1.4	1.4	1.7	1.8	1.7	2.0	1.8	1.4	1.3	0.7	1.1	1.6

Note: Nigeria's ratios are distorted for 1994-95 because of official exchange rate over-valuation affecting oil exports and oil value added (see chapter 3).

12-12. Net ODA from all donors as share of recipient GDI

	Percentage of GDI											Annual average		
	1980	1988	1989	1990	1991	1992	1993	1994	1995	1996	1997	75-84	85-89	90-MR
SUB-SAHARAN AFRICA	11.4	30.0	33.0	39.7	32.0	39.3	34.3	36.2	30.7	27.0	23.8	12.5	30.2	32.9
excluding South Africa	18.3	46.4	53.6	59.0	45.0	61.8	56.8	64.4	58.6	45.5	38.5	20.0	45.0	53.7
excl. S. Africa & Nigeria	32.5	54.2	62.7	68.7	54.2	82.2	68.7	77.4	68.5	52.1	46.1	31.3	52.1	64.7
Angola	..	17.0	15.0	22.4	17.7	167.0	21.0	48.0	33.1	31.5	24.4	..	12.7	45.6
Benin	42.4	62.6	151.5	102.6	98.6	121.0	89.4	109.0	71.5	77.5	56.9	40.9	91.4	90.8
Botswana	26.1	18.0	16.6	12.9	10.7	9.6	11.0	7.2	6.9	5.7	8.7	29.9	27.1	9.1
Burkina Faso	72.9	62.5	52.8	58.9	73.7	104.1	116.0	135.1	100.3	62.3	57.6	64.1	60.5	88.5
Burundi	91.9	124.0	113.0	161.3	154.0	191.9	142.6	320.3	300.3	187.8	154.5	89.3	108.0	201.6
Cameroon	18.7	10.6	23.8	22.5	25.0	43.9	27.8	60.6	38.4	29.5	34.0	15.0	11.3	35.2
Cape Verde		73.7	75.5	83.9	114.3	90.3	100.3	84.3	76.9	84.4	85.0	..	91.6	89.9
Central African Republic	198.7	154.5	129.7	137.1	100.3	101.9	131.2	166.7	207.4	354.4	101.6	129.1	115.2	162.6
Chad	104.5	319.4	281.3	144.6	274.0	217.0	201.6	138.5	126.9	134.9	95.4	281.8	277.3	166.6
Comoros	105.7	114.5	129.2	94.3	129.5	82.2	92.4	102.5	101.6	99.5	68.2	114.1	120.1	96.3
Congo, Democratic Rep. of	..	43.3	56.7	106.1	94.0	47.5	112.6	43.4	32.8	40.0	38.7	36.6	47.2	64.4
Congo, Republic of	15.1	21.1	27.1	49.0	23.9	17.9	21.8	37.6	16.2	28.1	44.8	19.5	22.2	29.9
Côte d'Ivoire	7.8	32.8	45.5	95.5	82.0	98.1	88.6	165.7	89.7	67.3	27.1	8.9	25.3	89.2
Djibouti	..	..	..	..	165.6	126.3	164.6	226.2	253.0	217.4	183.0	..	..	190.9
Equatorial Guinea	..	..	..	269.3	95.2	166.4	159.0	35.6	28.9	11.2	8.0	7.8	..	96.7
Eritrea	..	..	..	..	..	0.0	110.4	174.7	135.8	85.1	46.0	..	..	92.0
Ethiopia	..	64.5	69.5	126.0	208.0	231.0	123.1	144.8	93.4	74.0	52.3	37.2	70.3	131.6
Gabon	4.7	7.4	12.1	10.3	10.0	5.5	10.4	19.9	12.9	9.6	2.9	4.1	7.7	10.2
Gambia, The	84.7	195.0	172.9	141.3	148.1	146.7	112.4	107.7	61.8	45.5	57.7	100.5	225.0	102.7
Ghana	76.7	98.4	103.5	66.3	84.2	74.7	46.6	41.9	50.5	43.9	30.0	60.8	78.5	54.8
Guinea	..	63.0	87.4	59.9	70.1	78.6	70.1	53.7	55.0	38.1	45.2	..	69.1	58.8
Guinea-Bissau	190.8	139.5	140.8	177.7	144.9	96.0	130.8	342.1	205.6	288.5	215.5	158.2	161.6	200.1
Kenya	22.3	48.7	61.9	70.6	12.4	80.8	103.3	57.6	46.1	39.0	28.1	27.3	42.0	54.8
Lesotho	60.2	51.7	44.2	32.4	26.9	27.9	27.2	19.1	16.2	14.0	11.5	73.5	60.7	21.9
Liberia	32.1	..	..	..	..	..	..	..	..	..	..	44.5	94.0	..
Madagascar	38.1	91.8	104.4	76.4	208.4	107.0	94.1	89.2	87.7	78.4	199.4	47.1	101.1	117.6
Malawi	46.8	150.0	134.6	142.2	117.6	159.8	158.4	136.6	178.6	178.1	112.7	49.5	125.0	148.0
Mali	96.7	104.9	103.4	87.7	83.0	70.0	62.8	92.1	96.7	83.1	88.1	103.7	117.1	82.9
Mauritania	94.3	68.9	138.7	117.8	108.5	83.0	158.0	180.7	135.1	130.2	129.9	106.9	97.3	130.4
Mauritius	14.1	8.7	8.9	10.9	8.3	4.9	2.6	1.3	2.2	1.8	3.6	15.1	11.6	4.4
Mozambique	80.8	290.0	238.7	257.2	267.3	481.2	441.8	274.2	201.5	170.3	146.8	99.7	215.3	280.0
Namibia	0.0	6.0	16.0	18.4	39.5	23.1	35.2	19.4	27.4	26.3	25.6	0.0	8.0	26.9
Niger	24.1	87.3	102.4	198.3	176.4	291.7	377.3	232.3	191.3	134.8	170.1	84.2	127.1	221.5
Nigeria	0.3	2.9	8.2	6.0	4.1	3.6	5.6	4.1	4.7	4.3	3.3	0.6	3.2	4.5
Rwanda	82.8	71.7	71.1	77.4	135.6	124.9	119.6	2,231.1	622.6	471.6	317.2	85.9	68.5	512.5
São Tomé and Principe	26.6	260.4	344.1	..	289.5	323.6	258.4	224.2	312.1	208.5	153.6	66.1	191.1	252.8
Senegal	75.1	95.0	129.6	104.6	90.3	75.5	65.9	109.1	87.9	69.6	50.5	81.6	116.5	81.7
Seychelles	38.5	28.6	23.7	39.7	27.5	20.9	14.4	10.2	8.4	7.3	7.8	43.6	43.9	17.0
Sierra Leone	..	99.8	86.5	74.3	123.3	237.1	350.3	377.5	426.1	222.8	..	128.4	149.1	258.8
Somalia	169.3	174.6	128.9	347.8	..	..	..	..	..	..	..	156.0	166.2	347.8
South Africa	0.0	0.0	0.0	0.0	0.0	0.0	1.5	1.4	1.4	1.5	2.1	0.0	0.0	1.0
Sudan	55.9	..	..	..	..	..	..	..	..	..	..	44.3	55.2	..
Swaziland	28.4	22.6	16.8	32.7	29.7	21.2	20.1	16.4	12.8	8.3	6.3	25.1	30.8	18.5
Tanzania	..	107.0	110.7	122.9	86.7	102.1	80.4	92.5	81.2	84.8	83.9	..	108.3	91.8
Togo	28.1	93.2	89.6	60.4	73.7	83.5	104.0	123.7	91.3	68.7	55.2	39.6	82.6	82.6
Uganda	148.3	56.6	77.3	122.7	132.3	159.9	124.7	128.9	89.2	69.7	83.6	106.9	59.9	113.9
Zambia	35.2	115.8	86.7	84.6	237.4	273.7	177.1	158.5	421.9	125.4	108.1	34.1	112.2	198.3
Zimbabwe	14.5	18.7	21.3	22.3	23.8	58.0	33.5	33.7	27.6	16.9	14.9	9.3	22.6	28.8
NORTH AFRICA	7.2	7.0	6.7	17.7	21.8	16.0	11.4	11.9	8.3	9.3	7.6	9.4	7.2	13.0
Algeria	1.1	1.1	1.0	1.5	2.4	2.8	2.4	3.1	2.4	2.6	2.0	1.1	1.0	2.4
Egypt, Arab Republic	22.0	12.2	12.3	43.8	64.2	47.3	31.4	31.3	19.5	19.7	14.6	33.9	15.9	34.0
Libya	0.2	..	..	..	..	..	..	..	..	..	..	0.2	..	..
Morocco	19.7	9.8	8.3	16.2	19.5	14.3	11.8	9.7	7.3	9.0	6.7	14.4	12.1	11.8
Tunisia	9.1	15.2	11.7	11.8	10.5	8.6	5.3	2.8	1.6	2.6	3.9	11.3	10.9	5.9
ALL AFRICA	9.6	19.5	20.6	28.7	28.0	29.1	24.6	26.4	22.2	20.1	17.4	10.8	18.8	24.6

Note: Nigeria's ratios are distorted for 1994-95 because of official exchange rate over-valuation affecting oil exports and oil value added (see chapter 3).

12-13. Net ODA from DAC donors as share of recipient GDI

	Percentage of GDI										Annual average		
	1980	1988	1989	1990	1991	1992	1993	1994	1995	1996	1997	75-84	85-89	90-MR
SUB-SAHARAN AFRICA	6.5	19.8	20.6	25.3	19.7	23.3	20.7	20.5	17.0	15.7	13.8	7.1	19.1	19.5
excluding South Africa	10.4	30.7	33.5	37.5	27.8	36.6	34.3	36.2	32.0	26.1	21.9	11.4	28.4	31.6
excl. S. Africa & Nigeria	18.4	35.8	38.8	43.6	33.4	48.8	41.9	43.8	37.6	30.1	26.4	17.8	32.8	38.2
Angola	..	11.3	9.7	13.7	10.1	92.4	10.8	23.8	19.1	17.0	12.7	..	8.7	25.0
Benin	16.8	36.8	84.2	48.0	58.8	76.6	45.6	60.2	45.0	43.6	37.4	21.0	50.1	51.9
Botswana	20.5	15.0	12.5	10.5	8.2	7.9	6.6	4.6	4.1	4.8	3.9	23.1	20.4	6.3
Burkina Faso	51.9	46.5	39.0	42.0	47.0	63.5	62.9	82.0	51.8	40.1	33.9	43.3	41.5	52.9
Burundi	46.8	51.2	48.8	95.8	73.0	91.6	82.1	111.0	112.0	62.5	49.5	48.1	49.4	84.7
Cameroon	12.1	9.2	15.8	17.1	18.2	35.5	26.9	33.0	29.9	20.0	22.4	10.1	8.7	25.4
Cape Verde	..	50.9	52.2	57.8	85.4	59.1	69.2	56.6	49.5	54.4	52.7	..	64.4	60.6
Central African Republic	134.5	80.8	68.0	54.5	56.3	61.2	88.4	94.4	151.5	256.9	67.8	84.4	65.2	103.9
Chad	59.7	177.2	143.6	83.8	141.9	133.8	129.0	66.8	67.3	53.8	40.9	155.1	154.6	89.6
Comoros	32.8	76.1	92.0	62.2	60.9	39.0	53.1	45.5	50.5	54.7	37.1	43.0	67.4	50.4
Congo, Democratic Rep. of	..	31.5	33.7	74.8	67.6	28.7	62.6	17.2	19.7	25.4	24.1	25.3	29.5	40.0
Congo, Republic of	9.1	18.8	24.0	45.4	21.0	16.1	20.5	26.2	13.6	25.8	43.5	11.8	19.5	26.5
Côte d'Ivoire	5.6	17.4	29.9	73.5	56.3	68.3	82.0	85.3	53.7	31.3	14.2	7.0	18.0	58.1
Djibouti	..	..	..	..	126.7	102.7	115.6	164.6	189.5	157.9	131.2	..	..	141.2
Equatorial Guinea	..	..	..	189.8	53.2	96.1	83.0	19.4	18.5	8.4	5.8	0.0	..	59.3
Eritrea	..	..	..	..	..	0.0	78.0	105.7	85.5	67.6	30.2	..	..	61.2
Ethiopia	..	37.5	35.2	63.0	88.1	89.3	46.9	76.4	55.3	38.8	30.6	13.6	39.5	61.0
Gabon	4.2	6.9	11.0	9.8	9.8	5.2	9.9	17.6	12.1	8.6	2.2	3.4	6.7	9.4
Gambia, The	25.6	125.4	97.0	80.4	79.3	65.5	64.9	58.1	32.6	20.3	24.3	46.6	128.1	53.2
Ghana	42.8	40.2	50.8	31.2	42.8	40.5	23.6	25.5	27.7	23.5	17.6	32.8	32.1	29.0
Guinea	..	39.1	45.9	28.1	31.8	40.8	31.6	27.8	29.1	17.4	14.8	..	38.8	27.7
Guinea-Bissau	110.4	70.1	79.6	103.2	78.2	51.9	77.3	240.8	135.6	200.1	100.5	92.8	81.4	123.5
Kenya	15.6	35.5	36.1	43.7	8.2	47.4	48.4	34.1	28.9	22.3	18.5	21.1	30.4	31.4
Lesotho	40.7	32.7	23.7	19.4	15.8	13.3	14.0	7.5	8.7	6.4	5.5	43.9	35.9	11.3
Liberia	19.7	..	..	..	..	..	..	..	..	..	..	32.5	66.7	..
Madagascar	15.0	65.8	52.5	51.3	125.3	63.6	59.0	58.5	56.4	49.4	130.6	25.0	57.7	74.3
Malawi	24.7	72.5	56.4	60.8	46.8	58.0	50.5	73.0	90.7	93.8	56.3	26.2	61.3	66.2
Mali	47.5	62.6	69.0	56.2	50.7	38.4	37.9	50.5	50.5	49.0	49.6	55.7	73.4	47.9
Mauritania	28.7	42.6	88.8	52.3	54.4	47.8	94.4	86.0	73.8	47.0	49.6	25.5	53.1	63.2
Mauritius	10.8	6.8	7.7	9.3	7.6	3.7	2.7	0.7	0.9	-0.1	0.2	9.8	9.7	3.1
Mozambique	54.8	231.1	168.5	191.6	192.1	330.0	303.5	163.3	127.8	101.9	94.7	74.1	164.0	188.1
Namibia	0.0	4.6	9.8	5.9	20.3	15.8	27.9	15.8	20.9	19.0	19.0	0.0	5.4	18.1
Niger	14.9	55.7	67.0	126.7	123.7	206.4	276.2	160.9	134.2	85.0	90.4	51.1	80.2	150.4
Nigeria	0.1	2.4	7.3	4.1	2.7	1.9	1.4	1.0	1.6	1.1	0.9	0.4	2.6	1.8
Rwanda	51.5	39.5	40.7	48.4	86.9	66.2	67.2	1,521.8	296.1	176.2	95.8	54.3	39.2	294.8
São Tomé and Principe	8.2	91.5	169.4	..	135.0	148.1	156.0	118.0	227.8	128.1	97.1	17.6	75.2	144.3
Senegal	51.9	58.2	97.8	74.9	59.6	50.7	47.6	80.4	52.2	46.9	34.6	50.5	73.0	55.9
Seychelles	32.4	24.5	18.0	36.1	20.1	16.8	5.1	5.8	7.1	3.0	3.3	38.5	31.2	12.1
Sierra Leone	..	51.2	62.5	47.2	79.8	130.3	177.4	73.4	122.8	76.3	..	49.4	83.7	101.0
Somalia	54.4	125.4	80.6	189.7	..	..	..	..	..	..	..	49.5	107.6	189.7
South Africa	0.0	0.0	0.0	0.0	0.0	0.0	1.0	1.0	1.2	1.3	1.8	0.0	0.0	0.8
Sudan	24.4	..	..	..	..	..	..	..	..	..	..	17.0	29.8	..
Swaziland	18.5	13.8	6.9	21.4	17.2	10.5	12.7	8.0	8.7	5.6	3.7	16.1	20.4	11.0
Tanzania	..	82.8	83.5	88.4	61.3	62.0	54.8	54.5	54.0	57.5	49.5	..	84.0	60.3
Togo	16.1	58.0	48.3	35.8	45.4	50.4	82.3	62.3	55.8	40.2	33.7	21.5	46.6	50.7
Uganda	55.2	26.8	28.0	44.7	56.6	56.0	70.8	58.9	45.4	37.7	43.7	45.8	21.2	51.7
Zambia	25.9	98.7	72.8	72.0	156.7	184.7	103.7	95.7	91.1	72.3	64.2	26.1	88.8	105.0
Zimbabwe	9.9	16.0	18.3	19.4	21.8	39.2	20.7	16.8	19.5	12.7	10.1	7.2	19.8	20.0
NORTH AFRICA	4.4	6.3	5.7	10.4	16.7	13.1	8.1	9.5	6.8	7.4	5.3	4.5	6.2	9.7
Algeria	0.7	0.8	0.6	1.3	2.1	2.5	1.8	2.8	2.2	2.2	1.6	0.9	0.7	2.1
Egypt, Arab Republic	18.8	11.7	11.2	25.5	53.1	39.4	23.8	26.9	16.3	17.2	11.2	15.3	14.9	26.7
Libya	0.1	..	..	..	..	..	..	..	..	..	..	0.1	..	..
Morocco	4.1	8.7	7.4	9.2	9.6	11.1	7.0	4.9	5.1	5.4	3.1	5.5	8.3	6.9
Tunisia	6.1	11.3	7.5	6.4	7.8	6.6	3.0	1.9	1.2	0.8	1.4	8.0	7.7	3.6
ALL AFRICA	5.6	13.7	13.6	17.9	18.5	18.9	15.4	16.0	13.1	12.5	10.4	5.8	12.7	15.3

Note: Nigeria's ratios are distorted for 1994-95 because of official exchange rate over-valuation affecting oil exports and oil value added (see chapter 3).

12-14. Net ODA from multilateral donors as share of recipient GDI

| | Percentage of GDI | | | | | | | | | | Annual average | | |
	1980	1988	1989	1990	1991	1992	1993	1994	1995	1996	1997	75-84	85-89	90-MR
SUB-SAHARAN AFRICA	3.7	9.9	12.1	13.6	12.0	15.9	13.5	15.7	13.7	11.2	9.9	4.0	10.3	13.2
excluding South Africa	6.0	15.4	19.7	20.2	16.9	25.0	22.4	28.2	26.5	19.2	16.3	6.4	15.4	21.8
excl. S. Africa & Nigeria	10.6	18.0	23.5	23.5	20.4	33.2	26.6	33.6	30.8	21.8	19.3	10.0	17.9	26.2
Angola	..	5.4	5.1	8.6	7.6	74.3	10.0	24.1	14.0	14.5	11.7	..	3.9	20.6
Benin	24.8	25.4	64.5	54.8	40.7	44.5	43.7	47.4	24.8	32.3	19.1	19.5	39.7	38.4
Botswana	5.5	2.9	4.4	2.5	2.4	1.9	3.8	2.5	2.8	1.0	5.1	6.2	6.6	2.8
Burkina Faso	21.0	15.6	13.8	15.0	24.9	40.1	53.1	52.9	47.4	21.9	20.6	20.1	17.9	34.5
Burundi	42.2	70.7	61.9	65.4	82.6	101.3	62.0	212.3	191.3	126.4	115.8	39.0	54.8	119.6
Cameroon	5.0	1.5	8.0	5.6	6.9	8.4	0.9	27.7	8.4	9.7	9.2	4.3	2.6	9.6
Cape Verde	..	21.8	22.9	25.9	28.6	31.5	30.6	27.7	27.3	28.1	32.6	..	26.3	29.0
Central African Republic	60.5	72.0	62.1	81.3	42.4	40.7	42.8	73.3	55.4	94.3	37.9	42.9	48.1	58.5
Chad	44.8	142.2	137.7	59.8	129.9	83.2	70.2	71.1	59.3	79.8	50.1	117.9	122.7	75.4
Comoros	32.7	38.2	36.5	31.7	68.6	43.2	39.1	56.9	51.1	44.7	31.8	43.1	49.0	45.9
Congo, Democratic Rep. of	..	11.8	23.0	22.2	26.4	18.5	50.0	26.2	13.1	14.0	12.6	11.3	17.7	22.9
Congo, Republic of	3.6	2.2	3.0	3.6	2.9	1.9	1.2	11.3	2.6	2.3	1.3	5.7	2.8	3.4
Côte d'Ivoire	2.2	15.3	15.6	22.0	25.6	29.8	6.5	80.4	35.9	36.1	12.9	1.9	7.3	31.2
Djibouti	..	..	..	..	34.5	24.7	37.1	40.8	55.9	48.7	42.0	..	..	40.5
Equatorial Guinea	..	..	..	79.1	32.6	70.3	76.0	16.2	10.4	2.8	2.9	5.3	..	36.3
Eritrea	..	..	..	..	..	0.0	31.3	55.6	45.5	16.0	11.0	..	..	26.6
Ethiopia	..	27.1	34.5	54.6	119.8	141.6	76.0	68.4	38.1	35.2	21.7	20.4	30.6	69.4
Gabon	0.6	0.6	1.1	0.4	0.2	0.4	0.5	2.2	0.9	1.1	0.9	0.5	0.7	0.8
Gambia, The	48.0	74.3	78.3	60.2	65.7	84.0	50.3	52.8	31.2	28.1	44.5	43.2	98.4	52.1
Ghana	23.7	55.9	52.4	35.0	40.5	34.7	23.4	16.9	23.3	20.6	18.7	24.9	46.2	26.6
Guinea	..	20.5	37.2	30.9	38.5	38.2	39.2	26.2	25.2	18.1	23.7	..	27.1	30.0
Guinea-Bissau	75.9	61.3	58.4	74.5	65.5	41.7	52.0	100.6	69.9	86.0	105.9	54.6	71.6	74.5
Kenya	6.7	13.0	25.8	26.6	4.2	33.8	55.4	23.9	17.1	16.9	13.8	5.8	11.2	24.0
Lesotho	19.5	19.3	20.6	13.1	11.2	14.4	13.0	11.6	7.5	7.1	5.6	29.1	24.5	10.4
Liberia	9.4	..	..	..	..	..	..	..	..	..	..	10.9	27.3	..
Madagascar	15.1	26.5	52.7	25.3	83.2	43.4	35.1	30.6	31.3	29.0	68.5	19.9	44.3	43.3
Malawi	22.1	77.5	78.1	81.3	70.8	101.9	108.0	63.6	87.8	84.1	59.1	23.3	63.7	82.1
Mali	37.4	41.0	33.8	28.7	31.5	30.9	25.6	43.8	48.6	35.4	35.0	38.7	38.1	34.9
Mauritania	19.3	27.6	52.4	53.4	53.7	38.2	66.3	101.7	70.8	88.7	79.2	30.4	32.4	69.0
Mauritius	3.4	1.4	1.4	1.5	0.9	1.2	-0.1	0.7	1.4	2.1	2.5	4.9	1.4	1.3
Mozambique	16.3	57.9	69.3	65.5	75.1	150.5	137.0	110.4	73.4	68.0	49.3	22.5	49.6	91.1
Namibia	0.0	1.4	6.2	12.5	19.1	7.3	7.3	3.6	6.5	7.3	6.6	0.0	3.4	8.8
Niger	9.0	30.3	34.6	69.8	50.7	85.4	99.2	68.4	56.8	49.8	65.9	26.4	45.2	68.2
Nigeria	0.1	0.6	0.8	1.9	1.4	1.7	4.2	3.1	3.1	3.2	2.5	0.2	0.6	2.6
Rwanda	30.6	31.5	28.5	26.4	47.5	58.7	51.6	706.3	326.9	294.6	222.4	29.7	27.7	216.8
São Tomé and Principe	18.4	168.9	174.7	..	154.5	175.5	102.3	106.2	84.3	80.4	57.6	48.5	115.9	108.7
Senegal	22.6	33.0	29.6	29.4	27.7	22.9	16.5	28.5	34.1	21.5	14.5	25.0	36.9	24.4
Seychelles	6.1	3.4	5.7	3.7	7.4	4.5	8.8	4.5	1.6	3.2	3.1	4.4	10.9	4.6
Sierra Leone	..	38.8	23.7	27.0	43.5	106.8	172.8	304.0	302.2	142.3	..	49.4	58.7	157.0
Somalia	65.0	47.5	48.1	100.5	..	..	..	..	..	..	..	58.5	56.2	100.5
South Africa	0.0	0.0	0.0	0.0	0.0	0.0	0.5	0.4	0.2	0.2	0.4	0.0	0.0	0.2
Sudan	17.2	..	..	..	..	..	..	..	..	..	..	12.0	14.3	..
Swaziland	9.9	8.8	9.9	11.2	12.5	10.7	7.5	8.4	4.1	2.7	2.4	9.0	10.4	7.4
Tanzania	..	24.2	27.1	34.2	25.6	40.3	25.6	37.5	26.8	27.6	29.5	..	24.3	30.9
Togo	12.0	35.9	41.6	24.7	28.5	33.9	21.5	61.3	35.4	29.3	20.5	17.2	33.4	31.9
Uganda	91.3	29.8	44.6	70.2	65.6	100.7	53.7	68.2	43.0	31.2	39.4	60.3	37.4	59.0
Zambia	6.8	17.1	13.9	12.7	80.8	89.0	73.4	62.7	330.8	53.1	41.5	6.2	23.4	93.0
Zimbabwe	4.2	2.9	3.1	2.3	2.1	19.0	12.8	17.0	8.3	4.3	4.9	1.7	2.9	8.8
NORTH AFRICA	0.8	0.6	0.8	0.7	2.0	1.5	2.0	2.1	1.2	1.8	2.2	1.6	0.6	1.7
Algeria	0.1	0.2	0.3	0.1	0.2	0.2	0.6	0.3	0.3	0.3	0.4	0.1	0.1	0.3
Egypt, Arab Republic	3.1	0.6	1.2	0.7	4.6	2.6	2.6	3.4	2.1	2.0	3.0	7.2	0.9	2.6
Libya	0.1	..	..	..	..	..	..	..	..	..	..	0.1	..	..
Morocco	1.4	0.7	0.9	1.4	2.4	2.4	4.5	4.4	1.9	3.2	3.2	1.3	0.7	2.9
Tunisia	1.0	3.7	2.5	2.4	2.7	2.2	2.6	1.3	1.0	2.5	2.8	1.4	2.2	2.2
ALL AFRICA	2.5	5.7	6.8	7.1	8.1	9.6	8.7	10.2	8.9	7.6	6.8	2.9	5.5	8.4

Note: Nigeria's ratios are distorted for 1994-95 because of official exchange rate over-valuation affecting oil exports and oil value added (see chapter 3).

12-15. Net ODA per capita from all donors

	U.S. dollars (current prices)											Annual average		
	1980	1988	1989	1990	1991	1992	1993	1994	1995	1996	1997	75-84	85-89	90-MR
SUB-SAHARAN AFRICA	20	29	30	34	33	34	31	32	31	26	23	15	25	31
excluding South Africa	21	31	32	37	35	37	32	34	32	28	24	17	27	32
excl. S.Africa & Nigeria	26	39	39	46	43	45	40	42	40	34	30	21	34	40
Angola	7	18	19	29	29	35	29	42	38	48	37	7	16	36
Benin	26	36	59	57	55	54	56	48	51	52	39	21	36	52
Botswana	117	126	129	116	103	84	96	62	63	54	81	91	114	83
Burkina Faso	30	35	31	38	47	47	49	45	49	41	35	24	32	44
Burundi	28	39	39	49	46	54	37	52	47	32	19	23	37	42
Cameroon	31	25	41	39	44	59	44	57	34	30	36	22	24	43
Cape Verde	223	268	264	323	305	344	325	327	295	308	273	144	276	312
Central African Republic	48	73	66	85	58	58	55	52	51	50	27	34	59	54
Chad	8	48	46	55	45	40	36	33	36	44	31	18	40	40
Comoros	129	127	106	107	146	107	107	83	88	79	54	119	123	97
Congo, Democratic Rep. of	16	16	20	24	12	7	4	6	4	4	4	12	16	8
Congo, Republic of	55	41	42	98	58	48	51	145	49	163	99	49	49	89
Côte d'Ivoire	26	39	35	59	53	61	60	121	90	70	31	17	25	68
Djibouti	260	199	153	376	203	206	237	222	177	157	136	212	215	214
Equatorial Guinea	43	140	163	176	175	168	140	78	85	76	58	27	116	119
Eritrea	0	0	0	0	0	0	20	45	42	43	33	0	0	23
Ethiopia	6	20	15	20	21	22	21	20	16	15	11	5	16	18
Gabon	81	118	143	138	145	68	98	170	132	112	35	73	105	112
Gambia, The	85	101	114	109	107	113	83	66	43	34	35	58	109	74
Ghana	18	41	50	38	58	39	38	33	38	37	28	13	33	39
Guinea	20	47	65	51	64	74	65	56	63	44	55	15	42	59
Guinea-Bissau	75	109	122	133	116	104	92	166	107	162	110	64	100	124
Kenya	24	38	47	50	38	35	35	26	27	22	16	19	31	31
Lesotho	70	68	81	83	72	80	77	62	60	54	46	53	66	67
Liberia	52	28	25	46	64	47	47	24	45	74	33	40	34	47
Madagascar	26	27	31	34	38	30	29	22	23	27	59	16	27	33
Malawi	23	47	53	59	60	64	54	49	44	50	34	19	36	52
Mali	41	55	55	58	53	49	40	47	56	51	44	29	51	50
Mauritania	113	96	128	118	106	94	149	119	99	114	102	115	115	113
Mauritius	34	55	58	84	63	42	24	13	20	17	36	37	51	37
Mozambique	14	66	58	71	74	100	79	80	70	57	58	11	45	74
Namibia	0	18	45	91	133	101	106	92	123	119	102	0	19	108
Niger	30	52	41	52	47	45	41	43	30	27	35	30	47	40
Nigeria	1	1	4	3	3	3	3	2	2	2	2	1	1	2
Rwanda	30	38	34	42	51	48	48	115	111	100	75	26	34	74
São Tomé and Principe	44	228	403	478	437	468	374	389	638	347	242	72	208	422
Senegal	47	87	100	112	85	88	64	80	80	68	49	45	84	78
Seychelles	337	301	286	513	325	268	266	174	172	248	194	242	338	270
Sierra Leone	28	27	26	16	26	32	49	63	46	42	27	16	23	38
Somalia	74	62	59	64	23	78	105	64	23	11	12	50	68	47
South Africa	0	0	0	0	0	0	7	8	10	9	12	0	0	6
Sudan	33	41	33	34	36	22	18	16	9	8	7	29	42	19
Swaziland	89	51	38	71	68	66	63	64	62	33	30	60	48	57
Tanzania	37	42	37	46	41	50	34	34	30	29	31	28	34	37
Togo	35	62	59	74	56	60	25	32	47	39	29	31	50	45
Uganda	9	26	29	41	39	42	34	41	43	35	41	7	20	40
Zambia	55	65	50	62	110	125	103	82	227	67	65	35	58	105
Zimbabwe	23	30	28	35	39	77	47	52	45	33	29	15	29	45
NORTH AFRICA	31	22	22	63	60	45	30	31	23	26	22	31	24	37
Algeria	9	7	6	11	13	15	13	15	11	11	8	8	8	12
Egypt, Arab Republic	34	30	30	104	94	66	43	47	35	37	32	44	34	57
Libya	5	1	4	5	6	1	1	1	2	2	2	3	2	2
Morocco	46	20	19	44	50	38	28	24	19	24	17	28	22	31
Tunisia	36	40	36	48	43	46	26	12	8	14	21	36	33	27
ALL AFRICA	22	28	28	39	38	36	31	32	30	26	23	18	25	32

12-16. Net ODA per capita from DAC donors

	U.S. dollars (current prices)											Annual average		
	1980	1988	1989	1990	1991	1992	1993	1994	1995	1996	1997	75-84	85-89	90-MR
SUB-SAHARAN AFRICA	11	19	18	21	20	20	18	18	17	15	13	9	16	18
excluding South Africa	12	20	20	23	21	21	19	19	18	16	13	10	17	19
excl. S.Africa & Nigeria	15	25	24	28	26	27	24	24	22	20	17	12	21	24
Angola	5	12	12	18	17	20	15	21	22	26	19	4	11	20
Benin	10	21	33	27	33	34	29	27	32	29	26	11	20	29
Botswana	92	105	97	95	79	69	58	40	37	45	36	69	87	57
Burkina Faso	22	26	23	27	30	29	27	27	25	26	21	16	22	26
Burundi	14	16	17	29	22	26	21	18	17	11	6	12	17	19
Cameroon	20	22	27	30	32	48	42	31	26	21	24	15	19	32
Cape Verde	135	185	183	222	228	225	224	219	190	198	169	95	188	210
Central African Republic	32	38	35	34	33	35	37	29	37	36	18	22	34	32
Chad	5	27	23	32	23	25	23	16	19	18	13	10	22	21
Comoros	40	84	76	71	69	51	62	37	44	44	30	45	69	51
Congo, Democratic Rep. of	12	12	12	17	9	4	2	2	3	2	2	8	10	5
Congo, Republic of	33	37	38	91	51	43	48	102	41	150	96	30	43	78
Côte d'Ivoire	19	21	23	46	36	43	56	62	54	32	16	13	18	43
Djibouti	114	152	130	171	156	167	166	161	132	114	98	125	138	146
Equatorial Guinea	5	72	102	124	98	97	73	42	54	57	42	9	66	73
Eritrea	0	0	0	0	0	0	14	27	26	34	21	0	0	15
Ethiopia	2	12	8	10	9	8	8	10	9	8	6	2	9	9
Gabon	71	110	130	132	142	64	93	151	124	101	26	61	91	104
Gambia, The	26	65	64	62	57	50	48	36	23	15	15	25	62	38
Ghana	10	17	24	18	29	21	19	20	21	20	16	7	14	21
Guinea	7	29	34	24	29	38	29	29	33	20	18	4	23	28
Guinea-Bissau	43	55	69	77	63	56	55	117	71	112	51	37	50	75
Kenya	17	28	27	31	25	21	17	15	17	12	11	15	22	19
Lesotho	47	43	44	50	42	38	40	24	32	25	22	32	39	34
Liberia	32	21	16	17	23	10	9	13	11	40	11	27	24	17
Madagascar	10	19	16	23	23	18	18	15	15	17	39	8	16	21
Malawi	12	23	22	25	24	23	17	26	23	26	17	10	17	23
Mali	20	33	37	37	32	27	24	26	29	30	25	16	32	29
Mauritania	35	60	82	53	53	54	89	57	54	41	39	29	62	55
Mauritius	26	43	50	72	58	32	24	7	9	-1	2	24	42	25
Mozambique	9	52	41	53	53	69	54	48	44	34	37	8	34	49
Namibia	0	13	28	29	69	69	84	75	93	86	76	0	12	73
Niger	19	33	27	33	33	32	30	30	21	17	18	18	30	27
Nigeria	0	1	3	2	2	1	1	0	1	0	0	0	1	1
Rwanda	19	21	19	26	33	26	27	78	53	37	23	16	20	38
São Tomé and Principe	14	80	198	270	204	214	226	205	466	213	153	22	84	244
Senegal	33	53	75	80	56	59	46	59	48	46	33	28	52	53
Seychelles	284	258	217	468	237	215	94	98	145	102	81	213	247	180
Sierra Leone	18	14	18	10	17	18	25	12	13	14	9	8	13	15
Somalia	24	45	37	35	14	59	81	52	15	5	5	16	44	33
South Africa	0	0	0	0	0	0	5	6	8	8	10	0	0	5
Sudan	15	22	18	17	15	7	6	7	5	4	3	11	22	8
Swaziland	58	31	16	47	39	33	39	31	42	22	17	39	31	34
Tanzania	28	33	28	33	29	30	23	20	20	20	18	21	26	24
Togo	20	39	32	44	34	36	20	16	29	23	17	18	29	27
Uganda	3	12	10	15	17	15	19	19	22	19	22	2	7	18
Zambia	41	56	42	53	73	85	60	50	49	38	39	27	46	56
Zimbabwe	16	25	24	30	36	52	29	26	32	25	19	11	25	31
NORTH AFRICA	19	20	19	37	46	37	22	25	19	20	15	16	21	28
Algeria	6	5	4	9	12	14	10	14	10	9	7	6	5	11
Egypt, Arab Republic	29	29	27	60	78	55	33	40	29	33	25	23	31	44
Libya	3	0	2	2	1	0	0	0	1	0	0	1	1	1
Morocco	10	18	17	25	25	29	17	12	13	15	8	10	16	18
Tunisia	25	30	23	26	32	35	15	8	6	5	8	25	23	17
ALL AFRICA	13	19	18	24	24	23	19	19	17	16	14	10	17	20

12-17. Net ODA per capita from multilateral donors

	U.S. dollars (current prices)											Annual average		
	1980	*1988*	*1989*	*1990*	*1991*	*1992*	*1993*	*1994*	*1995*	*1996*	*1997*	*75-84*	*85-89*	*90-MR*
SUB-SAHARAN AFRICA	6	10	11	12	13	14	12	14	14	11	10	5	9	12
excluding South Africa	7	10	12	13	14	15	13	15	15	12	10	5	9	13
excl. S.Africa & Nigeria	8	13	15	16	17	18	16	18	18	14	13	6	12	16
Angola	2	6	6	11	12	16	14	21	16	22	18	3	5	16
Benin	15	14	25	30	23	20	27	21	18	22	13	10	16	22
Botswana	25	21	34	23	23	17	33	22	26	10	47	19	27	25
Burkina Faso	9	9	8	10	16	18	23	18	23	14	13	7	9	17
Burundi	13	22	21	20	25	29	16	34	30	22	14	10	19	24
Cameroon	8	4	14	10	12	11	1	26	7	10	10	6	5	11
Cape Verde	81	79	80	100	76	120	99	107	105	102	105	46	84	102
Central African Republic	15	34	32	51	25	23	18	23	14	13	10	12	25	22
Chad	3	21	22	23	21	15	13	17	17	26	17	7	18	19
Comoros	40	42	30	36	77	56	45	46	44	36	25	45	50	46
Congo, Democratic Rep. of	4	4	8	5	3	3	2	3	2	1	1	3	6	3
Congo, Republic of	13	4	5	7	7	5	3	44	8	13	3	14	7	11
Côte d'Ivoire	7	18	12	14	17	19	4	59	36	37	15	4	7	25
Djibouti	31	39	21	35	42	40	53	40	39	35	31	27	44	40
Equatorial Guinea	37	68	60	52	60	71	67	36	31	19	21	17	50	45
Eritrea	0	0	0	0	0	0	6	14	14	8	8	0	0	6
Ethiopia	3	8	8	9	12	13	13	9	6	7	4	3	7	9
Gabon	10	10	13	6	3	4	4	19	9	13	10	8	10	9
Gambia, The	48	39	52	46	47	65	37	32	22	21	27	26	48	37
Ghana	6	23	25	20	28	18	19	13	18	18	17	5	19	19
Guinea	13	15	28	26	35	36	37	27	29	21	29	8	17	30
Guinea-Bissau	30	48	51	56	53	45	37	49	36	48	54	23	45	47
Kenya	7	10	19	19	13	15	19	11	10	9	8	4	8	13
Lesotho	23	25	38	34	30	41	37	37	28	28	23	20	27	32
Liberia	15	7	8	29	41	37	38	11	34	34	22	11	10	31
Madagascar	10	8	16	11	15	12	11	8	8	10	20	7	12	12
Malawi	11	24	31	34	36	41	37	23	22	24	18	8	18	29
Mali	16	21	18	19	20	22	16	22	28	22	18	11	17	21
Mauritania	23	39	48	54	52	43	63	67	52	78	62	32	38	59
Mauritius	8	9	9	12	7	11	-1	7	13	20	25	12	7	12
Mozambique	3	13	17	18	21	31	24	32	25	23	19	3	10	24
Namibia	0	4	17	62	64	32	22	17	29	33	26	0	6	36
Niger	11	18	14	18	14	13	11	13	9	10	13	9	17	13
Nigeria	0	0	0	1	1	1	2	1	1	1	1	0	0	1
Rwanda	11	16	14	14	18	23	20	36	58	63	53	9	14	36
São Tomé and Principe	30	148	204	208	233	254	148	185	172	134	91	50	125	178
Senegal	14	30	23	32	26	27	16	21	31	21	14	14	28	23
Seychelles	53	36	69	48	87	58	164	78	34	107	77	25	79	82
Sierra Leone	9	10	7	6	9	15	24	51	32	27	17	7	8	23
Somalia	28	17	22	18	9	17	23	12	9	6	6	19	23	13
South Africa	0	0	0	0	0	0	2	2	2	1	2	0	0	1
Sudan	10	14	13	17	20	14	11	9	4	4	4	8	13	10
Swaziland	31	20	22	25	29	33	23	33	20	11	11	21	17	23
Tanzania	7	10	9	13	12	20	11	14	10	10	11	6	8	12
Togo	15	24	27	30	22	24	5	16	18	17	11	13	20	18
Uganda	5	14	17	24	20	26	15	21	21	15	19	4	12	20
Zambia	11	10	8	9	37	41	43	33	178	28	25	6	12	49
Zimbabwe	7	5	4	4	4	25	18	26	13	9	9	3	4	14
NORTH AFRICA	4	2	3	3	6	4	5	5	3	5	6	5	2	5
Algeria	1	1	2	1	1	1	3	2	1	1	1	1	1	1
Egypt, Arab Republic	5	2	3	2	7	4	4	5	4	4	7	9	2	4
Libya	2	1	2	3	5	1	1	1	1	2	1	2	1	2
Morocco	3	1	2	4	6	6	11	11	5	9	8	2	1	7
Tunisia	4	10	8	10	11	12	13	6	5	14	16	4	7	11
ALL AFRICA	6	8	9	10	11	12	11	12	12	10	9	5	7	11

Figure 12-1. Total net ODA as a share of recipient GDP, 1997*

(percent)

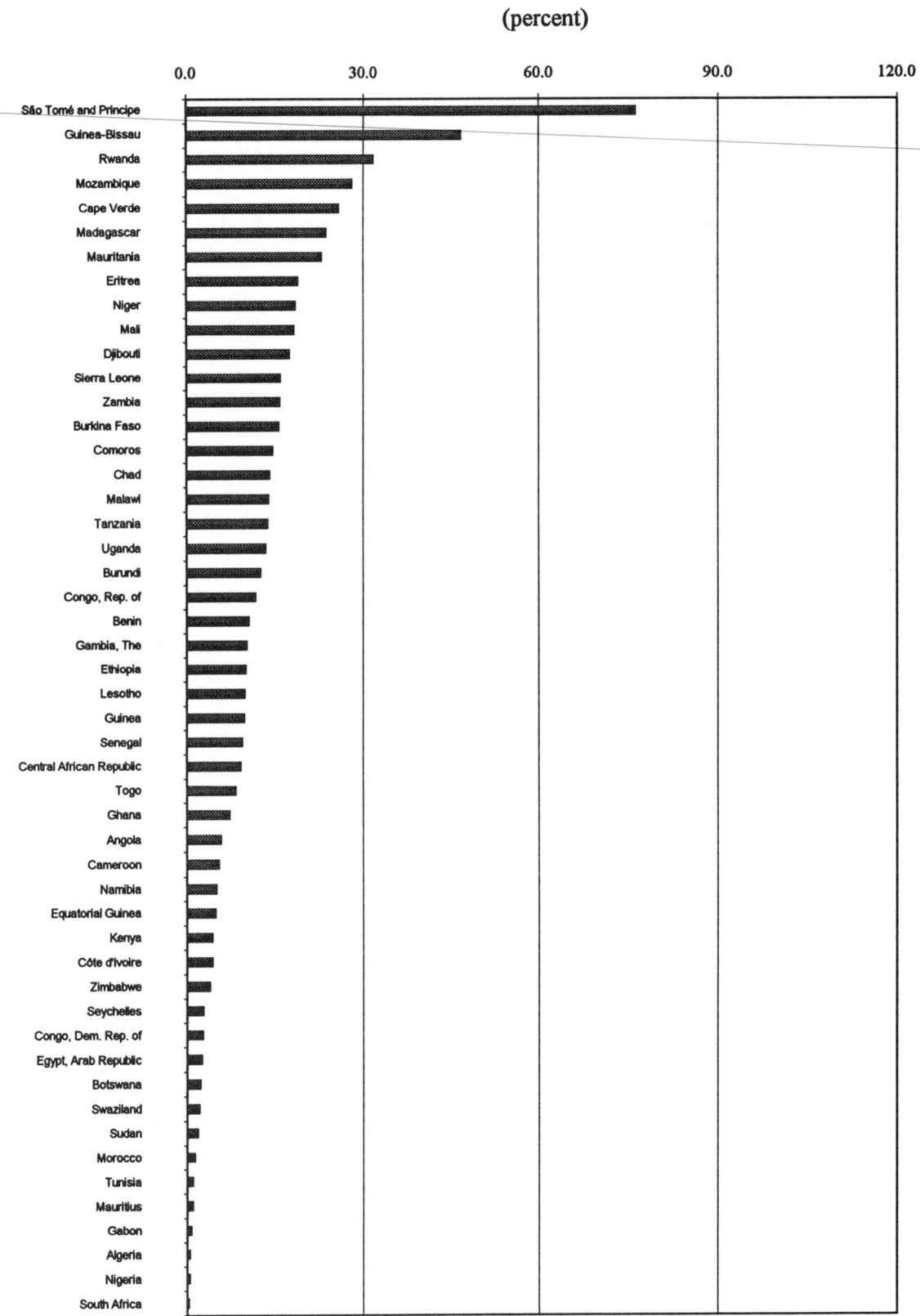

* Or most recent year available.

Note: Nigeria's ratio is distorted because of official exchange rate over-valuation affecting oil exports and oil value added.

Figure 12-2. Total net ODA per capita, 1997

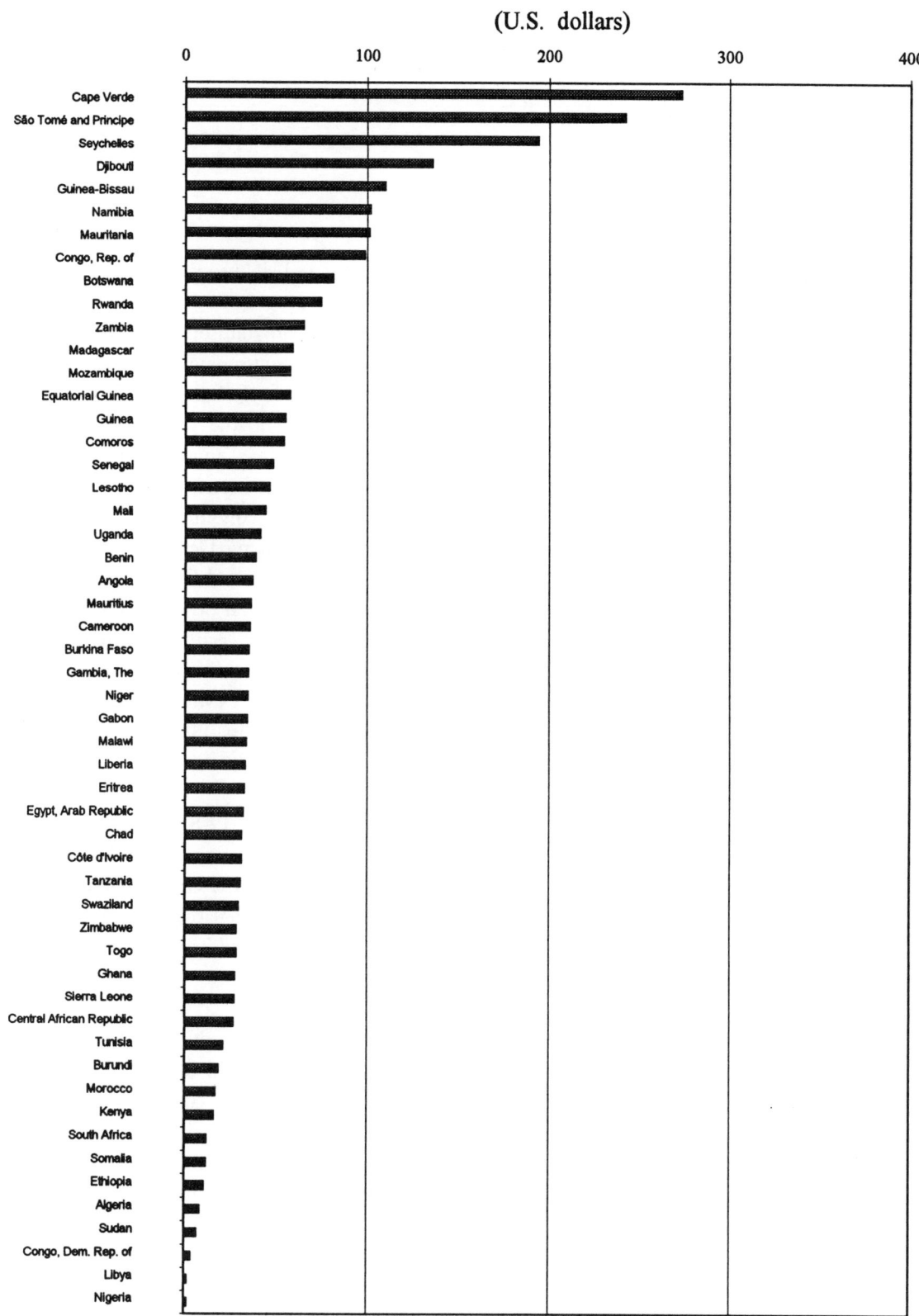

Technical Notes

Tables

Table 12-1. Net ODA from all donors, nominal. This table represents the total of Tables 12-2 through 12-4.

Table 12-2. Net ODA from DAC donors, nominal. This table (OECD data) includes net ODA from Australia, Austria, Belgium, Canada, Denmark, Finland, France, the Federal Republic of Germany before reunification, Italy, Japan, the Netherlands, Norway, Sweden, Switzerland, the United Kingdom, and the United States (OECD data). (Ireland and New Zealand have been excluded in compilation because their ODA to Africa is negligible.)

Table 12-3. Net ODA from non-DAC bilateral donors, nominal. This is net ODA from Organization of Petroleum Exporting Countries (OPEC), the former Council for Mutual Economic Assistance (CMEA) countries, and China (OECD data). OPEC countries are Algeria, Iran, Iraq, Kuwait, Libya, Nigeria, Qatar, Saudi Arabia, the United Arab Emirates, and Venezuela. The former CMEA countries are Bulgaria, Czechoslovakia, the former German Democratic Republic, Hungary, Poland, Romania, and the former Soviet Union.

Table 12-4. Net ODA from multilateral donors, nominal. This includes net ODA (OECD data), most notably from the African Development Fund, the European Development Fund for the Commission of the European Communities, the International Development Association (IDA), the International Fund for Agricultural Development, Arab/OPEC-financed multilateral agencies, and UN programs and agencies (OECD data). The UN programs and agencies include mainly the UN regular program of Technical Assistance, the UN Development Programme (UNDP), the UN High Commissioner for Refugees, the UN Children's Fund (UNICEF), and the World Food Programme. Arab/OPEC-financed multilateral agencies include the Arab Bank for Economic Development in Africa, the Arab Fund for Economic and Social Development (AFESD), the Islamic Development Bank, the OPEC Fund for International Development, the Arab Authority for Agricultural Investment and Development, the Arab Fund for Technical Assistance to African and Arab Countries, and the Islamic Solidarity Fund. ODA flows from the IMF Trust Fund and Structural Adjustment Facility (SAF) are also included.

Tables 12-5, 12-6, 12-7, and 12-8. Net ODA from all donors, from DAC donors, from non-DAC bilateral donors, and from multilateral donors, real. These tables are obtained by deflating data in Tables 12-1 through 12-4 by the World Bank LIMIC import price deflator.

Tables 12-9, 12-10, and 12-11. Net ODA from all donors, from DAC donors, and from multilateral donors as a share of recipient's GDP. These tables show the relative importance of these aid flows to recipients' economies. They are obtained by dividing figures in Tables 12-1, 12-2, and 12-4 by GDP data from Table 2-5, which reflect current prices and exchange rates. For a given level of aid flows, devaluation of a recipient's currency may inflate the ratios shown in the table. Thus, trends for a given country and comparisons across countries that have implemented different exchange rate policies should be interpreted carefully.

Tables 12-12, 12-13, and 12-14. Net ODA from all donors, from DAC donors, and from multilateral donors as a share of recipient GDI. These tables are obtained by dividing figures in Tables 12-1, 12-2, and 12-4 by GDI (World Bank country desks). These tables highlight the relative importance of the indicated aid flows in maintaining and increasing investment in these economies. The same caveats mentioned above apply to their interpretation. Furthermore, aid flows do not exclusively finance investment (for example, food aid finances consumption), and the share of ODA going to investment varies across countries.

Tables 12-15, 12-16, and 12-17. Net ODA per capita from all donors, from DAC donors, and from multi- lateral donors. These tables are calculated by dividing figures in Tables 12-1, 12-2, and 12-4 by midyear population (Table 1-2). These ratios offer some indication of the importance of aid flows in sustaining per capita income and consumption levels (shown in Tables 2-19 and 2-20, respectively), although comparisons must be done carefully because exchange rate fluctuations, the actual rise of ODA flows, and other factors vary across countries and over time.

Figures

The following indicators have been used to derive the figures in this chapter.

Figure 12-1. Total net ODA as a share of recipient's GDP (Table 12-9).

Figure 12-2. Total net ODA per capita (Table 12-15).

Methodology used for regional aggregations and period averages in chapter 12

Table	Aggregations[a]		Period averages[b]	
	(1)	*(2)*	*(1)*	*(2)*
12-1	x		x	
12-2	x		x	
12-3	x		x	
12-4	x		x	
12-5	x			x
12-6	x			x
12-7	x			x
12-8	x			x
12-9		x	x	
12-10		x	x	
12-11		x	x	
12-12		x	x	
12-13		x	x	
12-14		x	x	
12-15		x	x	
12-16		x	x	
12-17		x	x	

Note: Regional aggregations are shown in the rows for Sub-Saharan Africa, North Africa, and All Africa. Period averages are shown in the last three columns. This table shows only the methodologies used in this chapter.

a. Regional aggregations: (1) simple total; (2) simple total of the first indicator divided by the simple total of the second indicator (same country coverage); (3) simple total of the gap-filled indicator; (4) simple total of the gap-filled main indicator divided by the simple total of the gap-filled secondary indicator; (5) simple total of the first gap-filled main indicator less the simple total of the second gap-filled main indicator, all divided by the simple total of the secondary indicator; (6) weighted total; (7) median; (8) no aggregation; (9) simple arithmetic mean.

b. Period averages: (1) arithmetic mean (using the same series as shown in the table, i.e., ratio if the rest of the table is shown as ratio, level if the rest of the table is shown as level, growth rate if the rest of the table is shown as growth rate); (2) least-squares growth rate (using main indicator); (3) least-squares growth rate (using main indicator in constant terms, with the rest of the table in current terms).

13

Social Indicators

This chapter provides indicators in the areas of demography, health, education, and gender issues in development. These indicators can be useful in evaluating and monitoring the social impact of development progress, aid flows, and structural adjustment policies.

The chapter presents such indicators as dependency ratio, urbanization, crude death rate, life expectancy at birth, infant mortality rate, child mortality rate, immunization rates for children, maternal death rate, and number of population per physician. These indicators are an indirect measure of the physical well-being of the population. In the same vein, such indicators as literacy rate among adults, school enrollment ratios by gender, and pupil-teacher ratio give some picture of the progress being made in education and training. Social indicators refer to phenomena that are inherently more qualitative than macroeconomic variables and thus need to be interpreted cautiously. Further caution is called for because of the particular limitations of the data. One of these limitations is the paucity—or even nonexistence—of data on certain indicators in many of the countries covered. This is especially true of indicators dealing with gender issues. Many countries have no data showing the gender breakdown of several social indicators.

Even when data are available, comparison among countries is limited due to varied practices in data gathering and reporting. Often the countries report survey data that cover different portions of the nation. Sometimes surveys are limited to just the urban areas to cover only the largest cities or the capital city alone. This is especially true of the health indicators. Such indicators as immunization rates for children under one year of age, percentage of births attended by health personnel, infant mortality rate, child mortality rate, and maternal death rate are often based on surveys of a handful of hospitals in the urban areas.

Another source of limitation is the definition of terms, which may differ from country to country. Some countries, for example, consider an institution as a "private school" only if it receives no form of financial support from the government, while others classify as "private" all schools not run by the government, whether or not they receive financial support from the government. In like manner, some countries include personnel other than doctors and trained nurses in the term "medical personnel."

Cultural norms may also affect the reported data. This is especially true for gender issues. In some countries, it is assumed that no woman can be the head of any household that also contains an adult male. In population censuses, therefore, enumerators and respondents simply take such assumptions for granted, reporting a male rather than a female as head of the household or family (see United Nations, *The World's Women, 1970–90*). This distorts the true picture of the percentage of households headed by women.

The main source for this chapter is the *World Development Indicators* in the World Bank Statistical Information Management Analysis Database (SIMA), which contains electronic information as reported by a number of institutions and agencies in the socioeconomic field, such as the United Nations, UNICEF, UNESCO, World Health Organization (WHO), the UNDP, and the ECA. Other sources of data also include reports and publications on children, health, human development, education, and population from various agencies including the World Bank.

In this chapter, columns headed by a period (for example, 1992–97) show data for the latest available year within the period.

13-1. Age and gender structure of the population

	Females as percentage of total population		Age groups as percentage of total population						Age dependency ratio	
			1980			1997				
	1980	1996	0-14	15-64	65+	0-14	15-64	65+	1980	1997
SUB-SAHARAN AFRICA	50.2	50.5	45.1	51.3	2.9	44.5	52.3	2.9	0.9	0.9
excluding South Africa	50.2	50.4	45.6	50.9	2.8	45.3	51.6	2.8	0.9	0.9
excl. S.Africa & Nigeria	50.1	50.3	45.4	50.8	2.9	45.4	51.4	2.8	1.0	0.9
Angola	50.9	50.6	44.6	52.4	3.0	47.5	49.4	2.9	0.9	1.0
Benin	50.7	50.7	45.1	50.8	4.1	46.9	50.0	2.9	1.0	1.0
Botswana	52.2	51.1	48.7	49.8	2.0	42.7	53.9	2.3	1.0	0.8
Burkina Faso	50.5	50.6	47.4	49.8	2.8	47.0	50.3	2.8	1.0	1.0
Burundi	51.9	51.0	44.7	51.8	3.5	46.0	51.5	2.7	0.9	0.9
Cameroon	50.6	50.4	44.3	52.0	3.6	44.1	52.4	3.5	0.9	0.9
Cape Verde	54.0	53.4	45.5	47.2	6.2	41.3	55.5	4.4	1.1	0.8
Central African Republic	..	51.5	41.7	54.4	4.0	42.8	53.2	3.7	0.8	0.9
Chad	50.8	50.5	41.9	54.5	3.6	50.4	45.2	3.1	0.8	1.2
Comoros	49.9	50.2	48.2	49.2	2.6	45.5	51.6	2.7	1.0	0.9
Congo, Democratic Rep. of	51.1	50.6	46.0	51.1	2.8	47.4	49.9	2.8	1.0	1.0
Congo, Republic of	51.2	51.2	45.0	51.5	3.4	46.0	50.7	3.2	0.9	1.0
Côte d'Ivoire	48.9	49.0	46.6	51.0	2.5	43.8	52.4	2.7	1.0	0.9
Djibouti	50.5	50.7	44.1	54.1	2.5	40.6	56.1	3.2	..	0.8
Equatorial Guinea	51.2	51.2	40.6	53.9	4.1	43.1	53.6	4.0	0.8	0.9
Eritrea	50.4	50.4	..	..	..	44.8	52.6	2.7	..	0.9
Ethiopia	50.6	49.8	44.6	52.5	2.9	46.0	50.9	2.7	1.0	1.0
Gabon	50.9	50.7	34.1	59.5	6.4	38.9	55.1	5.8	0.7	0.8
Gambia, The	50.7	50.6	42.6	54.4	3.0	41.7	54.9	2.9	0.8	0.8
Ghana	50.4	50.3	45.0	52.2	2.8	44.1	52.8	3.1	0.9	0.9
Guinea	50.1	49.7	45.8	51.6	2.6	45.6	51.6	2.6	0.9	0.9
Guinea-Bissau	50.9	50.8	39.0	57.2	4.0	42.6	52.9	4.0	0.8	0.9
Kenya	50.0	49.9	50.1	46.5	3.4	44.9	51.9	2.9	1.1	0.9
Lesotho	51.8	50.9	41.9	53.9	4.2	40.3	55.9	4.1	0.9	0.8
Liberia	49.5	49.6	44.3	52.0	3.6	45.1	52.5	2.7	0.9	0.9
Madagascar	50.7	50.2	44.4	51.7	4.0	45.4	51.6	3.0	0.9	0.9
Malawi	51.6	50.7	47.5	50.3	2.3	46.3	51.0	2.5	1.0	1.0
Mali	51.2	50.7	46.8	50.7	2.6	47.1	49.6	3.3	1.0	1.0
Mauritania	50.7	50.5	43.7	53.1	3.0	44.0	52.9	3.1	0.9	0.9
Mauritius	50.7	50.0	35.7	60.9	3.7	26.2	67.0	6.0	0.6	0.5
Mozambique	50.8	51.6	43.4	53.4	3.1	45.0	50.1	4.0	0.9	1.0
Namibia	50.6	50.2	43.2	53.4	3.7	41.9	54.2	3.7	0.9	0.8
Niger	50.8	50.6	46.8	50.8	2.5	48.6	48.9	2.4	1.0	1.0
Nigeria	50.6	50.8	46.1	51.2	2.6	44.7	52.7	2.5	0.9	0.9
Rwanda	50.6	50.6	48.7	48.8	2.4	41.5	47.4	1.9	1.0	0.9
São Tomé and Principe	..	50.0	..	..	..	38.3	54.8	6.3	..	0.8
Senegal	50.0	50.1	45.3	51.8	2.8	45.1	52.3	2.6	0.9	0.9
Seychelles	..	48.7	..	..	..	30.9	63.5	6.9	..	0.6
Sierra Leone	51.0	51.0	43.0	53.9	3.1	45.6	51.1	2.6	0.9	0.9
Somalia	50.6	50.4	46.7	50.3	2.9	47.7	49.8	2.5	1.0	1.0
South Africa	50.2	52.0	39.5	57.2	3.4	33.8	61.1	4.8	0.8	0.6
Sudan	49.9	49.8	44.9	52.4	2.7	40.2	56.9	3.1	0.9	0.8
Swaziland	50.9	52.2	45.9	51.3	2.9	42.6	54.5	2.6	1.0	0.8
Tanzania	50.8	50.5	47.6	50.1	2.3	45.7	51.4	2.5	1.0	0.9
Togo	50.7	50.5	44.6	52.4	3.2	45.7	50.8	3.0	0.9	1.0
Uganda	50.5	50.3	47.8	49.7	2.5	48.7	48.9	2.2	1.0	1.0
Zambia	51.1	50.4	49.4	48.2	2.4	46.1	51.3	2.2	1.1	0.9
Zimbabwe	50.4	50.4	47.9	49.5	2.6	42.2	54.8	2.8	1.0	0.8
NORTH AFRICA	49.5	49.3	42.2	53.9	3.9	36.2	59.5	4.2	0.9	0.7
Algeria	50.4	49.4	46.5	49.6	3.9	37.9	58.3	3.7	1.0	0.7
Egypt, Arab Republic	49.2	49.1	39.5	56.5	4.0	36.5	58.9	4.4	0.8	0.7
Libya	47.1	48.0	46.6	51.2	2.2	40.0	57.2	2.9	1.0	0.8
Morocco	49.9	50.0	43.2	52.7	4.1	34.1	61.8	4.3	0.9	0.6
Tunisia	49.3	49.5	41.6	54.6	3.8	32.8	61.7	5.6	0.8	0.6
ALL AFRICA	50.1	50.2	44.6	51.8	3.1	43.0	53.6	3.1	0.9	0.9

Note: Some age groups may not add up to 100 due to rounding up error.

13-2. Poverty

	GDP per capita, based on PPP, 1997	Percentage of population living under US$ 1 a day, 1984-1997	National poverty headcount as % of population, 1984-1997	% of the population below 2/3 of national mean per capita income, 1991-97		Gini coefficients, 1991-96		Percentage of household income spent on food, 1991-97
				Urban	Rural	Urban	Rural	
SUB-SAHARAN AFRICA	1566	..	..	22	37	..	..	64
excluding South Africa	1137	..	..	22	37	..	..	64
excl. S. Africa & Nigeria	1186	..	..	22	37	..	..	64
Angola	1461	..	..	..	..	..	..	..
Benin	1287	..	33	..	..	..	..	..
Botswana	8393	33	..	..	..	..	..	..
Burkina Faso	1016	..	..	13	65	38	46	57
Burundi	637	..	36	..	..	..	..	..
Cameroon	1927	..	40	..	..	..	..	55
Cape Verde	3032	..	..	..	..	..	..	..
Central African Republic	1307	..	..	33	77	51	63	60
Chad	978	..	64	..	..	..	..	..
Comoros	1548	..	..	..	..	..	..	..
Congo, Democratic Rep. of	866	..	..	..	..	..	..	..
Congo, Republic of	1658	..	..	..	..	..	..	..
Côte d'Ivoire	1861	18	..	29	51	39	33	48
Djibouti	..	..	..	38	84	38	39	43
Equatorial Guinea	3395	..	..	..	..	..	..	..
Eritrea	828	..	..	..	..	..	..	..
Ethiopia	544	..	..	21	50	56	40	72
Gabon	7751	..	..	..	..	..	..	..
Gambia, The	1486	..	64	21	73	43	35	60
Ghana	1662	..	31	22	37	34	36	39
Guinea	1833	26	..	18	57	..	..	56
Guinea-Bissau	1170	88	49	30	65	55	56	..
Kenya	1199	50	42	14	53	51	52	71
Lesotho	1976	49	49	..	..	..	..	..
Liberia	..	..	..	..	..	..	..	..
Madagascar	935	72	..	21	57	..	..	70
Malawi	707	..	54	..	..	..	57	..
Mali	750	..	..	8	64	53	55	75
Mauritania	1752	31	57	18	56	34	33	70
Mauritius	9424	..	11	..	..	..	..	..
Mozambique	877	..	..	..	..	..	..	..
Namibia	5087	..	..	..	..	..	..	..
Niger	851	62	63	14	55	39	31	60
Nigeria	954	31	34	32	52	44	46	67
Rwanda	666	46	51	..	..	..	..	..
São Tomé and Principe	1559	..	..	..	..	..	..	..
Senegal	1753	54	33	14	66	..	..	61
Seychelles	11306	..	..	..	..	..	..	..
Sierra Leone	415	..	68	..	..	..	..	..
Somalia	..	..	..	..	..	..	..	..
South Africa	7466	24	..	40	86	..	..	56
Sudan	1628	..	..	..	..	..	..	..
Swaziland	3427	..	..	36	70	..	..	65
Tanzania	522	11	51	20	51	..	..	70
Togo	1502	..	32	..	..	..	..	..
Uganda	1174	69	55	16	46	35	44	63
Zambia	976	85	68	28	70	40	46	64
Zimbabwe	2385	41	26	..	..	..	..	..
NORTH AFRICA	3644	..	..	..	..	..	..	..
Algeria	4517	2	23	..	..	..	..	..
Egypt, Arab Republic	3084	8	..	..	..	..	..	..
Libya	..	..	..	..	..	..	..	..
Morocco	3358	1	13	..	..	..	..	..
Tunisia	5379	4	14	..	..	..	..	..
ALL AFRICA	1927	..	..	22	37	..	..	64

13-3. Income distribution

	Share of income held by population groups			
	Richest 10%	Richest 20%	Poorest 10%	Poorest 20%
	1986-96	1986-96	1986-96	1986-96
SUB-SAHARAN AFRICA	..	..	..	..
excluding South Africa	..	..	..	..
excl. S. Africa & Nigeria	..	..	..	..
Angola	..	..	..	..
Benin	..	..	..	..
Botswana	42.9	58.9	..	3.6
Burkina Faso	39.5	55.0	2.2	5.5
Burundi	..	..	..	..
Cameroon	..	..	..	..
Cape Verde	..	..	..	..
Central African Republic	..	..	..	..
Chad	..	..	..	..
Comoros	..	..	..	..
Congo, Democratic Rep. of	..	..	..	..
Congo, Republic of	..	..	..	..
Côte d'Ivoire	28.5	44.1	2.8	6.8
Djibouti	..	..	..	..
Equatorial Guinea	..	..	..	..
Eritrea	..	..	..	..
Ethiopia	33.7	47.7	3.0	7.1
Gabon	..	..	..	..
Gambia, The	37.6	52.8	1.5	4.4
Ghana	27.3	42.2	3.4	7.9
Guinea	32.0	47.2	2.6	6.4
Guinea-Bissau	42.3	58.9	0.5	2.1
Kenya	34.9	50.2	1.8	5.0
Lesotho	43.4	60.1	0.9	2.8
Liberia	..	..	..	..
Madagascar	36.7	52.1	1.9	5.1
Malawi	..	..	..	..
Mali	40.4	56.2	1.8	4.6
Mauritania	29.9	45.6	2.3	6.2
Mauritius	..	..	..	..
Mozambique	..	..	..	..
Namibia	..	..	..	..
Niger	35.4	53.3	0.8	2.6
Nigeria	31.3	49.3	1.3	4.0
Rwanda	..	..	..	..
São Tomé and Principe	..	..	..	..
Senegal	42.3	57.9	1.0	3.1
Seychelles	..	..	..	..
Sierra Leone	43.6	63.4	0.5	1.1
Somalia	..	..	..	..
South Africa	45.9	64.8	1.1	2.9
Sudan	..	..	..	..
Swaziland	..	..	..	..
Tanzania	30.1	45.5	2.9	6.9
Togo	..	..	..	..
Uganda	31.2	46.1	2.6	6.6
Zambia	39.2	54.8	1.6	4.2
Zimbabwe	46.9	62.3	1.8	4.0
NORTH AFRICA	..	..	..	..
Algeria	26.8	42.6	2.8	7.0
Egypt, Arab Republic	26.7	41.1	3.9	8.7
Libya	..	..	..	..
Morocco	30.5	46.3	2.8	6.6
Tunisia	30.7	46.3	2.3	5.9
ALL AFRICA	..	..	..	..

13-4. Urbanization

	Total population (millions)			Average annual percentage growth of total population			Urban population as percentage of total population			Average annual percentage growth of urban population		
	1980	1989	1997	1975-79	1980-89	1989-97	1980	1989	1997	1975-79	1980-89	1989-97
SUB-SAHARAN AFRICA	380.7	493.7	612.3	2.8	2.9	2.7	23.0	27.5	32.3	4.9	4.8	4.7
excluding South Africa	353.2	459.2	571.7	2.9	2.9	2.7	21.0	26.0	31.1	5.4	5.2	5.0
excl. S. Africa & Nigeria	282.0	365.7	453.8	2.9	2.9	2.7	19.6	23.9	28.5	5.2	5.0	5.0
Angola	7.0	8.9	11.7	2.6	2.7	3.3	20.9	26.9	32.3	5.9	5.5	5.6
Benin	3.5	4.6	5.8	2.6	3.1	2.9	27.3	33.8	40.0	7.2	5.6	5.0
Botswana	0.9	1.2	1.5	3.5	3.5	2.7	15.1	38.2	65.4	8.5	13.5	9.8
Burkina Faso	7.0	8.7	10.5	2.2	2.5	2.4	8.5	13.2	16.9	7.8	7.4	5.5
Burundi	4.1	5.3	6.4	2.1	2.8	2.4	4.3	6.1	8.1	8.1	6.7	6.0
Cameroon	8.7	11.2	13.9	2.8	2.8	2.8	31.4	39.4	46.4	6.2	5.4	4.9
Cape Verde	0.3	0.3	0.4	0.7	1.6	2.2	23.5	42.0	57.5	2.6	7.8	6.3
Central African Republic	2.3	2.9	3.4	2.3	2.4	2.2	35.1	37.3	39.9	3.3	3.1	3.1
Chad	4.5	5.6	7.2	2.0	2.6	3.0	18.8	20.9	22.8	6.0	3.8	4.1
Comoros	0.3	0.4	0.5	..	2.5	2.6	23.2	27.4	31.5	..	4.4	4.3
Congo, Democratic Rep. of	27.0	36.2	46.7	2.9	3.2	3.2	28.7	27.9	29.3	2.4	2.9	3.8
Congo, Republic of	1.7	2.2	2.7	2.8	2.8	2.9	41.0	52.2	60.0	5.9	5.6	4.7
Côte d'Ivoire	8.2	11.3	14.2	3.9	3.6	3.0	34.8	39.8	44.6	5.7	5.1	4.4
Djibouti	0.3	0.5	0.6	6.3	6.3	3.3	73.6	79.7	82.6	7.8	7.3	3.8
Equatorial Guinea	0.2	0.3	0.4	-2.8	5.6	2.3	27.4	34.5	44.6	-2.5	8.0	5.6
Eritrea	2.4	3.0	3.8	2.6	2.7	2.7	13.5	15.6	17.7	4.6	4.3	4.3
Ethiopia	37.7	49.3	59.8	2.7	2.9	2.3	10.5	13.1	16.3	4.7	5.3	5.0
Gabon	0.7	0.9	1.2	3.1	3.3	2.7	34.0	43.5	52.1	6.2	6.1	5.0
Gambia, The	0.6	0.9	1.2	3.2	3.4	3.8	19.6	25.1	30.4	6.0	6.1	6.2
Ghana	10.7	14.4	18.0	1.7	3.3	2.8	31.2	33.6	36.9	2.4	4.1	3.9
Guinea	4.5	5.6	6.9	1.3	2.4	2.7	19.1	25.0	30.6	4.5	5.5	5.3
Guinea-Bissau	0.8	1.0	1.1	5.0	2.1	2.2	16.9	19.7	22.5	6.2	3.8	3.8
Kenya	16.6	22.8	28.6	3.7	3.5	2.9	16.1	23.2	30.4	8.2	7.6	6.3
Lesotho	1.3	1.7	2.0	2.5	2.5	2.3	13.4	19.4	25.6	6.9	6.6	5.8
Liberia	1.9	2.4	2.9	3.0	2.8	2.3	35.0	41.5	46.2	6.0	4.8	3.6
Madagascar	8.9	11.3	14.1	2.5	2.7	2.8	18.3	23.0	27.6	5.1	5.2	5.1
Malawi	6.2	8.2	10.3	3.3	3.1	2.8	9.1	11.5	14.3	6.9	5.8	5.5
Mali	6.6	8.2	10.3	2.2	2.4	2.8	18.5	23.2	28.1	4.8	5.0	5.2
Mauritania	1.6	2.0	2.5	2.4	2.6	2.8	27.4	41.8	53.8	8.7	7.4	6.0
Mauritius	1.0	1.0	1.1	1.6	0.9	1.1	42.4	40.7	40.8	1.3	0.5	1.1
Mozambique	12.1	14.0	16.6	2.8	1.8	2.0	13.1	25.2	36.4	11.4	9.1	6.8
Namibia	1.0	1.3	1.6	2.7	2.7	2.7	22.8	30.1	38.0	4.7	5.7	5.6
Niger	5.6	7.5	9.8	3.1	3.3	3.3	12.6	15.7	19.2	6.7	5.8	5.8
Nigeria	71.1	93.5	117.9	3.0	3.1	2.9	26.9	34.1	41.3	5.8	5.7	5.3
Rwanda	5.2	6.8	7.9	3.3	3.1	0.4	4.7	5.2	5.9	6.7	4.4	1.9
São Tomé and Principe	0.1	0.1	0.1	1.2	2.4	2.7	30.7	38.1	44.4	3.9	4.9	4.7
Senegal	5.5	7.1	8.8	2.8	2.8	2.6	35.9	39.9	45.0	3.7	4.0	4.1
Seychelles	0.1	0.1	0.1	1.7	0.8	1.4	40.0	48.8	56.0	5.5	3.1	3.1
Sierra Leone	3.2	3.9	4.7	2.0	2.1	2.4	24.1	29.4	34.6	4.6	4.3	4.5
Somalia	5.9	7.3	8.8	7.2	2.3	2.1	22.2	24.0	26.4	8.0	3.1	3.3
South Africa	27.6	34.5	40.6	2.1	2.5	2.1	48.1	48.7	49.7	2.2	2.6	2.3
Sudan	18.7	23.6	27.7	3.1	2.6	2.0	20.0	25.8	33.2	4.5	5.3	5.3
Swaziland	0.6	0.7	1.0	3.2	3.1	3.1	17.8	25.5	32.9	8.3	7.1	6.4
Tanzania	18.6	24.7	31.3	3.1	3.2	3.0	14.8	20.2	25.6	11.0	6.7	6.0
Togo	2.6	3.4	4.3	2.6	2.9	3.1	22.9	28.1	31.7	9.3	5.5	4.6
Uganda	12.8	15.8	20.3	2.7	2.2	3.2	8.8	10.9	13.2	3.8	4.6	5.5
Zambia	5.7	7.5	9.4	3.4	3.1	2.8	39.8	41.8	43.6	6.1	3.7	3.4
Zimbabwe	7.0	9.5	11.5	2.8	3.4	2.5	22.3	27.8	33.2	5.5	5.8	4.7
NORTH AFRICA	88.4	111.5	131.4	2.5	2.6	2.1	44.6	48.6	52.4	3.5	3.6	3.0
Algeria	18.7	24.4	29.3	3.1	3.0	2.3	43.4	50.9	57.1	4.4	4.8	3.8
Egypt, Arab Republic	40.9	51.3	60.3	2.3	2.5	2.1	43.8	43.9	45.1	2.5	2.6	2.4
Libya	3.0	4.3	5.2	4.3	4.0	2.4	69.3	80.8	86.2	7.4	5.7	3.3
Morocco	19.4	23.6	27.3	2.3	2.2	1.9	41.1	47.5	53.2	4.0	3.8	3.3
Tunisia	6.4	8.0	9.2	2.5	2.6	1.8	51.5	57.1	63.3	3.3	3.6	3.1
ALL AFRICA	469.1	605.2	743.7	2.8	2.8	2.6	27.1	31.4	35.9	4.4	4.5	4.3

Note: Minus sign indicates population outflow.

13-5. Components of population change

	Total fertility rate			Crude birth rate			Crude death rate		
	1982	*1992*	*1997*	*1982*	*1992*	*1997*	*1982*	*1992*	*1997*
SUB-SAHARAN AFRICA	..	5.9	5.5	46.5	43.0	40.8	17.0	15.4	14.8
excluding South Africa	..	6.1	5.7	47.4	43.9	41.9	17.4	15.9	15.3
excl. S. Africa & Nigeria	..	6.1	5.8	46.8	44.1	42.3	17.5	16.3	16.1
Angola	7.0	7.2	6.8	50.8	50.8	48.4	22.8	19.2	18.8
Benin	7.0	6.3	5.8	49.3	43.9	42.8	18.1	15.3	13.2
Botswana	6.0	4.9	4.4	44.1	36.8	33.9	·9.5	8.0	15.4
Burkina Faso	7.5	6.9	6.6	46.9	47.3	44.8	19.9	18.3	19.1
Burundi	6.8	6.8	6.3	46.2	46.2	42.8	17.9	21.5	20.3
Cameroon	6.4	5.7	5.3	43.9	40.6	39.2	15.7	12.8	11.2
Cape Verde	6.3	3.9	3.6	38.4	33.9	32.4	11.3	7.6	6.9
Central African Republic	5.7	5.3	4.9	42.4	39.6	36.9	18.6	17.4	19.1
Chad	7.1	6.9	6.5	44.2	47.0	45.1	21.4	18.2	16.5
Comoros	7.2	5.2	4.6	45.5	37.0	34.9	16.8	10.2	9.1
Congo, Democratic Rep. of	6.7	6.7	6.4	47.9	46.2	46.6	15.2	14.7	14.9
Congo, Republic of	6.3	6.3	6.1	43.9	44.7	43.7	15.7	16.1	16.3
Côte d'Ivoire	7.4	5.7	5.1	50.1	38.9	37.4	16.0	14.9	16.4
Djibouti	6.6	5.8	5.3	44.2	39.0	37.9	19.1	16.2	15.0
Equatorial Guinea	5.8	5.9	5.5	43.3	43.5	41.0	21.1	18.0	16.5
Eritrea	7.5	6.5	5.8	..	42.4	40.5	..	16.4	11.8
Ethiopia	7.0	6.6	6.5	48.0	49.0	45.8	22.1	20.2	20.0
Gabon	4.5	5.2	5.2	33.1	36.6	36.5	18.1	16.1	16.0
Gambia, The	6.5	6.0	5.7	48.2	43.5	43.0	23.1	19.2	13.4
Ghana	6.5	5.5	4.9	45.0	38.4	35.5	13.1	10.6	9.3
Guinea	6.2	5.7	5.5	46.8	45.0	40.9	23.5	19.0	17.3
Guinea-Bissau	6.0	6.0	5.8	44.7	43.3	42.0	25.1	21.4	21.0
Kenya	7.7	5.2	4.7	49.7	36.1	36.5	12.1	9.4	12.9
Lesotho	5.4	5.0	4.8	38.9	36.4	35.3	13.8	11.3	12.4
Liberia	6.8	6.8	6.3	47.0	48.2	45.7	16.7	24.8	17.4
Madagascar	6.6	6.0	5.8	46.5	45.9	42.1	15.5	12.6	11.2
Malawi	7.6	6.7	6.4	53.5	50.2	47.6	21.6	22.1	23.2
Mali	7.1	..	6.6	49.0	51.1	47.2	21.6	17.5	16.0
Mauritania	6.1	5.9	5.5	42.3	42.6	40.6	18.5	14.7	13.5
Mauritius	2.5	2.3	1.9	22.2	20.4	17.4	6.0	6.7	7.0
Mozambique	6.5	6.3	5.3	45.7	44.9	40.6	20.1	18.6	19.5
Namibia	5.8	5.3	4.9	40.3	38.5	35.8	13.5	11.8	11.9
Niger	7.5	7.4	7.4	51.7	52.1	52.4	22.2	19.2	18.4
Nigeria	6.9	5.9	5.3	49.6	43.3	40.4	17.1	14.2	12.3
Rwanda	8.1	6.6	6.2	50.4	40.0	45.9	18.6	26.6	21.5
São Tomé and Principe	..	5.0	4.7	38.7	43.0	32.5	10.2	9.0	9.5
Senegal	6.7	5.9	5.6	45.5	40.0	39.7	17.7	13.0	12.7
Seychelles	3.5	2.7	2.1	24.1	22.9	20.8	7.4	7.2	6.5
Sierra Leone	6.5	6.5	6.1	48.9	49.1	45.7	28.5	29.8	25.5
Somalia	7.3	7.3	7.3	51.8	52.1	52.3	22.0	25.1	18.5
South Africa	4.2	3.2	2.8	35.5	31.2	25.0	11.1	8.8	7.9
Sudan	6.4	5.0	4.6	43.5	34.9	33.3	15.8	13.9	11.6
Swaziland	6.0	5.1	4.7	43.1	40.2	37.3	13.7	10.7	10.3
Tanzania	6.7	6.0	5.5	46.5	42.8	41.2	14.8	13.5	15.6
Togo	6.6	6.6	6.1	45.0	41.6	41.0	15.8	15.5	15.7
Uganda	7.3	6.9	6.6	49.1	50.2	47.9	17.6	18.2	19.8
Zambia	6.9	6.2	5.6	49.0	44.6	42.3	14.8	15.1	18.9
Zimbabwe	6.2	4.3	3.8	43.0	35.5	31.4	11.8	10.9	12.4
NORTH AFRICA	..	3.8	3.3	38.9	28.2	25.4	11.6	7.5	6.4
Algeria	6.4	4.0	3.6	40.6	28.2	27.1	10.7	5.9	4.9
Egypt, Arab Republic	5.1	3.8	3.2	39.1	28.5	24.5	12.7	8.6	7.0
Libya	7.2	4.2	3.8	45.6	28.8	29.1	10.9	5.2	4.5
Morocco	5.1	3.8	3.1	37.3	28.2	25.7	11.4	7.5	6.8
Tunisia	4.9	3.2	2.8	33.7	25.7	22.5	8.4	6.3	6.8
ALL AFRICA	..	5.4	5.0	45.1	40.3	38.1	16.0	13.9	13.4

13-6. Survival prospects

	Life expectancy at birth (years)		Infant mortality (per thousand)		Mortality of children under 5 years (per thousand)	Maternal mortality (per 100,000 live births)	Adult HIV-1 seroprevalence (per 100 adults)
	1982	1997	1982	1997	1997	1995 or MR available	1997
SUB-SAHARAN AFRICA	48	51	111	91	147	..	7.5
excluding South Africa	48	50	114	93	151	..	7.0
excl. S. Africa & Nigeria	48	49	119	97	158	..	7.8
Angola	42	46	149	125	209	1,500	2.1
Benin	49	53	115	88	149	500	2.1
Botswana	59	47	67	58	88	250	25.1
Burkina Faso	45	44	117	99	169	930	7.2
Burundi	47	42	118	119	200	1,300	8.3
Cameroon	51	57	88	52	78	500	4.9
Cape Verde	62	68	84	56	72	..	..
Central African Republic	47	45	114	98	160	700	10.8
Chad	43	49	120	100	182	900	2.7
Comoros	50	60	106	65	93	460	0.1
Congo, Democratic Rep. of	50	51	109	92	148	..	4.4
Congo, Republic of	50	48	88	90	145	890	7.8
Côte d'Ivoire	50	47	105	87	140	600	10.1
Djibouti	45	50	132	106	175	570	10.3
Equatorial Guinea	44	50	138	108	177	820	1.2
Eritrea	44	51	91	62	95	1,400	3.2
Ethiopia	42	43	159	107	175	1,400	9.3
Gabon	49	52	112	87	136	500	4.3
Gambia, The	41	53	154	78	..	1,000	2.2
Ghana	54	60	90	66	102	740	2.4
Guinea	40	46	177	120	182	880	2.1
Guinea-Bissau	39	44	164	130	220	910	2.3
Kenya	56	52	66	74	112	650	11.6
Lesotho	54	56	117	93	137	610	8.4
Liberia	51	47	144	116	194	560	3.7
Madagascar	51	57	112	94	158	660	0.1
Malawi	45	43	163	133	224	620	14.9
Mali	43	50	180	118	235	580	1.7
Mauritania	47	53	117	92	149	800	0.5
Mauritius	67	71	28	20	23	112	0.1
Mozambique	44	45	133	135	201	1,500	14.2
Namibia	54	56	84	65	101	220	19.9
Niger	42	47	146	118	..	593	1.5
Nigeria	46	54	96	77	122	1,000	4.1
Rwanda	46	40	124	124	209	1,300	12.8
São Tomé and Principe	..	64	80	50	74	..	..
Senegal	46	52	112	70	110	510	1.8
Seychelles	69	71	19	15	18	..	..
Sierra Leone	35	37	189	170	286	1,800	3.2
Somalia	43	47	143	122	205	1,600	0.3
South Africa	58	65	63	48	65	230	12.9
Sudan	49	55	92	71	115	370	..
Swaziland	53	60	94	65	101	560	18.5
Tanzania	51	48	104	85	136	530	9.4
Togo	50	49	105	86	138	640	8.5
Uganda	48	42	116	99	162	550	9.5
Zambia	51	43	88	113	189	230	19.1
Zimbabwe	56	55	76	69	108	280	25.8
NORTH AFRICA	59	68	97	44	56	..	0.0
Algeria	60	70	88	32	39	140	0.1
Egypt, Arab Republic	57	66	112	51	66	170	0.0
Libya	62	70	60	24	30	220	0.1
Morocco	60	67	92	51	67	372	0.0
Tunisia	63	70	59	30	33	..	0.0
ALL AFRICA	50	54	109	86	136		6.0

13-7. Immunization and ORT use

	Percentage of children (0-1 years) immunized against						ORT use among the under five (percent)
	DPT			Measles			
	1986	1994	1997	1986	1994	1997	1992-93
SUB-SAHARAN AFRICA	32	51	53	36	52	58	..
excluding South Africa	30	51	53	34	52	58	50
excl. S. Africa & Nigeria	34	53	55	40	53	55	..
Angola	10	31	41	60	44	78	48
Benin	17	86	78	20	78	82	28
Botswana	65	78	76	64	71	79	64
Burkina Faso	34	41	70	64	45	68	15
Burundi	65	47	..	41	41	..	49
Cameroon	..	31	44	..	31	43	84
Cape Verde	54	..	78	59	..	82	5
Central African Republic	19	40	..	24	37	..	24
Chad	10	18	24	..	24	30	15
Comoros	24	58	48	26	..	49	70
Congo, Democratic Rep. of	39	29	18	39	33	20	46
Congo, Republic of	68	..	23	86	..	18	67
Côte d'Ivoire	30	41	70	..	47	68	16
Djibouti	26	57	62	19	59	59	56
Equatorial Guinea	3	..	81	17	..	82	40
Eritrea	..	36	60	..	27	53	..
Ethiopia	7	37	63	10	28	52	68
Gabon	48	48	..	58	50	..	25
Gambia, The	73	78	96	62	68	91	51
Ghana	15	48	60	31	49	59	44
Guinea	2	73	53	9	69	56	82
Guinea-Bissau	29	74	63	..	68	51	26
Kenya	72	50	36	65	47	32	69
Lesotho	73	58	57	72	82	53	78
Liberia	15	..	..	39	..	..	15
Madagascar	22	66	..	18	55	..	26
Malawi	70	98	95	65	99	87	50
Mali	3	39	52	5	46	56	41
Mauritania	11	50	28	40	53	20	54
Mauritius	86	89	..	75	85	..	..
Mozambique	32	55	61	39	65	70	60
Namibia	..	80	63	..	68	57	75
Niger	5	..	28	..	..	42	17
Nigeria	16	44	45	17	50	69	80
Rwanda	77	..	77	63	..	66	36
São Tomé and Principe	65	..	73	58	..	60	50
Senegal	..	57	65	..	50	65	27
Seychelles	94	96	98	95	92	100	..
Sierra Leone	..	41	26	..	44	28	60
Somalia	17	..	..	25	..	..	78
South Africa	70	..	..	64	..	..	..
Sudan	14	77	79	11	86	92	47
Swaziland	73	74	67	66	62	57	85
Tanzania	74	83	74	97	79	69	83
Togo	..	71	33	..	59	38	33
Uganda	21	79	58	32	79	60	45
Zambia	66	86	70	36	89	69	90
Zimbabwe	75	80	78	74	79	73	..
NORTH AFRICA	71	87	91	68	85	88	24
Algeria	..	75	79	..	69	74	27
Egypt, Arab Republic	80	92	94	78	92	92	34
Libya	53	..	96	52	..	92	80
Morocco	54	87	95	48	87	92	14
Tunisia	72	91	96	67	87	92	22
ALL AFRICA	37	57	58	41	57	62	48

Notes: ORT = Oral re-hydration therapy; DPT = diphtheria, pertussis (whopping cough), and tetanus.

13-8. Child malnutrition

Social Indicators

	Percentage of children (1990-97)			Percentage of infants with low birth weight		Percentage of under-five (1990-97) suffering from moderate to severe		
	Exclusively breastfed, (0-3 months)	Breastfed, plus other food, (6-9 months)	Still breastfeading, (20-23 months)	1988	1993-96	Underweight	Wasting	Stunting
SUB-SAHARAN AFRICA	29	63	..	..	..	..	..	..
excluding South Africa	29	63	..	..	..	..	..	..
excl. S. Africa & Nigeria	37	67	..	..	..	..	..	..
Angola	12	70	49	21	..	35	6	53
Benin	15	97	65	8	..	29	14	25
Botswana	39	82	23	8	8	27	11	29
Burkina Faso	12	44	81	..	21	33	13	29
Burundi	89	66	73	..	16	38	9	43
Cameroon	7	77	35	10	13	15	3	26
Cape Verde	18	..	..	..	..	..	6	16
Central African Republic	23	93	52	15	..	23	7	34
Chad	2	81	62	..	..	39	..	40
Comoros	5	87	45	7	..	26	8	34
Congo, Democratic Rep. of	32	40	64	10	..	34	10	45
Congo, Republic of	43	95	27	..	16	24	..	..
Côte d'Ivoire	3	65	45	15	14	24	8	24
Djibouti	..	..	..	11	..	23	13	26
Equatorial Guinea	..	..	..	..	..	..	..	..
Eritrea	66	45	60	..	..	44	16	38
Ethiopia	74	..	35	..	16	48	8	64
Gabon	57	..	..	10	10	..	..	..
Gambia, The	..	8	58	..	..	26	..	..
Ghana	19	63	48	17	17	27	11	26
Guinea	52	..	15	25	13	24	12	29
Guinea-Bissau	..	..	..	13	20	23	5	..
Kenya	17	90	54	15	16	23	6	34
Lesotho	54	47	52	10	..	16	5	44
Liberia	15	17	25	..	..	20	..	..
Madagascar	61	93	49	10	15	34	7	48
Malawi	11	78	68	20	..	30	7	48
Mali	13	33	60	17	17	40	23	30
Mauritania	90	64	59	..	9	23	7	44
Mauritius	16	29	..	9	..	15	14	10
Mozambique	37	..	..	20	20	26	8	36
Namibia	22	65	23	..	..	26	9	29
Niger	1	67	52	..	15	43	15	41
Nigeria	2	52	43	20	16	39	9	43
Rwanda	90	68	85	..	17	29	4	42
São Tomé and Principe	..	..	..	7	3	16	..	26
Senegal	16	69	50	..	..	22	7	23
Seychelles	..	..	..	10	9	6	..	..
Sierra Leone	..	94	41	13	..	29	9	35
Somalia	..	..	..	..	16	39	..	30
South Africa	..	..	..	..	..	9	3	23
Sudan	14	45	44	15	15	34	17	34
Swaziland	37	51	20	..	..	10	..	..
Tanzania	41	93	53	13	14	31	7	43
Togo	15	25	99	20	20	19	..	34
Uganda	70	64	40	..	..	26	5	38
Zambia	27	88	43	..	13	24	4	42
Zimbabwe	16	93	26	5	14	16	6	21
NORTH AFRICA	45	34	..	..	..	14	..	..
Algeria	48	29	21	9	9	13	9	18
Egypt, Arab Republic	53	37	..	12	12	15	5	30
Libya	..	..	..	5	5	5	3	15
Morocco	31	33	20	..	4	10	2	24
Tunisia	12	53	16	8	16	9	4	23
ALL AFRICA	32	59	..	..	..	..	..	..

13-9. Access to sanitation facilities

	Percentage of population with access to sanitation facilities					
	1985			1993-96		
	Total	*Urban*	*Rural*	*Total*	*Urban*	*Rural*
SUB-SAHARAN AFRICA	..	..	..	47	..	..
excluding South Africa	..	45	..	47	..	..
excl. S. Africa & Nigeria	..	..	20	42	..	..
Angola	18	27	16	15	71	4
Benin	10	45	4	24	60	11
Botswana	36	79	13	55	91	41
Burkina Faso	9	38	5	..	..	..
Burundi	52	90	25	48	71	47
Cameroon	36	..	..	40	73	21
Cape Verde	10	36	9	..	..	..
Central African Republic	19	36	9	45	..	..
Chad	14	..	..	21	74	7
Comoros	..	..	..	23	40	16
Congo, Democratic Rep. of	..	..	10	..	53	7
Congo, Republic of	40	..	..	9	15	4
Côte d'Ivoire	..	..	..	51	..	..
Djibouti	37	43	19	50	..	..
Equatorial Guinea	..	28	..	42	33	40
Eritrea	..	..	..	..	12	0
Ethiopia	..	..	5	8	..	..
Gabon	50	..	..	76	79	67
Gambia, The	77	..	..	37	..	..
Ghana	26	47	17	32	75	11
Guinea	..	..	..	14	24	10
Guinea-Bissau	25	..	..	21	32	17
Kenya	44	75	39	45	69	35
Lesotho	..	..	..	..	76	32
Liberia	21	24	20	..	..	..
Madagascar	..	8	..	34	64	25
Malawi	60	88	56	64	94	61
Mali	21	90	5	37	61	22
Mauritania	..	7	..	32	44	19
Mauritius	97	100	95	100	..	..
Mozambique	..	..	..	23	68	12
Namibia	..	..	..	42	78	37
Niger	9	36	3	..	..	..
Nigeria	..	30	..	57	82	48
Rwanda	..	60	60	94	..	..
São Tomé and Principe	15	..	..	19	..	..
Senegal	..	87	..	..	68	12
Seychelles	99	..	..	98	..	99
Sierra Leone	21	43	10	..	..	..
Somalia	15	60	5	18	..	..
South Africa	..	..	..	53	78	12
Sudan	5	20	1	22	79	4
Swaziland	63	100	25	..	..	..
Tanzania	..	90	78	86	97	83
Togo	14	34	8	41	76	22
Uganda	13	40	10	67	60	50
Zambia	47	56	41	51	66	37
Zimbabwe	26	100	5	66	99	48
NORTH AFRICA	..	..	..	..	..	..
Algeria	..	..	..	..	..	..
Egypt, Arab Republic	..	..	..	70	95	49
Libya	91	100	53	86	90	75
Morocco	46	..	..	68	97	39
Tunisia	52	84	16	80	100	50
ALL AFRICA	..	..	..	..	..	..

13-10. Access to safe water

	Percentage of population with access to safe water					
	1988			1993-96		
	Total	*Urban*	*Rural*	*Total*	*Urban*	*Rural*
SUB-SAHARAN AFRICA	..	..	..	47	74	32
excluding South Africa	..	..	..	47	74	32
excl. S. Africa & Nigeria	..	..	..	49	76	39
Angola	..	75	18	32	69	15
Benin	..	79	35	72	82	69
Botswana	56	100	33	70	100	77
Burkina Faso	35	50	26	..	..	..
Burundi	..	92	27	58	97	55
Cameroon	..	47	27	41	71	30
Cape Verde	..	100	49	67	..	..
Central African Republic	19	29	14	23	20	25
Chad	..	..	..	24	48	17
Comoros	..	..	..	48	74	41
Congo, Democratic Rep. of	36	62	16	..	89	26
Congo, Republic of	..	..	..	..	50	11
Côte d'Ivoire	..	60	77	72	97	73
Djibouti	..	30	14	80	..	..
Equatorial Guinea	..	..	..	33	41	31
Eritrea	..	..	..	7	..	..
Ethiopia	10	..	..	26	90	20
Gabon	52	..	50	67	80	30
Gambia, The	..	..	..	50	64	39
Ghana	..	93	40	65	88	52
Guinea	27	62	15	55	55	44
Guinea-Bissau	21	19	22	53	38	57
Kenya	..	..	..	45	74	43
Lesotho	40	..	40	62	64	60
Liberia	..	50	25	30	58	8
Madagascar	..	..	..	16	54	4
Malawi	51	66	49	60	97	52
Mali	..	48	17	48	56	20
Mauritania	..	..	..	64	87	41
Mauritius	95	100	92	100	..	..
Mozambique	19	50	12	24	44	40
Namibia	..	..	..	60	62	45
Niger	..	..	..	52	58	..
Nigeria	16	..	..	50	80	39
Rwanda	70	..	..	..	79	44
São Tomé and Principe	..	..	..	60	..	..
Senegal	..	..	..	50	90	44
Seychelles	90	..	..	83	99	80
Sierra Leone	..	86	20	34	58	21
Somalia	..	..	..	37	..	..
South Africa	..	..	..	59	90	33
Sudan	35	100	20	60	84	41
Swaziland	..	..	..	60	80	46
Tanzania	..	80	..	49	65	45
Togo	..	..	..	55	82	41
Uganda	..	45	12	42	60	36
Zambia	70	..	..	53	66	37
Zimbabwe	65	100	14	77	99	64
NORTH AFRICA	79	91	64	..	..	..
Algeria	77	86	55	..	..	..
Egypt, Arab Republic	95	100	90	84	95	74
Libya	90	..	..	95	90	91
Morocco	47	74	17	57	97	20
Tunisia	78	100	52	90	100	76
ALL AFRICA	..	..	..	47	..	..

13-11. Health expenditure

	Public expenditure as % of GDP, 1990-96	Private expenditure as % of GDP, 1990-96	Total expenditure		
			as % of GDP, 1990-96	per capita, US$, 1990-96	per capita PPP, international $, 1990-96
SUB-SAHARAN AFRICA	2.6	..	..	..	..
excluding South Africa	1.4	..	..	..	..
excl. S.Africa & Nigeria	..	..	..	..	..
Angola	3.9	..	..	..	..
Benin	1.8	..	..	..	..
Botswana	1.8	1.4	3.1	..	..
Burkina Faso	4.7	3.2	5.5	17	49
Burundi	1.0	..	..	..	..
Cameroon	1.0	0.4	1.4	7	24
Cape Verde	3.3	..	..	..	..
Central African Republic	2.0	..	..	..	..
Chad	1.6	0.1	2.7	6	33
Comoros	1.1	0.2	1.2	..	..
Congo, Democratic Rep. of	0.2	..	..	..	..
Congo, Republic of	1.8	3.2	6.3	77	116
Côte d'Ivoire	1.4	2.1	3.5	25	57
Djibouti	..	..	..	..	..
Equatorial Guinea	5.8	1.3	7.2	27	65
Eritrea	1.1	0.9	2.0	..	..
Ethiopia	1.6	1.0	2.6	3	13
Gabon	0.6	..	..	..	..
Gambia, The	2.0	..	..	..	..
Ghana	2.9	0.1	1.7	6	31
Guinea	1.2	..	..	..	..
Guinea-Bissau	1.1	..	..	..	..
Kenya	1.9	1.0	2.6	8	28
Lesotho	3.7	..	..	..	..
Liberia	..	..	..	..	..
Madagascar	1.4	..	..	..	..
Malawi	2.3	..	..	..	..
Mali	2.0	1.3	2.7	8	17
Mauritania	1.8	4.1	5.2	28	81
Mauritius	2.2	1.7	4.0	116	304
Mozambique	4.6	..	..	..	..
Namibia	4.1	3.4	6.8	127	315
Niger	1.6	..	..	..	..
Nigeria	0.3	0.7	1.0	5	11
Rwanda	1.9	..	..	..	..
São Tomé and Principe	9.9	..	..	..	..
Senegal	1.2	..	..	..	..
Seychelles	4.1	..	..	..	..
Sierra Leone	1.6	2.0	..	..	..
Somalia	..	..	..	..	..
South Africa	3.6	4.3	7.9	258	542
Sudan	..	1.9	0.2	4	..
Swaziland	2.5	..	..	..	..
Tanzania	2.5	..	..	..	..
Togo	1.6	2.2	3.4	15	59
Uganda	1.9	2.2	3.9	9	34
Zambia	2.9	0.7	3.3	17	31
Zimbabwe	1.7	3.1	4.7	41	133
NORTH AFRICA	2.2	1.8	4.0	63	121
Algeria	3.3	1.3	9.9	85	210
Egypt, Arab Republic	1.7	2.1	3.7	38	103
Libya	..	..	..	..	..
Morocco	1.2	2.4	3.6	49	124
Tunisia	3.0	2.8	5.9	99	260
ALL AFRICA	2.3	..	..	..	..

13-12. Health care

	Population per physician		Population per hospital bed		Percentage of births attended by trained health personnel	Percentage of population with access to health services
	1981	1990-95	1981	1990-95	1990-94	1990-94
SUB-SAHARAN AFRICA	..	..	..	1,304	..	..
excluding South Africa	..	..	..	1,304	..	..
excl. S.Africa & Nigeria	..	..	..	1,523	..	..
Angola	..	23,728	..	774	17	24.0
Benin	16,989	12,443	886	4,281	34	42.0
Botswana	7,451	3,916	..	635	..	..
Burkina Faso	55,744	27,364	..	3,341	41	..
Burundi	..	17,033	..	1,508	24	80.0
Cameroon	..	11,950	..	392	58	..
Cape Verde	..	4,274	..	631	49	..
Central African Republic	22,777	27,400	..	1,145	..	..
Chad	..	30,065	..	1,389	..	26.0
Comoros	..	8,816	..	362	..	..
Congo, Democratic Rep. of	..	15,133	..	701	..	59.0
Congo, Republic of	..	3,822	..	299	..	..
Côte d'Ivoire	..	11,407	..	1,232	45	..
Djibouti	4,291	6,155	266	394	..	..
Equatorial Guinea	..	3,556	..	..	5	..
Eritrea	..	..	..	..	6	..
Ethiopia	88,119	35,051	..	4,141	8	55.0
Gabon	2,189	1,998	..	313	80	..
Gambia, The	..	..	..	1,637	44	..
Ghana	..	..	..	685	44	25.0
Guinea	45,463	7,340	..	1,816	31	45.0
Guinea-Bissau	..	..	528	677	50	..
Kenya	10,095	..	..	607	45	..
Lesotho	..	16,895	..	..	50	..
Liberia	9,454	..	..	..	..	..
Madagascar	10,060	8,356	..	1,068	57	..
Malawi	53,913	45,737	..	645	57	..
Mali	25,992	18,103	..	..	46	..
Mauritania	..	7,255	..	1,503	40	..
Mauritius	1,813	1,169	..	325	97	99.0
Mozambique	36,970	..	..	1,153	29	..
Namibia	..	4,321	..	..	68	..
Niger	..	54,444	..	..	15	30.0
Nigeria	..	5,208	..	599	31	67.0
Rwanda	32,318	31,029	677	605	26	..
São Tomé and Principe	2,388	1,885	..	212	63	..
Senegal	12,687	13,016	..	1,371	47	40.0
Seychelles	..	..	..	..	99	99.0
Sierra Leone	18,975	..	..	..	..	..
Somalia	22,103	..	..	1,327	2	..
South Africa	..	..	..	..	..	..
Sudan	9,581	..	1,110	919	86	70.0
Swaziland	..	9,277	..	..	67	55.0
Tanzania	..	23,454	..	1,123	44	93.0
Togo	21,355	12,607	..	662	..	..
Uganda	21,405	..	661	1,092	..	..
Zambia	7,913	13,403	287	..	51	..
Zimbabwe	7,074	6,869	..	1,959	69	..
NORTH AFRICA	5,936	1,283	570	574	52	..
Algeria	..	1,218	..	475	77	..
Egypt, Arab Republic	733	546	483	476	45	99.0
Libya	611	930	207	239	68	100.0
Morocco	18,558	2,743	814	895	40	62.4
Tunisia	3,642	1,757	..	566	50	90.0
ALL AFRICA	..	..	..	1,132	..	..

13-13. Illiteracy rate

	Percentage of population 15 years of age and above that is illiterate								
	1985			*1990*			*1997*		
	Total	*Male*	*Female*	*Total*	*Male*	*Female*	*Total*	*Male*	*Female*
SUB-SAHARAN AFRICA	56	45	65	50	40	59	42	34	50
excluding South Africa	59	48	70	53	43	63	44	35	53
excl. S. Africa & Nigeria	59	48	70	54	43	64	46	37	55
Angola	..	..	..	..	..	..	..	..	..
Benin	78	68	87	74	62	85	66	52	79
Botswana	37	39	35	32	34	30	26	28	23
Burkina Faso	87	79	94	84	75	92	79	70	89
Burundi	68	56	79	62	52	72	55	46	64
Cameroon	45	34	56	38	28	47	28	21	35
Cape Verde	43	28	53	38	25	47	29	18	38
Central African Republic	72	58	84	67	53	79	58	44	70
Chad	..	..	..	..	..	..	..	..	..
Comoros	48	40	55	46	39	54	45	37	52
Congo, Democratic Rep. of	..	..	..	..	..	..	..	..	..
Congo, Republic of	41	29	52	33	23	42	23	15	30
Côte d'Ivoire	72	63	82	67	57	77	57	49	66
Djibouti	..	..	..	..	..	..	..	..	..
Equatorial Guinea	34	19	48	27	15	39	20	9	30
Eritrea	..	..	..	..	..	..	..	..	..
Ethiopia	76	68	85	72	64	80	65	59	71
Gabon	..	..	..	..	..	..	..	..	..
Gambia, The	80	74	85	75	68	80	67	60	74
Ghana	50	37	63	43	31	55	34	23	43
Guinea	..	..	..	..	..	..	..	..	..
Guinea-Bissau	78	63	91	73	58	88	66	50	82
Kenya	36	24	48	29	19	39	21	13	28
Lesotho	25	38	13	22	34	11	18	29	7
Liberia	67	51	82	61	45	77	52	35	68
Madagascar	..	..	..	..	..	..	..	..	..
Malawi	52	34	68	48	31	64	42	27	57
Mali	81	75	87	75	68	82	65	57	72
Mauritania	68	56	79	65	54	76	62	51	72
Mauritius	23	17	29	20	15	25	17	13	21
Mozambique	71	56	86	67	51	82	60	43	75
Namibia	30	26	33	25	23	28	20	19	22
Niger	90	84	96	89	82	95	86	78	93
Nigeria	59	48	70	51	41	62	40	31	49
Rwanda	53	43	64	47	37	56	37	29	44
São Tomé and Principe	..	..	..	..	..	..	..	..	..
Senegal	75	66	85	72	62	81	65	55	75
Seychelles	..	..	..	..	..	..	..	..	..
Sierra Leone	..	..	..	..	..	..	..	..	..
Somalia	..	..	..	..	..	..	..	..	..
South Africa	21	20	22	19	18	20	16	15	17
Sudan	61	47	76	55	42	69	47	35	59
Swaziland	34	32	36	29	26	30	23	21	24
Tanzania	44	29	57	37	24	49	28	18	38
Togo	62	46	77	56	40	71	47	31	62
Uganda	49	35	63	44	31	57	36	25	47
Zambia	37	25	47	32	22	41	25	17	33
Zimbabwe	17	11	22	13	9	18	9	6	12
NORTH AFRICA	57	43	71	52	38	66	45	33	58
Algeria	53	39	67	47	34	61	40	27	52
Egypt, Arab Republic	57	43	71	53	40	67	47	35	60
Libya	39	22	59	32	17	49	24	11	37
Morocco	67	53	80	61	47	75	54	41	67
Tunisia	47	34	61	41	28	54	33	22	44
ALL AFRICA	56	45	67	50	40	61	43	33	51

13-14. Primary school gross enrollment ratio

	Total			Males			Females		
	1980	1990	1994-96	1980	1990	1994-96	1980	1990	1994-96
SUB-SAHARAN AFRICA	78	76	77	87	83	84	66	68	69
excluding South Africa	77	72	72	87	80	80	66	64	64
excl. S. Africa & Nigeria	68	67	63	77	73	70	58	59	57
Angola	..	92	..	..	96	..	..	88	..
Benin	67	58	78	91	78	98	43	39	57
Botswana	91	113	108	83	109	107	100	117	108
Burkina Faso	18	33	40	22	41	48	13	26	31
Burundi	26	73	51	32	79	55	21	66	46
Cameroon	98	101	89	107	109	93	90	93	84
Cape Verde	114	121	..	119	..	..	110	..	..
Central African Republic	71	65	..	92	80	..	51	51	..
Chad	..	54	58	..	75	76	..	34	39
Comoros	86	75	75	100	87	..	72	63	..
Congo, Democratic Rep. of	92	70	72	108	81	86	77	60	59
Congo, Republic of	141	133	114	148	141	120	135	124	109
Côte d'Ivoire	75	67	71	90	79	82	60	56	61
Djibouti	37	38	39	..	45	45	..	32	33
Equatorial Guinea	135	..	..	..	..	..	..	..	..
Eritrea	..	..	53	..	..	59	..	..	48
Ethiopia	37	33	38	48	39	48	27	26	27
Gabon	..	..	..	..	..	..	..	..	..
Gambia, The	53	64	77	70	76	87	36	52	67
Ghana	79	75	..	88	82	..	71	68	..
Guinea	36	37	48	48	50	62	25	24	33
Guinea-Bissau	68	..	62	94	..	79	43	..	45
Kenya	115	95	85	120	97	85	110	93	85
Lesotho	104	112	108	85	100	102	122	123	114
Liberia	48	..	..	61	..	..	35	..	..
Madagascar	130	103	92	131	103	92	129	103	91
Malawi	60	68	89	72	74	..	49	62	..
Mali	26	26	45	34	33	55	19	19	35
Mauritania	37	49	79	48	56	84	26	41	75
Mauritius	93	109	107	94	109	107	91	110	106
Mozambique	..	67	60	..	77	70	..	57	50
Namibia	..	129	131	..	123	130	..	135	132
Niger	25	29	29	33	37	36	18	21	22
Nigeria	109	91	98	123	104	109	95	79	87
Rwanda	63	70	..	66	70	..	60	69	..
São Tomé and Principe	..	..	..	..	..	..	..	..	..
Senegal	46	59	68	56	68	75	37	50	61
Seychelles	..	..	..	..	..	..	..	..	..
Sierra Leone	52	50	..	61	60	..	43	41	..
Somalia	22	..	..	28	..	..	15	..	..
South Africa	90	122	131	..	123	133	..	121	129
Sudan	50	53	51	59	60	55	41	45	47
Swaziland	103	111	118	104	114	122	102	109	115
Tanzania	93	70	66	99	70	67	86	69	66
Togo	118	109	120	144	132	140	93	87	99
Uganda	50	75	74	56	83	81	43	66	68
Zambia	90	99	89	98	..	91	83	..	86
Zimbabwe	85	116	119	..	117	115	..	115	111
NORTH AFRICA	84	91	100	97	100	107	69	83	93
Algeria	95	100	108	108	108	113	81	92	102
Egypt, Arab Republic	73	94	101	84	101	107	61	86	94
Libya	125	105	..	129	109	..	121	102	..
Morocco	83	67	86	102	79	97	63	54	74
Tunisia	102	113	117	117	120	120	87	107	113
ALL AFRICA	79	79	78	89	86	85	67	71	72

13-15. Pupil progression

	Pecentage of cohort reaching grade 5 (1992-95)			Progression to secondary school 1992		
	Total	*Male*	*Female*	*Total*	*Male*	*Female*
SUB-SAHARAN AFRICA	..	..	..	..	..	..
excluding South Africa	..	..	..	..	..	..
excl. S. Africa & Nigeria	..	..	..	..	..	..
Angola	..	..	..	..	..	..
Benin	61	64	57	..	..	..
Botswana	90	87	93	84	84	85
Burkina Faso	75	74	77	27	27	27
Burundi	..	..	..	..	..	..
Cameroon	..	..	..	..	..	..
Cape Verde	..	..	..	..	..	..
Central African Republic	..	..	..	..	..	..
Chad	59	62	53	..	..	..
Comoros	80	..	..	39	..	..
Congo, Democratic Rep. of	..	..	..	27	25	30
Congo, Republic of	55	40	78	..	..	..
Côte d'Ivoire	75	77	71	..	..	..
Djibouti	79	..	..	38	..	..
Equatorial Guinea	..	..	..	..	..	..
Eritrea	71	73	67	77	84	70
Ethiopia	55	57	53	80	82	77
Gabon	59	58	61	..	..	..
Gambia, The	80	78	83	..	..	..
Ghana	..	..	..	..	..	..
Guinea	54	85	68	50	51	47
Guinea-Bissau	..	..	..	..	..	..
Kenya	..	..	..	41	..	..
Lesotho	80	72	87	62	..	..
Liberia	..	..	..	..	..	..
Madagascar	40	49	33	35	35	35
Malawi	..	..	..	10	..	..
Mali	82	87	82	63	64	60
Mauritania	64	61	68	32	34	28
Mauritius	99	98	99	51	49	54
Mozambique	46	52	39	39	39	39
Namibia	79	80	84	86	..	..
Niger	73	72	74	..	..	..
Nigeria	..	..	..	..	..	..
Rwanda	..	..	..	..	..	..
São Tomé and Principe	..	..	..	..	..	..
Senegal	85	89	81	..	..	..
Seychelles	100	99	96	100	..	..
Sierra Leone	..	..	..	..	..	..
Somalia	..	..	..	..	..	..
South Africa	75	72	79	..	..	..
Sudan	..	..	..	..	..	..
Swaziland	87	85	89	80	81	79
Tanzania	83	81	85	12	..	..
Togo	..	..	..	..	..	..
Uganda	..	..	..	..	..	..
Zambia	..	..	..	..	..	..
Zimbabwe	79	78	79	66	..	..
NORTH AFRICA	..	..	..	..	..	..
Algeria	94	94	95	79	77	83
Egypt, Arab Republic	..	..	..	83	82	85
Libya	..	..	..	..	..	..
Morocco	78	79	77	..	..	..
Tunisia	91	90	92	58	57	59
ALL AFRICA	..	..	..	..	..	..

Notes: In Seychelles a policy of automatic promotion is practiced at the primary level of education. Tanzanian figures refer to mainland only.

13-16. Net primary enrollment ratio

	Total			Males			Females		
	1980	1990	1994-96	1980	1990	1994-96	1980	1990	1994-96
SUB-SAHARAN AFRICA	..	..	..	..	..	..	..	..	..
excluding South Africa	..	..	..	..	..	..	..	..	..
excl. S. Africa & Nigeria	..	..	..	..	..	..	..	..	..
Angola	..	..	63	..	..	80	..	..	47
Benin	..	..	63	..	..	80	..	..	47
Botswana	76	93	81	69	90	79	82	97	83
Burkina Faso	15	27	31	18	33	37	11	21	24
Burundi	20	..	..	23	..	..	16	..	..
Cameroon	..	..	..	..	..	..	..	..	..
Cape Verde	90	..	..	93	..	..	88	..	..
Central African Republic	56	53	..	73	64	..	41	42	..
Chad	..	..	46	..	..	59	..	..	33
Comoros	..	..	..	..	..	..	..	..	..
Congo, Democratic Rep. of	..	54	..	..	61	..	..	48	..
Congo, Republic of	96	..	..	99	..	..	93	..	..
Côte d'Ivoire	..	47	55	..	..	63	..	..	47
Djibouti	..	32	32	..	..	36	..	..	27
Equatorial Guinea	..	..	..	..	..	..	..	..	..
Eritrea	..	..	30	..	..	32	..	..	29
Ethiopia	..	..	28	..	..	29	..	..	18
Gabon	..	..	..	..	..	..	..	..	..
Gambia, The	50	..	65	66	..	72	34	..	57
Ghana	..	..	..	..	..	..	..	..	..
Guinea	..	..	..	..	..	..	..	..	..
Guinea-Bissau	47	..	..	63	..	..	31	..	..
Kenya	91	..	..	92	..	..	89	..	..
Lesotho	67	73	70	55	65	64	79	81	76
Liberia	..	..	..	..	..	..	..	..	..
Madagascar	..	..	61	..	..	60	..	..	62
Malawi	43	50	..	48	52	..	38	48	..
Mali	20	18	28	..	23	33	..	14	22
Mauritania	..	..	57	..	..	61	..	..	53
Mauritius	79	95	98	80	95	98	79	95	98
Mozambique	..	47	40	..	..	45	..	..	34
Namibia	..	..	91	..	..	..	..	..	..
Niger	21	24	25	..	31	30	..	18	19
Nigeria	..	..	..	..	..	..	..	..	..
Rwanda	59	66	..	62	66	..	57	66	..
São Tomé and Principe	..	..	..	..	..	..	..	..	..
Senegal	37	..	58	44	..	64	30	..	52
Seychelles	..	..	..	..	..	..	..	..	..
Sierra Leone	..	..	..	..	..	..	..	..	..
Somalia	16	..	..	20	..	..	12	..	..
South Africa	..	..	..	..	..	..	..	..	..
Sudan	..	..	..	..	..	..	..	..	..
Swaziland	80	88	91	..	88	90	..	88	91
Tanzania	68	51	48	..	51	47	..	52	48
Togo	..	75	85	..	87	98	..	62	72
Uganda	..	..	..	..	..	..	..	..	..
Zambia	77	..	75	81	..	76	73	..	74
Zimbabwe	..	..	..	..	..	..	..	..	..
NORTH AFRICA	..	..	89	..	..	95	..	..	84
Algeria	81	93	94	91	99	97	71	87	91
Egypt, Arab Republic	..	..	93	..	..	98	..	..	88
Libya	..	..	..	..	..	..	..	..	..
Morocco	62	58	74	75	68	83	47	48	65
Tunisia	82	94	98	92	97	99	72	90	96
ALL AFRICA	..	..	..	..	..	..	..	..	..

13-17. Number of school teachers

	Primary						Secondary					
	Total teaching staff			Percentage females			Total teaching staff			Percentage females		
	1980	1990	1994-96	1980	1990	1994-96	1980	1990	1994-96	1980	1990	1994-96
SUB-SAHARAN AFRICA	..	..	..	30	35	38	..	..	..	..	..	..
excluding South Africa	..	..	..	30	35	36	..	..	..	..	..	..
excl. S. Africa & Nigeria	..	..	..	28	32	36	..	..	..	..	..	..
Angola	..	31,062	..	..	..	..	..	..	..	..	..	..
Benin	7,994	13,556	13,957	23	25	24	..	..	..	..	..	..
Botswana	5,316	8,956	12,785	72	80	77	1,137	3,716	6,670	37	40	43
Burkina Faso	3,700	8,903	14,037	20	27	24	..	..	..	..	..	..
Burundi	4,805	9,465	10,316	47	46	50	..	2,026	..	..	21	..
Cameroon	26,763	38,430	40,970	20	30	32	8,926	19,820	..	..	..	..
Cape Verde	1,436	..	..	..	..	..	184	..	..	..	..	..
Central African Republic	4,130	4,004	..	25	25	..	724	..	..	16	..	..
Chad	..	7,980	10,151	..	6	8	..	..	2,792	..	..	4
Comoros	1,292	1,995	1,508	7	..	..	449	..	..	20	..	..
Congo, Democratic Rep. of	..	114,000	121,054	..	24	22	..	..	..	..	..	..
Congo, Republic of	7,186	7,578	7,060	25	32	36	5,117	6,851	7,173	..	..	16
Côte d'Ivoire	26,460	39,002	40,529	15	19	21	..	..	10,929	..	..	..
Djibouti	419	742	1,096	..	37	30	278	..	628	..	..	..
Equatorial Guinea	647	..	..	..	..	..	..	..	..	..	..	..
Eritrea	..	2,895	5,476	..	45	36	..	..	2,071	..	..	14
Ethiopia	33,322	68,370	89,189	22	24	28	..	23,319	25,984	..	10	10
Gabon	3,441	..	4,943	27	..	39	1,587	..	3,094	24	..	18
Gambia, The	1,932	2,757	4,118	32	31	29	620	756	1,547	25	..	17
Ghana	47,921	66,946	..	42	36	..	31,636	..	..	21	..	..
Guinea	7,165	8,699	11,875	14	22	25	..	5,976	..	..	12	..
Guinea-Bissau	3,257	..	..	24	..	..	462	..	..	21	..	..
Kenya	102,489	172,117	181,975	..	37	40	17,081	..	..	..	..	..
Lesotho	5,097	6,448	7,898	75	80	79	1,299	..	2,878	..	..	53
Liberia	9,099	..	..	23	..	..	..	..	..	..	..	..
Madagascar	39,474	38,933	44,145	..	..	51	..	..	..	..	..	..
Malawi	12,540	22,942	49,138	..	31	39	953	..	3,172	..	..	1
Mali	6,862	8,156	8,718	20	23	23	..	5,748	..	..	14	..
Mauritania	2,183	3,741	6,225	9	18	20	..	..	2,067	..	..	..
Mauritius	6,379	6,507	5,215	43	44	51	..	..	4,737	..	..	45
Mozambique	17,030	23,107	24,575	22	..	23	..	4,657	5,615	..	..	17
Namibia	..	..	..	..	..	..	..	..	..	..	..	..
Niger	5,518	8,835	11,376	30	33	32	1,284	2,775	5,258	21	18	14
Nigeria	343,551	331,915	435,210	34	43	46	41,581	141,377	152,596	29	33	36
Rwanda	11,912	19,183	..	38	46	..	1,454	2,802	..	16	20	..
São Tomé and Principe	588	..	..	..	..	..	..	..	..	..	..	..
Senegal	9,175	13,394	16,567	24	..	26	4,302	..	..	..	..	..
Seychelles	658	..	577	80	..	88	127	328	689	37	..	50
Sierra Leone	9,528	10,850	..	..	..	..	..	5,969	..	..	18	..
Somalia	8,122	..	..	29	..	..	2,089	..	..	7	..	..
South Africa	160,286	..	224,896	..	..	74	..	..	128,784	..	..	64
Sudan	43,451	60,047	102,987	31	51	62	18,831	33,628	15,504	..	35	45
Swaziland	3,278	5,083	5,975	79	79	78	..	2,213	3,087	..	46	43
Tanzania	81,386	96,850	108,874	37	41	44	3,837	7,944	12,751	..	24	26
Togo	9,201	11,105	18,535	21	19	14	..	4,492	5,389	..	12	12
Uganda	38,422	84,149	82,745	30	30	32	3,833	16,881	16,235	..	..	19
Zambia	21,455	33,200	38,528	40	..	43	4,882	..	..	..	..	..
Zimbabwe	28,118	59,154	63,718	..	39	44	3,782	24,547	28,254	..	29	36
NORTH AFRICA	..	..	..	..	45	46	..	..	..	..	..	39
Algeria	88,481	151,262	170,956	37	39	45	41,137	127,024	151,948	..	39	45
Egypt, Arab Republic	..	279,315	356,499	..	52	49	121,999	286,797	424,586	31	..	39
Libya	36,591	85,537	..	47	..	..	24,323	..	..	24	..	..
Morocco	56,908	91,680	114,406	30	37	38	36,526	79,657	84,202	..	29	32
Tunisia	27,375	50,609	60,101	29	45	49	14,328	33,058	45,411	29	32	38
ALL AFRICA	..	..	..	30	37	40	..	..	..	..	..	..

Note: Figures include both part-time and full-time teachers.

13-18. Pupil / teacher ratio

	Number of pupils per teacher					
	Primary			Secondary		
	1980	1990	1994-96	1980	1990	1994-96
SUB-SAHARAN AFRICA	..	39	..	..	..	..
excluding South Africa	..	39	..	..	..	..
excl. S. Africa & Nigeria	..	38	..	..	..	..
Angola	..	32	..	..	..	..
Benin	48	36	52	..	..	..
Botswana	32	32	25	18	17	17
Burkina Faso	54	57	51	..	..	..
Burundi	37	67	50	..	..	..
Cameroon	52	51	..	26	..	..
Cape Verde	40	..	..	..	..	..
Central African Republic	60	77	..	..	..	..
Chad	..	66	67	..	..	35
Comoros	46	..	52	..	..	..
Congo, Democratic Rep. of	..	40	45	..	..	..
Congo, Republic of	54	65	70	..	..	..
Côte d'Ivoire	39	36	41	..	..	..
Djibouti	40	43	34	..	..	..
Equatorial Guinea	..	..	..	..	..	..
Eritrea	..	38	44	..	..	43
Ethiopia	64	36	38	..	..	..
Gabon	45	..	51	..	..	..
Gambia, The	24	..	30	..	..	..
Ghana	30	29	..	..	..	..
Guinea	36	40	49	..	..	..
Guinea-Bissau	23	..	..	10	..	..
Kenya	38	31	30	..	..	..
Lesotho	48	55	47	19	..	24
Liberia	16	..	..	..	..	..
Madagascar	38	40	37	..	..	..
Malawi	65	61	59	..	..	16
Mali	42	42	70	..	14	..
Mauritania	41	45	50	..	..	..
Mauritius	20	21	24	..	..	..
Mozambique	..	55	58	..	..	33
Namibia	..	..	..	..	..	..
Niger	41	42	41	30	28	19
Nigeria	..	41	37	..	..	29
Rwanda	59	57	..	..	25	..
São Tomé and Principe	28	..	..	..	..	..
Senegal	46	53	58	..	..	..
Seychelles	22	..	17	..	..	13
Sierra Leone	..	..	..	..	..	..
Somalia	33	..	..	21	..	..
South Africa	..	..	36	..	..	28
Sudan	34	34	29	..	..	5
Swaziland	34	33	34	..	..	18
Tanzania	41	35	36	..	..	..
Togo	55	58	51	..	28	..
Uganda	..	29	35	..	..	..
Zambia	49	..	39	..	..	..
Zimbabwe	44	36	39	..	..	0
NORTH AFRICA	33	28	25	21	17	16
Algeria	35	28	27	25	17	17
Egypt, Arab Republic	..	..	23	..	..	16
Libya	18	..	..	12	..	..
Morocco	38	27	28	22	..	..
Tunisia	39	28	24	20	..	..
ALL AFRICA	..	37	..	..	..	..

Note: Figures include both part-time and full-time teachers.

13-19. Secondary school gross enrollment ratio

	Total			Males			Females		
	1980	*1990*	*1994-96*	*1980*	*1990*	*1994-96*	*1980*	*1990*	*1994-96*
SUB-SAHARAN AFRICA	15	23	27	20	26	29	10	21	24
excluding South Africa	15	19	21	20	22	24	10	16	18
excl. S. Africa & Nigeria	14	17	17	18	21	19	9	14	14
Angola	21	12	..	..	..	..	..	..	..
Benin	16	12	17	24	17	24	8	7	10
Botswana	19	43	65	17	41	62	21	45	68
Burkina Faso	3	7	..	4	9	..	2	5	..
Burundi	3	6	7	4	7	..	2	4	..
Cameroon	18	28	27	24	33	32	13	23	22
Cape Verde	8	21	..	9	..	..	7	..	..
Central African Republic	14	12	..	21	17	..	7	7	..
Chad	..	8	10	..	13	15	..	3	4
Comoros	22	18	21	30	21	24	15	14	19
Congo, Democratic Rep. of	24	..	26	35	..	32	13	..	19
Congo, Republic of	74	53	53	89	63	62	60	44	45
Côte d'Ivoire	19	22	24	26	30	33	11	14	16
Djibouti	12	12	14	15	14	17	9	9	12
Equatorial Guinea	..	..	..	..	..	..	..	..	..
Eritrea	..	..	20	..	..	24	..	..	17
Ethiopia	9	14	12	12	16	13	7	13	10
Gabon	..	..	..	..	..	..	..	..	..
Gambia, The	11	19	25	16	25	30	7	12	19
Ghana	41	36	..	50	45	..	31	28	..
Guinea	17	10	12	24	15	18	10	5	6
Guinea-Bissau	6	..	..	10	..	..	2	..	..
Kenya	20	24	24	23	28	26	16	21	22
Lesotho	18	25	31	14	20	25	21	30	37
Liberia	22	..	..	31	..	..	13	..	..
Madagascar	..	18	16	..	18	16	..	18	16
Malawi	5	8	17	7	11	21	3	5	12
Mali	8	7	10	12	9	13	5	4	7
Mauritania	11	14	16	18	19	21	4	9	11
Mauritius	50	53	65	51	53	63	49	53	66
Mozambique	5	8	7	8	10	9	3	6	6
Namibia	..	44	61	..	39	56	..	49	66
Niger	5	7	7	7	9	9	3	4	5
Nigeria	18	25	33	24	29	36	12	21	30
Rwanda	3	8	..	4	9	..	3	7	..
São Tomé and Principe	..	..	..	..	..	..	..	..	..
Senegal	11	16	16	15	21	20	8	11	12
Seychelles	..	..	..	..	..	..	..	..	..
Sierra Leone	14	17	..	20	22	..	8	13	..
Somalia	9	..	..	13	..	..	5	..	..
South Africa	..	74	94	..	69	87	..	80	102
Sudan	16	24	21	20	27	23	12	21	20
Swaziland	38	44	54	39	44	55	37	43	54
Tanzania	3	5	5	4	6	6	2	4	5
Togo	33	24	27	50	35	40	16	12	15
Uganda	5	13	12	7	17	15	3	10	9
Zambia	16	24	27	22	..	34	11	..	21
Zimbabwe	8	50	49	9	53	52	7	46	45
NORTH AFRICA	41	62	64	49	68	68	31	54	60
Algeria	33	61	63	40	67	65	26	54	62
Egypt, Arab Republic	51	76	75	61	84	80	39	68	70
Libya	76	86	..	89	..	..	63	..	..
Morocco	26	35	39	32	41	44	20	30	34
Tunisia	27	45	65	34	50	66	20	40	63
ALL AFRICA	20	31	34	26	35	37	15	28	31

Note: "Secondary" refers to secondary general education.

13-20. Public expenditure on education

	As percentage of Total public expenditure			As percentage of GDP		
	1980	*1990*	*1993-95*	*1980*	*1990*	*1993-95*
SUB-SAHARAN AFRICA	..	..	..	..	..	..
excluding South Africa	..	..	..	..	..	..
excl. S. Africa & Nigeria	..	..	..	..	..	..
Angola	..	..	..	..	..	..
Benin	..	..	..	..	..	2.6
Botswana	22.2	20.5	24.5	..	..	..
Burkina Faso	15.5	18.3	17.9	1.8	..	..
Burundi	..	..	14.1	..	3.2	4.5
Cameroon	12.4	15.6	14.6	..	..	..
Cape Verde	..	..	..	..	..	..
Central African Republic	..	..	..	3.5	1.9	1.5
Chad	..	..	..	..	..	1.1
Comoros	..	..	..	..	3.4	3.7
Congo, Democratic Rep. of	18.9	..	0.8	..	..	..
Congo, Republic of	..	..	..	5.3	..	5.3
Côte d'Ivoire	..	..	..	5.7	..	4.3
Djibouti	..	..	..	..	3.2	..
Equatorial Guinea	..	..	..	..	..	..
Eritrea	..	..	..	..	..	..
Ethiopia	10.2	9.9	14.0	..	2.6	3.6
Gabon	..	..	..	..	..	..
Gambia, The	12.3	12.3	..	2.3	2.4	2.7
Ghana	..	..	..	..	..	..
Guinea	..	..	..	..	..	1.5
Guinea-Bissau	..	..	..	..	..	..
Kenya	19.6	19.9	20.6	5.2	5.4	6.1
Lesotho	..	17.5	..	6.5	..	8.8
Liberia	11.9	..	..	..	..	..
Madagascar	..	15.0	11.3	3.5	..	..
Malawi	9.0	10.4	..	2.0	1.9	3.8
Mali	15.7	..	..	..	..	1.8
Mauritania	..	..	..	4.1	3.7	3.4
Mauritius	17.6	14.3	17.8	4.1	3.0	2.9
Mozambique	..	..	..	..	1.5	..
Namibia	..	..	..	..	..	7.0
Niger	18.0	..	..	..	..	..
Nigeria	..	..	..	..	..	..
Rwanda	..	..	..	2.2	..	..
São Tomé and Principe	..	..	..	..	..	..
Senegal	23.0	..	..	4.1	3.6	..
Seychelles	..	..	12.2	..	6.1	4.7
Sierra Leone	..	13.3	..	..	..	..
Somalia	..	..	..	..	..	..
South Africa	..	..	..	..	..	..
Sudan	9.8	..	..	3.8	..	..
Swaziland	24.6	27.4	..	3.9	3.9	5.1
Tanzania	13.3	..	..	..	..	..
Togo	..	..	..	4.7	4.4	4.0
Uganda	14.9	..	..	..	..	..
Zambia	11.4	9.0	17.6	3.5	..	1.6
Zimbabwe	15.5	..	..	4.8	7.3	6.8
NORTH AFRICA	..	..	..	..	..	..
Algeria	..	..	..	..	..	..
Egypt, Arab Republic	8.1	14.0	13.8	..	..	..
Libya	..	..	..	..	..	..
Morocco	17.3	18.2	16.6	4.8	4.8	4.8
Tunisia	17.0	17.0	18.3	4.5	5.0	5.5
ALL AFRICA	..	..	..	..	..	..

13-21. Economic opportunities of women

	Female / male ratio of participation in economic activity 1994	Female as percentage of male in occupational group, 1990			
		Administrative and managerial	Professional and technical	Clerical and sales	Services
SUB-SAHARAN AFRICA	57	11	42	..	..
excluding South Africa	57	10	37	..	..
excl. S.Africa & Nigeria	58	..	..	..	..
Angola	58	..	..	..	..
Benin	85	..	..	..	..
Botswana	49	57	159	151	238
Burkina Faso	81	16	35.	168	28
Burundi	82	16	44	..	..
Cameroon	46	11	32	59	46
Cape Verde	36	30	94	170	134
Central African Republic	74	10	23	146	13
Chad	25	..	..	..	..
Comoros	63	..	29	..	..
Congo, Democratic Rep. of	52	10	20	..	..
Congo, Republic of	61	7	40	..	..
Côte d'Ivoire	54	..	..	..	..
Djibouti	64	2	25	..	..
Equatorial Guinea	63	2	37	..	..
Eritrea	..	..	..	..	..
Ethiopia	56	13	31	..	..
Gabon	55	..	..	..	..
Gambia, The	62	18	31	..	..
Ghana	63	10	56	..	..
Guinea	61	..	..	..	..
Guinea-Bissau	61	..	..	..	..
Kenya	62	..	..	..	..
Lesotho	69	50	130	144	209
Liberia	41	..	..	..	..
Madagascar	60	..	..	..	..
Malawi	62	5	53	58	39
Mali	17	25	23	130	71
Mauritania	29	8	26	33	81
Mauritius	35	17	71	44	70
Mozambique	85	13	26	..	..
Namibia	30	26	69	..	..
Niger	83	9	..	..	..
Nigeria	51	6	35	140	13
Rwanda	83	9	47	48	35
São Tomé and Principe	..	..	..	..	..
Senegal	60	..	..	..	..
Seychelles	72	40	139	143	141
Sierra Leone	45	9	47	191	18
Somalia	59	..	..	..	..
South Africa	54	21	88	..	196
Sudan	30	3	40	..	..
Swaziland	60	17	119	116	82
Tanzania	85	..	..	..	..
Togo	52	9	27	..	..
Uganda	65	..	..	..	..
Zambia	41	6	47	136	29
Zimbabwe	49	18	67	52	42
NORTH AFRICA	16	19	39	31	14
Algeria	11	6	38	13	23
Egypt, Arab Republic	12	19	40	40	9
Libya	12	..	..	..	..
Morocco	26	34	46	..	..
Tunisia	33	8	21	..	..
ALL AFRICA	49	13	41	..	..

13-22. Household and economic participation of women

	Percentage of households headed by women (latest available between 1991-98)	Percentage of women in occupational group 1991-93					
		Agriculture	Mining	Utilities & manufacturing	Construction, transport, storage & communications	Service industries	Community, social & personal services
SUB-SAHARAN AFRICA	..	..	..	..	..	..	..
excluding South Africa	..	..	..	..	..	..	..
excl. S.Africa & Nigeria	..	..	..	..	..	..	..
Angola	..	..	..	..	..	..	..
Benin	..	..	..	..	..	..	..
Botswana	..	2	1	12	9	35	41
Burkina Faso	6	..	..	..	..	..	..
Burundi	..	..	..	..	..	..	..
Cameroon	18	..	..	..	..	..	..
Cape Verde	..	..	..	..	..	..	..
Central African Republic	16	..	..	..	..	..	..
Chad	..	14	0	14	14	14	43
Comoros	..	..	..	..	..	..	..
Congo, Democratic Rep. of	..	..	..	..	..	..	..
Congo, Republic of	..	..	..	..	..	..	..
Côte d'Ivoire	12	..	..	..	..	..	..
Djibouti	17	..	..	..	..	..	..
Equatorial Guinea	..	..	..	..	..	..	..
Eritrea	..	..	..	..	..	..	..
Ethiopia	18	10	0	24	6	10	50
Gabon	..	..	..	..	..	..	..
Gambia, The	1	..	..	..	..	..	..
Ghana	14	..	..	..	..	..	..
Guinea	8	..	..	..	..	..	..
Guinea-Bissau	10	..	..	..	..	..	..
Kenya	15	20	0	8	5	11	57
Lesotho	..	..	..	..	..	..	..
Liberia	..	..	..	..	..	..	..
Madagascar	18	..	..	..	..	..	..
Malawi	..	73	0	7	2	4	14
Mali	6	..	..	..	..	..	..
Mauritania	24	..	..	..	..	..	..
Mauritius	..	12	0	64	2	7	15
Mozambique	..	..	..	..	..	..	..
Namibia	..	..	..	..	..	..	..
Niger	6	5	5	20	25	25	25
Nigeria	13	..	..	..	..	..	..
Rwanda	..	..	..	..	..	..	..
São Tomé and Principe	..	..	..	..	..	..	..
Senegal	8	..	..	..	..	..	..
Seychelles	..	..	..	..	..	..	..
Sierra Leone	..	..	..	..	..	..	..
Somalia	..	..	..	..	..	..	..
South Africa	27	..	..	..	..	..	..
Sudan	..	..	..	..	..	..	..
Swaziland	26	23	1	16	4	20	36
Tanzania	11	..	..	..	..	..	..
Togo	..	..	..	..	..	..	..
Uganda	2	..	..	..	..	..	..
Zambia	19	..	..	..	..	..	..
Zimbabwe	..	38	1	6	3	10	..
NORTH AFRICA	..	36	0	21	2	8	32
Algeria	..	..	..	..	..	..	..
Egypt, Arab Republic	..	52	0	10	2	7	29
Libya	..	..	..	..	..	..	..
Morocco	..	3	0	45	2	11	39
Tunisia	..	..	..	..	..	..	..
ALL AFRICA	..	..	..	..	..	..	..

13-23. Relative prices of consumption and investment in PPP terms, 1993

	International price level	Relative price level (price level of GDP=100)									
					Private consumption					Government consumption	Gross Fixed capital formation
	Ratio of PPP rate to $ exchange rate	Total	All food	Bread and cereals	Clothing and footware	Fuel and power	Health care	Education	Transport and communications		
SUB-SAHARAN AFRICA	..	..	..	..	..	..	..	..	..	..	..
excluding South Africa	..	..	..	..	..	..	..	..	..	..	..
excl. South Africa & Nigeria	..	..	..	..	..	..	..	..	..	..	..
Angola	..	..	..	..	..	..	..	..	..	..	..
Benin	..	..	..	..	..	..	..	..	..	..	..
Botswana	37	125	103	113	157	256	105	98	65	113	108
Burkina Faso	..	..	..	..	..	..	..	..	..	..	..
Burundi	..	..	..	..	..	..	..	..	..	..	..
Cameroon	50	93	87	98	102	173	88	60	97	123	141
Cape Verde	..	..	..	..	..	..	..	..	..	..	..
Central African Republic	..	..	..	..	..	..	..	..	..	..	..
Chad	..	..	..	..	..	..	..	..	..	..	..
Comoros	..	..	..	..	..	..	..	..	..	..	..
Congo, Democratic Rep. of	..	..	..	..	..	..	..	..	..	..	..
Congo, Republic of	64	98	115	105	109	288	58	55	67	78	193
Côte d'Ivoire	52	98	101	112	97	..	89	60	78	116	151
Djibouti	..	..	..	..	..	..	..	..	..	..	..
Equatorial Guinea	..	..	..	..	..	..	..	..	..	..	..
Eritrea	..	..	..	..	..	..	..	..	..	..	..
Ethiopia	..	..	..	..	..	..	..	..	..	..	..
Gabon	80	126	147	95	131	284	90	119	79	152	91
Gambia, The	..	..	..	..	..	..	..	..	..	..	..
Ghana	..	..	..	..	..	..	..	..	..	..	..
Guinea	33	97	106	118	75	173	37	68	94	80	127
Guinea-Bissau	..	..	..	..	..	..	..	..	..	..	..
Kenya	21	90	91	123	85	140	45	41	71	72	196
Lesotho	..	..	..	..	..	..	..	..	..	..	..
Liberia	..	..	..	..	..	..	..	..	..	..	..
Madagascar	..	..	..	..	..	..	..	..	..	..	..
Malawi	34	87	98	109	54	148	31	50	73	79	279
Mali	38	90	92	131	86	..	59	31	90	63	179
Mauritania	..	..	..	..	..	..	..	..	..	..	..
Mauritius	39	93	81	65	72	111	59	87	67	108	134
Mozambique	..	..	..	..	..	..	..	..	..	..	..
Namibia	..	..	..	..	..	..	..	..	..	..	..
Niger	..	..	..	..	..	..	..	..	..	..	..
Nigeria	36	101	150	171	58	56	46	40	47	61	115
Rwanda	..	..	..	..	..	..	..	..	..	..	..
São Tomé and Principe	..	..	..	..	..	..	..	..	..	..	..
Senegal	48	90	87	119	74	227	75	45	79	81	237
Seychelles	..	..	..	..	..	..	..	..	..	..	..
Sierra Leone	29	115	141	192	107	185	34	39	76	37	147
Somalia	..	..	..	..	..	..	..	..	..	..	..
South Africa	..	..	..	..	..	..	..	..	..	..	..
Sudan	..	..	..	..	..	..	..	..	..	..	..
Swaziland	35	92	84	100	138	187	53	66	54	91	..
Tanzania	..	..	..	..	..	..	..	..	..	..	..
Togo	..	..	..	..	..	..	..	..	..	..	..
Uganda	..	..	..	..	..	..	..	..	..	..	..
Zambia	43	113	126	185	98	282	29	46	89	34	213
Zimbabwe	26	105	81	97	91	221	51	77	62	89	..
NORTH AFRICA	..	..	..	..	..	..	..	..	..	..	..
Algeria											
Egypt, Arab Republic	35	90	88	97	124	80	54	49	92	92	106
Libya	..	..	..	..	..	..	..	..	..	..	..
Morocco	37	93	83	77	68	282	81	81	77	106	182
Tunisia	39	92	81	62	142	105	80	109	79	124	159
ALL AFRICA	..	..	..	..	..	..	..	..	..	..	..

13-24. Structure of household consumption in PPP terms, 1997

	Ratio of PPP rate to $ exchange rate	Household consumption per capita PPP	Food		Clothing and footware	Fuel and power	Health care	Education	Transport and communications	Other consumption
			All food	Bread and cereals						
SUB-SAHARAN AFRICA	..	..	..	..	..	..	..	..	..	..
excluding South Africa	..	..	..	..	..	..	..	..	..	..
excluding South Africa & Nigeria	..	..	..	..	..	..	..	..	..	..
Angola		..	45	..	..	..	..	..	..	..
Benin	..	1,100	45	13	8	3	3	8	14	17
Botswana	43	3,084	25	9	4	1	7	22	21	19
Burkina Faso		..	..	..	..	..	..	..	..	..
Burundi		..	..	..	..	..	..	..	..	..
Cameroon	34	1,277	38	7	14	2	6	9	8	24
Cape Verde		..	..	..	..	..	..	..	..	..
Central African Republic		..	..	..	..	..	..	..	..	..
Chad		..	..	..	..	..	..	..	..	..
Comoros		..	..	..	..	..	..	..	..	..
Congo, Democratic Rep. of		..	..	..	..	..	..	..	..	..
Congo, Republic of	52	791	36	5	3	1	10	15	18	17
Côte d'Ivoire	39	1,393	35	8	9	..	8	26	11	11
Djibouti		..	..	..	..	..	..	..	..	..
Equatorial Guinea		..	..	..	..	..	..	..	..	..
Eritrea		..	..	..	..	..	..	..	..	..
Ethiopia		..	..	..	..	..	..	..	..	..
Gabon	59	2,468	37	7	3	2	8	8	20	23
Gambia, The		..	..	..	..	..	..	..	..	..
Ghana		..	..	..	..	..	..	..	..	..
Guinea	30	1,456	32	6	19	2	14	9	9	15
Guinea-Bissau		..	..	..	..	..	..	..	..	..
Kenya	30	872	38	11	8	2	5	22	10	16
Lesotho		..	..	..	..	..	..	..	..	..
Liberia		..	..	..	..	..	..	..	..	..
Madagascar		..	..	..	..	..	..	..	..	..
Malawi	34	607	45	17	18	2	8	9	8	10
Mali	33	655	48	13	13	..	2	7	14	15
Mauritania		..	..	..	..	..	..	..	..	..
Mauritius	41	6,533	24	4	8	3	10	5	19	30
Mozambique		..	..	..	..	..	..	..	..	..
Namibia		..	..	..	..	..	..	..	..	..
Niger		..	..	..	..	..	..	..	..	..
Nigeria	37	692	48	15	8	6	3	4	5	27
Rwanda		..	..	..	..	..	..	..	..	..
São Tomé and Principe		..	..	..	..	..	..	..	..	..
Senegal	30	1,536	52	11	14	2	2	11	6	13
Seychelles		..	..	..	..	..	..	..	..	..
Sierra Leone	42	267	48	13	12	3	13	14	8	2
Somalia		..	..	..	..	..	..	..	..	..
South Africa		..	..	..	..	..	..	..	..	..
Sudan		..	..	..	..	..	..	..	..	..
Swaziland	41	2,579	27	6	6	4	10	17	18	19
Tanzania		..	..	..	..	..	..	..	..	..
Togo		..	..	..	..	..	..	..	..	..
Uganda		..	..	..	..	..	..	..	..	..
Zambia	42	625	47	7	8	1	3	12	10	19
Zimbabwe	33	1,572	28	7	11	2	9	23	14	12
NORTH AFRICA		..	..	..	..	..	..	..	..	..
Algeria		..	..	..	..	..	..	..	..	..
Egypt, Arab Republic	41	1,962	44	11	7	3	8	8	5	26
Libya		..	..	..	..	..	..	..	..	..
Morocco	37	2,360	45	11	9	2	5	10	10	18
Tunisia	38	3,687	35	7	6	2	6	7	15	29
ALL AFRICA		..	..	..	..	..	..	..	..	..

Figure 13-1.   Life expectancy, 1997

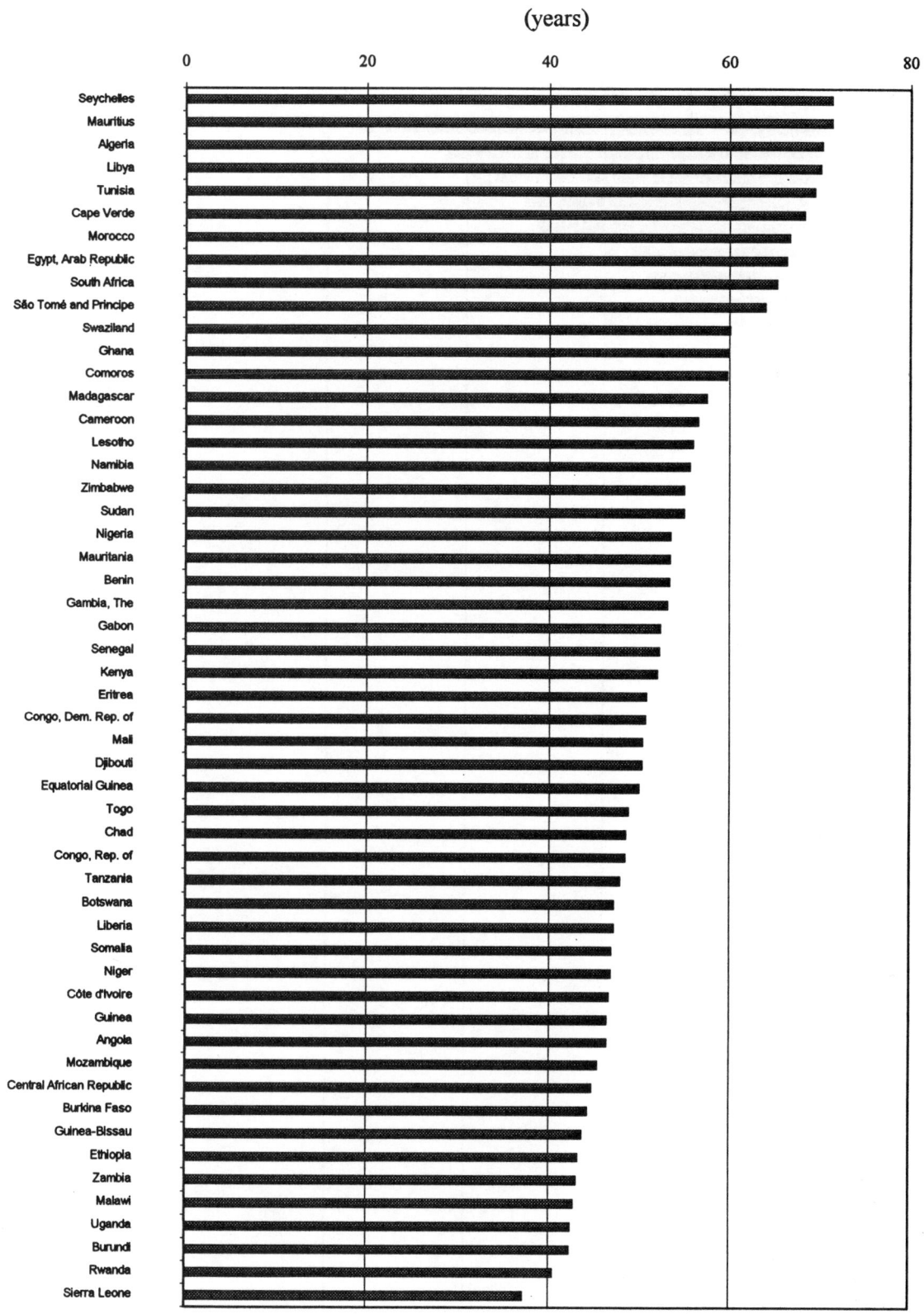

Figure 13-2. GDP per capita based on PPP, 1997

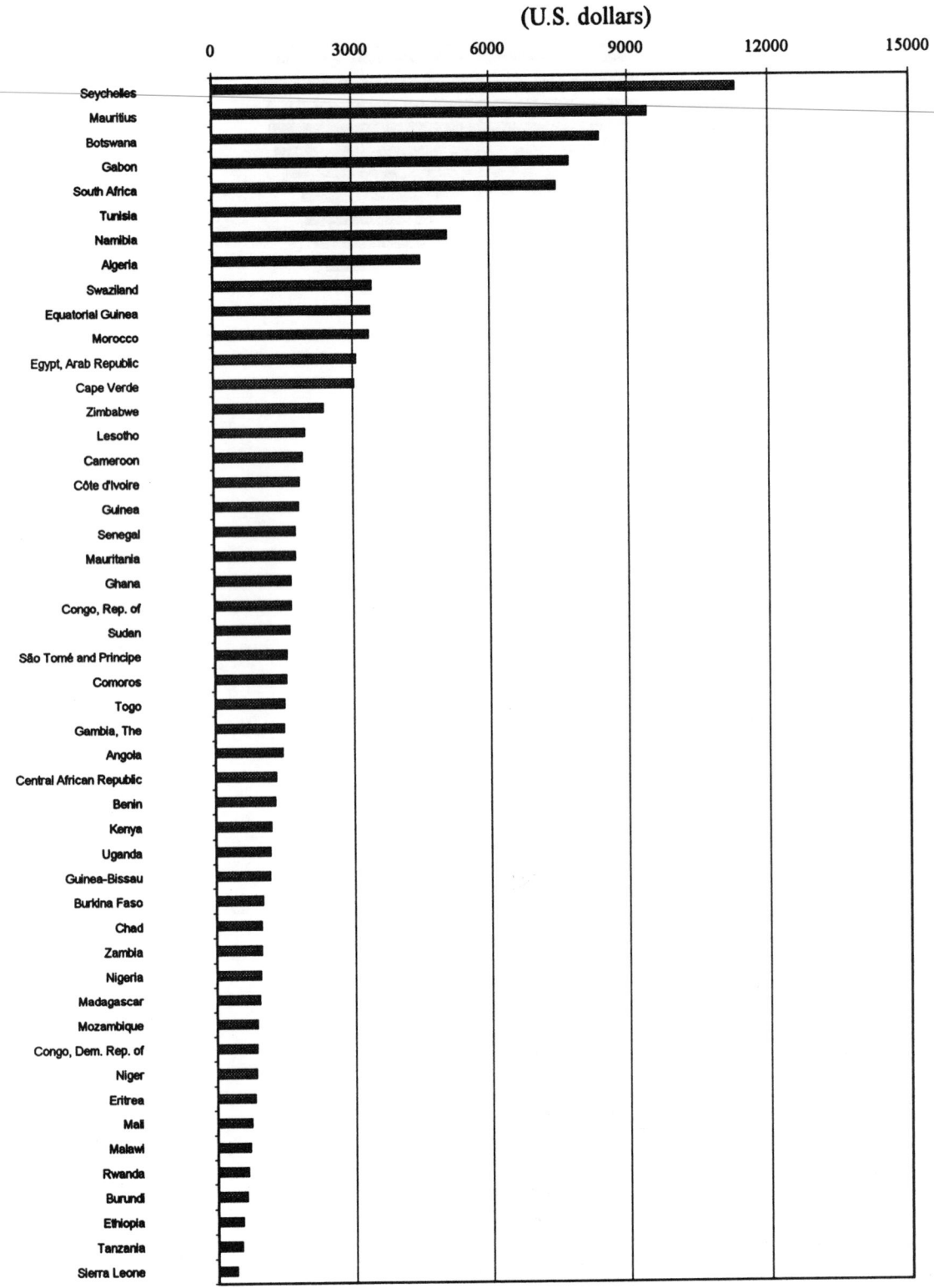

Figure 13-3. Urban population as percentage of total population, 1997*

(percent)

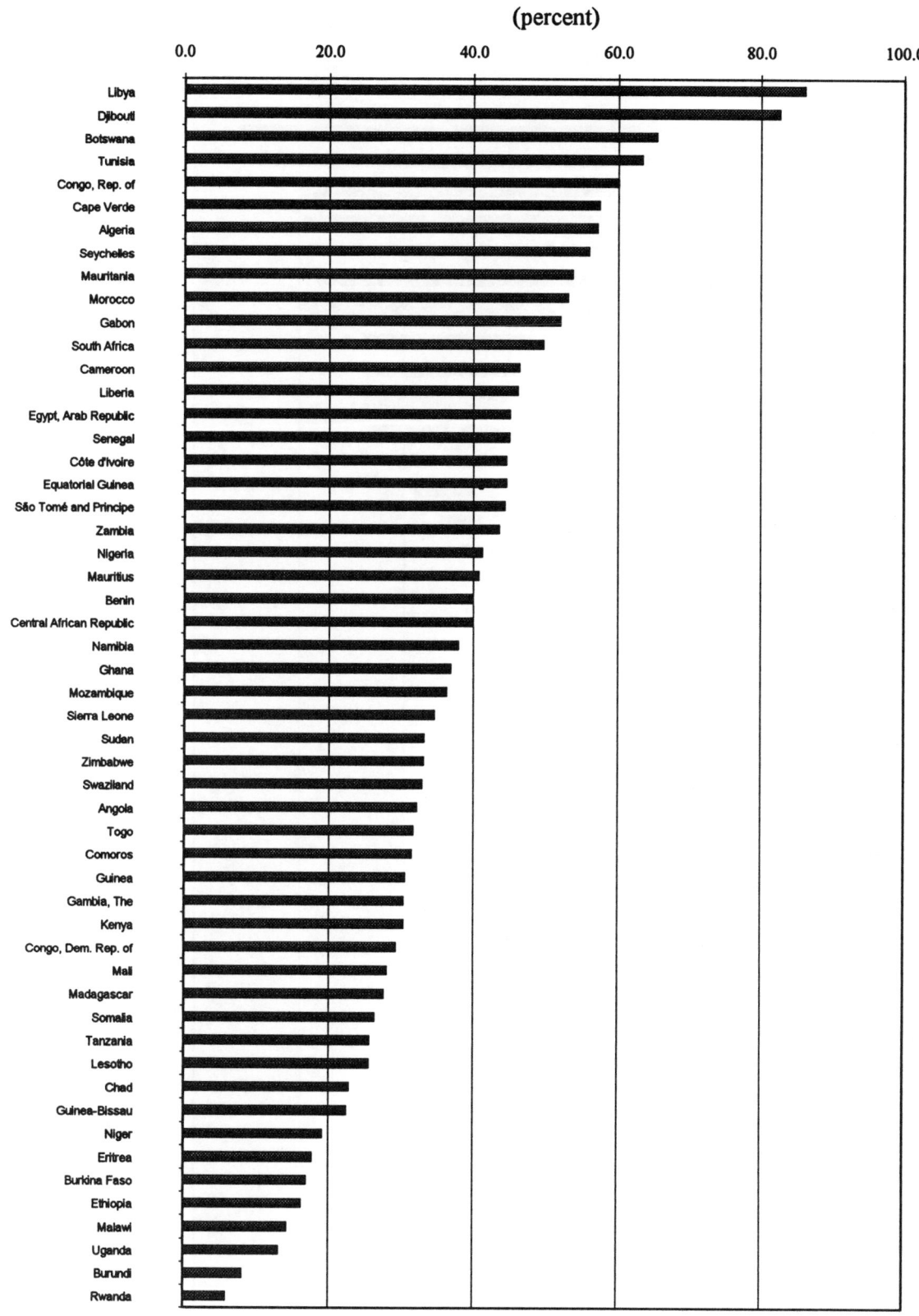

* Or most recent year available.

Figure 13-4.   Primary school gross enrollment ratio, 1996*

(percent)

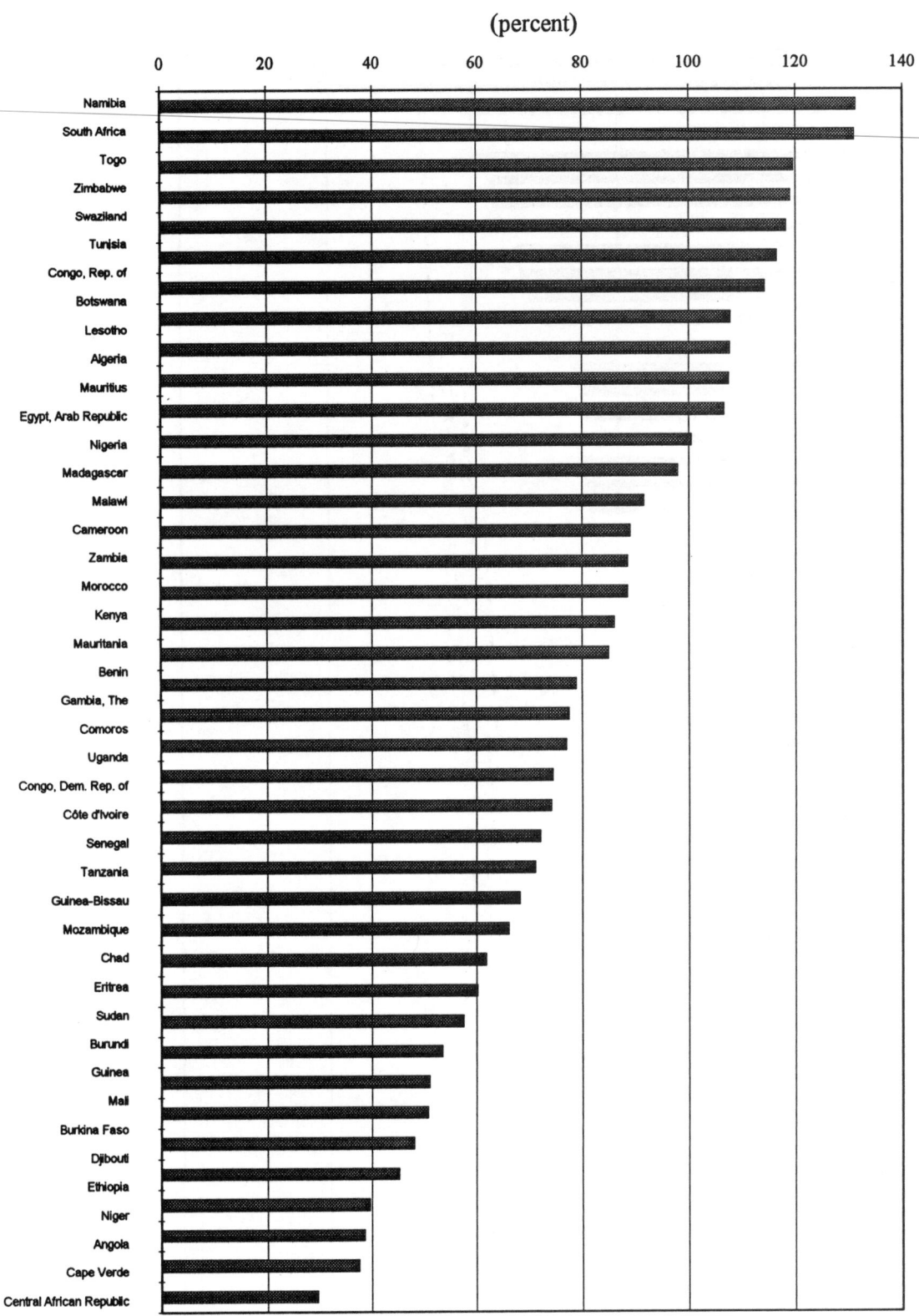

*Or most recent year available

Figure 13-5. Maternal mortality, 1995*

(per 1,000,000 live births)

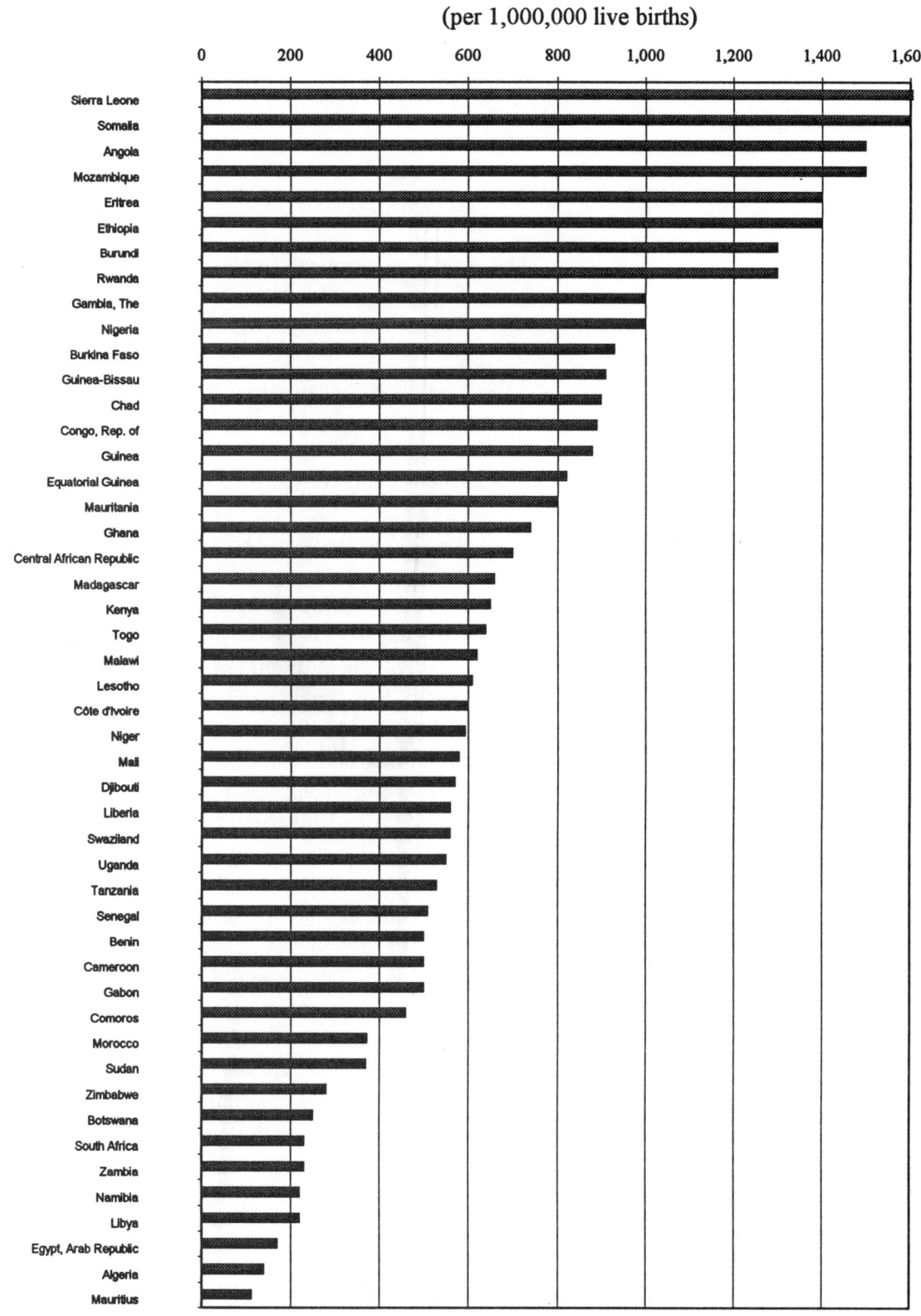

* Or most recent year available.
** Maternal mortality is greater than 1600.

Technical Notes

Tables

Table 13-1. Age and gender structure of the population. Age and gender structure of the population (UN and World Bank data) is the distribution of the total population according to age and gender. Only the female composition of the population is presented, as the male composition can easily be figured as the residual. Figures relate to midyear populations as estimated from the latest censuses. Age dependency ratio is calculated as the ratio of dependents—population under age 15 and above age 65—to the working age population—those aged 15 to 64.

Table 13-2. Poverty. This table presents selected indicators for comparing the incidence and extent of urban and rural poverty. The first indicator uses purchasing power parities rather than official exchange rates to calculate GDP per capita: a measure of the overall mean level of poverty at the national level. The next indicator is the national poverty headcount, which shows the percentage of the population living below the poverty line deemed appropriate for the country by its authorities. The poverty line is defined as the below which adequate standards of nutrition, shelter, and personal amenities cannot be assured. Since these levels are country specific, cross-country comparisons cannot be made. The next indicator, however, uses a relative concept of poverty, which does allow such comparisons. It shows the percentage of the urban and rural populations living on less than two-thirds of the mean national per capita income. Associated with these indicators are the urban and rural Gini coefficients, which describe the level of inequality in urban and rural income distributions.

The last indicator shows the percentage of household income spent on food (UNDP, World Bank, Penn World Tables, National Household Surveys).

Table 13-3. Income distribution. This table presents the share of income held by the richest and poorest population groups in a country (World Bank data and national household surveys).

Table 13-4. Urbanization. This table presents the number of persons living in urban areas as a percentage of the total population. Average annual percentage growth rates are shown separately for the urban population and the total population. The urban population percentages are based on the number of persons living in areas defined as "urban" according to national definitions of this concept. Since national definitions differ, cross-country comparisons should be made with caution (World Bank data).

Table 13-5. Components of population change. This table presents three determinants of population change: total fertility rate, crude birth rate, and crude death rate. Crude birth rate is the number of births per 1,000 population in a given year. Crude death rate is the number of deaths per 1,000 population in a given year. Total fertility rate is the average number of children that would be born alive to a woman during her lifetime, if she were to bear children at each age in accordance with prevailing age-specific fertility rates (World Bank data).

Table 13-6. Survival prospects. This table shows five health-related indicators: life expectancy at birth, infant mortality rate, child mortality rate, maternal mortality rate, and adult HIVs sero prevalence.

Life expectancy at birth is the number of years a newborn infant would live if prevailing patterns of mortality at the time of its birth were to stay the same throughout its life. Infant mortality rate is the number of deaths of infants under one year of age per 1,000 live births in a given year. Child mortality rate is the number of deaths of children under five years of age per 1,000 live births in a given year. Maternal mortality rate is the annual number of deaths of women from pregnancy-related causes per 100,000 live births. Adult HIV-1 sero prevalence reflects the estimated rate of infection in each country's adult population (aged 15 to 49) (UNAIDS).

Table 13-7. Immunization and ORT use.

This is the percentage of children under one year of age immunized against tuberculosis, DPT, polio, and measles. It also gives the use rate of oral rehydration therapy (ORT) among children under five years of age. DPT refers to diphtheria, pertussis (whooping cough), and tetanus. ORT use is the percentage of all cases of diarrhea in children under five years of age treated with oral rehydration salts or an appropriate household solution (WHO data).

Table 13-8. Child malnutrition.

Data reported on this table give the percentage of children and babies suffering from nutrition-related problems of low birthweight, underweight, wasting, and stunting. Figures are also given on the extent of breastfeeding among nursing mothers.

Low birthweight refers to babies born weighing less than 2,500 grams. Underweight refers to children under the age of five weighing two standard deviations below the median weight for age of the reference population. Wasting refers to children of ages 12 through 23 months weighing two standard deviations below the median weight for height of the reference population. Stunting refers to children of ages 24 through 59 months standing two standard deviations below the median height-for-age of the reference population (UNDP various years, WHO and World Bank data).

Table 13-9. Access to sanitation facilities.

Table 13-9 shows the percentage of the population with access to sanitation facilities (WHO data). Urban areas with access to sanitation facilities are defined as urban populations served by connections to public sewers or household systems, such as pit privies, pour-flush latrines, septic tanks, communal toilets, and other such facilities. Rural populations with access were defined as those with adequate disposal, such as pit privies and pour-flush latrines. Application of these definitions may vary, and comparisons can therefore be misleading.

Table 13-10. Access to safe water.

This table refers to the percentage of the population with reasonable access to safe water supply, which includes treated surface waters or untreated, but uncontaminated water, such as that from springs, sanitary wells, and protected boreholes. In an urban area, this may be a public fountain or standpost located not more than 200 meters away. In rural areas, it implies that members of the household do not have to spend a disproportionate part of the day fetching water. Data are presented separately for total, urban and rural population (WHO data).

Table 13-11. Health expenditure.

This table shows total health expenditure as percentage of GDP and on a per capita basis—both in current $ and PPP terms. The ratio to GDP is also shown for public and private expenditure. *Total health expenditure* is the sum of public and private health expenditures. It covers the provision of health services (preventive and curative), family planning activities, nutrition activities, and emergency aid designated for health but does not include provision of water and sanitation. *Public health expenditure* consists of recurrent and capital spending from government (central and local) budgets, external borrowings and grants (including donations from international agencies and nongovernmental organizations, and social (or compulsory) health insurance funds. *Private health expenditure* includes direct household (out-of-pocket) spending, private insurance, charitable donations, and direct service payments by private corporations (WHO, IMF, and World Bank data).

Table 13-12. Health care. Indicators presented here are population per physician, population per hospital bed, the percentage of births attended by trained health personnel, and access to health services. The figure for physicians includes, in addition to the total number of registered practitioners in the country, medical assistants whose medical training is less than that of qualified physicians, but who nevertheless dispense similar medical services, including simple surgical operations. The definition of recognized medical practitioners differs among countries. Hospital beds include inpatient beds available in public, private, general, and specialized hospitals and in rehabilitation centers. In most coases acute and chronic care are included. Births attended refers to births attended by physicians, nurses, midwives, trained primary healthcare workers, or trained traditional birth attendants. Access to health services refers to the percentage of the population that can reach appropriate local health services by the local transport in no more than one hour (WHO and World Bank data).

Table 13-13. Illiteracy rate. This table shows the share of illiterate adults in total adult population aged 15 years and over. Literacy is defined as the ability to read and write. A person who can, with understanding, both read and write a short, simple statement about his everyday life is literate. Persons who can read, but cannot write, are included with illiterates. Figures are shown separately for males, females, and both genders combined (UNESCO data).

Tables 13-14. Primary school gross enrollment ratio. This is the total number of pupils enrolled at the primary level of education, regardless of age, expressed as a percentage of the population corresponding to the official school age of primary education in a given country. Data are given separately for males, females, and both genders combined. Figures shown may be more than 100 percent since total enrollment

includes pupils above and pupils below the primary school age, as well as repeaters (UNESCO data).

Tables 13-15. Pupil progression. This table provides two education indicators. *Percentage of cohort reaching grade 5 of primary school* shows the percentage of children starting primary school, who eventually attain grade 4. The estimate is based on the Reconstructed Cohort Method, which uses data on enrollment and repeaters for two consecutive years. Progression to secondary school (general) is the number of new children in the first grade of secondary school (general) divided by the number of children enrolled in the final grade of primary school in the previous year (according to the country's duration of primary education (UNESCO and World Bank data).

Table 13-16. Net primary enrollment ratio. This is the ratio of the number of children of official school age enrolled in school to the number of children of official school age in the population (UNESCO data).

Table 13-17. Number of school teachers. Teachers in both public and private schools are covered in this table. Data refer to both full-time and part-time teachers, excluding other instructional personnel without teaching functions. Figures are shown here separately for primary and secondary schools. Percentage females means the number of female teachers expressed as a percentage of total teaching staff (UNESCO data).

Table 13-18. Pupil/teacher ratio. This ratio gives the average number of pupils per teacher. Figures are given separately for primary and secondary schools. As teaching staff includes both full-time and part-time teachers, comparability of this ratio between countries may be affected as the proportion of part-time teachers varies greatly from one country to another (UNESCO data).

Table 13-19. Secondary school gross enrollment ratio. This is the secondary school equivalent of the data presented in Table 13-14. It gives the total number of students enrolled at the secondary level of education, regardless of age, expressed as a percentage of the population corresponding to the official school age of secondary education. Data are presented separately for males, females, and both genders combined. Second level, general refers to education in secondary schools that provides general or specialized instruction based upon at least four years of previous instruction at the first or primary level, which do not specifically aim at preparing the pupils directly for a given trade or occupation. Such schools may be called high schools, middle schools, or lyceums and offer courses of study whose completion is a minimum condition for admission into universities. In some countries, some of these schools provide both academic and vocational training. These composite secondary schools are considered as equivalent to the academic type of secondary school and are thus classified as second level, general (UNESCO data).

Table 13-20. Public expenditure on education. This table presents the public expenditure on education (UNESCO) first as a percentage of total public expenditure (IMF/GFS) and then as a percentage of current GDP (Table 2-5).

Table 13-21. Economic opportunities of women. This table shows two indicators. Female/male ratio of participation in economic activity shows the number of female workers in relation to the number of male workers. Females as percentage of males in occupational group shows the breakdown of the first indicator for occupational categories (UNDP data).

Table 13-22. Household and economic participation of women. This table presents indicators on gender issues in development. Households headed by women (World Bank data) refers to families in which a woman is acknowledged as the head by the other members. The occupational statistics are based on UN, *Statistical Yearbook 1992–93*.

Table 13-23. Relative prices of consumption and investment in PPP terms, 1993. This table shows

1993 relative prices of consumption and investment using purchasing power parity (PPP). PPP measures the cost of goods in one country relative to a numeraire country, in this case the United States. An international price level above 100 means that the general price level in the country is higher than that in the United States. For example, Kenya's price level of 21 means that a bundle of goods and services purchased for $100 in the United States costs only $21 in Kenya.

The relative prices of components of GDP shown in the table are calculated from their international prices measured relative to each country's price level of GDP. A figure above 100 indicates that the price of that component is higher than the average price level of GDP. This is not the same as saying that the component is more expensive in that country than in the United States. It indicates only that the price for that component is higher than the general price level prevailing in the country.

International price level is the ratio of a country's PPP rate to its official exchange rate for U.S. dollars. Private consumption includes the consumption expenditures of individuals, households, and nongovernmental organizations. *All food* includes all food purchased for household consumption. *Bread and cereals* comprise the main staple products: rice, flour, bread, all other cereals; and cereal preparations. *Clothing and footwear* include purchases of new and used clothing and footwear and repair services. *Fuel and power* exclude energy used for transport (rarely reported to be more than 1 percent of total consumption in low- and middle-income economies). *Health care and education* include government as well as private expenditures. *Transport and communications* cover all personal costs of transport, telephones, and the like. *Government consumption* includes spending on goods and services for collective consumption less spending on recreational and other related cultural services, education, health, and housing. Expenditure on governmental final consumption consists of compensation of employees, consumption of intermediate goods and services, and consumption of fixed capital and indirect taxes paid less proceeds from sales of goods and services to other sectors such as fees charged by municipalities and other government agencies, school fees, fees for medical and hospital treatment and drug sales, and sales of maps and charts. *Gross fixed capital formation* comprises expenditures on construction, producer durables, and changes in stocks. Construction includes residential and nonresidential buildings and roads, bridges, and other civil engineering activities. Producer durables include machinery and nonelectrical equipment, electrical machinery and appliances, and transport equipment. Changes in stocks cover increases in the value of materials and supplies, works in progress, and livestock (including breeding stock and dairy cattle) (ICP and World Bank data).

Table 13-24. Structure of household consumption in PPP terms, 1997. This table reflects shares based on real values of items that make up household consumption. Because the goods and services that make up consumption are valued at uniform prices, PPP-based expenditure shares also provide a consistent view of differences in the real structure of consumption between countries. The shares shown in the table reflect the relative quantities of goods and services consumed rather than their nominal cost.

Although PPPs are more useful than official exhcnage rates in comparing consumption patterns, caution should be used in interpreting PPP results. PPP estimates are based on price comparisons of comparable items, but not all items can be matched perfectly in quality across countries and over time. Services are particularly difficult to compare, in part because of differences in productivity. Many services, such as government services, are not sold on the open market in all countries, so they are compared using input prices (mostly wages). Because this approach ignores productivity differences, it may inflate estimates of real quantities in lower-income countries (ICP and World Bank data).

Figures

The following indicators have been used to derive the figures in this chapter.

Figure 13-1. Life expectancy (Table 13-6).

Figure 13-2. GDP per capita, based on PPP, 1997 (Table 13-2).

Figure 13-3. Percentage of urban population in total population (Table 13-4).

Figure 13-4. Primary school enrollment ratio (Table 13-14).

Figure 13-5. Maternal mortality (Table 13-6).

Methodology used for regional aggregations and period averages in chapter 13

Table	Aggregations[a]					Period averages[b]	
	(1)	(2)	(6)	(7)	(8)	(1)	(2)
13-1							
Col. 1–8		x					
Col. 9–10			x				
13-2							
Col. 1, 3			x				
Col. 4, 5, 8				x			
Col. 2, 6-7					x		
13-3					x		
13-4							
Col. 1–3	x						
Col. 4–6							x
Col. 7–9			x				
Col. 10–12			•				x
13-5							
Col. 1–3			x				
Col. 4–6		x					
Col. 7–9		x					
13-6			x				
13-7			x				
13-8			x				
13-9			x				
13-10			x				
13-11							
Col. 1–4			x				
Col. 5					x		
13-12			x				
13-13			x				
13-14			x				
13-15			x				
13-16			x				
13-17							
Col. 1–3, 7–9					x		
Col. 4–6, 10–12			x				
13-18			x				
13-19			x				
13-20			x				
13-21			x				
13-22					x		
13-23					x		
13-24					x		

Note: Regional aggregations are shown in the rows for Sub-Saharan Africa, North Africa, and All Africa. Period averages are shown in the last three columns. This table shows only the methodologies used in this chapter.

a. Regional aggregations: (1) simple total; (2) simple total of the first indicator divided by the simple total of the second indicator (same country coverage); (3) simple total of the gap-filled indicator; (4) simple total of the gap-filled main indicator divided by the simple total of the gap-filled secondary indicator; (5) simple total of the first gap-filled main indicator less the simple total of the second gap-filled main indicator, all divided by the simple total of the secondary indicator; (6) weighted total; (7) median; (8) no aggregation; (9) simple arithmetic mean.

b. Period averages: (1) arithmetic mean (using the same series as shown in the table, i.e., ratio if the rest of the table is shown as ratio, level if the rest of the table is shown as level, growth rate if the rest of the table is shown as growth rate); (2) least-squares growth rate (using main indicator); (3) least-squares growth rate (using main indicator in constant terms, with the rest of the table in current terms).

14

Environmental Indicators

This chapter was drawn entirely from the World Resources Institute and reflects tables published in their *World Resources 1998–99*. It includes data on natural resources—their use by sector and the trends in their use—protected resources and those in danger of extinction, commercial energy production and its components, globally threatened species and protection and management programs.

Until the early 1970s, environmental issues were mainly focused on problems of industrial countries and on such issues as water and air pollution, acid rain, and greenhouse gas emissions. Since the publication of the Club of Rome's *The Limit to Growth* in 1972, however, issues of natural resource depletion and degradation have received considerable attention in assessing environmental factors and their impacts on the development prospects of developing nations. At the national level, environmental concerns revolve around population expansion, desertification, deforestation, and the by-products of energy consumption.

Environmental destruction is not, however, confined by geographic borders. For instance, global warming, said to be caused by greenhouse gas emissions, has become a major global environmental concern. The issue of the greenhouse effect may be subject to controversy at the theoretical level and difficult to prove at the practical level. The fact that industrial wastes generated in one country cross frontiers and cause environmental damage to other nations is, however, widely acknowledged. Common interests, therefore, compel the international community to jointly work toward a common goal of preserving the environment.

Increasing emphasis on the links between the environment and development, both at the national and international levels, is reflected in the growing number of scientific and analytical studies. Challenging the hegemony of the SNA national income accounting convention, numerous scholarly endeavors are under way to internalize environmental consequences in national income calculations. The argument is made that the SNA methodology overstates national income levels for two reasons. First, it does not account for both the direct and indirect costs of drawing down natural resources. Second, it counts expenditure on resources for environmental protection activities as income. The changes both in methodology and emphasis have created an urgent demand for physical data. The information in this chapter aims to meet this growing demand, notwithstanding the limitations in data coverage and reliability.

The rate of deforestation is of particular concern because the cost of deforestation goes far beyond the loses of forest products, such as timber and fuelwood. There are equally significant indirect costs, including soil erosion; the substitution of animal and agricultural residues for cooking, which would otherwise be used for fertilizer; and climate changes. Deforestation is caused by many factors, including increased demand for settlement area, cultivation, woodfuel, or a combination thereof. The information in this chapter provides an empirical framework for assessing policy alternatives in reversing the continuing depletion of natural resources.

Data on roundwood production and consumption are important in monitoring the causes of deforestation. In addition, since roundwood is a primary source of energy in developing nations, data on roundwood consumption is essential in analyzing air pollution. For instance, for 1985–87, Africa used close to 88 percent of its roundwood production for fuel and charcoal production, while approximately 12 percent of the roundwood production went to industrial uses. To put these figures in perspective, the corresponding figures for Europe are 16 and 84 percent.

Information on fresh water resources available and on the extent and the methods of their uses can provide a partial basis for analyzing Africa's agricultural performance, its potential hydroelectric power, and its populations' health conditions. Almost all Sub-Saharan African countries use a very small fraction of their internal renewable water resources. For instance, Ethiopia, a nation that has suffered from repeated droughts, uses only 2 percent of its water resources. The major problem rests in the uneven geographic distribution of water resources with respect to population density and the state of freshwater drawing technology. The quality of water is as important as the quantity of water available. Water-related disease accounts for 80 percent of all sicknesses and for 90 percent of the 15 million deaths in developing countries each year.

Data on energy production are shown because of related environmental consequences. Biomass fuel, comprising woodfuel and animal and agricultural residues, accounts for 40 to 90 percent of total energy used in Sub-Saharan Africa.

Data on protected areas and endangered species indicate the intentions of countries to safeguard the environment and protect the use of natural resources for future generations.

14-1. Land area and use, 1982-94

	Land area (000 hectares)	Population density (per 1,000 hectares) 1996	Domesticated land as a % of land area a/ 1994	Cropland		Permanent pasture		Forest and woodland		Other land	
				1992-94	Percentage change since 1982-84	1992-94	Percentage change since 1982-84	1992-94	Percentage change since 1982-84	1992-94	Percentage change since 1982-84
SUB-SAHARAN AFRICA	..	..	..	..	..	..	..	..	..	..	..
excluding South Africa	..	..	..	..	..	..	..	..	..	..	..
excl. S. Africa & Nigeria	..	..	..	..	..	..	..	..	..	..	..
Angola	124,670	90	46	3,500	2.9	54,000	0.0	23,000	-0.9	44,170	0.2
Benin	11,062	503	21	1,880	3.9	442	0.0	3,400	-11.0	5,340	7.0
Botswana	56,673	26	46	420	5.0	25,600	0.0	26,500	0.0	4,153	-0.5
Burkina Faso	27,360	394	34	3,465	18.0	6,000	0.0	13,800	0.0	4,082	-11.7
Burundi	2,568	2,423	86	1,120	-5.1	1,080	9.1	325	0.0	43	-41.1
Cameroon	46,540	291	19	7,040	1.2	2,000	0.0	35,900	0.0	1,600	-4.9
Cape Verde	..	..	..	..	..	..	..	..	..	..	..
Central African Republic	62,298	54	8	2,020	2.5	3,000	0.0	46,700	0.0	10,578	-0.5
Chad	125,920	52	38	3,256	3.4	45,000	0.0	32,400	0.0	45,264	-0.2
Comoros	..	..	..	..	..	..	..	..	..	..	..
Congo, Dem. Rep. of	34,150	78	30	170	9.9	10,000	0.0	19,900	0.0	4,080	-0.4
Congo, Rep. of	226,705	206	10	7,900	2.5	15,000	0.0	166,000	0.0	37,805	-0.5
Côte d'Ivoire	31,800	441	54	4,031	22.5	13,000	0.0	9,600	-5.9	5,149	-3.0
Djibouti	..	..	..	..	..	..	..	..	..	..	..
Equatorial Guinea	2,805	146	12	230	0.0	104	0.0	1,830	0.0	641	0.0
Eritrea	10,000	328	75	366	..	4,622	..	523	..	1,155	..
Ethiopia	100,000	582	31	12,197	..	28,267	..	13,633	..	49,269	..
Gabon	25,767	43	20	460	1.8	4,700	0.0	19,900	-0.4	707	11.3
Gambia, The	1,000	1,141	37	165	-10.6	194	2.1	94	-6.0	547	4.1
Ghana	22,754	784	57	4,407	15.0	8,400	0.0	9,300	-3.1	647	-29.7
Guinea	24,572	306	47	787	10.2	10,700	0.0	6,700	0.0	6,385	-1.1
Guinea-Bissau	2,812	388	50	340	10.3	1,080	0.0	1,070	0.0	322	-9.0
Kenya	56,914	488	45	4,520	5.6	21,300	0.0	16,800	0.0	14,294	-1.6
Lesotho	3,035	685	76	320	10.6	2,000	0.0	..	..	715	-4.1
Liberia	9,632	233	25	371	-0.1	2,000	0.0	4,600	0.0	2,661	0.0
Madagascar	58,154	264	47	3,105	3.1	24,000	0.0	23,200	0.0	7,849	-1.2
Malawi	9,408	1,046	38	1,700	19.9	1,840	0.0	3,700	-1.1	2,168	-10.0
Mali	122,019	91	27	2,569	25.1	30,000	0.0	11,800	-1.7	77,650	-0.4
Mauritania	102,522	23	38	208	6.7	39,250	0.0	4,410	-2.0	58,654	0.1
Mauritius	203	5,562	56	106	-0.9	7	0.0	44	-24.1	46	48.4
Mozambique	78,409	227	60	3,180	3.2	44,000	0.0	17,300	0.0	13,929	-0.7
Namibia	82,329	19	47	704	6.6	38,000	0.0	12,500	0.0	31,125	-0.1
Niger	126,670	75	12	4,035	13.9	10,440	13.1	2,500	0.0	109,695	-1.5
Nigeria	91,077	1,263	80	32,579	6.1	40,000	0.0	14,300	-10.6	4,198	-3.9
Rwanda	2,467	2,188	75	1,150	5.4	695	-0.7	250	0.0	372	-12.7
São Tomé and Principe	..	..	..	..	..	..	..	..	..	..	..
Senegal	19,253	443	42	2,355	0.2	5,700	0.0	7,467	-1.8	3,731	3.6
Seychelles	..	..	..	..	..	..	..	..	..	..	..
Sierra Leone	7,162	600	38	540	4.4	2,201	-0.1	1,947	2.5	2,474	-2.6
Somalia	62,734	157	70	1,026	1.1	43,000	0.0	16,000	6.7	2,708	-27.2
South Africa	122,104	347	79	15,200	15.4	81,433	0.1	8,200	0.0	17,271	-10.8
Sudan	237,600	115	52	12,975	3.3	110,000	12.2	42,367	-1.5	72,258	-14.0
Swaziland	1,720	512	73	191	24.3	1,070	-5.1	119	16.6	340	0.9
Tanzania	88,359	349	44	3,660	23.7	35,000	0.0	33,067	-1.9	16,632	-0.4
Togo	5,439	772	48	2,420	2.5	200	0.0	900	-11.8	1,919	3.2
Uganda	19,965	1,015	43	6,780	9.1	1,800	0.0	6,300	5.0	5,085	-14.6
Zambia	74,339	111	47	5,273	2.2	30,000	0.0	32,000	6.7	7,066	-23.0
Zimbabwe	38,685	296	52	2,876	2.5	17,190	0.5	8,800	-7.4	9,819	5.8
NORTH AFRICA	..	..	..	..	..	..	..	..	..	..	..
Algeria	238,174	121	17	8,088	9.1	31,024	-2.8	3,949	-10.0	195,197	0.4
Egypt	99,545	636	3	3,137	26.5	..	..	34	9.7	96,374	-0.7
Libya	175,954	32	9	2,170	3.1	13,300	0.3	840	33.0	159,644	-0.2
Morocco	44,630	605	68	9,686	13.9	20,933	0.2	8,613	9.9	5,397	-28.8
Tunisia	15,536	589	51	4,882	-0.1	3,416	1.8	666	17.1	6,602	-1.8
ALL AFRICA	2,963,468	249	36	189,803	6.5	889,350	0.0	713,405	-0.3	1,171,024	-0.8

Source: Food and Agriculture Organization of the United Nations, the United Nations Statistical Commission, the United Nations Economic Commission for Europe, and other sources.

Notes: a. Domesticated land is the sum of cropland and permanent pasture.

0 = zero or less than half the unit of measure;   .. = not available.

14-2. Forest resources, 1980-95

	Forest area								Plantation	
	Total forest				Natural forest				Extent (000 ha)	Annual % change
	Extent (000 ha)		Annual % change		Extent (000 ha)		Annual % change			
	1990	1995	1980-90	1990-95	1990	1995	1980-90	1990-95	1990	1990-95
SUB-SAHARAN AFRICA	..	..	..	..	..	..	..	..	..	..
excluding South Africa	..	..	..	..	..	..	..	..	..	..
excl. S. Africa & Nigeria	..	..	..	..	..	..	..	..	..	..
Angola	23,385	22,200	-0.6	-1.0	23,265	22,080	-0.6	-1.0	120	0.8
Benin	4,923	4,625	-1.4	-1.2	4,909	4,611	-1.4	-1.3	14	5.1
Botswana	14,271	13,917	-0.5	-0.5	14,270	13,916	-0.5	-0.5	1	0.0
Burkina Faso	4,431	4,271	-0.7	-0.7	4,411	4,251	-0.7	-0.7	20	8.2
Burundi	324	317	2.2	-0.4	232	225	-0.6	-0.6	92	19.4
Cameroon	20,244	19,598	-0.6	-0.6	20,228	19,582	-0.6	-0.6	16	13.6
Cape Verde	16	..	7.8	..	6	..	..	..	10	..
Central African Republic	30,571	29,930	-0.4	-0.4	30,565	29,924	-0.4	-0.4	6	47.9
Chad	11,496	11,025	-0.7	-0.8	11,492	11,021	-0.7	-0.8	4	5.8
Comoros	..	..	..	..	..	..	..	..	..	..
Congo, Dem. Rep. of	112,946	109,245	-0.7	-0.7	112,904	109,203	-0.7	-0.7	42	9.8
Congo, Rep. of	19,745	19,537	-0.2	-0.2	19,708	19,500	-0.2	-0.2	37	11.5
Côte d'Ivoire	5,623	5,469	-7.7	-0.6	5,560	5,403	-7.8	-0.6	63	7.0
Djibouti	1,320	..	..	..	22	..	..	..	0	..
Equatorial Guinea	1,829	1,781	-0.4	-0.5	1,826	1,778	-0.4	-0.5	3	0.0
Eritrea	282	282	..	0.0	233	233	..	0.0	..	..
Ethiopia	13,891	13,579	..	-0.5	13,751	13,439	..	-0.5	189	10.1
Gabon	18,314	17,859	-0.6	-0.5	18,293	17,838	-0.6	-0.5	21	4.6
Gambia, The	95	91	-1.1	-0.9	94	90	-1.1	-0.9	1	0.0
Ghana	9,608	9,022	-1.3	-1.3	9,555	8,969	-1.3	-1.3	53	2.2
Guinea	6,741	6,367	-1.1	-1.1	6,737	6,363	-1.2	-1.1	4	4.6
Guinea-Bissau	2,361	2,309	0.8	-0.4	2,360	2,308	0.8	-0.4	1	0.0
Kenya	1,309	1,292	-0.4	-0.3	1,191	1,174	-0.5	-0.3	118	1.5
Lesotho	6	6	14.6	0.0	0	0	0.0	0.0	7	16.1
Liberia	4,641	4,507	-0.5	-0.6	4,635	4,501	-0.5	-0.6	6	1.0
Madagascar	15,756	15,106	-0.9	-0.8	15,539	14,889	-1.0	-0.9	217	1.5
Malawi	3,612	3,339	-1.2	-1.6	3,486	3,213	-1.4	-1.6	126	8.1
Mali	12,154	11,585	-0.8	-1.0	12,140	11,571	-0.8	-1.0	14	27.3
Mauritania	556	556	0.0	0.0	554	554	0.0	0.0	2	24.1
Mauritius	12	12	1.2	0.0	3	3	-0.7	1.4	9	1.7
Mozambique	17,443	16,862	-0.7	-0.7	17,415	16,834	-0.7	-0.7	28	4.3
Namibia	12,584	12,374	-0.3	-0.3	12,584	12,374	-0.3	-0.3	0	0.0
Niger	2,562	2,562	0.0	0.0	2,550	2,550	0.0	0.0	12	10.3
Nigeria	14,387	13,780	-1.6	-0.9	14,236	13,629	-1.7	-0.9	151	2.8
Rwanda	252	250	1.7	-0.2	164	162	-0.2	-0.2	88	6.6
São Tomé and Principe	..	..	..	..	..	..	..	..	..	..
Senegal	7,629	7,381	-0.6	-0.7	7,517	7,269	-0.7	-0.7	112	25.5
Seychelles	..	..	..	..	..	..	..	..	..	..
Sierra Leone	1,522	1,309	-2.8	-3.0	1,516	1,303	-2.8	-3.0	6	3.0
Somalia	760	754	-0.3	-0.2	756	750	-0.3	-0.2	4	0.0
South Africa	8,574	8,499	-0.1	-0.2	7,279	7,204	-0.8	-0.2	965	1.7
Sudan	43,376	41,613	-1.0	-0.8	43,173	41,410	-1.0	-0.8	203	5.6
Swaziland	146	146	0.0	0.0	74	74	0.0	0.0	72	0.1
Tanzania	34,123	32,510	-1.1	-1.0	33,969	32,356	-1.1	-1.0	154	8.1
Togo	1,338	1,245	-1.6	-1.4	1,317	1,224	-1.8	-1.5	17	12.0
Uganda	6,400	6,104	-0.9	-0.9	6,380	6,084	-0.9	-1.0	20	0.0
Zambia	32,720	31,398	-0.9	-0.8	32,677	31,355	-0.9	-0.8	48	5.8
Zimbabwe	8,960	8,710	-0.7	-0.6	8,876	8,626	-0.7	-0.6	84	1.8
NORTH AFRICA	..	..	..	..	..	..	..	..	..	..
Algeria	1,978	1,861	-1.2	-1.2	1,493	1,376	-2.6	-1.6	485	4.8
Egypt	34	34	1.8	0.0	0	0	0.0	0	34	1.8
Libya	400	400	3.2	0.0	190	190	0.0	0	210	7.4
Morocco	3,894	3,835	-0.3	-0.3	3,573	3,514	-0.6	-0.3	321	3.5
Tunisia	570	555	0.9	-0.5	369	354	-1.6	-0.8	201	8.1
ALL AFRICA	538,978	520,237	-0.8	-0.7	534,226	515,455	-1	-0.7	4,416	4.4

Sources: Food and Agriculture Organization of the United Nations and the United Nations Economic Commission for Europe.

Notes: 0 = zero or less than half the unit of measure; negative numbers indicate reduction in forest area; .. = not available.

14-3. Forest ecosystems, 1996

	Land area (000 hectares)	Original Forest as a % of land area a/	Closed forests Forests as a % of original forest Current forests b/ 1996	Frontier forests c/ 1996	Percent frontier forests c/ threatened 1996	Mangroves Area (000 ha)	Mangroves Percent protected	Forest ecosystems (1996) Tropical forests Area (000 ha)	Tropical forests Percent protected	Nontropical forests Area (000 ha)	Nontropical forests Percent protected	Sparse trees and parkland Area (000 ha)	Sparse trees and parkland Percent protected
SUB-SAHARAN AFRICA	..	..	..	..	..	..	..	..	..	..	..	..	..
excluding South Africa	..	..	..	..	..	..	..	..	..	..	..	..	..
excl. S. Africa & Nigeria	..	..	..	..	..	..	..	..	..	..	..	..	..
Angola	124,670	20	15	0	111	0	0	37,564	3	0	0	0	0
Benin	11,062	16	4	0	0	0	0	1,516	18	0	0	585	2
Botswana	56,673	2	100	0	0	0	0	12,123	2	0	0	0	0
Burkina Faso	27,360	0	0	0	0	0	0	0	0	0	0	5,667	16
Burundi	2,568	46	3	0	0	0	0	219	18	0	0	139	3
Cameroon	46,540	80	42	8	97	227	2	20,009	6	0	0	2,416	22
Cape Verde	..	..	..	..	..	..	..	..	..	..	..	..	..
Central African Republic	62,298	52	16	4	100	0	0	17,101	20	0	0	1,451	48
Chad	125,920	0	0	0	0	0	0	3,516	4	0	0	2,857	1
Comoros	..	..	..	..	..	..	..	..	..	..	..	..	..
Congo, Dem. Rep. of	226,705	83	60	16	70	22	0	135,071	7	0	0	172	40
Congo, Rep. of	34,150	100	68	29	65	19	76	24,321	4	0	0	0	0
Côte d'Ivoire	31,800	75	10	2	100	0	0	2,702	23	0	0	625	18
Djibouti	..	..	..	..	..	..	..	..	..	..	..	..	..
Equatorial Guinea	2,805	96	38	0	0	25	0	1,749	0	0	0	0	0
Eritrea	..	..	..	..	..	0	0	1	0	0	0	0	0
Ethiopia	110,000	25	17	0	0	0	0	11,937	19	0	0	4,804	21
Gabon	25,767	100	90	32	100	147	3	21,481	4	0	0	0	0
Gambia, The	1,000	39	62	0	0	51	5	188	5	0	0	244	2
Ghana	22,754	66	9	0	0	0	0	1,694	7	0	0	336	17
Guinea	24,572	76	5	0	0	316	0	3,073	1	0	0	2,723	1
Guinea-Bissau	2,812	100	34	0	0	317	0	1,141	0	0	0	550	0
Kenya	56,914	17	19	0	0	0	0	3,423	8	0	0	2,754	3
Lesotho	3,035	2	0	0	0	0	0	89	9	0	0	0	0
Liberia	9,632	100	44	0	0	0	0	3,149	3	0	0	1	0
Madagascar	58,154	93	13	0	0	310	0	6,940	6	0	0	0	0
Malawi	9,408	12	0	0	0	0	0	3,830	9	0	0	0	0
Mali	122,019	0	0	0	0	0	0	6,132	2	0	0	336	0
Mauritania	102,522	0	0	0	0	..	..	..	..	..	..	..	..
Mauritius	203	..	..	..	..	..	..	..	..	..	..	..	..
Mozambique	78,409	33	14	0	0	565	4	20,863	7	0	0	14,414	7
Namibia	82,329	0	95	0	0	0	0	3,436	11	0	0	0	0
Niger	126,670	0	0	0	0	0	0	27	16	0	0	0	0
Nigeria	91,077	45	11	1	100	1,145	0	11,634	7	0	0	10,588	4
Rwanda	2,467	36	16	0	0	0	0	291	77	0	0	162	2
São Tomé and Principe	..	..	..	..	..	..	..	..	..	..	..	..	..
Senegal	19,253	14	16	0	0	158	3	2,076	7	0	0	8,816	13
Seychelles	..	..	..	..	..	..	..	..	..	..	..	..	..
Sierra Leone	7,162	100	10	0	0	176	1	260	20	0	0	104	0
Somalia	62,734	4	0	0	0	0	0	11,800	1	0	0	1,530	1
South Africa	122,104	13	0	0	0	0	0	10,333	5	52	26	0	0
Sudan	237,600	1	0	0	0	0	0	12,288	12	0	0	5,870	9
Swaziland	1,720	22	0	0	0	0	0	286	3	0	0	0	0
Tanzania	88,359	22	9	0	0	323	0	14,356	16	0	0	583	3
Togo	5,439	33	7	0	0	0	0	224	3	0	0	91	9
Uganda	19,965	70	4	0	0	0	0	3,772	17	0	0	1,850	65
Zambia	74,339	7	70	0	0	0	0	21,989	32	0	0	39	14
Zimbabwe	38,685	7	67	0	0	0	0	15,397	12	0	0	0	0
NORTH AFRICA	..	..	..	..	..	..	..	..	..	..	..	..	..
Algeria	238,174	5	12	0	0	0	0	0	0	2,694	4	1	83
Egypt	99,545	1	0	0	0	0	0	134	0	4	0	0	0
Libya	175,954	1	0	0	0	0	0	0	0	53	0	0	0
Morocco	44,630	22	7	0	0	0	0	0	0	1,862	3	0	0
Tunisia	15,536	18	5	0	0	0	0	0	0	300	2	0	0
ALL AFRICA	2,963,468	23	34	8	77	3,801	1	448,197	9	8,249	2	69,710	11

Source: Food and Agriculture Organization of the United Nations.

Notes:
a. Original forest is that estimated to have covered the planet 8000 years ago given current climate conditions
b. Includes frontier and nonfrontier forests.
c. Frontier forests are large, relatively undisturbed forest ecosystems
0 = zero or less than half of the unit of measure; .. = not available

14-4. Wood production and trade, 1983-95

	Average annual roundwood production						Average annual production				Average annual net trade in roundwood a/	
	Total		Fuel and charcoal		Industrial roundwood		Sawnwood		Paper			
	(000 cubic meters) 1993-95	Percent change since 1983-85	(000 cubic meters) 1993-95	Percent change since 1983-85	(000 cubic meters) 1993-95	Percent change since 1983-85	(000 cubic meters) 1993-95	Percent change since 1983-85	(000 cubic meters) 1993-95	Percent change since 1983-85	(000 cubic meters) 1993-95	Percent change since 1983-85
SUB-SAHARAN AFRICA	..	..	..	..	..	..	..	..	..	..	..	..
excluding South Africa	..	..	..	..	..	..	..	..	..	..	..	..
excl. S. Africa & Nigeria	..	..	..	..	..	..	..	..	..	..	..	..
Angola	6,794	32	5,830	33	964	28	5	15	0	0	3926	..
Benin	5,725	36	5,413	36	312	44	24	227	..	..	..	..
Botswana	1,538	39	1,443	39	95	39	..	..	..	..	..	..
Burkina Faso	9,770	31	9,328	31	442	30	2	-10	..	..	..	..
Burundi	4,828	36	4,725	35	104	145	21	681	..	..	..	..
Cameroon	15,263	30	12,065	32	3,197	24	1,088	136	5	0	82	-732
Cape Verde	..	..	..	..	..	..	..	..	..	..	..	..
Central African Republic	3,795	15	3,250	15	545	13	68	16	..	..	-24	..
Chad	4,407	26	3,773	26	633	28	2	135	..	..	..	..
Comoros	..	..	..	..	..	..	..	..	..	..	..	..
Congo, Dem. Rep. of	3,668	46	2,288	34	1,380	73	57	-3	..	..	20	..
Congo, Rep. of	45,830	43	42,599	44	3,231	28	95	-19	3	29	-2	-323
Côte d'Ivoire	14,298	18	11,204	44	3,094	-29	667	-7	..	..	-81	..
Djibouti	..	..	..	..	..	..	..	..	..	..	..	..
Equatorial Guinea	721	26	447	0	274	122	5	-83	..	..	190	0
Eritrea	..	..	..	..	..	..	..	..	..	..	..	..
Ethiopia	46,002	24	44,279	25	1,724	-4	35	-21	8	-21	..	..
Gabon	4,717	36	2,813	35	1,905	37	165	59	..	..	0	..
Gambia, The	1,206	41	1,094	31	112	442	1	0	..	..	..	-15
Ghana	25,990	59	24,331	58	1,660	67	727	141	..	..	413	..
Guinea	4,794	39	4,191	44	603	16	74	-18	..	..	38	0
Guinea-Bissau	577	4	422	0	155	16	16	0	..	..	..	..
Kenya	40,353	42	38,462	42	1,891	28	185	7	132	81	-99	-234
Lesotho	690	32	690	32	..	..	..	..	..	..	..	..
Liberia	6,181	45	5,200	38	981	101	90	-44	..	..	171	..
Madagascar	10,455	48	9,950	59	506	-37	94	-60	5	-49	56	..
Malawi	10,196	56	9,669	55	527	70	45	133	..	..	..	..
Mali	6,341	36	5,937	36	404	38	13	151	..	..	..	16
Mauritania	13	33	8	33	5	33	..	..	..	..	..	-7
Mauritius	18	-10	8	-45	10	98	4	167	..	..	841	..
Mozambique	17,852	19	16,844	20	1,008	8	34	-6	1	-42	630	..
Namibia	..	..	..	..	..	..	..	..	..	..	..	-49
Niger	5,672	38	5,322	38	350	39	4	..	..	..	..	..
Nigeria	108,074	32	99,811	34	8,263	9	2,723	7	56	129	-4	..
Rwanda	5,660	1	5,392	1	268	17	36	209	..	..	..	..
São Tomé and Principe	..	..	..	..	..	..	..	..	..	..	..	..
Senegal	5,107	25	4,405	23	702	38	23	54	..	..	14	..
Seychelles	..	..	..	..	..	..	..	..	..	..	..	-1066
Sierra Leone	3,249	23	3,126	25	124	-12	5	-69	..	..	..	..
Somalia	8,648	19	8,543	19	105	13	14	0	..	..	-100	..
South Africa	23,978	23	7,162	1	16,816	35	1,485	-6	1755	19	..	0
Sudan	24,747	31	22,456	31	2,291	30	3	-75	3	-67	..	-9
Swaziland	1,469	-34	560	0	909	-45	75	-27	..	..	..	-1
Tanzania	35,680	36	33,533	35	2,147	67	29	-71	25	..	1429	0
Togo	2,053	175	1,836	207	217	47	8	381	..	..	-318	-111
Uganda	16,684	41	14,466	41	2,218	43	83	262	3	275	..	-4
Zambia	14,422	39	13,341	35	1,081	111	351	601	3	-20	-443	-6
Zimbabwe	8,075	15	6,269	10	1,806	41	250	79	79	16	256	..
NORTH AFRICA	..	..	..	..	..	..	..	..	..	..	..	..
Algeria	2,489	35	2,081	29	408	81	13	0	86	-27	-79	74
Egypt	2,643	27	2,520	27	123	27	..	..	220	65	-11	-1
Libya	650	2	536	0	114	16	31	0	6	15	..	376
Morocco	2,263	14	1,432	14	831	13	83	-29	103	1	103	40
Tunisia	3,502	26	3,293	23	209	80	20	363	87	147	42	-2051
ALL AFRICA	567,133	33	502,378	34	64,754	23	8,761	18	2580	24	42	

Source:　Food and Agriculture Organization of the United Nations.

Notes:　a. Imports of roundwood are shown as positive numbers; exports are represented by negative numbers.

　　　() = zero or less than half of the unit of measure; .. = not available

14-5. Freshwater resources and withdrawals, 1970-98

	Annual internal renewable water resources		Annual river flows			Annual withdrawals			Sectoral withdrawals (percent)		
	Total (cubic km)	Per capita 1998 (cubic meters)	From other countries (cubic km)	To other countries (cubic km)	Year of data	Total (cubic km)	Percentage of water resources	Per capita (cubic meters)	Domestic	Industrial	Agricultural
SUB-SAHARAN AFRICA	..	..	..	..	..	..	..	..	..	..	..
excluding South Africa	..	..	..	..	..	..	..	..	..	..	..
excl. S. Africa & Nigeria	..	..	..	..	..	..	..	..	..	..	..
Angola	184	15,376	..	..	1987	0.48	0	57	14	10	76
Benin	10	1,751	15.5	..	1994	0.15	1	28	23	10	67
Botswana	3	1,870	11.8	..	1992	0.11	4	84	32	20	48
Burkina Faso	18	1,535	..	..	1992	0.38	2	39	19	0	81
Burundi	4	546	..	..	1987	0.10	3	20	36	0	64
Cameroon	268	18,711	0.0	0.0	1987	0.40	0	38	46	19	35
Cape Verde	..	..	..	..	..	..	..	..	..	..	..
Central African Republic	141	40,413	..	..	1987	0.07	0	26	21	5	74
Chad	15	2,176	28.0	..	1987	0.18	1	34	16	2	82
Comoros	..	..	..	..	..	..	..	..	..	..	..
Congo, Dem. Rep. of	935	19,001	84.0	..	1990	0.36	0	10	61	16	23
Congo, Rep. of	222	78,668	610.0	..	1987	0.04	0	20	62	27	11
Côte d'Ivoire	77	5,265	1.0	..	1987	0.71	1	67	22	11	67
Djibouti	..	..	..	..	..	..	..	..	..	..	..
Equatorial Guinea	30	69,767	0.0	..	1987	0.01	0	15	81	13	6
Eritrea	3	789	6.0	..	..	..	..	..	..	..	..
Ethiopia	110	1,771	0.0	..	1987	2.21	2	51	11	3	86
Gabon	164	140,171	0.0	..	1987	0.06	0	70	72	22	6
Gambia, The	3	2,513	5.0	..	1982	0.02	1	29	7	2	91
Ghana	30	1,607	22.9	..	1970	0.30	1	35	35	13	52
Guinea	226	29,454	0.0	..	1987	0.74	0	142	10	3	87
Guinea-Bissau	16	14,109	11.0	..	1991	0.02	0	17	60	4	36
Kenya	20	696	10.0	..	1990	2.05	10	87	20	4	76
Lesotho	5	2,395	0.0	..	1987	0.05	1	30	22	22	56
Liberia	200	72,780	32.0	..	1987	0.13	0	54	27	13	60
Madagascar	337	20,614	0.0	0.0	1984	16.30	5	1,579	1	0	99
Malawi	18	1,690	1.1	..	1994	0.94	5	98	10	3	86
Mali	60	5,071	40.0	..	1987	1.36	2	162	2	1	97
Mauritania	0	163	11.0	..	1985	1.63	408	923	6	2	92
Mauritius	2	1,915	0.0	0.0	1974	0.36	16	410	16	7	77
Mozambique	100	5,350	116.0	0.0	1992	0.61	1	40	9	2	89
Namibia	6	3,751	39.3	..	1991	0.25	4	179	29	3	68
Niger	4	346	29.0	..	1988	0.50	14	69	16	2	82
Nigeria	221	1,815	59.0	..	1987	3.63	2	41	31	15	54
Rwanda	6	965	..	..	1993	0.77	12	135	5	2	94
São Tomé and Principe	..	..	..	..	..	..	..	..	..	..	..
Senegal	26	2,933	13.0	..	1987	1.36	5	202	5	3	92
Seychelles	..	..	..	..	..	..	..	..	..	..	..
Sierra Leone	160	34,957	0.0	..	1987	0.37	0	98	7	4	89
Somalia	6	563	7.5	..	1987	0.81	14	99	3	0	97
South Africa	45	1,011	5.2	..	1990	13.31	30	359	17	11	72
Sudan	35	1,227	119.0	65.5	1995	17.80	51	666	4	1	94
Swaziland	3	2,836	1.9	..	1980	0.66	25	1,171	2	2	96
Tanzania	80	2,485	9.0	..	1994	1.16	1	40	9	2	89
Togo	12	2,594	0.5	..	1987	0.09	1	28	62	13	25
Uganda	39	1,829	27.0	..	1970	0.20	1	20	32	8	60
Zambia	80	9,229	35.8	..	1994	1.71	2	216	16	7	77
Zimbabwe	14	1,182	5.9	..	1987	1.22	9	136	14	7	79
NORTH AFRICA	..	..	..	..	..	..	..	..	..	..	..
Algeria	14	460	0.4	0.7	1990	4.50	32	180	25	15	60
Egypt	3	43	55.5	0.0	1993	55.10	1,968	921	6	8	86
Libya	1	100	0.0	0.0	1994	4.60	767	880	11	2	87
Morocco	30	1,071	0.0	0.3	1992	10.85	36	433	5	3	92
Tunisia	4	371	0.6	0.0	1990	3.07	87	376	9	3	89
ALL AFRICA	3,996	5,133	..	..	1995	145.14	4	202	7	5	88

Source: Food and Agriculture Organization of the United Nations.

Notes: 0 = zero or less than half of the unit of measure; .. = not available.

14-6. Marine and freshwater catches, aquaculture, balance of trade, and fish consumption

	Average annual marine catch a/ (000 metric tons)		Average annual freshwater catch a/ (000 metric tons)		Average annual aquaculture production 1993-95 (metric tons)				Average annual balance of trade b/ 1993-95 (million US$)			Per capita annual food supply from fish and seafood	
	1993-95	% change since 1983-85	1993-95	% change since 1983-85	Marine fish	Dia-dromous fish	Fresh-water fish	Molluscs & Crus-taceans	Fish	Molluscs & crustaceans	Fish meal	Total 1993-95 (kg)	% change since 1983-85
SUB-SAHARAN AFRICA	..	..	..	..	..	..	..	..	..	..	..	..	..
excluding South Africa	..	..	..	..	..	..	..	..	..	..	..	..	..
excl. S. Africa & Nigeria	..	..	..	..	..	..	..	..	..	..	..	..	..
Angola	78	-1	6.7	-11	..	..	..	..	-6.6	-2.7	0.0	12.4	-51.1
Benin	14	192	25.2	-18	..	..	98	..	-9.0	0.6	0.0	10.2	-5.8
Botswana	..	..	2.0	41	..	..	..	..	-4.6	-0.6	-0.1	7.1	98.4
Burkina Faso	..	..	7.7	5	0	0	0	0	-3.6	0.0	0.0	1.3	-22.3
Burundi	21	246	0.4	-92	0	0	53	0	-0.6	0.0	0.0	3.8	39.3
Cameroon	42	-25	23.2	15	0	0	51	0	-22.2	1.7	-0.3	8.5	-41.2
Cape Verde	..	..	..	..	..	..	..	..	..	..	..	..	..
Central African Republic			13.3	1	0	0	367	0	-0.7	0.0	0.0	4.5	-19.7
Chad	..	..	75.8	57	..	..	..	..	-0.3	0.0	0.0	5.9	102.1
Comoros	..	..	..	..	..	..	..	..	..	..	..	..	..
Congo, Dem. Rep. of	4	140	166.7	27	0	0	733	0	-40.1	-0.1	0.0	5.1	-44.1
Congo, Rep. of	18	-8	18.8	38	0	0	5	0	-18.5	0.0	0.0	31.4	-23.9
Côte d'Ivoire	58	-22	14.1	-41	0	0	255	0	12.1	4.4	0.8	12.5	-22.6
Djibouti	..	..	..	..	..	..	..	..	..	..	..	..	..
Equatorial Guinea	3	15	0.4	48	..	..	..	..	-1.6	0.0	0.0	..	..
Eritrea	2	..	0.0	..	..	..	..	..	0.0	..	0.0	..	..
Ethiopia	0	..	5.0	..	0	0	39	0	-0.3	0.0	0.0	..	..
Gabon	24	28	2.5	39	0	0	6	0	-10.3	3.2	0.0	44.0	-18.8
Gambia, The	19	124	2.5	-9	0	0	0	0	0.8	3.1	0.0	17.5	8.2
Ghana	300	34	52.7	24	0	0	505	0	17.7	5.9	-0.9	22.8	5.5
Guinea	60	130	4.1	130	0	0	5	0	2.0	4.8	0.0	6.7	-18.0
Guinea-Bissau	5	75	0.3	317	..	..	..	..	0.6	0.1	0.0	5.6	149.4
Kenya	108	86	86.0	112	0	314	823	68	20.1	0.9	-0.3	5.7	12.4
Lesotho	0	367	0.0	66	0	5	12	0	0.0	0.0	0.0	4.0	13.7
Liberia	4	-61	3.9	-3	0	0	0	0	-0.9	0.3	0.0	..	..
Madagascar	85	180	32.0	-12	0	0	2,521	911	17.6	60.5	0.5	7.3	21.4
Malawi	..	..	57.5	-11	0	0	231	5	0.1	0.0	-0.6	6.8	-25.9
Mali	5	53	81.6	53	0	0	84	0	-1.5	0.0	0.0	6.4	-12.4
Mauritania	87	0	5.2	-14	..	..	..	..	19.7	127.0	0.0	16.2	23.4
Mauritius	19	74	0.1	270	29	0	42	72	6.9	-3.7	-2.2	27.7	56.4
Mozambique	25	-27	3.4	-15	0	0	54	0	-10.7	69.8	-0.1	2.1	-40.6
Namibia	305	2,336	1.1	183	0	0	4	42	58.7	0.0	6.7	10.8	5.0
Niger	..	..	2.8	0	0	0	29	0	-1.6	0.4	0.0	0.4	-28.1
Nigeria	187	14	114.2	19	1,053	14	15,179	0	-138.6	35.4	-1.3	6.9	-27.1
Rwanda	..	..	3.5	247	0	0	51	0	-0.2	0.0	0.0	..	..
São Tomé and Principe	..	..	..	..	..	..	..	..	..	..	..	..	..
Senegal	330	43	30.7	45	0	0	29	14	88.7	32.2	0.6	26.8	22.1
Seychelles	..	..	..	..	..	..	..	..	..	..	..	..	..
Sierra Leone	47	34	14.7	-10	0	0	22	0	3.4	10.6	0.0	15.0	-16.8
Somalia	15	-3	0.3	-6	..	..	..	..	5.0	2.5	0.0	..	..
South Africa	552	-32	0.9	16	23	937	117	2,942	119.5	50.2	-56.1	7.6	-14.7
Sudan	4	70	39.6	50	0	0	467	0	-2.4	0.0	0.0	1.7	23.9
Swaziland	..	..	0.1	29	0	0	23	0	..	..	..	0.0	..
Tanzania	243	68	100.1	-21	0	0	183	0	9.8	6.9	0.0	11.8	-8.5
Togo	9	-23	5.9	69	0	0	607	0	-12.4	1.5	0.0	10.7	-12.0
Uganda	96	6	117.6	29	0	0	153	0	18.9	0.0	0.0	10.4	-17.6
Zambia	11	-1	57.1	3	0	0	4,422	0	-1.0	0.0	-0.4	9.2	-17.1
Zimbabwe	20	72	1.1	-74	0	100	37	13	-8.4	-0.7	-0.5	2.2	7.1
NORTH AFRICA	..	..	..	..	..	..	..	..	..	..	..	..	..
Algeria	114	74	0.3	862	53	14	254	31	-6.7	2.3	-0.3	3.5	1.8
Egypt	116	225	190.0	33	11,732	0	26,859	0	-64.4	0.4	-5.4	6.9	4.0
Libya	33	162	0.1	..	0	0	90	0	16.2	-0.5	-0.8	3.9	19.1
Morocco	739	59	1.7	40	1,030	198	200	148	241.0	399.2	-0.4	7.6	8.7
Tunisia	84	7	0.4	..	676	206	174	108	17.7	56.3	0.0	7.9	-18.6
ALL AFRICA	3,917	31	1373.1	19	14,597	1,788	54,785	4,511	299.6	868.2	-62.4	6.8	-13.6

Source: Food and Agriculture Organization of the United Nations.

Notes: a. Aquaculture production is included in country totals.

b. Exports minus imports.

0 = zero or less than half of the unit of measure; .. = not available

14-7. Commercial energy production, 1985-95

	Total		Solid fuels		Liquid fuels		Gaseous fuels		Primary electricity	
	Peta-joules, 1995	Percent change since 1985	Peta-joules, 1995	Percent change since 1985	Peta-joules, 1995	Percent change since 1985	Peta-joules, 1995	Percent change since 1985	Peta-joules, 1995	Percent change since 1985
SUB-SAHARAN AFRICA	..	..	..	..	..	..	..	..	..	..
excluding South Africa	..	..	..	..	..	..	..	..	..	..
excl. S. Africa & Nigeria	..	..	..	..	..	..	..	..	..	..
Angola	1,121	129	0	0	1,109	131	7	56	5	4
Benin	4	-68	0	0	4	-68	0	0	0	0
Botswana	..	..	..	..	..	..	..	..	..	..
Burkina Faso	0	0	0	0	0	0	0	0	0	0
Burundi	1	220	0	-100	0	0	0	0	0	-100
Cameroon	222	-43	0	-100	213	-45	0	0	10	20
Cape Verde	..	..	..	..	..	..	..	..	..	..
Central African Republic	0	-100	0	0	0	0	0	0	0	-100
Chad	0	..	0	0	0	0	0	0	0	0
Comoros	..	..	..	..	..	..	..	..	..	..
Congo, Dem. Rep. of	72	-21	3	-15,	48	-31	0	0	21	19
Congo, Rep. of	385	57	0	0	383	57	0	-100	2	141
Côte d'Ivoire	19	-60	0	0	15	-65	0	0	4	-18
Djibouti	..	..	..	..	..	..	..	..	..	..
Equatorial Guinea	10	138,789	0	0	10	0	0	0	0	-100
Eritrea	..	..	..	..	..	..	..	..	..	..
Ethiopia	7	56	0	0	0	0	0	0	7	204
Gabon	799	119	0	0	764	112	764	38,642	3	25
Gambia, The	0	0	0	0	0	0	0	0	0	0
Ghana	22	93	0	0	0	-100	0	0	22	104
Guinea	1	70	0	0	0	0	0	0	1	70
Guinea-Bissau	0	0	0	0	0	0	0	0	0	0
Kenya	22	21	0	0	0	0	0	0	22	21
Lesotho	..	..	..	..	..	..	..	..	..	..
Liberia	1	-23	0	0	0	0	0	0	1	6
Madagascar	1	8	0	0	0	0	0	0	1	8
Malawi	3	74	0	0	0	0	0	0	3	75
Mali	1	88	0	0	0	0	0	0	1	107
Mauritania	0	-100	0	0	0	0	0	0	0	-100
Mauritius	0	-100	0	0	0	0	0	0	0	-100
Mozambique	1	-36	1	-3	0	0	0	0	0	-100
Namibia	..	..	..	..	..	..	..	..	..	..
Niger	5	14	5	14	0	0	0	0	0	0
Nigeria	4,054	26	1	-75	3,857	24	174	59	22	180
Rwanda	1	65	0	0	0	0	0	-100	1	69
São Tomé and Principe	..	..	..	..	..	..	..	..	..	..
Senegal	0	0	0	0	0	0	0	0	0	0
Seychelles	..	..	..	..	..	..	..	..	..	..
Sierra Leone	0	0	0	0	0	0	0	0	0	0
Somalia	..	..	..	..	..	..	..	..	0	0
South Africa (a)	4,931	27	4,379	14	373	0	72	0	108	137
Sudan	3	-10	0	0	0	0	0	0	3	62
Swaziland	..	..	..	..	..	..	..	..	..	..
Tanzania	6	157	0	-100	0	0	0	0	5	125
Togo	0	-100	0	0	0	0	0	0	0	-100
Uganda	3	31	0	0	0	0	0	0	3	29
Zambia	37	-24	9	-29	0	0	0	0	28	-22
Zimbabwe	71	-31	62	-32	0	0	0	0	9	-19
NORTH AFRICA	..	..	..	..	..	..	..	..	..	..
Algeria	4,997	55	1	326	2,565	24	2,431	109	1	-57
Egypt	2,530	23	0	0	1,961	4	530	279	39	34
Libya	3,130	38	0	0	2,884	37	246	43	0	0
Morocco	22	-23	19	-16	0	-100	1	-70	2	16
Tunisia	185	-24	0	0	179	-21	6	-65	0	-100
ALL AFRICA	22,667	35	4,480	12	14,364	31	3,499	117	324	46

Source: United Nations Statistical Division.

Notes: a. Data are for the South Africa Customs Union (Botswana, Lesotho, Namibia, South Africa, and Swaziland).

1 petajoule = 1,000,000,000,000,000 joules = 947,800,000,000 Btus = 163,400 "U.N. standard" barrels of oil = 34,140 "U.N. standard" metric tons of coal.

0 = zero or less than half of the unit of measure; .. = not available or indeterminate.

Environmental Indicators

14-8. Energy balances, 1985-95

| | Industry | | Iron and steel | | Transportation | | Air | | Road | | Agriculture | | Commercial and public services | | Residential | |
| | Total (% of total final consumption) | | (% of total final consumption) | | Total (% of total final consumption) | | (% of total final consumption) | | (% of total final consumption) | | (% of total final consumption) | | (% of total final consumption) | | (% of total final consumption) | |
	1995	1985	1995	1985	1995	1985	1995	1985	1995	1985	1995	1985	1995	1985	1995	1985
SUB-SAHARAN AFRICA	..	..	..	..	..	..	..	..	..	..	..	..	..	..	..	..
excluding South Africa	..	..	..	..	..	..	..	..	..	..	..	..	..	..	..	..
excl. S. Africa & Nigeria	..	..	..	..	..	..	..	..	..	..	..	..	..	..	..	..
Angola	26.5	23.9	0.0	0.0	50.6	58.6	27.1	26.2	23.6	32.4	0.0	0.0	18.0	14.0	0.0	0.0
Benin	14.7	7.2	0.0	0.0	58.2	74.8	21.0	10.8	37.2	64.0	0.0	0.0	25.4	14.4	0.7	0.4
Botswana	..	..	..	..	..	..	..	..	..	..	..	..	..	..	..	..
Burkina Faso	..	..	..	..	..	..	..	..	..	..	..	..	..	..	..	..
Burundi	..	..	..	..	..	..	..	..	..	..	..	..	..	..	..	..
Cameroon	17.5	14.5	0.0	0.0	43.7	53.9	4.8	5.0	38.9	48.9	0.0	0.1	16.3	9.0	0.0	0.5
Cape Verde	..	..	..	..	..	..	..	..	..	..	..	..	..	..	..	..
Central African Republic	..	..	..	..	..	..	..	..	..	..	..	..	..	..	..	..
Chad	..	..	..	..	..	..	..	..	..	..	..	..	..	..	..	..
Comoros	..	..	..	..	..	..	..	..	..	..	..	..	..	..	..	..
Congo, Dem. Rep. of	8.7	10.5	0.0	0.0	66.1	70.5	22.6	11.9	43.5	58.6	0.0	0.0	18.6	7.7	0.0	0.0
Congo, Rep. of	29.1	24.7	0.0	0.0	38.6	43.5	8.8	8.8	29.8	34.6	0.0	0.0	16.7	17.7	0.0	0.0
Côte d'Ivoire	21.6	17.8	0.0	0.0	49.5	49.1	9.0	9.6	38.7	34.8	3.0	4.1	14.2	13.2	6.3	7.3
Djibouti	..	..	..	..	..	..	..	..	..	..	..	..	..	..	..	..
Equatorial Guinea	..	..	..	..	..	..	..	..	..	..	..	..	..	..	..	..
Eritrea	..	..	..	..	..	..	..	..	..	..	..	..	..	..	..	..
Ethiopia	24.8	19.3	0.0	0.0	51.9	59.1	20.8	20.6	31.1	36.1	2.3	3.8	6.5	7.8	2.6	3.7
Gabon	29.0	46.3	0.0	0.0	42.5	19.8	13.9	4.2	24.5	15.6	0.0	0.0	12.9	19.2	2.6	0.3
Gambia, The	..	..	..	..	..	..	..	..	..	..	..	..	..	..	..	..
Ghana	34.5	29.7	0.0	0.0	44.4	47.2	4.4	3.9	38.4	39.8	1.7	3.8	13.0	10.8	2.0	2.3
Guinea	..	..	..	..	..	..	..	..	..	..	..	..	..	..	..	..
Guinea-Bissau	..	..	..	..	..	..	..	..	..	..	..	..	..	..	..	..
Kenya	26.4	24.3	0.0	0.0	51.6	54.9	16.7	14.8	33.0	37.7	3.1	2.8	11.8	8.9	1.1	4.9
Lesotho	..	..	..	..	..	..	..	..	..	..	..	..	..	..	..	..
Liberia	..	..	..	..	..	..	..	..	..	..	..	..	..	..	..	..
Madagascar	..	..	..	..	..	..	..	..	..	..	..	..	..	..	..	..
Malawi	..	..	..	..	..	..	..	..	..	..	..	..	..	..	..	..
Mali	..	..	..	..	..	..	..	..	..	..	..	..	..	..	..	..
Mauritania	..	..	..	..	..	..	..	..	..	..	..	..	..	..	..	..
Mauritius	..	..	..	..	..	..	..	..	..	..	..	..	..	..	..	..
Mozambique	12.0	15.0	0.0	0.0	16.4	17.2	7.6	7.4	8.8	9.9	3.5	0.0	6.7	5.5	0.1	0.0
Namibia	..	..	..	..	..	..	..	..	..	..	..	..	..	..	..	..
Niger	..	..	..	..	..	..	..	..	..	..	..	..	..	..	..	..
Nigeria	16.0	17.9	0.6	0.6	51.6	56.5	4.9	5.0	46.2	50.1	0.0	0.6	13.5	18.2	2.3	0.7
Rwanda	..	..	..	..	..	..	..	..	..	..	..	..	..	..	..	..
São Tomé and Principe	..	..	..	..	..	..	..	..	..	..	..	..	..	..	..	..
Senegal	29.4	26.0	0.0	0.0	55.0	61.2	20.5	22.5	31.1	31.1	0.2	3.2	11.0	5.6	2.6	1.5
Seychelles	..	..	..	..	..	..	..	..	..	..	..	..	..	..	..	..
Sierra Leone	..	..	..	..	..	..	..	..	..	..	..	..	..	..	..	..
Somalia	..	..	..	..	..	..	..	..	..	..	..	..	..	..	..	..
South Africa	45.8	59.9	13.3	25.7	27.6	24.0	2.0	1.7	23.9	19.9	4.2	3.1	5.5	7.0	3.6	4.8
Sudan	29.6	28.6	0.0	0.0	43.4	45.1	11.5	6.6	30.4	34.4	8.9	12.0	7.0	3.2	2.2	2.6
Swaziland	..	..	..	..	..	..	..	..	..	..	..	..	..	..	..	..
Tanzania	15.2	30.6	0.0	0.1	44.4	32.5	6.3	6.1	34.0	19.7	4.6	3.7	28.0	25.3	4.3	3.9
Togo	..	..	..	..	..	..	..	..	..	..	..	..	..	..	..	..
Uganda	..	..	..	..	..	..	..	..	..	..	..	..	..	..	..	..
Zambia	57.5	63.4	0.0	0.0	20.1	18.7	3.8	4.1	16.3	13.3	2.9	2.3	4.3	5.4	7.9	6.6
Zimbabwe	52.2	48.9	14.1	17.6	20.3	25.3	2.3	3.1	13.8	15.9	10.2	12.0	5.8	5.1	8.3	6.8
NORTH AFRICA																
Algeria	23.1	24.9	4.2	8.6	22.2	39.4	2.3	4.2	16.1	34.3	0.0	0.3	29.2	21.5	0.0	2.3
Egypt	49.7	46.0	2.9	4.0	19.9	24.2	2.8	2.6	17.1	20.0	0.7	3.3	20.6	18.7	0.0	1.0
Libya	31.9	36.2	0.0	0.0	40.2	39.0	3.6	6.0	36.7	33.0	0.0	0.0	7.5	3.2	0.0	0.0
Morocco	22.9	40.3	0.0	0.0	12.9	27.7	3.9	5.9	6.4	19.4	0.7	5.0	18.7	16.0	2.4	6.5
Tunisia	33.5	34.1	2.0	3.2	31.3	31.1	5.9	3.9	24.8	21.5	7.3	5.7	15.0	18.4	8.6	7.5
ALL AFRICA	37.5	43.3	6.1	11.6	29.3	32.2	3.9	4.0	24.1	26.2	2.4	2.8	13.2	12.3	2.3	3.2

Source: United States Geological Survey.

14-9. Production of selected minerals and materials, 1995

	Bauxite (Al content) (000 metric tons)	Iron ore (Fe content) (000 metric tons)	Copper ore (Cu content) (metric tons)	Silver ore (Ag content) (metric tons)	Gold (Au content) (kilograms)	Sulfur (000 metric tons)	Salt (000 metric tons)	Nitrogen (ammonia) (000 metric tons)	Phosphorus (P2O5) (000 metric tons)	Potassium (potash) (000 metric tons)	Sand and gravel (000 metric tons)	Hydraulic cement (000 metric tons)
SUB-SAHARAN AFRICA	..	..	..	..	..	..	..	..	..	..	..	..
excluding South Africa	..	..	..	..	..	..	..	..	..	..	..	..
excl. S. Africa & Nigeria	..	..	..	..	..	..	..	..	..	..	..	..
Angola	..	..	..	..	..	..	30	..	..	..	..	300
Benin	..	..	..	..	..	..	1	..	..	..	..	380
Botswana	..	..	21,029	..	86	..	208	..	..	..	..	..
Burkina Faso	..	..	..	..	6,000	..	7	..	..	..	..	..
Burundi	..	..	..	..	10	..	..	..	..	..	..	..
Cameroon	..	..	..	..	560	..	..	..	..	..	..	520
Cape Verde	..	..	..	..	..	..	..	..	..	..	..	..
Central African Republic	..	..	..	..	700	..	..	..	..	..	..	..
Chad	..	..	..	..	..	..	..	..	..	..	..	..
Comoros	..	..	..	..	..	..	..	..	..	..	..	..
Congo, Dem. Rep. of	..	..	28,800	10	9,500	..	..	..	..	..	..	100
Congo, Rep. of	..	..	..	..	5	..	..	..	..	..	..	100
Côte d'Ivoire	..	..	..	..	3,200	..	..	..	..	..	..	500
Djibouti	..	..	..	..	..	..	..	..	..	..	..	..
Equatorial Guinea	..	..	..	..	..	..	..	..	..	..	..	..
Eritrea	..	..	..	..	59	..	255	..	..	..	1,334	350
Ethiopia	..	..	..	..	4,500	..	5	..	..	..	1,600	611
Gabon	..	..	..	..	70	..	..	..	..	..	..	130
Gambia, The	..	..	..	..	..	..	..	..	..	..	..	..
Ghana	123	..	..	3	52,200	..	50	..	..	..	..	1,400
Guinea	3,600	..	..	..	7,863	..	..	..	..	..	..	..
Guinea-Bissau	..	..	..	..	..	..	..	..	..	..	..	..
Kenya	..	..	..	..	170	..	74	..	..	..	..	1,500
Lesotho	..	..	..	..	..	..	..	..	..	..	..	..
Liberia	..	..	..	..	500	..	..	..	..	..	..	..
Madagascar	..	..	..	..	500	..	30	..	..	..	..	60
Malawi	..	..	..	..	..	..	..	..	..	..	..	139
Mali	..	..	..	..	7,800	..	5	..	..	..	..	20
Mauritania	..	7,000	..	..	..	..	6	..	..	..	..	375
Mauritius	..	..	..	..	..	..	6	..	..	..	..	..
Mozambique	3	..	..	..	900	..	40	..	..	..	..	20
Namibia	..	..	22,530	66	2,099	..	300	..	..	..	..	..
Niger	..	..	..	..	..	..	3	..	..	..	..	30
Nigeria	..	100	..	..	..	..	..	350	..	..	..	2,600
Rwanda	..	..	..	..	100	..	..	..	..	..	..	5
São Tomé and Principe	..	..	..	..	..	..	..	..	..	..	..	..
Senegal	..	..	..	..	..	..	120	..	600	..	..	590
Seychelles	..	..	..	..	..	..	..	..	..	..	..	..
Sierra Leone	70	..	..	..	50	..	100	..	..	..	..	..
Somalia	..	..	..	..	..	..	1	..	..	..	..	25
South Africa	..	19,806	199,600	174	523,820	509	313	600	1,087	..	..	9,071
Sudan	..	..	..	..	3,000	..	75	..	..	..	..	250
Swaziland	..	..	..	..	..	..	..	..	..	..	..	..
Tanzania	..	..	..	..	44	..	7	..	7	..	..	800
Togo	..	..	..	..	..	..	..	..	720	..	..	350
Uganda	..	..	..	..	..	..	5	..	..	..	..	130
Zambia	..	..	329,200	14	79	..	..	10	..	..	..	300
Zimbabwe	..	160	9,500	10	24,344	..	..	70	45	..	..	1,000
NORTH AFRICA												
Algeria	..	1,000	..	3	..	..	178	380	232	..	..	6,200
Egypt	..	2,100	..	..	..	..	1,000	940	390	..	32,800	16,000
Libya	..	..	..	..	..	..	12	200	..	..	..	2,300
Morocco	..	40	13,000	330	..	..	175	..	..	..	..	6,500
Tunisia	..	128	..	1	..	..	400	..	2,182	..	..	4,300
ALL AFRICA	..	..	..	..	..	..	..	..	..	..	..	..

Source: United States Geological Survey.

14-10. CO$_2$ emissions from industrial processes, 1995

| | Carbon dioxide emissions (000 metric tons) | | | | | | Per capita carbon dioxide | |
	Solid	Liquid	Gas	Gas flaring	Cement manufacture	Total	Emissions (metric tons)	Bunker fuels a/ (000 metric tons)
SUB-SAHARAN AFRICA	..	..	..	..	..	..	..	..
excluding South Africa	..	..	..	..	..	..	..	..
excl. S. Africa & Nigeria	..	..	..	..	..	..	..	..
Angola	0	1,667	322	2,460	149	4,602	0.4	2,561
Benin	0	443	0	0	189	634	0.1	59
Botswana	2,242	0	0	0	0	2,242	1.5	0
Burkina Faso	4	956	0	0	0	956	0.0	4
Burundi	18	198	0	0	0	213	0.0	18
Cameroon	4	3,880	0	0	259	4,144	0.3	48
Cape Verde	..	..	..	..	..	..	..	..
Central African Republic	0	234	0	0	0	234	0.1	40
Chad	0	95	0	0	0	95	0.0	59
Comoros	..	..	..	..	..	..	..	..
Congo, Dem. Rep. of	854	1,194	0	0	50	2,099	0.0	476
Congo, Rep. of	0	1,048	7	167	50	1,268	0.5	33
Côte d'Ivoire	0	10,113	0	0	249	10,362	0.8	260
Djibouti	..	..	..	..	..	..	..	..
Equatorial Guinea	0	132	0	0	0	132	0.3	0
Eritrea	..	..	..	..	..	..	..	..
Ethiopia	11	3,045	0	0	29	3,525	0.7	315
Gabon	0	1,894	1,583	0	65	3,543	3.3	418
Gambia, The	0	216	0	0	0	216	0.2	0
Ghana	7	3,342	0	0	698	4,045	0.2	161
Guinea	0	1,081	0	0	0	1,081	0.1	40
Guinea-Bissau	0	231	0	0	0	231	0.2	18
Kenya	253	5,683	0	0	747	6,683	0.3	172
Lesotho	..	..	..	..	..	..	..	..
Liberia	0	319	0	0	0	319	0.1	51
Madagascar	44	1,048	0	0	30	1,125	0.1	55
Malawi	44	612	0	0	69	725	0.1	37
Mali	0	454	0	0	10	465	0.0	51
Mauritania	15	2,865	0	0	187	3,067	1.4	70
Mauritius	176	1,315	0	0	0	1,491	1.3	861
Mozambique	150	835	0	0	10	993	0.1	216
Namibia	..	..	..	..	..	..	..	..
Niger	458	645	0	0	15	1,118	0.1	48
Nigeria	150	29,217	8,563	51,493	1,296	90,717	0.8	2,301
Rwanda	0	484	0	2	3	491	0.1	29
São Tomé and Principe	..	..	..	..	..	..	..	..
Senegal	0	2,770	0	0	294	3,063	0.4	784
Seychelles	..	..	..	..	..	..	..	..
Sierra Leone	0	443	0	0	0	443	0.1	315
Somalia	0	0	0	0	12	11	0.0	0
South Africa (a)	250,453	47,291	3,543	0	4,520	305,805	7.4	7,236
Sudan	0	3,375	0	0	125	3,499	0.1	139
Swaziland	454	0	0	0	0	454	0.5	0
Tanzania	15	2,026	0	0	399	2,440	0.1	158
Togo	0	572	0	0	174	744	0.2	0
Uganda	0	978	0	0	65	1,044	0.0	0
Zambia	795	1,462	0	0	149	2,404	0.3	110
Zimbabwe	5,738	3,495	0	0	498	9,735	0.9	..
NORTH AFRICA	..	..	..	..	..	..	..	..
Algeria	3,243	22,134	47,222	15,578	3,089	91,267	3.3	1,411
Egypt	2,451	55,205	26,055	0	7,973	91,684	1.5	5,108
Libya	15	25,564	9,255	3,424	1,146	39,403	7.3	751
Morocco	6,247	19,764	48	0	3,239	29,294	1.1	249
Tunisia	238	8,849	3,818	261	2,143	15,308	1.7	586
ALL AFRICA	274,078	269,355	100,416	73,386	27,932	745,595	1.1	25,326

Sources: Carbon Dioxide Information Analysis Center.

Notes: a. Bunker fuels are stored fuels to be used for ship or air transport.

Estimates are of the carbon dioxide emitted, 3.664 times the carbon it contains.

0 = zero or less than half the unit of measure, .. = not available.

14-11. Globally threatened species: mammals, birds, and higher plants, 1990s

	Mammals				Birds				Higher plants			
	Total number of known species			No. of species	Total number of known species			No. of species	Total number of known species			No. of species
	All species	Endemic species	Threatened species	per 10,000 km² a/	All species	Endemic species	Threatened species	per 10,000 km² a/	All species b/	Endemic species	Threatened species	per 10,000 km² a/
SUB-SAHARAN AFRICA	..	..	..	..	..	..	..	..	..	..	..	..
excluding South Africa	..	..	..	..	..	..	..	. ..	..	..	..	..
excl. S. Africa & Nigeria	..	..	..	..	..	..	..	..	..	..	..	..
Angola	276	7	17	56	765	13	13	156	5,000	1,260	25	1,017
Benin	188	0	9	85	307	0	1	138	2,000	..	3	899
Botswana	164	0	5	43	386	0	7	101	..	17	4	..
Burkina Faso	147	0	6	49	335	0	1	112	1,100	..	0	369
Burundi	107	0	5	76	451	0	6	322	2,500	..	1	1,783
Cameroon	297	13	32	83	690	8	14	193	8,000	156	74	2,237
Cape Verde	..	..	..	..	..	..	..	..	..	..	..	..
Central African Republic	209	2	11	53	537	0	2	137	3,600	100	0	921
Chad	134	1	14	27	370	0	3	75	1,600	..	12	322
Comoros	..	..	..	..	..	..	..	..	..	..	..	..
Congo, Dem. Rep. of	415	28	38	69	929	22	26	153	11,000	1,100	7	1,817
Congo, Rep. of	200	1	10	62	449	0	3	140	4,350	1,200	3	1,356
Côte d'Ivoire	230	1	16	73	535	0	12	170	3,517	62	66	1,118
Djibouti	..	..	..	..	..	..	..	..	..	..	..	..
Equatorial Guinea	184	3	12	131	273	3	4	194	3,000	66	9	2,135
Eritrea	112	..	6	49	319	0	3	140	..	..	..	..
Ethiopia	255	31	35	54	626	28	20	133	6,500	1,000	153	1,378
Gabon	190	2	12	64	466	0	4	157	6,500	..	78	2,197
Gambia, The	108	0	4	104	280	0	1	269	966	..	0	928
Ghana	222	1	13	78	529	1	10	186	3,600	43	32	1,264
Guinea	190	1	11	66	409	0	12	142	3,000	88	35	1,043
Guinea-Bissau	108	0	4	71	243	0	1	159	1,000	12	0	655
Kenya	359	21	43	94	844	6	24	221	6,000	265	158	1,571
Lesotho	33	0	2	23	58	0	5	40	1,576	2	7	1,093
Liberia	193	0	11	87	372	1	13	168	2,200	103	1	1,037
Madagascar	105	84	46	27	202	104	28	53	9,000	6,500	189	2,347
Malawi	195	0	7	86	521	0	9	230	3,600	49	61	1,592
Mali	137	0	13	28	397	0	6	81	1,741	11	14	355
Mauritania	61	1	14	13	273	0	3	59	1,100	..	3	239
Mauritius	4	2	4	7	27	9	10	46	700	325	222	1,183
Mozambique	179	1	13	42	498	0	14	117	5,500	219	92	1,294
Namibia	154	3	11	36	469	1	8	109	3,128	..	23	729
Niger	131	0	11	27	299	0	2	60	1,170	..	0	237
Nigeria	274	6	26	62	681	2	9	153	4,614	205	9	1,036
Rwanda	151	0	9	110	513	0	6	373	2,288	26	0	1,662
São Tomé and Principe	..	..	..	..	..	..	..	..	..	..	..	..
Senegal	155	0	13	58	384	0	6	144	2,062	26	32	771
Seychelles	..	..	..	..	..	..	..	..	..	..	..	..
Sierra Leone	147	0	9	77	466	0	12	243	2,090	74	12	1,091
Somalia	171	11	18	43	422	10	8	107	3,000	500	57	761
South Africa	247	27	33	51	596	8	16	122	23,000	..	953	4,711
Sudan	267	11	21	43	680	0	9	110	3,132	50	8	506
Swaziland	47	0	5	39	364	0	6	303	2,636	4	41	2,197
Tanzania	316	12	33	70	822	24	30	183	10,000	1,122	406	2,229
Togo	196	1	8	110	391	0	1	220	2,000	..	0	1,128
Uganda	338	6	18	118	830	3	10	290	5,000	..	6	1,762
Zambia	229	3	11	55	605	1	10	145	4,600	211	9	1,105
Zimbabwe	270	1	9	81	532	0	9	159	4,200	95	94	1,253
NORTH AFRICA	..	..	..	..	..	..	..	..	..	..	..	..
Algeria	92	2	15	15	192	1	8	32	3,100	250	145	509
Egypt	98	7	15	21	153	0	11	33	2,066	70	84	452
Libya	76	5	11	14	91	0	2	17	1,800	134	57	327
Morocco	105	4	18	30	210	0	11	60	3,600	625	195	1,028
Tunisia	78	1	11	31	173	0	6	69	2,150	..	24	855
ALL AFRICA	..	..	..	..	..	..	..	..	..	..	..	..

Source: World Conservation Monitoring Centre (WCMC).

Notes: a. Values are standardized using a species-area curve.

b. Flowering plants only.

Threatened species data are as of June 1993. .. = not available.

14-12. Globally threatened species: reptiles, amphibians, and fish, 1990s

	Reptiles				Amphibians				Freshwater fish	
	Total number of known species			No. of species per 10,000 km² a/	Total number of known species			No. of species per 10,000 km² a/	Total number of known species	
	All species	Endemic species	Threatened species		All species	Endemic species	Threatened species		All species	Threatened species b/
SUB-SAHARAN AFRICA	..	..	..	..	..	..	..	..	..	..
excluding South Africa	..	..	..	..	..	..	..	..	..	..
excl. S. Africa & Nigeria	..	..	..	..	..	..	..	..	..	..
Angola	..	18	5	..	..	22	0	..	..	0
Benin	..	1	2	..	..	0	0	..	..	0
Botswana	157	2	0	41	38	0	0	10	92	0
Burkina Faso	..	3	1	..	..	0	0	..	..	0
Burundi	..	0	0	..	..	2	0	..	..	0
Cameroon	..	20	3	..	..	66	1	..	..	26
Cape Verde	..	..	..	..	..	..	..	..	..	..
Central African Republic	..	0	1	..	..	0	0	..	..	0
Chad	..	1	1	..	..	0	0	..	..	0
Comoros	..	..	..	..	..	..	..	..	..	..
Congo, Dem. Rep. of	..	33	3	..	..	53	0	..	..	1
Congo, Rep. of	..	1	2	..	..	1	0	..	..	0
Côte d'Ivoire	..	3	4	..	..	3	1	..	..	0
Djibouti	..	..	..	..	..	..	..	..	..	..
Equatorial Guinea	..	3	2	..	..	2	1	..	..	0
Eritrea	..	..	3	..	..	0	0	..	..	0
Ethiopia	..	8	1	..	..	34	0	..	..	0
Gabon	..	3	3	..	..	4	0	..	..	0
Gambia, The	..	1	1	..	..	0	0	..	79	0
Ghana	..	1	4	..	..	4	0	..	..	0
Guinea	..	3	3	..	..	3	1	..	..	0
Guinea-Bissau	..	2	3	..	..	1	0	..	..	0
Kenya	187	17	5	49	88	11	0	23	..	20
Lesotho	..	2	0	..	..	1	0	..	8	1
Liberia	62	2	3	28	38	4	1	17	..	0
Madagascar	252	227	17	66	144	149	2	38	40	13
Malawi	124	6	0	55	69	3	0	31	..	0
Mali	16	3	1	3	..	1	0	..	..	0
Mauritania	..	1	3	..	..	0	0	..	..	0
Mauritius	11	8	6	19	0	0	0	0	..	0
Mozambique	..	5	5	..	62	1	0	15	..	2
Namibia	..	26	3	..	32	2	1	7	102	3
Niger	..	..	1	..	..	..	0	..	..	0
Nigeria	>135	7	4	..	>109	1	0	..	260	0
Rwanda	..	1	0	..	..	1	0	..	..	0
São Tomé and Principe	..	..	..	..	..	..	..	..	..	..
Senegal	..	1	7	..	..	1	0	..	83	0
Seychelles	..	..	..	..	..	..	..	..	..	..
Sierra Leone	..	1	3	..	..	2	0	..	..	0
Somalia	193	49	2	49	27	3	0	7	..	3
South Africa	299	91	19	61	95	48	9	19	94	27
Sudan	..	7	3	..	..	1	0	..	..	0
Swaziland	102	1	0	85	40	0	0	33	40	0
Tanzania	284	64	4	63	124	48	0	28	..	19
Togo	..	1	3	..	..	3	0	..	..	0
Uganda	149	2	1	52	50	1	0	17	291	28
Zambia	..	2	0	..	83	1	0	20	..	0
Zimbabwe	153	2	0	46	120	3	0	36	112	0
NORTH AFRICA	..	..	..	..	..	..	..	..	..	..
Algeria	..	4	1	..	..	0	0	..	..	1
Egypt	83	0	6	18	6	0	0	1	70	0
Libya	..	1	3	..	..	0	0	..	..	0
Morocco	..	11	2	..	..	1	0	..	..	1
Tunisia	..	1	2	..	..	0	0	..	..	0
ALL AFRICA	..	..	..	..	..	..	..	..	..	..

Source: World Conservation Monitoring Centre (WCMC).

Notes: a. Values are standardized using a species-area curve.

b. Threatened species include a few marine species.

Threatened species data are as of 1996.   ..= not available.

14-13. National protection of natural areas, 1997

	All protected areas (IUCN categories I-V)			Totally protected areas (IUCN categories I-III)		Partially protected areas (IUCN categories IV-V)		% of protected areas (IUCN cat. I-V) at least	
	Number	Area (000 ha)	Percent of land area	Number	Area (000 ha)	Number	Area (000 ha)	100,000 ha in size	1 million ha in size
SUB-SAHARAN AFRICA	..	..	..	..	..	..	..	..	..
excluding South Africa	..	. ..	..	..	..	..	..	..	..
excl. S. Africa & Nigeria	..	..	..	..	..	..	..	..	..
Angola	12	8,181	6.6	6	5,423	6	2,758	50	..
Benin	2	778	7.0	2	778	0	0	100	..
Botswana	8	10,497	18.5	4	4,551	4	5,945	88	37.5
Burkina Faso	12	2,855	10.4	3	534	9	2,321	50	8.3
Burundi	9	144	5.6	0	0	9	144	..	..
Cameroon	16	2,097	4.5	7	1,032	9	1,066	50	..
Cape Verde	..	..	..	..	..	..	..	..	..
Central African Republic	13	5,110	8.2	5	3,188	8	1,922	85	15.4
Chad	9	11,494	9.1	2	414	7	11,080	100	22.2
Comoros	..	..	..	..	..	..	..	..	..
Congo, Dem. Rep. of	11	10,191	4.5	10	10,187	1	4	82	36.4
Congo, Rep. of	9	1,545	4.5	2	513	7	1,032	56	..
Côte d'Ivoire	11	1,986	6.2	10	1,891	1	95	36	9.1
Djibouti	..	..	..	..	..	..	..	..	..
Equatorial Guinea	..	..	..	..	..	..	..	..	..
Eritrea	3	501	5.0	0	0	3	501	67	..
Ethiopia	20	5,518	5.5	12	3,036	8	2,482	70	..
Gabon	5	723	2.8	1	15	4	708	20	..
Gambia, The	4	22	2.2	3	18	1	4	..	..
Ghana	9	1,104	4.8	7	1,097	2	7	33	..
Guinea	3	164	0.7	3	164	0	0	33	..
Guinea-Bissau	..	..	..	..	..	..	..	..	..
Kenya	36	3,504	6.2	32	3,451	4	52	19	2.8
Lesotho	1	7	0.2	0	0	1	7	..	..
Liberia	1	129	1.3	1	129	0	0	100	..
Madagascar	36	1,119	1.9	16	744	20	375	3	..
Malawi	9	1,059	11.3	5	696	4	362	33	..
Mali	13	4,532	3.7	2	750	11	3,782	62	15.4
Mauritania	4	1,746	1.7	3	1,496	1	250	75	25.0
Mauritius	3	12	6.0	1	7	2	6	..	..
Mozambique	11	4,779	6.1	5	1,967	6	2,812	64	18.2
Namibia	16	10,616	12.9	10	9,775	6	841	44	18.8
Niger	6	9,694	7.7	2	1,500	4	8,194	67	33.3
Nigeria	20	3,020	3.3	7	2,276	13	745	45	..
Rwanda	5	362	14.7	2	264	3	98	20	..
São Tomé and Principe	..	..	..	..	..	..	..	..	..
Senegal	9	2,180	11.3	5	1,012	4	1,168	33	..
Seychelles	..	..	..	..	..	..	..	..	..
Sierra Leone	2	82	1.1	0	0	2	82	..	..
Somalia	1	180	0.3	0	0	1	180	100	..
South Africa	232	6,578	5.4	35	4,262	197	2,316	4	0.4
Sudan	11	8,642	3.6	8	8,499	3	143	64	36.4
Swaziland	2	35	2.0	0	0	2	35	..	..
Tanzania	30	13,816	15.6	12	4,100	18	9,716	67	10.0
Togo	8	428	7.9	3	357	5	71	25	..
Uganda	32	1,910	9.6	7	876	25	1,034	19	..
Zambia	21	6,364	8.6	21	6,364	0	0	52	4.8
Zimbabwe	25	3,068	7.9	11	2,704	14	364	24	4.0
NORTH AFRICA	..	..	..	..	..	..	..	..	..
Algeria	18	5,891	2.5	13	5,762	5	129	11	11.1
Egypt	12	793	0.8	4	99	8	695	8	..
Libya	6	173	0.1	3	51	3	122	17	..
Morocco	7	316	0.7	2	9	5	307	14	..
Tunisia	6	44	0.3	6	44	0	0	..	..
ALL AFRICA	746	154,043	5.2	300	90,091	446	63,952	28	4.8

Source: World Conservation Monitoring Centre (WCMC).

Notes: 0 = zero or less than half the unit of measure.   .. = not available or indeterminate.

14-14. International protected areas, 1997

| | International protection systems | | | | | |
| | Biosphere reserves | | World heritage sites | | Wetlands of international importance | |
	Number	Area (000 ha)	Number	Area (000 ha)	Number	Area (000 ha)
SUB-SAHARAN AFRICA	..	..	..	..	..	..
excluding South Africa	..	..	..	..	..	..
excl. S. Africa & Nigeria	..	..	..	..	..	..
Angola	0	..	0	0	0	..
Benin	1	880	0	0	0	..
Botswana	0	..	0	0	1	6,864
Burkina Faso	1	16	0	0	3	299
Burundi	0	..	0	0	0	..
Cameroon	3	850	1	526	0	..
Cape Verde	..	..	..	..	..	..
Central African Republic	2	1,640	1	1,740	0	..
Chad	0	..	0	0	1	195
Comoros	..	..	..	..	..	..
Congo, Dem. Rep. of	3	298	5	6,855	2	866
Congo, Rep. of	2	172	0	0	0	..
Côte d'Ivoire	2	1,480	3	1,484	1	19
Djibouti	..	..	..	..	..	..
Equatorial Guinea	0	..	0	0	0	..
Eritrea	0	..	0	0	0	..
Ethiopia	0	..	1	22	0	..
Gabon	1	15	0	0	3	1,080
Gambia, The	0	..	0	0	1	20
Ghana	1	8	0	0	6	178
Guinea	2	133	1	13	6	225
Guinea-Bissau	1	110	0	0	1	39
Kenya	5	1,335	0	0	2	49
Lesotho	0	..	0	0	0	..
Liberia	0	..	0	0	0	..
Madagascar	1	140	1	152	0	..
Malawi	0	..	1	9	1	225
Mali	1	771	1	400	3	162
Mauritania	0	..	1	1,200	2	1,189
Mauritius	1	4	0	0	0	..
Mozambique	0	..	0	0	0	..
Namibia	0	..	0	0	4	630
Niger	1	728	2	7,956	1	220
Nigeria	1	0	0	0	0	..
Rwanda	1	15	0	0	0	..
São Tomé and Principe	..	..	..	..	..	..
Senegal	3	1,094	2	929	4	100
Seychelles	..	..	..	..	..	..
Sierra Leone	0	..	0	0	0	..
Somalia	0	..	0	0	0	..
South Africa	0	..	0	0	15	486
Sudan	2	1,901	0	0	0	..
Swaziland	0	..	0	0	0	..
Tanzania	2	2,338	4	7,380	0	..
Togo	0	..	0	0	2	194
Uganda	1	220	2	132	1	15
Zambia	0	..	1	4	2	333
Zimbabwe	0	..	2	1,095	0	..
NORTH AFRICA	..	..	..	..	..	..
Algeria	2	7,276	1	..	2	5
Egypt	2	2,577	0	0	2	106
Libya	0	..	0	0	0	..
Morocco	0	..	0	0	4	11
Tunisia	4	32	1	13	1	13
ALL AFRICA	46	24,033	30	29,910	72	13,522

Source: World Conservation Monitoring Centre (WCMC), United Nations Educational, Scientific, and Cultural Organization (UNESCO), and Ramsar Convention Bureau, Switzerland.

Notes: 0 = zero or less than half the unit of measure.   .. = not available or indeterminate.

14-15. Endangered species management programs, 1996

Species — Common name	Scientific name a/	Distribution b/	IUCN status c/	Species management programs d/	Estimated wild population	Zoo census, 1996 — Number of zoos housing species	Number of captive animals	Number of captive births	Crude rate of change e/
Reptiles									
Boa, Dumeril's Ground	Acrantophis dumerili	Madagascar	VU	S	..	43.0	188	13	0.99
Boa, Madagascan Tree	Sanzinia madagascariensis	Madagascar	VU	UK	..	32.0	193	21	1.13
Boa, Madagascar	Acrantophis madagascariensis	Madagascar	VU	A	..	10.0	57	7	1.09
Crocodile, W. African Dwarf	Osteolaemus tetraspis	Central and West Africa	VU	A, UK	..	45.0	141	2	1.03
Gecko, Standing's Day	Phelsuma standingi	Madagascar	VU	UK	..	37.0	315	68	1.21
Lizard, Giant Girdled	Cordylus giganteus	South Africa	VU	A	>150,000	16.0	55	6	1.02
Tortoise, African Pancake	Malacochersus tornieri	Kenya, Tanzania	VU	UK	>20,000	47.0	228	11	1.05
Tortoise, Aldabra Giant	Geochelone gigantea	Seychelles	VU	Au	155,000	85.0	278	0	..
Tortoise, Geometric	Psammobates geometricus	South Africa	EN	A	2,000-4,000	1.0	10	0	1.03
Tortoise, Radiated	Geochelone radiata	Madagascar, Mauritius, Reunion	VU	A, S	2-2.5 million	54.0	412	25	1.00
Birds									
Crane, Wattled	Grus carunculatus	Africa	VU	J, S, UK	13,000-15,000	37.0	109	8	1.00
Griffon, Cape	Gyps coprotheres	Southern Africa	VU	A	..	5.0	36	2	1.05
Ibis, Northern Bald	Geronticus eremita	N.Africa and Middle East	CR	E, J	..	55.0	708	94	1.04
Ibis, Southern Bald	Geronticus calvus	Lesotho, S.Africa, Swaziland	VU	A	10,000	5.0	47	4	1.34
Peafowl, Congo	Afropavo congensis	Dem. Rep. of Congo	VU	E, S	..	18.0	96	41	0.99
Pigeon, Mauritius Pink	Columba mayeri	Mauritius	CR	E, S	77	32.0	233	51	1.14
Mammals									
Addax	Addax nasomaculatus	North Africa and the Sahel	EN	Au, E, S, UK	<250	62.0	514	93	1.02
Ass, Somali Wild	Equus africanus somaliensis g/	Ethiopia, Somalia	CR	E	100-250	8.0	29	2	0.96
Cheetah	Acinonyx jubatus f/	Africa	VU	A, Au, E, J, S,	9,000-12,000	117.0	666	70	0.82
Chimpanzee	Pan troglodytes f/	Africa	EN	J, S, UK	105,000	146.0	2,697	76	1.01
Chimpanzee, Pygmy (Bonobo)	Pan paniscus	Dem. Rep. of Congo	EN	E, S	10,000-20,000	17.0	98	5	1.04
Dog, African Wild	Lycaon pictus f/	Africa	EN	A, E, S	3,000-5,000	43.0	241	60	1.03
Drill	Mandrillus leucophaeus f/	Cameroon, Eq. Guinea, Nigeria	EN	E, J, S	<10,000	8.0	46	5	1.02
Elephant, African	Loxodonta africana f/	Africa	EN	E, S	581,175	101.0	282	1	0.81
Fossa	Cryptoprocta ferox	Madagascar	VU	E	..	7.0	29	2	1.03
Fox, Rodrigues Flying	Pteropus rodricensis	Mauritius (Rodrigues)	CR	S	350	17.0	557	156	1.16
Gazelle, Dama	Gazella dama	North Africa and the Sahel	EN	E	..	15.0	62	5	0.84
Gorilla, Western Lowland	Gorilla gorilla gorilla	West Central Africa	EN	E, S	>110,000	95.0	643	38	..
Hippopotamus, Pygmy	Hexaprotodon liberiensis f/	West Africa	VU	E, S, UK	..	61.0	164	11	0.98
Lechwe, Kafue	Kobus leche kafuensis	Zambia	VU	UK	..	13.0	133	24	0.95
Lemur, Black	Eulemur macaco macaco	Madagascar	VU	E, J, S, UK	..	42.0	171	14	0.95
Lemur, Mongoose	Eulemur mongoz f/	Comoros, Madagascar	VU	E, S	..	23.0	173	28	1.03
Lemur, Ring-tailed	Lemur catta	Madagascar	VU	S	..	167.0	1,087	128	1.00
Lemur, Ruffed	Varecia variegata f/	Madagascar	EN	Au, E, J, S	..	158.0	895	135	1.05
Lion, African	Panthera leo e/	Africa	VU	S	30,000-100,000	192.0	825	97	1.04
Monkey, Diana	Cercopithecus diana f/	West Africa	VU	E, UK	..	47.0	144	12	0.97
Oryx, Scimitar-horned	Oryx dammah	Israel [int.], North Africa	CR	Au, E, S	..	80.0	897	165	0.81
Rhinoceros, Black	Diceros bicornis f/	Africa	CR	Au, E, J, S, UK	2,400	57.0	170	5	1.07
Zebra, Grevy's	Equus grevyi	Ethiopia, Kenya	EN	E, J, S	..	70.0	332	25	0.99
Zebra, Hartman's Mountain	Equus zebra hartmannae g/	Angola, Namibia, S.Africa	EN	E, S	7,350	21.0	77	7	0.92

Source: World Conservation Union, International Species Information System, and other sources

Notes: a. Scientific names follow the "1996 IUCN Red List of Threatened Animals" nomenclature

b. From the "1996 IUCN Red List": [int] = introduced; [re-int] = reintroduced; [ex?] = believed to be extinct; [?] = unknown if the species is currently found in the area

c. IUCN threatened status: CR = critically endangered; EN = endangered; EW = extinct in the wild; VU = vulnerable

d. A = African Propagation Program (APP); Au = Australasian Species Management Program (ASMP); B = Zoological Society of Brazil Species Program (SZB); E = European Endangered Species Programs (EEP); J = Species Survival Committees Japan (SSCJ); S = North America Species Survival Plan (SSP); UK = United Kingdom Joint Management of Species UK = United Kingdom Joint Management of Species Committee (JMSC).

e. A rate > 1 indicates a net population increase; a rate < 1, a net population decrease; and a rate = 1 indicates that the captive population is stable.

f. Zoo census data include all subspecies being held in captivity

g. IUCN status listed applies to the species; the subspecies is not listed separately under the "1996 IUCN Red List."

Technical Notes

Tables

These notes are based on technical notes for each table as presented in WRI 1998–99. They have been edited and shortened for this volume. Readers are urged to consult the original source for details.

Table 14-1. Land area and use, 1982–94. Land area and land use data are provided to the FAO by national governments in response to annual questionnaires. The FAO also compiles data from national agricultural censuses. The FAO often adjusts the definitions of land use categories and sometimes substantially revises earlier data.

Land use data are periodically revised and may change significantly from year to year. For the most recent land use statistics, see the latest *FAO Production Yearbook.*

Land area data are for 1994. They exclude major inland water bodies, national claims to the continental shelf, and Exclusive Economic Zones.

Population density was derived by using the population figures for 1996 published by the United Nations Population Division and 1994 land area data from the FAO. Although the population figures were published in 1994, actual censuses and estimates were made in prior years.

Cropland includes land under temporary and permanent crops, temporary meadows, market and kitchen gardens, and land that is temporarily fallow. Permanent crops are those that do not need to be replanted after each harvest, such as cocoa, coffee, rubber, fruit, and vines. This category excludes land used to grow trees for wood or timber.

Permanent pasture is land used for five or more years for forage, including natural crops and cultivated crops. This category is difficult for countries to assess because it includes wildland used for pasture. In addition, few countries regularly report data on permanent pasture. As a result, the absence of a change in permanent pasture area may indicate differences in land classification and data reporting rather than actual conditions. Grassland not used for forage is included under other land.

Domestic land is the sum of cropland and permanent pasture.

Forest and woodland includes land under natural or planted stands of trees, as well as logged-over areas that will be reforested in the near future.

Other land includes uncultivated land, grassland not used for pasture, built-up areas, wetlands, wastelands, and roads.

Table 14-2. Forest resources, 1980–95. *Total forest* consists of all forest area for temperate countries and the sum of natural forest and plantation area categories.

FAO defines a *natural forest* as a forest composed primarily of indigenous (native) tree species. Natural forests include closed forest, where trees cover a high proportion of the ground and where grass does not form a continuous layer on the forest floor (e.g., broadleaved forests, coniferous forests, and bamboo forests), and open forest, which FAO defines as mixed forest/grasslands with at least 10 percent tree cover and a continuous grass layer on the forest floor. Natural forests encompass all stands except plantations and include stands that have been degraded to some degree by agriculture, fire, logging, and other factors.

Plantations refer to forest stands established artificially by afforestation and reforestation for industrial and nonindustrial usage. Reforestation does not include regeneration of old tree crops (through either natural regeneration or forest management), although some countries may report regeneration as reforestation. Many trees are also planted for nonindustrial uses, such as village wood lots. Reforestation data often exclude this component. The data presented here reflect plantation survival rates as estimated by FAO.

Average annual percent change is shown as a percentage of the exponential growth rate. If negative (in parentheses), these figures reflect net deforestation, which is defined as the clearing of forest lands for all forms of agricultural uses (shifting cultivation, permanent agriculture, and ranching) and for other land uses such as settlements, other infrastructure, and mining. In tropical countries, this entails clearing that reduces tree crown cover to less than 10 percent. Deforestation, as defined here, does not reflect changes within the forest stand or site, such as selective logging (unless the forest cover is permanently reduced to less than 10 percent).

Table 14-3. Forest ecosystems, 1996. *Closed forests* exclude some woodlands and wooded savannah.

Original forest as a percentage of land area refers to the estimate of the percentage of land that would have been covered by closed forest about 8,000 years ago, assuming current climatic conditions, before large-scale disturbance by human society began.

Current forests refer to estimated closed forest cover within the past 10 years or so (this varies by country). Only closed moist forests are given for Africa.

Frontier forests are large, relatively intact forest ecosystems. They represent undisturbed forest areas that are large enough to maintain all of their biodiversity, including viable populations of wide-ranging species associated with each forest type.

Percentage of frontier forests threatened refers to frontier forests where ongoing or planned human activities such as logging, mining, and other large-scale disturbances will eventually degrade the ecosystem through

species decline or extinction, drastic changes in the forest's age structure, etc., and would result, if continued, in the violation of one of the above-mentioned criteria.

Tropical forests include all forests located between the Tropics of Cancer and Capricorn. All other forests are put into the *nontropical* category.

Percentage protected includes forest areas that fall within the protected areas in the world that are listed as the World Conservation Union's (IUCN) management categories I-V.

Table 14-4. Wood production and trade, 1983–95.

Total roundwood production refers to all wood in the rough, whether destined for industrial or fuelwood uses.

Fuel and charcoal production covers all rough wood used for cooking, heating, and power production. Wood intended for charcoal production, pit kilns, and portable ovens is included.

Industrial roundwood production comprises all roundwood products other than fuelwood and charcoal.

Processed wood production includes sawnwood and panels.

Paper production includes newsprint, printing and writing paper, and other paper and paperboard.

Average annual net trade in roundwood is the balance of imports minus exports.

Table 14-5. Freshwater resources and withdrawals, 1970–98. Annual internal renewable water resources refers to the average annual flow of rivers and groundwater generated from endogenous precipitation. Caution should be used when comparing different countries because these estimates are based on differing sources and dates. These annual averages also disguise large seasonal, inter-annual, and long-term variations. When data for annual river flows from and to other countries are not shown, the internal renewable water resources figure may include these flows. Per capita annual internal renewable water resource data were calculated using 1995 population estimates.

Annual withdrawals as a percentage of water resources refer to total water withdrawals, not counting evaporative losses from storage basins, as a percentage of internal renewable water resources and river flows from other countries. Water withdrawals also include water from desalination plants in countries where that source is a significant part of all water withdrawals.

Per capita annual withdrawals were calculated using national population data for the year of data shown for withdrawals.

Sectoral withdrawals are classified as domestic (drinking water, homes, commercial establishments, public services [for example, hospitals], and municipal use or provision); industry (including water withdrawn to cool thermoelectric plants); and agriculture (irrigation and livestock).

Table 14-6. Marine and freshwater catches, aquaculture, balance of trade, and fish consumption. *Marine and freshwater catch* data refer to marine and freshwater fish, killed, caught, trapped, collected, bred, or cultivated for commercial, industrial, and subsistence use (catches from recreational activities are included where available). Crustaceans and molluscs are included. Statistics for mariculture, aquaculture, and other kinds of fish farming are included in the country totals. Figures are the national totals averaged over a 3-year period; they include fish caught by a country's fleet anywhere in the world. Catches of freshwater species caught in low-salinity seas are included in the statistics of the appropriate marine area. Marine catch includes catches of diadromous (migratory between saltwater and freshwater) species.

Data are represented as nominal catches, which are the landings converted to a live-weight basis, that is, the weight when caught.

Landings for some countries are identical to catches.

Aquaculture is defined by FAO as "the farming of aquatic organisms, including fish, molluscs, crustaceans, and aquatic plants. Farming implies some form of intervention in the rearing process to enhance production, such as regular stocking, feeding, and protection from predators, etc. [It] also implies ownership of the stock being cultivated. . . ." Aquatic

organisms that are exploitable by the public as a common property resource are included in the harvest of fisheries.

Marine fish include a variety of species groups such as mullets, seabasses, groupers, snappers, tunas, mackerels, etc. *Diadromus fish* include surgeons, river eels, salmons, trouts, etc. *Freshwater fish* include carps, perches, catfish, and tilapias, among others. Molluscs include freshwater molluscs, oysters, mussels, scallops, clams, abalones, and cephalopods. *Crustaceans* include, among others, freshwater crustaceans, crabs, lobsters, shrimps, and prawns. Data on whales and other marine mammals are excluded from this table.

Balance of trade is defined as exports minus imports. Figures are the national totals averaged over a 3-year period in millions of U.S. dollars. Imports are usually on a cost, insurance, and freight basis (c.i.f.) (i.e., insurance and freight costs added in). Exports are generally on a free-on-board basis (FOB) (i.e., not including insurance or freight costs). A surplus of imports over exports is shown in parentheses. Trade in *fish* includes fish that is fresh, frozen, chilled, salted, or smoked as well as fish products and preparations. Trade in *molluscs and crustaceans* includes molluscs and crustaceans that are fresh, chilled, smoked, derived products, etc. Trade in *fish meal* includes meals, solubles, etc.

Per capita annual food supply from fish and seafood is the quantity of both freshwater and marine fish, seafood, and derived products available for human consumption. Data on aquatic plants and whale meat are excluded from the totals. The amount of fish and seafood actually consumed may be lower than the figures provided, depending on how much is lost during storage, preparation, and cooking, and on how much is discarded. Data are presented in kilograms per capita. Years shown are 3-year averages.

Table 14-7. Commercial energy production, 1985–95. Total production of commercially traded fuels includes solid, liquid, and gaseous fuels and primary electricity production. Solid fuels include bituminous coal, lignite, peat, and oil shale burned directly. Liquid fuels include crude petroleum and liquid natural

gas. Gas includes natural gas and other petroleum gases.

Primary electricity is valued differently depending on its source. Wind, tide, wave, solar, and hydroelectric power generation is expressed at the energy value of electricity (1 kilowatt hour = 3.6 million joules). Nuclear and geothermal power generation is valued on a fossil-fuel-avoided basis rather than an energy-output basis. Electricity production data generally refer to gross production. Data for Zambia and Zimbabwe refer to net production. Gross production is the amount of electricity produced by a generating station before consumption by station auxiliaries and transformer losses within the station are deducted. Net production is the amount of electricity remaining after these deductions. Typically, net production is 5 to 10 percent less than gross production. Energy production from pumped storage is not included in gross or net electricity generation. Electricity production includes both public and self-producer power plants. Fuelwood, charcoal, bagasse, animal and vegetal wastes, and all forms of solar energy are excluded from production figures, even when traded commercially.

One petajoule (1,015 joules) is the same as 0.0009478 quads (1,015 British Thermal Units) and is the equivalent of 163,400 "UN standard" barrels of oil or 34,140 "UN standard" metric tons of coal. The heat content of various fuels has been converted to coal-equivalent and then to petajoule-equivalent values using country-specific and other conversion factors.

South Africa refers to the South Africa Customs Union: Botswana, Lesotho, Namibia, South Africa, and Swaziland.

Table 14-8. Energy balances, 1985–95. *Total final consumption* is the sum of consumption by the different sectors. Backflows from the petrochemical industry are not included. *Industry sector* includes the *iron and steel* industry, chemical industry, nonferrous metals basic industries, nonmetallic mineral products (e.g., glass, ceramics, cement, etc.), transport equipment, machinery, mining and quarrying, food and tobacco, paper, pulp and print, wood and wood prod-

ucts, construction, textile and leather, and any non-specified industry. The *transportation sector* includes all fuel used for transportation except international marine bunkers. Fuel used for ocean, coastal, and inland fishing is not included. *Air transportation* includes both international civil aviation and domestic air travel. *Road transportation* includes all human and cargo transportation taking place on a nation's road network. *Agriculture* includes all agricultural activity, including ocean, coastal, and inland fishing. *Commercial and public services* include service sectors such as stores, repair shops, restaurants, etc. *Residential* includes energy use by residences. IEA reports that it can be difficult to accurately distinguish among the agriculture, commercial, and public services sectors, and that a total of the three is more accurate than values for the individual sectors.

Table 14-9. Production of selected minerals and materials, 1995. *Bauxite* is the primary ore from which aluminum is derived, although these data also contain the dry bauxite equivalents of the minerals nepheline syenite and alunite. To allow comparisons with other extraction activities, the bauxite equivalent is reported here in terms of its content of aluminum, which is 25 percent of the mass of bauxite. Not all bauxite is used for the production of aluminum, however; it can also be used in the production of such items as abrasives, chemicals, and refractories.

Iron ore is reported as the elemental iron contained in the production of iron ore, iron ore concentrates, and iron ore agglomerates and in principle contains no double-counting of ores traded rather than produced.

Copper ore is the world mine production in terms of the copper content of ores produced. Where possible, the copper content was calculated from actual analysis of the relevant ores or concentrates.

Silver ore is commonly produced as a byproduct of gold, copper, and other metals production, although it is also mined directly.

Gold production is based on the actual reported production of the element. It does not necessarily capture small-scale artisanal production nor production that, to escape taxation, enters illegal channels.

Sulfur is produced from elemental deposits, from the production of other minerals, or as a by-product of other industrial processes. It is counted here as produced in the country of origin if production is from native sulfur, pyrites, gypsum, byproducts from the extraction of crude oil and natural gas, or tar sands. It is counted as produced in the country of recovery if it is obtained from metallurgical operations, petroleum refineries, or spent oxides.

Salt here refers to sodium chloride, or common salt, and is derived from mines, oceans, and seas through evaporation and by the extraction of brines. It is used to season and preserve foods, as an essential raw material for the chemical industry, and for several other industrial uses.

Nitrogen is measured as the amount (82.2 percent) contained in anhydrous *ammonia* produced by combining nitrogen from the air with hydrogen (derived from several potential sources) and water. Ammonia, in turn, provides the essential input to a variety of nitrogen-based fertilizers that together provide more than 50 percent of the nitrogen required for the world's food and fiber production.

Phosphorus, another of the three essential elements for plant growth, is obtained primarily from phosphate rock and is measured in terms of the quantity of phosphorus pentoxide (P_2O_5) or its equivalent.

Potassium, the final of the three elements essential for plant growth, is derived from a variety of mined and manufactured salts.

Sand and gravel for construction are basic raw materials produced everywhere for local use. Because of the local nature of these resources, data on sand and gravel should be used with caution and can significantly understate the amount actually produced in a country. These data are presented here to illustrate the relative magnitude of reported production. Sand and gravel are used in the production of concrete, asphalt paving materials, road building, fill, concrete products, and in a variety of other applications.

Hydraulic cement is a product that can set underwater and is the dominant form of cement manufactured in the world. It use in concrete and in masonry is critical to the construction industry. Portland and masonry cements are made by burning calcareous rocks such as limestone with lesser quantities of other materials.

Table 14-10. Carbon dioxide emissions from industrial processes, 1995. This table includes data on industrial additions to the carbon dioxide flux from solid fuels, liquid fuels, gas fuels, gas flaring, and cement manufacture. The Carbon Dioxide Information Analysis Center (CDIAC) annually calculates emissions of CO_2 from the burning of fossil fuels and the manufacture of cement for most of the countries of the world. Estimates of total and per capita national emissions do not include bunker fuels used in international transport because of the difficulty of apportioning these fuels among the countries benefiting from that transport. Emissions from bunker fuels are shown separately for the country where the fuel was delivered.

Emissions of CO_2 are often calculated and reported in terms of their content of elemental carbon. CDIAC reports them that way. For this table, CDIAC's figures were converted to the actual mass by 3.664 (the ratio of the mass of carbon to that of CO_2).

Solid, liquid, and gas fuels are primarily, but not exclusively, coals, petroleum products, and natural gas. Gas flaring is the practice of burning off gas released in the process of petroleum extraction, a practice that is declining. During cement manufacture, cement is calcined to produce calcium oxide. In the process, 0.498 metric ton of CO_2 is released for each metric ton of cement produced. Total emissions consist of the sum of the CO_2 produced during the consumption of solid, liquid, and gas fuels, and from gas flaring and the manufacture of cement.

Combustion of different fossil fuels releases CO_2 at different rates for the same level of energy production. Burning oil releases about 1.5 times the amount of CO_2 released from burning natural gas; burning coal releases about twice as much CO_2 as natural gas.

Table 14-11. Globally threatened species: mammals, birds, and higher plants, 1990s. The total number of known species may include introductions in some instances. Data on mammals exclude cetaceans (whales and porpoises), except where otherwise indicated. Threatened bird species are listed for countries included within their breeding or wintering ranges. Higher plants refer to numbers of native vascular plant species. Total plant species numbers may differ from earlier estimates published in previous editions of WRI (1994), as totals are of full species only, rather than of species and subspecies. The number of endemic species refers to those species known to be found only within the countries listed. Figures are not necessarily comparable among countries because taxonomic concepts and the extent of knowledge vary (for the latter reason, country totals of species and endemics may be underestimates). In general, numbers of mammals and birds are fairly well known, while plants have not been as well inventoried.

The World Conservation Union classifies threatened and endangered species in six categories.

Endangered. "Taxa in danger of extinction and whose survival is unlikely if the causal factors continue operating."

Vulnerable. "Taxa believed likely to move into the endangered category in the near future if the causal factors continue operating."

Rare. "Taxa with world populations that are not at present endangered or vulnerable, but are at risk."

Indeterminate. "Taxa known to be endangered, vulnerable, or rare but where there is not enough information to say which of the three categories is appropriate."

Out of danger. "Taxa formerly included in one of the above categories, but which are now considered relatively secure because effective conservation measures have been taken or the previous threat to their survival has been removed."

Insufficiently known. "Taxa that are suspected but not definitely known to belong to any of the above categories."

The number of threatened species listed for all countries includes full species that are endangered, vulnerable, rare, indeterminate, and insufficiently known, but excludes introduced species or those known to be extinct.

Number of species per 10,000 square kilometers provides a relative estimate for comparing numbers of species among countries of differing size. Because the relationship between area and species number is non-linear (that is, as the area sampled increases, the number of new species located decreases), a species-area curve has been used to standardize these species numbers.

Table 14-12. Globally threatened species: reptiles, amphibians, and fish, 1990s. Threatened marine turtles and marine fish are excluded from country totals. Endangered fish species numbers do not include approximately 250 haplochromine and 2 tilapiine species of Lake Victoria cichlids, since the ranges of these species are undetermined.

The number of species per 10,000 square kilometers provides a relative estimate for comparing numbers of species among countries of differing size.

Table 14-13. National protection of natural areas, 1997. All protected areas combine natural areas in five World Conservation Union (formerly the International Union for Conservation of Nature and Natural Resources, IUCN), management categories (areas at least 1,000 hectares).

Totally protected areas are maintained in a natural state and are closed to extractive uses. They encompass the following three management categories: *category I,* scientific reserves and strict nature reserves; *category II,* national parks and provincial parks; and *category III,* natural monuments and natural landmarks.

Partially protected areas are areas that may be managed for specific uses, such as recreation or tourism, or areas that provide optimum conditions for certain species or communities of wildlife. Some extractive use within these areas is allowed. They encompass two management categories: *category IV,* managed nature reserves wildlife sanctuaries; and *category V,* protected landscapes and seascapes.

Protected areas between at least 100,000 hectares and 1 million hectares in size refer to all IUCN category I–V protected areas that fall within these two classifications.

The values in this table do not include locally or provincially protected sites, or privately owned areas.

Table 14-14. International protected areas, 1997.
Internationally protected areas usually include sites that are listed under national protection systems.

Biosphere reserves are representative of terrestrial and coastal environments that have been internationally recognized under the Man and the Biosphere Programme of UNESCO.

World heritage sites represent areas of "outstanding universal value" for their natural features, their cultural value, or for both natural and cultural values. The table includes only natural and mixed natural and cultural sites.

Any party to the Convention on Wetlands of International Importance, Especially as Waterfowl Habitat that agrees to respect the site's integrity and to establish wetland reserves can designate wetlands of international importance.

Marine and coastal protected areas refer to all protected areas greater than 1,000 hectares with littoral, coral, island, marine, or estuarine components. The area given is the whole protected area.

Table 14-15. Endangered species management programs, 1996.
Species: in this table are those mammals, birds, amphibians, and reptiles that (a) have an ongoing management plan recognized and approved by regional zoo associations, (b) are listed as threatened or extinct in the wild under the *1996 IUCN Red List of Threatened Animals*, and (c) are housed in zoos that are members of the International Species Information System (ISIS). The species' common and scientific names follow the *IUCN Red List* nomenclature, and thus species may have been given different names by ISIS and the Conservation Breeding Specialist Group (CBSG).

Distribution: the countries or regions where species are found in the wild follow the *IUCN Red List.* For birds, regions include migratory ranges. Where possible, the table indicates if a species has been reintroduced ("re-int.," i.e., the species has been reestablished after disappearing from that particular area), intro-

duced ("int.," i.e., the species was not found in that area before its introduction), is believed to be extinct ("ex?"), or whether it is unknown if the species is currently found in the area ("?").

IUCN status refers to species that fall within the IUCN category of Critically Endangered (CR), Endangered (EN), Vulnerable (VU), or Extinct in the Wild (EW). The category EW is described by IUCN as species "known only to survive in captivity or as a naturalized population well outside the past range." The status of several subspecies being managed in captivity was not listed separately under the *IUCN Red List*; therefore, the status for the whole species was listed in this table.

Species management programs are active, regionally organized efforts of managed cooperation among zoos, usually for species at risk in the wild, although a few programs were initiated as a result of a need to maintain the species in captivity and not because of the species' threatened status. According to the AZA, species management programs breed species in captivity to "maintain a healthy and self-sustaining captive population that is both genetically diverse and demographically stable." It is important to note, however, that for many taxa, zoos are past the first stage of trying to breed the species and are into the second stage of trying not to breed them too fast, because the available space in many zoos is full or because space needs to be made for more threatened taxa. Several species management programs include reintroduction of the species into the wild, and in some cases, these programs have been responsible for returning a species to its former habitat. However, species reintroduction is not the goal of all species management programs.

Estimated wild population: accurate numbers for wild populations are known for only a few well-studied species. Most figures presented here are estimates based on a number of different methodologies from extrapolating population estimates using remaining habitat to actual population counts; therefore, caution is recommended when using these figures.

Zoo census data include data from ISIS-member zoos exclusively. As of 1996, 495 institutions (about half of the world's recognized zoos) were ISIS members. This table underestimates the number of institutions, animals, and births in the world because other institutions that are breeding species in captivity are not members of ISIS.

Number of zoos housing species is number of ISIS-member zoos housing the species.

Number of captive animals includes all living individuals of a species housed in ISIS-member zoos as of December 1996. Not all individual animals participate in the species management programs. For many species, the figures include all subspecies being held in zoos, and this is indicated as such in the table.

Number of captive births refer to the total births minus deaths within the first 30 days of life that occurred during the past 6 months of 1996.

Crude rate of change is an indicator of captive population stability or the annual population increase or decrease per 100. A figure of 1.00 means the captive population is stable, whereas 0.90 indicates a 10 percent decrease in the captive population. This indicator is the net result of all processes including births, deaths, imports, exports, capture, escapes, etc.

15

Household Welfare Indicators for Selected Countries

The absence of reliable information on poverty in Sub-Saharan Africa has led to the implementation of poverty monitoring programs. Major components of these programs included data collection and policy analysis through capacity building of statistical offices. This chapter presents a set of standardized household welfare indicators derived from household surveys carried out and analysed during FY98 in 22 African countries: Burkina Faso, Central African Republic, Côte d'Ivoire, Djibouti, Ethiopia, the Gambia, Ghana, Guinea, Guinea-Bissau, Kenya, Madagascar, Mali, Mauritania, Niger, Nigeria, Senegal, South Africa, Sierra Leone, Swaziland, Tanzania, Uganda, and Zambia. Most of these countries are among the 37 countries that were assisted in establishing a poverty monitoring program under the Social Dimensions of Adjustment (SDA) project.

In the previous edition of the ADI, the welfare indicators produced were divided into five main groups: demographic indicators, education and literacy, household structure, household expenditure and poverty incidence ,and household amenities. While these indicators provided a wide array of information on living standards, a few aspects of poverty and individual welfare were not taken into account, in particular, the determinants of household income (labor market structure and income sources) and anthropometric indicators (stunting, wasting, and underweight).

After a review of the quality of the data files, a new set of standardized data files was produced. Additional welfare indicators were identified from the surveys: labor force participation, branch of activity, malnutrition, and age dependency ratio. (A new set of indicators were produced and published in the 1997 annual SPA Report on poverty in Sub-Saharan Africa).

The changes made to the data base are reflected in the welfare indicators, country coverage, and number of standardized data files. The number of household and individual welfare indicators will increase from 37 in the previous edition to 52 in a future edition. Similarly, the coverage is expanded to include 5 additional countries, increasing the total number of countries published in the report from 17 in the last edition to 22 in the 1998 edition. These additional countries include: Djibouti, Ethiopia, Mali, Mauritania, and Swaziland. Compared to the previous edition, this volume is more representative of Sub-Saharan African countries.

Out of the 22 countries, 4 Sub-Saharan African countries that appeared in a much earlier edition of the ADI recently carried out a new survey: Ghana, Guinea Bissau, Senegal, and Zambia. This occurrence of two time points for a set of standardized data files for few countries has increased the scope of information and size of the Bank's Poverty Monitoring Unit data base which now has 26 standardized data sets. In countries with more than one survey, welfare indicators will be estimated from the most recent survey to better reflect the changes in living standards.

All statistics are based on nationally representative household surveys. Survey results have been disaggregated by urban and rural expenditure quintiles. Welfare indicators are grouped into seven classes: demographic, education and literacy, household structure, labor markets and employment status, household expenditure, household amenities and anthropometrics indicators. The technical notes provide definitions of indicators, which sometimes differ from country to country. Differences in definitions and in the way in which variables have been computed may cause discrepancies between indicators published by the national statistical offices and the ones given here. The robustness and completeness of expenditures and household variables vary according to the type of survey used to collect the data.

The four types of household surveys referred to are traditional household budget surveys (HBS) integrated surveys (IS) or living standards measurement surveys (LSMS), priority surveys (PS), and Core Welfare Indicators Questionnaire surveys (CWIQ). Household budget surveys involve multiple visits to a household during a year, provide the most complete record of expenditures, and capture seasonal variations in expenditure patterns. They are limited, however, in terms of additional social indicators. The integrated and Living Standards Measurement surveys involve two visits to the household within a fortnight and provide a more complete picture of household living standards. The expenditure data are generally complete, but seasonal and month-to-month variation in expenditure patterns are not well captured, which can bias in the results. The priority surveys were designed to provide a rapid way to collect socioeconomic indicators, involve one visit to a household, and may underestimate expenditure levels. The CWIQ survey is an automated data entry and editing survey program that rapidly monitors key indicators using optical scanner technology. Like the PS, data on households and individual living conditions are collected on a single visit, and attempts are not always made to accurately estimate total household expenditure.

While the absolute expenditure levels may be affected by type of survey used, the relative ranking of households within a country-the grouping of households into expenditure quintiles-is less affected. Expenditure surveys were used in Ethiopia, Niger, Nigeria, Sierra Leone, and Swaziland. Integrated or Living Standards Measurement surveys were used in Madagascar, Mauritania, South Africa, Tanzania, and Uganda. Priority surveys were used in Burkina Faso, Central African Republic, Côte d'Ivoire, Djibouti, the Gambia, Guinea, Guinea-Bissau, Kenya, Mali, Senegal, and Zambia. The Core Welfare Indicators Questionnaire was used in Ghana.

Generic definitions

Household is defined as a group of related or unrelated people, who live in a dwelling unit or its equivalent, eat from the same pot, and share common housekeeping arrangements.

Expenditure quintiles are derived by ranking sample households according to per capita expenditure. Individuals rather than households are used as the basis for estimating expenditures quintiles. Quintiles are constructed such that the first quintile represents the poorest 20 percent, the second quintile the next poorest 20 percent (less poor), and so on; the fifth quintile represents the wealthiest group.

Price deflators, when available, are used to adjust expenditures for regional price differences. In many countries, deflators were not available. Urban-rural differences are overestimated when price deflators are not used.

Demographic indicators

Population below 15 years is estimated by taking the ratio of all individuals below age 15 to the total number of individuals in the population. The calculation is repeated for men and women.

Number of households in each quintile varies due to differences in household size, although the total number of individuals in each quintile is the same.

Average household size is estimated for each quintile as well as for regional and national levels by taking the weighted average household size in each quintile.

Age dependency ratio is estimated as the number of individuals with age less than or equal to 14 or above 65 years over the number of individuals with age between 15 and 64 years of age, weighted by the population weights.

Number of males per 100 females is estimated as the total number of males aged 15 years or older as a proportion of total female population in the same age range.

Education and literacy indicators

Net primary enrollment rate is defined as the total number of children of primary school age (6 to 13 years) enrolled as a proportion of the total number of children of primary school age.

Net secondary enrollment rate is the total number of children of secondary school age (14 to 18 years) enrolled as a proportion of the total number of children of secondary school age.

Literacy rate is the proportion of the population above 15 years old able to read and write. When the literacy level is not specified, however, the individual is considered illiterate.

Head of household indicators

Monogamous male-headed refers to a male-headed household having no more than one spouse.

Polygamous male-headed refers to a male-headed household with more than one spouse. However, differences exist in the way in which countries define polygamous households. In few a countries, the term refers to the households where all the wives live under the same roof.

Single male-headed refers to a male-headed house-hold where the head is either divorced or has never been married.

Defacto female-headed refers to a household where the husband is not present and the wife the main decision-maker in his absence and is thus the head by default.

Dejure female-headed is a single female-headed household where the head has never been married or is divorced or widowed.

Educational level of the head shows the percentage of household heads who have completed primary or secondary education or who have never attended any school.

Labor market indicators

Labor market indicators have been computed for population aged 15 years and above.

Employment of head follows the international standard industrial classification of all economic activities and is divided into five broad categories: agriculture and fishing, manufacture/mining/construction, commerce, civil servant/army, and other sectors. Agropastoralist is used when the main source of income of the household is farming and/or livestock. Similarly, in other sectors, the employment status of the head is determined by the share of income derived from the sector in total household income. For household heads who work in more than one sector, the sector from which the largest income share is derived will prevail.

Proportion of employed refers to the share of the population aged between 15 and 64 years which is currently employed.

Labor force participation is the proportion of the population aged 15-64 which supplies labor to produce goods and services during a given period. The labor force population includes currently employed people and job seekers.

Household expenditure indicators

These indicators provide information on per capita expenditure in local currency (including the value of own-produced food consumed in the household) and the share of food in household expenditures. Price deflators, when available, are used to compensate for regional price differences.

Mean per capita expenditure, in local currency, is estimated as the weighted average per capita household expenditure. It includes the value of own-produced food consumed in the household.

Poverty line is a relative poverty line defined as 2/3 of the national mean per capita expenditure. This definition may differ from country-specific definitions used by national statistical offices.

Food share in total expenditure provides a weighted estimate of total per capita household expenditure allocated to food, including a valuation of own-produced food consumed by the household.

Household amenities indicators

These indicators provide estimates of the percentage of households using different household amenities.

Type of fuel for cooking includes firewood, gas and kerosene, charcoal, and electricity.

Access to safe sanitation refers to households equipped with a flush toilet or pit latrine.

Access to water indicates the percentage of households with access to different sources of drinking water.

Anthropometrics indicators

Stunting refers to children under 59 months of age who have height-for-age Z-scores below minus two standard deviations from the median of the reference population.

Wasting refers to children under 59 months of age who have weight-for-height Z-scores below minus two standard deviations from the median of the reference population.

Underweight refers to children under 59 months of age who have weight-for-age Z-scores below minus two standard deviations from the median of the reference population.

Age pyramids

These indicators represent the population derived from each survey by age group. Unlike the tables, which describe literacy rates for adults over age 15, the shaded area shows the proportion in each age group that is attending or has attended school. Therefore, the shaded areas of the pyramids do not represent literacy rates. These pyramids have been adjusted for age misreporting using the methodology of the U.S. National Academy of Science.

15-1. Burkina Faso: household welfare indicators

| | | | | | | Expenditure quintile | | | | | | | | |
| | | | Rural | | | | | | Urban | | | | | |
Indicator	Unit of measure	National total	All	1	2	3	4	5	All	1	2	3	4	5
Demographic indicators														
Sample size (households)	Number	8610	5897	944	989	1119	1293	1552	2713	427	480	497	542	767
Total population	000s	9385	7863	1576	1573	1571	1575	1569	1522	305	304	304	305	304
Population below 15 years	Percent	48	49	53	52	50	47	44	43	49	47	43	42	35
Population 60 years and above	Percent	5	6	6	5	6	6	6	3	5	4	4	2	2
Age dependency ratio	Percent	106	112	132	123	115	102	91	83	107	96	85	78	56
Number of males per 100 females (age 15 and over)	Number	88	85	78	81	79	87	96	107	90	100	105	114	124
Average household size	Number	7.8	8.1	11.2	9.6	8.6	7.2	5.9	6.5	8.7	7.7	6.9	6.4	4.4
Education and literacy														
Net primary enrollment rate (total)	Percent	33	27	17	20	24	33	44	69	53	66	73	79	80
Male	Percent	38	32	22	27	31	39	45	74	58	69	78	85	87
Female	Percent	28	21	12	12	15	26	42	65	48	62	68	74	74
Net secondary enrollment rate (total)	Percent	12	6	2	2	5	6	14	36	18	25	38	43	57
Male	Percent	14	7	2	2	7	8	17	42	23	29	46	46	70
Female	Percent	10	4	1	2	2	3	10	31	14	21	30	39	47
Literacy rate (total)	Percent	19	12	6	8	10	12	21	52	24	40	49	58	79
Male	Percent	27	19	11	14	18	19	31	62	34	51	60	67	85
Female	Percent	11	6	3	4	3	6	13	41	15	29	37	49	72
Head of household														
Marital status of head														
Monogamous male-headed	Percent	52	51	42	50	49	55	54	56	51	56	59	60	55
Polygamous male-headed	Percent	30	33	45	39	37	31	22	15	29	22	17	13	5
Single male-headed	Percent	10	8	7	6	7	6	13	15	7	8	9	15	28
Defacto female-headed	Percent	3	2	3	2	2	2	3	4	5	5	5	4	4
Dejure female-headed	Percent	6	5	3	4	5	5	8	9	8	9	10	8	8
Education level of head														
No level	Percent	82	89	94	95	92	92	78	53	84	74	59	50	20
Primary not completed	Percent	6	5	4	4	5	5	6	11	9	9	14	12	11
Completed primary, no secondary	Percent	5	3	2	2	3	3	6	12	5	9	16	14	13
Secondary not completed	Percent	5	2	0	0	0	1	7	16	2	8	10	19	29
Completed secondary / higher level	Percent	2	1	0	0	0	0	3	9	0	0	1	5	26
Labor market (population aged 15 to 64)														
Number of employed people in sample	Number	30238	24441	5251	4920	5073	4858	4339	5797	1483	1206	1023	979	1106
Proportion of employed	Percent	50	42	39	41	42	44	44	29	33	29	27	27	31
Branch of activity														
Agriculture/fishing	Percent	87	94	97	98	97	95	85	32	67	41	27	17	5
Manufacturing/mining/construction	Percent	4	2	1	1	2	3	4	16	9	16	19	22	18
Commerce	Percent	5	2	1	1	1	2	5	25	15	27	31	33	22
Civil servant/army	Percent	3	1	0	0	0	1	5	20	6	13	15	23	44
Other sector	Percent	1	1	0	0	0	0	2	6	3	4	8	5	12
Labor force participation (total)	Percent	84	89	91	91	91	90	85	58	71	62	54	52	54
Male	Percent	91	95	96	97	96	96	93	73	82	76	71	68	70
Female	Percent	77	84	86	87	86	85	77	43	61	48	38	33	35
Household expenditure														
Mean per capita expenditure (CFAF)	000s	67	49	18	27	36	50	112	161	39	73	112	171	412
Population below relative poverty line	Percent	56	65	100	100	100	24	0	13	67	0	0	0	0
Share of food in total expenditure	Percent	57	59	62	65	62	59	50	43	50	46	45	41	32
Household amenities														
Type of fuel for cooking														
Firewood	Percent	88	91	89	90	92	92	91	77	94	92	85	80	51
Gas, kerosine	Percent	3	1	1	1	0	0	2	10	1	2	3	5	26
Charcoal	Percent	2	1	0	0	0	0	2	5	0	2	3	4	12
Electricity	Percent	0	0	0	0	0	0	0	0	0	0	0	1	0
Other	Percent	7	7	10	9	7	7	5	8	5	5	8	10	11
Access to sanitation	Percent	30	16	7	8	9	15	32	88	72	85	88	93	96
Access to water														
Pipe/borne	Percent	17	4	1	1	3	3	9	74	50	68	77	78	86
Well	Percent	73	85	86	88	85	86	81	24	48	31	21	20	12
Other	Percent	9	11	12	12	12	11	10	2	2	1	3	1	2
Owner occupancy rate	Percent	86	91	95	96	96	93	81	64	78	77	69	63	46
Malnutrition (children aged 0 to 59 months)														
Stunting	Percent	41.0	43.9						19.1					
Wasting	Percent	17.9	18.0						17.0					
Underweight	Percent	39.6	41.6						24.1					

Source: Household Priority Survey, *Enquête prioritaire sur les conditions de vie des ménages, 1994/95.*

15-2. Central African Republic: household welfare indicators

						Expenditure quintile										
				Rural						Urban						
	Unit of measure	National total	All	1	2	3	4	5	All	1	2	3	4	5		
Demographic indicators																
Sample Size	Number	7417	4462	815	701	773	943	1230	2955	578	539	514	547	777		
Total population	000's	3340	2085	417	417	416	417	417	1257	251	251	251	251	251		
Female	Percent	49	49	50	50	50	50	48	50	51	50	50	50	48		
Population below 15 years	Percent	47	46	52	50	47	44	40	48	49	48	51	49	44		
Female	Percent	49	49	48	47	51	50	49	49	50	48	50	49	49		
Number of households	000's	682	466	76	81	89	98	121	215	44	40	37	40	54		
Average household size	Number	5	5	6	5	5	4	3	6	6	6	7	6	5		
Education and literacy																
Net primary enrollment (total)	Percent	48	37	29	35	37	40	48	65	46	65	69	73	76		
Male	Percent	54	46	39	42	46	48	58	68	50	70	71	74	78		
Female	Percent	41	28	19	27	27	33	38	62	42	59	66	71	74		
Net secondary enrollment (total)	Percent	36	23	21	27	19	27	22	52	42	49	52	57	62		
Male	Percent	50	39	35	48	36	42	32	64	53	62	63	71	72		
Female	Percent	23	9	8	8	6	13	13	42	28	36	43	46	54		
Literacy rates (total)	Percent	41	30	22	26	26	32	40	61	43	55	61	70	73		
Male	Percent	57	47	39	43	41	51	55	75	59	74	76	83	80		
Female	Percent	27	14	8	12	12	13	24	48	29	39	47	58	64		
Head of household																
Marital status of head																
Monogamous male-headed	Percent	51	54	58	58	56	60	42	46	48	48	46	46	42		
Polygamous male-headed	Percent	8	9	11	11	11	7	7	5	7	6	6	4	2		
Single male-headed	Percent	13	13	5	8	11	11	25	12	9	9	10	9	20		
Defacto female-headed	Percent	12	10	10	9	10	9	10	17	13	17	19	20	16		
Dejure female-headed	Percent	16	14	16	15	12	13	16	21	23	20	19	21	20		
Education level of head																
Completed primary	Percent	27	22	16	17	19	27	28	39	26	38	46	46	40		
Completed secondary	Percent	4	1	0	0	1	1	4	10	2	4	6	14	20		
Illiterate	Percent	69	77	84	83	80	73	68	52	73	58	48	40	40		
Employment of head																
Agro-pastoral activities	Percent	68	82	94	92	89	85	62	38	80	54	31	18	10		
Household expenditure																
Per capita expenditure (FCFA)	000's	54	35	4	10	16	28	118	84	13	33	56	87	230		
Population below poverty line	Percent	61	77	100	100	100	87	0	33	100	65	0	0	0		
Food share in total expenditure	Percent	60	61	52	60	64	65	62	59	58	62	62	60	53		
Household amenities																
Type of fuel for cooking																
Firewood	Percent	99	99	100	99	100	100	99	97	99	99	99	99	90		
Gas, kerosine	Percent	1	0	0	0	0	0	1	2	0	1	0	1	6		
Charcoal	Percent	0	0	0	0	0	0	0	1	0	0	0	0	3		
Electricity	Percent	0	0	0	0	0	0	0	0	0	0	0	0	0		
Other	Percent	0	0	0	0	0	0	1	1	1	1	1	1	1		
Access to Sanitation																
Access to Water																
Pipe	Percent	10	1	2	1	1	1	2	27	11	22	27	35	40		
Wells/borne	Percent	39	33	34	31	29	33	35	53	53	52	54	54	52		
Other	Percent	51	66	64	68	70	67	63	19	36	26	19	11	8		
Malnutrition (children aged 0 to 59 months)																
Stunting	Percent	.														
Wasting	Percent	.														
Underweight	Percent	.														

Source: Household Priority Survey, 1993.

15-3. Côte d'Ivoire: household welfare indicators

			Expenditure quintile											
Indicator	Unit of measure	National total	Rural						Urban					
			All	*1*	*2*	*3*	*4*	*5*	*All*	*1*	*2*	*3*	*4*	*5*
Demographic indicators														
Sample size (households)	Number	1000	520	63	79	90	109	179	480	77	77	91	89	146
Total population	000s	14400	8318	1610	1690	1656	1641	1721	6082	1174	1194	1163	1240	1311
Population below 15 years	Percent	44	46	56	51	47	46	31	41	49	48	46	36	26
Population 60 years and above	Percent	5	7	6	5	5	5	13	2	1	1	2	2	3
Age dependency ratio	Percent	95	101	144	115	100	97	66	71	98	94	90	59	37
Number of males per 100 females (age 15 and over)	Number	95	98	94	86	87	100	119	92	90	76	86	93	108
Average household size	Number	5.5	5.4	8.0	6.8	6.1	5.4	3.3	5.6	7.2	7.2	6.0	5.9	3.6
Education and literacy														
Net primary enrollment rate (total)	Percent	38	30	17	33	30	34	39	50	40	41	50	69	53
Male	Percent	40	32	20	36	24	38	45	55	43	43	51	78	75
Female	Percent	35	26	13	30	37	25	31	45	35	40	50	60	42
Net secondary enrollment rate (total)	Percent	18	9	3	7	14	10	11	28	20	20	22	35	38
Male	Percent	22	12	5	7	20	18	14	37	28	32	29	43	53
Female	Percent	14	4	0	8	6	0	7	20	15	11	14	28	30
Literacy rate (total)	Percent	45	29	20	32	31	30	31	65	56	55	60	72	76
Male	Percent	56	41	29	43	50	39	42	76	67	68	79	81	81
Female	Percent	35	17	10	23	14	20	18	55	47	46	44	64	69
Head of household														
Marital status of head														
Monogamous male-headed	Percent	57	58	65	60	54	59	55	56	65	61	59	54	49
Polygamous male-headed	Percent	12	14	15	19	24	18	5	8	14	15	6	9	1
Single male-headed	Percent	17	17	8	8	14	12	29	17	5	9	12	18	30
Defacto female-headed	Percent	2	2	4	0	3	1	2	3	5	3	2	2	3
Dejure female-headed	Percent	12	9	7	13	5	9	9	16	11	11	20	18	17
Education level of head														
No level	Percent	60	72	80	72	67	75	71	42	62	58	41	39	26
Primary not completed	Percent	5	6	4	6	4	4	8	3	3	1	6	1	5
Completed primary, no secondary	Percent	14	13	13	15	14	15	9	17	22	18	17	16	13
Secondary not completed	Percent	11	6	1	3	10	6	7	19	9	13	22	28	20
Completed secondary / higher level	Percent	10	4	3	5	5	1	5	20	3	10	14	17	37
Labor market (population aged 15 to 64)														
Number of employed people in sample	Number	.	.	.	.	.	.	.	.	.	.	.	.	.
Proportion of employed	Percent	.	.	.	.	.	.	.	.	.	.	.	.	.
Branch of activity														
Agriculture/fishing	Percent	.	.	.	.	.	.	.	.	.	.	.	.	.
Manufacturing/mining/monstruction	Percent	.	.	.	.	.	.	.	.	.	.	.	.	.
Commerce	Percent	.	.	.	.	.	.	.	.	.	.	.	.	.
Civil servant/army	Percent	.	.	.	.	.	.	.	.	.	.	.	.	.
Other sector	Percent	.	.	.	.	.	.	.	.	.	.	.	.	.
Labor force participation (total)	Percent	.	.	.	.	.	.	.	.	.	.	.	.	.
Male	Percent	.	.	.	.	.	.	.	.	.	.	.	.	.
Female	Percent	.	.	.	.	.	.	.	.	.	.	.	.	.
Household expenditure														
Mean per capita expenditure (CFAF)	000s	126	102	43	65	85	120	196	160	57	87	122	170	361
Population below relative poverty line	Percent	42	51	100	100	57	0	0	29	100	47	0	0	0
Share of food in total expenditure	Percent	48	53	52	52	51	56	52	41	45	47	43	38	33
Household amenities														
Type of fuel for cooking														
Firewood	Percent	66	89	91	97	94	93	80	32	55	52	32	25	16
Gas, kerosine	Percent	7	1	0	0	0	1	1	17	0	3	9	15	37
Charcoal	Percent	18	2	3	1	2	4	2	41	39	42	54	51	28
Electricity	Percent	0	0	0	0	0	0	0	0	0	0	0	0	0
Other	Percent	9	8	7	2	5	2	16	10	6	3	5	9	19
Access to sanitation	Percent	57	33	25	37	26	32	40	91	83	88	92	92	94
Access to water														
Pipe/borne	Percent	52	41	49	42	43	35	39	69	49	59	69	70	83
Well	Percent	34	37	29	40	31	37	42	30	51	41	30	27	16
Other	Percent	13	22	22	18	26	27	19	1	0	0	1	3	1
Owner occupancy rate	Percent	54	75	74	81	82	78	68	22	22	18	24	24	22
Malnutrition (children aged 0 to 59 months)														
Stunting	Percent	.	.						.					
Wasting	Percent	.	.						.					
Underweight	Percent	.	.						.					

Source: Household Priority Survey, *Enquête prioritaire sur les dimensions sociales de l'ajustement*, 1995.

15-4. Djibouti: household welfare indicators

| | | | Expenditure quintile | | | | | | | | | | | |
| | | | Rural | | | | | | Urban | | | | | |
Indicator	Unit of measure	National total	All	1	2	3	4	5	All	1	2	3	4	5
Demographic indicators														
Sample size (households)	Number	2380	397	67	65	75	85	105	1983	387	360	368	383	485
Total **sedentary** population	000s	259	15	3	3	3	3	3	244	49	49	49	49	49
Population below 15 years	Percent	38	43	51	50	40	42	33	37	45	40	38	34	30
Population 60 years and above	Percent	4	4	4	2	3	6	6	4	3	4	4	4	4
Age dependency ratio	Percent	67	85	119	106	71	82	59	66	90	75	66	57	46
Number of males per 100 females (age 15 and over)	Number	80	84	81	98	78	64	102	80	80	81	80	79	80
Average household size	Number	6.7	5.8	6.9	7.1	6.2	5.5	4.4	6.8	7.5	7.6	7.3	6.8	5.3
Education and literacy														
Net primary enrollment rate (total)	Percent	68	64	48	65	74	65	82	68	54	70	70	75	79
Male	Percent	73	77	64	79	82	78	87	73	59	74	77	78	82
Female	Percent	62	50	32	52	62	53	73	63	48	65	64	71	74
Net secondary enrollment rate (total)	Percent	30	7	3	7	7	11	9	31	10	25	35	39	52
Male	Percent	34	12	3	13	14	13	14	35	12	29	44	41	61
Female	Percent	26	2	2	0	0	9	0	27	8	22	26	38	45
Literacy rate (total)	Percent	52	33	20	28	34	32	45	53	36	50	53	58	63
Male	Percent	70	47	30	43	44	50	63	71	50	67	74	78	83
Female	Percent	37	20	12	12	26	19	26	38	24	36	37	42	46
Head of household														
Marital status of head														
Monogamous male-headed	Percent	63	58	51	69	53	52	63	64	63	59	68	62	66
Polygamous male-headed	Percent	10	15	11	17	19	16	14	9	10	11	8	10	8
Single male-headed	Percent	4	4	5	2	0	3	8	4	1	3	3	3	8
Defacto female-headed	Percent	5	6	9	0	9	11	2	5	8	7	6	3	4
Dejure female-headed	Percent	17	18	25	12	19	19	14	17	17	20	15	22	14
Education level of head														
No level	Percent	61	81	97	86	93	80	61	60	84	75	62	56	32
Coranic	Percent	3	2	1	3	3	2	2	3	3	5	2	2	4
Primary not completed	Percent	5	2	0	5	0	3	4	6	3	4	5	5	9
Completed primary, no secondary	Percent	14	8	2	6	3	13	14	14	7	10	15	20	18
Secondary not completed	Percent	11	5	0	0	1	1	16	11	2	5	13	11	21
Completed secondary / higher level	Percent	5	1	0	0	0	1	3	6	0	1	3	4	16
Labor market (population aged 15 to 64)														
Number of employed people in sample	Number	2585	276	32	44	44	56	100	2309	296	379	448	500	686
Proportion of employed	Percent	17	11	7	9	9	11	20	17	10	13	16	19	26
Branch of activity														
Agriculture/fishing	Percent	0	0	4	0	0	0	0	0	1	0	0	0	0
Manufacturing/mining/construction	Percent	5	5	4	10	9	0	4	5	3	8	7	4	4
Commerce	Percent	21	19	16	30	22	16	14	21	31	26	17	23	16
Civil servant/army	Percent	42	50	56	45	38	46	57	41	33	34	45	41	46
Other sector	Percent	32	26	20	15	30	38	24	32	32	31	31	31	35
Labor force participation (total)	Percent	48	38	28	31	36	45	47	49	43	50	49	49	53
Male	Percent	64	61	49	45	57	72	76	64	55	65	64	63	71
Female	Percent	36	19	12	16	19	27	17	37	33	38	37	37	38
Household expenditure														
Mean per capita expenditure (FDJI)	000s	190	87	25	50	69	98	195	197	66	109	153	213	442
Population below relative poverty line	Percent	41	84	100	100	100	100	17	38	100	92	0	0	0
Share of food in total expenditure	Percent	43	61	78	66	62	55	46	42	55	46	41	37	30
Household amenities														
Type of fuel for cooking														
Firewood	Percent	4	44	77	60	44	37	18	1	4	1	0	0	0
Gas, kerosine	Percent	90	48	21	33	45	55	73	93	90	95	96	92	93
Charcoal	Percent	0	5	1	8	9	4	3	0	0	0	0	1	0
Electricity	Percent	4	1	0	0	1	2	1	4	2	3	3	5	5
Other	Percent	2	2	0	0	0	2	6	2	3	1	1	2	1
Access to sanitation	Percent	18	3	2	3	2	2	5	19	4	6	12	21	43
Access to water														
Pipe/borne	Percent	79	45	24	42	52	50	52	81	63	75	82	90	91
Well	Percent	3	38	61	40	38	32	27	1	4	1	1	0	0
Other	Percent	18	17	15	18	10	18	21	18	33	25	17	10	9
Owner occupancy rate	Percent	68	88	98	91	93	86	76	66	77	71	65	66	56
Malnutrition (children aged 0 to 59 months)														
Stunting	Percent	27.1	35.8						26.6					
Wasting	Percent	14.6	8.2						15.0					
Underweight	Percent	18.0	20.4						17.9					

Source: Household Priority Survey, *Enquête Djiboutienne auprès des des ménages. Indicateurs sociaux*, 1996.

15-5. Ethiopia: household welfare indicators

| Indicator | Unit of measure | National total | Expenditure quintile | | | | | | | | | | | |
| | | | Rural | | | | | | Urban | | | | | |
			All	1	2	3	4	5	All	1	2	3	4	5
Demographic indicators														
Sample size (households)	Number	10948	6569	1036	1141	1233	1412	1747	4379	666	801	813	1008	1091
Total population	000s	55607	47236	9402	9449	9432	9449	9503	8372	1663	1678	1677	1674	1680
Population below 15 years	Percent	45	46	50	49	48	44	37	39	47	44	39	34	28
Population 60 years and above	Percent	5	5	5	4	5	6	7	6	6	5	6	6	5
Age dependency ratio	Percent	92	96	115	106	104	92	71	73	103	92	75	63	45
Number of males per 100 females (age 15 and over)	Number	105	100	102	98	103	95	101	137	140	131	117	146	150
Average household size	Number	5.0	5.1	5.9	5.6	5.2	4.8	4.2	4.7	5.4	5.3	4.7	4.4	3.9
Education and literacy														
Net primary enrollment rate (total)	Percent	21	13	11	12	14	14	18	67	59	66	68	71	74
Male	Percent	24	17	14	15	17	18	23	67	62	66	66	74	75
Female	Percent	18	10	8	9	10	10	13	66	56	67	70	69	74
Net secondary enrollment rate (total)	Percent	6	1	0	0	0	1	1	30	20	28	34	30	34
Male	Percent	6	1	0	0	0	1	1	35	23	36	42	31	41
Female	Percent	6	0	0	0	0	1	1	25	17	22	26	29	29
Literacy rate (total)	Percent	26	19	13	17	19	20	25	63	47	58	63	67	75
Male	Percent	36	30	21	27	30	31	36	76	61	72	77	83	85
Female	Percent	17	8	4	7	8	8	13	53	35	48	51	57	68
Head of household														
Marital status of head														
Monogamous male-headed	Percent	72	76	77	80	77	75	73	49	55	57	46	48	44
Polygamous male-headed	Percent	0	0	0	0	0	0	0	0	0	0	0	0	0
Single male-headed	Percent	5	5	2	4	4	5	7	6	1	3	7	7	10
Defacto female-headed	Percent	5	5	4	5	4	5	6	8	5	5	6	10	12
Dejure female-headed	Percent	18	14	16	12	15	15	14	37	39	35	41	36	34
Education level of head														
No level	Percent	78	83	90	88	82	81	76	54	77	60	57	49	36
Primary not completed	Percent	12	12	8	9	13	12	14	12	11	13	15	11	11
Completed primary, no secondary	Percent	2	2	1	1	1	2	2	5	3	7	4	6	5
Secondary not completed	Percent	5	3	1	2	3	4	6	15	6	14	14	14	23
Completed secondary / higher level	Percent	3	1	0	0	0	1	2	14	3	6	11	20	25
Labor market (population aged 15 to 64)														
Number of employed people in sample	Number	17685	11836	2052	2163	2303	2357	2961	5849	829	980	1179	1244	1617
Proportion of employed	Percent	60	71	73	72	72	71	69	46	43	43	46	44	51
Branch of activity														
Agriculture/fishing	Percent	79	89	91	91	89	90	87	9	15	8	11	7	4
Manufacturing/mining/construction	Percent	4	2	3	2	2	2	2	16	15	15	19	15	15
Commerce	Percent	8	4	4	3	4	4	4	42	44	49	39	40	41
Civil servant/army	Percent													
Other sector	Percent	8	5	3	4	5	5	7	33	25	27	30	38	41
Labor force participation (total)	Percent	85	92	90	92	90	95	92	51	49	50	52	51	52
Male	Percent	88	93	92	92	93	93	93	60	58	58	57	62	64
Female	Percent	82	91	89	92	87	97	90	44	42	43	48	43	43
Household expenditure														
Mean per capita expenditure (Ethiopian birrs)	Unit	1743	1495	606	889	1155	1538	3279	3155	857	1392	1991	2929	8603
Population below relative poverty line	Percent	46	50	100	100	53	0	0	21	100	6	0	0	0
Share of food in total expenditure	Percent	72	74	80	78	76	73	61	65	74	70	67	66	48
Household amenities														
Type of fuel for cooking														
Firewood	Percent	73	75	74	75	74	76	77	61	63	65	67	62	51
Gas, kerosine	Percent	3	0	0	0	0	0	1	20	11	17	16	22	31
Charcoal	Percent	1	0	0	0	0	0	0	4	2	3	3	5	7
Electricity	Percent	18	19	20	19	20	19	17	10	15	11	12	9	8
Other	Percent	5	5	6	5	6	5	5	4	9	5	2	2	2
Access to sanitation	Percent	14	5	3	4	4	5	8	59	43	53	52	69	74
Access to water														
Pipe/borne	Percent	36	30	30	28	29	31	33	61	59	65	55	66	60
Well	Percent	6	6	4	7	6	6	8	7	10	10	7	6	4
Other	Percent	58	64	66	66	65	63	60	32	31	26	38	29	35
Owner occupancy rate	Percent	90	97	98	97	97	97	97	51	55	56	49	49	49
Malnutrition (children aged 0 to 59 months)														
Stunting	Percent	66.6	67.8						57.5					
Wasting	Percent	8.3	8.7						5.6					
Underweight	Percent	43.3	44.8						31.9					

Source: Ethiopia Household Income, *Consumption and Expenditure Survey* (HBS/WMS-1995/96), Central Statistical Authority.

15-6. The Gambia: household welfare indicators

Indicator	Unit of measure	National total	Rural						Urban					
			All	1	2	3	4	5	All	1	2	3	4	5
Demographic indicators														
Sample size (households)	Number	2009	1181	191	204	209	233	344	828	108	107	133	169	311
Total population	000s	.												
Population below 15 years	Percent	46	49	48	51	51	48	44	42	45	45	47	43	33
Population 60 years and above	Percent	5	6	6	6	6	6	7	4	4	5	4	4	5
Age dependency ratio	Percent	97	111	111	121	124	108	94	82	90	91	96	82	56
Number of males per 100 females (age 15 and over)	Number	98	88	87	77	84	94	97	111	119	92	105	103	136
Average household size	Number	8.8	11.3	13.9	13.1	12.7	11.4	7.7	6.9	10.1	10.1	8.1	6.6	4.0
Education and literacy														
Net primary enrollment rate (total)	Percent	31	19	9	15	16	25	33	49	34	49	54	49	60
Male	Percent	35	23	13	18	19	30	38	51	42	58	58	45	53
Female	Percent	28	15	6	11	14	19	28	47	26	41	51	52	68
Net secondary enrollment rate (total)	Percent	16	8	3	7	7	11	11	25	19	25	28	29	26
Male	Percent	20	11	6	9	9	13	17	30	24	26	29	38	35
Female	Percent	12	5	0	5	6	8	6	20	13	23	27	21	18
Literacy rate (total)	Percent	41	33	31	33	28	33	38	50	38	44	47	50	65
Male	Percent	54	46	43	47	41	47	51	62	50	57	62	61	75
Female	Percent	28	21	20	21	17	21	24	36	23	32	31	40	53
Head of household														
Marital status of head														
Monogamous male-headed	Percent	55	58	63	54	56	62	57	53	48	45	60	62	48
Polygamous male-headed	Percent	21	32	33	39	36	32	25	12	19	27	12	11	3
Single male-headed	Percent	14	6	3	6	5	3	12	20	20	10	12	11	33
Defacto female-headed	Percent	10	3	2	2	4	2	6	15	12	15	15	13	16
Dejure female-headed	Percent	1	0	0	0	0	0	0	1	1	3	1	2	1
Education level of head														
No level	Percent	46	34	32	29	31	37	39	55	48	55	56	53	58
Coranic	Percent	49	64	67	70	69	62	56	38	48	39	39	43	30
Primary not completed	Percent	2	1	1	1	0	0	1	3	1	5	3	1	5
Completed primary, no secondary	Percent	0	0	0	0	0	0	0	0	0	0	0	0	0
Secondary not completed	Percent	0	0	0	0	0	0	0	0	0	0	0	0	1
Completed secondary / higher level	Percent	2	1	0	0	0	0	3	4	3	1	2	3	6
Labor market (population aged 15 to 64)														
Number of employed people in sample	Number	7994	6098	1312	1181	1202	1168	1235	1896	370	344	334	336	512
Proportion of employed	Percent	40	37	40	36	36	36	40	30	31	27	28	26	38
Branch of activity														
Agriculture/Fishing	Percent	.	.	.	.	.	.	.	.	.	.	.	.	.
Manufacturing/mining/construction	Percent	.	.	.	.	.	.	.	.	.	.	.	.	.
Commerce	Percent	.	.	.	.	.	.	.	.	.	.	.	.	.
Civil servant/army	Percent	.	.	.	.	.	.	.	.	.	.	.	.	.
Other sector	Percent	.	.	.	.	.	.	.	.	.	.	.	.	.
Labor force participation (total)	Percent	70	80	84	79	82	76	78	59	63	56	61	53	63
Male	Percent	62	70	75	69	72	65	68	55	55	47	57	48	63
Female	Percent	78	89	92	88	90	87	88	64	74	64	64	57	64
Household expenditure														
Mean per capita expenditure	Number	105	57	17	34	49	67	119	164	48	82	116	161	415
Population below relative poverty line	Percent	50	73	100	100	100	63	0	21	100	5	0	0	0
Share of food in total expenditure	Percent	60	60	60	61	63	61	57	60	69	65	60	57	50
Household amenities														
Type of fuel for cooking														
Firewood	Percent	89	97	98	99	99	99	93	83	88	93	91	93	68
Gas, kerosine	Percent	2	1	0	0	0	1	2	3	1	0	0	1	9
Charcoal	Percent	1	1	0	0	0	0	1	1	0	0	1	1	1
Electricity	Percent	0	0	0	0	0	0	0	0	0	0	0	0	1
Other	Percent	8	1	1	1	1	0	4	12	11	7	8	5	21
Access to sanitation	Percent	.	.						.					
Access to water														
Pipe/borne	Percent	42	7	2	7	6	8	9	68	55	52	58	71	84
Well	Percent	58	93	98	93	94	92	91	31	45	45	41	28	16
Other	Percent	1	0	0	0	0	0	0	1	0	3	2	1	1
Owner occupancy rate	Percent	68	93	96	96	97	93	87	48	75	66	62	41	29
Malnutrition (children aged 0 to 59 months)														
Stunting	Percent	35.4	40.2						27.9					
Wasting	Percent	8.1	7.9						8.3					
Underweight	Percent	26.2	30.3						19.8					

Source: Household Priority Survey, 1992.

15-7. Ghana: household welfare indicators

							Expenditure quintile							
						Rural					Urban			
Indicator	Unit of measure	National total	All	1	2	3	4	5	All	1	2	3	4	5
Demographic indicators														
Sample size (households)	Number	14511	9160	1032	1309	1502	1860	3457	5351	559	749	902	1111	2030
Total population	000s	12431	8521.1	1705	1705	1705	1702	1703	3909.8	782.9	782.1	782	782	781
Population below 15 years	Percent	42	44	50	52	49	43	27	36	45	42	39	35	22
Population 60 years and above	Percent	7	7	6	5	5	8	13	6	6	5	6	6	9
Age dependency ratio	Percent	87	97	120	121	111	94	57	69	95	82	75	63	40
Number of males per 100 females (age 15 and over)	Number	81	81	86	79	74	74	92	81	71	71	70	79	115
Average household size	Number	4.1	4.3	8.3	6.4	5.4	4.2	2.2	3.8	7.3	5.4	4.6	3.7	2.0
Education and literacy														
Net primary enrollment rate (total)	Percent	63	61	57	55	62	66	71	68	62	67	71	70	73
Male	Percent	64	62	60	56	60	67	71	69	60	71	73	72	71
Female	Percent	62	60	53	54	63	65	70	67	65	63	68	68	76
Net secondary enrollment rate (total)	Percent	38	35	32	33	37	34	40	45	40	44	47	48	49
Male	Percent	41	37	36	36	38	36	44	48	40	49	50	49	56
Female	Percent	36	32	28	30	35	31	37	43	40	41	44	48	44
Literacy rate (total)	Percent	48	40	37	39	41	38	46	63	52	58	64	68	71
Male	Percent	62	54	52	52	54	53	60	77	70	72	79	82	79
Female	Percent	37	29	25	29	30	27	33	52	39	47	54	57	62
Head of household														
Marital status of head														
Monogamous male-headed	Percent	52	52	52	59	60	58	44	50	45	55	60	60	41
Polygamous male-headed	Percent	14	16	21	22	20	18	9	10	20	17	12	9	4
Single male-headed	Percent	9	7	1	0	1	2	15	13	1	1	2	7	30
Defacto female-headed	Percent	12	12	14	11	8	9	15	12	20	14	12	10	11
Dejure female-headed	Percent	14	14	12	8	11	13	17	14	14	14	13	15	14
Education level of head														
No level	Percent	41	47	60	52	46	48	41	31	54	41	30	26	23
Primary not completed	Percent	6	6	7	6	10	6	6	4	5	7	5	3	3
Completed primary, no secondary	Percent	3	4	3	3	5	3	4	3	3	3	2	2	3
Secondary not completed	Percent	36	35	26	34	35	34	38	39	31	37	44	42	39
Completed secondary / higher level	Percent	13	8	4	6	5	9	12	23	7	12	19	26	32
Labor market (population aged 15 to 64)														
Number of employed people in sample	Number	10936	14513	2284	2435	2616	3011	4162	7359	1054	1214	1350	1571	2169
Proportion of employed	Percent	36	33	24	27	30	34	50	34	24	28	31	36	51
Proportion of employed in formal sector		13	8	3	6	5	7	13	23	10	16	20	27	32
Proportion of employed in informal sector		87	92	97	94	95	93	87	77	90	84	80	73	68
Branch of activity														
Agriculture/Fishing	Percent	52	69	77	76	72	69	60	15	29	21	15	10	9
Manufacturing/mining/construction	Percent	8	6	5	5	6	6	7	12	10	11	13	12	14
Commerce	Percent	24	15	14	12	15	16	18	42	43	47	45	45	35
Other sector	Percent	16	10	4	7	7	9	15	31	18	21	28	33	42
Labor force participation (total)	Percent	68	68	56	63	67	71	80	66	57	61	62	68	79
Male	Percent	69	71	55	64	68	74	85	67	53	56	60	69	83
Female		66	67	57	63	65	68	76	66	60	64	63	67	74
Household expenditure														
Mean per capita expenditure (CIDI)	000s	206	175	83	116	146	191	342	272	105	164	225	315	555
Population below relative poverty line	Percent	37	44	100	100	22	0	0	20	100	1	0	0	0
Share of food in total expenditure	Percent	.	.	.	.	.	.	.	.	.	.	.	.	.
Household amenities														
Type of fuel for cooking														
Firewood	Percent	69	92	99	98	96	94	85	25	53	40	28	17	16
Gas, kerosine	Percent	4	1	0	0	0	0	1	12	0	2	5	13	20
Charcoal	Percent	26	7	1	2	4	5	14	62	47	59	67	68	61
Electricity	Percent	0.3	0.1	0.0	0.0	0.1	0.0	0.1	1	0	0.0	0.1	0.8	1.7
Other	Percent	0.2	0.2	0.1	0.2	0.1	0.1	0.2	0.3	0	0.1	0.0	0.3	0.7
Access to sanitation	Percent	25	17	10	12	15	19	20	42	31	36	40	43	47
Access to water														
Pipe/borne	Percent	37	14	9	10	11	12	19	82	71	75	81	88	86
Well	Percent	35	46	43	45	47	48	44	13	17	20	13	10	11
Other	Percent	28	40	48	45	41	39	37	4	12	6	5	2	3
Owner occupancy rate	Percent	37	47	67	60	51	50	34	19	34	24	19	15	16
Malnutrition (children aged 0 to 59 months)														
Stunting	Percent													
Wasting	Percent													
Underweight	Percent													

Source: Core Welfare Indicator Questionnaire (CWIQ), 1997.

15-8. Guinea: household welfare indicators

| | | | Expenditure quintile | | | | | | | | | | | |
| | | | Rural | | | | | | Urban | | | | | |
Indicator	Unit of measure	National total	All	1	2	3	4	5	All	1	2	3	4	5
Demographic indicators														
Sample size (households)	Number	4416	1680	228	273	318	359	502	2736	425	413	485	574	839
Total population	000s	6450	4326	865	869	867	863	863	2124	425	423	426	424	425
Population below 15 years	Percent	46	48	53	52	49	46	40	44	49	45	44	42	37
Population 60 years and above	Percent	7	8	8	7	8	9	9	4	5	5	4	4	4
Age dependency ratio	Percent	102	112	137	125	117	104	85	85	107	93	86	78	66
Number of males per 100 females (age 15 and over)	Number	80	70	67	76	69	67	73	98	91	95	92	100	110
Average household size	Number	6.6	6.5	8.5	7.4	7.0	6.2	4.6	6.9	8.7	8.8	7.8	6.7	4.7
Education and literacy														
Net primary enrollment rate (total)	Percent	29	18	13	14	15	22	28	56	38	55	57	66	71
Male	Percent	35	23	21	17	18	34	31	65	46	63	69	74	77
Female	Percent	23	12	5	9	12	12	24	48	29	47	46	58	65
Net secondary enrollment rate (total)	Percent	12	3	1	2	3	6	3	25	16	24	26	28	34
Male	Percent	16	5	2	4	6	10	4	33	18	33	35	39	41
Female	Percent	7	1	0	0	0	2	1	17	12	12	16	17	28
Literacy rate (total)	Percent	14	7	4	5	8	8	8	27	21	28	28	30	29
Male	Percent	21	13	7	10	17	17	14	35	32	38	37	38	30
Female	Percent	8	2	1	1	1	2	3	20	11	18	20	22	27
Head of household														
Marital status of head														
Monogamous male-headed	Percent	48	44	42	41	41	43	52	54	44	50	53	59	59
Polygamous male-headed	Percent	32	36	46	42	42	38	22	24	37	33	29	20	10
Single male-headed	Percent	4	3	1	4	2	2	6	7	3	2	3	4	16
Defacto female-headed	Percent	8	9	5	7	9	10	10	7	6	7	7	8	7
Dejure female-headed	Percent	8	7	5	6	6	7	11	8	10	8	8	10	7
Education level of head														
No level	Percent	82	91	95	92	91	93	87	61	81	65	68	60	44
Primary not completed	Percent	6	4	3	6	5	4	5	8	6	13	8	8	7
Completed primary, no secondary	Percent	0	0	0	0	0	0	0	1	1	2	1	1	2
Secondary not completed	Percent	9	4	2	2	4	3	7	19	10	14	17	19	28
Completed secondary / higher level	Percent	4	0	0	0	0	0	1	11	2	6	6	12	20
Labor market (population aged 15 to 64)														
Number of employed people in sample	Number	13037	6073	1093	1140	1225	1303	1312	6964	1402	1279	1315	1421	1547
Proportion of employed	Percent	53	44	40	41	43	46	49	34	31	33	33	36	38
Branch of activity														
Agriculture/fishing	Percent	71	93	96	96	94	95	86	11	25	14	8	6	4
Manufacturing/mining/construction	Percent	7	2	2	1	3	1	3	19	20	21	17	19	18
Commerce	Percent	17	3	1	2	3	3	8	51	44	51	58	54	48
Civil servant/army	Percent	2	0	0	0	0	0	1	7	3	4	7	7	12
Other sector	Percent	4	0	0	0	0	0	1	13	9	11	11	14	19
Labor force participation (total)	Percent	83	93	94	92	93	94	91	67	68	67	66	67	67
Male	Percent	86	94	97	93	94	94	94	73	72	70	70	71	79
Female	Percent	82	92	92	91	93	94	89	62	64	65	62	62	55
Household expenditure														
Mean per capita expenditure (FG)	000s	468	342	136	207	281	388	698	724	241	394	542	769	1675
Population below relative poverty line	Percent	44	57	100	100	85	0	0	18	88	0	0	0	0
Share of food in total expenditure	Percent	56	62	60	62	63	65	61	45	55	48	46	40	34
Household amenities														
Type of fuel for cooking														
Firewood	Percent	81	99	99	100	99	100	97	42	71	52	39	36	27
Gas, kerosine	Percent	0	0	0	0	0	0	0	1	0	0	1	0	3
Charcoal	Percent	17	1	0	0	0	0	2	53	29	46	60	61	59
Electricity	Percent	0	0	0	0	0	0	0	1	0	0	0	0	2
Other	Percent	1	0	1	0	0	0	0	3	0	1	0	2	8
Access to sanitation	Percent	55	40	41	39	43	34	42	86	78	86	85	89	90
Access to water														
Pipe/borne	Percent	25	1	0	0	0	0	4	59	35	50	59	66	71
Well	Percent	75	98	100	100	100	99	95	40	64	49	41	32	28
Other	Percent	1	0	0	0	0	1	1	1	2	1	0	1	1
Owner occupancy rate	Percent	74	89	90	91	90	91	85	41	60	56	40	35	27
Malnutrition (children aged 0 to 59 months)														
Stunting	Percent	28.9	32.7						20.1					
Wasting	Percent	12.4	13.2						10.6					
Underweight	Percent	22.3	25.3						15.4					

Source: Household Integrated Survey, *Enquête intégrale budget et consommation, 1994/95.*

15-9. Guinea Bissau: household welfare indicators

Indicator	Unit of measure	National total	Expenditure quintile											
			Rural						Urban					
			All	1	2	3	4	5	All	1	2	3	4	5
Demographic indicators														
Sample size (households)	Number	1625	1185	229	230	227	252	247	440	103	88	77	94	78
Total population	000s	1060	741	148	148	149	148	148	319	64	64	63	64	63
Population below 15 years	Percent	44	43	41	45	45	44	43	46	43	47	45	46	47
Population 60 years and above	Percent	8	9	11	10	9	8	9	4	7	3	3	5	3
Age dependency ratio	Percent	96	97	95	104	102	94	91	93	93	96	90	93	96
Number of males per 100 females (age 15 and over)	Number	86	83	82	80	84	88	81	95	95	87	101	92	101
Average household size	Number	6.5	6.3	6.2	6.7	6.4	5.9	6.2	7.2	6.8	7.5	7.4	7.0	7.2
Education and literacy														
Net primary enrollment rate (total)	Percent	.	.	.	.	.	.	.	.	.	.	.	.	.
Male	Percent	.	.	.	.	.	.	.	.	.	.	.	.	.
Female	Percent	.	.	.	.	.	.	.	.	.	.	.	.	.
Net secondary enrollment rate (total)	Percent	.	.	.	.	.	.	.	.	.	.	.	.	.
Male	Percent	.	.	.	.	.	.	.	.	.	.	.	.	.
Female	Percent	.	.	.	.	.	.	.	.	.	.	.	.	.
Literacy rate (total)	Percent	23	12	8	10	12	15	17	50	43	43	52	51	62
Male	Percent	35	22	15	19	21	27	28	66	55	63	71	65	75
Female	Percent	13	4	3	2	3	4	6	35	31	25	34	38	48
Head of household														
Marital status of head														
Monogamous male-headed	Percent	52	50	45	47	51	58	49	58	36	59	69	57	70
Polygamous male-headed	Percent	9	6	8	8	7	5	5	14	25	11	12	14	7
Single male-headed	Percent	1	0	0	0	0	0	1	3	2	2	3	4	5
Defacto female-headed	Percent	28	33	35	34	31	28	37	17	25	21	7	17	11
Dejure female-headed	Percent	10	10	12	11	10	9	9	8	12	6	9	7	7
Education level of head														
No level	Percent	67	77	86	83	79	70	67	40	55	44	40	34	24
Coranic school	Percent	2	2	1	2	2	4	3	2	2	0	0	4	4
Primary not completed	Percent	18	14	9	11	13	17	19	30	25	36	38	22	28
Completed primary, no secondary	Percent	5	4	3	4	3	5	5	6	2	7	5	8	9
Secondary not completed	Percent	7	2	1	0	3	2	4	20	14	14	15	28	31
Completed secondary / higher level	Percent	1	1	0	0	0	2	2	2	1	0	1	4	5
Labor market (population aged 15 to 64)														
Number of employed people in sample	Number	.	.	.	.	.	.	.	.	.	.	.	.	.
Proportion of employed	Percent	.	.	.	.	.	.	.	.	.	.	.	.	.
Branch of activity														
Agriculture/fishing	Percent	.	.	.	.	.	.	.	.	.	.	.	.	.
Manufacturing/mining/construction	Percent	.	.	.	.	.	.	.	.	.	.	.	.	.
Commerce	Percent	.	.	.	.	.	.	.	.	.	.	.	.	.
Civil servant/army	Percent	.	.	.	.	.	.	.	.	.	.	.	.	.
Other sector	Percent	.	.	.	.	.	.	.	.	.	.	.	.	.
Labor force participation (total)	Percent	.	.	.	.	.	.	.	.	.	.	.	.	.
Male	Percent	.	.	.	.	.	.	.	.	.	.	.	.	.
Female	Percent	.	.	.	.	.	.	.	.	.	.	.	.	.
Household expenditure														
Mean per capita expenditure	Number	242	191	18	59	108	194	578	360	68	164	249	381	940
Population below relative poverty line	Percent	54	65	100	100	100	24	0	30	100	49	0	0	0
Share of food in total expenditure	Percent	.	.	.	.	.	.	.	.	.	.	.	.	.
Household amenities														
Type of fuel for cooking														
Firewood	Percent	10	2	2	4	2	2	3	31	18	21	25	43	46
Gas, kerosine	Percent	3	1	1	0	1	1	2	7	2	3	4	10	15
Charcoal	Percent	69	76	73	77	72	78	78	52	65	69	60	37	30
Electricity	Percent	2	1	0	1	1	0	3	6	7	5	4	7	9
Other	Percent	16	20	25	18	24	19	15	4	9	2	7	2	0
Access to sanitation	Percent	.	.	.	.	.	.	.	.	.	.	.	.	.
Access to water														
Pipe/borne	Percent	8	2	1	1	1	3	3	26	20	22	26	27	33
Well	Percent	81	86	84	86	87	85	86	69	78	75	71	60	61
Other	Percent	11	13	15	13	11	12	11	5	2	4	2	13	6
Owner occupancy rate	Percent	80	92	94	94	93	88	90	49	59	39	57	42	48
Malnutrition (children aged 0 to 59 months)														
Stunting	Percent	.	.						.					
Wasting	Percent	.	.						.					
Underweight	Percent	.	.						.					

Source: Priority survey, *Inquerito ligeiro junto às familias, 1992*.

15-10. Kenya: household welfare indicators

Indicator	Unit of measure	National total	Rural						Urban					
			All	1	2	3	4	5	All	1	2	3	4	5
Demographic indicators														
Sample size (households)	Number	10857	9171	1623	1507	1734	1823	2484	1686	309	326	316	349	386
Total population	000s	26424	22293	4459	4459	4457	4457	4460	4131	826	826	828	825	825
Population below 15 years	Percent	49	51	55	54	52	50	43	40	50	45	42	36	27
Population 60 years and above	Percent	4	5	4	4	4	4	6	2	1	1	2	2	2
Age dependency ratio	Percent	107	116	138	128	120	112	87	70	101	85	76	60	40
Number of males per 100 females (age 15 and over)	Number	90	87	81	88	85	85	94	103	89	92	94	118	119
Average household size	Number	5.2	5.6	7.0	6.5	5.9	5.5	3.9	4.0	5.8	5.0	4.4	3.7	2.6
Education and literacy														
Net primary enrollment rate (total)	Percent	76	75	66	73	78	80	80	84	73	85	83	92	95
Male	Percent	77	76	67	75	79	82	80	84	71	82	88	94	98
Female	Percent	75	74	64	72	78	78	81	84	76	90	80	89	91
Net secondary enrollment rate (total)	Percent	11	9	3	7	9	12	16	27	15	25	25	26	44
Male	Percent	12	9	3	7	9	13	15	33	12	28	33	30	66
Female	Percent	11	8	3	6	8	11	16	22	17	22	21	22	29
Literacy rate (total)	Percent	75	71	60	72	73	75	75	92	87	92	90	93	95
Male	Percent	83	80	72	79	82	83	83	95	94	95	93	95	97
Female	Percent	68	64	50	65	65	68	68	88	81	90	87	91	92
Head of household														
Marital status of head														
Monogamous male-headed	Percent	61	61	59	63	62	61	58	64	65	67	61	64	62
Polygamous male-headed	Percent	8	9	12	9	9	9	6	5	10	5	5	6	2
Single male-headed	Percent	6	5	3	2	3	3	9	13	4	8	15	13	19
Defacto female-headed	Percent	9	11	10	12	11	11	9	4	3	4	4	5	4
Dejure female-headed	Percent	15	16	15	13	16	16	17	14	18	15	14	13	13
Education level of head														
No level	Percent	32	37	51	38	36	33	33	9	17	9	11	8	6
Primary not completed	Percent	28	29	30	35	32	29	24	21	32	27	23	18	14
Completed primary, no secondary	Percent	13	13	11	13	15	14	13	14	16	17	15	11	12
Secondary not completed	Percent	11	9	5	9	8	12	11	17	16	16	16	18	18
Completed secondary / higher level	Percent	17	11	4	6	9	12	19	39	18	30	35	45	50
Labor market (population aged 15 to 64)														
Number of employed people in sample	Number	.	.	.	.	.	.	.	.	.	.	.	.	.
Proportion of employed	Percent	.	.	.	.	.	.	.	.	.	.	.	.	.
Branch of activity														
Agriculture/fishing	Percent	.	.	.	.	.	.	.	.	.	.	.	.	.
Manufacturing/mining/construction	Percent	.	.	.	.	.	.	.	.	.	.	.	.	.
Commerce	Percent	.	.	.	.	.	.	.	.	.	.	.	.	.
Civil servant/army	Percent	.	.	.	.	.	.	.	.	.	.	.	.	.
Other sector	Percent	.	.	.	.	.	.	.	.	.	.	.	.	.
Labor force participation (total)	Percent	.	.	.	.	.	.	.	.	.	.	.	.	.
Male	Percent	.	.	.	.	.	.	.	.	.	.	.	.	.
Female	Percent	.	.	.	.	.	.	.	.	.	.	.	.	.
Household expenditure														
Mean per capita expenditure (KSH)	000s	13	11	3	6	9	12	23	29	7	13	19	28	77
Population below relative poverty line	Percent	47	53	100	100	64	0	0	14	71	0	0	0	0
Share of food in total expenditure	Percent	71	72	73	75	75	72	67	61	70	64	64	58	46
Household amenities														
Type of fuel for cooking														
Firewood	Percent	76	93	98	98	97	95	85	9	26	9	8	6	3
Gas, kerosine	Percent	13	2	1	1	1	2	6	56	35	44	53	63	70
Charcoal	Percent	9	4	1	1	2	3	9	30	38	46	36	27	17
Electricity	Percent	1	0	0	0	0	0	0	4	0	1	2	3	9
Other	Percent	0	0	0	0	0	0	0	0	0	0	1	0	0
Access to sanitation	Percent	79	75	62	74	77	79	79	95	89	91	96	97	99
Access to water														
Pipe/borne	Percent	32	17	10	16	15	17	24	90	87	90	89	90	93
Well	Percent	33	40	42	41	41	41	36	5	8	5	7	4	2
Other	Percent	35	43	47	43	44	42	40	5	5	5	3	6	5
Owner occupancy rate	Percent	77	93	96	94	96	94	87	16	26	19	14	16	11
Malnutrition (children aged 0 to 59 months)														
Stunting	Percent	35.5	36.2						31.2					
Wasting	Percent	6.7	6.9						6.7					
Underweight	Percent	22.6	23.1						20.1					

Source: Welfare Monitoring Survey, 1994

15-11. Madagascar: household welfare indicators

| | | | Expenditure quintile | | | | | | | | | | | |
| | | | *Rural* | | | | | | *Urban* | | | | | |
Indicator	Unit of measure	National total	*All*	*1*	*2*	*3*	*4*	*5*	*All*	*1*	*2*	*3*	*4*	*5*
Demographic indicators														
Sample size (households)	Number	4500	2648	455	457	500	560	676	1852	254	322	377	389	510
Total population	000s	12344	10193	2039	2039	2039	2036	2039	2151	429	432	429	431	431
Population below 15 years	Percent	45	46	53	51	48	43	36	40	50	45	39	37	30
Population 60 years and above	Percent	5	5	4	4	5	6	7	4	4	3	5	5	4
Age dependency ratio	Percent	93	98	124	115	103	89	67	75	113	86	72	67	49
Number of males per 100 females (age 15 and over)	Number	95	96	98	94	88	95	105	92	85	91	89	95	95
Average household size	Number	4.9	4.9	6.0	5.7	5.3	4.7	3.7	5.0	6.5	5.6	4.9	4.7	3.9
Education and literacy														
Net primary enrollment rate (total)	Percent	31	26	12	21	28	36	43	57	38	51	68	68	68
Male	Percent	30	25	10	22	26	31	44	57	38	50	69	69	66
Female	Percent	32	28	13	19	31	42	41	57	37	53	67	67	70
Net secondary enrollment rate (total)	Percent	15	8	1	5	4	12	23	41	15	25	47	59	64
Male	Percent	15	9	2	5	6	10	26	42	15	26	45	69	66
Female	Percent	15	8	0	5	3	13	20	40	15	25	49	51	61
Literacy rate (total)	Percent	93	92	90	91	90	93	95	96	90	96	97	98	98
Male	Percent	94	93	92	91	92	94	95	97	92	98	97	99	99
Female	Percent	93	92	89	91	88	93	96	95	88	94	96	96	97
Head of household														
Marital status of head														
Monogamous male-headed	Percent	72	73	72	75	74	76	70	67	64	67	67	70	66
Polygamous male-headed	Percent	0	0	0	1	0	0	0	0	0	0	0	1	0
Single male-headed	Percent	8	8	7	6	6	7	13	7	5	6	6	7	11
Defacto female-headed	Percent	2	2	2	1	1	1	3	2	3	2	1	2	3
Dejure female-headed	Percent	18	17	18	17	18	16	15	23	28	24	26	20	21
Education level of head														
No level	Percent	29	33	48	37	31	30	23	11	20	19	11	8	4
Primary not completed	Percent	49	51	47	54	56	54	46	39	63	50	46	30	20
Completed primary, no secondary	Percent	4	4	1	3	5	3	6	5	5	6	6	6	4
Secondary not completed	Percent	15	11	4	5	8	13	21	31	12	21	34	40	40
Completed secondary / higher level	Percent	3	1	0	0	1	0	3	13	1	4	4	17	32
Labor market (population aged 15 to 64)														
Number of employed people in sample	Number	10368	6907	1348	1292	1377	1433	1457	3461	602	658	687	701	813
Proportion of employed	Percent	49	44	39	40	43	46	51	35	32	35	35	36	39
Branch of activity														
Agriculture/fishing	Percent	81	90	96	95	95	90	78	29	51	45	26	17	10
Manufacturing/mining/construction	Percent	6	4	2	3	2	5	6	17	10	15	21	20	16
Commerce	Percent	5	2	1	0	2	2	6	18	15	15	20	19	20
Civil servant/army	Percent	3	2	0	0	1	1	6	12	3	5	9	19	23
Other sector	Percent	5	2	1	1	1	2	4	24	21	20	24	26	31
Labor force participation (total)	Percent	84	88	88	87	89	89	86	67	74	70	66	64	62
Male	Percent	89	92	91	91	94	93	92	74	78	78	74	71	71
Female	Percent	79	83	84	84	85	84	80	60	70	63	58	57	55
Household expenditure														
Mean per capita expenditure (FMG)	000s	237	191	56	102	142	204	451	454	115	204	310	466	1177
Population below relative poverty line	Percent	51	57	100	100	87	0	0	21	100	3	0	0	0
Share of food in total expenditure	Percent	70	72	74	74	74	73	65	62	70	70	64	58	48
Household amenities														
Type of fuel for cooking														
Firewood	Percent	85	94	100	98	99	94	86	37	68	58	39	26	12
Gas, kerosine	Percent	0	0	0	0	0	0	0	2	0	0	0	1	9
Charcoal	Percent	14	5	0	2	1	5	14	57	28	41	60	70	73
Electricity	Percent	1	0	0	0	0	1	1	3	4	1	1	3	6
Other	Percent	0	0	0	0	0	0	0	0	0	0	0	0	0
Access to sanitation	Percent	33	26	11	21	26	29	37	67	46	50	67	78	83
Access to water														
Pipe/borne	Percent	18	7	4	5	5	7	11	71	52	55	72	81	86
Well	Percent	21	22	20	18	14	26	29	19	22	31	20	16	11
Other	Percent	61	71	76	78	82	68	60	9	26	14	8	3	3
Owner occupancy rate	Percent	75	81	87	87	81	78	74	46	63	57	43	41	36
Malnutrition (children aged 0 to 59 months)														
Stunting	Percent	50.0	50.8						45.4					
Wasting	Percent	12.8	13.2						10.3					
Underweight	Percent	42.5	44.1						32.9					

Source: Household Integrated Survey, *Enquête permanente auprès des ménages*, 1993/94.

15-12. Mali: household welfare indicators

| | | | Expenditure quintile | | | | | | | | | | | |
| | | | Rural | | | | | | Urban | | | | | |
Indicator	Unit of measure	National total	All	1	2	3	4	5	All	1	2	3	4	5
Demographic indicators														
Sample size (households)	Number	9312	3863	627	632	747	833	1024	5449	803	911	1010	1199	1526
Total population	000s	7934	6640	1270	1303	1341	1300	1426	1294	257	255	256	261	265
Population below 15 years	Percent	35	35	36	36	36	34	33	33	36	35	32	32	29
Population 60 years and above	Percent	5	6	6	5	6	6	6	4	4	4	4	4	3
Age dependency ratio	Percent	61	62	66	66	65	59	57	54	61	59	54	52	45
Number of males per 100 females (age 15 and over)	Number	92	92	90	93	92	96	90	94	92	93	97	95	95
Average household size	Number	9	9	14	13	10	8	6	8	10	9	8	7	5
Education and literacy														
Net primary enrollment rate (total)	Percent	23	21	17	13	20	21	31	57	57	55	51	58	64
Male	Percent	29	27	24	14	26	28	38	58	62	57	50	61	64
Female	Percent	17	14	9	11	14	13	23	55	51	53	52	55	63
Net secondary enrollment rate (total)	Percent	5	4	2	2	1	5	8	18	12	19	19	19	23
Male	Percent	7	6	4	3	2	9	8	23	18	23	20	22	35
Female	Percent	4	3	0	2	0	0	7	14	6	15	17	17	13
Literacy rate (total)	Percent	4	4	4	4	4	4	5	2	1	2	2	3	3
Male	Percent	6	7	7	7	6	6	8	3	2	3	3	4	5
Female	Percent	1	1	2	1	1	1	2	1	1	1	1	1	2
Head of household														
Marital status of head														
Monogamous male-headed	Percent	4	4	3	1	3	3	6	5	1	1	3	6	12
Polygamous male-headed	Percent	32	34	43	39	37	33	28	24	33	29	25	21	16
Single male-headed	Percent	57	56	51	55	55	57	58	60	53	60	62	62	62
Defacto female-headed	Percent	1	1	1	0	0	1	2	2	2	2	2	2	3
Dejure female-headed	Percent	6	5	3	5	5	6	6	9	11	8	9	9	8
Education level of head														
No level	Percent	76	81	92	93	89	80	66	57	77	70	60	52	39
Primary not completed	Percent	8	7	3	4	5	9	11	10	8	10	9	11	11
Completed primary, no secondary	Percent	3	2	2	1	1	3	3	5	4	4	5	5	4
Secondary not completed	Percent	10	7	2	3	4	6	14	21	9	13	22	24	29
Completed secondary / higher level	Percent	4	3	1	1	1	3	5	8	2	3	4	9	17
Labor market (population aged 15 to 64)														
Number of employed people in sample	Number	7953	6727	1455	1029	1275	1250	1718	1226	226	209	229	236	326
Proportion of employed	Percent	17	14	14	9	11	14	20	3	3	3	3	3	4
Branch of activity														
Agriculture/fishing	Percent	93	96	95	99	97	97	93	42	47	61	36	38	31
Manufacturing/mining/construction	Percent	2	1	1	0	0	0	2	17	16	11	22	13	23
Commerce	Percent	1	1	1	0	1	0	2	12	9	8	13	16	16
Civil servant and other sector	Percent	4	3	3	1	2	2	4	28	29	21	29	33	30
Labor force participation (total)	Percent	19	22	23	15	19	22	32	5	5	5	5	4	6
Male	Percent	22	25	28	17	20	24	35	6	6	6	6	6	8
Female	Percent	17	20	18	13	17	20	29	3	3	4	3	3	4
Household expenditure														
Mean per capita expenditure (Franc CFA)	000s	60	44	13	22	31	45	109	143	42	71	100	145	359
Population below relative poverty line	Percent	55	64	100	100	100	25	0	8	39	0	0	0	0
Share of food in total expenditure	Percent	75	77	78	78	76	78	76	64	70	66	66	63	53
Household amenities														
Type of fuel for cooking														
Firewood	Percent	95	97	99	98	98	97	95	85	97	94	91	84	70
Gas, kerosine	Percent	0	0	0	0	0	0	0	1	0	0	0	0	2
Charcoal	Percent	3	0	0	0	1	0	1	13	3	6	8	14	26
Electricity	Percent	0	0	0	0	0	0	0	0	0	0	0	0	0
Other	Percent	2	2	1	1	2	3	4	1	0	0	1	1	1
Access to sanitation	Percent	.	.		.		.	.	.		.		.	.
Access to water														
Pipe/borne	Percent	32	25	29	25	25	24	25	58	38	51	55	64	70
Well	Percent	58	64	66	70	66	63	58	35	53	42	35	29	24
Other	Percent	11	11	5	5	9	13	17	8	10	8	9	7	6
Owner occupancy rate	Percent	78	85	94	94	92	84	72	48	58	57	52	43	40
Malnutrition (children aged 0 to 59 months)														
Stunting	Percent	.	.						.					
Wasting	Percent	.	.						.					
Underweight	Percent	.	.						.					

Source: Enquête Malienne de onjoncture Économique et Sociale, 1994.

15-13. Mauritania: household welfare indicators

Indicator	Unit of measure	National total	Rural All	1	2	3	4	5	Urban All	1	2	3	4	5
Demographic indicators														
Sample size (households)	Number	3412	1219	165	165	243	270	376	2193	359	342	362	458	672
Total population	000s	1162	653	127	128	131	132	134	509	99	99	101	103	107
Population below 15 years	Percent	32	35	39	37	36	34	27	30	39	35	34	26	18
Population 60 years and above	Percent	7	8	5	6	8	8	10	5	4	4	5	7	6
Age dependency ratio	Percent	57	64	72	68	69	65	49	49	70	59	59	42	28
Number of males per 100 females (age 15 and over)	Number	89	85	92	93	91	73	82	94	81	85	82	96	122
Average household size	Number	5	5	7	7	6	5	4	5	7	7	6	5	3
Education and literacy														
Net primary enrollment rate (total)	Percent	44	34	22	33	36	39	46	58	49	59	62	57	65
Male	Percent	45	36	25	32	35	42	52	59	48	55	65	62	71
Female	Percent	42	32	18	35	37	35	38	57	51	62	59	52	58
Net secondary enrollment rate (total)	Percent	15	6	1	3	6	10	11	26	17	23	29	32	33
Male	Percent	17	9	2	6	10	13	15	28	17	26	29	36	35
Female	Percent	13	3	0	1	2	8	7	24	17	19	29	28	31
Literacy rate (total)	Percent	39	30	23	27	24	30	42	49	38	45	49	54	54
Male	Percent	46	34	25	29	30	37	49	58	45	56	58	64	62
Female	Percent	32	26	22	24	20	26	36	40	33	36	42	45	44
Head of household														
Marital status of head														
Monogamous male-headed	Percent	60	65	71	77	66	61	59	54	58	57	66	58	41
Polygamous male-headed	Percent	3	3	5	2	4	4	1	2	5	2	4	1	0
Single male-headed	Percent	12	9	7	4	9	10	12	16	5	6	4	13	34
Defacto female-headed	Percent	1	1	0	0	0	0	1	1	2	1	2	1	1
Dejure female-headed	Percent	24	22	17	17	21	26	26	27	31	34	25	27	23
Education level of head														
No level	Percent	0	0	0	0	0	1	0	1	1	0	0	2	1
Primary not completed	Percent	89	95	99	99	97	95	90	80	88	86	83	78	74
Completed primary, no secondary	Percent	4	1	0	1	1	1	3	7	6	6	9	10	6
Secondary not completed	Percent	0	0	0	0	0	1	0	1	0	1	0	1	2
Completed secondary / higher level	Percent	7	3	0	0	2	3	7	11	5	7	8	10	17
Labor market (population aged 15 to 64)														
Number of employed people in sample	Number	1960	628	95	76	124	151	182	1332	212	179	198	281	462
Proportion of employed	Percent	11	9	8	7	9	9	13	11	8	8	9	12	19
Branch of activity														
Agriculture/fishing	Percent	38	67	74	76	66	69	56	7	10	8	8	5	7
Manufacturing/mining/construction	Percent	17	8	7	12	7	5	10	26	37	38	24	23	20
Commerce	Percent	15	10	14	6	6	13	10	19	13	15	17	18	25
Civil servant	Percent	10	6	3	2	4	7	11	14	12	12	11	23	13
Other sectors	Percent	21	9	1	5	17	7	14	32	27	27	39	31	34
Labor force participation (total)	Percent	19	18	17	14	18	18	22	20	16	14	18	20	27
Male	Percent	33	33	30	28	33	35	36	34	29	25	33	32	43
Female	Percent	6	5	4	2	4	5	10	7	6	6	5	7	9
Household expenditure														
Mean per capita expenditure (Franc CFA)	000s	69	50	18	31	42	57	101	95	35	57	76	106	200
Population below relative poverty line	Percent	39	56	100	100	83	0	0	18	94	0	0	0	0
Share of food in total expenditure	Percent	70	77	73	75	80	77	78	62	64	62	62	61	60
Household amenities														
Type of fuel for cooking														
Firewood	Percent	48	76	85	75	77	81	67	14	37	17	11	7	8
Gas, kerosine	Percent	30	13	7	14	13	13	17	52	27	44	55	63	59
Charcoal	Percent	19	10	8	9	8	5	16	30	32	37	32	28	28
Electricity	Percent	1	0	0	0	1	0	0	1	1	1	1	1	2
Other	Percent	2	1	0	3	2	1	1	2	3	1	1	1	4
Access to sanitation	Percent	35	16	7	12	16	21	20	58	39	49	58	65	66
Access to water														
Pipe/borne	Percent	44	9	8	12	8	9	10	88	73	85	87	91	94
Well	Percent	47	77	70	76	77	77	82	10	26	13	10	6	3
Other	Percent	9	13	22	12	14	14	9	3	2	2	3	3	3
Owner occupancy rate	Percent	76	94	95	96	95	96	90	54	70	61	60	52	41
Malnutrition (children aged 0 to 59 months)														
Stunting	Percent	.	.						.					
Wasting	Percent	.	.						.					
Underweight	Percent	.	.						.					

Source: Enquête Permanente sur les Conditions de Vie des Ménages, 1995.

15-14. Niger: household welfare indicators

Indicator	Unit of measure	National total	Expenditure quintile												
			Rural						Urban						
			All	1	2	3	4	5	All	1	2	3	4	5
Demographic indicators														
Sample size (households)	Number	4377	1697	260	289	316	387	445	2680	528	464	474	514	700
Total population	000s	9063	7607	1500	1520	1526	1527	1535	1456.2	291.4	291.5	291.2	291.3	290.7
Population below 15 years	Percent	48	47	47	50	49	46	45	50	53	52	50	50	43
Population 60 years and above	Percent	5	5	6	5	5	5	6	3	4	4	3	3	3
Age dependency ratio	Percent	103	102	102	111	107	98	93	107	126	117	107	108	82
Number of males per 100 females (age 15 and over)	Number	89	88	97	85	86	88	83	93	91	96	91	91	95
Average household size	Number	7.1	7.1	8.1	7.7	7.7	6.7	5.9	7.2	8.2	8.3	8.0	7.3	5.2
Education and literacy														
Net primary enrollment rate (total)	Percent	21	15	11	15	19	14	14	50	36	45	55	54	63
Male	Percent	25	20	14	22	26	17	20	54	42	50	59	57	65
Female	Percent	16	10	8	8	14	12	9	45	29	42	50	50	60
Net secondary enrollment rate (total)	Percent	7	3	1	1	4	4	3	24	13	24	27	29	29
Male	Percent	9	4	3	3	5	6	4	27	17	24	29	33	32
Female	Percent	5	1	0	0	2	2	3	22	9	24	24	25	27
Literacy rate (total)	Percent	.	.	.	.	.	.	.	.	.	.	.	.	.
Male	Percent	.	.	.	.	.	.	.	.	.	.	.	.	.
Female	Percent	.	.	.	.	.	.	.	.	.	.	.	.	.
Head of household														
Marital status of head														
Monogamous male-headed	Percent	64	65	65	61	67	69	64	59	60	57	58	61	59
Polygamous male-headed	Percent	24	25	25	28	27	23	22	21	22	25	24	22	15
Single male-headed	Percent	4	3	4	3	2	3	5	5	3	3	3	3	11
Defacto female-headed	Percent	2	2	1	2	0	2	3	2	2	2	3	2	2
Dejure female-headed	Percent	6	5	6	6	4	4	5	13	13	14	12	12	13
Education level of head														
No level	Percent	54	58	70	63	50	50	57	36	43	38	35	37	31
Coranic school	Percent	33	33	26	29	37	38	33	31	39	40	34	28	19
Primary (completed or not)	Percent	9	8	4	6	12	11	7	15	10	15	18	18	16
Secondary (completed or not) and higher	Percent	4	1	0	1	1	1	3	18	8	8	13	17	35
Labor market (population aged 15 to 64)														
Number of employed people in sample	Number	6664	2933	479	532	570	701	651	3731	754	658	721	727	871
Proportion of employed	Percent	23	20	18	20	20	22	19	17	14	15	16	18	23
Branch of activity														
Agriculture/fishing	Percent	.	.	.	.	.	.	.	.	.	.	.	.	.
Manufacturing/mining/construction	Percent	.	.	.	.	.	.	.	.	.	.	.	.	.
Commerce	Percent	.	.	.	.	.	.	.	.	.	.	.	.	.
Civil servant/army	Percent	.	.	.	.	.	.	.	.	.	.	.	.	.
Other sector	Percent	.	.	.	.	.	.	.	.	.	.	.	.	.
Labor force participation (total)	Percent	.	.	.	.	.	.	.	.	.	.	.	.	.
Male	Percent	.	.	.	.	.	.	.	.	.	.	.	.	.
Female	Percent	.	.	.	.	.	.	.	.	.	.	.	.	.
Household expenditure														
Mean per capita expenditure (CFA)	000s	66	56	7	20	38	65	150	118	34	66	93	130	265
Population below relative poverty line	Percent	48	55	100	100	76	0	0	14	69	0	0	0	0
Share of food in total expenditure	Percent	60	60	37	49	67	70	73	59	58	65	63	59	51
Household amenities														
Type of fuel for cooking														
Firewood	Percent	90	90	82	86	91	90	96	90	90	95	93	93	83
Gas, kerosine	Percent	2	1	1	3	0	1	1	4	2	2	4	4	9
Charcoal	Percent	0	0	0	0	0	0	0	0	0	0	0	0	0
Electricity	Percent	0	0	0	0	0	0	0	1	0	0	0	1	3
Other	Percent	8	9	17	11	9	8	3	4	8	3	3	2	5
Access to sanitation	Percent	19	8	2	6	7	10	13	77	59	71	76	82	90
Access to water														
Pipe/borne	Percent	29	18	14	16	24	21	13	90	83	90	89	92	94
Well	Percent	65	76	84	79	69	71	79	7	14	8	8	5	4
Other	Percent	6	6	3	5	7	8	8	3	3	3	3	3	2
Owner occupancy rate	Percent	90	97	99	97	97	97	95	54	68	59	61	55	39
Malnutrition (children aged 0 to 59 months)														
Stunting	Percent	.	.						.					
Wasting	Percent	.	.						.					
Underweight	Percent	.	.						.					

Source: Household Priority Survey, *Enquête permanente de conjoncture économique et sociale,* 1995.

15-15. Nigeria: household welfare indicators

Indicator	Unit of measure	National total	*Expenditure quintile*											
			Rural						*Urban*					
			All	*1*	*2*	*3*	*4*	*5*	*All*	*1*	*2.*	*3*	*4*	*5*
Demographic indicators														
Sample size	Number	8937	5276	686	817	917	1100	1756	3661	479	616	658	702	1206
Total population	Thousands	107000	65861	13183	13160	13177	13178	13163	41139	8220	8226	8251	8220	8221
Female	Percent	50	50	50	50	50	51	50	50	47	49	52	51	49
Population below 15 years	Percent	50	50	50	50	50	51	50	50	47	49	52	51	49
Female	Percent	48	47	48	47	47	47	48	49	49	50	50	49	47
Number of households	Thousands	22739	13654	1863	2190	2486	2962	4153	9085	1119	1425	1541	1777	3223
Average household size	Number	4.7	4.8	7.1	6	5.3	4.4	3.2	4.5	7.3	5.8	5.4	4.6	2.6
Education and literacy														
Net primary enrollment (total)	Percent	56	51	48	50	55	58	67	63	55	63	69	69	74
Male	Percent	60	56	48	51	54	59	71	66	56	62	71	72	74
Female	Percent	58	54	47	49	56	56	62	64	55	65	66	67	73
Net secondary enrollment (total)	Percent	46	38	26	34	40	45	46	58	41	59	64	63	61
Male	Percent	48	40	23	38	43	49	50	59	42	67	67	61	64
Female	Percent	45	36	29	30	37	42	42	56	39	50	61	66	58
Literacy rates (total)	Percent	44	33	23	27	28	39	43	62	43	47	65	70	74
Male	Percent	51	39	28	33	34	44	51	70	55	60	71	77	81
Female	Percent	36	27	19	21	23	34	35	53	31	36	59	63	66
Head of household														
Marital status of head														
Monogamous male-headed	Percent	53	56	59	62	64	61	44	49	52	58	60	59	33
Polygamous mlc-headed	Percent	15	17	30	26	19	13	8	12	31	18	12	9	4
Single male-headed	Percent	16	13	4	3	5	10	29	21	5	8	11	15	41
Defacto female-headed	Percent	2	2	2	1	3	2	2	2	2	1	2	2	2
Dejure female-headed	Percent	13	12	4	7	9	14	17	16	11	14	15	14	21
Education level of head														
Completed primary	Percent	28	26	24	20	23	27	30	32	28	30	36	39	29
Completed secondary	Percent	20	11	5	4	7	13	18	33	19	19	29	33	47
Illiterate	Percent	52	63	71	76	70	60	52	35	53	52	35	29	23
Labor market														
Employment of head														
Agro-pastoral activities	Percent	52	73	91	84	80	69	57	20	40	26	18	17	13
Household expenditure														
Per capita expenditure (Naira)	Value	744	708	161	328	483	702	1866	802	264	471	657	891	1729
Population below poverty line	Percent	44	52	100	100	59	0	0	32	100	61	0	0	0
Food share in total expenditure	Percent	67	68	76	76	76	70	65	66	80	78	71	67	61
Household amenities														
Type of fuel for cooking														
Firewood	Percent	..	..	..	..	..	..	..	..	..	..	..	..	..
Gas, kerosine	Percent	..	..	..	..	..	..	..	..	..	..	..	..	..
Charcoal	Percent	..	..	..	..	..	..	..	..	..	..	..	..	..
Electricity	Percent	..	..	..	..	..	..	..	..	..	..	..	..	..
Other	Percent	..	..	..	..	..	..	..	..	..	..	..	..	..
Access to sanitation		..	..	..	..	..	..	..	..	..	..	..	..	..
Access to water														
Pipe	Percent	..	..	..	..	..	..	..	..	..	..	..	..	..
Wells/borne	Percent	..	..	..	..	..	..	..	..	..	..	..	..	..
Other	Percent	..	..	..	..	..	..	..	..	..	..	..	..	..
Malnutrition (children aged 0 to 59 months)														
Stunting	Percent	.	.						.					
Wasting	Percent	.	.						.					
Underweight	Percent	.	.						.					

Source: Consumer Expenditure Survey, 1992.

15-16. Senegal: household welfare indicators

Indicator	Unit of measure	National total	Rural All	1	2	3	4	5	Urban All	1	2	3	4	5
Demographic indicators														
Sample size (households)	Number	3277	1314	217	232	247	272	346	1963	323	333	367	396	544
Total population	000s	7599	4619	923	919	925	923	929	2980	592	592	595	600	600
Population below 15 years	Percent	45	47	52	50	48	45	41	42	45	45	43	39	35
Population 60 years and above	Percent	6	7	6	6	7	8	8	5	4	4	5	4	5
Age dependency ratio	Percent	97	108	128	117	112	99	88	82	104	90	86	71	63
Number of males per 100 females (age 15 and over)	Number	123	129	123	134	139	136	117	115	126	123	116	112	103
Average household size	Number	10	11	13	12	11	10	8	9	11	11	10	9	7
Education and literacy														
Net primary enrollment rate (total)	Percent	37	22	21	18	21	23	28	63	49	60	55	72	83
Male	Percent	39	25	21	20	27	27	32	65	47	64	60	76	84
Female	Percent	35	20	22	17	15	19	25	61	50	57	51	68	82
Net secondary enrollment rate (total)	Percent	13	3	1	2	2	3	6	25	11	17	17	30	52
Male	Percent	16	4	1	3	4	6	8	31	18	23	24	35	58
Female	Percent	10	1	1	1	0	1	3	20	4	12	12	25	48
Literacy rate (total)	Percent	27	17	17	18	16	15	18	42	36	41	42	47	44
Male	Percent	39	30	31	34	29	27	30	51	50	53	51	56	47
Female	Percent	18	7	7	6	6	6	8	34	25	31	34	39	41
Head of household														
Marital status of head														
Monogamous male-headed	Percent	48	46	44	49	43	45	50	49	47	46	46	47	55
Polygamous male-headed	Percent	30	37	40	39	42	39	27	21	24	24	24	21	15
Single male-headed	Percent	3	3	2	3	2	3	3	3	2	2	3	2	5
Defacto female-headed	Percent	12	10	8	7	11	10	12	15	17	15	17	15	13
Dejure female-headed	Percent	8	4	6	2	2	3	6	12	9	13	10	15	13
Education level of head														
No level	Percent	78	93	90	94	95	94	91	58	79	73	65	57	32
Primary not completed	Percent	4	3	7	3	2	3	3	6	6	6	6	7	5
Completed primary, no secondary	Percent	7	2	3	3	2	1	2	13	10	14	17	12	13
Secondary not completed	Percent	6	1	1	1	1	2	2	12	5	5	9	16	20
Completed secondary / higher level	Percent	5	1	0	0	0	0	2	11	1	1	4	8	29
Labor market (population aged 15 to 64)														
Number of employed people in sample	Number	9193	4433	815	854	833	946	985	4760	876	914	936	992	1042
Proportion of employed	Percent	56	68	68	70	65	69	66	48	51	49	47	47	47
Branch of activity														
Agriculture/fishing	Percent	36	60	68	65	57	60	54	4	8	6	4	2	1
Manufacturing/mining/construction	Percent	9	4	1	3	5	5	5	16	17	18	16	17	14
Commerce	Percent	13	8	5	7	7	9	10	20	18	19	21	21	21
Civil servant/army	Percent	2	0	0	0	0	0	1	4	1	2	3	5	8
Other sector	Percent	40	28	26	25	31	27	29	56	56	56	56	56	56
Labor force participation (total)	Percent	64	70	72	70	66	68	72	56	54	55	57	56	57
Male	Percent	72	81	81	82	81	84	79	60	62	62	61	59	57
Female	Percent	57	61	65	61	56	58	66	52	48	50	52	53	56
Household expenditure														
Mean per capita expenditure (FCFA)	000s	148	96	41	63	81	106	187	231	88	127	170	234	535
Population below relative poverty line	Percent	45	66	100	100	100	28	0	14	69	0	0	0	0
Share of food in total expenditure	Percent													
Household amenities														
Type of fuel for cooking														
Firewood	Percent	56	84	82	86	83	87	81	18	33	28	18	13	6
Gas, kerosine	Percent	21	2	0	1	2	1	4	48	23	28	41	56	74
Charcoal	Percent	22	12	13	12	13	11	14	34	43	45	40	31	20
Electricity	Percent	0	0	0	0	0	0	0	0	0	0	0	0	0
Other	Percent	1	2	5	2	2	1	1	0	1	0	0	0	0
Access to sanitation	Percent	65	45	32	45	45	47	52	93	83	91	94	95	98
Access to water														
Pipe/borne	Percent	53	30	16	22	32	35	38	84	76	78	82	84	94
Well	Percent	44	67	79	77	64	63	57	14	22	20	15	13	4
Other	Percent	3	4	4	2	4	2	5	2	2	2	3	3	2
Owner occupancy rate	Percent	75	91	92	96	90	91	86	55	52	58	65	61	44
Malnutrition (children aged 0 to 59 months)														
Stunting	Percent	.	.						.					
Wasting	Percent	.	.						.					
Underweight	Percent	.	.						.					

Source: *Enquete senegalaise aupres des menages, Direction de la prevision et de la statistique, 1994/95.*

15-17. Sierra Leone: household welfare indicators

Indicator	Unit of measure	National total	Expenditure quintile												
			Rural						Urban					
			All	*1*	*2*	*3*	*4*	*5*	*All*	*1*	*2*	*3*	*4*	*5*
Demographic indicators														
Sample size	Number	3407	2244	202	363	596	713	370	1163	200	186	234	244	299
Total population	Thousands	4580	2426	471	486	468	517	484	2154	431	429	436	429	431
Female	Percent	48	48	49	46	47	50	50	47	49	51	45	47	44
Population below 15 years	Percent	45	44	48	50	42	40	44	47	43	49	49	48	46
Female	Percent	47	48	49	46	47	49	48	.45	50	49	41	46	39
Number of households	Thousands	796	410	36	60	96	127	91	386	68	61	72	78	105
Average household size	Number	5.8	5.9	13.1	8.2	4.9	4.1	5.3	5.6	6.3	7	6	5.5	4.1
Education and literacy														
Net primary enrollment (total)	Percent	55	48	63	66	66	29	23	62	62	55	77	68	75
Male	Percent	63	53	66	70	67	34	24	72	65	61	78	71	81
Female	Percent	54	47	59	61	64	23	22	63	59	50	75	65	66
Net secondary enrollment (total)	Percent	47	42	50	62	50	17	17	53	42	46	63	62	58
Male	Percent	53	48	59	66	58	22	17	59	45	49	65	72	69
Female	Percent	40	35	40	56	40	12	17	46	39	42	60	52	40
Literacy rates (total)	Percent	32	27	36	41	37	19	9	38	36	33	41	39	40
Male	Percent	42	37	48	53	46	27	15	47	43	45	53	48	48
Female	Percent	23	19	26	28	29	11	4	28	29	23	29	29	29
Head of household														
Marital status of head														
Monogamous male-headed	Percent	57	55	30	57	71	51	53	59	63	56	57	60	60
Polygamous male-headed	Percent	19	22	57	29	9	17	25	16	17	22	22	12	10
Single male-headed	Percent	11	10	2	2	5	20	9	12	5	11	6	14	19
Defacto female-headed	Percent	1	1	1	0	1	1	0	1	0	1	1	2	0
Dejure female-headed	Percent	12	13	11	11	15	12	13	12	14	10	14	13	10
Education level of head														
Completed primary	Percent	8	7	5	8	7	7	8	9	8	8	9	10	8
Completed secondary	Percent	29	25	28	35	35	24	8	34	30	33	33	33	38
Illiterate	Percent	63	68	67	58	58	69	84	57	62	58	58	57	53
Labor market														
Employment of head														
Agro-pastoral activities	Percent	33	45	35	24	20	49	82	20	24	27	23	17	15
Household expenditure														
Per capita expenditure (Leone)	Value	2275	1551	117	157	226	1117	6083	3091	303	1231	2280	3585	8057
Population below poverty line	Percent	56	74	100	100	100	72	0	36	100	83	0	0	0
Food share in total expenditure	Percent	64	69	51	62	71	80	79	58	51	58	60	60	61
Household amenities														
Type of fuel for cooking														
Firewood	Percent	..	..	..	..	..	..	..	..	..	..	..	..	..
Gas, kerosine	Percent	..	..	..	..	..	..	..	..	..	..	..	..	..
Charcoal	Percent	..	..	..	..	..	..	..	..	..	..	..	..	..
Electricity	Percent	..	..	..	..	..	..	..	..	..	..	..	..	..
Other	Percent	..	..	..	..	..	..	..	..	..	..	..	..	..
Access to sanitation														
Access to water														
Pipe	Percent	..	..	..	..	..	..	..	..	..	..	..	..	..
Wells/borne	Percent	..	..	..	..	..	..	..	..	..	..	..	..	..
Other	Percent													
Malnutrition (children aged 0 to 59 months)														
Stunting	Percent	.	.						.					
Wasting	Percent	.	.						.					
Underweight	Percent	.	.						.					

Source: Survey of Household Expenditure and Household Economic Activities (SHEHEA), 1989/90.

15-18. South Africa: household welfare indicators

Indicator	Unit of measure	National total	Expenditure quintile											
			Rural						Urban					
			All	1	2	3	4	5	All	1	2	3	4	5
Demographic indicators														
Sample size (households)	Number	7963	3638	503	540	596	748	1251	4325	540	680	847	1022	1236
Total population (extrapolated)	000s	41650	21208.5	4241.1	4237.7	4243.1	4235.8	4250.9	20441.5	4084.3	4089.2	4086.7	4083.1	4098.2
Population below 15 years	Percent	33	37	45	41	38	34	26	29	38	35	30	25	19
Population 60 years and above	Percent	7	8	7	8	9	9	8	7	7	6	5	6	10
Age dependency ratio	Percent	61	72	97	85	78	67	45	51	73	61	41	35	
Number of males per 100 females (age 15 and over)	Number	108	107	120	124	116	114	78	109	124	124	111	101	95
Average household size	Number	4.7	5.5	8.2	7.6	6.8	5.4	3.1	4.1	7.0	5.4	4.3	3.4	2.6
Education and literacy														
Net primary enrollment rate (total)	Percent	.	.	.	.	.	.	.	.	.	.	.	.	.
Male	Percent	.	.	.	.	.	.	.	.	.	.	.	.	.
Female	Percent	.	.	.	.	.	.	.	.	.	.	.	.	.
Net secondary enrollment rate (total)	Percent	.	.	.	.	.	.	.	.	.	.	.	.	.
Male	Percent	.	.	.	.	.	.	.	.	.	.	.	.	.
Female	Percent	.	.	.	.	.	.	.	.	.	.	.	.	.
Literacy rate (total)	Percent	.	.	.	.	.	.	.	.	.	.	.	.	.
Male	Percent	.	.	.	.	.	.	.	.	.	.	.	.	.
Female	Percent	.	.	.	.	.	.	.	.	.	.	.	.	.
Head of household														
Marital status of head														
Monogamous male-headed	Percent	56	49	52	58	56	52	41	60	48	53	62	64	65
Polygamous male-headed	Percent	0	1	1	0	1	0	0	0	0	0	0	0	0
Single male-headed	Percent	16	18	4	5	5	8	40	14	4	10	11	16	20
Defacto female-headed	Percent	1	1	2	0	1	0	1	1	1	2	2	1	1
Dejure female-headed	Percent	27	31	41	37	38	39	18	24	46	36	25	19	14
Education level of head														
No level	Percent	23	38	56	54	46	40	20	11	28	17	10	7	5
Primary not completed	Percent	67	58	44	46	53	59	71	74	72	82	88	82	57
Completed primary, no secondary	Percent	4	1	0	0	0	0	3	7	0	0	1	3	19
Secondary not completed	Percent	6	3	0	0	0	1	7	8	0	1	1	8	19
Completed secondary / higher level	Percent	0	0	0	0	0	0	0	0	0	0	0	0	0
Labor market (population aged 15 to 64)														
Number of employed people in sample	Number	11929	4441	505	580	709	892	1755	7488	728	1182	1523	1868	2187
Proportion of employed	Percent	32	14	6	8	10	14	34	30	11	20	28	39	52
Branch of activity														
Agriculture/fishing	Percent	8	33	66	67	36	32	0	1	0	0	0	1	2
Manufacturing/mining/construction	Percent	30	25	0	17	25	21	45	32	26	35	42	32	26
Commerce	Percent	13	2	0	0	0	0	6	16	9	18	22	20	10
Civil servant/army	Percent	25	33	34	17	20	47	42	23	41	26	18	24	14
Other sector	Percent	24	7	0	0	19	0	7	29	24	21	18	23	48
Labor force participation (total)	Percent	41	29	17	18	23	27	52	51	29	40	49	60	71
Male	Percent	38	25	16	17	24	26	42	50	28	40	48	59	69
Female	Percent	43	33	18	19	21	29	60	53	29	41	50	60	74
Household expenditure														
Mean per capita expenditure (rands)	Number	468	190	47	80	115	171	535	623	98	206	352	670	1788
Population below relative poverty line	Percent	44	86	100	100	100	100	30	40	100	100	0	0	0
Share of food in total expenditure	Percent	56	55	61	59	58	56	41	39	55	48	41	30	18
Household amenities														
Type of fuel for cooking														
Firewood	Percent	22	49	80	75	64	50	20	2	7	4	1	0	0
Gas, kerosine	Percent	24	23	14	15	23	31	26	25	55	41	30	18	7
Charcoal	Percent	5	5	1	5	8	8	4	4	11	9	5	3	0
Electricity	Percent	48	21	1	2	4	10	50	69	27	45	63	79	93
Other	Percent	1	2	3	3	2	1	0	0	0	0	0	0	0
Access to sanitation	Percent	84	77	53	65	76	78	90	89	64	82	88	96	99
Access to water														
Pipe/borne	Percent	79	53	32	39	48	50	72	99	98	99	99	100	100
Well	Percent	10	22	40	30	25	22	12	0	0	1	0	0	0
Other	Percent	11	24	28	31	27	28	17	0	2	0	1	0	0
Owner occupancy rate	Percent	63	69	86	83	81	75	48	59	52	56	52	54	70
Malnutrition (children aged 0 to 59 months)														
Stunting	Percent	.	.						.					
Wasting	Percent	.	.						.					
Underweight	Percent	.	.						.					

Source: Living Standards and Development Survey, 1993

15-19. Swaziland: household welfare indicators

			Expenditure quintile											
			Rural						Urban					
Indicator	Unit of measure	National total	All	1	2	3	4	5	All	1	2	3	4	5
Demographic indicators														
Sample size (households)	Number	6246	4612	852	844	853	926	1137	1634	201	274	306	344	509
Total population	000s	863	680	137	136	136	136	136	183	37	36	36	37	37
Population below 15 years	Percent	38	40	40	41	40	39	37	30	37	31	31	26	25
Population 60 years and above	Percent	5	5	5	5	5	6	6	3	3	4	3	3	3
Age dependency ratio	Percent	69	75	77	80	78	76	67	47	66	48	48	39	36
Number of males per 100 females (age 15 and over)	Number	94	91	91	94	89	91	90	106	92	102	99	100	140
Average household size	Number	6.3	7.6	8.4	8.4	8.1	7.5	6.2	3.9	6.1	4.8	3.8	3.5	2.7
Education and literacy														
Net primary enrollment rate (total)	Percent	.	.	.	.	.	.	.	.	.	.	.	.	.
Male	Percent	.	.	.	.	.	.	.	.	.	.	.	.	.
Female	Percent	.	.	.	.	.	.	.	.	.	.	.	.	.
Net secondary enrollment rate (total)	Percent	.	.	.	.	.	.	.	.	.	.	.	.	.
Male	Percent	.	.	.	.	.	.	.	.	.	.	.	.	.
Female	Percent	.	.	.	.	.	.	.	.	.	.	.	.	.
Literacy rate (total)	Percent	76	72	67	70	72	75	77	87	82	84	89	90	89
Male	Percent	77	73	68	71	72	76	79	87	86	82	90	88	88
Female	Percent	75	71	66	69	72	74	76	87	78	86	89	93	90
Head of household														
Marital status of head														
Monogamous male-headed	Percent	57	62	61	63	62	62	60	47	59	56	55	44	34
Polygamous male-headed	Percent	1	2	2	2	2	2	1	1	1	1	0	1	0
Single male-headed	Percent	14	6	5	5	5	6	9	30	12	24	21	31	47
Defacto female-headed	Percent	2	2	4	3	3	1	1	1	2	0	0	0	1
Dejure female-headed	Percent	26	28	28	27	28	30	28	21	26	19	24	24	17
Education level of head														
No level	Percent	33	43	52	47	44	41	32	15	22	21	12	10	15
Primary not completed	Percent	33	36	35	35	37	36	36	26	29	32	27	26	21
Completed primary, no secondary	Percent	4	5	3	4	4	6	6	2	6	4	2	1	2
Secondary not completed	Percent	27	16	10	14	14	16	23	49	39	40	54	54	50
Completed secondary / higher level	Percent	3	1	1	1	1	1	2	7	3	3	5	10	11
Labor market (population aged 15 to 64)														
Number of employed people in sample	Number	9961	7582	1233	1331	1551	1639	1828	2379	338	440	426	498	677
Proportion of employed	Percent	26	22	17	19	22	23	27	39	27	35	38	43	51
Branch of activity														
Agriculture/fishing	Percent	53	50	54	58	51	46	47	59	63	67	61	59	50
Manufacturing/mining/construction	Percent	13	14	14	11	18	14	12	9	4	8	9	11	12
Commerce	Percent	10	11	9	11	10	13	12	7	6	3	7	5	11
Civil servant/army	Percent	0	0	0	0	0	0	0	0	0	0	0	0	0
Other sector	Percent	24	24	23	20	21	27	28	25	27	21	23	24	27
Labor force participation (total)	Percent	43	38	30	34	40	41	45	57	45	52	56	60	70
Male	Percent	52	46	40	42	48	47	53	67	56	62	67	68	78
Female	Percent	34	31	21	27	32	36	37	46	35	41	44	52	58
Household expenditure														
Mean per capita expenditure (Emalangeni)	000s	5.1	3.4	0.6	1.4	2.2	3.4	9.3	11.4	1.1	2.8	5.4	10.2	37.5
Population below relative poverty line	Percent	63	70	100	100	100	51	0	36	100	81	0	0	0
Share of food in total expenditure	Percent	65	69	81	76	69	64	54	52	78	64	52	39	29
Household amenities														
Type of fuel for cooking														
Firewood	Percent	13	2	1	1	1	2	5	34	20	26	33	37	45
Gas, kerosine	Percent	7	2	1	1	2	2	4	15	12	12	15	17	17
Charcoal	Percent	67	93	96	97	96	93	87	16	26	23	15	15	10
Electricity	Percent	5	1	1	0	0	0	1	14	9	14	13	16	16
Other	Percent	8	2	2	1	1	2	2	20	32	26	24	15	12
Access to sanitation	Percent	80	71	63	68	70	74	75	97	90	98	98	97	98
Access to water														
Pipe/borne	Percent	39	14	10	13	14	14	19	86	82	80	84	90	91
Well	Percent	17	23	23	22	26	24	23	5	10	8	6	3	3
Other	Percent	44	62	67	66	60	62	58	8	8	12	11	7	6
Owner occupancy rate	Percent	93	100	100	100	100	100	99	69	74	73	68	67	63
Malnutrition (children aged 0 to 59 months)														
Stunting	Percent	.	.						.					
Wasting	Percent	.	.						.					
Underweight	Percent	.	.						.					

Source: Swaziland Household Income Expenditure Survey, 1994.

15-20. Tanzania: household welfare indicators

			colspan across *Expenditure quintile*												
			Rural							*Urban*					
Indicator	Unit of measure	National total	All	1	2	3	4	5	All	1	2	3	4	5
Demographic indicators															
Sample size (households)	Number	5177	2259	320	383	419	502	635	2918	277	404	425	728	1084
Total population	000s	27530	19566	3900	3926	3898	3908	3914	7964	1596	1590	1584	1597	1592
Population below 15 years	Percent	47	49	54	53	50	48	41	43	51	47	44	40	35
Population 60 years and above	Percent	4	4	4	4	5	4	5	4	4	4	4	3	4
Age dependency ratio	Percent	100	106	128	125	109	101	77	85	113	98	88	75	61
Number of males per 100 females (age 15 and over)	Number	87	86	83	77	89	93	90	87	78	78	85	98	96
Average household size	Number	6.1	6.3	7.8	6.9	6.6	5.9	4.9	5.6	7.2	6.5	6.1	5.3	4.1
Education and literacy															
Net primary enrollment rate (total)	Percent	.	.	.	.	.	.	.	.	.	.	.	.	.
Male	Percent	.	.	.	.	.	.	.	.	.	.	.	.	.
Female	Percent	.	.	.	.	.	.	.	.	.	.	.	.	.
Net secondary enrollment rate (total)	Percent	.	.	.	.	.	.	.	.	.	.	.	.	.
Male	Percent	.	.	.	.	.	.	.	.	.	.	.	.	.
Female	Percent	.	.	.	.	.	.	.	.	.	.	.	.	.
Literacy rate (total)	Percent	74	71	63	67	73	73	76	82	71	81	80	85	89
Male	Percent	83	81	76	76	84	83	84	89	82	88	85	91	96
Female	Percent	66	62	53	60	63	64	69	76	62	76	75	80	82
Head of household															
Marital status of head															
Monogamous male-headed	Percent	77	78	72	76	82	80	77	75	80	78	75	73	71
Polygamous male-headed	Percent	8	10	15	10	8	9	7	3	5	3	6	2	1
Single male-headed	Percent	3	3	2	2	1	2	5	5	1	3	3	7	8
Defacto female-headed	Percent	1	1	0	1	1	0	1	3	1	4	1	3	4
Dejure female-headed	Percent	11	9	10	10	8	9	10	15	13	12	16	15	16
Education level of head															
No level	Percent	23	25	34	31	23	22	21	17	24	17	23	15	11
Primary not completed	Percent	58	60	57	57	63	62	61	53	57	52	52	55	51
Completed primary, no secondary	Percent	6	5	3	3	6	6	4	9	9	10	11	8	7
Secondary not completed	Percent	7	4	2	2	4	5	7	12	7	9	9	15	18
Completed secondary / higher level	Percent	7	6	5	8	4	5	7	9	4	12	5	7	13
Labor market (population aged 15 to 64)															
Number of employed people in sample	Number	4153	537	48	83	87	134	185	3616	307	457	500	902	1447
Proportion of employed	Percent	8	4	2	3	3	4	6	18	11	13	17	21	30
Branch of activity															
Agriculture/fishing	Percent	.	.	.	.	.	.	.	.	.	.	.	.	.
Manufacturing/mining/construction	Percent	.	.	.	.	.	.	.	.	.	.	.	.	.
Commerce	Percent	.	.	.	.	.	.	.	.	.	.	.	.	.
Civil servant/army	Percent	.	.	.	.	.	.	.	.	.	.	.	.	.
Other sector	Percent	.	.	.	.	.	.	.	.	.	.	.	.	.
Labor force participation (total)	Percent	16	8	4	7	7	9	10	35	25	27	34	38	49
Male	Percent	25	13	7	12	11	15	17	51	35	41	50	55	69
Female	Percent	9	3	2	3	3	4	5	21	16	16	20	21	31
Household expenditure															
Mean per capita expenditure (KSH)	000s	106	86	33	52	70	96	178	154	53	84	116	164	356
Population below relative poverty line	Percent	42	51	100	100	57	0	0	20	97	0	0	0	0
Share of food in total expenditure	Percent	70	73	73	73	73	73	70	63	69	66	60	64	55
Household amenities															
Type of fuel for cooking															
Firewood	Percent	79	96	100	98	98	97	93	42	69	59	46	37	18
Gas, kerosine	Percent	2	0	0	0	0	0	1	7	1	3	4	8	14
Charcoal	Percent	17	3	0	2	2	3	6	47	30	37	50	51	59
Electricity	Percent	1	0	0	0	0	0	0	3	0	1	1	4	7
Other	Percent	0	0	0	0	0	0	0	0	0	0	0	0	1
Access to sanitation	Percent	94	92	88	93	91	93	93	97	96	98	98	95	98
Access to water															
Pipe/borne	Percent	12	2	1	1	1	2	4	35	13	20	27	40	57
Well	Percent	31	38	34	43	33	38	39	17	38	17	24	11	5
Other	Percent	57	61	65	57	66	60	57	49	48	64	49	49	38
Owner occupancy rate	Percent	83	94	97	96	97	92	89	59	78	74	63	52	43
Malnutrition (children aged 0 to 59 months)															
Stunting	Percent	.	.						.					
Wasting	Percent	.	.						.					
Underweight	Percent	.	.						.					

Source: Human Resource Development Survey, 1993

15-21. Uganda: household welfare indicators

| | | | Expenditure quintile | | | | | | | | | | | |
| | | | Rural | | | | | | Urban | | | | | |
Indicator	Unit of measure	National total	All	1	2	3	4	5	All	1	2	3	4	5
Demographic indicators														
Sample size (households)	Number	9924	6396	1081	1114	1207	1250	1744	3528	688	637	693	682	828
Total population	000s	18620	16313	3262	3264	3261	3263	3263	2307	461	463	458	465	462
Population below 15 years	Percent	50	50	57	54	52	49	40	46	55	53	48	43	34
Population 60 years and above	Percent	5	5	5	5	5	6	6	2	2	3	2	2	1
Age dependency ratio	Percent	114	117	152	132	126	111	80	91	132	119	95	76	53
Number of males per 100 females (age 15 and over)	Number	88	88	77	82	86	90	101	91	76	74	98	105	100
Average household size	Number	4.6	4.7	6.0	5.5	4.9	4.5	3.4	3.9	5.3	4.6	4.0	3.7	2.8
Education and literacy														
Net primary enrollment rate (total)	Percent	.	.	.	.	.	.	.	.	.	.	.	.	.
Male	Percent	.	.	.	.	.	.	.	.	.	.	.	.	.
Female	Percent	.	.	.	.	.	.	.	.	.	.	.	.	.
Net secondary enrollment rate (total)	Percent	.	.	.	.	.	.	.	.	.	.	.	.	.
Male	Percent	.	.	.	.	.	.	.	.	.	.	.	.	.
Female	Percent	.	.	.	.	.	.	.	.	.	.	.	.	.
Literacy rate (total)	Percent	63	59	46	56	60	62	69	86	71	83	89	90	94
Male	Percent	76	74	64	72	75	76	78	91	82	88	94	93	95
Female	Percent	51	47	32	42	47	49	60	82	62	79	84	87	93
Head of household														
Marital status of head														
Monogamous male-headed	Percent	65	66	66	66	68	68	63	60	63	57	65	64	54
Polygamous male-headed	Percent	3	4	5	5	4	4	2	1	2	0	1	1	0
Single male-headed	Percent	5	5	1	2	3	4	10	10	1	5	6	10	19
Defacto female-headed	Percent	23	23	26	25	23	22	21	23	30	32	23	18	18
Dejure female-headed	Percent	2	2	1	2	1	2	3	6	4	4	5	7	9
Education level of head														
No level	Percent	31	35	46	37	34	32	30	11	26	14	8	10	4
Primary not completed	Percent	41	43	41	46	43	44	41	32	35	43	37	33	20
Completed primary, no secondary	Percent	9	9	8	8	11	9	9	13	14	11	14	11	13
Secondary not completed	Percent	7	7	3	5	6	8	8	13	11	16	15	12	11
Completed secondary / higher level	Percent	10	7	2	4	5	7	12	32	14	16	26	34	53
Labor market (population aged 15 to 64)														
Number of employed people in sample	Number	21528	14786	3142	2871	2783	2779	3211	6742	1590	1299	1306	1222	1325
Proportion of employed	Percent	49	40	35	37	39	41	49	44	37	39	43	48	53
Branch of activity														
Agriculture/fishing	Percent	83	90	96	93	92	88	82	37	57	48	35	33	20
Manufacturing/mining/onstruction	Percent	4	3	1	2	2	3	4	15	14	13	18	13	15
Commerce	Percent	7	3	1	2	2	4	6	28	16	27	25	32	34
Civil servant/army	Percent	5	4	1	2	3	4	7	13	9	9	14	15	18
Other sector	Percent	2	1	1	1	1	1	1	7	3	3	8	6	13
Labor force participation (total)	Percent	87	88	89	87	88	87	88	84	86	86	83	85	81
Male	Percent	83	83	81	81	84	82	84	82	79	82	80	82	85
Female	Percent	92	93	94	92	92	92	92	86	92	88	86	89	78
Household expenditure														
Mean per capita expenditure (shillings)	Number	13	12	4	7	9	13	24	25	7	12	17	25	63
Population below relative poverty line	Percent	42	46	100	100	30	0	0	16	78	0	0	0	0
Share of food in total expenditure	Percent	63	65	64	65	65	66	63	51	57	54	54	51	41
Household amenities														
Type of fuel for cooking														
Firewood	Percent	85	94	98	97	96	94	90	27	61	36	29	19	8
Gas, kerosine	Percent	2	2	1	1	1	2	2	5	2	1	3	3	11
Charcoal	Percent	12	4	1	2	2	3	7	62	35	62	65	74	66
Electricity	Percent	1	0	0	0	0	0	0	5	2	1	2	3	13
Other	Percent	0	0	0	0	0	0	0	1	0	0	0	0	2
Access to sanitation	Percent	78	75	61	69	78	79	81	95	89	95	95	96	98
Access to water														
Pipe/borne	Percent	7	2	1	1	2	2	3	35	19	26	28	41	49
Well	Percent	54	55	53	55	55	54	57	51	56	57	59	46	44
Other	Percent	39	43	46	44	43	44	40	14	24	17	13	13	7
Owner occupancy rate	Percent	82	91	96	95	93	91	84	26	44	30	25	21	20
Malnutrition (children aged 0 to 59 months)														
Stunting	Percent	.	.						.					
Wasting	Percent	.	.						.					
Underweight	Percent	.	.						.					

Source: Household Integrated Survey, 1992/93.

15-22. Zambia: household welfare indicators

Indicator	Unit of measure	National total	Rural						Urban					
			All	*1*	*2*	*3*	*4*	*5*	*All*	*1*	*2*	*3*	*4*	*5*
Demographic indicators														
Sample size (households)	Number	11754	5234	805	905	985	1099	1440	6520	1045	1052	1191	1385	1847
Total population	000s	9546	6026	1205	1207	1206	1203	1206	3520	701	707	704	704	705
Population below 15 years	Percent	44	45	50	48	46	45	38	43	49	46	44	41	33
Population 60 years and above	Percent	4	5	5	5	5	5	6	2	3	2	2	1	1
Age dependency ratio	Percent	88	95	112	103	99	92	72	78	102	90	83	71	52
Number of males per 100 females (age 15 and over)	Number	105	109	113	111	110	112	103	98	101	99	100	99	91
Average household size	Number	5.0	4.8	6.1	5.4	5.1	4.6	3.7	5.3	7.0	6.5	5.7	4.9	3.7
Education and literacy														
Net primary enrollment rate (total)	Percent	67	60	52	58	62	65	70	78	70	78	80	82	83
Male	Percent	66	60	54	55	62	64	68	79	69	81	82	83	84
Female	Percent	67	61	50	60	62	65	72	78	72	76	78	82	83
Net secondary enrollment rate (total)	Percent	20	12	8	11	10	14	17	33	23	28	30	40	46
Male	Percent	22	13	10	12	9	17	19	37	23	29	31	49	53
Female	Percent	18	10	7	9	11	10	15	30	23	27	29	32	41
Literacy rate (total)	Percent													
Male	Percent													
Female	Percent													
Head of household														
Marital status of head														
Monogamous male-headed	Percent	61	59	57	61	63	61	54	67	70	72	71	71	57
Polygamous male-headed	Percent	6	8	9	8	7	8	7	3	5	5	4	3	2
Single male-headed	Percent	8	7	3	3	5	5	14	11	5	5	8	9	20
Defacto female-headed	Percent	5	7	6	7	6	6	7	2	2	2	3	2	1
Dejure female-headed	Percent	19	20	25	22	20	20	18	17	19	17	16	14	20
Education level of head														
No level	Percent	19	24	30	28	23	23	20	9	14	9	10	7	6
Primary not completed	Percent	29	36	40	39	38	35	31	14	28	19	13	11	7
Completed primary, no secondary	Percent	19	21	19	20	22	21	21	16	22	19	20	13	12
Secondary not completed	Percent	20	14	10	11	14	15	18	31	27	36	33	35	27
Completed secondary / higher level	Percent	14	5	1	3	4	6	10	30	9	18	24	34	48
Labor market (population aged 15 to 64)														
Number of employed people in sample	Number	18684	9463	1668	1757	1816	1957	2265	9221	1620	1512	1673	1958	2458
Proportion of employed	Percent	56	69	70	70	70	69	67	47	45	43	45	48	54
Branch of activity														
Agriculture/fishing	Percent	65	87	95	91	91	85	76	11	29	14	10	6	3
Manufacturing/mining/construction	Percent	8	3	2	2	2	5	5	21	15	22	22	24	20
Commerce	Percent	15	5	2	4	3	5	10	39	36	39	41	39	38
Civil servant/army	Percent	7	3	1	2	3	3	6	16	8	13	14	17	21
Other sector	Percent	5	1	1	1	1	2	3	14	12	12	13	14	17
Labor force participation (total)	Percent	72	73	71	68	73	72	77	71	68	66	70	73	78
Male	Percent	74	77	76	73	78	77	79	71	69	66	70	72	74
Female	Percent	70	69	67	64	69	68	75	72	67	67	70	74	81
Household expenditure														
Mean per capita expenditure (Kwacha)	000s	24	16	4	7	11	16	44	37	9	17	24	36	97
Population below relative poverty line	Percent	55	70	100	100	100	52	0	28	100	38	0	0	0
Share of food in total expenditure	Percent	64	69	81	76	70	65	53	56	64	60	58	54	45
Household amenities														
Type of fuel for cooking														
Firewood	Percent	63	89	98	96	93	89	77	13	32	16	11	8	5
Gas, kerosine	Percent	0	0	0	0	0	0	0	0	0	0	0	0	0
Charcoal	Percent	23	9	1	4	6	9	18	51	57	60	56	50	41
Electricity	Percent	13	1	0	0	0	0	3	36	10	25	32	42	54
Other	Percent	1	1	1	1	0	1	1	0	0	0	0	0	0
Access to sanitation	Percent	69	56	42	54	57	60	63	93	87	91	93	94	95
Access to water														
Pipe/borne	Percent	31	6	1	4	3	7	12	77	61	74	75	82	86
Well	Percent	45	60	63	60	59	59	60	15	30	18	16	11	8
Other	Percent	25	34	36	36	37	34	28	8	9	9	9	7	6
Owner occupancy rate	Percent	68	86	95	90	90	85	76	35	60	45	35	28	20
Malnutrition (children aged 0 to 59 months)														
Stunting	Percent	.	.											
Wasting	Percent	.	.											
Underweight	Percent	.	.											

Source: Zambian Living Conditions and Monitoring Survey. Central Statistical Office, Zambia, 1996.

Technical Notes

Burkina Faso

Data source. The Burkina Faso Priority Survey [Enquête prioritaire sur les conditions de vie des ménages au Burkina] was carried out under the SDA project by the Institut national de la statistique et de la démographie, the Statistical Unit of the Ministry of Finance and Planning. Initiated in October 1994, the data collection process was completed in September 1995. The project was funded by the World Bank, the African Development Bank (ADB), and the United Nations through the UNDP.

Sample. The survey used a two-stage stratified random sample and was nationally representative. The country was divided into seven strata (two urban and five rural), and data were collected in all urban and rural regions. Approximately 20 households were sampled without repeat and with equal probability from 434 enumeration areas, producing a sample size of 8,442, of which 2,718 were urban households and 5,724 rural.

Expenditure data. Total household expenditures on health, food, and nonfood items were recorded for the 30 days preceding the enumerator's visit, while expenditure on education covered the 1993/94 academic year. However, the number of household expenditure items was limited to 55, of which 23 were food items and 22 nonfood items. Household owned-produced and consumed food was accounted for in the aggregate total expenditure. Data were collected on a single visit to the household. Price deflators were applied to adjust for spatial differences.

Household. A household was defined as a basic socioeconomic unit made up of different members, not necessary related, who reside in the same compound, share their resources and meals, and recognize one member as head.

Literacy. Household members who could read and write a sentence in any language were considered literate.

Central African Republic

Data source. The Central African Republic Priority Survey [L'Enquête prioritaire sur les conditions de vie des ménages] was carried out under Le Projet dimensions sociales de l'ajustement et du développement by the Statistics Department of the Ministry of Finance and Planning. The data collection process started in the urban area in September 1992 and was completed in the rural area in June 1994.

Sample. The survey was a nationally representative household survey, based on the enumeration areas of the 1988 General Population Census (which delineated the urban and rural areas). The sample size was 7,500 households. Approximately 2,960 households were selected from urban and 4,540 from rural areas.

Expenditure data. Expenditure information was collected during a single visit to the household. The survey collects data on 36 expenditure items, of which 25 were nonfood items and 11 food items. The recall period was two weeks for food and frequently purchased items and a month for educational and clothing expenses. Household owned-produced and -consumed food was not accounted for in total household expenditure aggregate. No adjustments were made to correct for regional price differences.

Household. This was defined as a group of related or unrelated people who live in the same dwelling unit, have been sharing meals for at least 6 of the 12 months preceding the data collection, and recognize one member as head.

Literacy. Persons were considered literate if they had either attended any school and had completed elementary education level or were older than 15 and could read and write a short note in French, even though they may never have attended any school.

Côte d'Ivoire

Data source. The Côte d'Ivoire 1995 Priority Survey [Enquête Niveau de Vie] was carried out under the SDA project by the Direction de la Statistique, unit of the Ministry of Economics, Finance, and Planning. The project was jointly funded by the government of Côte d'Ivoire, IDA, and the ADB.

Sample. This was a nationwide household survey based on the priority survey 1993 master sample. It was a two-stage, self-weighted, stratified random sampling. In the first stage, 100 clusters were randomly selected from the 480 clusters of households. In the second stage, 10 households were selected from each cluster, producing a total sample size of 1,000 households.

Expenditure data. Expenditure data collected detailed information on household expenditure on health during the past three months preceding the enumerator's visit. Detailed information on other household expenditure items was collected either over a 1-month or 12-month recall period. Expenditure information was collected during a single visit on 69 items, of which 28 were food items and 41 nonfood items. Regional price indices were used to account for spatial differences, with the Abidjan CPI as base.

Household. This was defined as a person or a group of people who have been living under the same roof for the past 12 months, share the same meal, and recognize one member as head.

Literacy. Household members who could read and write a sentence in any language were considered literate.

Djibouti

Data source. The Enquête Djiboutienne auprès des ménages (EDAM), was carried in 1996 (from April 2 to July 15) by the National Statistical Office [Direction Nationale de la Statistique] under the Ministry of Commerce. The project was funded by several donors, including the World Bank, United Nations, ADB, and the governments of Belgium and Norway. Technical assistance was received from the World Bank.

Sample. The EDAM was a nationwide household survey, with full coverage of urban and rural areas. However, the nomad population was not sampled. Urban households were slightly over sampled, 2,000 households were drawn in urban strata, and 400 in rural areas. Initially 2,400 households were sampled, but following correction for non response, the total number of households in the sample was reduced to 2,380.

Sample design. The survey was drawn on a master sample and enumeration areas obtained from the sampling frame revised in 1994. A multistage stratified random sampling design was used to select the sample. Three strata (urban and rural) were identified, and households were selected with systematic sampling within each enumeration areas in the strata.

Expenditure data. Data collection on household and individual expenses was carried out on a single visit to the household, based on weekly and monthly reference periods. Expenditure data were collected on 35 items, of which 9 were nonfood items and 26 food items. Special consideration and emphasis were put on the consumption of khât in the overall household total expenditure.

Household. This was defined as a person living alone or any group of people staying together, related or not, and sharing the same catering arrangements.

Household head. This was defined as the person whose authority is recognized and fully accepted by other household members.

Ethiopia

Data source. The 1995 Household Income, Consumption, and Expenditure Survey (HICES) was carried out by the Central Statistical Office. The data collection process was spread over six months, from July 1995 to January 1996. The project was funded by the World Bank, which provided technical assistance in the data collection and analysis.

Sample. The HICES was a nationwide household survey that covers all administrative regions, including urban and rural. However, nonsedentary population was not covered. The overall sample was relatively large, with 11,687 at the national level, of which 6,569 were rural households and 4,379 urban households. Data were collected on multiple visits to the households. In particular, households were visited twice for nonfood items. To take into account the slack season and the peak/dry (harvest) season, surveyed households were visited 16 times for food items.

Sample design. The data were collected using a multistage stratified random sampling. The country was divided into 21 rural and 11 urban domains. A total of 943 enumeration areas (EAs) were identified in the administrative regions, and 929 were surveyed. Using systematic random sampling, 15 households were sampled from urban EAs, and 12 households were sampled from each rural EA.

Expenditure data. The HICES was an income expenditure type survey, which collects information on

most households expenditure items, including food and nonfood consumption. Food expenditure include 200 items, both purchased and home-produced. The total expenditure variable was calculated by aggregating all estimates of expenditure items extrapolated to the annual value. Prices deflators were not used to account for regional and spatial differences.

Literacy. Persons were considered as literate if they could read and write a sentence in national language.

The Gambia

Data source. The Gambia Priority Survey was carried out under the SDA program by the Central Statistics Department of the Ministry of Finance and Economic Affairs. The data collection was spread over four months, from late February to early May 1992. The project was funded by the government of the Gambia, the World Bank, and the ADB. Technical assistance was provided by the World Bank.

Sample. A multistage sample using probability proportional to size was used in the sample selection. The survey has a national coverage, both urban and rural areas, with low rates of nonresponse. The data were collected on a single visit to the household. The total sample size was 2,031 households, of which 1,185 were rural and 846 urban.

Expenditure data. The survey collected information on household expenditure incurred during the previous month on selected items, and/or over a year for educational expenses. Total household expenditure on food was collected on five items, and home-produced and -consumed food was not accounted for in estimating total household expenditure.

Household. This was defined as a group of people who normally live and eat together and accept the authority of one member as head. A household may also consist of one person, and its members may or may not be related.

Literacy. Literacy was defined as the ability to read and write a simple sentence in any language (English/Arabic).

Access to sanitation. This priority survey did not collect data on household access to sanitation and type of toilet facilities.

Ghana

Data source. The Core Welfare Indicator Questionnaire (CWIQ) Survey is a rapid monitoring instrument designed to provide evolution and trends of key social indicators for different population groups. The survey was carried out by the Ghana Statistical Service in July 1997. Funding was provided by the World Bank and the Ghanaian government. The World Bank also provided technical assistance.

Sample. This was a nationwide household survey based on the master sample of enumeration areas as defined by the 1984 population census. A multistage sampling design was used to select the sample. The enumeration areas (EAs) were selected with probability proportional to size. Initially 14,514 households were sampled with systematic random sampling within the EAs. But following correction for nonresponse and underreporting, the total sample size was reduced, and the revised sample contained 14,511 households, of which 9,160 wererural and 5,351 urban.

Coverage. National coverage and relatively large sample allowed for a much finer analysis disaggregated at the regional and district level. Data were collected on single visit to the household and in a relatively short period of time, averaging 45 minutes.

Expenditure data. The 1997 Ghana CWIQ did not include an expenditure module to the core, and no information was collected on household and individual expenditures. However, a set of poverty predictors was used to estimate a predicted total expenditure function. This function was estimated as the weighted sum of poverty predictors, with the coefficients de-

rived from GLSS 3 survey. In the absence of price deflators, no attempt was made to correct for regional and spatial differences.

Expenditure quintiles. Expenditure quintiles for household ranking were constructed from expenditure proxies or poverty predictors, carefully identified in the previous round of Ghana living standards surveys, GLSS3. These poverty predictors were used to impute for total household per capita expenditure.

Household. This was defined as a person living alone or any group of people staying together and sharing the same catering arrangements.

Literacy. Persons were considered literate if they could read and write. In the CWIQ context, literacy question was referred to household members 15 years of age and older only.

Coranic school. Coranic education was not considered as part of the basic curricula during the data collection, which emphasizes formal education and schooling.

Total population estimates. Household weights constructed in the CWIQ design to extrapolate total population from household to national level tends to underestimate the total population. Despite successive rate of growth over the past 10 years, national population estimates from the CWIQ appear to be smaller than the figures obtained in the 1984 population census.

Guinea

Data source. The Guinean Integrated Survey [Enquête Integrale sur les Conditions de Vie des Ménages] was carried out under *Le Project Dimensions Sociales de l'Ajustement Structurel* by the Statistical Unit of the Ministry of Finance and Planning. The data collection was carried out between January 1994 and February 1995. The project was funded by the government of Guinea, IDA, CIDA, and the ADB.

Technical assistance was provided by the World Bank.

Sample. The Guinean Integrated Survey was a nationwide household survey with extended coverage. The data were collected in urban and rural areas on a relatively large and representative sample. The total sample size was 4,416 households, of which 1,680 were rural and 2,736 urban. The data were collected on multiple visits to the household.

Sample design. A multistage stratified random sample was used to draw households from the master sample. The strata were defined as the main agroeconomic regions. The survey was based on the sampling frame used in the priority survey context and derived from the 1983 general population census.

Expenditure data. The survey collected expenditure data during two visits. Expenditure data were adjusted to correct for regional and seasonal price differences.

Household. This was defined as a group of related or unrelated people who have been living in the same dwelling unit and sharing meals for at least 6 of the 12 months preceding the data collection and who recognize one member as head.

Literacy. Persons were considered literate if they had completed at least primary education.

Guinea-Bissau

Data source. The Guinea-Bissau Priority Survey [Inquérito Ligeiro Junta as Familias] was part of the SDA project. The survey was implemented by the Direcção General de Estatistica under the Ministério de Economica e Financas in 1991. Funding for the survey was provided by the UNDP, ADB, the World Bank, and a number of donors and organizations. Technical assistance was provided by the World Bank.

Sample. The 1991 Priority Survey was nationally representative, with extended coverage in both urban and rural areas. A total of 1,060 households were surveyed, of which 720 were rural and 340 urban households. The sample was based on administrative boundaries in regions and sectoral subdivisions. The data were collected on a single visit to the household.

Expenditure data. The Guinea Bissau Priority Survey was a PS+ type survey, with an expanded expenditure module. Total expenditure was estimated as the sum of cash expenditure on consumption goods and services; the value of own-produced food, transfers, and remittances received (in cash and in kind); and goods received in barter. Items excluded from the household expenditure data include the purchase of buildings, land, and the imputed value of owner-occupied houses and vehicles.

Household. This was defined as a group of people who have been living in the same dwelling unit and sharing meals for at least 6 of the past 12 months preceding the data collection and who recognize one member as head.

Literacy. Persons were considered literate if they could read and write a simple sentence.

Access to sanitation. Information on household sanitation was not collected during the survey.

Kenya

Data source. The National Welfare Monitoring Survey I was a household priority survey carried out in November/December 1992 by the Central Bureau of Statistics in the Ministry of Planning and National Development. The data were collected in 44 districts, excluding Turkana, Marsabit, and Samburu. In the North Eastern province, the data were collected only from the urban clusters.

Sample. A total of 1,205 clusters were sampled, with 10 households sampled from each cluster, providing a sample of 12,050 households. Implementation difficulties led to the loss of a significant number of responses, approximately 4,000 households. The final sample size was 8,123 households.

Expenditure data. The survey collected information on household expenditure on essential commodities incurred during the month before the data collection. The data were collected on a single visit to the household and does not account for seasonality. Price deflators were used to correct for regional price differences.

Household. This was defined as a person or a group of people living in the same compound (fenced or unfenced), answerable to the same head, and sharing a common source of food and/or income.

Literacy. Persons were considered literate if they could read and write a sentence in English.

Madagascar

Data source. The Madagascar Integrated Survey [Enquête permanente Aupres des Menages] was carried out under the Project Dimensions Sociales de l'Ajustement Structurel by the Statistical Service [Office Statistique et informatique pour la Programmation du Développement]. Initiated in April 1993, the data collection was completed in October 1993. The project was funded by the government of Madagascar, the World Bank, and the UNDP.

Sample. The survey used a three-stage stratified random sample. The sample was stratified by urban and rural areas. The sample size was 4,500 households, of which 2,557 were rural and 1,943 urban.

Expenditure data. The survey collects data on all aspects of household expenditures (food and nonfood). In urban areas, a daily diary was used to record consumption expenditure to reduce nonsampling and recall errors.

Household. This was defined as a person or group of people living together and sharing the same food, as well as other household items and facilities.

Literacy. Household members were considered literate if they had completed primary education, attended any literacy course, or could read and write a sentence in French.

Mali

Data source. The Enquête Malienne de Conjoncture Economique et Sociale (EMCES) was a priority type survey. The survey was carried out in 1994 by the national statistical office, Direction Nationale de la Statistique et de l'Informatique (DNSI) right in the aftermath of the devaluation. The survey was funded by the World Bank, the United Nations, and the European Union. Technical assistance was provided by the Bank.

Sample. The EMCES was a nationwide survey. However, due to strike, the rural population located in the northern regions of Gao, Kayes, and Tombouctou were not sampled. Therefore the urban population is slightly over-sampled. Initially 9,700 households were sampled with systematic random sampling within the enumeration areas (EAs). But following correction for nonresponse and underreporting on few household items and data editing, the total sample size was reduced, and the revised sample contained 9,312 households, of which 3,863 were rural and 5,449 urban. Data were collected on a single visit to the household and therefore do not account for seasonality.

Sampling design. The 1987 census EAs were used as the primary sampling unit, and households were used as the secondary sampling unit. A two-stage stratified random sampling was used to draw households. The EAs were selected with probability proportional to size.

Total expenditure variable. Data on household expenses and consumption were gathered on a limited number of items: education, health, clothing, housing, transportation, transfers, and food. Overall, estimated values of total expenditure were collected on 35 household items, of which 10 were food items.

Household owned-produced and -consumed food, which represents a large share of consumption in rural areas, was not taken into account in the EMCES. This may have produced an underestimation of rural total expenditure. However, a correction factor was used to reduce the bias toward underestimation of total expenditure estimates in rural areas. Price deflators were used to adjust for regional price differences.

Literacy. Persons were considered literate if they could communicate in one of the local languages.

Formal and informal sector. Although information was collected on industry, type of economic and professional activity, the questionnaire did not allow for disaggregation into formal and informal sector activities.

Mauritania

Data source. The 1995 Mauritania survey [Enquête Permanente sur les Conditions de Vie des Ménages (EPCV)] was carried out by Central Statistical Office [Office National de la Statistique (ONS)] over 9 months, from October 1994 to June 1995. The survey was part of the Social Dimensions Adjustment program initiated by the World Bank. The survey was funded by the World Bank and the government of Mauritania. The World Bank provided technical assistance.

Sample. The EPCV was a nationwide survey, with 99.9 percent coverage in the first round and 96.4 percent in the second round. However, due to migrations and sampling issues, the nomadic population could not be sampled. Initially 3,540 households spread over four stratum were sampled with systematic random sampling within the enumeration areas (EAs). But following correction for nonresponse and underreporting on few household items and data editing, the total sample size was reduced, and the revised sample contains 3,412 households. Urban households were slightly oversampled, and the breakdown shows that 1,219 households were located in

rural areas and 2,193 in urban areas. Data were collected on two visits to the household.

Sampling design. The 1987 census EAs were used as the primary sampling unit, and households were used as the secondary sampling unit. A two-stage stratified random sampling was used to draw households. The EAs were selected with probability proportional to size.

Household total expenditure. Expenditure and consumption modules were comprehensive. Data on household expenses and consumption were gathered on a large number of items, including durable goods, food and consumption of owned production, construction, health and education, expenditure on clothing, housing, transportation, and transfers. Overall estimated values of total expenditure was collected on 133 household items, of which 79 were food items, and data on owned-produced and -consumed food was collected on 34 items.

Price deflators. To account for variations in the cost of living across regions and changes in prices that may have resulted from extended data collection during multiple visits to the households, price deflators were used to correct for regional price differences.

Data issues. The estimated weighting coefficients available and produced in the context of the 1995 EPCV survey were slightly bias, and the overall population derived from applying the weights to the sample does not yield the total population as estimated from the census. Therefore, to reduce the sampling bias, demographic and household welfare indicators are estimated at the level of the sample and not the total population. The National Statistical Office is updating the sampling frame and design to revise these weights.

Industry variable. The industry variable was constructed using the list or nomenclature of industrial and professional codes provided by the National Income Account. These codes were regrouped into eight categories available in the instruction manual for creating standardized files.

Literacy. Persons were considered literate if they could read and write a sentence in any language.

Niger

Data source. The Household Budget Consumption Survey [Enquête nationale du budget et de la consomation des ménages] was carried out in two phases by the Statistical Unit [Direction de la Statistique et des Comptes Nationaux] under the Ministry of Finance and Planning between 1989 and 1993. The survey was part of the Programme d'appui à la gestion économique et financière and was funded by the World Bank, PNUD, and the governments of France and the Netherlands.

Sample. This was a two-stage nationwide household survey based on a master sample drawn from the 1988 population census. The survey was based on a multistage stratified random sample. A total of 3,799 households were selected at the national level, of which 1,775 were from urban areas and 2,024 from rural areas.

Expenditure data. The survey used three reference periods: day, month, and year. Household diaries were used to reduce errors associated with the recall period. The urban and rural data initially collected in two different periods were consolidated after adjustment for regional and over-time price differences and are expressed in 1992 constant CFAF.

Household. This was defined as a group of people who live together in the same dwelling unit, share meals, and recognize one member as head.

Literacy. Persons were considered literate if they had attended any school. However, since primary school students below a certain class may not be able to read or write, these figures are likely to be high.

Access to sanitation. Households with access to safe sanitation refer to those equipped with a flush toilet.

Nigeria

Data source. The National Consumer Survey was part of the National Integrated Survey of Households, sponsored by the United Nations through the National Household Survey Capabilities Programme. The data collection started in April 1992 and was completed in March 1993. The survey and data collection process was conducted by the Federal Office of Statistics.

Sample. This was a nationwide household survey based on enumeration areas defined by the 1991 population census. The survey used a two-stage stratified random sample with extended coverage. Overall, a sample of about 10,000 households was drawn from 120 enumeration areas selected from each of the 21 states and the Federal Capital territory. But following correction for nonresponse and data editing, the total sample size was reduced to 8,937 households, of which 5,276 wererural households and 3,661 urban households.

Expenditure data. The survey included information on most household expenditure items: food, nonfood, and own-produced and -consumed food items. Data collection was carried out on multiple visit to the household to capture changes and variations in household total expenditure. Price deflators were used to adjust for regional price differences.

Household. This was defined as a group of related or unrelated people, living in a dwelling unit or its equivalent, eating from the same pot, and sharing common housekeeping arrangements.

Literacy. Persons were considered literate if they had completed primary education.

Access to sanitation. Information on household sanitation was not collected during this survey.

Access to water. Information on household access to water was not collected during this survey.

Senegal

Data source. The 1994 Income Expenditure Type Survey [Enquête Senegalaise auprès des ménages (ESAM)] was carried out under the Projet Dimensions Sociales de l'Ajustement Structural, by the statistical division, Direction de la Prevision et de la Statistique of the Ministry of Economic and Finance. Initiated in April 1994, the data collection was completed in May 1995. The project was funded by the government of Senegal, the World Bank, and CIDA. Technical assistance was provided by the World Bank and the Canadian International Development Agency (CIDA).

Sample. A two-stage stratified random sample was used. In the first stage, the districts de recensement were sampled with probability proportional to size, and households were sampled in the second stage. The strata were divided along the main geographical regions. The total sample size was 3,277 households, of which 1,314 were rural and 1,963 urban. The survey was conducted nationwide.

Expenditure data. The survey collects information on most household and individual expenditure items and food and nonfood items. A diary was used in the household to reduce nonsampling errors associated with a long recall period. To reduce variation and changes in price over time, the data were collected on multiple visits to the household. However, expenditures were not deflated by regional CPI to account for spatial differences.

Household. This was defined as a person or group of people living in the same compound, answerable to the same head, and sharing a common source of food and/or income.

Literacy. People were considered literate if they could read and write a sentence in French.

Access to sanitation. The survey did not collect data on household access to sanitation and type of toilet facilities.

Sierra Leone

Data source. The Survey of Household Expenditure and Household Economic Activities was carried out between October 1989 and September 1990 by the Central Statistics Office. Funding and technical assistance were provided by the UNDP, ECA, UNICEF, ILO, UNFPA, and FAO.

Sample. The survey covered the entire country, including provinces in urban and rural areas, and was based on administrative subdivisions and enumeration areas of the 1985 population census. A two-stage stratified random sample was used. A total sample size of 2,800 households was drawn. A total of 1,940 households were selected from the urban area (1,560 from large towns and 380 from the small towns), and 860 households were from rural areas.

Expenditure data. These include consumption expenditures on food, imputed value of consumption of own-produced goods, and monetary value of gifts received, purchased, and other acquisition of nonfood items. The nonconsumption component of taxes, insurance premiums, income transfers, and remittances were left out. Nominal figures were not deflated with a regional price index.

Household. This was defined as a group of people living in the same dwelling unit or its equivalent, eating from the same pot, and sharing the common housekeeping arrangements.

Literacy. People were considered literate if they had completed primary education.

Access to sanitation. Information on household sanitation was not collected during the survey.

Access to water. Information on household access to water was not collected during the survey.

South Africa

Data source. The South African Living Standards and Development Survey was a nationwide household survey conducted between July 1993 and April 1994 by the Southern Africa Labor and Development Research Unit in the School of Economics at the University of Cape Town. Funding for the project was provided by the governments of Denmark, Netherlands, and Norway through the World Bank.

Sample. The sampling frame was based on the existing census enumeration areas. The sample was a two-stage, self-weighting design in which the first stage units were the Census Enumerators Sub-Districts, and the second stage units were households. Enumerators collected detailed information on 9,000 households, of which approximately 4,230 were rural and 4,770 urban.

Expenditure data. The survey collected data on household key expenditure items classified into two groups: food and nonfood. Nearly 748 households failed to report nonfood consumption, and only 1,462 households provided information on remittances expenditure. No price adjustment was made to account for seasonality and regional price variation.

Household. Two definitions of households were used to avoid double counting. One was used in the first part of the questionnaire (household roster), which referred to individuals who lived under one roof or within the same compound at least 15 days during the past year, shared food from a common source, and contributed to a common resource pool. Visitors were not included. The second was used in the second part of the questionnaire and included household members who had lived "under this roof for more than 15 of the past 30 days."

Literacy. People were considered literate if they had completed a standard form 7 or higher.

Swaziland

Data source. The 1994 Swaziland Household Income and Expenditure Survey (SHIES) was a nationwide household survey. The data collection was spread over 12 months, from November 1994 to October 1995. The survey was carried out by the Central Statistical Office, with technical assistance from Statistics Sweden and the Board of Investment and Technical Support. The project was funded by the World Bank.

Sample. The data were collected nationwide, with urban areas household slightly over-sampled. Initially 6,350 homesteads were sampled with systematic random sampling within the enumeration areas (EAs). But following correction for nonresponse and underreporting, the total sample size was reduced to 6,246 households, of which 4,612 were rural and 1,634 urban. The data collection was performed on multiple visits to the household.

Sampling design. The SHIES used the 1986 population census as the basis for sampling frame. A two-stage stratified random sampling was used to draw households. The census EAs were used as the primary sampling unit. The homesteads were used as the secondary sampling unit. Out of 1,079 EAs, 216 were sampled with probability proportional to size.

Expenditure data. The SHIES was an income expenditure survey, which collects information on most household and individual expenditure items, including food and nonfood. However, food consumption and home-produced food was underestimated during the data collection. Moreover, over 20 percent of households lack information on rent. For these households, expenditure on food, owned-produced food, and rent expenses were imputed for households missing this information in rural areas.

Correction for seasonality. To account for these variations, price deflators were used to adjust for over-time and regional price differences. In particular, a regression model with a host of independent variables and total expenditure as dependent variable was used to estimate seasonal differences. Independent variables include months, education, housing, and demographic. The intercept and monthly parameters were used to calculate the monthly weights, which were then used as the basis for accounting for these variations.

Homestead. This refers to a house or collection of houses found in a common yard or home, normally in rural areas. In urban areas, a homestead will be a built-in plot.

Household. This consists of one or more persons, related or unrelated, who live together in one, or part of one, or more than one housing unit/dwelling and have common catering arrangements.

Tanzania

Data source. The Human Resource Development Survey was carried out by the World Bank with the University of Dar es Salaam and the Tanzanian Planning Commission. The data collection was carried out over seven months, from September 1993 to March 1994. The project was funded by the British Overseas Development Administration (ODA), the government of Japan, and the World Bank.

Sample. This was a nationwide household survey based on the national master sample revised in 1990. The sample was based on a two-stage stratified random sample. Approximately 25 households were randomly selected from each enumeration area, which produced a sample of 5,184 households, of which 2,262 were rural and 2,922 urban.

Expenditure data. The survey collected information on household expenditure incurred over different reference periods (day, week, and month). The data collection was carried out during a single visit to the household. No adjustment was made for regional and seasonal price differences.

Household. This was defined as a person living alone or any group of people staying together and sharing the same catering arrangements.

Literacy. People were considered literate if they could read a newspaper, write a letter, or perform written calculations.

Uganda

Data source. The Uganda Integrated Household Survey was conducted by the Statistics Department of the Ministry of Planning and Economic Development. It consists of three surveys: the integrated survey, the small-scale enterprise survey, and the community survey. Except for a few parishes, the integrated survey covered most districts in Uganda and was implemented over 12 months between 1992 and 1993.

Sample. This was based on a two-stage stratified sample. The sample size was 9,921 households, of which 6,398 were rural and 3,523 urban. The sample was representative, and data were collected on multiple visits to the household to account for over-time differences and variations in the level of consumption in the household.

Expenditure data. The survey collected data on all household expenditures, including food and nonfood items. The data were collected from multiple visits to the household. Adjustments were made to correct for regional and seasonal price differences.

Household. This was defined as a group of people who normally eat and live together. These people may or may not be related by blood, but make common provision for food and other essentials for living and have one person whom they regard as the head of the household.

Literacy. Persons were considered literate if they had completed primary education.

Zambia

Data source. The 1996 Zambia Living Conditions and Monitoring Survey (LCMS) was part of the statistical program initiated in Zambia under the Social Dimensions and Adjustment project. The survey was carried over one month, between September and October 1996, by the Central Statistical Office in the Ministry of Planning. Technical assistance and funding were provided by Statistics Norway and the World Bank.

Sample. This was a nationwide survey, which collected data at the household and individual levels. The LCMS was a Priority Plus type survey (PS+), which is a PS with expanded consumption module. The data were collected on a single visit to the household in both urban and rural areas. The overall sample size was relatively large, 11,601 households. Households in urban areas were slightly over-sampled; of 11,601 households, 6,508 were urban and 5,093 rural.

Sampling design. A multi-stage stratified random sample was used to draw households. A total of 57 districts were identified in the nine provinces, and census supervisory areas (CSAs) were selected in the first stage. Standard enumeration areas were identified within the CSAs, which were designed so that each CSA contains about 3 SEAs. The sampling frame was based on the 1990 population census.

Expenditure data. The survey collected data on household consumption and expenditure on food and nonfood items. Food expenditure included 31 items, both purchased and home-produced. Household expenditures recorded during one month were aggregated to obtain a household monthly consumption expenditure. Since data were collected on a single visit, expenditure data do not capture seasonality. No adjustment was made for regional price differences.

Household. This was defined as a group of people who normally eat and live together and have one person whom they regard as the head of household.

Literacy. People were considered literate if they had completed the standard grade 5 or higher.

Bibliography

Association for the Development of African Education. 1995. *A Statistical Profile of Education in Sub-Saharan Africa, 1990–93*. Paris.

Candoy-Sekse, Rebecca. 1988. *Techniques of Privatization of State-Owned Enterprises. Volume III. Inventory of Country Experience and Reference Materials*. World Bank Technical Paper 90. Washington, D.C.

Central African Republic, Division of Statistics and Economic Studies. 1994. "Enquete prioritaire sur les conditions de vie des menages." Bangui.

Club of Rome. 1972. *The Limit to Growth*. Rome.

Côte d'Ivoire, Institut National de Statistique. 1994. "Enquete prioritaire." Abidjan.

Currency Data & Intelligence Inc. Monthly. *Global Currency Report*. New York.

Floyd, Robert, Clive Gray, and R. P. Short. 1984. *Public Enterprise in Mixed Economies: Some Macroeconomic Aspects*. Washington, D.C.: International Monetary Fund.

Food and Agriculture Organization (FAO). 1987. *Agrostat Code Book*. Rome.

___. annual. *Fertilizer Yearbook*. Rome.

___. annual. *Food and Agriculture Organization Production Yearbook*. Rome.

___. annual. *Food Aid in Figures*. Rome.

___. annual. *Trade Yearbook*. Rome.

___. annual. *Yearbook of Forest Products*. Rome.

Galal, Ahmed. 1990. "Public Enterprise Reform: A Challenge for the World Bank." PRE Working Paper 407. World Bank, Country Economics Department, Washington, D.C. Processed.

___. 1991. *Public Enterprise Reform: Lessons from the Past and Issues for the Future*. World Bank Discussion Paper 119. Washington, D.C.

The Gambia, Ministry of Finance. 1993. "Report on the 1992 Priority Survey." Banjul.

Grootaert, Christian, and Timothy Marchant. 1991. *The Social Dimensions of Adjustment Priority Survey: An Instrument for the Rapid Identification and Monitoring of Policy Targeting Groups*. SDA Working Paper 12. Washington, D.C.: World Bank.

Guinea, Ministry of Planning and Finance. 1991. "Rapport Final: Enquete sur les informations prioritaire: Dimensions Sociales de l'Adjustment Structurel." Conakry.

417

Guinea-Bissau, National Institute of Statistics and Census. 1992. "Relatorio Final: Inquerito Ligeiro Junto as Familias." Bissau.

Hemming, Richard, and Ali M. Mansoor. 1988. *Privatization and Public Enterprises.* IMF Occasional Paper 56. Washington, D.C.

International Energy Agency (IEA). 1996. *Energy Statistics and Balances of Non-OECD Countries, 1993–94.* Paris.

International Labour Organization (ILO). annual. *Yearbook of Labor Statistics.* Geneva.

___. 1968. *International Standard Classification of Occupations.* Geneva.

___. 1987. *World Labor Report* 1. Oxford: Oxford University Press.

International Monetary Fund (IMF). 1986. *Manual on Government Finance Statistics.* Washington, D.C.

___. 1993. *Balance of Payments Manual,* Fifth ed. Washington, D.C.

___. annual. *Balance of Payments Yearbook.* Washington, D.C.

___. annual. *Government Finance Statistics Yearbook.* Washington, D.C.

___. monthly. *International Financial Statistics.* Washington, D.C.

___. various issues. *Recent Economic Development.* Washington, D.C.

International Road Federation. 1995. *World Road Statistics, 1990–94.* Geneva.

International Telecommunication Union (ITU). 1995. *World Telecommunication Development Report.* Geneva.

Jager, William, and Charles Humphreys. 1988. "The Effect of Policy Reforms on Africa." *American Journal of Agricultural Economics* 70 (50): 1036–43.

Kenya, Central Bureau of Statistics. 1993. "Welfare Monitoring Survey." Nairobi.

Metallgesellschaft AG. annual. *Metallstatistik.* Frankfurt am Main.

Mukui, John Thinguri. 1994. "Kenya: Poverty Profiles, 1982–92." Prepared for the Office of the Vice-President and Ministry of Planning and National Development, Nairobi, Kenya.

Nair, Govindan, and Anastosios Filppides. 1988. "How Much Do State-Owned Enterprises Contribute to Public Sector Deficits in Developing Countries?" PPR Working Paper 45. World Bank, Development Economics Vice Presidency, Washington, D.C. Processed.

Organisation for Economic Cooperation and Development (OECD). Various issues. *Geographical Distribution of Financial Flows to Developing Countries.* Paris.

Republic of South Africa. 1990. *South Africa Statistics.* Pretoria: Government Printer.

Swanson, Daniel, and Teferra Wolde-Semait. 1989. *Africa's Public Enterprise Sector and Evidence of Reforms.* World Bank Technical Paper 95. Washington, D.C.

Uganda, Ministry of Finance and Economic Planning. 1993. "Report on the Uganda National Integrated Household Survey 1992–93." Entebbe.

United Nations. 1950. *Index Numbers of Industrial Production.* New York.

___. 1989. *Compendium of Statistics and Indicators on the Situation of Women.* New York.

___. 1992. *The World's Women, 1970–90.* New York.

___. annual. *Population and Vital Statistics Report.* New York.

___. annual. *Yearbook. G., International Trade Statistics.* New York.

United Nations Children's Fund (UNICEF). annual. *The State of the World's Children.* New York.

United Nations Development Programme (UNDP). 1994. *Human Development Report 1994.* New York.

United Nations Development Programme and the World Bank. 1989. *African Economic and Financial Data.* Washington, D.C.

___. 1992. *African Development Indicators.* Washington, D.C.

United Nations Program on HIV/AIDS (UNAIDS). 1998. "Report on the Global HIV/AIDS Epidemic." Geneva.

United Nations Statistical Office (UNSO). 1975, 1986. "United National Standard International Trade Classification," revisions 2 and 3 (SITC, rev. 2 and 3). Statistical Papers, series M. no. 34, rev. 2 and 3. New York.

___. *United Nations International Standard Classification of All Economic Activities*, revision 2 (ISIC, rev. 2). New York.

___. annual. *Energy Statistics Yearbook*. New York.

United Nations Educational, Scientific, and Cultural Organization (UNESCO). 1982. *Conferences of Ministers of Education and Those Responsible for Economic Planning in African Member States*. Paris.

___. 1986. *Regional Bulletin of Education Statistics BREDA – STAT*. Regional Office for Education in Africa. Paris.

___. 1989. *Trends and Projections of Enrollment by Level of Education and by Age, 1960–2025 (as assessed in 1989)*. Division of Statistics on Education. Paris.

___. 1990. *Basic Education and Literacy: World Statistical Indicators*. Paris.

___. annual. *Statistical Yearbook*. Paris.

Wadda, Rohey, and Russel Craig. 1993. "Report on the 1992 Priority Survey." Central Statistics, Ministry of Finance and Economic Affairs, Banjul, The Gambia.

World Bank. 1988. *Education in Sub-Saharan Africa: Policies for Adjustment, Revitalization, and Expansion*. Washington, D.C.

___. 1993a. "Africa Adjustment Study P.E. Sector Reform: Case Studies." Washington, D.C. Processed.

___. 1993b. "Public Enterprise Reform and Privatization in Africa." Washington, D.C. Processed.

___. 1994a. "Kenya Poverty Assessment." Eastern Africa Department, Africa Region. Washington, D.C.

___. 1994b. "A Statistical Profile of Education in Sub-Saharan Africa in the 1980s." Africa Technical Department. Washington, D.C. Processed.

___. 1994c. *World Population Projections, 1994-95*. Washington, D.C.

___. 1994d. "Zambia Poverty Assessment." Southern Africa Department. Washington D.C.

___. 1995. *Bureaucrats in Business*. New York: Oxford University Press.

___. annual. *Commodity Trade and Price Trends*. Washington, D.C.

___. annual. *Global Development Finance* (was *World Debt Tables* up to 1996).

___. annual. *World Bank Atlas*. Washington, D.C.

___. annual. *World Debt Tables* (until 1996; now *Global Development Finance*). Washington, D.C.

___. annual. *World Development Indicators*. Washington, D.C.

___. annual. *World Development Report*. New York: Oxford University Press.

World Resources Institute. 1998. *World Resources, 1998–99*. Washington, D.C.

___. 1996. *World Resources 1996–97*. Washington, D.C.

World Bureau of Metal Statistics. monthly. *World Metal Statistics*. London.

World Health Organization (WHO). annual. *World Health Statistics Annual*. Geneva.

___. various issues. *World Health Statistics Quarterly*. Geneva.

Zambia, Central Statistical Office. 1993. "Social Dimensions of Adjustment: Priority Survey I, 1991." Lusaka.

DISTRIBUTORS OF WORLD BANK PUBLICATIONS

Prices and credit terms vary from country to country. Consult your local distributor before placing an order.

ARGENTINA
Oficina del Libro Internacional
Av. Cordoba 1877
1120 Buenos Aires
Tel: (54 1) 815-8354
Fax: (54 1) 815-8156
E-mail: olilibro@satlink.com

AUSTRALIA, FIJI, PAPUA NEW GUINEA, SOLOMON ISLANDS, VANUATU, AND SAMOA
D.A. Information Services
648 Whitehorse Road
Mitcham 3132
Victoria
Tel: (61) 3 9210 7777
Fax: (61) 3 9210 7788
E-mail: service@dadirect.com.au
URL: http://www .dadirect.com.au

AUSTRIA
Gerold and Co.
Weihburggasse 26
A-1011 Wien
Tel: (43 1) 512-47-31-0
Fax: (43 1) 512-47-31-29
URL: http://www .gerold.co/at.online

BANGLADESH
Micro Industries Development
    Assistance Society (MIDAS)
House 5, Road 16
Dhanmondi R/Area
Dhaka 1209
Tel: (880 2) 326427
Fax: (880 2) 811188

BELGIUM
Jean De Lannoy
Av. du Roi 202
1060 Brussels
Tel: (32 2) 538-5169
Fax: (32 2) 538-0841

BRAZIL
Publicações Tecnicas Internacionais Ltda.
Rua Peixoto Gomide, 209
01409 Sao Paulo, SP.
Tel: (55 11) 259-6644
Fax: (55 11) 258-6990
E-mail: postmaster@pti.uol.br
URL: http://www .uol.br

CANADA
Renouf Publishing Co. Ltd.
5369 Canotek Road
Ottawa, Ontario K1J 9J3
Tel: (613) 745-2665
Fax: (613) 745-7660
E-mail: order .dept@renoufbooks.com
URL: http:// www .renoufbooks.com

CHINA
China Financial & Economic Publishing House
8, Da Fo Si Dong Jie
Beijing
Tel: (86 10) 6333-8257
Fax: (86 10) 6401-7365

China Book Import Centre
P.O. Box 2825
Beijing

Chinese Corporation for Promotion of Humanities
52 You Fang Hu Tong,
Auan Nei Da Jie
Beijing
Tel: (86 10) 660 72 494
Fax: (86 10) 660 72 494

COLOMBIA
Infoenlace Ltda.
Carrera 6 No. 51-21
Apartado Aereo 34270
Santafé de Bogotá, D.C.
Tel: (57 1) 285-2798
Fax: (57 1) 285-2798

COTE D'IVOIRE
Center d'Edition et de Diffusion Africaines (CEDA)
04 B.P. 541
Abidjan 04
Tel: (225) 24 6510; 24 6511
Fax: (225) 25 0567

CYPRUS
Center for Applied Research
Cyprus College
6, Diogenes Street, Engomi
P.O. Box 2006
Nicosia
TTel: (357 2) 59-0730
Fax: (357 2) 66-2051

CZECH REPUBLIC
USIS, NIS Prodejna
Havelkova 22
130 00 Prague 3
Tel: (420 2) 2423 1486
Fax: (420 2) 2423 1114
URL: http://www .nis.cz/

DENMARK
SamfundsLitteratur
Rosenoerns Allé 11
DK-1970 Frederiksberg C
Tel: (45 35) 351942
Fax: (45 35) 357822
URL: http://www.sl.cbs.dk

ECUADOR
Libri Mundi
Libreria Internacional
P.O. Box 17-01-3029
Juan Leon Mera 851
Quito
Tel: (593 2) 521-606; (593 2) 544-185
Fax: (593 2) 504-209
E-mail: librimu1@librimundi.com.ec
E-mail: librimu2@librimundi.com.ec

CODEU
Ruiz de Castilla 763, Edif. Expocolor
Primer piso, Of. #2
Quito
Tel/Fax: (593 2) 507-383; 253-091
E-mail: codeu@impsat.net.ec

EGYPT, ARAB REPUBLIC OF
Al Ahram Distribution Agency
Al Galaa Street
Cairo
Tel: (20 2) 578-6083
Fax: (20 2) 578-6833

The Middle East Observer
41, Sherif Street
Cairo
Tel: (20 2) 393-9732
Fax: (20 2) 393-9732

FINLAND
Akateeminen Kirjakauppa
P.O. Box 128
FIN-00101 Helsinki
Tel: (358 0) 121 4418
Fax: (358 0) 121-4435
E-mail: akatilaus@stockmann.fi
URL: http://www .akateeminen.com/

FRANCE
Editions Eska
5, avenue de l'Opéra
75001 Paris
Tel: (33 1) 42-86-56-00
Fax: (33 1) 42-60-45-35

GERMANY
UNO-Verlag
Poppelsdorfer Allee 55
53115 Bonn
Tel: (49 228) 949020
Fax: (49 228) 217492
URL: http://www.uno-verlag.de
E-mail: unoverlag@aol.com

GHANA
Epp Books Services
P.O. Box 44
TUC
Accra
Tel: 223 21 778843
Fax: 223 21 779099

GREECE
Papasotiriou S.A.
35, Stoumara Str.
106 82 Athens
Tel: (30 1) 364-1826
Fax: (30 1) 364-8254

HAITI
Culture Diffusion
5, Rue Capois
C.P. 257
Port-au-Prince
Tel: (509) 23 9260
Fax: (509) 23 4858

HONG KONG, CHINA; MACAO
Asia 2000 Ltd.
Sales & Circulation Department
302 Seabird House
22-28 Wyndham Street, Central
Hong Kong, China
Tel: (852) 2530-1409
Fax: (852) 2526-1107
E-mail: sales@asia2000.com.hk
URL: http://www .asia2000.com.hk

HUNGARY
Euro Info Service
Margitszgeti Europa Haz
H-1138 Budapest
Tel: (36 1) 350 80 24, 350 80 25
Fax: (36 1) 350 90 32
E-mail: euroinfo@mail.matav.hu

INDIA
Allied Publishers Ltd.
751 Mount Road
Madras - 600 002
Tel: (91 44) 852-3938
Fax: (91 44) 852-0649

INDONESIA
Pt. Indira Limited
Jalan Borobudur 20
P.O. Box 181
Jakarta 10320
Tel: (62 21) 390-4290
Fax: (62 21) 390-4289

IRAN
Ketab Sara Co. Publishers
Khaled Eslamboli Ave., 6th Street
Delafrooz Alley No. 8
P.O. Box 15745-733
Tehran 15117
Tel: (98 21) 8717819; 8716104
Fax: (98 21) 8712479
E-mail: ketab-sara@neda.net.ir

Kowkab Publishers
P.O. Box 19575-511
Tehran
Tel: (98 21) 258-3723
Fax: (98 21) 258-3723

IRELAND
Government Supplies Agency
Oifig an tSoláthair
4-5 Harcourt Road
Dublin 2
Tel: (353 1) 661-3111
Fax: (353 1) 475-2670

ISRAEL
Yozmot Literature Ltd.
P.O. Box 56055
3 Yohanan Hasandlar Street
Tel Aviv 61560
Tel: (972 3) 5285-397
Fax: (972 3) 5285-397

R.O.Y. International
PO Box 13056
Tel Aviv 61130
Tel: (972 3) 649 9469
Fax: (972 3) 648 6039
E-mail: royil@netvision.net.il

Palestinian Authority/Middle East
Index Information Services
P.O.B. 19502 Jerusalem
Tel: (972 2) 6271219
Fax: (972 2) 6271634

ITALY, LIBERIA
Licosa Commissionaria Sansoni SPA
Via Duca Di Calabria, 1/1
Casella Postale 552
50125 Firenze
Tel: (39 55) 645-415
Fax: (39 55) 645-415
E-mail: licosa@ftbcc.it
URL: http://www .ftbcc.it/licosa

JAMAICA
Ian Randle Publishers Ltd.
206 Old Hope Road, Kingston 6
Tel: 876-927-2085
Fax: 876-977-0243
E-mail: irpl@colis.com

JAPAN
Eastern Book Service
3-13 Hongo 3-chome, Bunkyo-ku
Tokyo 113
Tel: (81 3) 3818-0861
Fax: (81 3) 3818-0864
E-mail: orders@svt-ebs.co.jp
URL: http://www .bekkoame.or.jp/~svt-ebs

KENYA
Africa Book Service (E.A.) Ltd.
Quaran House, Mfangano Street
P.O. Box 45245
Nairobi
Tel: (254 2) 223 641
Fax: (254 2) 330 272

KOREA, REPUBLIC OF
Dayang Books Trading Co.
International Division
783-20, Pangba Bon-Dong, Socho-ku
Seoul
Tel: (82 2) 536-9555
Fax: (82 2) 536-0025
E-mail: seamap@chollian.net

Eulyoo Publishing Co., Ltd.
46-1, Susong-Dong
Jongro-Gu
Seoul
Tel: (82 2) 734-3515
Fax: (82 2) 732-9154

LEBANON
Librairie du Liban
P.O. Box 11-9232
Beirut
Tel: (961 9) 217 944
Fax: (961 9) 217 434

MALAYSIA
University of Malaya Cooperative
    Bookshop, Limited
P.O. Box 1127
Jalan Pantai Baru
59700 Kuala Lumpur
Tel: (60 3) 756-5000
Fax: (60 3) 755-4424
E-mail: umkoop@tm.net.my

MEXICO
INFOTEC
Av. San Fernando No. 37
Col. Toriello Guerra
14050 Mexico, D.F.
Tel: (52 5) 624-2800
Fax: (52 5) 624-2822
E-mail: infotec@rtn.net.mx
URL: http://rtn.net.mx

Mundi-Prensa Mexico S.A. de C.V.
c/Rio Panuco, 141-Colonia Cuauhtemoc
06500 Mexico, D.F.
Tel: (52 5) 533-5658
Fax: (52 5) 514-6799

NEPAL
Everest Media International Services (P.) Ltd.
GPO Box 5443
Kathmandu
Tel: (977 1) 472 152
Fax: (977 1) 224 431

NETHERLANDS
De Lindeboom/Internationale Publicaties b.v.–
P.O. Box 202, 7480 AE Haaksbergen
Tel: (31 53) 574-0004
Fax: (31 53) 572-9296
E-mail: lindeboo@worldonline.nl
URL: http://www .worldonline.nl/~lindeboo

NEW ZEALAND
EBSCO NZ Ltd.
Private Mail Bag 99914
New Market
Auckland
Tel: (64 9) 524-8119
Fax: (64 9) 524-8067

Oasis Official
P.O. Box 3627
Wellington
Tel: (64 4) 499 1551
Fax: (64 4) 499 1972
E-mail: oasis@actrix.gen.nz
URL: http://www.oasisbooks.co.nz/

NIGERIA
University Press Limited
Three Crowns Building Jericho
Private Mail Bag 5095
Ibadan
Tel: (234 22) 41-1356
Fax: (234 22) 41-2056

NORWAY
SWETS Norge AS
Book Department, Postboks 6512 Etterstad
N-0606 Oslo
Tel: (47 22) 97-4500
Fax: (47 22) 97-4545

PAKISTAN
Mirza Book Agency
65, Shahrah-e-Quaid-e-Azam
Lahore 54000
Tel: (92 42) 735 3601
Fax: (92 42) 576 3714

Oxford University Press
5 Bangalore Town
Sharae Faisal
PO Box 13033
Karachi-75350
Tel: (92 21) 446307
Fax: (92 21) 4547640
E-mail: ouppak@TheOffice.net

Pak Book Corporation
Aziz Chambers 21, Queen's Road
Lahore
Tel: (92 42) 636 3222; 636 0885
Fax: (92 42) 636 2328
E-mail: pbc@brain.net.pk

PERU
Editorial Desarrollo SA
Apartado 3824, Ica 242 OF. 106
Lima 1
Tel: (51 14) 285380
Fax: (51 14) 286628

PHILIPPINES
International Booksource Center Inc.
1127-A Antipolo St, Barangay, Venezuela
Makati City
Tel: (63 2) 896 6501; 6505; 6507
Fax: (63 2) 896 1741

POLAND
International Publishing Service
Ul. Piekna 31/37
00-677 Warzawa
Tel: (48 2) 628-6089
Fax: (48 2) 621-7255
E-mail: books%ips@ikp.atm.com.pl
URL: http://www .ipscg.waw.pl/ips/export/

PORTUGAL
Livraria Portugal
Apartado 2681, Rua Do Carmo 70-74
1200 Lisbon
Tel: (1) 347-4982
Fax: (1) 347-0264

ROMANIA
Compani De Librarii Bucuresti S.A.
Str. Lipscani no. 26, sector 3
Bucharest
Tel: (40 1) 613 9645
Fax: (40 1) 312 4000

RUSSIAN FEDERATION
Isdatelstvo <Ves Mir>
9a, Kolpachniy Pereulok
Moscow 101831
Tel: (7 095) 917 87 49
Fax: (7 095) 917 92 59

SINGAPORE; TAIWAN, CHINA
MYANMAR; BRUNEI
Hemisphere Publication Services
41 Kallang Pudding Road #04-03
Golden Wheel Building
Singapore 349316
Tel: (65) 741-5166
Fax: (65) 742-9356
E-mail: ashgate@asianconnect.com

SLOVENIA
Gospodarski Vestnik Publishing Group
Dunajska cesta 5
1000 Ljubljana
Tel: (386 61) 133 83 47; 132 12 30
Fax: (386 61) 133 80 30
E-mail: repansekj@gvestnik.si

SOUTH AFRICA, BOTSWANA
For single titles:
Oxford University Press Southern Africa
Vasco Boulevard, Goodwood
P.O. Box 12119, N1 City 7463
Cape Town
Tel: (27 21) 595 4400
Fax: (27 21) 595 4430
E-mail: oxford@oup.co.za

For subscription orders:
International Subscription Service
P.O. Box 41095
Craighall
Johannesburg 2024
Tel: (27 11) 880-1448
Fax: (27 11) 880-6248
E-mail: iss@is.co.za

SPAIN
Mundi-Prensa Libros, S.A.
Castello 37
28001 Madrid
Tel: (34 91) 4 363700
Fax: (34 91) 5 753998
E-mail: libreria@mundiprensa.es
URL: http://www .mundiprensa.com/

Mundi-Prensa Barcelona
Consell de Cent, 391
08009 Barcelona
Tel: (34 3) 488-3492
Fax: (34 3) 487-7659
E-mail: barcelona@mundiprensa.es

SRI LANKA, THE MALDIVES
Lake House Bookshop
100, Sir Chittampalam Gardiner Mawatha
Colombo 2
Tel: (94 1) 32105
Fax: (94 1) 432104
E-mail: LHL@sri.lanka.net

SWEDEN
Wennergren-Williams AB
P. O. Box 1305
S-171 25 Solna
Tel: (46 8) 705-97-50
Fax: (46 8) 27-00-71
E-mail: mail@wwi.se

SWITZERLAND
Librairie Payot Service Institutionnel
Côtes-de-Montbenon 30
1002 Lausanne
Tel: (41 21) 341-3229
Fax: (41 21) 341-3235

ADECO Van Diermen EditionsTechniques
Ch. de Lacuez 41
CH1807 Blonay
Tel: (41 21) 943 2673
Fax: (41 21) 943 3605

THAILAND
Central Books Distribution
306 Silom Road
Bangkok 10500
Tel: (66 2) 235-5400
Fax: (66 2) 237-8321

TRINIDAD & TOBAGO
AND THE CARRIBBEAN
Systematics Studies Ltd.
St. Augustine Shopping Center
Eastern Main Road, St. Augustine
Trinidad & Tobago, West Indies
Tel: (868) 645-8466
Fax: (868) 645-8467
E-mail: tobe@trinidad.net

UGANDA
Gustro Ltd.
PO Box 9997, Madhvani Building
Plot 16/4 Jinja Rd.
Kampala
Tel: (256 41) 251 467
Fax: (256 41) 251 468
E-mail: gus@swiftuganda.com

UNITED KINGDOM
Microinfo Ltd.
P.O. Box 3, Omega Park, Alton,
Hampshire GU34 2PG
England
Tel: (44 1420) 86848
Fax: (44 1420) 89889
E-mail: wbank@microinfo.co.uk
URL: http://www .microinfo.co.uk

The Stationery Office
51 Nine Elms Lane
London SW8 5DR
Tel: (44 171) 873-8400
Fax: (44 171) 873-8242
URL: http://www.theso.co.uk/

VENEZUELA
Tecni-Ciencia Libros, S.A.
Centro Cuidad Comercial Tamanco
Nivel C2, Caracas
Tel: (58 2) 959 5547; 5035; 0016
Fax: (58 2) 959 5636

ZAMBIA
University Bookshop, University of Zambia
Great East Road Campus
P.O. Box 32379
Lusaka
Tel: (260 1) 252 576
Fax: (260 1) 253 952

ZIMBABWE
Academic and Baobab Books (Pvt.) Ltd.
4 Conald Road, Graniteside
P.O. Box 567
Harare
Tel: 263 4 755035
Fax: 263 4 781913

BOOKSELLERS OF WORLD BANK PUBLICATIONS

Prices vary from country to country. Consult your local bookseller for prices and availability.

BULGARIA
Humanities Research Center
P.O. Box 1784
1784 Sofia
Tel: (359 2) 76 81 57
Fax: (359 2) 76 35 34; 76 27 84
E-mail: chr@mgu.bg

CHINA
China National Publications Import & Export Corporation
16 Gongti East Road
Post Code 100020
Beijing

HUNGARY
Foundation for Market Economy
112 Pf 249
1519 Budapest
Tel: (36 1) 204 2951; 204 2948
Fax: (36 1) 204 2953
E-mail: ipargazd@hungary.net

JORDAN
Global Development Forum
P.O. Box 941488
Amman 11194
Tel: (962 6) 5537701
Fax: (962 6) 5537702
E-mail: gdf@index.com.jo

KENYA
Legacy Books
Loita House, Loita Street, Mezz. 1
P.O. Box 68077
Nairobi
Tel: (254 2) 330853/221426
Fax: (254 2) 330854/561654
E-mail: Legacy@form-net.com

KOREA, Republic of
Sejong Books, Inc.
81-4 Neung-dong
Kwangjin-ku
Seoul 143-180
Tel: (82 2) 498-0300
Fax: (82 2) 3409-0321
E-mail: sjbk@mail.nuri.net
URL: http://203.248.78.1/sejong/

NEPAL
Bazaar International
GPO Box 2480
Kathmandu
Tel: (977 1) 22-29-83
Fax: (977 1) 22-94-37

SLOVAK REPUBLIC
Slovart G.T.G. Ltd.
Krupinská 4
P.O. Box 152
852 99 Bratislava 5
Tel: (42 7) 839471; 839472; 839473
Fax: (42 7) 839485
E-mail: gtg@internet.sk

THAILAND
Chulalongkorn University Book Center
Phyathai Road
Bangkok 10330
Tel: (66 2) 218 7292
Fax: (66 2) 255 4441

TURKEY
Dünya Infotel, A.S.
100 Yil Mahallesi
34440 Bagcilar-Istanbul
Tel: (90 212) 629 0808
Fax: (90 212) 629 4689; 629 4627
E-mail: dunya@dunya-gazete.com.tr
URL: http://www.dunya.com/

UNITED ARAB EMIRATES
Al Hamim Stationary & Bookshop
P.O. Box 5027
Sharjah
Tel: (971 6) 734687
Fax: (971 6) 384473
Pager: (971 6) 9760976

URUGUAY
Librería Técnica Uruguaya
Colonia 1543, Piso 7, Of. 702
Casilla de Correo 1518
Montevideo 11000
Tel: (598 2) 490072
Fax: (598 2) 41 34 48